Techniques for Wildlife Habitat Management of Uplands

McGraw-Hill Biological Resource Management Series

A Series of Primers on the Conservation and Exploitation of Natural and Cultivated Ecosystems
Wayne M. Getz, Series Editor

NEIL F. PAYNE • *Techniques for Wildlife Habitat Management of Wetlands*

CARL WALTERS • *Adaptive Management of Renewable Resources*

ANTHONY STARFIELD AND A. L. BLELOCH • *Building Models for Wildlife Management*

PETER B. R. HAZELL AND ROGER D. NORTON • *Mathematical Programming for Economic Analysis in Agriculture*

JOHN P. WORKMAN • *Range Economics*

JOSEPH BUONGIORNO AND J. KEITH GILLESS • *Forest Management and Economics: A Primer in Quantitative Methods*

GORDON L. SWARTZMAN AND STEPHEN P. KALUNZY • *Ecological Simulation Primer*

RAOUL A. ROBINSON • *Host Management in Crop Pathosystems*

C. RONALD CARROLL, JOHN H. VANDERMEER, AND PETER M. ROSSET • *Agroecology*

CHADWICK D. OLIVER AND BRUCE C. LARSON • *Forest Stand Dynamics*

RICHARD E. PLANT AND NICHOLAS D. STONE • *Knowledge-Based Systems in Agriculture*

Herd of elk crossing the rangelands of Montana. (Photo by Mark F. J. Payne.)

Techniques for Wildlife Habitat Management of Uplands

Neil F. Payne

College of Natural Resources
University of Wisconsin
Stevens Point, Wisconsin

Fred C. Bryant

Department of Range
and Wildlife Management
Texas Tech University
Lubbock, Texas

McGraw-Hill, Inc.

New York   San Francisco   Washington, D.C.   Auckland   Bogotá
Caracas   Lisbon   London   Madrid   Mexico City   Milan
Montreal   New Delhi   San Juan   Singapore
Sydney   Tokyo   Toronto

Library of Congress Cataloging-in-Publication Data

Payne, Neil F.
  Techniques for wildlife habitat management of uplands / Neil F.
Payne, Fred C. Bryant.
      p.   cm.—(McGraw-Hill biological resource management series)
  Includes bibliographical references (p.) and index.
  ISBN 0-07-048963-7 (cloth)—ISBN 0-07-048966-1 (paper)
  1. Wildlife habitat improvement 2. Forest management. 3. Range
management. 4. Habitat conservation. I. Bryant, Fred. II. Title.
III. Series.
  SK355.P39   1994
  639.9'2—dc20   93-34866
                                                                      CIP

1 2 3 4 5 6 7 8 9 0   DOC/DOC   9 0 9 8 7 6 5 4

ISBN 0-07-048963-7 (cloth)

ISBN 0-07-048966-1 (paper)

*The sponsoring editor for this book was Sybil P. Parker, the editing
supervisor was Joseph Bertuna, and the production supervisor was
Suzanne W. Babeuf. It was set in Century Schoolbook by
McGraw-Hill's Professional Book Group composition unit.*

Printed and bound by R. R. Donnelley & Sons Company.

This book is printed on acid-free paper.

Dedicated to our parents
Forrest and Ruth Payne
John and Ruth Bryant

Contents

Part 2. Rangelands

Part 3. Farmlands

Part 4. Artificial Improvements

Foreword

In his appreciation of Gifford Pinchot, Roderick Nash spoke of Pinchot's inspirational power, emphasizing that "to arouse men, and move them to action, one cannot speak only to their minds; one must touch their hearts as well."

This lesson has been applied with ever increasing fervor, until today the issues of conservation surge back and forth through public affairs on floods of emotion. So the hearts are touched. What now of the minds?

In these days, enthusiasts of all sorts take their hearts to war, and leave their minds behind. Their emotional attacks provoke emotional counterattacks. Each side has the same motto: Win or Die.

But in real life few win entirely or die entirely. A peace table is found, treaties are hammered out, concessions are made. To gain advantage in mediation, a negotiator must know the value, for his or her cause, of each concession granted or gained. But if all the negotiator brings to the table is fervor, the negotiation takes place in a vacuum, when what the negotiator should have in hand is a rich supply of relative values and demonstrable facts.

So now is the time to rephrase Nash and say: "To strengthen the ability of the emotionally committed to act effectively, one cannot appeal only to their hearts; one must arm them with the tools of reason as well."

This book is about the tools of reason, applied in the interests of wildlife welfare to upland habitats. It is concerned with concepts, methods, and structures, all aimed at encouraging wild creatures to do what they have been genetically selected to do—prosper, multiply, and spread into suitable new habitats.

Hardly anyone, worldwide, would quarrel with the concept of healthy, productive wildlife populations, if blatant conflicts with other human interests were minimized. So what is the problem? The problem is that every upland is under some human program of management, and most of these programs are carried out without the welfare of wildlife as one objective. At worst, wildlife populations are deliberately liquidated for immediate financial gain. More often, wildlife populations are affected incidentally by programs without ill intent, but also without an informed interest in wildlife welfare.

One solution, often tried, is to eliminate management programs and "let nature take care of its own." So we, and our neighbors everywhere, have parks and wildlife refuges which, inevitably, begin to show wildlife-related problems and so to generate managerial programs.

In the real world, therefore, upland habitats will be managed. Plans will be made, budgets drawn up, funds alloted and spent. And wildlife will be affected.

One solution, often tried, is to mitigate the damage done, after it has been done. But cure is a much more expensive proposition than prevention, and budgets seldom stretch to satisfactory after-the-fact remedies. More often, the managerial bulldozer lunges ahead while a low-budget crew of biologists follows along behind, practicing what French military doctors of World War I called *triage*: ignoring the hopeless and those who would recover without help, and focusing on those for whose need they have a remedy.

Since management of some sort is going to proceed endlessly, it would seem a reasonable advance to integrate wildlife goals with other managerial goals as the plans are being developed.

A biologist or two as members of the planning team will face several handicaps. The first, of course, is that the managerial program already has a long history. People involved have long established habits and thoughts concerning it. The often unstated assumptions on which it is based might be obsolete, but since they are seldom examined, this is not immediately evident. There is the strong human tendency to say, "We've always done it this way." One year's budget looks much like another, as next year's budget is usually constructed by tinkering with last years's budget. Zero-based budgeting is not the usual practice in land-management planning. The persons hired to carry out the budgeted tasks are permanent employees. They will display the common human tendency to do today much the same as they did yesterday. Their behavior is highly territorial—they are most comfortable within their accustomed professional habitat, and they will resent, resist, and if possible repel or at least evade, any outside effort to change their ways.

Next, our imaginary biologists will be handicapped by their ignorance of the workings of the managerial apparatus that they are instructed to improve.

And finally, their biological expertise will be deficient.

This brings us to the present volume, which addresses the last two problems admirably. The text takes up each upland type under management—forestlands, rangelands, farmlands—and describes the elements of present managerial procedures. This sets the stage—the reader can now understand what long-term traditional managers consider the tools of their trade, and the various conditions under which they apply them.

In addition, the book brings together in an orderly fashion information on how wildlife conservation has been found, through hundreds of studies, to fit into each sort of managerial pattern. This volume, in short, takes the reader into the workings of the managerial system and the many ways that efforts have been made to influence that system to be more responsive and effective on behalf of wildlife welfare. Our planning-group biologist, well-versed in what this volume has to offer, is likely to be a much more effectual person than he or she would be without it.

Further, the volume brings much to the public interest sector. In the United States and Canada, at least, there is much public interest and participation in upland management. Partly this is due to the public ownership of vast upland areas, partly it is due to the public's legal ownership of wildlife, and partly it is due to the intense interest in wildlife on the part of the public.

Interest and enthusiasm are not wanting. But when public pressures are exerted on managerial agencies, sometimes resistance is justified by the argument that "we know of no studies supporting your assertions." On examination, this statement parallels that of the Kurds who, when exhorted by Turkish foresters to care better for the deteriorating watersheds, can apparently neither read, write, nor understand Turkish; they cultivate a willful ignorance.

The environmental activist faced by willful ignorance on the part of a managerial agency will find this volume useful. Like the young biologist, he or she will learn the professional land manager's language, aims, and procedures. And he or she will learn how, in other settings, these have been modified in favor of wildlife welfare. A stronger base for informed negotiation will be established.

The authors of this volume must be complimented upon the successful completion of a demanding task. Their contribution has many immediate uses, not least of which is in the land-management schools. We can look forward to its establishment on the shelf of perennial reference, advancing through periodic revision as knowledge grows and values change.

Richard D. Taber

Preface

Efforts have been made to discredit what wildlife ecologists have defined as critical habitat to sustain minimum viable populations of certain species because the calculations are not precise enough or statistically perfect. But why must wildlife ecology be so precise when dealing with wildlife, especially threatened or endangered wildlife and their habitat? Has it come to this? Why a *minimum* viable population? That's taking a huge risk that the minimum might be too small and that our generation will be taken to task by our grandchildren because our stewardship of their resources was lousy. Why not a better balance of wildlife population levels than a mere minimum viable population? Is too much space needed? What kind of argument is that when the habitats left in much of North America, especially the contiguous United States, are mere remnants of pre-settlement habitats of just 300 years ago?

A healthy ecosystem is the foundation of society. The environmental crisis is a situation no age has faced before. That we are at a crossroads requiring precise calculations of critical habitat for minimal allowance to sustain a minimum viable population is in itself sad testimony of society's weak stewardship of natural resources for future generations of people. Decreased amounts of habitat must be managed better and protected from human exploitation, mainly encroachment. When research on wildlife has gaps in the results, it behooves society to err on the side of caution in maintaining habitat for a healthy ecosystem and for future generations of wildlife and humans to enjoy. And it behooves society to allow more habitat to exist than the bare minimum.

Wildlife ecologists have been powerful in obtaining biological information about wildlife populations and addressing their needs. Wildlife ecologists have been weak in addressing environmental literacy, biodiversity, biopolitics, and bioeconomics, e.g., the monetary clout of the tourist industry as it pertains to the outdoors, and other economic environmental incentives to manage wildlife habitat. Wildlife ecologists have been notoriously weak in addressing human population growth—the crux of environmental degradation. Even the famed "Earth Summit" on environmental concerns held in 1992 in Rio de Janeiro, with representatives from around the world, lacked the guts to touch it.

We wildlifers talk about "carrying capacity." We know how many deer a given habitat can support, and what happens when the carrying capacity is exceeded. Society fails to recognize a carrying capacity relative to humans and a given quality of life. We hear the cry "We need more jobs," without an accompanying realization that we are eliminating more and more habitat as our populations grow, that we are producing more people than we have jobs for, and that the problem can't be solved by producing more jobs. That defies common sense.

Society talks about "extinction" and "minimum viable populations" of plants and animals, which we know occur naturally but are accelerated by high human populations and resource use, among other things. Cultural and religious attitudes about human population control and distribution must be changed. Many of the world's social ills are a function of human populations stressing and exceeding their carrying capacity. How will we answer our grandchildren when they want to know why our generation doomed a species to extinction because we did not adequately protect and manage habitat from human population growth and encroachment? If the habitat is removed, the species becomes extinct; it cannot be brought back even if the habitat is.

So who should take a stand on human population growth? The professionals involved with managing the natural resource base as the life support system for a healthy society, that's who. And that's us. We've known it all along. The powerful quote at the top of Chapter 1 sums it up well, but is not news. We need to enlist the aid of developers, demographers and economists, among others, if we are going to do our job right. We need more training in these subjects in the university. We urgently need to improve environmental literacy of societies of the world, with required ecological courses for *everyone* at the primary, secondary, and university levels. And some of us need to step into politics.

But this book is not about biopolitics or bioeconomics; it's about habitat management. We recognize that protecting habitats from loss and excessive fragmentation is central to the challenge of saving wildlife. Solutions will be found in the arenas of politics, economics, human demography, and in reshaping religious, cultural, and ethnic values. Our mission is to provide a book which emphasizes techniques to manage the habitats we have left. We also want to foster the principle of *active* habitat management. Simply erecting a fence around a refuge or sanctuary to keep people out does not ensure that wildlife can be maintained. Using the technologies, tools, and techniques of active and passive habitat management will promote biodiversity in most ecosystems.

The wildlife profession seems to have concentrated its efforts more on the glamour of single-species research and management than on the more mundane areas of habitat research and management. Hence this book. Many species-specific books exist, but where are the habitat books? They're tough to write, we'll tell you that. As the world departs from its fascination with game species predominantly, habitat management for biodiversity gains impetus. That means the emphasis on other products, predominantly wood and livestock, will be reduced or made more compatible with wildlife management and general biodiversity. As A. W. Allen wrote in 1987, "Active habitat managment and attempts to mitigate habitat losses cannot be delayed until all the required and appropriate data are collected. Applicable research may take generations to formulate and complete...."

In a way we are surprised that habitat techniques books such as this one haven't been published previously, habitat being the basis of the wildlife profession and the support system for all society. In another way, we can understand why. It is hard, tedious, unglamorous work, subject to much criticism in the end because of a broad scope in content and continent. The material presented has to have broad application or the material has to be presented such that it is useful locally either because the management procedure is standard or the example can be adjusted or stimulate ideas for local use.

We constantly had to remind ourselves to focus on general habitat management for interior wildlife and edge wildlife, and avoid the tendency to discuss species-specific wildlife habitat management procedures—such discussion being beyond the scope of this book and generally impractical in a book dealing largely with habitat management for biodiversity. So little has been written about habitat management for nongame species and so much for game species that we were tempted to pursue the literature on game species almost exclusively.

This book is a companion volume to *Techniques for Wildlife Habitat Management of Wetlands,* published in 1992. Originally, the two-volume set was designed to be one volume. But space restrictions would have resulted in a book with less "how to" and mostly literature review, or too large a volume. As the first volume developed, the need for a volume on uplands became increasingly clear.

Management of uplands and wetlands cannot be separated entirely, for they support each other, especially in riparian areas and other ecotones. For example, many ducks nest in grass uplands and most wildlife of uplands requires wetlands for drinking water. So there is a certain amount of overlap between the two books.

The volume on wetlands differed somewhat in approach, in that wetlands management generally involves direct management for wildlife. Uplands management practices generally involve indirect management for wildlife as a by-product of direct management for timber, livestock, or crops. Because of professional and societal interest in biodiversity, this volume on uplands emphasizes more direct management for wildlife. But management for other products provides the means for expensive habitat improvement far more extensive than affordable with direct habitat improvement.

As with the volume on wetlands, this volume on uplands is designed for use mainly in the United States and Canada, although its principles, examples, and ideas have worldwide application. Again, the design was to sweep the literature thoroughly and present the best information that could be applied broadly or could stimulate ideas for different areas by the examples presented. Again we strove for a relatively self-contained book. But sometimes the detail required was unmanageable, and references were provided for additional detail. Thus, these two books are (1) techniques books and (2) sourcebooks for literature on habitat management.

Of the literature reviewed, about 1500 references were used for this volume. Despite computer searches, which are influenced by the key words used, our constant fear is that we have missed something important out there. We'd like to think not, but we probably have, and we hope it's minimal.

In the preface to *Techniques for Wildlife Habitat Management of Wetlands* we asked whether a book on wildlife habitat management that incorporates information from across North America could be useful locally. We answered "yes," and we say again here that we think it can, "especially if wildlife managers are not too provincial in outlook and avoid the temptation to dismiss summarily the techniques successfully used elsewhere with the notion that they don't apply locally and then proceed to reinvent the wheel. If not directly applicable, techniques usually can be modified for local use or at least to stimulate ideas. Although many published wildlife maps seem to dipect North America as ending ecologically along the 49th parallel between the United States and Canada, this is hardly the case, as migratory and even resident wildlife readily attest. Nonetheless, local conditions must be understood in order to practice the art of accurate and efficient management. Thus we have the compromise of implementing the broad approach modified by local conditions."

This book is a techniques manual on upland habitat improvement. It is a how-to book, emphasizing technique and minimizing principle. It is meant to serve as (1) a training guide (college textbook) for aspiring wildlife managers and (2) a practical guide and sourcebook of ideas and techniques for resource managers to adapt and modify regionally in the United States and Canada, and elsewhere where applicable, as they plan and develop habitat-improvement projects. Details impractical to include are provided in the references.

Thanking those who helped with the manuscript is awkward because a simple "thank you" seems a weak expression of the deep gratitude we feel. For reviews we thank Fred B. Samson (U.S. Forest Service, Missoula, MT), Toni Rinaldi (U.S. Forest Service, Rhinelander, WI), Carolyn Seig (U.S. Forest Service, Rapid City, SD), Keith Severson (U.S. Forest Service, Tempe, AZ), David R. Patton (Northern Arizona University), Eric M. Anderson and Alan Haney (University of Wisconsin—Stevens Point), William R. Clark (Iowa State University), Carlton Britton and R. Scott Lutz (Texas Tech University), Fred S. Guthery (Texas A&M University-Kingsville), Phillip J. Urness (Utah State University), Keith R. McCaffery and Ron G. Eckstein (Wisconsin Department of Natural Resources, Rhinelander). We benefited from stimulating and enlightening discussions with Eric M. Anderson (University of Wisconsin—Stevens Point), Clive A. David (University of Wisconsin—Stevens Point), Steve Demarais (Texas Tech University), D. Lynn Drawe (Welder Wildlife Foundation), and Tim Fulbright (Texas A&M University-Kingsville).

We are grateful to Richard D. Taber (formerly College of Forest Resources, University of Washington) who wrote the Foreword.

At the University of Wisconsin—Stevens Point, Dean Alan Haney and Associate Dean Rick Wilke of the College of Natural Resources provided administrative support. Dorothy Synder requested materials and duplicated figures, Carole Van Horn conducted computerized literature searches and ordered books, Christine Neidlein obtained interlibrary loans, Victoria Billings, Marg Whalen, and Theresa Chao located federal and state documents, Donna Carpenter assisted with checkout and located "lost" books. Janet Snedeker and Christopher H. Danou proofread appendixes and checked scientific names with botanist Frank Bowers. Mark Payne provided photographs and Dan Shaw provided illustrations of wildlife.

At Texas Tech University Chair Ronald E. Sosebee of the Department of Range and Wildlife Management, Dean Samuel E.

Curl, and Associate Dean Robert C. Albin of the College of Agricultural Sciences and Natural Resources provided release time and administrative support. Lisa Bradley helped assemble references and reprints and compiled appendixes of scientific names. John R. Thomasson provided illustrations. Greg Huber and Ann Hild helped verify scientific names and Morty Ortega made maps, checked references and scientific names, and generally perused the manuscript for typographical errors and inconsistencies. Amy Harrison helped with the typing. Gretchen Scott watched over other projects so time could be spent on this book.

Virginia Crandell (University of Wisconsin—Stevens Point) and Karen Davis (Texas Tech University) spent hour upon hour on revision after revision. We could not have done this without them.

For support, understanding, and patience, we extend our deepest thanks to our families: Adam, Mark, and Erin Payne; Lisa, Clint, and Coy Bryant; and especially our loving wives, Janis Payne and Janis Bryant.

Neil F. Payne
Fred C. Bryant

Conversion Table

The relation of SI units (International System of Modernized Metric Units) and U.S. Customary System Units

SI (metric) unit	Equivalent U.S. Customary System unit
Centimeter (cm)	0.394 inch (in)
Decimeter (dm)	0.328 foot (ft)
Meter (m)	1.094 yards (yd) or 3.281 feet (ft)
Kilometer (km)	0.622 mile (mi)
Square centimeter (cm^2)	0.155 square inch (in^2)
Square meter (m^2)	1.197 square yards (yd^2)
Hectare (ha)	2.473 acres
Square kilometer (km^2)	0.386 square mile (mi^2)
Cubic centimeter (cm^3)	0.061 cubic inch (in^3)
Cubic meter (m^3)	1.309 cubic yards (yd^3) or 35.320 cubic feet (ft^3)
Liter (L)	0.908 quart (qt) or 0.227 gallon (gal) or 0.028 bushel (bu)
Milliliter (mL)	0.068 tablespoon (tblsp)
Gram (g)	0.035 ounce (oz)
Kilogram (kg)	2.205 pounds (lb)
Metric ton (t)	1.103 tons or 2205 pounds (lb)
Degree Celsius (°C)	9/5 + 32 = degrees Fahrenheit (°F)

Principles, Concepts, Terms, and Management Considerations of Biodiversity

Finally, and most important, none of these recommendations will be practical if we continue to pack more and more of mankind and his works into the landscape of North America. The control of human populations is the first necessity if the multitude of populations of other forms of life is to survive.

TABER ET AL. (1970)
No Deposit—No Return

*The law locks up both man and woman
Who steals the goose from off the common,
But lets the greater felon loose
Who steals the common from the goose.*

MEDIEVAL ENGLISH QUATRAIN

We do not inherit the land from our ancestors, we borrow it from our children.

CHIEF SEATTLE

A thing is right when it tends to preserve the integrity, stability, and beauty of the biotic community. It is wrong when it tends otherwise. ...To keep every cog and wheel is the first precaution to intelligent tinkering.

ALDO LEOPOLD
A Sand County Almanac

This book is intended to provide some guidelines to practical management for biodiversity of upland wildlife in the United States and Canada. It is divided into four parts, discussing, respectively, forestlands, rangelands, farmlands, and artificial improvements. Initially we considered organizing the book by forestland, rangeland, and farmland types. Rangeland types were few enough and habitat techniques varied enough to facilitate that arrangement in this book. Techniques for farmlands did not vary substantially by farmland type, so we ignored the types. A review of the literature convinced us that a division by forest type was impractical because of the many types involved, and because of the lack of information on many types and the repetition of techniques required in many cases. An attempt to divide forestlands by region proved impractical for the same reasons. Instead, we focused on forestlands with and without fragmented interiors. The best information published is presented for a certain vegetative type or region so that imaginative wildlifers might use it, modify it, adapt it, test it, or glean ideas for use elsewhere. In some cases conflicting information is presented to reveal the nonspecific nature of this information as it might apply to various vegetative types or regions.

Forest and range managers traditionally have managed and often mismanaged public lands for wood and livestock as the main products (e.g., Lansky 1992). The economics of outdoor recreation (e.g., Decker and Goff 1987, Whelan 1991), other values (Ehrenfeld 1976, 1988), and concern for an environmentally sustainable global economy and balanced and healthy ecosystems, especially within the past decade, have produced a concept, *biodiversity,* resulting in greater emphasis on wildlife as a product of the land. Biodiversity is the variety of life and associated ecological processes (Wilcove and Samson 1987, Keystone Center 1991). Control of natural processes has resulted in loss of biodiversity at the ecosystem (Odum et al. 1987), community (Picket and White 1985), and species (Botkin 1990) levels of biological organization. Among other things, maintaining biodiversity will avoid creating endangered species and thus avoid the high social and economic costs of their recovery (Reid and Miller 1989, Scott et al. 1993).

The U.S. Congress has passed an Endangered Species Act, which has had modest and variable success, but does not prevent species from becoming endangered. Congress has yet to pass an *endangered ecosystems act,* which would do just that (Grumbine 1992). Protection of biodiversity, i.e., the application of conservation biology, will reduce the number of threatened and endangered species, thus obviating the triage approach to their recovery with limited budgets (Norton 1987).

Humans tend to be anthropocentric in their view of the world. Anthropocentrism elevates humans over other animals, plants, greater ecosystems, and the rest of the world (Grumbine 1992). Thus, nonhumans become resources for humans. Resourcism must improve its assumptions, to wit:

1. Planning for human demands must be done for the long term.
2. The world's abundance is exhaustible.
3. Technology cannot continue to extend limits to growth.

To sustain itself, society will have to accept the notion that wood and forage are secondary products to managing for biodiversity, because society depends on a healthy ecosystem for survival. That philosophy will entail a reversal in the way forestlands and rangelands have been managed in the past. Forest and range management should be coordinated closely with wildlife habitat-management strategies to enhance biodiversity and sustain production of commercial timber and livestock along with that of wildlife for balanced ecosystems and for recreation and tourism. In some cases this will mean land managers of forest and range ecosystems on public and even private land must reverse their philosophy of the land to that of managing for biodiversity with wood and livestock as a byproduct, with the cost for management borne by the private sector or the public till. Public lands are a public resource, on which management for biodiversity usually can be accomplished if professional wildlifers are given the mandate to do it. The methods exist to enhance wildlife habitat on private uplands, too, with little or no disruption of income from other products such as wood, livestock, and crops. Lands also can be restored to enhance biodiversity (Jordan 1986, Buckley 1989). It is time to focus on what we leave on the land, rather than on what we take from it (Fairbanks 1991).

Wildlife habitat management can be direct or indirect. Indirect management tends to be incidental to other land use. Wildlife administrators must avoid the tendency to view incidental benefits as a substitute for carefully executed habitat-management projects, especially for threatened or endangered species (Millsap et al. 1987).

Ecosystem management involves complex forces (Grumbine 1992): conservation biology, gap analysis, a biodiversity-protection network, new forestry, restoration of damaged lands, interagency cooperation, local and regional long-term planning, scientific education of the public, activism. Business as usual on the landscape must change. This will not happen without broad-based public education, support, and participation. And it depends on how we manage ourselves, i.e., our economy, resource consumption, pollution, and population growth (Meffe et al. 1993). If social and political systems fail to address adequately the global threats of human population growth, poverty, pollution, and political instability, the best research and management of resources will have little lasting effect on biodiversity (Salwasser 1991).

Although this book discusses mainly forestlands, rangelands, and farmlands, in fact all lands need to be part of the overall management scheme to achieve true biodiversity. Biodiversity has to address the continuum of ecosystems, successional stages, and stand conditions on the landscape.

Much is known about habitat needs of many species of wildlife, especially game species, relative to silviculture, livestock grazing, and farming in various forestlands, rangelands, and farmlands. In recent decades, much has been learned about habitat management for nongame wildlife too. Piecing the literature together produces a mosaic of knowledge about habitat management for biodiversity of wildlife. Management for biodiversity, especially of forests, is long term, during which time new ideas will be formed and old ideas will be altered, abandoned, or reconfirmed. Yet, "to say we don't know enough is to take refuge behind a half-truth and ignore the fact that decisions will be made regardless of the amount of information available" (Thomas 1979a:6).

The term *wildlife* has had many definitions over the years, the narrowest being *game species* of birds and mammals. Now, *wildlife* tends to be defined to include all wild animals. Management for biodiversity includes all native animals and plants occurring naturally in a given area. Wildlife habitat managed for biodiversity must be managed on a landscape basis from large scale to small scale, which requires long-term planning.

In their management plans national forestlands and rangelands are legally required to maintain diverse plant and animal communities (Mealey 1984, Payne 1992: Table A.7). The term *multiple use* has been written into the legal mandate for at least three decades on public land in the United States and Canada. But most wildlifers would agree that until the recent interest in managing for biodiversity, management for wildlife has been mainly incidental to management for other resources, because the direct monetary profit from forest, range, and farm products was more visible than the indirect profit from recreation and tourism and the long-term benefits from maintaining biodiversity. Moreover, the concept of multiple use is based on economics rather than ecology, and thus is inappropriate to today's land-management problems (Grumbine 1992).

The philosophy of wildlife habitat management can be characterized as one of *protection* or *intervention* (Frankel 1983). Both are needed to maximize biodiversity in a human-dominated landscape with reduced amounts of habitat available for protection or natural disturbance. Wildlife biologists should design programs that use compatible natural processes with the least amount of human manipulation to achieve objectives, e.g., by reducing fire suppression to allow fire-dependent plants and animals to thrive in fire-adapted communities. Biologists need to recognize the effects that proposed habitat manipulation will have on all wildlife, not just the target species or community.

Management for wildlife has been described for *featured species* or for *species richness* (U.S. Forest Service 1971, 1973, 1975, Holbrook 1974, Hall and Thomas 1979, Capp et al. 1984, Lipscomb et al. 1984). Management for species richness should be related to management for biodiversity, although diversity includes species abundance and thus is a measure of average rarity within a community (Harris 1984). Unless endangered or threatened, the species featured generally is one with broad habitat needs, so that managing it for maximum population density also benefits many associated species of wildlife.

Wildlife-management goals must consider edge species, interior species, home ranges, minimum viable populations, habitat islands, and connecting corridors. Management for biodiversity is somewhat different from management for species richness. Species richness tends to be highest along edges (*ecotones*); thus, management for species richness implies maximizing edge effect, which excludes the less diverse interior species (Yahner 1988). Management for biodiversity emphasizes interior species by assuming enough ecotones for edge species will result from a mixture of natural features and natural and artificial disturbance of habitats (Fig. 1.1).

The terms *featured species* and *emphasis species* are synonymous, and tend to refer to game species and threatened or endangered

Figure 1.1 Elk grazing in a natural opening next to a coniferous forest in Montana. (*Photo by Mark F. J. Payne.*)

species. Game species typically are associated with edges (Leopold 1933), perhaps partly because they tend to be large and shy and need more food and cover, which edges provide (Hunter 1990). Thus, the terms *featured species* and *species richness* actually differ little in practical application because both often are associated with edge habitats. The term *indicator species* has been misused, with little or no ecological thought involved in their selection (Landres et al. 1988). An indicator species can be used to manage for species richness by representing the needs of other species adapted to similar habitat (Lipscomb et al. 1984). Hence the term can be synonymous with "featured species." In fact, the concept of *management indicator species* evolved from the featured-species concept (Graul and Miller 1984). But the concept of management indicator species seems to be an unproven theory which does little to protect ecosystem functioning (Grumbine 1992). The term *indicator species* can be used to mean a *stenotopic species,* i.e., an ecological indicator species, which is a species with an ecological tolerance so narrow that its abundance indicates certain environmental conditions (Graul et al. 1976, Hunter 1990). Alternatively, it can be used to indicate a *guild indicator species,* i.e., a specific species from a group of species that share a need for common resources in the environment. If *indicator species* refers to interior habitats by focusing on a wildlife species indicative of that habitat and associated wildlife, it relates to the term *biodiversity* because the natural occurrence of edge produces the edge species too.

Some wildlife species are *area-sensitive species* because they are associated with a certain size of habitat. The terms *area-sensitive species, size-dependent species,* and *obligate interior species* are related. Some species are not dominants, but have a role so important that the integrity of the ecosystem depends on it. Such species are called *keystone species* (Hunter 1990). Large animals often are rare in ecosystems but often are keystone species (Soulé 1991). Because their maintenance might be critical to the diversity and integrity of the ecosystem, large animals should be provided with habitat and landscape linkages. *Critical-link species* are vital to ecosystem function (Westman 1985). They might not be keystone species, and often are litter invertebrates and decomposer microorganisms rarely included as threatened or endangered species or in environmental impact statements (Westman 1990). *Indicator species* that are *stenotopic species* because they have a narrow ecological tolerance should be monitored as an index to the quality and quantity of various types of ecosystems. A *flagship species* has high public identity and support. Its management can indirectly facilitate the wise conservation of many other species (Hunter 1990). An *umbrella species* is one that needs a large area that contains hundreds or thousands of lesser known or even unknown species, and thus helps maintain them (Peterson 1988).

Organisms sometimes are referred to as *habitat specialists* or *habitat generalists* relative to their need for a diverse environment (Hunter 1990). Habitat specialists can be subdivided into those needing a diverse environment, such as the woodcock, and those needing a fairly uniform environment, such as the spotted owl and other small carnivores. Habitat generalists, i.e., *eurytopic species* such as large mammals, have a wide tolerance for environmental conditions and can inhabit various habitats. Virtually all species of wildlife with large home ranges are habitat generalists or else they can cross most types of habitat routinely. But the space needs of entire breeding populations should be considered, especially for relatively immobile species with potential for genetic isolation.

Because of the potentially severe contrasts in structural diversity of forests, wildlife will respond as *edge, interior,* or *ubiquitous* (generalist) species. The density and variety of edge species increase with forest fragmentation, interior species decrease, and ubiquitous species are unchanged because they can exploit either edge or interior habitats (Whitcomb et al. 1981). Forest management for biodiversity is a compromise between developing habitat for edge and interior wildlife. Information needed to assess changes in biodiversity can be obtained by (1) assessing the processes and patterns of presettlement vegetation, (2) inventorying the age classes of trees and community diversity, (3) analyzing the existing extent of corridors connecting communities, (4) assessing various wildlife guilds or indicator species to compare their future status resulting from any proposed habitat management (Hillis 1991), (5) determining minimum viable populations, distribution, and desirable population level of the indicator species, and (6) quantifying the habitat parameters for modeling the minimum viable population (Mealey and Horn 1981, Lehmkuhl 1984).

The Nature Conservancy estimates that a representative array of ecosystems will contain 85 to 90 percent of the wildlife species in the region (Noss 1987a). This is the *coarse-filter approach* to saving biological diversity. But some species still can be endangered, so a *fine-filter approach* focuses on preserving such species. Combined, the coarse-filter/fine-filter approach should work well (Hunter 1990).

Alpha diversity, also called species richness, is the diversity within a given habitat (Hunter 1990, Patton 1992). *Beta diversity* is the diversity between different habitats. *Gamma diversity* includes both alpha and beta diversity of a unit separated geographically from other such units, e.g., by latitude. Alpha and vertical (structural) diversity are related, as are beta and horizontal (spatial) diversity. Samson and Knopf (1982) summarized the level of resolution and potential management use for alpha, beta, and gamma diversity, and described case studies of alpha and beta diversity. Most wildlife agencies have emphasized alpha diversity, which favors edge species. Alpha diversity often is measured by the Shannon-Weaver index of abundance and evenness (Hair 1980). Wildlifers historically have focused on alpha and beta diversity; now gamma diversity must be addressed. Conservation of biological diversity will require an understanding of the processes that shaped the habitats and the maintenance of those same processes.

"Balance of nature" is a myth; nature is never balanced because it is changing constantly, if only because succession changes. Thus, management goals must be flexible to accommodate changes in environmental conditions (Landres 1992).

The concept of *dynamic equilibrium* is based on the assumption that a given ecosystem type has a normal composition, structure, and function to which the ecosystem will return once a stress is relieved. In fact, the ecosystem is merely a relatively stable set of species resulting from a unique series of events, but due to spatial variation, temporal variation, and chaotic change, the ecosystem has no single condition or state (Niering 1987, Landres 1992). Biological diversity can be enhanced or maintained by applying some general recommendations (Samson and Knopf 1982, Noss 1983, Probst and Crow 1991, Knopf 1992, Landres 1992, Samson 1992):

1. A regional perspective should be used, beyond the boundaries of specific landowners, and beyond individual forest stands, to assess the cumulative impact of individual projects on regional populations and resources. Biotic integrity must be emphasized; information about biodiversity must conform to biogeographic, rather than political, provinces. Ecosystem and multispecies management must substitute for tree and single-species management. Ecological surveys and inventories must occur to learn what and how much is on the land and where it is. Knowledge of presettlement biotic communities and natural processes should guide restoration and management decisions. Several communities are "natural" in a given area at a given time, with change playing a role (Sprugel 1991). Temporal variation in distribution and abundance of natural resources requires that management plans account for metapopulation structure, succession, cumulative and regional effects, and changing species composition. Practices promoting site-specific (alpha) diversity should be minimized in favor of between-habitat (beta) diversity. Management decisions should progress in a top-down ecological hierarchy, beginning with regional geographic (gamma) diversity of ecosystems.

2. Enough habitat should be provided to maintain species of concern such as large, wide-ranging mammals, not just enough to attract immigrants from more productive habitats. Large, contiguous forest stands, low contrast between adjacent areas, landscape linkages, and other spatial patterns should be created to reduce unnatural frag-

mentation. All stages of succession and all stand conditions should be provided for each forest and range type on a variety of sites.

3. Problem species and ecosystems should be monitored by using guilds if possible or ecosystem health indicators.

4. Biological diversity must be sustainable, because it is critical to a healthy, sustainable environment and human society.

5. Land managers must be kept informed to anticipate and correct problems.

Wildlife management for biodiversity on most forestlands is virtually the opposite of what it is on most wooded rangelands. On most forestlands, fragmentation and simplification (e.g., decline of old-growth characteristics such as large woody debris, snags, den trees, large-diameter trees, old trees, supercanopy trees, etc.) predominate and cause declines in forest-interior wildlife species and increases in edge wildlife species. On many rangelands, lack of fragmentation often predominates and results in increases of interior wildlife species and reductions of edge wildlife species. Important considerations for managing landscapes for biodiversity include (1) assessing successional stages; (2) evaluating the extent of fragmentation as it produces edge habitat and reduces interior habitat; (3) examining the potential to manage wildlife by guild or by ecosystem health indicators; (4) assessing, crudely or otherwise, the minimum viable population needed for the most demanding species; (5) determining the approximate size, shape, distribution, and abundance of habitat reserves needed; and (6) habitat monitoring and gap analysis.

Succession and Stand Condition

Whereas forestlands can have at least three layers of vegetation (ground layer, shrub layer, and canopy), rangelands and farmlands tend to have one or two (ground layer and perhaps shrub layer). Farming is an effort to maintain the plant community in the early successional stage of grass/forb for crops and pasture. Range-management efforts generally try to sustain rangelands in grassland stages that promote high forage, watershed, and recreational values. Such efforts are highly successful on farmlands, which are privately owned, and less successful on rangeland, much of which is publicly owned and contains a substantial shrub component. For wildlife, a variety of habitat conditions is needed, some of which must be extensive to include viable populations of interior wildlife.

Unless the process is interrupted, shade-intolerant plant communities ultimately are replaced by more tolerant plant communities in a process called *succession,* until the climax community is attained. The climax community for a given region usually is limited by climate. *Climax* refers to the last stage of plant succession in a given biome. It is the tundra in the tundra biome, the desert in the desert biome, the grassland in the grassland biome, the coniferous forest in the coniferous forest biome, the deciduous forest in the deciduous forest biome, and so forth. More specifically, the climax flora comprises a particular group of dominant plants, e.g., the sugar maple–basswood community and associated trees in northern areas of the deciduous forest biome or the blue grama–buffalograss community, and associated grasses and forbs of the shortgrass prairie. The transition zone where edges mix is an *ecotone.* A specific animal community associates with a specific stage (*sere*) of succession and its ecotone. As plant communities succeed to other plant communities, so too do the associated animal communities. Replacing one sere by another, e.g., via silvicultural treatment on forestlands or brush control on rangelands, will replace one animal community by another. Succession can proceed by *autogenic* forces caused by plants and animals, or by *allogenic* forces caused by outside influences such as fire or wind.

Grassland successional stages usually include a progression from bare soil to annual plants (grasses and forbs) to perennial forbs to short-lived perennial grasses to sod-forming grasses or bunchgrasses that eventually maintain a relatively stable equilibrium (Coupland 1992). Succession of plant communities and assemblages is strongly influenced by soil type and soil moisture gradients. Such gradients affect topographic position in the rolling, undulating terrain characteristic of grasslands. Topographic positions which affect plants that grow on them and their associated successional stages include top slopes (more xeric knolls and upper slopes), midslopes (xeric to mesic), and lower slopes and valleys (mesic). Differences in intensity of insolation between north-facing and south-facing slopes increase with increasing latitudes so that the effects of aspect are more evident in the Canadian portion than farther south.

In shrubland and woodland vegetation types, succession advances from bare soil to grass/forb stages to shrub or woody plant dominance. In the pinyon-juniper ecosystem for example, secondary succession after fire is as follows: (1) bare soil; (2) annual stage; (3) annual/ perennial forb stage; (4) perennial forb/grass half-shrub; (5) shrub stage or perennial grass stage; (6) pinyon-juniper woodland.

Biodiversity is complicated in grassland types because of the highly developed ecotypic differentiation (Risser 1988), but certainly habitat size and horizontal and vertical diversity are major determinants. Biodiversity of shrubland and woodland types would be determined by the amount of habitat saved for interior species as well as the size and arrangement of openings created for edge species.

Forest plant communities progress through four seral stages of succession (Patton 1992): bare soil, grass/forb, shrub, and tree. The tree seral stage progresses through four general stages of stand development (Oliver and Larson 1990):

1. *Stand initiation stage,* whereby new species and individuals continue to appear for several years after a disturbance.
2. *Stem exclusion stage,* whereby after several years no new individuals appear, some die, and survivors grow larger and variably in this brushy stage, shading the forest floor.
3. *Understory reinitiation stage,* whereby shade-tolerant herbs, shrubs, and tree seedlings again appear from 60 to 150 years later, depending on site and forest type, but grow little.
4. *Old-growth stage,* whereby overstory trees die in an irregular fashion and some of the understory trees grow to the overstory.

The understory reinitiation stage generally contains fewer animal species than the stand initiation stage but more than the stem exclusion stage. The old-growth stage generally contains more plant and animal species than the stem exclusion or understory reinitiation stages, but less than the stand initiation stage (Manuwal and Huff 1987, Oliver and Larson 1990). [Species richness of plants and animals does not differ among unmanaged Douglas-fir forests in the young (25–80 years), mature (80–200 years), and old-growth (more than 200 years) stages in western Oregon and Washington (Hansen et al. 1991) and perhaps elsewhere.] These four stages of stand development often are further divided into six structural stages, also called *stand conditions* (Thomas et al. 1979d, Hall et al. 1985a): grass/forb, shrub, open sapling/pole, closed sapling/pole sawtimber, large sawtimber, and old growth (Table 1.1). These can be further refined (Towry 1984): grass/forb, shrub/seedling, sapling/pole with less than 40 percent canopy closure, sapling/pole with 40 to 70 percent canopy closure, sapling/pole with more than 70 percent canopy closure, mature with less than 40 percent canopy closure, mature with 40 to 70 percent canopy closure, mature with more than 70 percent canopy closure, old growth. Wildlife species are distributed by these stand conditions and their edges (Table 1.2) (Crawford and Titterington 1979).

Wildlife species richness is enhanced mostly by early (grass/forb and shrub) and late (large sawtimber and old growth) forest successional stages and stand conditions, with relatively few species in the intermediate (open sapling/pole and closed sapling/pole sawtimber) conditions (Hall and Thomas 1979, Hall et al. 1985a). Stand condition also can be categorized as in Table 1.3 (Harris 1984).

TABLE 1.1   Forest Stand Conditions and Related Environmental Variables in a
Temperate Coniferous Forest

			Stand condition			
Environmental variable	Grass/ forb	Shrub	Open sapling/ pole	Closed sapling/ pole saw- timber	Large saw- timber	Old growth
Plant diversity	3	4	4	1	3	5
Vegetation height	1	2	3	4	5	5
Canopy volume	1	2	3	4	5	4
Canopy closure	1	2	3	5	4	4
Structural diversity	1	2	4	2	3	5
Herbage production	5	4	3	1	2	3
Browse production	1	5	3	1	2	3
Animal diversity	2	5	4	1	3	4
Woody debris (natural)	5	4	3	2	3	5
Woody debris (intensive management)	1	1	1	2	2	5

Note: Higher numbers indicate better development.
SOURCE: Adapted from Hall et al. (1985a).

Succession and stand condition are influenced by such environmental factors as soil type, moisture, microclimate, slope, aspect, elevation, and temperature (Hall et al. 1985a). These conditions can be advanced or retarded by natural or human means, e.g., mechanical, chemical, fire, wind, flooding, insects, disease, grazing, irrigating, planting, fertilizing (Table 1.4) (Thomas et al. 1979d). For maximum biodiversity, all successional stages and stand conditions that occur in each forest type in a given biome must be represented in various size, shape, and distribution. Such representation influences distribution and abundance of plants and animals. Ecosystems on some sites are more prone to disturbance by wind, fire, landslide, disease, and insects. A species' presence or absence might depend more on topographic position or aspect than on the age or condition of the forest occurring there (Harris 1984).

For plant species diversity, *distribution* refers to the spatial arrangement of species, individuals, or age classes (Mealey 1984). Spatial patterns have two dimensions: vertical and horizontal (Whittaker 1975). Wildlife diversity, particularly of birds, correlates

TABLE 1.2   **Response of Birds to Habitat Modification, by Response Time, Bird Habitat Group, and Silvicultural Treatment**

				Treatment				
Response time (yr)	Un-even-age	Large-diameter limit	Thinning sawlogs	Thinning poles	Shelter-wood cut	Commercial clearcut and small-diameter limit	Silvicultural clearcut	Cut, site preparation, and plant
Slash/Open Ground Group								
0 to 5 ±	R	R	R-O	O	A-C	A-C	A	O
5 to 30 ±	R	R	R	R	R	O	O	O
30 to 100 ±	R	R	—	R	R	R	R	R
Bramble/Herbaceous Group								
0 to 5 ±	O	O	O	O	O	A-C	A	R-O
5 to 30 ±	O	O	R-O	R-O	C	R-O	R-O	R-O
30 to 100 ±	O	O	—	O	R	O	C	O
Shrub/Sapling Group								
0 to 5 ±	R	O	O	R	O	R-O	R-O	O
5 to 30 ±	R	O	R-O	R-O	C	A-C	A-C	C-R
30 to 100 ±	R	O	—	O	R	R-O	O	O
Lower-Canopy Group								
0 to 5 ±	A	R	R	C	C	R-O	O	O
5 to 30 ±	A	R	C	C	O	R-O	R	R
30 to 100 ±	A	C	—	A-C	C-R	R-O	C	C
Upper-Canopy Group								
0 to 5 ±	A	R	R	R	C	R-O	O	O
5 to 30 ±	A	R	C	C	O	R-O	O	O
30 to 100 ±	A	C	—	A-C	C-R	R-O	C	C
Cavity-Nesting Group								
0 to 5 ±	O	R	R-O	R-O	O	R	R-O	O
5 to 30 ±	O	R	R-O	R-O	O	R	O	O
30 to 100 ±	O	R	—	R	O	R	O	O

Note: Response in the number of species and density: A = abundant, C = common, R = regular, O = occasional.

SOURCE: Adapted from Crawford and Titterington (1979).

positively with vertical structure. Wildlife distribution correlates positively with horizontal structure. On rangelands, vertical structure involves layers of bare soil, forbs, shortgrasses, midgrasses, tallgrasses, and sometimes shrubs or other woody plants; horizontal structure is the arrangement of bare ground and patches of different-sized

TABLE 1.3   Stand Condition of Douglas-Fir Forests Relative to Approximate Age and Size of Trees

Stand condition	Age (yr)	Size (cm)*
Regeneration	0–10	—
Seedling/sapling	10–50	13
Pole timber	50–100	25
Sawtimber	100–150	40
Large sawtimber	150–250	55
Old growth	250–450	75

*Depends on site conditions and climate.
SOURCE: Adapted from Harris (1984).

TABLE 1.4   Anticipated Changes in Stand Condition Due to Management Activities

Management action	Stand condition					
	Grass/ forb	Shrub/ seedling	Pole/ sapling	Young	Mature	Old growth
Shrub control						
Herbicides	>	>	>	<	<	<
Mechanical control	<	<	NA	<	<	<
Controlled burn						
Cold burn	<	<	>	>	<	<
Hot burn	<	<	<	<	<	<
Fertilization	<	>	>	>	>	O
Grazing and browsing (moderate rates)						
Cattle and sheep	<	>	O	O	<	<
Goats	O	<	O	O	<	<
Deer and elk	<	>	O	O	<	<
Planting						
Trees	>	>	NA	NA	>	>
Shrubs	>	<	NA	NA	NA	NA
Grasses/forbs	>	<	NA	>	>	O
Regeneration cut						
Clearcut	NA	NA	NA	<	<	<
Shelterwood	NA	NA	NA	>	<	<
Seed tree	NA	NA	NA	<	<	<
Salvage	NA	NA	<	<	<	<
Thinning (including single-tree selection harvest)	NA	>	>	>	>	O

Note: > = advances succession; < = retards succession; O = no effect on succession; NA = not applicable.
SOURCE: Adapted from Thomas et al. (1979d).

TABLE 1.5   Contrast of Edges between Plant Ecosystems and Structural Stages of Timbered Stands

Successional stage or stand condition	Edge contrast						
	OG	M	P	SSS	GF	Shr	Gra
Old growth (OG)	—	L	M	H	H	M	H
Mature (M)	L	—	M	M	H	M	H
Pole (P)	M	M	—	M	H	M	H
Seedling/sapling/ shrub (SSS)	H	M	M	—	L	L	L
Grass/forb (GF)	H	H	H	L	—	M	L
Shrublands (Shr)	M	M	M	L	M	—	M
Grasslands (Gra)	H	H	H	L	L	M	—

Note: H = high edge contrast, M = medium edge contrast, L = low edge contrast, — = no edge contrast.
SOURCE: Adapted from Mealey (1984).

grasses, or it can be intermixed grazed and ungrazed patches of grasslands. On forestlands, vertical structure involves layers of vegetation in uneven-aged forests; horizontal structure or patchiness involves trees occurring in even-aged stands, each stand of a different age (Mealey 1984). The stands can be in different structural conditions. The more successional stages or stand conditions in an area, the greater will be the edge effect. Conversely, the fewer successional stages or stand conditions in an area, the greater will be the interior effect, i.e., interior wildlife species will prosper and edge species will not. The degree of edge contrast between two successional stages or stand conditions generally can be referred to as high, medium, or low (Table 1.5) (Mealey 1984). Low contrast would benefit interior wildlife more, and edge wildlife less, than high contrast.

Standard indices used to measure wildlife species diversity can be used to estimate the diversity of landscapes by treating each successional stage or kind of stand (e.g., oak stand or large stand or old stand) as if it were a different species and by using its total area to represent its abundance (Hunter 1990). But comparisons between landscapes must be consistent; the more fine the division of successional stages or kinds of stands, the more "diversity" will be calculated.

Edge Versus Interior

Managing or preserving large habitat areas for interior wildlife species generally conflicts with that for game species (Faaborg 1980, Yahner 1988). Management for game species generally favors forest fragmentation to increase edge (Leopold 1933, Hunter 1990). A landscape that seems fragmented to some small animals will seem unfragmented to some large animals (Harris and Silva-Lopez 1992).

Fragmented forest and *patchy forest* are not synonymous (Harris and Silva-Lopez 1992). A patchy forest contains heterogeneous natural gradations of forest patches and associated plants and animals. A fragmented forest contains segregated forested tracts in a formerly forested landscape. A naturally patchy forest can be transformed into a fragmented forest.

Regressive fragmentation results when habitat is cleared from one direction and the front edge of the habitat is simply pushed back. *Enveloping fragmentation* results when clearing surrounds the habitat, causing it to contract. *Divisive fragmentation* results when a road or other right-of-way bisects habitat and obstructs movement of organisms. *Intrusive fragmentation* results when habitat is removed or greatly altered from within, as from patchcuts or food plot cuttings. *Encroaching fragmentation* occurs when habitat is removed from both sides of a linear habitat, leaving a corridor of riparian or other linear habitat connected to larger patches at each end (Harris and Silva-Lopez 1992).

The two components of habitat fragmentation are *habitat loss* and *habitat insularization* (Wilcove et al. 1986). Fragmentation can lead to local extinction via four means (Wilcove 1987):

1. A species can be excluded initially from the protected fragments.

2. A decrease in fragment size or heterogeneity can eliminate suitable habitat.

3. Smaller, isolated populations in fragments risk extirpation from catastrophes, demographic variability, genetic deterioration, or social dysfunction.

4. Fragments can disrupt important ecological relationships, causing deleterious effects of edge environments and external alien environments, and loss of key species that leads to secondary extirpation of other species dependent on the key species.

Fragmentation can be hard or soft. *Hard fragmentation* produces the most contrast and edge because it involves the interruption or separation of a contiguous ecosystem by another ecosystem—for example, by intermixing agricultural land with a forest, or by roads and powerlines cutting through forestland, or even by severe patchy alteration of age classes, e.g., patchcuts. *Soft fragmentation* involves, for example, different age classes or forest types within a contiguous forest, or different grassland types within a contiguous rangeland. Extensive fragmentation is natural in some regions. For example, habitats in the northern Rocky Mountains were highly fragmented due to numerous small fires; old-growth lodgepole pine might not have occurred in some areas but the structural characteristics (large trees and logs, snags) of other old-growth types survive repeated burns (pers. comm. F. B. Samson, U.S. Forest Service, Missoula, MT, 1992). Due to excessive unnatural hard fragmentation of wildlife habitat in North America and elsewhere and consequent proliferation of edge species at the expense of interior species, the wildlife goal should be to manage for biodiversity, which means deemphasizing edge and emphasizing interior in some regions to achieve a more natural balance of habitat and wildlife. Presettlement vegetation is a good template but not an absolute model for modern distribution and abundance of wildlife.

Some ecotones are abrupt, as a lake and forest separated by a cliff, and some are extensive, as one forest or range type extending into another. The internal structure of a forest edge next to an open area is dominated by a zone of shrubs and small trees called a *mantel,* that reduces the impact of outside weather into the forest (Forman and Godron 1986). A perennial herbaceous zone called the *saum* lies just outside the mantel next to the open area. Edges can be high- or low-contrast, and abrupt, feathered, or mosaic (Fig. 1.2). Edges can be inherent or induced (Thomas et al. 1979c). *Inherent edges* are relatively stable and permanent features of the landscape resulting from the meeting of at least two plant communities or topographic features. If altered, inherent edges ultimately return to their earlier veg-

Figure 1.2 Black bear (blond color phase) exploiting feathered grassland/shrubland/ forestland edge in Montana. (*Photo by Mark F. J. Payne.*)

etative state. *Induced edges* result from the meeting of successional stages caused by alteration of vegetation naturally (e.g., by wildfires, wind, insects, disease) or by humans (e.g., logging, grazing, herbicides). Induced edges are relatively temporary and often abrupt; they can be a barrier to the dispersal and distribution of wildlife.

In hilly and mountainous areas, north and south slopes generally show large differences in microclimate and habitat diversity. But where precipitation is abundant and cloudy weather ameliorates climatic differences between north and south slopes, such as on the west side of the North Cascades, habitat is similar on both slopes (Emmingham et al. 1992).

Wildlife diversity tends to be high along edges because some animals need access to two habitats or even three or more (places where three or more habitats meet are called *coverts*), some use only the ecotone, and some extend into the ecotone from adjacent habitats (Hunter 1990). Many species of plants and animals avoid edges. But edges can be ecological traps (Gates and Gysel 1978) because predation rates can be higher (Gates and Gysel 1978, Chasko and Gates 1982, Wilcove et al. 1986, Temple 1987, Andren and Angelstam 1988, Prins and Iason 1989, Yahner et al. 1989) and more nests are parasitized by brown-headed cowbirds (Gates and Gysel 1978, Brittingham and Temple 1983). Evidently not all edges sustain predation rates higher than the interior (Yahner and Wright 1985, Angelstam 1986, Ratti and Reese 1988, Small and Hunter 1988, Noss 1991a). Nonetheless, wildlife management practices maximizing habitat fragmentation for interspersion have threatened numerous species of eastern forest birds with extinction due to nest predation and parasitism, e.g., Kirtland's warbler and Bachman's warbler (Harris and Silva-Lopez 1992). Forest fragmentation also evidently reduces decomposition rates (Klein 1989). Schonewald-Cox and Buechner (1992) listed other major effects of landscape fragmentation.

Ungulates such as elk and white-tailed deer can reduce or eliminate regeneration of many plants that support other wildlife (e.g., Harmon and Franklin 1983, Alverson et al. 1988, Anderson and Katz 1993). Even for game species, no more edge should be maintained than the cutting option for woodlands produces (Gullion 1984). Hunters and predators hunt along edges, game and many nongame species are attracted to edges, and that is where most of them will die. Feathered edges have lower predation rates than abrupt edges do (Ratti and Reese 1988). The longer the edge is around a forested area, the more likely will be the intrusion of exotic plants and animals, poachers, fire, pesticides, and other disruptive agents (Janzen 1986, Usher 1988).

The relationship of all vertebrate wildlife to stand size is assumed to be reasonably indicated by bird species richness (Thomas et al. 1979c).

Species of birds intolerant of fragmentation tend to be highly migratory and specialized for forest interior habitat, where they build open nests on or near the ground, and have small clutch sizes and numbers of clutches per year (Greenberg 1980, Whitcomb et al. 1981). They might be especially vulnerable to high rates of nest predation and brood parasitism (Askins et al. 1990). Factors influencing the number of bird species breeding in interior forests include size, isolation, structure, and floristics of the habitat (Lynch and Whigham 1984). Effects of forest and rangeland fragmentation are species-specific.

The extensive fragmentation which has occurred in eastern forests generally has produced a patchy landscape of woodlots surrounded by agricultural land, providing relatively static and simple systems (Lehmkuhl and Ruggiero 1991). By contrast, western forests are at an early stage of fragmentation, with dynamic and complex systems. Boundaries between old growth and clearcuts in eastern and western forests are distinct initially but become increasingly ambiguous as succession and stand conditions develop; woodlot boundaries remain distinct and relatively unchanged.

In western forests, abundance and richness of vertebrates are weakly related to stand size and isolation, although some negative effects have been identified for some species (Rosenberg and Raphael 1986). The lack of a better relationship might be due to the packing of animals into remaining habitat before populations ultimately decline, as Whitcomb et al. (1981) found in eastern forests. Nevertheless, Rosenberg and Raphael (1986) recommended excluding less than 20 ha of Douglas-fir forest as a viable stand because it tends to lack the full complement of vertebrate species. This should be increased to 50 ha for stands more than 50 percent isolated. Thus, for example, no stand less than 20 ha (or 50 ha with more than 50 percent insularity) could be considered representative old growth because some of the old-growth characteristics are missing from so small a stand.

The minimum size of forest blocks that must be maintained for best biodiversity is not well defined, and it varies substantially with adjacent habitat. Some patches (woodlots) of forestland in agricultural landscapes must be at least 97 ha for at least a 50 percent chance of supporting a breeding population of birds (Table 1.6) (Temple 1988). Neotropical migrant birds restricted to the forest interior for breeding are most abundant on large forested areas of over 70 ha on agricultural land, much less common on intermediate fragments of 6 to 14 ha, and rare on small forest fragments of 1 to 5 ha (Table 1.7) (Whitcomb et al. 1981). Ubiquitous species are equally abundant in forest tracts of all sizes. Most permanent residents use edge and interior. Of 25 species of area-sensitive neotropical migrants for which estimates of 50 percent probability of occurrence are available,

TABLE 1.6   Minimum Size of Woodlot That Has
a 50 Percent Chance of Supporting a Breeding
Population of Some Birds

Species	Woodlot size (ha)
Wood thrush	8
Hairy woodpecker	16
Yellow-throated vireo	16
Scarlet tanager	16
Veery	24
Tufted titmouse	32
Blue-gray gnatcatcher	32
Ovenbird	32
Least flycatcher	64
Chestnut-sided warbler	64
Mourning warbler	64
Cerulean warbler	81
Hooded warbler	81
American redstart	97
Acadian flycatcher	97
Pileated woodpecker	97

SOURCE: Adapted from Temple (1988).

Robbins (1988) predicted that 20 can use areas as small as 250 ha, 15 can use 100 ha, 13 can use 40 ha, 10 can use 20 ha, and 4 can use 4 ha. Area and structural characteristics of the habitat must be considered when comparing breeding bird densities in small woodlands and in more extensive forests (Oelke 1966).

Askins et al. (1987) reported four of seven forest-interior birds studied were not found in areas of less than 187 ha (Table 1.8). At least 3000 ha are needed to retain all species of the forest-breeding birds in the eastern deciduous forest of North America (Table 1.9) (Robbins et al. 1989). Each order of magnitude that reduces the area will reduce the number of area-sensitive birds by about 50 percent (Robbins 1988). Birds breeding in small woodlots might incorporate several patches within 2 km of their territory (Howe 1984, Robbins et al. 1989). Large reserves (over 300 km^2 on the island of Java) are needed for viable populations of all species of forest raptors (Thiollay and Meyburg 1988).

Unlike closed-forest, shrubland, or woodland ecosystems, where the native consumers are generally less mobile, grassland species are highly mobile because their food, water, and cover are more variably impacted by weather patterns and climatic extremes. Patch sizes needed vary considerably among wildlife forms occupying grasslands. Size of the area needed to support 100 wide-ranging pronghorns might be 2000 ha, whereas meadowlarks need less than 1 ha, horned larks and grasshopper sparrows more than 1 ha, Henslow's sparrows

TABLE 1.7   Tolerance of Forest Birds to Fragmentation in Deciduous Forestland on Agricultural Land

	Island size*			Tolerance to fragmentation†
	1–5 ha	6–14 ha	>70 ha	
Forest-interior species				
Black-and-white warbler	0	0	9	0.00
Worm-eating warbler	0	0	8	0.00
Pileated woodpecker	0	0	2	0.00
Ovenbird	0	2	21	0.10
Hooded warbler	1	1	4	0.25
Kentucky warbler	0	2	6	0.33
Scarlet tanager	5	6	14	0.43
Acadian flycatcher	4	4	9	0.44
Hairy woodpecker	0	1	2	0.50
White-breasted nuthatch	0	2	2	1.00
Forest-interior and edge species				
Blue-gray gnatcatcher	0	0	6	0.00
Yellow-throated vireo	0	0	2	0.00
Yellow-billed cuckoo	1	1	7	0.14
Red-eyed vireo	6	8	23	0.35
Wood thrush	14	14	23	0.61
Tufted titmouse	10	13	15	0.87
Mourning dove	6	8	9	0.89
Blue jay	8	10	10	1.00
Red-bellied woodpecker	7	9	9	1.00
Cardinal	14	13	11	1.18
Eastern wood pewee	6	12	10	1.20
Carolina chickadee	11	11	9	1.22
Downy woodpecker	8	10	8	1.25
Rufous-sided towhee	9	12	9	1.33
Great crested flycatcher	2	10	6	1.67
Carolina wren	9	16	9	1.78
Common flicker	9	11	6	1.83
Gray catbird	14	7	3	2.33
Field-edge species‡				
Common crow	10	9	9	1.00
American robin	8	5	3	1.67
Common grackle	6	6	3	2.00
Starling	11	10	3	3.33

*Numbers of presumed territories in 60-min point surveys on the 10 islands of each given size class.

†Number of presumed territories per point sampled on the 6- to 14-ha islands divided by the number per point sampled on the >70-ha islands.

‡No edge species were considered to be true island inhabitants. But the four species in the field-edge category were abundant enough that their residence in islands could not be excluded.

SOURCE: Adapted from Whitcomb et al. (1981).

TABLE 1.8 Some Forest-Interior Birds Found Only in Larger Forests

Species	Patch size (ha)		No. forests
	Minimum	Average	
Worm-eating warbler	21	477	23
Blue-gray gnatcatcher	50	1086	7
Brown creeper	50	818	13
Black-throated green warbler	187	354	5
Hermit thrush	323	791	3
Yellow-throated vireo	347	1366	7
Cerulean warbler	647	1634	5

SOURCE: Adapted from Askins et al. (1987).

and upland sandpipers more than 10 ha, and greater prairie chickens more than 150 ha (Sampson 1980, Risser 1988). Proximity of patches to each other also plays an important role in determining presence or absence of a species. For example, greater prairie chickens need patches of 300 ha in size within 14 km of each other (Sampson 1980). In shrubland and woodland types, 40 to 100 ha probably would support most interior bird species. For a species such as sage grouse, at least 3 to 4 km (1000 to 2300 ha) surrounding a lek might be needed to support a breeding population (Autenrieth et al. 1982). Of all bird species breeding on tallgrass prairies, nearly 67 percent are habitat-size-dependent (Samson 1980). West (1993) discussed other considerations for biodiversity of rangelands.

The minimum size at which the forest-edge woody plant community can be differentiated from the forest-interior community seems to be about 2.3 ha (Vestal and Heermans 1945, Forman and Elfstrom 1975, Levenson 1981), depending on shape (Temple 1986). The forest edge is more exposed than the forest interior to the drying and other effects of sun and wind, so the forest interior is more mesic and shade-tolerant, with different plant and animal communities. Islands of forest less than about 2.3 ha function essentially as edge communities of mixed intolerant and residual tolerant species of woody plants, with a decline in their species richness of woody plants until the island's size reaches about 3.8 ha (Levenson 1981). Thus, management efforts must include protecting the less disturbed woodlots larger than about 4 ha (Levenson 1981). Forest vegetative edge effects extend at least 10 to 15 m into a forest stand on the east, north, and south sides, and up to 30 m on the west side (Ranney et al. 1981). Simulations indicate that reducing island size below 4 to 5 ha leads to a loss of shade-tolerant species in predictable sequence.

The U.S. Forest Service has limited clearcut size to 16.3 ha, which does mean that distances to edge are generally less than 70 m

TABLE 1.9 Forest Areas Where Probability of Occurrence (PO) Is at Maximum (100%) and at 50% of Maximum (Suggested Minimum Area for Breeding) for 26 Species of Area-Sensitive Birds

Species	Area (ha) 100% PO	Area (ha) 50% PO	Area (ha) of 3 smallest isolated forests where a species was detected on ≥ 2 visits 1	2	3
Permanent residents					
Tufted titmouse	52	0.5	0.8	0.6	0.2
Red-bellied woodpecker	85	0.3	1.8	1.6	0.2
Hairy woodpecker	200	6.8	26.7	16.1	10.4
Pileated woodpecker	3000 +	165.0	65.2	64.3	42.2
Short-distance migrants					
American crow	10	0.2	0.5	0.2	0.2
White-breasted nuthatch	300	3.0	4.2	3.0	1.6
Red-shouldered hawk	3000	225.0	52.0	40.5	39.7
Neotropical migrants					
Great-crested flycatcher	72	0.3	2.5	0.8	0.8
Veery	250	20.0	24.1	11.3	9.3
Kentucky warbler	300	17.0	11.0	10.4	9.3
Ovenbird	450	6.0	2.5	1.2	0.8
Wood thrush	500	1.0	0.8	0.8	0.2
Acadian flycatcher	3000 +	15.0	4.5	2.6	0.2
Black-and-white warbler	3000 +	220.0	493.0	208.0	208.0
Black-throated blue warbler	3000 +	1000.0	1500.0	1500.0	1120.0
Blue-gray gnatcatcher	3000 +	15.0	23.0	10.1	6.8
Canada warbler	3000 +	400.0	883.0	883.0	187.0
Cerulean warbler	3000 +	700.0	1500.0	637.0	138.0
Louisiana waterthrush	3000 +	350.0	184.1	24.7	24.7
Northern parula	3000 +	520.0	516.0	415.0	10.1
Northern waterthrush	3000 +	200.0	187.0	187.0	24.1
Red-eyed vireo	3000 +	2.5	0.7	0.5	0.5
Rose-breasted grosbeak	3000 +	1.0	123.0	24.1	11.3
Summer tanager	3000 +	40.0	47.8	47.8	24.7
Worm-eating warbler	3000 +	150.0	30.4	29.1	21.0

Note: Area-sensitive species are those species whose probability of occurrence increases with area.

SOURCE: Adapted from Robbins et al. (1989).

(Williamson and Hirth 1985). Wind and sun dry out edges exposed to them, and turn mesic forest into xeric edge (Ranney et al. 1981). Tree species on south and west edges are the most xeric and rarely extend into mesic forest interiors. Species on north and east edges are more shade-tolerant and might extend into island interiors. Other tree species are ubiquitous. Except for ubiquitous tree species, the proportion of these edges depends on the shape, orientation, and minimum width of forest islands. Islands that are small, narrow, irregularly shaped, or with much exposure to the south, west, or southwest will contain a relatively high proportion of tree species in the most xeric, edge-oriented group. In addition to edges transverse to the prevailing wind, other conditions that increase edge effect include habitats located at high elevations on slopes, high contrast of structure and species composition of adjacent habitats, the edge structure itself, and habitats (Morrison et al. 1992).

Edges of forest stands can be divided into three general types (Oliver and Larson 1990):

1. Those resulting from adjacent stands of the same age caused by the same disturbance, but with different growth rates and/or spacings due to different site conditions

2. Those resulting from a forest stand next to an area that does not support a forest (e.g., field, stream)

3. Those resulting from adjacent forest stands of different ages

Edge effects on vegetation generally extend at least two tree heights into the forest stand. For example, that is about 120 m for 60-m-high Douglas-fir; thus, a forest fragment of less than 30 ha consists only of edge (Franklin and Forman 1987, Morrison et al. 1992). Thus, to provide interior habitat in old-growth forests of the western Douglas-fir forests, patch size would have to be at least 30 ha, although smaller patches are important as a network of dispersal for many wildlife species.

The "three-tree-height" rule of thumb has been used to estimate how far climactic effects of a surrounding clearcut will penetrate an adjacent old-growth stand (Fritschen et al. 1971, Harris et al. 1982, Harris 1984). But because such penetration is influenced by the shape of the clearcut, the distance, or threshold thickness, at which a central point would be buffered from winds from any direction is about six tree heights—i.e., three tree heights from each direction (Harris 1984). A circular 10-ha stand of old growth with trees 60 m tall surrounded by a clearcut would contain no interior because the strip to buffer wind would be 360 m in diameter, which is about 10 ha. If trees are 60 m high, the buffer zone of three tree heights from any direction would be 180 m, so that a circular stand of old growth next to a clearcut would have to be 3847 ha (7000 m in diameter) to reduce the 180-m buffer strip to 10 percent of the total area. But the surrounding buffer strip can be mature rather than old growth so long as the trees are tall and dense enough to prevent light and wind from penetrating below the canopy of the enclosed old-growth stand (Harris 1984).

The edge width is best defined by the functional use of edges by wildlife (Yahner 1988). Edge effects typically can be measured 200 m into a forest (Temple and Cary 1988). Some evidence indicates that the detrimental edge effects of parasitism by brown-headed cowbirds or predation on open nests of forest birds might extend 600 m into the forest, requiring forest tracts to be more than 100 ha before forest-interior habitat is found (Wilcove 1985, 1990, Wilcove et al. 1986, Robinson 1990), although major vegetation changes caused by edges extend only 10 to 30 m inside the forest, depending on exposure (Wales 1972, Ranney et al. 1981). Gates and Mosher (1981) found that the vegetative structural width of a field/forest edge was less than 13 m but that the spatial distribution of bird nests was more than 64 m. A similar trend operates from the forest edge into an adjacent grassland (Johnson and Temple 1986). Shape of the forest influences the interior core of it; long, narrow forests could have no core or interior wildlife while a more square or circular shape of the same area would have a core and interior wildlife (Levenson 1981, Temple 1986).

Forests of less than 30,000 to 50,000 ha might show considerable edge effect (Wilcove 1987). Alverson et al. (1988) recommended that some large (200 to 400 km^2) contiguous blocks of mature forest be established to reduce white-tailed deer populations to the two to four deer per square kilometer of presettlement time in Wisconsin. Their abnormally high densities can eliminate much of the ground and shrub layers on which various other wildlife depend. Such a low deer density might allow the reintroduction of the indigenous moose, which cannot survive brainworm infections contracted as a result of high deer densities (>3.9 deer per 1 km^2) (Parker 1990).

Edge effect will be increased with (1) edges transverse to prevailing windstorms; (2) high contrast of structure and species composition of adjacent vegetation types (the greater the contrast of vegetation height, e.g., stand age, the greater the edge effect); (3) the structure of the edge itself; and (4) forests located at high elevations on slopes (Morrison et al. 1992).

Most large tracts of forestland in the United States occur on federal lands (U.S. Forest Service 1981). But most forestland (61 percent) is not federally owned, and much of that 61 percent is privately owned small parcels. Most management for interior wildlife species in the United States tends to occur on the federal lands, but most of that is fragmented with logging roads; logging and pulping operations; rights-of-way for highways, railroads, and powerlines; and interspersed private ownership. To complicate matters, many interior species are neotropical migrating birds dependent on winter habitat outside North America. Interior habitat should be large enough to provide at least four major functions (Forman 1990): (1) linking headwaters or low-order stream networks; (2) maintaining habitat for wide-ranging species or those with a large home range that do not readily cross fragments; (3) maintaining habitat for species requiring interior or remoteness; (4) enhancing the natural disturbance regimes in which most species evolved.

Forest types that historically have been influenced by extensive natural disturbance such as wildfire are likely to be extensive enough to have an interior relatively uninfluenced by edge effects. Such forests will contain obligate interior wildlife species. Forest types that historically have been influenced by patchy natural disturbance such as wind are less likely to be extensive enough to have vast interiors devoid of edge effects. Obligate interior wildlife species might not have evolved with such forest types; managing such forests for interior habitat might be superfluous. Fast-growing, shade-intolerant forest types also might contain no substantial interior habitat because their fast dynamics produce patchiness. Likewise, forested areas with substantial topographical variation in a relatively small area or forests growing on a variety of glacial soils left in a relatively small area might not develop any substantial interior in which obligate interior wildlife species could have evolved. Management for biodiversity should be geared to emulate natural disturbance for a given forest type.

A circle is the surface with the least amount of edge per unit area. The less a stand's shape diverges from a circle, the less edge it will have per unit area—an important consideration in managing for interior or edge species. Also, a circular shape minimizes reduction of patch size by windthrow (Samson et al. 1989). When the long axis of a rectangle is much longer than the short axis, the edge-to-area ratio becomes substantially larger. Harvest units in forests or habitat treatment on rangelands with shapes approximating such a rectangle, but with convoluted edges, have the greatest edge-to-area ratio, and have more public appeal because such edges appear more natural than straight edges. The size of a stand, harvest operation, or rangeland habitat treatment affects how much edge it has. The amount of edge is increased by dissecting a forest or rangeland into a mosaic of many small stands. Such dissection, as noted above, is called *fragmentation*.

An index can be calculated to relate edge length to area for various shapes of harvest units planned or in place (Patton 1975):

$$\text{Index} = \frac{\text{edge length}}{2\sqrt{\text{area} \times \pi}}$$

The index for a circle is 1, so the closer the index is to 1, the less edge and the more interior (if large enough) it would have. The lengths of natural and induced edges must be added together (Thomas et al. 1979c). The equation can be modified for an ellipse, which still allows access to the edge from the center of large clearcuts, and serves as a gauge to measure optimal stand shape with given area (Marcot and Meretsky 1983). An ellipse is a more probable shape of home range for wildlife.

Guilds

Practical habitat management for diverse wildlife populations suggests that they be grouped into *guilds* by life-form based on habitat needs for reproduction and feeding (Hall and Thomas 1979, Short and Burnham 1982, Verner 1984, Hunter 1990). For example, the 327 species of amphibians, reptiles, birds, and mammals in a mixed conifer community in Oregon can be reduced to 16 life-forms, of which only 8 *stenotopic* (narrow-tolerance) life-forms show a clear association with successional stage or stand condition (Hall and Thomas 1979). The rest are *eurytopic* (wide-tolerance) life-forms influenced little by habitat modification because they are so versatile in habitat needs. But guilds must correspond to natural ecological subdivisions of plant communities (Terborgh and Robinson 1986). A guild might contain only one species. Although members of individual guilds do not respond consistently to habitat modification (Mannon et al. 1984, Verner 1984), such modification generally is not definitive enough to allow the adjustment of management for the nuances of individual species of wildlife within a managed guild of wildlife. But to preserve the ecosystem, habitat management must be modified if any native wildlife species is threatened.

Verner (1984) proposed managing environments for breeding birds, which management probably provides for migrants and winter residents that use basically the same sets of resources in the same zones of the habitat. The life-forms of Hall and Thomas (1979) and Thomas et al. (1979d) are essentially guilds, but contain so much variety in habitat zones that consistency of response by various species in each life-form to habitat changes can be poor (Verner 1984). The approach by Short and Burnham (1982), as modified by Verner (1984), probably provides the most applicable structuring of guilds for wildlife management, but is still too complex for practical application (Morrison et al. 1992). Although the concept of management guilds has been criticized (Landres et al. 1988), it probably has not been tested properly (Finch 1991). The typical composition of guilds is based on species' similarities in microhabitat, food, reproduction, or substrate selection rather than on abrupt macrohabitat changes like those caused by fragmentation.

Probably more practical and effective than guilds are ecosystem health indicators that relate more to the frequency and types of natural processes causing the development of a given ecosystem (pers. comm. F. B. Samson, U.S. Forest Service, Missoula, MT, 1992). For example, some insect or other invertebrate populations might be monitored, because they can change dramatically when natural processes are altered.

Minimum Viable Population

Fragmentation is likely to produce isolated populations which may be either self-sustaining *sources* or nonsustaining *sinks* due to varying environmental conditions at each site (Landres 1992). These local populations, called *demes,* interact via dispersal as a *metapopulation.* An understanding of the complexity of metapopulation dynamics is needed to provide the correct amount, quality, and distribution of habitat at various scales, and should guide habitat rehabilitation and land acquisition (Morrison et al. 1992).

The degree to which a landscape managed for biodiversity can tolerate fragmentation is influenced by the home range, mobility, seasonal movement, and social behavior of individuals of interior wildlife species. But home ranges overlap and some mobile species will cross fragmented areas. To preserve genetic variability, the minimum size of unfragmented (interior) forest is best determined by the minimum viable population size of interior species of wildlife that do not cross fragmented areas. Such definition generally is lacking, or the area defined might be too large to be possible now for some species, such as certain large carnivores with low density and extensive areal needs (e.g., Florida panther), although large, wide-ranging resident species such as cougars tend to be habitat generalists—i.e., they tend not to have specific habitat needs except for minimal road density and other human disturbance (Harris 1984, Noss 1992). Even for a species such as the red-cockaded woodpecker, the minimum viable population has been calculated at 509 breeding pairs requiring at least 25,450 ha (Reed et al. 1988), which is larger than the estimates of population size and area contained in the species-recovery plan (U.S. Fish and Wildlife Service 1985). Koenig (1988) calculated a minimum viable population of red-cockaded woodpeckers even larger than that calculated by Reed et al. (1986, 1988).

A viable population has a high probability (say, 95 or 99%) of persisting a long time (say, 100 to 1000 years) (Noss 1992). With few exceptions, viable populations generally contain thousands of individuals (Thomas 1990). Determining viability is complex. Estimates depend on the mathematical model used, e.g., values for key population parameters such as birth rates, death rates, and population density. Species at most risk of extirpation in a region merit the most concern about population viability. Such species typically include those with (1) small populations of limited or patchy distribution or low density, (2) poor dispersal ability, (3) large home ranges, (4) low reproductive potential, (5) dependence on rare or threatened habitats, and (6) high exploitation or persecution rates (Noss 1992).

Small populations are vulnerable to extirpation or extinction from factors such as environmental and demographic stochasticity, social dysfunction, and genetic deterioration (Shaffer 1981, Soulé 1987a). Samson (1983) reviewed other variables influencing the determination of minimum viable populations. Because all populations fluctuate over time, small populations are more likely to fluctuate down to zero (Noss 1992). Thomas (1990) reviewed empirical studies and concluded that species with average levels of population fluctuation must maintain an average of 1000 individuals to assure population viability. Species of birds and mammals with highly variable populations might need average populations of about 10,000 individuals for long-term persistence (Noss 1992).

Management plans should maintain populations above minimum viability to be ecologically functional (Conner 1988). Determining specific levels of minimum population viability for most species is impractical. If it is impractical for indicator species too, enough usually is known about them to hazard at least an educated guess about a minimum viable population size and its need for space. If enough data do not exist for an educated guess, get the data. Towry (1984) estimated minimum viable population size, areal needs, and habitat needs of 60 wildlife species. Thomas (1990) estimated that minimum viable populations are several thousand to ten thousand, or a little higher than that estimated by Soulé (1987b). But populations smaller than the minimum calculated might be critically important (Soulé 1987b), especially as large populations need large areas which might be unavailable. In fact, the minimum viable population size of species such as the northern spotted owls (20 pairs) (Thomas et al. 1990) and the expansion of introduced populations from small gene pools suggest that the minimum viable population is much smaller than Soulé (1987b) and Thomas (1990) indicated. As a practical working model, a realistic goal to preserve the gene pool of birds might be to maintain enough area to maintain 50% of the bird's maximum probability of occurrence (Robbins 1988).

Several studies indicate that short-term survival of a wildlife species needs a population of about 50 *breeding* individuals, and continuing adaptation needs about 500, although for most situations the number of individuals will range from the upper hundreds to the thousands, maybe rarely to the ten thousands for 95% probability of persistence for 100 or 1000 years, given no strong potential for environmental or catastrophic uncertainty (Franklin 1980, Shaffer 1987). Most biologists probably agree with Lande and Barrowclough (1987) that 500 is about the right order of magnitude—i.e., as high as 5000 and as low as 50 individuals (Grumbine 1990a) to avoid inbreeding depression (Lacy 1992). Wilcox et al. (1986) and Shaffer (1991) discussed management and analysis of viable populations.

Models for extinction (Belovsky 1987) indicate that (1) the largest mammalian carnivores (10 to 100 kg) will persist 100 years in 0 to 22 percent of the world's current parks, but no park is large enough to guarantee persistence for 1000 years; (2) the largest mammalian herbivores (100 to 1000 kg) will persist for 100 years in 4 to 100 percent of the world's parks, and for 1000 years in 0 to 22 percent of the parks; (3) regions of 10^6 to 10^9 km^2 are needed for larger mammals (over 50 kg) to persist in evolutionary time (10^5 to 10^6 years), given no major climatic change. Patchiness of ecosystems probably is manageable in many situations, although minimum critical size might be about 10^4 km^2 (Lovejoy and Oren 1981).

Trends in populations are indicators of sustainability. Even if the population is relatively high, if that level reveals a severe decrease from the previous population level, some action must be taken to prevent possible extirpation if the trend so indicates (pers. comm. F. B. Samson, U.S. Forest Service, Missoula, MT, 1992). Risk analysis should promote spreading the risk of extirpation or extinction across the landscape; it should consider the importance of stochastic events in evaluating viability (Samson et al. 1985). Stochastic (uncertain) processes can be grouped into four broad categories (Grumbine 1992):

1. *Genetic uncertainty,* i.e., random changes from inbreeding, etc., which alter reproductive and survival capability of individuals

2. *Demographic uncertainty,* which results from random events that affect the reproduction and survival of populations

3. *Environmental uncertainty,* which results from unpredictable changes in climate, weather, food supply, and the populations of predators and competitors that affect reproduction and survival of populations

4. *Catastrophic uncertainty,* which results from tornadoes, hurricanes, avalanches, landslides, volcanic eruptions, fires, floods, etc., occurring at random intervals, that affect reproduction and survival of populations

Reserves

Biological diversity cannot be conserved effectively in natural reserves alone because the reserve network is too small, major expansion is unlikely, and the species in reserves are susceptible to global climate changes as the isolation of the reserves acts to bar migration between them (Wilcove 1989, Westman 1990). To date, most of the effort in biological conservation has focused on protecting national parks that cover only about 3.2 percent of the earth's land area (Reid and Miller 1989). Protecting biodiversity is equally important in the vast man-

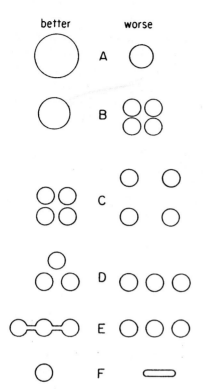

better   worse

A

B

C

D

E

F

Figure 1.3 Geometric design principles for nature reserves. Those on the left probably would hold more species at equilibrium and have lower extinction rates than those on the right. (*Diamond 1975, Margules et al. 1982, Hunter 1990.*)

aged forest ecosystems, agricultural ecosystems, and human settlements (Pimental et al. 1992) that combined cover about 95 percent of the earth's land area (Western and Pearl 1989).

A combination of area and isolation of habitat is one of the most important considerations to maintain natural diversity of breeding bird populations (Robbins et al. 1989). Reserves should be large, circular, and undivided—and if divided, connected by dispersal corridors or located close to each other (Pickett and Thompson 1978, Kobayashi 1985, Shafer 1990). Populations of obligate forest-interior wildlife species are conserved better in a single large reserve than in several small reserves (Robbins et al. 1989).

Six design features have been proposed to help maintain species diversity in nature reserves surrounded by human-dominated landscapes (Fig. 1.3) (Diamond 1975, Margules et al. 1982, Hunter 1990). Diamond (1975) and Wilson and Willis (1975) suggested general principles for managing habitat islands: (1) one large island is better than many small islands; (2) several islands close together are better than several islands far apart; (3) a cluster of islands is better than a line of islands; (4) an island linked to another island by an isthmus or corridor of habitat generally is better than two isolated islands; (5) a compact (circular) island with a low ratio of edge to area is better than an elongated island with a high ratio of edge to area. The compromise is to create reserves of a variety of sizes (Hunter 1990). Very small reserves would be excluded because their biota typically comprises common, widely distributed, mostly edge species that would inhabit the periphery of larger reserves. Very large reserves should be avoided if their protection conflicts with establishing smaller reserves and they far exceed the size needed by any indigenous population of wildlife. Yet larger reserves are preferred because they will become rarer with human encroachment and fragmentation of the landscape, which is essentially irreversible. Parks, refuges, nature preserves, and other worldwide protected areas comprise less than 3 percent of the world's surface (Reid and Miller 1989, Samson et al. 1991). This percentage will not change substantially and cannot sustain all worldwide species and ecosystems, thus emphasizing the need to manage other lands for biodiversity.

Carrying capacity refers to the maximum number of a given species of wildlife that a habitat can support without damage. *Dynamic equilibrium* means that natural processes maintain the communities and species present in an ecosystem, with no human interference. The reserve must be large enough to include all successional stages for all vegetation types present (White 1987). Communities and species need more active stewardship and monitoring in smaller preserves. Simulation models indicate that minimum areas for dynamic equilibrium to occur in Appalachian forests subject only to tree-fall disturbance (affecting less than 1000 m^2) are 100 to 10,000 ha (Shugart 1984). For Appalachian forests subject to wildfires, minimum area is about 100,000 ha. For Australian forests subject to large wildfires, minimum areas are 1 million to 1 billion ha. Dynamic equilibrium probably is barely obtainable in Yellowstone National Park (895,600 ha) (Romme and Knight 1982), and probably is obtainable in Great Smoky Mountains National Park (200,000 ha) for tree-fall disturbance and possibly wildfire (White 1987). Robbins et al. (1989) suggested that some reserves in eastern deciduous forests should contain at least 3000 ha to be protected in perpetuity. Schonewald-Cox (1983) estimated that viable populations of small herbivorous and omnivorous mammals might need reserves of 10,000 to 100,000 ha, but ungulates and large carnivores need reserves of 1 million to 10 million ha. Hummel (1990) estimated that 50 grizzly bears need about 49,000 km^2, 50 wolverines about 42,000 km^2, and 50 wolves about 20,250 km^2. If 1000 is considered the minimum viable population, the size of reserves needed for grizzly bears, wolverines, and wolves would be 20 times as large. Such immense areas would have to involve regional and interregional systems of interlinked reserves, e.g., the Greater-Yellowstone Ecosystem linked to the Northern Continental Divide Ecosystem and to the Canadian Rockies (Noss 1992).

The greater ecosystem concept to protect biodiversity must provide (1) habitat for viable populations of all native species, (2) areas large enough to accommodate regimes of natural disturbance, (3) protection over centuries to allow species and ecosystems to continue evolving, and (4) integration of human use at sustainable levels that prevent ecological degradation (Grumbine 1990b). These considerations determine the ecosystem's boundaries.

The design of a nature reserve should be based on the smallest area with a natural disturbance regime which balances rates of emigration from external sources with rates of internal extinctions (Pickett and Thompson 1978). Shugart (1984) suggested that a landscape can maintain its equilibrium conditions if it is about 50 times larger than the area disturbed, i.e., the landscape can absorb disturbances if about 50 times larger than the area disturbed. Thus, a manager might have to alter the scale of disturbance or increase the area under management to maintain equilibrium conditions.

Landscape processes can be biotic and abiotic (Morrison et al. 1992). Abiotic natural disturbances such as climatic changes, can be slow. They can be fast, as with fire, storms, floods, landslides, and volcanoes. Biotic processes include species invasion, epidemics of disease and parasites, and human disturbance. Landscape processes can be classified generally by type (physical, biological, physical-biological) and regime (size, frequency, timing) (Karr and Freemark 1985, Morrison et al. 1992).

Ecosystem is a somewhat nebulous term meaning the network of interactions of communities of plants and animals (the biotic part) with energy, minerals, and nutrients from the sun, air, soil, and water (the abiotic part) in a manner that sustains life (Anderson 1985, Robinson and Bolen 1985, Hunter 1990, Patton 1992). Ecosystems have arbitrary boundaries, and are not closed systems. Thus, ecosystem management is difficult to define.

Landscape management of ecosystems probably is more definitive because a line can be drawn on a map more readily to define the management unit. The landscape is a recognizable, distinct entity (Forman and Godron 1986, Crow 1991, Hansen and di Castri 1992). The study of the response of communities to patterns across more than one patch is called *landscape ecology* (Morrison et al. 1992). A local-regional watershed approach probably is best (Samson et al. 1989, Grumbine 1992, Morrison et al. 1992).

Selection of natural areas for reserves requires consideration of a list of attributes that apply to the biology of the most demanding or threatened wildlife species (Adamus and Clough 1978). They include the species' endemism, site tenacity, areal size needs, seasonal mobility, spatial distribution, reproductive capacity, habitat scarcity, and tolerance to humans. Kirkpatrick and Brown (1991), Margules et al. (1988, 1991), and Pressey and Nicholls (1991) described methods to identify species and their reservation needs, and to select networks of reserves for maximum biodiversity. Hoose (1981) described several approaches to protect important areas, including leases, rights of first refusal, easements, acquisition, registration, dedication, organizing a statewide protection plan, and lobbying. Grumbine (1992) suggested some practical strategies to incorporate private lands immediately into ecosystem management; in order of likely short-term success, these are zoning law changes, purchase and/or condemnation, leasing, tax incentives, conservation easements, land trusts, stewardship programs, and education.

Wildlife species prone to extinction in small, isolated reserves tend to be ecological specialists, large animals with large home ranges (i.e., top carnivores), and species with variable populations that depend on patchy or unpredictable resources (Noss 1987a). But small carnivores probably need the largest areas of uniform habitat (Hunter 1990) because they cannot cross extensive fragmented areas as readily as the more mobile large carnivores. Home range and habitat size for carnivores (including insectivores) are larger than for omnivores and herbivores. Home ranges (in hectares) for mammals can be predicted from body weight W (in grams), percentage of flesh in the diet, and mode of life (McNab 1963, Harestad and Bunnell 1979, Gittleman and Harvey 1982, Mace and Harvey 1983, Harris 1984):

$$\text{Home range of herbivores} = 0.002W^{1.02}$$

$$\text{Home range of carnivores} = 0.022W^{1.30}$$

$$\text{Home range of omnivores} = 0.059W^{0.92}$$

The least-squares equation that describes the species-area curve for mammals is

$$S = 16.3A^{0.16}$$

where S = the number of species and A = area in hectares (Harris 1984). The exponent (0.16) is remarkably similar to the lower limit calculated for continental islands by MacArthur and Wilson (1967). Thus, a species-area curve with an exponent of 0.16 implies that, to double the number of species, an area would have to be 76 times larger than it was—e.g., a 10-ha patch of habitat that supports 40 species of mammals would have to be 760 ha to support 80 species (Harris 1984). The species-area curve ($S = cA^z$) predicts that larger areas will

TABLE 1.10   Comparison of Estimated Size of Currently Surviving Populations and Now Extinct Populations of Wildlife at Time of Establishment of 24 National Parks in Western North America

Group	Surviving populations			Extinct populations		
	Median size	95% Cl	N	Median size	95% Cl	N
Lagomorphs	70,889	34,720–173,150	60	3,276	702–56,952	9
Artiodactyls	792	429–1504	88	241	3–1,273	7
Small carnivores	1,203	908–1704	127	256	122–880	26
Large carnivores	108	70–146	153	24	14–68	16

Note: Parks were established on average about 80 years ago. Cl means confidence limits; N means number of surviving populations.
SOURCE: Adapted from Newmark (1986) and Soulé (1987b).

contain more species than smaller areas when the exponent (z) values are positive (Harris and Silva-Lopez 1992). The relationship indicates that roughly 50 percent of the number of species disappears when 90 percent of the habitat disappears (MacArthur and Wilson 1967).

Comparing population estimates of mammals in 24 national parks when first established (averaging about 80 years ago) in western North America reveals that the median initial sizes for most surviving populations tend to range between one hundred and a few thousand (Table 1.10) (Newmark 1986, Soulé 1987b). The size of 14 national parks in the western United States is correlated positively with the number of resident large mammal species (Bekele 1980, Hunter 1990). Virtually all national parks were too small when established to maintain all mammal species found at the time of establishment (Newmark 1985, 1987). Studies by Schonewald-Cox (1983), Newmark (1985), and Salwasser et al. (1987) indicate that nature reserves (e.g., national parks) in the United States are inadequate for protecting large vertebrate species. To reduce future potential loss, wildlife will need active management in the parks, or the parks will have to be enlarged by cooperative management or leasing of surrounding areas or by outright acquisition (Agee and Johnson 1988).

Grumbine (1990a, 1992) suggested new legislation and described an ecosystem-management model for reform to address lack of landscape-level management, insufficient data, competition between federal land-management agencies, bureaucratic inertia, and other problems that thwart preservation of biodiversity. To restore habitat, roads must be closed, fences and other structures removed, natural disturbances and hydrologic processes restored, exotic plants and animals removed, and extirpated species reintroduced (Noss 1987b, Temple 1990). The process and pattern of presettlement vegetation should be reconstructed, and models developed to project the current natural composition. Natural processes, such as fire, can be reintroduced when the natural composition is restored. Otherwise the habitat might need preparatory habitat restoration—e.g., removal of excess shrubby growth accumulated from fire suppression, which might promote unnatural catastrophic burns. Except for the largest natural areas, disturbance must be managed indefinitely to produce a mix of successional stages or stand conditions that perpetually meet the needs of the native biota. Reserves of all sizes need active intervention to mitigate effects of water and air pollution, control exotic species, and control the impacts of human visitors. But the policy to remove all exotic species can be somewhat unnatural. Natural communities are subjected continually to new arrivals to which the resident population usually adjusts without a net loss of species (Westman 1990).

Ecological stewardship should mimic the natural regime as a delicate balance between overmanipulation and laissez faire neglect (Noss 1987b). Natural disturbances can be extensive or patchy in space and time. A landscape can be viewed as a shifting mosaic of disturbed patches in various stages of recovery (Bormann and Likens 1979). To determine size of reserves, regimes of natural disturbance must be considered for habitat diversity and maintaining all the plant and animal species associated with different seral stages (Noss 1992). Ecological factors for planning reserves include spatial distribution and patch size of disturbance, successional dynamics, potential undisturbed refuge areas within or near the reserve, and dispersal capabilities of species. Shugart and West (1981) estimated that landscapes would have to be 50 to 100 times larger than average disturbance patches to maintain relatively constant proportions of different seral stages that change over time.

Because natural disturbances shape landscapes, conservation strategies should not focus on species and populations, but should be expanded with two basic approaches (Grumbine 1992): (1) entire landscapes should be managed by using studies of viable populations and minimum dynamic areas, and/or (2) remaining native habitats should be protected and connected.

Noss (1992) proposed a regional reserve system consisting of three types of area: core reserves, multiple-use (buffer) zones, and corridors (Fig. 1.4). The core reserves are selected first. Then they are connected by corridors and buffered across the landscape from intensive land use. Important core reserves should be linked by corridors with roadless interiors. If road density and intensity of human activities are low, an archipelago of core reserves in a matrix will function well for most native species. Properly managed multiple-use zones at a landscape level (1:24,000 or larger) will function as corridors for

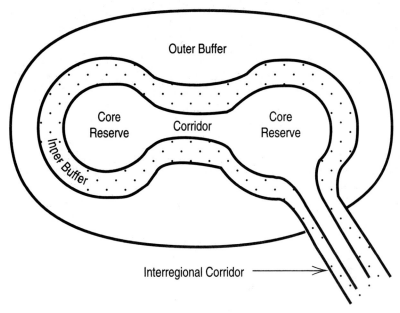

Figure 1.4   Core reserves, connecting corridors or linkages, and buffer zones comprising a regional wilderness recovery network. (*Noss 1992.*)

many species, especially at a regional level. In time, a well-designed wilderness network to preserve biodiversity should dominate a region, with human habitations as islands within the network (Noss 1992).

Core reserves

Selecting sites and drawing boundaries.   Where large national parks, wilderness areas, or other reserves already exist, boundaries should be enlarged to include adjacent and nearby roadless areas, old-growth stands, and other ecologically important areas (Noss 1992). Otherwise, boundaries should enclose geographic clusters of (1) managed areas (such as wildlife areas), (2) old-growth stands, (3) other natural (virgin) forest, (4) other natural areas and sensitive sites, (5) roadless areas, (6) underrepresented vegetation types, and (7) areas of rare species as determined from natural heritage program databases for each state in the United States, some Canadian provinces, and some Latin American countries. Gap analysis available for some states and provinces will provide information on unprotected and underprotected vegetation types. At a regional scale, the overall system of core reserves should include (1) representative examples of all major ecosystem types, vegetation types, and seral stages native to the region; (2) entire environmental gradients (all physical habitat types); (3) centers of endemism and species richness as determined perhaps from gap analysis; (4) population centers of large, wide-ranging species, especially large carnivores; (5) populations of other rare species.

At the landscape level (1:24,000 or larger), after the location of the core reserves is determined, boundaries must be defined more precisely, corridors added so that all sites that would be linked naturally are reconnected, and the entire network enveloped in a matrix of buffer zones. Various maps can be used, such as detailed road maps, plat books, wildlife maps such as those for ungulate winter range and dispersal corridors, and those showing land-use information such as proposed timber sales, grazing allotments, and mineral rights.

Size. Surrounded by adequate buffer zones and/or well interconnected by corridors, core reserves can be relatively small, maybe 4000 to 40,500 ha, and still serve most target species (Noss 1992). Surrounded by hostile habitat (urban areas, agricultures, tree farms), core reserves might need at least 1 to 10 million ha to sustain viable populations of large mammals. Large core reserves also are needed to maintain diversity of seral stages across a landscape of vegetation types prone to high-intensity fire. Where core reserves are too small, prescribed burns or silvicultural treatment will be needed to maintain diversity of seral stages.

Management. The smaller the reserve, the more management is needed. Core reserves should be roadless (wilderness) areas (Noss 1992). Management should emphasize restoration, to include (1) planting native species in all ecosystems and thinning plantations on forestlands to diversify species composition and structure; (2) thinning fire-suppressed and artificially dense stands of naturally open-structured forest types (e.g., ponderosa pine or longleaf pine) before reintroducing fire; (3) reintroducing fire to grasslands, shrublands, and forestlands without thinning by allowing natural fires to burn or by prescribed burns that mimic the seasonality, intensity, and frequency of natural fires; (4) inoculating soil with mycorrhizal fungi, where needed, to reestablish native vegetation; (5) eliminating livestock, and controlling or preferably eliminating other exotic species of plants and animals; (6) reintroducing extirpated native species of wildlife, including large carnivores; (7) permanently closing and revegetating all roads.

Corridors

Corridors connecting core reserves are extensions of the reserves and thus provide additional reserve-type habitat (Noss 1992). Among other considerations (see Chap. 6, "Corridors and Riparian Areas," for a full discussion of these) corridors should provide dispersal and genetic interchange between core reserves, and latitudinal and elevational range shifts with seasonal climate changes, e.g., seasonal movements from summer range to winter range caused by changes in temperature or precipitation. At the landscape level, small core reserves within a cluster of them should be connected by corridors; at the regional level, clusters of reserves should be connected by larger corridors. (See Chap. 6 for size considerations.)

Multiple-use (buffer) zones

Multiple-use (buffer) zones (Fig. 1.4 and see Fig. 4.4) have several functions, which include (1) insulating core reserves from hostile land use and ameliorating edge effects, (2) providing supplemental habitat and habitat linkages for some native species, (3) buffering intensively used human areas from depredating large mammals that reach relatively high densities in the core reserves, and (4) providing multiple use (Noss 1992). At least two zones are best to provide a gradation of use intensity, low near the core reserve and increasingly intense toward the intensively used human areas. Inner zones should have a road density of 0.3 km/km^2 or less. Human use should be low-intensity, such as nonconsumptive recreation including primitive camping, wilderness hunting and fishing, low-intensity silviculture (light selective cutting), and limited habitat manipulation for target species of plants and animals. Outer zones could have a road density up to 0.6 km/km^2. Human use can be more intensive, such as campgrounds and other heavier recreational use (but no off-road vehicles), biodiversity silviculture (e.g., partial-retention harvests, selection cuts), and more intensive habitat manipulation for target wildlife.

Habitat Monitoring and Gap Analysis

A landscape should be defined as a hydrologic (watershed) unit (Morrison et al. 1992). A landscape design for biodiversity must be evaluated as follows:

1. *Cumulative-effects analysis* predicts effects on the distribution and abundance of species and communities of plants and animals from on-site and off-site activities. Such analysis helps describe future options available under each alternative and provides more information to make management decisions.

2. *Assessment of disturbance processes and long-term productivity* describes the type, extent, frequency, intensity, and location of dis-

TABLE 1.11 Indicator Variables for Inventorying and Monitoring Terrestrial Biodiversity at Four Levels of Organization

| | Indicators | | | |
	Composition	Structure	Function	Inventory and monitoring tools
Regional (landscape)	Identity, distribution, richness, and proportions of patch (habitat) types and multipatch landscape types; collective patterns of species distributions (richness, endemism)	Heterogeneity; connectivity; spatial linkage; patchiness; porosity; contrast; grain size; fragmentation; configuration; juxtaposition; patch-size frequency distribution; perimeter-area ratio; pattern of habitat layer distribution	Disturbance processes (areal extent, frequency or return interval, rotation period, predictability, intensity, severity, seasonality); nutrient cycling rates; energy flow rates; patch persistence and turnover rates; rates of erosion and geomorphic and hydrologic processes; human land-use trends	Aerial photographs (satellite and conventional aircraft) and other remote sensing data; Geographic Information System (GIS) technology; time series analysis; spatial statistics; mathematical indices (of pattern, heterogeneity, connectivity, layering, diversity, edge, morphology, autocorrelation, fractal dimension)
Community (ecosystem)	Identity, relative abundance, frequency, richness, evenness, and diversity of species and guilds; proportions of endemic, exotic, threatened, and endangered species; dominance-diversity curves; life-form proportions; similarity coefficients; C4:C3 plant species ratios	Substrate and soil variables; slope and aspect; vegetation biomass and physiognomy; foliage density and layering; horizontal patchiness; canopy openness and gap proportions; abundance, density, and distribution of key physical features (e.g., cliffs, outcrops, sinks) and structural elements (snags, down logs); water and resource (e.g., mast) availability; snow cover	Biomass and resource productivity; herbivory, parasitism, and predation rates; colonization and local extinction rates; patch dynamics (fine-scale disturbance processes); nutrient cycling rates; human intrusion rates and intensities	Aerial photographs and other remote-sensing data; ground-level photo stations; time series analysis; physical habitat measures and resource inventories; habitat suitability indices (HSI, multispecies); observations, censuses and inventories, captures, and other sampling methodologies; mathematical indices (e.g., of diversity, heterogeneity, layering dispersion, biotic integrity)

Population (species)	Absolute or relative abundance; frequency; importance or cover value; biomass; density	Dispersion (microdistribution); range (macrodistribution); population structure (sex ratio; age ratio); habitat variables (see community-ecosystem structure, above); within-individual morphological variability	Demographic processes (fertility, recruitment rate, survivorship, mortality); metapopulation dynamics; population genetics (see below); population fluctuations; physiology; life history; phenology; growth rate (of individuals); acclimation; adaptation	Censuses (observations, counts, captures, signs, radio tracking; remote sensing; habitat suitability index (HSI); species-habitat modeling; population viability analysis
Genetic	Allelic diversity; presence of particular rare alleles, deleterious recessives, or karyotypic variants	Census and effective population size; heterozygosity; chromosomal or phenotypic polymorphism; generation overlap; heritability	Inbreeding depression; outbreeding rate; rate of genetic drift; gene flow; mutation rate; selection intensity	Electrophoresis; karyotypic analysis; DNA sequencing; offspring-parent regression; sib analysis; morphological analysis

SOURCE: Noss 1990.

turbance agents in shaping the composition, structure, and function of communities.

3. *Monitoring of the landscape design* should identify early warning signals that a plant or animal population is responding adversely to landscape conditions, so that remedial action can be taken.

Management for biodiversity must be monitored to identify the best procedures and designs (Table 1.11) (Noss 1990, Goldsmith 1991, Margules and Austin 1991, Williams and Marcot 1991, Morrison et al. 1992). (For an example, see Davis 1989.) Habitat management objectives should be specific and measurable (Ripley 1980). Management practices should be monitored to determine effectiveness and alterations needed (Cooperrider et al. 1986). To facilitate statistical analysis of results, monitoring should involve a sound experimental design (e.g., monitoring of control and treatment areas and/or pre- and post-treatment sampling, with suitable replication) (Millsap et al. 1987). Results should be shared with other managers through publication in appropriate journals or symposia proceedings (Baskett 1985).

As a coarse-filter approach to conservation planning, *gap analysis* identifies the gaps among areas managed for the biodiversity of native species and natural ecosystems (Scott et al. 1993). The gaps then are filled via land acquisition or management changes so that all ecosystems are represented. Gap analysis is a method to identify gaps in protecting biodiversity at statewide or provincewide, regional, national, and international levels. Gap analysis uses vegetation types and species of vertebrates, butterflies, and/or other taxa as indicators of biodiversity. Maps of existing vegetation are prepared from satellite imagery (LANDSAT) and other sources for entry into a Geographic Information System (GIS), and verified by examining aerial photos and by field checks. Distribution maps for individual species of biological or political interest and maps of land ownership and management are overlaid in the GIS to identify gaps in biodiversity-management areas. Gap analysis cannot identify areas smaller than 100 ha.

Gap analysis should be used to compare today's landscape to the historic conditions in order to emulate historic conditions and natural processes as much as feasible and establish habitat-management and conservation priorities (pers. comm. F. B. Samson, U.S. Forest Service, Missoula, MT, 1992). For example, a regionwide gap analysis might reveal disproportionate use of one tree species or age class, or one range, versus another. Therefore, a manager might reduce or eliminate tree harvest or shift to another species or size class, an approach which seems obvious but is rarely implemented.

Forestlands

Forest Types

The federal government owns about 33 percent of the 8,625,000 km^2 in the United States (Committee on Agricultural Land Use and Wildlife Resources 1970, Bailey 1978, Yonce 1983). Forests and woodlands occur on 307 million ha, of which 36 percent is noncommercial due to low productivity or reservation for parks, wilderness areas, or other nontimber uses. Of the commercial forestland, 22 percent is federally owned, states and counties own 6 percent, private industry owns 14 percent, farmers own 24 percent, and 34 percent is in other private ownership. Of the noncommercial forestland, over 75 percent is federally owned, mostly in Alaska and other western states. Of the commercial and noncommercial forestland combined in the United States, 61 percent is nonfederal, the U.S. Forest Service owns 19 percent, the U.S. Bureau of Land Management owns 16 percent, and other federal agencies own 4 percent (U.S. Forest Service 1981). Of the commercial forestland, 74 percent is east of the 100th meridian and 26 percent is west of it in the contiguous United States (Shaw 1967, Yonce 1983).

In Canada, most forests are virgin; the main disturbance has been fire (Eyre 1980). Forests cover about 45 percent of Canada's total land area of 9,997,000 km^2. About half is commercial forest, of which 80 percent is provincially owned, 11 percent is federal, and 9 percent is private (Forestry Canada 1988).

Forests can be classified as *noncommercial* or *commercial,* where commercial means capable of yielding at least 1.4 m^3 of wood per hectare per year and suitable for timber harvest (Duffield 1990). Where annual precipitation is at least 40 cm, trees grow close enough together to comprise a *forest.* Trees in drier regions are more widely spaced, comprising what is often referred to as a *woodland* rather than a forest. Trees do not grow in areas with less than about 30 cm of annual precipitation, where no soil occurs, where soil is frozen permanently, or where human or other disturbance prevents their reestablishment.

Forests can be classified as follows (Duffield 1990):

1. Evergreen forests, mainly:
   a. Coniferous forests (in cooler climates mainly)
   b. Broad-leaved evergreen forests (in warmer climates mainly)

2. Deciduous forests, mainly:
   a. Cold-deciduous forests (leaves shed in winter)
   b. Drought-deciduous forests (leaves shed in dry season)

Little agreement exists on a standard approach to forest-habitat classification because of its complexity (Bailey 1977, Thomas and Verner 1986). The 100th meridian separates forests in the United States and Canada broadly into eastern and western regions, distinguished basically by rainfall and elevation, which influence growth. Thus, forests in the West are mainly coniferous; forests in the East are mostly deciduous or mixtures of both (Patton 1992). In western North America, large areas of trees extend over the main ranges of the Rocky Mountains and Pacific Coast from Alaska to California. Many relatively small, widely scattered forested areas occur on higher plateaus and ridges, intermingled with treeless areas in large arid areas, especially in parts of the central and southern Rocky Mountains. Large unbroken forest areas occur in most of Canada, northern New England, and the Appalachian section of the South Atlantic and Gulf states. Elsewhere the forestlands occur mainly in small areas on farms and other small properties. Texas and Florida contain small areas of tropical forest.

Based on the extent of the dominant vegetation, forests in the United States can be grouped broadly into seven regions (U.S. Department of Agriculture 1968, Patton 1992). Each forest region contains several major and minor forest types of the dominant tree association:

I.   Alaska Coast and Interior (hemlock/spruce/hardwoods)

II. Pacific Coast and Interior (Douglas-fir/ponderosa pine/redwood)

III. Northern Rocky Mountains (lodgepole pine/Douglas-fir/larch)

IV. Southern Rocky Mountains (pinyon-juniper/ponderosa pine/fir-spruce)

V.   Lake States and Northeast (aspen-birch/maple-beech-birch/spruce-fir)

VI.   Central Mountains and Plateaus (oak-hickory/oak-pine)

VII. Southern States (loblolly-shortleaf/longleaf-slash pine)

Forest regions also can be classified as (1) northern coniferous forest, (2) northern hardwoods forest, (3) Pacific Coast forest, (4) Rocky Mountain forest, (5) central broad-leaved forest, (6) oak-pine forest (southern), (7) bottomland hardwoods forest, and (8) tropical forest (Fig. 2.1) (Duffield 1990).

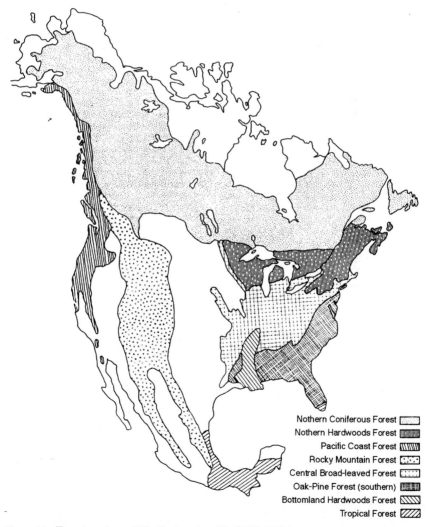

Nothern Coniferous Forest

Nothern Hardwoods Forest

Pacific Coast Forest

Rocky Mountain Forest

Central Broad-leaved Forest

Oak-Pine Forest (southern)

Bottomland Hardwoods Forest

Tropical Forest

Figure 2.1   Forest regions of North America. (*Duffield 1990.*)

TABLE 2.1   Classification Scheme for World Vegetation

Symbol	Description	Example
I.	Class	a. Forest
		b. Woodland
A.	Subclass	a. Evergreen forest
		b. Evergreen woodland
1.	Group	a. Temperate and subpolar needle-leaved
		b. Needle-leaved
a.	Formation	a. Conical crowns
		b. Rounded crowns
(1).	Series	a. Engelmann spruce–subalpine fir
		b. Ponderosa pine
(a).	Association	a. Engelmann spruce–subalpine fir/grouse whortle-berry
		b. Ponderosa pine/antelope bitterbrush

SOURCE: United Nations (1973).

Smith (1980) described broad forest groups based on continental subdivisions by seas, mountain ranges, deserts, grasslands, and glaciers: (1) boreal forest; (2) western conifer forest (Pacific coastal complex, Sierra Nevadan complex, Rocky Mountain complex); (3) eastern deciduous forest (Appalachian forest, northern hardwood forest, midland hardwood forest, Ozark-Piedmont forest, southeastern pine forest, bottomland hardwood forest, northeastern coniferous forest. The U.S. Department of Agriculture (1968) recognized 25 major forest types of over 850 native tree species.

Using plant physiognomic characteristics (appearance, life-form), the United Nations (1973) developed a worldwide vegetation system that is open-ended and hierarchical with five mutually exclusive vegetative classes: forest, woodland, shrubland, dwarf-shrubland, and herbaceous vegetation. These are further subdivided (Table 2.1). The distinction between forest and woodland concerns canopy closure, with 25 to 60 percent closure for woodland and 60 percent or more for forest (Driscoll et al. 1984, Patton 1992).

Forest-cover types contain tree crowns which cover at least 25 percent of the area. They must occupy fairly large areas (usually tens of thousands of hectares), but not necessarily in continuous stands (Eyre 1980). Forest types are named after dominant tree species as determined from basal area, or stem density where the stand contains only seedlings and saplings. The species named in the type must comprise at least 20 percent of the total basal area. Sometimes a trinomial or a general descriptive name is used for the type.

In the United States and Canada, 20 forest-type groups (Table 2.2) of 145 forest-cover types are recognized: 90 in the East (Table 2.3)

TABLE 2.2   Forest-Type Groups of Canada and the United States

Eastern	Western
1. White pine–red pine–jack pine	11. Douglas-fir
2. Spruce-fir	12. Hemlock–Sitka spruce
3. Longleaf pine–slash pine	13. Ponderosa pine
4. Loblolly pine–shortleaf pine	14. Western white pine
5. Oak-pine	15. Lodgepole pine
6. Oak-hickory	16. Larch
7. Oak-gum-cypress	17. Fir-spruce
8. Elm-ash-cottonwood	18. Redwood
9. Maple-beech-birch	19. Noncommercial
10. Aspen-birch	20. Hardwoods

SOURCE: Adapted from Eyre (1980).

and 55 in the West (Table 2.4) (Eyre 1980). In Canada, eight forest regions are divided into 90 forest sections (Table 2.5) (Rowe 1972). A *region* is defined as a major geographic belt or zone broadly uniform in physiognomy, composed of dominant tree species. Sections relate the dominant tree species to the physiography. In the *Forestry Handbook,* Hook et al. (1984) described various forest types in seven eastern and five western forest regions of North America (Table 2.6). For wildlife-habitat improvement, Halls et al. (1984) combined the various forest types into broader categories (Table 2.7). A simpler arrangement, developed by the U.S. Department of the Interior Geological Survey, mainly for national use of remote-sensor data, is to have three categories of rangeland (herbaceous, shrub and brush, mixed), three categories of forestland (deciduous, evergreen, mixed), and two categories of wetland (forested, nonforested) (Anderson et al. 1976, Hook et al. 1984).

Perhaps the simplest classification system for forests is to distinguish just three forest types (coniferous, deciduous, and mixed) and three successional stages of each type by height class (e.g., less than 5 m, 5 to 15 m, and over 15 m) (Hunter 1990). Recognizing forest stands by their dominant species or group of species is more definitive. Even better is developing a forest-stand classification into a forest-ecosystem classification by recognizing differences in physical sites that support certain forest types, for the physical environment provides the foundation for communities. The most efficient way to manage wildlife for diversity is to manage by ecosystem (Hunter 1990). Major climactic zones, called "biomes," are too large to distinguish ecosystems. But physiographic regions, based on integrated information about climate, soils, and topography, will help define ecosystems. Allen (1987b) listed 18 vegetative zones in North America (Fig. 2.2, Table 2.8).

TABLE 2.3   Eastern Forest-Cover Types of Canada and the United States

Type group and type name	Type group and type name
Boreal forest region	White oak
Boreal conifers	Black oak
Jack pine	Northern red oak
Balsam fir	Other central types
Black spruce	Black locust
Black spruce–tamarack	Yellow poplar
White spruce	Yellow poplar–eastern hemlock
Tamarack	Yellow poplar–white oak–northern
Boreal hardwoods	red oak
Aspen	River birch–sycamore
Pin cherry	Silver maple–American elm
Paper birch	Sassafras–persimmon
	Pin oak–sweetgum
Northern forest region	Pitch pine
Spruce-fir types	Eastern redcedar
Red spruce	
Red spruce–balsam fir	**Southern forest region:**
Red spruce–Fraser fir	Southern yellow pines
Red spruce–yellow birch	Sand pine
Red spruce–sugar maple–beech	Longleaf pine
Paper birch–red spruce–balsam fir	Longleaf pine–slash pine
Northern white cedar	Shortleaf pine
Pine and hemlock types	Virginia pine
Red pine	Loblolly pine
Eastern white pine	Loblolly pine–shortleaf pine
White pine–hemlock	Slash pine
Eastern hemlock	South Florida slash pine
White pine–northern red oak –red	Pond pine
maple	Oak-pine types
White pine–chestnut oak	Longleaf pine–scrub oak
Hemlock–yellow birch	Shortleaf pine–oak
Northern hardwoods	Virginia pine–oak
Sugar maple	Loblolly pine–hardwood
Sugar maple–beech–yellow birch	Slash pine–hardwood
Sugar maple–basswood	Bottomland types
Black cherry–maple	Cottonwood
Beech–sugar maple	Willow oak–water oak–diamondleaf
Red maple	oak
Other northern types	Live oak
Northern pin oak	Swamp chestnut oak–cherrybark
Gray birch–red maple	oak
Black ash–American elm–red maple	Sweetgum–willow oak
Hawthorn	Sugarberry–American elm–green
	ash
Central forest region	Sycamore–sweetgum–American elm
Upland oaks	Black willow
Post oak–blackjack oak	Overcup oak–water hickory
Bur oak	Bald cypress
Bear oak	Bald cypress–tupelo
Chestnut oak	Water tupelo–swamp tupelo
White oak–black oak–northern red	Sweetbay–swamp tupelo–redbay
oak	

TABLE 2.3   Eastern Forest-Cover Types of Canada and the United States (*Continued*)

Other southern types	Sweetgum–yellow poplar
Ashe juniper–redberry (Pinchot) juniper	Atlantic white cedar
Mohr ("shin") oak	Pondcypress
Mesquite	**Tropical forest region (Florida only)**
Southern scrub oak	Tropical hardwoods
Southern redcedar	Mangrove
Cabbage palmetto	

SOURCE: Adapted from Eyre (1980).

TABLE 2.4   Western Forest-Cover Types of Canada and the United States

Type group and type name	Type group and type name
Northern interior (boreal)	Western hemlock
White spruce	Western hemlock–Sitka spruce
White spruce–aspen	Coastal true fir–hemlock
White spruce–paper birch	Western redcedar–western hemlock
Paper birch	Western redcedar
Balsam poplar	Pacific Douglas-fir
Black spruce	Douglas-fir–western hemlock
Black spruce–white spruce	Port Orford cedar
Black spruce–paper birch	Redwood
High elevations	Oregon white oak
Mountain hemlock	Douglas-fir–tanoak–Pacific madrone
Engelmann spruce–subalpine fir	**Low elevations, interior**
Red fir	Cottonwood–willow
Whitebark pine	Bur oak
Bristlecone pine	Interior ponderosa pine
California mixed subalpine	Western juniper
Middle elevations, interior	Pinyon-juniper
Interior Douglas-fir	Arizona cypress
White fir	Western live oak
Western larch	Mesquite
Grand fir	**South Pacific, except for high mountains**
Western white pine	Sierra Nevada mixed conifer
Blue spruce	Pacific ponderosa pine–Douglas-fir
Aspen	Pacific ponderosa pine
Lodgepole pine	California black oak
Limber pine	Jeffrey pine
Rocky Mountain juniper	Knobcone pine
North Pacific	Canyon live oak
Red alder	Blue oak–digger pine
Black cottonwood–willow	California coast live oak
Sitka spruce	

SOURCE: Adapted from Eyre (1980).

TABLE 2.5   Forest Regions and Sections of Canada

Type group and type name	Type group and type name
Boreal forest region	**Montane forest region**
Laurentide-Onatchiway	Ponderosa Pine and Douglas-Fir
Chibougamau-Natashquan	Central Douglas-Fir
Gaspe	Northern Aspen
Gouin	Montane Transition
Northern Clay	Douglas-Fir and Lodgepole Pine
Hudson Bay Lowlands	
East James Bay	**Coast forest region**
Missinaibi-Cabonga	Strait of Georgia
Central Plateau	Southern Pacific Coast
Superior	Northern Pacific Coast
Nipigon	Queen Charlotte Islands
Upper English River	
Hamilton and Eagle Valleys	**Columbia forest region**
Northeastern Transition	Southern Columbia
Fort George	Northern Columbia
Lower English River	
Manitoba Lowlands	**Deciduous forest region**
Aspen-Oak	Niagara
Aspen Grove	
Mixedwood	**Great Lakes–St. Lawrence forest region**
Hay River	Huron-Ontario
Lower Foothills	Upper St. Lawrence
Northern Foothills	Middle St. Lawrence
Upper Foothills	Laurentian
Upper Churchill	Algonquin-Pontiac
Nelson River	Middle Ottawa
Northern Coniferous	Georgian Bay
Athabasca South	Sudbury-North Bay
Upper Mackenzie	Eastern Townships
Lower Mackenzie	Temiscouata-Restigouche
Upper Liard	Saguenay
Stikine Plateau	Haileybury Clay
Dawson	Timagami
Central Yukon	Algoma
Eastern Yukon	Quetico
Kluane	Rainy River
Northwestern Transition	
Grand Falls	**Acadian forest region**
Corner Brook	New Brunswick Uplands
Anticosti	Upper Miramichi-Tobique
Northern Peninsula	Eastern Lowlands
Avalon	Carleton
Newfoundland-Labrador Barrens	South Atlantic Shore
Forest-Tundra	East Atlantic Shore
Alpine Forest-Tundra	Cape Breton Plateau
	Cape Breton–Antigonish
Subalpine forest region	Prince Edward Island
East Slope Rockies	Fundy Coast
Interior Subalpine	Southern Uplands
Coastal Subalpine	Atlantic Uplands
	Central Lowlands
	Cobequid

SOURCE: Rowe (1972).

TABLE 2.6   Forest Regions and Types in the United States and Canada as Listed in the *Forestry Handbook*

Eastern forest regions

Southeastern pine–hardwood forest (12 types)
- Loblolly pine
- Longleaf pine
- Sand pine
- Shortleaf pine
- Slash pine
- Pitch pine
- Pond pine
- Virginia pine
- Oak
- Southern redcedar
- Yellow poplar
- Cabbage palmetto

Central hardwood forest (11 types)
- Post oak–blackjack oak
- Bur oak
- Chestnut oak
- Pitch pine
- Eastern redcedar
- Sugar maple
- White oak–black oak–northern red oak
- White oak
- Black oak
- Yellow poplar
- Sassafras–persimmon

Bottomland forest (16 types)
- Cottonwood
- Willow oak
- Swamp chestnut oak–cherrybark oak
- Sweetgum–willow oak
- Sugarberry–American elm–green ash
- Sycamore–pecan–American elm
- Black willow
- Overcup oak–water hickory
- Atlantic white cedar
- Pondcypress
- Bald cypress
- Water tupelo
- Sweetbay–swamp tupelo–redbay
- River birch–sycamore
- Silver maple–American elm
- Pin oak–sweetgum

Appalachian hardwood-conifer forest
- White pine–hemlock (11 types)
- Eastern hemlock
- Sugar maple
- Red spruce
- Fraser fir
- Chestnut oak
- White oak
- Northern red oak
- Yellow poplar
- Beech–sugar maple
- Virginia pine

Northern hardwood-conifer forest (17 types)
- Jack pine
- Balsam fir
- Northern pin oak
- Red pine
- Aspen
- Pin cherry
- Paper birch
- Gray birch–red maple
- Eastern white pine–northern red oak–red maple
- Eastern white pine
- Eastern hemlock
- Sugar maple
- Black cherry–maple
- Red spruce–sugar maple–beech
- Red spruce
- Paper birch–red spruce–balsam fir
- Beech–sugar maple

Northern spruce-fir forest (8 types)
- Jack pine
- Balsam fir
- Black spruce
- Black spruce–tamarack
- Aspen
- Pin cherry
- Paper birch
- Tamarack
- White spruce

Northern swamps and bogs (5 types)
- Balsam fir
- Black spruce
- Black spruce–tamarack
- Northern white cedar
- Tamarack

TABLE 2.6   Forest Regions and Types in the United States and Canada as Listed in the *Forestry Handbook* (*Continued*)

Western forest regions
  Northern Rocky Mountain conifer forest (12 types)
    Engelmann spruce–subalpine fir
    White bark pine
    Interior Douglas-fir
    Western larch
    Grand fir
    Western white pine
    Blue spruce
    Aspen
    Lodgepole pine
    Western hemlock
    Western redcedar
    Black cottonwood–willow
  Southern Rocky Mountain conifer forest (8 types)
    Engelmann spruce–subalpine fir
    Interior Douglas-fir
    White fir
    Blue spruce
    Aspen
    Lodgepole pine
    Limber pine
    Interior ponderosa pine
  Southwestern pinyon-juniper woodland (5 types)
    Western juniper
    Pinyon-juniper
    Arizona cypress
    Western live oak
    Mesquite

Northern coastal conifer forest (14 types)
    Mountain hemlock
    Engelmann spruce–subalpine fir
    Grand fir
    Western white pine
    Lodgepole pine
    Red alder
    Black cottonwood
    Sitka spruce
    Western hemlock
    True fir–western redcedar
    Douglas-fir
    Port Orford cedar
    Oregon white oak
    Redwood
  Southern coastal mountain forests (15 types)
    Lodgepole pine
    Limber pine
    Red alder
    Black cottonwood–willow
    Port Orford cedar
    Redwood
    Douglas-fir–tanoak–Pacific madrone
    Sierra Nevada mixed conifer
    Pacific ponderosa pine
    California black oak
    Jeffrey pine
    Knobcone pine
    Canyon live oak
    Blue oak–digger pine
    California coast live oak

SOURCE: Adapted from Hook et al. (1984).

TABLE 2.7   Forest Categories Described for Wildlife Habitat Improvement in the United States and Canada as Listed in the *Forestry Handbook*

Southern forests
  Pine and pine-hardwoods
  Bottomland hardwoods

Central hardwood forest
  Upland hardwoods

Western forests
  Pinyon-juniper
  Ponderosa pine
  Lodgepole pine
  Aspen

Douglas-fir and western larch
Spruce-fir

Northern and northeastern forests
  Appalachian oak and oak-hickory
  Oak-pine
  Northern hardwoods and
    conifer–northern hardwoods
  Northern spruce, spruce-fir and hardwood, northern white cedar

SOURCE: Adapted from Halls et al. (1984).

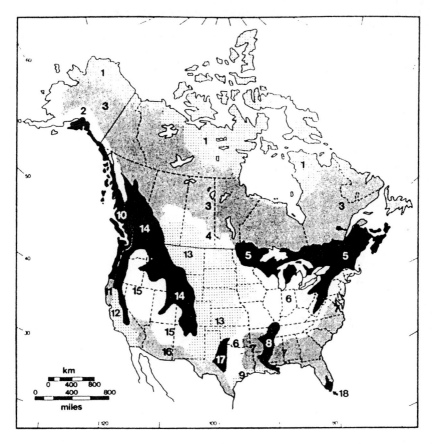

Figure 2.2 Major vegetation zones of North America: (1) arctic tundra, (2) subarctic and alpine tundra, (3) boreal forest (taiga), (4) parkland, (5) northeastern mixed forest, (6) deciduous forest, (7) southeastern mixed forest, (8) riverbottom forest, (9) Gulf coastal marshes, (10) Pacific Coast forest, (11) redwood forest, (12) California grassland and chaparral, (13) prairie, (14) coniferous forest, (15) sagebrush scrubland, (16) creosote scrubland, (17) mesquite, (18) Everglades. (*Allen 1987b.*)

Garrison et al. (1977) described 34 soil-vegetation units, called "ecosystems," for the conterminous United States (Table 2.9), followed by the Küchler (1964) system equivalents (phytocoenosis designations) (U.S. Geologic Survey 1967, 1970). The forest and woodland ecosystems are synonymous with broad geographic forest types described in U.S. Forest Service (1967). Each ecosystem contains descriptions of physiography, climate, soils, vegetation, fauna, and land use. In cooperation with the U.S. Fish and Wildlife Service, Bailey (1978) expanded these to include ecoregions of the United States relative to domain, division, province, and section (Table 2.10). For each province, Bailey (1978) described five categories of dominant

TABLE 2.8   Area and Percentage of North American Continent in Each of 18 Dominant Vegetation Zones

Vegetation zone	Area (km²)	% total North American area
Polar domain		
1. Arctic tundra	2,907,300	14.8
2. Subarctic and alpine tundra	467,700	2.4
3. Boreal forest	5,481,500	28.0
4. Parkland	220,600	1.1
Humid temperate domain		
5. Northeastern mixed forest	1,087,200	5.5
6. Deciduous forest	1,576,100	8.0
7. Southeastern mixed forest	900,900	4.6
8. Riverbottom forest	175,500	0.9
9. Gulf coastal marshes	99,000	0.5
10. Pacific Coast forest	351,700	1.6
11. Redwood forest	40,500	0.2
12. California grassland and chaparral	202,400	1.0
Dry domain		
13. Prairie	3,044,600	15.5
14. Coniferous forest	1,542,100	7.9
15. Sagebrush scrubland	918,600	4.7
16. Creosote scrubland	463,700	2.4
17. Mesquite	133,100	0.7
Humid tropical zone		
18. Everglades	35,100	0.2
Total	19,611,600	100.0

Note: Vegetation zone area data were provided by the Ontario Ministry of Natural Resources.
SOURCE: Allen (1987b).

physical and biological characteristics: land surface form, climate, vegetation, soils, fauna. Omernik (1987) developed and refined Bailey's (1977, 1978) description of ecoregions of the United States to produce a map with 76 ecoregions (Table 2.11). DeGraaf et al. (1988) compared five national land classification systems. Ecological (biophysical) land classification in Canada is based on a synthesis of information about geomorphology, soils, vegetation, and climate (Thie and Ironsides 1976).

Succession complicates classification systems because it is not perfectly predictable and it adds the dimension of time (Hunter 1990). Forest type classification tends to ignore the place of a forest type in a successional sequence because each type tends to be treated as an independent unit without regard to its place in succession. In an ecosystem classification system, the problem of successional stages can be avoided by focusing on the climax stage likely to develop on a particular site, without ignoring the various stages involved.

TABLE 2.9   Ecosystems of the United States

Forest and woodland ecosystems
White–red–jack pine
  Great Lakes pine forest
Spruce-fir
  Great Lakes spruce-fir forest
  Conifer bog
  Northeastern spruce-fir forest
  Southeastern spruce-fir forest
Longleaf–slash pine
  Southern mixed forest (seral stages)
  Subtropical pine forest (southern
    Florida)
Loblolly–shortleaf pine
  Northeastern oak-pine forest
  Oak-hickory-pine forest
  Pocosin
  Sand pine scrub
Oak-pine
  Oak-hickory-pine forest
  Southern mixed forest
Oak-hickory
  Oak savanna
  Mosaic of bluestem prairie and oak-
    hickory forest
  Cross Timbers
  Black Belt
  Oak-hickory forest
  Appalachian oak forest
Oak-gum-cypress
  Live oak–sea oats
  Cypress savanna
  Mangrove
  Southern floodplain forest
Elm-ash-cottonwood
  Northern floodplain forest
  Elm-ash forest
Maple-beech-birch
  Maple-basswood forest
  Beech-maple forest
  Mixed mesophytic forest
  Northern hardwoods
  Northern hardwoods-fir forest
  Northern hardwoods-spruce forest
Aspen-birch
  Northern hardwoods (seral stages)
  Northern hardwoods-fir forest
    (seral stages)
  Northern hardwoods-spruce forest
    (seral stages)
Douglas-fir
  Cedar–hemlock–Douglas-fir forest
  Douglas-fir forest
  Mosaic of cedar–hemlock–Douglas-
    fir forest and Oregon oakwoods

  California mixed evergreen forest
Ponderosa pine
  Mixed conifer forest
  Pine-cypress forest
  Western ponderosa forest
  Eastern ponderosa forest
  Black Hills pine forest
  Pine–Douglas-fir forest
  Arizona pine forest
Western white pine
  Cedar-hemlock-pine forest
Fir-spruce
  Silver fir–Douglas-fir forest
  Fir-hemlock forest
  Red fir forest
  Western spruce–fir forest
  Spruce-fir–Douglas-fir forest
  Southwestern spruce-fir forest
Hemlock–Sitka spruce
  Spruce-cedar-hemlock forest
Larch
  Grand fir–Douglas-fir forest
Lodgepole pine
  Lodgepole pine–subalpine forest
Redwood
  Redwood forest
Western hardwoods
  Oregon oakwoods
  California oakwoods
Shrubland ecosystems
Sagebrush
  Great Basin sagebrush
  Sagebrush steppe
  Wheatgrass-needlegrass shrub-
    steppe
Desert shrub
  Mesquite bosques
  Blackbrush
  Saltbush-greasewood
  Creosotebush
  Creosotebush-bursage
  Paloverde-cactus shrub
Shinnery
  Shinnery
Texas savanna
  Ceniza shrub
  Mesquite-acacia savanna
  Mesquite–live oak savanna
  Juniper-oak savanna
  Mesquite-oak savanna (seral
    stages)
Southwestern shrub steppe
  Grama-tobosa shrub steppe
  Trans-Pecos shrub savanna

TABLE 2.9   Ecosystems of the United States (*Continued*)

Chaparral–mountain shrub	Bluestem-grama prairie
Oak-juniper woodland	Mesquite-buffalograss
Transition between oak-juniper	Prairie
woodland and mountain-	Sandsage-bluestem prairie
mahogany-oak scrub	Bluestem prairie
Chaparral	Nebraska sand hills prairie
Coastal sagebrush	Blackland prairie
Mountainmahogany-oak shrub	Bluestem-sacahuiste prairie
Pinyon-juniper	Cedar glades
Juniper-pinyon	Fayette prairie
woodland	Desert grasslands
Grassland ecosystems	Grama-galleta steppe
Mountain grasslands	Grama-tobosa prairie
Fescue-oatgrass	Galleta-threeawn shrub steppe
Fescue-wheatgrass	Wet grasslands
Wheatgrass-bluegrass	Tule marshes
Fescue–mountain muhly prairie	Northern cordgrass prairie
Foothills prairie	Southern cordgrass prairie
Mountain meadows	Palmetto prairie
Plains grasslands	Everglades
Grama-needlegrass-wheatgrass	Annual grasslands
Grama-buffalograss	California steppe
Wheatgrass-needlegrass	Alpine ecosystem
Wheatgrass-bluestem-needlegrass	Alpine
Wheatgrass-grama-buffalograss	Alpine meadows and barren

SOURCE: Garrison et al. (1977).

TABLE 2.10   Land Area of the United States Classified by Ecoregion

	Percent
1000 Polar domain	
1200 Tundra division	
Lowland ecoregions	
1210 Arctic tundra province	2.2
1220 Bering tundra province	2.6
Highland ecoregion	
1230 Brooks Range province	1.6
1300 Subarctic (taiga) division	
Lowland ecoregion	
1320 Yukon forest province	5.7
Highland ecoregion	
M1310 Alaska Range province	3.1
2000 Humid temperate domain	
2100 Warm continental division	
Lowland ecoregion	
2110 Laurentian mixed-forest province	
2111 Spruce-fir forest section	1.0
2112 Northern hardwoods-fir forest section	0.6
2113 Northern hardwoods forest section	2.8

TABLE 2.10   Land Area of the United States Classified by Ecoregion (*Continued*)

	Percent
2114 Northern hardwoods-spruce forest section	1.8
Highland ecoregion	
M2110 Columbia forest province	
M2111 Douglas-fir forest section	0.4
M2112 Cedar–hemlock–Douglas-fir forest section	1.0
2200 Hot continental division	
Lowland ecoregions	
2210 Eastern deciduous forest province	
2111 Mixed mesophytic forest section	1.1
2112 Beech-maple forest section	1.9
2113 Maple-basswood forest and oak savanna section	1.3
2114 Appalachian oak forest section	3.1
2115 Oak-hickory forest section	3.7
2300 Subtropical division	
Lowland ecoregion	
2310 Outer coastal plain forest province	
2311 Beech-sweetgum-magnolia-pine-oak section	3.2
2312 Southern floodplain forest section	1.4
2330 Southeastern mixed-forest province	7.7
2400 Marine division	
Lowland ecoregion	
2410 Willamette-Puget forest province	0.4
Highland ecoregion	
M2410 Pacific forest province (in conterminous U.S.)	
M2411 Sitka spruce–cedar–hemlock forest section	0.2
M2412 Redwood forest section	0.2
M2413 Cedar–hemlock–Douglas-fir forest section	0.8
M2414 California mixed-evergreen forest section	0.1
M2415 Silver fir–Douglas-fir forest section	0.8
M2410 Pacific forest province (in Alaska)	0.2
2500 Prairie division	
Lowland ecoregions	
2510 Prairie parkland province	
2511 Oak–hickory–bluestem parkland section	3.8
2512 Oak and bluestem parkland section	2.4
2520 Prairie brushland province	
2521 Mesquite–buffalograss section	1.0
2522 Juniper–oak–mesquite section	0.7
2523 Mesquite–acacia section	0.9
2530 Tallgrass prairie province	
2531 Bluestem prairie section	3.3
2532 Wheatgrass–bluestem–needlegrass section	1.5
2533 Bluestem–grama prairie section	2.0
2600 Mediterranean division	
Lowland ecoregion	
2610 California grassland province	0.6
Highland ecoregions	
M2610 Sierran forest province	1.1
M2611 California chaparral province	1.0
3000 Dry domain	
3100 Steppe division	

TABLE 2.10   Land Area of the United States Classified by Ecoregion (*Continued*)

	Percent
Lowland ecoregions	
3110 Great Plains–shortgrass prairie province	
3111 Grama-needlegrass-wheatgrass section	2.6
3112 Wheatgrass-needlegrass section	3.1
3113 Grama-buffalograss section	3.9
3120 Palouse grassland province	0.5
3130 Intermountain sagebrush province	
3131 Sagebrush-wheatgrass section	2.8
3132 Lahontan saltbush–greasewood section	1.0
3133 Great Basin sagebrush section	1.4
3134 Bonneville saltbush–greasewood section	0.7
3135 Ponderosa shrub forest section	0.3
3140 Mexican highlands shrub steppe province	0.6
Highland ecoregion	
M3110 Rocky Mountain forest province	
M3111 Grand fir–Douglas-fir forest section	1.1
M3112 Douglas-fir forest section	2.8
M3113 Ponderosa pine–Douglas-fir forest section	1.8
M3120 Upper Gila Mountain forest province	1.1
P3130 Colorado plateau province	
P3131 Juniper-pinyon woodland and	
sagebrush-saltbush mosaic section	1.2
P3132 Grama-galleta steppe and	
juniper-pinyon woodland mosaic section	1.6
A3140 Wyoming Basin province	
A3141 Wheatgrass-needlegrass-sagebrush section	0.4
A3142 Sagebrush-wheatgrass section	1.0
3200 Desert division	
Lowland ecoregions	
3210 Chihuahuan Desert province	
3211 Grama-tobosa section	0.5
3212 Tarbush–creosote brush section	1.5
3220 American desert province (Mojave, Colorado, Sonoran)	
3221 Creosote bush section	1.2
3222 Cresote bush–bursage section	1.2
4000 Humid tropical domain	
4100 Savanna division	
Lowland ecoregion	
4110 Everglades province	0.2
4200 Rainforest division	
Highland ecoregion	
M4210 Hawaiian Islands province	0.3

Note: Total km^2 = 8,625,000
SOURCE: Bailey (1978).

TABLE 2.11   Ecoregions of the Conterminous United States

1. Coast Range	39. Ozark Highlands
2. Puget Lowland	40. Central Irregular Plains
3. Willamette Valley	41. Northern Montana Glaciated Plains
4. Cascades	42. Northwestern Glaciated Plains
5. Sierra Nevada	43. Northwestern Great Plains
6. Southern and Central California Plains and Hills	44. Nebraska Sand Hills
7. Central California Valley	45. Northeastern Great Plains
8. Southern California Mountains	46. Northern Glaciated Plains
9. Eastern Cascades Slopes and Foothills	47. Western Corn Belt Plains
10. Columbia Basin	48. Red River Valley
11. Blue Mountains	49. Northern Minnesota Wetlands
12. Snake River Basin/High Desert	50. Northern Lakes and Forests
13. Northern Basin and Range	51. North Central Hardwood Forests
14. Southern Basin and Range	52. Driftless Area
15. Northern Rockies	53. Southeastern Wisconsin Till Plains
16. Montana Valley and Foothill Prairies	54. Central Corn Belt Plains
17. Middle Rockies	55. Eastern Corn Belt Plains
18. Wyoming Basin	56. Southern Michigan/Northern Indiana Till Plains
19. Wasatch and Uinta Mountains	57. Huron/Erie Lake Plain
20. Colorado Plateaus	58. Northeastern Highlands
21. Southern Rockies	59. Northeastern Coastal Zone
22. Arizona/New Mexico Plateau	60. Northern Appalachian Plateau
23. Arizona/New Mexico Mountains	61. Erie/Ontario Lake Plain
24. Southern Deserts	62. North Central Appalachians
25. Western High Plains	63. Middle Atlantic Coastal Plain
26. Southwestern Tablelands	64. Northern Piedmont
27. Central Great Plains	65. Southeastern Plains
28. Flint Hills	66. Blue Ridge Mountains
29. Central Oklahoma-Texas Plains	67. Central Appalachian Ridges and Valleys
30. Central Texas Plateau	68. Southwestern Appalachians
31. Southern Texas Plains	69. Central Appalachians
32. Texas Blackland Prairies	70. Western Allegheny Plateau
33. East Central Texas Plains	71. Interior Plateau
34. Western Gulf Coastal Plain	72. Interior River Lowland
35. South Central Plains	73. Mississippi Alluvial Plain
36. Ouachita Mountains	74. Mississippi Valley Loess Plains
37. Arkansas Valley	75. Southern Coastal Plain
38. Boston Mountains	76. Southern Florida Coastal Plain

SOURCE: Omernik (1987).

3

Silvicultural Options and Impacts

Forestry Overview

Compared to other ecosystems, forests are tall, with at least three layers of vegetation: canopy, shrub layer, and ground layer. Sometimes the canopy contains an upper canopy and a lower canopy, i.e., it is at least two-tiered. If any of these layers is undeveloped, so will be the wildlife populations associated with it. Forests with well-developed layers of vegetation contain high vertical diversity of plants and animals. Vertical diversity generally requires uneven-aged management, i.e., selection harvesting (Hunter 1990). For maximum biodiversity, not all stands should be managed for vertical structure. After all, after an extensive natural disturbance like wildfire, a new stand of seedlings develops more or less as an even-aged forest. So a managed forest should be a compromise of even-aged and uneven-aged management in stands large enough to accommodate interior wildlife, where it occurred naturally, which will vary among forest types. The key to successful regulation of timber age classes for producing both timber and wildlife with minimum impact and cost is long-term planning of cutting schedules (Roach 1974). Once the distribution of cut areas is set, the pattern is difficult and expensive to alter (Halls 1973). The silvicultural system used has far-reaching detrimental or beneficial effects on wildlife, depending on species (Harlow and Van Lear 1981, 1987).

Forest systems are complex and more difficult to plan than most systems (Hunter 1990). They are more three dimensional than other terrestrial systems. Moreover, succession forces forests to change in species composition until the climax stage is achieved (Table 3.1) (Daniel et al. 1979), which disturbance constantly alters to an earlier successional stage. Not only are there many different forest types, the physical sites that support the various forest types also differ. The diversity of goals that characterize forest planning can conflict. This chapter and the next chapter focus on maintaining (1) interior wildlife and biological diversity with timber production, and (2) edge wildlife with timber production. Other goals could include recreation, aesthetics, livestock grazing, and preservation of water resources.

Because of the patchy nature of many forest landscapes, and because in perhaps most regions the whole forest tends to be isolated in a landscape dominated by human activities, managing forests for biodiversity is not so much a matter of producing more edge as it is of producing less. Managing forests for interior wildlife means reducing edge effects. Interior wildlife species need extensive unfragmented tracts of forest, few of which exist in most of North America due to human encroachment. Even relatively large forests tend to be fragmented and are subject to influences from surrounding lands. Edge wildlife will be accommodated by successional changes resulting from landscape differences (e.g., rivers, lakes, wetlands, meadows, cliffs, rock outcrops, changes in forest type), natural disturbance (fire, wind, landslide, insects, disease), silvicultural treatments, and other human disturbance (e.g., logging roads, rights-of-way for railroads, power-lines, pipelines). The rate of natural disturbance among various forest types over extensive periods is about 0.5 to 2 percent per year—i.e., each area in the forest will be disturbed about once every 50 to 200 years (Zackrisson 1977, Runkle 1985, Hunter 1990).

The three major owners of forestlands are governments, corporations, and private individuals. Because healthy ecosystems are the basic life support system to society, all of society benefits from managing for biodiversity. Thus, all taxpayers should pay for it. The two ways they can do so are through the management of public forests and by subsidizing certain costs on private lands, such as reduced property taxes (Hunter 1990). Four other groups also could bear the extra costs of managing for biodiversity: wildlife users, wood consumers, landowners, and taxpayers. Consumptive users of wildlife pay through license fees, equipment taxes, and property leases, but nonconsumptive users and landowners pay essentially nothing.

Softwoods produce more wood faster than hardwoods, but hardwoods generally produce more wildlife (Hunter 1990). A balance is needed. For example, Nova Scotia is committed to maintaining 65 percent of the forests in softwoods and 35 percent in hardwoods, which varies by site condition (Nova Scotia Department of Lands and Forests ca. 1989).

Public forests often are divided into ranger districts, which are divided into management units, which are divided into compart-

TABLE 3.1   Shade Tolerance of Some North American Trees

Eastern hardwoods
Very tolerant
  Eastern hophornbeam
  American hornbeam
  American beech
  American holly
  Flowering dogwood
  Sugar maple
Tolerant
  Basswood
  Blackgum
  Box elder†
  Red maple
  Silver maple
  Buckeye
  Persimmon†
  Sourwood
Intermediate
  American chestnut
  American elm*
  Rock elm
  Black oak
  White oak*
  Northern red oak*
  Southern red oak
  Black ash
  Green ash
  White ash
  Hackberry*
  Magnolia†
  Sweet birch
  Yellow birch
Intolerant
  Black walnut
  Butternut
  Hickory*
  Pecan
  Black cherry
  Catalpa
  Chokeberry
  Honeylocust
  Kentucky coffee tree
  Paper birch
  Pecan
  Pin oak
  Scarlet oak
  Sassafras†
  Sweetgum
  Sycamore†
  Tupelo*
  Yellow poplar
Very intolerant
  Bigtooth aspen

Quaking aspen
Cottonwood
Blackjack oak
Post oak
Turkey oak
Black locust
Gray birch
River birch
Osage orange
Willow

Eastern conifers
Very tolerant
  Atlantic white cedar*
  Balsam fir
  Eastern hemlock
Tolerant
  Northern white cedar
  Red spruce*
  Black spruce
  White spruce
Intermediate
  Bald cypress*
  Eastern white pine
  Slash pine*
Intolerant
  Loblolly pine
  Pitch pine*
  Pond pine
  Red pine
  Shortleaf pine
  Virginia pine
  Eastern redcedar
Very intolerant
  Jack pine
  Longleaf pine
  Sand pine
  Tamarack

Western hardwoods
Very tolerant
  Vine maple
Tolerant
  Canyon live oak
  Tanoak
  Bigleaf maple
  California laurel†
  Madrone†
Intermediate
  California white oak†
  Oregon white oak†
  Golden chinquapin†
  Bigleaf maple
  Oregon ash

Red alder†
Very intolerant
  Cottonwood
  Quaking aspen
  Willow

Western conifers
Very tolerant
  Alpine fir
  California torreya
  Pacific yew
  Western hemlock
  Western redcedar
Tolerant
  Alaska yellow cedar†
  Incense cedar
  Port Orford cedar
  Grand fir
  Pacific silver fir
  Subalpine fir
  White fir
  Engelmann spruce
  Sitka spruce
  Mountain hemlock
  Redwood
Intermediate
  Blue spruce
  Douglas-fir
  Giant sequoia
  Red fir†
  Monterey pine
  Sugar pine
  Western white pine
Intolerant
  Big-cone spruce
  Juniper
  Noble fir
  Bishop pine
  Coulter pine
  Jeffrey pine
  Knobcone pine
  Limber pine
  Lodgepole pine
  Piñon pine†
  Ponderosa pine
Very intolerant
  Alpine larch
  Western larch
  Bristlecone pine
  Digger pine
  Foxtail pine
  Whitebark pine

*Some uncertainty.
†Great uncertainty.
SOURCE: Adapted from Daniel et al. (1979), Hocker (1979), and Hook et al. (1984).

ments, which are divided into stands. Foresters refer to a *stand* as at least 2 ha of trees, but usually about 60 ha, reasonably similar in species composition and age structure, usually growing on a fairly homogeneous site (Gross and Dykstra 1989, Hunter 1990, DeGraaf et al. 1992). *Compartments* are usually 160- to 1200-ha administrative units (Fitzgerald 1984, Gross and Dykstra 1989).

Forest regulation is designed to produce sustained yields of wood, accomplished by area or volume control (Patton 1992). *Area regulation* (area control) involves an area of specific size but variable volume that is cut each year or other time period. The area to be cut is calculated by dividing the cutting interval by the rotation age. For example, if silvicultural treatment (cutting) is scheduled every 15 years in a stand on an 80-year rotation, 19% of the area would be cut every 15 years (i.e., 15 years ÷ 80 years = 0.19). *Volume regulation* (volume control) involves removing a specific volume of wood each year or other time period regardless of the size of the cut area, or until other resources are impacted.

Rotation time is the time interval between regeneration cuts on the same area of land to perpetuate an even-aged stand. In a compartment of 960 ha, for example, a 120-year rotation would result in 8 ha/year being cut (i.e., 960 ha ÷ 120 years), and 120 8-ha stands or 240 4-ha stands, etc., aged 1 to 120 years are designated. *Nonadjacency constraint* means that adjacent stands in even-aged management must be of different age/size classes. *Cutting cycle* is the time interval between cuts in an uneven-aged stand. For example, in a compartment of 960 ha, a 20-year cutting cycle would result in 48 ha in one stand to be cut annually (i.e., 960 ha ÷ 20 years) (Patton 1992).

Industrial forests tend to be managed in rotations of 40 to 60 years. Federal forests have more sociological and ecological constraints and tend to be managed usually in rotations of 60 to 100 years (Scott 1980, Brown and Curtis 1985). In intensively managed forests, any of these rotations eliminates those stand conditions with the greatest structural diversity, namely, the older seral stages of the mature forest and old growth. Early or late successional stages provide primary habitat for twice as many wildlife species as midsuccessional stages, which nonetheless often dominate the rotation time. For example, the two midsuccessional stages of Douglas-fir dominate about 60 percent of the standard rotation time of 80 years (Harris et al. 1982).

Four basic forest-management activities disturb habitat or rearrange vegetation (Stubblefield 1980): silvicultural systems, transportation systems, logging systems, and fuel (slash) management. Longer distances between the road and the designated timber tend to reduce the number of types of logging systems capable of removing the timber. Also, longer yarding distances usually require greater cable-holding capacities, which with conventional systems generally means larger equipment and wider roads with fewer curves, which is less compatible with wildlife.

Trees are felled (1) manually by chain saw or (2) mechanically by rubber-tired or tracked carrier vehicle usually, with a shearing head, or by fellerbuncher for whole-tree harvesting (Fig. 3.1) (Studier et al. 1984, Johnson et al. 1987). Transport of logs to the haul road is called "skidding" if logs are moved by animals or tractor, "forwarding" if moved in the bunk of an off-road carrier, or "yarding" if moved by cable, balloon, or helicopter.

Ground logging systems are used on relatively level terrain and include horse team, wheeled tractor, and crawler (tracked) tractor (Stubblefield 1980, Studier et al. 1984). Aerial logging systems include helicopters, balloons, and a combination of helicopter and air bag called a "helistat."

Cable logging systems use a machine called a "yarder" for winching in (yarding) logs from the felling site. They are used on mountainous terrain, and include highlead (Fig. 3.2), skyline with a non-slack-pulling carriage (Fig. 3.3), skyline with a slackpulling carriage (Fig.

Figure 3.1 Chip-harvesting system showing fellerbuncher, grappleskidder, whole-tree chipper, and chip van. (*Courtesy U.S. Forest Service North Central Forest Experiment Station.*)

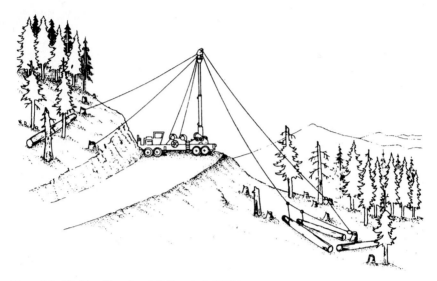

Figure 3.2 Highlead logging. (*Neitro et al. 1985.*)

Figure 3.3 Skyline logging—non-slackpulling carriage. (*Neitro et al. 1985.*)

3.4), and skyline with grapples (Fig. 3.5) (Studier et al. 1984, Neitro et al. 1985, Nyberg et al. 1989). A slackpulling carriage has a skidding line which is pulled out up to 45 m laterally to the side of the skyline and attached to logs. A non-slackpulling carriage and grapples allow

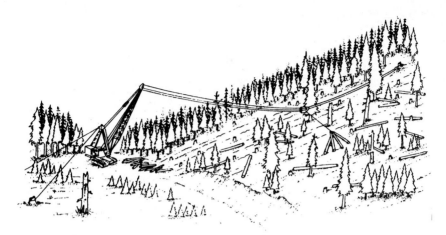

Figure 3.4 Skyline logging—slackpulling carriage. (*Neitro et al. 1985.*)

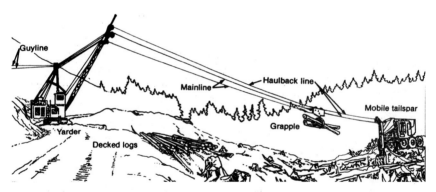

Figure 3.5 Typical skyline yarding system with grapples. (*Nyberg et al. 1989.*)

no lateral logging. Highleads drag the logs over the ground; maximum yarding distance is about 305 m uphill and 152 m downhill. Skylines mostly suspend logs aboveground during yarding, except during lateral yarding to a slackpulling carriage; maximum yarding distance is 1524 m. Multiple spans extend skylines, thus allowing large areas to be yarded with minimal site disturbance and road density. Cable yarding equipment will operate in a fan-shaped setting or where skyline roads are parallel for moving equipment (U.S. Forest Service 1986).

Some of the methods for fuel management include shaded fuel breaks, prescribed burning, piling and burning wood residue, chipping of slash, lopping and scattering slash, yarding unused residue to decking sites, constructing firelines to isolate hazards, felling snags, crushing brush and slash, windrowing logging debris, burying debris,

TABLE 3.2   Silvicultural Treatments

I. Regeneration Treatments: done to establish a stand

    A. Natural regeneration: establishing a stand from seed produced at the site, seed brought to the site by wind or animals, or from sprouts of root stocks already present on the site

Even-aged stands	Stands in which there are no more than two age classes.
Clearcutting	Establishing a new stand by first removing all of the previous stand; can be done in strips, patches, or blocks.
Seed tree	Establishing a new stand from seed derived from residual trees widely spaced as single trees or groups of two to three trees which are cut after seedlings are established.
Shelterwood	Establishing a new stand by gradually removing the existing stand so that new seedlings become established under the protection of the older trees; in strips, patches, or blocks, the first cut opens the canopy by about 50 percent, the second cut often removes 25 percent of the original stand, the third cut removes the rest.
Coppice	Establishing a new stand from sprouts or suckers derived from the previous stand; dimensions of clearings created are less than one-half the height of trees in the stand.
Coppice with standards	Mixture of sprouts or suckers with seedlings from reserving a few of the better trees, called standards.
Uneven-aged stands	Stands in which there are at least three age classes.
Selection	Maintaining an uneven-aged stand by repeated cuttings in a stand at regular intervals, typically every 5–10 years; may be organized as single tree or group designed to duplicate natural succession by selecting trees of all sizes and ages, large (> 0.4 ha) group selection resembles a small clearcut, i.e., even-aged management.

removing debris completely, and allowing public removal of debris for fuelwood. In addition to chain saws and fire, some of the tools used for fuel management include handwork, tractors, cable systems, and helicopters (Stubblefield 1980).

Silvicultural treatments (Table 3.2) are used in forest regulation. The structure, size, shape, and frequency of these treatments influence succession, edge and interior habitat, and biodiversity. The two general silvicultural treatments are *regeneration treatment* and *inter-*

TABLE 3.2   Silvicultural Treatments (*Continued*)

B. Artificial regeneration: establishing a stand by transplanting or seeding

Site preparation	Removing debris and/or competitors before planting or seeding: can be done manually, mechanically, chemically, or by burning.
Direct seeding	Establishing a stand by planting or spreading seed: seed can be broadcast or planted in spots.
Propagule	Establishing a stand by setting out seedlings, transplants, cuttings, or stumps.

II. Intermediate treatments: done between regeneration periods

A. Stands *not* past the sapling stage:

Release treatments	Freeing young trees from competitors manually, mechanically, chemically, by burning, mulching, grazing, or cultivation.
Weeding	Removing any competitor, regardless of position.
Cleaning	Removing overtopping competitors of same age.
Liberation	Removing overtopping competitors of older age.

B. Stands *past* the sapling stage:

Thinnings	Reduce the number of stems per hectare to reallocate growth, anticipate and capture mortality, and stimulate understory.
Low thinning	From below, removing weakest first.
Crown thinning	Within the main canopy (high thinning).
Dominant thinning	Above the main canopy.
Pruning	Remove limbs to improve wood quality and alter microclimate.
Prescribed burning	Controlled use of fire to control understory composition and fuel accumulation.
Sanitation cut	Remove insect and disease-bearing material.
Salvage cut	Remove dead trees killed by fire, wind, insects, or disease while still marketable.

SOURCE: Adapted from Hunter (1990), with additions from Thomas (1979), Smith (1986), and Patton (1992).

mediate treatment (Burns 1983, Hunter 1990). *Natural regeneration* involves producing even-aged or uneven-aged stands. Trees are harvested with plans for natural regeneration to perpetuate the forest. *Artificial regeneration* involves producing even-aged stands by planting seeds or propagules.

Timber stand improvement (TSI), or *stand improvement,* is a form of intermediate treatment that generally does not involve harvest of commercially valuable material (Beaufait et al. 1984). TSI is used mainly to improve the quality and value of trees on forestland newly acquired or not previously managed, usually via (1) precommercial thinning, (2) removing cull trees (weeding), (3) understory release by removing brush or less desirable larger trees to release saplings, and (4) site preparation for regeneration by removing trees, brush, and vines to release seedlings or favor seed dissemination and germination. TSI is most cost effective in relatively young forests capable of producing at least 3.5 m^3 of wood per hectare per year (Hill 1985).

Natural Regeneration

Shade-tolerant trees of different ages tend to comprise forests with small-scale, frequent disturbances, which usually are termed *uneven-aged* (Figs. 3.6 and 3.7) (Hunter 1990, Patton 1992). An even-aged

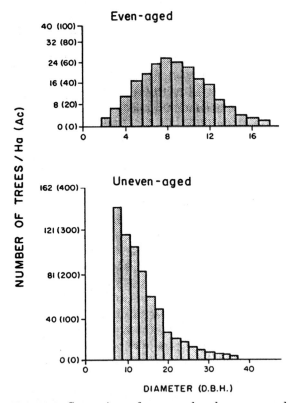

Figure 3.6 Comparison of even-aged and uneven-aged stands by diameter and number of trees per hectare. (*Patton 1992.*)

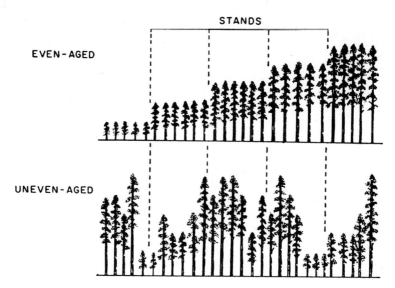

Figure 3.7 Visual schematic comparison of even-aged and uneven-aged stands. (*Patton 1992.*)

forest resulting from large-scale, infrequent disturbances tends to have one age class of either shade-tolerant or shade-intolerant trees, depending on stage of succession since the last disturbance. Stands in uneven-aged management have no rotation age because trees of various sizes and ages are always present (Hall et al. 1985b). The distinction between even-aged and uneven-aged stands can be ambiguous if the size of the stand is undefined, because virtually all uneven-aged stands consist of many very small even-aged stands.

Uneven-aged forests can be managed as small units of even-aged stands. Differences between even-aged and uneven-aged management include species composition and intensity and frequency of harvest, but the fundamental difference is the arrangement of the trees (Patton 1992). Emphasis on wood production truncates succession to favor rapid growth, short rotations, and economically valuable trees; early and late stages are shortened or eliminated (Edgerton and Thomas 1978).

Forest types that tend to have natural large-scale disturbance from fire should be managed by even-aged methods (Hunter 1990). Other forest types should be managed by uneven-aged methods. Even-aged management tends to support more wildlife species than uneven-aged management does in northern hardwoods, swamp hardwoods, spruce-fir, hemlock, oak-pine, and pine of northeastern forests (DeGraaf 1992, Hornbeck and Leak 1992).

Even-aged management

Even-aged management usually is used for shade-intolerant species (Wiley 1988b). Even-aged stands typically have single-storied canopies, and lack vertical (structural) diversity but have horizontal (spatial) diversity (Thomas 1979b, McAninch et al. 1984, Brown and Curtis 1985). Even-aged management is accomplished by clearcuts, seed-tree cuts, shelterwood cuts, coppice cuts, and coppice-with-standards cuts. Shelterwood and seed tree regeneration cuts might be multitiered for many years until cut when the new stand is established or until the uncut trees succumb to windthrow, sun-scald, insects, or disease (Thomas 1979b). A rotation age is established, e.g., 95 years, during which precommercial thinning might be used to space trees, and commercial thinnings are used to harvest trees that would die or compete with the desired stand density that maximizes height and diameter. Rotation age affects the amount of land in each successional stage. Even-aged forests provide all successional stages for associated wildlife, except that no old-growth habitat is produced in the rotation. Trees are mainly shade-intolerant. Douglas-fir and aspen, for example, need natural fire, clearcuts, or shelterwood cuts to regenerate because they cannot reproduce adequately in the shade of a multistoried stand produced by uneven-aged management (Hall et al. 1985b). Nonetheless, some professionals are calling for an end to even-aged management because of excessive loss of trees from windthrow and damage, excessive fragmentation of the forest (unless clearcuts are extensive), and reduced vertical diversity (Dodd and Adams 1989, Foss 1991).

Because even-aged management with seed tree and shelterwood cuts favors natural regeneration, these methods are preferred to clearcuts, which often require expensive artificial regeneration resulting in a monoculture (Smith and Martin 1974). But shelterwood cuts can resemble small clearcuts and require more heavily used roads for more entries into the forest ecosystem, and thus cause greater disturbance to wildlife (McAninch et al. 1984). Artificial regeneration with native seed mixtures will reduce the amount of time the land is in the grass/forb successional stage somewhat typical of the grassland biome and other grasslands, and thus expedite development of the forest and its wildlife. But a compromise in the use of seeding is needed if grasslands in the area are minimal, typically due to their conversion to agriculture and other uses.

Clearcuts. Clearcutting tends to favor shade-intolerant trees, and is the main method to produce even-aged stands. Clearcuts initially replace forest wildlife with grassland or brush wildlife. Foresters often plant propagules or seed clearcuts with preferred commercial species, practices which produce a monoculture undesirable for wildlife. The size of a cut which constitutes a clearcut is somewhat ambiguous, but *clearcut* can be defined as a cut at least 1 ha in area (Hunter 1990). *Patchcuts* are areas of 0.1 to 1 ha; the area is too small to be called a clearcut, but all the trees are removed, just as with a clearcut. Patchcuts can merge into group selection cuts which resemble small clearcuts if large enough. The term *patchcut* also is used to describe the relatively close placement of clearcuts of 16 to 20 ha or less. *Cutovers* are areas from which trees have been fairly recently harvested; the term often is used to describe a clearcut area in the grass/forb and seedling/shrub successional stages.

Clearcutting is the timber-cutting practice that alters wildlife habitat most because it completely removes the forest habitat, setting succession to an early stage, disturbing soil conditions, and modifying microclimatic conditions (McAninch et al. 1984). Often, slash is burned to prepare the site for forest regeneration, which can be by natural or, more commonly, by artificial means; the latter produces the least variation in age of the even-aged cuts, about 10 years compared to as much as 20 years for seed tree and shelterwood cuts (Brown and Curtis 1985). Brown and Curtis (1985) thought that diversity of wildlife habitat probably would be highest if at least two of the even-aged methods of harvest were used in the same watershed. Maximum edge contrast occurs when a clearcut is placed next to a mid-rotation-aged stand, because the contrast remains longer than the short-lived contrast between a clearcut and a mature forest scheduled for cutting (Harris and Marion 1982). Factors which influence wildlife use of the clearcut include nonadjacency constraint, size, shape, amount of precipitation, snow depth, amount of soil disturbance, and slash treatment (McAninch et al. 1984). The amount of precipitation influences rate of successional or structural change.

Traditional, even-aged methods fail to put enough back into the soil (Brooks 1991), especially if whole-tree harvesting is used. Biological reinvestment means leaving dead trees, woody debris, and a structure for the complex processes occurring below ground. Clearcutting tends to remove most of the snags and large woody debris which would have fed necessary organic matter to soils, served as water reservoirs, and provided habitat for a variety of organisms involved in reforestation (Brooks 1991). After logging, woody debris typically averages 6.7 to 11.2 t/ha, which is substantially less than needed for furbearers, small animals, or nutrient recycling (Hillis 1991). Clearcuts do not completely mimic the natural disturbance to which wildlife has adapted (Hunter 1990, Brooks 1991). Large openings created by clearcutting allow higher wind speed, which can condense water vapor fast, releasing heat which melts snowpacks, causing erosion, mudslides, floods, damaged water channels, increased sediment loads, and logging slash in streams (Brooks 1991). The increased wind speed and snow depth increase heat loss and reduce mobility of resident wildlife, except those insulated and concealed by snow, and bury forage deeply.

Clearcutting is the most controversial silvicultural method. Clearcuts should be located where few people will see them, for many people find them aesthetically displeasing and objectionable.

Seed tree cuts.   The seed tree method of even-aged management closely resembles the clearcut method, depending on the number and characteristics of trees left (McAninch et al. 1984). Usually about 25 to 60 trees per hectare are left (Yarrow 1990a). Seed dissemination is about three times the tree height (Smith 1986). Seed tree cuts are unfeasible where wet or thin soils produce root systems unable to withstand windthrow. Also, the small volume of timber left is difficult to sell (Jackson et al. 1984). After the new crop of trees is established, remaining trees might have to be felled and left as logs because they will retard the growth of the young trees if left standing.

Groups of seed trees provide more cover potential and edge than single seed trees do. Habitat is better for some wildlife species if the final removal cut of seed trees is not made, leaving a savannalike condition during the grass/forb successional stage. Seed trees provide excellent perches for some raptors hunting in the open area, and develop into snags. Wildlife associated with open tree canopies and open habitat will benefit, although some will receive heavier than normal predation from raptors. Impacts of seed tree cuts and clearcuts on wildlife are similar, although vertical diversity is substantially better and horizontal diversity slightly better with seed tree cuts (Crawford and Frank 1987).

Shelterwood cuts.   Shelterwood cuts cause minimal site disturbance and, for some wildlife species, the least habitat improvement of the even-aged methods of forest management (McAninch et al. 1984, Brown and Curtis 1985). Early successional stages are essentially lacking in shelterwood cuts. But various nongame birds and certain other tree-dwelling wildlife benefit from the multistoried canopy and variety of age classes produced. Intensive site preparation by bulldozers with rootrakes is impractical with shelterwood cuts, so stump holes remain to be enlarged by decay and burrowing, and then used by wildlife such as mice, chipmunks, rabbits, foxes, and other species (Jackson et al. 1984).

The length of the regeneration periods, the intensity of management, and the type of shelterwood cut influence wildlife use (McAninch et al. 1984). If shelterwood cuts are made in two or more operations at intervals of 5 to 25 years, the effects on birds are similar to those from group selection cuts, at least in spruce-fir stands (Crawford and Titterington 1979). More forest age classes result from shelterwood cuts with longer regeneration periods of 40 to 60 years than with periods of 10 to 20 years (McAninch et al. 1984). Intensive shelterwood management results in greater disturbance to wildlife due to more entries into the forest ecosystem and more heavily used roads.

Shelterwood cuts can be arranged in time and space uniformly, irregularly, in strips, or in groups (Smith 1986). Three-stage shelterwood cuts are better than two-stage cuts because of (1) smaller horizontal openings, which improves habitat for all but the most mobile wildlife species, (2) larger retention of vertical diversity, and (3) improved vertical diversity by producing two age classes of regeneration (Crawford and Frank 1987). The regeneration begins to provide some vertical diversity by the time the final cut removes the remaining overstory; the stand then resembles a clearcut.

Coppice cuts.   The coppice method of even-aged management is designed mainly to produce fuelwood, pulpwood, and animal browse from angiosperms (Smith 1986). Because stump sprouts and root suckers are the main source of regeneration, the stand is clearcut so that nothing is left to reduce sprouting vigor. Due to frequent cutting, the coppice method is most likely to deplete the soil by removing chemical nutrients, although harvesting trees when leafless and leaving slash can help. The coppice method is used most with quaking aspen and bigtooth aspen (Smith 1986).

Coppice-with-standards cuts.   Where a market for pulpwood or fuelwood exists, the coppice-with-standards method will build stand structure and maintain tree species diversity with a combination of (1) sprouting or suckering from cut trees and (2) seedlings from genetically superior crop trees (standards) that are left (Hunter 1990). Release work could be concentrated around each standard. Harvest could be staggered in time to improve vertical structure in the stand.

Uneven-aged management

Uneven-aged management is accomplished by group selection cuts and single-tree selection cuts. Uneven-aged management sometimes is called *all-age management.* Uneven-age management results in a more aesthetically pleasing forest environment than even-aged management. Mature trees usually dominate uneven-aged forests, with conditions resembling climax forests (McAninch et al. 1984). An almost continuous forest canopy of trees of various ages is produced with minimal disturbance to the site from timber removal. Cutting cycles exist, but no rotation age exists because trees of all sizes and ages are harvested selectively, and trees of various sizes and ages are always present (Hall et al. 1985b). No more than 15 percent of a stand should be cut at a time because too much wind damage will occur (Foss 1991). Stands have no obvious beginning or end because they are continuously or periodically regenerated, tended, and harvested (Alexander and Edminster 1977). Thus, no grass/forb, shrub, or sapling/pole successional stages exist, because only one kind of habitat exists—a multilayered forest of different tree sizes (Hall et al. 1985b).

Mature and old-growth trees, including snags, are usually more abundant than in even-aged stands (McAninch et al. 1984). Although deficient in horizontal (spatial) plant diversity, the multistoried crowns provide vertical (structural) diversity. A gradual reduction of shade-intolerant trees and understory plants results in a stand of shade-tolerant trees that can reproduce and grow under a canopy (Franklin 1976, Hall et al. 1985b). The value for wildlife relates to the target tree size, i.e., how much time a tree needs to reach a certain diameter (Hall et al. 1985b). For example, if the target tree size is 50 cm dbh (diameter at breast height), the stocking level is maintained by periodic harvest of all tree sizes until the largest trees reach 50 cm at perhaps 100 years. In this example, no old growth would develop. Forests under uneven-aged management tend to comprise groups of even-aged, shade-tolerant trees (Thomas 1979b, Smith 1986), especially from group selection cuts. In time, uneven-aged management benefits wildlife species adapted to more mature forest conditions (Thomas 1979b); but this is also true of even-aged management.

Group selection cuts.   Initially, group selection cuts increase the diversity of plants and animals because the small openings created temporarily increase shade-intolerant plants and forage plants (Thomas 1979b). Openings created produce clumped plant growth (Crawford and Frank 1987). Longer cutting sequences produce larger openings and clumps, increasing the mobility needed for animals to travel between treated and untreated areas, thus reducing horizontal habitat diversity for small mammals. Reduced horizontal diversity creates less habitat for birds that depend on openings, but increases it for canopy birds. Group selection generally increases populations of birds that prey on spruce budworm.

Openings over 0.4 ha tend to resemble even-aged management. Most are about 0.2 ha (Crawford and Frank 1987). Miller (1934) and Bromley et al. (1990) suggested that wildlife benefits most when group selection creates openings with diameters at least twice the height of the taller trees.

Single-tree selection cuts.   Single-tree selection tends to increase the proportion of shade-tolerant tree species (Edgerton and Thomas 1978). This method probably is best to preserve individual trees of high wildlife values—such as trees best for dens, nests, or roosts, or trees with high mast production—and to remove other trees encroaching on and competing with individual wildlife trees and groups of trees in important wildlife habitats such as riparian areas and winter ranges (McAninch et al. 1984). Removing only the most profitable trees, called *high-grading*, is widely discouraged because only poor-quality trees remain (Hunter 1990).

Single-tree selection maximizes vertical diversity by providing more canopy layers than other silvicultural treatments do (Crawford and Titterington 1979). But the ground and shrub layers are less developed even after a tree is cut because adjacent tree crowns spread out to reduce light penetration. This results in a relatively even distribution of a low but constant population of understory plants and associated wildlife.

Artificial Regeneration

Artificial regeneration often involves intensive management of plantations for wood. Such management typically involves some or all of the following (Hansen et al. 1991): clearcutting all live and dead trees; using fire or herbicides to control competing vegetation; replanting a single species; periodic thinning to maintain evenly spaced, vigorous trees; harvesting every 50 to 100 years.

Reforestation through artificial regeneration (planting) is not recommended for wildlife. Artificial regeneration accelerates succession that often produces stands of monocultures with low biodiversity. Converting stands of hardwoods to conifers generally reduces wildlife diversity (Hunter 1990). But in extensive hardwood stands, converting some sites to conifers can benefit wildlife. Converting an undesirable forest monotype to another monotype should be avoided. Even converting one type of conifer to another can harm wildlife (Repenning and Labisky 1985). Young conifer plantations are highly beneficial to wildlife in summer because ground vegetation is still present for forage and insect production and the conifers are large enough for cover. After that stage, wildlife use declines as the canopy closes and ground and shrub layers disappear.

Mature pine plantations have essentially no ground or shrub layers; only canopy wildlife inhabitants are present. Intermediate cuttings to minimum recommended stocking levels can help maintain a ground layer (Ohmann et al. 1978). Wildlife use of a pine plantation depends on its size and shape, species and spacing of the conifers, the associated neighboring habitats, and characteristics of the animals (Bailey and Alexander 1960). At 15 to 25 years (6 to 8 m high), plantation crowns close—this is the worst stage for wildlife. Conifers 15 m or higher allow light to filter through, which allows woody and herbaceous plants to establish, unless phytotoxins interfere. Plantations should be interspersed with openings, and with brush and/or hardwood areas, and should be no larger than 3 ha to benefit edge species of wildlife. Strips of mature hardwoods should be maintained through a coniferous plantation (Bromley et al. 1990).

Larger plantations benefit interior canopy-dwelling wildlife species. They contain greater variety and density of edge wildlife if stands are of uneven age with 0.1- to 0.8-ha openings scattered throughout and left unplanted. A checkerboard arrangement of conifers alternating with unplanted areas would duplicate natural openings (Smith 1958). Such coniferous plantations should not exceed 6 ha (Connecticut Department of Environmental Protection 1989). Where Christmas trees are no objective, 3-m spacing rather than 2-m spacing allows longer retention of live lower branches and herbaceous cover. Close planting and periodic removal of Christmas trees also improves habitat. Planting several rows of spruce around the plantation perimeter reduces windchill and snow depth within. The species composition of plantations should be mixed by alternating 20 rows of one type with 10 or more widely spaced rows of another. Hardwood thickets of aspen, cherry, and hawthorne should be retained within plantations (Smith 1958). Soft mast, especially *Rubus,* should be encouraged in openings.

To improve diversity in planted areas, a brush buffer should be retained around the perimeter of the clearcut (Wiley 1988b). Large trees, dead or alive, should be left in clumps of 0.1 to 0.2 ha distributed throughout the cut area where windthrow is unlikely. Wet areas, frost pockets, and poor sites should be unplanted. Open rows should be left unplanted at even intervals throughout the planting site to provide management access and herbaceous/shrub mixtures.

If planting is done, stocking should be low and irregular. Spacing seedlings 3.0 by 3.6 m or 3.6 by 3.6 m produces more herbaceous forage from sunlight penetration than the 1.8- by 1.8-m or 1.8- by 2.4-m spacing often used (Halls 1973). Forage production will be very low from crown closure to the first commercial thinning; a crown closes fast with a 1.8- by 1.8-m spacing. A reasonable compromise between the needs of wildlife and timber production probably would be to space 2.4 by 3.0 m (Halls 1973), but 3 by 3 m, 4.6 by 4.6 m, or 6.1 by 6.1 m is better for wildlife (Halls et al. 1984, Allen and Kennedy 1989). Other spacing configurations can be used to increase plant species richness and vertical diversity early in the rotation without reducing the final wood volume (Lewis et al. 1985).

Even without wide spacing, planting seedlings at time intervals as individuals, groups, or alternate rows will provide some vertical diversity (Fig. 3.8) (Hunter 1990). Planting a mixture of species improves vertical diversity of plantations. Species with similar

Figure 3.8 A planted stand with vertical structure established by planting groups of trees at time intervals. (*Adapted from Hunter 1990.*)

growth rates and shade tolerance should be planted so that each species is in blocks or double rows to reduce competitive exclusion. Such schemes are unnecessary if the mixture differs in growth rates (Smith 1986). Competing plants can be weakened or eliminated mechanically; chemically; or with a cover crop, especially of legumes (Hunter 1990). Tree shelters can be used to protect seedlings (Windell 1991). Other measures might be needed to protect seedlings from animal damage (Black 1992).

If stand conversion occurs, it should occur in strips or small blocks with natural stands between plantations, which benefits wildlife and reduces danger of widespread crown fires in conifer plantations (Rutske 1969). Firebreaks should be planted to clover to serve as wildlife openings in the area cleared for conversion. If maintaining openings is unfeasible, a buffer strip 1 to 3 chains wide should be reserved for natural regeneration between planted area and natural stand. Several species of conifers should be planted on conversion sites to improve diversity.

Block plantings can be designed in a checkerboard pattern of at least two species, each block containing at least four rows of four trees each, planted on 2.4-m centers (Fig. 3.9) (Perkins undated,

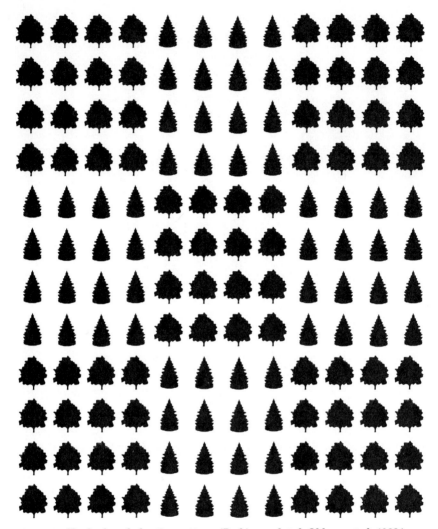

Figure 3.9 Checkerboard planting pattern. (*Perkins undated, Ohlsson et al. 1982.*)

Ohlsson et al. 1982). Block plantings also can be made in a row group planting of two or more species on 2.4-m centers by groups of rows (Fig. 3.10). Block plantings in rows consist of two or more species planted on 2.4-m centers by single rows (usually one species per row) in an aligned or staggered pattern (Figs. 3.11 and 3.12). The trees in Christmas tree and other single-species plantations can be planted and harvested in rotation to maintain an open portion of the understory. Such plantations can be improved for wildlife with a single or double row of shrubs planted around the perimeter (Rafaill and Vogel 1978, Ohlsson et al. 1982), unless damage to trees results from

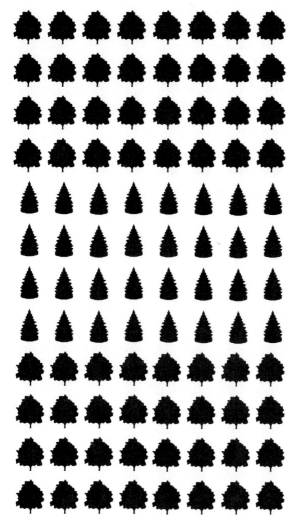

Figure 3.10 Row group planting. (*Perkins undated, Ohlsson et al. 1982.*)

attracting wildlife such as deer. Hardwood stands can be improved by planting conifers in blocks of 0.1 to 0.4 ha.

Strip plantings generally consist of strips of herbaceous ground cover alternated with strips of woody vegetation (Figs. 3.13 and 3.14) (Ohlsson et al. 1982, Herricks et al. 1982). Width of strips varies with size of area and land uses and cover types of surrounding area. On expansive areas such as wide benches and outslopes, mining sites, and mountaintop removal sites, strips of trees and/or shrubs should be 9 to 15 m wide alternated with strips of grasses and legumes 30 to 46 m wide, with all

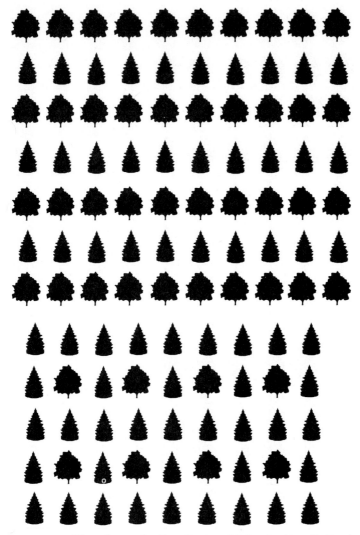

Figure 3.11 Aligned row planting (*top*) and interplanting (*bottom*). (*Perkins undated, Ohlsson et al. 1982.*)

strips planted on the contour. Woody strips should be connected with woody corridors on very large areas. A single or double row of woody vegetation provides enough edge on benches less than 30 m wide. Where seed drills can be used, seed can be planted on the contour in herbaceous strips 1.5 to 2.4 m wide, separated by open areas 1 m wide planted to single rows of woody vegetation. On steep slopes, fast-growing woody species should be planted 1 to 1.5 m apart in paired rows 1.5 to 1.8 m apart on the contour, with seedlings staggered in each row; the

Figure 3.12 Staggered row planting. (*Perkins undated, Ohlsson et al. 1982.*)

procedure should be repeated about every 6 m down the slope. Uniform strip width should not be maintained. Strips in oldfield or brush habitats should be about 6 m wide and about 20 percent of the area.

Clump or patch plantings consist of randomly spaced clumps of dense vegetation, usually of a single species and with irregular edges (Fig. 3.15) (Herricks et al. 1982, Ohlsson et al. 1982). Odd areas and small depressions are good sites for patches of shrubs and trees, and grasses and forbs. Woody patches should be about 3 to 6 m wide and 15 to 30 m long and of fast-growing food- and cover-producing types (see Tables A.1 through A.5). Herbaceous patches generally should be about 9 to 27 m^2.

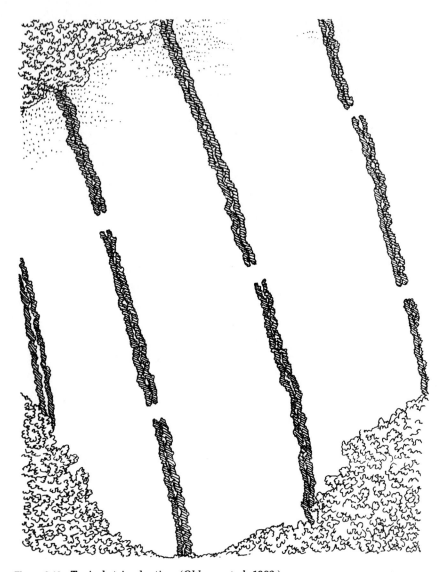

Figure 3.13 Typical strip planting. (*Ohlsson et al. 1982.*)

Edge or boundary plantings can improve habitat for edge species of wildlife, especially if combined with food patches and water areas (Fig. 3.16) (Ohlsson et al. 1982). Two methods can be used to develop edge. Several rows of shrubs can be planted along the edge between woods and field. Also, the edge of the woods can be feathered back by selectively cutting trees along the edge for perhaps 12 to 30 m back

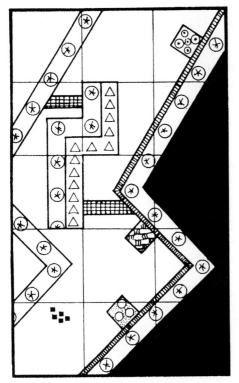

Planting Key:

- ■ Undisturbed forest
- □ Open Grasslands
- ▣ Deciduous Trees
- △ Coniferous Trees
- ▦ Corridor
- ▥ Edge
- ▢ Shrubs & Herbs
- ▨ Small & Large Shrubs
- ▦ Forbs & Grasses
- ▣ Clump Plantings

Figure 3.14 Strip planting. (*Herricks et al. 1982.*)

into the woods; this will allow more light to develop the ground and shrub layers. Den trees and snags should be uncut. Cut material can be used as logs and brush piles.

If a clearcut in hardwood were 16 ha and the policy insisted on planting, about 12 ha might be planted and the rest left to natural forest regeneration (Rutske 1969). Some area should be left open next to a road for recreational viewing (Fig. 3.17) or surrounded by an unplanted strip if not next to a road (Fig. 3.18). Openings larger than 4 ha could be planted as in Fig. 3.19, and long, narrow openings as in Fig. 3.20.

Spreading seed mixtures from the air can improve diversity because the patchy distribution that occurs produces stands of diverse composition and structure (Noble and Hamilton 1975). But

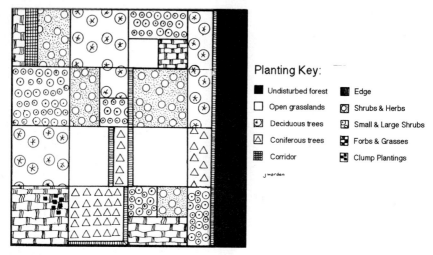

Figure 3.15 Patch planting. (*Herricks et al. 1982.*)

establishment often is reduced by adverse weather, seed predation by birds and small mammals, or competition from the other plants (Hunter 1990). Intensive mechanical site preparation, heavy seeding, and maybe even poison bait feeding stations and other animal control measures might be needed for success (Radvanyi 1970, 1973, 1974, Marsh and Steele 1992). Trees left in seed tree cuts and snags left in clearcuts will provide perches for raptors and corvines which will prey on the seed-eating birds and mammals.

Food plants for some upland wildlife species are listed in Martin et al. (1951), Chapman and Feldhamer (1982), Novak et al. (1987), and others. Halls (1977) described and illustrated 106 fruit-producing woody plants used by wildlife in the South. Halls et al. (1984) listed 191 species and genera of regional food plants of value to large carnivores, small carnivores, large herbivores, medium herbivores, small herbivores, game birds, and songbirds in North America (Table A.1). Cordell et al. (1984) and National Wildlife Federation (1984) listed grasses and forbs, low shrubs, tall shrubs, small trees, large deciduous trees, and large coniferous trees recommended for wildlife planting for five regions in North America (Tables A.2 and A.3). Hunt et al. (1978) listed collection and planting periods, region, life-form, and other characteristics of 361 plants recommended for habitat improvement on uplands (Tables A.4 and A.5). Campbell and Johnson (1981) recommended seeding six native species of evergreen forbs in new Douglas-fir clearcuts in late summer or early fall at 1.2 to 1.7 kg/ha for wildlife, and presented techniques for collecting, cleaning, and storing seed. U.S. Forest Service (1969, 1974), Hartman and Kester

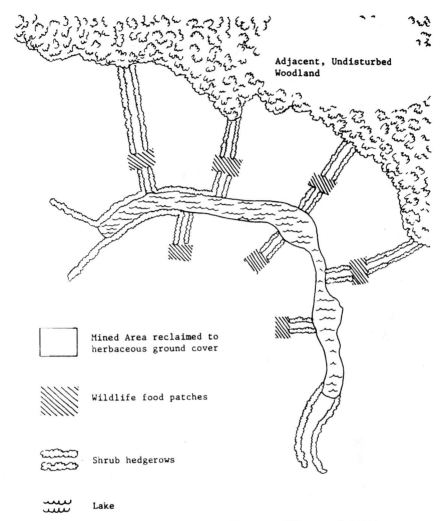

Adjacent, Undisturbed
Woodland

☐ Mined Area reclaimed to
herbaceous ground cover

▨ Wildlife food patches

〰️ Shrub hedgerows

〰️ Lake

Figure 3.16   Wildlife planting scheme. (*Russell 1978, in Ohlsson et al. 1982.*)

(1975), Williams and Hanks (1976), Hunt et al. (1978), Institute for Land Rehabilitation (1978), Rafaill and Vogel (1978), Jensen and Hodder (1979), Larson (1980), Dickson and Vance (1981), Proctor et al. (1983a), Beaufait et al. (1984), Cordell et al. (1984), Lantz (1984), Long et al. (1984), Smith (1986), Payne (1992), and others described details of planting techniques.

Site Preparation

Site preparation is a form of disturbance which sets back succession,

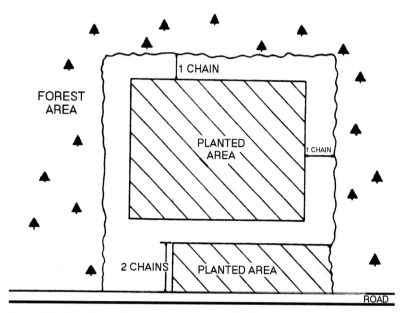

Figure 3.17 Possible pattern for planting a 4-ha forest opening next to a road. (*Rutske 1969.*)

but its net result is to accelerate succession by improving conditions for trees to grow. The three basic types of site preparation are mechanical, chemical, and prescribed burns.

Mechanical

Techniques for mechanical site preparation range from simple chopping and burning to the three-pass system of shearing, raking, and windrowing used mostly to convert mixed hardwood stands to pine plantations (Yarrow 1990a). In most cases, roller chopping and burning is adequate to establish conifers, relatively inexpensive, and best for wildlife. The fell-and-burn technique of site preparation involves felling in spring the standing residual trees left after a commercial clearcut, and then burning the area the following summer, often resulting in a mix of conifers and hardwoods excellent for wildlife. Rock raking (root raking), i.e., bulldozing rocks, stumps, sprouts, and ground cover into windrows to prepare the ground for planting, can remove much of the shrub and sprout growth that natural stand regeneration would promote (Rutske 1969). Moreover, windrows often contain large nutrient reserves and more topsoil than woody debris (Morris et al. 1983). A bulldozer with a K-G blade or towing two roller brush cutters also can be used (Smith 1986). Cabling or chaining, i.e., dragging heavy cables or anchor chains between two bulldozers,

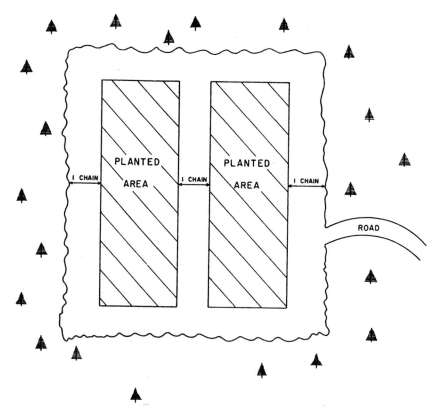

Figure 3.18 Possible pattern for planting a 4-ha forest opening not next to a road. (*Rutske 1969.*)

sometimes is used to remove trees and stumps in pinyon-juniper (Vallentine 1989). If the terrain permits, plowing, disking, and/or harrowing is done (Allen and Kennedy 1989). Mechanical site preparation is best done in late winter or early spring because then it favors large-seeded plants more than small, windborne-seeded plants, and thus a better variety and abundance of vegetation the following winter (Yarrow 1990a).

The benefits of mechanical site preparation are often temporary since plants develop from buried seeds, sprouts, and rhizomes to compete with tree seedlings (White et al. 1975, Hunter 1990). Mechanical treatment might produce greater species richness than chemical treatment (Marceau 1981, Martin 1981). Light site preparation increases fruit production (Stransky and Halls 1980) and can increase diversity (Swindel et al. 1983), production (Moore and Swindel 1981), and nutritional value (Stransky and Halls 1976) of forage plants eaten by large herbivores. Chaining in pinyon-juniper woodlands

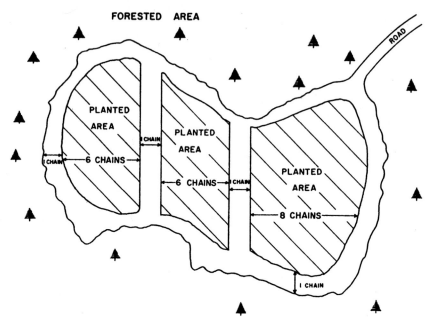

Figure 3.19 Possible pattern for planting forest openings larger than 4 ha. (*Rutske 1969.*)

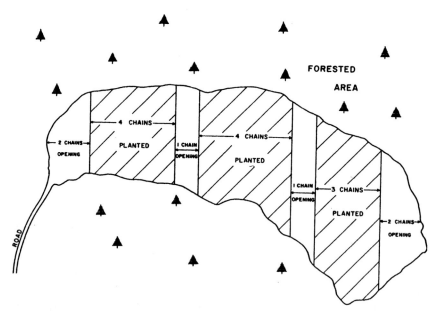

Figure 3.20 Possible pattern for planting long, narrow forest openings with conifers. (*Rutske 1969.*)

reduces bird species richness by two-thirds and breeding bird densities by one-half and increases small mammal populations 200 to 300 percent; effects last 8 to 15 years (O'Meara et al. 1981). Clearing widths should be no wider than 200 m, with some untreated strips or patches left (O'Meara et al. 1981, Swindel et al. 1983). (See "Woodlands," under "Mechanical Treatment," in Chap. 9.) Beaufait et al. (1984), Lantz (1984), Smith (1986), and others described techniques of site preparation on forest lands.

Chemical

Herbicides cause less structural damage to soil than mechanical treatment does, generally involve less off-site risk than fire does, and can be more selective than mechanical treatment or fire and just as selective as manual treatment (Hunter 1990). Nonetheless, other methods might be better than releasing toxic substances into the environment. (Also see "Herbicides" under "Intermediate Treatment" in this chapter, and "Herbicides" in Chap. 9.)

Prescribed burns

Fires can return nutrients to a site and raise soil pH (Wright and Bailey 1982). Prescribed burns are inexpensive. A disadvantage is that unlike mechanical and chemical treatment in site preparation, fire occurs naturally, stimulating many competing plants (Hunter 1990). Where commercial cutting is uneconomical, fire can be used to recycle aspen when stands are deteriorating and would convert to balsam fir or other shade-tolerant trees (Rutske 1969). But some deteriorating aspen stands are necessary habitat to some species of wildlife.

For site preparation, fires are used mostly for burning slash. Two general forms of prescribed burns are practiced (Pyne 1984). *Jackpot burning* removes heavy fuels or isolated clusters of debris. *Broadcast burning* removes continuous surface fuels over larger areas. It produces more food plants for species like elk and grizzly bears than other slash treatments do (Lyon and Basile 1980). For jackpot burning, heavy fuels must be dry and fine fuels moist. For broadcast burning, fine fuels must be dry. Back fires, with or without interior control lines, are used for most broadcast burns. If grass is the main fuel, a sequence around the perimeter may be used of back fire, flank fire, and head fire, to expedite burning larger areas. At least 670 to 1120 kg/ha of fine fuel is needed to burn grasslands with or without shrubs (Wink and Wright 1973, Beardall and Sylvester 1976). (Also see "Prescribed Burns" under "Intermediate Treatment" in this chapter, and "Prescribed Burns" in Chap. 10.)

Site Improvement

Fertilizer

Fertilizing forests is expensive, but fertilization can replace nutrients removed in harvesting and improve marginal sites (Hunter 1990). Fertilizers accelerate succession (Allen 1987c), which has negative effects on early successional wildlife and positive effects on mid to late successional wildlife. Fertilizer and lime increase the soil pH and bacteria, and thus affect the many invertebrates that eat soil microorganisms (Heliovaara and Vaisanen 1984). Tree vigor is improved, which improves resistance to defoliating insects but can render trees susceptible to sap-feeding insects due to increased turgor pressure. Applying industrial residues, ash, and municipal waste can increase understory biomass, reduce plant species richness, increase wildlife, and increase the amount of heavy metals and toxins in wildlife (Dressler and Wood 1976, West et al. 1981, Zasoski 1981, Anthony and Kozlowski 1982, Dressler et al. 1986, Martin et al. 1987). Smith (1986) described other aspects of applying fertilizer and mulch to forests. (See "Fertilizing" in Chap. 9.)

Drainage and irrigation

Drainage has been used to improve site conditions for certain species of trees (Smith 1986). It is expensive. It is also detrimental to those species of wildlife which depend on wet forests. For wildlife management and biodiversity, drainage should be avoided.

Irrigation is too expensive to be used extensively (Smith 1986). It accelerates succession.

Intermediate Treatment

Seedlings and saplings are released to develop faster if competing plants are weakened or eliminated, thus accelerating succession, an effect which might or might not be desirable. Opening the canopy increases fruit production, browse, forage, and nesting habitat. Most bird species nest between ground level and 3 m (Preston and Norris 1947), although many forest birds occupy other specific forest microhabitats (Dickson and Noble 1978, Conner et al. 1983a). Thus, the often shallow canopy and relatively simple structure of an even-aged stand has a simple bird and other wildlife community compared to a mature forest, in which natural thinning opens the canopy to allow sunlight to penetrate to develop the ground and shrub layers (Harlow et al. 1980, Lanyon 1981, Harris 1984, Hunter 1990).

Release treatments conducted early in the life of a stand are less likely to impact species diversity negatively (Hunter 1990). Yet early release can reduce the availability and size of snags, especially those of shade-intolerant tree species that form soft snags, such as birch and aspen.

Seedlings and saplings can be released with herbicides, fire, or cutting. Burning and cutting usually have a shorter-lived effect on target plants and plant species richness than herbicides. Herbicides that are activated through the soil or translocated to the roots can kill the roots, thus prolonging control, compared to fire and cutting (Walstad and Kuch 1987). Release also can be accomplished with the coppice-with-standards method of regeneration cut (see under "Even-Aged Management," above in this chapter).

Herbicides

Use of herbicides should be minimal. Trade names and common chemical names of herbicides commonly used in forestry include Dowpon M (dalapon), Aatrex 80 W (atrazine), Esteron 4 (2, 4-D), Roundup (glyphosate), Milogard (propazine), Princep (simazine), Asulox (asulam), Goal (oxyfluorfen), Modown (bifenox), Spike (tebuthiuron), Tordon (picloram), and Velpar (hexazinone) (Heidmann 1984). The Weed Science Society of America (1989) listed 148 major herbicides available in the United States and Canada. The U.S. Environmental Protection Agency (1974 plus updates) has listed herbicides approved for use in the United States, but some of these may not be approved by Canada or in individual states and provinces of the United States or Canada.

The list of herbicides approved for use by federal, state, and provincial governments varies annually or even more often as new herbicides are discovered and approved or as new information indicates approved herbicides are dangerous to public health and they are then disapproved. Hudson et al. (1984) described the toxicity to wildlife of 193 pesticides, including herbicides and insecticides. Federal, state, and provincial laws and regulations must be followed as well as the directions on the label of the product. Restricted-use pesticides may be applied in the United States only by applicators certified with the U.S. Environmental Protection Agency. Laws and regulations governing the use of herbicides are listed in U.S. Environmental Protection Agency (1974 plus updates). The U.S. Federal Aid Advisory Review Board must approve use of herbicides to be purchased with, or applied on lands purchased with, U.S. Federal Aid funds (Rutherford and Snyder 1983). Advance planning is needed because approval takes several months and probably will require an environmental impact assessment or an environmental impact statement.

Herbicides applied too early and vigorously could reduce the plant species richness for the entire rotation or longer if the seed bank is eliminated (Hunter 1990). Spraying herbicide over conifer plantations to eliminate competing shrubs and hardwood sprouts eliminates much of the benefit to wildlife derived from forest cutting (Rutske 1969). Aerial application can be adjusted by altering speed, or, alternately, by turning the spray boom on and off to create *skip areas* (patterns of untreated forest) as small as 1 to 1.5 ha or as narrow as 2.4 m; these serve as important refuge areas for brushland birds and mammals (McCormack et al. 1978, McCormack and Banks 1983, Santillo 1987). Skip areas should be marked before treatment. About 0.4 ha should be left untreated for every 8 ha treated (5 percent of the cut area) (Santillo 1988). Most skip areas should occur along logging roads and watercourses, within wet swale areas of cuts, in areas of unstable soils, in areas of low conifer stocking, and in patches within large treated blocks. To improve diversity, if a site larger than 40 ha is to be treated with herbicide to release conifers, half the area should be treated before brush overtops the conifers, and the other half 2 to 5 years later. Better precision is achieved when herbicide is applied by spot gun, boom wick, and ground tank with nozzle rather than by air (Minnesota Department of Natural Resources 1985). Types, characteristics, application, and timing of herbicides are described in DeVaney (1967), Miller and Craig (1979), Scifres (1980b), Holt and Fischer (1981), Newton and Knight (1981), Beaufait et al. (1984), Heidmann (1984), Lantz (1984), Smith (1986), Woehler (1987), Vallentine (1989), Michael and Neary (1990), Payne (1992), and others.

Cutting

Thinning.   Thinnings encourage the ground and shrub layer of herbs and shrubs for wild and domestic animals. Thinning too early or heavily can encourage too competitive an understory and worsen windthrow (Hunter 1990). Thinning too late or lightly causes overstocking and subsequent reduced growth and increased mortality. In coniferous forests, understory development and snow interception are functions of tree density and canopy closure in second-growth stands (Kessler 1984). Stocking guides used to prescribe thinnings for timber production can be used to enhance diversity. For example, in the stocking chart for even-aged northern hardwoods, the usual goal of thinning to the levels at line B in Fig. 3.21 promotes individual crop trees without sacrificing timber production (Carl et al. 1982, Hunter 1990). Thinning to the levels at line C will allow the stand to reach line B within 10 years. Thinning below the levels at line C would produce more vertical diversity within the stand by keeping the canopy open for at least 10 years.

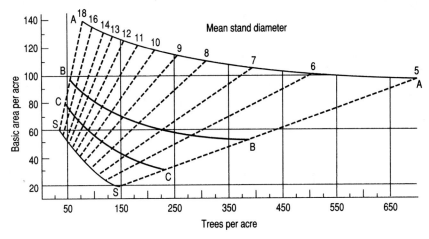

Figure 3.21 Stocking chart for even-aged northern hardwoods, based on basal area per 0.4 ha, number of trees in the main canopy, and average diameter. For timber objectives, stands above the A line are overstocked. Stands between A and B lines are stocked adequately. Stands between B and C lines should be stocked adequately within 10 years. Stands below the C line are understocked. For managing sugar maples, stands at the S line are at minimum stocking levels. (*Carl et al. 1982.*)

One heavy thinning early in the life of the stand should improve conditions for shade-intolerant and associated trees, thus increasing species richness. In some forest types, vertical structure can be enhanced with less severe, more frequent thinnings. Unlike the line pattern of thinning, the herringbone and chevron patterns remove fewer rows (spines) of trees and have short side rows (ribs) attached to each spine in a plantation (Fig. 3.22) (Anderson 1988). The juncture of each rib and spine forms an opening, which is enlarged when corner trees are lost as logs are dragged out. Many species of wildlife benefit when new plants colonize the scarified openings.

Precommercial thinnings can reduce food and cover. Such thinnings can increase diversity by creating openings in dense conifer or hardwood regeneration, or decrease diversity by removing hardwoods from conifer stands or by removing patches of conifers from hardwood stands (Crawford and Frank 1987). Thinning provides more available and nutritious food, especially for browsers, by concentrating nutrients in fewer plants.

Precommercial thinning should delay closure of the coniferous canopy to prolong the understory vegetation (Kessler 1984). For timber production, thinning commonly is delayed until canopy closure shades out conifer seedlings and competing plants. For wildlife production, thinning should be early enough to maintain a vigorous understory. Thinning too heavily can release conifers, which is undesirable for

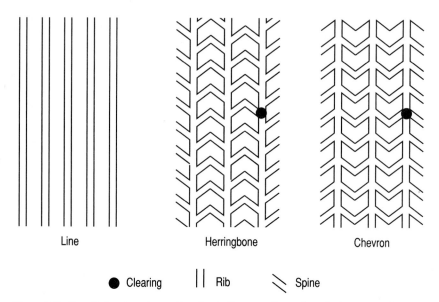

Line   Herringbone   Chevron

● Clearing || Rib   ＼ Spine

Figure 3.22 Small clearings in conifer plantations are formed at the juncture of each rib and spine with the herringbone and chevron patterns of tree thinning. (*Anderson 1989*)

wildlife and timber, and increase the snowpack in the forest, thus covering whatever forage was released. Too much precommercial thinning also produces too much slash for big game to negotiate (Wallmo 1969).

Commercial thinning in pole-size and sawlog-size stands allows use of trees that would otherwise die and decay, improves growth of remaining trees, and benefits associated wildlife (Crawford and Frank 1987) unless too many potential snags are removed. Maximum vertical diversity occurs when low, dominant, and crown thinnings are balanced to produce the shrub layer, midcanopy, and overstory in about equal volume, without removing too many potential snags (see "Snags and Live Den Trees" in Chap. 7).

Crown thinning can improve vertical diversity, but might decrease diversity of tree species (Crawford and Frank 1987). Heavy thinning can appear initially like group selection. Site quality influences the time needed for canopy closure after thinning. Intermediate sites maintain vertical and horizontal diversity longer. High-quality sites need thinning more often.

Crown thinnings open the canopy, develop the ground and shrub layers, and develop deeper crowns on the crop trees. The most practical way to encourage vertical diversity and plant species richness in plantations and natural stands of single species is with early and repeated thinnings, especially where even-aged management and short rotations prevent development of the open canopies of old growth.

Crown thinnings every 5 years or less can increase forage (Conroy et al. 1982), but with less protein, phosphorous, and calcium than preferred by some wildlife if the forage grows under heavy shade (Blair et al. 1983). Thus, some areas should not be thinned heavily. Thinnings can produce a second canopy of shade-tolerant trees that shade out the ground and shrub layers, which benefits canopy-using songbirds but not other wildlife (Blair and Feduccia 1977, Dickson 1982). Heavy crown thinnings also reduce thermal protection and increase snowpack (Nyberg et al. 1986).

Dominant and low thinnings reduce vertical structure and species richness (Hunter 1990). By killing low-quality trees with herbicide or girdling in groups rather than singly, ground and shrub layers will develop better while cavity trees develop (McComb 1982, McComb and Rumsey 1983). Some trees rot more slowly and stand longer if girdled rather than treated with herbicide (Conner et al. 1983c).

In southern industrial pine forests with a 30- to 35-year rotation, thinning should reduce basal area by 30 percent or more during ages 12 to 16 years and again during 20 to 25 years, or as early and often as economically feasible (Buckner and Landers 1980). Cutting all competing trees within 15 dm of selected crop trees (about 247 crop trees per hectare at 6 by 6 m) in a sapling-sized (2.5 to 13 cm dbh) stand of 90% northern hardwoods and 10% hemlock produces about 127 to 225 kg of fresh browse per square meter of basal area (Stoeckler et al. 1958). For best seedling and browse production, forests containing mixed oak and cove hardwoods should have a basal area of 20 to 23 m^2/ha (Knierim 1971). Loblolly–shortleaf pine forests should be thinned to a basal area of 14 m^2/ha to produce maximum deer browse. But 16 to 18 m^2/ha might be a reasonable compromise with timber production when repeated at 5- to 8-year intervals (Halls 1973). Food-producing trees, cavity trees, and uncommon trees that would add variety to the ecosystem should be preserved. Halls et al. (1984) described improvement practices mainly for edge wildlife of the major forest associations in North America. Smith (1986) described thinning practices for wood production.

Pruning.   Pruning reduces vertical structure. Removing live limbs close to the ground reduces forage and cover for wildlife associated with the ground and shrub layers. Removing dead limbs reduces availability of perching sites and insect prey. Restricting pruning to selected crop trees within a stand reduces impact to wildlife, especially songbirds (Hunter 1990). Smith (1986) described techniques.

Prescribed burns

Use. The terms *prescribed burns* and *controlled burns* are essentially synonymous (Smith 1986). In timber management, prescribed burns are used to eliminate heavy accumulations of litter that could fuel a wildfire, to control understory plants including maintenance of grassy understory and grasslands, to open pitch-sealed cones, to break the dormancy of buried seeds, to decrease water use of plants, to recycle nutrients, to prepare seedbeds for wind-disseminated seeds such as pine, and to control some diseases and insects (Komarek 1966, Wright and Bailey 1982, Chandler et al. 1983a, 1983b, Pyne 1984, Smith 1986). Such burns usually are set to burn fuel that naturally occurs on the forest floor beneath existing stands. In wildlife management, prescribed burns are used to improve habitat quality and quantity by increasing vertical diversity and quality and quantity of forage including grass, browse, and fruit. Such burns are not as hot as fires from burning slash in site preparation. But prescribed burns to reduce fuel are designed to interrupt vertical and horizontal diversity and thus reduce the incidence of crown fires (Smith 1986). Reduced vertical and horizontal diversity reduces wildlife diversity.

Until humans suppressed fire, stand replacement fires occurred every 435 years on average in Mount Rainier National Park (Hemstrom and Franklin 1982) and 150 to 276 years in the Cascades of central Oregon (Teensma 1987, Morrison and Swanson 1990). Most fires had uneven intensity. Severely burned patches were 0.2 to 100 ha in the Oregon Cascades; 86 percent were less than 16 ha. In the west central Cascades of Oregon, fires occurred every 166 years for partial or total stand replacement, and 114 years for all fires including low-severity fires. Canopy trees become snags and logs with fires of low to moderate intensity (Spies et al. 1990). Such fires also create canopy openings and/or bare soil for early successional herbs and shrubs and suppressed trees (Miles and Swanson 1986), and this improves species and structural diversity in all forest stages (Spies et al. 1988, Morrison and Swanson 1990). But some remnants of stands survive severe disturbances (Franklin et al. 1985). For example, mortality of canopy trees was less than 70 percent in 57 to 69 percent of the area burned between 1800 and 1900 in an area in the Oregon Cascades (Morrison and Swanson 1990.) Disturbances of high and low intensity are important agents of forest development.

Wildlife responds to fire effects as fire-intolerant, fire-impervious, fire-adapted, or fire-dependent (Kramp et al. 1983). Prescribed burns should be used in forest ecosystems where natural fire was common (Smith 1986). That generally excludes temperate and tropical rain forests, and perhaps to some extent bottomland hardwood forests and swamp coniferous forests. Improved quantity and quality of forage results from prescribed burning to maintain openings or dispose of slash (Taber 1973).

Thinning stimulates development of the ground and shrub layers. If the shrub layer consists of shade-tolerant tree seedlings or tall shrubs that shade out the ground layer, prescribed burning can be used to topkill some or most of this woody midstory (Komarek 1963). In the southeastern United States 1- to 2-year burning schedules will benefit turkeys, bobwhite quail, and other wildlife associated with the ground layer; 3- to 5-year burning schedules increase woody sprouts and fruit and benefit deer, bears, and other wildlife associated with the shrub layer (Buckner and Landers 1980, Hamilton 1981, Marion and Harris 1982). Selected thickets, brush piles, stream drains, etc., should be protected. Snags and large logs should be protected where silvicultural treatments have reduced their natural abundance (Horton and Mannon 1988). Burning should occur soon after thinning, and often enough to prevent excessive fuel accumulations. In the southeastern United States, grasses develop and most sprouting hardwoods decline with repeated summer burns; winter burns encourage woody sprouts (Stransky and Harlow 1981). Even the biomass and frequency of herbs can increase with winter burning (Moore et al. 1982). Such increases can persist for four growing seasons (Hallisey and Wood 1976). Fruit production and disease prevention to pines are best with burns every 3 years in the southeastern United States (Johnson and Landers 1978, Smith 1986), once the pines are 4.6 to 6.1 m tall (Bromley et al. 1990). In hardwood forests, burning before the acorns fall encourages development of oaks, which are thick-barked and relatively fire-resistant; oak forests in many areas resulted from repeated wildfires during the past 200 years (Bromley et al. 1990). Burns and scarification within a site often vary from patchy to complete; vegetative response varies accordingly (Taber et al. 1981). Cooler, more patchy site preparation fires or no fire at all on some sites could help maintain fire-sensitive species of plants (Spies 1991).

Prescribed burning on winter range for elk and deer reduces encroachment of conifers and stimulates grasses (Noste and Brown 1981). Spring burning of seral shrub fields in the West, when snowpacks and moist forest floors help control fires, resprouts old shrubs and stimulates forbs. Species that germinate from seed, such as willow and *Ceanothus,* should be burned during late summer and fall.

Fires on small areas of 4 to 8 ha can be used to improve browse conditions in aspen stands next to winter concentration areas of deer (Rutske 1969). Repeated fires in small areas can be used to create and maintain openings in the forest, but that promotes habitat fragmentation.

To reduce fire damage to foliage, the canopy must be well above the height of the flames (Smith 1986). Too much dry ground fuel results in too hot a fire and high risk of scorching and girdling trees. Only longleaf pine can withstand hot fires in North America, although certain other species can when their bark becomes rough and thick. Burning should be done during a gentle breeze which carries heat out of the forest. On steep slopes burning can be done on calm days because enough updrafts develop. Head fires (see Payne 1992) travel with the wind and damage trees less than back fires, which burn against the wind, because head fires dissipate heat better. But head fires spread to crowns more easily than back fires do, and must be avoided if crowns are likely to be damaged. Injury to trees depends on how long the temperature is maintained above the lethal threshold, generally 55°C. Lowest temperatures are achieved with winter burns.

Fire-adapted species of trees can be divided into five categories (Smith 1986).

1. Closed-cone pines, such as jack pine, lodgepole pine, Monterey pine, bishop pine, and sand pine, benefit when a crown fire kills the older trees, exposes the mineral soil, and opens the cones.

2. Cherries and certain shrubs like gooseberry and currant have hard-coated seeds that can survive a long time in the forest floor and germinate after fires.

3. Many broad-leaved trees and shrubs and a few conifers will be stimulated by fire to regenerate from sprouts.

4. Light-seeded species, such as birches, spruces, Douglas-fir, eastern white pine, western white pine, sweetgum, and yellow poplar, are not very resistant to fire but germinate and thrive on seedbeds of bare mineral soil exposed by fire, and produce a heterogeneous forest.

5. Species with fire-resistant bark, such as oak, longleaf pine, pitch pine, shortleaf pine, slash pine, and ponderosa pine, benefit from surface fires which arrest natural succession, expose favorable seedbeds, and prevent more destructive fires.

Prescribed burns generally are applied extensively to forest types with fire-resistant bark, but at times to sprouters like aspen if commercial harvest is uneconomical and to trees and shrubs with hard-coated seeds to stimulate browse and fruit production. To be protected, trees must be of fire-resistant size. Fire can be applied in uneven-aged forests only when the time between cutting and burning is at least the same as the time the reproduction needs to establish and develop resistance to fire (Smith 1986).

Fire should be prohibited in areas with many snags (Conner 1981). To create snags where few or none exist, a back fire can be used every 7 to 10 years. Combustible materials should be raked at least 3 m away from the tree base of known cavity trees to reduce risk of ignition. A fire lane should be plowed 60 m from the edge of colony sites for species like the red-cockaded woodpecker. Such fire lanes should be burned with a back fire every 3 years separately from the rest of the forest. Fire suppression equipment should be kept near cavity trees with heavy gum flows near their lower portion (see "Snags and Live Den Trees" in Chap. 7). To enhance fruit production from woody plants, prescribed burning is better than K-G blading or chopping in site preparation. Prescribed burning should be minimized in pine forests with an understory of fruit-producing woody plants. Prescribed fire can be used in bottomland hardwoods to enhance food production for wildlife. Leech (1982) presented examples of fire prescriptions for ponderosa pine.

Payne (1992) described types of prescribed burns, timing, site preparation, fuel, weather, smoke management, personnel and equipment, firing patterns, and report procedures. Smoke behavior and management are detailed in Southern Forestry Fire Laboratory Personnel (1976).

Weather and fuel. Flexibility in fire prescriptions increases with increased fine fuel. The closer the woody species grow in the shrub layer, the less fine fuel is needed (Wright and Bailey 1982). High-volatility fuels are explosive; low-volatility fuels are relatively safe to burn. Highly volatile fuels can cause firebrands and might need firelines up to 150 m wide (Green 1970, Bunting and Wright 1974). Grasses and most hardwoods are low-volatility fuels. Sagebrush, live aspen, oaks, rough beneath southeastern pines, and slash are moderately volatile fuels. Chaparral, dead aspen, dead juniper, and live conifers are high-volatility fuels.

Four sources of weather information generally are available (Wade and Lunsford 1989): National Weather Service, state or provincial forestry agencies, local observations, and private weather forecasting services. Wind, relative humidity, temperature, rainfall, and air mass stability are the most important considerations because they influence fuel moisture and fire and smoke behavior. An experienced prescribed burner can conduct a successful burn even when at least one factor is undesirable if other factors offset the undesirable one(s). Familiarity with local weather patterns is needed.

Conditions for winter burning often occur for several days after a cold front passes with 0.6 to 1.2 cm of rain. Summer weather conditions are less predictable.

Before burning, the latest weather forecast is obtained for the day of the burn, the following night, and the following day. Weather observations are made every 1 or 2 hours before, during, and after the burn to detect changes that might affect fire and smoke behavior. Readings must be made on a similar area upwind of the fire to avoid the fire's heating and drying effects. By using a belt weather kit that includes an anemometer and psychrometer, and observing cloud conditions, a competent prescribed burner can obtain a fairly complete picture of current weather conditions.

Underburning means to burn under a canopy. For most topography and fuel conditions, the preferred wind speed in the stand is 1.6 to 4.8 km/h, measured at eye level. Most forecasts give wind speed at a 6-m height in the open, which should be 10 to 32 km/h. Wind speed should be 13 km/h to burn standing debris, 8 to 13 km/h to burn chaparral, and 13 to 24 km/h to burn dead hardwood and volatile fuels and to top-kill shrubs (Britton and Wright 1971, Wink and Wright 1973). Easterly winds generally are undesirable for controlled burns, but sea and land breezes with expected arrival and departure times often are used along the coast. Steady and persistent winds are best, with higher wind speeds steadier in direction. Winds generally increase to a maximum in early afternoon then decrease to a minimum after sunset. Airstreams flow up slopes during day and down slopes at night.

Relative humidity should be 30 to 55 percent. Each 6°C rise in temperature decreases the relative humidity by half. The air behind a cold front is colder and drier.

Air temperature should be below 15.5°C for winter underburns (Wade and Lunsford 1989). During the growing season, air temperature should be above 26.6°C to control undesirable plants.

Burning should cease during prolonged drought, and resume after a soaking rain of at least 2.5 cm. Fine-fuel moisture should be 10 to 20 percent in the surface layer of freshly fallen needles and leaves. It should be 20 to 25 percent in areas of heavy fuel, especially with aerial ignition. A rough estimate of 15 to 20 percent moisture content can be obtained by bending a pine needle into a loop so that it snaps when the width of the closing loop is 0.6 to 1.2 cm (Wade and Lunsford 1989). A better estimate is obtained with 10-hour time-lag fuel moisture sticks (see Payne 1992). The lower litter always should be checked to be sure it is damp (Wade and Lunsford 1989). Burning on organic soil will dry it out and ignite it unless it is very wet.

The lowest risk of firebrands and crown fires and best smoke dispersion occur when the atmosphere is slightly unstable or air motion is neutral to vertical, causing an air inversion. The distance from the base of this inversion layer to the ground is called the *mixing height,* above which smoke mixes vigorously with air if the transport speed of the wind in the mixing layer is 14 to 32 km/h. Mixing heights should be 518 to 1981 m above ground.

For *debris burning,* wind speeds should be 1.6 to 4.8 km/h (eye level) for broadcast burning and up to 13 to 16 km/h for jackpot burning (see "Prescribed Burns" under "Site Preparation" earlier in this chapter). Humidity should be 30 to 55 percent.

Lack of an overstory allows improved smoke dispersion and higher temperatures for burning. The center perimeter fire (see Payne 1992) should be used when ambient air temperatures are high so that the heat is drawn into the cleared area to prevent heat damage to adjacent trees.

Burns should occur several days after a hard rain moistens the soil. Even then, intense, long-lasting fires should be avoided, especially on clay soils and steep slopes. Such fires are more likely with jackpot burning, which is one reason piling or windrowing slash is discouraged.

After logging, fuel is ready to burn when needles turn a greenish yellow and hardwood leaves wither. Ten-hour time-lag fuel moisture sticks (see Payne 1992) produce excellent results if left on the area and in the adjacent forest at least 2 weeks before reading. The sticks on the logged area should have a moisture content of 10 percent compared to over 15 percent in the forest. After several weeks of curing, fuels over 5 to 7.6 cm in diameter should be piled for adequate drying. Atmospheric stability is similar for underburning and debris burning.

Types of fires.   Types of fires are back fire, head fire, perimeter fire (center perimeter fire), flank fire, spot fire, and chevron fire (see Payne 1992). Martin and Dell (1978), Wade and Lunsford (1989), Wisconsin Department of Natural Resources (1990), and Payne (1992) described circumstances and uses for these fires. Head fires generally are used to kill shrubs and trees (Fahnestock and Hare 1964, Gartner and Thompson 1972, Sackett 1975), to burn low quantities of fine fuel (672 to 1120 kg/ha), and to clean up brush and debris (Heirman and Wright 1973, Wink and Wright 1973). Back fires are used when fuel exceeds about 2000 kg/ha to reduce heat damage to conifers and general overstory (Biswell et al. 1973, Wade and Lunsford 1989), and when weather is riskier than desired. Generally, center perimeter and, at times, spot fires are used to burn slash in clearcuts (Wright and Bailey 1982).

Topography.   Fires burn faster traveling up slopes. For example, a fire burns twice as fast up a 20 to 40 percent slope as on level ground (Southwest Interagency Fire Council 1968). Burns should be made along ridges rather than across them, because firewhirls usually develop on the lee side and might cause spot fires by throwing large firebrands ahead of the leading edge of the fire (Countryman 1971). On

TABLE 3.3   Ignition Methods for Prescribed Burning

Method	Where used	How used	Advantages	Disadvantages
Flamethrower	Slash or brush; broadcast or jackpot burning	Burner walks firelines or skid trails and ignites fuel combinations	Fastest hand-carried igniter; burner can reach several feet with flame to avoid walking in slash brush	Somewhat more expensive and complicated than drip torch, heavier to carry, and uses more fuel than drip torch does
Drip torch or drag torch	Almost any situation	Burner walks firelines, trails, or through fuels, dropping burning fuel	Simple, light, inexpensive, reliable equipment	Slower than flamethrower; burner often must move through heavy fuel
Helitorch	Clearcut slash; could be used in brush or other low vegetation	Helicopter carries large drip torch in sling; drips burning fuel	Fast ignition; not committed to predetermined firing	Helicopter expensive; safety not yet determined
Electrical ignition (primacord/jellied gasoline)	Clearcuts in west coast states; heavy slash and smoke dispersion considerations	Primacord is wrapped around metal or plastic containers of jellied gasoline and then electrically detonated in desired pattern	Extremely rapid ignition and convective buildup; excellent for smoke dispersal	Expensive to wire; once wired must burn
Fusees	Anywhere; best used as an auxiliary to other methods when needed	Burner walks fireline or trails, or through fuels; must hold flame to fuel for short period to ensure ignition	Inexpensive, light; can be carried in vest or pocket to use as auxiliary method	Very slow; must pause to hold flame to fuel; expensive in labor time to start fire

15-cm igniter cord-safety fuse (DAID'S)	Large or remote areas, from aircraft; Australia, Everglades	Ignited by cigarette lighter and then dropped from plane or helicopter to start spot fires; flames 15–20 seconds after ignition	Can ignite remote areas; intermediate expense; can cover large area	Dangerous if mishandled or in crash
Potassium permanganate/ethylene glycol capsules	Large or remote areas, from aircraft; Australia	Chemicals mixed by liquid injection, then dropped from plane or helicopter to start spot fires; ignites 30–60 seconds after mixing	Capsule and contents inexpensive; can easily cover large areas	Best only for large remote areas

SOURCE: Martin and Dell (1978).

calm days firewhirls can develop on flat terrain if the entire perimeter is lit (Haines and Updike 1971) or if head fires are burned into back fires. Other potential sites for firewhirls are edges of roads, corners of burns, curves in topography, and heavy fuel loads on forest sites.

Fireline. A *fireline* is a burned-over area between two firebreaks. A *firebreak* can be a natural break such as a road, pond, stream, or cultivated field, or a strip of ground plowed, disked, rotovated, or dozed down to mineral soil (McPherson et al. 1986, Payne 1992). Other methods of creating firebreaks can be used too (Payne 1992).

A 1.5- to 6.1-m fireline is wide enough in southeastern pine, slash, and grassland litter (Wright and Bailey 1982). A fireline 76 m wide is best in sagebrush/grass. A fireline 152 m wide is best for highly volatile fuels. Firelines can be narrower on ridgetops, especially if the south-facing slope is being burned and the north-facing slope is more moist, as is likely. Payne (1992) described other features of firebreaks, fire lines, and site preparation.

Ignition. Ignition methods vary with size of area and type of fuel to be burned (Table 3.3) (Dell and Ward 1970, Martin and Dell 1978, Tour 1991).

Managed Forests

Interior Habitats

Attention to structural complexity of forests to maximize biodiversity is advocated in the concept of "new forestry" and "new perspectives" (Franklin 1989, Gillis 1990, Kessler et al. 1992). Silvicultural texts mention techniques for developing structurally diverse mixed-species stands (e.g., Smith 1986), but the techniques have not been widely adopted (Hansen et al. 1991).

Managing complex forest ecosystems requires flexibility and various management practices that meet desired vegetation conditions (Evans 1974). For maximum biodiversity, all management practices should be sensitive to total plant composition, and maintain or develop it to ensure that all *native* plant and animal species survive. Systematic discrimination against any native species of plants or animals is ecologically unsound. Some species of wildlife will benefit more with treatment of habitat, some will benefit more with no treatment. The assumption should not be made that a managed forest is an improvement over an unmanaged forest (Maser 1988).

Management units

Every forest and other natural resource area should have a landscape ecological plan (Forman 1990). Plans should include five key spatially fixed characteristics: uncommon features, existing large patches, stream corridors, steep slopes, and links with other forests (Fig. 4.1). To tie a plan together into a basic spatial framework, three additional characteristics are added, which need more decision making: additional large patches, major natural land corridors, and main routes

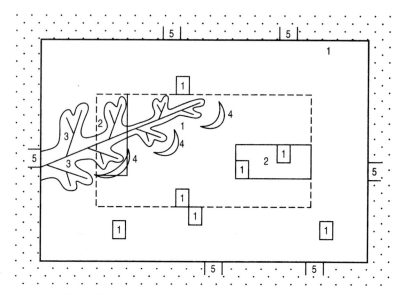

Figure 4.1 Spatially fixed characteristics needing special protection within a natural resource area such as a forest. Dotted area indicates the surrounding matrix; dashes separate the forest edge from the forest interior. 1 = uncommon features; 2 = large patches; 3 = stream/river corridors; 4 = steep slopes; 5 = links with other natural resource areas. (*Forman 1990.*)

for people (Fig. 4.2). Landscape boundaries usually are relatively distinct ecologically, due to geomorphology, natural disturbance, and human land use (Forman and Godron 1986). The natural resource area usually has administrative boundaries, based on previous land ownership, that do not correspond well with natural ecological boundaries (Lehmkuhl 1984, Schonewald-Cox and Bayliss 1986, Knopf 1992). But the landscape ecology plan must include the larger landscape mosaic. Expenses from effects between the natural resource area and surrounding area must be paid by society (Forman 1990).

To maintain biodiversity, natural disturbance must be emulated to provide the various-sized successional stages and stand conditions diversity requires (Samson et al. 1991). Regimes of natural disturbance, such as fire, wind, disease, and insects, might need to be mimicked with active management, such as planning of the extent and shape of prescribed burns and use of silvicultural treatments. Shade-intolerant old growth ultimately will succeed naturally to shade-tolerant old growth if such species are present, and the forest composition and structure will change; management must change with the changing forest. But some forests are too small for such mimicry.

The most important approach is integrating conservation planning with development planning, rather than relegating each to separate sections of the landscape (Harris 1984). For proper management for

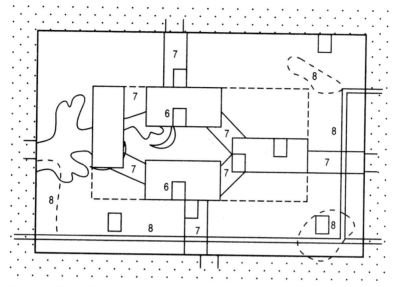

Figure 4.2 Example of the basic spatial framework that delimits areas needing special protection and areas appropriate for more intensive uses. Two character-istics, i.e., 6 = large patches (additional) and 7 = upland natural corridors, added to spatially fixed characteristics 1 to 5 (Fig. 4.1), delimit the area needing special protection; 8 = primary roads and paths for people. (*Forman 1990.*)

biodiversity, the extensive approach of landscape and regional ecology must complement the more intensive approach of reserving land specifically as national parks, wildlife refuges, etc.

Forestlands should be divided into an ecological hierarchy of units (Samson and Knopf 1982, Samson et al. 1989, Samson 1992). For example, a watershed might be needed for a wolverine's foraging habitat, a subdrainage for home range, a drainage for a few pairs, a river basin for a population, and an ecoregion for a metapopulation. The largest unit should be a physiographic *province* consisting of sev-eral watersheds (Samson et al. 1989). Provinces account for differ-ences in latitude, altitude, maritime versus terrestrial climates, and other geographic factors affecting the distribution of habitats and associated wildlife. Based mainly on percentage of an area that is forested and on slopes, watersheds should be divided into land types which produce a similar and predictable response to land-manage-ment activities (Hall and Thomas 1979). Forests on some land types are more open than on others (see Fig. 4.6); wildlife will respond dif-ferently to the same silvicultural treatment on different land types.

A system of old-growth islands should be integrated into the man-aged forest landscape; this system should be designed for the future, and evaluated as a *system* rather than as individual islands of habi-tat. To simplify planning, individual islands should be located perma-

nently rather than shifted in response to future human encroachment. To maintain genetic diversity and viability, the whole system
must involve travel corridors, i.e., landscape linkages, connecting the
habitat islands over an extensive area, if the corridors occurred naturally (see Chap. 6). Although all habitat types should be represented,
the system probably is served best if the interconnecting corridors are
riparian, associated with the dendritic pattern of streams within a
watershed. Thus, watersheds of different order should constitute a
management unit just as streams of different order constitute the corridors connecting old-growth islands within and between the watershed management units (see Fig. 6.16). Lower-elevation floodplain
sites support more wildlife per unit area than higher-elevation riparian areas do. Thus, floodplain forests as well as riparian corridors
should be heavily represented in the conservation strategy (Harris
1984). When sites and uses are chosen in certain combinations, the
concept of ecosystem synergism predicts a total desirable ecological
effect greater than the sum of the independent effects; for example,
such positive synergism results when old-growth sites are next to
mature forest sites or riparian sites.

Tree species have some indicator value of site quality, but understory plants are more commonly used for the final classification of
habitat types because they generally have more restrictive ecological
tolerance (Daubenmire and Daubenmire 1968, Pfister et al. 1977,
Kotar et al. 1988, Brooks 1989). The relationship of site quality also
can be quantified to an array of biological and physical factors in a
multiple-factor system that is simple and inexpensive to measure and
highly predictive of productivity (Thie and Ironsides 1976, Demarchi
and Chamberlain 1978, Leak 1980, 1982, Barnes et al. 1982).

Boundaries of stands in a compartment should conform to boundaries of site quality for each forest type (Roach 1974, Brooks 1989),
if such boundaries are large enough to prevent patchcuts or small
clearcuts (patchcuts and small clearcuts are acceptable if they
mimic natural disturbance or growth conditions). Then the age-class
distribution is decided and the appropriate rotation length and cutting sequence are selected for each site class or type class. The
planned regeneration cuts for each site class should be plotted
simultaneously on the same compartment map. Then adjustments
in cutting schedules can be made as needed. Silvicultural treatments must be coordinated with adjacent compartments throughout
the forest.

A variation of the ecological hierarchy (Samson et al. 1989) involves
two basic strategies to maintain the current distribution of each
species throughout its existing range (Fig. 4.3) (Lehmkuhl 1984).
These are the core population and dispersed-population strategies. In
the *core population (dispersal center) method* of distribution, popula-

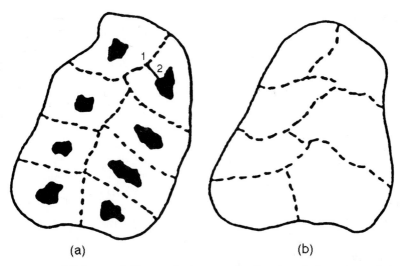

Figure 4.3 Minimum viable populations can be distributed throughout their existing range by (*a*) the core population or dispersal center method (distance between points 1 and 2 is average dispersal distance for the species), or (*b*) the dispersed-population method. (*Lehmkuhl 1984.*)

tions are distributed in cells, with a central core of habitat (Fig. 4.3*a*) that can be managed almost exclusively for wildlife, and a surrounding area managed for other uses. Each core is large enough to contain one minimum viable population (see Chap. 1). The area surrounding the habitat core in each cell ultimately might become suitable habitat, into which the population in the core area can then disperse. The distance between core areas of adjacent cells is determined by the mean dispersal distance of the population(s) within the cores, which is where the cell boundary is drawn. Thus, the distance between core areas is about twice the mean dispersal distance.

For species with large areal needs, the core areas can be reduced in size and separated by the mean dispersal distance rather than twice that distance; but the cores should be large enough to support at least 50 breeding individuals. This arrangement would provide adequate gene flow between the subpopulations in the cores and allow repopulation of cells with extirpated subpopulations. Patches or corridors of habitat between core areas might be needed to aid movement between subpopulations. Patches of suboptimal (*sink*) habitats should be arranged peripherally but close to optimal (*source*) habitats to allow recolonization of sink habitats when resources are good and populations high (Morrison et al. 1992). The core population method seems most applicable to relatively nongregarious and sedentary wildlife such as rodents and some birds that need relatively small areas of homogeneous habitat (Lehmkuhl 1984).

In the *dispersed-population method* of distribution, habitat is managed with other uses throughout the cell rather than in core areas (Fig. 4.3*b*). Most forests are managed this way. The dispersed-population method seems most applicable to wide-ranging territorial or gregarious (herd) species that need heterogeneous habitat (Lehmkuhl 1984).

Special situations need special approaches. On isolated mountain ranges producing an island effect, a wildlife species below the minimum viable population is managed as a subpopulation. It might need unrelated animals introduced at times to add variation to the gene pool. Where two forests or agencies share a population in time or space, each forest or agency would have to coordinate management of its subpopulation (Lehmkuhl 1984, Schonewald-Cox and Bayliss 1986, Knopf 1992).

Defining the areal distribution of a population is the first requirement in the decision to use the core population method or the dispersed-population method of animal distribution (Lehmkuhl 1984). Other important considerations include

1. Habitat needs in terms of diversity, interspersion, quality, and key features

2. Social behavior—i.e., territorial, gregarious, pairs, singly

3. Dispersal ability or mobility (migratory or resident) to exploit new habitat and find mates in subpopulations

4. Susceptibility to epidemics and natural catastrophes

5. Extent of habitat and population occurring on land managed by other landowners, and extent of their cooperation.

Multiple-use modules (MUMs) can be used to design a management unit for multiple use, including preserving old growth (Harris 1984). The old growth would be held in a core preserve surrounded by buffer zones of other uses, although the uses need not be addressed equally (Fig. 4.4) (Harris 1984, Noss 1987b). Roads, vehicles, and consumptive uses should be disallowed in the old-growth core. Use intensity of the various multiple-use objectives increases with distance from the core. Several clustered cores should be connected by corridors (inner buffer zones) surrounded by an outer buffer zone; these can be connected likewise to another cluster of cores (Fig. 4.5 and see Fig. 1.4) (Noss 1987b). At least 50 percent of the multiple-use module might be in the protected core (Noss 1991b). Flexible zoning laws are needed. (See "Old Growth" in this chapter.)

Lipscomb et al. (1984) recommended that the management area be no larger than 8100 ha to ensure that each kind of habitat produced will be well distributed within large areas. A management unit of about 3000 to 4000 ha might be a reasonable compromise for alpha (low mobility) species, as it generally includes about 80 to 90 percent of the wildlife

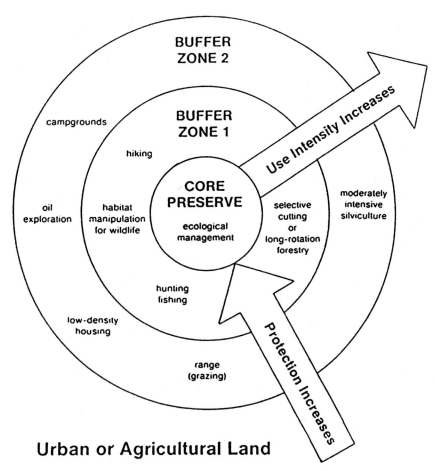

Figure 4.4 A multiple-use module (MUM), modified from Harris (1984) with an inviolate core preserve surrounded by a gradation of multiple-use buffer zones. Intensity of use increases outward through the buffer zones; intensity of protection increases inward. Important functions of an MUM are to (1) insulate sensitive elements in preserves from human threats including intensive land use, (2) provide marginal habitat for animals inhabiting a preserve, hence increasing effective preserve size, and (3) provide assorted human uses in the landscape with minimal conflict. (*Noss 1987b.*)

species inhabiting most forest types (Patton 1992). It would not include animals like the spotted owl, which needs 18,000 to 30,000 ha (see "Old Growth" in this chapter). Robbins et al. (1989) suggested that at least 3000 ha of contiguous forest canopy are needed to retain all forest-breeding birds in the eastern deciduous forest of North America.

Sizes of clearcuts, forest islands, and inter-island distances resulting from cutting sequences should be influenced by the home range, travel distance, and minimum viable population size of obligate interior species with the largest home range that might be contained

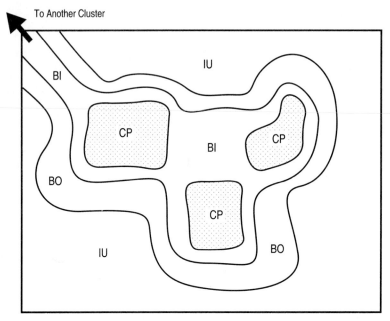

To Another Cluster

Figure 4.5 An integrated network of clustered reserves is created by combining the corridor and multiple-use zoning strategies. In this example, an inner buffer zone (BI) of low-intensity use surrounds and functionally interconnects three core preserves (CP). An outer buffer zone (BO) further buffers this complex from intensive land use (IU). A broad habitat corridor links this whole cluster of preserves to another cluster (not shown). (*Noss 1987b.*)

within the habitat patches (Harris 1984). (See "Minimum Viable Population" in Chap. 1.) Actually, size of the management unit should be large enough to contain more than the minimum viable population (Conner 1988).

Recommendations specific to eastern deciduous forests but perhaps generally applicable are as follows (Wilcove 1987): (1) clearings within the forest interior should be avoided; (2) forested tracts should be circular rather than irregular; (3) if 600 m is used as a measure of predation edge effect, then no true forest interior will occur within circular forestlands smaller than 100 ha (this finding is inconclusive) (see "Woodlots," Chap. 5); (4) forested tracts should be at least several hundred to several thousand hectares in size; (5) wildlife managers should broaden their perspective to include the area surrounding the managed area, in order to minimize deleterious external effects.

Among other things, a diverse landscape must have three basic characteristics: species composition resulting in a variety of cover types, balanced age structure, and spatial heterogeneity (Hunter 1990). After an array of communities is designed, they must be arranged on the landscape in time and space. The more closely the managed units can be arranged to reflect natural ecological communities, the better all resource prescriptions will be (Evans 1974).

Management strategy

Wildlife management can emphasize wildlife production or wildlife and other products combined (Samson et al. 1989). Some areas are so flat that the term *watershed* hardly has meaning compared to hilly or mountainous areas. But watershed can be defined as broadly or narrowly as desired to encompass terrain surrounding large rivers or small streams, even on flat terrain. If forests are divided into physiographic provinces containing several watersheds, at least one watershed within each province should be left intact (Schoen et al. 1984, Samson et al. 1989). In other watersheds, timber harvest should mimic the historical natural disturbance regime as much as possible.

With the dendritic pattern of streams and rivers dissecting the landscape, the land between two streams will be somewhat triangular, with the apex pointing downstream (Harris 1984) (see Fig. 6.16). In the upper reaches of the watershed, forest management might schedule clearcuts within these natural landscape units of adjacent watersheds so that the adverse affects of runoff, erosion, and nutrient loss would be shared by the two watersheds rather than concentrated in one. But confining operations to a single watershed reduces disturbance in an adjacent watershed because they are separated by a ridge (Black et al. 1976) (Fig. 4.6).

The dispersed-patch or checkerboard system of clearcutting on some federal forestlands tends to increase edge and reduce interior (Franklin and Forman 1987). For example, if the width of recently exposed edges is estimated conservatively by a measure equivalent to two tree heights, by the time a forest of 80-m-high Douglas-fir is 50 percent cut into 10-ha patches, no unmodified forest interior conditions exist. Obligate forest-interior wildlife would decline, but populations of edge species, including most game species, would be at maximum. (See "Edge versus Interior" in Chap. 1.)

Forest establishment should be no problem on large clearcuts in forests regularly experiencing large-scale disturbance, such as fire in some coniferous forests. But in forests used to small-scale disturbances (such as windthrow in tropical and temperate rain forests), or in temperate forests where seedlings of some shade-tolerant trees cannot survive in clearcuts or they have heavy seeds not easily transported into the middle of large clearcuts, the shelterwood and seed tree methods can be used to assure enough seeds and proper environment for regeneration (Hunter 1990), as can group selection (pers. comm. A. Haney, College of Natural Resources, University of Wisconsin—Stevens Point, 1993). These methods also can be used to

Figure 4.6 Adjacent watersheds separated by a ridge, with more open forest on some land types than on others. (*Photo by Mark F. J. Payne.*)

simulate large-scale disturbance (Van Lear 1991). Clearcuts should be accomplished such that soil erosion is reduced and enough slash remains to return nutrients to the soil and provide habitat for small animals. Otherwise chemical fertilization might be needed, although it cannot replace the organic matter so important to soil structure or the habitat that slash provides small animals.

In some areas, e.g., mixed hardwood stands, clearcuts often leave more than half the biomass (Van Lear 1991). By cutting most residual trees after merchantable trees have been removed, the appearance and functioning, to some degree, simulate areas impacted by high winds. Prescribed broadcast burning of logging slash after clearcutting can leave over 60% of large-diameter slash, thus simulating the fate of blow-downs in much of North America. Burn prescriptions can be modified to enhance patchiness of burns. Structure can be enhanced by the reserve seed-tree and irregular shelterwood methods (Smith 1986, Van Lear 1991), which leave the residual overstory trees indefinitely.

Clearcuts will develop into other stand conditions and successional stages. Extensive clearcuts ultimately become extensive contiguous forests with large interiors. Such clearcuts should be at least large enough to accommodate the minimum viable population of most if not all of the obligate interior wildlife species associated with the relatively uniform habitat of a given successional stage or stand condition of forest types that normally contain such species. Such clearcuts are larger than the public prefers aesthetically in some cases. The shape of a clearcut should be tailored to the landform, contours, and soil associations (Harris and Marion 1982). The size, shape, and distribution of patches cut in the forest are influenced by the existing landscape mosaic—that is, topography (e.g., drainage pattern and the length, evenness, and steepness of slopes), broad geographic patterns (e.g., differences in frequency of high winds between inland and coastal regions), and localized site conditions (e.g., poorly drained soils), all of which influence catastrophic events like fire and windthrow (Franklin and Forman 1987).

Forests that periodically experience natural large-scale disturbance, e.g., from wildfire, tend to establish readily after a clearcut. Forests that normally are maintained by small-scale disturbance, e.g., from windthrow, will have difficulty reestablishing soon after a large clearcut (Hunter 1990). Thus, clearcuts should not exceed the size of natural disturbances. A large natural disturbance, e.g., from fire, probably would be too large to mimic with a clearcut due to public sentiment, insufficient land to distribute such cuts equally in all successional stages of all forest types and site quality, and the different effects a fire and a clearcut have on the soil and the vegetation (Hunter 1990, Seymour and Hunter 1992).

Small-scale disturbances can be simulated with the individual tree selection and group selection methods of uneven-aged management (Van Lear 1991). The openings simulate canopy gaps in which regeneration develops. Small patchcuts could simulate larger small-scale disturbances.

Because local populations (demes) of plants and animals are distinct genetically from other demes of the same species, Pielou (1990) recommended that not more than 25 ha be cut in any 100-ha block of forest during a 50-year period, to save multitudes of demes of different species from obliteration. Individual tree selection is preferable to clearcutting. This approach might work in areas where a similar regime of natural disturbances occurs. In all cases, demes of plants and animals must be considered relative to tree harvest methods. Some demes no doubt evolved with large natural disturbances.

A key concept in managing forests for biodiversity is to emulate natural forest succession as much as possible at the landscape and stand levels (Samson et al. 1991).

Landscape level. Perhaps the most common approach to timber harvest in North America is a regular pattern of clearcuts and equal-sized leave strips between clearcuts (Samson et al. 1991). This creates edge but reduces interior. It also reduces large, contiguous stands of old growth. Two concepts in landscape management will allow timber harvest, provide habitat for size-dependent (area-sensitive) species, reduce edge, ensure a sustainable ecosystem, reduce road construction, maintain more old growth, and maintain a range of options for future resource management (Samson et al. 1991). These are progressive harvest and aggregated harvest.

Progressive harvest. In many areas, timber tends to be harvested in wide, continuous strips (Samson et al. 1989). Species richness is different and better at lower elevations (Harris 1984, Hansen et al. 1991), although management for biodiversity should occur at all elevations. Because lowland habitats are more productive for wildlife, the upper portion of the watershed should be harvested first to retain lowland habitats during most of the first rotation (Fig. 4.7) (Sampson et al. 1989), and old-growth islands should be larger in lowland areas (Harris 1984). North-facing slopes should be harvested in large, adjoining units before harvesting south-facing slopes, which provide critical winter habitat for many wildlife species. The south-facing slopes should be maintained as a contiguous unit of old-growth habitat where possible. Where harvest is scheduled for south-facing and southwest-facing slopes, the sun will reduce snow depth and early snowmelt will uncover herbaceous plants to aid winter survival of big game (McAninch et al. 1984), especially if adjacent cover is available.

Three factors determine the effective size of an old-growth stand which is essentially a habitat island (Harris 1984): size, distance from a similar old-growth stand, and extent of difference of the habitat separating old-growth stands. If the habitat between old-growth stands is similar to old growth, the entire area might be considered a composite which effectively increases the size of the old-growth stand. For example, a 25-ha old-growth stand of Douglas-fir should maintain its integrity if surrounded by mature timber (Harris et al. 1982). An old-growth stand surrounded by clearcut and regeneration stands should be perhaps 10 times larger than an old-growth stand surrounded by a buffer zone of mature timber (Fig. 4.8) (Harris et al. 1982, Harris 1984). Scheduling decisions will be affected by the amount of old growth to leave, and especially by the amount of large sawtimber to

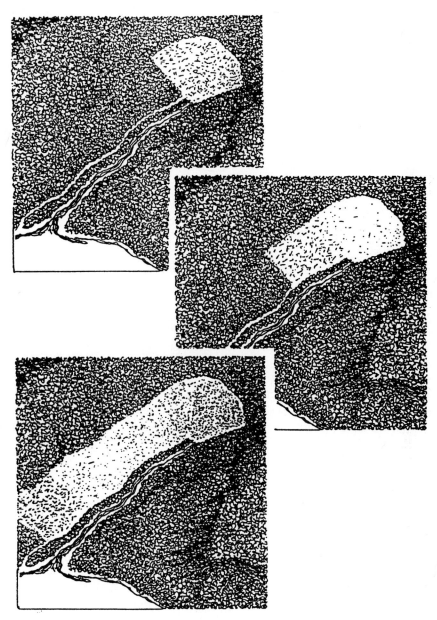

Figure 4.7 Recommended pattern of progressive timber harvest beginning in the upper portions of the watershed on north-facing slopes and proceeding toward the lower portion of the watershed. (*Samson et al. 1989.*)

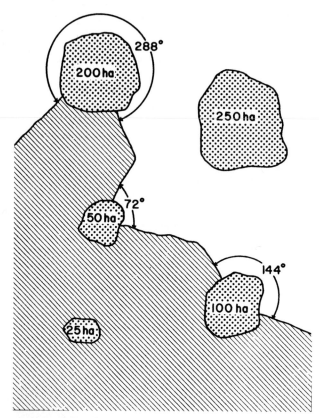

Figure 4.8 Size versus surroundings. An inverse relationship exists between the recommended size of old-growth stands (dotted) and the degree to which they are joined by second-growth (striped) and isolated in clearcuts (clear). (*Harris et al. 1982.*)

leave as a buffer that effectively increases the size of old-growth islands. (See "Old Growth" in this chapter.)

The best system to incorporate old growth into managed forests probably is a combination of long rotations surrounding reserves of old growth permanently withdrawn from harvest (Harris 1984, Hunter 1990). Advantages of the system are as follows (Harris 1984):

1. The effective size of the old-growth island is increased by the surrounding managed stands if most are mature. Such a buffer of wind, temperature, light, and relative humidity will effectively reduce the minimum size of old-growth stands needed to maintain the ecosystem processes and structural integrity. If surrounded by mature stands, the old-growth island will be protected more from

disturbance, especially from wind, and from fire in the West where mature stands are less susceptible than younger stands.

2. With the effective size of old growth increased without actually increasing the amount of area in old growth, more old-growth islands can be established with surrounding long-rotation stands.

3. The increased number of old-growth islands will facilitate conservation of endemic species in this unique habitat.

4. The increased number of islands geometrically increases two-way interactions between islands and geometrically reduces inter-island distances. This facilitates connecting the islands with corridors, thus improving movements, genetic interchange and colonization of wildlife and some plants, and conservation of large carnivores and other wide-ranging species.

5. The increased number of islands would increase the number of territorial species associated with old growth.

6. Surrounding an old-growth island with long-rotation stands can simplify planning of spatial patterns because replacement stands always will be near the old-growth island.

Long rotations probably should not be used in regions adapted to natural fragmentation, perhaps from numerous natural patchy fires. Long rotations would change the natural fragmentation of the landscape from a complex to a monotypic one (Knight 1987). Management of old-growth ponderosa pine and other conifers characteristic of the Rocky Mountains is being threatened by fire suppression. Aspen (and associated wildlife) also is disappearing in the West as fire is controlled.

Silvicultural treatments in some regions should involve large stands with substantial violation of age-class nonadjacency constraints (Robbins 1979, Franklin and Forman 1987, Gross and Dykstra 1989, Samson et al. 1989, 1991) and road rehabilitation and/or minimal road construction. Each of the large stands must represent a different successional stage or stand condition such that all successional stages or stand conditions are represented. Ideally, stands of old growth should be selected in all sites and forest types (Evans 1974), although shade-intolerant old-growth forest types (e.g., aspen) eventually would succeed to the climax stage of shade-tolerant old-growth forest types where they exist together.

Edge effect from human-caused fragmentation (e.g., roads, railroads, powerlines, housing construction, agriculture) is excessive to that from natural disturbance and habitat differences. Such excessive edge effect should be mitigated. For minimum edge effect, stands in even-aged management should be cut progressively—i.e., sequentially, referred to as the *locus method* of timber harvest (Robbins 1979,

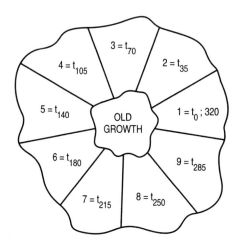

Figure 4.9 Island of old growth surrounded by long-rotation progressive cutting sequence (1–9) for minimal edge effect; t = time in years elapsed until area is cut. (*Adapted from Harris 1984.*)

Franklin and Forman 1987, Gross and Dykstra 1989, Samson et al. 1989, 1991, Becker et al. 1990) (Figs. 4.9, 4.10)—with maximum relaxation of nonadjacency constraints to minimize edge contrast. For example, Harris (1984) recommended that an old-growth island of Douglas-fir be surrounded by nine replacement stands. A rotation of 320 years instead of the usual 80 years for Douglas-fir allows the stands to survive another 120 years after the age of about 200 years when they begin to acquire the structural characteristics of old growth (Franklin et al. 1981). But the longer the rotation is, the less area will be in early successional stages with their associated wildlife (Hall and Thomas 1979). Prescriptions would need to consider potential problems from increased risks of fire, insect outbreaks, storm damage to trees, floods, landslides, excess runoff, and nutrient loss; land capability to produce and maintain particular environmental conditions must also be considered (Morrison et al. 1992).

To accommodate all wildlife species, Hunter (1990) proposed cutting equal amounts of forest by uneven-aged and even-aged (viz., clearcutting) management, omitting the amount in mature sawtimber. This should be modified by the historical natural disturbance regime in the area. Old growth should be preserved in as contiguous and circular a stand as possible, to reduce edge. Thus, species of wildlife needing the vertical structure of uneven-aged forests will benefit, as will those needing the various stand conditions and interiors with the reduced vertical structure of even-aged forests. Mature sawtimber in even-aged management will have developed some vertical structure.

Edges separating cuts should be as straight as possible in compliance with natural borders such as different soils, and within aesthetic

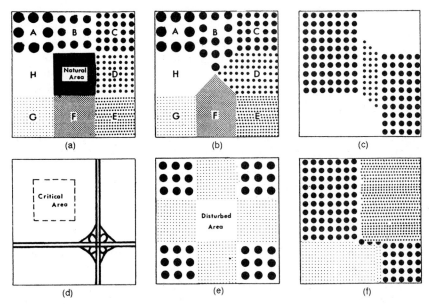

Figure 4.10 Management implications for forests surrounded by other land use (extent of shading simulates age of forest). (*a*) Ideal management, most likely preserving all bird species present. (*b*) Good management, with maximum adjacent habitat of each seral stage. (*c*) Birds can be preserved by planting trees to connect isolated woods with other forestland. (*d*) Presence of disturbances such as highways requires change in management strategy. (*e*) Severe fragmentation causes extinction of area-sensitive species. (*f*) If connected wooded corridors are left, effects of fragmentation can be reduced. (*Robbins 1979.*)

constraints, to minimize edge effect; the exception is when windthrow is a problem and feathering is needed (see "Stand Level" in this chapter). Adjacent stands similar in age and size will increase the effective size of a stand condition, thus benefiting interior species. The more stands there are, the more similar they and their edges will be, but the smaller they will be too. Thus, some compromise between number and size of stands is needed and will be influenced by spatial requirements and minimum viable populations of associated wildlife relative to the effects of natural disturbance. A Geographic Information System (GIS) is extremely useful, with historical (if possible), current, and accurate inventories of environmental conditions, habitats, and other landscape features (Morrison et al. 1992, Scott et al. 1993).

Insofar as possible, for each of the six stand conditions (see Tables 1.3 and 1.4) or nine or more stands recommended by Harris (1984) in the cutting sequence (see Fig. 4.9) in each of the forest types on poor, medium, and good sites (including topography and aspect), the home range, home range overlap, and minimum viable population should be calculated for those obligate interior species of wildlife with the largest home range, as described for the spotted owl (see "Old Growth" in this chapter). Some species with large home ranges can be ignored because they are habitat generalists or capable of routinely crossing most forest habitat types to reach the types they prefer. If space permits, stands larger than minimum should be clearcut in sequence, to reduce edge effect and produce extensive horizontal diversity and interiors of developing forests; otherwise, a decision must be made as to which wildlife species of large home range to ignore and how much smaller the stands to be clearcut must be.

Forests adapted to patchy natural disturbance should be managed by various-sized patchcuts emulating natural disturbance, with old growth protected (see "Edge Habitats" in this chapter). The effects of insects and diseases on tree mortality tend to be more extensive and continuous in simple forest types of one or two dominant tree species, and more dispersed or patchy in more complex forest types (pers. comm. H. Schabel, College of Natural Resources, University of Wisconsin—Stevens Point, 1992). The patchy distribution of different soils and topography in some areas might result in a naturally patchy distribution of forest types or stand conditions. Again, the regime of natural disturbance should be emulated in silvicultural operations.

The number of clearcuts of different sizes should be determined so that the total area of each size to be cut is about equal (Hunter 1990). Clearcuts should be smaller on steep slopes than on flat terrain (Harris and Marion 1982).

Franklin and Forman (1987) proposed reducing the emphasis on dispersing small clearcut patches throughout the forest (Fig. 4.11a, 4.11b, and 4.11c) to favor progressive or clustered cuts from scattered nuclei (Fig. 4.11d, 4.11e, and 4.11f). Within some of the clustered cutover areas, networks of small forest patches and corridors could be retained to increase cover and edge for game species, enhance interpatch movement of wildlife, and reduce wind fetch. Other cutover areas should be unfragmented to allow a contiguous forest to develop. Large patches of primeval forest should be identified and reserved for interior species, with no cutting preferably, or at least no even-aged cutting. Because most forests are surrounded by landscapes dominated by human activity, forest-interior wildlife should be managed in a core buffered from external effects, with edge wildlife living on the forest periphery (Hunter 1990). Clusters of small- and medium-sized forest stands could be located on the edge, surrounding a matrix of larger stands supporting interior wildlife species. Forest corridors (see Chap. 6) should be maintained to connect the reserves (Franklin and Forman 1987).

A program known as *minimum fragmentation* is being used in some national forests as part of a landscape-management approach based on

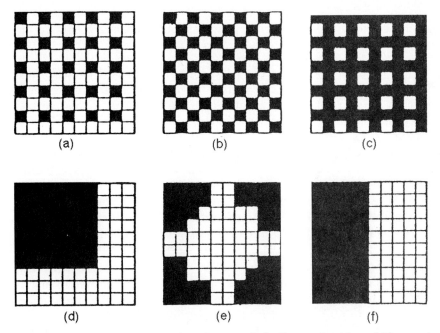

Figure 4.11 Progression of clearcutting from regularly dispersed patches of 25 percent (*a*), 50 percent (*b*), and 75 percent (*c*) cutover points; pattern of cutting at 50 percent point with single-nucleus (*d*), four-nucleus (*e*), and progressive-parallel (*f*) cutting systems. (*Franklin and Forman 1987.*)

the hypotheses of Franklin and Forman (1987) (Morrison et al. 1992). Broad landscape objectives are established and then desired future conditions for specific areas are described. Four general steps are followed:

1. The existing land allocations described in the forest-management plan are identified.
2. The current condition of the watershed is evaluated.
3. The desired conditions to meet management requirements are described (e.g., habitat needs of featured species).
4. The landscape is designed to meet future conditions.

The landscape is designed by specifying the timing, type, size, and location of management activities, such as timber harvesting and regeneration (Morrison et al. 1992). A focus on certain landscape features guides the management activities. Such features can be winter range for big game, scenic resources, naturally occurring forest stands, etc. Instead of 2- to 5-year project action plans or 10- to 15-year national forest land-management plans, landscape conditions spanning the next harvest cycle are planned. Timber harvest, regeneration, and other forest-management activities are located and scheduled to reduce the fragmentation effects of dispersed cuts and to produce large, contiguous forest blocks in the future.

Aggregated harvest.   Similar in some respects to Franklin and Forman's (1987) proposal, *aggregated harvest* means combining small (4 to 10 ha) harvest units into one or more large units; this method concentrates harvest activities that minimize fragmentation, thus reducing edge and increasing interior (Samson et al. 1991). For example, in the boreal forest, clustering clearcuts of less than 100 ha each could imitate the effects of much more extensive crown fires, especially if uncut buffers were left along shorelines to imitate stringers of unburnt lowland forest that often break up a large fire (Seymour and Hunter 1992). Aggregated harvest also maintains large, contiguous stands of old growth for an extended period in the rotation.

Stand level.   Young forests that follow harvest by clearcutting are dense and hard to improve for wildlife because of the limited industrial use of small trees. Three approaches at initial entry are more effective in maintaining habitat for some species of wildlife in areas to be cut (Samson et al. 1991): *gap development, securing (feathering) the edge,* and *green-tree retention.*
Temperate and tropical rain forests and perhaps some bottomland forests and other swamps tend to be relatively immune to fire; periodic and widespread disturbance from wind in such forests produces windthrow patches ranging from 0.4 to 70 ha in Alaska (Harris 1989). In contrast, other forests influenced by extensive fire tend to be contiguous (Samson et al. 1991). In some rain forests especially, patches of 0.4 to 1.0 ha are common. These low-impact, high-frequency gaps are caused by windthrow. Such forests should be harvested with group selection cuts of 0.4 to 1.0 ha to emulate natural forest dynamics and windthrow patterns. (See "Edge Habitats" in this chapter.)
Legacies include large windfirm trees, snags, and small green trees in the understory that survive natural catastrophic events such as fire or windthrow (Franklin 1989, Samson et al. 1991). Legacies can be retained by *feathering* a forest edge with selective harvests along the unit boundary to secure the newly created forest edge against windthrow. Feathering will channel wind above the forest canopy; otherwise the abrupt border of a harvest unit would be exposed to wind and might sustain substantial undesirable windthrow (see Fig. 4.14). A feathered edge also sustains lower predation rates than an abrupt edge does (Ratti and Reese 1988). Disruption of forest edges or interiors can be minimized by planting native conifers or other fast-growing native woody species along the newly created edge to speed development of buffer vegetation (Ranney et al. 1981).

About 10 to 40 percent of the living trees should be retained as small groups of old, live (green), windfirm trees within or extended into a clearcut (Franklin 1989, Franklin and Spies 1991, Samson et al. 1991, Spies et al. 1991). But these might serve as lightning rods on some sites and be undesirable in some areas. Such residual trees should be inherently long-lived, deep-rooted species that provide as little competition as possible to the developing stand (Seymour and Hunter 1992). Tall trees with narrow, medium-length crowns and continue to grow in height are best, although some wolf trees should be retained (see "Wolf Trees" in Chap. 5). Shallow-rooted species as residual trees should be left in clumps to resist wind better. (See "Snag Distribution" under "Snags and Live Den Trees" in Chap. 7.)

Partial cutting can be used to supplement or substitute for long rotations; they are not mutually exclusive, except that they produce irregular edges and less interior compared to circular or straight-edge cuts. Large conifers, hardwoods, snags, and logs should be retained. Old, windfirm trees will provide a two- or three-layered forest canopy, and also will provide snags and logs in later successional stages. If large structural legacies remain after the previous stand is partially cut, the structural characteristics of old growth can develop in less than 100 years in Douglas-fir, for example, although old-growth conditions begin to emerge naturally at 175 to 225 years (Fig. 4.12) (Franklin and Spies 1991). (See "Old Growth" in this chapter.) Combinations of natural regeneration, planting, and retaining advanced regeneration can produce mixed or pure stands.

Other harvest approaches and considerations. Tree harvest could be conducted so that old growth is maintained as large, contiguous blocks connected by travel corridors of trees along riparian areas and beach fringe (Fig. 4.13) (Samson et al. 1989). The blocks should be large enough for obligate interior wildlife species with large home ranges, and for species that have not been studied adequately. (See "Old Growth" in this chapter and "Riparian Areas" in Chap. 6.) Stands will be more persistent due to reduced edge exposed to windthrow. Most of the blocks of old growth will consist of several old-growth types. The blocks should be maintained from the riparian strip or shoreline up to treeline or the upper portions of the watershed to provide cover for seasonal movements of remaining animals between lower and higher elevations and increase the amount and variety of remaining forest.

Small management units, small forests, and small areal forest types should be harvested with selection cuts to avoid excessive fragmentation. Clearcuts there would not produce enough interior to accommodate many wildlife species; especially, they cannot provide for a minimum viable population of the most demanding area-sensitive obligate interior species with large home ranges.

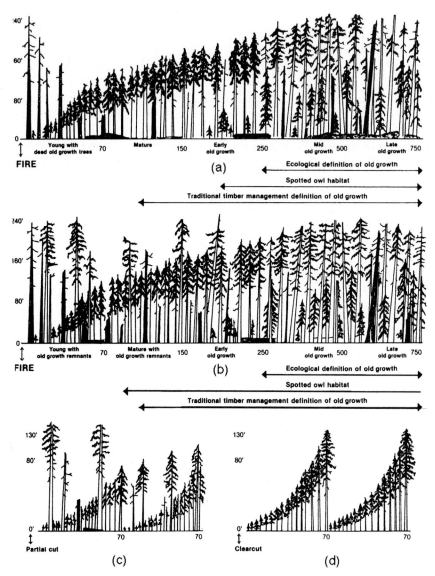

Figure 4.12 Successional series in Douglas-fir associated with (*a*) natural succession after total destruction of a stand of old growth, (*b*) natural succession after partial destruction of an old-growth stand, (*c*) succession under a partial-cutting regime to maintain two size and age classes of trees, and (*d*) succession under a clearcutting regime with a single age class. Structural similarities exist between (*b*) and (*c*). (*Franklin and Spies 1991.*)

Each forest landscape is unique. Biological diversity should include a compromise between clearcuts (for different forest conditions or successional stages, i.e., horizontal diversity) in some areas and selection cuts (for vertical diversity) in others, so that their ecological effects balance

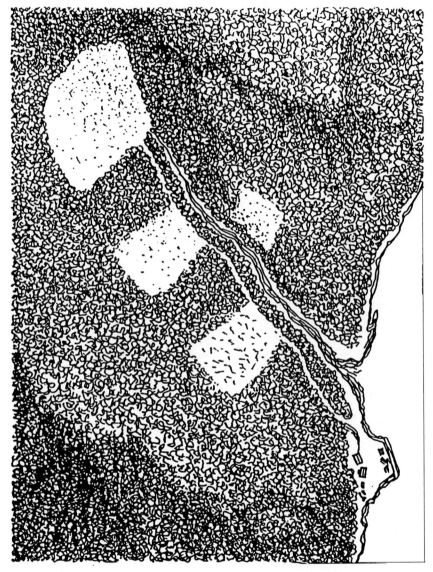

Figure 4.13 Pattern of timber harvest to maintain old growth in large, contiguous blocks connected by travel corridors of trees along riparian areas. (*Samson et al. 1989.*)

each other somewhat. For example, balancing various stands of oak and pine relative to the three basic characteristics of species composition, age, and area is easy conceptually, but becomes more complicated when oak is managed as an uneven-aged forest and pine as an even-aged forest—especially if stands vary in size (Table 4.1) (Hunter 1990).

TABLE 4.1   Management of a Hypothetical 9000-ha Forest Composed of Oak and Pine

Balanced Species, Age, and Area (ha)			
Oak	Young	Intermediate	Old
Small scale	500	500	500
Medium scale	500	500	500
Large scale	500	500	500
Pine	Young	Intermediate	Old
Small scale	500	500	500
Medium scale	500	500	500
Large scale	500	500	500

Different Rotation Age and Natural Disturbance			
Oak	<50 yr	50–100 yr	>100 yr
Small scale (single-tree selection)		1,500 ha of uneven-aged forest	
Medium scale (<1 ha)	500	500	500
Large scale (1–10 ha)	500	500	500
Pine	<40 yr	40–80 yr	>80 yr
Small scale (<1 ha)	500	500	500
Medium scale (1–10 ha)	500	500	500
Large scale (>10 ha)	500	500	500

More Diverse Array of Stands			
Oak	<50 yr	50–100 yr	>100 yr
Small scale (single-tree selection)		1,500 ha of uneven-aged forest	
Medium scale (< 1 ha)	700	500	—
Large scale (1–10 ha)	150	840	810
Pine	<40 yr	40–80 yr	>80 yr
Small scale (<1 ha)	560	670	40
Medium scale (1–10 ha)	880	80	800
Large scale (>10 ha)	910	560	—

SOURCE: Adapted from Hunter (1990).

Key wildlife areas in all forest types should be preserved such that natural corridors of cover connect them with other suitable habitat (see Chap. 6), unless the corridors fragment the open landscape unacceptably. Preference generally should be given to mast trees, den trees, and wolf trees in those areas (such as draws and hummocks) where trees will be left. Unique or sensitive habitat associated with the timber, such as a deeryard, can be treated as a separate type or site class and managed accordingly with more specific wildlife constraints assigned (Roach 1974). If the unique or sensitive habitat is more closely related to the geology than to the timber type (e.g., a spring seep), it should be surrounded with buffer zones, if needed, and perhaps excluded from cutting (but see "Water Holes" in Chap. 7). Critical forest habitat should be selectively cut or protected if it includes threatened or endangered species, ecologically sensitive species or communities, or a rare deeryard, spring seep, etc. Steep and/or rocky areas, often with fragile soils, should be withdrawn from forest cutting, as should some lands of low site index (Monthey 1984). Tree harvest should be balanced between areas of low and high site index because, just as with plant populations, better wildlife populations tend to be found on better soils.

All the needs of wildlife cannot be met readily in a forest managed for timber production. Hence, in each region some tracts of land should be established as parks or nature preserves—some of which should be hundreds and even thousands of square kilometers in size—representing the region's different ecosystems (Hunter 1990). Some areas that are prime sites for growing timber—i.e., flat, fertile, well-drained, and so forth—should be included in the preserve system because the associated plant and animal communities on good and poor sites differ.

Seymour and Hunter (1992) recommended a *triad approach* to forestland allocation: (1) High-productivity sites with no special ecological characteristics would be allocated to high-yield silviculture. (2) Lands with unique ecological value would be set aside as reserves. (3) New forestry silvicultural practices (Franklin 1989, Gillis 1990) maintaining structural complexity would be applied to lands that do not qualify for high-yield or reserve status. In the long run, increasing yields on relatively small, intensively managed areas would allow substantial areas to be set aside as reserves without threatening future wood supplies (Seymour and McCormack 1989). Where land is mostly private, incentive programs might be needed.

Plantations should be located close to mills and access roads. Because reserves must represent the entire range of ecosystems, some fertile, moderately well-drained, low-elevation sites good for timber must be included. Areas to be managed with new forestry might serve as buffers between plantations and reserves. Sensitive areas such as steep slopes and riparian areas also should be reserved from timber harvesting, even though spread out across the landscape.

For spruce-fir forests in the Northeast, Seymour and Hunter (1992) recommended a two-aged silvicultural system that mimics the small, patchy natural disturbance patterns there. The system is an irregular shelterwood method similar to conventional even-aged shelterwood management, except that in the final-removal cutting, some trees from the older cohort are not harvested. They are retained through part or all of the subsequent rotation of the younger cohort. Thus, vertical structure and economic value are enhanced during stand development. For example, just eight white pines retained to grow to large size above a cohort of spruce and fir can exceed the value of an entire hectare of spruce-fir pulpwood (Seymour and Hunter 1992).

Restoring the original tree species of pre-European settlement can be done by (1) natural seeding from any remaining trees and (2) artificially seeding or planting (Seymour and Hunter, 1992). Natural seeding requires seed tree cuts. It works well only for species that are windfirm as individuals and thrive after disturbance. Such trees also must be old enough to produce enough seed for regeneration; success often depends on timing the harvest with a good seed year. Only a few species, such as eastern white pine, meet these requirements. If the species is extirpated from the stand, enrichment planting should be used, not to create a monoculture, but to enrich the other regeneration by planting about 10 percent as many trees as in a standard plantation.

Old growth

In a normal rotation, forests managed mainly for wood are not allowed to develop old-growth stands because they are uneconomical; mature stands are cut before they reach an age when average net annual growth is close to zero. Forests managed for biodiversity must contain the old-growth successional stage. To maximize biodiversity in such areas, multiple use must be minimized to favor preserving some habitat that is not disturbed artificially. Old growth [see Patton (1992) for definition] tends to be self-perpetuating, with a stabilized species composition (Thomas et al. 1988b). In some areas, even fast-growing, shade-tolerant aspen stands of old growth can successfully regenerate repeatedly without major disturbance such as wildfire, given no competition from conifers (Mueggler 1985, Mehl 1992). Most forest stands in North America reach the old-growth stage in 100 to 500 years (Oliver and Larson 1990). Natural old growth generally is considered a nonrenewable resource because of the time needed for a stand to develop, the fact that it is primeval (virgin) timber, and the differences between primeval old growth and second-growth old growth (Kimmins 1987).

The best location for an old-growth stand in the Northwest and perhaps elsewhere is on a moist site containing surface water, preferably, a stream with a riparian strip, dominated by hardwoods, and connecting the old growth to at least one other old-growth stand (Harris 1984). The site should be at a lower elevation with north or east aspects, which are much less susceptible to fire than west or south exposures. It could extend over a ridgetop so that the ridge system could serve as a movement route, which would have to include some sunny, south-facing slope. Roads should be distant to reduce fragmentation and the probability of fire.

The amount of forest to maintain in old growth generally is reported as at least 5 percent (Harris 1984) to 10 percent (Evans 1974, Jerry 1984, Hays 1986, Thompson 1986). [The area of old growth in presettlement forests was probably about 50 percent (Harris 1984).] Determining the spatial requirements and minimum viable populations of wildlife attached to old growth will dictate how much of it to maintain in each forest type and site (Hunter 1990). Managing mature sawtimber with selection cuts next to old growth will increase the effective size of the old-growth areas for some species of interior plants and animals (Harris 1984) (see "Progressive Harvest" in this chapter).

Recommendations in a national forest used by pileated woodpeckers and caribou are to maintain at least 10 percent of the forested area in old growth, distributed so that at least 5 percent (about 200 ha) occurs in each third-order watershed (about 4000 ha), in largely contiguous stands (Jerry 1984). To provide for most native forest wildlife, the Missouri Department of Conservation recommends that 40 percent of a forest produce mast, 20 percent produce forage, and 10 percent be in old-growth areas of at least 60 ha (Evans 1974, Thompson 1986). Thompson (1986) suggested that this goal can be met simply by (1) maintaining 10 percent of the area in permanent openings to provide enough forage when combined with the 11 percent in regeneration, and (2) excluding at least 10 percent of the area from cutting to be maintained as old growth for cavity-users and to add to the mast production of pole-timber and sawtimber stands.

Harris (1984) recommended that old growth in the Northwest comprise 25 percent and recruitment stands 75 percent of the area in long-rotation management. Harris (1984) further recommended that 20 percent of the forest landscape be committed to long-rotation management so that 5 percent could be maintained perpetually in old-growth islands—i.e., in the 240- to 320-year age class for Douglas-fir, for example—in addition to the old-growth core.

Many species need old growth; examples from the Pacific Northwest include the northern spotted owl, marbled murrelet, ancient murrelet, Hammond's flycatcher, red tree vole, coast mole, and various plants (Hunter 1990). If the northern spotted owl is used as an indicator species for wildlife needing older coniferous forests (250 to 750 years old) in the northwestern United States and southwestern Canada, then the total size needed to maintain 20 pairs is

18,225 to 30,375 ha, or about 180 to 300 km^2. Twenty pairs is considered a minimum viable population, with a median home range per pair of 1215 to 2025 ha and a 25 percent overlap in home range (Thomas et al. 1990). The equation is:

$$
\begin{aligned}
\text{size of habitat} \ = \ &\text{median annual home range} \\
\text{conservation area} \quad &\text{of owl pairs} \\[6pt]
&\times \ (1 - \text{percentage home} \\
&\quad \text{range overlap}) \\[6pt]
&\times \ \text{minimum viable} \\
&\quad \text{population} \\[6pt]
= \ &1215 \text{ to } 2025 \text{ ha} \times 0.75 \times 20 \\
= \ &18,225 \text{ to } 30,375 \text{ ha}
\end{aligned}
$$

These blocks of late successional and/or old-growth habitat-conservation areas should not be too linear and should be spaced 19 km apart, which is within the dispersal distance of juveniles. Where habitat-conservation areas must be smaller, the distance between them should be only about 11 km. About half the federal forestland in western Washington and western Oregon might be suitable for owl management (Table 4.2) (Johnson et al. 1991). Juvenile spotted owls are unable to cross clearcuts and disperse successfully in a fragmented landscape, partly because great horned owls live in edge habitats and eat spotted owls, and barred owls outcompete and displace spotted owls in patchy landscapes (Marcot and Holthausen 1987, Grumbine 1992).

The two most prestigious ornithological organizations in North America, the American Ornithological Union and the Cooper Ornithological Society, convened a scientific committee to review the literature and recommend management. The committee concluded that to ensure population viability for 50 years, at least 2900 pairs of owls needed protection on federal lands, with an average of 930 ha to be allowed per pair in California and Oregon and 1700 ha per pair in Washington (Dawson et al. 1987).

Late successional and/or old-growth forest reserved as habitat-conservation areas for spotted owls and other wildlife and plants dependent on it should be managed to maintain and/or enhance its ecological integrity (Johnson et al. 1991). No merchantable timber (including salvage) should be removed. Other management activities might be appropriate, such as fire prescription and/or suppression, precommercial silvicultural treatments of young stands, restoring aquatic habitats, and perhaps ecotourism.

Connecting corridors seem unnecessary if at least 50 percent of the land outside the habitat-conservation areas contains timber with an

TABLE 4.2 Existing Area (in Hectares) in the Federal Land Base and Late Successional and/or Old-Growth Forest Withdrawn from Timber Production under Different Land Allocations on Nine National Forests in Western Washington and Western Oregon and Five U.S. Bureau of Land Management Districts in Western Oregon

Category	BLM	FS	Total
Federal land base			
Total land	915,000	3,929,000	4,844,000
Total forest	881,000	3,394,000	4,275,000
LS/OG forest*	437,000	1,619,000	2,056,000
LS/OG forest withdrawn, by land allocation			
FP	152,000	856,000‡	1,008,000
FP + LS/OG1	263,000	1,151,000	1,414,000
FP + LS/OG1 + owl additions†	275,000	1,192,000	1,467,000
FP + LS/OG1 + owl additions + LS/OG2	312,000	1,341,000	1,653,000
FP + LS/OG1 + owl additions + LS/OG2 + LS/OG3	437,000	1,619,000‡	2,056,000

Note: BLM = U.S. Bureau of Land Management. FS = U.S. Forest Service. LS/OG = late successional and/or old-growth forest (over 80 years old for BLM; potential old growth for FS). LS/OG1 = most significant late successional and/or old-growth forest. LS/OG2 = significant late successional and/or old-growth forest. LS/OG3 = all other late successional and/or old-growth forest. FP = forest plan for each national forest and BLM district.

*As of 1988.

†See "Provision for the Northern Spotted Owl," in Johnson et al. (1991).

‡Other information (an undated Forest Service fact sheet entitled "Vegetative Mapping for Determination of Old Growth") suggests that this estimate of potential old growth withdrawn from timber production by the Forest Plans is high. Rather than the 53 percent withdrawn estimated here (856,000/1,619,000), other information suggests that about 46 percent is withdrawn.

SOURCE: Johnson et al. 1991.

average dbh of at least 28 cm and at least 40 percent canopy closure (Thomas et al. 1990). Lands allocated to riparian corridors, streamside management zones, special management areas for species such as marten and pileated woodpeckers, and other such uses provide additional habitat for dispersing spotted owls. Minimum structural retention per hectare of such lands should average five large logs, five large snags, and fifteen live trees larger than the average stand diameter which have immediate wildlife value and serve as sources of snags and logs (see "Snags and Live Den Trees" and "Logs and Slash" in Chap. 7). Preferably, at least 10 percent of the forest outside the habitat-conservation areas should be over 180 years old and 10 percent should be 120 to 180 years old so that late successional stages and/or old growth can be replaced over time. The forest suitable for timber production should be managed with area regulation (area con-

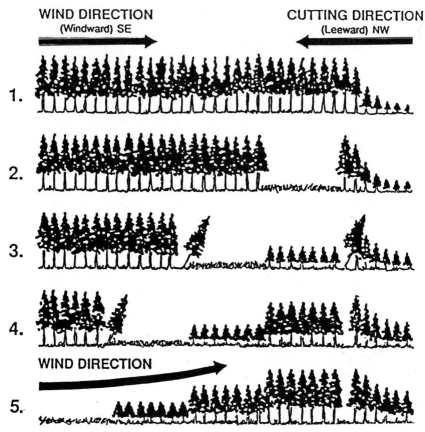

WIND DIRECTION
(Windward) SE

CUTTING DIRECTION
(Leeward) NW

WIND DIRECTION

Figure 4.14 Cutting is done progressively in strips, into the wind, to develop a windfirm stand border: (1) A stand windward of a naturally windfirm feature, for example, a scrub-cedar stand. (2) The first strip is cut close to the more windfirm stand. (3) The second strip is cut windward of the first strip; blowdown at the leeward edge of the uncut stand is salvaged. (4) Strips are cut to the windward; blowdown on the windward edge of the uncut stand is salvaged. (5) As strip cutting continues to windward, the developing stand increases in height, which helps to lift the wind gradually, thereby eliminating an abrupt windward edge. (*Harris 1989.*)

trol) on a rotation of 120 years; 180 years is better so that at most one-eighteenth of the area would be harvested every decade (Johnson et al. 1991). Cutting more than 15 percent at a time will result in excessive wind damage (Foss 1991). Timber should be harvested into the prevailing wind to reduce windthrow (Fig. 4.14) (Harris 1989). Furman et al. (1984), Harris (1989), and Oliver and Larson (1990) discussed guidelines to reduce wind damage.

Other arrangements for old growth include retaining strips of it along waterways connecting moderate-sized blocks of it to large parks and reserves (Recher et al. 1987), and retaining widely distributed portions of it as refugia from which wildlife can recolonize cut areas as they develop into new forests (Wilson and Johns 1982, Wong 1985). The U.S. Forest Service was considering a plan to establish a network of 400- to 1200-ha old-growth patches spaced 10 to 20 km apart, the patch size varying depending on the physiographic province (Swanson et al. 1990).

The complexity of old growth seems strongly associated with (1) vertical diversity produced by a multilayered canopy of different species and sizes of trees, (2) large trees, (3) large snags and logs, and (4) patchiness from small-scale disturbance and death of dominant trees (Thomas et al. 1988b). Large snags and logs are less common in regions such as the southeastern United States or the tropics and more common in regions such as the coastal conifer forests of the Pacific Northwest and the dry conifer forests of the Rocky Mountains, where trees grow large, the species are decay-resistant, and organic decomposition is slow (Oliver and Larson 1990). Because of overharvesting, not enough old growth remains to meet ecological needs in some areas, e.g., at low elevations (Harris et al. 1982). Also, protected old growth ultimately will succumb to natural disturbance regimes caused by fire, wind, insects, and diseases (Harris 1984). Younger stands should be managed in protected areas to replace such loss of old growth (Oliver and Larson 1990). Allowing naturally disturbed old growth to succeed back to old growth is more likely to preserve the natural diversity than letting clearcut areas succeed to old growth.

Old growth has been so drastically reduced in most forest types in the United States and much of Canada that long-rotation management with clearcuts surrounding an old-growth core will have to be arranged relative to existing old growth (Harris 1984)(see Fig. 4.9). In areas and forest types where no old growth exists, some extensive second growth should be set aside at intervals to be managed ultimately as old-growth cores surrounded by long-rotation even-aged and uneven-aged management. (See "Management Strategy" in this chapter.) In time, with no intervening disturbances, even-aged plantations or naturally regenerated stands of second growth will develop into old growth, or old-growth conditions (Franklin and Spies 1984, Newton and Cole 1987, Thomas et al. 1988b, Lennartz and Lancia 1989, Spies et al. 1991)—although perhaps somewhat different from natural old growth (Spies and Franklin 1988) due to differences in stand history (Fig. 4.15, alternative I) and to the different effects produced by clearcutting compared to natural disturbance. *Demes* are genetically distinct populations of plants or animals adapted to the peculiarities of the local environment. Herbs that reappear in a second-growth forest are not nearly so diverse genetically as those in the original forest (Pielou 1990). If a plant species reoccupies its original range, it often will be genetically impoverished due to the loss of many of its demes. Some demes might be lost forever.

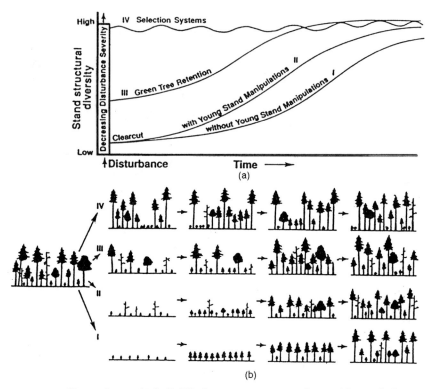

Figure 4.15 Alternative methods (I–IV) of management to accelerate old-growth characteristics of even-aged plantations or naturally regenerated stands of second growth. (*Spies et al. 1991.*)

Old-growth characteristics can be accelerated in young stands by planting density, precommercial thinning, and vegetation control (Fig. 4.15, alternative II). The planting density can be controlled so that desired species are not excluded through competition. Hardwoods can be grown in clumps so that conifers will not overtop them and reduce their vigor and potential mast production. Precommercial thinning prevents or delays stem exclusion and prolongs life of early seral species. Grouping hardwoods and thinning conifers to variable spacing enhances horizontal and vertical structure (Spies et al. 1991). Commercial thinning also will enhance vertical structure, but it can increase windthrow unless vigorous, windfirm trees are left. In addition to providing merchantable wood at advanced ages, commercial thinning can maintain much species diversity with large trees, thus providing some aspects of late successional forest ecosystems.

Where terrain suits logging and windthrow is minimal, green-tree retention can provide timber products and allow old-growth characteristics to develop in less time than the first two alternatives would (Fig. 4.15, alternative III). (See "Stand Level," under "Management Strategy," in this chapter.)

Uneven-aged stands with old-growth characteristics can be developed with selection cuts where site conditions, stand structure, and species mix allow (Fig. 4.15, alternative IV). But no early successional stages and associated wildlife will occur as they do with alternatives I, II, and III. Implementing these four alternatives, especially green-tree retention, requires stand-specific analysis of fuels and fire management; effects of pathogens, insects, and wildlife; layout of logging systems; costs; stand development and yield; and worker safety (Spies et al. 1991).

Edge Habitats

Management for edge wildlife mainly involves maximizing edge effect with horizontal diversity, which is produced by even-aged management—mainly clearcutting in relatively small units. Management units could emulate patchy natural disturbance. Such management often is geared toward featured species, especially some of the many game species associated with edges. These practices are used generally in areas designated for short-rotation, even-aged management following a planning process that begins on a regional level. These practices are unsuitable for areas designated for old growth and interior species of wildlife. They are suitable for most game species.

Many monographs and books are species-specific in providing details of habitat needs and management (e.g., Stoddard 1931, Bump et al. 1947, Hewitt 1967, Wallmo 1981, Thomas and Toweill 1982, Halls 1984, Novak et al. 1987). Habitat suitability index models on various species of North American wildlife (e.g., Schroeder 1983, Allen 1987a) are available from the U.S. Fish and Wildlife Service National Ecology Research Center, Fort Collins, CO. Recovery plans for over 200 endangered plants and animals in North America are available from the Fish and Wildlife Reference Service, Rockville, MD. The U.S. Army Corps of Engineers, Vicksburg, MS, is developing a comprehensive *Wildlife Resources Management Manual,* of which many species-specific and habitat technical reports are available (e.g., Doerr et al. 1986, Teaford 1986).

Capp et al. (1984) and Lipscomb et al. (1984) described detailed steps for wildlife habitat management, mainly for edge species of wildlife.

1. Identify and describe the management area.
2. Select featured species to be used as guides in the process to plan habitat needs.

3. Develop objectives for the habitat-management and habitat-treatment needs of the selected species.

4. Implement silvicultural treatment schedules to establish and maintain habitat size and conditions specified by the objectives.

Identify and describe management area

The first step is the taking of the initial inventory. Some details of this procedure are commonly overlooked, but they should not be. Yet, over-inventorying must be avoided to prevent waste of time, effort, and money.

Management area boundaries should be delineated on aerial photos and maps. These could be physiographic provinces or watersheds within the province (Samson et al. 1989). Within each management area, the boundaries of each forested ecosystem or land type (Hall and Thomas 1979) should be delineated on aerial photos and maps.

For each ecosystem or land type, operable and inoperable timber stands should be delineated relative to slope, rocks, wetlands, and other features which influence mechanical timber harvesting. Slopes over 40 percent generally are considered inoperable (Capp et al. 1984). The area to be influenced by tree harvest activities includes a zone influenced by the home range of wildlife. For deer and elk the distance is about 183 m extending beyond operable and inoperable timber (see Fig. 5.1). Nonforested areas, such as meadows, shrublands, water, and talus slopes, that occur within about 183 m of forested sites should be included as part of the nearest forested ecosystem. Inoperable timber areas are not cut, and will succeed to old growth.

The structural stages of operable timber stands and the habitat types should be identified and summarized. Special silvicultural characteristics should be recorded for operable timber stands to aid the manager designing and scheduling timber harvests. Wildlife should be inventoried, but that often is impractical.

Select featured species

Featured species are selected to guide management to improve or sustain species richness (Capp et al. 1984, Lipscomb et al. 1984). Their habitat needs should represent the needs of other species adapted to similar habitat. Featured species are specified because specifying habitat needs for all forest wildlife species is impractical. A list of featured species should include those which use the edges of all successional stages and stand conditions. Game species with broad habitat requirements, keystone species, and threatened or endangered species are commonly selected as featured species.

TABLE 4.3   Habitat Structural Options for Managing Units of Any Size for Featured Species

	Options	
	Feature species associated with early forest successional stages	Feature species associated with late forest successional stages
Forest structure objective	Horizontal structural diversity	Vertical structural diversity
Timber-management system	Even-aged	Uneven-aged preferred, even-aged possible
Rotation cycle	Short	Long (if even-aged management)
Individual treatment: size, edge, contrast, special and unique habitats	Varies with species selected	Varies with species selected

Note: Featured species associated with early successional stages include elk, mule deer, deer mouse, ground squirrels, white-crowned sparrows, and others. Featured species associated with late successional stages include pine marten, red-backed vole, goshawk, hairy woodpecker, ruby-crowned kinglet, hermit thrush, and others.
SOURCE: Lipscomb et al. (1984).

Develop habitat objectives

The general approach is to manage forests either (1) for early *or* late successional stages or stand conditions, or (2) for a combination of both early *and* late successional stages or stand conditions (Table 4.3) (Capp et al. 1984, Lipscomb et al. 1984). A specific area of forested land could be developed in early and/or late successional stages or stand conditions to be maintained in generally specific percentages over time (Table 4.4). Management options range from 80 percent horizontal and 20 percent vertical structure for early to midsuccessional species such as deer and elk (Fig. 4.16) to 70 percent vertical and 30 percent horizontal for late successional species such as some nongame birds. For species richness, 20 percent of the management unit should be in vertical structure, created by uneven-aged management or the latter part of long-rotation even-aged management; 30 percent in horizontal structure of at least three successional stages under even-aged management; and 50 percent in either vertical or horizontal structure.

Minimum wildlife population levels.   Habitat must be provided to accommodate at least the minimum wildlife population density desired.

TABLE 4.4　Habitat Structural Options for Managing Units of Any Size for Different Population Emphases

Management goals	Percent of area in		
	Vertical structure		Horizontal structure
Provide for species richness and feature early successional species	20	(Maximum)	80
	25		75
	30		70
	35		65
	40	(Minimum)	60
Provide for species richness and feature late successional species	45	(Minimum)	55
	50		50
	55		45
	60		40
	70	(Maximum)	30

SOURCE: Lipscomb et al. (1984).

Figure 4.16　If open enough to develop a ground layer, low vertical structure can benefit species such as mule deer. (*Photo by Mark F. J. Payne.*)

TABLE 4.5   Duration (in Years) of Each Stage of Some Forest Ecosystems under Average Natural Conditions

Ecosystem	Grass/ forb	Shrub/ seedling	Sapling/ pole	Mature	Old growth
Subalpine forest and Douglas-fir	10–15	15–40	40–60	100–200	90–100
Ponderosa pine	10–15	10–15	30–50	70–100	75–100
Lodgepole pine	5–10	15–20	20–50	50–100	50–75
Aspen	1–2	4–6	20–30	50–80	50–75
Pinyon-juniper	10–15	15–25	20–25	75–100	100–150
Gambel oak	1–2	6–10	20–40	30–50	30–50

Note: Structural stages for riparian ecosystems are not addressed in this table because these are usually managed as uneven-aged stands. The sapling/pole and mature stages each can be divided into (1) less than 40 percent canopy closure, (2) 40 to 70 percent, and (3) more than 70 percent.
SOURCE: Wills (1984).

Realistically, that density should be set at 20 percent or more of maximum density for each species, because that tends to be the minimum quality habitat usable to meet a species' needs. For the featured species, the minimum acceptable population level would likely be substantially higher than 20 percent of optimum. But objectives set too high might not be achievable.

Developing a prescription.   To develop a management plan, the expected duration of each structural or successional stage must be known (e.g., Table 4.5), especially as it relates to the future growth expectation for a particular stand condition (Wills 1984). Site conditions and the number and type of intermediate treatments will influence growing conditions.

A management plan needs prescriptions developed for the various stands of trees. Developing a prescription has six steps (Wills 1984).

1. The area in the management unit or stand is determined.

2. The age is determined at which the stand will be totally regenerated (the rotation period) and provide an even, sustained yield of the desired habitat conditions. Since old growth essentially cannot be regenerated for long-lived tree species, the age of regeneration usually extends at most through the mature stage.

3. The number of years between treatment entries is determined. The corresponding number of entries needed to treat the stand completely is determined by dividing the rotation period by the treatment interval. For example, for lodgepole pine, 190 years ÷ 10 = 19 entries needed to regenerate the stand to provide continuous 20 percent old growth.

4. The number of hectares to be treated in each period or entry is determined by dividing the total hectares to be managed by the number of entries. For lodgepole pine, 400 ha ÷ 19 entries = 21 ha treated every 10 years.

5. The treatments to provide the necessary structural stages are determined. For lodgepole pine, for example, clearcutting provides the grass/forb and later stages and regenerates the stand to provide an even-flow, sustained yield of wood and habitat conditions for the wildlife associated with each stand condition that the growing forest passes through. Other options also are available.

6. After a regeneration cut, if a different canopy closure is desired from the normally occurring closure, additional silvicultural practices are needed. For example, if the objective is to maintain 10 percent of the mature stands with a canopy closure of 40 to 70 percent, intermediate cuts would have to remove about 40 percent of the canopy in two entries 10 years apart, or 10 percent of the area would need 20 percent of the canopy removed over 20 years. Subsequent treatments must be adjusted to growth rates and the regeneration schedule. All treatments require the services of a knowledgeable silviculturist to reduce problems such as insects, disease, and windthrow.

Selecting a prescription.   A wide range of possible prescriptions along with a large number of selected wildlife species will require that relative values be assigned to the selected species to compare the benefit of increasing one species over another (Capp et al. 1984, Lipscomb et al. 1984). For example, if 1.0 is used for deer, 10.0 for bald eagles, and 0.1 for ruffed grouse, the manager would be equally satisfied to increase wildlife populations by 10 deer, 1 eagle, or 100 grouse. If the manager could increase grouse and decrease deer by modifying the management plan, the choice might be made only if 10 additional grouse to every deer lost could be expected. Many management practices involve this sort of trade-off.

The prescription best suited to maximize the population of featured species is determined from a function value. The equation to determine the function value F is

$$F = (V_1 \times P_1) + (V_2 \times P_2) + \cdots + (V_n \times P_n)$$

where V is the relative value of the featured wildlife species and P is the population density of that species which is expected if the habitat provided by a prescription is occupied at its normal level. With the relative values for eagles, deer, and grouse given above, a prescription providing habitat for 6.1 deer, 0.11 eagle, and 2.9 grouse per 40 ha has a higher function value $[(6.1 \times 1) + (0.11 \times 10) + (2.9 \times 0.1) = 7.49]$ than a prescription for 5.3 deer, 0.14 eagle, and 6.2 grouse per 40 ha $[(5.3 \times 1) + (0.14 \times 10) + (6.2 \times 0.1) = 7.32]$.

The animal itself is the best integrator of environmental factors. Selecting a prescription for operable timber and zone of influence begins with visual evaluation of wildlife densities and/or condition for summer and winter for the different prescriptions for each forest ecosystem (forest type), determined from field work including hunter check stations. Prescriptions might need alteration for several reasons, especially economic efficiency for feasibility and practicability (Capp and Mehl 1984). Implementing the management plan is most efficient economically when wood volumes harvested pay for the tree stand treatments, namely, logging and road building. The commercial timber sale is usually the most practicable and economical tool to manage forests for producing resources. Alterations also allow the manager to select the prescription that most likely will produce the types or number of trees needed by the selected wildlife species. Adjustments to the standard prescriptions and the associated numbers for wildlife produced are needed if (1) structural stages take more or less time than anticipated, (2) substantial amounts of permanent openings or shrublands occur, and (3) the prescription increases the amount of inoperable timber.

Implement silvicultural treatment

No matter which silvicultural treatment is used to manage wildlife, three variables must be considered (Hall et al. 1985b): (1) topography and land type, (2) stand condition, and (3) scheduling and arranging treatments.

Topography and land type.   Topography and land type influence the type and distribution of water, plants, wildlife, harvest, and transportation systems (Hall and Thomas 1979, Hall et al. 1985b). Some land types have a small forest component with a substantial grass/forb component. This would obviate the development of much additional grass/forb condition, although a shrub stage is still needed. Slopes under 35 percent generally allow ground yarding, and thus maximum flexibility in choosing even- or uneven-aged management, size of area, and scheduling and arranging treatment. Slopes over 80 percent, especially more than 610 m long, are more expensive to log if small regeneration units without midslope roads are desired; this is because they require cable, helicopter, or balloon yarding systems, with costs influenced by distance from roads and length and shape of slopes. (Cable yarding systems can economically harvest large sawtimber stands containing about 185,000 board feet per hectare 610 m from a road, but are not economical for commercial thinning where only about 12,000 to 17,000 board feet per hectare would be removed.) Old growth on slopes over 60 percent requiring cable yarding might be left along streams. The rest of the forest on the slope could be harvested in a 95-year rotation if species such as Douglas-fir predominate, because commercial thinning and yarding could occur from an upslope road. Old growth also could be maintained on unstable land forms, broken convex slopes difficult to cable yard, and other locations where commercial thinning is economically questionable.

Uneven-aged management is generally uneconomical on slopes too steep for ground yarding equipment without substantial damage to residual trees. Aspect also is influential because south-facing slopes provide more thermal cover and spring forage than north-facing slopes. Other topographic factors influencing the development of silvicultural treatment include the location of wetlands and free-flowing water.

Stand condition. Stand condition dictates the type of silvicultural treatment to apply. Stand condition includes characteristics of current vegetation, such as tree species, height, diameter, standing volume, and density; growth potential (site index) of the area; disease and insects in the stand; the vegetation's ecological reactions to the treatment; plant indicators of tree species best adapted to the area; and current wildlife habitat components such as number, size, and type of snags and cavity trees, and number, size, and type of logs and stumps. Reaction of the plant community to clearcutting determines the kind of early successional vegetation (grass, forbs, and shrubs) that will colonize the cutover; how much will be produced; and how long it will exist, i.e., how severely it will compete with tree regeneration.

Many modifications in standard silvicultural practices exist to achieve wildlife habitat objectives (Hall and Thomas 1979). For example, the grass/forb successional stage can be maintained longer by delaying planting in a clearcut where natural regeneration had failed, or by heavily seeding a new clearcut with a sod-forming grass mixture to delay forest regeneration. The shrub stage can be maintained longer by allowing shrubs to compete with seedlings. Wildlife requiring early successional stages would benefit. A clearcut that is well stocked with mixed conifer seedlings will remain in the grass/forb stage about 10 to 15 years (Hall and Thomas 1979). Precommercial thinning to a low tree density can maintain a 10- to 15-year-old regenerated clearcut in the grass/forb, shrub, or open sapling/pole stage 5 to 15 years longer (Hall et al. 1985b). If too much early successional stage exists, tree planting could be expedited in clearcuts along with elimination of competing grasses and forbs. In the closed conditions of sapling/pole/sawtimber stands, commercial thinning can be done earlier or more severely than warranted for maximum timber production to produce more rapid development of a multi-tiered forest canopy while leaving snags and also leaving live trees of low vigor to become snags. In relatively mature stands, foregoing commercial thinning will encourage the creation and maintenance of late mature or old-growth conditions.

Scheduling and arranging treatments. Scheduling and arranging treatments involves rotation age for even-aged management and target tree size for uneven-aged management (Hall et al. 1985b). With even-aged management, for example, in a 95-year rotation of Douglas-fir, a regeneration cut must be scheduled on 1 percent of the land every year—i.e., 10 percent every 10 years—resulting in 10 percent of the area in grass/forb and shrub conditions up to 10 years old. A 95-year rotation on site index 90, for example, requires scheduling two commercial thinnings—except on steep, long, broken, or convex slopes, where one heavy thinning or a harvest cut would suffice; old-growth conditions require three commercial thinnings and possibly reduced understory. (The culmination of mean annual increment is about 95 years for Douglas-fir on the site quality indicated, i.e., site index 90.) Clearcut regeneration units scheduled at least every 15 years in Douglas-fir will maintain open habitat for those wildlife species needing it to feed and breed. In uneven-aged management, the stand must be thinned periodically to increase the diameter of young trees. This involves harvesting some trees of each age class, including some that are target tree size.

As a result of wildfires, some areas are occupied by a single age class of timber. If wildlife habitat improvement objectives are to have 10 percent of the land in clearcuts less than 10 years old, some portions of such areas must be cut younger than rotation age, and other portions must be deferred until after rotation age.

The longer the rotation age, the less area will be in early successional stages (Hall and Thomas 1979). For example, rotations of Douglas-fir and white fir that optimize habitat for elk generally occur every 50 to 140 years, depending on site index (Figs. 4.17 and 4.18). For pileated woodpeckers, which require old growth, optimum habitat requires rotations of 240 years (Fig. 4.19). To balance habitat needs of elk and pileated woodpeckers, the amount of forage areas, hiding cover, thermal cover, and old growth must be proportioned correctly, perhaps by having 10 percent of the forested land in each of these conditions (Fig. 4.20). Except for old growth, rotation age will not affect wood volume production adversely; but rotation age alters the *type* of wood products produced.

Harris (1984) proposed a compromise that includes edge effect while providing habitat for interior species and old-growth species (Fig. 4.21). The compromise involves islands of old growth surrounded by a long-

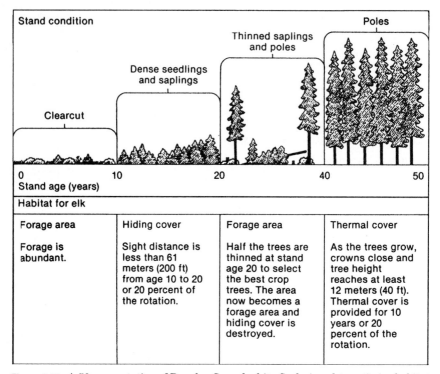

Figure 4.17 A 50-year rotation of Douglas-fir and white fir designed to optimize habitat for elk. (*Hall and Thomas 1979.*)

rotation cutting sequence of alternate stands that results in the maximum average age difference between adjacent stands over a complete cutting cycle. (Compare Fig. 4.9 and see discussion on long rotations surrounding reserves of old growth in section on "Progressive Harvest," under "Management Strategy" in this chapter.) A greater average age difference occurs between stands in long-rotation islands consisting of an odd number of stands than an even number of stands (Fig. 4.22). Selection of the next site to cut is more complex for even-numbered stands. Harris (1984) recommended nine replacement stands surrounding an old-growth core in Douglas-fir. If the old-growth core is or is not ever cut when equilibrium is reached, the system will ensure that 66 percent of the surrounding buffer stands are over 100 years old and that 33 percent are in regeneration condition that provides forage and cover for early successional species of wildlife.

New clearcut boundaries should minimize square corners and stringers (rows of tree stands), and follow natural topography and natural stand boundaries (Capp et al. 1984). Clearcuts should be perpendicular to storm winds to reduce windthrow of standing trees. On

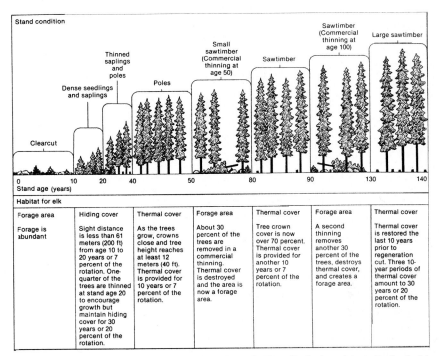

Stand condition							
Clearcut	Dense seedlings and saplings	Thinned saplings and poles / Poles	Small sawtimber (Commercial thinning at age 50)	Sawtimber	Sawtimber (Commercial thinning at age 100)		Large sawtimber

Stand age (years): 0 10 20 40 50 80 90 130 140

Habitat for elk							
Forage area	Hiding cover	Thermal cover	Forage area	Thermal cover	Forage area	Thermal cover	
Forage is abundant	Sight distance is less than 61 meters (200 ft) from age 10 to 20 years or 7 percent of the rotation. One-quarter of the trees are thinned at stand age 20 to encourage growth but maintain hiding cover for 30 years or 20 percent of the rotation.	As the trees grow, crowns close and tree height reaches at least 12 meters (40 ft). Thermal cover is provided for 10 years or 7 percent of the rotation.	About 30 percent of the trees are removed in a commercial thinning. Thermal cover is destroyed and the area is now a forage area.	Tree crown cover is now over 70 percent. Thermal cover is provided for another 10 years or 7 percent of the rotation.	A second thinning removes another 30 percent of the trees, destroys thermal cover, and creates a forage area.	Thermal cover is restored the last 10 years prior to regeneration cut. Three 10-year periods of thermal cover amount to 30 years or 20 percent of the rotation.	

Figure 4.18 A 140-year rotation of Douglas-fir and white fir designed to optimize habitat for elk. (*Hall and Thomas 1979.*)

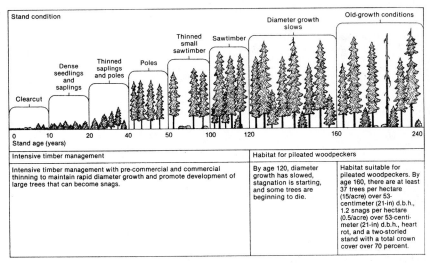

Stand condition						
Clearcut	Dense seedlings and saplings	Thinned saplings and poles / Poles	Thinned small sawtimber / Sawtimber	Diameter growth slows		Old-growth conditions

Stand age (years): 0 10 20 40 50 100 120 160 240

Intensive timber management	Habitat for pileated woodpeckers	
Intensive timber management with pre-commercial and commercial thinning to maintain rapid diameter growth and promote development of large trees that can become snags.	By age 120, diameter growth has slowed, stagnation is starting, and some trees are beginning to die.	Habitat suitable for pileated woodpeckers. By age 160, there are at least 37 trees per hectare (15/acre) over 53-centimeter (21-in) d.b.h., 1.2 snags per hectare (0.5/acre) over 53-centimeter (21-in) d.b.h., heart rot, and a two-storied stand with a total crown cover over 70 percent.

Figure 4.19 A 240-year rotation of Douglas-fir and white fir designed to attain optimum old-growth conditions for pileated woodpeckers. Commerical thinning is essential to stimulate diameter growth and produce the large trees needed for cavity excavation. (*Hall and Thomas 1979.*)

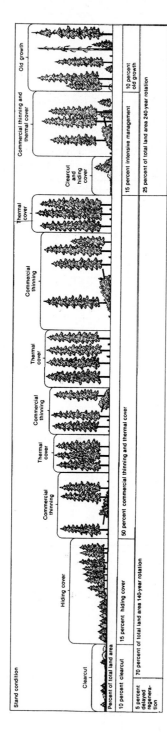

Figure 4.20 Silvicultural treatment in Douglas-fir and white fir to attain about 10 percent of the land area in each of the habitats critical for elk and pileated woodpeckers: clearcut, shrubland, hiding cover for elk, and old growth. A 140-year rotation is applied to 70 percent of the total land area, a 240-year rotation to 25 percent, and delayed regeneration to 5 percent. (Forested areas that provide suitable habitat for elk also will meet the habitat needs of deer.) (*Hall and Thomas 1979.*)

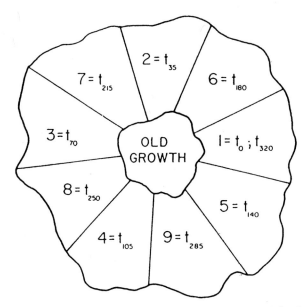

Figure 4.21 Schematic illustration of a long-rotation island of stands surrounding old growth, illustrating the cutting sequence (alternate stands) that leads to maximum average age difference between adjacent stands over a complete cutting cycle (t = years elapsed between first cut and subsequent cuts.) (*Harris 1984.*)

slopes steeper than 20 percent that face the prevailing wind, thinning should be reduced to 30 percent of the canopy. (See Furman et al. 1984, Harris 1989, and Oliver and Larson 1990 for cutting guidelines relative to wind.) On slopes steeper than 20 percent, placing the long axis of the clearcut up-and-downhill prevents or minimizes sidehill skidding.

The increased wind speed and snow depth which occur in clearcuts increase heat loss and reduce mobility of resident wildlife (except those insulated and concealed by snow), and bury forage deeply. Cutting in strips at right angles to the prevailing wind, sculpturing the perimeters of clearcuts, leaving stands of unthinned mature timber on the upwind side of clearcuts, and minimizing the size of openings will reduce heat loss and increase mobility (McAninch et al. 1984). Clearcuts to improve big-game winter ranges should be located on south- and southwest-facing slopes where the sun will reduce snow depth and early snowmelt will uncover herbaceous plants.

For maximum edge effect, harvest units must be planned in time and space to maintain a sustained edge effect throughout the timber rotation (Logan et al. 1985). Natural edges, rich in plant and animal species, need protection from human encroachment. Induced edges in

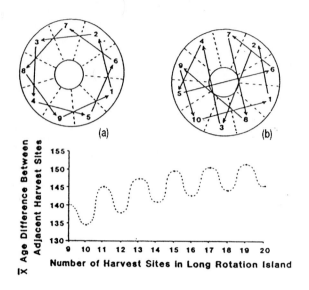

No. Harvest Sites	X̄ Age Between Adjacent Sites	No. Years Between Successive Cuts
9	140.0	35.0
10	134.4	32.0
11	145.0	29.0
12	137.8	26.6
13	147.6	24.6
14	140.6	22.9
15	149.3	21.3
16	142.6	20.0
17	150.6	18.8
18	144.2	17.8
19	151.6	16.8
20	145.6	16.0

Figure 4.22 A long-rotation island with an odd number of stands (e.g., nine, as in *a*) simply requires cutting alternative stands. If a long rotation of 320 years is assumed, the mean age difference between adjacent stands is always greater for islands with odd-numbered stands than for those with even-numbered stands and increases as the number of stands in the island increases. The cutting sequence for even-numbered stands is more complex (*b*), but involves cutting the second stand to the right, return to previous cut, then second to the left, etc. (*Harris 1984.*)

managed forests are caused mainly by timber harvest. Wide edges should be left undisturbed. Narrow edges should be widened by selectively leaving a variety of plants along the edge. Harvest boundaries should be placed so that the tallest vegetation is maintained along the edge to provide the most layers of foliage, which attracts the most wildlife. Harvest units should be separated to provide a mosaic of habitats and thus more interspersion of edge. Harvest units should be designed with mosaics and irregular boundaries to increase the length of edge habitat.

For maximum edge effect, all harvesting should be even-aged management, clearcutting preferably. For maximum edge effect, at least 80 percent of a stand's boundary should comply with the nonadjacency constraint (Salwasser and Tappeiner 1981, Gross and Dykstra 1989), with at least two decades of age difference, at least on the west slope of the Sierra Nevada mountains of the southwestern United States (Salwasser and Tappeiner 1981). Maximum age difference and edge contrast occur if stands are cut when adjacent stands are halfway through the rotation period (Mealey et al. 1982, Harris 1984, Hunter 1990). To obtain 80 percent, each stand can have no more than six adjacent neighboring stands (Gross and Dykstra 1989). Thus, by allowing one violation per stand for nonadjacency constraint, i.e., about one out of five shared boundaries, 80 percent of the boundaries will comply with the nonadjacency constraint. Since coverts are so valuable in attracting wildlife, in some cases stands should be shaped as hexagons, because when this is done each corner will join three habitat types (Giles 1978, Bromley et al. 1990).

In the national forests of the United States, a stand has to be at least 4.5 to 7.5 m tall, depending on region, before an adjacent stand can be cut (Hunter 1990), although Harris and Skoog (1980) recommended waiting until a stand is 60 to 70 percent as tall as adjacent stands. Height probably is better than age as an index of stand condition and successional stage (Hunter 1990).

Size of area treated is influenced by (1) the wildlife habitat objectives and other management objectives; (2) the area in a stand condition; and (3) the effect the topography has on road location and harvest systems, i.e., type of equipment used (Hall et al. 1985b). Species richness of birds apparently declines when stands exceed about 34 ha because less edge, with its higher species richness, is produced (Galli et al. 1976, Thomas et al. 1979c, Hall et al. 1985b). This implies that the size of the area to be treated should be about 34 ha, although some species of wildlife need a much larger area, and some larger areas should be included. But the size of the area to be treated should be modified to emulate the size and shape of natural disturbance.

Clearcuts in stands of conifers with nonserotinous cones should be no wider than five to seven tree heights, to ensure adequate seedfall over the entire clearcut and to improve moisture conditions for seedlings (Capp et al. 1984). Clearcuts in stands of conifers with serotinous cones can be wider than five to seven tree heights if cones from felled trees are left well scattered on the ground and slash is burned to improve regeneration.

The distance between stands must be considered to maintain viable wildlife populations: for example, a maximum of 75 m for flying squirrels, 366 m for deer and elk, 3.2 to 4.0 km for eagles, 4.8 to 19.3 km for spotted owls (Hall et al. 1985b, Bendel and Gates 1987). Otherwise, connecting corridors should be left unless the fragmentation caused by corridors is undesirable (see Rosenfield et al. 1992).

Small clearcuts no wider than 366 m are best (McGinnes 1969, Hall and Thomas 1979, Capp et al. 1984). Halls et al. (1984) recommended clearcutting strips up to 200 or 300 m wide in northern conifers; blocks or strips less than 60 to 90 m wide spaced 30 to 120 m apart are best in species like lodgepole pine. Stands or groups of stands should be at least 183 m wide to provide hiding and thermal cover for species such as deer and elk (Capp et al. 1984), and no larger than about 72 to 97 ha for moose (Bergerud and Manuel 1968, Peek et al. 1976). Clearcuts larger than 100 ha should have uncut shelter patches of 3 to 8 ha, or the cut should be shaped so that moose and other wildlife need to travel only 200 m or less to reach cover (Fig. 4.23) (Hogg 1990). A reserve of 120 m should be left around aquatic feeding areas, mineral licks, and calving areas. In areas of late winter habitat for moose, the size of cutovers and uncut areas should be equal; uncut areas may be cut when new growth in the cutovers is tall enough to provide overhead late winter cover.

The size of the cut is not as important as the width. The narrower and longer the clearcut is, the more wildlife home ranges will be affected (McGinnes 1969). Clearcuts benefiting edge wildlife, which includes most game species, probably should not exceed 50 ha (Nova Scotia Department of Lands and Forests ca 1989). Regeneration cuts should occur on areas 20 ha or less in eastern hardwoods and 40 ha or less in pine (Halls et al. 1984). Edge wildlife will benefit from clearcuts up to 81 ha, but patchcuts of 8 to 16 ha are better for most because wildlife tends to use them more evenly and thoroughly than larger units (U.S. Forest Service 1974a). Patchcuts should be irregularly shaped, and located no closer together than the width of the adjacent patchcut units. Clearcutting lodgepole pine and spruce-fir doubled the use by mule deer 10 years after logging if the clearcuts were in strips 1, 2, 3, and 6 chains wide with alternating uncut strips of the same width (Wallmo 1969).

Halls et al. (1984) said that at least 0.2 km of forest should remain between areas cut at the same time. Cutting units should be 1.5 to 2 times as long as they are wide, but based on needs of elk and deer, widths should be up to 366 m (Hall and Thomas 1979, Thomas et al. 1979b), which will occur if ratios of average length to average width fall within the range indicated by the shaded area in Fig. 4.24 (Mealey et al. 1982). Widths should be up to 400 m for moose (Hogg 1990). If regeneration will occur over $3N + 2$ or more decades, where N is the number of

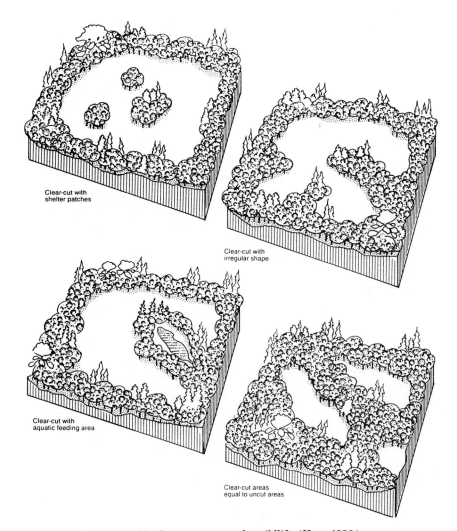

Labels within the figure:

Clear-cut with
shelter patches

Clear-cut with
irregular shape

Clear-cut with
aquatic feeding area

Clear-cut areas
equal to uncut areas

Figure 4.23 Some desirable clearcut patterns for wildlife. (*Hogg 1990.*)

decades a regenerated area needs to reach pole size for wildlife cover, higher length-to-width ratios are acceptable, because cover areas will always be two units wide in such cases. The general rule for laying out clearcuts to manage timber to produce wildlife is that the fraction of a stand to be regenerated in any decade should equal $1/R$, where R equals the desired stand rotation age in decades (Mealey et al. 1982).

To distribute treatments uniformly in time and space, about equal areas should be cut in each 10-year period, and scattered throughout the management area (Lipscomb et al. 1984). For best edge contrast,

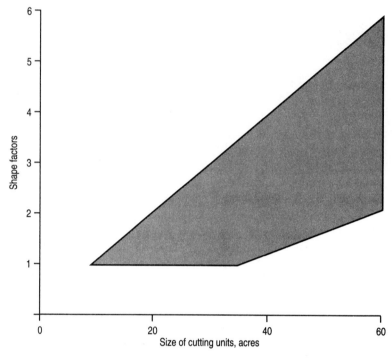

Figure 4.24 Relationships between size (in acres) of cutting units and the corresponding shape factors (ratio of average length to average width) desirable for big game habitat. Shape factors within the shaded area are preferred if a large stand is to be regenerated in less than $3N + 2$ decades (N = number of decades needed to establish wildlife cover after regeneration). (*Mealey et al. 1982.*) [For metric equivalence, see metric conversion table in the front of the book.]

no more than one-third of a stand's basal area should be scheduled within 183 m of any stand younger than pole size or within 183 m of a natural opening, unless the cut occurs next to a natural opening along a boundary less than 366 m long.

Generally, no more than one-seventh of the management area should be cut in any decade where trees reach pole size in 30 years (Mealey et al. 1982, Lipscomb et al. 1984). Where trees reach pole size in 20 years, about one-fifth or less of the area should be cut in any decade. Generally, the requirements for edge contrast can be met if the proportion of area regenerated in any decade does not exceed $1 \div (2N + 1)$.

Stands should be distributed as the left side of Fig. 4.25 illustrates (Lipscomb et al. 1984); this usually can be achieved by subdividing existing stands when their boundaries do not coincide with the new schedule. While shapes vary, corners form when boundaries cross, except for boundaries of perimeter stands. So that adjacent tree stands have a full number of decades to grow since last cut, successive entries must be made at about the same part of the decade to

For 2 decade edge contrast:

For 3 decade edge contrast:

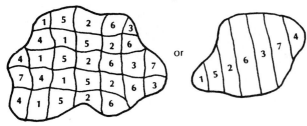

For 4 decade edge contrast:

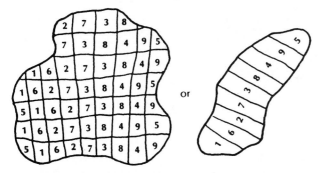

Figure 4.25 Cutting patterns which produce edge contrast (numbers indicate decade of regeneration). (*Lipscomb et al. 1984.*)

maximize edge effect. To maintain the desired mix of structural stages, the proportion of area assigned to regeneration in any decade should never differ substantially from the inverse of the number of decades in the rotation length. For example, if the rotation length is eight decades, one-eighth of the area should be cut (regenerated) in any one decade.

If an area is to be regenerated over a certain number of decades P, where $P \geq 2N + 1$, dispersion can be achieved with a repeating pattern of cutting units without violating edge contrast constraints, as

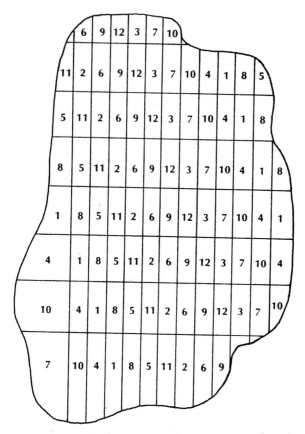

Figure 4.26 Cutting pattern which produces dispersion while maintaining a three-decade edge contrast over 120 years. (*Lipscomb et al. 1984.*)

the right side of Fig. 4.25 illustrates. If P exceeds $3N + 1$, the cutting pattern can be improved as in Fig. 4.26 to provide better scattering of the openings produced from the clearcuts (Lipscomb et al. 1984).

Maximum game populations generally occur when the cutover patchwork is about 50 percent of the forest (Franklin and Forman 1987). Managers can choose to create many openings of various sizes or few openings in long, narrow, contoured strips (Patton 1974). Either design would benefit most big game species, but a long, narrow strip probably would not benefit small game and nongame edge species because a larger number of small openings with the same area would provide more edge for them (Franklin and Forman 1987). A leave strip (corridor) of trees and shrubs at least 6 m wide should be left for every 137 m in length of clearcut or final shelterwood cut, or a 0.1- to 0.2-ha clump

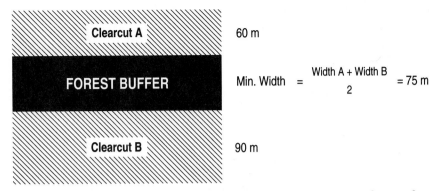

Figure 4.27 Method to determine the width of a forest buffer between two clearcuts less than 10 years old (*Connecticut Department of Environmental Protection 1989.*)

of trees should remain per 2 to 4 ha of clearcut or final shelterwood cut (Williamson undated, Connecticut Department of Environmental Protection 1989). The length of the clearcut or final shelterwood cut is unimportant as long as leave strips are maintained (see "Leave Strips" in Chap. 6). If a new clearcut or final shelterwood cut is scheduled parallel to a similar cut made less than 10 years earlier, the sites should be separated by a forest buffer at least as wide as the average width of the two cut areas (Fig. 4.27). If the cleared area exceeds 16 ha, the manager should leave travel lanes of 2 to 4 ha, thus creating an area which is large enough to be managed as a stand, or islands of at least 0.2 ha (Minnesota Department of Natural Resources 1985). The impact of clearcuts and final shelterwood cuts can be modified with planning and care (Figs. 4.28 and 4.29) (Hassinger et al. 1981).

Three habitat components, mast, forage, and old growth, can provide guidance in forest management for wildlife and produce habitat diversity when interspersed across a landscape containing a range of land sites and vegetation conditions (Evans 1974). About 40 percent of a compartment should be maintained in species and size classes that produce sustained yields of mast. In most forest ecosystems, *forage,* a broad term sometimes applied to all vegetation used as food by wildlife, occurs mainly where crown closure is less than 40 to 50 percent (Evans 1974, Wills 1984). Forage production declines with increasing canopy closure; little if any forage production occurs under stands with canopy closure over 70 percent. Light cuts removing 30 percent of the basal area can triple browse production after 1 year (Patton and McGinnes 1964). In some forests, forage production peaks for ungulates about 4 years after heavy cuts (Patton and McGinnes 1964); in others, forage production increases for about 10 to 20 years after logging (Scotter 1980).

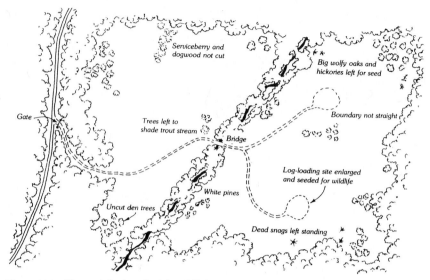

Figure 4.28   Clearcut designed with wildlife considerations. (*Hassinger et al. 1981.*)

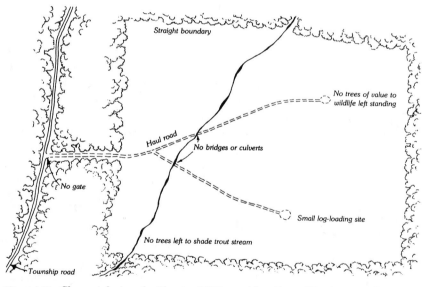

Figure 4.29   Clearcut designed without wildlife considerations. (*Hassinger et al. 1981.*)

About 20 percent of the area should be maintained in a sustained productive forage condition in all plant communities on all land sites (Evans 1974). On a rotation of 80 to 100 years in oak-hickory and oak-pine, for example, 10 to 12 percent of a managed forest will be in sus-

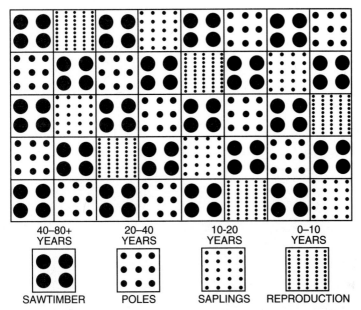

40–80+
YEARS

20–40
YEARS

10-20
YEARS

0-10
YEARS

SAWTIMBER   POLES   SAPLINGS   REPRODUCTION

Figure 4.30 Diagram of ultimate age-class distribution providing productive wildlife habitat in oaks on a 324-ha management unit, with each stand 8 ha, rotation age 80 years, and a 10-year cutting schedule. (*Shaw 1971.*)

tained forage production from regeneration cuts and other timber-management practices. The remaining 10 percent would be permanent forage provided from fields in various successional stages; old homesteads; rights-of-way; trails; firebreaks; and poor-quality sites for timber production, i.e., sparse sawtimber stands (see "Openings" in Chap. 7). About 10 percent of the area should be in old growth, with all other successional stages and forest conditions represented (Evans 1974). Optimum habitat for most species of forest birds occurs in hardwood stands with 57 percent canopy closure, a basal area of 1.5 m²/ha for small trees and 10 to 20 m²/ha for large trees, a density of 12,000 small trees per 40 ha and 6800 large trees per 40 ha, 78 percent ground cover, 27 percent shrub cover, 15 percent midstory cover, and 20 percent coniferous growth (Chadwick et al. 1986).

One of the most valuable forests for wildlife is an oak forest. As an example for modification, a management unit of 320 ha could be divided into 8-ha stands. With a rotation age of 80 years and a 10-year cutting schedule, eventually 50 percent of the area would be in sawtimber stands (40 to 80 years), 25 percent in pole stands, and 25 percent in seedling/sapling stands (Fig. 4.30) (Shaw 1971).

5

Woodlots

A *woodlot* is essentially a forest fragment, generally of less than 100 ha, in a nonforest area converted to other land use. Unlike extensive managed forests, woodlots tend to be privately owned nonindustrial lands; woodlots comprise 58 percent of all commercial forestlands in the United States, with 90 percent east of the 100th meridian, and 67 percent in hardwoods (Yonce 1983). For many years wildlife has been the main objective for most woodlot owners (Christensen and Grafton 1966). Wildlife improves property value and enjoyment. Recent agricultural economics have resulted in landowners high-grading many of the woodlots that escaped high-grading in the past. These often isolated islands of fragmented landscape tend to be surrounded by other land uses, usually agriculture. They should be managed to prevent further high-grading; restore previously high-graded woodlots; and maintain the integrity of the woodlot in general by preventing excessive fragmentation and ensuring regeneration of the trees, especially oak. One of the biggest problems is the landowner's desire to build a house in the woodlot or to sell it to someone else for that purpose. Land-management programs to help private landowners were described in Dumke et al. (1981).

Because woodlots tend to be relatively small, obligate interior species of wildlife tend not to occur in them unless they exceed about 100 ha (Wilcove 1987) or are next to larger forest tracts. Thus, managing woodlots for wildlife tends to be management for edge species because the edge effect extends throughout most woodlots. Maximizing diversity of habitat types will increase edge and maximize diversity of edge and ubiquitous species of wildlife; altering vegetation to maximize diversity will reduce timber production and could cause damage to gardens, ornamental plantings, orchard trees, and Christmas trees from animals such as deer and rabbits.

Managing woodlots for edge benefits many game species, which often is a goal of the owner, usually for personal use because of the small size of most woodlots, although some incentives exist (Wigley and Melchoirs 1987, Wilkins 1988, Yarrow 1990b, Yarrow and Smathers 1990). Selling or leasing hunting rights usually requires large areas (240 ha or more) to provide enough game (deCalesta 1983), unless several adjacent landowners combine their areas for lease. Even then they will compete with free hunting if public lands are nearby, unless the public land is so crowded that hunters will pay for exclusive use of private land managed for wildlife.

Habitat improvement might be impractical on land with a variety of woods, brush, meadows (fields), and wetlands. Wildlife in most woodlots can benefit from tree harvesting to release the best mast trees and shrubs, from creating snags and logs, from creating openings of forbs and grasses, from planting, and from construction of a farm pond (Payne 1992, and see Chap. 13). Woodlots should be fenced from grazing; cattle trample soil and plants, and rub against plants; they also create a browse line, eating as high as they can reach and virtually eliminating the ground and shrub layers, thus substantially reducing vertical diversity.

The woodlot should be viewed as part of the larger surrounding area (Decker et al. 1983). The woodlot's surroundings will be important as a source of wildlife, a barrier to wildlife movement, a contiguous expansion of similar habitat for area-sensitive wildlife, or a vital habitat requirement missing in the woodlot. Small woodlots cannot be managed for far-ranging species like turkeys unless surrounding land use is compatible. Habitat management for predators involves managing habitat for their prey and providing cover for the predator. Thus, habitat management of herbivores and predators is interrelated.

Inventory and Planning

Existing habitat and its arrangement should be inventoried and evaluated to determine how much is available, what species of wildlife currently are supported, what species and approximate densities are desired, and if the existing habitat has the potential for alteration to produce the desired wildlife species and densities. Deer probably are the largest wildlife species that can reasonably be expected to respond to woodlot management. An annual harvest of about two to three deer would need a combination of about 40 ha of woodlot and meadow if all parts of the meadow are within about 122 m of the woods (Fig. 5.1) (Blymer and Mosby 1977, deCalesta 1983, Witmer et al. 1985). Birding

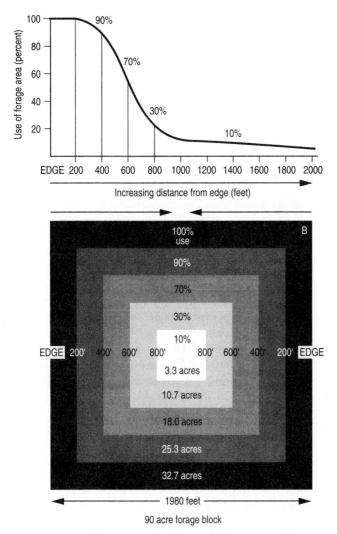

Figure 5.1 Use of forage areas by deer and elk relative to distance from edge of cover. (*Witmer et al. 1985.*)

and general wildlife watching and photography require more habitat diversity, with all successional stages represented if space permits. Wetlands, ponds, streams, and riparian vegetation should be protected, improved, or developed (Payne 1982, and see Chaps. 6 and 13).

Habitat manipulation for a specific habitat type and successional stage will encourage some species of wildlife and discourage others. The woodlot and surrounding land should be mapped, and habitat and wildlife inventoried and evaluated. The inventory should be as detailed as needed for management. Aerial photos, soils maps, and topographic maps should be obtained; potential for various species of wildlife assessed relative to soils, climate, and vegetation present and possible; objectives set; activities planned; and timetable set (Hassinger et al. 1979, Craven 1981, deCalesta 1983, Gutiérrez et al. 1984). The completed plan should include (1) landowner objectives; (2) inventory and arrangement of plants, plant communities, and wildlife; (3) list of plants needed for planting to enhance wildlife habitat, and procedures for planting and maintenance; (4) timber harvest methods and improvement for wildlife; and (5) program to protect the woodlot from fire, insects, disease, and livestock grazing (Bratton 1984). Controlled burns might be needed to regenerate species like oak or restore savanna. The plan must be biologically and economically feasible, should focus on native plants, and should increase wildlife productivity on a sustained basis.

After the inventory, the woodland should be divided into compartments of various sizes and shapes but similar vegetative, soil, topographic, productivity, or other important characteristics (Decker et al. 1983). Examples include a pine plantation, oak stand, wetland, stream and riparian strip, apple orchard, and abandoned homesite or other opening. Compartments should have easily identified and located boundaries. Otherwise painting boundary trees helps. Some compartments should receive exclusive emphasis for wildlife. Prescriptions for habitat improvement are scheduled by compartment. Records of inventory and habitat improvement should be maintained by compartment.

Because of the small size of most woodlots, they have a relatively low carrying capacity for many species of wildlife; the needs of highly mobile, wide-ranging species cannot be met, and relatively immobile narrow-ranging species are isolated with perhaps an inadequate gene pool. On property where establishment of woodlots is being considered, one large unfragmented woodlot is better than several small woodlots. Islands of woodlots should be connected with wooded corridors, especially riparian zones along streams. A wooded corridor also should extend from woodlot to isolated water hole. (See Chap. 6.)

The juncture of three or more desirable habitat types, called a *covert*, produces unusually dense and variable wildlife populations. The best coverts combine food, cover, and water. Coverts should be planned in woodlots managed for wildlife. This is not difficult because the woodlot generally is surrounded by another habitat type—often a field of some sort, which often provides some food. Thus, two habitat types—field and woods—are available already, and a proper cutting arrangement would join two different forest types or age classes with the field. A pond, stream, or wetland should be included in the covert system. Coverts are most efficiently designed when fields and woods are shaped in hexagons (Bromley et al. 1990). The smaller these hexagonal units are, the better they are for woodlot (edge) wildlife. But small units can produce too much edge and nuisance numbers of wildlife, and units less than about 10 ha for timber and about 2 ha for fuelwood can be uneconomical.

Cutting Strategy

One of the best ways to attract wildlife to a woodlot is to leave it alone rather than fragment it further, especially those larger than about 4 ha (Levenson 1981) (see "Edge versus Interior" in Chap. 1). But wood-lots managed for wildlife often can be improved in conjunction with the sale of commercial timber. In fact, that is usually the most efficient and economical way. Before a contract is signed to log the wood-lot, at least 38 specific trees per hectare should be flagged as "leave trees": large old trees, wolf trees, snags, live den trees, best mast trees, unusual trees, clumps of conifers (Hershey and Wiegers undated), as well as vigorous clumps of most shrubs such as *Rubus* and hazel. Patches of 0.4 to 2 ha should be preserved, especially near spring seeps, riparian zones, steep ravines, or along edges of coniferous stands (Devlin and Payne undated). Such patches should comprise 1 to 3 percent of the woodlot.

Lower branches of trees are leafier at the edge of the woodlot; some of the edge trees should be left unless their removal on the south and west sides is desired to enhance development of the ground and shrub layers by allowing sunlight to penetrate further into the woodlot. On sides of the woodlot facing prevailing winds, usually west and northwest sides, lower branches, especially of conifers, improve thermal cover by reducing windchill as snow accumulates on the branches and retards wind speed. Such perimeters should be uncut 15 m wide (Guljas undated). (See "Woodlot Borders and Other Brushy Areas," under "Mast, Browse, and Forage" in this chapter.)

A timber sales contract should be negotiated with a timber contractor to include location and description of the property; description and arrangement of the trees to be cut (i.e., species, size, groupings to create openings, etc.); price of timber, financial arrangements, and guaranteed title to products; termination date; special features such as location of roads, log-loading sites, bridges, and culverts; erosion prevention; seeding materials; and provision to settle disputes (Fig. 5.2) (Hassinger et al. 1981). Local wildlife biologists can assist in determining the specifics of a timber sales contract for wildlife habitat improvement. For woodlots managed as wildlife habitat, the goal should be to maintain or increase the mix of species and sizes of trees

I, Mark Hamilton of Masten, Pennsylvania (Purchaser) agree to purchase from Woodrow Meristem of Pomfret Center, Pennsylvania (Seller) the trees described below.

I. Location of Sale: The 42-acre woodland is in Derry Township, Tioga County, Pennsylvania, at the intersection of PA Route 804 and Legislative Route 7221, as shown on the attached map.

II. Trees to be Cut: Cut all designated trees and/or trees marked with yellow paint. Reserve all hemlock, hickory, dogwood, serviceberry, and black gum. Additional trees of special wildlife value to be left are marked with blue paint. Also not to be cut are any trees within 100 feet of Brougher Run except those marked with yellow paint by Seller.

III. Conditions of Sale:

A. The Purchaser agrees to the following:

(1) To pay the Seller the sum of $16,350 for the above designated or marked trees, and to make payment in advance of cutting.

(2) To waive all claim to the above described trees unless they are cut and removed on or before one calendar year from the date on this contract. In the event Purchaser is, due to circumstances beyond his control, unable to complete the sale in the time allowed, the Seller and Purchaser may agree on an extension of time for this contract.

(3) To construct a log-loading site approximately one-half acre in size in the southeast portion of the tract at a location agreed upon by the Seller and Purchaser.

(4) To do all in his power to prevent and suppress forest fires on, or threatening, the sale area.

(5) To avoid unnecessary injury to all trees not designated to be cut.

(6) To repair damages caused by logging to ditches, fences, bridges, roads, trails, or other improvements damaged beyond ordinary wear and tear.

(7) Not to assign this Agreement in whole or in part without the written consent of the Seller.

(8) All tops and slash from felled trees within 25 feet of the adjoining highway will be removed. No slash will be left across or on the public road, cleared field, or Brougher Run. Tops may be left on skid trails to prevent erosion.

(9) To leave standing all marked property boundary trees.

(10) Purchaser will take precautions to prevent soil erosion and other conditions detrimental to the property resulting from logging operation. Should such conditions occur, they will be corrected by the purchaser. He also will remove all oil cans, paper, and other trash resulting from the operation.

(11) To furnish to Seller 20 pounds of perennial rye grass seed, 2 pounds of timothy seed, and 6 pounds of innoculated birdsfoot trefoil which Seller will apply to the log-loading site and roads upon completion of this timber sale.

(12) To maintain public liability and workman's compensation insurance policies for the duration of this contract

B. The Seller agrees to the following:

(1) To guarantee title to the forest products covered by this Agreement, and to defend it against all claims at his expense.

(2) The property boundary lines shown to the Purchaser by the Seller are correct as located on the attached map. The Seller will save harmless the Purchaser from all trespass claims originating as a result of errors in the boundary line location made by the Seller.

(3) To allow the Purchaser to make necessary logging-road improvements such as bridges and gates which shall be removed or left in place as agreed upon by the Seller and the Purchaser. Trees designated for cutting may be used to construct such improvements.

(4) To grant freedom-of-entry and right-of-way to the purchaser and his employees on and across the area covered by this Agreement, and also other privileges usually extended to purchasers of timber which are not specifically covered, provided they do not conflict with specific provisions of this Agreement.

C. In case of dispute over the terms of this Agreement, we agree to accept the decision of an Arbitration Board of three selected persons as final. Each of the contracting parties will select one person, and the two selected will select a third to form this Board.

Signed this _____ day of _____ 19_____

Witness:

_____

_____

(Signed) _____
                                          Purchaser

_____
                                          Seller

Figure 5.2 A sample contract designed for a timber sale with wildlife considerations. (*Hassinger et al. 1981.*)

and shrubs, while improving the vertical diversity of the ground, shrub, and canopy layers on the property.

Jackson et al. (1984) highly recommended a two-cut shelterwood system for woodlots because of the diverse wildlife habitat produced. But except for shade-intolerant, fast-growing, short-lived species like aspen, selection cuts are preferable in woodlots because they create the most vertical structure for wildlife variety and are less expensive than even-aged systems in intensively managed woodlots (Hershey and Wiegers undated, Bratton 1984, Yarrow 1990a). Group selection is preferred to single-tree selection because high-grading is prevented and small openings are created. Cuts should be 0.04 to 0.4 ha (Yarrow 1990a), or at least twice the height of the trees (Bromley et al. 1990) (these can resemble small clearcuts), with at least an equal amount uncut. Stumps should be allowed to resprout. Stump sprouting of oak is enhanced when cutting occurs between December and May (Connell et al. 1973). Stump height should be over 46 cm to increase heart rot, if desired. With oaks, less than 40 percent of the merchantable trees over 36 cm dbh should be cut (Nixon and Hansen 1987). Thinnings and shelterwood cuts should leave a basal area of at least 9 m^2 of 30-cm dbh or larger oak sawtimber per hectare (Williamson undated).

Shaw (1967) thought that ideal habitat would exist if owners of small (32 to 36 ha) woodlots managed about 25 percent of it in a series of selectively cut units and about 75 percent in clearcut units. In the clearcut units, all woody stems over 5 cm dbh would be cut. Clearcuts should be scheduled so that 25 percent of the woodlot is in young stands (5 to 12 cm dbh), 25 percent in pole timber stands (13 to 25 cm dbh), and 50 percent in sawtimber stands (over 25 cm dbh) after a full rotation. In a woodlot of mostly hardwoods, about 10 percent of the clearcut area should be in conifer patches for cover, 5 percent in openings maintained to encourage early successional growth of native vegetation, and 2 percent planted with grass, legume, or grain crops. But openings are not needed in most woodlots surrounded by open land.

A typical 36-ha farm woodlot could be divided into 16 cutting units averaging about 2.25 ha each (Fig. 5.3) (Shaw 1967). Four units along roads and streams would be cut selectively (single-tree selection), three units would be clearcut now, three in 20 years, three in 40 years, and three in 60 years. In 80 years the first three units would be cut again, and so forth. Benefits to game would be greater if twice as many 1-ha units were clearcut every 10 years with nonadjacency constraints, selection cuts occurred every 10 years, and no cutting occurred in riparian areas. Old growth should be uncut; most woodlots will not contain it though. Some second growth should be allowed to develop into old growth—i.e., a section of the woodlot should never be cut, especially parcels isolated by swamps or water, riparian zones, timber of low economic value, eagle and osprey nest buffer zones, and areas where aesthetics are important (Henderson 1987, 1988).

Improvement for wildlife of a 32-ha woodlot consisting mainly of hardwood pole timber could proceed as in Fig. 5.4 (Shaw 1977) if single-tree selection cuts improve riparian areas as illustrated. Each numbered stand is 0.8 to 2 ha. The plan has an 80-year rotation with a 10-year cutting cycle. After the second or third harvest (in 20 or 30 years), (1) hardwoods comprise 85 percent, conifers 15 percent, and even-aged

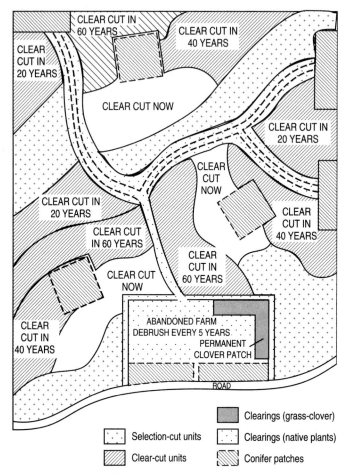

Figure 5.3 Timber-wildlife plan for a typical 36-ha farm woodlot in eastern hardwood country, with each cutting unit about 2.25 ha. (*Shaw 1967.*)

stands 70 percent of the wooded area; (2) selectively cut stands comprise 25 percent, and permanent openings (log landings and daylighted logging roads) 5 percent of the area; and (3) the age-class distribution is approaching 50 percent in sawtimber, 25 percent in pole timber, and 25 percent in the seedling/sapling stage. By dividing the 32-ha woodlot into four roughly equal sections, after the second cut each 8-ha section would contain a new clearcut, at least one conifer plantation, a selectively cut stand, and some daylighted logging road maintained in low, early successional plants. This example provides the ingredients of productive woodlot habitat: good diversity, good interspersion, good cover, continuous supply of ample food, balanced age classes of trees.

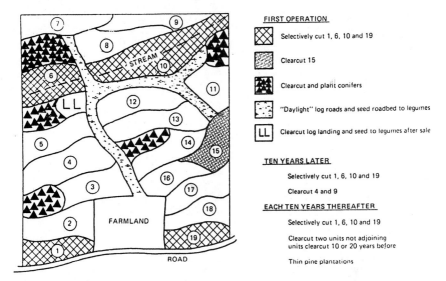

FIRST OPERATION

⊠ Selectively cut 1, 6, 10 and 19

▨ Clearcut 15

▲▲ Clearcut and plant conifers

⬚ "Daylight" log roads and seed roadbed to legumes

LL Clearcut log landing and seed to legumes after sale

TEN YEARS LATER

Selectively cut 1, 6, 10 and 19

Clearcut 4 and 9

EACH TEN YEARS THEREAFTER

Selectively cut 1, 6, 10 and 19

Clearcut two units not adjoining
units clearcut 10 or 20 years before

Thin pine plantations

Figure 5.4 A wildlife-oriented timber management plan for a typical 32-ha pole timber woodlot in northeastern hardwood country. (*Shaw 1977.*)

Quaking aspen is one of the most important tree species for wildlife, and for several species of wildlife aspen is more important than all other tree species combined (Johnson et al. 1987), partly because it is high in protein, it grows so fast on various sites, and it is so widespread. Quaking aspen has the widest distribution of any tree species in North America (Gullion 1984, Jones 1985).

Because aspen regeneration is so responsive to clearcutting and because the tree grows so fast, much can be done with it on small woodlots to benefit wildlife. Small cutting units to benefit ruffed grouse also benefit other wildlife (Figs. 5.5 and 5.6) (Gullion ca 1982, 1984, Yahner 1984, Henderson 1987). The heterogeneity of the 16 ha in Fig. 5.6 can be improved as in Fig. 5.7 (Hunter 1990). The cutting arrangement in Fig. 5.7 requires annual cutting. Some people might prefer to cut every 4 or 5 years (Fig. 5.8) (Hunter 1990). Large woodlots could be divided and treated as in Fig. 5.9 (Hunter 1990); the cutting pattern efficiently moves to a new parcel each year without sacrificing much diversity, and can be adapted readily to local conditions of different forest communities. On poorer sites or in colder climates where aspen grows more slowly, or where older trees are desired, the rotation age should be extended (Fig. 5.10) (Hunter 1990).

If timber is an objective, cutting should proceed in a fashion that enhances wildlife production. Shaw's (1967, 1977) patchiness seems to recognize the boundaries of natural mixes of forest types. Such patchiness is preferable to intensive, regular patchiness—except

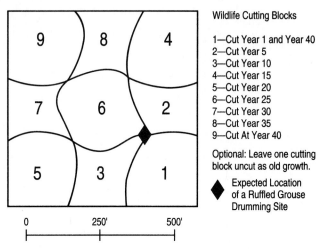

Figure 5.5 A timber-harvesting plan for a 4-ha woodlot. (*Gillion 1984, Henderson 1987.*)[See metric conversion table.]

that the whole woodlot is probably in itself enough of a patch within the usually agricultural landscape, and does not need further fragmentation.

Aspen can grow in pure stands, but often it is mixed with birch, oak, or pine. Where clones or individual aspen trees occur, 0.4-ha openings made into and immediately southwest of an aspen stand increase soil temperature and should encourage aspen sprouting into the opening (Williamson undated). Cutting several aspen stems from the clone on the side towards the opening will increase sprouting.

In large woodlots and forests, cuts up to 16 ha of aspen should be rectangular and about 100 to 200 m wide, with the space between cuts not over 300 m wide, and the long axis north-south (Kubisiak 1985). Cutting should proceed from south to north to facilitate sunlight penetration and responding aspen regeneration. Cutting during dormancy is best because more vigorous suckering will occur, but cutting in other seasons is acceptable if a complete clearcut is made (Brinkman and Roe 1975). Scattered clones of mature male aspen should be left for winter food (Williamson undated). Even 9.0 to 1.4 m^2 of residual basal area will retard sprout growth by 35 to 40 percent (Perala 1977). Cuts larger than 16 ha should leave clones of 50 to 60 mature aspen in every 8 ha (Kubisiak 1985). The upland edge of lowland aspen cover should be managed for long-range food-producing areas by maintaining about 25 percent of the lowland perimeter in openings and forest regrowth (Byelich et al. 1972).

Cutting schedules in the aspen parkland of western Canada vary somewhat for woodlots of 16 ha or more (Fig. 5.11) (Poston and

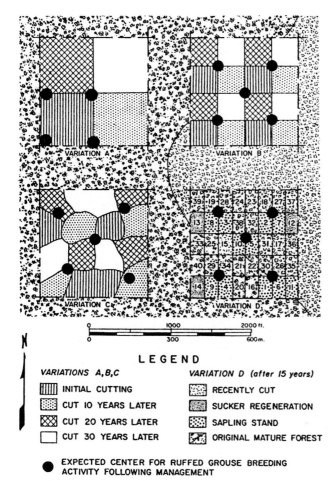

Figure 5.6 Management prescriptions for a 16-ha tract divided into 4-ha blocks (variation A); 2.5-ha blocks (variation B); variable 2.5-ha units (variation C); and 0.4-ha blocks with numbers indicating the year each block would be cut, shown 15 years after cutting began (variation D) (*Gullion 1984.*)

Schmidt 1981). Figure 5.12 illustrates an example of a simple wildlife habitat management plan for a 16-ha abandoned homestead area which includes aspen and oak (Henderson 1987). If no commercial market is available for aspen, burning is a feasible alternative (DeByle 1985). Units of 2 to 24 ha can be burned on a rotation of 60 to 100 years to provide a mixture of even-aged stands for wildlife. Many wildlife species depend on old-growth aspen. Aspen tends to regenerate by suckering rather than seeding. Aspen pole timber or sawtimber should be clearcut at 50- to 60-year rotations or earlier for rapid regeneration through suckering (DeGraaf et al. 1992). Aspen will die

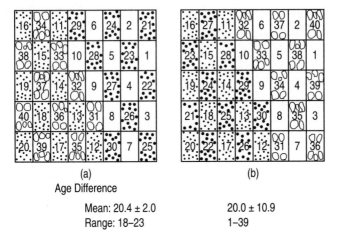

(a)   (b)

Age Difference

Mean: 20.4 ± 2.0   20.0 ± 10.9
Range: 18–23   1–39

Figure 5.7 Cutting patterns which maximize the average age difference between adjacent stands: (*a*) age differences deviate little from the overall average; (*b*) age differences range from 1 to 39 years. (*Adapted from Hunter 1990.*)

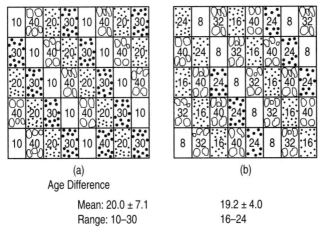

(a)   (b)

Age Difference

Mean: 20.0 ± 7.1   19.2 ± 4.0
Range: 10–30   16–24

Figure 5.8 Possible patterns for cutting only four (*a*) or five (*b*) times per 40 years. (*Adapted from Hunter 1990.*)

if not cut or otherwise removed before age 60 or 80 years, and the clonal stock will be lost (Perala and Russell 1983). Cutting the main stem stimulates suckering within 6 m of it, and sometimes within 12 to 15 m of it (Tubbs et al. 1987).

Oaks (acorns, buds, flowers, browse) are eaten by more birds and mammals than any other woody plant genus except perhaps *Rubus*. Oaks are also important as providers of cavities and other cover. In Canada and the United States, 80 species of oaks occur extensively, often mixed with other species, e.g., hickory. Oaks are slow-growing.

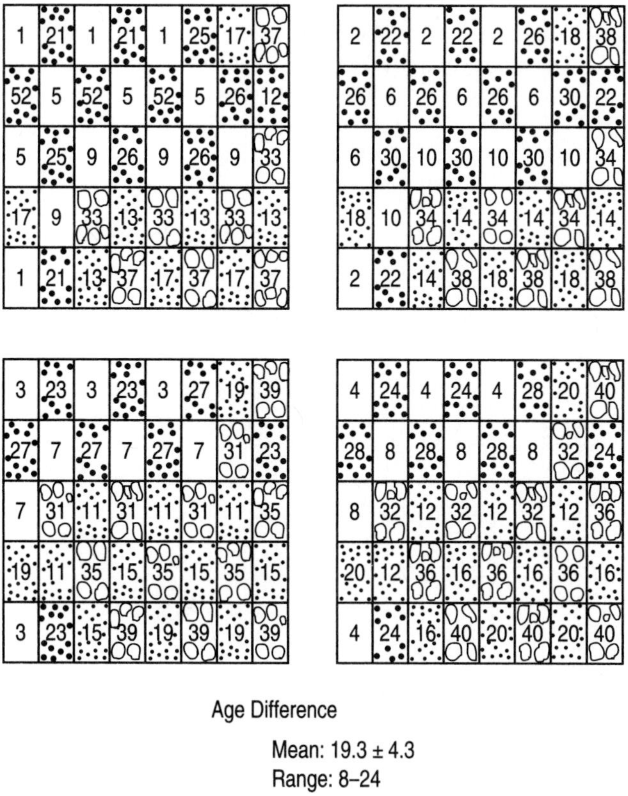

Age Difference

Mean: 19.3 ± 4.3

Range: 8–24

Figure 5.9 If the area were divided into four 16-ha management units, a high average age difference could be maintained by cutting each unit in sequence each year. (*Adapted from Hunter 1990.*)

Tree squirrels can be used as featured species perhaps representative of other wildlife requiring large old oaks or similar forest types. Thus, the optimal cutting pattern for clearcuts in a woodlot includes well-dispersed cuttings (Fig. 5.13) (Nixon and Hanson 1987). The interval for cutting 50 percent of the woodlot or stand varies with size of cut, rotation length, and size of woodlot (Table 5.1) (Nixon and Hanson 1987). After 50 percent of the woodlot or stand has been cut, the clearcuts might have to be deferred once during each rotation to avoid creating adjacent stands each less than 40 years old (Table 5.2) (Nixon and Hanson 1987). Shaw (1971) discussed a cutting schedule for large oak forests (see Fig. 4.30). Thinning of oaks can begin at age 10 years on a spacing of 4.5 to 6.1 m; commercial thinning should space trees about 8.2 m apart for full use of the site. Maximum sprouting for browse production occurs when oak is thinned to a basal area of 15 to 17 m^2/ha (Knierim et al. 1971). Stump sprouts should be thinned to one, two, or three sprouts per stump when 5 to 10 years old (Tubbs et al. 1987).

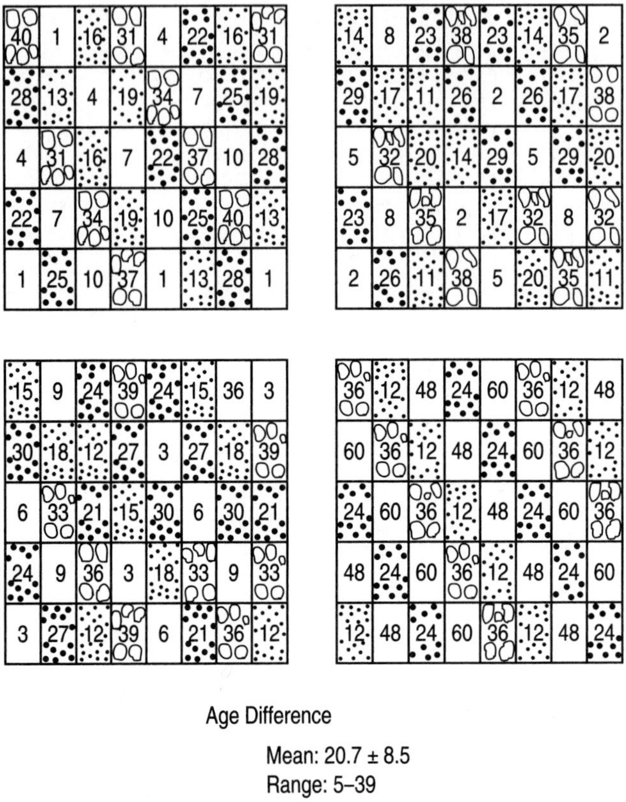

Age Difference

Mean: 20.7 ± 8.5

Range: 5–39

Figure 5.10 If the area were divided into four 16-ha management units, some habitat could be provided for wildlife needing older forests by managing one unit on a 60-year rotation. (*Adapted from Hunter 1990.*)

Stand Improvement

Timber stand improvement (TSI) can be called *wildlife stand improvement* (WSI) when stand improvement focuses on wildlife habitat improvement (Spencer 1988). Stand improvement should occur first on the most protected sites (east and south sides) with the lowest gradient, for they support the widest ecotones with the greatest area and variety of plants (Byelich et al. 1972). Thinning to a basal area of 14 to 16 m²/ha benefits deer and associated wildlife (Yarrow 1990a). A good compromise between wildlife and timber is to thin initially at age 12 to 20 years and every 5 to 7 years thereafter until final harvest.

During WSI, all standing dead trees, logs, and 2.5 to 10 den trees per hectare should be left (Bratton 1984, Bromley et al. 1990). (See "Snags and Live Den Trees" and "Logs and Slash" in Chap. 6.) Wolf trees and good mast trees should be left, and thinning should occur around them. Cull trees should be killed by girdling. Only the vines

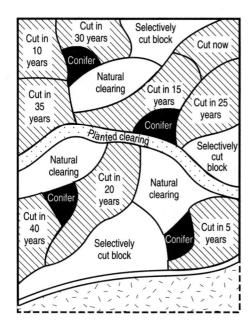

Figure 5.11 Cutting scheme for a large (≥16 ha) woodlot. (*Poston and Schmidt 1981.*)

damaging wildlife trees should be killed. Stumps should not be treated chemically, because this discourages stump sprouts for browse.

Thinning in plantations and woodlots in general should eliminate or avoid producing a rowlike appearance. Deciduous trees provide food and should not be removed from coniferous plantations (Hassinger et al. 1979, Decker et al. 1983). Competing trees should be removed within a circle around the selected tree to be preserved. The diameter of the circle in feet is determined by taking the preserved tree's diameter breast height in inches, multiplying by 2, and adding 1 for trees less than 10 in (25 cm) dbh, 2 for trees 10 to 17 in (25 to 43 cm), and 3 for trees over 17 in (43 cm) (Decker et al. undated). For example, a tree 14 in (36 cm) dbh would need a cleared circle 30 ft (9 m) in diameter ($2 \times 14 + 2 = 30$).

After the thinning is done, the preserved tree can be fertilized in spring to increase growth and/or mast production by applying a complete fertilizer such as a 5-10-5 formula at a maximum rate of 1 kg/cm dbh, or half that amount if a 10-10-10 fertilizer is used (Decker et al. undated). Placed under the crown, the fertilizer can be broadcast on the ground or poured in a series of holes 20 to 25 cm deep dug in the ground with a crowbar. The effects of fertilizer last about 3 years. But fertilizing every year is more productive, if less practical.

Mast production can be improved by pruning dead, damaged, or diseased branches. On some trees, such branches should be retained to serve as perches and produce cavities.

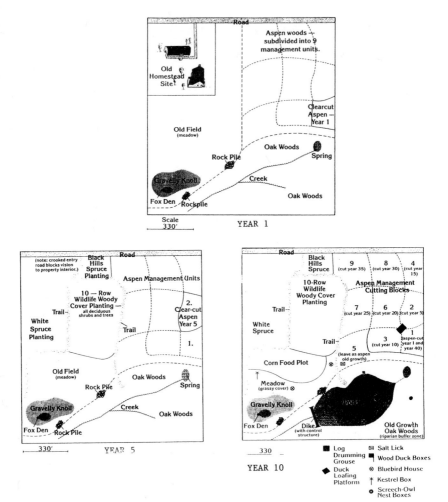

Figure 5.12 Wildlife habitat management plan for a 16-ha abandoned homestead area. (*Henderson 1987.*)[See metric conversion table.]

Tubbs et al. (1987) developed a somewhat complicated guide to management of wildlife trees in northern hardwoods, but it is oriented too much to timber production. It could be adapted to other forest types if simplified and oriented more to wildlife production.

If the woodlot lacks certain types of good wildlife plants normally found in the area, soil characteristics should be examined by the local soils office, where a published soil survey report also can be obtained. If the soil is suitable or can be made suitable with lime or fertilizer, seeding or transplanting of native species of plants can be accomplished (Burger 1973, Henderson 1987, Payne 1992). Tree shelters should be used to protect trees and shrubs from gnawing and brows-

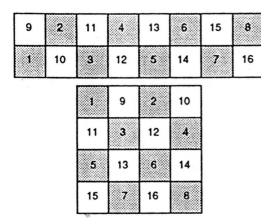

Figure 5.13 Cutting sequences (designated numerically) to benefit tree squirrels by avoiding adjacent clearcuts on rectangular or square units. (*Nixon and Hansen 1987.*)

TABLE 5.1   Minimum Clearcutting Intervals (in Years) for Various Woodlot Sizes, Cut Sizes, and Rotation Lengths

Size of cut (ha)	Rotation length for 8-ha woodlot (yr)			Rotation length for 16-ha woodlot (yr)			Rotation length for 24-ha woodlot (yr)		
	60	80	100	60	80	100	60	80	100
0.8	6	8	10	3	4	5	2	2	3
1.2	9	12	15	4	6	7	3	4	5
1.6	12	16	20	6	8	10	4	5	6
2.0	15	20	25	7	10	12	5	6	8

SOURCE: Nixon and Hansen (1987), modified from Roach and Gingrich (1968).

TABLE 5.2   Deferred Cutting Interval (in Years) Needed to Avoid Adjacent Stands, Both of Which Are <40 Years Old

Size of cut (ha)	Rotation length for 8-ha woodlot (yr)			Rotation length for 16-ha woodlot (yr)			Rotation length for 24-ha woodlot (yr)		
	60	80	100	60	80	100	60	80	100
0.8	22	16	10	16	8	0	16	8	4
1.2	31	28	25	24	16	12	16	8	0
1.6	28	24	20	22	16	10	20	15	10
2.0	25	20	15	19	10	4	20	16	8

Note: The deferral is needed only once during each rotation, after 50 percent of the stands (none adjacent) in the unit have been cut. In all instances here, shape of the unit is rectangular and the shape of the cut is square.
SOURCE: Nixon and Hansen (1987).

ing wildlife (Windell 1991). The U.S. Soil Conservation Service recommends that seed and transplants be planted within 160 km south, 320 km north, or 400 km east or west of their original source, and ideally within 40 to 80 km of their original source (Henderson 1987). State and provincial wildlife agencies can recommend suitable plants

Figure 5.14 A closed-canopy hardwood woodlot underplanted with shade-tolerant conifers. (*Decker et al. 1983.*)

(see Tables A.1 through A.5), and can provide the names of commercial suppliers if needed. If commercial suppliers are used, the origin of their stock should be ascertained so that nonregional stock can be avoided. Payne (1992) described plant propagation techniques for wetlands and associated uplands.

Evergreen Cover

An individual conifer has more cover value than an individual hardwood tree, especially if the conifer has developed into a wolf tree. In a predominantly hardwood woodlot, good cover is provided by 0.8 to 2 ha of conifers per 40 ha of woods, in clumps of 0.1 to 2 ha (Hassinger et al. 1979, Decker et al. 1983). Conifers should not be established near openings because raptors use the conifers for cover to prey on wildlife attracted to the opening (Gullion 1984).

Shade-tolerant native conifers can be underplanted in a closed-canopy woods (Fig. 5.14) (Decker et al. 1983). Results are best with trees such as spruce planted in clumps of about six trees, on 1.8-m centers (Hassinger et al. 1979, Decker et al. 1983).

Some openings in hardwood stands or at corners of old fields should be planted in a J-, C-, or S-shape with conifers spaced 3 by 3 m so that lower branches live longer (Fig. 5.15) (Decker et al. 1983). Evergreen cover is especially effective if tall, mature conifers and holly are located near low-growing evergreens such as rhododendron, mountain laurel, or young conifers (Hassinger et al. 1979). The outside row of a pine plantation should be planted with slow-growing, shade-tolerant spruce. The lower limbs of spruce will survive to reduce windchill in the pines.

Figure 5.15 Conifers planted between field edge and woodlot. (*Decker et al. 1983.*)

Wolf Trees

Wolf trees have large spreading branches developed from extensive exposure to sunlight. They are undesirable for forestry because they tend to be crooked with many branches and thus suppress development of nearby trees. They are desirable for wildlife because they provide an unusually large amount of food (mast) and cover for perching, nesting, denning, etc. Wolf trees should be preserved.

Mast, Browse, and Forage

Management predominantly for food often produces cover. Food for herbivores consists generally of mast, browse, and forage. *Mast* is produced by some trees and shrubs, and can be hard (nuts, seeds) or soft (fruit). *Browse* consists of the current annual growth including buds and flowers of woody plants. *Forage* consists of herbaceous vegetation (forbs, grasses, and grasslike plants such as sedges). Herbivores in turn attract the carnivores.

Mast trees

Mast trees provide important food in late summer, fall, and winter. At least 25 to 50 percent of the trees in the woodlot should be mast producers (Devlin and Payne undated).

In plantations of conifers, hardwood mast trees and shrubs should be preserved (Yarrow 1990a). Because some individual trees produce more mast than others of the same age and variety, age and mast yield should be determined generally, if not specifically, so that the top producers can be saved from cutting (Burger 1973). Fully exposed tree crowns produce the most seed; shaded portions of trees produce less seed (Tubbs et al. 1987). Large trees produce more seed than small trees. Some species vary in annual seed production. Some species are dioecious; only the females produce seed. Trees bear the most seed during their prime at mid-age.

Oak, hickory, beech, walnut, butternut, cherry, ash, and conifers are the most important mast trees. Trees and shrubs such as birch, hazel, alder, and aspen produce male catkins that are eaten by some wildlife species (Tubbs et al. 1987). Oak is the single most important tree because of its variety, abundance, distribution, and broad use by so many wildlife species (Table 5.3) (Goodrum et al. 1971). Oaks in the white oak group produce acorns every year and are preferred because the acorns have less tannin. Oaks in the black (red) oak group produce acorns every 2 years because their acorns need two seasons to develop. If poor spring weather kills the blossoms, the white oak group would produce no acorns that year, and the black oak group none the following year. Thus, a ratio of two or three trees in the black oak group to one tree in the white oak group is desirable (Williamson undated, Shaw 1971). This mix will produce about 112 kg of acorns per hectare from about 54 to 62 oaks per hectare of at least 35 cm dbh, an amount which should meet the needs of most wildlife (Shaw 1971, Verner 1980, Decker et al. 1983). To sustain high populations of gray squirrels, at least 168 kg of acorns per hectare is needed, which can be produced from a basal area of at least 13 m^2 of sawtimber-sized oaks per hectare. Production of acorns varies with species (Tables 5.4 through 5.6) (Shaw 1971, Payne and Copes 1988). Oak stands of different ages can be interspersed to provide optimal habitat diversity for wildlife (Table 5.7) (Goodrum et al. 1971). Stands with 60 to 100 percent stocking produce the most acorns (Williamson undated). Shaw (1971) discussed an age-class distribution and cutting schedule for best mast production in an oak forest (see Fig. 4.30). (Also see "Cutting Strategy" in this chapter.)

Apple trees

Wild or neglected apple trees are excellent wildlife trees for the fruit, browse, cavities, and nesting cover produced. Apple trees should be planted where they do not occur. Planting stock should be 15 to 18 dm high, protected by expandable plastic strips of 0.6-cm mesh hardware cloth buried 15 cm deep (Hassinger et al. 1979, Olson and Langer 1990).

Rejuvenating existing apple trees involves several steps (Connecticut Department of Environmental Protection 1988c, Olson and Langer

TABLE 5.3   Example of the Need for Acorns by Some Common Game Species

| Dietary needs | Species and population density (ha per animal) | | | | | |
	Bob-white quail (2.0)	Gray squirrel (0.8)	Fox squirrel (1.2)	Turkey (20.3)	White-tailed deer (8.1)	Total
Kilograms of food needed per animal per day	0.01	0.09	0.14	0.23	2.27	—
Kilograms of acorns needed per hectare						
180 days	0.40*	15.1†	14.8†	1.6†	25.2*	57.1
300 days	0.67*	25.2†	24.7†	2.6†	42.0*	95.2
Kilograms of acorns needed per animal						
180 days	0.81*	12.1†	17.8†	31.9†	204*	266.6
300 days	1.35*	20.2†	29.6†	52.3†	340*	443.5

*For 50 percent of diet.
†For 75 percent of diet.
SOURCE: Adapted from Goodrum et al. (1971).

TABLE 5.4   Kilograms of Fresh Acorns per Hectare Relative to Diameter at Breast Height of Various Species of Oak

dbh (cm)	Chest-nut oak	White oak	Post oak	North-ern red oak	South-ern red oak	Scar-let oak	Black oak	Water oak	Black-jack oak	Sand-jack oak
10	—	—	0.2	—	—	—	—	—	—	0.8
15	—	—	0.9	—	—	—	—	—	—	1.9
20	—	0.3	1.6	—	—	—	—	0.6	0.5	3.0
25	1.0	2.1	2.2	0.5	0.6	2.8	1.2	3.0	1.9	4.1
30	3.5	4.0	2.9	2.5	1.1	4.4	1.9	5.5	3.5	—
36	5.6	5.8	3.7	6.4	2.2	6.3	2.6	8.0	4.8	—
41	6.7	7.7	4.4	11.2	4.1	9.0	3.1	10.5	6.3	—
46	9.1	9.6	5.0	16.3	7.2	13.5	3.8	13.0	7.7	—
51	10.0	11.4	5.7	17.7	11.8	16.6	4.5	15.6	8.9	—
56	11.0	13.5	6.5	19.2	18.3	19.6	5.2	18.2	10.8	—
61	11.3	15.2	—	17.3	27.0	20.1	5.8	20.8	12.2	—
66	11.8	17.0	—	15.5	35.5	20.5	6.5	—	—	—

SOURCE: Shaw (1971).

TABLE 5.5   Kilograms of Fresh Acorns per Hectare Relative to Basal Area of Oaks in Southern Plains Forests

Basal area* per ha (m²)	Black oak group†		White oak group‡	
	23–36 cm	>36 cm	23–36 cm	>36 cm
0.2	2.2	5.6	6.7	6.7
0.4	4.5	10.1	12.3	13.5
0.6	6.7	15.7	19.1	19.1
0.7	9.0	21.3	25.8	25.8
0.9	12.3	26.9	32.5	32.5
1.1	14.6	31.4	38.1	39.2
1.3	16.8	37.0	44.8	46.0
1.5	19.1	42.6	51.6	52.7
1.7	21.3	47.1	57.2	58.3
1.9	23.5	52.7	62.8	65.0

*Applicable only to trees having healthy crowns extending at least one-third of total height.
†Includes southern red oak and blackjack oak.
‡Includes post oak and white oak.
SOURCE: Payne and Copes (1988).

1990). If more than one stem exists, the most vigorous stem should be retained by cutting off the others near the ground. All other shrubs and trees, including overtopping trees, should be removed back to the drip line of the apple tree. If the apple tree is growing in a competitive forest, it should be pruned before competing trees and shrubs are cleared from the area. All dead, diseased, and insect-infested branches should be removed. Dead branches with cavities should be retained. Diseased and insect-infested branches should be burned and cutting tools coated with bleach between cuttings. About one-third of the remaining growth should be removed, especially vertical branches which will shade the rest. Branches at a 45 to 90° angle are the best to retain, plus the short spur branches which grow on the side of the larger branches and produce the fruit. Other branches to remove include those in the center of the tree, those with narrow crotches, and those that hang below or across others. Drooping branches should be cut back. Pruning should occur in late winter or early spring.

Apple trees should be fertilized with calcium nitrate or a complete fertilizer such as 10-10-10 at the rate of 2.3 kg for a large tree, 1.4 kg for a small tree, and 0.5 kg for a sapling. Fertilizer should be applied in early spring. It may be scattered evenly from the drip line to within 1 m of the trunk, but that often encourages competing grass. Within the drip line, fertilizer can be poured into 10 to 15 holes dug 3 dm deep with a crowbar. Effects of fertilizing last about 3 years (Hassinger et al. 1979).

TABLE 5.6 Kilograms of Fresh Acorns per Hectare Relative to Basal Area of Dominant or Codominant Oak Trees in Mountain Forests

Basal area* per ha (m^2)	Black oak group†		White oak group‡	
	23–36 cm	>36 cm	23–36 cm	>36 cm
0.2	5.6	7.8	4.5	5.6
0.4	10.1	15.7	7.8	12.3
0.6	15.7	23.5	12.3	17.9
0.7	20.2	31.4	15.7	24.7
0.9	25.8	39.2	20.2	30.3
1.1	31.4	47.1	23.5	37.0
1.3	35.9	55.0	28.0	42.6
1.5	41.5	62.8	31.4	49.3
1.7	46.0	70.6	35.9	54.9
1.9	51.6	78.5	39.2	56.0
2.0	56.0	86.3	43.7	68.4
2.2	61.7	94.2	47.1	74.0
2.4	67.3	102.0	51.6	80.7
2.6	71.8	109.9	54.9	87.4
2.8	77.3	117.7	59.4	93.0
3.0	81.9	125.6	62.8	99.8
3.2	87.4	133.4	67.3	105.4
3.3	92.0	141.2	71.8	112.1
3.5	97.5	149.1	75.1	118.8
3.7	103.1	157.0	79.6	124.4
4.6	128.9	196.2	99.8	154.7
5.6	154.7	235.4	118.8	186.1

*Applicable only to trees having healthy crowns extending at least one-third of total height.

†Includes northern red oak, black oak, and scarlet oak.

‡Includes chestnut oak and white oak.

SOURCE: Payne and Copes (1988).

Woodlot borders and other brushy areas

The two basic types of brushy cover are (1) young trees of the brush-stage forest and (2) shrubs and vines (Hassinger et al. 1979). The brush-stage forest provides cover for 5 to 10 years after tree harvest. Practices that cause the least soil disturbance result in the best production of soft mast such as *Rubus* (Stransky and Roese 1984). Because of its variety of species, broad distribution, and vigor, *Rubus* probably is the most used woody plant in North America for its mast, browse, and cover.

Brushy borders can be established along woodlot edges by cutting all trees taller than 3 m or larger than 7.5 cm dbh in a border 6 to 9 m wide (Hershey and Wiegers undated, Husek 1970, Hassinger et al. 1979, Bratton 1984), especially on the east, south, and west sides, where they receive more sunlight (Kennedy undated). Such borders

TABLE 5.7   Percentage of Oaks Producing Acorns by Species and 5-cm Bole Diameter Class

Diameter class (cm)	Black oaks				White oaks		
	Southern red	Black-jack	Water	Sand-jack	White	Post	Cow
10	20	25	—	78	—	41	—
15	21	56	59	92	—	42	—
20	50	76	47	90	38	57	—
25	59	90	83	95	25	64	—
30	68	85	90	—	—	69	—
36	78	100	100	—	—	73	75
41	81	83	—	—	90	—	50
46	85	67	100	—	90	73	100
51	83	—	92	—	—	76	—
56	92	100	—	—	—	76	—
61	100	—	100	—	—	—	—
66	100	—	—	—	75	—	—

SOURCE: Adapted from Goodrum et al. (1971).

also can be established along logging roads, skid trails, log landings, and other openings (see "Openings" and "Logging Roads and Skid Trails" in Chap. 7). Brush piles should be built with the slash and spaced 30 to 60 m apart in sunny locations (Kennedy undated) (see "Brush Piles and Rock Piles" in Chap. 15).

Some openings should be constructed for shrubs by removing a group of trees. Natural openings with shrubs should be maintained. Brushy areas can be maintained by recutting every 5 or 6 years with a brush-hog (Hassinger et al. 1979). About half of the border should be cut each time to retain some wildlife habitat for fall and winter (Connors undated). Mowing should occur in late summer when most nesting is completed.

Female grapevines should be retained in at least four to six trees per hectare during selective harvest, preferably in mast trees (Sanderson et al. 1980). Male grapevines bear no fruit. Grapevines in noncommercial trees should be retained. Grapevine thickets on the ground hold snow and form pockets of shelter. They can be improved for cover and fruit by cutting adjacent trees to admit more sunlight (Hassinger et al. 1979).

When an alder thicket reaches 20 to 25 years old or the stems are 5 to 10 cm in diameter and begin to grow horizontally or lie down, about 25 percent of it should be cut every 5 years (Williamson undated, Hassinger et al. 1979). Large stands should be cut 21 m wide, separated by uncut strips 85 m wide. Winter cutting promotes the best

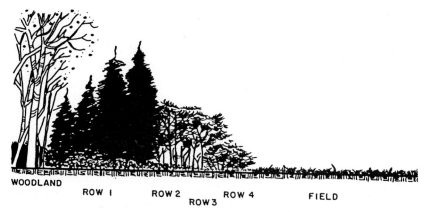

Figure 5.16 Cross section of a typical field and woodlot border planted for wildlife. (*Connors undated.*)

sprouting. Alder swales can sometimes be used as skid trails, with alders cut off at the ice line. Dense alders can be improved by grazing them lightly an average of 74 cow-days per hectare per year (e.g., 1 cow for 74 days or 74 cows for 1 day, etc.) (Husek 1970).

The most expensive method of developing a woodlot border is to plant shrubs and trees along the edge 9 to 15 m wide in one to four rows (Fig. 5.16) (Connors undated, Kennedy undated, Anderson 1969). Row 1 should contain coniferous trees, with the leaders pruned when the trees reach 4.5 to 6 m tall to reduce additional height and produce bushiness. Rows 2 and 3 should contain tall shrubs. Row 4 should contain short shrubs. Species of shrubs should be chosen that flower and fruit at different times of the year (see Table A.2). (Also see "Hedgerows" and "Shelterbelts" under "Linear Habitats" in Chap. 11.)

Herbaceous openings

The three main types of herbaceous cover are grains, grasses, and legumes (Van Hoey undated). All of these also provide food. They are most effective for wildlife when sewn in strips 9 to 15 m wide, preferably in mixtures of native species.

Undisturbed grassy cover can be provided by running a fence diagonally across the corner of a pasture next to a woodlot (unpub. rep., Kansas Fish and Game Commission). The woodlot border can be a suitable grass-legume mixture in a strip 5 m wide (Anderson 1969), which should be mowed 20 cm high in late summer the first year (Van Hoey undated). Then half of it should be mowed every 2 to 4 years in late summer (Connors undated). Other recommendations are presented in "Openings" in Chap. 7.

Food plots

Two to five rows or a strip 3 to 9 m wide of unharvested crops should be left along woodlot borders (Anderson 1969, Bratton 1984, Busch 1989). Root pruning of the woodlot border might be needed to invigorate the food strip; this is done by digging a trench, at least 46 cm and preferably 61 cm deep, along the edge of the woodlot with a ripper blade on a bulldozer or a single-row subsoiler or long-shanked chisel pulled by a farm tractor (unpub. rep., Kansas Fish and Game Commission). Two or three passes might be most efficient. Root pruning lasts at least 4 years. Otherwise, a strip can be disked along the field edge during routine seed bed preparation, and left idle for annual forbs to pioneer (Busch 1989).

Other types of food plots vary in size from 0.05 to 0.4 ha (Connors undated). The size and number needed vary with the size of the woodlot and the amount of food available within the woodlot and in surrounding fields. Mixed grain crops should be used (Decker and Kelley undated, National Audubon Society 1969, Woehler 1982). Food plots should be reestablished every 1 or 2 years with standard farming procedures. (See "Food Plots" in Chap. 11.)

Dusting Areas

Where there are no dusting areas for birds, these should be developed by choosing areas of fine, loose soil and spading an area 6 dm by 9 dm in a sunny spot (unpub. rep., Kansas Fish and Game Commission). Sunny areas should be located in herbaceous openings away from human disturbance such as hiking.

Water and Riparian Areas

Many woodlots contain natural springs or seeps, creeks, small ponds, or wetlands. Preserving and protecting these valuable wildlife areas and their buffers might be the only management needed. Because many wetland wildlife species use grassy areas for cover, at least 0.8 to 1.6 ha of nearby unmowed grassy cover should be maintained for each 0.4 ha of pond (Henderson 1987). This is best accomplished where pond adjoins field and woods in a highly productive covert. Overhanging limbs from adjacent trees provide hunting perches for species such as belted kingfishers and green-backed herons that prey on minnows. Rocks can be placed to create a small falls, beneficial because flowing or dripping water is more attractive than still water to wildlife (Hassinger et al. 1979, Henderson 1987). Other management techniques and considerations are presented in Chap. 13, under "Riparian Areas" in Chap. 6, and in Payne (1992).

Chapter

6

Corridors and Riparian Areas

Corridors

To maintain native animals and plants in perpetuity in fragmented, human-dominated landscapes, Harris and Scheck (1991) recommended that society adopt the principle of *faunal movement corridors,* i.e., *landscape linkages.* Only the largest parks in our society can fulfill the needs of wide-ranging species, especially the large carnivores (Noss and Harris 1986). Small and large areas connected by natural corridors can support a similar species composition (MacClintock et al. 1977). Although themselves a form of fragmentation, habitat corridors are needed to provide movement and gene flow between wildlife populations in habitat that otherwise would be isolated. Small, isolated populations cannot maintain genetic and demographic integrity indefinitely (Slatkin 1987). They ultimately will disappear as surely as if the isolated habitat were removed too. Populations of waterfowl and other migratory waterbirds have recovered from the brink of extinction as a result of the imposition of controls on hunting and the establishment of an integrated, continentwide system of refuges in migration corridors. No similar program exists for mammals because society has ignored the effects of fragmentation and has not recognized the need for mammals to move and interbreed (Harris 1985).

Much of the original landscape of North America was interconnected. But corridors are complicated, and they can be good or bad

(Simberloff et al. 1992). Corridors should be restricted to landscape connections that occurred naturally. This approach is always preferable to connecting landscapes with travel corridors that did not exist previously (e.g., drainage and irrigation ditches, windbreaks, and even introduced riparian strips) (Noss 1987c, Harris and Scheck 1991, Knopf 1992). When unnatural corridors are used, undesirable dispersal of both indigenous and exotic animals and plants will occur, seriously compromising biotic integrity. Isolated strips of windbreaks, hedgerows, riparian fragments, etc., are not movement corridors. Landscapes such as the Great Plains were effective barriers, allowing the evolution of distinct taxa in eastern and western forests. The fragmentation of the Great Plains by riparian corridors has resulted in hybridization and loss of species (Knopf 1992). The single most important factor in the evolution of species and communities has been barriers, whether at the microsite or continental level (pers. comm. F. B. Samson, U.S. Forest Service, Missoula, MT, 1992).

A wildlife movement corridor is a linear natural, restored, or cultural connection between at least two larger, similar habitat areas (Harris and Scheck 1991). It maintains gene flow, and is used for movement of animals and of plants pollinated or dispersed by animals. With forests, a strip of timber left during clearcutting will aid wildlife movements across areas too open at first and too dense later (Landers 1992). The main corridors that should be adapted for movement by native plants and animals are streamside management zones and linear riparian forests, landscape linkages that interconnect protected areas, roadways, utility rights-of-way, hedges and ownership boundaries such as fencelines, and recreational greenways (Harris and Scheck 1991).

The high edge-to-area ratio and high level of disturbance in corridors favor early successional plant associations (Loney and Hobbs 1991). Based on width, corridors can be classified as either (1) *line corridors,* so narrow that the two edges influence all parts of the corridor, or (2) *strip corridors,* which can be wide enough to have an interior (Forman and Godron 1986), although even the latter mostly are maximized edge habitat. Corridors can be higher than surroundings, e.g., windbreaks and hedgerows (see Chap. 11), or lower than surroundings, e.g., powerline rights-of-way and strip clearcuts. Hedgerows wider than about 12 m are strip corridors because of higher forest-herb diversity and abundance; those narrower are line corridors. Based on origin, corridors can be (1) natural—e.g., streams and rivers, riparian strips, mountain passes, isthmuses, and narrow straits, which are present in unfragmented landscapes and retained following fragmentation; (2) remnant—e.g., roadsides, railway edges, and fragmented natural corridors; (3) cultural, created for utilitarian and aesthetic use—e.g., shelterbelts, hedgerows, drainage and irrigation ditches, and forest clearings for utility rights-of-way (Loney and Hobbs 1991); or (4) cultural, created for wildlife movement—e.g., fish ladders, road underpasses, and elevated roads, pipelines, and overpasses (Harris and Scheck 1991).

Riparian areas are the best hope for creating a system of interconnecting corridors (Harris 1985), although they might not suit wildlife species of dry upland habitats (Forman 1983). Other types of corridors include abandoned railroad rights-of-way, and powerline, pipeline, and other easements for mammals mainly. Windbreaks (shelterbelts), greenbelts, wooded visual screens, canopy roads, and wooded median strips of interstate highways will be used as corridors mainly by birds. In urban areas, some animals could use jogging, bicycle, and equestrian trails, just as wooded fencerows can be used in rural areas (Harris 1985). Noss (1987c) listed potential advantages and disadvantages of corridors. Some of these, such as riparian areas, can be maintained as unique habitat and serve as movement corridors. An adequate movement corridor is a function of the movement requirements of the native species present in the area. Corridors must be restored where they are needed but have been removed or are otherwise inadequate.

The need for a corridor depends on the size of the habitat patches to be connected by it and the abundance of animals contained within the patches (Soulé 1991). Even abundant species are likely candidates for extinction when patches are small. Where average patch size is small, corridors must be able to transport normally abundant species including small mammals, certain birds, reptiles, amphibians, and insects (Fig. 6.1). However, narrow corridors might also provide habitat for farmland and edge wildlife species such as brown-headed cowbirds, common grackles, starlings, and red-winged blackbirds, thus funneling these competitors, predators, and brood parasites into a forest (Ambuel and Temple 1983).

Two indications of vulnerability to extinction are rarity of a wildlife species and the variability of its population size (or population growth rate, i.e., reproductive and mortality rates) from generation to generation or from year to year (Soulé 1991). Rarer and highly variable species are candidates for extinction, especially on small habitat patches. If patches are so small that the sum of their areas cannot support large animals, they might have to be ignored. Where the area of many small patches sums to an area large enough for large animals, a network of connecting corridors might work. (See "Reserves" and "Minimum Viable Population" in Chap. 1.)

Most users of corridors are *corridor travelers* or *corridor dwellers* (Beier and Loe 1992). Corridor travelers use corridors to pass between two areas for juvenile dispersal, seasonal migration, or movement between parts of a large home range. Typical corridor travelers are large herbivores, medium to large carnivores, and many migrato-

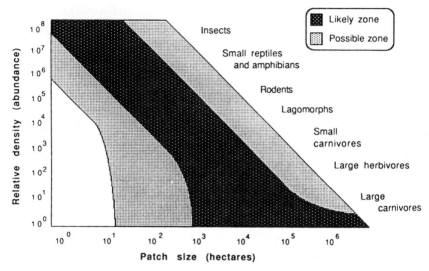

Figure 6.1 Zones of abundance and patch sizes (dark shading) for which a species is likely to need a corridor, and zones where corridors might be needed or helpful (light shading). (*Soulé 1991.*)

ry animals. Corridor dwellers need several days to several generations to pass through the corridor. Typical corridor dwellers are most plants, insects, amphibians, reptiles, small mammals, and birds with small dispersal ability. A corridor suitable for corridor dwellers must provide most or all of their life-history needs.

For corridor travelers, the topography, vegetation, and location relative to movement patterns should facilitate encountering the corridor entrance (Beier and Loe 1992). Then the habitat within it must attract the animal to enter and travel it for the time needed to reach the other end. Impediments must be removed or mitigated. These include type of road crossing, off-road vehicles, fences, dam construction, stream channelization, grazing, silviculture, dogs and cats, outdoor lighting, traffic and other noise, and other human activities. For corridor dwellers, additional considerations include the presence or absence of the species within the corridor. If the species is absent, the habitat has to be suitable for its introduction, and any gaps must be short enough to be crossed.

Roads are particular obstacles, as are corridors for entry of materials, edge species, and disturbances (Beier and Loe 1992, Noss 1992, Schonewald-Cox and Buechner 1992). Corridors should be located where the number of road crossings is minimal, and preferably zoned roadless in the center. Fencing should be used to guide animals away from high-speed roads and toward an underpass (preferable to a culvert), tunnel, bridge, viaduct, or other structure. Where low-use roads cross corridors, methods such as speed limits, signs, curves, grades, and speed bumps should be used to reduce vehicle speeds. Land uses next to the corridor should be considered before location, and controlled after location.

To facilitate movement of species as seasonal climate changes, corridors should be aligned upslope, north-south, and coast-inland (Noss 1992). Migration routes should be included. Corridors should extend up each slope of a river to each ridgeline and downslope on each side of the ridge to include riparian zones. Management activities, such as the location of campsites near water, should be minimal to facilitate animal movement. If such facilities as campgrounds are demanded, they should be spaced from the water relative to sensitivity of aquatic life, soil erodibility, and soil drainage (McReynolds et al. 1983).

Corridor width is influenced by edge effect (Soulé 1991). High mortality along edges requires a wide corridor. Corridors that are too wide confuse traveling animals, usually subjecting them to high mortality. If such mortality is low, corridors can be wider. Corridors should be straight, so that animals spend less time in edge habitat and are not confused by a maze of indirect routes. Corridors should have straight sides and a constant width.

Corridor length is determined by the travel speed and mortality rate of the wildlife species involved. Long corridors accommodate species that move fast. The range in speed among almost all species in a region has as many orders of magnitude (about 9) as the ranges in body size and density (Soulé 1991).

An effective approach to dimensions of corridors takes into account location, landform, distribution of natural vegetation, and movement and habitat needs of the most demanding native wildlife species and other species of interest, as well as adjacent human activities (Harris and Scheck 1991, Beier and Loe 1992). For example, cougars cross freeways through the underpass that is aligned best with a major drainage, rather than through the best-designed underpass located elsewhere (Foster and Humphrey 1991). Width can be narrow if the distance between tracts of habitat and the time of use are short. Harris and Scheck (1991) made the following general recommendations for width of movement corridors:

1. About 1 to 10 m for individual animals when much is known about their behavior and they will use the corridor only for several weeks or months

2. About 100 to 1000 m for movements of an entire species when much is known about its biology and it will use the corridor for years

3. About several kilometers for all species in the area and/or when little is known of the species' biology and/or they will use the corridor for decades

Harrison (1992) suggested that long corridors be at least 1 home range wide: e.g., 12–22 km for gray wolves, 5 km for cougars, 2.5 km for bobcats, 2 km for black bears, 0.6 km for white-tailed deer. If rectangular lifetime home ranges are twice as long as wide, a corridor connecting populations of grizzly bears should be at least 44.25 km wide (Noss 1992).

At the landscape level (1:24,000 or larger), Noss (1992) recommended that corridors be at least 3 times wider than the longest distance penetrated by edge effects. For example, if the edge effect extends 600 m into a forest (Wilcove 1985, 1990, Wilcove et al. 1986, Robinson 1990), the corridor would have to be 1800 m wide to have a 600-m-wide interior. (For other considerations of edge effect, see "Edge versus Interior" in Chap. 1.) Corridors at the regional level (perhaps longer than 16 km) should average at least 1.6 km wide, and much wider for large carnivores; bottlenecks should be no narrower than 0.4 to 0.8 km (Noss 1992), although preferably no bottlenecks should exist.

Corridors should be managed on a regional and local level. The regional—e.g., statewide or provincewide—strategy has five steps involving agency heads, decision makers, small private landowners, and concerned citizens (Harris 1985):

1. Clarify the corridor concept and illustrate its roles and the need for cooperation.

2. Illustrate the existing interconnections of habitat islands with streams and rivers, the need for more protection and enhancement to allow several subsystems to function for numerous species, that protecting one drainage system will interconnect several areas, and the feasibility of tying in other upland areas.

3. Develop a functional, interconnected, statewide habitat system with long-term leases, easements, tax incentives, management agreements, and zoning laws.

4. Develop guidelines for widths of corridors along various-sized streams to accommodate most vertebrates, especially mammals, which are the most sensitive to movement and areal needs.

5. Determine the need for road underpasses and bridge design to reduce movement barriers.

Finally, the use of corridors should be monitored to demonstrate their biological importance and the best designs (Nicholls and

Margules 1991, Beier and Loe 1992, Inglis and Underwood 1992). Monitoring programs can include counts of tracks or other sign, photography, radiotelemetry, or measures of gene flow. Equal sampling intensity should occur before and after developing the corridor, as well as within and next to the corridor.

Leave strips

Corridors higher than surroundings include *leave strips,* or *stringers,* which are strips of trees left after a clearcut to connect islands of old growth or mature forest. Such strips should be mature, of relatively closed canopy, and wide enough to resist windthrow (Harris 1984). A leave strip is needed most in a clearcut larger than 81 ha that does not contain a riparian corridor (Landers 1992). The wider the corridor is and the greater the contrast is between corridor and adjacent habitat, the more likely it is that the corridor interior will have characteristic plants and animals (Anderson et al. 1977, Johnson et al. 1979, Chasko and Gates 1982, Forman 1987, Gates 1991).

Leave strips should occur along prime locations for travel lanes. These are areas of least topographic resistance, such as saddles and gaps, bands around ridges, and stream courses; seeps, springs, and riparian zones; and cover areas in locations deficient in cover (Thomas et al. 1979b). Leave strips should be 137 to 183 m wide for deer and elk; noncontiguous patches of cover can serve as travel lanes if separated by 90 m or less (Black et al. 1976).

Gehrken (1975), Buckner and Landers (1980), Bromley et al. (1990), and Landers (1992) recommended that corridors be at least 100 m wide for species like turkeys, or at least wide enough so that an observer cannot see through. The Nova Scotia Department of Lands and Forests (ca 1989) recommended that at least one corridor at least 50 m wide be left after a clearcut over 50 ha, with any harvesting of the corridor limited to selection cuts removing less than 40 percent of the merchantable timber, and skidding trails located on high ground, narrow, and angled through the corridor rather than straight across. A leave strip at least 6 m wide should be left for every 137 m in length of clearcut or final shelterwood cut (Connecticut Department of Environmental Protection 1989). Leave strips should connect with uncut forest, not with another leave strip. At least 5 percent of clearcuts over 60 ha should be maintained as travel corridors; otherwise, clumps of trees 0.2 to 0.4 ha in area should be scattered throughout the clearcut, usually one clump per 2 to 4 ha (Oliveri 1988). For red-cockaded woodpeckers, Conner and Rudolph (1989) recommended corridors at least 400 m wide, consisting of trees at least 30 years old, and within 5 km of active colonies. Luman and

Neitro (1980) recommended corridor-type management zones 1.2 to 3.0 km wide, with blocks of older forests averaging 32 ha and spaced about 0.6 km apart throughout the corridor. These wide corridors should connect blocks of old growth and mid-aged stands of at least 259 ha (U.S. Bureau of Land Management 1981, Monthey 1984). Such wide corridors could be scheduled into the long-rotation sequential clearcuts advocated by Harris (1984) and Samson et al. (1989, 1991), or incorporated into the uneven-aged management strategy in coordination with the even-aged management strategy (see "Progressive Harvest," under "Management Strategy" in Chap. 4).

Rights-of-way

Corridors lower than surroundings generally produce undesirable fragmentation; such corridors include rights-of-way for powerlines, pipelines, railroads, and roads. But such corridors can be managed to create a vegetation structure changing from grasses and forbs in the center to shrubs and trees on the outside. Such ecotones should be feathered to avoid some edge effects (Gates 1991). A powerline corridor should be somewhat wider than 60 m to function as a strip corridor providing field-interior habitat for grassland birds (Anderson et al. 1977). The vegetation in rights-of-way is often U-shaped in cross section (Fig. 6.2) (Svenson 1966). With a road or trail usually needed under the wires for maintenance, the central third can be kept in low grasses, forbs, and shrubs, and the outer areas in shrubs or small trees which will not grow into the wires (Svenson 1966, Arner 1977), but which will provide food and cover for wildlife such as moose, deer, elk, grouse, and snowshoe hares. In southeastern mixed and eastern deciduous forests, about one-third of the corridor should be in a mixed shrub community and two-thirds in a grass-legume mixture for animals such as turkeys, quail, and cottontails (Fig. 6.3) (Arner 1977). Wildlife with small home ranges next to powerline corridors benefit most if the corridor contains a shrub community throughout, which is hard to establish but easy to maintain (Niering and Goodwin 1974, Morgan and Gates 1983, Gates 1991). However, the center of pipeline corridors should be in low vegetation so that leaks of oil and gas can be detected from the air (Svenson 1966).

Construction of the right-of-way corridor could begin with at least one clearcut or selection-cut strip along the corridor to create a parallel series of successional bands of vegetation (Gates 1991). The first band of vegetation could be a strip of shrubs less than 2.5 cm dbh, the next a strip of saplings at least 2.5 to 7.6 cm dbh, the next a strip of pole-sized trees 7.6 to 30.5 cm dbh, and the last a mature forest over 30.5 cm dbh. These strips should be 10 to 15 m wide, as many shrubby edge zones are; they should be maintained when regular

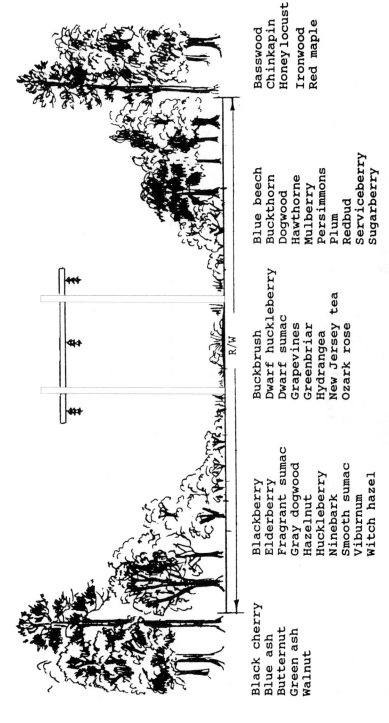

Figure 6.2 Example of vegetation for right-of-way (R/W), which is U-shaped in cross section with outer two-thirds in tall shrubs or small trees and center third kept in low grazing vegetation. (*Svenson 1966.*)

Black cherry	Blackberry	Buckbrush
Blue ash	Elderberry	Dwarf huckleberry
Butternut	Fragrant sumac	Dwarf sumac
Green ash	Gray dogwood	Grapevines
Walnut	Hazelnut	Greenbriar
	Huckleberry	Hydrangea
	Ninebark	New Jersey tea
	Smooth sumac	Ozark rose
	Viburnum	
	Witch hazel	

Blue beech	Basswood
Buckthorn	Chinkapin
Dogwood	Honey locust
Hawthorne	Ironwood
Mulberry	Red maple
Persimmons	
Plum	
Redbud	
Serviceberry	
Sugarberry	

R/W

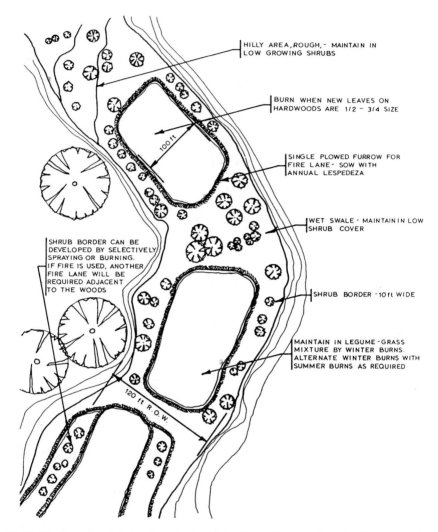

HILLY AREA, ROUGH, - MAINTAIN IN
LOW GROWING SHRUBS

BURN WHEN NEW LEAVES ON
HARDWOODS ARE 1/2 - 3/4 SIZE

100 ft

SINGLE PLOWED FURROW FOR
FIRE LANE - SOW WITH
ANNUAL LESPEDEZA

WET SWALE - MAINTAIN IN LOW
SHRUB COVER

SHRUB BORDER CAN BE
DEVELOPED BY SELECTIVELY
SPRAYING OR BURNING.
IF FIRE IS USED, ANOTHER
FIRE LANE WILL BE
REQUIRED ADJACENT
TO THE WOODS

SHRUB BORDER - 10 ft WIDE

MAINTAIN IN LEGUME - GRASS
MIXTURE BY WINTER BURNS.
ALTERNATE WINTER BURNS WITH
SUMMER BURNS AS REQUIRED

120 ft R.O.W.

Figure 6.3 Some possible treatments for rights-of-way in an eastern deciduous forest. (*Arner 1977.*)

corridor maintenance is done. Such a design would disperse prey and predator to reduce predation, and minimize the barrier effect of abrupt edges. But the wider edge would reduce the forest interior for area-sensitive species.

Plantings in clumps are best along areas bordering woodlands; plantings in rows are best along open areas such as grassland or cropland (U.S. Soil Conservation Service 1975). Isolated patches of shrubs with some small trees interspersed within the herbaceous opening might be ideal for songbirds (Chasko and Gates 1982), especially if the shrubs and trees produce soft or hard mast. In some cases, ponds could be constructed in a powerline right-of-way with no adverse effects to the maintenance of the powerline (Svenson 1966).

Extending small lobes or peninsulas of shrubby vegetation from the forest edge into the corridor tends to channel animals toward the tip of the peninsula to cross the corridor more readily (Forman 1987). Shrubby areas with small trees can be preserved in areas where the distance between ground and powerlines is large, such as across valleys (Chasko and Gates 1982). Openings wider than 30 m should contain scattered rough-barked trees to facilitate movement by flying squirrels (Mowrey and Zasada 1984). Animals also can move across a corridor if it is breached with alternate spraying, mowing, or burning of different sections to provide different seral stages (Chasko and Gates 1982, Gates 1991).

Woody plants should be used as screening along trails, roads, or other areas of public use that cross utility corridors (Ulrich 1976). Clumps of 10 or more conifers spaced 24 by 30 dm at each side of a road crossing will screen the right-of-way from travelers if desirable, and reduce poaching (U.S. Soil Conservation Service 1975). Small trees that bush out in open areas should be left standing after tall trees are removed (Ulrich 1976). The wooded edge next to roads and streams should be kept as continuous as possible. Only the trees that might contact the powerlines should be removed for 15 m into the woods on the right-of-way from the edge of the road or stream. Construction paths should be cleared near the centerline but at an angle to it (Fig. 6.4). Areas cleared for pipelines should be "plugged" at the road with dense plantings for at least 60 m along the right-of-way from the road (Fig. 6.5) (Downey 1976).

A screen should remain where a right-of-way crosses a wooded hilltop, peak, ridge, or other high and exposed area (Ulrich 1976). In a valley, ravine, or gorge where the conductors are at least 6 m above ground, tree removal in the right-of-way can be narrowed to the conductor width plus 6 m. Only an access path is needed where conductors are more than 6 m above the anticipated height of the mature forest. Where powerlines occur along the side of a hill, the area cleared of trees on the lower side of the right-of-way should not be as wide as the one on the upper side. Most fruit and nut trees and shrubs should remain.

Clearcuts tend to occur in a 15-m radius around metal poles and towers and a 6-m radius around wood poles. Access roads should be clearcut 4.6 m wide and meander near the center of the right-of-way for maintenance, including removal of tall-growing trees and construction of brush piles. Outside the basic working area, the right-of-way should be designed to produce islands of desirable species (Fig. 6.6) (Ulrich 1976), with irregular borders to increase edge effect if desirable, and to improve aesthetic appearance (Fig. 6.7) (Maser et al. 1979d).

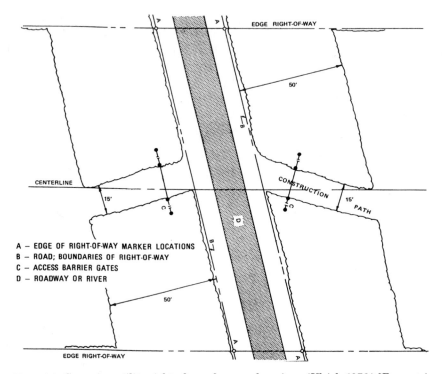

A – EDGE OF RIGHT-OF-WAY MARKER LOCATIONS
B – ROAD; BOUNDARIES OF RIGHT-OF-WAY
C – ACCESS BARRIER GATES
D – ROADWAY OR RIVER

Figure 6.4 Screening utility right-of-way from road or river. (*Ulrich 1976.*) [*For metric equivalents, see metric conversation table in the front of the book.*]

Figure 6.5 Pipeline right-of-way "plugged" with a screen of unobtrusive vegetation at road crossing. (*Downey 1976.*)

Figure 6.6 Island effect of selective clearing along powerline right-of-way. (*Ulrich 1976.*)

Figure 6.7 Powerline rights-of-way can be designed with irregular borders to enhance edge effect if desirable, and improve aesthetic appearance. (*Maser et al. 1979d.*)

Collisions of birds with powerlines can be reduced (1) by locating powerlines next to cliffs, windbreaks, or the base of low hills (Fig. 6.8); (2) by installing more towers and reducing the height of powerlines to that of the surrounding forest (Fig. 6.9); (3) by placing highly visible structures such as trees next to powerlines (Fig. 6.10); (4) by clustering lines at river crossings (Fig. 6.11); (5) by creating new feeding and/or resting areas so that birds do not have to cross powerline corridors (Fig. 6.12); (6) by reversing the locations of land uses attractive and unattractive to waterfowl (Fig. 6.13); and (7) by placing lines

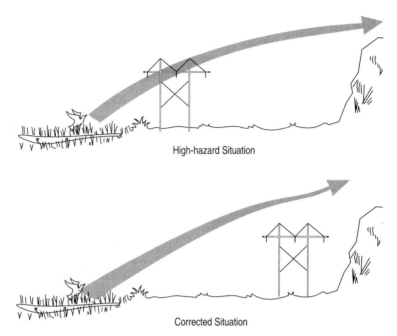

High-hazard Situation

Corrected Situation

Figure 6.8 Mitigation to reduce collisions of birds with powerlines by judicious line placement relative to local topography. (*Thompson 1978.*)

parallel rather than perpendicular to wind direction where winds are confined by topography, as in major river canyons (Fig. 6.14) (Thompson 1978). Collisions also can be reduced by improving visibility of wires. If possible, powerline corridors should be placed parallel rather than perpendicular to predominant flight paths, and away from wetlands, waterfowl concentration areas, flyways, roosting areas, feeding areas, breeding areas, low passes, and paths used for periodic feeding flights (Thompson 1978).

Riparian Areas

Riparian strips provide superior wildlife habitat and movement corridors because they are next to a source of water and consist mainly of hardwoods, which provide a food base (nectar, catkins, buds, fruit, seeds) unavailable from conifers (Harris 1984) (Fig. 6.15). Riparian ecosystems also receive water, nutrients, and energy from upstream, and return nutrients and energy against gravity through fish migration and the movement of other wildlife that ingest, digest, and transform the plants and animals they eat, and deposit them in uplands and wetlands (Harris 1984, 1985). Riparian strips are most valuable when they extend to upland habitats (Forman 1983).

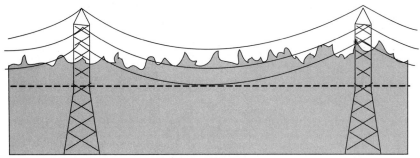

High-hazard Situation

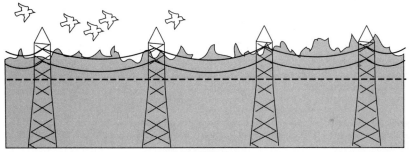

Corrected Situation

Figure 6.9 Wire strikes can be mitigated by placing the lines just below treetops in areas where flocks of birds commonly fly just above the forest canopy. The horizontal dashed line indicates minimum ground clearance of the conductors; more towers and shorter spans are needed to lower the line and maintain this clearance. (*Thompson 1978.*)

Wildlife species found in riparian areas are mainly ecological generalists (Knopf 1992). Introduced riparian corridors have fostered the ingress of plant and animal species historically alien to the region. In much of the West, riparian areas are largely sinks for widely distributed plant and animal generalists and travel corridors for Russian olive, purple loosestrife, and other undesirables. These might include, for example, raccoons with their negative impact on waterfowl populations. Such areas should be restored by removing the introduced riparian habitat.

Conventional tree harvesting can cause severe, perhaps irreparable, damage to sites characterized by steep slopes, wet soils, shallow soils, riparian zones, and other fragile features. Every landscape should have a reasonable area of old forests, some of which should occur on sensitive sites, especially in riparian zones (Hunter 1990). A riparian area is one of the most important types of wildlife habitat, and it can provide a system of movement corridors that will mitigate the effects of forest fragmentation by linking all the old forests of a region into a

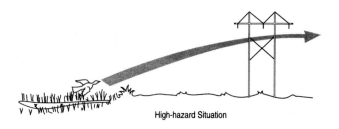

High-hazard Situation

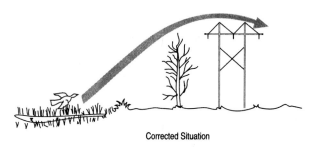

Corrected Situation

Figure 6.10 Mitigation to reduce collision by placing highly visible structures next to the line to alter flying height of birds. (*Thompson 1978.*)

network (Harris 1984, Noss and Harris 1986, Hunter 1990). If riparian areas or streamside zones do not connect larger tracts of habitat, they function mainly as long, narrow fragments of habitat rather than also serving as movement corridors (Harris and Scheck 1991).

The location of old-growth areas surrounded by long-rotation management areas is ideal only when the areas are connected by riparian strips or other suitable corridors (Harris 1984). Therefore, during the planning stage, regional (state or province) habitat maps should be studied for *gap analysis* to determine what pattern is ideal and possible at the regional level, and what is ideal and available at the forest level (Harris 1984, Scott et al. 1991, 1993). Decisions about which stands and corridors to maintain or develop must be made at the district level. The proposal and system will not work without higher-level guidance and integration into present planning operations and the landscape. Interagency cooperation and coordination are essential, as are a solid, bold approach and perseverance.

Drainage and river systems have a dendritic pattern of first-, second-, third-, and higher-order stream systems, the highest-order stream being the main river or stream in the watershed, with tributaries having progressively smaller numbers (Fig. 6.16) (Melton et al. 1984). First- to third-order streams (and watersheds) are considered small-sized streams, the fourth to sixth order are medium-sized, and seventh order and higher are large-sized rivers. (The Mississippi River

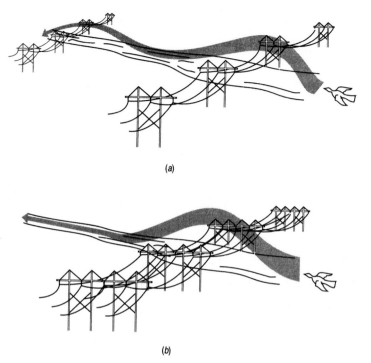

(a)

(b)

Figure 6.11 Mitigation to reduce collision of birds by clustering lines at river crossings. Two climbs and descents are needed at (a) but only one is needed at (b). (*Thompson 1978.*)

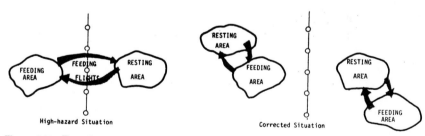

Figure 6.12 To reduce collision of waterfowl with powerlines, in some cases, local feeding-flight patterns might be changed by creating new feeding and/or resting areas. (*Thompson 1978.*)

is a twelfth-order stream.) Worldwide, 85 percent of streams are small, 12 percent are medium, and 3 percent are large (Leopold et al. 1964). Streams and riparian vegetation also can be classified by physical and biological characteristics (Table 6.1) (Melton et al. 1984). Permanent impoundment of streams has substantial impact on wildlife habitat in the inundated floodplain (Fig. 6.17) (Brinson et al. 1981).

The width of riparian strips should be scaled to stream order, with wider strips along the higher-order streams, i.e., those at lower, flat-

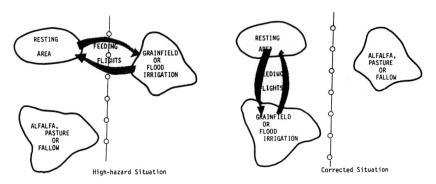

Figure 6.13 Reversing the locations of attractive and unattractive land uses near a powerline might change waterfowl feeding-flight patterns and reduce collisions with the powerline. (*Thompson 1978.*)

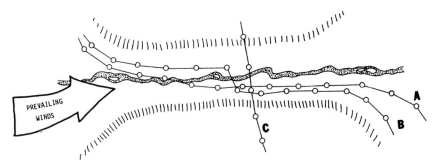

Figure 6.14 Where winds are confined by topography, as in major river canyons, collision of birds with powerlines can be reduced by placing lines parallel, rather than perpendicular, to wind direction and by crossing the river obliquely rather than perpendicularly. (A is preferable to B or C.) (*Thompson 1978.*)

ter elevations (Harris 1984). Long-rotation islands of forest placed near riparian strips at low elevations should be larger than the more numerous long-rotation islands placed near the riparian strips of the more numerous tributaries at higher elevations.

Managing most riparian areas mostly involves protection from human disturbance (Swift 1984, Oakley et al. 1985), specifically (1) road construction, (2) lumbering, (3) improper grazing, (4) agriculture, (5) stream channel modification, (6) reservoir development, (7) recreational development, and (8) urbanization. Groundwater pumping for industrial, municipal, and agricultural uses might become the most serious threat to riparian systems (Ohmart and Anderson 1986). Unrestricted tree cutting near a stream has substantial negative effects on the stream ecosystem, but buffer strips of riparian and adjacent upland forests can largely mitigate these negative effects (Hunter 1990).

Figure 6.15 Riparian area of hardwood trees and shrubs so beneficial to wildlife. (*Photo by Mark F. J. Payne.*)

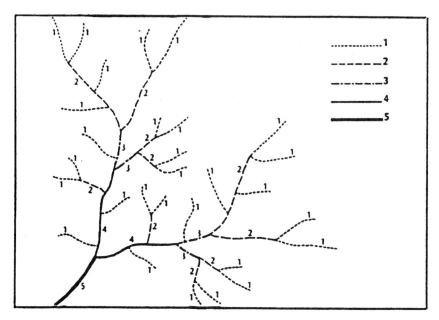

Figure 6.16 Hierarchical classification of streams (and drainages or watersheds) by stream order. (*Melton et al. 1984.*)

TABLE 6.1   Characteristics of Various Stream Types

Characteristic	Type A	Type B	Type C
Flood plain	Poorly defined	Some terraces	Multiple terraces
Sediment supply	Low	Moderate	High
Channel gradient	>3%	1 to 3%	<1%
Channel configuration			
Alignment	Straight	Nearly straight	Sinuous
Sinuousity ratio	1:1.1	1:1.1 to 1:1.4	1:1.5+
Entrenchment	Deep	Moderate	Shallow
Depth-to-width ratio	1:1 to 1:8	1:9 to 1:20	1:21+
Channel stability rating	Good to excellent	Good to fair	Fair to poor
Substrate particles	Boulders or large rocks	Small gravel to small boulders	Silt to small gravel
Trout productivity	Low	Moderate to high	Moderate to high
Riparian zone width	Narrow, often discontinuous	Moderate	Wide

SOURCE: Adapted from Melton et al. (1984).

General size

Although fixed riparian widths are easier to legislate and administer, variable widths can permit tailoring of streamside management practices to the specific conditions of the stream and its valley, such as meanders with undercut banks and floodplains with off-channel areas used for winter rearing (Bisson et al. 1987). Ideally, the width of buffer strips should be based on the stream width, topography, soil type, hydrologic regime, climate, and goals of the management policy (Budd et al. 1987). Practical determination of stream corridor widths can be made easily and efficiently by combining a simple field survey of selected stretches of a stream and analysis of soils, vegetation, physiography, and land-use characteristics. Actually, the width will vary relative to habitat structure and quality within the corridor, type of surrounding habitat, and the wildlife species expected to use the corridor (Noss 1987c).

The procedure for calculating habitat buffers for wetland wildlife is as follows (Brown et al. 1990):

1. The habitat type is determined for the particular regionally important wetland that is on or waterward from the proposed develop-

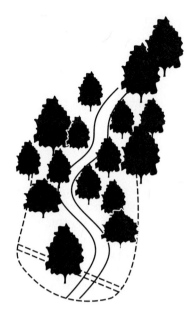 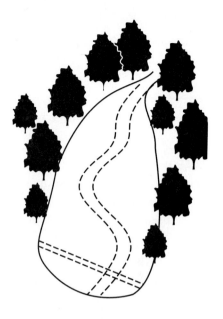

BEFORE IMPOUNDMENT

Habitat for stream-dwelling fish.

Predominantly floodplain/terrestrial wildlife habitat.

Streambank habitat for many specialized wildlife species.

Natural hydrologic regime provides exchange pathways for nutrients, detritus and organisms between channel and floodplain.

Downstream transport of detritus and sediments.

Corridor for fish and wildlife movements.

AFTER IMPOUNDMENT

Habitat for lake-dwelling fish.

Predominantly aquatic fish habitat.

Streambank habitat replaced by extensive, often unstable shoreline; altered spaces assemblage.

Permanent inundation eliminates floodplain vegetation and vital pathways of exchange.

Retention of detritus and sediments behind dam.

Corridor altered and interrupted.

Figure 6.17 Values to fish and wildlife of impounding small streams. (*Brinson et al. 1981.*)

ment site. For landscape situations where no vegetated wetland transitional area (e.g., marsh or swamp) occurs, the habitat determination should be made for the upland habitat (e.g., flatwoods, hummock, sandhill) that is next to the aquatic system.

2. The quality of the habitat is determined, as follows:

High.   The area is in a relatively natural state.

Medium.   The area has been cleared for silvicultural or agricultural purposes, but no permanent structures such as buildings and roads have been built.

Low.   The area has been cleared; buildings, roads, and other permanent structures have been built.

3. The buffer width found in Table 6.2 for the previously determined habitat type and quality is selected.

4. Wildlife buffers can include wetland and upland habitats. The wetland wildlife habitat buffer should begin at the waterward edge of the forested wetland or upland habitat that is next to the aquatic system. An upland buffer strip at least 15 m wide should be included in each buffer for nesting and overwintering of semi-aquatic reptiles. (If the swamp or marsh is wider than the recommended buffer, an upland buffer strip at least 15 m wide should be added to the landward edge of the wetland.)

5. If no trees are next to the marsh (e.g., open flatwoods), a buffer 98 m wide is needed to prevent disturbance from human activities.

6. Marsh areas often occur along flowing water systems (e.g., rivers). These marshes do not function as separate habitats if they are too small to support most wildlife species associated with marsh communities. These marshes must be at least 2 ha in area, and vegetation must extend at least 15 m waterward from the waterward edge of the adjacent upland or forested wetland community.

TABLE 6.2   Recommended Wetland Buffer Widths for Various Wildlife Habitats of High, Medium, and Low Quality

Habitat	Quality	Buffer width
Salt and fresh-water marshes	High	98 m
	Medium	98 m and revegetate buffer into natural habitat
	Low	As wide as possible up to 98 m
Cypress and hardwood swamps, hummocks, and flatwoods	High	168 m
	Medium	168 m and revegetate buffer into natural habitat
	Low	As wide as possible up to 168 m
Sandhills	High	223 m
	Medium	223 m and revegetate buffer into natural habitat
	Low	As wide as possible up to 223 m

SOURCE: Brown et al. (1990).

The procedure for calculating requirements for noise attenuation for riparian wildlife is as follows (Brown et al. 1990):

1. Information on the local noise threshold policies for important wetlands should be obtained or developed.

2. The maximum (not average) current noise level for the site, or potential noise level for a proposed site, should be assessed.

3. Noise reduction should be assessed under the proposed conditions after development occurs from the site to the waterward edge of the wetland (or upland if no wetland is present). Measurements of noise reduction should be conducted through vegetated areas during winter when most deciduous foliage is absent. The U.S. Department of Transportation (1981) and U.S. Department of Housing and Urban Development (1984) have described standardized methods for assessing noise levels.

4. The width should be determined for a vegetated buffer or some other attenuation means (e.g., barriers) capable of reducing the maximum expected sound level to the acceptable limit.

Until wildlife managers know more about the corridor needs of individual wildlife species, streamside zones of mature trees should be at least 30 m wide, and much wider if some harvesting occurs (Erman et al. 1977, Buckner and Landers 1980, Washington Department of Ecology 1981, Hunter 1990, Rudolph and Dickson 1990). For various reasons a 100-m strip on each side of the stream is better; for example, some waterfowl nest that far from water (Atlantic Waterfowl Council 1972, Bellrose 1980). Clearcutting closer results in the entire riparian strip being a clearcut edge with no interior. Riparian strips are 20 to 100 m wide on each side of all streams on the Yakima Indian Reservation in Washington, the size dependent on unique site-specific characteristics identified in an environmental assessment, rather than on the size of the stream (Bradley 1988). For slopes of 10 to 30°, 1 m should be added to the buffer zone for each degree of slope (Nova Scotia Department of Lands and Forests ca 1989). For slopes steeper than 30°, the buffer zone should begin 5 m back from the first regular break in the slope that is more than 5 m wide. Additional width is needed for unstable soils, poor drainage, or unique wildlife habitat. Wide zones or leave strips reduce windthrow and erosion, and provide snags, logs, and large organic debris for streams (Franklin et al. 1981, Bisson et al. 1987).

On each side of streams and rivers that drain more than 130 km^2 and around lakes and freshwater and coastal wetlands, buffer zones should be at least 75 m wide and even up to 100 m wide for some wildlife species (Elliott 1988, Wiley 1988b). The first 30 m should have either (1) no cutting, with all heavy equipment excluded, or (2) light selection cutting of stems over 15 cm dbh, with no heavy equipment permitted except with high flotation tires (Elliott 1988, Wiley 1988b, Nova Scotia Department of Lands and Forests ca 1989). The zone from 30 to 75 (or 100 m) should receive single-tree or group selection cuts, with no more than 40 percent of the volume removed per 10-year period.

Buffer zones should be at least 30 m wide on each side of streams draining less than 130 km², with the first 7.6 m uncut or treated with light selection cutting of stems over 15 cm dbh (Elliott 1988). The zone from 7.6 to 30 m should receive single-tree or group selection cuts, with no more than 40 percent of the volume removed per 10-year period.

Water tables tend to be high in riverbottom areas, resulting in trees with shallow root systems that are especially vulnerable to windthrow (Bisson et al. 1987). Such areas require larger buffer riparian zones. Some mature stands of 1000 ha or more should be maintained for forest bird communities in bottomlands, with connecting corridors of mature trees (Dickson 1978). In other bottomlands, no cutting should occur within 46 m of a stream (Halls et al. 1984). Where wetlands constitute less than 7 percent of the area (about 7 ha/km²) and are surrounded by forest, buffer zones with a radius of 183 m should remain uncut (Rogers et al. 1988).

Riparian corridors and associated habitats in Alaska are 150 m wide along beaches, 30 m wide along salmon streams, and 300 m wide along estuaries (Samson et al. 1991). The riparian area furnishes large woody debris at least 30 cm in diameter which is needed in stream channels for structural complexity and pool formation for aquatic invertebrates, fish, and their predators (Maser et al. 1988, Sedell et al. 1989). Henderson (1987, 1988) recommended buffer zones 60 m wide around wetlands over 0.4 ha and 30 m wide around smaller wetlands.

Other size considerations

Brinson et al. (1981) listed widths of riparian buffer strips for various purposes; the widest buffer they recommend is one 400 m wide, to maintain wild or scenic values of river corridors. (*Width* of the riparian strip refers to width at one side of the stream only.) Decker et al. (1983) recommended that the width of buffer zones along streams be 15 m on slopes less than 10 percent, 30 m on 10 to 30 percent slopes, 46 m on slopes over 30 percent, and 61 m between water sources and log landings. Small and Johnson (1986) recommended buffer strips 75 m wide along larger streams, rivers, and lakes, with no cutting in the first 25 m, and group selection cuts spaced at least 30 m apart removing 50 percent or less of the canopy in the rest of the buffer. All hardwood snags, live trees with cavities, wolf trees, some dominant live conifers, raptor and heron nest trees, and other potential wildlife trees should be uncut, consistent with operator safety (Elliott 1988). No harvesting should occur within any part of the buffer if shallow root systems or other conditions promote windthrow.

Howard and Allen (1989) recommended that protected zones at least 60 m wide be left on each side of perennial streams wider than about 10 m, and divided between the two sides on smaller streams. They thought a buffer 15 m wide would be adequate on each side of intermittent streams, small sloughs, and isolated wetlands. Limited selection cuts would encourage crown development and mast production, and development of a denser cover of herbaceous plants, shrubs, and tree seedlings for bank and water quality protection and wildlife use (Howard and Allen 1989). For example, gray squirrels and fox squirrels are more abundant in riparian zones wider than 55 m than in narrower zones (Dickson and Huntley 1987). Smith and Martin (1974) recommended no tree cutting for at least 50 m along each side of major or navigable streams, with selective cutting for the next 50 m; no cutting should occur for at least 25 m along minor, intermittent, or nonnavigable streams, with selective cutting for the next 25 m. Stumps 1 m high should be left to exclude machinery (Nova Scotia Department of Lands and Forests ca 1989).

Coniferous debris persists longer in streams than does hardwood debris (Anderson et al. 1978, Swanson and Lienkaemper 1978). In streams with channels wider than 15 to 25 m, large conifers are usually needed for stability and to anchor smaller debris (Lienkaemper and Swanson 1987). Smaller deciduous species can be stable in narrower channels (Bisson et al. 1987).

The following silvicultural guidelines, recommended by Rainville et al. (1986) for riparian areas of northern Idaho, have general application elsewhere although requiring modification in some cases:

1. For maximum recruitment of large organic debris to streams, riparian stands in the western hemlock and grand fir habitat types should be harvested at a rate of about 4 percent of the streambank length per decade. Harvesting 5 percent is preferable if a timber stand is managed on a 100-year rotation and is located between the riparian stand and road. If stands are managed on a 200-year rotation, a 5 percent entry rate would allow both types of stand to be managed while trade-offs are minimized. This approach requires coordinating riparian needs with timber harvest in the area between riparian strip and road, and leaving alternate riparian strips unharvested (Fig. 6.18). Standard timber rotations and leave strips for these habitat types generally are not recommended except along fifth-order or larger streams, where large trees are needed to create stable

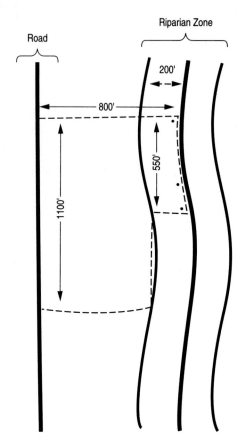

Figure 6.18 A possible approach to integrate management of riparian and adjacent timber areas. (*Rainville et al. 1986.*) [*For metric equivalents, see metric conversion table in the front of the book.*]

pools. Leave strips of 3 to 4 percent harvest rates are preferable in subalpine fir habitat types.

2. Riparian stands should not be harvested at recommended rates where soils are unstable or conifer regeneration would be inhibited—e.g., in openings which raise the water table, stimulate development of brush, or create frost pockets.

3. The normal high-water area should be cleared of logging debris. Dozer piling of slash should be avoided, as it can cause sedimentation. Western hemlock, subalpine fir, and grand fir forest types should not be thinned to less than 2195 trees per hectare after two thinnings. With sanitation or salvage cuts, the size of trees to leave should be over 30 cm dbh within 9 m from the stream, over 46 cm dbh from 9 to 18 m from the stream, and over 61 cm dbh from 18 to 27 m from the stream.

Idaho requires (1) hardwood trees, shrubs, grasses, and rocks left wherever they shade a stream or maintain soil integrity near a

TABLE 6.3   Minimum Number of Standing Trees to Be Left
per 305 m of Class I Streams in a Strip 15 m Wide

Tree dbh (cm)	Stream width		
	>6 m	3–6 m	<3 m
0–20	200	200	200
20.1–30.4	42	42	42
30.5–50.4	21	21	—
>50.4	4	—	—

Note: These are state of Idaho requirements. Class I streams
are streams used for domestic water supply or important for
spawning, rearing, or migration of fish.
    SOURCE: Idaho Department of Lands (1990), in Belt et al.
(1992).

stream; (2) 75 percent of the canopy cover left; (3) slash removed and
piled at least 1.5 m above the high-water line of Class I streams and
removed from Class II streams if it blocks the stream; and (4) hardwoods, conifers, and snags retained as indicated in Table 6.3 (Idaho
Department of Lands 1990). California requires 50 percent of the
overstory and 50 percent of the understory left on Class I streams,
and no slash burning in the buffer zone (California Department of
Forestry and Fire Protection 1991) due to increased nutrient loads in
streams (Skille 1990). Oregon requires the buffer strip to be three
times the average width of the stream at high flow, but between 7.6
and 30 m (Oregon Department of Forestry 1991). Belt et al. (1992)
compared the requirements for stream buffer strips in Idaho,
Washington, California, and Oregon.

The U.S. Forest Service, Region 10, probably has the most complete
set of standards and guidelines for large organic debris and riparian
management areas (the Region 10 *Aquatic Habitat Management
Handbook*) (Sedell et al. 1989). To produce enough large organic
debris for habitat suitability in streams, undisturbed habitat needs
13 to 24 trees over 30 cm dbh per 30 m of stream. Streams up to 6 m
wide need trees at least 30 cm dbh. Streams 6 to 15 m wide need
trees 51 cm dbh. Streams over 15 m wide need trees 76 cm dbh,
preferably with root wads attached. Trees should be at least 1.5 times
as long as the channel width.

For an area to be considered suitable for most wildlife in upland
buffer zones along the Wekiva River in Florida, Brown and Schaefer
(1987) recommended minimum standards of (1) tree canopy height
greater than 15 m, (2) tree canopy closure greater than 70 percent,
(3) average tree crown diameter greater than 70 percent, (4) more
than seven trees of at least 50 cm dbh per hectare, (5) more than 0.2
snags greater than 50 cm dbh per hectare, (6) average shrub height

greater than 6 dm but less than 46 dm, and (7) shrub canopy closure greater than 70 percent. In New Hampshire, at least 50 percent of the basal area must be retained within 15 to 30 m of a stream or pond edge to maximize accumulation of large woody debris in streams (Rabon and Weyrick 1989). The diameter at breast height of the leave trees must be (1) 30 cm for 3- to 6-m streams and 46 cm for wider streams, within 9 m of the streambank; (2) 46 cm for 3- to 6-m streams and 61 cm for wider streams, within 9 to 18 m of the stream-bank; (3) 61 cm for 3- to 6-m streams and 91 cm for wider streams, within 18 to 27 m of the streambank.

Regulations governing requirements for trees in riparian zones after timber harvest in Washington vary relative to geography, and might apply elsewhere too (Tables 6.4, 6.5) (Washington Forest Practices Board 1988, Bilby and Wasserman 1989). Western Washington receives much more precipitation than eastern Washington does, with more frequent washout of large organic debris. The regulations would prevent harvest in riparian zones at 21 per-cent of the gravel/cobble sites and 18 percent of the boulder/bedrock sites. Where harvest is allowed, 87 percent of the preharvest stems would remain in the riparian zone at gravel/cobble sites and 81 per-cent at boulder/bedrock sites (Bilby and Wasserman 1989). But with this selective cutting system, many buffer riparian strips do not pos-sess enough old-growth trees or other trees large enough to provide stable debris in third-order or larger streams (Bisson et al. 1987). Riparian zones managed in association with clearcutting in Washington average 15 m wide along each side of the stream, but vary from 9 to 90 m wide (Bilby and Wasserman 1989). Where the 7-day water temperature exceeds 15.5°C, 75 percent of the canopy must be left (Washington Forest Practices Board 1988). Young et al. (1990) recommended silvicultural prescriptions designed to enhance the structural complexity of riparian stands next to streams used for past drives of railroad ties that caused removal of shoreline conifers and scoured streambeds. (See "Snags and Live Den Trees" and "Coarse Woody Debris" in Chap. 7.)

To protect water areas, Welsch (1991) recommended that riparian areas be divided into three zones if they occur next to or downstream from grassland, pasture, or cropland:

1. Zone 1 is a strip that extends 4.6 m from the edge. Tree cutting and livestock are excluded. Removal of potential problem vegeta-tion and planting for streambank stability are allowed.

2. Zone 2 is a strip that extends 18.3 m from zone 1. Periodic tree harvesting and timber stand improvement are used to maintain vigorous growth replacement of leaf litter, and to remove nutrients

TABLE 6.4   Requirements for Numbers of Trees to be Left along Streams after Timber Harvest in Western and Eastern Washington*

Western Washington				
Water type† and average width	Maximum width of riparian zone (m)	Ratio of conifer to deciduous; minimum size of leave trees	No. of trees per 305 m each side	
			Gravel/ cobble‡	Boulder/ bedrock
Type 1 and 2 23 m and over	30	Representative of stand	50	25
Type 1 and 2 under 23 m	23	Representative of stand	100	50
Type 3 2 m and over	15	2:1; 30 cm or next largest available§	75	25
Type 3	8	1:1; 15 cm or next largest available§	25	25

Eastern Washington

Leave all trees up to 30.5 cm dbh.

Within the riparian management zone, leave all snags that do not violate the state safety regulations.

Leave 40 live conifer trees per hectare, 30.5 to 50.8 cm dbh, distributed by the size best representing the stand.

Leave 7 conifer trees per hectare at least 50.8 cm dbh.

Leave the 5 largest deciduous trees per hectare that are at least 40.6 cm dbh. If such trees do not exist, and if 5 snags per hectare, at least 50.8 cm dbh, do not exist, substitute 12 conifer trees per hectare, at least 50.8 cm dbh. If conifer trees of at least 50.8 cm dbh do not exist within the riparian zone, substitute the 5 largest conifer trees per hectare.

Leave 7 deciduous trees 30.5 cm to 40.6 cm dbh where they exist.

On streams with a boulder/bedrock bed, the minimum leave-tree requirement shall be 185 trees per hectare, at least 10.2 cm dbh.

On streams with a gravel/cobble (less than 25.4 cm in diameter) bed, the minimum leave-tree requirement shall be 335 trees per hectare, at least 10.2 cm dbh.

On lakes and ponds the minimum leave-tree requirement shall be 185 trees per hectare, at least 10.2 cm dbh.

*For wildlife habitat within the riparian management zone, an average of 12 undisturbed and uncut wildlife trees should be left per hectare in a ratio of one coniferous tree to one deciduous tree equal in size to the largest existing trees of those species within the zone. Where the 1:1 ratio is not possible, either species present may be substituted. At least 40 percent of the leave trees shall be live and undamaged after the harvest is done. Whenever possible, wildlife trees shall be left in clumps.
†See Table 6.5.
‡Gravel and cobble streambeds consist mainly of material <25 cm in diameter.
§The next largest trees to those specified in the rule will be left standing when those available are smaller than the sizes specified. Type 1, 2, or 3 waters of lakes or ponds shall have the same leave-tree requirements as boulder/bedrock streams.
SOURCE: Adapted from Bilby and Wasserman (1989).

TABLE 6.5 Water-Typing Criteria Used in Washington

Parameter	Type 1	Type 2	Type 3	Type 4	Type 5
			Water type		
Channel width	N/A	≥6 m between OHWM	Anadromous fish: ≥1.5 m between OHWM Resident game fish: ≥3 m wide between OHWM	≥6 dm between OHWM	<6 dm between OHWM
Gradient	N/A	Less than 4%	Anadromous fish: <12%, not upstream of a falls >3 m high Resident game fish: <12%	N/A	N/A
Flow	N/A	N/A	Anadromous fish: N/A Resident game fish: >9 dm³/s at summer low flow	N/A	N/A
Impoundment	N/A	Water surface area of ≤0.4 ha at seasonal low flow	Anadromous fish: surface area <0.4 ha at seasonal low flow Resident game fish: surface area <0.2 ha at seasonal low flow	N/A	N/A
Fisheries	N/A	Used by substantial numbers of anadromous or resident game fish for spawning, rearing, and migration	Used by many anadromous or resident game fish for spawning, rearing, or migration	Not used by many fish	Not used by many fish
Diversion	N/A	Domestic use for ≤100 residences or campsites, accommodation facility for ≥100 persons, includes upstream reach of 457 m or until the drainage area is <50%, whichever is less	Domestic use for ≥10 residences or camping units, or accommodation facility for ≥10 persons; includes upstream reach of 457 m or until the drainage area is <50%, whichever is less	N/A	N/A
Other	All water within the OHWM inventoried as "shorelines of the state" excluding related wetlands	Stream flowing through campgrounds available to the public having ≥30 campsites	Contributes ≥20% of the flow to a Type 1 or 2 water; anadromous fish impoundments have outlet to stream with anadromous fish	N/A	All natural waters not classified as Type 1, 2, 3, or 4; seepage areas, ponds and drainways having short runoff periods

Note: OHWM = ordinary high-water mark(s). N/A = not applicable.
SOURCE: Washington Forest Practices Board (1988).

and pollutants absorbed by the tree. Shade levels and production of leaf litter, detritus, and large woody debris must be maintained. Livestock are excluded.

3. Zone 3 is a strip that extends at least 6 m beyond zone 2. Ungrazed grassland will suffice, as will dense perennial grass and forbs. Vegetation must be maintained in vigorous condition by mowing, controlled grazing, and occasional burning.

Zone 2 should be wider in unstable or sandy and gravelly soils. Zone 2 should be adjusted for slope by increased width so that the combined width of zones 1 and 2 is equal to one-third of the slope distance from the stream bank to the top of the pollutant source area. The area of buffer strips around ponds or lakes should be at least one-fifth the drainage area of the pastureland and cropland source area. Open-water wetlands existing as seeps in fields along hill slopes should have a buffer of zones 1, 2, and 3 on sides receiving runoff, and zones 1 and 3 on other sides. Livestock may be controlled in zone 3, but must always be excluded from zones 1 and 2. Where only zones 1 and 3 are used, hay may be harvested in zone 3, but livestock must always be excluded from both zones (Welsch 1991).

Protecting riparian areas from overgrazing of livestock can be accomplished by adjusting the distribution of livestock (stocking rates and location), pasture design, livestock access points, amount of use, timing of use, duration of use, frequency of use, and kind of livestock (Kauffman and Krueger 1984, Kinch 1989). The loss of forage in riparian areas from exclusion fencing might be inconsequential, but fencing and maintenance are expensive and restrictive to some wildlife species. Fencing design should allow passage of wild ungulates. Small riparian areas can be protected by fencing springs and seeps and by piping the water to adjacent areas. Natural trailing or loafing by livestock in some riparian areas can be regulated by fencing gaps relative to gullies, cliffs, and other natural barriers, or by placing trees, brush, or at least 25- to 50-cm rocks along stream banks. Rocky areas used as water gaps will reduce loafing and trampling. Because livestock trail along fences, streams should be centered within a pasture. Otherwise the fence should be placed along but away from the stream, with water gaps to the stream. Panels of corrugated metal roofing can be suspended over the stream between ends of a fence to control livestock movement and swing with the flow of water, allowing debris to pass.

Livestock also can be attracted away from riparian areas by creating shade and water developments, and placing rubbing posts, oilers, salt, hay, grain, molasses, and other supplements only in upland areas at least 400 m and preferably 800 m or more from riparian areas and intermittent drainages (Kinch 1989). The entrances to live-stock-handling facilities and pastures or allotments should be located away from riparian areas, especially if adequate water exists elsewhere for the livestock. Livestock will be attracted to uplands planted with palatable forage species or that have been subjected to prescribed burning to enhance forage production and palatability. Frequent riding and herding improve distribution, and increase calf crops by improving opportunities for breeding. Some groups of cattle prefer riparian areas, some prefer uplands. Selective culling of cattle that prefer riparian areas might benefit the livestock owner and the riparian zone (Kinch 1989).

Kinch (1989) described grazing-management practices used successfully on specific riparian areas. Payne (1992) described physical, chemical, and biological techniques to improve wetlands and adjacent uplands for wildlife, including planting and controlled grazing in riparian areas. (See especially Payne 1992:Tables 5.2 and A.17 through A.21).

Chapter

7

Special Forest Habitats and Features

Openings

Forest openings are used heavily by edge wildlife, including most game species. Because such openings fragment the forest, they are avoided by interior species. In areas managed for biodiversity, construction of openings should be avoided, or else openings should be clumped to reduce fragmentation (Minnesota Department of Natural Resources 1985).

Two general types of openings occur in forest lands (McCaffery et al. 1981): *natural* (relict) and *constructed.* Natural openings tend to be permanent; constructed openings can be permanent or temporary (Connecticut Department of Environmental Protection 1988a). Permanent openings are maintained to encourage herbaceous vegetation or herbaceous/shrubby vegetation. Nixon et al. (1970) and Oliveri (1988) recommended that 10 percent of a forest be in openings at all times. The Connecticut Department of Environmental Protection (1988a) recommended that at least 2 percent of the forest be maintained in permanent herbaceous openings and at least 5 percent in permanent herbaceous/shrubby openings. McCaffery et al. (1981) recommended that 1 to 5 percent of the forest be maintained in permanent herbaceous openings, depending on deer density desired (Table 7.1). The Minnesota Department of Natural Resources (1985) recommended that at least 5 percent of the upland forests be in grass/forb openings of

TABLE 7.1   Example of Guidelines for Evaluating Forest Habitat Quality for White-Tailed Deer and Associated Wildlife

	Percent required to maintain specified fall densities		
Forest	4 deer/ km^2	8 deer/ km^2	≥12 deer/ km^2
Intolerant forest types	>25	>45	>65
Grass and upland brush	1	3–5	5
Oak and scrub oak	5	10	20
Aspen and off-site aspen	20	25	30
Jack pine or yarding cover*	10	15	15
Tolerant types† and plantations	<65	<45	<25

*Cedar, hemlock, swamp conifers, white spruce, balsam fir, and white pine.
†Northern hardwoods, mixed hardwoods (maple–red oak–aspen–birch), and balsam fir.
SOURCE: McCaffery et al. (1981).

0.2 to 4 ha with less than 10 percent trees and shrubs. Openings of 0.05 to 0.1 ha might be more suitable for some sites and small areas (Hershey and Wiegers undated). Connors (undated) and Hershey and Wiegers (undated) recommended that openings be considered only for forested areas larger than 4 to 8 ha. In fact, unless additional fragmentation is desired for game species, openings are unnecessary in woodlots (<100 ha) because woodlots usually are surrounded by openings, and the edge effect extends throughout (Wilcove 1987).

Natural openings

Natural openings consist of preexisting or maintained herbaceous openings with stocking rates of less than 10 percent trees and less than 30 percent brush (McCaffery et al. 1981). They usually result from historic disturbance such as homesteads (Fig. 7.1) (Giles 1978), old camps, log landings, or frost pockets, which were not mechanically constructed for wildlife but may have been reclaimed by herbicide treatment.

The openings system also should include abandoned gravel pits (Henderson 1987). At least 50 percent of the gravel pit floor should be bare ground for dusting and burrowing. Cut banks should be preserved for nesting, roosting, and denning.

Forest reconnaissance–type maps should be used to identify natural openings (McCaffery et al. 1981). Aerial photos usually are needed to identify openings smaller than 1.2 ha. Otherwise a special inventory is needed. Up to 3 percent should be maintained in each ¼-township-sized block (about 2330 ha). These can be developed and maintained by mowing every 2 to 3 years, burning about every 3 years,

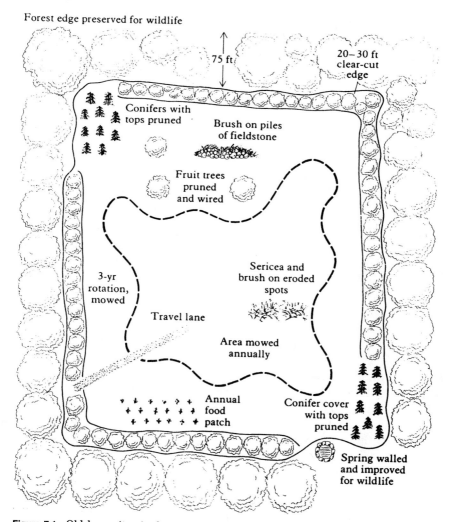

Forest edge preserved for wildlife

75 ft

20–30 ft
clear-cut
edge

Conifers with
tops pruned

Brush on piles
of fieldstone

Fruit trees
pruned
and wired

3-yr
rotation,
mowed

Sericea and
brush on eroded
spots

Travel lane

Area mowed
annually

Annual
food
patch

Conifer cover
with tops
pruned

Spring walled
and improved
for wildlife

Figure 7.1 Old homesites in forest areas, like other clearings, can be maintained as wildlife areas, but might need special work such as extending travel lanes toward the center of large clearings, which also reduces fields of view for hunters and poachers. (*Giles 1978.*)

and spot-treating shrubs with herbicide as needed. Stumps and boulders preclude most mechanical treatment, including mowing, which tends to reduce the natural beauty of natural openings anyway.

Areas larger than 4 ha scheduled for reforestation should have openings scheduled (Minnesota Department of Natural Resources 1985). Spot failures that show up 5 to 10 years after planting or after canopy closure should be developed and maintained as openings.

Constructed openings

Existing openings should be identified and preserved before new openings are programmed for construction. Stocking rates on sandy soils often are sparse enough to preclude concern about openings. Openings should be developed on loamy soils (McCaffery and Creed 1969).

If openings must be built, the best methods to establish long-lasting herbaceous clearings are enlarging log landings and bulldozing new clearings (Wunz 1987). Enlarging log landings is more practical and economical. For example, log landings occur in Pennsylvania at the rate of one landing per 20 ha; if each landing were enlarged to 0.4 ha, they would comprise 2 percent of the forest.

Openings should be selected ecologically to prolong their existence in the grass/forb/shrub stage and minimize maintenance. Secure, sod-covered openings near high-value summer range are preferred. Openings with aesthetic value or access are preferred. If few openings exist, they can be created by cutting a bunch of trees; preferably this cutting should be done where two forest or other habitat types meet, to create a covert as well as an opening. Such treatment should occur on areas of low site index where little or no advanced reproduction exists, in frost pockets, or on shallow soils that are poorly to somewhat poorly drained or excessively well drained (Decker and Kelley undated, Tubbs and Verme 1972). Soils maps, aerial photos, topographic maps, and forest-type maps are useful initially, followed by field examination. A change in species offers clues to potential sites for creating openings. Such sites will remain in the herbaceous/shrub stage 20 or 30 years. Preferably, openings should border logging trails, another timber type, a swamp, or a marsh.

Openings can be constructed where habitat comprises 15 to 55 percent intolerant upland forest types (McCaffery et al. 1981). Combined with the natural openings, constructed openings should comprise up to 5 percent of ¼-township-size blocks or compartments (about 2330 ha). They should be at least 0.3 ha and rarely more than 0.8 ha on any 16-ha tract (Hassinger et al. 1979, McCaffery et al. 1981). The width can vary from 0.5 to at least 2 times the height of uncut adjoining trees (Minnesota Department of Natural Resources 1985, Connecticut Department of Environmental Protection 1988a, Becker et al. 1990). Openings should be at least 60 m wide to enlist frost as an agent for natural maintenance (McCaffery and Creed 1969, McCaffery et al. 1981). The ratio of length to width can vary from 3:1 (Minnesota Department of Natural Resources 1985) to 6:1 (Becker et al. 1990). Openings should be spaced 0.5 km apart for short-ranging species such as quail and grouse to 0.9 km apart for wider-ranging species such as turkey and deer (McCaffery and Creed 1969, Halls et al. 1984, Payne and Copes 1988).

Openings can be developed from log landings, along the edges of cuts, on south- or southwest-facing slopes, and in an east-west direction for maximum sunlight, and should be S-shaped or J-shaped, with irregular edges (Minnesota Department of Natural Resources 1985, Connecticut Department of Environmental Protection 1988a), unless irregular shapes are too costly or difficult to maintain. Rectangular openings are easier to develop and maintain (Larson 1967). Openings should extend downslope of rock outcrops to maximize solar exposure (Becker et al. 1990). Once trees are cut, a bulldozer should remove stumps and rocks to facilitate site preparation and maintenance if a herbaceous opening is desired and funds are available. Site preparation involves disking, liming, fertilizing, disking again, and seeding with a suitable grass-legume mixture (Hassinger et al. 1979), unless the grasses will crowd out the legumes, as in some areas (Krusac and Michael 1979). A local soils office can test the soil for lime and fertilizer requirements (Table 7.2) (Wiley 1988b). Lime requirements should be checked every 5 years (Hassinger et al. 1979). To maintain openings where grasses predominate, 10-10-10 fertilizer can be broadcast by hand or with a cyclone seeder in late summer at 112 kg/ha every 2 years or as needed. Where legumes predominate, 10-20-20 fertilizer can be broadcast at 336 kg/ha every 3 to 5 years or as needed. Herbaceous openings should be mowed every 2 to 3 years as needed. Herbaceous/shrub openings should be mowed every 4 to 6 years.

Openings are best in hardwood forests. In coniferous forests, openings are used heavily by species such as turkey, deer, elk, and bear, but they often become ecological traps for birds using the plants and insects because conifers conceal raptors which prey on birds such as ruffed grouse (Gullion 1984). In hardwood forests, clumps of conifers should be removed in or next to openings.

TABLE 7.2   Recommended Fertilizer and Lime Applications for Seeding Herbaceous Plants

| Soil test for phosphorus | Fertilizer | | Lime | |
	Application rate (kg/ha)	Type*	Soil pH	Application rate (mt/ha)
Very low to low	896	5-20-20	<5.8	6.7
Medium to high	560	10-20-20	5.8–6.1	4.5
Very high	560	10-10-10	6.2–6.5	2.2
			6.6–6.8	0.0

Note: Phosphorus is the key nutrient to determine how much fertilizer to use when seeding. Fertilizer should be worked into the soil with drags and covered with mulch to prevent erosion into nearby stagnant lakes where phosphorus can trigger algal blooms.

*NPK (nitrogen-phosphorus-potassium) fertilizers.

SOURCE: Wiley (1988b).

Large openings need maintenance less often to control invasion of shrubs and trees (McCaffery and Creed 1969). Disturbance of the sod cover tends to increase maintenance requirements. Efforts to promote irregular brushy edge should be aimed at the opening's edge into the forest rather than within the opening. Grassy openings in aspen should be protected from invading aspen suckers by leaving a strip of aspen 1 chain wide around the edge of the opening when surrounding aspen is harvested. Aspen regeneration can be reduced by clearing with a rock rake and leveling with a heavy construction disk.

Where large stands of small pole timber occur, the number of openings should be as nearly optimal as possible. Sparse sawtimber stands do not need as many openings. Between these two extremes, spacing patterns should be developed to fit the terrain, cover, and wildlife requirements in the particular area (Fig. 7.2) (Giles 1978).

A system of even-aged timber management simplifies developing a system of wildlife openings. Good spacing of regeneration cuts (clearcuts) over the growing cycle might preclude the need for openings in some regions. After a final harvest cut, specified areas should be designated as permanent herbaceous openings and excluded from timber regeneration. Some timber regeneration can occur if some openings are not planted and other areas receive various silvicultural treatments (Rutske 1969). But clearcuts are no substitute for herbaceous openings on medium to heavy soils in some regions (e.g., Lake States). Utility rights-of-way, railroad rights-of-way, roadsides, firebrakes, log landings, trails, food patches, grass stubble, and ground cover should be included and managed as part of the openings system.

One pattern of cutting would be to cut an area and maintain it as a herbaceous/shrubby opening, surrounded by a transition zone of 30 m or so; mast and den trees would occupy 25 percent of the zone in strips or blocks, and early successional vegetation would occupy 75 percent of the zone (Fig. 7.3) (Connecticut Department of Environmental Protection 1989). One-fifth of the area could be cut every 10 years on a 50-year even-aged rotation for cordwood. The proposed opening could be included in the rotation if cost and labor prevent its maintenance.

To reduce costs, openings created by economic activities, such as log landings from timber harvesting and rights-of-way for transmission lines, should be used whenever possible (Wunz 1987). Sites should have no or few ferns and ericaceous shrubs (Wunz 1984). A proper seedbed should be prepared by scraping off ericaceous root mats and duff down to mineral soil, grading out wheel ruts, and loosening wheel-packed soil. Moderate amounts of soil amendments should be applied (about 3 to 4 mt/ha of lime and 300 to 400 kg/ha of 15-10-10 or similar fertilizer). Seed should be sowed during spring to midsummer

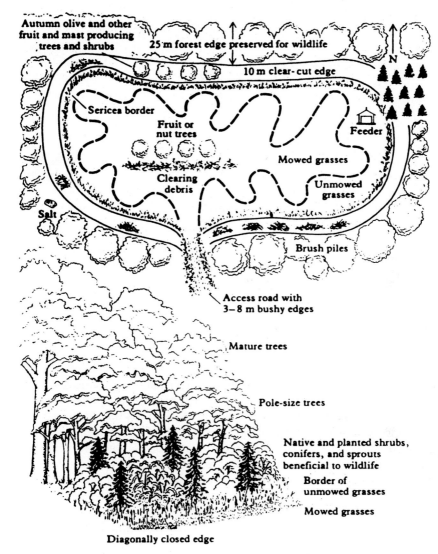

Autumn olive and other fruit and mast producing trees and shrubs

25 m forest edge preserved for wildlife

10 m clear-cut edge

Sericea border

Fruit or nut trees

Feeder

Mowed grasses

Clearing debris

Unmowed grasses

Salt

Brush piles

Access road with 3–8 m bushy edges

Mature trees

Pole-size trees

Native and planted shrubs, conifers, and sprouts beneficial to wildlife

Border of unmowed grasses

Mowed grasses

Diagonally closed edge

Figure 7.2 Features recommended for the design and edge management of forest wildlife clearings. (*Giles 1978.*)

immediately after seedbed preparation, and then disked lightly or dragged with a section of chain-link fence to cover seed. Free nitrogen always can be provided by including inoculated birdsfoot trefoil seed of early and late varieties in a mixture with one or more grasses at a rate of 10 kg/ha of trefoil plus 20 kg/ha of grass. Seed mixtures are more likely to establish a dense sod. Clumps of fruiting shrubs may be planted on the north edge of forest openings (Henderson 1988).

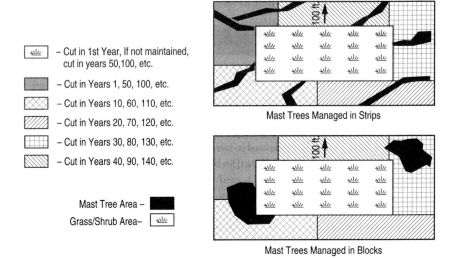

- Cut in 1st Year, If not maintained, cut in years 50,100, etc.

- Cut in Years 1, 50, 100, etc.

- Cut in Years 10, 60, 110, etc.

- Cut in Years 20, 70, 120, etc.

- Cut in Years 30, 80, 130, etc.

- Cut in Years 40, 90, 140, etc.

Mast Tree Area –

Grass/Shrub Area–

Mast Trees Managed in Strips

Mast Trees Managed in Blocks

Figure 7.3 Cutting schedule for wildlife-management zones to maintain an opening. (*Connecticut Department of Environmental Protection 1989.*)

Logging Roads and Skid Trails

Roads fragment forests and are lethal barriers to movement of wildlife, especially to large carnivores such as mountain lions, bears, and wolves (Harris 1985, Thiel 1985, Jensen et al. 1986, Mech et al. 1988, Brocke et al. 1990). Gray wolves fail to survive when road densities exceed about 0.6 km/km². Even small mammals do not cross roads readily (Oxley et al. 1974, Barnett et al. 1978, Mader 1984). Main roads, secondary roads, and primitive roads affect elk negatively if road density is 1 km/km² or more, especially on west- and south-facing slopes 0.2 to 0.8 km away from the road (Perry and Overly 1976, Lyon 1983). In intensively managed industrial forests, road density is about 4.3 km/km², 1 km of road serves about 40 ha, and 0.5 ha is cleared per kilometer of road right-of-way (Bennett 1962, Larsen 1974, Hynson et al. 1982). Excessive trails can result in undesirable exploitation by hunters of game species such as ruffed grouse and whitetail bucks. To protect species often subject to legal or illegal killing, such as large carnivores, roads should be closed in some areas, and in other areas road density should be less than perhaps 0.3 km/km² (Noss 1992).

Small-scale uneven-aged management costs more than large-scale even-aged management (Hunter 1990). With uneven-aged management, harvest operations extend over a relatively large area, requiring repeated returns to a stand, and a larger network of roads. Forest roads encourage overhunting, and even settlement and conversion of forests to agriculture. Yet some are needed for logging, recreation, and protection against undesirable damage from fire, insects, and disease.

Long-rotation management areas (see "Interior Habitats" in Chap. 4) should be located away from major human traffic arteries because fire incidence, roadkills, and poaching are correlated with proximity to roads and amount of human activity (Harris 1984). Roads should not follow stream gradients because of extensive destruction to riparian habitat. Roads should be located on upslope benches away from meadows; wetlands; riparian zones; key winter range; travel lanes, such as saddles or low divides used by elk to cross ridges between drainages (Thomas et al. 1988a); feeding sites; reproductive areas; and key habitats for threatened, endangered, or unique wildlife (Halls et al. 1984). Ridges often are used as wintering areas (Armleder et al. 1986).

Critical areas should be shielded with vegetation or topography. Silvicultural treatment in such areas should not open the areas closer than 122 m to the road (Thomas et al. 1979b). Straight stretches of road should not exceed 0.4 km in forested areas (Fig. 7.4). Circular routes should be avoided (Armleder et al. 1986). An unspaced strip of shrubby vegetation at least 10 m wide should be left along roads as security cover. Gates should be installed to close roads to protect a species during part or all of a year (Thomas et al. 1979b). Logging roads should be minimized. Logging roads and skid trails should be designed to avoid particularly vigorous patches of shrubs. Roads should be as narrow as possible. Culverts and bridges should be used for stream crossings, which should be minimal and at right angles to reduce disturbance to riparian vegetation. Construction of all roads should minimize erosion and stream siltation. Hynson et al. (1982) and Everest et al. (1985) presented detailed information about road construction on forest lands. Most skid road designs for logging have parallel, sunburst, or cloverleaf patterns relative to haul roads and landings (Fig. 7.5) (Studier et al. 1984).

Abandoned logging roads, skid trails, and landing sites should be seeded with a grass-legume mixture and treated as part of the openings system (Connecticut Department of Environmental Protection 1989) (see Fig. 4.28). For roads averaging 5 m wide, about 4.5 kg of 10-20-20 fertilizer and 45 kg of lime should be applied for every 30 m of road (Hassinger et al. 1981). Slash can be used to block illegal access to skid trails at intervals along the trail, with most of the trail exposed for growth of grasses and forbs. If slash is not windrowed or piled, a network of skid trails should be left free of slash for wildlife movement and growth of grasses and forbs.

Roads and trails through unlogged areas can be improved for edge wildlife by *daylighting,* i.e., cutting and releasing vegetation along

Location of Roads

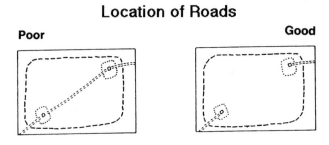

Design of Intersections

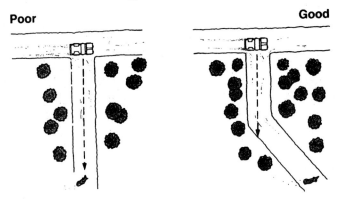

Figure 7.4 Location and design of logging roads to minimize impact on wildlife. (*Armleder et al. 1986.*)

areas within forests to increase sunlight on the forest floor (Connecticut Department of Environmental Protection 1988b). All woody vegetation should be removed within 3 m of both sides of a road or trail. All stumps and rocks should be removed within 1.5 m of the road or trail. Clearing and scarification allow planting and maintenance of a mixture of grasses and forbs. About half the trees should be removed within 7.6 to 9.1 m on each side of the road or trail to create a transition zone from herbaceous vegetation to forest. Every 3 to 5 years the grass and forb area should be mowed to remove invading brush. Every 12 to 15 years the outer areas should be cut to maintain the daylight effect.

Trails across south-facing slopes above a lowland brush area provide dusting and sunning sites, fill with snow to facilitate obstruction-free snow roosting by grouse, ensure early snow melt and thus early availability of green plants, and produce food-producing herbs and shrubs if the trail is wide enough (Rutske 1969). Site preparation usually includes liming, fertilizing, and harrowing before seeding.

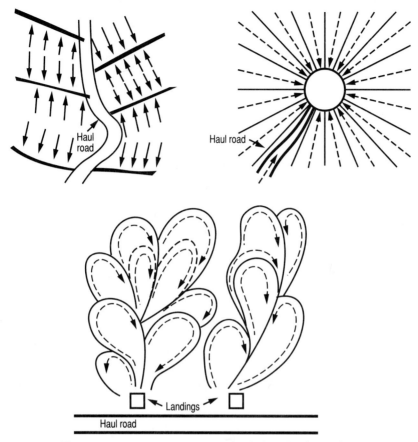

Figure 7.5 Three common systematic patterns for skid roads. (*Studier et al. 1984.*)

Fire management might require fuel breaks in forest cover, although they contribute to undesirable forest fragmentation. These fuel breaks should be treated as herbaceous forage areas (Thomas et al. 1979b). They should be as narrow as possible, with sight distances less than 0.4 km across, and substantially less than that where travel lanes cross.

Road and off-road use by snowmobiles, motorcycles, and other all-terrain vehicles must be regulated.

Snow

Chionophiles are animals which have evolved behavioral and morphological adaptations to snow that limit their distribution to snowy regions (Peek 1986). *Chionophores* can live in snowy regions but have no special adaptations to do so. *Chionophobes* cannot tolerate snow.

The four ecologically important characteristics of snow are depth, temperature (for insulation), hardness (crust), and density (compaction). Snow ages in a process called *firnification,* increasing in density and hardness as the time since snowfall passes, thus increasing its strength and support capability and reducing insulating quality. Tundra snows are shallow, strongly compacted by wind, and unmeltable during winter. Taiga (boreal forest) snows are deep and soft, unaffected by wind. Steppe snows are inconsistent, shallow, and generally not durable. Mountain snows are variable and generally durable. Snows in areas next to large bodies of water tend to be deeper than in similar latitudes and altitudes elsewhere.

Snow can have harmful or beneficial effects to wildlife; it insulates, cools, concentrates, hinders, conceals, exposes (Peek 1986). It covers forage and certain prey species, and facilitates capture of certain prey species. Shaping open ridgetops to retain snowfields helps caribou avoid insects and keep cool in summer. For deer and other wildlife confined by snow, cuts and clearcut strips should be about 23 to 30 m wide where snow is deep, perhaps with timbered strips at intervals for travel lanes (Krefting 1962, Rutske 1969) (see "Leave Strips" in Chap. 6). Strips oriented in an east-west direction improve tree regeneration and hold deeper snow for snow-roosting wildlife (e.g., ruffed grouse). Snow melts early along south-facing edges of such strips to provide green forage at a critical time.

Deeryards

Deer have a high political profile due to widespread public interest in viewing them for consumptive and nonconsumptive purposes and the associated substantial economic benefits. In northern areas where snow approaches 46 cm deep or day length shortens enough, white-tailed deer congregate on usually traditional wintering areas called *deeryards,* which constitute 5 to 10 percent of the total deer range and are thus especially sensitive to forest alteration (Telfer 1978, Wiley 1988a). Deeryards can range from 20 to 2800 ha—for example averaging 130 ha in spruce-fir in New Brunswick (Boer 1978) and 32 ha, 46 ha, and 112 ha in northern, central, and western Nova Scotia, respectively (Telfer 1978).

Deeryards have two basic components (Reay et al. 1990). The core range provides cover and usually consists of concentrations of softwoods with high crown closure, located preferably on south-facing slopes in hilly and mountainous country, and sometimes in low areas such as wetlands and stream corridors (e.g., in the Midwest). Often they are located in groups along major river valleys or coastlines of the Great Lakes or ocean (Gill 1957, Banasiak 1961, Telfer 1978). Of 350 deeryards surveyed in Maine, 85 percent were in spruce-fir forest patches along streams or ponds (Banasiak 1961), emphasizing the importance of riparian areas (see Chap. 6). Next to or surrounding the core area are mixed hardwoods and softwoods which provide browse (see Table A.6) (Gill 1957).

Five key factors influence deer on winter range (Nyberg et al. 1986): (1) snow depth and duration, (2) abundance and height of rooted forage, (3) composition and rate of lichen and foliage litterfall, (4) quality and quantity of security cover, and (5) quality and quantity of thermal cover. Forestry practices can modify at least 16 features of the overstory that influence snow interception (Bunnell et al. 1985), but 4 of these features are especially influential (Nyberg et al. 1986): species composition of the overstory, crown size and form, canopy closure, and patchiness of the stand.

Species composition influences branch angle and flexibility, interwhorl distance, and height-to-base ratio (ratio of length of live crown to maximum crown width). For maximum snow interception, overstory crowns should be long and wide, with interwhorl distances of about 70 cm for western conifers at least. Canopy closure should be 70 to 90 percent to reduce snow depth and duration the most. Patchiness of the stand affects snow distribution, melt rate, and browse production. Such openings on winter range should be one-half to one tree height wide, preferably with trees of intermediate canopy on the downwind side. These four features can be manipulated through establishment and tending practices of stands scheduled for rotations longer than 150 years on productive sites in Alaska (Nyberg et al. 1986, Kirchhoff and Schoen 1987).

For rooted forage, tall, dense, productive, digestible browse should be provided to feed the target number of overwintering deer. A crown closure of 30 to 60 percent provides optimum conditions for browse production.

Black-tailed deer and woodland caribou consume large amounts of litterfall forage as rooted browse becomes covered with snow. Most of this is from arboreal lichens, called "old man's beard," of the genera *Alectoria, Bryoria,* and *Usnea.* Most such lichens occur in old-growth trees.

Security cover can be provided by manipulating visual density, physical complexity, size, and shape of the vegetation, especially relative to topographic features. Security cover must be near forage areas.

Good thermal cover invariably precludes forage production, so the two must be juxtaposed. For best thermal cover, the coniferous canopy must have about 100 percent closure and be at least 4 m high to trap long-wave radiation at deer height. Such thickets should have nearby openings large enough to be unshaded at low solar angles to provide warmth during daytime.

Ideal winter sites in the West are on south-facing slopes of 30 to 80 percent at elevations below 800 m. Small rock outcrops or bluffs, which absorb thermal radiation, are present in portions of the stand.

In mountainous terrain of places like the coastal forests of southern British Columbia, four snowpack zones influence the management of winter, spring, and summer range for deer and elk (Becker et al. 1990). The shallow snowpack zone usually occurs between sea level and 300 m elevation, with less than 30 cm of snow lasting less than 2 weeks. The moderate snowpack zone usually occurs between 200 and 600 m elevation, with usually 30 to 60 cm of snow lasting up to 2 weeks. The deep snowpack zone usually occurs between 500 and 900 m elevation, with snow often more than 60 cm deep lasting 2 weeks or more. The very deep snowpack zone usually occurs above 800 m elevation, with snow often more than 60 cm deep and lasting most of the winter.

In the shallow snowpack zone, deer and elk can use most habitats in all seasons due to low snowfall and mild temperatures. Thus, managers have much flexibility.

In the moderate snowpack zone, when the trees reach 10 m high, areas with 60 to 70 percent crown closure should be thinned to maintain that degree of closure to develop the understory, preferably to the north, east, south, and southwest of openings for maximum penetration of the afternoon sun. Areas with 70 to 90 percent crown closure should be thinned to less than 70 percent closure to develop large crowns and understory forage, then maintained at 70 to 90 percent closure for maximum snow interception. Conifer thickets should be maintained, especially around openings, as should cover next to special habitats. Management should concentrate on upland south-facing slopes of 10 to 50 percent with an aspect of 90 to 270°. Old growth, with its snow interception and abundant litterfall of arboreal lichens, should be maintained.

Deer and elk usually migrate from the deep snowpack zone to lower snowpack zones for winter. If they winter in the deep snowpack zone, it is on range with southerly aspects and slopes of at least 40 percent that are exposed to winter sun. Elk winter on lowlands with slopes of 0 to 10 percent and on adjacent uplands with southerly aspects and slopes of 10 to 50 percent exposed to winter sun. Deer and elk rely much more on old growth for winter survival. Management is similar to that for the moderate snowpack zone.

In the very deep snowpack zone, severe winter and spring weather preclude winter use by deer and elk, which migrate to lower snowpack zones for winter (Becker et al. 1990).

In the eastern half of Canada and the United States, deeryards tend to be of three general types (Rutske 1969): (1) upland conifers (spruce, fir, hemlock); (2) lowland mixed (swamp) conifers (black spruce, balsam fir, hemlock, white cedar); (3) white cedar swamps. Hemlock stands also are used in some areas (Reay et al. 1990). Deeryards typically have more than 70 percent crown closure, stand heights over 10.7 m, and more than 23 m²/ha basal area (Wiley 1988a).

Deeryards first must be located by contacting local wildlife and forestry personnel and citizens, by examining aerial photos for likely areas, and by late winter aerial reconnaissance (Telfer 1978). After field checking, the information is plotted on forest inventory maps or 1:50,000 topographic maps.

A buffer strip 60 to 100 m wide should surround the deeryard and be managed for browse production on a maximum rotation of 100 years with a maximum cutting interval of 10 years (Rutske 1969, Reay et al. 1990). Thus, at least 10 percent of the area should be regenerated every 10 years. Another alternative is to cut the forest in units of 16 to 65 ha, with each unit cut in alternating strips 20 m wide (Fig. 7.6) (Krefting 1962, Verme 1965). Best browse production actually occurs with a 40-year rotation and 25 percent of the area regenerated every 10 years. Generally, patchcuts of 0.2 to 0.8 ha are best, cut preferably in winter when tops can be eaten by deer and stump sprouting will be best. Stumps should be cut low. Stumps 15 to 30 cm sprout more vigorously than stumps 46 to 61 cm high, and might remain in reach of deer longer (Morton and Sedam 1938, Krefting 1941). Hawthorn and apple trees should be retained. Where possible or practical, aspen should be cut within 0.8 km of known or potential deeryards (Perala 1977). One recommendation is to leave at least 25 oaks per hectare within 0.8 km of deeryards, the total number of hectares equal to the size of the deeryard or to 2.5 times the number of deer in the yard (Rutske 1969). Beyond 0.8 km from deeryards, at least 12 oaks per hectare should be left. A ratio of three red oaks to one white oak should be left near deeryards, and two red oaks to one white oak or bur oak on summer range.

Stands must be managed by area regulation to ensure that at least 50 percent of the wintering area always can provide functional shelter (Gill 1957, Reay et al. 1990). The rest of the area should have four to six age classes to provide hardwood browse and softwood regeneration for future cover (Verme 1965, Boer 1978, Wiley 1988a). Narrow deeryards must not be fragmented. Overmature, diseased, and insect-damaged trees should be cut first.

Travel corridors should be designed into each cutting plan. These should be unbroken, dense softwood cover at least 60 m (Reay et al. 1990) or 100 m (Wiley 1988a) wide, connecting all parts of the deeryard, preferably along streams. Travel corridors can be permanent or can be relocated as needed with careful planning. (See "Corridors" in Chap. 6.)

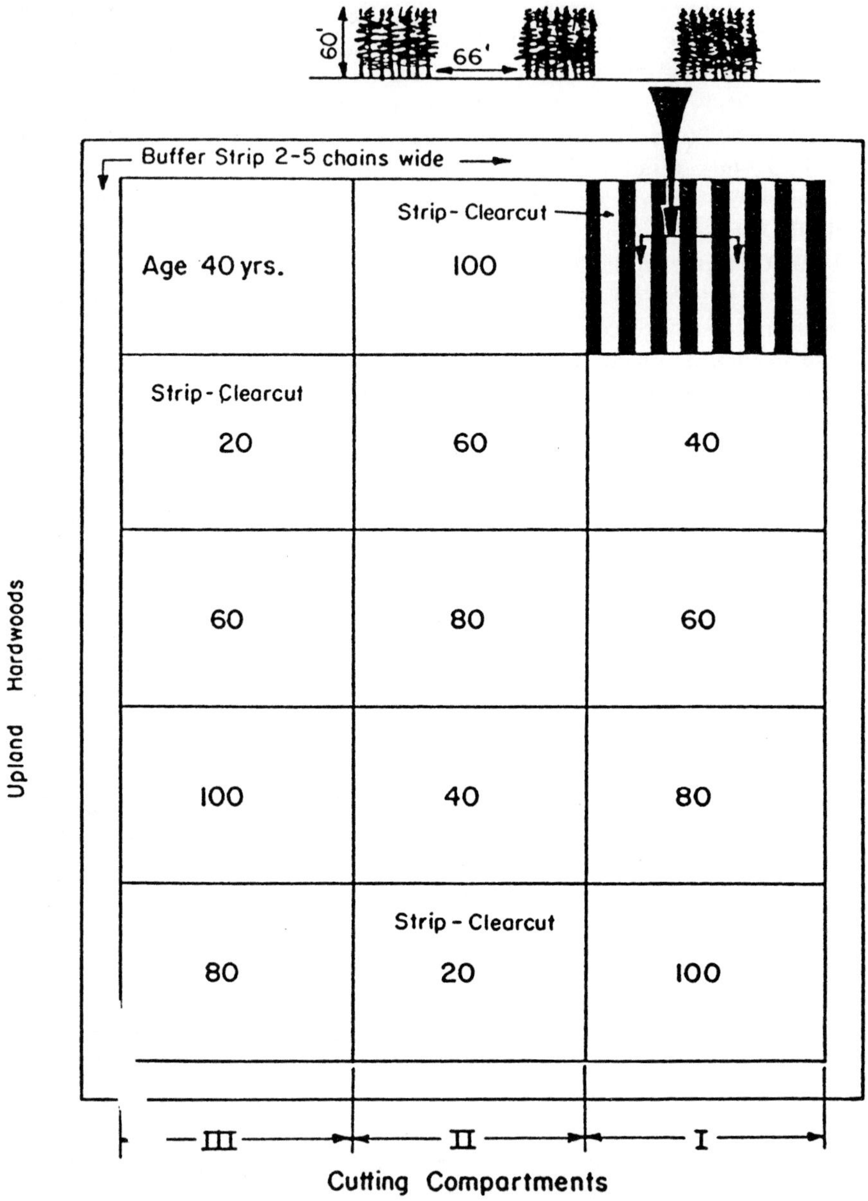

Figure 7.6 Arrangement and systematic cutting of upland hardwoods in the East for high sustained carrying capacity of nearby coniferous deeryards. (*Verme 1965.*) [*For metric equivalence, see metric conversion table in the front of the book.*]

Spruce-fir

In spruce-fir areas, uneven-aged management by group selection, with a stand entered every 10 to 20 years, is best (Reay et al. 1990). Group selection openings should be 6 to 12 m in diameter and uniformly distributed to distribute browsing pressure. Fir should be cut in preference to spruce, cedar, and hemlock, which are longer-lived, more windfirm, and more resistant to spruce budworm. Because of their value as cover and food, cedar and hemlock should be protected (Boer 1978). Except on sites and terrain that will not support disturbance of bare ground, summer logging is best because scarification favors regeneration of spruce (Reay et al. 1990). Thinning should not occur in patches of larger poles or sawtimber.

In wintering areas larger than 80 ha, even-aged management with a two- or three-stage shelterwood system is best. A two-stage system is used on secondary sites, with the first cut made in summer to remove 30 to 35 percent of the basal area, including merchantable and submerchantable hardwood; this induces sprouting for browse and encourages coniferous replacement for cover. Larger, more vigorous spruce, cedar, and hemlock should be left to provide seed and shade. The second (final) cut should occur after adequate regeneration, usually at least 5 years after the first entry, in winter. On primary sites where the risk of windthrow is high or the area of functional shelter is small, a three-stage shelterwood system is best. During the first entry, 20 percent of the basal area is removed, and another 20 percent is taken 5 to 10 years later. The final cut is made when regeneration is adequate. Because aspen coppice growth severely competes with spruce and fir regeneration, aspen should not be cut. Telfer (1978) considered an ideal stand interspersion to consist of blocks in each of four height classes differing by 5 to 7 m growing close together. Because rotations of spruce-fir pulpwood are usually 60 to 80 years, 10 to 40 percent of each compartment should be cut every 15 to 20 years.

Where the uniform shelterwood system is inappropriate, or in stands over 60 years old with at least 70 percent balsam fir, strip shelterwood cuts can be used to regenerate the area quickly. The stand then can be managed by group selection or shelterwood cuts. Cut strips should be 6 to 12 m wide and leave strips 12 to 24 m wide, with irregular borders and an east-west to northeast-southwest orientation, depending on windthrow hazard. In the first cut, 25 to 40 percent of the area to be regenerated should be cut. The rest of the area should be cut when regeneration growth is 3 to 6 dm tall in the residual strips.

Thinnings should occur early or not at all. Even-aged stands or patches of uneven-aged stands should be thinned before they are 4.6 m tall or 5 cm dbh (Reay et al. 1990). Deeryards can be expanded by underplanting species of conifers resistant to browsing, such as spruce (Telfer 1978) (see Fig. 5.14).

Swamp conifers

Even-aged management can be used in most of a deer-wintering area by using a 75-year rotation and 15-year cutting interval to produce five age classes to ensure at least 50 percent of the deeryard in perpetual winter cover (Wiley 1988a). Clearcuts should be no more than 2 ha in deeryards less than 162 ha, and no more than 4 ha in deeryards over 162 ha. Larger clearcuts might be acceptable if narrow and irregularly shaped. Clearcuts should be separated by an uncut strip at least 100 m wide. Small yards might need to be clearcut to keep deer away.

A less practical alternative is to use a two-stage shelterwood system. Stands are entered every 15 years; half of the cutting blocks scheduled for harvest receive a removal cut at each entry (Fig. 7.7) (Wiley 1988a). Logging yards should be located outside the deeryard.

To increase coniferous cover in 100-m riparian strips of the deeryard, uneven-aged management of single-tree or group selection cuts

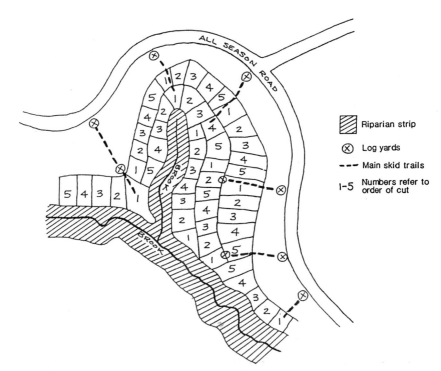

Figure 7.7 Example of a management scheme for a deer-wintering area in the East. (*Wiley 1988a.*)

be hand-planted if natural regeneration is too sparse (<60 percent), but deer are likely to eat them unless protected (Windell 1991). Large hardwoods should be removed or killed at least 5 years before clearcutting so that shade from overstory conifers will kill root suckers and stump sprouts. Because stump sprouts are a great source of browse, they should be allowed to develop where competition with cedar is no problem. Rehabilitating deeryards should be done only where (1) deer densities can be kept low with antlerless harvests, (2) annual logging of white cedar in some areas will attract deer away from regenerating areas, and (3) winter shelter for deer is eliminated by harvesting a large (16 to 65 ha) block of timber within 5 to 10 years. If strip clearcutting is used, uncut strips must be removed as soon as adjacent strips regenerate adequately, because existing shelter will provide travel lanes for deer to forage for white cedar on regenerated areas (Verme and Johnston 1986).

In addition to silvicultural methods, browse can be produced by applying herbicides, controlled burning, and bulldozing if budget allows. Bulldozing should be done about every 5 years in spring, on areas of 4 to 10 ha widely scattered to prevent concentrations of deer, in strips at least 30 m wide with irregular edges, about 20 ha/km^2 (Chase and Severinghaus 1949).

In Michigan, cedar deeryards less than 81 ha are too small to regulate deer activity efficiently, and probably cannot be managed by designated age classes. Clearcutting the entire stand at age 60 to 80 years, or even later, is recommended; clearcutting will force the herd elsewhere during the critical restocking stage (Verme 1965), which will be preferably at a time when other coniferous cover has developed nearby.

Snags and Live Den Trees

Many species of forest wildlife depend on snags and live den trees to meet a variety of needs (Scott et al. 1977, Neitro et al. 1985, Tubbs et al. 1987). Uses include cavity nest sites, nesting platforms, sources of feeding substrate, plucking posts, singing or drumming sites, food cache or granary, courtship locations, overwintering sites, roosting, lookout posts, hunting and hawking perches, fledging sites, dwellings or dens, loafing sites, nesting under bark, communal nesting or nursery colonies, anvil sites, and thermally regulated habitat. Snags are also used for the basic behavioral and physiological needs (Davis 1983). Snags are the main source of logs on the ground and in streams. Often, more snags are available than snag-using wildlife needs, especially where trees succumb to insects and disease (Swallow et al. 1986).

Management of insectivorous birds that use snags extensively can reduce insect infestations such as spruce budworm in forests if enough snags exist for the birds' needs (Evans and Conner 1979, Thomas et al. 1979a, Crawford and Titterington 1979, Takekawa et al. 1982, Neitro et al. 1985, Hunter 1990). Artificial nest boxes have been used extensively in Europe to substitute for snags normally used by cavity-nesting birds but which are eliminated in Europe's intensively managed forests. But leaving snags is cheaper than building, installing, and tending birdhouses.

Types of snags

Hardwoods provide more cavities than softwoods do because when large hardwood limbs drop off, cavities develop. Nonetheless, primary cavity users tend to use softwoods more because excavation is easier than in hardwoods.

Snags can be hard or soft and of nine different stages of decomposition (Fig. 7.9) (Maser et al. 1979a, Thomas et al. 1979a). Snags 1, 2, 3, and 4 are hard snags. Cull trees can be left during silvicultural treatment to become snags, but their seeds might be genetically inferior for reforestation. Cavity-nesting wildlife uses soft snags the most. Woodpeckers are strongly associated with snags. Still, about 40 percent of woodpecker nest trees in North America are live (Miller and Miller 1980). The endangered red-cockaded woodpecker prefers live

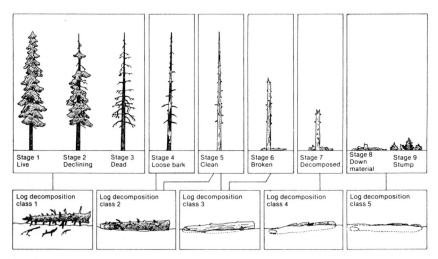

Figure 7.9 Upon falling, snags and trees enter log decomposition class 1, 2, 3, or 4. (*Maser et al. 1979a.*)

trees (Conner 1978), and the largest woodpecker, the pileated wood-pecker, does not use soft or rotted snags (Harris 1983).

Relative to logging safety, preferred types of snags and live defective trees have little or no lean and are as follows (Neitro et al. 1985, U.S. Forest Service 1986):

Type A. Recently dead trees with good root systems, and preferably tops already broken out or suitable for topping. Needles on conifers are red if present.

Type B. Windfirm live cull or defective trees with tops broken out one-half to two-thirds of tree height.

Type C. Live defective trees safe enough to be topped with explosives to reduce susceptibility to windthrow.

Type D. Snags over 30 cm dbh with bark still tight, preferably with tops broken out.

Type E. Snags with tops broken out and obvious loss of bark, preferably less than 18 m tall.

Unmerchantable trees are classified as culls. Sawlog-size cull trees of classes 3 and 4 can provide potential cavity sites (Tubbs et al. 1987). Trees in cull class 3 are live trees with two major defects. Trees in cull class 4 are live trees with at least three major defects and are most likely to be used by cavity users.

Cavities in trees are formed through natural decay and through excavation by woodpeckers (Neitro et al. 1985). Both processes might depend on infection of the tree by fungi, which softens wood for cavity formation. Snags decompose through interaction of fungi, bacteria, insects, and weather over time. Decomposition accelerates in live and dead trees when tops break off. Live and dead trees with broken tops stand longer because they are less susceptible to windthrow. Snags deteriorate (1) from top to bottom, resulting in decreased height and the sloughing of needles, branches, bark, and wood; and (2) from sap-wood to heartwood, resulting ultimately in soft snags. The rate of decomposition depends on size and species of snag. The larger the snag, the longer it will remain standing, the more wildlife value it has, and the less often it must be replaced. For example, Douglas-fir snags should be at least 60 cm dbh and 15 m tall (Mannan et al. 1980). Management for species with longer lives and harder wood will reduce the need for snag replacement.

Woodpeckers that excavate live trees prefer those with heart rot, caused by a fungus. Trees that have heart rot sometimes can be identified by the following characteristics (Conner 1978):

1. Fungal conks (fruiting bodies)

2. Stubs of broken branches

3. Wounds or scars resulting from lightning, fire, or mechanical damage

4. Dead areas on living trees

5. Woodpecker holes or cavities

6. Discolored or soft, decayed wood in samples taken by increment borer

7. Heart rot fungi in cultures of wood taken by increment borer

8. Indication of wood decay by testing the tree with a Shigometer

Impact of forestry

Forestry practices influence snag production and retention (Table 7.4) (Neitro et al. 1985). Maximum production of wood fiber and demands for firewood are inconsistent with snag management (Table A.7)

TABLE 7.4   Forestry Practices That Usually Impact Snag Production and Retention

| Forest practice | Potential adverse impact | | |
	None to slight	Moderate	High
Silvicultural system	Single-tree selection, extended rotation	Group selection, shelter-wood	Clear-cutting with short rotations
Utilization standard	All snags and culls retained	Some snags and cull trees retained for wildlife	Intensive salvage program
Harvest method	Balloon or horse logging	Skyline, full-sus-pension	Cat logging, extensive road system
Deadwood (fuels) management	No burn	Spot burn	Broadcast burn, preventive fire management
Fuelwood harvest	Highly restricted and regulated	Restricted to specific areas	Few restric-tions, low regulations
Herbicides	No treatment	Spot treatment with surface equipment	Aerial applica-tion (snags felled for aerial access)

SOURCE: Neitro et al. (1985).

(Carey and Gill 1980, Johnson et al. 1987). Bigger snags are better, but they generally require rotations and cutting cycles longer than acceptable for silvicultural treatment; others are removed for safety reasons (Neitro et al. 1985). Even-aged management ultimately removes all trees; leaving snags can increase populations of snag-using wildlife; it also might reduce some wildlife populations in clearcuts due to increased predation by raptors and corvines using the snags as perches. Uneven-aged management is more conducive to snag management.

In unmanaged forests, suppression (i.e., growth rate suppressed for trees below the canopy) is the main cause of mortality and snags. Such snags tend to be small. Young, unmanaged forests often have some large remnant snags and live trees remaining from forests removed by wildfire, insects, and diseases (Cline et al. 1980). Tree mortality and snag formation decrease with age (Neitro et al. 1985). In managed forests, thinning, salvage, short harvest rotations, and clearcut logging reduce or eliminate snag formation. These conflicts can be reduced by coordinating snag-management objectives with silvicultural practices. Allowance must be made for loss of snags to logging operations, firewood cutting, and windthrow, which typically is about 34 percent (Scott 1978).

Estimating snag abundance and wildlife needs

Before creating and/or designing the snags and live den trees to be left during the harvest, their numbers must be determined relative to the needs of associated wildlife (Zillgitt 1946, Cimon 1983, Yamasaki and Tubbs 1986, Bull et al. 1990).

The number of snags Y needed for excavators can be calculated (Bull and Meslow 1977, Raphael and White 1984, Neitro et al. 1985):

$$Y = A + B + C$$

where A = maximum density of cavity-nesting birds
B = number of snags used annually for nesting and roosting by each pair
C = a reserve of suitable snags (usually 4)

If the timber on an area is to be cut, the number of snags to be left can be calculated (Bull and Meslow 1977):

$$S = T(L - R) + Y$$

where S = density of snags to be left
T = years to next harvest

L = density of annual snag loss
R = density of annual snag recruitment
Y = number of snags needed

A snag suitability index (SSI) can be estimated (Raphael and White 1984):

$$\text{SSI} = 0.06D + B - 0.52T - 0.80$$

where D = snag dbh (cm)
B = decimal proportion of stem covered by bark
T = O if the top is broken and 1 if the top is intact.

A positive value indicates the snag is suitable for nesting. Values of -1.0 to 1.0 indicate borderline snags that cannot be classified reliably. A computer simulation model can be used to estimate tree mortality and snag retention (Rasmussen and Folliott 1983).

Falling rates must be estimated to determine the number of hard snags to be left to become soft snags in time (Raphael and White 1984). For example, on a burned area in the Sierra Nevada in California, 16 percent of the pines and 33 percent of the firs were standing after 15 years. Thus, to produce one standing soft snag of each species 15 years later, six hard pines and three hard firs were needed initially. To maintain woodpecker populations at 70 percent of their potential in a 130-year rotation of a Douglas-fir–ponderosa pine community, for example, the density of snags 31 to 50 cm dbh is 148 per 40 hectares; 11,640 live trees per 40 hectares are needed to furnish those snags because 34 snags per hectare per year fall and live trees sustain 0.4 percent mortality (Bull et al. 1980). For snags over 50 cm dbh, 9 snags per hectare and 103 live trees per 40 hectares are needed because 0.4 snags per hectare per year fall and live trees sustain 0.4 percent mortality.

Biologists studying forest types from nearly all regions of the United States and Canada recommend variable yet somewhat consistent snag densities; 5 to 10 large snags per hectare seems to be a good guide without using too sophisticated and complex a model (Hunter 1990).

In the southwestern United States, the policy of the U.S. Forest Service is to leave 7.4 snags per hectare within 152 m of water and forest openings, and 5 per hectare throughout the rest of the forest (Patton 1992). Good snags were considered to be over 46 cm dbh with over 40 percent bark cover. Generally, estimates of the density of large-diameter ($\geq$46 cm dbh) cavity/den trees needed for nesting and roosting sites for viable populations of large cavity-dwelling wildlife like raccoons, fishers, and pileated woodpeckers are 8 to 100 per 40

TABLE 7.5   Number of Snags and/or Den Trees Required per 40 Hectares to Maintain 50 to 100 Percent of the Populations of All Forest-Interior Species of Wildlife

Tree dbh (cm)	Percent of optimum					
	100	90	80	70	60	50
>48	100	90	80	70	60	50
25–48	400	360	320	280	240	200
<25	200	180	160	140	120	100

Note: Snag and den tree requirements are similar because many species would use either live or dead trees and the number of species needing live den trees approximated the number of species needing dead trees.

SOURCE: Titus (1983).

TABLE 7.6   Optimum Number of Snags and/or Den Trees per 40 Hectares by Three Broad Habitat Types

Tree dbh (cm)	Forest interior		Semiopen and open	Wooded watercourses
	Dens	Snags	Dens*	Dens*
>48	100	0	300	200
25–48	400	400	400	1400
<25	200	200	300	900

*Animals here need den trees because creating snags by deadening trees is not generally recommended in these land-use patterns.

SOURCE: Titus (1983).

hectares; a higher density is needed for foraging of cavity-dwelling species (Yamasaki and Tubbs 1986). Small wildlife, like downy woodpeckers, hairy woodpeckers, and nuthatches, can use decayed upper portions of large snags as well as medium (25–46 cm dbh) and small (15–25 cm dbh) snags (Evans and Conner 1979, Yamasaki and Tubbs 1986). Cordell et al. (1984) recommended the density of cavity and den trees needed as 400 per 40 hectares for small snags and 100 per 40 hectares for medium snags. About four hard snags are needed to produce one soft snag, varying with tree species (Raphael and White 1984). Densities of snags and den trees vary by habitat type and density of associated wildlife desired (Tables 7.5, 7.6) (Titus 1983).

For plains cottonwoods in bottomlands of the western Great Plains, Sedgewick and Knopf (1986) recommended (1) retaining live trees of at least 55 cm dbh, (2) retaining a diversity of heights and diameters of cavity trees but averaging a dbh of 69 cm at a density of 92 per 40 hectares, and (3) limiting the harvest of cottonwoods with dead limbs at least 10 cm in diameter and retaining cottonwoods with limbs over 15 cm in diameter. For average populations of primary cavity users in

Florida, McComb et al. (1986) recommended creating 4 to 9 surplus snags per primary cavity nester by stand improvement every 4 to 6 years or when 50 percent loss is reached; the aim is to produce snags at sustained densities of at least 120 per 40 hectares for snags 13 cm or more dbh, 84 per 40 hectares for snags 25 cm or more dbh, and 8 per 40 hectares for snags 50 cm or more dbh. As a general guide, about 423 suitable soft snags (15 years or older) per 40 hectares are needed to support maximum densities of birds on forests burned with wildfire, with 4 hard snags needed to produce 1 soft snag (Raphael and White 1984). On unburned forests, 342 suitable snags (one-third hard snags) are needed per 40 hectares.

Noncommercial land and withdrawn commercial land should be managed for 100 percent population level of cavity users (Neitro et al. 1985). For example, suppose snags are removed on half the area through silvicultural treatment or human encroachment (e.g., housing development, agriculture), and a decision is made to manage the other half at 50 percent population level; that actually amounts to 25 percent of the original population level, which might not be a viable population level.

Snag distribution

Individual snags or den trees should be evenly spaced along the forest edge and of various species and sizes in all forest types. Decker et al. (1983) recommended leaving at least three suitable snags for every 122 m of edge, within 15 m of the edge. In the forest interior, snags should be left in clumps and should not extend above the canopy of the nearly mature forest (Robbins 1979). Some clearcuts should have none as they develop into unfragmented forests. Windfirm trees should be selected for snags (Tubbs et al. 1987). The least windfirm trees and poorest locations can be identified as follows:

1. Shallow-rooted tree species, e.g., most conifers

2. Trees with root or butt rot, or shallow root systems due to high-water-table bedrock, or to soils with fragipans and hardpans. (These trees are often characterized by smaller than normal crowns.)

3. Trees located on saddles, on ridges, along stands that parallel storm directions, and on the leeward side of clearcuts

The most windfirm trees are young, with well-developed, long crowns and sharply tapering stems. Windfirm sites should be chosen before windfirm trees are chosen.

Clumps of snags and den trees are better than individual snags for withstanding windthrow and providing cover, but they might increase inter- and intraspecific competition for dens (Titus 1983). At least one clump of 15 closely spaced snags over 23 cm dbh should be retained on every 2 ha, with smaller clumps spaced more closely (Raphael and White 1984), or 0.1 ha of clumps per 2 ha of regeneration cuts (Evans and Conner 1979, Chadwick et al. 1986). Other snags can be left in old growth, riparian areas, and other uncut movement corridors (see "Old Growth" in Chap. 4 and "Corridors" and "Riparian Areas" in Chap. 6).

During clearcutting, snags should be left in clumps in draws, or along boundaries between adjacent clearcut areas (Neitro et al. 1985), except where management for interior wildlife requires unfragmented landscape. Such boundaries should be located in the lower one-half to two-thirds of each unit (Neitro et al. 1985). Snags can be more evenly distributed on clearcut units scheduled for tractor yarding on flat to moderate terrain. Snags should be preserved in some clearcuts to serve as perches for raptors and other birds, and to meet food, cover, and other needs for certain other wildlife. Snags should be eliminated in some clearcut areas to eliminate perches for raptors and corvines that would undesirably suppress populations of some ground-dwelling wildlife. Trees left in the interior of clearcuts should be less than 18 m tall.

During partial and intermediate cuts, snags can be more evenly distributed because loggers and machinery can avoid working around trees specified for wildlife habitat. Thinning unevenly throughout the stand will allow natural mortality of unthinned trees to occur, leaving snags (Conner 1978). Directional felling can be used to avoid hitting retained snags. Snags and other wildlife trees can be protected from slash burning by building firelines around them and in some cases by placing fire retardant on the snags before slash burning (Neitro et al. 1985). Such areas can be preburned before lighting the entire unit. Live trees damaged or killed during slash burning or prescribed burns should be left as wildlife trees. Trees left in the middle of clearcuts are least likely to spread fire to the adjacent forest. To retain snags in units to be slash-burned, three burning zones should be established (Fig. 7.10) (Neitro et al. 1985). (See "Prescribed Burns" under "Intermediate Treatment" in Chap. 3.)

State or provincial safety regulations might require removal of snags within 30 to 60 m of roads or other areas of high public use. Safe snags should be retained, especially below roads. Snags above roads are especially susceptible to unauthorized removal by woodcutters. Federal Occupational Safety and Health Administration (OSHA) regulations should be consulted concerning a compromise between snag removal for logging safety and snag retention for snag-dependent wildlife.

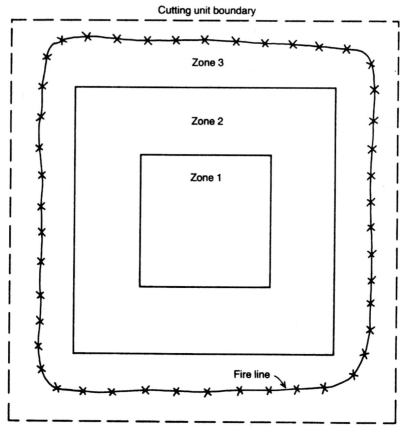

Cutting unit boundary

Zone 3

Zone 2

Zone 1

Fire line

Location	Types of Wildlife Tree	Reason
Zone-1	Best for tall snags, soft or hard	Long distance from fireline
Zone-2	Best for short soft and hard snags	Reduced danger of spot fires
Zone-3	Best for hard or green snags	Green trees don't start spot fires

Figure 7.10 Retention zones for wildlife trees in clearcut units scheduled for slash burning. (*Neitro et al. 1985.*)

Logging systems

Snags and defective live trees should be left around landings if they are windfirm and vertical or lean away, and are unlikely to blow over onto guylines or skylines, or into the landing (Neitro et al. 1985, U.S. Forest Service 1986). With tractor logging, skid trails should be located away from the snag a distance of one-third the height of it and opposite the direction of lean. With helicopter logging, snags of questionable stability, tops, or limbs should be removed where motor down-wash might dislodge them, unless a better landing site can be found.

With highlead and skyline clearcut logging, snag types A and B should be retained between skyline corridors, as well as D and E if less than 6 m tall and stable, and if snags will not be hit by moving lines. Type C and tall trees can be topped. (See "Types of Snags.")

With slackpulling carriages, snag types A, B, and C should be interspersed with leave trees in partial cuts if the snags are stable and have broken tops or sound tops. Snag types D and E should be left between corridors if snags are stable with sound limbs, less than 18 m tall, and will not be hit by moving lines (see Fig. 3.4).

High tree stumps (at least 2 m tall) left during logging operations will provide nesting and foraging sites for some wildlife species (Neitro et al. 1985). Closing roads or restricting firewood cutting to snags less than 20 cm dbh will help protect snags.

Large stick nests indicate raptor nests. During selection cuts, trees with large stick nests should be surrounded by an uncut buffer area of at least 1 chain, and during the nesting season (about April to June) no harvesting should occur within 5 chains of the nest (Krohn and Owen 1988). With clearcuts, a 5-chain buffer should surround all raptor nests, with selective thinning that retains most of the mature trees occurring in the outer 4 chains.

Creating snags artificially

On lands managed intensively for timber, artificially creating snags may be necessary to supplement snag recruitment and retention. Trees can be topped to provide entry for heart rot (Bull et al. 1980). Topping can be done safely with explosives before clearcutting (Bull et al. 1981). Primacord (200 grains) can be wrapped tightly around a tree just above a whorl of limbs so that the limbs are left to support nest construction for ospreys (Habitat Express, January 1983c, U.S. Forest Service Intermountain Region, Ogden, UT). Although experimental, in general the number of wraps is seven for a 25-cm-diameter tree, five for a 15-cm tree, and four for a 10-cm tree.

Snags also can be produced by girdling live trees at least 30 cm dbh; frill girdling and inoculating them with sap rots; or boring and inoculating them with a suitable heart rot fungus at sizes, heights, position, and orientation appropriate for woodpeckers (usually above 3 m) (Conner 1978, Conner et al. 1983c). Some herbicides will kill trees (Conner et al. 1981, McComb and Rumsey 1983). But girdling and herbicides decay trees from the outside in, often causing them to weaken and fall before they become suitable snags (Conner et al. 1983c, Bull and Partridge 1986). Goodell et al. (1986) suggested injecting a fungicide into the phloem of a tree to kill it and preserve the sapwood, after which the fungus inoculation technique can be used to decay the heartwood.

The best method of creating a snag is to climb a live tree, cut the top off 15 to 25 m above the ground, and remove the lower limbs (Bull and Partridge 1986). In some situations creating den trees might be better than creating snags; this can be done by cutting off 10- to 15-cm limbs about 15 cm from the trunk to expose the cut to rain and snow to accelerate decay, or by wounding the bark of a wolf tree of about 10 cm dbh by chopping out a section of bark 15 cm by 15 cm at the base to produce a large tree with a hollow (Decker and Kelley undated, Sanderson 1975, DeGraaf and Shigo 1985).

Holes 5 cm in diameter can be drilled under limbs 8 cm in diameter in snags to facilitate decay and use by wildlife (Decker and Kelley undated). Cavities in live or dead trees for secondary cavity users can be cut with a chain saw (Carey and Gill 1983, Gano and Mosher 1983) modified as described by Carey and Gill (1983) (see Payne 1992:361). Artificial cavities for red-cockaded woodpeckers can be built by drilling into live pines (Fig. 7.11) (Copeyon 1990, Taylor and Hooper 1991). Cavities also can be built by using a chain saw to cut a hole 10 cm wide by 25 cm high by 15 cm deep in a live pine with a diameter of over 38 cm at the height of the hole, and inserting a prefabricated cavity, preferably made from western redcedar, although other long-last-

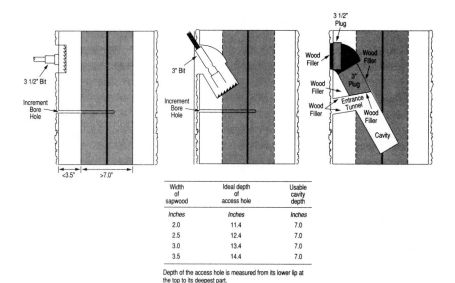

Width of sapwood	Ideal depth of access hole	Usable cavity depth
Inches	*Inches*	*Inches*
2.0	11.4	7.0
2.5	12.4	7.0
3.0	13.4	7.0
3.5	14.4	7.0

Depth of the access hole is measured from its lower lip at the top to its deepest part.

Figure 7.11 Cavity drilled into live pine for red-cockaded woodpeckers. (*Taylor and Hooper 1991.*) [*See metric conversion table.*]

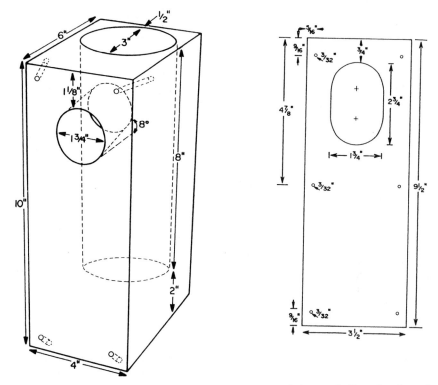

Figure 7.12 Cavity insert (*left*) and restrictor (*right*) for holes cut in live pine for red-cockaded woodpeckers. (*Allen 1991.*) [*See metric conversion table.*]

ing woods also work (Fig. 7.12) (Allen 1991). A cavity restrictor made of stainless steel should be installed to prevent larger woodpeckers from enlarging the entrance hole of the insert (Fig. 7.12) (Allen 1991).

In areas excessively vulnerable to firewood cutters, wildlife trees can be armored by nailing two or three twisted wire fence stays in an offset pattern on the bole (Styskel 1983). These are virtually invisible from a short distance, thus suitable even in visually sensitive areas. They can be seen readily close up. Because killing trees is costly, resulting snags should be protected from woodcutters by attaching the fence stays (Bull and Partridge 1986). Protecting existing snags is better than killing trees to produce a specific number of snags per unit area.

Nesting trees for threatened and endangered species

The U.S. Forest Service uses special management for nest trees of threatened and endangered wildlife such as the red-cockaded wood-pecker and bald eagle (Yoakum et al. 1980). Such management should continue until nest abandonment. The management protocol is as follows:

1. Maintain an inventory of all nest sites and identify in detail the location of each.

2. Check nests periodically and record a cumulative history of nest use.

3. Limit development activities within 5 chains of any nest tree to management measures that help maintain the nesting site.

4. Establish and mark on the ground around each nest site a special buffer zone 10 chains in radius.

5. Within the buffer zone during the period from November 1 to June 15, prohibit timber cutting, timber stand improvement, prescribed burning, road construction, recreation construction, and other intrusive activities.

6. Evaluate critically all practices, such as insecticide spraying, aquatic plant control, and the use of fish toxicants, for their effects on nesting sites within the forest and areas outside the forest but within 0.8 km of the forest's boundary.

7. Reserve three to five old-growth trees as roosting and potential nest trees within the buffer zone surrounding the nest. For red-cockaded woodpeckers, an aggregate of cavity-containing live pines, 25 to 64 cm dbh, 70 to 100 years old, is needed for each colony.

An example of a management plan for bald eagles and golden eagles involves concepts of buffer, territory, and region zones for nesting habitat (Fig. 7.13), and buffer zones for winter habitat (Fig. 7.14) (Stalmaster et al. 1985, Krohn and Owen 1988). With territory zonation, the width of the primary and secondary zones is still generally 100 m and 200 m, respectively, but width decisions are more site-specific. In the primary zone, only those actions essential to protect the site are allowed, and only outside the nesting period. In the secondary zone, selection cuts may be conducted when the birds are not in residence. From 200 to 400 m, high-disturbance activities, such as road construction, harvesting, and site preparation, are prohibited during the nesting period. Recommendations for a rookery of great blue herons are similar. The zoning approach (Fig. 7.14a) is often inadequate to protect nesting territories, and modifications are preferred (Fig. 7.14b, 7.14c).

All forestland within 1.6 km of major water bodies is potential eagle nesting habitat. Best management practices involve a multistoried uneven-aged stand with 20 to 40 percent crown closure on 50 percent of the zone; the stand should be maintained by selective harvest and thinning, with 25 tall potential nest trees at least 240 years

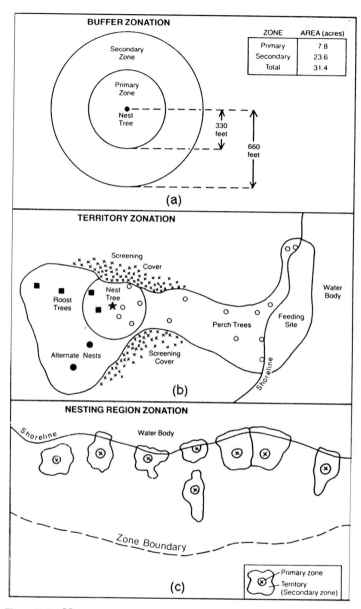

Figure 7.13 Management to protect nesting bald eagles has progressed from the buffer zone concept (*a*), to the territory zone concept (*b*), where all components of the nesting territory are protected by a zone extending beyond the primary buffer zone; the nesting-region zone plan (*c*) encompasses a large habitat area identified for protection and enhancement where multiple eagle nests occur. (*Stalmaster et al. 1985.*) [*For metric equivalence, see metric conversion table in the front of the book.*]

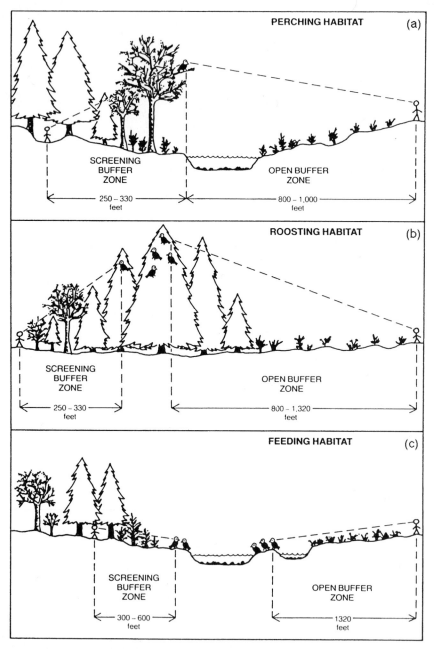

Figure 7.14 Buffer zones for bald eagles should be established to protect winter perching (*a*), roosting (*b*), and feeding (*c*) sites with zone lengths shortened as shown for screening zones if thick vegetative, topographic, or other visual barriers are present. (*Stalmaster et al. 1985.*) [*For metric equivalence, see metric conversion table in the front of the book.*]

old and 97 cm dbh left standing per hectare (in western North America). Logging should not occur in roosting areas unless it maintains or enhances the area. No logging should occur in or next to wintering areas when occupied by eagles.

Coarse Woody Debris

Under successive cycles of clearcutting in forests of coastal Oregon, the amount of coarse woody debris is predicted to decrease by 30 percent of the preharvest level at the end of the first 100-year rotation, and 6 percent after the second (Spies and Cline 1988). Thus, the amount of coarse woody debris is lower in managed than in unmanaged forests. This is because most snags and fallen trees are removed from the harvest site and because harvest truncates structural development before large amounts of coarse woody debris can accumulate (Hansen et al. 1991). More coarse woody debris is produced by high-severity than low-severity disturbances. Snags and live culls will add to future log recruitment if snag management is an objective of a stand (Eubanks 1989) (See "Snags and Live Den Trees" in this chapter).

Logs can be classified into five classes based on extent of decomposition (Table 7.7, and see Fig. 7.9) (Maser et al. 1979a, Maser and Trappe 1984, Bartels et al. 1985). A log goes through "internal succession" as it decays, and "external succession" as the surrounding plant community changes (Harmon et al. 1986). Internal succession, i.e., rate of decay, of a log is influenced by the tree species, its size, what killed the tree, origination as live tree or snag, placement on ground, surrounding microclimate, and associated biotic community (Maser and Trappe 1984). Various wildlife species are associated with each log class. Larger logs have more wildlife potential. For wildlife needs, management should consider the species composition of the timber stand, diameter of the trees, density of the trees, number and decay classes of logs on the ground, number and condition of snags, speed with which a new stand of trees can become established and reach a diameter of 30 to 43 cm (Maser et al. 1979a), and number and condition of tip-ups (blown-down trees with root wads). (Also see "Riparian Areas" in Chap. 6.)

Whole-tree harvesting has detrimental and beneficial effects on wildlife. Slash provides cover for big game, insects, small mammals, birds, and associated predators. But slash also hampers movement of big game. And slash deters tree-seedling production and survival by screening seedlings from sunlight and causing increased production of rodents, which eat seeds and seedlings.

Unnaturally high accumulation of logs and slash, i.e., dead and down woody material, can be detrimental in any habitat type. The general guideline is to retain or produce an amount distributed in a fashion similar to a naturally occurring accumulation of coarse woody debris.

TABLE 7.7   A Five-Class System of Log Decomposition Based on Work Done on Douglas-Fir

Log charac- teristic	Log decomposition class				
	1	2	3	4	5
Bark	Intact	Intact	Trace	Absent	Absent
Twigs <3 cm	Present	Absent	Absent	Absent	Absent
Texture	Intact	Intact to partly soft	Hard, large pieces	Small, soft blocky pieces	Soft and powdery
Shape	Round	Round	Round	Round to oval	Oval
Color of wood	Original color	Original color	Original color to faded	Light brown to faded brown or yellowish	Faded to light yellow or gray
Portion of log on ground	Log elevated on support points	Log elevated on support points but sagging slightly	Log is sagging near ground	All of log on ground	All of log on ground

SOURCE: Maser et al. (1979a).

At least five uncharred class 1 or 2 logs per hectare, and all other logs, should be retained. Ideally, logs should be from all tree species and at least 30 to 43 cm in diameter at the large end and 6 m or more long. They should lie perpendicular to slopes. Stable logs with one end in a stream should be retained. During logging, care should be taken to avoid shattering class 4 and 5 logs with heavy equipment, to reduce or eliminate removal of class 1 and 2 logs for salvage or firewood, and to avoid bunching or aligning class 3 logs along the direction of skidding (Maser and Trappe 1984). Some trees can be pulled down mechanically to create tip-ups (Crow et al. 1993). Logs do not need to be uniformly distributed. Some areas could be cleared for fire lanes, fuel breaks, or other human access; other areas could have a high density of logs.

Yarding of unmerchantable material should be reduced or eliminated (Eubanks 1989). Slash should be retained for cover on 10 percent of clearcuts (Dimock 1974, Garrison and Smith 1974, Pierovich et al. 1975, Maser et al. 1979a, Bartels et al. 1985), in 5 to 10 loose piles per hectare (Larson et al. 1986) to break long sight distances and provide cover in critical areas (Thomas et al. 1979b). Slash should be no higher than 20 cm on at least 75 percent of an area important for forage production for big game. Continuous concentrations of slash higher than 15 cm above ground or larger than 8 cm in diameter should be avoided to facilitate movement of big game. Chips from wood-chipping machines should be scattered less than 2.5 cm deep. Windrowed slash should not force big game more than 70 m away from established trails. Otherwise, breaks 3 m wide should be provided every 60 m or less. Slash should not be windrowed at right angles to a road because this practice facilitates shooting of big game by hunters and poachers.

Slash is often burned to remove a potential fire hazard and facilitate reforestation. In some clearcuts, slash and shrubs should be eliminated by burning to return nutrients to the soil, to reduce cover for microtines and their predation on tree seeds, and to promote early successional wildlife associated with the grass/forb stage. Some slash might be needed to reduce erosion. Logs can be retained best if burning occurs in the spring before winter moisture is lost, or after extended precipitation (Bartels et al. 1985), which also protects root systems of forage species. Fire retardants can be applied around logs, or readily combustible fuels can be raked away. (See "Prescribed Burns" in Chap. 3.)

Water Holes

Water holes about 0.2 ha in area and 1.8 to 2.7 m deep should be developed throughout dry forest areas at about 0.4 per square kilometer (Halls et al. 1984); the exception is on ungulate wintering range, where water might encourage animals to remain throughout summer, thus resulting in overuse of the site (Green and Salter 1987). Springs and seeps should be protected from cattle and logging, and perhaps developed for wildlife by cutting all trees at least 20 m back from them and removing all slash from the seep and clearing, leaving uncut all food-producing shrubs and small trees, and locating logging haul roads at least 50 m away (Wunz et al. 1983). The best seeps have consistent flows, a surface area greater than 40 m^2, a pH near neutral or above, and relatively high soil fertility. (See "Springs and Seeps" in Chap. 13.)

Livestock Pastures

Forests managed for interior or for edge wildlife should not be grazed by cattle due to the relative paucity of herbaceous cover typical of most forests; the competition with wildlife for the ground and shrub layers that provide cover and forage; the elimination of reproduction of the ground, shrub, and canopy layers through grazing, browsing, rubbing, and trampling of plants, and compaction of the soil; and pos-

sible type conversion of the forest due to survival only of tree
seedlings unpalatable to cattle. If grazing occurs, it should occur at
competitive prices rather than prices subsidized by the public; higher
prices will reduce demand and therefore reduce grazing pressure.
Cattle grazing should be allotted after measurement of forage and
allocation to wildlife have been made. Such allocation and allotment
require careful supervision and control. In general, livestock grazing
should occur between June 15 and September 15 to allow development of nesting cover in spring and residual nesting cover in late
summer and early fall for the following spring. The U.S. Soil
Conservation Service recommends that livestock pastured during the
growing season should remove less than 50 percent of the annual
herbage produced, based on the key grasses and forbs eaten. During
the dormant season, at least 35 percent of the key grasses, forbs, and
browse species within reach should be left ungrazed and unbrowsed.
Grazing by cattle and big game can reduce competitive impacts of
understory vegetation and thus benefit regeneration of trees in some
situations (Krueger 1983); however, cattle should not compete for forage needed by wildlife. Standard controlled grazing practices should
be used (Graham et al. 1992). (See "Controlled Grazing" in Chap. 10,
"Riparian Areas" in Chap. 6, and Payne 1992).

Savanna

One of the most threatened upland habitats in North America is the
savanna. There are two major reasons for this: one is that savanna
can be converted readily to agriculture and other uses but cannot be
recovered readily because of the long time needed to establish the
large, scattered trees; the other is that unconverted savanna has been
invaded by shrubs from fire suppression (Haney and Apfelbaum
1990). High-quality oak savannas are among the rarest ecosystems in
North America, comprising perhaps about 0.02 percent of their original extent (Nuzzo 1986). The most important management practice is
simply to preserve and protect existing savanna from human
encroachment, including overgrazing of livestock.

Savanna can be defined as transition land between forestland and
grassland, with at least 2.5 trees per hectare but less than 50 percent
canopy closure (Curtis 1959). Savanna includes land such as oak barrens and pine barrens. Savanna exists from repeated natural disturbance, mainly fire, which eliminates encroaching brush to maintain
the grass/forb stage with scattered thick-barked trees such as oak
that can withstand fire. Thus, a periodic prescribed burn (about every
3 to 5 year) is the most effective, efficient, and economical technique
for maintenance. Young replacement oaks might need protection from
fire by raking fuel at least 3 m away from them or applying a fire

retardant around them. (See "Prescribed Burns" in Chap. 3 and Chap. 10, and Payne 1992.) Controlled grazing of livestock is also useful. (See "Controlled Grazing" in Chap. 10.) Selective cutting of encroaching shrubs and undesirable trees can be combined with spot treatment of the stumps with herbicide to prevent sprouting.

Oak savannas in excellent condition, with few shade-tolerant trees and shrubs, should be burned every 3 to 5 years (Haney et al. 1993). Large savannas should be divided into at least two burn units, with each unit burned a different year. Spring and summer fires tend to discourage exotic plants and cool-season grasses more than fall fires do. Hot fires are needed to reduce the shrub layer.

Oak savannas in good condition have less than 20 to 50 percent canopy closure, but the larger oaks are dying. After a hot fire or several less intense fires, burning should be suspended for 10 to 15 years or until the newly recruited oak sprouts are 5 cm dbh. The savanna should be burned with a series of light to moderate burns when the young oaks have a density of one tree per 10 m^2, reducing the density to one tree per 100 m^2 or so. Then the savanna is burned every 3 to 5 years.

Oak savannas in fair condition have more of a shrub layer and many nonsavanna species in the herb layer, which should be eliminated or reduced with several successive fall burns after leaf fall adds fuel. When the canopy is opened to 50 percent or more and most exotic herbs are eliminated, maintenance burning every 3 to 5 years can be done.

Because of dense understory shading, oak savannas in poor condition often have insufficient fire fuels to carry a fire. Mechanical and chemical removal might be needed. Wick application of Garlon 4 or other suitable herbicide on stumps will prevent resprouting (see Chaps. 3 and 9). The savanna should be burned in spring. Excessive coarse woody debris unnatural to a savanna might need to be removed. Mechanical and chemical spot treatment still might be needed. Fire should be used annually until most undesirable vegetation is removed. Then planting with seeds—preferably from a nearby donor savanna, or alternatively from a local commercial source—might be necessary, perhaps with standard site preparation. Seed should be spread in fall so that freezing and thawing will work it into the soil. Then a spring fire will not destroy it. Annual burns are needed to control nonsavanna species until native species reestablish, when a maintenance fire regime (every 3 to 5 years) can be used.

Caves, Cliffs, and Talus

Caves provide a more stable environment of moisture and temperature than most terrestrial habitats do (Scharpf and Dobler 1985). Various wildlife species use them for roosting, perching, breeding, nesting, shelter, and hibernation. Coastal cliffs often are used by

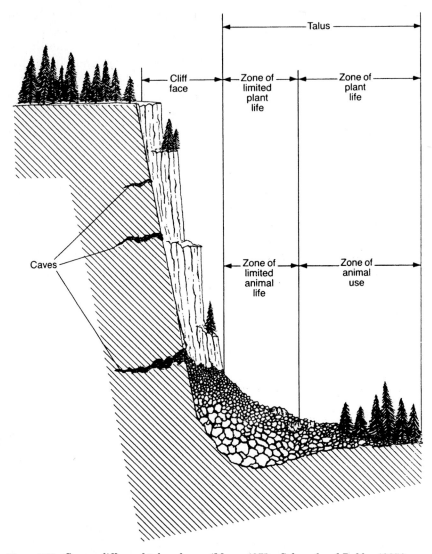

Figure 7.15 Caves, cliffs, and talus slopes. (*Maser 1979c, Scharpf and Dobler 1985.*)

spectacular numbers of seabirds. Caves can be (1) shallow caves and ledges, (2) cliff-face caves, (3) lava tubes and water-eroded underground caves, or (4) abandoned mine shafts and railroad tunnels (Maser et al. 1979b, 1979c, Scharpf and Dobler 1985). Cliffs can be classified by size (height and length) (Maser et al. 1979c).

The accumulation of dislodged rock fragments at the base of cliffs or other steep slopes is called *talus* (Fig. 7.15) (Maser et al. 1979c,

Scharpf and Dobler 1985). Taluslike structures of similar wildlife habitat include lava stringers, collapsed lava tubes, hardrock mine tailings, roadside and railroad fill, and riprap along streambanks and elsewhere. Class of talus is based on the most common diameter of rock: (1) less than 0.5 m, (2) 0.5 to 1 m, (3) 1 to 2 m, (4) 2 m or larger. Class of talus influences the spaces between rocks or the flatness of the topography that can accommodate various-sized animals as burrows, cover, or observation fields (Brown 1985). Talus slopes vary in steepness, class of talus, and wildlife.

Little or nothing beyond protection can be done to manage unique, fragile habitats such as caves, cliffs, and talus (Maser et al. 1979c). Caves might need to be sealed with gates to protect bats and other wildlife from vandals (Henderson 1987). Removal of adjacent timber should be avoided, as alterations could occur in light intensity, wind currents, temperature, drainage patterns, humidity, and food sources (Scharpf and Dobler 1985). Adjacent plant communities should be stabilized. Spelunking and rock climbing should be regulated. Incursion of roads, railroads, powerlines, mines, etc., into fragile or unique habitats should be avoided; these uses should be located in the poorest-quality habitat insofar as possible.

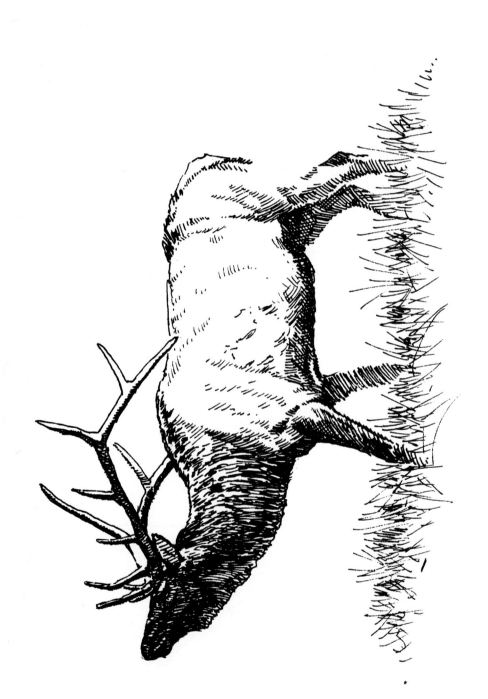

Rangelands

8

Types of
Rangeland and
General Management

Vegetation and community types on rangelands in the western United States and Canada have been classified in numerous ways by numerous authors during the past century (see Johnson et al. 1980, Kerr 1986, Short 1986). Vegetation classification and mapping have involved floristic, structural, hierarchical, and classless systems. This discussion of wildlife habitat management focuses on rangeland vegetation types as delineated by Holechek et al. (1989), and, to a lesser extent, Cooperrider et al. (1986) and Küchler (1964) (Fig. 8.1).

Rangelands are lands where the dominant potential vegetation is mainly native grasses, grasslike plants, forbs, and/or shrubs. Generally, rangelands are more suitable for management by ecological than by agronomic practices. Thus they encompass all uncultivated lands which provide forage and habitats for livestock and wildlife. Holechek et al. (1989) included forests in their definition of rangeland types; we combine grazable forests and mountain meadows into forestlands, which we discuss in Part 1 of this volume (and see Payne 1992). We separate forestlands from rangelands because of cultural practices associated with forests and their value as commercial sawtimber. Notable exceptions in this book are grazable woodlands, i.e., pinyon-juniper, oak, chaparral, mountain shrub, and mesquite-acacia woodland types, where fuelwood is sometimes harvested. We consider these as important woodland vegetation types of rangelands. In summary, we include four broad vegetation categories: grasslands, tun-

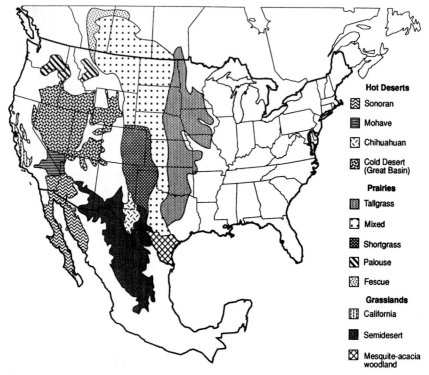

Figure 8.1   Deserts, prairies, and grasslands of North American rangelands. (*Cooperrider et al. 1986, Holechek et al. 1989, Coupland 1992.*)

dra, shrublands, and woodlands, separated into 15 major vegetative types (Table 8.1).

Generalizing habitat management is difficult within highly variable rangeland vegetation types, especially those in arid to semiarid climates, because many exceptions exist. Management goals, objectives, and techniques are usually site-specific, as are plant and animal responses to interventions and human-induced perturbations.

Grasslands

Grasslands occur in an environment with irregularities in weather patterns. Abnormal wet or dry spells occur often enough to impose severe stresses on wildlife. In a drought year, for example, reduced precipitation, higher than average temperatures, and increased wind movement occur, producing greater evapotranspiration. "Boom or bust" cycles in quail populations are a classic example of the wildlife response.

TABLE 8.1 Rangeland Vegetation Types and Communities of the Western United States and Canada: The Present Extent of Distribution, and Dominant Genera

Category/ vegetation type	Area (millions of ha)	Primary herbaceous genera	Primary woody genera
Grasslands			
Tallgrass prairie	15	Sorghastrum, Panicum, Andropogon, Schizachyrium	Artemisia, Rhus
Northern mixed prairie	30	Festuca, Buchloe, Agropyron, Poa, Stipa, Elymus	Quercus, Prosopis, Juniperus
Southern mixed prairie	20	Bothriochloa, Stipa, Bouteloua	Prosopis, Artemisia, Rhus
Shortgrass prairie	20	Bouteloua, Buchloe	Artemisia, Eriogonum
California annual grasslands	3	Stipa, Avena, Bromus, Hordeum	Artemisia, Rosa
Palouse prairie	3	Festuca, Agropyron	Prosopis, Acacia, Larrea, Celtis
Semidesert grasslands	15	Hilaria, Bouteloua, Aristida, Bothriochloa	
Tundra			
Canada	240	Carex, Selaginella, Cladonia, Eriophorum, Poa	Salix
United States	76	Carex, Selaginella, Cladonia, Eriophorum, Poa	Salix
Shrublands			
Cold deserts (Great Basin)	73	Agropyron, Sitanion, Festuca, Elymus	Artemisia, Purshia, Chrysothamnus
(Sagebrush community)	(56)		
(Saltbush community)	(17)	Hilaria, Sitanion, Oryzopsis	Artiplex, Eurotia, Sarcobatus
Hot deserts (Mojave, Sonoran, Chihuahuan)	30		
(Creosote community)	(26)	Hilaria, Oryzopsis, Bouteloua, Aristida	Larrea, Acacia, Prosopis
(Blackbush community)	(1)	Hilaria	Coleogyne, Artemisia
(Paloverde-cactus-bursage community)	(3)	Aristida, Bouteloua	Cercidium, Ambrosia, Mimosa, Acacia, Prosopis
Woodlands			
Pinyon-juniper	17	Agropyron, Oryzopsis, Elymus	Juniperus, Artemisia, Pinus, Purshia
Oak; scrub oak (shinnery and Gambel)	16	Site specific	Quercus
Chaparral	13	Bromus, Stipa, Poa	Arctostaphylos, Quercus, Ceanothus, Adenostoma
Mountain shrub	?	Bromus, Stipa, Festuca	Prunus, Purshia, Cercocarpus, Ceanothus
Mesquite-acacia	7	Schizachyrium, Panicum, Stipa	Prosopis, Acacia

SOURCE: Adapted from Kuchler (1964), Cooperrider et al. (1986), Institute for Land Rehabilitation (1978), Holechek et al. (1989).

TABLE 8.2   Relative Bird Richness and Densities of Several Rangeland Vegetation Types

Community	Species present (N/4.6-ha plot)	Population density (pairs/40 ha)
Alpine tundra	3 or 4	15–20
Saltbush	3 or 4	15–20
Creosotebush	3 or 4	15–20
Grassland	5 ±	25–100
Sagebrush	10–12	50–100
Paloverde-cactus-bursage	10–12	50–100
Chaparral	10–12	50–100
Pinyon-juniper	20 ±	40–80

SOURCE: Johnson et al. (1980).

Except for alpine tundra and two shrubland communities (saltbush of cold deserts and creosotebush of hot deserts), grasslands generally have the lowest bird richness and densities of the rangeland types (Table 8.2) (Johnson et al. 1980). Thus, grassland bird communities are small assemblages of species of broadly distributed forms (Wiens and Dyer 1975). Standing herbaceous biomass of grasslands is greater than other major vegetation types, but the vegetation is simple floristically and physiognomically.

The Palouse prairie, the semidesert grasslands, and the California grasslands historically did not have much animal impact from large herbivores, although they might have been present. The remaining major grassland communities evolved with substantial impact from large herbivores like American bison; thus they are resilient when grazed (Table 8.3) (Holechek et al. 1989). Other rangeland community types vary in their resiliency to grazing. How resilient these communities are or how soon they recover from overgrazing might sug-

TABLE 8.3   Resiliency of Rangeland Communities to Grazing

Resilient*	Moderate resilience†	Low resilience‡
Tallgrass prairie	Mountain shrub	Palouse prairie
Northern mixed prairie	Oak woodland	Pinyon-juniper
Southern mixed prairie	Chaparral	Cold desert
Shortgrass prairie	Chihuahuan semi-	Hot desert
Mesquite-acacia woodland	desert grasslands	Tundra
	California grassland	Sonoran semidesert grasslands

*Resilient = will recover from overgrazing within 3 to 10 years.
†Moderate resilience = will recover from overgrazing within 10 to 30 years.
‡Low resilience = over 30 years before any substantial recovery from overgrazing; some locations show no recovery after 50 years.
SOURCE: Adapted from Holechek et al. (1989).

TABLE 8.4   Rangeland Communities and Their Tolerance to Fire

Tolerant*	Moderate tolerance†	Low tolerance‡
Tallgrass prairie	Shortgrass prairie	Cold desert
Northern mixed prairie	California annual grassland	Hot desert
Southern mixed prairie	Pinyon-juniper	Alpine tundra
Chaparral	Mountain shrub	Arctic tundra
Palouse prairie		Semidesert grasslands
Oak woodland		
Mesquite-acacia woodland		

*Tolerant = interval between fire and recovery is 2 to 5 years.
†Moderate tolerance = interval between fire and recovery is 5 to 15 years.
‡Low tolerance = interval between fire and recovery is 20 to 80 years.

gest the relative role of livestock and the importance of their presence in managing rangeland habitats. In some rangeland communities, their presence is questionable; in others, livestock are needed as a disturbance agent and could be an important, cost-effective management tool. Because grasslands evolved with fire, their relative tolerance to burning is greatly influenced by historical frequency. Some rangeland communities burned often; others burned less often and are less tolerant of fire (Table 8.4).

Classification systems usually refer to "potential natural vegetation," which causes confusion because habitats are managed based on existing, not potential, vegetation. For example, today the southern mixed prairie of Texas' Edwards Plateau has a woodland overstory dominated by live oak, juniper, or both. The same southern mixed prairie in Texas' Rolling Plains might have a woodland overstory dominated by mesquite. Therefore the direction of habitat management should not always be toward a return to prehistoric natural vegetation. Optimum habitat management for these two "prairie" regions might not mean a return to a domination of mid-grass vegetation, but instead would retain some of the overstory as thermal or hiding cover for deer or old-growth juniper as nesting habitat for an endangered species, such as the golden-cheeked warbler.

Tundra

Tundra refers to a treeless vegetation type in arctic or high-elevation (greater than 2800 m) regions (Figs. 8.2 and 8.3) (Lent 1986). Because the soil might be frozen to a depth of 1 to 2 m for as long as 7 months of the year, low-growing, herbaceous perennial plants, mosses and lichens, and prostrate shrubs dominate. In the United States, most tundra is in Alaska. About 51 percent (39 million ha) is arctic tundra, 45 percent (35 million ha) is alpine tundra. The remaining 4 percent

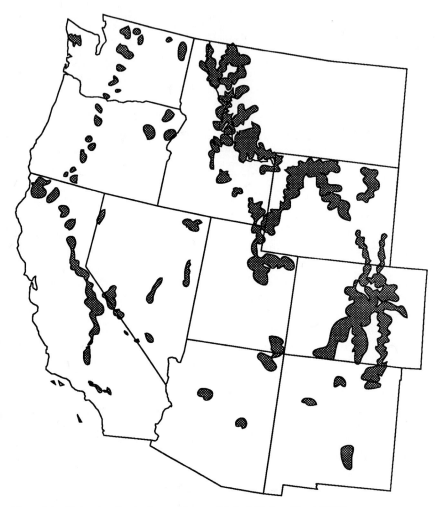

Figure 8.2 Alpine tundra in the contiguous United States. (*Lent 1986.*)

or 3 million ha of alpine tundra occurs in the lower 48 states (Fig. 8.2). Canada has about 240 million ha of tundra (Klein 1970). Fundamental ecological differences exist between arctic and alpine tundra. All tundra is fragile and not resilient to overgrazing, or tolerant of fire (see Tables 8.3 and 8.4).

Shrublands

Cold deserts

Shrublands include habitat in cold and hot deserts (see Table 8.1). *Cold deserts,* referred to by some authors as the *Great Basin* or *shrub-*

Figure 8.3 Tundra (stippled) in Canada and Alaska. (*Bailey 1984, Lent 1986.*)

steppe, might be dominated by shrubs such as sagebrush (Fig. 8.4) or saltbush; sagebrush usually occurs at higher elevations than saltbush, which dominates the salt desert shrub type (Fig. 8.5). Blackbrush also has been included in the cold desert type. These cold desert associations recover slowly from abusive grazing, but control of big sagebrush speeds recovery of grasses in sagebrush vegetation types (Holechek et al. 1989).

Hot deserts

Hot deserts include vegetation types and associations in the Mohave, Chihuahuan, and Sonoran (including the Arizona Upland subdivision and the Lower Colorado subdivision) deserts. Many vegetation subtypes occur in these deserts. The Mohave Desert has lower floral diversity and richness than the Chihuahuan Desert. The Sonoran, especially the Arizona Upland subdivision, is rich in flora because it is virtually frost-free and some areas have adequate (73 cm) precipitation. The Lower Colorado subdivision of the Sonoran Desert is relatively low in diversity. All hot deserts are fragile in their response to overgrazing or fire (see Tables 8.3 and 8.4). Hot deserts did not evolve with grazing pressure by large herbivores, except for scattered popu-

Figure 8.4 Distribution of sagebrush types. (*Holechek et al. 1989, Branson et al. 1967.*)

lations of mule deer, pronghorns, or bighorn sheep. Fuel loads are relatively low, so fire frequency was low.

Many current shrublands were formerly grasslands or a mix of
shrubs and grasses, according to numerous historic reports, diaries,
and other records. Disagreement exists regarding causes of these
changes to shrublands; overgrazing, climatic shifts, fire suppression,
and seed dissemination by domestic animals are proposed agents.
Because vegetation of hot deserts apparently did not evolve with
heavy grazing by large ungulates, overgrazing by livestock at the
turn of this century had a major impact. Recovery from overgrazing is

slow and the consequence of abuse is severe. Livestock grazing is not practical over much of the Mohave and Sonoran deserts, but it will continue to be an important land use in the Chihuahuan Desert (Holechek et al. 1989).

Woodlands

Sometimes referred to as *pigmy conifer woodland,* the *pinyon-juniper vegetation type* is found mainly in Utah, New Mexico, Nevada, Arizona, and Colorado; but California, Oregon, Idaho, and Texas also contain pinyon and/or juniper (Fig. 8.6). This woodland occurs on at

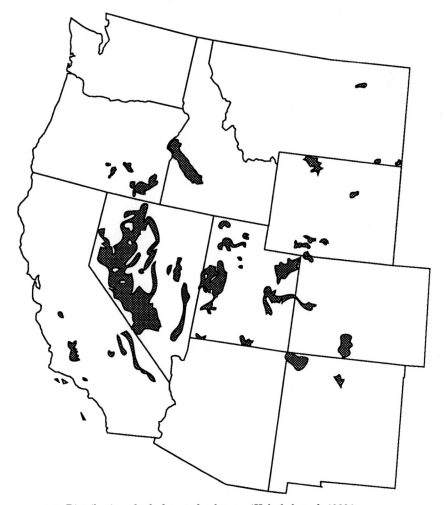

Figure 8.5 Distribution of salt desert shrub type. (*Holechek et al. 1989.*)

Figure 8.6 Distribution of the pinyon-juniper type. (*Holechek et al. 1989.*)

least 17 million ha (see Table 8.1); it is best developed at elevations of
1500 to 2100 m, but some trees can occur as low as 900 m or above
2700 m. Other estimates of distribution vary from 19 million ha
(Evans 1988) to 30.7 million ha (Terrell and Spillet 1975) to 32.5 million ha (West et al. 1975, Institute of Land Rehabilitation 1978).
Foliar ground cover can be as great as 60 percent, with juniper domi-
nating lower elevations and xeric sites; the percentage of pinyon pine
usually increases with elevation. Pinyon-juniper often overlaps at ecotones with other rangeland vegetation types, including sagebrush,
saltbush, Gambel oak, and chaparral–mountain shrub types. Its history has been punctuated by overuse by livestock and suppression of

fire; encroachment into grasslands and foothills and increased density of trees have resulted. Although amounts of herbaceous forage are generally low, pinyon-juniper remains a valuable habitat for wintering large ungulates, a resource for recreationists, and a source of fence posts, fuelwood, pulpwood, and Christmas trees.

Oak woodlands include shinnery oak (1.4 million ha) in Oklahoma, Texas, and eastern New Mexico; Gambel oak (3.75 million ha) in the Rocky Mountains; oak savanna of California and Oregon; and the Madrean Evergreen woodlands of southern Arizona. The latter was described as the "ecological metropolis" of the Coues deer (Severson and Medina 1983). We include post oak savanna of Texas and Oklahoma and the live oak savanna of Texas' Edwards Plateau as components of the tallgrass or southern mixedgrass prairies. Oak woodlands vary in their importance to wildlife, but all provide mast, browse, thermal and hiding cover, and nest and perch sites. Oaks generally are fire-tolerant. Oak woodlands are moderately used by livestock.

Because of the confusing chaparral types, chaparral in California and Arizona is treated separately from the mountain shrub vegetation type. *California chaparral* refers to dense stands of shrubby plants dominated by broadleaf and narrowleaf nondeciduous species (Vallentine 1989). Most are vigorous sprouters. Chapparal occurs in foothills and is also mixed with woodlands at higher elevations. Common species are chamise, ceanothus, California scrub oak, interior live oak, and manzanita. Regenerative characteristics include prolific seed production, rhizomes, and sprouting from crowns following top-kill. Arizona interior chaparral is dominated by species such as shrub live oak, pointleaf manzanita, Wright silktassel, mountainmahogany, and skunkbush.

Mountain shrub woodlands tend to be transition zones between foothills and forestlands. Thus they have scattered distribution, rendering their area of occurrence difficult to determine. Mountain shrub woodlands of the Rocky Mountains contain an array of many important low-growing (1 to 10 m tall), woody species such as mountainmahogany, bitterbrush, willow, maple, serviceberry, chokecherry, snowberry, elderberry, currant, squawbush, and buckbrush. They are important to mule deer and elk.

Mesquite is a dominant tree or shrub in semidesert grasslands and southern mixed prairie vegetation types, but it occurs as the mesquite-acacia woodland in the southern tip of Texas. Severe brush encroachment has occurred in the past century, and its density sometimes makes this brush thicket impenetrable. Habitat management usually favors wildlife species such as white-tailed deer, northern bobwhite quail, and Rio Grande turkey.

TABLE 8.5 Rangeland Practices and Their Potential‡ as Tools in Wildlife Habitat Management

	Controlled grazing		Woody plant control			Cultural practices		
	Strategic grazing*	Environmental protective grazing†	Fire	Mechanical	Herbicide	Disking	Reseeding	Fertilizing
Grasslands and tundra								
Tallgrass prairie	Yes	Yes	+	−	−	+	0	+
Northern mixed prairie	Yes	Yes	+	−	−	0	0	0
Southern mixed prairie	Yes	Yes	+	+	−	+	0	−
Shortgrass prairie		Yes	0	+	−	0	0	−
California annual grassland		Yes	0	0	−	0	0	−
Palouse prairie		Yes	0	0	−	0	0	−
Semidesert grassland		Yes	0	0	−	−	0	−
Alpine tundra		Yes	−	−	−	−	−	−
Arctic tundra		Yes	−	−	−	−	−	−
Shrublands								
Cold desert		Yes	0	0	−	−	+	−
Hot desert		Yes	−	0	−	−	+	−
Woodlands								
Pinyon-juniper	Yes	Yes	+	+	0	−	+	−
Oak	Yes	Yes	+	+	0	0	0	−
California chaparral	Yes	Yes	+	+	0	0	0	−
Mountain shrub	Yes	Yes	0	+	0	−	+	−
Mesquite-acacia	Yes	Yes	+	+	+	+	+	0

*Strategic grazing = livestock are used as a manipulative tool to create specific habitat conditions.
†Environmental protective grazing = livestock are cautiously managed and strictly controlled to protect fragile environments and prevent overuse of wildlife habitats.
‡+ = good potential; 0 = moderate potential; − = low potential

Rangeland Management Practices:
An Overview

Of all the habitat-management techniques used on rangelands today, only two occurred as natural components in ecosystem development: herbivory and fire. Cultural practices used include mechanical tree or shrub removal, herbicides, seeding, and fertilizing. Their relative value as habitat-management techniques varies with vegetation type (Table 8.5). In an attempt to reclaim and improve rangeland habitats, cultural practices have been necessary mostly because new stable states have been reached. Climate change, excessive herbivory, and/or fire changes in impact or frequency commonly are attributed to vegetation changes in rangeland ecosystems. Fire's impact was reduced directly through active suppression or indirectly through loss of herbaceous fuel to carry a fire.

In the following chapters, we present these six practices as potential techniques for rangeland-habitat management. Integrative management, i.e., using a variety of techniques (grazing, prescribed burning, mowing, herbicides) in sequential or spatial pattern or design to accomplish habitat objectives, was beyond the scope of this book. Such detailed planning is intimately site-specific, extremely complex, and requires creativity and a thorough understanding of the potential plant responses to each technique.

9

Rangeland Management Techniques: Mechanical, Chemical, and Seeding

Mechanical Treatments

Over the past five decades, philosophies regarding woody plant conversions evolved from eradication to control to management (Scifres 1980b), and more recently to integrated-management systems (Scifres 1986). Changing attitudes have been shaped by the elevated status of wildlife in the planning process.

For wildlife habitat management, in many shrubland and woodland vegetation types, total conversion and total protection rarely produce abundant, diverse fauna, although total protection is needed for some parts of all habitat types. For example, eradication of woody plants will have adverse effects on obligate species (Table 9.1), species needing structural and floral diversity, species needing hiding or thermal cover, or obligate interior species that need untreated stands of shrublands or woodlands. At the other extreme, dense, closed canopies of woody plants, succulents, shrubs, or noxious weeds over expansive areas might not promote optimum biodiversity because edge species need openings created in such stands. Prudent, well-designed mechanical treatments should be considered in habitat management. One management goal should involve a mosaic of patches in different stages of disturbance, successional recovery, and community maturation. Another goal should involve expansive habitat types. All management should mimic natural processes and habitat regimes.

TABLE 9.1   Examples of Typical Bird Species and Obligate Wildlife Dependent on Woody Plants in Some Rangeland Habitats

Vegetation type	Typical breeding species	Obligate or near-obligate species	Woody plants important to obligate species
Grasslands			
Tallgrass prairie	Prairie chicken Sharp-tailed grouse Meadowlark Horned lark Grasshopper sparrow Upland sandpiper		
Mixed prairie	Horned lark Savannah sparrow Vesper sparrow Meadowlark Lark bunting	Golden-cheeked warbler Black-capped vireo	Ashe juniper, live oak Shinnery oak, live oak, sumac, Texas persimmon
Shortgrass prairie	Burrowing owl Lark bunting Scaled quail Horned lark Meadowlark Cassin's sparrow Rufous-crowned sparrow Sharp-tailed grouse		
Alpine tundra	Water pipit Horned lark Rosy finch		
Shrublands			
Cold desert		Brewer's sparrow Vesper sparrow Sage grouse Sage sparrow Sage thrasher Piute ground squirrel	Sagebrush Sagebrush Sagebrush Sagebrush Sagebrush Sagebrush
Hot desert Mohave	Gambel's quail Roadrunner Lecoute's thrasher Scott's oriole		
Chihuahuan	Roadrunner Ladderback woodpecker		

TABLE 9.1   Examples of Typical Bird Species and Obligate Wildlife Dependent on Woody Plants in Some Rangeland Habitats   (Continued)

Vegetation type	Typical breeding species	Obligate or near-obligate species	Woody plants important to obligate species
Sonoran			
Paloverde-cacti	Elf owl Costa's hummingbird Verdin Cactus wren Curve-billed thrasher		
Creosotebush	Roadrunner Verdin Lecoute's thrasher Mockingbird Pyrrhuloxia Black-throated sparrow		
Woodlands			
Pinyon-juniper		Scrub jay	Pinyon pine/juniper
		Gray flycatcher	Pinyon pine/juniper
		Screech owl	Pinyon pine/juniper
		Plain titmouse	Pinyon pine/juniper
		Gray vireo	Pinyon pine/juniper
		Wrentit	Pinyon pine/juniper
California chaparral	Black-throated gray warbler		
Gambel oak (northern Utah)	Blue-gray gnatcatcher Black-headed grosbeak Lazuli bunting Rufous-sided towhee		
Mountain brush	Scrub jay Bushtit Rufous-sided towhee Blue-gray gnatcatcher		

SOURCE: Johnson et al. 1980, Harper et al. 1985, Coupland 1992.

To evaluate mechanical treatment, a wide array of factors must be considered (Table 9.2). Also, because of aesthetics, landscape design should become a fundamental component in planning rangeland conversion projects (Forman and Godron 1986, Rodiek and Bolen 1991). Kinds of equipment to use is another consideration. Range Seeding and Equipment Committee (1970), Roby and Green (1976), Brown (1977), Larson (1980), Scifres (1980b), Long et al. (1984), Payne and Copes (1988), Vallentine (1989), and others have provided details on the many kinds of equipment used in mechanical manipulation of rangeland habitats. Inter- and multidisciplinary planning is the key to successful projects.

In general, patches of treated and untreated areas are recommended for edge species of wildlife (Fig. 9.1); large, unfragmented, and untreated areas are best for interior wildlife species. The distribution, pattern, and structural heterogeneity that woody plants provide remains the critical factor for wildlife. Woody draws, ravines, rough ridges, and shallow, rocky sites are best left untreated. Deer use wooded areas on northwesterly exposures in summer and southern exposures in winter (Vallentine 1989); these sites might remain untreated. Treatments at or along riparian zones usually are not recommended (see Chap. 6). Certain rangeland vegetation types do not lend themselves to mechanical treatments (see Chap. 8).

Mechanical treatment can have several objectives: (1) control or remove existing or undesirable vegetation; (2) disrupt compacted soil; (3) remove debris (e.g., stumps, rocks, and litter) to allow access and smooth operation of seeding equipment; (4) smooth and firm the seedbed before seeding; (5) manipulate the soil microtopography to improve stand establishment; (6) make clearings in otherwise dense shrub or woody canopies. Some techniques and equipment include the following (Doerr et al. 1986):

1. *Blading or dozing:* Large cutting blades are attached to the front or rear of a bulldozer tractor to push and uproot woody plants, or cut them off at the ground.

2. *Rootplowing:* A V-shaped or U-shaped blade 2 to 3 m long is mounted on the rear of a bulldozer tractor to uproot plants.

3. *Chaining:* Two bulldozers pull between them a ship's anchor chain that is 30 to 150 m long, with each link weighing 10 to 35 kg (Fig. 9.2). The chain is pulled in a U-shaped or J-shaped loop to uproot and crush woody plants.

4. *Cabling:* Two bulldozers pull a cable between them that is 60 to 185 m long and 4 to 5 cm in diameter. Treatment is similar to chaining, but is lighter and used for smaller and sparser vegetation.

TABLE 9.2   Factors to Be Considered in Planning Mechanical Manipulation for Wildlife Habitat Improvement

Wildlife factors	Watershed/soil factors	Vegetation factors
Obligate wildlife species present	Soil fertility	Need for reseeding or plant propagation
Resident and migratory species	Soil type	Invasion of noxious, secondary plants
	Soil depth	
Riparian zones	Soil moisture relationships	Phenological stage of target and nontarget plants, and basal diameter
Area of influence	Debris and slash removal	
Size of openings	Control of domestic livestock grazing	Size, density, and basal diameter of target plants
Width of openings		
	Erodibility	Resiliency of plants released by overstory removal
Ecological requirements of wildlife species	Aspect	
Native plants released by overstory removal or mechanical disturbance	Slope	Season of treatment
		Sprouting potential of shrubs
	Heterogeneity	
Planned travel corridors, travel and escape routes, and widths thereof	Site potential	Taxon to be saved
	Topography	Maintenance of openings created (longevity) and need for follow-up treatments
Forage-to-cover ratios	Season of treatment	
Proximity of treated sites to important habitat components for breeding, display, feeding, hiding, or thermal balance		Control of domestic livestock grazing
		Apical dominance
Influence on vertical structure		Impact on floral diversity
Control of wild ungulate spot-grazing		
Control of domestic livestock spot-grazing		

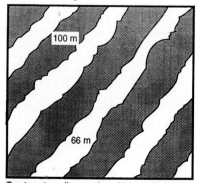

Treatments as linear strips with irregular borders

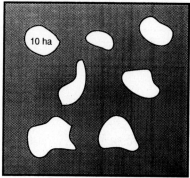

Treatments as openings

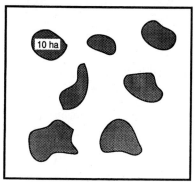

Treatments as mottes

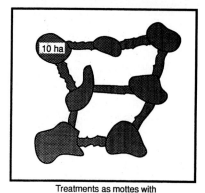

Treatments as mottes with interconnected travel lanes

Figure 9.1 "Managing" brush could involve several treatment designs.

5. *Railing:* Two bulldozers pull a heavy railroad rail between them in a U-shaped design to uproot or crush vegetation.

6. *Rollerchopping:* A tractor, bulldozer, or two bulldozers pull a steamroller drum that has chopper blades welded parallel to each other on the outer surface of the drum. Weight of the drum can be varied by filling with water to different levels. Rollerchoppers chop and crush vegetation and usually can handle trees and shrubs up to 15 cm in diameter.

7. *Shredding and rotobeating:* A tractor or bulldozer pulls a shredder or rotobeater designed to cut woody plants and debris and chop material into mulch. Most available rotobeater shredders can handle trees up to 5 cm in diameter, while some can handle trees up to 25 cm in diameter.

8. *Mowing:* A tractor pulls a mower that works as a flail (blades cut in a downward action), rotary (blades cut horizontally), reel (blades slice in a downward movement), or sickle bar (blades cut in a scissorlike motion) design.

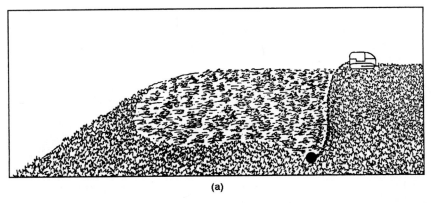

(a)

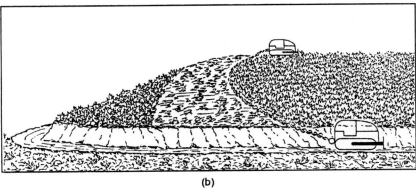

(b)

Figure 9.2 Chaining with (*a*) a ball-and-chain or (*b*) a chain pulled between two tractors is a popular technique for preparing California chaparral for burning. (*Roby and Green 1976.*)

9. *Plowing:* A tractor pulls a unit with several disks attached that are facing the same way to move the soil in one direction.

10. *Harrowing:* A tractor pulls a unit with several disks attached in opposite ways to move the soil in opposite directions.

11. *Furrowing:* A tractor pulls a unit of disks or blades that make furrows (channels) in the soil 60 to 150 cm apart.

12. *Pitting:* A tractor or bulldozer pulls a disk pitter or rotary drum pitter to make small pits or basins which hold rain or runoff water.

13. *Imprinting:* A tractor or bulldozer pulls a unit with disks attached that are notched or offset to provide intermittent soil contact for forming shallow holes. A steamroller drum also can be used that has geometric-shaped pads that protrude and make prints or shal-

low depressions in the soil. The drum imprinter is similar to a rollerchopper, except that pads are used rather than blades.

Grasslands

Tallgrass prairie. Woody plants can invade idle tallgrass prairies or those not burned, hayed, or mowed. To some extent the increase in structural layering enhances bird diversity, but true grassland species benefit little from shrub invasion. For example, Kirsch (1974) reported woody plants to be detrimental to greater prairie chickens. Where eastern redcedar has invaded prairie habitats, mechanical methods such as tractor-mounted saws, tree shears, and plow blades are used as control agents (Wilson and Schmidt 1990).

Mowing is the most common mechanical treatment to control noxious weeds such as ragweed, hoary vervain, goldenrod, common yarrow, and western ironweed in the tallgrass prairie (Vallentine 1989). Care must be taken to protect some ragweed because of its importance to birds. Rotation mowing at 3- to 5-year intervals can be used to manage greater prairie chicken habitat if prescribed burning is not possible (Kirsch 1974). Unmowed areas of at least 0.3 ha should be left about every 800 m. Although mowing reduces growth of competitively dominant grasses, allowing the persistence of less competitive plant species, it does not create openings for recruitment of seedlings as grazing does (Hobbs and Huenneke 1992). Mowing also creates habitat conditions with less heterogeneity than grazing, and nutrient cycling takes a different form (Rizand et al. 1989). In short, advantages and disadvantages of mowing versus grazing should be considered. In South Dakota, mowing was generally ineffective in controlling undesirable marsh elder, mustard, gumweed, and mullein, and desirable wildlife plants such as sunflower, common ragweed, and western ragweed (Vallentine 1989).

A four-step process has been used to restore natural grasslands, or glades, invaded by eastern redcedar in southwestern Missouri. Because of the economic importance of eastern redcedar, the first phase of glade restoration is to open a site of 10 to 75 ha to commercial tree harvest. The second phase is to fell all remaining trees with a chain saw. Next, the glade is allowed to recover 1 to 2 years for fine fuels (grasses) to become established. Finally, the glades are burned every 3 to 5 years in fall or spring, to maintain the desired vegetation complex. Burning also serves to clean up debris and kill smaller trees that were missed by mechanical methods. March burns are better for forbs important to wildlife; April burns benefit grasses (Lewis et al. 1964). Native grasses such as little bluestem, big bluestem, switchgrass, and forbs such as Missouri evening primrose increase on restored glades. In some instances, grass productivity increases 100 percent; species diversity also increases (Martin and Houf 1993). Wildlife species such as Bachman's sparrow, grasshopper mouse, Texas brush mouse, pygmy rattlesnake, and collared lizards are favored by habitats created in glade restoration and management. Livestock grazing generally favors wildlife and plant species diversity on restored glades compared to ungrazed sites (Martin and Houf 1993).

Restoration of Florida prairies invaded by saw-palmetto and other shrubs suggests that bird richness and abundance is affected negatively by rollerchopping large areas, but not by prescribed burning (Fitzgerald and Tanner 1992). Conversion to original prairie vegetation probably requires some mechanical treatments and fire, with scattered wetlands providing the habitat mosaic to support a mixture of grassland birds.

Southern mixed prairies.   Southern mixed prairies have been invaded by two tenacious woody plants: mesquite and juniper. Mechanical techniques for mesquite control include chaining and rootplowing; chaining and dozing are used most commonly for juniper control. Rootplowing kills woody plants, but it results in severe soil disturbance and is not recommended. Repeated shredding is also effective and can be used on young mesquite (Wright and Stinson 1970). Follow-up treatments usually are needed if openings are to be maintained.

In southern mixed prairies dominated by mesquite, openings made in dense stands by chaining or shredding increase edge, enhance structure, and increase production of herbaceous plants. Darr and Klebenow (1975) recommended leaving mesquite-dominated bottomland sites untreated because of high use of the areas by white-tailed deer for cover and feeding. Treating uplands and not bottomlands also benefits Rio Grande turkeys, which roost in mesquite bottomlands. Rio Grande turkeys avoided cleared areas greater than 200 ha in north-central Texas (Quinton et al. 1980). Therefore, only uplands should be treated by chaining small (10 ha) clearings of mesquite or narrow (30- to 50-m wide) strips, but clumps (or mottes) should be left for hiding cover (Litton 1977). For bobwhite quail, habitat management includes disking in March to increase natural foods, and providing brush piles and mesquite half-cuts for loafing, roosting, and escape cover. These combined management guidelines increased populations twofold over unmanaged mesquite uplands, yet did not negatively impact nongame birds (Webb and Guthery 1983).

Where redberry juniper dominates, small clearings are needed to open the habitat; sites and treatments should be selected carefully. Steep slopes (greater than 20 percent) should be avoided; small 3- to

6-ha clearings can be chained or bulldozed to benefit species such as white-tailed deer and mule deer. Chaining large clearings (greater than 50 ha) is not recommended. Removing individual trees by dozing can be used to thin stands if canopy cover exceeds 20 to 25 percent.

Habitat management guidelines for edge species in dense ashe juniper–live oak communities in the Edwards Plateau (Bryant 1990) include:

1. Chaining in dense stands (25 percent canopy cover or greater) to open the habitat

2. Individual tree dozing to thin moderately dense stands (15 to 25 percent canopy cover)

3. Treating 50 percent of an area in 10-ha clearings to increase deer distribution, herbaceous production, edge, and vertical structure (Rollins et al. 1988)

4. Preparing linear openings 30 to 100 m wide with irregular borders to enhance edge

5. Leaving all oaks on treated sites for perches and acorn production

6. Avoiding or carefully planning treatments on riparian areas

7. Treating only on slopes 20 percent or less to prevent erosion

8. Burning mechanically treated openings at 7- to 20-year intervals to maintain them

9. Protecting and retaining large (5- to 8-m tall), overmature juniper and maintaining undisturbed tracts (larger than 200 ha) occupied by the golden-cheeked warbler

10. Maintaining dense shrub canopies that extend from the ground up to 1- to 2-m tall where black-capped vireos occur (Hayes et al. 1987)

11. Leaving slash and downed trees on 10 percent of a clearing to be used by other wildlife species such as cottontail rabbits and jackrabbits

12. Ensuring aesthetic landscape designs of treatment patterns to preserve land values

Shortgrass prairies.   Wildlife species in shortgrass prairies usually prefer open habitats. Mechanical control for pronghorns in the southern Great Plains should be chaining rather than plowing, and size of treated areas should be less than 400 ha; some shrub cover (5 to 10 percent) should be maintained (Holechek et al. 1989). Except for dense cholla or mesquite, mechanical treatment of shortgrass prairie is rarely practiced. Disking strips (6 m wide) during late February to early March might promote annual and perennial forbs as food sources and edge for many wildlife species. Scaled quail and sharp-tailed grouse benefit from some shrubs in their habitat.

In the grasslands of the northern Great Plains, wooded draws constitute extremely valuable habitat for many wildlife species (Bjugstad and Sorg 1984, Hodorff et al. 1988). Mechanical removal of woody plants by firewood cutting should be applied cautiously. Furthermore, Rocky Mountain juniper woodlands associated with shortgrass prairies also should be perpetuated because they contribute nesting habitat, migration corridors, and winter food and cover for many birds (Sieg 1991) and enhance small mammal diversity (Sieg 1988). In the eastern prairies of Montana, sagebrush-grasslands are extremely important to pronghorns (MacCracken and Uresk 1984). Mechanical treatments should be applied cautiously to woody plants in each of these habitats.

Fescue prairies. Invasion of willow and aspen into Canadian fescue prairies can be controlled by bulldozing (Vallentine 1989). Grass production can increase threefold after mechanical treatments on aspen-dominated sites, and these treatments should be used if increased grass production is desired for wildlife. Anchor chaining also has been used in Canada for brush control, as has rollerchopping to break down and cut up poplar and willow (Vallentine 1989). The fragile, delicate tundra does not lend itself to mechanical treatment of any kind.

Semidesert grasslands. Three principal shrubland species targeted for control in southwest deserts are honey mesquite, velvet mesquite, and creosotebush. These, and other woody shrubs, have increased, and now dominate desert grasslands. For example, on a site in Arizona, mesquite increased from 60 to 360 plants per hectare between 1922 and 1965 (Reynolds and Martin 1968). Greater shrub density usually decreases grasses and forbs through loss of a soil horizon suitable for grass growth, loss of seed sources, and competition for moisture. Furthermore, these shrubs make microclimates more xeric and increase runoff and decrease infiltration, conditions which generally prohibit increases in herbaceous plants (Roundy and Jordan 1988).

Many kinds of mechanical treatments have been attempted in semidesert grasslands. Even though rootplowing is capable of killing mesquite and creosotebush, rootplowing without subsequent seeding seldom improves rangeland productivity (Roundy and Jordan 1988, Vallentine 1989). Rootplowing should not be used in areas with good grass cover under the shrub or tree canopy. Rollerchopping is ineffective on mesquite; effects of chaining seem temporary (Vallentine 1989). Undisturbed and partially cleared mesquite stands were better than totally cleared habitat for black-tailed jackrabbits and Gambel's quail (Germano et al. 1983).

Railing, shredding, chaining, imprinting, and rollerchopping remove the tops of creosotebush, but usually kill fewer plants than disking or rootplowing (Morton and Melgoza 1991). Designed to increase amounts of water retained in the soil, furrowing and imprinting did not increase grasses and forbs in the Sonoran Desert (Morton and Melgoza 1991). Mechanical disturbance in harsh desert environments does not always result in an orderly succession of vegetation to climax (Roundy and Jordan 1988). Mechanical treatments also can spread cactus and other succulents; detached cladophylls and joints of succulents can send down roots if moisture and other environmental conditions are adequate.

Shrublands

Cold desert. The literature on cold desert wildlife indicates that too much sagebrush is nearly as great a problem as too little (Urness 1979). Most wildlife species do best where stands have good mixtures of shrubs, grasses, and forbs, and/or a variety of cover types occurring in a relatively small area. Such cover types vary from fairly dense brush to grassy openings. Mechanical treatments can create grassy openings where too much sagebrush is a problem. Also, these treatments eliminate the uncertainty of size and shape of treatment that is common with prescribed burning (Urness 1979). Because different sagebrush species vary in their importance to wildlife, mechanical treatments can be designed to avoid important species. The distribution of sagebrush species is influenced by soil temperature and soil moisture gradients (Fig. 9.3) (West 1987).

Mechanical methods to alter sagebrush habitats include plowing, disking, rotobeating, chaining, railing, shredding, and harrowing (Table 9.3). Plummer et al. (1968) recommended chaining because it does not completely kill out sagebrush and retains native grasses and forbs. Early studies in Idaho suggest that railing resulted in the greatest sagebrush kill and that railing and rotobeating favored forbs, compared with burning and herbicides (Mueggler and Blaisdell 1958). Killing big sagebrush by some mechanical methods can release rabbitbush, a generally undesirable plant and more difficult to kill than sagebrush. In general, big sagebrush should be controlled only when it is overmature, decadent, not needed as forage, or not important as upland bird habitat (Pechanec et al. 1965). But songbirds also occupy sagebrush habitats. Medin (1990) found breeding birds in much greater richness and density in upper sagebrush-grass (22 to 23 species; 7 to 8 individuals per hectare) community types than in neighboring pinyon-juniper (13 to 15 species; 3 to 4 individuals per hectare), lower sagebrush (5 to 6 species; 3 to 3.5 individuals per hectare), and shadscale (2 to 3 species; 1 to 5 individuals per hectare)

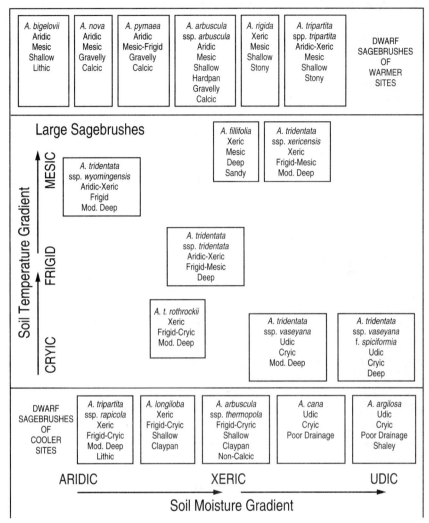

Figure 9.3 Ordination of major sagebrush taxa against gradients of soil temperature and soil moisture. (*West 1987.*)

types. Mechanical treatments are advocated on big game winter range with methods that will thin the stand but leave enough sagebrush to balance other shrub species, grasses, and forbs.

Extensive encroachment of juniper and pinyon trees onto sagebrush and grassland sites also might need treatment. Tree overstories benefit many wildlife species. But dense stands eliminate understory plants (Urness 1979). The objective would not be to eliminate trees, but to leave islands, travel lanes, and fingerlike projections in small, irregular-shaped treatments.

TABLE 9.3   Summary of Limitations and Advantages of the Four Most Common Mechanical Methods of Big Sagebrush Control

	Method of control			
	Anchor chaining	Cutting, beating, or shredding	Harrowing	Plowing or disking once over
Kill of big sagebrush	60–80 percent of old rigid brush, 10–20 percent each additional time over; 10–40 percent of young flexible brush	50–90 percent of large, old; 30–60 percent of young, flexible	30–70 percent of old, rigid; 10–30 percent of young, flexible	70–99 percent of old; slightly less of young
Kill of associated undesirable plants	Not effective on sprouting perennials or on annuals	Not effective on sprouting shrubs or herbaceous species	Not effective on sprouting shrubs or annuals	Usually not effective on sprouting shrubs; good on cheatgrass
Effect on desirable forage plants	Nonsprouting shrubs are damaged; sprouters recover; little damage to herbaceous species	Little damage to herbaceous plants; nonsprouting shrubs damaged	10–20 percent of bunchgrasses uprooted; damage to bitterbrush slight	Kills all except those that sprout or spread by rootstocks
Ease of seeding after treatment	Broadcast before second chaining, or drill after final chaining where feasible	Broadcast before cutting or beating heavy brush; drill after treating light brush	Seed broadcast ahead of harrow well covered; drilling difficult	Easily done with drills; seedbed may require packing
Adaptability to terrain and soil	Feasible on all soils and on slopes exceeding 30 percent; breakage rare	Limited to sites without protruding rocks	Particularly suited to rocky ground and rough terrain	Limited to little or no rock except with brushland plow
Availability of equipment	Commercially available through coastal salvage companies, or new	Commercially available	Not commercially available; can be built in machine shops	Plows and disks commercially available; brushland plow is custom-made
Effect on erosion hazard	Erosion usually decreased when approximate contours followed	Mulch left decreases hazard	Usually decreases hazard	Expose soil to moderate degree

SOURCE: Pechanec et al. (1965).

Of all the species for which habitat-management guidelines have been proposed, no set of guidelines is more detailed than those for sage grouse. For example, because Vasey big sagebrush and Wyoming big sagebrush are more palatable to sage grouse than basin big sagebrush, even the subspecies treated must be considered (Autenrieth et al. 1982). In general, habitat management should:

1. Provide an optimum habitat of 2000 sagebrush plants per hectare or similar areas nearby to provide sage grouse with ready access

2. Maintain at least 20 percent canopy cover of sagebrush, and 15 percent canopy cover for nesting and winter habitat (Wallestad 1975)

3. Protect other associated sagebrush species including dwarf sagebrush, fringed sagebrush, Louisiana sagebrush, and black sagebrush

4. Avoid treating sagebrush within 1.6 km of brooding areas and 90 m of streams and meadows

5. Avoid treating slopes greater than 20 percent

6. Chain in strips rather than blocks, by using natural terrain features to maximize edge effect (Autenrieth et al. 1982)

Other recommendations for manipulating sagebrush vegetation types also exist. Treatments should not exceed 30 percent of a large area and should be made in alternating strips of disturbed and undisturbed sagebrush. Leaving at least 30 percent of a large area undisturbed is recommended for raptors (Howard and Wolfe 1976). Width of disturbed strips should be 100 m or less with 200-m strips undisturbed. Evidently 100-m treated strips maintain bird species diversity (Castrale 1982). Irregular borders are best, unless the management goal is to reduce edge for interior species. Restricting the size of each disturbed strip to 16 ha or less would satisfy sage grouse needs and not be detrimental to the 100 or so nongame birds that forage and nest in sagebrush communities (Baker et al. 1976). Ungulates such as pronghorn, mule deer, and elk should benefit from the herbaceous forage produced from these management suggestions for sage grouse, although extreme care must be taken when interpreting research results for passerine breeding birds (Wiens et al. 1986). If seeding is needed after mechanical treatments, important sage grouse forbs such as alfalfa, yellow sweetclover, western yarrow, sainfoin, small burnet, vetch, goatsbeard, Chinese lettuce, and dandelion should be planted (Autenrieth et al. 1982).

Saltbush communities might be treated similarly without detrimental effects. Greasewood and shadscale flats are important feeding areas for kit fox and their prey, black-tailed jackrabbits (Spowart and

Samsom 1986). More research is needed relative to habitat requirements of wildlife in saltbush and greasewood communities.

Hot desert. In hot desert habitats, the Arizona pocket mouse inhabits
creosote flats; the Bailey pocket mouse and rock pocket mouse prefer
paloverde habitats dominated by white bursage; jackrabbits like
mesquite-catclaw-cacti habitats; and Merriam's kangaroo rat prefers
a mix of shrubs and grasses where vegetation cover is less than 10
percent (Cooperrider et al. 1986, Institute of Land Rehabilitation
1978). Gambel's quail seem to prefer dense stands of desert shrub
where cover shades 50 to 75 percent of the ground and where 60 to 80
percent of those shrubs are taller than 2 m (Cooperrider et al. 1986).

Mechanical modification of these habitats should be considered
with caution. Treatments should be avoided along riparian habitats,
dry washes, brushy draws used by Gambel's quail, and mesquite-
dominated drainageways used by deer and other wildlife. For example, as many as 29 guilds of wildlife could be affected negatively if the
shrub midstory canopy is removed (Short 1983). In fact, until more
definitive work is done which produces more positive results for
wildlife, mechanical treatments in the hot desert environments rarely
should be used as a technique for habitat management. Eliminating
the limited midstory vegetation of creosotebush-bursage communities
in Arizona will deleteriously affect three guilds of primary consumers
and two guilds of secondary consumers (Short 1983). Even more
guilds would be affected in Joshua tree–creosotebush communities.
Because the tree bole layer is the most fragile habitat layer in the
saguaro-paloverde community, mechanical treatment should be
avoided and habitat management should protect regenerating and
mature saguaro cactus (Short 1983).

Woodlands

Pinyon-juniper. Various mechanical methods using heavy equipment
are employed to chain, cable, crush, and bulldoze large areas of pinyon-juniper woodlands (Vallentine 1989). Extensive modifications
over large areas should be avoided. Short (1983) reported that six
guilds of primary consumers and eight guilds of secondary consumers
could be deleteriously affected in Arizona. Potentially, large-scale
clearing of pinyon-juniper woodlands could negatively impact over 75
percent of the wildlife guilds using them. But tree superdominance
across expansive areas also might be undesirable. Opening dense
stands of pinyon-juniper woodland benefits edge species and ground-
feeding and ground-nesting fauna; dense woodlands promote interior
species and tree and bole gleaners and feeders. Mule deer also need

pinyon-juniper. For example, about 54 percent of mule deer winter range in Utah is pinyon-juniper woodland (Terrell and Spillet 1975). These woodlands serve as food and security cover. Thermal cover is an important habitat component to retain (Leckenby 1978). Management guidelines for mule deer have been suggested by several researchers (Table 9.4).

General habitat-management guidelines should be followed which try to minimize the impact on all wildlife, not just mule deer, because pinyon-juniper woodlands are rich in wildlife species. In central Oregon, western juniper habitat supports larger bird populations and more species than ponderosa pine, lodgepole pine, or sagebrush habitats (Maser and Gashwiler 1978). Balda and Masters (1980) reported that 73 bird species breed in pinyon-juniper woodlands, 31 regularly. Average density is about 95 breeding pairs per 40 hectares (Balda and Masters 1980). Typically, 35 to 40 percent of birds are permanent residents. Rodents, lagomorphs, mammalian predators, ungulates, raptors, and other wildlife also use and even require pinyon-juniper woodlands.

Openings of 100 ha or less created by mechanical means benefit deer (Short et al. 1977, Rutherford and Snyder 1983), small mammals (Baker and Frischnecht 1973, O'Meara et al. 1981), and lagomorphs (Howard et al. 1987). Increases in small mammals would improve food sources for raptors and other terrestrial predators (Howard and Wolfe 1976). In the short term, breeding and migrant birds in Arizona are affected by removal of the pinyon-juniper overstory. Reducing pinyon-juniper dominance and increasing grass cover favors bird richness (Table 9.5). In New Mexico, decreasing the pinyon-juniper overstory increased a warm-season grass (blue grama) but decreased cool-season grasses (New Mexico muhly and pinyon ricegrass) (Pieper 1990). In Northwestern Colorado, breeding bird densities were lower but ground nesters were more prevalent than tree-nesting birds on chained versus unchained pinyon-juniper woodlands (O'Meara et al. 1981), implying that well-designed openings can enhance biodiversity.

To open dense stands (more than 400 trees per hectare), cabling has been recommended to optimize survival of shrubs (O'Meara et al. 1981, Howard et al. 1987, Skousen et al. 1989). Dozing individual trees is recommended to thin other sites. Treatment during the warmer months of late summer and early fall is best for nongame wildlife (O'Meara et al. 1981). For nesting birds, especially hawks, treatment before March 15 and after June 15 is best (Howard and Wolfe 1976).

Leaving slash, debris, and downed trees aids watershed protection (Gifford 1975), nitrogen cycling (Evans 1988), desert cottontails (Kundaeli and Reynolds 1972), and songbirds (Maser and Gashwiler 1978). For deer, slash and debris should cover 20 percent or less of the treated site (Terrell and Spillet 1975). Windrowing debris after

TABLE 9.4 Comparison of Recommended Guidelines for Conversion of Pinyon–Juniper Woodlands to Benefit Certain Wildlife

Habitat parameter/ treatment pattern	Lamb and Pieper (1971) (NM/deer)	Leckenby (1978) (OR/deer)	McCulloch (1979) (AZ/deer)	Terrell (1973) (UT/deer)	Terrell and Spillet (1975) (UT/deer)	Bright (1978) (OR/deer)	Institute of Land Rehabilitation (1978) (NM/deer)	Short et al. (1977) (NM/deer)	O'Meara et al. (1981) (CO/ nongame)	Scott and Boeker (1977) (AZ/ turkey)	Skousen et al. (1989) (UT/all)
Proportion of total area treated	50–75%	<33%	<33%	<20%	<25%		<20%				
Width of clearing	240–480 m	<120 m	36–240 m	385–775 m	<385 m		<440 m	30–200 m	<200 m	<90 m	30–200 m
Width of untreated woodland	>240 m		36–240 m	960–1925 m	960 m						
Sites avoided*	a,b,c,d,e,h,i		a,b	g	c,p						
Sites treated*	m,n	k		i,j,m,o	k,m,n,o		f,i,m,o				
Desired canopy cover remaining				15%	15%	25%					

*a = steep slopes
b = rocky slopes
c = ridges
d = shallow soil
e = slopes >15%
f = slopes <20%

g = slopes >20%
h = recreation sites
i = valleys
j = protected hillsides
k = create numerous small openings

l = northeasterly exposures
m = southerly exposures
n = easterly exposures
o = westerly exposures
p = northerly exposures

SOURCE: Severson and Medina (1983).

TABLE 9.5   Number of Bird Species on 4-ha Study Plots in Pinyon-Juniper Woodland

Bird classification	Pinyon-juniper woodland ($n = 4$)	Pinyon-juniper grassland ($n = 1$)	Pinyon-juniper, newly cleared ($n = 1$)	Pinyon-juniper, old clearing ($n = 1$)
Breeding species	7	13	5	10
Summer visitors	5	5	3	6
Summer species	13	18	8	16
Migrants and wintering species	10	19	3	14

Note: n = number of 4-ha plots.
SOURCE: Carothers and Johnson (1975).

chaining is not recommended because of increased erosion potential (Gifford 1975) and barriers to ungulates.

Desirable shrub densities vary from 60 shrubs per hectare for deer (Terrell and Spillet 1975) to 210 shrubs per hectare for desert cottontails (Kundaeli and Reynolds 1972). Howard and Wolfe (1976) recommended a 20 percent shrub cover for ferruginous hawks and their prey.

The following are general recommendations for opening up dense stands of pinyon-juniper or juniper woodlands through mechanical treatments:

1. Maintain a mosaic pattern of successional stages.
2. Confine treatments to extensive, dense stands which are more than 400 m wide, with an average crown cover of 20 percent and an overall tree density of 180 trees per hectare (Short and McCulloch 1977).
3. Create numerous, small narrow openings with irregular borders, 3 to 10 ha in size; clearing width should be less than 200 m, preferably 100 m; where possible, openings should be 200 to 400 m apart.
4. Leave 500-ha blocks untreated for optimum use by interior species.
5. Use commercial or private fuelwood harvest to reduce treatment cost; use chaining, cabling, or dozing of individual trees where appropriate.
6. Leave 50 to 75 percent of an area or winter range untreated.
7. Avoid selective removal of pinyon pine.
8. Identify and retain trees for cavity-nesting birds and as perches.
9. Leave slash and debris on no more than 20 percent of ground cover in a treated opening.

10. Leave perches.
11. Retain strips and blocks as travel lanes (at least 150 m wide) to and from preferred habitats.
12. Seed mixtures of forbs, shrubs, and grasses following mechanical disturbance.
13. Consider aesthetics where the target area is less than 5 km from a road or an area of high human activity (Schreyer and Royer 1975). Recommended guidelines (Short and McCulloch 1977) for aesthetic considerations include:

    (a) Use individual tree removal methods.
    (b) Leave trees in openings to create a savannalike appearance.
    (c) Protect major land forms.
    (d) Leave buffer zones 400 m wide along highways, by scenic and recreational areas, and at archeological sites.
    (e) Restrict treatments to gentle slopes.

Oak. Oak woodlands of California produce a larger population and greater diversity of birds (29 species) than mature chapparal (7 species) (Buttery and Shields 1975). Thus, oak woodlands must be managed cautiously. Furthermore, because woodland birds select breeding habitat based on the recognition of foliage patterns and densities, the removal or modification of vegetative strata can reduce bird diversity. The success of mechanical treatments, or type conversions, as a habitat improvement tool in California oak woodlands depends upon the extent, pattern, availability, state of maturity and/or successional stage, and if the treatment provides special habitat requirements for certain bird species. In the grassy areas of oak woodlands, disking strips or meandering paths every 2 to 3 years was superior to burning in the production of key foods for California quail (Blakely et al. 1990).

Gambel oak woodlands are important to wildlife in the intermountain West. Over 40 species of birds and 20 species of mammals have been reported to use the Gambel oak vegetation type (Harper et al. 1985). Steinhoff (1978) reported five species to depend upon Gambel oak in Colorado: jays, green-tailed towhee, Merriam's turkey, gray flycatcher, and Abert squirrel. Management objectives which might need mechanical treatment are (1) to increase oak sprouts as ungulate forage; (2) to reduce oak dominance to favor grasses, forbs, and more palatable shrubs; and (3) to protect oak stands by reducing invading plants such as ponderosa pine, Rocky Mountain juniper, or white fir. Lack of disturbance can limit the distribution, vigor, and growth of Gambel oak, as many plant stems die before they are 80 years old (Vallentine 1989). Management to stimulate suckering and stump sprouting involves removing substantial amounts of overmature oakbrush (Rutherford and Snyder 1983). In Arizona, when Gambel oak tops were cut in winter, all stumps sprouted. Dozing yielded greater browse production than hand cutting, although both produced more browse than uncut oakbrush did in Colorado (Rutherford and Snyder 1983). Although results from patchcutting have shown promise for stimulating deer and elk forage in Colorado (Kufeld 1983), such practices might not be applicable to all western states. Selective cutting of Gambel oak thickets should leave acorn-producing trees of at least 5 cm dbh, because maximum acorn yield is from trees of 5 to 6 cm dbh. Thus, management would be aimed at producing nutritious sprouting by winter cutting, while identifying and protecting mast-producing trees as well as snags for perching and cavity-nesting birds. Chaining has been used in Utah to reduce Gambel oak and increase herbaceous forage (Plummer et al. 1968). Twice-over chaining seems to be the best treatment to prepare stands for reseeding (Harper et al. 1985). Response of wildlife in southern Colorado to cutting and other habitat treatments varies with taxa (Table 9.6) (Harper et al. 1985).

If applicable, mechanical treatments in the Madrean evergreen woodland of Arizona can be directed at maintaining habitat for Mearn's quail.

In shinnery oak habitats of west Texas, western Oklahoma, and eastern New Mexico, lesser prairie chickens have declined by 97 percent during the past century (Taylor and Guthery 1980). Most of the decline has been attributed to cultivation that removed native habitats. Generally, management of shinnery oak vegetation with mechanical means is not recommended. Rather, protecting shinnery oak mottes (groups of trees) and other areas would benefit deer, scaled quail, northern bobwhite quail, and lesser prairie chickens and other animals in this region. Where shinnery oak is too thick or has an expanded distribution, shredding or mowing shinoak thickets while leaving 10 percent of the area in 0.1- to 0.2-ha mottes would be acceptable for quail. Mast-producing trees should be protected.

California chaparral.   Mechanical treatment (type conversion) has been used to intersperse grassy patches with dense stands of California chaparral. Some of these conversions have increased bird use, possibly due to edge effect (Carothers and Johnson 1975, Johnson et al. 1980), and some probably have reduced populations of interior birds and other wildlife. Most species of birds reach at least two-thirds of their highest percent occurrence in chapparal patches of at least 20 ha (Soulé et al. 1988). Small, irregular areas of chaparral-type conversions, or large areas mechanically treated but leaving islands of untreated chaparral,

TABLE 9.6   Estimated Tolerance of Selected Animals to Severe Disturbance of a Gambel Oak Community by Fire, Cutting, Grazing, or Herbicides in Colorado

Dependent species	Zone of occurrence* PPO	OSO	PJO	Seral stage of best development†	Fire	Disturbance‡ Cutting	Grazing	Herbicide
Dependent taxa								
Jays		x	x	L	T	T	T	–
Green-tailed towhee	x	x	x	NP	T	T	T	–
Steller's jay	x	x	x	L	T	T	–	–
Gray flycatcher	x	x		E–M	T	T	T	T
Turkey	x	x		NP	I	I	I	–
Abert squirrel	x			M–L	I	I	–	–
Influenced taxa								
Ruffed grouse		x		M–L	–	–	–	–
Ferruginous hawk	x	x	x	L	I	I	I	I
Band-tailed pigeon			x	L	–	–	–	–
Flycatcher		x	x	L	T	–	T	–
Hermit thrush	x			M	I	I	I	–
Junco	x			M	T	T	–	–
Lazuli bunting		x		M	T	T	T	–
Poorwill		x		M	T	T	T	T
Magpie		x		L	–	T	–	–
Rock wren			x	M**	–	T	–	–
Goldfinch	x	x		L	I	I	–	I
Sparrow	x			M–L	T	T	–	–
Virginia's warbler	x			L	T	T	–	–
Orange-crowned warbler	x			L	T	–	I	–
Mourning dove	x	x	x	E	T	T	T	T
Elk	x	x	x	M	T	T	I	T
Ermine	x	x	x	M**	T	T	–	T
Weasel	x	x		M**	T	T	–	T
Mule deer	x	x	x	M	T	T	T	T
Cottontail rabbit	x	x	x	M	T	T	–	T
Black bear	x			M	T	T	–	T

*Zones of occurrence are: PPO = dense ponderosa pine–oak; OSO = oak–serviceberry–Oregon-grape; PJO = pinyon-juniper–oak.
†Seral stages are: E = early; M = medium; L = late; NP = no preference.
**Slight preference for this stage.
‡Animal tolerance classes are: T = tolerant; I = intolerant; – = more data needed.
SOURCE: Harper et al. (1985).

can increase diversity of edge birds. Treatments leaving islands of untreated chaparral had more bird species than areas where chaparral was treated in large segments but no islands were left (Buttery and Shields 1975). Bleich and Holl (1982) recommended a ratio of brush to foraging areas for mule deer at about 1:9. Brush patches should be about 10 ha in size to be optimally useful as escape cover, and should be well distributed throughout the foraging areas.

Because many chaparral species sprout vigorously from root crowns, cutting can be used as a forage quality enhancement technique because it temporarily stimulates more nutritious new growth. Offset disking also can be used to control chaparral where open stands of light brush or dense stands of brush sprouts are present (Vallentine 1989). Mechanical conversion in the California chaparral is used to prepare sites for burning (Taber and Dasmann 1958). Equipment used has included bulldozers with an anchor chain, a straight-blade bulldozer, a bulldozer with a Tomahawk crusher, and rollerchoppers (Roby and Green 1976). A ball-and-chain technique (see Fig. 9.2) was effective on steep (30 percent or greater) slopes. Small, irregular-shaped clearings or strips are recommended for creating openings in dense chaparral for edge species of wildlife, but not for interior species.

Mountain shrub. Mountain shrub types usually are found on slopes too steep for mechanical manipulation. Fire has been used more often as a tool (see "Prescribed Burns" in Chap. 10). Cutting tall shrubs results in bringing forage down to a level more efficiently used by grazing ungulates (Leege 1969). For example, browse production from mature and overmature curlleaf mountainmahogany was doubled in Utah by top pruning in spring or autumn (Vallentine 1989).

Interior chaparral. In Arizona, dense stands of interior chaparral have been treated mechanically to increase grass production and facilitate use by grazing animals (Severson and Medina 1983). Rootplowing was unfavorable for mule deer because cover was removed (Urness 1974), but the size and shape of treatments might have been an important factor. Mechanical treatment that reduces midstory structure of the chaparral over large areas will negatively impact five guilds of primary consumers and five guilds of secondary consumers (Short 1983). Other interior wildlife species also might be affected.

Periodic regeneration of small units of chaparral should increase production of current annual growth, which is advantageous to the wildlife community (Short 1983). Stimulation of forbs by mechanical means also could improve forb availability. Recommendations for mechanical manipulation of Arizona chaparral could include treating 33 to 50 percent of a management unit with many 8- to 16-ha clearings and leaving undisturbed corridors and buffer zones of chaparral along and around gullies, ravines, rocky areas, natural travel routes, and water (Severson and Medina 1983). If smaller clearings (2 ha) are developed, untreated areas of at least 16 ha should be left 200 m apart (Reynolds 1972). For interior species, untreated areas larger than 200 ha should be left.

Mesquite-acacia. Because woody plants are important as food (Varner et al. 1977) and cover (Table 9.7), mechanical treatment should be aimed at maintaining high species richness, adequate screening and loafing cover, and diversity in age of woody plants. Rollerchopping is better than rootplowing because rootplowing decreases preferred woody plants such as bluewood, bumelia, guayacan, and spiny hackberry, while increasing such less desirable plants as mesquite and twisted acacia (Fulbright and Beasom 1987).

Like rootplowing, chaining is unpopular because of its potential to spread and increase the density of pricklypear (Dodd 1968). For chaining to be effective, each treatment must be done twice, and must include raking and stacking (Vallentine 1989). Shredding or mowing brush is also not recommended because it lowers shrub diversity (Fulbright 1987). Although disking (large disk plows pulled by crawler tractors) can spread pricklypear and tasajillo, it is effective in treating the undesirable whitebrush and agarito while maintaining other woody plants preferred by white-tailed deer (Fulbright et al. 1989, Bozzo et al. 1989). Mechanical treatments in general can be used to increase the abundance and diversity of forbs, but such treatments drastically affect structure and cover screen of the shrub community (Scifres 1980b) if done in large blocks. Rollerchopping is recommended as the preferred mechanical treatment in the mesquite-acacia woodland. If carefully planned and executed, managers can maintain floral density and diversity and enhance nutrient flow temporarily to browsing animals through stimulations of nutritious sprouts (Everitt 1983, Fulbright and Beasom 1987).

Opening dense thickets of woody plants creates edge and stimulates herbaceous forage production. Because of economic returns to private landowners, most research has been targeted at game species such as white-tailed deer, Rio Grande turkey, and northern bobwhite quail (Table 9.8). Although habitat-management guidelines are site-specific (Box 1964, Stoddart et al. 1975), leaving woody plant cover in strips with irregular borders is suggested for northern bobwhite quail, rather than in clumps or mottes (Guthery 1986). For white-tailed deer, northern bobwhite quail, Rio Grande turkey, and other wildlife, it is important to leave stands of old brush (more than 20 years old) while converting, in mosaic patterns, other brush patches to younger stands (less than 5 years). For northern bobwhite quail, such stands of old brush are recommended to be left 200 m apart (Jackson 1969, Guthery 1986). Up to 85 percent of brush cover can be removed safely if north-

TABLE 9.7   Wildlife Value Ratings for Selected Woody Plants of the Mesquite-Acacia Woodland

Common name, local name	Browse rating*	Protein rating†	Phosphorus rating*	Cover rating* (species, if known)
Lime pricklyash, colima	1			1 (bobwhite quail), 2 (deer)
Spiny bumelia, coma	1			1 (mature bucks)
Guajillo, guajillo	1			1 (deer)
Guayacan, guayacan	1	1	3	1 (mature bucks)
Spiny hackberry, granjeno	1			3 (deer), 1 (mature bucks)
Hackberry, palo blanco	1			
Blackbrush acacia, chaparro prieto	2	1	1	2 (deer)
Desert yaupon, capul	2	3	3	
Mesquite, mesquite	2			2
Lotebush, clapany	2	3	3	1 (bobwhite quail)
Texas colubrina, hogplum	2			
Twisted acacia, huisachillo	2	3	3	2 (bobwhite quail), 3 (deer)
Persimmon, chapote	2			
Catclaw, uña de gato	1	1	1	
Huisache, huisache	2			1 (white-wing dove)
Wolfberry, cilindrillo	3			
Retama, retama	2	1	1	3
Fiddlewood, fiddlewood		3	3	
Whitebrush, reventador	3			
Bluewood, brasil	1			1 (bobwhite quail)
Allthorn goatbush, amargoso	3			
Coyotillo, coyotillo	3	3	3	
Lantana, lantana	2	3	2	
Paloverde, paloverde	2	1	1	

*Rating: 1 = high; 2 = medium; 3 = low.
†Protein rating: 1 = >16%; 2 = 12–16%; 3 = <12%.
SOURCE: Everitt (1983); Nelle (1984).

TABLE 9.8 General Guidelines for Mechanically Treating Large Dense Areas of Mesquite-Acacia Woodlands for White-Tailed Deer, Rio Grande Turkey, and Northern Bobwhite Quail*

Animal species	Brush cover to be left (%)	Drainages left as brush (%)	Upland treatments as strips		Upland treatments as openings			Upland treatments as mottes†	
			Treated width (m)	Untreated width (m)	Max. width (m)	Size of opening (ha)	Openings per 1000 ha	Size of motte (ha)	Mottes per 1000 ha
White-tailed deer, turkey	40	≥70	100	66	200	10	60	10	40
Bobwhite quail	5–15	30–50	100	15	200	20	45	2.5	40

*Rollerchopping is the currently suggested mechanical treatment of choice.

†Where turkeys are present, travel lanes 30 m wide should be left to interconnect all mottes; areas of guayacan, coma, spiny hackberry, and bluewood should be flagged to be left as hiding cover for mature male deer.

ern bobwhite quail are the main consideration (Reid et al. 1980, Guthery 1986). But fragmented habitats or clearing of such large percentages of older brush could negatively influence interior species.

Small openings can be created for deer as long as not more than 50 to 60 percent of the total area is in clearings (Steuter and Wright 1980). White-tailed deer preferred openings of 10 ha when presented with sizes ranging from 4 to 32 ha (Drawe 1981). Treated blocks larger than 400 ha should be avoided (Davis and Winkler 1968, Inglis et al. 1986). If brush is cleared in strips, a belt or block of brush 50 to 75 m wide should be left every 200 to 250 m to break up open spaces to provide covered travel lanes for wildlife (Hailey 1979). Untreated strips should be 50 to 75 m wide; no mosaic of clearings should be further than 75 m from a cover screen (Inglis 1985).

All natural travel ways should be left, including saddles between ridges, headers or canyon beginnings, and extensions of ridges (Hailey 1979). Riparian areas should not be treated in their entirety, but maintained as important to all wildlife for travel corridors and other biological functions. If treatments occur near riparian areas, buffer strips 50 to 75 m wide should be left on each side of the waterway (see Chap. 6 and Payne 1992). Selective thinning or small clearings can be used to produce feeding sites along riparian areas (Inglis et al. 1986). In more arid climates, northern bobwhite quail prefer such mesic habitats as riparian areas (Campbell-Kissock et al. 1985). Disking to create early successional stages dominated by annual and perennial forbs is recommended for northern bobwhite quail (Guthery 1986).

For Rio Grande turkeys, mottes of old brush should be left near permanent water (Hauke 1975). In addition, large, open-canopied trees should be spared as roost trees; brush corridors and thickets of screening cover should be spared near roosts to permit undisturbed movement of birds.

Herbicides

In wildlife habitat management, herbicides should be one of the last options as a manipulative technique. However, they do offer an alternative to mechanical plant control for:

1. Controlling poisonous and other unwanted plants
2. Releasing closed communities over which tree canopies have gained dominance to stimulate herbaceous plant growth
3. Preventing invasion of grasslands and meadows by woody plants
4. Maintaining openings created by other techniques

5. Altering habitat structure

6. Top-killing strong sprouters to stimulate palatable regrowth

7. Manipulating plant succession

Advantages and disadvantages should be considered carefully (Table 9.9). Vallentine (1989) discussed advantages and disadvantages of herbicides in detail. Habitat managers should understand completely the properties of herbicides and their respective LD_{50}s (Table 9.10). An LD_{50} is the single dosage by mouth that kills 50 percent of the test animals, expressed as milligrams per kilogram of body weight. Several chemicals listed as mildly toxic have LD_{50} levels similar to aspirin and table salt.

The future use of herbicides on rangelands is uncertain. Their use as a habitat-management tool is questionable. During the last two decades the use of herbicides was greatly reduced on public lands and private lands. Even chemicals widely and effectively used in the 1960s and 1970s are now banned. Two examples are 2,4,5-T and its relative Silvex (2,4,5-TP). Furthermore, rangeland herbicides might become too expensive when cost-benefit analyses are examined. Even though their use in habitat management could have potential benefits, public pressures could cause more drastic restrictions of herbicide use on rangelands. Also, corporations might reject any testing of new rangeland herbicides because of the time constraints (greater than 10 years) and expense (greater than $1.5 million) of obtaining U.S. Environmental Protection Agency registration under the Federal Insecticide, Fungicide, and Rodenticide Act of 1972.

Herbicides that are used in the future probably will be nontoxic (LD_{50} greater than 5000 mg per kilogram of body weight), highly selective (will kill or damage only a particular plant species or group of species), and/or applied to individual plants or specific sites. Broadcast spraying over large areas rarely will be practiced.

Herbicides differ widely. Preemergent (soil-applied) herbicides normally are more persistent than contact herbicides. Some act as soil sterilants when applied at high rates. Many preemergents are not recommended on sandy soils or soils with low organic matter. Triazine-based preemergents (e.g., atrazine) are persistent in high-alkaline soils. Almost all herbicides have some drawback. They can be expensive (glyphosate), highly toxic (paraquat), and damage forbs (2,4-D), especially if used incorrectly. Herbicides should not be used in riparian habitats. Thus, the pros and cons of herbicide application must be weighed carefully when they are considered as a habitat-management technique.

The indirect effects of wildlife habitat alteration from herbicide application are of far greater concern than the direct (toxic) effects (Morrison

TABLE 9.9   Advantages and Disadvantages of Herbicides Compared to Other Forms of Plant Control

Advantages	Disadvantages
1. Can be used where mechanical methods are impossible, such as on steep, rocky, muddy, or many timbered sites, particularly with aerial application.	1. No chemical control has yet proven fully satisfactory for some noxious plant species.
2. Provides a variety of application methods ranging from individual plant treatment to aerial broadcasting.	2. Herbicides provide a desirable, noncompetitive seedbed for artificial seeding only under certain situations.
3. Provides a rapid control method from the standpoint of plant response and area covered when broadcast-applied.	3. Costs of control might outweigh expected benefits on low-potential rangeland habitats; this also is true of many other treatment methods.
4. Has low labor and fuel requirements in application.	4. Careless use of chemicals can be hazardous to nontarget plants in the stand and to cultivated crops or other nontarget sites nearby, or might contaminate water supplies.
5. Phenoxy herbicides are generally cheaper than mechanical control methods, but might cost more than prescribed burning.	5. Lack of selectivity might result in killing associated forbs and shrubs important for wildlife.
6. Most herbicides are selective or can be selectively applied so that damage to desirable plant species can be minimized.	6. The effective time period for applying foliage-applied herbicides is usually restrictive.
7. Maintains a grass and litter cover and does not expose soil to erosion.	7. Herbicides generally decrease plant diversity.
8. Safe and reliable when proper safeguards are followed.	8. Abundance and diversity of forbs, important to many wildlife species, are often drastically reduced.
9. Can often use regular farm and ranch spray equipment.	9. Herbicides can directly kill wildlife or have other undesirable effects on wildlife.
10. Soil-applied, but not foliage-applied, herbicides can be applied over a relatively long time period for brush control.	

SOURCE: Adapted from Vallentine (1989).

TABLE 9.10 Properties of Herbicides Used on Rangeland or Proposed for Rangeland Use

Common name (trade name)	Group and type of herbicide*	Uses, restrictions, LD_{50}†	Range and pasture uses, comments
Amitrole (Aminotriazole and Weedazole)	Triazole; foliage; nonselective, translocated	Noncropland use; LD_{50}, 15,000.	Effective on Canada thistle, field bindweed, horsetail, leafy spurge, whitetop, cattails, poison ivy. Suggested for patch treatment. Persists 2–4 weeks in soil.
Atrazine (AAtrex)	Triazine; selective, soil-active herbicide	Rangeland and pasture; LD_{50}, 5100.	Kills annual grasses and broadleaf weed seedlings, providing chemical fallow on range. Persists for over 1 year in dry soil. May increase protein content in perennial grasses. About 1:12 kg a.e./ha‡ has damaged established wheatgrasses.
Clopyralid (Lontrel, Reclaim)	Phenoxy-picolinic; selective, translocated, foliage applied	Limited clearance for range; LD_{50}, 5000.	Excellent control of honey mesquite, Russian knapweed, poison milkvetch, musk thistle, Canada thistle; minimal residue after 1 year.
Dalapon (Dowpon)	Aliphatic; translocated, selective, foliage applied	Pasture or noncropland use; LD_{50}, 3860.	Foliage spray on emerged aquatics such as cattails and rushes, also medusahead and foxtail barley.
Dicamba (Banvel)	Benzoic; selective, translocated, foliage or soil applied	Cleared for pasture and range at rates up to 9 kg a.e./ha; LD_{50}, 566–1028.	Controls difficult plants such as Russian knapweed, whitetop, saltcedar, field bindweed, Canada thistle, leafy spurge. Also useful in brush control. Persists in soil for up to a few months. Low volatility. Often mixed with 2,4-D.
2,4-D (several trade names)	Phenoxy; selective, translocated, foliage applied	Pasture and range; LD_{50}, 300–1000.	Effective as foliage spray on many broad-leaved herbaceous plants and some shrubs: bitterweed, arrowgrass, death camas, halogeton, locoweed, mulesear, rabbitbrush (partly), big sagebrush, sand sagebrush, tarweed, false-hellebore, common burdock.

Herbicide	Properties	Use/Toxicity	Remarks
2,4-DB (Butoxone, Butyrac)	Same as 2,4-D	Cleared for wide use; LD_{50}, 1960.	Used for broadleaf weed control in legumes (0.56–2.25 kg/ha); most weeds convert readily to 2,4-D; legumes except sweetclover convert slowly, and effects slight.
Fenac (Fenatrol)	Phenylacetic; translocated by roots; partly selective, temporary soil sterilant	Spot treatment on range; LD_{50}, 1040.	Used on Canada thistle, leafy spurge, Russian knapweed, and woody plants. Persists 1 year or longer in soil.
Glyphosate (Roundup)	Aliphatic; nonselective, translocated, foliage applied	Range and pasture; broad-spectrum herbicide; LD_{50}, 5000.	Used in total plant control; often applied with 2,4-D. Kills many brush and weed species, including foxtail barley and saltgrass. Can be applied selectively. Persists 1–3 weeks in soil, no apparent soil activity.
Hexazinone (Velpar)	Triazine; nonselective, translocated, foliage or root (mostly used as latter) applied	Rangeland use; LD_{50}, 1690 (available as wet-table powder, liquid, or large pellets).	Effective for individual woody plant wetting or patch spraying; useful in basal spraying and stem injection; grid application as large pellets permits selective brush control.
Kerosene or diesel oil	Organic compound; nonselective, foliage or trunk applied	Unrestricted	Mostly used in basal trunk spraying; minimum persistence in soil; mostly too costly for use now.
Paraquat (Paraquat, Gramoxone)	Bipyridyl; selective to nonselective, contact, foliage applied	Spot treatment on non-cropland, or pasture or range renovation; LD_{50}, 150.	Selectively kills annual grasses by application at 0.28–1.12 kg/ha; can be applied just before to range seeding. Rapid acting, nonvolatile. Soil contact inactivates. Has minor effect on broadleaf perennials. Low rate chemically cures but does not kill perennial grasses.

TABLE 9.10 Properties of Herbicides Used on Rangeland or Proposed for Rangeland Use (Continued)

Common name (trade name)	Group and type of herbicide*	Uses, restrictions, LD_{50}†	Range and pasture uses, comments
Picloram (Tordon)	Picolinic; selective, translocated, foliage or soil applied	Range and pasture; LD_{50}, 8200.	Effective as foliage spray or pellets on leafy spurge, pricklypear. Macartney rose, broom snakeweed, musk thistle, Russian knapweed, low larkspur, tall larkspur, whorled milkweed, and also many shrubs such as saltcedar, chamise, huisache, cholla, rabbitbrush, and oaks. Also effective on juniper and creosotebush with pellet application. Basal stem treatment. Nonvolatile. Rates over 1.12 kg/ha may persist for 2 or 3 years. Often synergic with 2,4-D.
Tebuthiuron (Spike; Grassland)	Substituted urea; partly selective, translocated, soil-active herbicide	Cleared for range use; LD_{50}, 286–644.	Controls a wide spectrum of woody plants including juniper, whitebrush, oaks, yaupon, big sagebrush, sand shinnery, creosotebush, tarbush, and buckbrush. Spot-apply or broadcast as pellets. Persists in soil up to several months to 2 years. Selective at 0.56 kg/ha rate or when high rates applied selectively.
Triclopyr (Garlon; Remedy)	Phenoxy-picolinic; selective, translocated, foliage applied	Cleared for rangelands; LD_{50}, 713.	Shows promise on broadleaf weeds such as tall larkspur and locoweed, and shrubs including oaks, maples, mesquite, saltcedar, Russian olive, and other root sprouters. Also effective in basal spray and trunk injection. Degraded rapidly in soil. Can be mixed with 2,4-D.

*For mode of action of individual herbicides, refer to Ashton and Crafts (1981); for symptoms of herbicide injury, refer to Sharma (1986).

†Registration of herbicides for range and pasture uses and the accompanying restrictions are subject to continual change. Current clearance and restrictions at both state and federal levels should be complied with; check current labels for permitted uses. Silvex and 2,4,5-T have been removed from the market in the United States and Canada. LD_{50} taken from Weed Science Society of America (1983). See Woodward (1982) for herbicide tolerance of trout.

‡a.e. = acid equivalent.

SOURCE: Vallentine (1989).

and Meslow 1983) because residues are usually of low concentration and short-lived (Vallentine 1989). So regardless of the chemical discussed and in the hope that new, nontoxic herbicides will be developed, the focus herein is on the *management application* of herbicides not the herbicides themselves. (See Payne 1992 for methods of application and "Herbicides" under "Intermediate Treatment" in Chap. 3.)

Grasslands and tundra

Eastern redcedar invades tallgrass prairies, reducing the herbaceous biomass (Engle et al. 1987). While this tree can benefit some wildlife species, grassland species could be affected negatively. Eastern redcedar should be controlled where canopy cover substantially depresses the phytomass that is an important wildlife habitat component. Chemicals effective in controlling it include picloram and tebuthiuron.

Prairie threeawn is a herbaceous invader on degraded, tallgrass prairie range sites; it colonizes bare soil and maintains dominance for many years. Its value to wildlife is minimal. Atrazine effectively controls prairie threeawn (Engle et al. 1990), but has been banned in some states because it contaminates groundwater. Suppression of native plants by glyphosate can promote establishment of big bluestem in seeded pastures or remnant native species on rangeland (Samson and Moser 1982). This might be an important consideration if big bluestem were needed as nesting or winter cover for birds.

Mesquite has been a tenacious invader on millions of hectares of shortgrass and mixed-grass prairies of the Southwest. The expanded range of mesquite has increased the distribution of white-tailed deer and perhaps other wildlife. Where dense canopies are a problem, treatment with herbicides might be needed. For wildlife habitat, no more than 60 percent of a mesquite-dominated habitat should be treated; treatments should be in strips 200 m wide or less, or as a patchwork of openings, with untreated strips 250 m wide and brush clumps left as security cover. For optimum biodiversity, large, untreated blocks should be left for interior species. Bottomland and riparian areas should be left untreated in southern mixed prairie habitats (Darr and Klebenow 1975). Triclopyr and clopyralid are two herbicides that could be used. Except for mockingbirds and golden-fronted woodpeckers, most nongame birds in northern Texas were unaffected by herbicide-treated areas designed to improve habitat for mourning doves and bobwhite quail, as long as stems and tree skeletons were left standing (Gruver 1984). Total density of nongame birds increased 54 percent on managed versus unmanaged sites; species diversity and richness were similar (Gruver and Guthery 1986). Forbs might decline 1 to 2 years posttreatment. Preemergent and postemergent herbicides also have been used to increase success of seeding by reducing competition. Efforts to establish fourwing salt-bush were improved by using metolachlor and alachlor as preemer-gents, and acifluorfen, clopyralid, and fluazifop-P as postemergent herbicides (Petersen et al. 1990).

In northern prairies, leafy spurge is a troublesome, introduced perennial which can be controlled with picloram, dicamba, and glyphosate (Hickman et al. 1990). Because forbs and other broad-leaved plants are important to many wildlife species, patchwork treatments of herbicides should be applied.

To improve success of perennial grass seedings, invading annuals in grasslands of California and elsewhere can be controlled with paraquat and glyphosate. These should be used in the fall (Vallentine 1989).

Herbicides used in semidesert grasslands have been targeted for plants such as mesquite, burroweed, creosotebush, tarbush, cholla, yucca, and pricklypear. Total control or large-block treatments of mesquite are not recommended in semidesert grasslands because these are valuable habitat for many species. Applications for use in habitat management should be restricted to small areas of patchwork design on sites of low erosion potential. Creation of 5- to 20-ha clear-ings in dense mesquite with herbicides can benefit some wildlife. Pre-scribed fire could be considered for maintenance if enough fine fuels occur (600 to 800 kg/ha) and controlled burns are spaced more than 15 years apart. In creosotebush communities, tebuthiuron treatments were more effective than mechanical treatments in killing these plants, but changes in grasses and forb density were the same whether creosotebush was chemically or mechanically treated (Morton and Melgoza 1991).

Herbicides must be avoided in alpine tundra (Braun 1980) and arc-tic tundra. Forbs valuable to many tundra wildlife species would be reduced substantially.

Shrublands

Cold desert. Sagebrush rangelands often are treated with herbicides to increase herbaceous plants. Herbicides such as 2,4-D killed 85 to 98 percent of the sagebrush in Oregon; rate of reinvasion was affected mainly by range condition (Hedrick et al. 1966). The herbicide 2,4-D has variable effects on other plant species (Table 9.11). Leaving nar-row strips and/or partially controlled areas also accelerates reinva-sion of treated sites (Vallentine 1989), but prescribed fire could be used to control reinvasion. But reinvasion might be desirable up to a point, especially on mule deer and pronghorn range.

Seeding of treated sites is widely practiced. Planting monocultures of crested wheatgrass is generally unsound wildlife management, but

TABLE 9.11   Effect of 2,4-D on Forbs and Shrubs Associated with Big Sagebrush

Genera reduced 67–100% in density	Genera reduced 34–66% in density	Genera reduced <33% in density	Genera not affected
Astragalus	Agoseris	Agastache	Achillea
Balsamorrhiza	Lithospermum	Antennaria	Aplopappus
Castilleja	Lupinus	Arnica	Astragalus
Helianthella	Artemisia cana	Comandra	Calochortus
Lupinus		Erigeron	Crepis
Mertensia		Eriogonum	Delphinium
Pentstemon		Penstemon	Geranium
Potentilla		Phlox	Linum
Geum		Senecio	Rumex
Zygadenas		Viola	Solidago
Amelanchier*		Chrysothamnus	Perideridia
		Pinus	Ceanothus*
		Populus	Opuntia
		Prunus	Potentilla
		Salix	Pseudotsuga
		Symphoricarpos*	Purshia
			Tetradymia

*Aerial portions severely damaged.
SOURCE: Peek (1986).

it provides valuable forage for deer and elk and succeeds at the lower spectrum of precipitation where other perennial grasses fail (Urness 1986). Mixtures are best. Whenever chemical seedbed preparation before seeding (detailed in Vallentine 1989) is used, managers should be cautious because forbs important to most wildlife are reduced by chemicals. If undesired weeds or shrubs dominate the treated site, chemical seedbed preparation might be considered. For example, Hedrick et al. (1969) recommended combined treatments of rotobeating sagebrush-rabbitbrush areas in year 1, spraying with 2,4-D in year 2, and seeding in year 3 for successful plant establishment.

Introduced into the western United States in the 1890s, cheatgrass brome is a problem invader over much of the Intermountain Region. Vallentine (1989) discussed several herbicides effective in combating cheatgrass where it dominates sites to the exclusion of other important plants. Two effective herbicides are paraquat and atrazine.

Even though untreated areas are important sources of seed that can reinfest treated areas, thus reducing the treatment's life expectancy (Johnson and Payne 1968), spraying large, entire units of sagebrush to increase grass for livestock (Vallentine 1989) is *not* recommended for wildlife habitat management. Howard and Wolfe (1976) recommended patterned treatments of small tracts instead of large tracts for species such as ferruginous hawks because such treatments improve the prey base. Generally, herbicides such as 2,4-D have an adverse impact on most birds, especially if treated areas are large. Brewer's sparrows and Vesper sparrows lose nesting habitat and food supplies (Institute of Land Rehabilitation 1978); Vesper sparrows are less sensitive than Brewer's sparrows (Best 1972). While partial control of sagebrush with 2,4-D did not affect Brewer's sparrows, total kill of sagebrush decreased the sparrow population by 54 percent in Montana (Wiens and Dyer 1975) and by 99 percent in Wyoming (Schroeder and Sturges 1975).

Habitats of sage grouse can take 10 years to recover after *total* sagebrush eradication with herbicides (Institute of Land Rehabilitation 1978). For example, sage grouse did not return to nest until 5 years after big sagebrush was sprayed over large tracts with 2,4-D (Klebenow 1970).

In general, mechanical treatments are recommended over herbicides for improving sage grouse habitat. But spraying areas with over 39 percent big sagebrush cover can benefit sage grouse, as long as treatments are in small blocks, strips, or patches (Holechek et al. 1989). To reduce losses of forbs, applications of 2,4-D in Idaho were recommended in early spring (early April) (Autenrieth et al. 1982), or when there is adequate snow cover during application. In either case, spraying must be conducted before forbs emerge. Braun et al. (1977) reported that spraying should be avoided along meadows, riparian areas, where big sagebrush cover is less than 20 percent, and where slopes are greater than 20 percent. Furthermore, 100-m or wider buffer strips of living sagebrush should remain. In the eastern portion of their range, Braun et al. (1977) recommended that sagebrush control not occur within a 3.2-km radius of sage grouse leks, nesting areas, wintering grounds, or breeding grounds. In the western portion, Urness (1979) believed that such recommendations were far too restrictive and limit our ability to improve sage grouse habitat. Herbicides could be used to prevent shrub invasion onto strutting grounds, clear shrubs that have encroached on meadows, and alter size and density of sagebrush to more closely approximate nesting requirements. Moreover, spraying more productive north-facing slopes in the 20- to 25-cm rainfall zone might enhance brood-rearing habitat (Autenrieth et al. 1982). The chemical Roundup (glyphosate) can be applied to sagebrush in winter months to kill only sagebrush above the snow.

Response by small mammals varies with herbicide treatment. Deer mice seem unaffected, northern pocket gophers and least chipmunks can decrease, badgers might decrease initially should gophers or ground squirrels be affected negatively (Cooperrider et al. 1986), and mountain voles usually increase (Institute of Land Rehabilitation

1978). Once preferred forbs return to an area, small mammals apparently return to pretreatment levels.

Elk apparently benefit from conversion of sagebrush to grass-dominated sites. Elk use increased 89 percent on chemically treated versus untreated sites in Wyoming (Severson and Medina 1983), and chemical treatments effectively influenced distribution (Wilbert 1963). Elk calving and feeding behavior was unaffected by herbicide control of sagebrush (Ward 1973). Mule deer used sagebrush less in Colorado after it was sprayed with 2,4-D (Severson and Medina 1983).

Pronghorns rely heavily upon browse diets during fall and winter, but forbs are important in spring and summer. They seem to do best where shrub cover is moderate and fairly low in stature (Vale 1974, Yoakum 1975). Potential exists to use herbicides in extensive dense stands of tall sagebrush with poor understories (Urness 1979). Such treatments can increase herbaceous species and improve the overall mix of plants.

For optimum biodiversity of wildlife habitat, herbicide applications to control sagebrush should be limited to 16 ha or less in a patchwork design, with 200-ha areas of untreated sagebrush as a buffer between treated sites and to retain untreated areas for interior species. Based on current knowledge, total treatment should be less than 20 percent of an area. Treatments on ridges, slopes, meadows, and riparian areas must be carefully planned; sagebrush flats are the most likely target area, as are sites dominated by rabbitbrush. Little benefit from any habitat modification can be expected unless livestock grazing is closely regulated after treatment.

Hot desert. Cautious and guarded use of herbicides in hot desert communities is recommended. Aside from the semidesert grasslands, herbicides probably have little application, particularly in the Sonoran and Mojave deserts.

Woodlands

Pinyon-juniper. Broad-scale herbicide use in pinyon-juniper woodlands has not been popular over the past three decades, especially as the sole technique to open them up. Characteristics of juniper make them resistant to foliage application of herbicide, but soil-to-root translocation holds promise. Tebuthiuron or picloram kills pinyon pine and Utah juniper less than 2 m tall. Tebuthiuron, but not picloram, kills one-seed juniper, but neither herbicide kills alligator juniper consistently (Johnsen and Dalen 1990).

Wildlife responses to herbicide treatments have not been adequately evaluated in pinyon-juniper woodlands. In one study, mule deer use was greater in a 146-ha chemically treated plot than on a 146-ha mechanically treated plot because herbicide caused greater interspersion and greater retention of screening cover (Severson and Medina 1983). Therefore, if herbicides could be used safely, aerial broadcast could create numerous, small, irregularly-shaped openings in terrain that is too rough for mechanical operations (Short and McCulloch 1977).

Evans et al. (1975) suggested that herbicides be used with mechanical treatment to manipulate pinyon-juniper. Small trees that escape chaining, cabling, or dozing can be treated effectively with picloram to ensure that the opening created is free of trees, if that is the management objective. Treating individual plants can be practical. Unwanted invaders of mechanically prepared openings, e.g., cheatgrass brome, might be controlled with atrazine or paraquat. Paraquat and glyphosate can be used to desiccate leaves or needles, rendering them more susceptible to prescribed burning (Evans et al. 1975).

The possibility of destroying midstory shrubs important as food sources, and the distasteful appearance of dead snags, are major disadvantages to herbicide use. The greatest danger is the gross misuse of chemicals in a woodland type that is very important to wildlife in the western United States and Canada (Short and McCulloch 1977).

Oak. Herbicides can be a valuable tool to improve elk habitat by top-killing Gambel oak in areas where dense stands occur. Elk use increased dramatically after Gambel oak was sprayed with herbicides (Kufeld 1977). Mule deer response was minimal. Small areas of 30 ha or less should be treated to create diversity and feeding sites. Tebuthiuron and triclopyr are effective for treating almost all oak species. Large trees should be protected for their mast-producing potential because acorns are relished by turkey, bear, deer, elk, and other wildlife species.

Treating shinnery oak with tebuthiuron can improve habitat for lesser prairie chickens by increasing forbs and tall grasses (Olawsky and Smith 1991). Tall grasses are used for concealment, especially for loafing and roosting during cool seasons (Davis et al. 1979, Taylor and Guthery 1980). Untreated areas provide acorns (Crawford and Bolen 1976b) and shade (Copelin 1963). A mosaic of treated and untreated shinnery oak is recommended to provide both shinnery oak and grass habitats for lesser prairie chickens (Olawsky and Smith 1991).

Extensive research about herbicides has been conducted, but little quantitative information is available on wildlife use of manipulated oak woodland habitats in the Southwest (Severson and Medina 1983).

California chaparral. Phenoxy herbicides have been used in the California chaparral to stimulate shrub regrowth and increase production of grass and forbs (Vallentine 1989). Species composition, population size, and relative abundance of birds did not change 2 years after herbicide treatment of chaparral (Beaver 1976). Sites of dense chaparral treated as a patchwork mosaic should benefit most edge wildlife. Herbicide treatment might be followed by prescribed burning.

Mountain shrub. The use of herbicides in mountain shrub communities to manipulate wildlife habitat has not received appropriate attention. Inferences drawn from herbicide effects elsewhere might be useful. Snowbrush ceanothus, chokecherry, and snowberry were top-killed when 2,4-D was used to kill sagebrush in Idaho (Vallentine 1989); most plants sprouted from the crown, producing palatable forage. Whisenant (1987) successfully treated big sagebrush with clopyralid, leaving bitterbrush and serviceberry relatively unharmed. Treating areas with 2,4-D resulted in different responses from bitterbrush. In Idaho, bitterbrush was unharmed or damaged only slightly; in Oregon and California, bitterbrush was damaged severely (Vallentine 1989). Damage to bitterbrush could be reduced if an area targeted for sagebrush were treated early, before bitterbrush elongated twigs or began to flower. Bitterbrush plants less than 30 cm tall and those that are flowering will be severely damaged or killed by 2,4-D (Vallentine 1989).

Mesquite-acacia. Because of the wide use of herbicides in this rangeland community type, wildlife responses have received considerable attention. Spraying 400-ha blocks significantly reduced use by white-tailed deer (Beasom and Scifres 1977). But up to 80 percent of a woodland treated in alternating strips of treated and untreated woodland with tree skeletons left standing for screening cover produced no long-term adverse effects for white-tailed deer (Beasom and Scifres 1977, Tanner et al. 1978) or Rio Grande turkeys (Beasom and Scifres 1977), although forb biomass and abundance decreased for 1 to 2 years. Populations of javelina declined after the strip treatments (Beasom and Scifres 1977), probably because their primary food source, pricklypear, also declined (Tanner et al. 1978). Leaving 5- to 10-ha thickets of brush near pricklypear stands seems to benefit javelina (Inglis 1985).

Criss-crossed application at variable rates of tebuthiuron caused interspersed patterns of brush. The resulting patches were shrub-dominated (no herbicide), shrub-herb dominated (one-half rate of herbicide), and herb-dominated (full rate of herbicide) (Fig. 9.4)

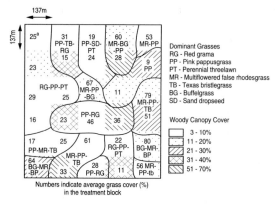

Figure 9.4 Variable rates of herbicide applied by aircraft or tractor designed to achieve a five-dosage-rate pattern for woody plant control. Resultant distribution of herbaceous plants, percent grass cover and woody canopy cover two years after treatment. (*Scifres and Koerth 1986.*)

(Scifres and Koerth 1986). Forbs were relatively unaffected but deer screening cover declined. Therefore, herbicide alteration of mesquite-acacia upland habitat should be acceptable for most wildlife as long as 20 percent of an area is left as old, mature woodland and tree skeletons remain as screening cover. Treating 20 percent and leaving 80 percent of a mesquite bottomland or drainage plus leaving black-brush-acacia uplands untreated did not cause consistent differences in deer use of the habitat (Beasom et al. 1982). Where live oak competes with herbaceous plants, treating live oak with tebuthiuron increased yields of grass by 2 to 4 times and forbs by 5 times compared with untreated oak (Fulbright and Garza 1991). The negative impact on desirable woody plants should be carefully considered in the planning process to avoid treating specific sites where desirable species dominate.

Where soil is disturbed in fall by disking to promote weedy sites, selected herbicides can be cost-effective to enhance production of foods for northern bobwhite quail and mourning doves. Diuron increased croton; metolachlor enhanced sunflower in Texas (Guthery et al. 1987), as did low rates of 2,4-D in Kansas (Pletscher and Robel 1979).

Seeding and Fertilizing

Seeding

Habitat management sometimes requires artificial revegetation such as seeding (Table 9.12) (Vallentine 1989), which usually involves preparing a seedbed followed by drilling or broadcasting seed. Such revegetation often is needed after land is treated with mechanical

TABLE 9.12   Considerations for Successful Seeding

Variable	Requirement
Rainfall	>27 cm per year general (Plummer et al. 1955); >37 cm in California chaparral (Bentley 1967); >50 cm on shallow or rocky soils.
Soil depth	60 cm best (Cook 1966); 30 to 60 cm moderate success.
Soil type	Medium-texture soils are best; heavy clays and fine sands most difficult to get establishment. Saline and alkali soils difficult unless adapted species are used.
Terrain	Bottomland sites are best. Avoid slopes >30% (30 cm rise for every 100 cm on the horizontal). Costs and equipment needs greater on slopes >20%.
Elevation and latitude	Higher altitude and more northerly latitude reduce the length of the growing season and might prevent seed set of less adapted species. Elevations >3500 m were best sites for seeding in hot desert ranges in Arizona.
Density of desirable plants	In the Intermountain Region, revegetation is recommended where less than one desirable bunchgrass exists per 64 cm^2 or a desirable sod-forming grass per 95 cm^2 (Plummer et al. 1955). One desirable shrub per 625 cm^2 also suggests seeding.

SOURCE: Adapted from Vallentine (1989).

TABLE 9.13   **Principal Causes of Revegetation Failure**

Germination of seed
1. Poor-quality seed (low germination, hard seed)
2. Unfavorable temperature
3. Insufficient soil moisture
4. Insufficient soil oxygen
5. High soil salinity
6. Depredation by birds and rodents
7. Insufficient soil coverage

Emergence of seedlings
1. Seeding too deep
2. Soil crusting
3. Desiccation
4. Wind and water erosion
5. Rodent and insect damage
6. Poor-quality seed (low vigor, shriveled, damaged)
7. High soil salinity
8. Frost-heaving

Seedling establishment
1. Drought
2. Competition from weeds
3. Competition of companion crops
4. Soil infertility
5. Insect, disease, and rodent damage
6. Lack of inoculation of legumes
7. Winter-killing and frost-heaving
8. Poor soil drainage and flooding
9. High temperatures
10. Grazed too soon—i.e., before plants become established
11. Wind and water erosion (including wind shear)

SOURCE: Vallentine (1989).

manipulation, herbicides, or fire, or on habitats that are denuded because of overuse, abuse, or neglect.

Why seeding fails.   Seeding fails for many reasons. Habitat managers should be cognizant of the causes for seeding failure (Table 9.13) (Vallentine 1989) before undertaking any seeding effort. In the western United States, drought and improper seed coverage were considered the two common causes of failure (Hyder et al. 1955). Lack of soil moisture and frost-heaving also account for lack of establishment. Frost-heaving, resulting from a buildup of ice crystals near the soil surface, is reduced by providing mulch cover before freezing weather (Biswell et al. 1953).

Plant species selection.   Adaptable plant species (Tables A.8, A.9) will be the ultimate criterion that determines success or failure of a revegetation effort. Selection should be made as follows:

1. Suitability as food or cover for wildlife
2. Drought tolerance
3. Cold hardiness
4. Tolerance of soil salinity
5. Soil texture adaptation
6. Tolerance of high water tables and wet soil conditions
7. Ease of establishment, aggressiveness, longevity, or seed production
8. Season of maximum growth or seed production and length of green growing period
9. Site selection—native plants are better than introduced plants

Perennial grasses have been more widely used than other kinds of plants and more information is available on them. Grasses are useful for wildlife, especially where nesting, loafing, or fawning cover is limiting or grass seeds are eaten by wildlife. Grass forage is commonly consumed by ungulates, especially in early spring or when nutritious regrowth is available (Willms et al. 1981, Bryant et al. 1981, Urness 1986).

Shrub seeding can increase quantity and quality of forage for wild ungulates and provide unique microhabitats for nesting, breeding, and perching birds. Difficulties in using shrubs for revegetation are availability of the seed source (McKell 1975) and lack of information on seeding requirements and suitability (Vallentine 1989). Native shrubs whose seeds are available in the West include bitterbrush, cliffrose, winterfat, mountainmahogany, selected varieties of sagebrush, and fourwing saltbush and other saltbush species.

Forbs and legumes benefit wildlife. Alfalfa, clovers, milkvetches, trefoil, sainfoin, and sweetclovers are among a few legumes available and show promise in the western United States and Canada (Plummer et al. 1968, Wilton et al. 1978). Forbs seeded for ungulates in the intermountain West include small burnet, arrowleaf balsamroot, and penstemons (Plummer et al. 1968). Annual legumes such as rose clover, burclover, and subterranean clover have been used in foothill habitats of California (Kay 1969) and western Oregon.

Establishing legumes might depend on effective nodulation and nitrogen fixation over other factors. Seed should be inoculated with *Rhizobium* bacteria if a strain is available for the legume being planted. Further, treating all seeds with an insecticide, fungicide, or rodenticide might be needed to ensure adequate germination and establishment. Pelleting seeds has proven largely unsuccessful.

Mixtures usually provide better results than single species because they increase the chance of getting a stand established (Table 9.14) (Vallentine 1989). In arid regions, mixtures might be impractical due to poor success.

Seeding often is recommended after mechanical disturbance of pinyon-juniper woodlands because seed sources and shrubs could be absent. Seeding mixtures produce the best results, although results are unpredictable. When 9 grasses, 7 forbs, and 10 shrubs were seeded onto a chained site in Utah, only 4 grasses (fairway, intermediate, bluebunch wheatgrasses, and orchardgrass) and 5 forbs (Lewis flax, alfalfa, yellow sweetclover, sainfoin, and small burnet) became established (Davis and Harper 1990). Aerial seeding might not produce satisfactory results for all plant species, but could be acceptable for shrubs and forbs (Clary 1988) and might be the only practical method to use on some sites. Drilling or imprinting is best. In Utah, seeding was most successful on south-facing hillsides, followed by ridgetops; level sites became dominated by cheatgrass (Christensen et al. 1966).

TABLE 9.14   Advantages of Mixtures and Single-Species Plantings for Revegetation

Advantages of complex mixtures	Advantages of single species
1. Establishing a stand where soil is heterogeneous.	1. Easier to seed evenly.
2. Longer green and succulent period.	2. More uniform grazing because of more uniform palatability.
3. Higher yield.	3. Provide feed at season most needed.
4. Provide a varied diet.	4. Similar growth/regrowth characteristics.
5. Stand less liable to total loss from adverse climatic conditions or insect damage.	5. More precise site adaptation.
6. Occupancy of land more rapid; better ground cover.	6. More stable plant composition.
7. Better adapted to variable canopy, soil, terrain, and climatic conditions.	7. Cheaper to establish.
8. More efficient use of the total soil profile.	8. More rapid establishment of primary species.
9. Provide more multiple uses, i.e., for livestock and big game.	9. Only one species might be fully adapted to the site or intended use.
10. Species can be included when seed is too scarce or limited for full seeding.	

SOURCE: Adapted from Vallentine (1989).

Specific seeding recommendations vary (Table 9.15). Skousen et al. (1989) used several mixtures and seeding rates to evaluate seeding and chaining in pinyon-juniper woodlands of Utah. Some sagebrush accessions are preferable to others and should be used (Rosenstock et al. 1989). Mule deer seem to prefer *Poa* spp. (Terrell and Spillet 1975),

TABLE 9.15 Plant Species Recommended for Seeding Mechanically Treated Pinyon-Juniper Woodlands

	Reference				
	Clary (1988)		Evans	Rosenstock et al.	Stevens et al.
Plant species	USFS*	BLM†	(1988)	(1989)	(1975)
Grasses					
Crested wheatgrass	x (3.4)	x (4.5)			x
Desert wheatgrass					x
Intermediate wheatgrass	x (1.7)			x (1.8)	x
Pubescent wheatgrass		x (2.2)		x (1.8)	
Fairway wheatgrass				x (3.5)	
Smooth brome	x (1.1)			x (0.9)	x
Grama (blue, black, sideoats)			x		
Lovegrass (Boer, Lehmann, weeping)			x		
Orchardgrass			x		
Russian wildrye	x (1.7)	x (2.2)	x	x (0.9)	x
Basin wildrye			x		
Winter rye		x (2.2)			
Indian ricegrass			x		
Spike muhly			x		
Sheep fescue			x		
Forbs					
Alfalfa	x (2.0)	x (1.1)	x	x (0.9)	x
Yellow sweetclover	x (0.3)	x (1.1)		x (0.4)	x
Small burnet	x (1.1)		x		x
Arrowleaf balsamroot					x
Lewis flax			x		
Palmer penstemon			x		
Rocky Mountain penstemon			x		
Shrubs					
Bitterbrush			x		x
Cliffrose			x		x
Winterfat			x		x
Fourwing saltbush		x (1.1)	x		x
Big sagebrush			x	x (0.4)	x
Rabbitbrush			x	x (0.4)	x

*USFS = U.S. Forest Service.
†BLM = U.S. Bureau of Land Management.
Note: Seeding rates (kg/ha) when known are in parentheses.

and these also should be included. For wildlife, recommended seeding rates of forbs and shrubs should be at least equal to those for grasses.

Site and seedbed preparation. The purpose of seedbed preparation is to ensure that the soil (1) is firm below the seeding depth, (2) is well pulverized, (3) is free from plant competition, (4) is free of seeds from competing plants, and (5) has mulch on the surface (Vallentine 1989). Plant competition limits germination and habitat revegetation. Habitat managers have many choices as to the type of equipment used (Tables 9.16 through 9.18) (Long et al. 1984, Doerr et al. 1986).

While grass seeders, press seeders, and pasture drills work well on relatively flat, smooth terrain (Doerr 1986a, 1986b, 1986c), other seeding techniques are needed for steeper, rougher, and rockier habitats. The rangeland drill (Fig. 9.5) (Doerr 1986d), the steep-slope seeder (Fig. 9.6) (Doerr 1986e), and the hydroseeder (Fig. 9.7) (Doerr 1986f) are better adapted to difficult seeding conditions affected by terrain and rocky sites.

Optimum seeding depth for most grass, forb, legume, and shrub seeds is 0.6 to 1.25 cm. Some species, e.g., winterfat, do best when planted 0.15 cm deep (Springfield 1970). Where drills are used, optimum row spacings vary from 15 to 60 cm, but 25 to 40 cm is most common. Seeding rates, seeding mixtures, and selection criteria vary (Tables A.9 through A.12).

Mulch and/or cover crops might be needed to stabilize soil and control erosion or to reduce weed competition. Mulch techniques vary with slope, costs, and labor (Table 9.19) (Long et al. 1984). Cover crops used vary from region to region (Table 9.20) (Long et al. 1984).

Interseeding. Seeding can require complete renovation (plowing and seedbed preparation) that *replaces* habitat vegetation. Or seeding can simply be applied locally to burned, mechanically treated, or chemically treated sites. *Interseeding* is another alternative. Interseeding is accomplished in strips placed through the native stand such that the stand becomes modified or augmented by the addition of supplemental plant species. Site and seedbed preparation, and perhaps even mulch, are needed, but only in linear strips. Interseeding should be considered where (1) the erosion hazard is high, (2) the preparation of a complete seedbed is too costly or impractical, or (3) the purpose is to augment rather than replace the plant stand (Vallentine 1989).

Interseeding is a compromise between slow, natural successional development and the rapid establishment through complete artificial revegetation. Normally, plant species native to the area should be used to complement and improve diversity and productivity of existing habitats. Grass species interseeded into habitats could improve

TABLE 9.16 Summary of Capabilities and Limitations of Site Preparation Equipment

Equipment	Site preparation	Capabilities	Limitations	Power requirements (hp)
Dozer blades	Bush clearing	Removes stumps and large trees.	Does not control rhizomatous and stump-sprouting species. Not suited for shallow or rocky soils. Least efficient clearing method.	39–700
Grubbers	Brush control	Removes individual rhizomatous and stump-sprouting species.	Not appropriate for dense stands.	65–200
Rootplows	Brush control	Controls stump-sprouting species on large areas.	Areas must be reseeded to increase herbaceous production.	60–170
Chains and cables	Brush control	Prepares rough seedbed for broadcast seeding or covering seed. Thins or clears dense extensive mature tree stands. Most economical tree-felling method.	Limited to tree diameters from 15 to 60 cm. Does not severely affect undergrowth with flexible stems. Does not control rhizomatous species.	190–290
Rotobeaters, shredders, and brush-hogs	Brush control	Shreds woody vegetation and creates a mulch material.	Not appropriate for rocky, shallow soils. High maintenance requirements.	60–250
Rollerchoppers	Brush control	Crushes and chops non-root-sprouting species.	Surface treatment only. Not appropriate for rocky soils. Does not control rhizomatous species.	60–370
Mowers	Herbaceous weed control	Removes top growth. Can reduce seed production.	Not generally suited for woody vegetation. Limited application on non-intensive management areas.	60–84
Standard and one-way disks	Seedbed preparation	Plows normal and deep, and controls herbaceous weeds.	Not suited for rocky or uneven terrain.	20–215
Offset and tandem disks	Seedbed preparation	Removes sparse brush. Useful for deep plowing dry, heavy soils.	Not suited for rocky or uneven terrain.	60–315
Brushland plows	Brush control, seedbed preparation	Suited for plowing rocky soils on uneven terrain and destroying brush.	Not widely available. Initial cost is high. Difficult to transport.	40–124
Disk-chains	Seedbed preparation	Good for herbaceous weed control and primary tilling.	Must be relatively brush- and rock-free; not widely available.	300

TABLE 9.16 Summary of Capabilities and Limitations of Site Preparation Equipment (Continued)

Equipment	Site preparation	Capabilities	Limitations	Power requirements (hp)
Chisel plows	Seedbed preparation	Relieves shallow compaction. Incorporates fertilizers and mulch.	Furrows do not last long.	30–315
Subsoilers and rippers	Soil compaction	Alleviates deep soil compaction. Creates deep furrows.	Not appropriate for rocky soils or steep slopes.	55–315
Soil sifters	Seedbed preparation	Clears stumps, logs, and other debris; reduces large soil clumps.	Must reseed rapidly to avoid erosion. Not suited for highly rocky soils.	100
Disk harrows	Secondary seedbed preparation	Controls annual vegetation and incorporates soil amendments.	Not adapted to rough, rocky, uneven terrain.	40–315
Spike-toothed harrows	Secondary seedbed preparation	Smooths roughly plowed soils. Useful on debris-laden soils and for covering broadcast seed.	Provides a surface treatment only. Not adapted to rough terrain.	+20
Spring-toothed harrows	Secondary seedbed preparation	Incorporates soil amendments and smooths moderately rocky and debris-laden soils.	Not adapted to extremely rough range sites without prior brush control and site preparation.	20–315
Klodbusters	Steep-slope seedbed preparation	Prepares steep slopes for broadcast seeding and hydroseeding.	Slopes must be >20%.	Low
Furrowers and trenchers	Erosion control	Creates furrows that collect moisture and improve infiltration. Trenchers are useful on slopes up to 45%.	Furrows must be on the contour. Furrows must last to be useful. Furrowers should not be used on slopes >20%.	42–60 (trenchers) 55–120 (furrowers)
Land imprinters	Seed environment improvement	Creates small pits for moisture collection and improved infiltration. Useful on rough land, up to 45% slope. Soil structure is not completely destroyed.	Cannot be used on dense brushy areas.	60–105
Gougers and pitters	Seed environment improvement	Creates small pits to collect moisture and increase infiltration.	Not adapted to slopes >20%.	+50
Basin blades	Seed environment improvement, erosion control	Used to create large basins (pits) for moisture collection and soil moisture concentration; best on slopes.	Low availability. High initial cost. Other techniques better on level ground.	290–370

SOURCE: Doerr et al. (1986).

TABLE 9.17 Techniques and Constraints for Seedbed Preparation

Technique	Primary purpose	Constraints					Normally associated seeding techniques	Remarks
		Steep slopes	Rocky soils	Wet soils	Compacted soils	Alternate equipment uses		
Cultipacking	To firm and pack seedbeds, break surface clods	x	See "Remarks"	x	NA	Cover broadcast seed	Broadcast	Special cultipackers available for rough, moderately rocky ground, not applicable to clayey soils.
Disking	To break surface soil clods, relieve surface compaction	x	See "Remarks"	x	—	Turn under stubble; weed control, mulch anchoring (hay, straw), incorporate soil amendments	Drill	Special disks available for moderately rough, rocky land; does not treat subsoil compaction.
Dozer tracking	To roughen seedbed surface to trap seed fertilizer, etc., and to decrease erosion	—	x	x	NA	Grading, creating dozer basins, ripping	Broadcast	Not applicable to unstable slopes.
Gouging	To enhance soil moisture in arid areas	x	—	x	x	None	Broadcast	Designed for arid and semi-arid areas; leaves very rough surface—can limit subsequent mulch application.
Harrowing	To break surface soil clods and smooth the seedbed	x	See "Remarks"	x	—	Control small weeds, incorporate soil amendments, cover broadcast seed	Drill, broadcast	Generally, equipment not adapted to extremely rocky soils—spring-tooth harrow adapted to sites too rocky for disking; flexible fine harrow adapted to soils too rocky for other harrow implements.
Klodbuster	To prepare the seedbed and fill in gullies on steep slopes	—	Large surface rocks	x	x	Cover broadcast seed and incorporate soil amendments on steep slopes	Broadcast	Not effective on slopes <20%; slopes must be free of stumps and large obstructions for efficient use.

TABLE 9.17 Techniques and Constraints for Seedbed Preparation *(Continued)*

Technique	Primary purpose	Constraints					Normally associated seeding techniques	Remarks
		Steep slopes	Rocky soils	Wet soils	Compacted soils	Alternate equipment uses		
Land imprinting	To improve moisture infiltration in arid areas	See "Remarks"	–	x	NA	Brush control, soft-rock crushing, and soil compaction	Broadcast	Designed for arid areas; leaves rough surface—could limit subsequent mulch application; can be cable-towed up steep slopes.
Ripping, chiseling	To decrease compaction and improve moisture infiltration	To the limit of dozer capability	–	x	–	Roughen subgrade before applying topsoil	Drill, broadcast	Can improve soil structure and aggregation of alkaline-affected soils; leaves a rough, cloddy seedbed.
Rotary tiller	To provide a loose seedbed; to break up sod	x	x	x	–	Incorporate soil amendments into the seedbed	Drill, broadcast	Limited to slopes <30%; effective topsoil incorporation of organic amendments.

Note: x = constraint applies to technique; – = no constraint is involved with this technique; NA = not applicable.
SOURCE: Long et al. (1984).

TABLE 9.18 Techniques and Constraints for Seeding and Planting

Technique	Primary purpose	Constraints						Remarks
		Steep slopes	Rough seed-bed	Labor inten-sive	High equip-ment cost	Possible high site mainte-nance	Low rate-to-time ratio	
Broadcast seeding	To rapidly seed disturbed areas	–	–	–	See "Remarks"	–	–	Requires high seeding rate; establishment risk higher than with drill seeding; equipment costs dependent on methods.
Drill seeding	To seed disturbed areas by placing the seed in intimate contact with the soil	x	See "Remarks"	–	x	–	–	Requires less seed than broadcast seeding; high success rate; some drills capable of seeding rough terrain.
Dryland tubeling planter	To plant containerized stock on harsh sizes	x	–	–	x	Possible	–	Requires containerized stock and specialized equipment.
Grass seeder	To seed disturbed areas without creating drill rows	x	x	–	x	–	–	Promotes even seed distribution.
Hand planting of seedlings	To promote rapid establishment of shrubs, trees, and vines	–	–	x	–	x	x	More costly than seeding; requires good-quality stock and proper implementation for success.
Hydraulic seeding (hydroseeding)	See "Broadcast Seeding"	–	–	–	x	–	–	See "Broadcast seeding"; can also apply fertilizer, lime, and mulch in one application if advisable.
Planting shrub and tree stock—manual	To establish mature tree stock	x	–	x	–	x	x	See "Hand-planting seedlings."
Seeding planters	To plant a high volume of seedlings in a short time	x	See "Remarks"	–	x	–	–	Cannot operate over large obstructions.
Sodding—manual	To establish plant species rapidly for immediate erosion and/or aesthetic concerns	–	x	x	–	x	x	Very useful for drainageways; high success rate if properly implemented; precludes seeding on treated sites.

TABLE 9.18 Techniques and Constraints for Seeding and Planting (Continued)

Technique	Primary purpose	Constraints						Remarks
		Steep slopes	Rough seed-bed	Labor intensive	High equipment cost	Possible high site maintenance	Low rate-to-time ratio	
Sodding—mechanical	To transplant native sodpads intact to stabilize highly erosion prone areas	x	–	x	x	x	x	Makes use of local plant materials; can use front-end loaders; shows promise.
Sprigger	To lift root systems of native shrubs and transplant to prepared sites	x	–	–	x	–	x	In testing phase; makes use of local plant materials.
Sprigging	To establish plant species from root cuttings	x	–	x	x	–	x	Makes use of local plant materials; need high density of native stock on site.
Steep-slope containerized planter	To plant containerized stock on steep cut-and-fill slopes	–	–	–	x	x	–	Recently developed, does not appear compatible with mulching.
Steep-slope scarifier-seeder	To scarify a seedbed, broadcast and cover seed, and firm the seedbed in one operation	–	–	–	x	–	x	In testing phase, compatible with mulching techniques.
Transplanting wild shrub and tree stock—mechanical	To establish large tree stock obtained on site	x	–	x	x	x	x	High success rate possible if implemented properly; makes use of local plant materials.

Note: x = constraint applies to technique; – = No constraint is involved with this technique.
SOURCE: Long et al. (1984).

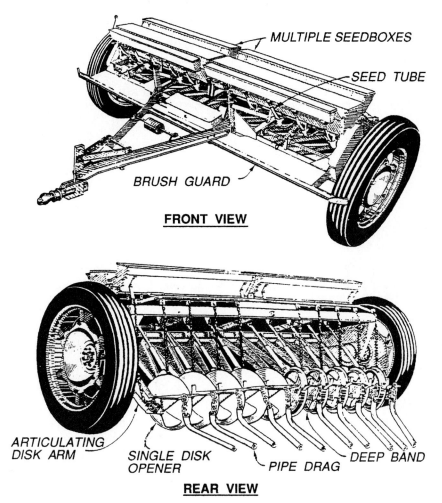

Figure 9.5 Front and rear views of the rangeland drill, showing major features. (*Doerr 1986d.*)

conditions for ground-nesting birds. In native prairies, sweetclover and alfalfa have been interseeded with grasses to improve forage production for livestock (Nichols and Johnson 1969, Kartchner et al. 1983), and probably for some wildlife species.

Erickson and Currie (1985) developed a versatile range interseeder, referred to as the Range Improvement Machine (RIM). In a single operation, RIM tills 4-cm strips, forms a 2-cm-deep V-furrow in the center of each tilled strip, and places seeds in the bottom of each furrow. Interseeding into grass sod might require such equipment. Distance between furrow centers has commonly been 10 cm on mesic

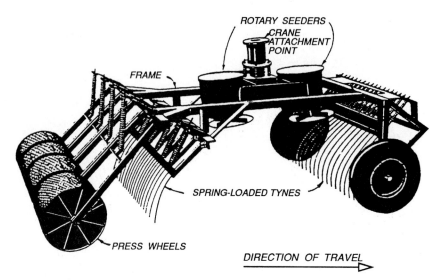

Figure 9.6 Diagram of steep-slope seeder showing tynes, press wheels, and rotary seeders. (*Doerr 1986e.*)

meadows, 60 to 120 cm on subhumid rangelands, and 180 to 240 cm on semiarid rangeland (Vallentine 1989).

Interseeding of browse plants has been used successfully on some intermountain rangelands to improve habitat for wild ungulates. Release from competition is critical the first year of seedling growth. Pendry and Provenza (1987) concluded that competition between species of plants was more important to establishment than protection from grazing by wild ungulates. In Utah, 60-cm scalp widths were superior to narrower widths for shrub survival (Giunta et al. 1975). For interseeding shrubs and forbs into heavy grass sod, 75-cm-wide scalps, 23 cm deep are needed in the intermountain area (Stevens et al. 1981). Strips cleared 100 cm wide for direct seeding and 150 cm wide for transplanted seedlings are needed to establish fourwing saltbush in semi-arid areas (Van Epps and McKell 1977).

Management after revegetation or interseeding greatly affects success and longevity of the stand. Pest and weed control might be needed. Where herbivory can be controlled, a conservative rule of thumb is to delay grazing until after the second full growing season after seeding (Vallentine 1989). When cattle can be carefully controlled, Launchbaugh (1976) recommended grazing to reduce competing weeds, which are a major deterrent to seedling establishment. Launchbaugh (1976) suggested (1) grazing when new weeds were 5 to 8 cm high, (2) basing the stocking rate on weed production, and (3) discontinuing grazing after midseason to allow reseeded plants to com-

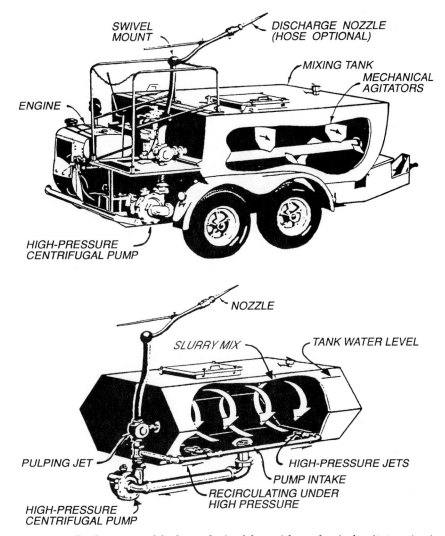

SWIVEL
MOUNT

DISCHARGE NOZZLE
(HOSE OPTIONAL)

MIXING TANK
MECHANICAL
AGITATORS

ENGINE

HIGH-PRESSURE
CENTRIFUGAL PUMP

NOZZLE

SLURRY MIX

TANK WATER LEVEL

PULPING JET

HIGH-PRESSURE JETS

PUMP INTAKE

RECIRCULATING UNDER
HIGH PRESSURE

HIGH-PRESSURE
CENTRIFUGAL PUMP

Figure 9.7 Trailer-mounted hydroseeder/mulcher with mechanical agitators (*top*). Bottom diagram shows a high-pressure jet agitation system which keeps the slurry mix in suspension. (*Doerr 1986f.*)

plete growth. In aspen, cattle grazing following burning suppressed regenerating suckers and enhanced broadcast seeding (Fitzgerald and Bailey 1983). Similarly, goats were used in Arizona to suppress shrub regrowth following prescribed burning and broadcast seeding. To improve establishment of vegetation, control of large ungulates through heavier harvest might be needed before revegetation. In Idaho, drastic reduction in deer numbers was unnecessary in a revege-

TABLE 9.19 Techniques for Providing Mulch in Artificial Revegetation

Technique	Constraints								Remarks
	Rough, rocky seedbeds	Steep slopes	Requires nitrogen supplement	Requires special machinery	High materials cost	Labor intensive	Inhibits revegetation techniques	Maintenance difficulty	
Annual cover crops	–	x	x	–	–	–	–	–	Site erosion-prone until crop established; apply before permanent seeding; allows delay of permanent seeding; very economical.
Chemical soil stabilizers and mulch tackifiers	–	–	–	x	x	–	Possible	–	Best when used with straw, hay, etc., as a tackifier; can increase surface water runoff; requires careful application.
Erosion control matting	x	–	–	–	x	x	x	x	Must have good soil-mulch contact; most applicable for steep slopes.
Fiberglass mulch	–	–	–	–	x	x	x	–	Good for stabilizing watercourses.
Gravel mulch	–	x	–	–	x	x	x	x	Permanent, long-lasting treatment; useful under woody plantings.
Jute netting	x	–	–	–	x	x	Possible	x	Best when used to anchor straw, hay, etc., mulch; must have good soil-mulch contact.
Paper mat mulch	x	–	–	–	x	x	x	x	Slow degradation in arid areas; must have good soil-mulch contact.
Plastic netting (plus organic mulch)	x	–	–	–	x	x	Possible	–	Must have good netting, mulch-soil contact; useful under woody plantings.
Straw/hay mulch (crimped)	x	x	x	–	–	–	–	–	Cost effective, widely used; avoid moldy or decayed materials; can introduce weed seeds to site, can be applied by many methods.
Wood chip mulch	–	–	Possible	Possible	–	Not if mechanically applied	x	–	Adequate supplies often limited; not as cost effective as crimped straw/hay; heavy applications can inhibit plant establishment.
Wood fiber mulch (Hydromulch)	–	–	–	x	x	–	x	–	Best with tackifier; may not be applicable for arid areas; common technique in humid areas; requires local water source.

Note: x = constraint applies to technique; – = no constraint is involved with this technique.
SOURCE: Long et al. (1984).

TABLE 9.20 Cover Crops for Artificial Revegetation

Representative state*	Species and dryland seeding rate per ha when seeded alone†
Alabama	Barley (1.5 bu), millet (14 kg), oats (2.5 bu), rye (1.5 bu), annual ryegrass (11 kg), wheat (1.5 bu).
New Mexico	Warm season = green sorghum (excluding dwarf varieties) (2–4 kg), forage sorghum (4–5 kg), Sudan grass (4–7 kg), millet (5–7 kg), broomcorn (4–7 kg); cool season = wheat, oats, barley, rye, speltz, triticale (all 20–27 kg).
North Dakota	Flax (as a wind barrier), oats (0.5 bu), barley (0.5 bu)
Oregon	Western Oregon = winter-hardy cereal grains (45 kg), annual ryegrass (14 kg); eastern Oregon = winter-hardy cereal grains (45 kg); southwestern Oregon = cereal rye (36 kg), barley (45 kg), oats (45 kg), annual ryegrass (7 kg).
Wisconsin	Oats (1–2 bu), rye (1–1.5 bu), winter wheat (1 bu), triticale (1.5 bu), annual ryegrass (7 kg).
Wyoming	Winter cover = winter rye (18–27 kg), winter wheat (18–27 kg); summer cover = spring small grain (18–27 kg), Sudan grass (4–7 kg), sorghum (4–7 kg).

*Representative states selected on the basis of differing climatic conditions to show variation in cover crop planting specifications.
†Species and rate selection depend on site climate and soil conditions.
SOURCE: Long et al. (1984).

tation program if plants normally were moderately grazed and heavy use occurred only during the most severe winters (Ferguson 1968).

Fertilizing

Fertilizing native rangeland habitats is practical and economical only where soil moisture is adequate (McKell et al. 1959, Wight and Black 1979) and plant response is guaranteed. Responses are area-, site-, and species-specific (Goetz 1975). Types of fertilizer, equipment, and application techniques vary (Tables 9.21 and 9.22) (Long et al. 1984).

Fertilizers have potential for mesic sites and high rainfall areas of the prairie regions. In habitat management, fertilizer can benefit large ungulates (Carpenter and Williams 1972).

Site selection. Basile (1970) recommended fertilizing only ridgetops on elk winter range because of the 250 percent increase in forage yields compared with a benchland site where fertilizer produced a 50 percent increase. In another example, twig growth of wavyleaf oak responded better to nitrogen on upper and middle slopes than lower slopes (Howard et al. 1980). In the arctic tundra, upland soils possess greater

TABLE 9.21   Equipment Commonly Used to Fertilize for Wildlife Habitat Management

Type	Description	Function and use
Aerial applicators	Hopper-mounted on small fixed-wing aircraft or helicopter; application rate controlled by operator-adjusted flow gate.	Large inaccessible, steep sites; may be cost-prohibitive on small areas.
Fertilizer blasting gun	Metal nozzle with trigger mechanism; two hoses, one connecting to portable air compressor, other is suction hose feeding fertilizer to gun; operated from vehicle (such as 3/4–1 ton truck) with one or two operators.	Distributes granular and pelletized fertilizer; good on steep, rugged terrain or confined areas having vehicular access; for spot treatments of individual trees or shrubs; applicator rate somewhat difficult to control; fertilizer as grains or pellets requires rainfall activation; phosphorus fertilizers may not solubilize and become accessible to deeper rooted species.
Fertilizer spreaders	Truck- or trailer-mounted hopper with sloped sides; hopper contains conveyor system which feeds fertilizer to rotating spreader blades; blades powered hydraulically or from vehicle power take-off; size of gate opening to blades or speed of conveyor controls application rate.	Large capacity; distribute dry materials such as granular fertilizer and/or lime; smaller versions can be used for broadcast seeding; not suited to very steep, rough, or brush land.
Wide (longitudinal) hoppers	Two types: self-contained and tillage implemented-mounted; self-contained unit similar to seed drill construction with side-wheels and transverse hopper, but lacking disks, chain drags, or packer-wheels; implement-mounted applicator mounts to seed drill or other tillage implement; both are driven by wheel-linked running gear; internal agitators control flow; implement-mounted applicator is similar to seedbox on a seed drill.	Self-contained unit broadcasts granular fertilizer in closely controlled, uniform pattern; fertilizer application not limited to narrow drill rows; broadcast fertilizers subject to blowing, washing unless covered; implement-mounted unit places fertilizer in bands; favorable for immediate contact with germinating seed; not subject to blowing or water transport across surface; fertilizer application limited to narrow drill rows.

absorptive capacity for phosphorus than sandy soils (McKendrick et al. 1980), so phosphorus might be more appropriate on upland arctic soils.

Plant and animal responses.   Generally, grasses, shrubs, and forbs respond to nitrogen; legumes respond to phosphorus (Vallentine 1989). In some examples, forbs respond more to nitrogen fertilizer

TABLE 9.21   Equipment Commonly Used to Fertilize for Wildlife Habitat Management (*Continued*)

Type	Description	Function and use
Liquid spray applicators	Truck-mounted tank with pumps and row of nozzles at rear of vehicle; sprays liquid mix of fertilizers; for foliar application or soil application.	Restricted to more level sites with good vehicular access; container tank lined with steel, plastic, or aluminum depending on type of fertilizer solution; good in arid areas where rainfall activation of granular fertilizers is limited; good in high-altitude or exceptionally cold areas where temperatures limit nutrient release and uptake; can be combined with pesticide application; best with micronutrients; application of macronutrients can burn leaves.
Manure spreaders	Tractor-attached wheeled hopper with conveyor on floor; manure spreaders at rear of hopper operate with conveyor off power take-off.	Spread manure or straw mulch; limited to nearly level areas accessible to vehicles; manure adds nutrients, improves soil structure.

SOURCE: Long et al. (1984).

than grasses do (Huffine and Elder 1960, Cosper and Thomas 1961). Legumes might respond to nitrogen as seedlings, but once nodules are well formed, additional nitrogen can be wasted (Carpenter and Williams 1972). Legumes also respond to sulfur (Bentley and Green 1954). In another example, sulfur caused preferential deer browsing on wedgeleaf ceanothus but not on mariposa manzanita (Gibbens and Pieper 1962). Because fertilizer affects grass-legume ratios in grasslands, a wildlife manager should be cautious about nitrogen fertilizer depressing legumes in the habitat. Plants and animals respond to fertilizer in many ways (Table 9.23). As a habitat-management technique, fertilizer can be used in as follows:

1. To increase palatability of forages
2 To increase available nutrients to plants and animals
3. To alter plant species composition
4. To affect distribution patterns of wild ungulates
5. To extend the period of green forage into late autumn
6. To induce early green-up of grass in spring

Fertilizers can produce variable effects. Blue grama, dwarf sagebrush, and wolfberry decreased in North Dakota (Goetz 1969), and

TABLE 9.22 Average Composition of Fertilizer Materials

Fertilizer	%N	%P	%K	%P$_2$O$_5$	%K$_2$O	% P solubility in water	%S	CaCO$_3$ equivalence* Basicity	Acidity
Nitrogen fertilizers									
Ammonia, anhydrous	82								147
Ammonium nitrate	33.5								60
Ammonium phosphate sulfate	16	9		20		> 75	16		88
Ammonium sulfate	20						24		110
Diammonium phosphate	21	22		50		> 75			75
Monoammonium phosphate	11	21		48		> 75	2.6		58
Potassium nitrate	14		38		46			23	
Urea	45								71
Sodium nitrate	16							28	
Phosphorus fertilizers (see also under nitrogen fertilizers)									
Calcium metaphosphate		28		64		Slight		Neutral	
Rock phosphate		15		33		≤ 1		Basic	
Superphosphate, single		9		20		> 75	12	Neutral	
Superphosphate, triple		20		46		> 75	1	Neutral	
Phosphoric acid		24		54		> 75			
Monopotassium phosphate		23	29	52	35	> 75		Neutral	110
Potassium fertilizers (see also under nitrogen and phosphorus fertilizers)									
Potassium chloride (muriate of potash)			50		60			Neutral	
Potassium sulfate			44		53		18	Neutral	

TABLE 9.22 Average Composition of Fertilizer Materials (Continued)

Organic fertilizers								
Manure, dairy (fresh)	0.7	0.13	0.54	0.30	0.65	50		Slight
Manure, poultry (fresh)	1.6	0.55	0.75	1.25	0.9	50		Slight
Manure, steer (fresh)	2.0	0.24	1.59	0.54	1.92	40		Slight
Sulfur fertilizers								
(see also under nitrogen and phosphorus fertilizers)								
Calcium sulfate (gypsum)							18.6	Acidic
Magnesium sulfate							13	Acidic
Soil sulfur							99	Acidic
Sulfate potash magnesia			21.5		26		18	Acidic
Liming fertilizers								
Calcium oxide								178
Dolomite								110
Limestone, ground								95
Shell meal								95

*Compared to 100 basicity for $CaCO_3$.
SOURCE: Vallentine (1989).

TABLE 9.23   Potential Uses and Benefits of Using Fertilizer in Wildlife Habitat Management on Rangelands

Potential benefit	Reference
Plant response	
1. Increased nutrient content of shrubs:	
Bitterbrush (nitrogen)	Bayoumi and Smith (1976)
Wavyleaf oak (urea/ammonium sulfate)	Severson and Medina (1983)
Wedgeleaf ceanothus (nitrogen)	Gibbens and Pieper (1962)
Big sagebrush (nitrogen)	Smith (1963), Bayoumi and Smith (1976), Barrett (1979)
2. Increased shrub leader length of:	
Wavyleaf oak (nitrogen)	Howard et al. (1980)
Hairy cercocarpus (urea)	Severson and Medina (1983)
Sagebrush (nitrogen)	Barrett (1979)
Wedgeleaf ceanothus (nitrogen)	Gibbens and Pieper (1962)
Bitterbrush and sagebrush (nitrogen but not phosphorus)	Bayoumi and Smith (1976)
3. Increased shrub biomass of:	
Wedgeleaf ceanothus seedlings (nitrogen)	Schultz et al. (1958), Gibbens and Pieper (1962)
Deerbrush ceanothus seedlings (nitrogen—first year only)	Schultz et al. (1958)
Chamise seedlings (nitrogen)	Schultz et al. (1958)
Western mountainmahogany (nitrogen)	Schultz et al. (1958)
4. Extended periods of green-forage availability	Humphrey (1962), Stroehlein et al. (1968), Baldwin et al. (1974)
5. Changed and improved chemical content of herbaceous forage, particularly increase in protein content and decrease in silica	Reid et al. (1966), Cosper et al. (1967), Jones and Handreck (1967), Burzlaff et al. (1968), Pieper et al. (1974), Barrett (1979)
6. Increased forage production	Cosper et al. (1967), Hubbard and Mason (1967), Mason and Mittimore (1969), Wight (1976), Barrett (1979)
7. Changed floral composition	Goetz (1969), Drawe and Box (1969), Johnston et al. (1967), Rauzi et al. (1968), Wight (1976)
8. Increased forbs	Rauzi (1979)
9. Increased plant growth and vigor	Lavin (1967), Barrett (1979), McKendrick et al. (1980)
10. Increased sexual reproduction of tundra grasses, forbs, and shrubs	McKendrick et al. (1980)
11. Increased forage palatability	Schultz et al. (1958), Brown and Mandery (1962), Gibbens and Pieper (1962), Smith (1963), Thomas et al. (1964)

TABLE 9.23 Potential Uses and Benefits of Using Fertilizer in Wildlife Habitat Management on Rangelands (Continued)

Potential benefit	Reference
12. Improved forage conditions	Thomas et al. (1964), Powell et al. (1979)
13. Increased browse yields	Schultz et al. (1958), Gibbens and Pieper (1962)
14. Increased browse seed production	Bayoumi and Smith (1976)
Animal reponse	
1. Greater area-specific ungulate use:	
Mule deer attracted to fertilized areas treated (urea) (no response to ammonium sulfate)	Severson and Medina (1983)
Mule deer attracted to fertilized crested wheatgrass	McGinnies (1968)
Elk attracted to fertilized hayfields in Washington	Brown and Mandery (1962)
Elk attracted to meadows in Oregon (nitrogen)	Geist et al. (1973)
Pronghorn attracted to fertilized plots (nitrogen)	Barrett (1979)
2. Greater mule deer preference for:	
Wedgeleaf ceanothus (sulfur)	Schultz et al. (1958), Gibbens and Pieper (1962)
Deerbrush ceanothus	Schultz et al. (1958)
Birchleaf mountainmahogany	
Mariposa manzanita (n,p,s)	Gibbens and Pieper (1962)
Bitterbrush	Bayoumi and Smith (1976)
Big sagebrush	Bayoumi and Smith (1976)
Mountainmahogany	Howard et al. (1980)
3. Increased deer cover	Gibbens and Pieper (1962), Curlin (1962)
4. Increased carrying capacity	Basile (1970)
5. Caused selective browsing	Gibbens and Pieper (1962)
6. Increased forage consumption by ungulates	Thomas et al. (1964), Longhurst et al. (1968)
7. Better livestock and cervid distribution	Brown and Mandery (1962), Hooper et al. (1969)

SOURCE: Adapted from Severson and Medina (1983).

some species were killed by heavy fertilizer application in Alberta (Smith et al. 1968). Forbs were unaffected in Oregon by nitrogen fertilization at high rates (Baldwin et al. 1974). Invader species can increase at a faster rate than desirables (Powell and Box 1967). Warm-season grass yields in Wyoming were unaffected by nitrogen fertilization; results for cool-season grasses were variable (Rauzi et al. 1968). Wavyleaf oak and fourwing saltbush did not respond to fertilizer (Severson and Medina 1983); shrubs and grasses did not respond to phosphorus in Utah (Bayoumi and Smith 1976). In the arctic tundra, four or more growing seasons might be needed for full effect of fertilization treatments (McKendrick et al. 1980).

Timing.   Season of fertilizer application depends upon the target species, amount and distribution of rainfall, and the kind of fertilizer. In rangeland habitats, fertilizers are applied in spring or fall. Nitrogen should not be applied in fall to lowlands subject to flooding in winter or spring (Vallentine 1989). Fertilizing later in the year (July, August) might delay initiation of green-up (Stroehlein et al. 1968). Where cool-season grasses predominate and are the target plants on the Great Plains, fertilization in March to April is recommended; warm-season grasses should be fertilized in May or June. In the Southwest, where rainfall peaks in late summer, timing should be near the beginning of the rainy season (Stroehlein et al. 1968).

10

Rangeland Management Techniques: Controlled Grazing and Prescribed Burning

Controlled Grazing

Herbivores, whether wild or domestic, influence vegetation development. They alter the appearance, productivity, and composition of plant communities. The role of herbivory and subsequent impacts depends in part on the evolutionary history of grazing in an ecosystem. For example, the midcontinent grasslands of North America have a long evolutionary history of grazing by large ungulates. The semidesert grasslands did not. Such regions with no recent history of grazing were dominated by plants that lacked tolerance mechanisms. The excessive buildup of introduced livestock between 1860 and 1920 helped change these wildlife habitats. While the devastation actually improved habitats for some wildlife species, many habitats and wildlife forms suffered. So it is today. Some species and habitats are highly sensitive (e.g., riparian areas and hot deserts). Some species and habitats are enhanced; some are unaffected.

As the need to manage ecosystems for biodiversity becomes greater, it is important to discuss grazing in this context. Ecologists and conservationists have come to recognize that many forms of disturbance are important components of natural systems. Both theory, e.g., the intermediate-disturbance hypothesis (Connell 1978), and growing empirical evidence suggest that moderate frequencies or intensities of disturbance foster maximum species richness (Hobbs and Huenneke 1992). Indeed, herbivores mediate species abundance and diversity by differential use of plants commonly susceptible to defoliation. Certain levels and combinations of grazing increase overall plant species diversity by decreasing the ability of competitive dominants to exclude other species and by creating gaps available for occupation by other plant species (Archer and Smeins 1991). Petraitis et al. (1989) and Pickett and White (1985) suggested that this is true in both equilibrium and nonequilibrium environments. Disturbance is important for within-patch diversity (alpha diversity) and for creating diversity at the landscape level (beta diversity). Indeed, Pickett and Thompson (1978) suggested that the recurrent nature of disturbances necessitates the preservation of a "minimum dynamic area," an area large enough to contain within it multiple patches in various stages of disturbance and recovery. Thus, small-scale perturbations associated with grazing contribute to the development of fine-grained mosaics of varying successional stages across landscapes (Archer and Smeins 1991).

Milchunas et al. (1988) suggested that grazing is a disturbance only where the evolutionary history of grazing is short; Hobbs and Huenneke (1992) suggested that, in any situation, a substantial change in grazing regime will constitute a disturbance. For example, the imposition of grazing animals on a system not previously subject to that type of grazing will constitute a disturbance. Species diversity can be affected by the direction of change in a grazing regime compared to the historical regime (van der Maarel 1971, Milchunas et al. 1990). Hobbs and Huenneke (1992) reported that many authors have noted maximum species diversity under intermediate levels of grazing, particularly in mesic grasslands.

Unfortunately, the impacts of livestock grazing on wildlife habitats have generally been regarded as negative (Severson and Urness 1993). If grazing is not managed correctly or is managed without the needs of wildlife species in mind, livestock can:

1. Remove all residual cover needed for ground-nesting birds
2. Create undesirable, and maybe irreversible, shifts in succession, with loss of habitat for wildlife favored by more advanced stages in succession
3. Alter habitat characteristics so that habitat selection mechanisms are not triggered (Buttery and Shield 1975)
4. Become direct competitors with wild ungulates, causing reduction in wild populations through lower reproduction and starvation
5. Reduce floral diversity needed for mammal, bird, and insect communities

6. Damage shrubs by reducing biomass or mast production, important diet and cover requirements for some birds and mammals

This chapter assumes that for the vegetation type in question, controlled livestock grazing has been determined an appropriate use. Furthermore, we assume that if livestock grazing has been deemed appropriate, these herbivores will be managed to promote or maintain biodiversity and that their presence and role is important to society. We further assume that controlled grazing also considers vegetation impacts of wild ungulates.

Grazing, overuse, and overgrazing

Two misconceptions apply to grazing (Severson and Medina 1983): (1) *grazing, overuse,* and *overgrazing* are synonymous, and (2) the mere presence of livestock equals direct conflict with wildlife species.

The first misconception can be understood if we define our terms: *grazing* is the consumption of standing forage by domestic or wild ungulates, *overuse* is grazing that leads to excessive removal of the current year's growth, and *overgrazing* is continued overuse which results in a regressive change in plants and soils. Figure 10.1 (Scifres et al. 1983, Archer 1989) illustrates changes in a grassland community as a function of grazing pressure and changes in fire frequency.

Overgrazing, not grazing or overuse, results in (1) altered proportions of plant species which would normally be present or (2) alteration of a site that supports a completely different plant complex from its ecological potential (e.g., California annual grasslands). It is generally a slow, often insidious, process caused by continued overuse of the forage over a period of years. *Overgrazing* is also a relative term. A "moderately" overgrazed range site might contain a slightly altered flora, while a "heavily" overgrazed range would support a completely different plant complex (Severson and Urness 1993).

At the worst, overgrazed rangelands might be irreversibly altered if major loss or damage to soils and soil properties occurs. At the best, they might need no treatment. Simply removing herbivory or grazing might not restore pristine vegetation to hot desert, cold desert, or woodland vegetation types. Removing herbivory from grasslands might even reduce wildlife populations that evolved under grazing pressure. For example, some passerines evidently coevolved with bison (Owens and Myres 1973). In another example, fire improves tundra for willow ptarmigan in Newfoundland by removing reindeer moss from ericaceous shrubs and other ptarmigan food plants. Because reindeer moss is also a preferred caribou food, ptarmigan might have coevolved with the heavy grazing of caribou (pers. comm. W. Skinner, Newfoundland Wildlife Division, 1991). Furthermore, the effects of climate in range-

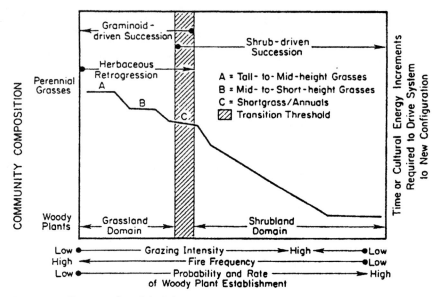

Figure 10.1 Conceptual model of changes in community structure as a function of grazing pressure. Within the grassland domain, grazing alters herbaceous composition while decreasing fire frequency. If grazing pressure is relaxed before some critical threshold(s), succession toward higher-condition grasslands can occur. In some cases such changes require decades. If enough woody plants become established, new successional processes and positive feedbacks might drive the system to a new steady state. Once in the shrubland or woodland domain, the seed bank and the vegetative regeneration potentials are altered, and the site might not revert to grassland or savanna, even after terminating grazing. Herbicides and grazing management that allow subsequent use of fire at regular intervals might be needed to reduce woody cover and enhance herbaceous production. (*Scifres et al. 1983, Archer 1989.*)

land habitats are as important as the effects of grazing. Changes in percent basal cover of shortgrass prairie vegetation were more a function of climate than livestock grazing (Fig. 10.2) (Branson 1985).

Severson and Urness (1993) concluded that the process of grazing, and even overgrazing, is not always undesirable. They gave examples of possible uses of livestock as a habitat-management tool and reported instances in which even overgrazing might be important to restoring certain habitat conditions. Such situations led Urness (1990) to conclude that overgrazing is bad only if it leads succession away from management objectives or if it degrades site integrity.

Use of overgrazing will be rare in wildlife habitat management. It cannot be considered or initiated capriciously. Its implementation requires an intimate knowledge of the ecological processes controlling rangeland biota (Severson and Urness 1993). One example illustrates its use for a featured species. Black-tailed prairie dogs tend to be more

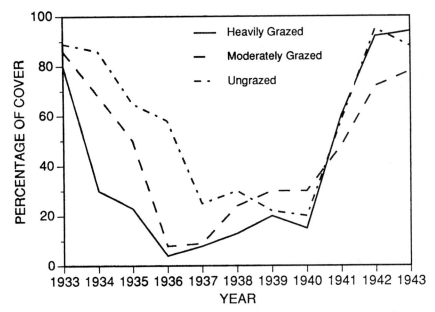

Figure 10.2 Changes in percentage basal cover in the shortgrass steppe vegetation type during and after drought. (*Branson 1985.*)

abundant in areas heavily grazed by livestock (Koford 1958) and the distribution of the endangered black-footed ferret generally is limited to prairie dog towns. Recommendations for ferrets include maintaining enough large prairie dog towns (Hillman et al. 1979), a situation which could involve management of livestock (Uresk and Bjugstad 1983). With careful, deliberate planning, correct allocation of resources, and strategic design and flexibility of grazing plans (Klebenow 1980), managing and maintaining wildlife on most rangelands is possible through controlled grazing that best mimics a natural grazing regime.

Herbivory by livestock could be used as a habitat-management technique under the concept of controlled grazing, because livestock are capable of modifying plant biomass, plant structure, and floral composition. *Controlled grazing* is defined as managing the degree and timing of removal or protection of the current year's growth which is consistent with habitat-management objectives. As a habitat-management technique, *controlled grazing* is further defined as either *environmental protective grazing* or *strategic grazing*.

Environmental protective grazing. *Environmental protective grazing* (EPG) implies livestock are cautiously managed and strictly controlled to protect fragile environments and prevent overuse and/or overgrazing of wildlife habitats. This is especially true in arid and semi-arid environments. Guidelines for EPG would ensure that rangelands (1) are conservatively stocked; (2) receive adequate, planned rest and deferment from grazing; (3) have grazing plans which are carefully timed around wildlife life cycles and phenological development of plants; (4) are closely monitored to prevent overuse of key plants and key areas important to wildlife; and (5) are dutifully managed to leave a certain amount of residual cover for wildlife— rather than following a "take-half, leave-half" policy. In specific cases, livestock might be excluded from "key" wildlife use areas.

Generally, six factors influence plants when they are grazed by herbivores (Table 10.1). The most overwhelming of factors is stocking rate; it is the factor of most concern, particularly where EPG is applied most appropriately. Stocking rate is expressed in animal units, animal unit months, or animal unit equivalents. An *animal unit* (AU) is the amount of forage consumed by a 454-kg cow and calf, or about 9 kg/day (Table 10.2) (Holechek et al. 1989). An *animal unit month* (AUM) is the amount of forage consumed by an animal unit during 1 month. An *animal unit equivalent* (AUE) is the proportion of *animal units* of different animal species based on their relative consumption (Table 10.2). Animal unit equivalency erroneously assumes a constant rate of intake and that all animals eat the exact same plant species in the exact same proportions. Nonetheless, AUs, AUMs, and AUEs provide a convenient thread of continuity for

TABLE 10.1   The Six Main Factors Affecting Plants Grazed by Herbivores

Factor	Definition or description
Stocking rate	Number of animal units* of a given kind of animal per total area grazed
Duration of grazing	Time a given area of land is occupied
Frequency of grazing	How often a plant or an area is grazed
Rest	Length of time plants are allowed to recover after defoliation (grazing)
Timing	Grazing or rest relative to important events in the life cycle (nesting, fawning, breeding) of wildlife species and/or to the phenological stage of plant species or plant groups
Kind of animal	Animal species†

*One animal unit (AU) = one 454-kg cow or the animal unit equivalent (AUE) (see Table 10.2).

†Animal species differ in their selection of plant species, plant parts, plant groups, and their mechanical impact (trampling). Thus, they affect habitats in different ways.

TABLE 10.2   Daily Dry-matter Consumption by Various Range Animals Based on Their Body Weight and Their Respective Animal Unit Equivalents (AUEs)

Animal	Animal weight (kg)	Daily dry-matter intake (% body weight)	Daily dry-matter intake (kg)	AUE
Cattle (mature)	455	2	9.1	1.00
Cattle (yearling)	318	2	6.8	0.75
Sheep	68	2	1.4	0.15
Goat	45	2	0.9	0.10
Horse	545	3	10.9	1.80
Donkey	318	3	6.4	1.05
Bison	818	2	16.4	1.80
Elk	318	2	6.4	0.70
Moose	545	2	10.9	1.20
Bighorn sheep	82	2	1.6	0.18
Mule deer	68	2	1.4	0.15
White-tailed deer	45	2	0.9	0.10
Pronghorn	55	2	1.1	0.12
Caribou	182	2	3.6	0.40

Note: Animal weight here means average weight of mature male or female animal.
SOURCE: Holechek et al. (1989).

assessing and implementing stocking-rate guidelines over a large area, particularly where proper use of key species is known (Table 10.3) (Holechek et al. 1989).

Also useful to habitat managers implementing EPG are stocking-rate guidelines for cattle only, based on annual herbage production (Table 10.4). These guidelines can be determined for a specific area using the formula

$$R = \frac{I}{Pvu}$$

where R = hectares per AU

$\quad\;\; I$ = cattle intake per year or season based on individual animal weight in kg and daily consumption as a percent of body weight

$\quad\; P$ = herbaceous biomass in kg/ha

$\quad\; v$ = proportion of herbaceous biomass that is actually eaten or used by cattle: (biomass of herbage used by cattle)/(biomass of all herbaceous plant species)

$\quad\; u$ = proportion of usable biomass allocated to cattle as light, moderate, or heavy grazing based on a management decision

TABLE 10.3   Guidelines for Use of Key Species on Rangeland Vegetation Types

Rangeland type	Percent use	Reference
Tallgrass prairie	45–55	Herbel and Anderson (1959)
Northern mixed prairie	40–50	Willms et al. (1986)
Southern mixed prairie	40–50	Heitschmidt et al. (1987)
Shortgrass prairie	40–50	Hart et al. (1988)
California annual grasslands	50–60	Bartolome et al. (1980)
Palouse prairie	30–40	Skovlin et al. (1976)
Semidesert grasslands	30–40	Valentine (1970), Martin and Cable (1974)
Cold desert		
Sagebrush type	30–40	Laycock and Conrad (1981)
Saltbush type	25–35	Hutchings and Stewart (1953)
Hot desert		
Creosotebush type	25–35	Hughes (1982)
Paloverde-cactus-bursage type	20–30	
Pinyon-juniper woodlands	30–40	
Oak woodlands		
Gambel oak type	30–40	
Shinnery oak type	40–50	
Mountain shrub	30–40	
Mesquite-acacia woodland	40–50	
Tundra		
Arctic	25–35	
Alpine	20–30	Thilenius (1979)

SOURCE: Adapted from Holechek et al. (1989).

This example assumes cattle eat very little amounts of brush or shrubs. The last term, u, would be determined differently if a manager wanted to preserve residual biomass for ground-nesting birds. The proportion would then become

$$u = \frac{Pv - B}{Pv}$$

where B is residual biomass to be preserved (pers. comm. F. S. Guthery, Texas A&I University, 1991). The formula then becomes

$$R = \frac{I}{Pv - B}$$

For example, if a residual biomass of 300 kg/ha were required in an area where $P = 1000$ kg/ha and $v = 0.45$, then

TABLE 10.4   Hypothetical Stocking-Rate Guidelines Based on Annual Herbage Production, Estimated Usable Forage, and Percent Use of Key Forage Species

Herbaceous forage production [kg/(ha · yr)]	Estimated usable forage* [kg/(ha · yr)]	Stocking rate (ha/AU)†		
		Light (25% use)	Moderate (45% use)	Heavy (60% use)
100	55	212.4	117.9	88.5
200	110	106.2	58.9	44.2
500	260	44.9	24.9	18.7
750	375	31.1	17.3	12.9
1000	520	22.5	12.5	9.3
1250	600	19.5	10.8	8.1
1500	755	15.5	8.6	6.4
2000	1100	10.6	5.9	4.4
2500	1250	9.3	5.2	3.9
3000	1600	7.3	4.1	3.0
3500	1800	6.5	3.6	2.7
4000	2100	5.6	3.1	2.3

*This example assumes that about 50% of the standing crop is species consumed by cattle and is considered usable forage. Values are hypothetical and depend on the vegetation type. In this example, values are estimated to vary between 48 and 55%. This example also assumes normal rainfall patterns.

†Based on a 400-kg cow eating 2% of body weight per day for 365 days (2920 kg forage per cow per year).

$$\text{Stocking rate} = \frac{2920 \text{ kg}}{(\text{kg usable forage/ha}) \, (\% \text{ use})}$$

$$R = \frac{2920}{(1000 \times 0.45) - 300}$$

$$= 19.46 \text{ ha/AU}$$

In this example, the proportion allocated to cattle was about 0.33:

$$\frac{(1000 \times 0.45) - 300}{1000 \times 0.45}$$

From these guidelines, four habitat-management principles emerge in areas where EPG is used. First, habitat managers should note that the greatest danger (or smallest margin for error or miscalculation) for overstocking rangeland would be on rangeland producing 2000 kg/(ha · yr) or less of herbage. For example, at 1500 kg/(ha · yr) if the stocking rate on 1000 ha of southern mixed prairie were permitted to increase from light to moderate, the AUs more than double from 65 to

116 (a 78 percent increase). Second, the relative danger of overstocking increases as herbaceous biomass decreases, especially in arid regions. For example, in the hot desert vegetation type of southern New Mexico, Herbel et al. (1972) reported that herbage production declined from 661 kg/ha before a drought to 173 kg/ha during a drought when averaged across four range sites. Thus, if herbaceous biomass on 2000 ha of a lightly grazed site decreased from 500 to 200 kg/(ha · yr) the number of AUs would have to be reduced from 45 to 19 (a 58 percent reduction in stocking rate). The impact of cattle on this brittle environment would be devastating if EPG were not implemented by concomitantly decreasing the cattle stocking rate. Indeed, livestock managers must build flexibility into their programs to be able to destock rapidly if local environmental conditions dictate. Long-term rangeland deterioration and damage probably occurs more often during drought or times of low rainfall. Third, determination of forage usable to livestock improves the manager's ability to determine stocking rates accurately. Finally, consideration of stocking rates in wildlife habitat management should be designed to leave certain heights, density, or biomass of residual cover for wildlife, rather than basing stocking rates strictly on percent use. Although the following cannot be applied uniformly or without designating a target wildlife species or groups of species, residual cover guidelines have been recommended at 30 to 35 cm for tallgrasses, 15 to 20 cm for midgrasses, and 5 to 8 cm for shortgrasses (Holechek et al. 1982).

Strategic grazing.   *Strategic grazing* is the use of livestock as a manipulative tool in wildlife habitat management to create specific habitat conditions. Several rangeland vegetation types are suitable for strategic grazing of livestock (see Chap. 8). Livestock grazing has been suggested as a tool to manage habitats for wildlife species as diverse as mule deer (Urness 1990), northern bobwhites (Guthery et al. 1990), and Canada geese (Kie and Loft 1990). Strategic grazing can precondition forage for elk by grazing cattle early in the growing season and removing them in fall to provide regrowth of nutritious forage (Fig. 10.3) (Anderson et al. 1990).

Strategic grazing can incorporate any or all of the six factors in Table 10.1 affecting vegetation (Fig. 10.4). Thus livestock can be used to:

1. Create weedy patches as feeding sites for upland birds (Guthery 1986) or concentrate ungulate feeders (deer, pronghorn)

2. Through planned rest periods, maintain sites of tall residual grass cover as nesting sites for upland birds (Guthery 1986) and waterfowl (Kantrud 1990)

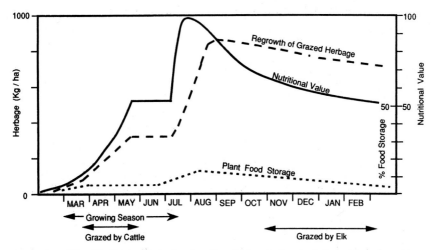

Figure 10.3 Hypothetical effect of using livestock grazing to interrupt and postpone plant physiological functions so as to improve the nutritional value of mature regrowth forage. (*Anderson et al. 1990.*)

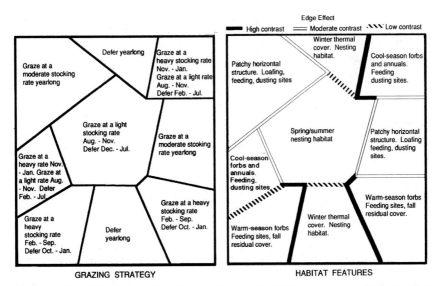

Figure 10.4 Hypothetical grazing scheme of a central Oklahoma site to achieve habitat objectives with strategic grazing. Strategic grazing would be rotated among pastures in subsequent years.

3. Promote regrowth of grasses, which are more nutritious for grass-eating wild ungulates than standing dead material

4. Reduce the volume of unwanted, standing dead material to increase access by wildlife to forbs or lower green leaves

5. Stimulate lateral sprouting of shrubs as desired forage for wintering ungulates

6. Create horizontal structural diversity (patchiness) of the herb layer as desired edge effect for birds [mean height of grass and its standard deviation is a good predictor of bird diversity (Balda 1975)]

7. Prevent shifts to seral stages which do not meet habitat requirements so that habitats for selected wildlife species are maintained

8. Cause shifts to lower seral stages which might be more suitable habitat for species favoring grazing disturbance

9. Create bare ground as feeding, dusting, and display sites for upland and passerine birds

10. Create bushier forms of trees and shrubs as better concealment for escape

11. Increase production of shrubs by removing competing understory (Urness 1990)

Grazing systems

Grazing systems provide planned grazing and deferment periods (Tables 10.5 and 10.6) so grazed plants can produce seed and photosynthetic material and permit seedlings to establish. Bryant (1982) reviewed numerous studies to evaluate effects of grazing systems on wildlife and noted that systems tend to benefit wildlife when compared to yearlong or season-long grazing. There are exceptions, but generally any grazing system is better for wildlife than continuous grazing.

The oldest and most popular grazing systems are the Merrill system of deferred rotation (Merrill 1954) and the rest-rotation system (Hormay 1961). Grazing systems vary relative to number and length of rest periods (Fig. 10.5); flexibility to accomplish wildlife habitat management depends upon objectives. Unfortunately, if fencing is needed to implement the system, fences can impede wildlife movements and costs can be high, even prohibitive. Other grazing systems not detailed in Table 10.5 but described in Table 10.6 include (1) deferred-rotation (Sampson 1913), (2) seasonal suitability based on elevation and subsequent phenological plant development (Holechek et al. 1981), (3) best-pasture (Valentine 1967, Pieper et al. 1978), and (4) the Santa Rita system (three-pasture rest rotation) (Martin and

TABLE 10.5 Grazing-System Characteristics that Provide Graze and Rest Periods to the Habitat or Vegetation

Grazing system	Number of pastures	Grazing period or length of occupation (days)	Rest period (days)	Number of rest periods in a completed cycle	Number of days in a completed cycle	Number of rest periods for the total area in a calendar year
Yearlong grazing (12 mo)						
Merrill, deferred-rotation	4			4	1460	
Year 1, Pasture A		245	120			1
Pasture B		305	60			0.5
Pasture C		245	120			1
Pasture D		305	60			0.5
South African Switchback	2					
Pasture A		21	42	3	168	6
Pasture B		42	21	3	168	6
High-intensity–low-frequency	8					
Plan A		21	147	7	158	2
Plan B		28	196	7	224	1
Short-duration	8					
Plan A		3	21	7	24	15
Plan B		7	49	7	56	6
Continuous, yearlong	1	365	0	0	365	0
Season-long grazing (4 mo)						
Rest-rotation	4	Varied	Varied	3	1460	0 to 1
Year 1, Pasture A		60	60			1
Pasture B		0	120			1
Pasture C		120	0			0
Pasture D		60	60			1
Continuous, season-long	1	120	0	0	120	0

Note: Completed cycle = each pasture is given the same total number of days of rest and grazing in each season of the year.

TABLE 10.6 Grazing Systems and Description

Grazing system	Description	Regional adaptability[a]	Effects on wildlife and/or wildlife habitat	Comments
Continuous (a.k.a. continuous year-long, continuous season-long)	To graze a particular unit of land throughout the season or year, year after year; no scheduled movement of livestock.	Any, annual grasslands, shortgrass prairie	Creates structural and spatial heterogeneity (patchy environments) at the herb layer that is conducive for some wildlife at light to moderate stocking rates; accentuates competition for desired forages with wild ungulates; intensifies social interactions between wild and domestic ungulates.	Accentuates plant species and area selectivity of livestock; best livestock performance; can distribute grazing pressure only with salting and water developments.
Rotation	To move livestock from one pasture to another on a scheduled basis.	Any	Varied.	Usually requires fences.
Deferred-rotation	To delay grazing until seed maturity of important forage species (deferment).	Any, mountain rangelands, stringer meadows, riparian zones	Ungrazed pastures permit greater forage selectivity and provide nonuse areas for wild ungulates to avoid livestock.	Might require fences.
Rest-rotation (a.k.a. Hormay grazing system)	To rest one pasture for 12 months; one pasture receives 12 months of nonuse while the other pastures receive some grazing use; usually involves 3 to 5 pastures.	Mountain rangelands, any	Residual herbaceous cover for nesting is provided in at least 2 pastures; wild ungulates are provided an area free from livestock for 1 year so they can avoid social interaction; forage selectivity by wildlife enhanced in the nonuse pasture.	Reduced livestock performance; light to moderate stocking rates are recommended.

System	Description	Suitable region	Wildlife/production notes	Comments
Merrill, deferred rotation (a.k.a. Merrill, three-herd, four-pasture grazing system)	To graze each pasture for 12 months, followed by 4 months of nonuse; with four pastures, each receives 4 months of nonuse during each season of the year once the cycle is completed after 4 years; where year-round growth is possible, plants that grow in different seasons have the opportunity to grow until seed maturity.	Mixed-grass prairies, short-grass prairies, southern rangelands	Good for combined wildlife and livestock production; good for combinations of livestock (sheep, goats, deer); good for integrating other forms of habitat management (fire, mechanical) if done in the vacant pasture.	Works best where opportunity for forage growth is year-round; light to moderate stocking rates recommended; fences required; livestock performance better or as good as short-duration grazing.
Three-pasture, two-herd	To graze each pasture 6 months and rest 3 months or graze 12 months and rest 6 months.	Any	Similar to deferred rotation.	Might require fences.
Seasonal suitability (a.k.a. best pasture system)	To partition the rangeland into pastures based on vegetation types; the best pasture is used for each season of the year.	Intermountain rangelands, arid rangelands	Might create problems for mobile wildlife moving to areas after recent rains.	Fences might be needed; suitable for areas of spotty rainfall patterns.
Short-duration grazing (a.k.a. Savory grazing method, cell grazing, high-performance grazing, time-controlled grazing)	To partition a land area into eight or more pastures and permit one herd of livestock to graze each pasture (usually in sequence) for a short, intensive period; objective is to achieve high stock density; grazing periods usually are 7 days or less, with rest periods of 60 days or less.	Mesic grasslands, tallgrass and mixed-grass prairies, flat terrain	Allows good flexibility for strategic grazing; creates uniform herb layer; rest period too short for recovery of shrubs after defoliation; problems if centrally located watering facilities are the only water source available to wildlife; does not increase trampling of ground nests; could benefit wildlife species limited by ground cover that is too tall and dense.	Fences required; potential for soil compaction because soil might take 90 days to recover; poor choice for arid, semi-arid regions; usually accompanied by recommendation of unrealistically high stocking rates; inappropriate in habitats of low resiliency to grazing; can control frequency and intensity of defoliation.

TABLE 10.6 Grazing Systems and Description (Continued)

Grazing system	Description	Regional adaptability	Effects on wildlife and/or wildlife habitat	Comments
High-intensity–low-frequency (a.k.a. high-utilization grazing, HILF)	To partition a land area into several pastures and permit one herd of livestock to graze each pasture in sequence; grazing periods usually are longer than 14 days, with rest periods of 100 days or more.	Mesic grasslands, tallgrass and mixed-grass prairies, flat terrain	Allows good flexibility for strategic grazing; creates uniform herb layer; rest period permits recovery of shrubs after defoliation; problems if centrally located watering facilities are the only water source available to wildlife; does not increase trampling of ground nests; could benefit wildlife species limited by ground cover that is too tall and dense.	Fences required; potential for soil compaction; inappropriate in habitats of low resilience to grazing; can control frequency of defoliation; livestock performance usually inferior.
South African switchback	To partition a land area into two pastures and move livestock back and forth according to varied schedules; grazing/rest periods usually are 21 days graze–42 days rest–42 days graze–21 days rest.	Mesic grasslands	Rest period too short for recovery of shrubs after grazing; moderate to high levels of social interaction between livestock and wild ungulates.	Minimal fencing required.
Santa Rita system (three-pasture, rest-rotation)	To partition a land area into three pastures and move livestock to achieve long rest periods.	Arid, semi-arid deserts and grasslands	Similar to rest-rotation.	Minimal fencing required.

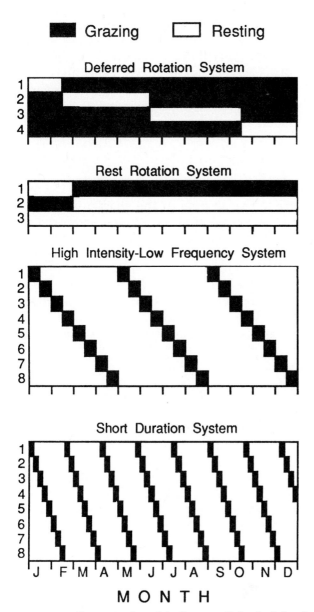

Figure 10.5 Conceptual model of sequential schedule of graze-rest periods for deferred-rotation (DR), rest-rotation (RR), high-intensity–low-frequency (HILF), and short-duration (SD) grazing systems. (*Kothmann 1980.*)

Ward 1976). In all cases, grazing systems were developed to provide an alternative to continuous season-long or yearlong grazing, systems which, in the long term, rarely provide range improvement. Valentine (1967), Stoddart et al. (1975), Holechek et al. (1989), Vallentine (1990), and Heitschmidt and Stuth (1991) provided a thorough discussion of the response of rangeland vegetation to grazing systems.

Effects of stocking rates and grazing systems

Grasslands. Potential loss of ground nests because of intensive grazing systems has concerned researchers in the shortgrass, mixed-grass, and tallgrass prairies. Bryant et al. (1982) first addressed the concern with short-duration grazing because of higher than moderate stocking rates and short-term concentration of livestock in smaller pastures. Koerth et al. (1983) reported that at heavy stocking rates (twice the moderate rate) under short-duration grazing, cattle trampling of simulated ground nests on a shortgrass prairie was not different from trampled nests under a moderately stocked, continuous yearlong pasture. Under short-duration grazing, Jensen et al. (1990) expressed major concern for disturbance of ground nests in tallgrass prairies if stock densities exceeded 2.5 AU per hectare.

Generally, prairie passerines would be expected to be present in substantial numbers if rangelands were in good condition (Wiens and Dyer 1975). Because birds seem to define their niches in terms of habitat structure, grazing pressures (stocking rates) have important consequences for birds, more so in mixed-grass and tallgrass than shortgrass prairies. In fact, in shortgrass prairies, grazing intensity (stocking rate) does not have as much an impact on breeding birds as does season (timing) of use (Wiens and Dyer 1975).

Management of some mixed-grass and tallgrass prairies should be directed toward uniformity of structure for interior species of prairie wildlife. Other mixed-grass and tallgrass prairies should be managed for heterogeneous mosaics (patchiness) of grass and forbs because such habitats are better suited for some nongame birds than uniform stands are (Verner 1975). Stocking-rate adjustments help achieve such habitat conditions. For example, in a mixed-grass community in Kansas, moderate (one steer per 1.42 ha) continuous grazing produced a distinct mosaic of overused and underused patches (Fig. 10.6) (Ring et al. 1985). Therefore, in terms of landscape diversity, light to moderate stocking rates are beneficial in creating small-scale environmental heterogeneity (Wiens and Dyer 1975) and in promoting greater diversity of plant species than heavy grazing or no grazing is

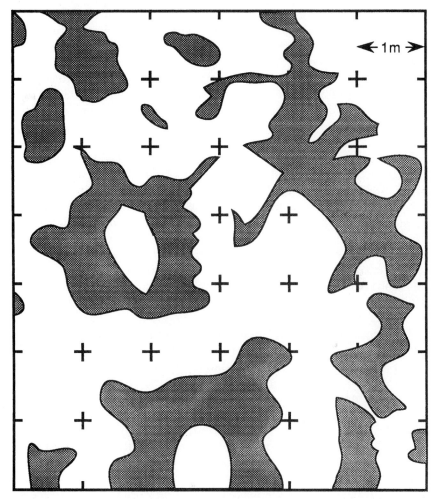

Figure 10.6 Effect of patch-grazing on native grasslands in Kansas. Darkened areas were grazed selectively and more intensively by cattle and created structural heterogeneity of the habitat landscape. (*Ring et al. 1985.*)

(Risser 1988). In fact, light to moderate grazing increased bird richness more than heavy grazing did in the northern Great Plains (Kantrud and Kologiski 1982).

Kirsch (1974) recognized the need for residual cover of 50 cm for greater prairie chickens in the tallgrass prairie. But these birds also need low successional stages. Neither annually grazed nor long-term ungrazed areas produced these desired effects simultaneously. Kirsch (1974) recommended burning or intensive rotational grazing of 65-ha blocks every 3 to 4 years, or one-third to one-fourth of a management unit 5 km² in size. Graul (1980) also suggested applying grazing to separate units as an appropriate technique to enhance grassland habitats. But if such a technique produces a matrix of many small habitat units, stenotopic species could be eliminated because their very restrictive habitat requirements are not met (Graul 1980). Thus, managers should maintain units of grassland large enough to accommodate stenotopic species. Samson (1980a) reported that the number of breeding bird species increased with increasing size of blocks of tallgrass prairie up to 5 to 7 km². This relationship was strongest for area-sensitive species when block-size was at least 1 to 1.5 km². Graul (1980) recommended using land trades to connect public blocks in a habitat corridor concept to achieve adequate block sizes for the integrity of prairie habitats. Samson (1980b) recommended block sizes of 300 ha for prairie chickens, with no more than 20 km between blocks. In general, when their respective habitats are fragmented, the area-sensitive species face local extirpations (Samson 1980a).

For prairie chickens in the northern mixed prairies, Manske et al. (1988) found that neither season-long, midseason grazing (June to September), or a three-pasture grazed only once in the season, benefited the vegetation or prairie chickens. A three-pasture system, with each pasture grazed twice during the grazing year, was recommended on the Sheyenne National Grasslands (Manske et al. 1988). Uresk (1986) reported that use rates of less than 40 to 55 percent of the prevailing recommended rate would be needed to improve key cool-season grasses on rangeland dominated by blue grama and buffalograss in northern mixed prairies. Kantrud (1981) found that total bird density was highest on heavily grazed plots, intermediate on moderately grazed plots, and lowest on lightly grazed plots. But heavy grazing reduces species richness because it increases dominance of a few species. Birds seemingly unaffected by grazing were the western meadowlark, upland sandpiper, and Sprague's pipit. Horned larks and chestnut-collared longspurs preferred heavily grazed sites and the lark bunting favored moderately grazed areas. But six species—bobolink, savannah sparrow, common yellowthroat, red-winged blackbird, LeConte's sparrow, and short-billed marsh wren—were greatly reduced or extirpated by heavy grazing. Heavy grazing should be avoided for optimum diversity of birds in northern mixed prairies (Kantrud 1981).

A relatively new grazing practice, referred to as *intensive early stocking,* is used today in tallgrass and southern mixed prairies. By design, a range is stocked intensively from April through mid-July. After mid-July, stocking rate is reduced. Although tallgrasses might benefit under this system, intensive early stocking reduced tallgrass residual cover (nesting cover) and forbs during the April–July period

(McCollum et al. 1990). By October, biomass of residual cover and forbs returned to similar biomass levels under season-long grazing. Even though biomass recovered after the April–July period, the impact of intensive early stocking on wildlife might be negative because of reduced grass biomass for nesting cover and a smaller amount of forbs available as food.

After reviewing research results on grazing systems used in the southern mixed prairie, Bryant et al. (1982) recommended the Merrill deferred-rotation grazing system for dual production of wildlife and livestock. Moderate stocking rates of less than 20 ha per AU are recommended under the Merrill system. Range improvement attained will benefit white-tailed deer (Bryant et al. 1981) and associated wildlife.

Short-duration grazing has been examined in the northern mixed prairies and the tallgrass prairies. In the northern mixed prairie, forbs disappeared at a rate 2 to 3 times faster with short-duration grazing than with continuous season-long grazing (Kirby et al. 1986). If such forbs were important to wildlife, the impact might be negative. On the other hand, short-duration grazing of tallgrass prairie in Oklahoma produced more forbs on the grazed site than on an ungrazed site (Gillen et al. 1991). One forb that responded dramatically was western ragweed, an important food source for many wildlife species. Impacts of short-duration grazing on wildlife in the southern mixed prairies have not been investigated adequately.

Grazing practices at the turn of the century changed California grasslands from perennial grasses to annual grasses (Holechek et al. 1989). Populations of California quail were adversely affected by the abusive grazing that occurred (Ryder 1980). Today, livestock can be compatible with California quail (Duncan 1980) and might be needed to maintain California quail habitat (pers. comm. S. Mastrup, California Department of Game and Fish, 1992). Moderate grazing has been compatible with several grassland species of wildlife, as long as grazing management achieves an interspersion of suitable and sizable areas of ungrazed climax grassland coupled with pastures managed in successional stages (Brown 1978). Kie and Loft (1990) used livestock in their model as a tool to reduce plant height from a tall-herb to a short-herb structural class. This alteration of structure would have a positive effect on 50 wildlife species (mostly birds and reptiles), no effect on 171 species, and a negative effect on 29 species (mostly mammals and amphibians) (Table 10.7). Duncan (1976) recommended grazing or mowing every 2 weeks to increase turkey mullein, an important food for mourning doves and quail.

In California wet meadows, livestock effectively open up shrub stands to benefit wildlife species. One method of strategic grazing in annual grasslands would be to graze livestock in late winter and

TABLE 10.7   Numbers of Wildlife Species Using Annual Grassland and Wet-Meadow Habitats Reduced from Tall-Herb to Short-Herb Structural Condition by Livestock Grazing in California

Class	Positive effect		No effect		Negative effect	
	Annual grass-land	Wet mea-dow	Annual grass-land	Wet mea-dow	Annual grass-land	Wet mea-dow
Birds	44	53	61	71	18	26
Mammals	2	2	84	72	8	9
Amphibians	0	1	5	16	3	2
Reptiles	4	3	21	10	0	0
Total	50	59	171	169	29	37

SOURCE: Kie and Loft (1990).

spring to create a short-herb structural class for the 50 species that are benefited and eliminate grazing in late fall and early winter to allow deer total access to forbs and acorns. A modified rest-rotation grazing system at light stocking rates (0.5 to 1.2 AUM per hectare) is recommended for wet meadows (Kie and Loft 1990). Payne (1992) discussed grazing management of wetlands.

In fescue grasslands of Alberta, grazing practices which maintain rangeland in good condition generally will favor the full range of prairie passerines that was known to occur, including Sprague's pipit and Baird's sparrow (Owens and Myres 1973). Under heavier stocking rates, chestnut-collared longspurs and horned larks will predominate and Sprague's pipits and Baird's sparrows will be rare. Thus, added grazing pressure will create a shift in population mixes of passerine birds, but no grassland passerines will be eliminated as long as native grassland remains unaltered by cultivation (Owens and Myres 1973).

In semidesert grasslands, long-term overgrazing, climate change, cessation of fire, and influence of rabbits and rodents have been hypothesized to have caused changes in vegetation composition (Hastings and Turner 1965). In general, semidesert grasslands have shifted from a monotypic grass type with low structural diversity to areas dominated by woody and succulent vegetation (Schmutz et al. 1992). Such drastic changes in structure improved conditions for some species. Wood (1969) reported a mean biomass of 807 g/ha for rodents on mesquite dunes—a deteriorated condition of black grama grassland—and 412 g/ha in an area dominated by black grama. Balda (1975) reported only 4 species of breeding birds present in a well-managed grassland, compared to 20 species in a severely overgrazed grassland supporting succulent plants and shrubs. But such habitat changes also hurt species like masked bobwhite quail, Montezuma quail, alpomado falcon, Sonoran pronghorn, and desert bighorn sheep (Snyder and Snyder 1975, Ryder 1980, Severson and Medina 1983). Some believe the impact of cattle might have been greater here than in any other rangeland vegetation type (Hastings and Turner 1965). In Arizona, Short (1983) suggested that the best management policy is to restrict livestock use of surface vegetation to that portion that does not impact the structure over time. At least twelve guilds could be affected negatively. Cassin's sparrows and grasshopper sparrows do best on protected or lightly grazed areas; horned larks and lark sparrows seem to prefer grazed areas (Bock and Webb 1984).

The masked bobwhite might be the most classic case history of a semidesert grassland species affected by abusive grazing. This upland bird formerly occupied semidesert grasslands of southern Arizona and northern Sonora, Mexico. It disappeared from Arizona by 1900, presumably because nesting and security cover declined as a result of a series of droughts coupled with excessive grazing. Evidently, masked bobwhite quail need more open grasslands of dense grass-forb mixtures than other hot desert quail, which prefer more broken, wooded terrain (Eng 1986). By comparison, Mearn's quail prefer wood cover in winter, but generally use areas with a mosaic of grasslands and shrublands.

One result of heavy grazing in semidesert grasslands has been the loss of herbaceous vegetation and also plants such as fourwing saltbush (Orodho et al. 1990). Jackrabbit populations generally were favored (Cooperrider et al. 1986, Schmutz et al. 1992).

A second result of heavy grazing in semidesert grasslands has been the increase in woody plants and succulents. Removal of livestock might not be enough to restore herbaceous cover to these invaded grasslands. Roundy and Jordan (1988) found that density of perennial grasses did not increase after 19 years of grazing exclusion. Woody plants make conditions more xeric, which increases the amount of bare soil, increases runoff, decreases infiltration, and creates a microclimate unsuitable for perennial grasses, especially if the seed source is lost. Some other form of habitat manipulation might be needed to restore the herbaceous component. Although Brady et al. (1989) found an increase in plains lovegrass cover on an ungrazed site compared to a grazed site, total cover and species richness were the same. They reported that grazing exclusion did not improve vegetative conditions, and neither did they support the theory that animal impact was needed to prevent further deterioration.

Diversity of animal groups generally increases after livestock are removed from semidesert grasslands, but the effect depends on the type of wildlife. Grazing favors birds; protected sites favor rodents

(Bock et al. 1984, Heske and Campbell 1991). Other dilemmas are apparent when the impact of livestock grazing is considered for all wildlife. Although desert mule deer generally favor ungrazed areas over grazed areas, especially in dry washes, Ragotzkie and Bailey (1991) suggested that rest-rotation grazing can be compatible with mule deer. Hughes (1990) reported that rest-rotation grazing can improve habitat conditions only if use rates by cattle are low (below 50 percent). Leaving some areas periodically ungrazed is a contingency measure that can prevent negative impacts by cattle during drought. Nonetheless, deer also heavily use pastures that are grazed the previous year (Wallace and Krausman 1987). For Mearn's quail, heavy livestock grazing in certain areas can increase preferred foods (pers. comm. R. Brown, Arizona Game and Fish Department, 1992). But use rates on grasses needed for nesting must not exceed 45 percent, particularly in spring. Mearn's quail could benefit from correct stocking rates that achieve less than 45 percent use, coupled with strategic grazing to produce desired forbs on certain areas (pers. comm. R. Brown, Arizona Game and Fish Department, 1992). Such discrepancies prevent generalizing about livestock grazing in semidesert grasslands. But some observations can be made.

Balda (1975) found a correlation between bird diversity and floral diversity. Thus, grazing practices which promote floral diversity (low levels of disturbance) might improve habitats for birds, whereas grazing that reduces floral diversity impinges negatively on their habitat. Habitat selection cues for birds in desert grasslands might have as much to do with plant species physiognomy as horizontal structure. Grazing which alters physiognomy might affect habitat selection. Leaving residual cover through planned rest and deferment or leaving some sites ungrazed could help support rodent densities at desired population levels. Creative grazing strategies could minimize livestock-wildlife conflicts in semidesert grassland habitats.

In Florida grasslands, livestock grazing is recommended to maintain suitable habitat for the widest variety of bird species. Grazing alters structure and composition of prairies and can improve habitat conditions (White 1975).

Tundra. In fragile alpine and arctic tundra, introduced livestock grazing is not recommended as a tool for wildlife habitat management. If alpine tundra is grazed at all, stocking rates should be light (Braun 1980). Wild ungulates, such as bighorn sheep, Dall sheep, and mountain goats, provide enough grazing pressure in alpine environments; livestock use probably is unwarranted. Even though native reindeer are used as livestock on arctic tundra, reindeer promote invasion of shrub species and only about 25 percent of reindeer winter ranges are really usable (Lent 1986). Reindeer grazing and trampling is destructive to lichens in tundra environments, and 10 years of rest might be needed before full recovery takes place (Pegau 1970). Muskoxen reduce lichen and shrub standing crop (Lent 1986), as do caribou, but sedges increase under heavy grazing (McKendrick 1981). Muskoxen could be used to shift tundra to lower successional stages if that were the management goal (McKendrick 1981). Tundra requires years to recover from any intensive impact, whether caused by humans (Bell and Bliss 1973) or ungulates.

Shrublands

Cold desert. Overgrazing of sagebrush rangelands has created conflicts with wildlife-management interests. Historical grazing greatly reduced palatable bunchgrasses and changed the composition of these vegetation types. But overgrazing alone was not totally responsible for the apparent expansion of big sagebrush (Ryder 1980). Suppression of natural fires aided the establishment and subsequent dominance of this plant on many cold desert sites. Innovative controlled grazing practices must also be developed to reduce impacts on and conflicts with wildlife species.

Livestock exclusion might be needed in specific cases. But livestock exclusion alone does not always prevent big sagebrush from increasing (Daddy et al. 1988). Some sagebrush species might in fact benefit from grazing. Evanko and Peterson (1955) found fringed sagebrush in Idaho to be more prevalent on a site grazed by livestock than in a 15-year exclosure.

Stocking rates must be strictly controlled. Increased stocking rates can decrease diversity and density of passerines (Ryder 1980). Heavy grazing by cattle can increase their use of browse species and increase diet overlap with mule deer (Lucich and Hansen 1981). Stocking rates are recommended at light to moderate rates unless specifically designed to meet habitat-management objectives. For example, heavy grazing in late fall followed by spring deferment can reduce sagebrush and increase grasses and forbs (Mueggler 1950, Laycock 1967). Moderate to heavy winter grazing by cattle can open up shrub and herb layers and facilitate raptors' ability to find prey during summer (Olendorff et al. 1980), and can maintain shrub dominance on sagebrush sites used by mule deer in winter (Smith 1949). Moderate cattle grazing (24 ha per AU) permitted an increase in herbaceous cover in New Mexico (Daddy et al. 1988). Where sagebrush has been controlled through mechanical, herbicidal, or prescribed burning treatments, livestock grazing should be regulated carefully to prevent overuse on treated sites (Baker et al. 1976).

The kind of animal grazed also influences sagebrush habitats. Long-term use by cattle can shift succession from grass toward a

TABLE 10.8   Mean Use Rates (Percent) of Important Herbaceous Forages and Shrubs on Deer Winter Ranges by Season, Stocking Intensity, and Kind of Livestock in Northern Utah

Grazing period and forage class	Cattle (Smith and Doell 1968)		Sheep (Jensen et al. 1972)		Horses (Reiner and Urness 1982)	
	Moderate	Heavy	Moderate	Heavy	Moderate	Heavy
Early						
Grasses	31	41	16	28	45	74
Forbs	28	32	21	45	8	18
Bitterbrush	5	13	23	39	0	0
Other shrubs	–	–	10	33	–	–
Middle						
Grasses	22	32	17	31	42	75
Forbs	12	17	36	43	7	20
Bitterbrush	20	36	69	84	0	0
Other shrubs	–	–	27	46	–	3
Late						
Grasses	22	35	27	39	41	79
Forbs	8	10	26	45	8	18
Bitterbrush	31	41	40	63	0	0
Other shrubs	–	–	18	32	–	3

Note: Grazing periods are defined as follows. Early: generally late May to late June. Middle: generally late June to early July. Late: generally late July to mid August.
SOURCE: Urness (1990).

browse-forb mix; sheep have the opposite effect (Ellison 1954). Continued early season use by cattle causes grasslands to shift to more shrub cover, a positive factor if the management goal is to benefit mule deer winter range (Stoddart et al. 1975). Stevens (1986) reported an increase in basin big sagebrush and black sagebrush where cattle, deer, and rabbits grazed an area that was chained 20 years earlier. Where cattle were excluded, basin big sagebrush decreased substantially. Based on use rates (Table 10.8), Urness (1990) recommended strategic grazing by cattle or sheep in late summer and horses at any time to shift the sagebrush community toward shrubs, particularly bitterbrush. Alternating these kinds of livestock each year or combining sheep and cattle also might improve mule deer habitat (Urness 1990), but some strategy of alternating use patterns should be designed to assure relative stability identified as desirable for a given array of wildlife species (Urness 1979). Furthermore, by using selective feeding behavior and other characteristics, different kinds of livestock have the potential to alter community composition, forage production and availability, and nutritional value for specific wildlife (Smith et al. 1979). Winter grazing by sheep at 50 percent use of current growth increased black sagebrush (Ellison 1969), an important forage plant for wild ungulates. Stevens (1986) also reported that black sagebrush was tolerant of grazing by rabbits, mule deer, and cattle. But Clary (1986) and Behan and Welch (1985) cautioned against overuse of black sagebrush because it is severely impacted by sheep defoliation, and such overuse can impact mule deer populations. Moderate grazing during midwinter or alternate years is compatible with maintenance of black sagebrush stands (Clary 1986). The lower-elevational distribution of black sagebrush must be watched carefully if sheep are grazing it. Sheep grazing, particularly in late winter, has a negative effect on growth and survival of budsage (Wood and Brotherson 1986). Heavy winter grazing by sheep can completely eliminate budsage from a shadscale-bursage complex (Wood and Brotherson 1986). In a northern Arizona sagebrush zone, a high correlation existed between sheep grazing and paucity of bird populations (Carothers and Johnson 1975), but in Idaho sheep grazing was compatible with nesting and nonnesting birds (Ryder 1980). Smith and Doell (1968) and Jensen et al. (1972) showed that livestock can be managed in a complemental way so as to make their impacts negligible.

Grazing systems, particularly the commonly used rest-rotation systems, could be helpful or harmful depending on the wildlife species involved, size of grazed units, and how the units are planned relative to wildlife needs. Elk move to rested units, but deer apparently do not (Urness 1979). Short-duration grazing apparently accelerates sagebrush invasion compared with continuous, season-long grazing (Owens and Norton 1990), and such an impact could be desirable or undesirable depending on the management goal.

Where sage grouse are a primary concern, EPG should be practiced. Because wet meadows, mesic sites, and riparian zones constitute a key sage grouse habitat for brood-rearing and summer use, these sites should be protected from excessive grazing (Crawford et al. 1992). Dense, grassy meadows that are grazed lightly or moderately by cattle can be attractive to sage grouse (Klebenow 1982). But as grazing intensity increases, sage grouse might be forced to use the meadow edge. Heavily grazed meadows in poor condition, with few grasses and forbs, are avoided by sage grouse except as a water source (Klebenow 1982). Such meadows might need burning or mechanical treatment to reduce dense sagebrush. Treatment should be followed by grazing exclusion until grasses and forbs reestablish. Fencing the stream meadow and leaving fence gaps to provide livestock access to water can provide protection from grazing (Fig. 10.7) (Autenrieth et al. 1982). Payne (1992) provided other considerations for protecting riparian areas from cattle.

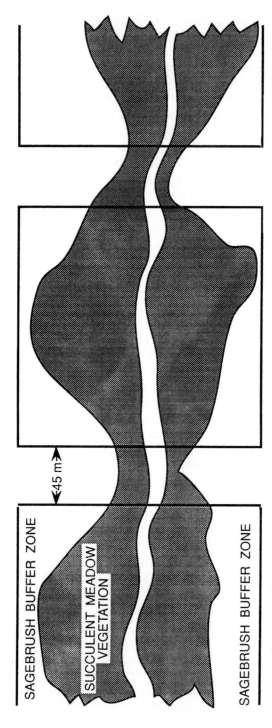

Figure 10.7 Stream meadow fencing allowing livestock access to water. (*Autenrieth et al.* 1982.)

SAGEBRUSH BUFFER ZONE

SUCCULENT MEADOW VEGETATION

SAGEBRUSH BUFFER ZONE

45 m

Timing of grazing in sage grouse habitats also should be considered. Grazing might be allowed after mid-August depending on the rainfall zone and the condition of the mesic site. On poor-condition mesic sites in a 15- to 25-cm rainfall belt, grazing should be allowed only once every 3 years or more until the sites begin to recover (Autenrieth et al. 1982).

Specific sites in sage grouse habitat should be managed carefully relative to livestock grazing. Nesting areas are the key to sage grouse reproduction and require special attention. Sage grouse are known to nest at the base of sagebrush plants, particularly those that are taller than the surrounding plants (Roberson 1986). Crawford et al. (1992) found sage grouse in Oregon prefer to nest in areas with greater cover of medium-height (40 to 80 cm) shrubs and tall (greater than 18 cm) residual grasses. They recommended stands be maintained or developed that consisted of 8 to 12 percent cover of Wyoming big sagebrush and 15 to 20 percent cover of mountain sagebrush and basin big sagebrush. The structural characteristics of medium-height shrubs and residual grass cover were important elements to nesting sage grouse.

Strategic grazing or EPG can be used to maintain residual grass cover. Use of grazing systems might achieve the desired habitat characteristics. For example, in the heavy-use pasture in a rest-rotation grazing system, the residual grasses required by nesting sage grouse might not be left. But, through careful planning, the system could be designed so that the heavy-use pastures would not be in areas where sage grouse are known to nest.

Brooding areas are also key to sage grouse survival. Grazing that protects, maintains, or encourages forbs would be important for hens with broods, particularly during early brood rearing (Crawford et al. 1992). Crawford et al. (1992) recommended grazing programs that achieve a more favorable balance of shrub canopy and herbaceous understory. Thinning dense sagebrush by fire or mechanical means might be needed in addition to controlled livestock grazing (Crawford et al. 1992). In 30-cm rainfall belts, annual post-August grazing probably could be allowed. Springs and seeps should not be disturbed by livestock. Livestock use should not exceed 50 percent of the forage in any pasture where sage grouse occur (Autenrieth et al. 1982). Problem areas, such as the heavy-use pasture in a rest-rotation grazing system, must be watched closely.

Hot desert. If grazing is considered at all in hot desert habitats, cautious, prudent, and conservative EPG should be practiced. Short (1983) reported that heavy grazing will deleteriously impact many wildlife guilds in creosotebush-bursage, Joshua tree–creosotebush, saguaro-paloverde, and mixed-scrub arroyo vegetation types.

Carothers and Johnson (1975) suggested that livestock should not graze desert habitats. If livestock graze desert habitats, use rates should not exceed 25 to 30 percent of current year's growth of key species (Holechek et al. 1989).

Hot desert environments are brittle, fragile, and slow to recover even after grazing exclusion. Some researchers have found that perennial grasses recover slowly after livestock are removed. In the Sonoran Desert, 50 years of livestock exclusion did not cause an appreciable change in species composition (Ryder 1980). In the Chihuahuan Desert, vegetation structure did not differ between transects exposed to or protected from cattle grazing (Heske and Campbell 1991).

Results of studies on grazing and wildlife in hot desert habitats vary. Grazing herbaceous biomass in excess of 55 percent use by weight can eliminate escape and hiding cover (Brown 1982). Management for residual cover to be left is the best approach because use rates of 46 to 50 percent are marginal for maintaining optimum Mearn's quail habitat (Brown 1982). No more than 30 to 40 percent use probably would be acceptable.

The Merriam's kangaroo rat prefers areas where vegetation cover is less than 10 percent (Institute for Land Rehabilitation 1978). It was more numerous in a grazed than in an ungrazed area (Reynolds 1950), yet it was the only member of a rodent community negatively affected by the presence of cattle in the Chihuahuan Desert (Heske and Campbell 1991).

For ungulates, decreased stocking rates could enhance reproduction of Coues white-tailed deer (Smith 1984) and fawn survival of white-tailed deer because of improved residual grass cover in marginal habitats (Brown 1984a). Livestock grazing at light to moderate stocking rates apparently had little impact on desert mule deer during normal-precipitation years (Horejsi 1982). But immediate and substantial stocking-rate reductions during drought years could improve cover and alleviate some fawn mortality (Horejsi 1982). Residual grass cover conceals fawns and might make them less vulnerable to predation. Because Coues deer avoid areas of high cattle use, especially at lower elevations, cattle should be managed to minimize spatial overlap with deer (Brown 1984b). Similar suggestions of reduced spatial overlap with cattle and sheep were proposed for desert bighorn sheep (Dodd and Brady 1986). Dodd and Brady (1986) discouraged distribution techniques which push cattle onto steeper slopes, although this is contrary to current thinking in range management. Using salt placement to attract livestock to ridges and butte tops should be avoided where desert bighorns occur. This reduces negative impacts on perennial grasses and shrubs and would maintain spatial segregation between cattle and desert bighorn sheep (Dodd and Brady 1986).

The dilemma in hot desert types is that (1) even though grazing probably should be excluded, exclusion might not result in improved habitats and (2) woody plant control might not increase herbaceous vegetation. Whatever habitat-management techniques are considered, careful planning with well-defined objectives is essential when dealing with vegetation types in hot deserts.

Woodlands

Pinyon-juniper. Overgrazing by cattle, sheep, and wild ungulates, spread of seeds by livestock, lack of fire, and changing climate have caused pinyon-juniper woodlands to increase (Stevens et al. 1975, Balda and Masters 1980). Because of the superdominance of trees, attempts to improve herbaceous production through grazing management alone have little chance of success (Dwyer 1975). Heavy grazing of herbaceous vegetation can negatively impact almost 40 guilds of primary and secondary consumers in Arizona (Short 1983). Heavy spring grazing might be most damaging (Skousen et al. 1989). Although a spring and fall cattle rotation might stimulate grasses, winter sheep grazing can be detrimental (Institute of Land Rehabilitation 1978).

Cattle were judged to be compatible with chained openings of pinyon-juniper in Utah but sheep were not (Terrell and Spillet 1975). Stevens et al. (1975) reported that the key to preventing reinvasion of chained juniper sites is to have a healthy grass, forb, and shrub complex. They found that combined use by mule deer, rabbits, and livestock was the best way to maintain this healthy complex. In Colorado, deer grazing combined with cattle and sheep grazing had no adverse effects on pinyon-juniper woodlands as long as stocking rates were moderate (Severson and Medina 1983). A grazing-management goal should be to maintain a healthy complex of grasses, forbs, and shrubs in openings created; livestock forage consumption must be controlled carefully to provide wild ungulate forage that is needed in fall, winter, and early spring (Severson and Medina 1983).

Strategies for livestock use in habitat management have not been explored adequately for pinyon-juniper woodlands. Brown (1990) reported on the effects of the Savory Grazing Method (SGM) (see Table 10.6 for explanation) on wild ungulates in an Arizona pinyon-juniper habitat. Excessively high stocking rates of cattle associated with this grazing system caused the range condition to decline. Although the elk population increased in the region, the grazing program had an adverse local impact on wild ungulates compared with rest-rotation grazing. Food availability declined within the SGM cell more rapidly than on the rest-rotation pastures, inducing a shift in elk use out of the cell to the rest-rotation pastures. Brown (1990) concluded that doubling, or near doubling, of original stocking rates is not advisable on Arizona's rangelands.

Oak. Oak woodlands in California receive fairly intensive grazing pressure, producing one-third of the forage used by the livestock industry in California (Huntsinger and Fortmann 1990). Generally, California quail benefit from livestock grazing if moderate stocking rates are used; similarly, deer are abundant and have good annual survival of fawns where moderate grazing is practiced (Klinger et al. 1989).

Grazing practices in the Madrean evergreen woodland of Arizona should be controlled carefully. Cattle grazing conflicts with Mearn's quail if excessive (greater than 55 percent use of available biomass) (Brown 1982), and with Coues white-tailed deer. Because 46 to 50 percent use by weight of forage is marginal for Mearn's quail, 35 to 40 percent use is preferable (Brown 1982). Strategic grazing by goats in the live oak–mixed-shrub community is not recommended because of reduced floral diversity and negative impact on shrubs (Severson and Debano 1991).

Shinnery oak rangelands of west Texas and eastern New Mexico might require manipulation of shin oak canopies. Herbicidal plant control is the technique most often used, and enhances habitat for ground-nesting birds such as lesser prairie chickens. Because residual grasses are favored nesting areas (Taylor and Guthery 1980), good grazing management (controlled stocking rates, grazing systems) must provide residual grass cover.

Gambel oak woodlands are more important to wildlife than to livestock. As an example of strategic grazing for habitat management, goats can be used to manipulate Gambel oak to increase the quality of winter mule deer diets under snow-covered conditions (Riggs et al. 1990). Strategically grazed at heavy stocking rates in summer, goats open up the dense canopy of oak stands, creating sites for herbaceous forage production and deer use of other shrubs (Urness 1990).

Chaparral and mountain shrub. Livestock grazing has not been studied as a management tool in the California chaparral. Mountain shrub vegetation types are grazed intermittently by livestock because they are usually in the transition zones between foothills and forested lands. EPG of light to moderate stocking rates should be applied to maintain the herbaceous understory. Because herbaceous species are usually more palatable to livestock, overuse can easily occur on any mountain shrub vegetation type. Bitterbrush and mountainmahogany occur in mountain brush types. These two species also occur in pinyon-juniper woodlands, sagebrush shrublands, and others. Strategic grazing, especially by cattle, can be used to stimulate basal

TABLE 10.9   Maximum Use Rates by Herbivores of Shrubs Found in Many
Rangeland Vegetation Types

Species	Use rate (%)	Reference
Serviceberry	60	Young and Payne (1948)
Bitterbrush	60	Ferguson and Basile (1966)
		Lesperance et al. (1970)
		McConnell and Smith
		(1977)
Mountainmahogany	60	Garrison (1953)
Rabbitbrush	50	Garrison (1953)
Redstem ceanothus	60	Swank (1958)
Evergreen ceanothus	40	Garrison (1953)
Big sagebrush	60	Wright (1970)
Chamise	50	Bedell and Heady (1959)
Willow	80	Telfer and Scotter (1975)
Aspen	70	Telfer and Scotter (1975)
Utah honeysuckle	65	Young and Payne (1948)
Rose	65	Young and Payne (1948)

Note: Use rate refers to present use of current annual growth.

sprouting of bitterbrush for deer (Thilenius and Hungerford 1967). Intensive cattle grazing every 15 to 20 years in a bitterbrush community decreases the competitive advantage of bunchgrasses and enhances bitterbrush seedling establishment and survival (Neal 1982). Cattle grazing from May to June does not affect bitterbrush, nor does fall use in years of greater than normal precipitation (Severson and Medina 1983). Total livestock exclusion did not accelerate bitterbrush regeneration in Idaho (Bunting et al. 1985). If sheep are used, EPG should be designed to avoid heavy spring use; it should be planned to achieve light use of bitterbrush in summer or fall. But Jensen et al. (1972) found spring use by sheep to be compatible with bitterbrush growth on mule deer winter range.

Use rates of many rangeland shrubs, whether by domestic or wild ungulates, vary according to species, but 50 percent use is generally acceptable (Table 10.9). Use rates for key grass species vary by rangeland types (Vallentine 1989).

Mesquite-acacia.   Recently, because of reduced livestock use, some parts of the mesquite-acacia woodland have advanced successionally, resulting in reduced populations of some wildlife species. For example, on the Welder Wildlife Refuge, where plant communities have gone from 19 to 40 percent climax vegetation to 50 to 60 percent climax, populations of small mammals, jackrabbits, white-tailed deer, northern bobwhite quail, and Rio Grande turkey declined between

1960 and 1980 (Drawe 1981). Songbird populations remained unchanged, largely because of vertical structure provided by trees and shrubs (pers. comm. D. L. Drawe, Welder Wildlife Refuge, 1992). Disturbance, such as strategic livestock grazing, could be used to stimulate open spaces, forbs, and grasses. In other parts of the mesquite-acacia woodland that have been overgrazed, more cautious grazing such as EPG should be practiced.

Because stocking rate is the overwhelming factor affecting habitat, the livestock enterprise should be integrated with habitat-management objectives. Stocking rates recommended for northern bobwhite quail include (1) light stocking in the more xeric (<50 cm rainfall) portions of their range, (2) light stocking when inadequate rainfall has created a short spring growing season, (3) light stocking on more xeric sites within higher-rainfall areas, (4) moderate stocking on areas with more than 75 cm of rainfall, and (5) heavier stocking rates on areas with more than 100 cm of rainfall (Guthery 1986).

Because northern bobwhite quail need nesting clumps of residual grass between 20 cm (Guthery 1986) and 50 cm (Johnsgard 1973) tall, light to moderate stocking rates are suggested, especially during the growing season, to retain enough biomass of warm-season grasses (pers. comm. F. S. Guthery, Texas A&I University, 1991). Moderate grazing was also best for ground-foraging birds—except mourning doves, which were more abundant with heavy than moderate grazing (Baker and Guthery 1990). Because northern bobwhite quail favor mesic habitats along bottomlands and stream systems in arid regions (Campbell-Kissock et al. 1985), EPG should be directed at riparian areas to provide suitable, but moderately disturbed, habitat.

Short-duration grazing has been widely practiced over the past 10 years in the mesquite-acacia woodlands. On clay loam sites, short-duration grazing provided better structure of ground cover for quail than continuous yearlong grazing did in dry years (Guthery et al. 1990). In the western portion of the mesquite-acacia woodland, quail densities were unaffected by short-duration grazing, but were affected by continuous grazing (Campbell-Kissock et al. 1985). During dry years, the Merrill deferred-rotation and short-duration grazing systems provided better nesting and protective cover than continuous grazing (Campbell-Kissock et al. 1984). Although short-duration grazing has the potential to disturb ground-nesting birds (Bryant et al. 1982), trampling of nests might not be a problem if stocking rates are below 2.5 AU per hectare (Bareiss et al. 1986). Nongame bird richness was improved with short-duration grazing, bird richness under continuous grazing was lowest, and cottontail rabbits and rodents were unaffected by either grazing practice (Guthery et al. 1990).

Central watering points that concentrate cattle can be a problem, but are an integral part of short-duration grazing. Several wildlife species avoid them (Prasad and Guthery 1986).

The presence of cattle might cause white-tailed deer to shift their use areas (Ellison 1969, Hood and Inglis 1974). Cohen et al. (1989a, 1989b) reported dramatic deer responses to cattle. Deer avoided herd movements under short-duration grazing, but they did not change the size of, nor did they leave, their home range. Short-duration grazing might not be a concern in white-tailed deer habitat (Cohen et al. 1989a, 1989b). In a dry year, Hyde et al. (1987) reported 0.0 fawns per female under short-duration grazing compared to 0.27 fawns per female under continuous, yearlong grazing. Hyde et al. (1987) suggested that coyote predation increased because of a decrease in hiding cover. Yet during the other 2 years, fawn-to-doe ratios were similar in both areas. Limited data on wild turkeys suggest no adverse affects of short-duration grazing (Bareiss et al. 1986, Schulz and Guthery 1987).

In zones of higher (more than 75 cm) rainfall, short-duration grazing is a potentially important habitat-management technique because of the flexibility it provides (Guthery et al. 1990). It might be the main means to practice strategic grazing. For example, Guthery (1986) recommended heavy spot-grazing to provide early successional stages for northern bobwhite quail in mesic regions of the mesquite-acacia woodland. This technique uses salt, water, hay, or supplements to concentrate cattle for short-term heavy grazing and is especially useful within 100 m of brush cover.

Prescribed Burns

Fire is the most ubiquitous agent of disturbance that releases energy and renews habitat (Landers 1989). The high flammability of herbaceous vegetation of grasslands plus the prevalence of lightning storms made the central prairies of North America a fire-dominated region. Aside from livestock grazing as a tool to enhance habitat, fire is more practical to use ecologically and economically than cultural alternatives. Fire is irreplaceable to many organisms. Fire has a natural role in the ecological development of most habitats, i.e., in promoting and maintaining interior, edge, interspersion, and diversity. Thus, it is natural to consider it as an ecological wildlife-management tool (Komarek 1971). Vallentine (1989) concluded that use of fire probably benefits wildlife more than any other resource, and no tool is more appropriate for manipulating wildlife habitat.

Prescribed burning is the judicious use of fire for a constructive purpose and according to a management plan. It can be used to achieve the following objectives:

1. Increase abundance of forbs

2. Change the kind and abundance of insects

3. Manage the invasion of shrubs and woody plants

4. Increase, temporarily, the palatability and nutrient content of forage plants like grass and browse

5. Create edge

6. Increase vegetation diversity

7. Retard succession or maintain a seral stage

8. Alter distribution patterns of ungulates

9. Improve accessibility of forage

10. Reduce litter and remove old, dead material

11. Rejuvenate woody plants for browse production

12. Stimulate earlier growth and green-up of fire-tolerant grasses

Without careful and thoughtful planning, fire can:

1. Exacerbate severely overgrazed areas if domestic or wild ungulates are not controlled

2. Destroy fire-sensitive plant species

3. Remove cover for ground-nesting wildlife

4. Increase erosion on highly erodible sites.

Factors influencing a prescribed burn (or the damage it can cause) include:

1. Size of burn

2. Frequency of burn

3. Timing

4. Rate of fire spread

5. Amount of fine fuel

6. Intensity of fire

7. Kind of fuel

8. Fuel moisture content

9. Soil moisture

Careful planning of prescribed burns is essential because plant species important to wildlife are affected by fire (Table 10.10). Wright and Bailey (1982), Chandler et al. (1983a, 1983b), Wade and Lunsford

TABLE 10.10 Important Ungulate Forage Plants and Their Relationship to Fire

Location	Forage species	Ungulate
Fire tolerant*		
Central United States	Live oak	White-tailed deer
	Vasey shinnery oak	White-tailed deer
	Sand shinnery oak	Pronghorn, mule deer
	Skunkbush sumac	Pronghorn, mule deer, white-tailed deer
	Littleleaf sumac	White-tailed deer
	Fragrant sumac	Pronghorn, mule deer
	Sand sagebrush	Pronghorn, mule deer
Intermountain West	Willow	Moose
	Sumacs	Mule deer
	Winterfat	Pronghorn, mule deer, elk
	Fourwing saltbush	Mule deer
	Chokecherry	Mule deer
	Desert bitterbrush	Mule deer
	Gambel oak	Elk, mule deer
	Snowberry	Mule deer
	True mountain-mahogany	Elk, mule deer
	Western mountain-mahogany	Mule deer
	Serviceberry	Mule deer
	Snowbrush ceanothus	Mule deer
	Redstem ceanothus	Mule deer
	Shrub live oak	Mule deer
	Oceanspray	Mule deer
	Syringa	Mule deer
	Mountain maple	Mule deer
Fire intolerant†		
Central United States	Forbs (late spring burns)	Deer, pronghorn
	Scarlet globemallow	Pronghorn
	Cacti	Javelina, white-tailed deer
	Texas wintergrass	White-tailed deer
Intermountain West	Antelope bitterbrush	Mule deer, pronghorn
	Mountain snowberry	Mule deer
	Cliffrose	Mule deer
	Big, fringed, black, low sagebrush	Mule deer
	Curlleaf mountain-mahogany	Mule deer, elk
	Desert ceanothus	Mule deer
	Threadleaf sedge	Mule deer, elk
	Scarlet globemallow	Pronghorn, mule deer
	Forbs (late spring burns)	All
Alpine and arctic tundra	Lichens	Caribou

*Not usually harmed by fire; usually resprout vigorously from the crown after fire.
†Moderately to severely damaged by fire.

(1987), McPherson et al. (1986), Higgins et al. (1989), and Payne (1992) described the various types of prescribed burns and the details of planning and implementing a prescribed burn. The different types of prescribed burns are illustrated in Payne (1992). (Also see "Prescribed Burns" in Chap. 3.)

Grasslands and tundra

Tallgrass prairies. Even though some recommendations call for normal and above-normal rainfall, the tallgrass prairie burns when the soil surface is wet or in years when much residual grass is available as fuel (Vallentine 1989). Prescriptions call for backfires and head fires (Launchbaugh and Owensby 1978).

In general, frequency of prescribed fire is a function of rainfall; burns could be every 5 to 8 years in a 51-cm precipitation zone but can be as often as every 1 to 3 years in an 89- to 102-cm precipitation zone (Wright and Bailey 1980). Vogl (1965) reported that unburned tallgrass prairie in Wisconsin leaves a mantle of dead and decaying vegetation that stifles growth of plants. In fact, 90 percent of the total herbage was dead material. Compared to an enclosure that had not been burned in 25 years, burning in March and April after snows melted resulted in a three- to fourfold increase in forbs for 1 to 2 growing seasons and a twofold increase in water content of forbs (Vogl 1965).

Most burning has been directed at increasing livestock forage or perennial warm-season grasses. For example, annual late spring burns in Kansas generally increased big bluestem and leadplant, while controlling cool-season grasses such as Kentucky bluegrass, Japanese brome, and snowberry (Vallentine 1989). Productivity of burned and unburned grasslands is variable, depending upon grassland type (Table 10.11) (Peek 1986).

In terms of plant diversity, annually burned grasslands have fewer species than unburned or periodically burned grasslands (Collins and Gibson 1990). Plant species diversity increases for 6 to 7 years after burning (Fig. 10.8) (Collins and Gibson 1990).

Late spring burning is generally detrimental to woody plants and forbs; those plants can enhance vegetative structure and food diversity for wildlife. Thus, burning less often than annually should be desirable for some wildlife species because it permits woody plants to establish. At least in Wisconsin, burning every 4 to 6 years retained herbaceous ground cover and burning every 10 years maintained a brush-prairie savanna (Vogl 1965). Within only 15 years without fire, woody species dominated mesic grasslands in Oklahoma (Collins and Gibson 1990).

To enhance wildlife habitat generally, burns conducted in winter

TABLE 10.11 Comparison of the Productivity of Burned and Unburned Grasslands

Type of vegetation	Location	Species	Productivity (g/m²)		Year of peak productivity after burning	Remarks
			Burned	Unburned		
Desert-grass-shrubs	Arizona	Perennial grasses	45	50	3d	
Tobosa grasslands	Texas	Tobosagrass	310	125	<1	Wet year
Tobosa grasslands	Texas	Tobosagrass	95	105	1st	Dry year
Tallgrass prairie	Wisconsin	Little bluestem–dominated	300	220	1st	Prairie depression
Tallgrass prairie	Wisconsin	Little bluestem–dominated	90	90	1st	Prairie upland
Rangeland	South Florida	Pineland threeawn	300	—	2d	May burn
Longleaf pine–tallgrass	Louisiana	Pinchill bluestem	250	250	2d	March burn
Longleaf pine–tallgrass	Louisiana	Pinchill bluestem	215	250	2d	May burn
Coastal prairie	Texas	Indiangrass	210	200	<1	Fall burn, midspring production
Midgrass prairie	North Dakota	Little bluestem	431	335	<1	Spring burn, late summer production
Ponderosa pine	Arizona	Native perennial grasses	17	7	2d	Unthinned pine
Ponderosa pine	Arizona	Native perennial grasses	65	50	1st	Thinned pine

TABLE 10.11 Comparison of the Productivity of Burned and Unburned Grasslands (Continued)

| Type of vegetation | Location | Species | Productivity (g/m^2) | | Year of peak productivity after burning | Remarks |
			Burned	Unburned		
Sage-grassland	Idaho	Idaho fescue	2	2	12th	Light burn
Sage-grassland	Idaho	Idaho fescue	2	2	12th	Moderate burn
Sage-grassland	Idaho	Idaho fescue	1	2	12th	Heavy burn
Sage-grassland	Idaho	Bluebunch wheat-grass	21	13	2d	Suppression 1st year
Sage-grassland	Idaho	14 species	55	33	3d	
Palouse prairie	Washington	Bluebunch wheat-grass	81	34	2d	
Palouse prairie	Washington	Cusick's bluegrass	2	4	1st	
Palouse prairie	Washington	Thurber needle-grass	1	2	2d	Little difference 1st and 2nd years

SOURCE: Peek (1986).

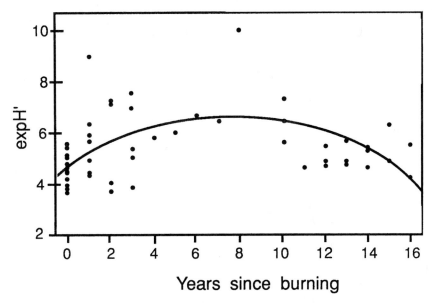

Figure 10.8 Changes in species diversity (expH') during postfire succession at Konza Prairie Research Natural Area, Kansas. $r^2 = 0.26$; $P = 0.001$. Note: expH' denotes the diversity index of Shannon-Weaver. (*Collins and Gibson 1990.*)

promote forbs more than late spring burns do (Bidwell et al. 1990). But spring backfires with a slower rate of fire (0.2 km per 6 h) produced 26 percent more forbs than a faster-moving headfire (2.7 km per 6 h). Spring backfires also can be used to manage tallgrass prairie habitat if restricted to small areas (Bidwell et al. 1990).

Heterogeneous mosaics of grasses and forbs are a more suitable habitat for some nongame birds than uniform stands of either (Verner 1975). Heterogeneous patchworks of burned and unburned areas benefit some insects, some small mammals, and some birds more than large burns do. But interior species of grassland wildlife prefer homogeneous areas. Kirsch (1974) recommended burning at 3- to 5-year intervals to restore vigor and retard succession to optimize habitat for greater prairie chickens. Generally, burns can be conducted in spring (between May 15 and June 15 in South Dakota). Earlier burns are better in warm springs. Prescribed burns increase height and density of warm-season grasses such as big bluestem, little bluestem, Indiangrass, and switchgrass (Payne 1992).

Prescribed burning is strongly recommended in habitats of the endangered Attwater's prairie chicken (Lehmann 1965, Chamrad and Dodd 1973). Habitats containing burns 1 to 3 years old are desirable because (1) burns at least 3 years old are needed for nesting because of the 2-dm cover heights, (2) burns at least 2 years old are needed for early (before June 15) brooding, and (3) burns at least 1 year old are needed for late (after June 15) brooding (Morrow 1986).

Small mammals respond to grassland burning as fire-negative, fire-positive, or fire-neutral. *Fire-negative* mammals are those associated with plant debris and/or feed in foliage (Table 10.12) (Kaufman et al. 1990). Fire-negative mammals include (1) species that forage on invertebrates in litter, (2) species that live in and eat dense plant foliage, and (3) species that nest in plant debris. *Fire-positive* mammals include (1) species that use ambulatory locomotion in habitats open at the herbaceous layer, (2) species that feed on seeds and insects, and (3) species that use saltatorial locomotion. Regardless, most mammal populations recover by the third year after fire (Kaufman et al. 1990). Thus, fire frequency of 2 to 10 years should create a cycle of varying population densities of small mammals and associated predators in tallgrass prairie. Such periodic burning generally increases small-mammal density (Fig. 10.9) (Kaufman et al. 1990). Because small mammals have limited mobility to take advantage of burned areas, small (10 to 50 ha) burns are better. Prescribed burns which create a mosaic of burned and unburned patches produce more of a mixture of fire-negative and fire-positive small mammals than burned or unburned prairie. Fires that move quickly across the landscape tend to burn more in patches. This probably will be better for small mammals. Fires that move slowly consume a greater percentage of fuel present, and can produce large-scale burns valuable to grassland interior wildlife.

Few studies have focused on the best season to burn for small mammals. For fire-negative mammals requiring the protective cover of litter or standing vegetation, an early fall to winter fire would have greater impact than a spring fire (Kaufman et al. 1990). Either a fall or spring fire would benefit fire-positive species. The interactive effects of grazing and burning have not been studied for small mammals. But natural disturbances such as grazing and burning increase heterogeneity in grasslands; a combination of grazing and burning apparently increases plant diversity (Table 10.13) (Collins and Gibson 1990). Enhanced plant diversity could influence small mammals in a positive way. But because wild and domestic ungulates are attracted to recently burned areas and preferentially graze them, the movement and impact of grazing animals within a landscape will be tied to the spatial distribution of burned patches. These grazing patterns following fire provide feedback to the ecology of the system and will lead to variable fire effects in future years (Risser 1990).

TABLE 10.12   General Population Responses of Small Mammals to Fires in Grasslands of North America

Mammal	Grassland type	Response
Shrews		
Masked shrew	Minnesota tallgrass prairie	0
Northern short-tailed shrew	Illinois tallgrass prairie (restored)	– ?
	Illinois tallgrass prairie (restored)	–
	Illinois tallgrass prairie (restored)	–
Elliot's short-tailed shrew	Kansas tallgrass prairie	–
Southern bog lemming	Kansas tallgrass prairie	–
Cricetine rodents		
Deer mouse	Minnesota tallgrass prairie	+
	Illinois tallgrass prairie (restored)	+
	Kansas tallgrass prairie	+
	Wisconsin brush prairie savanna	+?
	Kansas tallgrass prairie	+
Western harvest mouse	Kansas tallgrass prairie	–
	Kansas tallgrass prairie	–
White-footed mouse	Illinois tallgrass prairie (restored)	+
	Illinois tallgrass prairie (restored)	+
	Wisconsin brush prairie savanna	+?
	Kansas tallgrass prairie	0
Microtine rodents		
Meadow vole	Minnesota tallgrass prairie	–
	Illinois tallgrass prairie (restored)	– ?
	Illinois tallgrass prairie (restored)	– ?
	Illinois tallgrass prairie (restored)	–
	Illinois tallgrass prairie (restored)	–
	Nebraska tallgrass prairie	–
Prairie vole	Illinois tallgrass prairie (restored)	– ?
	Illinois tallgrass prairie (restored)	+
	Kansas tallgrass prairie	–
Sciurid rodents		
Thirteen-lined ground	Wisconsin brush prairie savanna	+?
squirrel	Kansas tallgrass prairie	+
Zapodid rodents		
Meadow jumping mouse	Illinois tallgrass prairie (restored)	+?
	Illinois tallgrass prairie (restored)	0
	Illinois tallgrass prairie (restored)	+

Note: + denotes fire-positive response; – denotes fire-negative response; 0 denotes fire-neutral response; ? denotes observations suggestive of the listed response, but data available were not or could not be tested statistically.
SOURCE: Kaufman et al. (1990).

Mixed-grass prairies.   Burning of northern mixed prairies should occur between late March and mid-May or about August 15 to September 15 (Payne 1992). But landscape mosaic diversity was highest with fall burns (Biondini et al. 1989), which would be preferable for heterogeneity but not homogeneity of habitat.

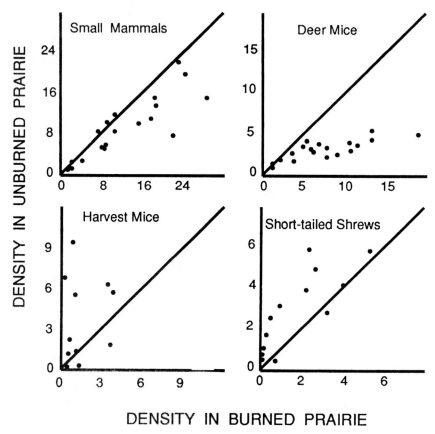

Figure 10.9 Relative density (number of individuals per trapline) of all small mammals, deer mice, western harvest mice, and Elliot's short-tailed shrews in burned and unburned areas on Konza Prairie, Kansas. Censuses in which densities in burned and unburned prairie are equal would fall on the diagonal lines. (*Kaufman et al. 1990.*)

Burning in northern mixed-grass prairies usually is directed at controlling cool-season grasses (Kirsch and Kruse 1972). Generally grass yields decreased in Kansas mixed-grass prairies after burning (Launchbaugh 1964), and fire had limited potential in Nebraska, especially on poor-condition rangeland where remnant plants of true mixed-grass prairie were absent (Schacht and Stubbendieck 1985). Density of important wildlife forbs like western ragweed remained unchanged after a March wildfire in western Kansas, but total forb yield was reduced (Launchbaugh 1964). In contrast, where litter accumulations were heavy at the time of an early spring burn, numbers and yield of western ragweed increased considerably (Hopkins et al. 1948).

TABLE 10.13   Average Values ($N = 3$) of Diversity (expH'), Evenness, and Richness for Plant Species in Four Disturbance Treatments in Tallgrass Prairie in Central Oklahoma

Variable	Year	Treatment			
		− G, − B	+ G, − B	− G, + B	+ G, + B
Diversity	1985	7.7	8.6	4.7	9.1
	1986	8.3	8.3	5.1	9.0
Evenness	1985	0.57	0.56	0.43	0.44
	1986	0.61	0.61	0.46	0.51
Richness	1985	26.7	30.7	31.1	32.7
	1986	24.3	24.7	27.7	29.0

Note: Richness is the number of species per unit area (the greater the number, the more rich). Evenness is the distribution of dominance among species (the greater the number, the more one or a few species dominates). Diversity (expH') is the relationship between richness and evenness (the greater the number, the more diverse). + G = grazed; − G = ungrazed; + B = burned; − B = unburned.

SOURCE: Collins and Gibson (1990).

In other southern mixed-prairie habitats, burning is recommended between December and February at 10- to 15-year intervals, but only after a wet fall and winter produces good soil moisture (McPherson et al. 1986). Burning prescriptions are usually directed at controlling woody plants like mesquite and juniper (Wright and Bailey 1982). Fire increases some rangeland grasses, but not the dominant ones (Whisenant et al. 1984). But an important cool-season deer forage, Texas wintergrass, is harmed by fire, particularly if burned in January or March (Whisenant et al. 1984). Shrubs used by birds for loafing or perching should be protected. Renwald et al. (1978) recommended that when burning large pastures, at least 10 large mesquite and 4 to 6 large lotebushes per hectare should be ringed with 7-m firebreaks to ensure adequate cover for quail and nongame birds. Grasses, such as blue grama, sideoats grama, and little bluestem, desired by ground-nesting birds, respond differently to fire. Generally, gramas are unharmed or decrease slightly in abundance if burned in wet years, but grama grasses are harmed if burned in dry years. Burning also can damage the rhizomatous form of sideoats grama. Little bluestem usually increases in abundance after burning in wet years, but can decrease by 50 percent if burned in dry years (Wright 1974). Burning can affect ungulate movement patterns. Distribution of bison can be influenced by prescribed burning (Shaw and Carter 1990).

Where mesquite dominates the overstory of southern mixed prairies, fire has been tested as a control measure (Wright et al. 1976). Seedlings less than 3.5 years old are killed or severely harmed, but those 3.5 years or older are very tolerant of fire. These are top-killed and readily sprout from the crown. Burning is most effective in March for controlling young mesquite; burning at 5- to 10-year intervals can help control older trees as well (Wright et al. 1976). For habitat management, fire can be used to maintain openings created by mechanical means or herbicides. Wildlife species such as mourning doves would be enhanced because they readily feed on recently burned sites (Wright and Bailey 1982).

Fire also has been used to control cholla and pricklypear (Bunting et al. 1980, Vallentine 1989). Because blossoms of cholla and fruits of pricklypear are eaten readily by deer and pronghorns, eradication of these plants is not recommended. During dry periods, deer and javelina also consume cladophylls of pricklypear.

The southern mixed prairie of the Edwards Plateau of Texas contains live oak and shinnery oak and has been invaded by ashe juniper. Fire has been used as a wildlife habitat enhancement technique in these situations (Harmel et al. 1991). Oaks readily sprout after fire but ashe juniper is killed by scorching 70 percent of the crown of older trees. Young ashe juniper seedlings less than 1 m are also killed. Forbs increase dramatically in burned areas, whereas grasses decrease slightly in live oak areas and in post oak areas (Hutchenson et al. 1989). White-tailed deer ate more high-quality forbs in burned than in unburned areas (Cross 1984), and deer densities were highest in burned areas. Prescribed burns are highly recommended for bobwhite quail (Jackson 1965).

Thus, fire can be used independently of other techniques or in conjunction with mechanical treatments that create openings in mature stands of juniper. Burning mature, live ashe juniper has been tested as a way to create openings in dense stands at lower cost (Bryant et al. 1983). Once openings are created, prescribed burning should be used to maintain openings, create early successional stages, and stimulate forage production of oaks and forbs (Bryant 1990). Prescribed burns should be at intervals of 7, 20, and 35 years to keep ashe juniper from reinvading habitat openings (Bryant 1990).

Shortgrass prairie. Shortgrass prairies should not be burned often, and only during or after moist periods (Wright and Bailey 1982, Kjellsen and Higgins 1990). Burning reduces grass production on shortgrass prairie regardless of season of burn in Texas (Vallentine 1989).

From Texas to North Dakota to southern Alberta, recovery of grass biomass after burning can take up to 4 years. Wildfires are especially damaging to shortgrass prairie. As a wildlife habitat tool for birds and pronghorns in shortgrass prairie, fire should be limited to small, localized burns to stimulate weedy sites. For southern shortgrass prairies, late winter to early spring burning is recommended over fall burning because fall burns can increase erosion. Recovery from fire is quickest after summer burning (Trlica and Schuster 1969).

For scaled quail and bobwhite quail, shrubs like lotebush, skunkbush, and wild plum should be protected and managed as loafing or escape cover. Livestock grazing must be controlled carefully to prevent heavy concentrations on burned sites that result in soil loss and damage to forage plants (Vallentine 1989). Deferment of livestock grazing until after the growing season on areas burned reduces the potential impact. Information is scant concerning the enhancement of forbs and shrubs; most research on burning has been concerned with their control to encourage grasses.

California annual grasslands.   In California annual grasslands, July burning increased burclover and filaree, desirable wildlife food plants (Vallentine 1989). Late burns, when soft chess seed is shattering, act to control medusahead in favor of soft chess and filaree (Vallentine 1989).

Palouse prairie.   Shrubs can increase bird richness 10-fold. Burns which remove all shrub cover should be avoided (Wiens and Dyer 1975).

Semidesert grasslands.   Where mesquite overstory dominates desert grasslands, fire has been used to control mesquite, but fire is effective only on small seedlings or saplings (Vallentine 1989). Thus, openings to enhance wildlife habitat cannot be created by fire where mesquite overstory exists. However, openings can be maintained. Mosaic sites with varying densities of mesquite maintain high reptilian diversity (Germano and Hungerford 1981); scattered mesquites benefit mourning doves, scaled quail, Gambel's quail (Bock and Bock 1990), and songbirds (Renwald et al. 1978). Important deer forage, such as false-mesquite calliandra and velvetpod mimosa, sprout after fire (Severson and Medina 1983).

Tundra.   Because tundra vegetation is fragile, burning is not generally recommended. Burning alpine tundra was questioned by Seip and Bunnell (1985) as a tool to enhance habitat for stone sheep. Although distribution of bighorn sheep can be affected, fire might not necessarily increase populations. Burning to remove lichens that smother ericaceous plants on the tundra in Newfoundland has been used to improve habitat for willow ptarmigan (pers. comm. W. Skinner, Newfoundland Wildlife Division, 1991).

Shrublands

Cold desert. For wildlife habitat management, mosaic-patterned fires are recommended as long as 50 to 60 percent of the sagebrush survives. Burned sites should be less than 16 ha (Baker et al. 1976). Time between prescribed burns in sagebrush communities should be 15 to 20 years or more on the same site. Apparently the frequency of natural fire varied considerably, from a fire every 20 to 25 years in Wyoming (Houston 1973) to every 50 years in Idaho (Wright et al. 1979).

Where the preburn understory is poor, seeding with mixtures of grasses and legumes is recommended (Plummer et al. 1968, Heady and Bartolome 1977). Success of seeding is highly variable, but it might work best if tied to specific habitat types where plants are known to be adaptable (Urness 1979).

Prescribed burns (Wright and Bailey 1992) should always be conducted at times of above average soil moisture. Burned sites must be protected from livestock grazing the first fall and for at least 1 year after the burn; light grazing could be applied the second year (Vallentine 1989). Wright and Bailey (1982) recommended that domestic grazing be withheld for two seasons. Indeed, livestock grazing might have to be deferred a season before burning to ensure that adequate fuels are present.

Fire effects in sagebrush community types have been studied for many years. Fire kills big sagebrush, low sagebrush, black sagebrush (Vallentine 1989), and other important plants (Table 10.14) (Pechanec et al. 1954 *in* Young 1983) (Table 10.15) (Vallentine 1989). Also, many bird species are obligates (sage grouse, sage thrasher, sage sparrow, Brewer's sparrow) or near obligates (green-tailed towhees and Vesper sparrows) of sagebrush and associated saltbrush flora (Baker et al. 1976). Therefore, prescribed burning must be used with caution in sagebrush plant associations. If fire effects and limitations are considered (Table 10.16), fire could be used where sagebrush stands become decadent and unproductive through time and require rejuvenation (Peek 1986). Some decadent stands should not be burned. An interspersion of grassy patches within sagebrush stands could improve habitat quality as long as prescribed burns are not too large in size, fragmentation does not result, and key habitats remain (e.g., sage grouse nesting or brooding habitats). Increased grass production benefits bighorn sheep (Lauer and Peek 1976) and mule deer (Willms et al. 1981).

Fire generally increases grasses and forbs, but several important shrubs such as black sagebrush, cliffrose, and curlleaf mountainmahogany can be eliminated (Vallentine 1989). Bitterbrush, an important ungulate browse plant in sagebrush communities, exhibits considerable

TABLE 10.14   Summary of Relative Response to Fire of Forbs in Sagebrush
Grasslands of Upper Snake River Plains of Idaho

Severely damaged	Slightly damaged	Undamaged
Hairy fleabane	Astragalus	Arrowleaf balsamroot
Hoary phlox	Matroot penstemon	Common comandra
Littleleaf pussytoes	Monroe globemallow	Sunflower
Low pussytoes	Pinnate tanseymustard	Coyote tobacco
Mat eriogonum	Plumeweed	Douglas knotweed
Uinta sandwort	Red globemallow	Flaxleaf plainsmustard
Wyeth eriogonum	Sticky geranium	Flaxweed tanseymustard
	Tailcup lupine	Foothill deathcamus
	Tapertip hawksbeard	Gayophytum
	Timber milkvetch*	Goldenrod
	Tongueleaf violet	Goosefoot
	Tumblemustard	Green ephedra*
	Wavyleaf thistle	Horsebrush*
	Whitlow-wart	Lambstongue groundsel
	Wild lettuce	Longleaf phlox
		Mulesear*
		Orange arnica
		Pale alyssum
		Purpledaisy fleabane
		Russian thistle
		Velvet lupine
		Western yarrow
		Wild onion

*From Vallentine (1989).
SOURCE: Pechanec et al. (1954) *in* Young (1983).

regional variation in response to fire (Britton and Clark 1985). Fire can
stimulate bitterbrush in a mountain big sagebrush community, but seriously damages bitterbrush in a basin big sagebrush community
(Bunting et al. 1985). Fire can be used to rejuvenate bitterbrush-saska-
toon stands in British Columbia, as well as climax stands of bitterbrush, Stansbury cliffrose, or true mountainmahogany in the Great
Basin (Peek 1986).

Autumn burns appear most damaging to sagebrush (Vallentine
1989); summer burns are most damaging to bitterbrush (Britton and
Clark 1985). Because spring burns damage bitterbrush least (Britton
and Clark 1985, Bunting et al. 1985), spring might be an optimum
time to burn where bitterbrush is a component of the plant community. When prescribed burns were to be used to manage for elk on rough
fescue grasslands of foothills, spring burns were recommended in
Montana during years of above normal precipitation (Jourdonnais
and Bedunah 1990). Fall burning impacts forbs lightly, and mule deer
preferred fall-burned grasses to grasses grazed by cattle in fall

TABLE 10.15   General Response to Fire of Flora in Sagebrush Communities

Harmed	Unharmed	Favored
Bitterbrush	Bluebunch wheatgrass	Arrowleaf balsamroot
Broom snakeweed	Indian paintbrush	Cheatgrass brome
Cliffrose	Indian ricegrass	Crested wheatgrass
Curlleaf mountain-	Needle-and-thread	Douglas sedge
mahogany	Penstemon	Foothill deathcamus
Eriogonum	Prairie junegrass	Green ephedra
Idaho fescue	Squirreltail	Horsebrush
Pussytoes	Tapertip hawksbeard	Lambstongue groundsel
Big sagebrush	Thurber needlegrass	Medusahead
Black sagebrush	Timber milkvetch	Mulesear
Low sagebrush		Purple pinegrass
Threetip sagebrush		Rabbitbrush
Threadleaf sedge		Sandberg bluegrass
		Serviceberry
		Snowbrush ceanothus
		Sticky currant
		Subalpine needlegrass
		Thickspike wheatgrass
		True mountainmahogany
		Velvet lupine
		Western wheatgrass
		Western yarrow

SOURCE: Adapted from Vallentine (1989).

TABLE 10.16   Some Limitations and Considerations Related to Fire Effects in Sagebrush Habitats

Fire effect	Limitations and considerations
Kill of big sagebrush	95–100% of all ages.
Kill of associated undesirable plants	Not effective on sprouting shrubs and some annuals.
Effect on desirable forage plants	Low kill of grass, 30–40% loss in vigor first year. Nonsprouting shrubs killed. Loss of forage and cover.
Ease of seeding after treatment	Easily done with drills; seed can be aerially broadcast and covered with anchor chain or pipe harrow; firm seedbed.
Adaptability to terrain and soil	No limit except as imposed by fire danger and erosion hazard.
Availability of equipment	Equipment generally available; brush rake useful; experience primary need.
Effect on erosion hazard	Exposes soil, destroys litter (unsuited to highly erosive areas).

(Willms et al. 1981). Whether burning is done in spring or fall, soils should be wet so the fire will be cool and do minimal damage to root collars (Peek 1986).

Some wildfires should be suppressed (Baker et al. 1976, Petersen and Best 1987); some natural wildfires should be allowed to burn. Repeated burning or larger, hot fires that remove extensive amounts of cover can be detrimental to sage grouse (Peek 1986) and other species of wildlife, but beneficial to others. The desirable impacts from using prescribed burns in habitat management of cold deserts would be (1) opening up of dense, monotypic sagebrush stands; (2) stimulation of selected shrub species; (3) increasing forbs (Urness 1979; Pyle 1992); (4) enhancement of floral diversity (Loope and Gruell 1973, Pyle 1992); (5) creation of edge; and (6) prevention of invasion by juniper.

Mosaic burns generally increase bird species richness as long as removal of sagebrush does not exceed 40 to 50 percent (Petersen and Best 1987). Bird density might decrease on some sites. Dominance of sage sparrows and Brewer's sparrows might decrease after fire (Castrale 1982, Petersen and Best 1987); the density of sage sparrow and sage thrashers seems unaffected (Petersen and Best 1987). Return rates, fledgling production, and nestling growth also seemed to be unaffected by mosaic-patterned fires (Petersen and Best 1987). Narrow-strip and small-block burns also might be acceptable, especially in a rainfall zone of at least 30 cm (Autenrieth et al. 1982).

April burns in strips 45 m by 90 m are best for sage grouse (Autenrieth et al. 1982). Pyle (1992) evaluated fall and spring burns on sage grouse foods in Oregon and found that fall burning increased Chichorieae but had no apparent effect on most other primary foods including microsteris, desert parsley, June beetles, and darkling beetles. Spring burns apparently were more severe, but again did not greatly influence primary food availability. The utility of burning as a food enhancement practice is limited if too much sagebrush is removed (Pyle 1992). Spot burns are suitable in brood-rearing areas. Historically, stand replacement fires periodically burned brood-rearing habitat, but extensive sagebrush reduction by burning could reduce these areas' value as foraging habitats (Pyle 1992). Where a diversity of cover can be created by prescribed burning, sage grouse habitat can be restored (Peek 1986). Burned areas which created openings in dense sagebrush stands were used as new leks for sage grouse in Idaho (Connelly et al. 1981).

Hot desert. Fuel accumulations in the Mojave, Sonoran, and Chihuahuan deserts are generally too sparse to carry a fire except after wet winters and springs (Severson and Medina 1983) or on more localized sites like sacaton flats and tobosagrass swales (Humphrey

1963, Vallentine 1989). Fire usually adversely affects grass herbage production for 2 to 3 years after a spring burn, and postfire recovery time for most species is long (up to 20 years) (Bock and Bock 1990). Wildfires and controlled burns in the Sonoran Desert cause substantial mortality of woody plants (bursage, creosotebush, paloverde) and of cacti like saguaro. Mortality of these plants would have a highly negative impact on wildlife species needing them. Thus, prescribed burning is seldom used and rarely recommended as a wildlife habitat management tool in the hot desert vegetation types, particularly in the Sonoran and Mojave deserts.

In the Chihuahuan Desert, fire can be an integral and natural part of wildlife management to stimulate herb, seed, and perhaps grass production, especially if burns can restore prehistoric conditions (Bock and Bock 1990). Any use of fire depends on a sufficient grass understory. Excluding livestock for 1 to 2 years might permit fuel buildup. Schmutz (1978) suggested a grazing system based on the desire to implement rotational burning. His system would provide 1 year of rest to allow fine-fuel buildup to carry a fire, followed by 2 years of deferred grazing after burning.

Fire affects desert wildlife by altering vegetative structure, and could increase wildlife species diversity if prescribed burns result in patchy mosaics in some areas and extensive unfragmented areas nearby. In the Sonoran Desert, Brown (1984a) proposed that fire would benefit white-tailed deer only when it increased the herbaceous understory to conceal fawns from predation. Generally, increased nutrient content of selected grasses following fire lasted only 1 year; nutrients in Fendler ceanothus were unaffected by prescribed fire (Severson and Medina 1983). Because of the severe erosion potential of steep to moderately steep slopes in desert habitats, any use of prescribed burning should be restricted to flat or level topography.

Woodlands

Pinyon-juniper. Fire is generally accepted as a major force in the distribution of pinyon-juniper woodlands. Cessation of fires has led to increased densities and contributed to the spread of pinyon and juniper trees (Severson and Medina 1983). Over the past five decades, most fire research has been directed at controlling woody plants and increasing livestock forage. Little emphasis has been given to using fire to enhance wildlife habitats in this plant community, even though wildlife species abound. For example, in the five western states of Nevada, Utah, Colorado, Arizona, and New Mexico, 73 species of birds are known to breed in pinyon-juniper woodlands—31 breed there regularly and 5 are obligate breeders (Balda and Masters 1980). Pinyon pine seems to be an important factor in determining bird populations. Mule deer and elk also are important as seasonal or yearlong inhabitants.

In central Oregon, juniper supports more species and larger populations of birds than community types dominated by ponderosa pine, lodgepole pine, or sagebrush (Maser and Gashwiler 1978). At least 83 bird and 23 mammal species use this community type in Oregon. As trees mature, the following changes in wildlife use have been noted (Maser and Gashwiler 1978):

1. *Seedling (less than 1 m)*. Used as shade and wind protection; foliage might be used as food.

2. *Sapling (1 to 2 m)*. Used as hiding cover and thermal cover, for food, for singing and perches, for nesting occasionally.

3. *Young-mature (greater than 2 m)*. Used as thermal and hiding cover; branch nesting and cavity nesting occurs; used for nest materials; food gleaning of insects, foliage, and berries occurs; provides perches for territory establishment and maintenance; provides sites for courtship and mating.

4. *Decadent*. Provides natural cavities for nesting by birds and hibernation by bats, shelter for ground dwellers, and nest materials.

Exclusive use of fire as a habitat-management tool in pinyon-juniper woodland is rare, although prescriptions are available (Wright and Bailey 1982). In most instances, fire is incorporated with mechanical treatment (see Chap. 10). Even so, fire could be used to (1) increase mule deer use of burned areas (McCulloch 1969); (2) create different successional stages in otherwise monotypic stands (Severson and Medina 1983, Evans 1988); (3) prevent juniper domination, which decreases understory shrubs (e.g., bitterbrush) (Bunting et al. 1985) and/or herbaceous plants; (4) extend the period of use for wild ungulates during critical times; or (5) maintain a perennial grass/forb stage (Peek 1986). Severson and Medina (1983) suggested the possibility of burning 30 percent of a unit in optimum patch sizes at 25-year intervals for mule deer. Short and McCulloch (1977) also recommended small burns because they create a greater variety of food and cover conditions than do larger burned or unburned areas. But some unburned areas are needed for species of wildlife that depend on unfragmented habitats.

Fire effects depend on plant species (Tables 10.17 and 10.18). Managers should avoid damaging important shrubs such as cliffrose, sagebrush, and bitterbrush. Large, older trees should be maintained for mast production of juniper berries and pinyon nuts because of their nutritional value (Balda and Masters 1980) and their importance to birds (Balda 1975). Igniting small (1.0 to 1.6 ha) spot burns

TABLE 10.17 Summary of Fire Effects on Major Shrub Species of Sagebrush and Pinyon-Juniper Zones of the Intermountain Region

Species	Preburn regeneration	Response to fire	Postburn regeneration; recovery time	Comments
Antelope bitter-brush Cliffrose	Heavy seed, animal-dispersed	Moderately to severely damaged	Seed germination from rodent caches, basal stem sprouting; slow.	Effect of fire on bitterbrush determined by growth form—decumbent form might sprout vigorously, upright form is a weak sprouter. Severely damaged by summer and fall burns. Spring burns enhance sprouting; burn when wet.
Big sagebrush Black sagebrush Low sagebrush	Light seed, wind-dispersed	Severely damaged	Seed germination nonsprouting; slow to rapid.	Frequent, heavy seed crops; readily dispersed over large areas. Good seed production before burning speeds reinvasion, especially in poor-condition ranges. Big sagebrush subspecies important relative to postburn community response. Black sagebrush and low sagebrush rarely burn due to low fuel loads—can be used as fuel breaks.
Threetip sage-brush	Light seed, wind-dispersed	Slightly to severely damaged	Resprouts (variable), seed germination; moderate to rapid.	Sprouting is strongest when burned with moist soils. Weak resprouting reported in Idaho; strong response reported in Oregon.
Silver sagebrush	Light seed, wind-dispersed	Slightly damaged to unharmed	Vigorous sprouting, seed germination; moderate to rapid.	Might be difference in degree of resprouting between the two subspecies.
Greasewood	Light seed, wind-dispersed	Slightly damaged to unharmed	Vigorous basal stem and some root sprouting; rapid.	Vigorous resprouting might result in increased density of stems. Poor seed production the first year after burning. Some stands burn infrequently if at all due to low amounts of fine fuels.

Species	Seed	Fire effect	Regeneration	Comments
Rubber rabbitbrush Green rabbitbrush Spineless horsebrush	Light seed, wind-dispersed	Unharmed to enhanced	Vigorous stem sprouting, seed germination; rapid to very rapid.	Reproduces abundantly from heavy seed crop, especially in low-condition ranges. Rubber rabbitbrush might be more susceptible to injury, especially if burned after heavy grazing or in early summer. Horsebrush is toxic to sheep.
Broom snakeweed	Light seed, wind-dispersed	Severely damaged	Seed germination, weak resprouting; moderate to rapid.	Might be completely removed from an area, but new plants invade open areas rapidly by seed.
Gambel oak	Heavy seed, gravity-dispersed	Enhanced	Vigorous stem and root sprouting; very rapid.	Fire stimulates suckering and thickens stands. Tends to thin out when protected from fire.
Common snowberry Mountain snowberry	Rhizomes, seed	Slightly damaged to unharmed	Weak to vigorous resprouting from basal buds and rhizomes; moderate to rapid.	Might be enhanced by cool fires, but hot fires can damage shallow rhizomes. Mountain snowberry is a weak sprouter.
True mountain-mahogany	Moderately heavy seed, wind-dispersed	Slightly damaged to enhanced	Vigorous sprouting, seed germination; recovery time unknown.	Little information available on this species. Recovery time probably moderate to rapid, based on its response.
Curlleaf mountain-mahogany	Moderately heavy seed, wind-dispersed	Moderately to severely damaged	Seed germination, weak sprouting; recovery time unknown.	Little information available on this species. Reported to be weak sprouter, but shoots died within 2 to 3 years. Recovery from seed probably slow to moderate.
Ninebark Oceanspray Spiraea	Light seed, wind-dispersed	Unharmed to enhanced	Basal stem sprouting; moderate.	Adapted to fire. Best response when burned with moist soils. Usually poor reproduction from seed.

TABLE 10.17 Summary of Fire Effects on Major Shrub Species of Sagebrush and Pinyon-Juniper Zones of the Intermountain Region (*Continued*)

Species	Preburn regeneration	Response to fire	Postburn regeneration; recovery time	Comments
Bittercherry Chokecherry Currant Rose Serviceberry	Heavy fleshy seed, animal-dispersed	Unharmed to enhanced	Basal stem sprouting; moderate.	Adapted to fire. Best response when burned with moist soils. Usually poor reproduction from seed except for currants that are heat-scarified, and germination is stimulated.
Snowbrush ceanothus	Heavy seed	Unharmed to enhanced	Vigorous sprouting from stems, seed is heat scarified; rapid.	Seedling establishment enhanced by fall burns. Spring burns produce fewer resprouts. Common pioneer on high-intensity burns.

Note: Postburn recovery time is based on the number of years needed to regain preburn plant frequency or canopy coverage: slow = greater than 10 years; moderate = 5 to 10 years; rapid = 2 to 5 years; very rapid = 1 to 2 years.
SOURCE: Wright et al. (1979), Payne and Copes (1988), Vallentine (1989).

TABLE 10.18 Summary of Fire Effects on Major Grass and Grasslike Species of the Sagebrush and Pinyon-Juniper Zones of the Intermountain Region

Species	Growth form	Response to fire	Postburn recovery time	Comments
Big bluegrass	Bunchgrass	Slightly to moderately damaged	Rapid to very rapid	Bluegrasses are mostly small bunchgrasses with densely clustered, medium- to fine-textured leaves. Little injury occurs with late summer or fall burns; most damage results from spring burns after initiation of growth. Heavy seed crops produced after burning.
Cusick bluegrass	Bunchgrass	Slightly to moderately damaged	Rapid to very rapid	
Muttongrass	Bunchgrass	Slightly to moderately damaged	Rapid to very rapid	
Nevada bluegrass	Bunchgrass	Slightly damaged	Rapid to very rapid	Same as above.
Sandberg bluegrass	Bunchgrass	Undamaged to slightly damaged	Rapid to very rapid	Same as above.
Kentucky bluegrass	Rhizomatous sodgrass	Slightly damaged	Rapid to very rapid	Increases mainly by vegetative spread.
Cheatgrass	Annual	Undamaged	Rapid to very rapid	Soil seed reserves are reduced and litter loss results in decreased plant density in the first year after fire. But plants are large and produce abundant seed. Stand reduction is short-lived, and density might exceed preburn levels within a few years.
Idaho fescue	Bunchgrass	Slightly to severely damaged	Slow to rapid	Densely tufted and fine-stemmed. Can sustain severe damage from hot summer or fall burns, but spring or fall burns with good soil moisture injure plants much less.
Indian ricegrass	Bunchgrass	Slightly damaged	Rapid	Slow to increase in density.
Junegrass	Bunchgrass	Undamaged	Rapid to very rapid	Small size and coarse-textured foliage result in little or no injury. Heavy seed production; might increase in density after burning.

TABLE 10.18 Summary of Fire Effects on Major Grass and Grasslike Species of the Sagebrush and Pinyon-Juniper Zones of the Intermountain Region (Continued)

Species	Growth form	Response to fire	Postburn recovery time	Comments
Columbia needlegrass	Bunchgrass	Moderately damaged	Moderate to rapid	Densely tufted stems make the needlegrasses one of the least fire resistant bunchgrasses. Large plants are most severely damaged, but reduction in basal area is likely among all size classes.
Needle-and-thread	Bunchgrass	Severely damaged	Moderate to rapid	
Thurber needlegrass	Bunchgrass	Severely damaged	Moderate to rapid	
Western needlegrass	Bunchgrass	Moderately damaged	Moderate to rapid	
Douglas sedge	Rhizomatous	Undamaged	Very rapid	Responses seem to be related to open growth habit and regrowth from rhizomes. Threadleaf sedge responds like fine-stemmed, densely tufted bunchgrasses.
Threadleaf sedge	Tufted bunch	Severely damaged	Moderate to slow	
Bottlebrush squirreltail	Bunchgrass	Undamaged to slightly damaged	Rapid to very rapid	Coarse-stemmed, loosely tufted. One of the most fire resistant bunchgrasses. Basal areas might be reduced from burning in dry years, but it might increase.
Bluebunch wheatgrass	Bunchgrass	Slightly damaged	Rapid to very rapid	Bluebunch wheatgrass is susceptible to injury when burned in dry years. Rhizomatous species might increase density. Other wheatgrasses are hard to burn when needed in monocultures.
Crested wheatgrass	Bunchgrass	Undamaged	Rapid	
Tall wheatgrass	Bunchgrass	Undamaged	Rapid	
Intermediate wheatgrass	Weakly rhizomatous	Undamaged	Rapid	
Thickspike wheatgrass	Rhizomatous	Undamaged	Rapid	
Western wheatgrass	Rhizomatous	Undamaged	Rapid	

Note: Postburn recovery time is based on the number of years required to regain preburn frequency or canopy coverage: slow = greater than 10 years; moderate = 5 to 10 years; rapid = 2 to 5 years.
SOURCE: Wright et al. (1979).

has been used to increase biodiversity in the Kaibab National Forest (Severson and Rinne 1990).

Oak. Gambel oak vegetation types offer important fall, winter, and spring habitat and winter foraging areas for elk and mule deer. As oak brush plants become older, they grow beyond reach of these ungulates. Gambel oak habitats can become so dense they physically exclude large animals and suppress understory growth. Tall, dense stands need to be opened to increase forage production and make stands more accessible. Prescribed burning, when compared to chaining and herbicides, was recommended to manage Gambel oak habitats in Colorado (Kufeld 1983). Shrubs and forbs respond positively to chaining, but ungulates generally respond to burning (Table 10.19) (Kufeld 1983). Burning should be done in the fall or immediately after oak leaf-fall. Under wet conditions and light winds (less than 24 km/h) during burning, the resulting burn will be patchy with natural openings and nearby cover areas. If burning is done in dry, windy weather, burned patches should not exceed 12 ha and 50 percent or less of the area should be burned. Cattle should be excluded for at least 2 years after treatment (Kufeld 1983).

Habitats dominated by shinnery oak of New Mexico, Oklahoma, and Texas are too fragile for burning because such oak types occur on sandy soils where exposure to wind and rain can result in erosion. Fire can be used in shinnery oak habitats only with caution. Burning only after wet fall and winter is recommended on sites where sand bluestem or little bluestem dominates.

In the Madrean evergreen woodlands of Arizona, fire can be used to control one-seed juniper and alligator juniper (Severson and Medina 1983). One-seed juniper suffers the greatest mortality when burned and does not sprout (send up basal shoots) readily; alligator juniper is harder to kill with fire and sprouts more readily than one-seed juniper (Johnson et al. 1962). Emory oak and Arizona white oak sprout readily after fire and are usually unaffected by burning (Bock and Bock 1988). Fire effects on grasses disappear after 2 years. Birds were about 18 percent more abundant on a burn for 18 months postburn, but rodents were 40 percent less common on burned sites (Bock and Bock 1988). Coues white-tailed deer evidently respond favorably for at least 6 years after fire, which indicates potential as a deer habitat management tool.

Arizona chaparral. In the interior chaparral of Arizona, fire is the main management tool to open dense shrub canopies for edge wildlife. Prescriptions have been suggested by Wright and Bailey (1982). Fire can be used to (1) enhance palatability and nutrient content of shrubs, (2) increase forbs, and (3) create mosaics of different-aged

TABLE 10.19   Rank of Vegetation and Wild Ungulate
Response to Burning, Chaining, and Spraying
Gambel Oak Habitats 2, 5, and 10 Years
Posttreatment

Treatment variable	Burn	Chain	Herbicide
2 years posttreatment			
Forbs	3	1	2
Grasses	3	2	1
Shrubs (general)	3	1	2
Gambel oak	2	1	3
Serviceberry	3	1	2
Chokecherry	3	1	2
Snowberry	3	2	1
Big sagebrush	3	2	1
Elk use	1	3	2
Mule deer use	1	1	1
5 years posttreatment			
Forbs	1	2	3
Grasses	2	3	1
Shrubs (general)	3	1	2
Gambel oak	1	2	3
Serviceberry	2	1	3
Chokecherry	2	3	1
Snowberry	3	2	1
Big sagebrush	3	2	1
Elk use	1	2	3
Mule deer use	2	2	1
10 years posttreatment			
Forbs	3	1	2
Grasses	2	3	1
Shrubs (general)	3	1	2
Gambel oak	2	1	3
Serviceberry	2	1	3
Chokecherry	1	2	3
Snowberry	3	1	2
Big sagebrush	3	1	2
Elk use	1	2	2
Mule deer use	2	2	1

Note: 1 = most productive or best response; 2 = intermediate response; 3 = worst response.
SOURCE: Kufeld (1983).

shrublands. Care must be taken to prevent damage to important, intermingled cover types (Severson and Medina 1983) and to preserve unburned areas for interior wildlife.

Most shrubs in the Arizona chaparral sprout vigorously from the crown (Severson and Medina 1983) and recover in 5 to 10 years (Pase and Granfelt 1977). Species like oak and skunkbush respond dramatically, even to repeated burning. But repeated fires are impractical; silktassel and buckthorn were damaged by burning two times in 3 years. Desert ceanothus, a desirable deer browse plant, is killed by a single burn (Vallentine 1989). Fire plus herbicides also eliminates birchleaf mountainmahogany, a primary deer food (Severson and Medina 1983). Although desert ceanothus produced seedlings, neither it nor manzanita sprouted from the crown (Pase and Lindenmuth 1971).

Small burns (10 ha) should be conducted under a 10- to 20-year rotation (Bock and Bock 1988). Vallentine (1989) recommended even smaller burns; burns 2.4 ha in size have the advantage of increasing deer use while reducing erosion, a major concern in the Arizona interior chaparral (Vallentine 1989). Burning narrow (15 to 30 m) contours on 20 percent of a watershed can increase fair- to good-quality browse (sprouts of shrub live oak and desert ceanothus seedlings) and forbs for mule deer.

Prescribed burns should be conducted when conditions are as cool as possible. Debano (1990) recommended burning when (1) cooler temperatures and higher humidities prevail, (2) live and dead fuel moistures are high, and (3) wind speeds are low. More specifically, (1) vegetation must be dormant or nearly dormant, (2) wind should not exceed 6.4 km/h, (3) relative humidity should be between 14 and 35 percent, and (4) fuel stick moisture should be between 8 and 18 percent (Cable 1975).

California chaparral.   Burning has been used for more than four decades to create habitat for black-tailed deer in chamise chaparral of California (Biswell 1969, Klinger et al. 1989). Use of fire to manage chaparral has been attributed to early studies by Taber and Dasmann (1958), who found a 300 to 400 percent increase in black-tailed deer use after a wildfire in pure chaparral. Deer numbers returned to preburn levels within 4 years. To permit seed production from nonsprouting shrubs, the site should not be reburned for 15 to 20 years (Biswell 1969, Severson and Medina 1983). Mule deer were compatible with burns conducted on parcels of 8 to 10 ha (Thornton 1981). Where burned chaparral was seeded with herbaceous species, deer numbers stabilized at 3 times preburn levels. Furthermore, Taber and Dasmann (1958) reported that deer reproduction improved.

Biswell (1969) recommended several techniques for opening up dense chaparral to improve deer habitat and populations. He suggested mechanical means, as well as spot-burning followed by reseeding and strip-burning with natural regeneration of herbaceous forage. Klinger et al. (1989) found that where deer had oak woodlands or grassland near burned chaparral, deer use increased for only 1.5 years after the burn and use was greatest only during the wet season. Also, they reported no improvement in deer reproduction.

The best use of fire for deer in the chaparral is to decrease dense stands of shrubs associated with manzanita (blue oak, black oak, and bigberry manzanita) and increase deer accessibility to shrubs associated with chamise (chamise, buckbrush) in the oak woodland near chaparral (Klinger et al. 1989). Thus, management objectives for fire differ where oak woodlands or grasslands are associated with dense chaparral compared to pure chaparral habitats.

In general, fall or spring burns are recommended rather than summer burns. Vallentine (1989) discussed advantages and disadvantages of spring versus fall burning in chaparral types.

Managers should leave at least 30 percent of the unit in dense brush to provide cover, maintain structural attributes of the stand, and maintain diversity of bird species (Buttery and Shields 1975). Woodland birds evidently recognize foliage patterns and density; thus, complete removal or modification will reduce the diversity of bird species (Buttery and Shields 1975).

Prescriptions (Wright and Bailey 1982) should incorporate evenly scattered, 2- to 4-ha burns over 20 percent of a managed deer herd unit. Large, clean burns are not good for deer or birds in chaparral habitats (Buttery and Shields 1975). Too much fragmentation is not desirable. Thus, small openings and/or brush islands in larger burns can increase the diversity of bird species (Buttery and Shields 1975).

Mountain shrub.   Prescribed fire offers several advantages in managing mountain shrub vegetation types. Burning shrubs increased nutrient content in the northwest (Leege 1969) and diet quality was improved for ungulates such as mountain sheep and mule deer in Colorado (Hobbs and Spowart 1984). Burning also increased the number and biomass of sprouts in the northwest (Leege 1969). Such species as willow, mountain maple, and serviceberry grow beyond reach, and burning will promote availability by reducing plant height. Palatability of unused browse plants such as oceanspray, syringa, and bittercherry is improved by burning (Leege 1969). Shrub response to burning was variable in Idaho (Table 10.20) (Merrill et al. 1982).

Burning also can enhance edge and structural diversity, which benefits edge birds if burns create small openings. But burns should be large enough to prevent concentration of ungulates. Such concentrations damage the site and increase competitive interactions among ungulate species (Spowart and Hobbs 1985). Adequately distributed over the habitat, openings can decrease localized overgrazing. Burns interspersed with unburned areas offer the best alternative. Unburned areas should be large enough to accommodate interior species for optimum biodiversity.

TABLE 10.20   Production of Shrubs Following Burning, Upper Selway, Idaho
(In Grams per Square Meter)

| | | Year after burning | | | |
Shrub	Unburned mean	1st	2d	3d	4th
Serviceberry	0.2	0.4	0.5	0.7	0.7
Redstem ceanothus	3.6	0.01	0.1	0.1	0.1
Ninebark	1.9	1.2	0.8	0.9	1.2
Rose	0.6	0.5	0.8	0.9	1.1
Spiraea	0.3	2.1	1.1	1.1	1.0
Snowberry	2.8	8.1	5.0	5.9	7.1
Total	9.5	12.0	8.2	9.6	11.0

SOURCE: Merrill et al. (1982).

Although generalizations do not apply everywhere, sprouting shrubs in the northwest that were burned in spring produced more sprouts than fall-burned plants, even though fall-burned sprouts were longer. This was true for species such as *Ceanothus, Prunus, Holodiscus, Philadeus,* and *Amelanchier* (Leege 1969). Thus, even though total biomass might be the same, spring burning could be more beneficial for ungulates because it produces more sprouts. In addition, most sprouting shrubs receive more use by ungulates the first winter after a spring burn than after a fall burn (Leege 1969). For a species like redstem ceanothus, fall burning apparently stimulates more seedlings.

Bitterbrush and mountainmahogany are found in the mountain shrub, sagebrush, and pinyon-juniper vegetation types. Where these plants occur, prescribed burns should be used with caution. Mountainmahogany is a weak sprouter and its reproduction depends entirely on seedling establishment; thus, prescribed burns should be restricted to sites where mountainmahogany is absent (Gruell et al. 1985). Because fire suppression permits communities to reach advanced seral stages and enhances mountainmahogany, fire should be excluded where (1) mountainmahogany is climax, (2) stands are less than 50 years old, (3) stands are vigorous and healthy, and (4) mountainmahogany stands are small (<0.2 ha) and scattered in and among cold desert vegetation types such as sagebrush (Gruell et al. 1985). Fire could be used in seral mountainmahogany stands.

Carefully planned burns (Fig. 10.10) (Wright and Bailey 1992) can be used to maintain bitterbrush on a long-term basis. Fires should be (1) conducted to minimize mortality to bitterbrush, (2) restricted in the

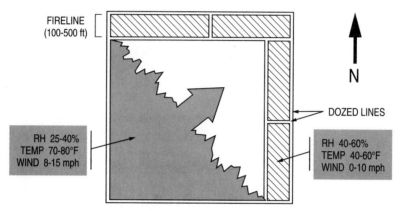

Figure 10.10 Generalized fire plan for conducting prescribed burns. Fireline width depends on fuel type and amount. (Wright and Bailey 1982.) [For metric equivalence, see metric conversion table in the front of the book.]

pinyon-juniper vegetation type, and (3) used at infrequent intervals (every 30 years or more on the same site). Variations in bitterbrush sprouting ability after fire are a function of several factors: growth form, season of burn, vegetation type in which the burn occurs, and fire severity (Fig. 10.11) (Bunting et al. 1985). Disturbance affects the density of bitterbrush, but it usually decreases initially after a fire (Bunting et al. 1985). Fire suppression ultimately might result in low rates of reproduction and declining productivity.

Mesquite-acacia. Prescribed burns can be used to (1) suppress woody plants, (2) remove litter and rough forage plants, (3) promote legumes and other valuable forbs, (4) promote uniform ungulate grazing, and (5) expedite secondary succession (Scifres 1980a). Prescribed burns also can be combined with mechanical brush treatment to maintain openings by reducing shrub canopy (Box et al. 1967); to stimulate forbs for songbirds, quail, and deer; to reduce litter accumulation; and to increase bare ground. Along with grazing and disking as potential disturbance factors for habitat management, burning also has been suggested as a management tool for northern bobwhite quail in this region (Guthery 1986). Burning during December to February promotes early successional stages, bare ground, insect diversity, legume abundance (Mutz 1980), and forb diversity (Springer et al. 1987), all of which are essential to songbirds, bobwhites, and some other species of wildlife. Early winter burns (December) stimulate more forbs than late spring burns (March) (Hansmire et al. 1988). Winter burns in general are recommended because they produce more forbs than

Growth Form:	Columnar		Sub-columnar	Conifer	Decumbent
Season of burn:	summer		fall		spring
Vegetation type:	Pinyon-juniper	Basin Big Sagebrush	Mountain Big Sagebrush	Conifer	Mountain shrub

Increased sprouting

Low →   Moderate   ↑   High

Vegetation type:	Pinyon-juniper	Basin Big Sagebrush	Mountain Big Sagebrush	Mountain	Conifer

Increased density of seedlings and mature plants

Low →   Moderate   ↑   High

Figure 10.11 Fire effects on sprouting of mature bitterbrush plants and seedling density as affected by growth form, timing, and vegetation type. (*Bunting et al. 1985.*)

spring, summer, or fall burns. Fall burns produce the most grass (Box and White 1969) if grass cover is needed to improve nesting or other grass-dominated habitat conditions. Cool fires at 4.5 to 15.5°C, relative humidity between 40 and 50 percent, and wind speed less than 13 km/h are recommended where brush cover is less than 5 percent (Guthery 1986).

Farmlands

11

Cultivation
and Cropping

Of the 607 million ha of non-federally owned land in the United States, 63 percent is in agriculture (Karr 1981): 27 percent is cropland (Dumke et al. 1981), 27 percent is rangeland, and 9 percent is pastureland.

Historically, agricultural practices created many different kinds of habitat. Small family farms were characterized by diverse crops and crop rotations, including interspersion of odd areas, shelterbelts, and hedgerows. Changes in land-use practices to intensive farming since the 1940s have resulted in a decline of wildlife populations. Habitat losses are attributed to "clean farming," fencerow-to-fencerow farming, larger instead of smaller farms, and row crops instead of cover crops, among other factors (Vance 1976, Taylor et al. 1978, Brady 1985, Carlson 1985, Schmutz 1987). The challenge for the wildlife habitat manager is to encourage the incorporation of proven techniques that affect wildlife populations in a positive way into existing farming practices (Table 11.1).

Farming Techniques

Conservation tillage

Conservation tillage is designed to leave protective amounts of residue on the soil surface to reduce wind erosion or kinetic energy of raindrops. This approach varies from *reduced-till*, whereby about 20 percent of the previous year's crop residue is left, to *no-till*, where at least 90 percent of the previous year's crop remains on the soil sur-

TABLE 11.1   Suggested Farm-Management Practices to Improve Wildlife Habitat in Crop Fields

Establish conservation-tillage systems

If fall plowing is needed on particular bottomland soils, plow only a portion of the field, leaving unplowed borders or strips for spring tillage.

Minimize herbicide application.

Use rotation of forage and small-grain crops.

Use winter cover crops.

Establish 5-m-wide field border strips around all or a portion of the field. Plant grass and legume species that benefit wildlife. Mow or disk grass strips at 3- to 5-year intervals to control woody vegetation.

Allow shallow draws to revegetate naturally, or plant warm-season grasses or a grass-legume mixture.

Delay mowing until after July 15 to avoid nesting losses.

Seed waterways to grasses and legumes beneficial to wildlife.

Establish grass filter strips around ponds which are in or near fields to reduce sedimentation and add cover.

Preserve existing woody draws or plant such areas to shrubs, deciduous trees, or evergreen trees to provide winter cover.

Plant field corners to evergreen trees to provide winter cover.

Leave at least 0.1 ha of grain crops unharvested for each 15 ha of crop field.

Leave blocks of undisturbed native grassland of at least 16 ha for every 200–300 ha of cultivated land.

Leave crop residues standing for winter cover in southern farmlands.

face (Wooley et al. 1985). Other terms include *mulch tillage* (other tillage implements used between harvest and planting) and *ridge-till* (ridge cultivated along row and next year seeds planted on ridge) (Brady 1985). In addition to the potential cover and food value of the residue remaining, nest destruction and/or abandonment can be reduced if fewer passes are made by farm machinery across a field. But this depends upon several factors, including nest position (between versus within rows) relative to the crop row, duration of the nesting cycle and the breeding season, propensity to renest, and timing of the breeding season (Wooley et al. 1985, Best 1986).

Most results show greater songbird and upland bird richness and higher nest densities with no tillage than with conventional tillage techniques (Basore et al. 1986, Castrale 1985, Warburton and Klimstra 1984). Northern bobwhite quail were less affected by tillage than by other habitat-management techniques (Minser and Dimmick 1988). Capture rates of small mammals were influenced weakly by

TABLE 11.2   Relative Value of Various Midwest Habitat Types
for Nesting by Ring-Necked Pheasants and Nongame Birds

Habitat	Nest density per 40 ha
Ring-necked pheasants	
Conventional corn	0
Narrow-row soybeans	0
Conventional soybeans	0
No-till row crops*	1
Row crops*	7
Strip cover†	13
Grassed terraces	35
Pasture	5–70‡
Waterways	90
Fencerows	97–163
Roadsides	20–200§
Nongame birds	
Conventional corn	2
Narrow-row soybeans	4
Conventional soybeans	13
No-till row crops*	13¶
Grassed terraces	14
Strip cover†	142
Fencerows	174
Osage-orange hedge	223
Idle pastures	122–259
Shrub plantings	627
Farmstead shelterbelts	3781

*Row crops include corn and soybeans.
†Strip cover includes waterways, roadsides, terraces and fencerows.
‡Range of densities from Joselyn et al. (1968), Baxter and Wolfe (1973), Gates and Hale (1975), Trautman (1982).
§Range of densities from Joselyn et al. (1968), Baxter and Wolfe (1973), Wolfe (1973), Mead (1973), Trautman (1982).
¶Does not include birds nesting in woody vegetation.
SOURCE: Wooley et al. (1985).

tillage practices in Indiana (Castrale 1985), but relative abundance of deer mice was greater with no tillage than with conventional tillage in Illinois (Warburton and Klimstra 1984).

Concern about increased crop damage by rodents probably is not warranted (Castrale 1985, Clark and Young 1986). Warburton and Klimstra (1984) found more invertebrates in no-tillage fields; duck production was 3.8 times greater on no-tillage than on conventional-tillage fields (Cowan 1982). No tillage is superior to conventional-tillage techniques, but it is inferior to native habitats in various successional stages and other habitats such as fencerows, shelterbelts, and idle pastures (Best 1986) (Table 11.2) (Wooley et al. 1985) (Table 11.3) (Basore

TABLE 11.3   Nesting Outcomes of 16 Species of Birds in Crop Fields and Strip Cover Associated with Crop Fields in Iowa, 1982–1984 (Values Represent Numbers of Nests)

Nest fate	No-tillage fields*			Tilled corn	Strip cover†
	Corn-corn	Corn-sod	Soybean-corn		
Successful‡	10	10	6	2	33
Predation	8	52	6	1	90
Desertion	2	0	1	1	20
Weather	0	1	0	0	11
Farming implements	0	4	3	0	2
Cowbird parasitism§	1	0	1	0	10
Unknown¶	0	10	5	1	33
Total	21	77	22	5	199

*Corn-corn = corn planted in corn residue; corn-sod = corn planted in sod residue; soybean-corn = soybeans planted in corn residue.
†Strip cover = fencerows, roadsides, terraces, waterways.
‡Nests fledging ≥ 1 young, excluding brown-headed cowbirds.
§Nests deserted after being parasitized or nests fledgling only cowbird young.
¶Nests inactive when located.
SOURCE: Basore et al. (1986).

et al. 1986). Efforts to maintain and manage these linear habitats will increase wildlife populations more than promoting no-tillage practices (Wooley et al. 1985).

Birds that traditionally nest mainly in grass cover (e.g., ring-necked pheasant, grasshopper sparrow, meadowlark) prefer no-tillage fields where maximum amounts of residue are available. As the amount of crop residue remaining decreases, the variety and density of nesting birds decrease. More versatile nesters such as killdeer and Vesper sparrow are attracted to fields with intermediate forms of reduced tillage. Other birds, such as the horned lark, might prefer fields with minimum residue and even bare ground (Castrale 1985, Basore et al. 1986).

Other advantages to reduced tillage in farmland management include improved grain and weed seed availability, insect abundance, and vegetation structure. But during severe winters, no tillage traps more snow than conventional tillage. Snow renders food sources unavailable (Wooley et al. 1985) and insulates small mammals.

Important characteristics which influence use of cultivated fields by wildlife include the kind of crop condition of the field at the time of planting, and the timing and frequency of disturbance. Conservation-

TABLE 11.4   Bird Species Known to Nest in Corn or Soybean Fields

Species	Crop
Ring-necked pheasant	Corn (NT)
	Soybeans (T,NT)
Killdeer	Corn (T,NT)
	Soybeans (T,NT)
Mourning dove	Corn (T,NT)
	Soybeans (T,NT)
Horned lark	Corn (T)
	Soybeans (T)
American robin	Corn (NT)
Common yellowthroat	Corn (NT)
Bobolink	Corn (NT)
Eastern meadowlark	Corn (NT)
Western meadowlark	Corn (NT)
	Soybeans (NT)
Red-winged blackbird	Corn (T,NT)
Brown-headed cowbird*	Corn (T,NT)
	Soybeans (T,NT)
Dickcissel	Corn (NT)
	Soybeans (T)
Savannah sparrow	Corn (NT)
Grasshopper sparrow	Corn (NT)
Vesper sparrow	Corn (T,NT)
	Soybeans (T,NT)
Field sparrow	Corn (NT)
	Soybeans (NT)

Note: T = tilled field, NT = no-tillage field.
*Reported cowbird parasitism of nests.
SOURCE: Best (1986).

tillage techniques affect condition of the field and timing of disturbance, and, thus, can result in ecological traps for nesting birds (Best
1986). *Ecological traps* are managed areas that attract wildlife
because they appear to be suitable habitat (e.g., for nesting) but can
become population sinks because of predation or human disturbance
(Gates and Gysel 1978). Standing residue of no-tillage fields might
attract nesting birds, and if fields are tilled within 30 days, nests
might be destroyed before they are completed. Birds nest in no-tilled
crops more readily than tilled crops (Table 11.4) (Best 1986).
Ecological traps could be avoided by delaying use of farm machinery
or widening the interval between machinery passes to more than 40
days. These suggestions might not be practical given the traditional
timing of farm operations (Fig. 11.1) (Best 1986).

Another concern is that conservation tillage creates an incentive for
landowners to cultivate previously unplowed areas, which are far

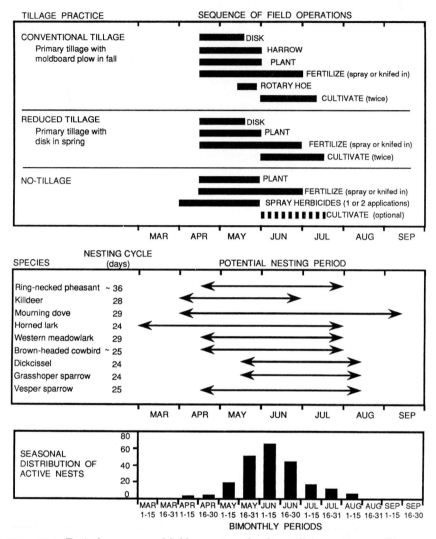

Figure 11.1 Typical sequences of field operations for three tillage systems used in corn and soybean fields, seasonal distribution of all active nests found in row-crop fields, and nesting phenologies for the major bird species nesting in corn and soybean fields in Iowa. (*Best 1986.*)

more productive habitat than conservation-tilled fields (Carlson 1985). Moreover, farmers might increase use of chemicals for weed and pest control to compensate for the reduction in tillage. No tillage might increase chemical concentrations in surface runoff water and eroded sediments, which would then become nonpoint sources of pollution (Laflen and Baker 1982).

Fallowing for wheat—i.e., leaving stubble standing overwinter—is practiced over much of the semi-arid regions of the United States. Higgins (1975) found that sharp-tailed grouse, five species of shorebirds, and four species of ducks nested in standing stubble of North Dakota. Because of the potential for an ecological trap, protection of nests might be achieved by using an undercutter. The undercutter plow is a farm implement used for weed control on wheat stubble or fallowed fields. Blades are pulled 7.5 to 15 cm beneath the soil surface. Using an undercutter could save bird nests and flightless birds in the stubble. If mulch treaders (an implement similar to a rotary hoe with sharp, twirling blades) are used with undercutters, wildlife habitat benefits are lost. Thus, mulch treaders should be removed. Rodgers (1981, 1985) reported that 53 percent of all bird nests were intact following undercutting (Table 11.5) (Rodgers 1985), when all would have been lost had the fields been disked. But in Colorado, Snyder (1984) found that undercutting in April or May did not save ring-necked pheasant nests from destruction.

Major factors related to farming practices influencing pheasant production (and probably that of other ground-nesting birds) are relative qualities of green wheat and stubble, timing of stubble cultivation, and timing of wheat harvest. Timing of stubble cultivation is the practice most easily manipulated (Snyder 1984). Options for the farmer are to cultivate before incubation (mid-May) or after the main nesting season has ended (early July), or to use herbicides to control early weed growth (Snyder 1984). Using herbicides instead of no tillage of wheat stubble for weed control would benefit ring-necked pheasants and other wildlife as long as herbicides are safe for wildlife.

Crop rotation

Ecofallow is a system of controlling weeds, and conserving soil moisture with crop rotation and minimum tillage, that holds promise for nesting birds, especially pheasants (Baxter 1982, Nason 1984). A 3-year rotation of wheat (year 1), row crop (e.g., sorghum) (year 2), and fallow (year 3), where corn or grain sorghum is planted directly into herbicide-treated stubble, might cause nest losses, but renests will not be jeopardized by farming operations (Snyder 1984). Suggested habitat management in Illinois includes 6-year rotations of crops in fields (Fig. 11.2) (Bailey 1984).

Crop diversity

Good interspersion, high contrast of vertical structure, small field size (1- to 5-ha units), high crop diversity (more than four crops), and non-cultivated areas (25 percent of area in permanent cover) will enhance

TABLE 11.5 Fate of Nests after Undercutting of Wheat Stubble

Species	Destroyed by tillage, n	Left intact, n	Fate of nests				
			Attendance resumed, n (%)*	Successful, n (%)	Lost to predators, n (%)	Abandoned, n (%)	
Ring-necked pheasant	2	9	8 (89)	8 (89)	—	1 (11)	
Bobwhite†	0	1	—	—	1 (100)	—	
Mourning dove	22	19	18 (95)	11 (58)	4 (21)	4 (21)	
Grasshopper sparrow	3	1	1 (100)	1 (100)	—	—	
Horned lark	2	0	—	—	—	—	
Western meadowlark	2	6	5 (83)	3 (50)	1 (17)	2 (33)	
All species	31	36	32 (89)	23 (64)	6 (17)	7 (19)	

*Percent of intact nests in parentheses.
†Incidence of resumed incubation was not determined.
SOURCE: Rodgers (1985).

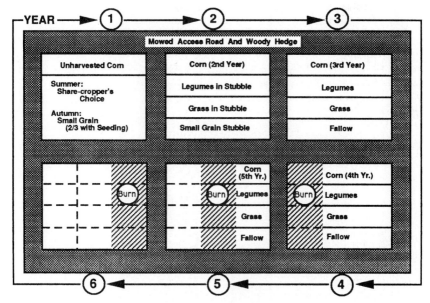

Figure 11.2 Habitat management for terrestrial wildlife in Illinois. Developmental stages of succession are maintained by rotating sharecropping activity and prescribed burning among fields on a 6-year schedule. Note the great diversity of habitat resulting when six contiguous fields are in the rotation. (*Bailey 1984.*)

wildlife (Fig. 11.3) (Rutherford and Snyder 1983). For example, farmland habitat plans for pheasants can be elaborate (Fig. 11.4 and Table 11.6) (Rutherford and Snyder 1983) or simple (Fig. 11.5) (Guthery et al. 1984). Guthery et al. (1984) also reported the relative value of cover crops (Table 11.7).

Small grains and meadows are recommended to improve habitat in intensively farmed areas. Intensive row cropping without small grains or grass meadow development in a rotation causes broods to range over an area 3 times larger than if small grains and meadows are available (Brady 1985). Although reduction in row-crop intensity, by including small grain or meadow in the rotation, can reduce farm income, such efforts provide lasting benefits to wildlife. Some government incentive, such as reduced property tax, or incentives from recreation might be needed. Using legumes in crop rotation systems would enhance soil nutrients as well as wildlife (Madsen 1981).

Organic farming

As an alternative production system, organic farming offers a possibility of improving the compatibility between crop and animal production practices and wildlife conservation (Papendick and Elliott 1985).

Tall Grass Mix   Green Wheat

Alfalfa/Grass Mix   Sweet Clover

Tall Sorghum   Shrub Thicket

Wheat Stubble   Snow Barrier

Scale (meters)   Weed Strip

0   100   200   300   400

Figure 11.3 A design to modify a quarter section of northeastern Colorado tablelands for pheasants and other wildlife by using chemical fallow and minimum tillage of wheat to increase nesting cover. (*Rutherford and Snyder 1983.*)

Organic farmers usually use less inversion tillage, avoid fertilizers and pesticides, have greater crop diversification, include livestock as an integral component, make more extensive use of small grains and meadows, and use crop rotations (especially legumes) more often (Cacek 1984a). But organic farmers cultivate more often than conventional farmers for weed control, which, with inopportune mowing, could create death traps for nesting and flightless birds (Carlson 1985). The potential benefits to wildlife would be associated with increased diversity of crops and increased area of cover, brooding, and

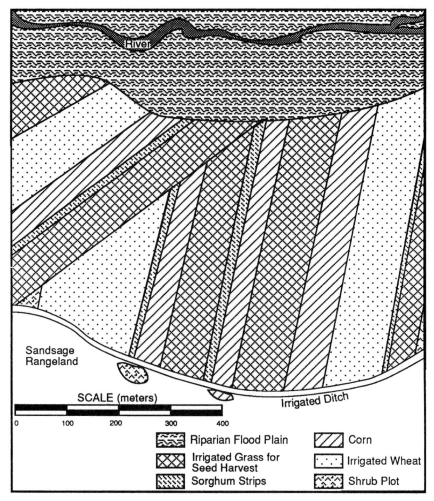

Figure 11.4 A hypothetical arrangement of irrigated land along a riverbottom managed with primary emphasis on pheasants and other nesting birds. (*Rutherford and Snyder 1983.*)

feeding sites. Research results indicate a positive effect of organic farming on breeding bird territories and populations (Gremaud and Dahlgren 1982, Papendick and Elliott 1985).

Field borders

Planting or leaving narrow strips of permanent, fast-growing, resilient vegetation (usually grasses and legumes) between fields and around the perimeter creates horizontal and vertical diversity in a

TABLE 11.6   Relative Proportions, Size, and Shape of Habitat Components for Ring-Necked Pheasants

Use type	Vegetation type	Percent of total	Unit size (ha)	Shape
Nesting, night roosting	Perennial herbaceous	30–60	2–5	Varied, rectangular to block
Nesting, feeding, night roosting	Small grains and their stubble	20–40	5–10	Wide strips to blocks
Total nesting cover	—	50–80	—	—
Winter resting, feeding, and harvest escape	Sorghums and corn	5–15	0.5–2	Small patches, strips
Brood cover, winter resting, night roosting, feeding	Annual weeds	5–10	0.5–1	Narrow strips, small patches
Display, sunning, loafing, flushing barriers	Fallowed (bare ground)	5–10	0.5	Narrow strips, small patches
Winter resting, protective, and harvest	Woody thick-ets, block plantings, or other winter cover	1–2	0.5	Small patches and blocks

SOURCE: Rutherford and Snyder (1983).

farmland operation. Field borders should be at least 5 m wide (Brady 1985). Added advantages to providing wildlife habitat include reduced erosion, reduced planting costs, and improved water quality.

Field borders 6 to 30 m wide next to riparian zones would reduce nonpoint sources of pollution; such wetland borders provide good nesting habitat for pheasants (Dumke and Pils 1979) and other wildlife. Field borders of alfalfa would benefit grassland songbirds and some species of gallinaceous birds as nesting cover. The extent of nest predation likely will depend on the width of the field border. Although unpopular with most farmers (Kirby et al. 1981), leaving or planting two to five rows or a strip 3 to 9 m wide of unharvested grain crops next to fencerows and wooded areas for wildlife would enhance food and cover values (Anderson 1969, Bratton 1984, Busch 1989).

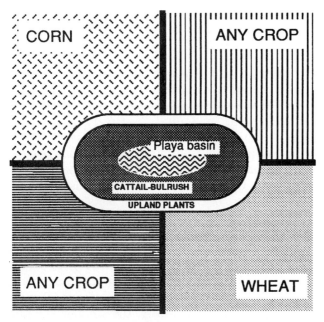

Figure 11.5 A simplified, habitat-management plan for wildlife next to a playa lake. Fields should be 45 ha or larger. Upland plants are left or planted around the playa basin. (*Guthery et al. 1984.*)

TABLE 11.7   Value of Crops and Native Habitats in Fulfulling Food and Cover Requirements of Pheasants in the Southern High Plains of Texas

Cover type	Nesting	Brooding	Food	Wintering
Playa	Excellent	Excellent	Fair	Excellent
Roadsides	Excellent	Excellent	Fair	Poor
Weedy tailwater pits	Good	Good	Fair	Fair
Weedy equipment parking areas	Good	Good	Fair	Fair
Corn	Poor	Fair	Excellent	Fair*
Grain sorghum	Poor	Fair	Excellent	Excellent
Forage sorghum	Poor	Excellent	Fair	Poor
Wheat	Excellent	Good	Good	Poor
Cotton	Poor	Fair	Poor	Poor
Soybeans	Poor	Fair	Good	Poor
Sugar beets	Poor	Good	Poor	Poor
Alfalfa	Good	Good	Fair	Poor
Vegetables	Poor	Fair	Fair	Poor
Rangeland	Fair	Poor	Poor	Poor

*The value of corn as winter cover is poor if all stubble is removed.
SOURCE: Guthery et al. (1984).

Food Plots and Odd Areas

Food plots

Food can be a limiting factor for wildlife populations, especially for resident wildlife in the arid West and Great Plains during winter and early spring (Robel 1984). If other habitat requirements are met, plantings of nutritious foods to supplement inadequate natural supplies can increase animal dispersion and distribution, enhance observational opportunities for wildlife enthusiasts, maintain greater wildlife populations, and ensure healthier, more productive animals. Food plots can be an alternative for strategic delivery of nutrients to animals at critical times of the year. In the Midwest or corn belt, food plots might not be an important habitat-management technique in farmland areas.

Besides restrictions placed on the habitat manager by edaphic, topographical, and climatic factors, planning food plots requires that the habitat manager be innovative. Where possible, food plots should always be rectangular to linear to maximize edge and interspersion (Table 11.8). Width should not exceed 100 m for ungulates or 50 m for ground-dwelling birds or mammals. Generally, the smaller the animal the narrower the food plot should be. For example, maximum width for quail management would be 3 to 6 m. Types and characteristics of grain plants available for food plots vary (Table 11.9) (Rutherford and Snyder 1983).

The number, location, and size of food plots are influenced by key habitats or critical microhabitats (woodlots, hedgerows, grassy areas, abandoned homesteads), travel corridors, proximity to water and cover, and distance from areas of high human activity. Size of the food plot hinges on the target species; 0.2 to 2.0 ha might be acceptable for Galliformes and granivorous songbirds; 4 to 8 ha would be better for ungulates. Food plot size for ungulates can depend heavily upon ani-

TABLE 11.8   Area-Edge Relationships Based on 1 ha of Land

Shape	Dimensions (m)	Perimeter (m)	Edge increase over a circle (%)	Interspersion index
Circle	Diameter = 113	354	—	1.000
Square	100 × 100	400	12.9	1.129
Rectangle	65 × 154	438	23.7	1.237
Rectangle	30 × 333	726	205.0	2.050
Strip	15 × 666	1362	384.7	3.847
Strip	10 × 1000	2020	570.6	5.706

Note: Figures for interspersion index based on Patton's (1975) formula.

TABLE 11.9 Some Considerations in Selecting Grain for Use in Food and Food/Cover Plantings in Colorado

Grain type	Species preferences and applications	Planting recommendations	Value to wildlife	Problems and limitations	Comments and special treatments	Comments and special treatments
Sorghum	Grain sorghum	Does best in sandy loams with at least 38 cm annual precipitation. Summer fallow or irrigation preferred.	Disk and apply 0.23 kg atraizine May 1 (Greb 1978). Plant around June 1 in rows 60–90 cm wide at 2–5 kg/ha. Combine with forage sorghums in most sites at 1/3 normal rate.	Food and limited feeding cover. Attains 0.8 m height in dryland sites.	Lodges under high winds and wet snow. Blackbirds consume in some locations.	Select early-maturing, lodge-resistant, dark-seeded varieties. Don't drill in less than 50 cm rows. Can be used in combination with forage sorghums, millets, and corn. Summer fallowing recommended on dryland sites.
Tall sorghums	Forage sorghum, Sudan grasses Hybrids of above, Broomcorn	Same as above.	Same as above. Combine with grain sorghums. Sudan seed should be planted at 17–22 kg/ha. Plant at 2/3 normal rate when combining with milo.	Serves mainly as protective overstory for feeding and as tall feeding cover during heavy snows.	Might get too tall under irrigation to allow hunter use. Lodges at 0.8 m height under heavy snow. Sudan is fine-stemmed and shorter. Food value often marginal.	Select for early-maturing, lodge-resistant, dark-seeded varieties. Use hybrid forage sorghums or sorghum-Sudan crosses on most sites. The grain-forage mixture is highly recommended for plains upland gamebird use. Use a summer-fallow/planted/idle-3-yr rotation on dryland sites.

TABLE 11.9 Some Considerations in Selecting Grain for Use in Food and Food/Cover Plantings in Colorado (Continued)

Grain type	Species preferences and applications	Planting recommendations	Value to wildlife	Problems and limitations	Comments and special treatments	Comments and special treatments
Cereal grains (winter annuals)	Rye	Adapted to use on sandy, poor soils with at least 38 cm annual precipitation.	Summer-fallow and drill in rows 25–35 cm wide at about 33 kg/ha in Sept.	Late fall/winter green food. Seed not preferred. Limited late spring nesting attains 0.8 to 1.2 m height.	Provides little over-winter cover 1st yr. Subject to ergot (poisonous fungus) in seed heads. Lodges under heavy snow with limited winter cover value. Volunteers back readily.	Use sweep tillage to undercut in late summer after it matures to promote volunteer regrowth if not already present. Leave second year for winter food/cover and nesting/brood use.
	Wheat (winter)	Better loam soils with minimum 38 cm annual precipitation.	Same as above. Seed at 33–44 kg/ha.	Late fall/winter green food. High protein seed. Provides marginal late spring nesting with 0.8 m height.	No winter cover first year. Lodges with limited cover value.	Same as above. Heads can be clipped after maturity to increase lodge resistance. Does not volunteer as readily as rye so sweep tillage undercutting may be necessary most years.
	Triticale (wheat-rye hybrid)	Same as for rye and wheat.	Same as for wheat.	Excellent green fall growth for winter greens. Better-quality seed than rye but attains taller growth than rye. (Mainly for pheasants and grouse.)	Same as for wheat and rye. Not subject to ergot.	Recommended as a replacement for rye on poorer soils. Treat like rye or wheat, allowing to stand over a second winter or longer if volunteering can be retained.
	Winter barley	Same as for wheat but adapted to high-alkaline sites.	Same as for wheat and rye seed at 55–87 kg/ha.	Same as above but seed not as highly preferred as wheat.		Same as for wheat.

TABLE 11.9 Some Considerations in Selecting Grain for Use in Food and Food/Cover Plantings in Colorado (Continued)

Cereal grains (spring annuals)	Spring wheat; spring oats; spring barley	Plant on loam to sandy soils receiving 38 cm annual precipitation or more and use barley in high-alkaline soils.	Plant in early to mid-April in plains region in 25- to 35-cm-wide drill rows.	Limited midsummer nesting and brood cover. Fall/winter food and limited feeding cover.	Will not stand up under heavy snows to provide protective feeding cover.	Use sweep tillage, undercutting in subsequent springs to attain volunteer regrowth with minimum tillage while retaining residual for nesting/brood cover.
Millets	Proso	Sandy loams to loams in sites receiving 30 cm or more annual precipitation.	Plant June 1–30 in rows 50–60 cm wide at 13–22 kg/ha. Use atrazine preemergent at 0.5 kg/ha applied 1 month before seeding (Greb 1978).	Late summer dove food. Waterfowl food when flooded or planted next to water.	No cover value of its own and not recommended for upland gamebirds other than doves except when added to sorghum mixtures. Flattened and buried under winter snows.	Plant small amounts in combination with grain sorghum and forage sorghum for late summer/early fall and spring consumption.
	Foxtail (German)	Same as above.	Same as above.	Same as above.	Produces more forage but less and smaller seed than Proso (Proso recommended).	Can be broadcast in disturbance tillage stips to supplement naturally occurring annuals.
	Japanese	Sandy wet sites.	Plant in late May or early June.	Mainly for waterfowl in wet sites or sites to be flooded. Limited use by doves and quail.	Same as for Proso.	Irrigate or temporarily flood to germinate and keep soil wet, if possible. Almost like barnyard grass.
Buckwheat	Tame buckwheat	Variable sandy to loam with 38 cm annual precipitation. Irrigation preferred.	Plant June 1–15 at 40–55 kg/ha.	Same as for millets, especially Japanese. Mainly for waterfowl.	Same as for millets. Seed doesn't persist.	Can be used to supplement forbs in disturbance-tillage sites in rangelands and riparian zones.

TABLE 11.9 Some Considerations in Selecting Grain for Use in Food and Food/Cover Plantings in Colorado (Continued)

Grain type	Species preferences and applications	Planting recommendations	Value to wildlife	Problems and limitations	Comments and special treatments	Comments and special treatments
Sunflower	Numerous varieties available	Better loam soils with at least 38 cm annual precipitation. Irrigation preferred.	Plant in rows 60–106 cm wide in May or early June.	Large nutritious seeds.	Stands are too open to provide feeding protection in fall and winter. Seeds devastated by blackbirds and other passerines. Requires 1 or more postplanting cultivation. Insect problems common.	Not recommended for seeding except in mixtures with corn, sorghums, or spring grains. Prevents use of herbicides in corn, sorghums, and millets, so use opportunities limited.
Safflower		Same as for sunflower.	Same as for sunflower. Broadcast at 28 kg/ha.	Seeds and limited cover.	Has not been evaluated in Colorado.	Possibly could be seeded in combination with sunflower, buckwheat, and field peas, but evaluations needed.
Legumes	Field peas	Loam soils with 38 cm or more of annual precipitation and irrigation preferred.	Plant in combination with spring cereal grains or sunflowers. Seed at up to 67 kg/ha. Use either with drilled grains or row crops.	Mainly in flooded sites for waterfowl. No cover value in fall or winter.	Value restricted to doves and waterfowl when planted alone. Must be planted in combination with other vegetation for use by quail, pheasants, and grouse.	

TABLE 11.9 Some Considerations in Selecting Grain for Use in Food and Food/Cover Plantings in Colorado (*Continued*)

| Legumes (*Continued*) | Hairy vetch | Better sandhill sites with 38 cm or more annual precipitation. | Seed in 36- to 60-cm rows in early May at 44–50 kg/ha. Plant in combination with sweetclover. | Provides fall/winter greens and seeds for prairie grouse and cottontails. | No important cover value other than for nesting and broods. | Biennial but tends to reseed readily, especially if shallow tillage is applied every few years. Can be seeded in combination with sweetclover, small grains (spring annuals), or sunflowers and safflowers. |

SOURCE: Rutherford and Snyder (1983).

mal density, to prevent ungulates from overgrazing the food plot and to determine the numbers of animals the manager wants to supplement.

Spacing and number of food plots also depend on the total area of the habitat and the mobility of the target species. In most instances, only 1.0 to 3.0 percent of the total area in question needs to be intensively managed in food plots. For example, on 500 ha, fifteen widely scattered 1-ha food plots is better for quail than one 15-ha food plot, because quail beyond 900 m from a food plot apparently are restricted from its use by mobility (Robel et al. 1974). Thus, fifteen food plots on 500 ha would have a distribution of one per 33 ha. At this spacing, quail would never be further than 400 m from a food plot, definitely within the 600-m limit proposed for healthier birds (Robel et al. 1974). For pheasants, eleven 1.5-ha food plots should be spaced at one per 50 ha, so that birds would never be more than 500 m away. Two 6- to 8-ha food plots per 500 ha would be best for deer, even though deer might travel far to feed on food plots. Mule deer in the Texas panhandle traveled more than 5 km from their traditional summer range to graze winter wheat (Sowell et al. 1985).

In farmland/cropland areas, alternatives are available for establishing food plots. Managers could convert abandoned cropland or odd areas to food plots, or simply reserve areas already cultivated, such as field borders, for wildlife food plants. Food plots also can be planted between woody plantings and riparian areas (Fig. 11.6) (Henderson 1987).

Although recommendations vary by region and animal, plants most useful for all wildlife are grain sorghum, legumes, and cereal grains (Table 11.10). Grain sorghum is ranked over corn because it usually is easier to establish under nonirrigated conditions, its seed is small,

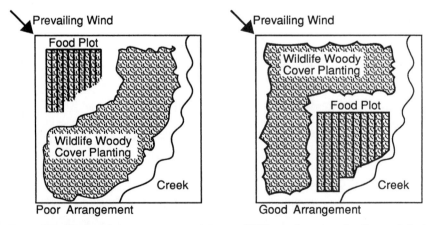

Figure 11.6 Good and poor arrangement for a wildlife woody cover planting and food plot. (*Henderson 1987.*)

TABLE 11.10   Principal Plants for Wildlife Food Plots

Upland wildlife species	Plants for food plots
Granivorous songbirds	Sunflower Sorghum Millet
Cottontail rabbit	Legumes (alfalfa, clovers, sweetclover, wheat/barley, vetch) Grass (bluegrasses, wheatgrass, timothy) Annual grains (wheat, rye, triticale)
Bobwhite quail	Grain sorghum Corn Sunflower
Pheasant	Corn Grain sorghum Alfalfa Soybeans
Mourning dove	Millet Grain sorghum Sunflower
Deer and turkey	Legumes (alfalfa, clovers, sweetclovers, vetch, peas, cow peas) Grain sorghum Annual grains (wheat, oats, triticale)

Note: Local soils, precipitation, temperature extremes, and elevation will dictate which plants will grow successfully.

its energy content is similar to corn, and it is acceptable to most birds (Robel et al. 1979, Shuman et al. 1988). Energy value of plant species should be considered before planting (Table 11.11) (Robel et al. 1979).

The amount of seed planted varies. In the eastern United States for example, a mixture of buckwheat (3 kg/ha), foxtail millet (3 kg/ha), Sudangrass (3 kg/ha), soybeans (4.5 kg/ha), and cow peas (5.5 kg/ha) should be sowed at a total of 19 kg/ha (National Audubon Society 1969). Further west, seedings can be as little as 15 kg/ha or as high as 30 kg/ha.

Food plots used as a year-round nutrient source should be designed to have plants of high nutrient content available at all times of the year, i.e., a constant flow of available food throughout the year. Based on production traits of some of these species, such a "feed flow" can be designed (Fig. 11.7) (Schweitzer et al. 1993). Other considerations for food plots have been recommended for the western Great Plains (see Table 11.9).

Food plots are not preferred to other forms of habitat management. Similar to direct feeding, food plots should be considered for man-

TABLE 11.11   Metabolizable Energy in Seeds of Plants Commonly Used for Food Plots for Seed-Eating Birds

Seed	Metabolizable energy content (kcal/g)
Excellent (greater than 4.14 kcal/g)	
Giant ragweed	4.32
Good (3.48 to 4.14 kcal/g)	
Western ragweed	3.88
Corn	3.87
Soybean	3.78
Sunflower	3.65
Sorghum	3.59
Low (2.61 to 3.48 kcal/g)	
German millet	3.47
Prostrate lespedeza	3.42
Korean lespedeza	3.14
Wheat	3.06
Thistle	2.70
Shrub lespedeza	2.69
Poor (less than 2.61 kcal/g)	
Patridgepea	2.42
Smartweed	2.30
Multiflora rose hips	2.02
Switchgrass	1.86
Smooth sumac	1.48

SOURCE: Robel et al. (1979).

agers wanting to intensify their management program. Disadvantages of food plots include (1) concentrating wildlife, which increases their vulnerability to disease transmission and predation; (2) attracting pests such as red-winged blackbirds, feral hogs, etc.; (3) expense; (4) for ungulates, necessity to monitor populations closely and regulate harvest to prevent deterioration of native food sources and animal health; and (5) in arid and semi-arid regions, failure of plantings in extremely dry years and lack of need in wet years. (See "Food Plots" in Chap. 5.)

Odd areas

Odd areas include eroded areas in crop fields, bare knobs, sinkholes, sand blowouts, gullies, rock piles, rock outcrops, borrow pits, gravel pits, and pieces of good land cut off from the rest of the field by stream, drainage ditch, gully, or center-pivot irrigation (Fig. 11.8) (Henderson 1984). These might need little or no improvement, except protection from fire and grazing. If food or cover plants are lacking,

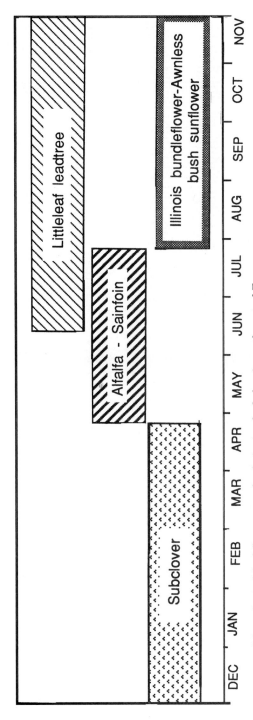

Figure 11.7 A hypothetical feed flow system for designing food plots in north-central Texas to provide year-round forage. (*Schweitzer et al. 1993.*)

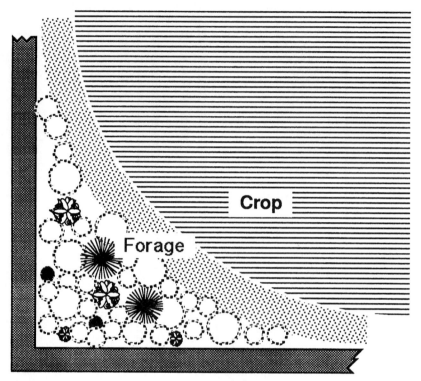

Figure 11.8 Planting trees, shrubs, grasses, and forbs to create wildlife habitat for odd areas of a center-pivot irrigating system. (*Henderson 1984.*)

they should be added. At least half the odd area should be in good ground cover of grasses and legumes. Cover height should be managed depending on nesting requirements of upland birds (Table 11.12). Site preparation on untillable lands is limited to scalping or herbicides (Woehler and Dumke 1982). Granular herbicides should be applied in fall on strips scalped 46 cm wide and 5 cm deep for planting shrub seedlings. But use of this technique is limited and depends upon local conditions.

Where winters are severe, 25 to 50 adapted conifers can be planted in such areas about 2.4 m apart in a clump so that they retain lower limbs for cover close to the ground as long as possible. One to three rows of fruit-producing shrubs should be planted 0.9 to 1.2 m apart around the conifers for nesting cover, food for songbirds, and escape cover (if the shrubs are thorny) (Anderson 1969). Shrub lespedezas, a useful legume, should be in rows 0.9 m apart, with the plants 0.6 m apart in the row. Another plan is to leave at least half the odd area in grass-legume openings, with the other 20 percent in spruce and 30

TABLE 11.12   Cover Height Requirements for Several
Gallinaceous Birds

Species	Cover height (cm)
Northern bobwhite quail	10–13
Gray partridge	13–15
Chukar partridge	13–15
Blue grouse	18–20
Sage grouse	18–46
Sharp-tailed grouse	20–25
Prairie chicken	25–30
Ring-necked pheasant	25–30

SOURCE: Payne and Copes (1988).

percent in deciduous fruit-bearing shrubs and small trees (e.g., saskatoon, crabapple, wild plum, chokecherry) (Poston and Schmidt 1981).

In farmlands west of the Mississippi, the odd area could be planted as a windbreak. To improve such areas for wildlife, two rows of such hardy shrubs as wild plum, sand cherry, Russian olive, or honeysuckle can be planted on the west and north sides. Then a 30-m-wide strip of switchgrass, sweetclover, or alfalfa could be planted next to the shrubs. A block of at least 100 conifers or hardwood trees (like boxelder, green ash, or soft maple) might be planted in the southwest corner. This type of planting should be at least 0.4 ha in area.

Leaving 16-ha blocks of undisturbed rangeland in a farmland area will promote prairie passerine species. In Alberta, the number of pairs per 40 ha was greatest in fescue rangeland (Table 11.13) (Owens and Myres 1973).

East of the Great Plains, native shrubs often will establish themselves naturally in odd areas protected from fire and grazing, and only a grass-legume mixture might need to be planted. Half the herbaceous area should be sprayed or mowed every 2 years to reduce invasion of woody plants. Burning also could be used as a management technique. Conversions of brush to grass should be planned. Islands and travel lanes of brush cover should be left.

Uncropped wet areas should be preserved. Such areas add to the diversity of any cropland.

Abandoned homesteads in farmland should be protected. Such nonintervention allows unaltered processes of natural disintegration to take place and costs nothing. Vegetation usually is a diverse array of plants including trees, shrubs, grasses, and forbs, some of it associated with old buildings. Habitat diversity is long-lasting (70 + years) and the mix changes over time (Bohn et al. 1980), accommodating many different wildlife forms.

TABLE 11.13 Number of Territories of Each Passerine Species on Each (16.2 ha) Study Plot

| | Plot description and number | | | | | | | | | | | | |
| Species | Undisturbed | | | | Mowed | | Grazed | | Fallow | | Seeded | | Total |
	1	2	3	4	5	6	7	8	9	10	11	12	
Baird's sparrow	7	9	3	8	0	0	0	0	0	0	0	0	27
Sprague's pipit	11	11	4	12	5	5	0	0	0	0	0	0	48
Savannah sparrow	3	4	5	3	2	0	2	0	0	0	0	0	19
Western meadowlark	1	2	1	0	0	0	1	1	0	0	0	0	6
Chestnut-collared longspur	0	0	0	0	0	20	5	6	0	0	0	0	31
Clay-colored sparrow	1	0	1	1	0	0	2	0	0	0	0	0	5
Horned lark	0	0	0	0	0	0	3	2	5	1	2	2	15
Vesper sparrow	0	0	0	0	0	0	0	0	0	0	0	1	1
Red-eyed vireo	0	0	0	0	1	0	0	0	0	0	0	0	1
Total	23	26	14	24	8	25	13	9	5	1	2	3	153
Number of species	5	4	5	4	3	2	5	3	1	1	1	2	9
Number of pairs per 42 ha	57.5	65.0	35.0	60.0	20.0	62.5	32.5	22.5	12.5	2.5	5.0	7.5	
Mean number of pairs per 42 ha		54.4				41.5		27.5		7.5		6.3	

SOURCE: Owens and Myres (1973).

Linear Habitats

So-called "waste" areas, surrounding cultivated fields and along fencerows, as well as ditches along roads, constitute important linear habitat available to passerine birds, small mammals, and raptors in areas where agriculture is widespread (Owens and Myres 1973). Along with hedgerows and shelterbelts, these habitats supply shelter, nest sites, and food, but also provide important habitats that were rare or lacking in pure native grassland areas. But creation of such corridors or landscape linkages must be avoided where they encourage the spread of native and exotic plant and animal species into areas not occupied naturally.

Roadways

Similar to fencerows, roadways (the area between the edge of the maintained road surface and the adjacent field on both sides of the road) might be the only remnant or even potential source of wildlife habitat in intensively farmed regions. Advantages of managing roadways include providing nesting cover, travel corridors, and foraging areas, and aesthetics. The most detailed studies of wildlife management related to roadways have been those that link pheasant nesting cover with roadways (Joselyn et al. 1968, Joselyn and Tate 1972). Generally, the juxtaposition of other key habitats in an area greatly influences the use of roadways by nesting hens (Warner and Joselyn 1986); the most influential adjacent habitat is hayfields (Warner et al. 1987). Roadway management should occur within blocks of 40 to 50 km^2 to be successful.

Communities of small mammals, mostly grassland rodents, were richer along interstates than county roads, and along roads than in adjoining habitats (Table 11.14) (Adams and Geis 1979). This obser-

TABLE 11.14   Number of Small Mammal Species Relative to Roads in Three Geographical Areas of the United States

Geograph- ical area	Road type	Distance from road		
		Roadside	80–160 m	240–320 m
Southeast	Interstate	10	7	6
(Virginia/	County road	8	7	6
North				
Carolina)				
Midwest	Interstate	12	7	5
(Illinois)	County road	8	6	5
Northwest	Interstate	13	14	14
(Oregon)	County road	14	12	10

SOURCE: Adams and Geis (1979).

vation might not have general application because mammal presence would depend on specific vegetation structure and composition, width of roadsides, and surrounding roadsides and habitats.

Where roadsides are mowed, mowing should preferably occur only once per year and a strip-mowing program should be adopted. Mowing a single strip next to the pavement and leaving the rest unmowed is best for small mammals (Wilkins and Schmidly 1979). Full-width mowing every 3 or 4 years should be enough to keep woody vegetation from encroaching on the roadside.

Because managed roadways encourage nesting of ring-necked pheasants (Joselyn and Tate 1972), roadways should not be mowed until after the nesting season. Mowing is costly and precludes use of roadways by most wildlife, particularly ground nesters (Verner 1975). Although predator activity might increase in linear habitats and affect nest success, the average success rate of nests on unharvested hayfields (25 percent) was similar to the success rate on seeded roadways (29 percent) (Warner et al. 1987). Roadway development can include several options for habitat management (Figure. 11.9) (Leedy and Adams 1982).

Monotypic stands of grass are sparse and lack structural heterogeneity. Thus they are suboptimal nest habitats for pheasants and other ground-nesting birds (Warner et al. 1987). Roadsides planted to grass-legume mixtures are best for pheasants (Joselyn et al. 1968). In Illinois, such mixtures would include brome with alfalfa or red clover (Warner et al. 1987).

A mixture of tame hay planted on roadsides for songbirds and pheasants is acceptable to farmers (David and Warner 1979). For the midwest, such a mixture includes smooth brome, alfalfa, red clover, timothy, and orchardgrass. Farmers dislike mixtures that disseminate weed seeds into their fields.

In farmlands of eastern Colorado, mixtures might include alfalfa, little bluestem, and various wheatgrasses (Rutherford and Snyder 1983). Economic returns justified seeding, fertilizing, and associated costs in the Midwest (Joselyn and Tate 1972).

Fencerows

In many areas of the Midwest and Great Plains, fencerows represent one of the last traces of wildlife habitat. Clean farming has removed fencerows, reduced their width, or eliminated their weedy and shrubby vegetation. Few landowners recognize the extent to which wildlife species depend upon fencerows. In Iowa, Best (1983) reported 12 different bird species in herbaceous fencerows, 38 in fencerows with scattered trees and shrubs, and 48 in fencerows with continuous trees and shrubs. In Michigan, the density and diversity of bird nests

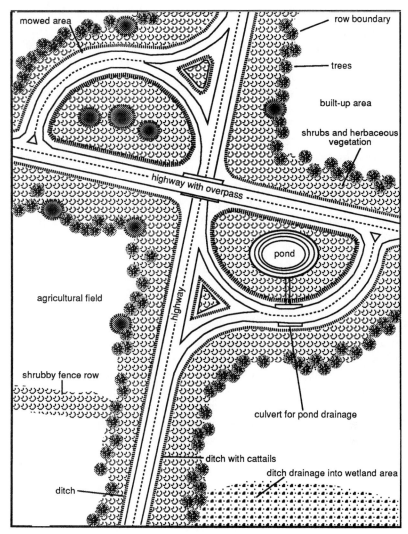

Labels in figure: mowed area; row boundary; trees; built-up area; shrubs and herbaceous vegetation; highway with overpass; agricultural field; pond; highway; shrubby fence row; culvert for pond drainage; ditch with cattails; ditch drainage into wetland area; ditch

Figure 11.9 Planting pattern for highway right-of-way vegetation for wildlife habitat enhancement. (*Leedy and Adams 1982.*)

increase with shrub abundance by adding diversity and layers of understory structure (Shalaway 1985). Fencerows in farmlands and croplands should be preserved, maintained, and restored, even though they can provide travel lanes for predators.

Specific recommendations include (1) ensuring a minimum width of 3 m, (2) creating mosaics through selective mowing and woodcutting, and (3) retaining or creating one to two tall snags (>46 cm dbh, 10 to 15 m tall) per kilometer of fencerow (Shalaway 1985). Protection of fencerows from grazing and fire encourages development of shrubs. Planting shrubs enhances habitat value for songbirds, gallinaceous birds, and small mammals. Patches of natural cover containing trees or shrubs strategically distributed in farmland areas would benefit Swainson's hawks; in contrast, ferruginous hawks need grassy areas to be successful (Schmutz 1987).

In glaciated areas, farmers pick stone (rocks) from their fields annually, as frost heave brings more stones to the surface. Farmers deposit these stones along field borders, along fencerows, or in a large pile in the center of the field. Reptiles and small mammals will burrow among these rocks if the rocks are piled high and wide enough. Shrubs and trees should be allowed to grow along the edge of the rock pile to improve habitat for other wildlife, especially birds. In such landscapes, lone trees should be left in pastures to serve mainly as resting perches for birds flying across the area. (See "Rock Piles" in Chap. 15.)

Hedgerows

Hedgerows grow naturally along fences, if protected. Where no fence occurs, a 3-m-wide strip should be plowed or disked where a hedgerow is desired. Fence posts should be set in a line or staggered about 6 m apart down the center of the plowed strip. Wire or twine string should be run 1 m high between the posts for bird perches. Bird droppings are laden with viable seed. Plants can grow from such depositions almost as fast as those growing from rootstock. For such species as northern bobwhite quail and cottontails, at least a 200-m hedge for every 16 ha of open country should be established (Dumke 1982). Hedgerows also can reestablish naturally from remnant stands.

Hedgerows with shrubs or a shrub-conifer mixture should be planted. After site preparation, two to four shrub stems per hole should be planted, with 1 to 2 m between holes. Conifers should be planted at a rate of one stem per hole, with 1 to 3 m between holes. Shrub rows should be spaced 2 m apart and conifer rows 3 m apart to provide contiguous cover in 8 to 12 years (Dumke 1982). Conifers will need thinning at 10 to 15 years. A three-row hedge of one row of shrubs and two of conifers will provide a 7-m-wide strip. Protection from grazing and fire is needed. Without site preparation, plantings can be made along fencerows, in gullies, along streams, and around ponds, springs, food patches, nesting grounds, breeding grounds, and other well-used wildlife sites.

For hedgerows consisting of shrubs only, at least four rows 8 m long, spaced 2 m apart, should be planted in early spring, and weed control should be established the first or second year. Weeds are controlled most often with herbicides, but cultivation, mulches, clipping,

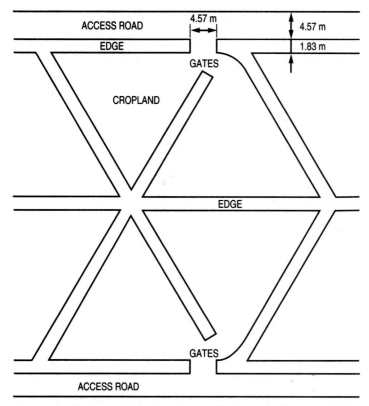

Figure 11.10 Recommended arrangement of hedgerows. (*Powers 1979.*)

and hand weeding also are effective. A triangular arrangement of fields, hedgerows, access roads, and gates was recommended by Powers (1979) (Fig. 11.10).

Hedgerows should be planted on south-facing slopes first, with the second choice being either east- or west-facing slopes. On leveled ditch banks, planting north and west edges is preferred. Where large fields are to be divided, exposure to the southeast, south, and east should be considered, in that order. On slopes exceeding 3 to 4 percent, hedgerow and row crops should be separated with a 2-m sodded border. Across a natural waterway, shrubs should be spaced to allow a vigorous grass/forb understory to develop. Woehler and Dumke (1982) described species selection and characteristics for Wisconsin.

Hedgerows should be 1.4 m high and 1.2 m wide if trimmed. Sides of ditches should not be trimmed every year. Only the current year's growth should be trimmed (Arnold 1983).

Based on a time budget to quantify use of various woody plants by nongame birds, Robel and Browning (1981) recommended multiflora rose, multiflora rose x *rugosa,* cardinal autumnolive, manchu cherry, Sargent crabapple, and buffaloberry as excellent woody plants for wildlife in Kansas. In the midwest, multiflora rose is considered an unwanted weedy species that spreads with bird droppings (pers. comm., W. Clark, Iowa State University, 1992). Native species such as plum and dogwood should be used. Woody plants have been recommended for Colorado (Table 11.15); some of these recommendations are based on growth characteristics (Table 11.16) (Rutherford and Snyder 1983). Woody plants also have been recommended regionally for North America (Tables A.1 through A.5). Where hedgerows compete for soil moisture with crops, root pruning is recommended (Capel 1984). In the Great Plains, woody hedgerows have been recommended as travel lanes, food, and escape and thermal cover for sharp-tailed grouse, bobwhites, ring-necked pheasants, gray partridge, mourning doves, and cottontails (Henderson 1984).

Shelterbelts

Farmland shelterbelts (windbreaks) are human-made habitats created by planting rows of trees and shrubs (Yahner 1983a). Changing land-use patterns have resulted in a decline of shelterbelts over much of the Midwest. Shelterbelts are deteriorating (Schaefer et al. 1987) and many are being removed (Cook and Cable 1990) to accommodate circular irrigation units and for other reasons, such as use of fertilizer in areas that do not require the protection and preservation of topsoil from wind erosion. Few new windbreaks are being planted (Harris et al. 1989), even though the Great Plains is less than 3 percent wooded (Griffith 1976) and represents a unique habitat used by game and nongame species. But locations for shelterbelts must be selected carefully. Shelterbelts can be unnatural travel corridors that did not exist previously, causing undesirable dispersal of both indigenous and exotic animals and plants and undesirable fragmentation, seriously compromising biotic integrity (Noss 1987c, Harris and Scheck 1991, Knopf 1992). (See "Corridors" in Chap. 6.)

Yahner (1983a, 1983b) found 11 species of small mammals and 87 species of birds using shelterbelts in Minnesota. Robel and Browning (1981) recorded 44 bird species in woody plantings in Kansas. In addition, numerous aspects of wildlife ecology have been associated with shelterbelts and are documented for birds (Weiser and Hlavinka 1956, Rotzein 1963, Field 1971, Martin and Vohs 1978, Martin 1980, Cassel and Wiehe 1980, and Yahner 1982a) and mammals (Van Deusen and Kaufman 1977, Swihart and Yahner 1982, Yahner 1982c). In summary, these unique habitats (1) preserve wildlife species able to survive

TABLE 11.15 Wildlife Values, Characteristics, and Limitations of Some Shrubs, Trees, and Vines in Colorado

Value classification	Species	Primary wildlife species value	Priority use locations	Planting form	Plant characteristics	Limitations	Comments
Shrubs recommended for priority use in wildlife plantings.	Wild plum	All plains upland game	Rangelands, farmlands, and riparian zones. Prefers sandy soils	Thickets	Excellent growth form and root-sprouting perpetuation. Excellent height, closed canopy yet open growth form near ground, fruits consumed by numerous wildlife.	Subject to winter browsing by rabbits and rodents.	Chokecherry can be substituted in better moisture sites.
	Squawbush sumac (quailbush or skunkbush)	Quail, cottontails, prairie grouse	Dry rangelands and farmlands	Scattered or thickets, shelterbelt edges	Long-lived, drought-tolerant, and high survival rate. Dense spreading growth form.	9- to 12-dm height. Limited spreading and root sprouting.	Not highly susceptible to browsing. Limited food value to lesser prairie chickens and others.
	Willow	Bobwhite, cottontails, pheasants, deer	Riparian and permanently wet sites	Thickets or small clumps	Attains good height, but rather open canopy. Rapid growth and spreading characteristics.	Requires perpetually wet sites.	Slips can be cut and stuck in mud to start new thickets easily and economically.
Alternates to the priority shrubs	Lilac	Pheasants, quail	Better farmlands and sandy ranges	Thickets and shelterbelt edges	Long-lived, drought-tolerant at once established. Medium height.	Tight V-shaped growth form and limited spreading.	*S. villosa* is similar but does not regenerate from suckers.
	Tartarian honeysuckle	Pheasants, quail, prairie grouse	Better farmlands and sandy ranges	Thickets and shelterbelt edges	Growth characteristics similar to lilac but faster growing.	Not spreading.	Not readily damaged by cottontails.

TABLE 11.15 Wildlife Values, Characteristics, and Limitations of Some Shrubs, Trees, and Vines in Colorado (Continued)

Value classification	Species	Primary wildlife species value	Priority use locations	Planting form	Plant characteristics	Limitations	Comments
Alternates to the priority shrubs (Continued)	Tamarisk (saltcedar)	Quail (three species), mourning doves, cottontails, deer	Alkaline, riparian and sandy ranges	Thickets or small clumps	Very drought-tolerant and alkaline-tolerant.	May need supplemental water to establish in dry sites.	T. hispida is a non-seeding species used in northern Colorado, can be a tenacious invader
	Caragana	Pheasants, quail, deer	Northeast Colorado better farmlands and sandy ranges.	Thickets and shelterbelt edges	Drought-tolerant, moderate height. Not adapted to southeast Colorado.	Tight V-shaped form offers poor protective cover. Loses leaves in summer.	Other species of Caragana may have better growth form.
Shrub species which need further evaluation	Cotoneaster	Mourning doves, pheasants, deer, bobwhite	Sandy riparian or better ranges and farmlands with supplemental water	Thickets or small blocks	Tall shrub or small tree with spreading growth form.	Moisture and alkalinity may be primary factors.	Peking cotoneaster (C. adultifolia) has a growth form similar to liliac and honeysuckle.
	Buffaloberry	Deer, doves, bobwhite, pheasants, sharp-tailed grouse	Riparian or with supplemental water	Small clumps or thickets	Moderately tall, spreading growth form highly suited for deer, doves, cottontails.	Apparently needs some supplemental water as in riparian zones.	Beautiful specimens can devolop.
	Elderberry	Mourning doves, quail, grouse, pheasants, deer	Sandy ranges or riparian zones	Small clumps or thickets	Moderately tall and shabby with overhanging growth form.	Uncertain.	Should be tested further.

TABLE 11.15 Wildlife Values, Characteristics, and Limitations of Some Shrubs, Trees, and Vines in Colorado   (Continued)

	Wildlife value	Site	Growth form	Characteristics	Limitations	Remarks
Willow	Scaled quail, bobwhite	Sandy ranges in southeast Colorado	Thickets		Possible winter hardiness.	Used in northeast Texas ranges for quail. Needs testing in southeast Colorado
Fragrant sumac	Scaled quail, bobwhite	Sandy ranges in southeast Colorado	Thickets or small clumps	Short to medium height.	Same as above.	Same as above.
Bristly locust	Scaled quail, bobwhite, mourning doves	Sandy ranges in southeast Colorado	Thickets or small clumps	Reportedly forms thickets similar to wild plum. Adapted to poor soils.	Unknown.	Recommended by some seed suppliers in Oklahoma.
Fourwing saltbush	Scaled quail, cottontails	Southeast Colorado shortgrass ranges	Scattered to thickets	Excellent low growth form and extremely drought-tolerant for use in marginal areas.		Difficult to transplant.
Sand cherry	Limited for Plains sharptails	Sandhills in northeast Colorado	Scattered to thickets	Short, open with no significant cover value (3–6 dm tall).	Poor growth and survival.	Direct-seed for prairie grouse. Not otherwise recommended.
Shrubs not recommended for general wildlife use						
Nanking cherry	Limited for pheasants, bobwhite	Irrigated or riparian sites	Thickets	Medium-height tight bush.	Subject to borers and drought.	Not recommended except under irrigation.
Rose	Bobwhite, cottontail	Riparian zone	Scattered to thickets	Low thorny stands with moderate drought tolerant and root sprouting.	Short growth form and considerable die-back. Insects.	Not recommended except for direct seeding in riparian as a supplement.
Multiflora rose	Bobwhite, pheasants, cottontails	Low-alkalinity wet sites	Thickets	Medium height, spreading, thorny.	Not suited for alkaline soils.	Use in loams and sands under irrigation. Spreads uncontrollably in some regions.
Oldman wormwood	Not recommended	Blowouts, bare ground	Rows or thickets	Medium-tall tight shrub. Dies back to base in winter.	Little new growth after the first die-back.	Not recommended.

TABLE 11.15 Wildlife Values, Characteristics, and Limitations of Some Shrubs, Trees, and Vines in Colorado (Continued)

Value classification	Species	Primary wildlife species value	Priority use locations	Planting form	Plant characteristics	Limitations	Comments
Shrubs for supplement to taller species and for direct seeding	Buckbrush or snowberry, currant, wild rose, fourwing saltbush, rabbit-brush	Quail, cottontails	Varied riparian to dry rangeland	Scattered to thickets	Generally short (0.6–1.2 m) growth-form for supplemental shrub protection.	Generally not tall enough for protection during winter snows.	Suggested for supplemental direct seeding in riparian and rangeland locations.
Trees for use in wildlife plantings	Russian olive	Doves, deer, bobwhite, pheasants	Alkaline riparian and northeast Colorado farmlands	Small clumps to shelterbelts	Spreading, thornlike branches of a low-growing treeform. Seed abundant and utilized. Moderately drought-tolerant and adapted for alkaline sites.	A short life span in dryland sites (15–30 years)	Reseeds itself in riparian alkaline.
	Russian mulberry	Doves, deer, pheasants	Better farmlands in northeast Colorado	Small clumps to shelterbelts	Growth form similar to Russian olive. Seedling survival and life span greater than Russian olive.	Rather slow growing unless supplemental water is provided.	Should be used instead of Russian olive in upland windbreaks and block plantings.
	Siberian and Chinese elm	Mourning doves, non-game birds	Farmlands. Use Siberian in northeast Colorado	Shelterbelts. Snow barrier	Good survival, rapid growth, not long-lived.	Marginal ground cover, leaf beetles defoliate.	Periodic half-cutting or coppicing stimulates basal growth for ground cover.
	Rocky Mountain juniper	Mourning doves, deer, pheasants, non-game birds	Northeast Colorado better farmlands	Clump plantings, snow barriers, shelterbelts	Long-lived, fair survival, retains dense, low cover for wildlife.	Sometimes difficult to establish. Slow-growing. Needs supplemental water.	Subject to destruction by wildfires.

TABLE 11.15 Wildlife Values, Characteristics, and Limitations of Some Shrubs, Trees, and Vines in Colorado (Continued)

Other trees for potential consideration	Osage-orange	Mourning doves, pheasants, non-game birds.	Farmlands in east edge of Colorado, preferably under irrigation	Clump plantings, shelterbelts.	Hardy, long-lived, spreading growth form similar to mulberry.	Adapted to more eastern farmlands.	Use in farmlands (preferably irrigated) along eastern tier of counties.
	Boxelder	Mourning doves, pheasants, non-game birds	Same as above	Same as above	Short-lived, fast-growing, substitute for elms.	Needs better soil and moisture conditions.	Same as above.
	Golden willow	Deer	Wet areas	Visual barriers in hunting areas.	Fast-growing, medium to tall.	Needs wet sites.	Not of major importance.
Woody vines recommended for use as wildlife plantings	Frost grape and Virginia creeper	Bobwhite, cottontails	Riparian zones	Scattered next to shrubs.	Form a canopy of protection over shrubs or low-growing vegetation.	Needs riparian or supplemental moisture.	Shrub-vine combination provides excellent cover.
Woody vines for potential consideration	Trumpet vine and vining honeysuckle	Bobwhite, cottontails	Riparian zones	Scattered next to shrubs.	Same as above.	Same as above.	Needs evaluation in various sites and moisture situations.

SOURCE: Rutherford and Snyder (1983).

TABLE 11.16 Characteristics of Shrub and Tree Species for Use in Hedgerows in Plains Areas of Colorado

Species	General height (m)	Root sprouting	Growth form	Tolerances			Soil preference	Suggested planting pattern	
				Cold	Drought	Alkaline		In rows (m)	Between rows (m)
Wild plum	2–3	E	Thicket	G	F	G	Sandy	3.6–5.4	3.6–4.8
Squawbush sumac	1–1.5	P	Low, spreading	G	E	E	Loam	3.6–5.4	3.6–4.8
Lilac	2–2.5	Some	Erect, spreading	G	G	G	Loam	5.4–7.2	3.6–4.8
Honeysuckle	2–3	Some	Erect, spreading	G	G	G	Sandy	1.8–2.4	3.6–4.8
Tamarisk*	3.6	Some	Erect, spreading	G	E	E	Sandy	1–1.8	3.6–4.8
Caragana*	3	None	Erect V-shaped	G	E	G	Loam	1–1.8	3.6–4.8
Willow	2–3	G	Thicket	G	P	E	Sandy	1–1.8	4.8–7.3
Cotoneaster	3.6	?	Tall, spreading	G	F	F–G	Sandy loam	2.4–4.8	4.8–7.3
Buffaloberry	3.6	Some	Tall, spreading	G	F	G	Sandy loam	1.8–4.8	4.8–7.3
Elderberry	3.6–6.0	?	Tall, spreading	G	G	G	Sandy	1.8–4.8	4.8–7.3
Russian olive	7.5	Little	Spreading	G	G	E	Any	1.8–4.8	4.8–6.0

Note: G = good; P = poor; F = fair; E = excellent.
*Caragana is not recommended for general use; tamarisk is a tenacious invader.
SOURCE: Rutherford and Snyder (1983).

in small areas, (2) ensure a unique habitat that contrasts with crop-lands and pastures, and (3) provide linkages to other types of wooded habitats used by dispersing or migrating birds.

Guidelines for managing shelterbelts (Yahner 1983a, 1983b) in areas where associated plants and animals occurred naturally include the following:

1. Preserve all existing shelterbelts.

2. Ensure that space within and between rows is greater than 5 m to permit shrub and herbaceous growth.

3. Establish shelterbelts that are greater than 0.6 ha in area and contain eight rows of plantings.

4. Shelterbelts should be long and narrow (280 m by 36 m or the ratio of length to width should be 7:1 or 8:1), even though linear configuration of shelterbelts might attract predators (Gates and Gysel 1978, Yahner 1982a).

5. Discontinue mowing and cultivation in shelterbelts over 25 years old as well as in new plantings, to improve structural diversity. Mowing or cultivation in recently established shelterbelts mini-mizes competition for soil moisture.

6. Retain snags as nesting, perching, and foraging sites.

7. Position new shelterbelts near cropland rather than pastureland.

8. Leave rows of standing crops unharvested or provide food plots or artificial feeders next to shelterbelts. A few rows of corn, sorghum, or sunflowers could be planted between rows of trees to improve food value. Artificial nest boxes can be added for certain species (see Chap. 15).

9. Maintain adjacent cropped areas in no-tillage or minimum-tillage farming systems.

10. Encourage woody (logs, stumps) and cultural (storage sheds, etc.) debris for small mammals.

11. Control livestock grazing to avoid grazing out herbaceous under-story.

12. Encourage vertical stratification through herbaceous, shrub, and tree establishment (Yahner 1982b).

Selecting the right species for planting will improve use by a variety of wildlife species in the southern Great Plains (Table 11.17) (Capel 1988). In Minnesota, Yahner (1983a) recommended inclusion of shrubs (*Lonicera*) and trees (*Picea, Populus, Acer,* and *Ulmus*) to increase ver-tical complexity for birds. In Kansas, Robel and Browning (1981) pro-

TABLE 11.17   Shelterbelts for the Southern Great Plains

State	Species	Comments
Texas panhandle	Evergreen: eastern red-cedar, Austrian pine, Rocky Mountain juniper Deciduous trees: honeylocust, black locust, bur oak Shrubs: skunkbush sumac, Russian olive, rainbow plum, fragrant sumac	Two-row to five-row most common; two rows evergreen trees, one row deciduous trees, one row shrubs; rows 7 m apart; 225 to 500 m minimum length; plant shrubs on east or south side.
Western Oklahoma, Kansas, Nebraska	Eastern redcedar, American plum, chokecherry	Two-row high-density plantings on north or west side; 17-m-wide grass planting on south or east side for snow storage; four-row planting of junipers or shrubs on south and east side of grass strip.
Eastern Nebraska	Peking cotoneaster, American plum, chokecherry, multiflora rose, Tartarian honeysuckle, fragrant sumac, bristly locust, American maple, eastern redcedar, jack pine, hackberry, osage-orange	Five-row plantings typical.
Colorado	American plum, chokecherry, fragrant sumac, Russian olive, mulberry, black locust, Rocky Mountain juniper	Used to achieve thicket-type plantings.

SOURCE: Capel (1988).

vided similar recommendations for nongame birds. Capel (1988) ranked woody plants for shelterbelts (Table 11.18). Henderson (1987) suggested several species (Table 11.19) for an eight-row shelterbelt; Norrgard (1989) offered a broader selection (Table 11.20). The Alberta Fish and Wildlife Division (1984) suggested a wide variety of species for shelterbelts with their value to wildlife (Table 11.21). For the northern Midwest, some plants have undesirable characteristics. These include barberries, trumpet vine, peashrubs, Russian olive, leafy spurge, green ash, honeysuckles, purple loosestrife, white sweetclover, yellow sweetclover, white mulberry, red mulberry, Lombardy poplar, buckthorn, black locust, poison ivy, reed canarygrass (Henderson 1987), and multiflora rose. Tables A.1 through A.5 list

TABLE 11.18   Relative Value of Woody Plants for Wildlife Food and Cover for
Kansas Shelterbelts

Conifers	Tall shrubs
1. Eastern redcedar	1. Russian olive
2. Rocky Mountain juniper	2. Autumn olive
3. Oriental arborvitae	3. Tartarian honeysuckle
4. Spruce	4. Hawthorn
5. Pine	5. Viburnum
6. Fir	6. Winterberry
	7. Dogwood
Deciduous trees	**Short shrubs**
1. Black locust	1. Multiflora rose
2. Bur oak	2. Fragrant sumac
3. Osage-orange	3. American plum
4. Hackberry	4. Common chokecherry
5. Pecan	5. Chickasaw plum
6. Black walnut	6. Sargent crabapple
7. Russian mulberry	7. Lilac
8. Green ash	8. Cotoneaster
9. Maple	9. Bristly locust
	10. Amur maple

Note: Species with lower numbers are more valuable.
SOURCE: Capel (1988).

plant species of regional value to wildlife; some of these plants could be used in shelterbelts.

The number of rows in a shelterbelt varies from north to south on the Great Plains. Two- to four-row shelterbelts are common in southern plains states such as Texas and Oklahoma. Farther north, more rows are needed for thermal protection and to control drifting snow. In South Dakota and Minnesota, an eight-row shelterbelt might be needed and a twenty-row, 33-m-wide shelterbelt might be needed in North Dakota and Manitoba (Capel 1988). Any shelterbelt less than 33 m wide in northern regions will not be wide enough to create an area free of snow drift and thus will lack any winter value for wildlife (Podol 1979). A 10-row planting with a variety of different shrubs and trees can be used as wildlife habitat and for snow accumulation (Fig. 11.11) (Norrgard 1989). Windbreaks of 16 rows have been designed (Fig. 11.12) (Henderson 1987), as have those with natural plantings (Fig. 11.13). Norrgard (1989) prepared a conceptual design of an ideal shelterbelt (Fig. 11.14).

Shelterbelts should be at least 30 m away from the area to be protected (Anderson 1969). Shelterbelts planted as windbreaks of single rows of trees or shrubs usually are repeated at 200-m intervals (Capel 1988). Preferably, shelterbelts should have an undulating design (Fig. 11.15) (PFRA Tree Nursery undated) so that wildlife entering open areas will be protected from view on three sides.

TABLE 11.19   Suggested Species Arrangements for an Eight-Row Farm Shelterbelt in the Upper Midwest

Row	Example 1	Example 2	Example 3	Example 4
			Species	
1 (outside)*	Silver maple Hybrid poplar	Silver maple Hybrid poplar	Silver maple Hybrid poplar	Silver maple Hybrid poplar
2	Hybrid poplar Male boxelder	Hybrid poplar Male boxelder	Hybrid poplar Male boxelder	Hybrid poplar Male boxelder
3	Hybrid poplar Hackberry	Green ash Male boxelder	Hybrid poplar Hackberry	Green ash
4	Norway spruce	Green ash Norway spruce	Green ash Hackberry	Hackberry
5	Douglas-fir Norway spruce	Douglas-fir Norway spruce	Douglas-fir Norway spruce	Douglas-fir Norway spruce
6	White spruce Black Hills spruce	White spruce Black Hills spruce	White spruce Black Hills spruce Douglas-fir Norway spruce	White spruce Black Hills spruce Douglas-fir Norway spruce
7 (inside)	Eastern red- cedar White spruce Black Hills spruce	Eastern red- cedar White spruce Black Hills spruce	White spruce Black Hills spruce	White spruce Black Hills spruce
8	Shrub row either 20 m to the windward of the outside tree row or 9 m to the leeward of the inside conifer row			

*Tall trees on outside row.
SOURCE: Henderson (1987).

TABLE 11.20   Recommended Species and Spacing for Shelterbelt and Wildlife Plantings in Minnesota

Deciduous shrubs: Spacing of plants within rows for shelterbelts and wildlife plants = 1.2 m
 Ninebark
 Cotoneaster
 Honeysuckle
 Late lilac
 Redosier dogwood
 Siberian peashrub
  (Caragana)
 Viburnum
 Nannyberry
 Wayfaringbush
 Cranberry

Small deciduous trees: Spacing of plants within rows for shelterbelt and wildlife plantings = 2 to 3 m
 Washington Hawthorne (rust-suscep-
  tible—do not plant with cedars)
 American plum
 Amur maple
 Chokecherry
 Crabapple
 Russian olive
 Mountain ash
 Nanking cherry
 Sandbar willow

Tall deciduous trees: Spacing of plants within rows for shelterbelts and wildlife plantings = 6 to 7 m
 Black walnut
 Hackberry
 Cottonwood
 Green ash
 Honey locust
 Oak
 Poplar
 Siberian elm
 Boxelder
 Silver maple
 White ash
 Willow

Conifers: Spacing of plants within rows for shelterbelts and wildlife = 3 to 4 m
 Eastern redcedar
 Northern white cedar
 Austrian pine
 Black Hills spruce
 Blue spruce
 Douglas-fir
 Jack pine
 Red pine
 Scotch pine
 White spruce

SOURCE: Norrgard (1989).

TABLE 11.21   Tree and Shrub Species Useful for Planting Shelterbelts for Wildlife in Alberta

Species	Site conditions	Wildlife species benefited
Northwest poplar, P3838 poplar, Brooks poplar (Space 3–4 m)	Grows slowly in dry areas, very fast in wetter areas.	Deer, rabbits, upland birds, raptors, songbirds.
Manitoba maple (Space 2.6 m)	Grows to 13 m, full sun. Grows well everywhere; not drought-tolerant. Hard, long-lived, seeds persist to spring.	Provides nesting cover, escape cover for birds. Young shoots browsed by deer.
Laurel willow, Acute willow (Space 2 m)	Grows well everywhere; not drought-tolerant.	Provides nesting cover, escape cover for birds. Young shoots browsed by deer.
Green ash (Space 2 m)	Grows slowly, drought-tolerant.	Seeds eaten by songbirds. Shoots browsed by deer.
Siberian elm (Space 2–6 m)	Grows well under drought conditions; winterkills in wet sites.	Browsed by deer; nesting cover for songbirds.
Blue spruce (Space 3.3 m)	Grows well under shade conditions; drought-tolerant.	Provides thermal cover for wintering birds.
White spruce (Space 3.8 m)	Grows well in moist, well-drained sites and under shade conditions.	Provides thermal cover for wintering birds.
Scotch pine (Space 3.8 m)	Grows well on sandy, dry soils and under shade conditions.	Provides thermal cover for wintering birds.
Caragana (Space 1 m)	Very drought-tolerant; will not tolerate excessive moisture.	Provides nesting cover, escape cover for songbirds and upland birds.
Chokecherry (Space 1.3 m)	Grows to 2 to 6 m. Grows well on moist, well-drained sites; drought-tolerant; will tolerate shading. Blackberries persist until winter.	Fruit eaten by sharp-tailed grouse, ruffed grouse, and songbirds; browsed by deer.
Hawthorn (Space 2 m)	Grows well on moist, well-drained sites; is drought-tolerant.	Fruit eaten by upland birds and songbirds; browsed by deer.
Russian olive (Space 2 m)	Grows well in dry sites; winterkills. Fruit September to spring.	Provides cover and berries late into winter to upland birds and songbirds.
Sea buckthorn (Space 1 m)	Drought- and salt-tolerant; growth is slow.	Berries eaten by upland birds and songbirds.

TABLE 11.21   Tree and Shrub Species Useful for Planting Shelterbelts for Wildlife in Alberta   (*Continued*)

Species	Site conditions	Wildlife species benefited
Honeysuckle (Space 1.3 m)	Rapid growth. Grows well on moist, well-drained sites; drought-tolerant. Red berries June to November.	Berries eaten by upland birds and songbirds.
Dogwood (Space 1 m)	Shrubs 1 to 10 m. Grows well on moist, well-drained sites; shade-tolerant.	Berries eaten by upland birds and songbirds; twigs, leaves eaten by deer.
Buffaloberry (Space 1 m)	Grows well on moist, well-drained sites; drought-tolerant.	Berries eaten by upland birds and songbirds; provides nesting and escape cover.
Villosa lilac (Space 1–2 m)	Grows well on moist, well-drained sites; drought-tolerant.	Provides escape and nesting cover for upland birds and songbirds.
Hansen's hedge rose (Space 1 m)	Grows well on moist, well-drained sites; drought-tolerant. Fruit July through winter.	Provides escape and nesting cover for upland birds and songbirds, fruit eaten by upland birds and songbirds.
Red elder (Space 1 m)	Berries July to September. Grows rapidly on moist, well-drained sites; winter-kills slightly. Best in full sun.	Berries eaten by songbirds and upland birds, deer browse on branches.
Saskatoon (Space 1 m)	Prefers moist, well-drained soils; drought- and shade-tolerant.	Berries eaten by songbirds and upland birds, deer browse on branches.
Siberian crabapple (Space 2 m)	Best in full sun. Prefers moist, well-drained soils; drought-tolerant. Fruit persistent to March.	Fruit eaten by songbirds and upland birds, deer browse on branches.

SOURCE: Alberta Fish and Wildlife Division (1984).

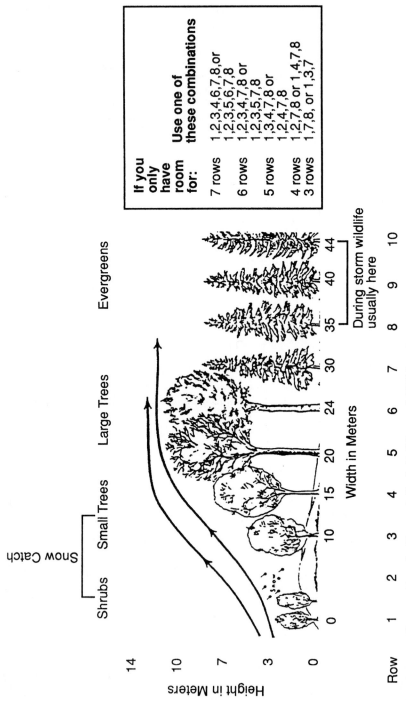

Figure 11.11 Cross section of a 10-row shelterbelt. (*Norrgard 1989.*)

If you only have room for:	Use one of these combinations
7 rows	1,2,3,4,6,7,8,or
6 rows	1,2,3,5,6,7,8
	1,2,3,4,7,8 or
	1,2,3,5,7,8
5 rows	1,3,4,7,8 or
	1,2,4,7,8
4 rows	1,2,7,8 or 1,4,7,8
3 rows	1,7,8, or 1,3,7

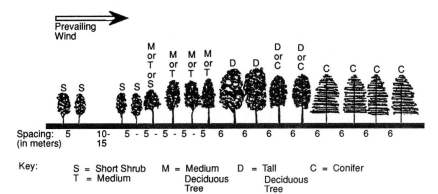

Figure 11.12 Side view of a 16-row woody cover planting for wildlife in Minnesota. (*Henderson 1987.*)

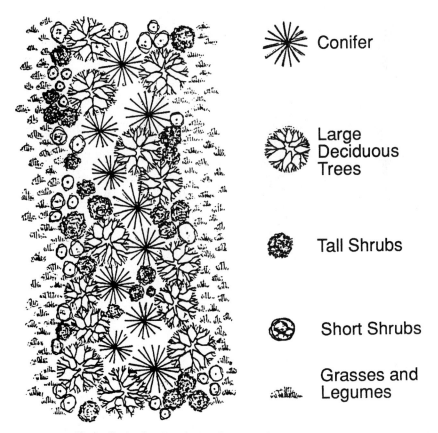

Figure 11.13 Naturalistic planting design for a woody cover planting for wildlife (no straight rows). (*Henderson 1987.*)

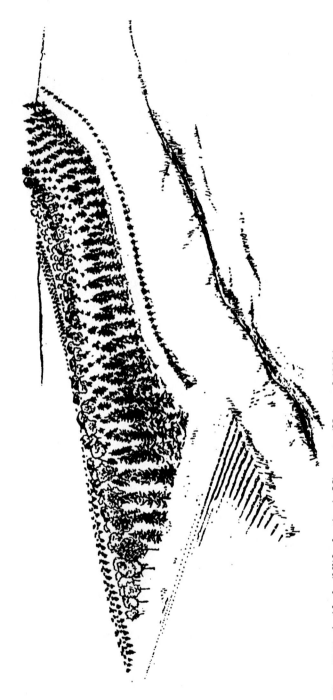

Figure 11.14 An ideal wildlife planting in Minnesota. (*Norrgard 1989.*)

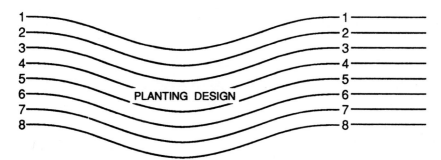

Figure 11.15 Undulating design of windbreaks that protect wildlife from view on three sides in opening. (*PFRA Tree Nursery undated.*)

12

Farm Programs, Pastures, and Cultural Inputs

Federal Programs

Wildlife and wildlife habitat are important but often overlooked components of national farm policy; yet while some wildlife populations have benefited incidentally, others have been negatively affected. Wildlife species highly dependent upon grassland and wetland habitats have been the most negatively affected (Berner 1987). Large areas of land idled under the Soil Bank program were partly responsible for the "boom" in the 1950s and 1960s of farmland wildlife in general (Carlson 1985) and pheasants in particular (Warner and Etter 1989). Set-aside programs of the U.S. Department of Agriculture also have been useful in creating or establishing wildlife habitat (Cacek 1984b). Shortcomings include (1) the uncertainty as to how much land will be diverted from one year to the next, (2) the planting of small grains unattractive to nesting birds until after midsummer, (3) untimely mowing, and (4) tillage in early fall that prevents habitat development for use in winter and spring (Warner and Etter 1989).

In the United States, the Federal Feed Grain Program of 1961 was an attempt to increase the area of forage crops to control production of corn and grain sorghum by creating "diverted areas"; that program added substantially to the availability of sites for pheasant nesting in Illinois (Joselyn and Warnock 1964). Land retirement programs such as the Payment in Kind (PIK) program in the United States have proven meaningless for wildlife because of their short-term nature

(Burger 1985). In general, shortcomings of set-aside programs have manifested themselves in three general areas. First, the existence of programs that divert farmlands is uncertain from one year to the next (Berner 1987). Second, contracts for fields enrolled in these programs have encouraged the planting of crops or forages that might be unsuitable as nesting habitat for many birds, and allowed mowing at inopportune times during the nesting season. Last, some programs encouraged tillage practices that did not permit fields to persist long enough to develop as habitat (Warner and Etter 1989), thus creating large areas of unsafe wildlife habitat. In short, multi-year (3 or more) cropland diversion programs (e.g., Soil Bank) generally improve wildlife habitats; annual cropland set-aside programs (e.g., 1986 and 1987 Field Grain and Wheat programs) can be devastating (Berner 1987), but windows of opportunity for habitat stability do exist in short-term programs (Brady and Hamilton 1987).

In 1985, the U.S. Congress implemented the Conservation Reserve Program (CRP) through Title XII of the Federal Food Security Act. Under provisions of CRP, farmers were paid to plant permanent cover in highly erodible cropland for a 10-year period. Even though Congress listed wildlife habitat as one of CRP's objectives, only about 4 percent of the 9.2 million ha enrolled in CRP through August 1987 was enrolled in Establishment of Permanent Wildlife Habitat (CP-4) (Isaacs and Howell 1988). For wildlife, other provisions of CRP include permanent cover established in introduced grasses and legumes (CP-1) or native grasses (CP-2), annual food plots (CP-12), shallow-water areas (CP-9), and shrub plantings (CP-4). Benefits of CRP on the southern high plains of Texas include (1) improved nesting for many songbirds, (2) distribution of ring-necked pheasants from formerly concentrated habitats vulnerable to nest loss, (3) improved pheasant production and recruitment, and (4) secure winter cover for many species of birds (Berthelsen et al. 1990). Schramm et al. (1987) proposed potential benefits to wildlife in general and guidelines for management. Real benefits depend upon (1) vegetative cover management practices (haying, grazing, and mowing) and the frequency with which political pressures open CRP lands to haying, grazing, or mowing; (2) the longevity of CRP payments to farmers; (3) the extent to which income is realized from wildlife-related recreation (Bryant and Smith 1988); and (4) the implementation of ancillary conservation practices (e.g., CP-4, CP-9, CP-12). Conservation reserve areas that are harvested, mowed, burned, or heavily grazed during the peak nesting season will provide few benefits for ground-nesting birds (Carlson 1985).

Even though active management can improve wildlife habitat on CRP lands, the greatest fear is that the current CRP program will not be renewed in a manner to encourage farmers to keep their lands in permanent cover. For example, unless a new Farm Bill continues CRP in its current or similar form, at least 64 percent of the farmers who have highly erodible lands enrolled in the High Plains Region of Texas will expect to return those lands to agricultural production the year after CRP is terminated (pers. comm., R. T. Ervin, Dep. Agric. Econ., Texas Tech Univ., Lubbock, 1993). The loss of wildlife habitat could be substantial because over 80 percent of the 1.7 million hectares of CRP lands currently enrolled in Texas are located in the High Plains Region. Indeed, this would be a tragic loss of not just wildlife habitat, but of permanent cover on fragile lands subject to high soil erosion potential.

Managing Pastures

Forage crops, hayfields, and pastures represent vital food and cover for insects, birds, herbivores, and their predators in farmland regions. Pasture management depends upon the forage type (alfalfa, oats, wheat), type of disturbance (haying, mowing, grazing), and timing of disturbance. For example, most nests and hens of pheasants in Illinois were destroyed when hay was cut between days 158 and 172 of the Julian calendar (Warner and Etter 1989). Over the last three decades, the dates of first hay cuttings have gradually shifted to earlier in the year, before nests are begun (Warner and Etter 1989). This early cutting benefits nesting birds because fewer nests are disturbed.

Protecting areas nearby as unmowed nesting cover is essential (Warner and Etter 1989). Raising the mowbar to 25 cm when cutting alfalfa hay saves pheasants. But unless incentives to the farmer are developed, relatively little wildlife management will occur. In 1981, raising the mowbar 25 cm at cutting time would have reduced farm income by $85 per pheasant produced (Bishop 1981).

Switchgrass planted as grazable pasture in Iowa is sought by pheasants (Wooley et al. 1982) and readily accepted by songbirds as nesting cover (George et al. 1979), as long as grazing and hay harvest are delayed until after most nesting is completed (June 20) and the height of grazed or hayed stubble remains taller than 20 to 25 cm (George et al. 1981). Small (2 to 8 ha) switchgrass plantings resulted in noticeable increases in pheasant numbers in grain-farming areas (George 1984). But switchgrass also can become so dense that birds use it only as winter cover, preferring to nest in brome-alfalfa mixtures (pers. comm. W. R. Clark, Iowa State University, 1992). Grazing techniques (see Chap. 10), could be applied to many regions of the farm belt. Other pasture species suitable as wildlife cover include Kleingrass, weeping lovegrass, Johnson grass (although considered a pest in southern croplands), smooth brome, orchardgrass, alfalfa, red clover, and sweetclover (George 1984).

Management alternatives depend on the vegetation type in the planted stands (Table 12.1) (Rutherford and Snyder 1983).

TABLE 12.1   Some Management Alternatives to Select Perennial Grasses, Legumes, and Mixtures to Seed on a Nesting Tract

Vegetation type	Primary species	Values to wildlife for	
		Nesting	Other
Warm-season mid- and tall grasses	Switchgrass; sand lovegrass; sand, silver, big, and little bluestems; Indiangrass	Lodge-resistant standing residual provides early spring nesting cover.	Night roosting, winter escape, loafing (especially for prairie grouse). Snow barrier to protect resting and feeding sites.
Cool-season mid- and tall grasses	Tall, intermediate, crested wheatgrass ryegrasses	Combination of new growth and partially lodged residual for mid- to late spring use.	Resting, roosting, and escape unless or until lodged by winter snows.
Legumes	Alfalfa; Cicer milkvetch	Mid- to late spring and summer nesting in new growth.	Early spring to late fall greens for food. Brood habitat (no winter cover).
Warm-season legume mix	Switchgrass; alfalfa	Standing residual and new spring growth combined. (good to excellent).	Night roosting, winter escape, and loafing. Snow barrier to resting and feeding
Cool-season legume mix	Tall wheatgrass; alfalfa	Good to excellent combination from early spring to summer. Use in preference to grass or alfalfa alone.	Limited brood and early spring to late fall feed. Limited winter resting, roosting, and escape.
Warm-season cool-season legume mix	Switchgrass; tall wheatgrass; alfalfa	Considered optimum for early spring to summer use.	Limited brood, night roosting, resting, and escape. Snow barrier to protect resting and feeding sites.

TABLE 12.1   Some Management Alternatives to Select Perennial Grasses, Legumes, and Mixtures to Seed on a Nesting Tract   (*Continued*)

Vege-tation type	Primary species	Management options		
		Standing-unharvested	Harvested for seed	Harvested for hay
Warm-season mid- and tall grasses	Switchgrass; Sand lovegrass Sand, silver, big, and little bluestems Indiangrass	Recommend for prairie grouse. Other wildlife in riparian sites.	Recommended in irrigated or riparian sites. High income potential. Herbicides recommended.	Not recommended. No residual for nesting or early spring growth.
Cool-season mid- and tall grasses	Tall, intermediate, crested wheatgrasses ryegrasses	Recommended in loam soil farmland for pheasants and riparian for other species. Limited use in rangelands to increase diversity.	Highly recommended. Reduces lodging. Herbicides and irrigation recommended.	Not recommended. Limited regrowth will provide marginal mid- to late spring nesting cover but not residual.
Legumes	Alfalfa; Cicer milkvetch	Needs old residual removed and a renovation applied at least every 2–3 years.	Limited potential due to noxious weeds. Recommended on weed-free sites.	One late summer cutting per year may help sustain vigor. Reduces value for broods. Irrigate after cutting to attain new fall growth.
Warm-season legume mix	Switchgrass; Alfalfa	Recommended. Alfalfa will gradually decrease as switchgrass increases.	Questionable due to weed-control difficulties in alfalfa.	Not recommended. Residual nesting and winter cover will be destroyed.
Cool-season legume mix	Tall wheatgrass; Alfalfa	Recommended in loam uplands and riparian areas.	Same as above.	Not recommended but limited regrowth will provide fair mid-spring nesting.
Warm-season cool-season legume mix	Switchgrass; Tall wheatgrass; Alfalfa	Highly recommended in all better soil and moisture sites. Priority for all species.	Questionable as above and due to varying grass seed maturity.	Not recommended but limited regrowth will provide fair mid-spring nesting.

TABLE 12.1   Some Management Alternatives to Select Perennial Grasses, Legumes, and Mixtures to Seed on a Nesting Tract   (Continued)

Vege- tation type	Primary species	Options for renovation		
		Priority 1	Priority 2	Priority 3
Warm-season mid- and tall grasses	Switchgrass; sand lovegrass sand, silver, big, and little bluestems; Indiangrass	Prescribed burn in April once every 5–8 years.	Gyromower shredding and shallow disking (March– April).	Late winter intensive grazing once every 5–8 years.
Cool-season mid- and tall grasses	Tall, intermedi- ate, crested wheatgrasses; ryegrasses	Same as above on all treatments. Use deep chiseling or deep rototilling to break up root-bound sodded stands, when present, to supplement burning.		
Legumes	Alfalfa; Cicer milkvetch	Deep-chisel and control-burn in early spring.	Prescribed early spring burning alone every 3–4 years.	Gyromower shredding and shallow disking in early spring.
Warm-season legume mix	Switchgrass; alfalfa	Prescribed burn once every 5–8 years (April).	Gyromower shredding and shallow disking (March– April)	Late winter intensive grazing once every 5–8 years.
Cool-season legume mix	Tall wheatgrass; alfalfa	Same as above on all treatments. Supplement with deep chiseling to thin grass stands.		
Warm-season cool-season legume mix	Switchgrass; tall wheatgrass; alfalfa	Same as above on all treatments.		

SOURCE: Rutherford and Snyder (1983).

Rutherford and Snyder (1983) recommended grasses (Table 12.2) and legumes (Table 12.3) for the western Great Plains. For the eastern Great Plains, big bluestem, Indiangrass, and switchgrass are acceptable; little bluestem, sideoats grama, and western wheatgrass are native grasses adaptable to the moderate-rainfall areas of the central Great Plains (George 1984). On sandy soils, sand bluestem and sand lovegrass should be planted. Payne (1992) presented information on planting warm-season and cool-season grasses on uplands associated with wetlands of the prairie pothole region of North America. Where native reestablished pastures are not grazed or cut for hay, prescribed burns every 3 to 5 years might be needed to remove litter, restore plant vigor, and control invasion of unwanted plants.

Chemicals and Irrigation

Fertilizer

Use of fertilizers for habitat management in noncultivated areas of farmlands is restricted to pastures, odd areas, field borders, grass terraces, and vegetative islands. Because of problems of nonpoint sources of pollution, managers should not use excess fertilizer, and should use no fertilizer near streams, lakes, wetlands, and riparian zones. Nitrogen fertilizer is not recommended when attempting to establish perennial grasses in dryland situations. Nitrogen applied to grass-legume mixtures will crowd out and speed the disappearance of the legume (Rutherford and Snyder 1983). Fertilizers should be used when soil nutrients are low (Table 12.4) (Rutherford and Snyder 1983). (See "Fertilizing" in Chap. 9; also see Payne 1992.)

Pesticides

Laboratory studies have documented the effects of certain chemicals on wildlife (Hoffman and Eastin 1982, Fleming et al. 1983, Hudson et al. 1984), but the immediate or long-term effect on wildlife under natural conditions is unknown. Wooley et al. (1985) suggested that possible routes of chemical exposure include (1) contact transfer from parents; (2) direct spraying on eggs, young, and adults; or (3) contamination through poisoned plant and insect foods. The insecticide Furadan (carbofuran) can kill birds (Balcom et al. 1984); paraquat (a herbicide) damages embryos of mallards (Hoffman and Eastin 1982) and could injure deer mice (Wooley et al. 1985). Northern bobwhite quail apparently are unaffected by paraquat (Castrale 1985). Organophosphorous and carbamate pesticides have relatively low environmental persistence; their chronic toxicity is of lesser importance in their overall

TABLE 12.2 Grass Species Recommended for Use in Plains Areas of Colorado

Common name	Recom-mended variety	Grass type	Region	Soil	Average height (m)	Seeds/kg (thou-sands)	Seeding rate (kg/ha)
Warm Season Grasses							
Switchgrass	Nebraska 28	Bunch to sod	Northern Plains	Sandy	0.8–1.5	856	4
Indiangrass	Holt Llano	Bunch to sod	Northern Plains	Sandy	0.6–1.5	156	10–13
Sand bluestem	Woodward	Bunch	Northern Plains	Sandy	0.8–1.8	249	13
Big bluestem	Kaw	Bunch to sod	Northern Plains, foothills	Sandy	0.8–1.8	286	10
Little bluestem	Pastura	Bunch	Northern Plains	Tight to sandy	0.6–1.2	561	6–9
Sand lovegrass	Nebraska 27	Bunch	Northern Plains	Sandy	0.5–0.9	2860	2
Prairie sandreed	—	Bunch to sod	Northern Plains	Sandy	0.5–1.5	601	5–6
Silver bluestem	—	Bunch	Southern Plains	Sandy	0.6–0.9		
Cool-Season Grasses							
Tall wheatgrass	Jose	Bunch	Northern Plains	Sandy to alkaline	0.8–1.5	174	8–10
Intermediate wheatgrass	Amur Oahe	Sod	Foothills, mountains	Sandy loam	0.6–1.2	220	7
Basin wildrye	C-43	Bunch	Foothills	Deep to heavy alkaline	0.6–1.2	363	5–6
Crested wheatgrass	Nordan	Bunch	Foothills, Northern Plains	Loam, dry	0.3–0.9	385	5

TABLE 12.2   Grass Species Recommended for Use in Plains Areas of Colorado   (*Continued*)

Common name	Recom- mended variety	Grass type	Region	Soil	Average height (m)	Seeds/kg (thou- sands)	Seeding rate (kg/ha)
			Cool-Season Grasses (*Continued*)				
Fairway crested wheatgrass	Commercial	Bunch	Foothills	Loam, dry	0.3–0.8	440	4–5
Pubescent wheatgrass	Huna	Sod	Foothills, mountains	Loam, dry	0.6–1.2	200	7
Smooth brome	Achenbach, Manchar	Sod	Mountains	Clayloam	0.5–0.9	275	9
Western wheatgrass	Barton	Sod	Foothills, Northern Plains	Clayloam	0.3–0.8	242	7
Mammoth wildrye	Volga	Bunch	Foothills	Sandy	0.9–1.8	121	2–4

SOURCE: Rutherford and Snyder (1983).

TABLE 12.3 Legume Species Recommended for Use in Plains Areas of Colorado

Common name	Recommended variety	Growth form	Survival persistence	Soil preference	Seed characteristics		Adaptation and use
					Seeds/kg (thousands)	Recommended rate (kg/ha)	
Alfalfa	Lakak Ranger	Erect	Perennial 7 years	Loam to sandy	495	4	Dryland, irrigated and meadow sites
Cicer milk-vetch	Lutana	Erect	Perennial	Sandy	264	9	Same as above
Ladino clover	—	Decumbent	Perennial	Sandy loam	1760	5–7	Pasture type
Strawberry clover	—	Short erect	Annual to perennial	Clay loam	—	—	Wet alkaline
Red clover	Lakeland	Erect	Biennial, short perennial	Heavy fertile	618	8–12	High altitude and elsewhere
Hairy vetch	—	Decumbent	Winter annual	Sandy	40	40–45	Sandy ranges
White sweet-clover	—	Erect	Biennial	Varied	576	4	Widespread
Yellow sweet-clover	Goldtop common	Erect	Biennial	Varied	572	4	Widespread

SOURCE: Rutherford and Snyder (1983).

TABLE 12.4 Relative Availability of Soil Nutrients for Growing Field Crops in Colorado

Nutrient	Field status	Level (ppm)				
		Very low	Low	Marginal to medium	Adequate to high	Very high
Phosphorus	Dryland	—	0–7	8–14	15–22	—
	Irrigated	0–7	8–14	15–22	23–30	>30
Potassium	Dryland	—	0–60	0–60	61–120	—
	Irrigated	—	0–60	61–120	121–180	>180
Zinc	Dryland	—	0.0–0.25	0.26–0.50	0.51–1.00	—
	Irrigated	0–0.25	0.26–0.50	0.51–1.00	>1.00	—
Iron	Dryland	—	0–1.5	1.6–3.5	>3.5	—
	Irrigated	—	—	—	—	—

SOURCE: Rutherford and Snyder (1983).

hazard to wildlife populations compared to the more persistent organochlorines (Smith 1987). Wildlife die-offs caused by organophosphates and carbamates are generally incidences of acute poisoning.

A major concern about conservation tillage is the greater use of chemicals to control weeds and insect pests (Castrale 1985). Generally, herbicides are less toxic than insecticides. Guarded use is still recommended until research reveals acceptable application rates or demonstrates less toxic chemicals, e.g., glyphosate instead of paraquat (Hoffman and Alders 1984). The hazard of any chemical is based not only on its toxicity but also its application rate, time of application, type of formulation and spray mixture, persistence, environmental conditions (Stinson and Bromley 1991), and bioconcentration in food chains (Smith 1987). General toxicities of some pesticides to some wildlife forms are known (Tables 12.5, 12.6)(pers. comm. J. Haukos, National Pesticide Hotline, Health Sciences Center, Texas Tech University, Lubbock, 1992). Tables A.13 through A.17 (Stinson

TABLE 12.5   Examples of Pesticides Toxic to Animals

Chemical	Animal	Recommended use
Extremely harmful		
Parathion	Mammals and birds	No
Methyl parathion	Mammals and birds	No
Carbofuran	Mammals and birds	No
Aldicarb	Mammals and birds	No
Methomyl	Mammals and birds	No
Dicrotophos	Mammals and birds	No
Fonophos	Mammals and birds	No
Azinphos-methyl	Mammals and birds	No
Terbufos	Mammals and birds	No
Dimethoate	Birds	No
Chlorpyrifos	Birds	No
Trichlorfon	Birds	No
Cypermethrin	Fish	No
Fenvalerate	Fish	No
Moderately harmful		
Malathion	Mammals and birds	Guarded
Carbaryl	Mammals and birds	Guarded
Picloram	Fish	Guarded
Trichlorfon	Mammals	Guarded
Dimethoate	Mammals	Guarded
Chlorpyrifos	Mammals	Guarded
Relatively safe		
Glyphosate	Mammals/birds/fish	OK
Cypermethrin	Mammals and birds	OK
Fenvalerate	Mammals and birds	OK
Picloram	Mammals and birds	OK
Insect growth regulators	Mammals and birds	OK

TABLE 12.6   Toxicity of Most Common Insecticides and Herbicides Used in Agriculture within the United States
Toxicity Measured by LD_{50} (mg/kg)

Chemical	Birds*	Mammals*
Insecticides		
Malathion	1,485	1,375
Chlorpyrifos (Dursban)	75	270
Azinphos-methyl	136	15
Parathion	13	22
Aldicarb (Temik)	3	1
Carbofuran (Furadan)	0.5	11
Disulfoton	7	6
Methomyl	16	17
Dicrotophos	2	17
Fenvalerate	10,000	451
Herbicides		
Trifluralin (Treflan)	>2,000	10,000
Glyphosate (Roundup)	4,640	4,300
Pendimethalin (Prowl)	10,000	1,250
2,4-D	>2,000	600
2,4-DP	10,000	800
Dicamba	10,000	1,700
Picloram	>2,000	8,200
Triclopyr	1,700	630
Clopyralid	1,500	>5,000
Paraquat	200	150

*Relative toxicity to birds (waterfowl) and mammals is given for each compound.
SOURCE: Hudson et al. (1984), Smith (1987), Hartley and Kidd (1990), Meister (1990).

and Bromley 1991) provide more detail for relative toxicities of insecticides, acaricides, nematocides, herbicides, and fungicides. Methods of application and precautions relating to herbicides are listed in Payne (1992). (See "Herbicides" in Chaps. 3 and 9.)

General considerations and recommendations include the following:

1. Avoid using chemicals during the nesting season (April–July). Apply when potential hazards to wildlife are lowest.

2. Avoid treatments near riparian zones.

3. Avoid treatments near wildlife concentration areas (e.g., goose feeding sites).

4. Avoid treatments during presence of wildlife (migration periods and concentrations) and in specific habitats (e.g., birds nesting in alfalfa).

5. Avoid using highly toxic insecticides in center-pivot irrigation systems (because of lack of control of application rates and drift potential).

6. Avoid chemicals in nontilled weedy areas (field borders, ditchways, fencerows, borrow pits). These usually are prime wildlife use areas in farmland communities

Irrigation

Irrigation of farmland has been a boon to some wildlife, such as pheasants in central Washington and the Texas panhandle. Corn and grain sorghum, produced under irrigation on lands too arid to support those crops otherwise, are important for many birds and critical to pheasants. As the area of irrigated land declines, bird use could decline as well. Yet, as irrigated croplands expand in Wisconsin, for example, white-tailed deer populations decline because deer distribution is restricted and winter range reduced on these lands (Murphy et al. 1985).

The recent expansion in the use of center-pivot irrigation systems and water cannons in agriculture suggests the potential for promoting plant growth for wildlife use. Generally, the expense involved does not justify irrigation, but situations could occur where wildlife values warrant it (Payne and Copes 1988).

Potential for habitat improvement includes timely irrigation of food plots to establish and promote grains and forages for wildlife, and irrigation of field borders, grass terraces, or pastures to enhance cover and food value. Conversion from ditch to sprinkler irrigation could save nests because of flooding caused by ditch irrigation (Rutherford and Snyder 1983), but such conversion would reduce populations of other wildlife as the aquatic and riparian habitats disappear.

Artificial Improvements

13

Water Developments

Importance of Water

Compared to the eastern United States and Canada, where water seldom limits upland wildlife, habitat management of the arid and semiarid regions of the central plains and western states and provinces might require water developments. Drought commonly affects reproduction through insufficient forage quality and quantity for species like deer (Brown 1984a, Smith 1984). Daily water needs also increase in xeric versus mesic habitats. For example, Oregon mule deer drank only 3.2 L per visit compared with 6.3 L per visit by mule deer in Arizona (Roberts 1977). Water availability also influences wildlife distribution. When mule deer were excluded from watering points in west Texas, deer use in that area declined by 66 percent (pers. comm., J. Brownlee, Texas Parks and Wildlife Department, 1990).

Properly placed and designed water supplies can be used to increase numbers of animals, distribute them across habitats or into unused portions of the habitat, mitigate habitat loss (Remington et al. 1984), or alter traditional movement patterns. Conversely, removal or closure of water points could be used to restrict use of habitats to avoid conflicts with humans or reduce excessive animal density or impact. Remington et al. (1984) used water developments to deter mule deer from a canal in Arizona, one of their traditional water sources. By the third year after the development of a new water source, mule deer use increased 400 percent at this new source.

Water needs are known for some gallinaceous birds (Table 13.1) and ungulates (Table 13.2). For birds like chickens, egg laying increases the water turnover rate by 69 percent compared to those in a nonreproduc-

TABLE 13.1 Importance of Water to Selected Gamebirds in the Western United States and Canada

Species	Need for open water	Movements relative to known water source	Optimum spacing of water developments	References
Native				
Scaled quail	Uncertain: succulent vegetation might supply needs.	Range 0.4 to 2.4 km from water.	1.6 km	Schemnitz (1961) Campbell et al. (1973)
Gambel's quail	Might congregate at water sources; might require open water if succulent vegetation is unavailable.	Range 1.6 to 3.2 km from water.	1.6 to 3.2 km	MacGregor (1950) Hungerford (1962) Hungerford (1960)
California quail	Might need open water if succulent vegetation is unavailable.	Broods: 0.4 km from water. Adults: 0.8 to 1.2 km from water.	1.6 km or less	Leopold (1977)
Mountain quail	Might need open water if succulent vegetation is unavailable.	Range 3.2 km from water.	1.6 to 3.2 km	MacGregor (1950)
Northern bobwhite quail	Use free water in hot, dry periods; succulent vegetation usually is adequate; need 3.47 percent of body mass per day.	Range 0.4 to 1.2 km from water.	1.6 km or less	Prasad and Guthery (1986) Koerth and Guthery (1991) Goodwin and Hungerford (1977) McNabb (1969)
Blue grouse	May need open water during nesting and brooding in drier areas of the cruising range.	None reported.	Might be beneficial on dry ranges	
Sage grouse	Open water used when and where available.	None reported.	3.2 to 8.0 km	Dalke et al. (1963)

TABLE 13.1 Importance of Water to Selected Gamebirds in the Western United States and Canada *(Continued)*

Native

Lesser prairie chicken	Open water used when and where available.	None reported.	1.6 to 3.2 km	
Greater prairie chicken	Open water used when and where available.	None reported.	1.6 to 3.2 km	
Wild turkey	Open water used when and where available; 1900 L per flock per summer.	Most hens nest within 0.8 to 1.6 km of open water.	1.6 to 3.2 km in arid regions	Payne and Copes (1988)

Introduced

Chukar partridge	Open water influences distribution; 2800 L per covey per year.	None reported.	0.8 to 1.6 km	Christensen (1954) Mackie and Buechner (1963)
Gray partridge	Might need open water if succulent vegetation is unavailable.	No major distribution patterns associated with water; usually found within 0.4 to 1.6 km of water.	0.8 to 1.6 km	Porter (1950) Oliver (1969)
Ring-necked pheasant	Usually food supplies water needs; 4 to 15.	Might nest near water sources.	0.8 to 1.6 km	Payne and Copes (1988)

TABLE 13.2 Importance of Water to Selected Ungulates in the Western United States and Canada

Species	Daily water requirements*	Seasonal cruising range	Spacing of water developments	References
Pronghorn	25–33 ml/kg BW, normal conditions; 95–190 ml/kg BW, dry conditions; dependable water needed during periods of dry forage; can meet requirements from preformed or metabolic water.	95% of 12,000 Wyoming pronghorn were within 4.8–6.4 km of water.	1.6 to 8 km	Boyd et al. (1986) Beale and Smith (1970) Robbins (1983) Sundstrom (1968) Yoakum (1978)
Desert mule deer	100–200 ml/kg BW.	3–5 km; pregnant females usually are within 0.8 km of open water.	4 to 4.8 km gentle terrain; <3.2 km rough terrain	Hanson and McCulloch (1955) Roberts (1977) Severson and Medina (1983) Elder (1954)
Mule deer	42–63 ml/kg BW, normal conditions; 100–200 ml/kg BW, dry conditions; move to open water if supply diminishes.	Migratory.	0.8 to 3.2 km	Mackie (1970) Roberts (1977)
White-tailed deer	16 ml/kg BW, dry vetetation; 31 ml/kg BW, succulant vegetation.	1.6 to 3 km; associated with riparian habitats and areas with water uniformly distributed.	1.6 to 3.2 km	Nichol (1936) Boyd et al. (1986)
Coues white-tailed deer	Might survive on moisture in succulent vegetation.			Severson and Medina (1983)

TABLE 13.2 Importance of Water to Selected Ungulates in the Western United States and Canada *(Continued)*

Desert bighorn	Dependable water required.	In dry seasons, most bighorns were within 1.6–2.4 km of water.	Minimal, 8 km; optimal, 2 km	Graff (1980) Boyd et al. (1986) Halloran and Deming (1958)
Elk	42–63 ml/kg BW.	Migratory.	1.6 to 3.2 km	Mackie (1970) Roberts (1977)
Javelina	Do not depend entirely on free water; will use if available.			Boyd et al. (1986)
Bison	Need water daily.	Areas inhabited by bison have readily available water sources.	3.2 to 8 km	Meagher (1978) Boyd et al. (1986)
Caribou	Free water is not an important limiting factor.	Found near riparian habitats at least most of the year; migratory.	Water developments rarely needed	Bergerud (1978)
Moose	Riparian zones important though not indispensable for habitat use; use aquatic plants in summer.	Along and around riparian zones.	Water developments rarely needed	Boyd et al. (1986)
Muskoxen	Drinking free water is rare among adults; snow is adequate.	Unrelated to free water.	Water developments rarely needed	Lent (1978)
Mountain goat	Free water is not an important limiting factor; snowbanks are adequate.	If introduced, water might restrict goat movements in southern ranges.		Rideout (1978)

*Note: BW = body weight.

tive state. Moreover, smaller birds have a much higher water requirement relative to body weight than larger birds. Robbins (1983) discussed major physiological differences between birds and mammals.

For Galliformes, requirements are met by metabolic water (byproduct of food metabolism), preformed water or succulence (water bound in plant and animal matter), dew, and free water (surface water). Preformed water can vary from 0 to 3 percent in dry seeds to 60 percent in insects and 90 percent in leafy greens. Among ungulates, ruminants can withstand water deprivation more easily than nonruminants because of the water held in the rumen.

Planning Water Developments

The needs of the target species as well as proper location are important considerations in the planning process. General guidelines are provided for optimum spacing of potential water development for some selected birds (Table 13.1) and ungulates (Table 13.2). Giles (1985) provided a formula to compute the number of watering points needed in a habitat based on optimal spacings. But whether water is truly limiting should be investigated adequately before installing any water development. Artificial water supplies did not increase long-term populations of several small desert rodents, nor was water determined to be the resource limiting Gambel's quail in Utah or Nevada (Robbins 1983).

Placement of water without regard for food or cover availability is a waste of time and money. Desert mule deer were abundant where density of forage species was high and perennial springs were present, but deer densities were low on areas of abundant forage that lacked year-round water (Leopold and Krausman 1991). Artificial water without adequate forage might not guarantee the presence of deer in arid regions.

Other undesirable locations for water development include in gullies or arroyos (Roberts 1977); on sandy soils; close to a natural water source; in unnatural places like summits or ridges; near roads, trails, or other sources of human activity; and, if the water supplement is rain-fed, in rain shadows (localized spots where less rain falls) (Halloran and Deming 1958). More suitable sites might include in ecotones and coverts; away from prevailing winds; on north-facing slopes (Roberts 1977); and in locations accessible to target wildlife but not competing animals, e.g., desert bighorn versus feral burros.

Facilities for watering livestock have benefited many wildlife species in the western United States and Canada (Prasad and Guthery 1986, Holechek et al. 1989, Heady and Bartolome 1977). Stock ponds might even enhance drought survival of a threatened species, such as the lesser prairie chicken in Texas (Crawford and

Bolen 1976a). But where livestock or feral animals share existing or potential water sources, care should be taken to exclude animals which can compete with or interrupt use of water sources.

Livestock disturb wildlife and denude and trample shoreline vegetation not only because they come and go to drink but also because they loaf at ponds and tanks (Buttery and Shields 1975). Prasad and Guthery (1986) demonstrated that livestock under short-duration grazing (see Chap. 10) disturbed several wildlife species at stock-watering ponds in Texas. Short-duration grazing was more intensive than continuous grazing because cattle were concentrated more. Water at the center of a short-duration cell was essentially unavailable to white-tailed deer, javelinas, mourning doves, and Rio Grande turkeys. Deer leave a water facility without drinking or before finishing when disturbed by cattle. Coyotes and raccoons apparently are unaffected by cattle at watering points under a short-duration grazing system. Except for Rio Grande turkeys and mourning doves, 64 other bird species were unaffected (Prasad and Guthery 1986). Water sources away from the cell center were used by all wildlife species. Livestock water facilities in areas under continuous grazing also were used by all wildlife. Recommendations for planning livestock water facilities include:

1. Use fencing to restrict livestock use at principal water sources to less than one-fourth of the shoreline (Fig. 13.1). This strategy minimizes social interactions, prevents trampling of all the shoreline vegetation, and might decrease water turbidity. High turbidity is detrimental to aquatic plants, amphibians, and possibly reptiles (Johnson 1983).

2. Develop ponds or tanks for independent use by wildlife. Fence to exclude livestock or feral ungulates.

3. Develop waterlines (spurlines) or trickle feeders off storage tanks or windmills to supply watering areas for wildlife (Fig. 13.2). Water catchment locations should be more than 200 m from the principal water source and fenced to exclude livestock or feral ungulates (McCarty 1986).

4. Fenced areas surrounding stockwater ponds or tanks, independent wildlife ponds, or catchments from spurlines should be at least 0.5 ha (50 m on a side), with a three-strand fence, 1.5 m tall, the bottom strand of smooth wire 45 cm off the ground, and constructed with pointed fence posts to discourage perching by avian predators (Bird 1977, McCarty 1986).

5. Even if unfenced, water sources should be maintained away from primary water supplies of any livestock operation for enhancement of wildlife species present.

ACCESS FOR
LIVESTOCK

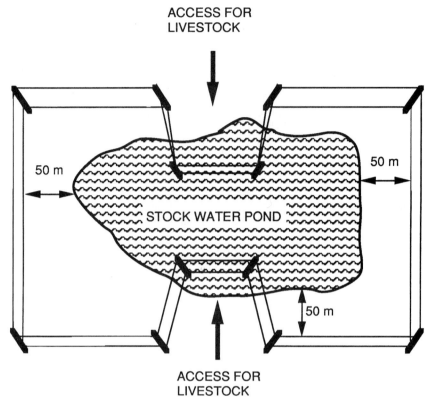

Figure 13.1   Fencing design around a pond to avoid trampling of shoreline vegetation by livestock.

6. Fence natural springs and seeps to prevent damage by wild and domestic ungulates (Rutherford and Snyder 1983), while using pipelines to provide free water (Yoakum et al. 1980).

Graul (1980) recommended fencing half of the shoreline to accommodate wildlife preferring short vegetation next to the water. To make livestock watering sites compatible with wildlife, the habitat manager should consider the following (Yoakum et al. 1980):

1. Ensure that troughs and other water basins are over 50 cm high.

2. Install safety barricades (bars) in water developments to prevent possible entry and drowning by wildlife. The horizontal distance from the rim of the trough to the barricade should not be over 50 cm high.

3. Install escape ramps for ungulates in facilities where water depth exceeds 50 cm.

Figure 13.2 Waterlines can be developed off storage tanks to provide wildlife watering points.

4. Construct wildlife escape ladders which lead into and out of water facilities. Slope of escape ladders should be 30 to 45 degrees. One escape ladder per 10 m of perimeter is preferable.

5. Provide a floating platform in large, open storage tanks for birds to drink and escape (Fig. 13.3) (Wilson and Hannans 1977).

Discussion of management of livestock ponds, reservoirs, and other watering facilities relative to waterfowl and other waterbirds is found in Payne (1992). U.S. Bureau of Land Management (1967) and U.S. Forest Service (1972, 1974b) provided additional descriptions and illustrations of watering facilities for livestock, many of which could apply or be adapted to wildlife.

Managing Natural Watering Points

Management guidelines for naturally occurring water sources such as water holes, seeps and springs, and ponds include the following:

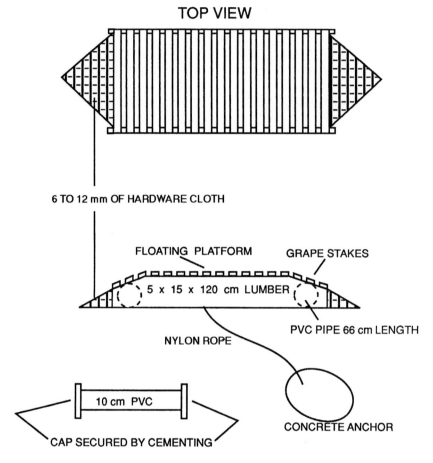

TOP VIEW

6 TO 12 mm OF HARDWARE CLOTH

FLOATING PLATFORM   GRAPE STAKES

5 x 15 x 120 cm LUMBER

PVC PIPE 66 cm LENGTH

NYLON ROPE

10 cm PVC

CAP SECURED BY CEMENTING

CONCRETE ANCHOR

Figure 13.3 Floating wildlife platform recommended for large, open, water storage tanks. (*Wilson and Hannans 1977.*)

1. Provide a natural drinking environment.
2. Maintain vegetation around the watering area.
3. Provide a large enough water development to supply water in all necessary seasons.
4. Fence the development from livestock (Fig. 13.4).
5. Provide such safety features as gentle basin slopes, ramps, and escape ladders (Figs. 13.5 and 13.6) (Payne and Copes 1988) (Figs. 13.7 and 13.8) (Wilson and Hannans 1977).

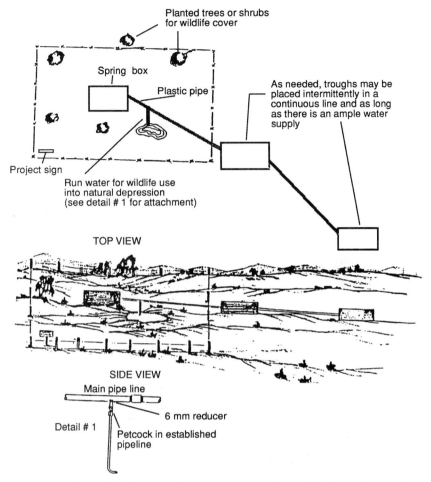

Planted trees or shrubs
for wildlife cover

Spring box

Plastic pipe

As needed, troughs may be
placed intermittently in a
continuous line and as long
as there is an ample water
supply

Project sign

Run water for wildlife use
into natural depression
(see detail # 1 for attachment)

TOP VIEW

SIDE VIEW

Main pipe line

6 mm reducer

Detail # 1

Petcock in established
pipeline

Figure 13.4 Water development for many uses can be modified for the benefit of
wildlife. This drawing of a spring improvement for livestock in Nevada included a side
basin installation for chukar partridge. (*Nevada State Office, U.S. Bureau of Land
Management.*)

Water holes are open water storage structures that occur naturally
in many habitats. Valuable water holes might need protection
through fencing. Water holes also can be improved by excavating the
basin itself or trenching runoff directly to the basin. In rocky areas
where rainfall is caught in rock basins, a sealer can even be used to
prevent percolation through porous rock.

Conflicts between domestic or feral ungulates can be remedied by
fencing designs (see Figs. 13.1, 13.2). Conflicts with people might
mean relocating campgrounds, trails, or roads.

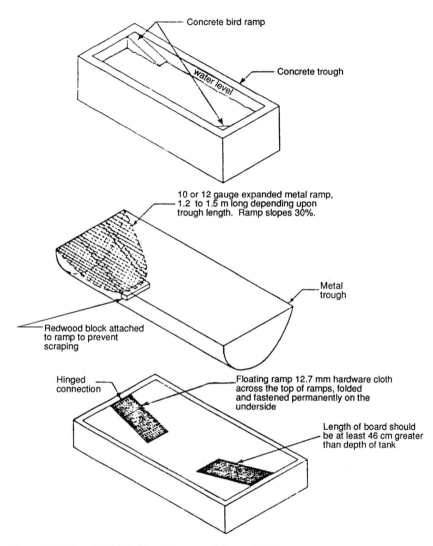

Figure 13.5 Trough bird ladder. (*Payne and Copes 1988.*)

Springs and seeps

Springs and seeps are among the most important watering points for terrestrial wildlife. Goerndt et al. (1985) described the difference between them. Springs have free-flowing water, while seeps usually keep soil moist or boggy. Springs and seeps can be found in secluded spots where water flows from them at lower temperatures and usually at higher quality than found standing in basins. Not only do wildlife species seek these areas for water, but associated microcli-

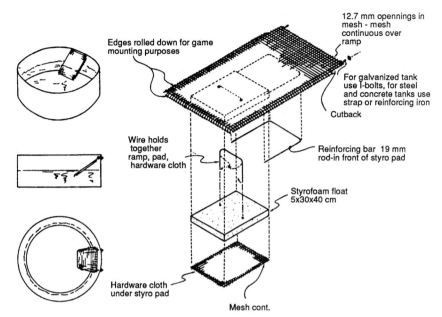

Figure 13.6 Small wildlife escape ramp. (*Payne and Copes 1988.*)

mates and food also make them attractive. Goerndt et al. (1985) reported that Merriam's turkey in New Mexico heavily used common watercress, which is usually associated with seeps and springs. They recommended locating, preserving, and protecting these and ensuring that suitable security cover exists near turkey habitat. To encourage productivity of watercress, they also recommended various techniques to slow water velocity, spread or diffuse water, and increase the area and depth of the substrate upon which watercress grows. Where natural ponds occur, management might be adaptable to guidelines previously mentioned. Use of guidelines depends on potential problems or conflicts with or between domestic, feral, and wild ungulates.

A spring or seep often needs an installation to make it a dependable water source (Figs. 13.9 and 13.10) (Rutherford and Snyder 1983, Payne and Copes 1988). The installation should be fenced to prevent trampling damage by animals. Payne and Copes (1988) provided construction procedures for springs and seeps. (See "Water and Riparian Areas" in Chap. 5, and "Water Holes" in Chap. 7.)

Riparian areas

See "Riparian Areas" in Chap. 6 and Payne (1992) for habitat management for rivers, creeks, and other free-flowing water sources and streamside vegetation.

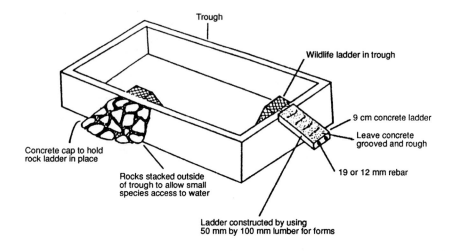

Trough

Wildlife ladder in trough

9 cm concrete ladder

Leave concrete
grooved and rough

Concrete cap to hold
rock ladder in place

19 or 12 mm rebar

Rocks stacked outside
of trough to allow small
species access to water

Ladder constructed by using
50 mm by 100 mm lumber for forms

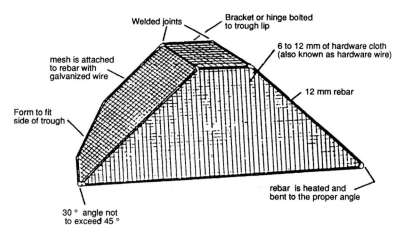

Welded joints

Bracket or hinge bolted
to trough lip

6 to 12 mm of hardware cloth
(also known as hardware wire)

mesh is attached
to rebar with
galvanized wire

12 mm rebar

Form to fit
side of trough

rebar is heated and
bent to the proper angle

30 ° angle not
to exceed 45 °

Figure 13.7   Concrete ramps for providing wildlife escape in livestock water trough (*top*) and details for a triangular-shaped wildlife ladder (*bottom*). (*Wilson and Hannans 1977.*)

Horizontal wells

Horizontal wells can be developed where historical springs and seeps occurred, where phreatophytes indicate a high water table, or where appropriate geological formations exist (Fig. 13.11) (Welchert and Freeman 1973, Bleich et al. 1982). Both dike-formation and contact-formation springs can occur. Drilling equipment to tap the aquifer must be relatively light and portable (about 400 to 600 kg) to be towed or heli-

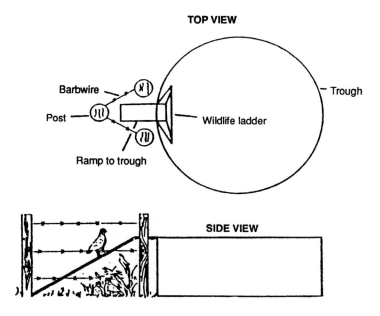

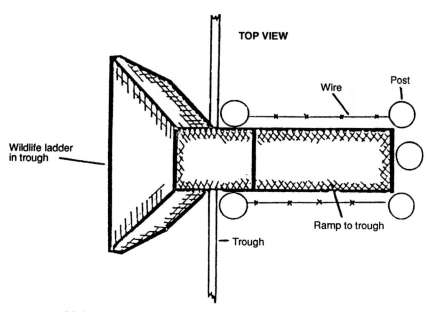

Figure 13.8 Modification of a livestock water trough with outside and inside ladder. (*Wilson and Hannans 1977.*)

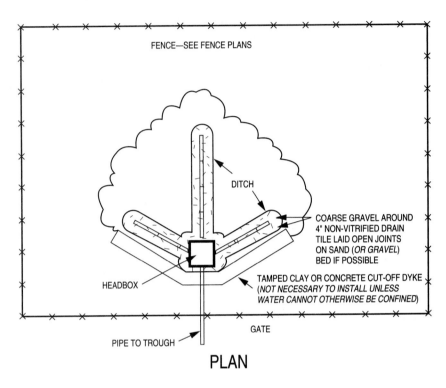

FENCE—SEE FENCE PLANS

DITCH

COARSE GRAVEL AROUND
4" NON-VITRIFIED DRAIN
TILE LAID OPEN JOINTS
ON SAND (*OR GRAVEL*)
BED IF POSSIBLE

TAMPED CLAY OR CONCRETE CUT-OFF DYKE
(*NOT NECESSARY TO INSTALL UNLESS
WATER CANNOT OTHERWISE BE CONFINED*)

HEADBOX

GATE

PIPE TO TROUGH

PLAN

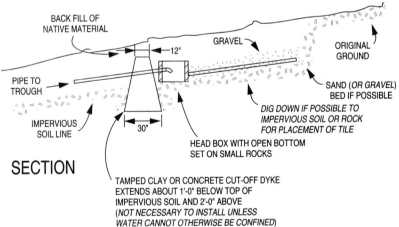

BACK FILL OF
NATIVE MATERIAL

GRAVEL

ORIGINAL
GROUND

12"

PIPE TO
TROUGH

SAND (*OR GRAVEL*)
BED IF POSSIBLE

DIG DOWN IF POSSIBLE TO
IMPERVIOUS SOIL OR ROCK
FOR PLACEMENT OF TILE

IMPERVIOUS
SOIL LINE

30"

HEAD BOX WITH OPEN BOTTOM
SET ON SMALL ROCKS

SECTION

TAMPED CLAY OR CONCRETE CUT-OFF DYKE
EXTENDS ABOUT 1'-0" BELOW TOP OF
IMPERVIOUS SOIL AND 2'-0" ABOVE
(*NOT NECESSARY TO INSTALL UNLESS
WATER CANNOT OTHERWISE BE CONFINED*)

Figure 13.9 Development designed to tap water in seeps or spring. (*Payne and Copes 1988.*)

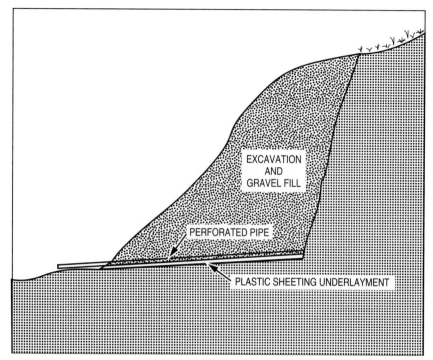

Figure 13.10 Simple construction technique to tap springs and seeps. (*Rutherford and Snyder 1983.*)

copter-lifted into rugged terrain. Where water is found, a 5-cm pipe is cemented in place, and a pipeline up to 16 km long can be run to a concrete drinking basin or commercial steel cattle trough with float valve.

Artificial Watering Points
Reservoirs and ponds

In the eastern United States, reservoirs and ponds are used often by wildlife. Construction of ponds in Alabama and Wisconsin is similar for depth (1.5 m), surface length (12 m), bottom dimensions (2.4 m by 4.8 m), and slope (1:1). A flat watering ramp should be provided at one end, the bottom of which should always reach the water level. Sod-forming grasses should be planted out to 6 m from the shoreline to reduce erosion potential; below the dam, planted vegetation cover should extend out 15 m. Birds prefer to water at earthen reservoirs more than at concrete troughs (Prasad and Guthery 1986).

In arid areas of the western United States and Canada, water development for livestock benefits wildlife (Crawford and Bolen 1976,

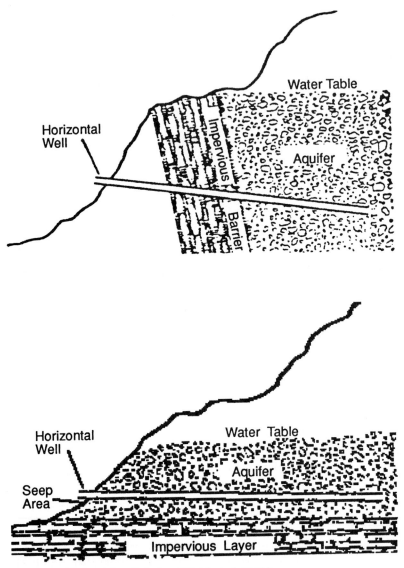

Figure 13.11   Horizontal well design. (*Bleich et al. 1982.*)

Holechek et al. 1989). In Arizona, ranchers excavated floodplains and built dams in canyons to catch and store flood waters. Although these might improve conditions for desert bighorns, their value was questionable because few attempts were made to keep water cool, prevent pollution, and retard evaporation (Halloran and Deming 1958).

Wildlife habitat below large reservoirs can degrade slowly over the years (Ohmart and Anderson 1986).

Another concern with ponds and reservoirs developed for livestock is intensive grazing and trampling of vegetation that can occur nearby (Soltero et al. 1989). Such trampling can reduce diversity, phytomass, vertical structure, and escape cover. Historically, this same effect might have been produced by bison (Holechek et al. 1989). Under proper livestock management around water sources in Texas, reservoirs received use by 66 bird and at least 4 mammal species (Prasad and Guthery 1986).

Ponds and reservoirs can be excavated or dammed, but they usually are located in focal points of a watershed to catch rainwater or snowmelt. Site selection is critical, as is the size of the drainage area needed for a desired storage capacity. The number of hectares of watershed or drainage area needed for the storage capacity of a reservoir 1 ha in size and 0.75 m deep varies across the United States and Canada. In the central plains of North America, drainage area varies from 5 ha in the eastern portion to 20 ha in the western part. In the drier, mountainous regions, drainage areas might exceed 50 ha. Payne and Copes (1988) offered guidelines for site selection:

1. When reservoirs are for livestock and wildlife only, they should be no larger than is needed to serve the forage base in which they are located.

2. The most suitable soils for dams are clays with a fair proportion of sand and gravel (1 part clay to 2 or 3 parts grit). Total clay soils crack badly upon drying and are apt to slip when wet.

3. The watershed above the dam should be large enough to provide enough water to fill the dam without excessive danger of flood damage.

4. The most economical site is one along a natural drainage where the channel is narrow and relatively deep, and the bottom is easily made watertight. The channel grade immediately above the dam should be as flat as possible.

5. Wildlife should have easy access.

6. If possible, the dam should be located to take advantage of natural spillway sites.

Consultation with engineers, soil scientists, and rangeland hydrologists is needed in the planning stages. Usually, state or provincial laws require such consultation before construction. A local government will know water laws concerning excavation and dams for ponds and reservoirs. Payne (1992) gave specifications for dam and spillway construction.

Sand dams

Sand dams are inexpensive and control evaporation of collected waters. Sites for sand dams include ephemeral streams in small- to medium-sized rocky canyons. Loose sand and gravel should be cleared from the rock bottom and a 2.5-cm galvanized outlet pipe should be built into the lowest point of a masonry dam at least 1 m high, and anchored to the rock base (Fig. 13.12) (Sivils and Brock 1981).

Numerous lengths of 30-cm-diameter aluminum pipe, with or without 1.3-cm holes drilled in the top third about 2.5 cm apart, should be placed upslope from the masonry dam to develop the holding basin. These could be attached to the outlet pipe (Bleich and Weaver 1983). A few large rocks or heavy wire screens over the end of the pipes will allow adequate filling and drainage. With a higher dam, the pipes should be layered to increase storage capacity, bolted together, and the bottom layer attached to the rock substrate with rebar or other

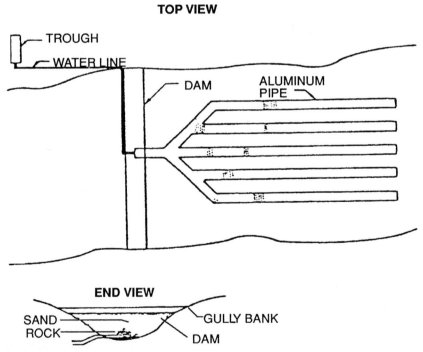

Figure 13.12   A schematic design of a sand dam for harvesting overland flow. (*Sivils and Brock 1981.*)

suitable material by drilling into the rock; this will anchor the system against heavy floods. The pipes must be covered with about 3 dm of coarse gravel and small rock, then 1 m of sand.

Plastic pipe connects the outlet pipe to a small trough with a float valve. To prevent jamming of the float valve by foreign objects, which would drain the trough, a 15-cm-diameter well screen (Johnson screen) 3 dm long should be capped with a bell reducer to a 5-cm outlet pipe on the upstream side of the dam. The water storage capacity of various-sized pipes that can be used in a sand dam water development is as follows (Sivils and Brock 1981): 4.3 L/dm in 15-cm (6-in) pipe, 8.7 L/dm in 30-cm (12-in) pipe, 12.9 L/dm in 46-cm (18-in) pipe, 17.2 L/dm in 61-cm (24-in) pipe. Gray (1974) provided additional guidelines for bighorns.

Dugouts

Smaller in size than reservoirs and ponds, *dugouts* (Fig. 13.13) (Yoakum et al. 1980) and *potholes* are artificial water developments which are excavated usually on flat, well-drained terrain. Payne (1992) described characteristics of dugouts (also called *pit tanks* or *pit reservoirs*) and potholes, and improvements for waterfowl. Rain-traps can be developed by using a storage pit (Fig. 13.14) (Payne and Copes 1988) or a storage bag (Fig. 13.15).

In playa basins of the southern high plains, dugouts have been excavated and are locally called *tailwater pits* because they are designed to receive overflow irrigation (see Payne 1992). Although poorly designed for wildlife use because of overall depth and steep shorelines, waterfowl and other birds use tailwater pits in periods when playa basins are dry.

In southeast Colorado, potholes have been blasted in wet meadows with dynamite (see Payne 1992) to provide sites for free water to accumulate for elk, mule deer, and Merriam's turkey, and in large slick rocks at least 1 m thick and 3 to 3.6 m in diameter that are sealed later with bentonite or commercial clay, if needed.

Guzzlers: permanent, self-filling water developments

For over four decades, the provision of guzzlers has been a popular technique for providing free water to wildlife in arid and semi-arid regions. First designed by Glading (1943), guzzlers have been modified many times. Even with all the modifications, a guzzler usually has three main components: (1) an apron to catch and channel water, (2) a cistern or storage tank, and (3) the basin ("guzzler") from which wildlife drink. Most guzzlers were designed initially for gallinaceous

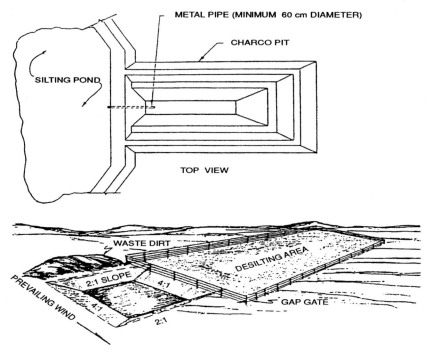

Figure 13.13 Schematic sketch of a "dugout" or charco pit used in the West for providing water on rangelands for livestock and wildlife. (*Nevada State Office, U.S. Bureau of Land Management.*)

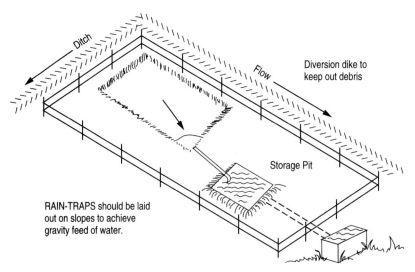

Figure 13.14 Design for a rain-trap that feeds a storage pit and trough. (*Payne and Copes 1988.*)

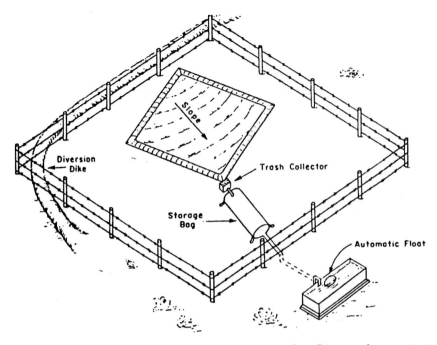

Figure 13.15 Design of a water trough that uses a storage bag. Diagram shows protected and sloped ground cover which collects precipitation for storage bag. Float maintains proper water level in tank.

birds (Glading 1947); hence the term *gallinaceous guzzler* was applied. Guzzlers probably were developed next as water sources for desert bighorn sheep (Halloran and Deming 1958). Today, they are constructed for many wildlife species (Remington et al. 1984, McCarty 1986).

Site location of the guzzler is critical. They should not be located where the terrain is too steep or in gullies where the guzzler could be washed out, damaged, or silted in by flood waters (Yoakum et al. 1980). If a natural apron is used instead of an artificial one, the area should not be so flat that rainfall or snowmelt is not properly trapped and channeled. The storage tank or cistern must be located where excavation is easiest. Other steps in the planning process were discussed earlier in this chapter.

The apron or catchment can be either natural or artificial. Natural aprons can include a large, slick rock to divert water to the cistern or the guzzler (Fig. 13.16) (U.S. Forest Service 1983), or simply a hillside steep enough and cleared of enough debris for runoff to occur (Elderkin and Morris 1989). The advantages of using natural aprons are that they are maintenance-free and cost less.

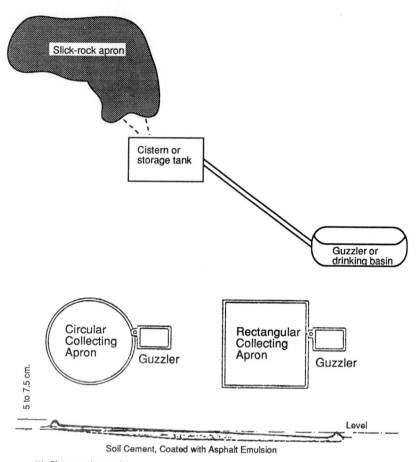

(1) Shape and smooth area
(2) Cover evenly with dry cement of rate of 1 sack for each 4.6 square meters, except on heavy clay soils, where use 1 sack for each 2.8 square meters
(3) Rake in thoroughly 64 - 76 mm
(4) Sprinkle thoroughly until soil wet 152 mm deep
(5) Paint or spray with asphalt emulsion as soon as possible after cement is set–always within 24 hours.

Figure 13.16   Slick-rick apron for guzzler (*top*), and water-collecting aprons for self-filling wildlife watering facility (*bottom*). (*U.S. Forest Service 1983.*)

Artificial aprons usually are constructed from corrugated sheets of fiberglass or galvanized iron. An *apron* is an elevated, rooflike structure that is pitched at about 5 percent at one end to catch rainwater and snow (Figs. 13.17 and 13.18) (Johnson and Jacobs 1986). Pitch should not be so great as to create rapid runoff or to permit heavy snow accumulations to slide off before they melt.

The formula to predict the size of the apron based on rainfall and storage capacity is as follows:

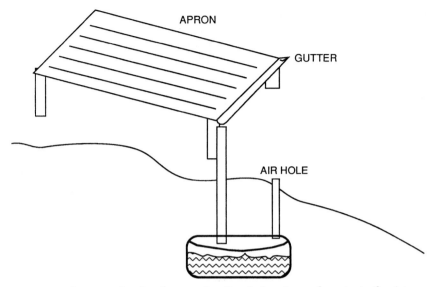

Figure 13.17 Apron can be of various construction designs to supply water to the cistern.

$$\text{Area (m}^2) = \frac{\text{capacity of cistern (L)} \times 0.99}{\text{minimum level of rainfall (mm)}}$$

Apron sizes for 2271-, 2650-, and 3407-L cisterns in various rainfall zones can be determined (Table 13.3) (Yoakum et al. 1980). Roberts (1977) developed an equation to predict the amount of water that is caught by a known-sized apron for every 2.5 cm of rainfall. Generally, an apron 14 m × 0.6 m would be fine for a rainfall zone of 20 to 30 cm/yr (McCarty 1986). A gutter usually is attached to collect and divert water to the cistern.

Cisterns should be made of galvanized iron. To prevent the stored water from freezing, they are buried or partially buried beneath the apron or at the point where the apron diverts maximum water flow. Water can be piped or channeled from the apron to the cistern if the terrain prohibits close proximity of the apron and cistern. Screens are used to prevent debris and animal matter from entering the cistern. Screens should be checked regularly. Cisterns should be dark to inhibit sunlight and algae growth, buried to prevent freezing, and cleaned every 2 years.

Water levels in the drinking basin usually can be controlled manually or automatically. A float valve in a container box separate from

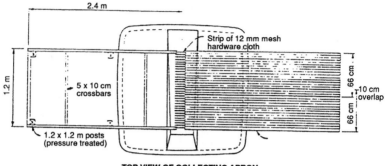

TOP VIEW OF COLLECTING APRON

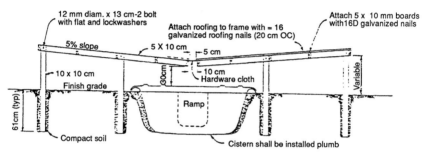

SIDE VIEW OF APRON AND CISTERN

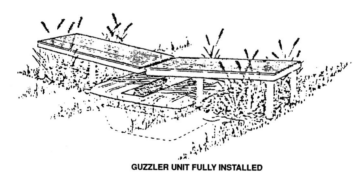

GUZZLER UNIT FULLY INSTALLED

Figure 13.18 A guzzler design with two aprons that feed water to the guzzler. (*Johnson and Jacobs 1986.*)

the basin works best (Fig. 13.19). This box and valve are buried in the ground below the cistern.

The basin from which animals drink is usually constructed of concrete. Although basin size is dictated by the kinds and sizes of animal to be watered, dimensions might be 70 to 76 cm in diameter and 15 to 20 cm deep. The basin also can consist of used tire sidewalls with

TABLE 13.3   Size of Apron Needed for 2271-, 2650-, and 3407-L Guzzlers

Mini-mum annual rainfall (cm)	Collecting surface required (m²)			Apron dimension (dm)					
				Square apron			Circular apron (diameter)		
	2271 L	2650 L	3407 L	2271 L	2650 L	3407 L	2271 L	2650 L	3407 L
2.5	90	105	135	93	102	114	108	114	129
5.1	45	54	68	66	72	81	75	81	93
7.6	30	35	45	54	57	66	60	66	75
10.2	23	26	34	48	51	57	54	57	66
12.7	18	21	27	42	45	51	48	51	57
15.2	15	18	23	39	42	45	45	48	54
17.8	13	15	19	36	39	42	39	42	48
20.3	11	13	17	33	36	42	36	39	45
22.9	10	12	15	33	36	39	36	39	42
25.4	9	11	14	30	33	36	33	36	42
27.9	8	10	12	27	30	33	30	33	39
30.5	7	9	11	27	30	33	30	33	36

SOURCE: Yoakum et al. (1980).

Cistern

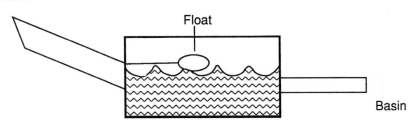

Figure 13.19 Float valve installed to regulate flow from the cistern to the drinking basin, or guzzler.

"corten" plate steel, concrete, or clay bottom (Figs. 13.20, 13.21, 13.22), or a fiberglass dish can be manufactured to fit any specifications (Elderkin and Morris 1989).

A self-contained guzzler of a single unit can be constructed from a heavy-equipment tire, partly buried in a hillside steep enough for runoff (35 percent slope or less) (Fig. 13.23) (Elderkin and Morris 1989). The runoff is channeled directly into the tire, which serves as cistern and drinking basin. The apron is a natural area at least 15 m by 6 m. Designed for chukar partridge, the basin is covered to prevent large animals from drinking and to shade the cistern–water basin to decrease algal growth.

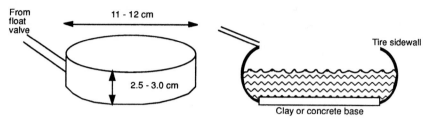

Figure 13.20   Guzzler design.

Pipelines, spurlines, and overflow pipes

Managers often develop secondary water sources for wildlife by tapping into ponds, reservoirs, water wells, or storage tanks (Fig. 13.24) (U.S. Forest Service, undated pamphlet). Pipe and gravity flow are combined to deliver water to drinking basins for wildlife. Unless gopher damage is a potential problem, plastic pipe usually is preferred to galvanized pipe because it can be transported easily to remote sites (Yoakum et al. 1980). Pipe specifications vary (see Table A.18). Several spurlines can be developed off one pipeline to distribute water. Pipelines and spurlines are expensive and might need extra maintenance, because they are usually buried for aesthetics or to prevent freezing or trampling.

The drinking basin must be fenced where damage or disturbance could arise from domestic, feral, or wild ungulates. Such basins should be 50 to 100 m from the source. At least 0.5 m of steel pipe should be used at the point of entry into the pipeline (storage tank or pond) and at the point of delivery (drinking basin). Plastic pipe should be used in between. A float valve and container box might be needed to regulate water levels in the drinking basin. Pipe must be laid to grade to prevent air blocks (Yoakum et al. 1980).

Overflow pipes must be installed on livestock drinking troughs or storage tanks. They can be so simple as to permit water to puddle or run over on the surface. More sophisticated designs include a water basin constructed 50 to 100 m away with a pipeline, connected to the overflow pipe to deliver water to the basin. Overflow pipes work well in dry regions where livestock water is pumped by windmill into a large storage tank. If overflow is unavailable, turkeys, songbirds, or even small mammals often drown in the concrete or metal storage tank by attempting to drink from the tank when the water level is low.

In Texas, where northern bobwhite quail are managed intensively, pipelines, spurlines, and overflow pipes are used to deliver water to specially designed drinking basins. Sometimes, temporary wildlife watering facilities are used (Fig. 13.25). Providing free water for

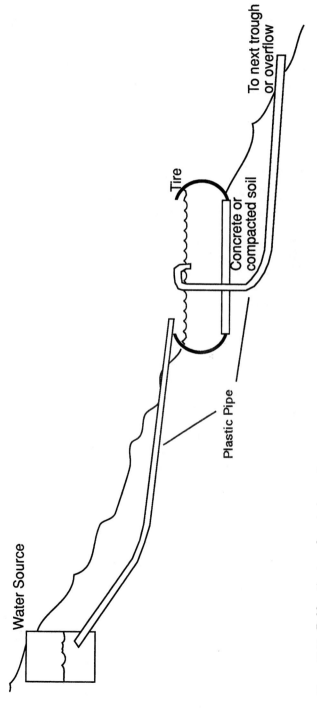

Figure 13.21 Rubber tire trough watering system.

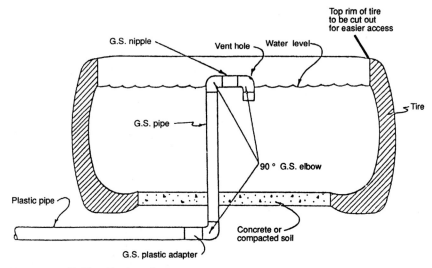

Figure 13.22 Rubber tire trough.

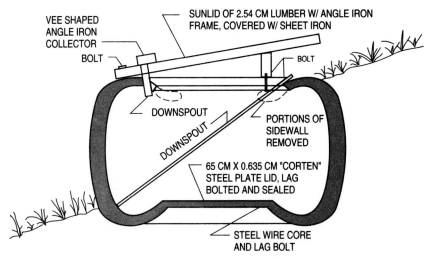

Figure 13.23 A simple guzzler with a tire to catch runoff water from an upland slope. (*Elderkin and Morris 1989.*)

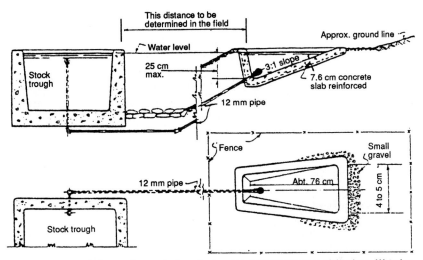

Note: This installation can be used where the troughs are kept full most of the time. Watering stations are to be fenced from stock.

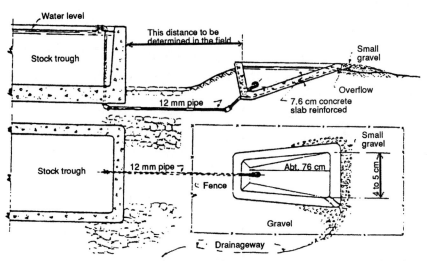

Note: This installation can be used when a fairly constant overflow can be expected from the throughs. A very good watering station for Sagehens.

Figure 13.24 Wildlife watering facility near stock trough. (*U.S. Forest Service.*)

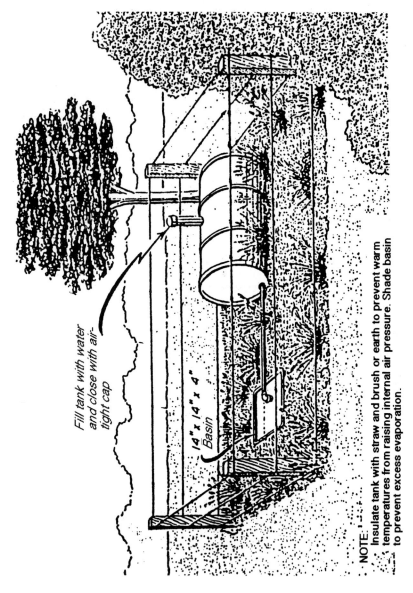

Fill tank with water and close with air-tight cap

14" x 14" x 4" Basin

NOTE:
Insulate tank with straw and brush or earth to prevent warm temperatures from raising internal air pressure. Shade basin to prevent excess evaporation.

Figure 13.25 Temporary wildlife watering facility. (*U.S. Soil Conservation Service.*)

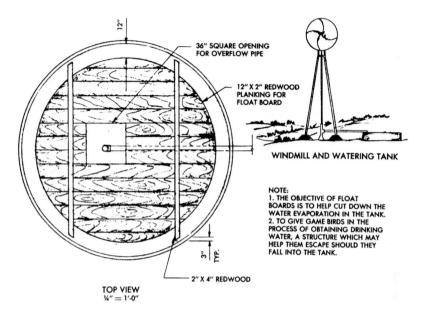

36" SQUARE OPENING
FOR OVERFLOW PIPE

12" X 2" REDWOOD
PLANKING FOR
FLOAT BOARD

WINDMILL AND WATERING TANK

NOTE:
1. THE OBJECTIVE OF FLOAT
BOARDS IS TO HELP CUT DOWN THE
WATER EVAPORATION IN THE TANK.
2. TO GIVE GAME BIRDS IN THE
PROCESS OF OBTAINING DRINKING
WATER, A STRUCTURE WHICH MAY
HELP THEM ESCAPE SHOULD THEY
FALL INTO THE TANK.

2" X 4" REDWOOD

TOP VIEW
¼" = 1'-0"

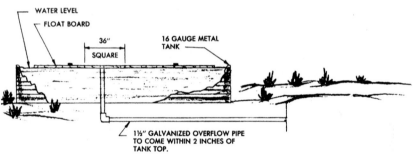

WATER LEVEL

FLOAT BOARD

36"
SQUARE

16 GAUGE METAL
TANK

1½" GALVANIZED OVERFLOW PIPE
TO COME WITHIN 2 INCHES OF
TANK TOP.

SIDE VIEW
¼" = 1'-0"

Figure 13.26 The simple round float board illustrated prevents drowning of wild birds by providing an area for them to drink at round water troughs. (*Nevada State Office, U.S. Bureau of Land Management*) [For metric equivalence, see metric conversion table in the front of the book.]

northern bobwhite quail in drier areas (less than 80 cm rainfall) might increase populations by dispersing quail into unused habitats.

Safety devices and special features

To avoid drowning small birds and mammals and to enhance water availability, adequate water levels should be maintained in concrete or metal water troughs and storage tanks. The water level should be no less than 5 cm from the lip of the tank or trough (Prasad and Guthery 1986). Escape ramps or ladders must be provided in any facility and installed so they cannot be damaged by domestic or wild ungulates (Yoakum et al. 1980). Yoakum et al. (1980) illustrated how a "wildlife saver" float board can be installed to prevent wildlife from drowning (Fig. 13.26).

Water quality

Water quality standards for upland wildlife have seldom been studied. The suggested upper limits for total dissolved solids and pH are 5000 mg/L and 9.2, respectively. Quality standards which will support aquatic organisms probably will not be detrimental to upland wildlife. Cuplin (1986a, 1986b) reported acceptable standards of most chemical elements and compounds for aquatic organisms. Managers need not worry about water quality for ungulates unless evidence suggests otherwise (Boyd et al. 1986).

14

Fences and Underpasses

Fences usually are used to control domestic livestock. For wildlife, fences have various effects: they can (1) hinder wildlife movements; (2) concentrate livestock in critical wildlife habitats; (3) entangle large animals, causing death or crippling; (4) protect wildlife habitat from livestock overgrazing or trampling; and (5) exclude nuisance wildlife from areas such as cropland, orchards, airports, and highway rights-of-way. Seamans (1951), Longhurst et al. (1962), Spillet et al. (1967), the U.S. Forest Service (1972), the U.S. Bureau of Land Management (1974, 1975), Karsky (1988), and others presented thorough descriptions and illustrations of various types of fences, passes, and enclosures suitable or adaptable to wildlife. Summaries of different kinds of fences are found in Table A.19 and A.20.

Fence Design
To aid wildlife movement

General guidelines for fence design and construction that do not hinder wildlife movements include the following:

1. Avoid using net wire or woven wire. These are the most difficult fences for wildlife to cross.

2. Avoid loose wire on a fence. It is easier for animals to become entangled in a fence that is loosely constructed or not maintained. Properly tightened wire is much easier for animals to cross.

3. Use smooth wire rather than barbed wire to prevent cuts and scrapes on animals crossing the fence. Because white-tailed and

mule deer prefer to jump a fence or go under it, and pronghorns prefer to go under it, replacing the top and bottom strands of a barbed wire fence with smooth wire is recommended.

4. Use as few strands of wire as possible. Two strands are better than three, and three are better than four.

5. Fence dimensions and wire spacings are critical so as not to impede wildlife movement. Several designs for spacing were developed for livestock and pronghorns (Fig. 14.1) (Karsky 1988). Maximum height of the top wire should be 120 cm (Karsky 1988, Howard 1991). Autenrieth (1978) suggested a maximum height of 86 cm for buck-and-pole fences. Because white-tailed deer and mule deer nor-

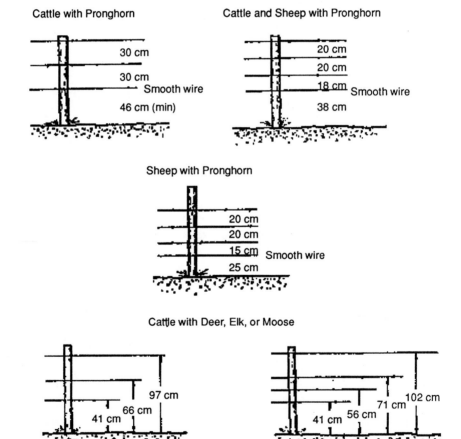

Figure 14.1 Spacing of fence wire to accommodate wild ungulates and livestock. (*Karsky 1988.*)

mally jump with their hind legs forward, the distance between the top and next wire should be at least 25 cm. This reduces the chance of their hind legs becoming entangled as they cross. Elk and moose drag their hind legs over the top wire, so entanglement is not as much of a concern. Minimum height from the ground to the bottom wire should be 40 cm for deer and 46 cm for pronghorns. Otherwise, antelope passes using cattleguards should be located in fence corners or offsets (Mapston and Zobell 1972, Yoakum et al. 1980).

6. In areas of heavy seasonal movements, along migration routes, or where topographical or habitat features restrict or concentrate wildlife movements, the preferred fence is a wood fence. Wood fences improve visual appraisal of fence location and dimensions so wildlife can negotiate the fence without causing damage to themselves. But wooden buck-and-pole fences are difficult for elk and bison to negotiate unless gates are left open (Scott 1992). Replacing the top wire with a top rail log or wood stay will help ungulates pass at known animal crossing points.

7. Fence adjustments greatly assist wildlife movements. These include adjustable fence segments (Fig. 14.2) (Karsky 1988), let-down fences (Fig. 14.3) (Karsky 1988), swing-back fences, and gate modifications. If such adjustments are planned during fence construction, fences are easily manipulated during harsh conditions or during times when livestock are absent and restricting their movements is unnecessary.

8. Use snowfences to reduce snow depths in shrub stands, thus facilitating deer use and creating drifts deep enough to protect overused and newly seeded areas (Regelin et al. 1977).

To restrict wildlife movement

Fencing to restrict or exclude wild ungulates and bears might be needed to protect them, and humans, from harm (e.g., along highways); to reduce agricultural damage; or to protect critical habitats from excessive grazing and browsing by wild ungulates (e.g., to improve forest regeneration or reduce degradation of riparian zones). In instances where wild ungulates must be excluded, some useful guidelines include the following:

1. To exclude white-tailed deer and mule deer, a fence must be at least 200 cm high (Karsky 1988). Twelve strands of single wire or three strands of net or woven wire, with each fence 70 cm tall, would exclude deer. Electric fences also have application; some designs are slanted at an angle to provide an even more effective barrier (Fig. 14.4) (Karsky 1988). The Cooperative Extension Service at Pennsylvania State

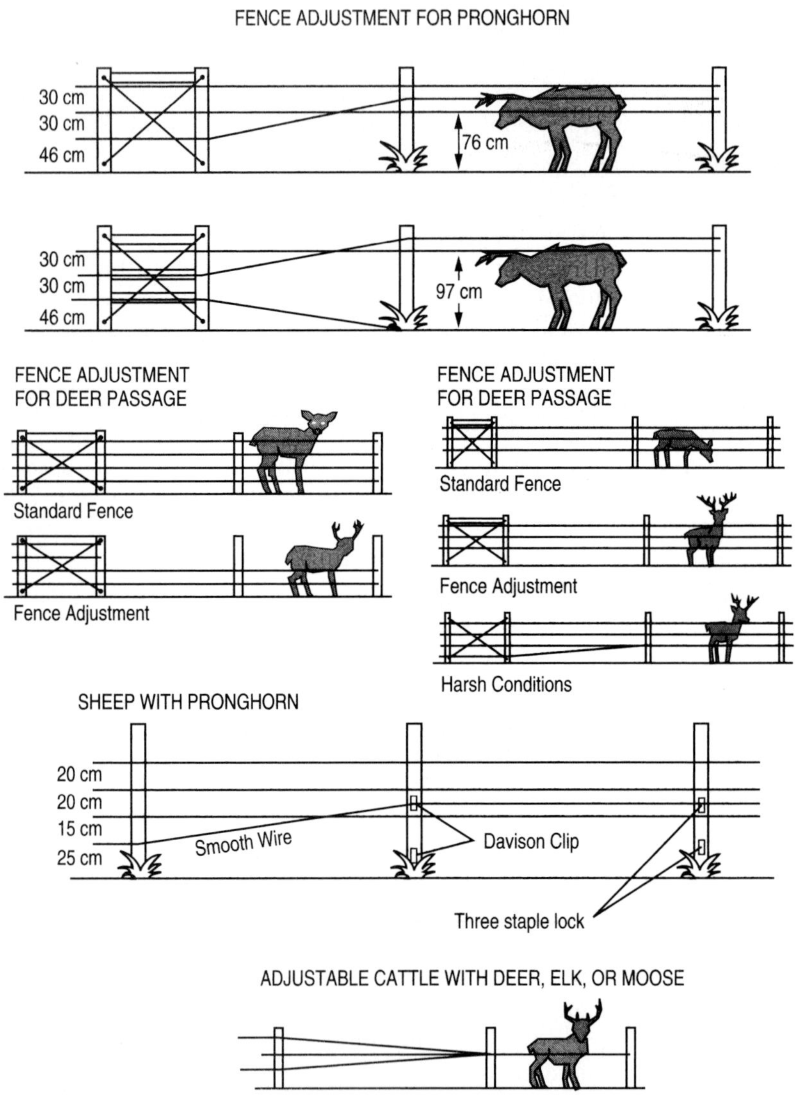

Figure 14.2 Fence adjustment to accommodate wild ungulates and livestock. (*Karsky 1988.*)

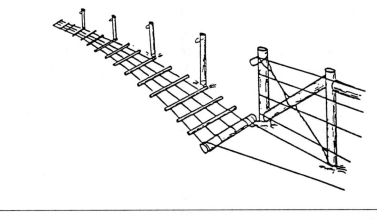

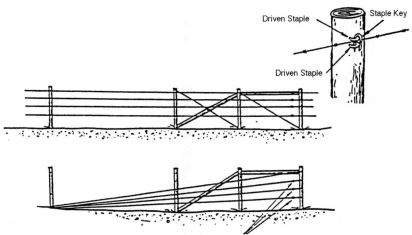

Figure 14.3 Let-down fences to permit wildlife to cross. (*Karsky 1988.*)

University developed a five-strand, high-tensile 12½-gauge steel wire fence electrified by a high-voltage, low-impedance, New Zealand–style energizer. The bottom wire is 25 cm off the ground, the other wires are 30.5 cm apart. Hollows should be filled, humps graded, and brush removed from the fence line. An open strip 2 to 2.67 m outside the fence should be maintained so that deer will walk toward the fence and not jump brush and fence alike. Temporary flagging should be attached to any new fence.

2. Bison will be excluded by a 12-strand fence and elk by a 15-strand fence. To deter elk from jumping, minimum height should be about 250 cm.

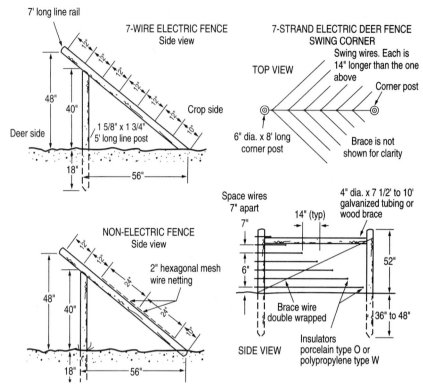

Figure 14.4   Design for slanted antideer electric fence. (*Karsky 1988.*) [For metric equivalence, see metric conversion table in the front of the book.]

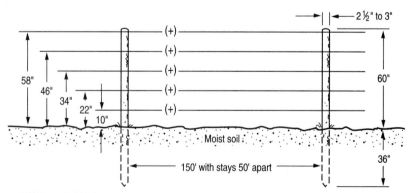

Figure 14.5   A five-strand electric fence to protect areas from bears. (*Karsky 1988.*) [For metric equivalence, see metric conversion table in the front of the book.]

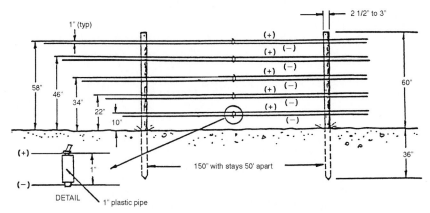

Figure 14.6 A bear fence with five sets of hot and ground wires. (*Karsky 1988.*) [For metric equivalence, see metric conversion table in the front of the book.]

3. Bears can be deterred if electric fence is used. Two fence designs are commonly used: one with five strands of wire, all charged electrically (Fig. 14.5) (Karsky 1988), the other with ten strands of wire, arranged as five sets of hot wire and ground wire connected by a plastic separator which keeps them 2.5 cm apart (Fig. 14.6) (Karsky 1988). Height of both fences should be 145 cm.

4. Anticoyote fences have been designed with 8 to 14 strands of alternating hot and ground wires at 10- to 20-cm spacings (Fig 14.7) (Karsky 1988). Recommended number of strands is 12 to 14. Recommended heights vary from 180 to 240 cm. One design includes a trip wire 20 cm from the fence, placed at a height of 15 cm to deter coyotes from crawling under. Howard (1991) determined that a seven-strand electrified anticoyote fence was a major barrier to mule deer in New Mexico. These types of fences should not be used in areas that serve as major movement or migration corridors.

Fence Location

Many types of habitat can be protected and enhanced with the help of a livestock fence. Fencing that permits grazing systems to be applied (see Chap. 10) or permits livestock exclusion on unique and critical habitats for all or part of the year can reduce or eliminate damage associated with trampling and grazing. Fencing around sloughs, riparian zones, and other wetland sites allows these areas to be rested or deferred from use by livestock or wild ungulates if needed. Livestock can be excluded periodically any time of the year or when desired use rates have been achieved.

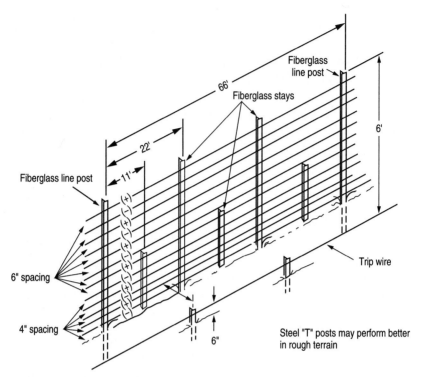

Figure 14.7 An electrically charged, 12-wire anticoyote fence. (*Karsky 1988.*) [For metric equivalence, see metric conversion table in the front of the book.]

Fencing livestock out of woodlots can make the areas more productive for several wildlife species. Similarly, fencing the perimeter of selected areas of meadow, pastures, and rangeland can help provide critical winter and spring forage for wild ungulates. Nesting waterfowl benefit from fencing if a 30- to 60-m buffer is left around the wetland perimeter (Payne 1992). Suggestions for locating fences include the following:

1. Avoid placing a fence on a steep hillside. A fence located on a hillside can be very difficult for animals to cross. The steeper the slope, the more difficult a barrier the fence becomes (Fig. 14.8) (Karsky 1988). If a hillside must be fenced, locate the fence straight up the slope rather than along the slope contour.

2. Where possible, in pronghorn range, locate fences in areas which are naturally windswept, to keep the fence clear of snow.

3. Place fences at least 4 to 6 m from the edge of brushy cover, so that animals will see the fence and avoid entanglement.

Figure 14.8 The barrier height of any fence is increased with the increase of ground slope for deer, elk, or moose. (*Karsky 1988.*) [For metric equivalence, see metric conversion table in the front of the book.]

4. Leave a margin of 4 to 6 m of natural vegetation next to a new fence line in farmland habitats. A band of native cover will provide travel corridors and nesting cover for many wildlife species.

5. When locating a new fence in a forested or brushy area, keep the sight line (the distance that can be seen down the fence line) to less than 360 m. Wild ungulates will be less resistant to crossing the fence and less vulnerable to human harassment (Alberta Fish and Wildlife Pub. No. 1/131, No.10).

Underpasses

Highways fragment habitat and disrupt or impede animal movements. Where highways cross migration routes or travel corridors of large mammals, mortality can be high and damage to vehicles and injury to humans frequent. Underpasses offer a solution. General recommendations for underpasses include the following. (Singer and Doherty 1985):

1. Locate bridges and underpasses on traditional crossing routes.

2. Do not make underpasses confining by making them too small or placing them in inappropriate locations.

TABLE 14.1   Dimensions of Underpasses Used by Mule Deer in Wyoming

Underpass	Length (m)	Width (m)	Height (m)
Machinery 1	60	9	4.5
Machinery 2	33	9	4
Box 1	46	3	3
Box 2	85	3	3
Box 3	119	3	3

Note: Machinery underpasses had dirt floors. Box underpasses had concrete roofs, floors, and sides.
SOURCE: Ward (1982).

3. Locate underpasses where shielding cover is present to reduce disturbance from vehicle traffic; plant shielding cover such as conifers at or near the areas where animals approach the underpass.

4. Place fences in the general direction of ungulate movements.

Two underpass designs used in Wyoming reduced vehicle-deer accidents by 90 percent (Ward 1982). Ward (1982) evaluated deer use of a machinery underpass, a bridge with supports that hold up the road above and with a dirt floor beneath. These are places where farm machinery often passes under highways. Also evaluated were box underpasses that have concrete walls and floors and are similar to a square culvert. Dimensions varied (Table 14.1) (Ward 1982). Concrete box underpasses, 3 m by 3 m by 30 m, were used by deer in Colorado (Pojar et al. 1973, Reed et al. 1975). Mountain goats readily use underpasses in Glacier National Park (Singer and Doherty 1985). Dimensions of underpasses built exclusively for mountain goats were 3 to 8 m high by 2.3 m wide by 11 m. Goats also used an underpass of 3 by 3 by 11 m. Moose need a path at least 3.5 m high; bridge designs for Florida panthers called for lengths of 30 m and heights of 3 m (Harris and Scheck 1991). Foster and Humphrey (1991) also reported on use of underpasses by panthers.

Mule deer in Wyoming used the machinery overpass more than the box design, probably because one of the machinery overpasses was nearest the traditional migration route (Ward 1982). At first, deer might have to be baited to the underpasses. But once they are accustomed to using them, deer use will continue. Fencing designs at least 2.4 m tall, with 1.6-km extension wings and one-way gates installed were effective in directing deer movements to underpasses (Reed et al. 1974, Ward 1982).

15

Brush Piles,
Rock Piles,
Nests, and Dens

Brush Piles and Rock Piles

For some species of wildlife, construction of brush piles and rock piles is one of the easiest and quickest means of providing security, thermal, and loafing cover where natural cover is limited. Quail, grouse, turkey, and various songbirds use brush piles. Mammals also use brush piles and rock piles. These include skunks, raccoons, opossums, river otters, woodchucks, ground squirrels, rabbits, woodrats, and small mammals (Yoakum et al. 1980, Webb and Guthery 1982, 1983, Mettler 1984, Martin and Steele 1986).

Placement and spacing

Brush piles and rock piles should be located near sources of food and other types of cover. Nearby locations could include:

1. Food plots
2. Unused fence/field corners
3. Other rock piles and brush piles
4. Fencerows, hedgerows, and shelterbelts
5. Large clearings
6. Woodland field borders

7. Sides of gullies

8. Unused cropland

9. Grazed pastures

10. Open rangeland

11. Water developments (reservoirs, ponds, dugouts, guzzlers)

Generally, 2 to 10 brush piles per hectare are enough for smaller, less mobile wildlife such as quail or rabbits (Giles 1978). Brush piles and rock piles should be 30 to 60 m apart (U.S. Army Corps of Engineers 1977, Martin and Steele 1984). If placed in areas devoid of conceal-ment cover or shelter, brush piles provide stepping stones or travel corridors to connect other suitable habitats for many wildlife species. For most wildlife, brush piles and rock piles should be within 0.5 km of water and within 50 to 150 m of food or cover (Martin and Steele 1984).

Brush piles should not be placed in the middle of an eroding gully, where they might be washed away, or along well-used roadsides (Allen 1969). Roadside locations place wildlife and vehicles in jeop-ardy from each other. Brush piles used as roosts for California quail are recommended within 15 m of brushy cover and within 1 km of water (Kosciuk and Peloquin 1986). Platform roosts for northern bob-white quail and Gambel's quail should be within 90 m of escape cover (Goodwin and Hungerford 1977).

Materials and construction

Brush piles.   Brush piles can be constructed with just about any material (Fig. 15.1) (Connors undated). Slash and debris from tree-harvesting, -pruning, or -clearing operations make excellent brush piles. Unmerchantable logs and poles, old fence posts, and downed trees also can be used. Most brush piles are 1.5 to 2.5 m tall and 4 to 10 m across (Steele 1984, Martin and Steele 1986).

Ground-level clearance should be 15 to 30 cm depending upon tar-get wildlife species. Metal grills (2.5 by 2.5 m), supported by cinder blocks or pipe and piled with brush, were used by northern bobwhite quail and scaled quail in Texas (Guthery 1980) (Fig. 15.2) (MacGregor 1950, Kosciuk and Peloquin 1986). Raised platform roosts topped with brush have been used by California quail and Gambel's quail (Figs. 15.3 and 15.4) (U.S. Army Corps of Engineers 1979, Kosciuk and Peloquin 1986). Brush platforms designed for javelina were 1 m tall and 2 m long by 2 m wide (Yoakum et al. 1980). Besides brush mounds and platforms, tepee shelters also are used. These are made by stacking 2-m-high logs together perpendicular to the ground and

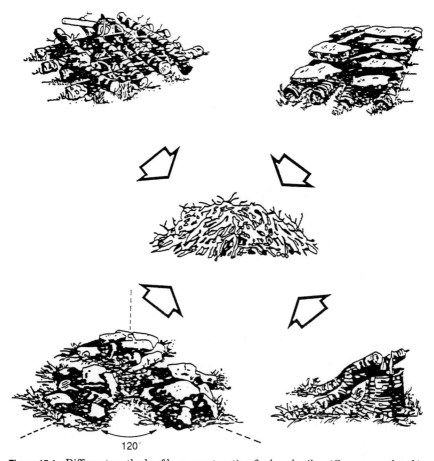

Figure 15.1   Different methods of base construction for brush piles. (*Connors undated.*)

joined at the top. Tepee structures might be more effective on sites with little woody cover; brush mounds and platforms might prove more useful in taller herbaceous cover (Boyer et al. 1988).

Rock piles.   Rock piles provide cover for various wildlife if the piles are large enough to provide an interior climate with a fairly stable temperature and humidity (Ambrose et al. 1983, Proctor et al. 1983a, 1983b). Rocks of any size larger than 20 to 30 cm in diameter can be used to construct rock piles. Coarse rocks over 50 cm in diameter should be on the bottom so that a maze of spaces occurs within the pile. Three rock piles 2 m apart, each 3 to 4 m across, and 1 to 2 m tall, provide adjoining microhabitats for small mammals and herp-

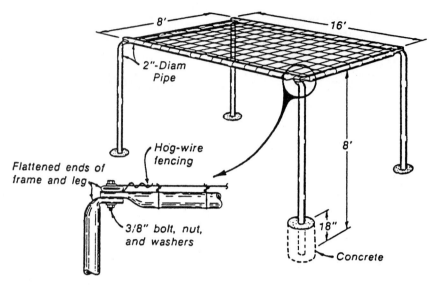

Figure 15.2   Construction and assembly details for pipe roost. (*MacGregor 1950.*) [For metric equivalence, see metric conversion table in the front of the book.]

tiles. Thus, several such rock piles are better than one large pile. Rock piles should occupy an area of about 10 m² (Green and Salter 1987).

Burger (1969) constructed an igloo-shaped rock and brush pile and left a 10- to 15-cm-wide tunnel system with two to three exits for rabbits. Similar structures of stones, iron, and brush have been used (National Audubon Society 1969, Giles 1978).

The more irregular the edge of the rock pile, the more value it will have for wildlife. Rocks are placed with use of a front-end loader and dump truck. About three to five rock piles should be built per hectare near habitat such as other cover, feeding areas, or water.

Rock piles intended as raptor perches or nests should be located on the leeward side of hills near ridgetops. Rock piles for small mammals should be placed along valley bottoms, in draws, on protected hillsides, and in other protected areas (Green and Salter 1987).

Artificial teepees.   In grassland and prairie habitats, artificial structures such as teepees are used by ground-dwelling fauna. Teepees are constructed with 10 to 20 railroad ties or wooden fenceposts, wired together at the top and spread out at the bottom to form a base. Teepees are cooler, more humid, and block solar radiation and light intensity better than unsheltered areas (Boyer et al. 1988). Northern

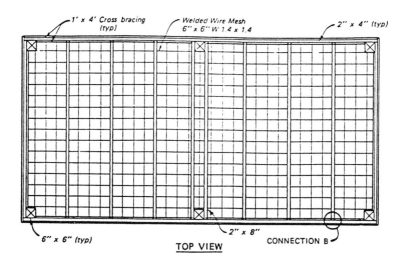

1' x 4' Cross bracing (typ)

Welded Wire Mesh 6" x 6" W 1.4 x 1.4

2" x 4" (typ)

6" x 6" (typ)

2" x 8"

CONNECTION B

TOP VIEW

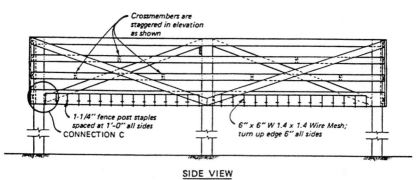

Crossmembers are staggered in elevation as shown

1-1/4" fence post staples spaced at 1'-0" all sides
CONNECTION C

6" x 6" W 1.4 x 1.4 Wire Mesh; turn up edge 6" all sides

SIDE VIEW

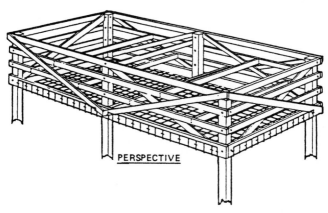

PERSPECTIVE

Figure 15.3 Roost plan, showing top view of wire mesh floor, side view of frame, and perspective of the completed roost. (*U.S. Army Corps of Engineers 1979, Kosciuk and Peloquin 1986.*) [For metric equivalence, see metric conversion table.]

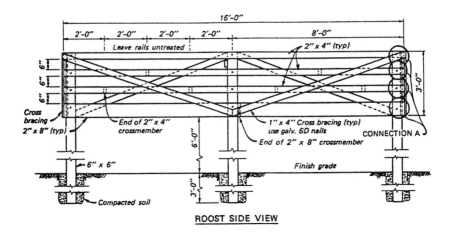

ROOST SIDE VIEW

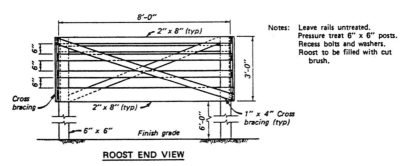

ROOST END VIEW

Figure 15.4 Construction and assembly details for elevated quail roost. (*U.S. Army Corps of Engineers 1979, Kosciuk and Peloquin 1986.*) [For metric equivalence, see metric conversion table in the front of the book.]

bobwhite quail prefer teepees to other forms of artificial shelter. Clusters of four to six teepees spaced 10 m apart were used by northern bobwhite quail (Beasom et al. 1991). Such clusters had a neutral to positive effect for nongame birds (Guthery et al. 1991).

Living brush piles. *Living brush piles,* or *half-cuts,* are constructed by cutting partway through the trunks of saplings or small deciduous trees (Fig. 15.5). The objective is to provide cover on or near the ground without killing the plant. For trees to be cut, diameter at breast height should be at least 10 cm. Normally, a cluster of four to six trees or a multistemmed tree (e.g., mesquite) can be cut at a height of 15 to 90 cm, depending upon tree species, wildlife species, and desired access at ground level.

Figure 15.5   A living brush pile. (*Connors undated.*)

TABLE 15.1   **Potential Trees for Living Brush Piles**

South	Midwest	West
Willow	Willow	Willow
Mesquite	Chinaberry	California live oak
Live oak	Yaupon	Buckthorn
Hackberry	Hackberry	Toyon
Elm	Post oak	Chokecherry
Blackjack oak	Blackjack oak	Aspen
Post oak	Ash	Maple
Ash	Maple	
	Hawthorn	
	Birch	
	Elm	
	Soapberry	
	Aspen	

SOURCE: Adapted from Steele and Martin (1986).

Once trees are cut, the treetops are bent toward a common center (Fig. 15.5). To ensure that the tree does not die immediately, a hinge of wood and bark must be left intact. Trees must be selected which are not so brittle as to break off cleanly when the top is felled (Table 15.1) (Leopold 1977, Steele and Martin 1986). To increase the food value of half-cuts, trees that harbor such fruit-producing vines as grape, greenbrier, and rattan could be selected (Lay 1965, National Audubon Society 1969). Cuts should be made in the spring after sap has risen and leaves have matured (Steele and Martin 1986). The cut trunk will lie almost parallel to the ground when properly cut.

Another type of living brush pile can be made by slicing partway into the top of each limb in the bottom two or three whorls of branches on a conifer, and pushing the branches down to form a "teepee" (Decker and Kelly undated, Gutiérrez et al. 1984). Large branches of deciduous trees can be cut partway and bent down too.

Maintenance and longevity

Brush piles should be inspected periodically and refurbished with new limbs and branches as old material rots and limbs become dislodged (Martin and Steele 1986). Though unnecessary in the Southwest and arid regions, one-third to one-fourth of the brush piles in mesic regions should be replaced annually (Chapman et al. 1982). Structures that have lost their value can be removed by burning.

Living brush piles of American elm lasted 3 years in Oklahoma (Steele and Martin 1986). In Texas, mesquite half-cuts lived 5 years (Webb and Guthery 1982).

Nest Structures and Perches

Squirrel nest boxes

Tree cavities are superior nest sites for gray squirrels and fox squirrels (Teaford 1986a). Artificial nesting structures can increase squirrel use of an area and increase carrying capacity (Flyger and Cooper 1967, Burger 1969, Nixon and Donohoe 1979) if natural den sites are inadequate. Other mammals known to use squirrel nest boxes are opossums, red squirrels, southern flying squirrels, and mice (*Peromyscus* spp.) (Hesselschwerdt 1942, McComb and Noble 1981).

Placement.   Nest boxes for squirrels are most effective when placed in immature pole-timber hardwood stands (20 to 30 dbh) where food is present but den sites are lacking (Burger 1969, Nixon and Donohoe 1979). Even-aged oak-hickory stands 30 to 60 years old are excellent candidates (Nixon and Donohoe 1979); mixed hardwood-pine stands with adequate food also show increases in squirrels.

The number of squirrel nest boxes per hectare varies from 0.5 for optimum benefits to 6 to 12 where squirrels are the highest priority. Most boxes should be placed 6 to 8 m above the ground (Teaford 1986b) (Fig. 15.6) (Barkalow and Soots 1965).

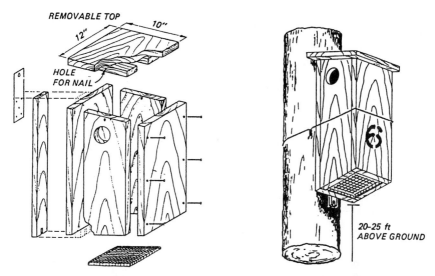

Figure 15.6 Assembly and installation details for a wooden nest box for squirrels. (*Barkalow and Soots 1965.*) [For metric equivalence, see metric conversion table.]

Design and construction.   Wooden nest boxes are recommended. The most desirable boxes (longevity = 15 to 25 years) are constructed from bald cypress heartwood, redwood, western redcedar, incense cedar, Port Orford cedar, or pressure-treated pine (Teaford 1986b). Construction details and assembly and installation detail vary (Figs. 15.6 and 15.7) (Barkalow and Soots 1965).

Songbird and raptor nest boxes

Artificial nests should be used to alleviate temporary local inadequacies in snag, den, and nest tree management. They are not an entirely suitable substitute because they might only partially provide one of the 40 uses of snags listed by Davis (1983), be sources for predators that learn to search for nest boxes, have high maintenance costs, lead to blowfly parasitism due to their shape (Miller and Miller 1980), and be unattractive.

The list of wildlife species using songbird and raptor nest boxes is extensive (Table 15.2) (Mitchell 1988) (Table 15.3) (Millsap et al. 1987). Almost 50 species of birds in North America are known to use boxes. Primary cavity users such as woodpeckers excavate a hole and seem to need the stimulus of excavation for nesting; secondary cavity users take advantage of holes previously excavated by primary cavity users (Mitchell 1988). Thus, nest box management is directed mainly

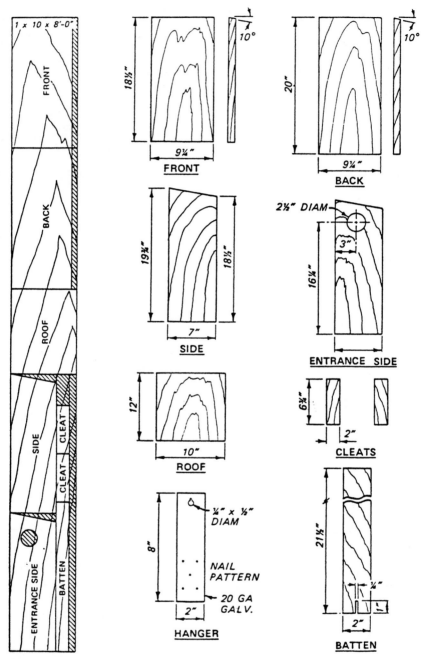

Figure 15.7   Construction details for a wooden nest box for gray squirrels and fox squirrels. (*Barkalow and Soots 1965.*) [For metric equivalence, see metric conversion table.]

TABLE 15.2   Wildlife Species Known to Use Boxes Designed for Cavity-Nesting Birds

Songbirds
American robin (shelves only)
Bluebirds
  Eastern bluebird
  Mountain bluebird
  Western bluebird
Brown creeper (infrequent use)
Chickadees and titmice
  Black-capped chickadee
  Carolina chickadee
  Mountain chickadee
  Tufted titmouse
  (Other species of chickadees and titmice probably will use nest boxes if provided.)
European starling
Flycatchers
  Ash-throated flycatcher
  Eastern phoebe (shelves only)
  Great-crested flycatcher
House finch
House sparrow
Nuthatches
  Brown-headed nuthatch
  Pygmy nuthatch
  White-breasted nuthatch
  Red-breasted nuthatch
Prothonotory warbler
Swallows
  Barn swallow (shelves only)
  Purple martin
  Tree swallow
  Violet-green swallow
Woodpeckers
  Downy woodpecker
  Golden-fronted woodpecker
  Hairy woodpecker
  Lewis woodpecker
  Northern flicker
  Pileated woodpecker
  Red-bellied woodpecker
  Red-headed woodpecker
  Yellow-bellied sapsucker
  (Other species of woodpecker will occasionally use boxes.)
Wrens
  Bewick's wren
  Carolina wren
  House wren

TABLE 15.2   Wildlife Species Known to Use Boxes Designed for Cavity-Nesting Birds (*Continued*)

Raptors (primarily use specially designed larger boxes)
American kestrel
Owls
  Barred owl
  Common barn owl
  Eastern screech owl
  Flammulated owl
  Northern saw-whet owl
  Whiskered screech owl

Waterfowl (primarily use specially designed larger boxes)
Black-bellied whistling duck
Common goldeneye
Barrow's goldeneye
Bufflehead
Common merganser
Hooded merganser
Wood duck

Mammals
Bats (several species will use songbird nest boxes)
Mice
  Deer mouse
  Eastern woodrat
  Golden mouse
  White-footed mouse
Ringtail (large boxes only)
Squirrels
  Arizona gray squirrel
  Eastern gray squirrel
  Fox squirrel
  Red squirrel
  Northern flying squirrel
  Southern flying squirrel
Opossum (large boxes only)

Amphibians and reptiles
Amphibians
  Gray treefrog
  Green treefrog
  Squirrel treefrog
Lizards
  Green anole
  Skinks
    Broadhead skink
    Five-lined skink
    Southeastern five-lined skink
Snakes
  Rat snakes
    Black rat snake
    Texas rat snake

SOURCE: Adapted from Mitchell (1988).

TABLE 15.3   Some North American Raptors That Have Used Nestboxes, and Selected References with Information on Nestbox Construction and Maintenance

Species	Comments	References
American kestrel	Design	Henderson and Holt (1962)
American kestrel	Nestbox sanitation	Hamerstrom et al. (1973)
American kestrel	Design, construction, effectiveness	Heintzelman (1971)
American kestrel	Design, construction	Yoakum et al. (1980)
American kestrel	Design, construction	Henderson (1992)*
Common barn owl	Design, placement, effectiveness	Marti et al. (1979)
Common barn owl	Design, effectiveness	Bunn et al. (1982)
Common barn owl	Design, construction, placement	Colvin (1983)
Flammulated owl	Design	Hasenyager et al. (1979)
Eastern screech owl	Design	Henderson and Holt (1962)
Eastern screech owl	Design	VanCamp and Henny (1975)
Eastern screech owl	Design	Henderson (1992)*
Barred owl	Design, construction, placement	Johnson and Follen (1984)
Barred owl	Design, construction	Henderson (1992)*
Saw-whet owl	Design	Rever and Miller (1973)
Saw-whet owl	Design, construction	Henderson (1992)*
Several	Design, placement, effectiveness	Soucy (1980)

SOURCE: Millsap et al. (1987).
*Updated.

at secondary cavity users. Habitat-management objectives include the following (Mitchell 1988):

1. Reestablish a local or regional population that has declined or been eliminated.

2. Attract birds to areas where food is adequate but nest sites are lacking.

3. Maintain a remnant population of woodpeckers during forest regeneration and snag development.

4. Increase public enjoyment and appreciation of wildlife.

5. Provide shelter and nest sites for multiple species in such spatially limited areas as urban areas.

Nest box programs should not try to (1) establish a population of primary cavity nesters, (2) mitigate the loss of natural nest sites, (3) replicate bird communities in the absence of natural habitat, or (4) substitute for the preservation and management of wildlife habitat.

Timing and placement.   Nest boxes should be installed before the nesting season, which is late winter for most songbirds. Late January to mid-February is best.

Good locations for nest boxes include pastures and field borders, fencerows, shelterbelts, orchards, road or powerline rights-of-way, and clearcut areas for birds using more open habitats (Mitchell 1988). Cavity nesters in woodland areas can use nest boxes in woodland clearings (edge wildlife species) or extensive forest stands (interior wildlife species). Boxes should be spaced at appropriate intervals (e.g., 90 m for bluebirds, 25 to 30 m for tree swallows) to prevent territorial conflicts (Mitchell 1988, Henderson 1992). Small nest boxes should be spaced at about four to eight per hectare; one per 4 hectares is acceptable for large cavity nesters (Gary and Morris 1980).

Design and construction.   Many designs have been published (Peterson 1963, Kalmbach and McAtee 1969, Gary and Morris 1980, Henderson 1992). Top-opening (Fig. 15.8) and side-opening (Fig. 15.9) boxes are most common (Zeleny 1976, Mitchell 1988); they vary in dimensions (Table 15.4) (Poston and Schmidt 1981, Mitchell 1988). A design for barred owls was reported by Henderson (1992) (Fig. 15.10).

While most managers overbuild the cubic capacity, the most important dimension is the size of the entry hole (Mitchell 1988). The bottom of the entry hole should be at least 15 cm above the floor for most species (Zeleny 1978). If desirable and weather-resistant materials are used, a nest box should last 10 to 15 years. Wood is recommended. The most desirable woods are bald cypress, redcedar, and redwood. Lumber should be at least 1.8 cm thick (Henderson 1992). Mitchell (1988) provided construction details for nuthatches, chickadees, titmice, wrens, and purple martins.

Predator guards are recommended (see Henderson 1992 and Payne 1992:365–368). These barriers hinder attacks mainly from terrestrial predators. The Noel coon guard is made from hardware cloth that surrounds the nest box entrance and extends outward about 13 cm.

Maintenance.   Debris and existing nest materials should be removed before the nesting season (no later than mid-January). During the nesting season, frequent inspection is needed to remove such undesirable species as starlings and house sparrows (Zeleny 1976). Sometimes starling eggs might have to be removed five or six times before the birds will abandon the box (Mitchell 1988). Boxes should be examined regularly for insect infestations that might inhibit use by birds.

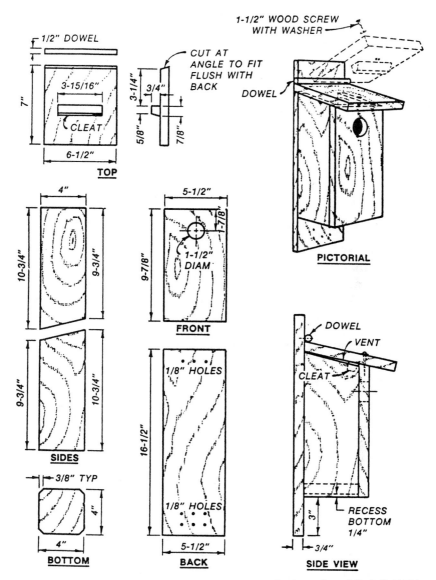

Figure 15.8 Construction details for a top-opening songbird nest box. (*Mitchell 1986.*)
[For metric equivalence, see metric conversion table in the front of the book.]

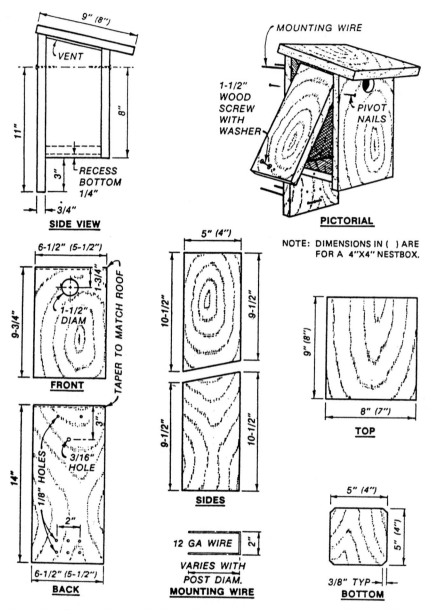

Figure 15.9 Construction details for a side-opening songbird nest box. (*Zeleny 1976.*) [For metric equivalence, see metric conversion table in the front of the book.]

TABLE 15.4   Nest Box Dimensions and Placement Heights

Species	Box floor (cm)	Box depth (cm)	Entrance height (cm)*	Entrance diameter (cm)	Box height (dm)
American robin†	18 × 20	20	—	—	18–45
Eastern bluebird	10 × 10	20–30	15–25	3.8	12–18
Mountain bluebird	13 × 13	20–30	15–25	3.8	12–18
Western bluebird	10 × 10	20–30	15–25	3.8	12–18
Chickadees	10 × 10	20–25	15–20	2.8	12–45
Titmice	10 × 10	20–25	15–20	3.2	15–45
Ash-throated flycatcher	15 × 15	20–25	15–20	3.8	15–45
Great-crested flycatcher	15 × 15	20–25	15–20	4.4	15–45
Phoebes†	15 × 15	15	—	—	24–36
Brown-headed nuthatch	10 × 10	20–25	15–20	3.2	15–45
Pygmy nuthatch	10 × 10	20–25	15–20	3.2	15–45
Red-breasted nuthatch	10 × 10	20–25	15–20	3.2	15–45
White-breasted nuthatch	10 × 10	20–25	15–20	3.5	15–45
Prothonotory warbler	13 × 13	15	10–13	3.5	12–24
Barn swallow†	15 × 15	15	—	—	24–36
Purple martin	15 × 15	15	3–5	6.4	18–60
Tree swallow	13 × 13	15–20	10–15	3.8	15–45
Violet-green swallow	13 × 13	15–20	10–15	3.8	15–45
Downy wood-pecker	10 × 10	20–25	15–20	3.2	15–45
Golden-fronted woodpecker	15 × 15	30–38	23–30	5.1	30–60
Hairy woodpecker	15 × 15	30–38	23–30	3.8	24–60
Lewis woodpecker	18 × 18	41–46	36–41	6.4	36–60
Northern flicker	18 × 18	41–46	36–41	6.4	18–60
Pileated woodpecker	20 × 20	41–61	30–51	7.6 × 10.2	45–75
Red-headed woodpecker	15 × 15	30–38	23–30	5.1	30–60
Yellow-bellied sapsucker	15 × 15	30–38	23–30	3.8	30–60
Bewick's wren	10 × 10	15–20	10–15	3.2	15–30
Carolina wren	10 × 10	15–20	10–15	3.8	15–30
House wren	10 × 10	15–20	10–15	3.2	15–30
Flicker	18 × 18	41–46	36–41	6.4	18–60
Screech owl‡	20 × 20	30–38	23–30	7.6	30–90
Saw-whet owl	15 × 15	25–30	20–25	6.4	36–60
Barn owl	25 × 46	38–46	10	15	36–54
Sparrow hawk	20 × 20	30–38	23–30	7.6	30–90

*Height of entrance hole above nest box floor.
†Use nesting shelf, which has open front.
‡Same dimensions for American kestrel.
SOURCE: Kalmbach and McAtee (1969), Mitchell (1988).

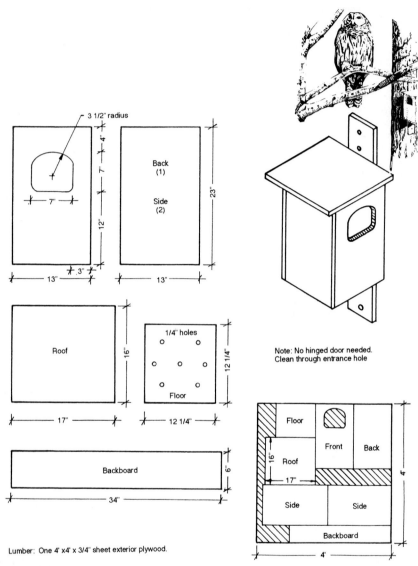

Figure 15.10 Instructions for making a barred owl nest box. (*Henderson 1992.*) [For metric equivalence, see metric conversion table in the front of the book.]

Other Nest Structures

Towers, platforms, and baskets can be used to alleviate nest deficiencies. Recommendations for artificial nests have been reported for raptors (Fig. 15.11) (Kahl 1972, Olendorff and Stoddart 1974, Van Daele

Figure 15.11 Artificial nest structure for raptors. (*Modified from Olendorff and Stoddart 1974 in Yoakum et al. 1980.*)

1980, Yoakum et al. 1980, Martin et al. 1986, Millsap et al. 1987, Payne 1992) (Table 15.5) (Millsap et al. 1987) (Fig. 15.12) (Henderson 1992), mourning doves (Fig. 15.13) (Cowan 1959), eagles (Fig. 15.14) (Nelson and Nelson 1976), and ospreys (Payne 1992). Mourning dove nests should be 2 to 5 m above the ground (Cowan 1959), although these doves also will nest on the ground.

Cliff-nesting raptors such as peregrine falcons and prairie falcons have nested on artificial ledges and excavated potholes (Fyfe and Armbruster 1977, Boyce et al. 1982). Artificial cavities should be placed at least halfway to the cliff top. These vary in size with species of raptor (Call 1979). For golden eagles, nest cavities should be 2 m long, 1.3 m deep, and 1.3 to 2 m high. For prairie falcons, the cliff face selected for an artificial cavity should be at least 6 m tall. The artificial nest hole or ledge should be at least 30 cm deep, 60 cm long, and 30 cm high (Fyfe and Armbruster 1977). Smith (1985) used blasting charges of explosives to create artificial nesting cavities for prairie falcons in Montana.

TABLE 15.5 Some North American Raptors That Have Used Artificial Nest Structures as Part of a Habitat-Management Project, and Selected References on Construction and Maintenance

Species	Structure type	Comments	References
Osprey	Tower and platform	Design, construction	Kahl (1972b)
	Tower and platform	Design, construction	Rhodes (1972)
	Tower and platform	Design, construction	Postupalsky and Stackpole (1974)
	Tower and platform	Effectiveness, design	Postupalsky (1978)
	Power pole platform	Design, construction	Van Daele (1980)
	Tower and platform	Design, construction	Henderson (1992)*
Snail kite	Basket	Design, placement	Sykes and Chandler (1974)
Bald eagle	Tower and platform	Effectiveness	Postupalsky (1978)
	Tower and platform	Design, placement, effectiveness	Grubb (1980)
Swainson's hawk	Tower and platform	Effectiveness	Schmutz et al. (1984)
Red-tailed hawk	Basket	Design, placement	Ellis and Kellett (1970)
	Basket	Effectiveness	Dunstan and Harrell (1973)
	Bohm (1977)	Basket	Design, placement
	Power pole platform	Effectiveness	Kochert et al. (1984)
Ferruginous hawk	Platforms	Placement, effectiveness	Fyfe and Armbruster (1977)
	Platform repair	Design, effectiveness	Craig and Andersen (1978)
	Tower and platform	Design, effectiveness	Howard and Hilliard (1980)
	Power pole platform	Effectiveness	Kochert et al. (1984)
	Tower and platform	Effectiveness	Schmutz et al. (1984)
Golden eagle	Power pole platform	Design, placement, effectiveness	Olendorff et al. (1981)
	Power pole platform	Effectiveness	Kochert et al. (1984)
Great horned owl	Basket	Effectiveness	Dunstan and Harrell (1973)
	Basket	Design, placement	Bohm (1977)
	Basket	Design, construction	Henderson (1992)*
Great gray owl	Basket	Design	Nero et al. (1974)
	Basket	Design, construction	Henderson (1992)*
Several	Tower and platform	Design, placement	Olendorff and Stoddard (1974)
	All	Design, effectiveness	Call (1979)
	Power pole platforms	Design, effectiveness	Olendorff et al. (1981)

SOURCE: Millsap et al. (1987).
*Updated.

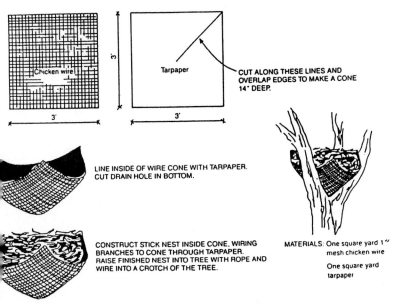

LINE INSIDE OF WIRE CONE WITH TARPAPER.
CUT DRAIN HOLE IN BOTTOM.

CONSTRUCT STICK NEST INSIDE CONE. WIRING
BRANCHES TO CONE THROUGH TARPAPER.
RAISE FINISHED NEST INTO TREE WITH ROPE AND
WIRE INTO A CROTCH OF THE TREE.

MATERIALS: One square yard 1″
mesh chicken wire

One square yard
tarpaper

15.12 Nest platform for great gray owls and great horned owls. (*Henderson*
) [For metric equivalence, see metric conversion table in the front of the book.]

vo techniques have been developed for artificial, in-tree cavities.
is the physical excavation of cavities with a chain saw and chisel
ne 1992:361); the other is to inject a tree with heart rot fungus
use a router to develop the cavity (Millsap et al. 1987).
storation of natural nest sites also should be considered. Millsap
. (1987) reported increased raptor productivity and use of natural
s after they were restored.

hes and Roosts

gs, dead limbs, fence posts, fence lines, utility poles, and utility
s can serve as perches and roosts. In rangeland and shrubland
ns, artificial perches and roosts can improve a habitat if they
ace natural ones that occurred historically. Otherwise they could
nd the range of some species of wildlife unnaturally, with unnat-
impact on other wildlife and perhaps plants.
rious perch designs have been explored for raptor species, includ-
artificial towers, transplanted snags, and girdled live trees (Table
) (Millsap et al. 1987). Effective designs vary, although higher
hes generally receive more raptor use than lower perches (Hall et
981).

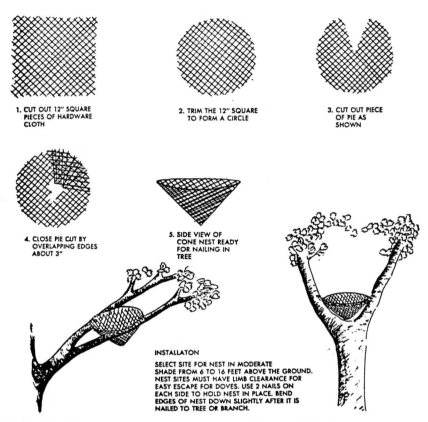

1. CUT OUT 12" SQUARE
PIECES OF HARDWARE
CLOTH

2. TRIM THE 12" SQUARE
TO FORM A CIRCLE

3. CUT OUT PIECE
OF PIE AS
SHOWN

4. CLOSE PIE CUT BY
OVERLAPPING EDGES
ABOUT 3"

5. SIDE VIEW OF
CONE NEST READY
FOR NAILING IN
TREE

INSTALLATON

SELECT SITE FOR NEST IN MODERATE
SHADE FROM 6 TO 16 FEET ABOVE THE GROUND.
NEST SITES MUST HAVE LIMB CLEARANCE FOR
EASY ESCAPE FOR DOVES. USE 2 NAILS ON
EACH SIDE TO HOLD NEST IN PLACE. BEND
EDGES OF NEST DOWN SLIGHTLY AFTER IT IS
NAILED TO TREE OR BRANCH.

Figure 15.13 Wire nest cones for mourning doves. (*Cowan 1959.*) [For metric equivalence, see metric conversion table in the front of the book.]

In open rangeland, raptors are sometimes electrocuted when using electric poles as roosts. About 95 percent of such mortality can be prevented by correcting only 2 percent of the electric poles (see Payne 1992:380). Gilmer and Wiehe (1977) found that while platforms and perches on powerline towers were used by nesting raptors, nesting success of ferruginous hawks was lower on towers than nests in any other substrate they studied. They attributed low success rate partly to high winds. Raptors made little use of wooden H-frame structures in Colorado (Stahlecker and Griese 1979).

Many powerline designs and corrective measures exist (U.S. Rural Electrification Administration 1972, Avery 1978, Bridges and McConnon 1981). Artificial perches for hawks and owls can be built on telephone poles, metal poles, or trees stripped of branches. Poles should be 6 to 15 m tall, planted at least 1 m deep, and spaced one

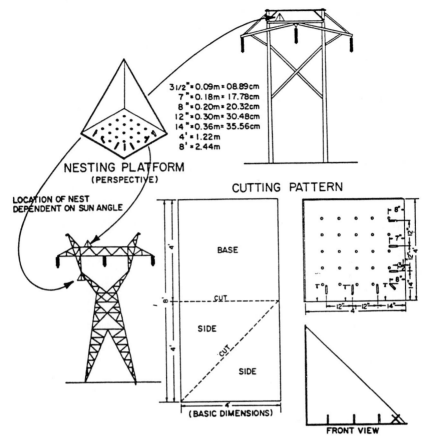

Figure 15.14   Eagle nesting platform. (*Nelson and Nelson 1976.*)

per 10 ha (Herricks et al. 1982). Brush piles provide suitable perches for smaller birds.

Artificial Burrows

Burrowing owls and ground-dwelling mammals can be attracted to subterranean boxes built of concrete or of wood such as oak or tulip poplar or warp-resistant exterior plywood (Fig. 15.15) (Decker and Kelley undated, Russell undated, Collins and Landry 1977, Herricks et al. 1982, Henderson 1992). Water-resistant lumber or exterior plywood at least 2 cm thick and nails or screws should be used. In pastures, lumber for tunnels should be 4 cm thick to withstand the weight of cows and horses. Protective coats of paint, creosote, or similar substance should

TABLE 15.6   Some North American Raptors That Have Used Artificial Perch Structures, and Selected References With Information on Construction and Placement

Species	Comments	References
Black-shouldered kite	Design, placement, effectiveness	Hall et al. (1981)
Sharp-shinned hawk	Design, effectiveness	Reinert (1984)
Cooper's hawk	Design, effectiveness	Reinert (1984)
Northern harrier	Design, placement, effectiveness	Hall et al. (1981)
	Design, effectiveness	Reinert (1984)
Harris' hawk	Design	Stumpf (1977)
Red-tailed hawk	Design	Stumpf (1977)
	Design, placement, effectiveness	Forren (1981)
	Design, placement, effectiveness	Hall et al. (1981)
	Design, effectiveness	Reinert et al. (1984)
Rough-legged hawk	Design, effectiveness	Reinert (1984)
Golden eagle	Design, placement, effectiveness	White (1974)
American kestrel	Design	Harrison (1977)
	Design, placement, effectiveness	Forren (1981)
Merlin	Design, effectiveness	Reinert (1984)
Peregrine falcon	Design, effectiveness	Reinert (1984)
Common barn owl	Design, placement, effectiveness	Hall et al. (1981)
Short-eared owl	Design, placement, effectiveness	Hall et al. (1981)
Snowy owl	Design, effectiveness	Reinert (1984)
Great horned owl	Design, placement, effectiveness	Forren (1981)
	Design, placement, effectiveness	Hall et al. (1981)
Burrowing owl	Design, effectiveness	Reinert (1984)

SOURCE: Millsap et al. (1987).

not be applied. Tunnels should be more than 1.3 m long with at least one 90 degree turn to increase darkness in the chamber. Less suitable are three or four connected field tiles buried at about a 45 degree angle, with a semicircle cut on opposite ends at the bottom of the box so that the tile will fit snugly into the box for two entrances/exits. The direction the entrances face is unimportant so long as cover is nearby.

The box chamber needs a removable top but no bottom. Boxes should be buried about 15 cm deep for insulation or at ground level with the top covered with brush to help keep the box interior dark. Boxes should be buried in areas of well-drained soil, near good cover such as a woods border, a weedy fencerow, or an irrigation ditch. Artificial burrows are especially important in areas devoid of abandoned burrows, and also in areas of sparse cover, and of hard or tightly packed soil. To minimize flooding, boxes placed on slopes or cut banks should be slightly higher than the entrance. For muskrats, burrows should be placed in banks of ponds supporting emergent vegetation, but above the high-water level to prevent flooding. A mound of soil built around the entrance helps attract burrowing animals to the site.

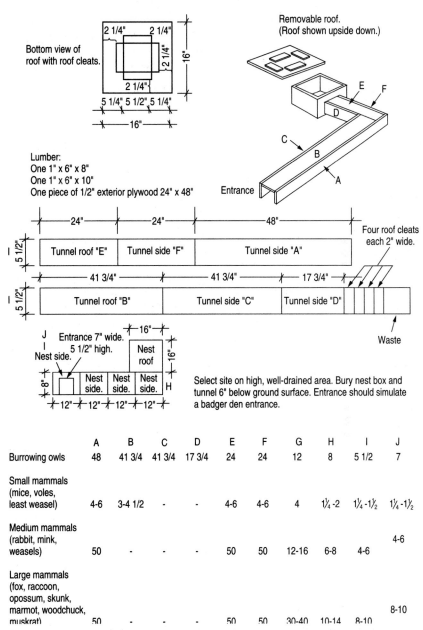

Bottom view of roof with roof cleats.

2 1/4"   2 1/4"
2 1/4"
16"
2 1/4"
5 1/4" 5 1/2" 5 1/4"
16"

Removable roof.
(Roof shown upside down.)

E
F
D
C
B
A

Lumber:
One 1" x 6" x 8"
One 1" x 6" x 10"
One piece of 1/2" exterior plywood 24" x 48"

Entrance

24"	24"	48"	Four roof cleats each 2" wide.
Tunnel roof "E"	Tunnel side "F"	Tunnel side "A"	

5 1/2"

41 3/4"	41 3/4"	17 3/4"	
Tunnel roof "B"	Tunnel side "C"	Tunnel side "D"	

5 1/2"

Waste

16"
J
Entrance 7" wide.
I   5 1/2" high.
Nest side.

| Nest side. | Nest side. | Nest side. | Nest roof | H |
16"
8"
12" 12" 12" 12"

Select site on high, well-drained area. Bury nest box and tunnel 6" below ground surface. Entrance should simulate a badger den entrance.

	A	B	C	D	E	F	G	H	I	J
Burrowing owls	48	41 3/4	41 3/4	17 3/4	24	24	12	8	5 1/2	7
Small mammals (mice, voles, least weasel)	4-6	3-4 1/2	-	-	4-6	4-6	4	$\frac{1}{4}$-2	$1\frac{1}{4}$-$1\frac{1}{2}$	$1\frac{1}{4}$-$1\frac{1}{2}$
Medium mammals (rabbit, mink, weasels)	50	-	-	-	50	50	12-16	6-8	4-6	4-6
Large mammals (fox, raccoon, opossum, skunk, marmot, woodchuck, muskrat)	50	-	-	-	50	50	30-40	10-14	8-10	8-10

Figure 15.15 Generic design for artificial burrow for burrowing owls and ground-dwelling mammals. (Dimensions in inches.) (*Henderson 1992, Herricks et al. 1982.*) [For metric equivalence, see metric conversion table in the front of the book.]

Deer Mouse Boxes

Insects can be controlled not only by insectivorous birds and bats (Yoakum et al. 1980) but also by deer mice preying on larvae and pupae of gypsy moths in young even-aged hardwood stands (Smith 1975) and probably elsewhere too. Deer mice also are an important prey base for various predators. Nest boxes for deer mice are 13-cm cubes of 1-cm (^{3}⁄$_8$-in) exterior plywood with a hinged lid and a 2.5-cm entrance hole (Nicholson 1941).

Bat Houses

Where the number of dead and dying trees with cavities has been reduced substantially, bat houses can be erected on a tree trunk 3 to 5 m above the ground, preferably near water, facing east to receive the morning sun and protected from the southern sun and the direction of prevailing winds (Greenhall 1982, Hastie 1990, Barnes 1991, Bat Conservation International 1991, Armstrong 1992, Henderson 1992).

Untreated, rough-sided lumber and galvanized nails should be used for construction (Fig. 15.16) (Bat Conservation International 1991). In cold climates, bat houses can be painted to absorb heat from sunlight. Roofing shingles can be used on the roof. The house can be larger to accommodate an entire colony. The house can be hung securely in various ways with nails, screws, hooks, and brackets.

Bat Gates for Caves

Vandalism and other human disturbance of caves might be the main cause for declines in populations of some species of bats. Steel closures called *bat gates* can be custom-made to fit individual caves or abandoned mine openings (Tuttle 1977, Powers 1985, Pollio 1991, Johnson 1992). Horizontally placed 10.3-cm angle iron welded 15.4 cm apart is the best design. Horizontally placed 1.9-cm round steel bars welded 15.4 cm apart can be used, but such a gate is more easily breached by vandals. Johnson (1992) provided details of construction, including welding.

Snake Hibernacula

An artificial *hibernaculum* for hibernating snakes is essentially an underground brush pile (Henderson 1987). Hibernacula can be built on south-facing slopes to receive sunlight along woods roads, log landings, and other forest openings where slash and stumps are abundant.

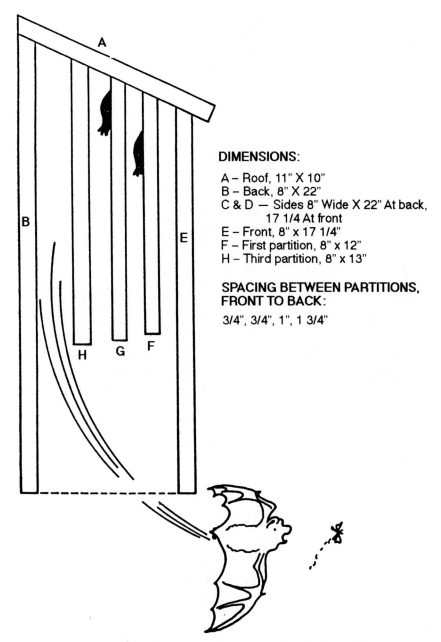

DIMENSIONS:

A – Roof, 11" X 10"
B – Back, 8" X 22"
C & D — Sides 8" Wide X 22" At back,
          17 1/4 At front
E – Front, 8" x 17 1/4"
F – First partition, 8" x 12"
H – Third partition, 8" x 13"

**SPACING BETWEEN PARTITIONS,
FRONT TO BACK:**

3/4", 3/4", 1", 1 3/4"

Figure 15.16 Bat house. (*Bat Conservation International 1991.*) [For metric equivalence, see metric conversion table in the front of the book.]

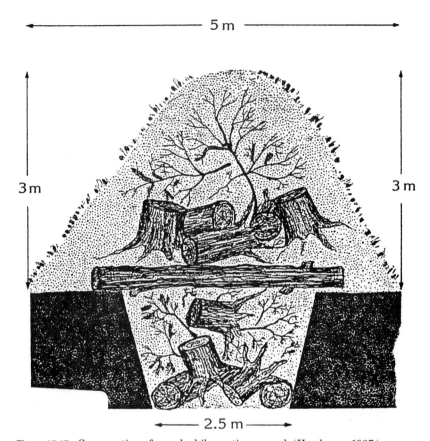

Figure 15.17   Cross section of a snake hibernation mound. (*Henderson 1987.*)

A trench 2.4 m deep and 2.7 m across on top should be dug, with excavated soil stockpiled at the edge. A layer of logs should be placed on the bottom of the trench, which then should be filled with stumps and branches. Then soil should be pushed into the trench to ground level. Then logs 3 m long should be placed side by side across the top of the trench, with more soil placed on top of the logs, more stumps placed on top of the soil, and more soil and branches placed on top of the stumps to form a mound about 3 m high and 5 m wide (Fig. 15.17) (Henderson 1987).

Tables

TABLE A.1 Food Plants of Value to Forest Wildlife

Common name	Scientific name[a]	Region[b]	Site[c]	Plant parts used[d]	Periods of greatest use[e]	Documented animal use[f]
Trees						
Firs	*Abies* spp. (EV)	NE, NC, NW, SW, IN	M, W	F L	F, W W	SB, LH, SH LH, GB
Maples	*Acer* spp.	NE, NC, NW, SE, SC, IN	M, W	F L, T B	F SP, W F, W, SP	SP, GB LH, SH MH
Birches	*Betula* spp.	SE, SC, NW, NC, NE, IN	D, M, W	L, T F B	F, W F, W F, W, SP	LH, GB GB, SB MH
American hophornbeam, blue-beech	*Carpinus caroliniana*	NE, SE, SC, NC	M, W	B	F, W, SP	MH
Hickory, pecan	*Carya* spp.	NE, NC, SE, SC	M, W	T, F	F, W	LH, SH, GB, SB
Dogwoods	*Cornus* spp.	AR	M, W	L, T, F F	F, W F, SU	LH GB, SB, LC LH, LC, SH, SC, SB, GB
Common persimmon	*Diospyros virginiana*	SE, SC	D, M	F	F	GB, MH LH, MH
American beech	*Fagus grandifolia*	NE, NC, SE, SC	M	T, B L, T, B	F, W SP, F, W	SH, GB, SB LH, MH
Ash	*Fraxinus* spp.	AR	M, W	F	F	SH, GB, SB
Honeylocust	*Gleditsia triacanthos*	SE	M	F	F, W	LH, SH, GB
American holly	*Ilex opaca* (EV)	NE, NC, SE, SC	M, D	F L	F, W W	LH, LC, SB, SB LH
Cedars (red)	*Juniperus* spp. (EV)	AR	D, M	F	S, F, W	LH, SC, SH, GB
Larch, tamarack	*Larix* spp.	NE, NC, NW	W	L, F	F	GB, SB
Incense-cedar	*Libocedrus decurrens* (EV)	N, W, SW	M, W	L	W	LH
Yellowpoplar, tulip tree	*Liriodendron tulipifera*	NE, NC, SE, SC	M	L, T F, B	F, W, SP	LH, SB, MH
Magnolia, cucumbertree	*Magnolia* spp.	SE	M	L, T	SP, W	LH

Common name	Scientific name	Region	Moisture	Part	Season	Wildlife
Sweetbay	*Magnolia virginiana* (EV)	SE	W	L	F, W	LH
Chinaberry	*Melia azedarach*	SE, SC	M	F	F, W	LH
Red mulberry	*Morus rubra*	NE, NC, SE, SL, SW	M	L, T, F	SP, S	LH, GB, SB
Blackgum, black tupelo, water tupelo	*Nyssa spp.*	NE, SE, SC	W, M	L, T B, F	SP, F, W F	LH, MH LH, LC, SC, GB
Sourwood	*Oxydendron arboreum*	SE	M	L, T L	SP, W F, W	LH LH, LC
Redbay	*Persea borbonia* (EV)	SE	W	F	F, W	LH
Spruce	*Picea spp.* (EV)	NE, NW, IN, NC	D, M, W	L, T, B L	W W	MH, LH LH
Pines	*Pinus spp.* (EV)	AR	D, M, W	L, T, B F	F, W, SP F, W	MH, LH GB, SB, SH
Bigtooth aspen, quaking aspen, cottonwood	*Populus spp.*	AR	M, W	L, T, F B	F, W, SP, SU	GB, LH, SH MH
Cherries, plums	*Prunus spp.*	AR	D, M, W	T F B	W F F, W, SP	GB, LH, MH LH, SH, LC, SC GB, MH
Douglas-fir	*Pseudotsuga menziesii* (EV)	NW, IN	M	L F B	F, W F, W F, W, SP	LH, GB GB MH
Oaks, oaks (EV)	*Quercus spp.*	AR SE, SC, SW	D, M, W D, M	L, T, F, B L, T, F	F F, W, SP	LH, SH, LC, GB, SB, LH SH, LC, GB, SB
Cabbage palmetto	*Sabal palmetto* (EV)	SE, SC	M, W	F	F, W	LC, SC, LH, SH, GB, SB
Willow	*Salix spp.*	AR	M, W	L, T	SU, F	LH, SB
Sassafras	*Sassafras albidum*	NE, NC, SE, SC	D, M	L, T, F F	SP, SU, F, W F	LH SH, SB, GB, LC, SC
Cypress	*Taxodium spp.*	SE, SC	W	F	F, W	GB
Cedars (white)	*Thuja spp.* (EV)	NE, NC	M, W	L L	W W	LH LH

TABLE A.1 Food Plants of Value to Forest Wildlife (Continued)

Common name	Scientific name[a]	Region[b]	Site[c]	Plant parts used[d]	Periods of greatest use[e]	Documented animal use[f]
Trees (Continued)						
Eastern hemlock	*Tsuga canadensis* (EV)	NE, NC	M	{ F, B	W, W	SB, MH
Elms	*Ulmus* spp.	AR	D, M	B	F, W, SP	MH
Shrubs						
Guajillo acacia	*Acacia berlandieri*	SW	D	L	F, W, SP	LH, GB
Chamise	*Adenostoma fasiculatum*	NW, SW, IN	D	L, T, F		LH, SH, SB
Alders	*Alnus* spp.	AR	W	{ L, B; F; T, B	SP, SU; F, W; W	MH; GB, SB, LH; MH, LH, SH
Serviceberry	*Amelanchier* spp.	NE, SE, SC, SW, NC, IN	D, M, W	L, T, F, B	F, W, SP	LH, GB, SB, MH, LC
Bearberry, manzanita	*Arctostaphylos* spp. (EV)	SW, NW, IN	D	L, T, F	W, SP, SU, F	LH, SH, LC, SC, GB, SB
Chokeberry	*Aronia* spp.	NE, NC, SE, SC	D, M	{ L, T; F	W; F	LH; GB, SB
Sagebrush	*Artemisia* spp. (EV)	SW, NW, IN	D, M	L, T, F	W	LH, SH, SB, GB
Oregon-grape	*Berberis aquifolium* (EV)	NW, SW, IN	D, M	{ L; F	W; F	LH; GB, LC
Bumelia	*Bumelia* spp.	SW	D, M	L, T	SP, F, W	LH
Calliandra, false-mesquite	*Calliandra eriophylla*	SW	D	L	W	LH
Jerseytea, deerbrush, buckbrush (EV), whitethorn (EV)	*Ceanothus* spp.	AR	D, M	L, T, F	F, W, SP, SU	LH, SH, SB
Spiny hackberry	*Celtis pallida*	SW, SC, NW, IN, NC	D, M	{ L, F; F	F, W; F	LH; SB, GB, SH, SC
Buttonbrush	*Cephalanthus occidentalis*	SW, SE, NE, SC	W	L, T, B	SU	MH, SB

Common name	Scientific name	Region	Moisture	Plant part	Season	Wildlife use
Curlleaf, mountainmahogany (EV), true mountainmahogany	*Cercocarpus* spp.	SW, NW IN, SW	D, M	{L F	W, SP	LH SB, SH, GB
Bearmat, misery mountain	*Chamaebatia foliolosa*	SW, NW	D, M	{L F	W, SP, SU	LH SB, SH, GB
Rabbitbrush	*Chrysothamnus* spp.	NW, SW, IN	D, M	L, T, F	SP, SU, F, W	LH, SH, SB, GB
Condalia	*Condalia* spp.	SW	D, M	L, T	SP	LH
Hazelnuts	*Corylus* spp.	NE, NW, SE, SW, NC	D, M	{T, F B	F, W, SP F, W, SP	GB, LC, LH MH, SH
Cliffrose	*Cowania mexicana*	SW, IN	D	L, T, F, E	F, W, SP	GB, SB
Hawthorns	*Crataegus* spp.	AR	D, M	L, T, F	F	GB
Swamp cyrilla, leatherwood	*Cyrilla racemiflora*	SE, SC	W	L, T	F, W	LH
Dalea	*Dalea* spp.	SW	D	L, T	SP, F, W	LH
Bush honeysuckle	*Diervilla lonicera*	NC	D, M	L, T	SP, SU, F	LH
Strawberry bush	*Euonymus* spp.	NE, SE, NC, SC	M	L, T	SP, F, W	LH
Winterfat	*Eurotia lanata*	SW, NW, NC, IN	M	L, T, F	F, W, SP	LH, SH, SB, GB
Apacheplume	*Fallugia paradoxa*	SW, IN	M, D	L, T, F	F, W, SP	
Silktassel	*Garrya* spp.	NW, SW, IN	M	L, T	F, W	LH
Huckleberries	*Gaylussacia* spp.	AR	D, M, W	{L, T, F F	SP, SU, F, W SU, F	LH GB, SB, LC, SC
Witch-hazel	*Hamamelis virginiana*	NE, SE, SC, SW	M, W	T, F	F, W	GB
Toyon, Christmas-berry	*Heteromeles arbutifolia* (EV)	SW	D	{B L, F	F, W, SP F, W	MH LH, GB, SB
Hollies,	*Ilex* spp. (EV)	SE, SC, NE, NC	M, W	L, F	F, W	LH, SH, LC, GB, SB
Dahoon holly,		SE, SC	M, W	{L, F	F, W	LH, GB, SB
Large gallberry,		SE, SC	M	{L, F	F, W	LH, GB, SB
Inkberry,		NE, SE, SC	M	{L, F	F, W	LH, GB, SB
Winterberry,		NE, NC, SE	M	{L, T, F	F, W	LH, LC, GB, SB
Yaupon		SE, SC	W, M	L	F, W	LH, SH

TABLE A.1 Food Plants of Value to Forest Wildlife *(Continued)*

Common name	Scientific name[a]	Region[b]	Site[c]	Plant parts used[d]	Periods of greatest use[e]	Documented animal use[f]
Shrubs (Continued)						
Common juniper, ground juniper, California juniper	Juniperus spp. (EV)	NE, NC, NW, SW	D, M	L	W	LH
		IN		F	F, W	GB, SB
Mountain laurel, lambkill	Kalmia spp. (EV)	NE, NC, SE, SC	M, W	L, T	F, W	LH, SH, SB
Wolfberry	Lycium berlandieri	SW, IN, NW	D, M	L, T, F	SP	LH
Alleghany menziesia	Menziesia pilosa	NE, SE	M, W	T	W	GB
Waxmyrtle, bayberry	Myrica spp.	NE, SE, SC	M, W	F	F, W, SP, SU	LH, SB, GB, SH
Cactus, pricklypear, cholla	Opuntia spp. (EV)	SE, SC, SW, IN	D	F, E	F, W	LH, SB, SH
Texas porlieria	Porlieria angustifolia	SW	D, M	L, T	SP	LH
Shrubby cinquefoil	Potentilla fruiticosa (EV)	NE, NC, NW, SW, IN	D, M	L, T		LH
Mesquite	Prosopis spp.	SW, IN	D	L, F	F, W	LH
Stonefruits	Prunus spp.	AR	D, M	L, T, F	SP, SU, F	LH, SH, SB, GB
Paperflower	Psilostrophe spp.	SW	D	L	SP	LH
Bitterbrush	Purshia tridentata	SW, NW, IN	D, M	L, T, F	W, SP, SU, F	LH, SH, SB, GB
Oaks (scrub, ground)	Quercus spp. (EV)	SE, SC, SW	M, D	L, T, F	F, W, SP	LH, LC, GB, SH, SB
Buckthorn	Rhamnus spp. (EV)	SW	D, M	L, T, F	W, SP, SU, F	LH, SH, LC
Rosebay, azalea	Rhododendron spp. (EV)	NE, NC, SE, SC	M, W	L, T	F, W	LH, GB
Sumac	Rhus spp.	AR	M, D	{ T F	F, W F	MH LH, SB, GB, MH
Gooseberry, currant	Ribes spp.	SW, NC	D, M	{ L, T, F L, T, F, E	SP, SU, F SP, F, W	LH, SH, SB, GB, LC, SC LH
Roses	Rosa spp.	AR	D, M, W	{ F T E	F, SU W F, SU	GB, SB, SH, LC, SC MH, LH MH

Blackberries, raspberries, dewberries	*Rubus* spp.	AR	D, M, W	L, T, F	SP, SU	LH, SH, LC, SC, SB, GB
Scrub palmetto	*Sabal* spp. (EV)	SE, SC	D, M	T	W	MH, LH
Willows	*Salix* spp.	AR	M, W	{ E { F	SU, F F, W	LC, LH MH
Elderberries	*Sambucus* spp.	AR	M, W	L, B L, T	SP, SU SP, W, F, SU	LH, SB, MH, SH MH, SH
Saw-palmetto	*Serenoa repens* (EV)	SE, SC	D, M	B L, T, F F	F, W, SP SP, F, W, SU SU	LH GB, SB, LC, SC, SH LH, SH
Coralberry, snowberry, wolfberry	*Symphoricarpos* spp.	NE, NC, NW, SW, IN	M, D	B	W	LC, LH
Blueberries, deerberries	*Vaccinium* spp.	AR	D, M, W	{ L, T, F { F	F, W SP, F, W, SU	LH GB, SB, SH
Rusty blackhaw, viburnum, possumhaw, arrowwood, nannyberry, witherod	*Viburnum* spp.	AR	M, W	L, T, F F L, T	F SP, F, W, SU SU, F	LH LC, SC, SB, GB LH
Vines						
Alabama supplejack	*Berchemia scandens*	SC, SE	M	F B L, T, F	W, SP F, W W, SP	GB, SB, SH SH LH, GB, SB
Yellow jessamine	*Gelsemium sempervirens* (EV)	SE, SC	M	L, T	SU	LH
Honeysuckles	*Lonicera* spp. (EV)	AR	D, M, W	L, T, F	F, W	LH, SH, SB
Poison ivy, poison oak	*Rhus* spp.	NE, SE, SC, NW, SW	M, W	L, T, F	F, W, SP, SU	GB, SB, LH, SH
Greenbriers	*Smilax* spp. (EV)	NE, SE, SC, SW, NC	D, M, W	{ F { L, T, F	F, W, SU F, W, SP	LH GB, SB
Grapes	*Vitis* spp.	AR	D, W, M	{ L, T, F { F	SP, SU F	LH GB, SB, SH, LC, SC

TABLE A.1   Food Plants of Value to Forest Wildlife   (Continued)

Common name	Scientific name[a]	Region[b]	Site[c]	Plant parts used[d]	Periods of greatest use[e]	Documented animal use[f]
Forbs						
Yarrow	Achillea spp.	SW	D, M, W	E	SP, SU, F, W	LH
Agoseris	Agoseris spp.	NW, NC	D, W	E	F	LH
Ragweed	Ambrosia spp.	SE, SW, IN, NC	M	{E, F}	{SP, SU, F; SU, F}	{LH, SH; GB, SB}
Pearly everlasting	Anaphalis spp.	NE, NC, NW, IN	D, M	E	SU, F	LH
Pussytoes, everlasting	Antennaria spp.	AR	M, D	F, E	SP, SU, F	LH
Lady's tobacco	Aphanostephus spp.	SW	D	E	SP	LH
Arnica	Arnica spp.	SW		F		SB, GB, SH
Asters	Aster spp.	NE, NC, SE, SC, IN	D, W, M	L, T, F, E	SP, SU, F	LH, SH, SB, GB
Balsamroot	Balsamorhiza spp.	IN, SW, NW	D, M	L	SU	LH
Brodiaea	Brodiaea spp.	NW, SW	D, M, W	E	SP, SU, W	LH, SH
Poppymallow	Callirhoe involucrata	SW	D	E	SP	LH
Pussypaws	Calyptridium umbellatum	NW, SW	D	E	SU	LH, SH, SB
Partridgepea	Cassia nictitans	SE	M, D	F	F	GB
Centella	Centella repanda	SE	M, W	E	SP, SU, F, W	LH, GB
Thistle	Cirsium spp.	SW	D, M	F	SU	SB, SH, GB, LH
Dwarf cornell, bunchberry	Cornus canadensis	NE, NC	M	F	F	GB
Croton	Croton spp.	AR	D	F	SU, F	GB, SB, SH
Pinnate tansymustard	Descuraina pinnata	AR	D, M	E	SP, SU, F	LH
Bundleflower	Desmanthus spp.	SE, SW	D, M	E	SP, SU, F	LH
Beggarweed, tick-trefoil	Desmodium spp.	SE	D, M	F	F	GB
Trailing-arbutus, mayflower	Epigaea repens (EV)	NE, SE, NC	M	E	F, W	LH, GB
Willowweed, fireweed	Epilobium spp.	AR	D, M, W	E	SP, SU, F	LH, SH, GB, SB

Common name	Scientific name	Region	Habitat	Part	Season	Birds
Turkey mullein	*Eremocarpus setigerus*	SW		F	F, W	GB
Fleabane	*Erigeron* spp.	SW		F		SB, SH, GB
Dog-tongue, wild buckwheat	*Eriogonum* spp.	NE, SE, IN, SW	M, W	L, T, F	F, SU W	GB, LH, SB, SH
Wooly sunflower	*Eriophyllum* spp.	SW		F		SB, SH, GB
Filaree, heronbill	*Erodium* spp.	NW, SW, IN	D, M	E	SP, SU	LH, SH
White snakeroot	*Eupatorium rugosom*	SE	M	E	SP, SU, F	LH
Strawberry	*Fragaria* spp.	NE, NC, NW, SE, IN	D, M, W	E	SP, SU, F	LH, GB, MH, SB, SH
Galax	*Galas aphylla* (EV)	SE	M	E	F, W	LH
Teaberry, wintergreen, checkerberry	*Gaultheria* spp.	NE, NW, NC, SE	M	E	F, W	LH, GB, SH
Avens	*Geum* spp.	SE, NE, IN, NC	M, W	L, F	F, W	GB, SB, SH, LH
Alumroot	*Heuchera villosa*	SE	M, W	L	F, W	GB
Mouseear, hawkweed	*Hieracium pilosella*	SE	M	E	SP, SU, F	LH
Jewelweed	*Impatiens carpensis*	NC	W	L	SU	LH
Lettuce	*Lactuca* spp.	AR	D, M	L, T, F	SP, SU, F	LH, GB
Peavine	*Lathyrus* spp.	NC, NW	M	L	SU, F, SP	LH, LC
Common lespedeza	*Lespedeza striata*	SE	M	F	F	GB, SB
Deervetch	*Lotus* spp.	AR	D, M, W	F	SP, SU, F, W	LH, GB
Ludwigia	*Ludwigia* spp.	SE	W	E	SP, SU, F, W	LH
Lupine	*Lupinus* spp.	AR	D, M, W	{F, E}	SU, F; SP, SU, F, W	LH, GB; LH
Medic	*Medicago* spp.	AR	D, M	E	SP, SU, F, W	LH, GB
Sweetclover	*Melilotus* spp.	SW	D, M, W	F, E	SP, SU, F, W	LH, GB
Moonseed	*Menispermum canadense*	NW	M, W	L	F	LH

TABLE A.1 Food Plants of Value to Forest Wildlife (Continued)

Common name	Scientific name[a]	Region[b]	Site[c]	Plant parts used[d]	Periods of greatest use[e]	Documented animal use[f]
Forbs (Continued)						
Partridgeberry	*Mitchella repens*	NE, NC, SE	M	E	F, W	LH, GB, SC
Waterlily	*Nymphaea odorata*	NE, SE	W	E	SP, SU, F, W	LH
Royal fern	*Osmunda regalis*	NE, SE	W	E	F, W	LH
Woodsorrel	*Oxalis* spp.	NE, NC, NW	M	E	F	LH, SB
Parthenium	*Parthenium* spp.	SW	D	E	SP	LH
Penstemon	*Penstemon* spp.	NW, IN, SW	D, M, W		SP, SU, W, F	SH, SB, GB, LH
Ground cherry	*Physalis* spp.	SW	D	E	SP	LH
		NC		L	SU	LH
Plantain	*Plantago* spp.	SE	M	F, E	W	LH, SB
Popcornflower	*Plagiobothrys* spp.	SW	D, M	E	W, SP	LH, SH, GB
Smartweed, knotweed, fringed bindweed	*Polygonum* spp.	AR	W, M	{F	SU	LH
				F	F, W	GB, SB
Western Christmas-fern, swordfern	*Polystichum* spp.	NE, SE, NC, NW	M, D	E	F, W	LH, GB, MH
Cinquefoil	*Potentilla* spp.	NE, SE, NC, SC, SW, NW, IN	M, W	{E	SP, SU, F	LH, GB, SB
				L	SP	LC
Buttercup	*Ranunculus* spp.	AR	M, W	{E	F	GB
				L	SP	LC
Sheep sorrel	*Rumex acetosella*	SE	M, W	L	F, W	GB
		SW	M, W	E	W, SP, SU	LH, SH
Goldenrod	*Solidago* spp.	NE, SE, SC, IN, NC	D, M, W	L, T, F, E	SP, SU, F	LH, SH, SB, GB
Dandelion	*Taraxacum vulgare*	AR	D, M, W	{E	SP, SU, F	MH, LC
				L, T, F	F, SP, SU	GB, SB, SH, LH
Clovers	*Trifolium* spp.	NE, NC, NW, SE	M, W	{E	SP, SU, F	GB, LH, MH, LC
			SW, IN	L, F	W	SH

562

Common name	Scientific name					
Vanilla trilisa, deer's tongue	*Trilisa odoratissima*	SE	M, W	E	F, W	LH
Vetch	*Vicia* spp.	NC	M	L	SU, F, SP	LH, LC
Violet	*Viola* spp.	NE, NC, NW, SE, SC, IN	M, W	E	SP, SU, F	GB, LH, SH, SB
Mulesear	*Wyethia* spp.	SW	D, M	L	SU	LH, SB, SH, GB
Grasses						
Wheatgrass	*Agropyron* spp.	IN, NW, SW	D	E	SU	LH
Giant cane	*Arundinaria gigantea*	SE	W	E	F, W, SP	LH
Bromegrass	*Bromus* spp.	SW, IN, NC	D, W		W, F, SP	LH, GB, SH, SB
Alkaligrass	*Distichlis spicata*	SW, NW, NC, IN	M, D, W	E	SU, F / W	SH / LH
Wild rye	*Elymus* spp.	AR	D, M	E	SP, SU, F, W	LH
Fescue	*Festuca* spp.	AR	D, M	E	SP, SU, F, W	LH, SH, SB
Prairie junegrass	*Koeleria cristata*	NW	D	E	SU	LH
Cutgrass	*Leersia* spp.	AR	W	L, F	SU	MH
Plantain	*Plantago* spp.	SE	M	F, E	W	LH, SB
Melic	*Melica* spp.	SW, IN, NW	D	F	SU	SB, GB, SH
Stoneyhills muhly	*Muhlenbergia cuspidata*	NW	D	E / F	SW	LH / SB, GB, SH
Panicgrass	*Panicum* spp.	SE, SC	M, W	L, T / F	W / SU	LH / GB, SB
Paspalums	*Paspalum* spp.	SE, SC, NE	W	L, F	SP, SU	LH, GB, SB
Bluegrass	*Poa* spp.	NW / NE, NE, NC, IN	M	E	W / F	LH / SH, SB, GB, LH
American cupscale	*Sacciolepis triata*	SE	W	E	W	LH
Bristle grass	*Setaria* spp.	AR	M	L, T, F	F	GB, SB
Squirreltail	*Sitanion* spp.	SW, SC, NC	D		F, SU	SH, SB, GB, LH

TABLE A.1 Food Plants of Value to Forest Wildlife (Continued)

Common name	Scientific name[a]	Region[b]	Site[c]	Plant parts used[d]	Periods of greatest use[e]	Documented animal use[f]
Grasses (Continued)						
Needlegrass	Stipa spp.	NW	D	{E, F}	F	LH SB, GB, SH
Grasslike species						
Sedges	Carex spp.	AR	D, M, W	{L, F, E}	SU, SP	MH LH, LC
Spikesedge	Eleocharis spp.	AR	W	L, F	SU	MH
Rush	Juncus spp.	AR	W, M	E	SP, SU, W	LH, SH
Bulrush	Scirpus americanus	SW	W	{E, F}	W W	LH SB
Other						
Horsetail	Equisetum spp.	NE, NC, NW	W	L	SP, SU, F, W	MH, LC
Mushrooms	Fungi	AR	M, W	E	SP, SU, F, W	LH, SH, LC, SC, GB, SB
Lichens	Osneacae	SW, NW	D, M, W	E	F, W	LH, SH
Mistletoes	Phoradendron spp.	SE, SW, SC, NW, IN	M, D	F, E	SP, S, F, W	LH, SB
Indianpipe	Monotropa spp.	SE, NE, NC, NW, IN	M	E	F	LH

[a]EV = evergreen. All other species are deciduous or have species that are both evergreen or deciduous.
[b]NE = Northeast, NC = North central, NW = Northwest, SE = Southeast, SC = South central, SW = Southwest, IN = Intermountain, AR = all regions.
[c]D = dry, M = medium, W = wet.
[d]L = leaves, T = twigs and buds, F = flowers and fruit, B = bark, E = entire plant.

[e]SP = spring, SU = summer, F = fall, W = winter.
[f]LC = large carnivores, SC = small carnivores, LH = large herbivores, MH = medium herbivores, SH = small herbivores, GB = game birds, SB = songbirds.
SOURCE: Adapted from Halls et al. (1984).

TABLE A.2 Food and Cover Plants Useful for Attracting Wildlife to Residential and Other Areas

Large trees	Small trees	Large shrubs	Low shrubs and vines	Forbs and grasses
		Northwest		
California black oak *Quercus kelloggii*	Dogwood *Cornus* spp.	Elderberry *Sambucus* spp.	Blackberry *Rubus allegheniensis*	Filaree *Erodium* spp.
Colorado spruce *Picea pungens*	Hawthorn *Crataegus* spp.	Golden currant *Ribes aureum*	Oregon-grape *Berberis aquifolium*	Sunflower *Helianthus* spp.
Douglas-fir *Pseudotsuga menziesioi*	Serviceberry *Amelanchier* spp.	Tartarian honeysuckle *Lonicera tartarica*	Snowberry *Symphoricarpos alba*	Tarweed *Madia* spp.
Lodgepole pine *Pinus contorta*	Mountain ash *Sorbus ameri-cana*	Multiflora rose *Rosa multiflora*	Coralberry *Symphoricarpos orbiculatus*	Timothy *Phleum* spp.
Ponderosa pine *Pinus ponderosa*	Thorn-apple *Crataegus columbiana*	Firethorn *Cotoneaster pyracantha*	Gooseberry *Ribes* spp.	Turkey mullein *Eremocarpus* spp.
Boxelder *Acer negundo*	Squaw-apple *Peraphyllum ramosissimum*	Highbush cranberry *Viburnum trilobum*	Buckthorn *Rhamnus* spp.	Bristlegrass *Setaria* spp.
		Russian olive *Elaeagnus angustifolia*	Sagebrush *Artemisia* spp.	Ragweed *Ambrosia* spp.
				Knotweed *Polygonum* spp.
		Southwest		
Live oak *Quercus virginiana*	Crabapple *Malus* spp.	Manzanita *Arctostaphylos* spp.	Blackberry *Rubus allegheniensis*	Filaree *Erodium* spp.

TABLE A.2 Food and Cover Plants Useful for Attracting Wildlife to Residential and Other Areas (Continued)

Large trees	Small trees	Large shrubs	Low shrubs and vines	Forbs and grasses
		Southwest		
Pin oak *Quercus palustris*	Sweet acacia *Acacia farnesiana*	Catclaw acacia *Acacia greggii*	Juniper *Juniperus* spp.	Sunflower *Helianthus* spp.
Pinyon pine *Pinus edulis*	Mesquite *Prosopis* spp.	Tartarian honeysuckle *Lonicera tartarica*	Pricklypear *Opuntia* spp.	Turkey mullein *Eremocarpus* spp.
Boxelder *Acer negundo*	Desert ironwood *Olneya tesota*	Multiflora rose *Rosa multiflora*	Virginia creeper *Parthenocissus quinquefolia*	Bristlegrass *Setaria* spp.
	Mulberry *Morus* spp.	Firethorn *Cotoneaster pyracantha*	Sagebrush *Artemisia* spp.	Ragweed *Ambrosia* spp.
		Cholla (cactus) *Opuntia* spp.		Knotweed *Polygonum* spp.
		Northeast		
Beech *Fagus grandifolia*	Cherry *Prunus* spp.	Autumn olive *Elaeagnus umbrellata*	Blackberry *Rubus allegheniensis*	Panic grass *Panicum* spp.
Birch *Betula* spp.	Crabapple *Malus* spp.	Dogwood *Cornus* spp.	Spicebush *Lindera* spp.	Sunflower *Helianthus* spp.
Colorado spruce *Picea pungens*	Dogwood *Cornus* spp.	Elderberry *Sambucus* spp.	Snowberry *Symphoricarpos albus*	Timothy *Phleum* spp.
Hemlock *Tsuga* spp.	Hawthorn *Crataegus* spp.	Sumac *Rhus* spp.	Coralberry *Symphoricarpos orbiculatus*	Bristlegrass *Setaria* spp.

Northeast

Sugar maple *Acer saccharum*	Eastern redcedar *Juniperus virginiana*	Winterberry *Ilex* spp.	Virginia creeper *Parthenocissus quinquefolia*	Ragweed *Ambrosia* spp.
White oak *Quercus alba*	Serviceberry *Amelanchier canadensis*	Tartarian honey-suckle *Lonicera tartarica*	Greenbrier *Smilax* spp.	Knotweed *Polygonum* spp.
White pine *Pinus strobus*	Mulberry *Morus* spp.	Highbush blueberry *Vaccinium corymbosum*	Mapleleaf viburnum *Viburnum acerifolia*	Pokeweed *Phytolacca americana*
Blackgum *Nyssa sylvatica*		Multiflora rose *Rosa multiflora*	Bittersweet *Celastrus* spp.	
Red maple *Acer rubrum*		Firethorn *Cotoneaster pyracantha*	Japanese honeysuckle *Lonicera japonica*	
Boxelder *Acer negundo*		Highbush cranberry *Viburnum trilobum*		

Southeast

Mountain ash *Sorbus americana*	Cherry *Prunus* spp.	Dogwood *Cornus* spp.	Bayberry *Myrica* spp.	Lespedeza *Lespedeza* spp.
Beech *Fagus grandifolia*	Crabapple *Malus* spp.	Elderberry *Sambucus* spp.	Blackberry *Rubus alleghen-iensis*	Panic grass *Panicum* spp.
Hackberry *Celtis* spp.	Dogwood *Cornus* spp.	Sumac *Rhus* spp.	Spicebush *Lindera benzoin*	Sunflower *Helianthus* spp.
Live oak *Quercus virginiana*	Hawthorn *Crataegus* spp.	Tartarian honeysuckle *Lonicera tartarica*	Virginia creeper *Parthenocissus quinquefolia*	Bristlegrass *Setaria* spp.
Loblolly pine *Pinus taeda*	Holly *Ilex* spp.	Highbush blueberry *Vaccinium corymbosum*	Greenbrier *Smilax* spp.	Ragweed *Ambrosia* spp.

TABLE A.2 Food and Cover Plants Useful for Attracting Wildlife to Residential and Other Areas (Continued)

Large trees	Small trees	Large shrubs	Low shrubs and vines	Forbs and grasses
		Northeast		
Pecan *Carya illinoensis*	Palmetto *Sabal* spp.	Multiflora rose *Rosa multiflora*	Mapleleaf viburnum *Virburnum acerifolia*	Knotweed *Polygonum* spp.
Slash pine *Pinus elliottii*	Persimmon *Diospyros virginiana*	Firethorn *Cotonester pyracantha*	Japanese honeysuckle *Lonicera japonica*	Pokeweed *Phytolacca americana*
Blackgum *Nyssa sylvatica*	Eastern redcedar *Juniperus virginiana*	Arrowwood *Viburnum dentatum*		
Red maple *Acer rubrum*	Serviceberry *Amelanchier* spp.			
Boxelder *Acer negundo*	Mulberry *Morus* spp.			

SOURCE: Adapted from Cordell et al. (1984).

TABLE A.3 Some Woody Plants Recommended for Planting to Attract Wildlife to Backyards and Elsewhere

Woody Plants†	Northeast/north central	Southeast	Region* Rockies/Great Basin	Northwest	Southwest
Low shrubs	Beach plum—MG‡ Blueberry—SGMB Coralberry—SH New Jersey tea—BM Huckleberry—SGMB	Beautyberry—SGM Saw-palmetto—BMS Cotoneaster—BS Blueberry-BSG Blackberry-BSG Smooth sumac—MSG	Rabbitbrush—MB Mormon tea—MG Prairie sagebrush—GM Smooth sumac—SGM	Salal—SGH Manzanita—SGM Mahala mat—BMG Evergreen huckleberry—MSG Rabbitbrush—MB	Beloperone—BH Brittlebush Buffaloberry—SGM Redberry buckthorn—SGBM Skunkbush—SM Trumpet bush—H
Tall shrubs	Pfitzer juniper—SG Winterberry—SGMB Arrowwood viburnum—SGM Redosier dogwood—SGMB Bayberry—SGM Spicebush—SGB	Yaupon—SB Red buckeye—H Southern blackhaw—GMB Wax myrtle—S Hercules club—BSM	Golden currant—SGMB Sand cherry—SGM Mountainmahogany—MB Chokecherry—SGMB Serviceberry—SGMB	Tall Oregon-grape—SM Red currant—SGMHB Serviceberry—SG Osoberry—SGM Cascara buckthorn—SG Blue elderberry-SGM	Creosotebush—M Bitterbrush—MB Desert-willow—H Sugar sumac—SGM Serviceberry—SG Shrub live oak—GMS
Small trees	Sassafras—SBGM Serviceberry—SGM Flowering dogwood—MGB Staghorn sumac-SGM Nannyberry—SGMB	Dahoon—SBG Flowering dogwood—SMGB Serviceberry—SGM American holly—SB Persimmon—MGS Cabbage palmetto—BM	Limber pine—MSG Western red birch—GMSB Rocky Mountain clump maple—MGS Utah juniper—SGMB Rocky Mountain juniper—SGMB	Pacific dogwood—MSGB Madrone—SGB Mountain ash—SGM Hawthorne—SGM Vine maple—SGM	Ironwood—MG Hackberry—SGB Paloverde—MH Velvet mesquite—MB Chokecherry—SGMB Madrone—SGB
Large trees (deciduous)	American beech—MGS Shagbark hickory—MBGS Northern red oak—MGSB White oak—MGSB Sugar maple—SGM Blackgum—SGM	Tulip poplar—HBSM Bald cypress—G Willow oak—MGS Pecan—MBG Hackberry-BSGM	Emory oak—MSB Quaking aspen—GSMB Fremont cottonwood—MGSB	Bigleaf maple—MGS Oregon white oak—MSG Red alder—SGMB	Arizona sycamore—B Bigtooth maple—MGS Gambel oak—MGSB New Mexico locust—BM
Large trees (evergreen)	White pine—MS Eastern hemlock—SGM Eastern redcedar—SBG White spruce—GSM Red pine—SGM White cedar—GSM	Longleaf pine—SM Live oak—MGSB Southern magnolia Loblolly pine—MS Carolina hemlock—SMG Eastern redcedar—SBGM	Lodgepole pine—MSB Ponderosa pine—MSB White fir—MSB Pinyon pine—MSG Douglas-fir—MSGB Subalpine fir—MSB	Western redcedar—SMB Western white pine—SM Douglas-fir—GMS Western hemlock—SGM White fir—GMSB	Emory oak—MSGB Rocky Mountain juniper—SGBM Blue spruce—MSG Ponderosa pine—MSB Pinyon pine—MSG

*Residents of the Great Plains can choose plants from the lists for the regions most similar in climate.

†All plants furnish shelter and reproductive cover for a variety of insects, birds, and perhaps some mammals; some are especially attractive as food. Low shrubs are 0.15 to 2.4 m, tall shrubs are 1.8 to 4.6 m, small trees are 3.7 to 18.3 m, and large trees are 15.2 to 61.0 m.

‡B = butterfly adult or caterpiller, H = hummingbird, S = songbird, G = game bird, M = mammal.

SOURCE: National Wildlife Federation (1984).

TABLE A.4 Selected Upland Plant Species for Habitat Development on Dredged-Material Sites and Various Other Areas

Species	Best propagule type	Collection periods*	Temporary storage requirements	Planting periods	Range†	Mature height	Growth habits	Remarks
Grasses								
American beachgrass (*Ammophila breviligulata*)‡,§,¶	Transplants	Oct–Mar	In wet sand beds or in pots of sand	Feb–May	MA, NE, GL	To 1.5 m	Perennial cool-season grass with stiff stems, full sun	Tolerates saline conditions, beach and dune areas, excellent for sandy beach and dune areas.
American dunegrass (*Elymus mollis*)‡,¶	Transplants	Sep–Mar	In wet sand beds or in pots of sand	Mar–Jun	NE, RNW	To 1.5 m	Strong, erect, fast-growing, full sun	Prefers sandy areas, good soil stabilizer.
Bahiagrass (*Paspalum notatum*)‡,¶	Seeds	Jul–Sep	Dry, cool area	Mar–Jun	SE, MA, FL, MS	To 0.5 m	Summer perennial, creeping base with upright stems, full sun	Cultivated for pasture, good cover, wide range of soils.
Barley (*Hordeum vulgare*)‡,§,¶	Seeds	May–Jul	Dry, cool area	Oct–Nov	Entire U.S.	To 1.3 m	Annual, winter cover crop grass, full sun	Extensively cultivated for cover and grain, requires good soil bed.
Barnyard grass (*Echinochloa crusgalli*)‡,¶	Seeds	Jun–Sep	Dry, cool area	May–Sep	Entire U.S. except FL	To 2 m	Annual grass, arching heads, full sun	Prefers moist soils, cultivated for waterfowl food.
Beach panic grass (*Panicum ararum*)‡	Transplants	Sep–Mar	In wet sand beds or in pots of sand	Mar–Jun	MA, SE, FL, MS	To 1.3 m	Perennial, few-flowered, full sun	Prefers sandy soils.
Beaked panic grass (*Panicum anceps*)	Seeds	Jul–Sep	Dry, cool area	Apr–Jun	MA, SE, FL, MS, MRV, SP, MP	To 2 m	Perennial, hardy, fast-growing, full sun	Prefers moist sandy soil.
Big bluestem (*Andropogon gerardii*)‡,¶	Seeds	Jul–Sep	Dry, cool area	Apr–Jun	Entire U.S. except PNW, CA	To 2 m	Perennial, robust, tufted, dense sod, full sun	Important forage grass, prefers well-drained soils.
Bromegrass (*Bromus inermus*)‡,¶	Seeds	Jul–Sep	Dry, cool area	Apr–Jun	Entire U.S. except SE, FL, MS, SP	To 2 m	Perennial, creeping rhizomes, erect stems, dense sod, full sun	Important forage grass, prefers well-drained soils.

Grasses (Continued)

Broomsedge (*Andropogon virginicus*)‡	Seeds	Sep–Oct	Dry, cool area	May–Sep	Entire eastern U.S. and CA	To 1 m	Perennial, dense culm, upright stems, full sun	Pest plant in pastures and crops, grows under most soil conditions.
Browntop millet (*Panicum ramosum*)¶	Seeds	Sep–Nov	Dry, cool area	Mar–Jul	SE, MA, MS, FL	To 0.6 m	Summer annual, erect stems, good seed producer, full sun	Prefers wet soils, excellent waterfowl food, no soil preparation necessary in many cases.
Bull paspalum (*Paspalum boscianum*)‡	Seeds	Jul–Oct	Dry, cold room	Mar–Jun	MA, SE, FL, MS	To 2 m	Stout summer annual, fast-growing, spreading, full sun	Prefers moist soils, good seed producer.
Bushy beardgrass (*Andropogon glomeratus*)‡	Seeds	Aug–Oct	Dry, cool area	Apr–Jun	NE, MA, SE, FL, MS, SP, SW, CA	To 2 m	Erect, dense, fast-growing, full sun	Prefers moist soils.
Calley Bermudagrass (*Cynodon dactylon* hybrid)¶	Transplants, rootstock	Year-round	In soil beds	Mar–Jun	SE, MS, SP, FL	To 0.5 m	Perennial, fast-growing, sterile, full sun	Vigorous new hybrid Bermuda, pasture use.
Coastal Bermudagrass (*Cynodon dactylon* hybrid)	Transplants, rootstock	Year-round	In soil beds	Mar–Jun	SE, MS, FL, SP, MS	To 0.5 m	Perennial, fast-growing, sterile, full sun	Planted extensively in southern pastures for grazing and hay, tolerates salt spray.
Common Bermudagrass (*Cynodon dactylon*)‡,¶	Seeds	Jun–Sep	Dry, cool area	Apr–Jun	Entire U.S. except MW, PNW, NP, NE	To 0.2 m	Perennial, fast-growing, abundant seeds, full sun	Pasture crop, lawns, pest in cultivated areas, tolerates wide range of conditions.
Common reed (*Phragmites australis*)‡	Rootstock, rhizomes	Sep–Mar	In sand beds or pots of sand	Feb–Jun	GL, NE, MA, SE, FL, MS, SP	To 4 m	Perennial, fast-growing, persistent, full sun	Pest plant in many areas, not recommended for any use other than soil stabilization.
Corn (*Zea mays*)‡,§,¶	Seeds	Jul–Oct	Dry, cool area	Mar–Jun	Entire U.S.	To 3 m	Summer annual, upright, heavy seed producer, full sun	Cultivated extensively for grain, silage, and human consumption.

TABLE A.4 Selected Upland Plant Species for Habitat Development on Dredged-Material Sites and Various Other Areas *(Continued)*

Species	Best propagule type	Collection periods*	Temporary storage requirements	Planting periods	Range†	Mature height	Growth habits	Remarks
Grasses *(Continued)*								
Dallisgrass (*Paspalum dilatatum*)‡,¶	Seeds	Jun–Sep	Dry, cool area	Year-round (MS, FL) Apr–May (north)	SE, MS, FL, MA, SP, SW	To 1.5 m	Dense perennial, full sun	Cultivated pasture grass.
Deertongue (*Muhlenbergia rigens*)‡	Seeds	Aug–Oct	Dry, cool area	Oct–Nov; Mar–Apr	NE, MA, SE, MS, MP, NP, MRV	To 1.6 m	Warm-season, full sun, dense clumps	Tolerates acid soils, seeds have strong dormancy.
European beachgrass (*Ammophila arenaria*)‡,¶	Transplants	Oct–Mar	Hold in wet sand beds or in sand pots	Feb–May	PNW, CA	To 1.5 m	Perennial, cool-season grass, rigid stems, full sun	Tolerates saline conditions, excellent for sandy beach and dune areas.
Fall panic grass (*Panicum dichotomiflorum*)‡	Seeds	Sep–Nov	Dry, cool area	Feb–Jun	Entire U.S. NP, PNW	To 1 m	Coarse, summer annual, fast-growing, good seed producer, full sun	Tolerates wide range of soil conditions including wet areas, considered crop pest.
Foxtail millet (*Setaria italica*)¶	Seeds	Jun–Sep	Dry, cool area	Apr–Jul	Entire U.S. except ME, FL, SP	To 2 m	Summer annual, upright, fast growth, full sun	Cultivated extensively for grain and silage, prefers moist soils.
Goose grass (*Eleusine indica*)‡	Seeds	Jun–Sep	Dry, cool area	Apr–Jul	Entire U.S. except NP, PNW	To 0.5 m	Small-culmed perennial, heavy seed producer, full sun	Pest plant in cultivated areas, grows in most soil conditions.
Green bristlegrass (*Setaria viridis*)‡	Seeds	Jul–Oct	Dry, cool area	Apr–Jul	Entire U.S.	To 1 m	Vigorous summer annual, clumped, full sun	Occurs in many soils, pest in crops, not palatable to browsers.
Italian ryegrass (*Lolium multiflorum*)‡	Seeds	May–Jul	Dry, cool area	Oct–Nov	Eastern U.S. and SP, NP, PNW, CA	To 1 m	Perennial in south, annual in north, hardy, forms dense root system, full sun	Cultivated for winter grazing, quick winter cover, and lawns.

Grasses (Continued)

Japanese millet (*Echinochloa crusgalli* hybrid)¶	Seeds	Jun–Sep	Dry, cool area	Apr–Sep	Entire U.S. except FL	To 1.5 m	Tall heavy annual, abundant seeds, full sun	Occurs in all soils, grown for waterfowl and cattle feed, is salt-tolerant to some extent.
Johnson grass (*Sorghum halepense*)‡,¶	Seeds	Jul–Oct	Dry, cool area	Apr–Sep	Entire U.S. except NP, MW, PNW	To 1.5 m	Hardy, fast-growing, erect, strong seed producers, full sun	Planted for pastures and hay, pest in cultivated areas.
Jungle rice (*Echinochloa colonum*)‡	Seeds	Jun–Sep	Dry, cool area	May–Sep	Entire U.S. except NP, MW	To 0.4 m	Perennial, prostrate to erect, full sun	Good seed producer, prefers wet to moist soils.
Large crabgrass (*Digitaria sanguinalis*)‡	Seeds	Jun–Sep	Dry, cool area	Apr–Sep	Entire U.S. except NP	To 0.3 m	Creeping annual, fast growing, full sun	Occurs in all soils, pest in cultivated areas, immune to herbicides.
Little hairgrass (*Aira praecox*)‡	Seeds	Jun–Aug	Dry, cool area	Apr–Jun	MA, PNW, CA	To 0.2 m	Annual, tufted culms, full sun	Prefers sandy, dry coastal soils.
Oats (*Avena sativa*)¶	Seeds	May–Jun	Dry, cool area	Sep–Oct	Entire U.S.	To 1 m	Cool-season annual, agronomic cereal crop, full sun	Occurs in almost all soil conditions, needs well-prepared seed bed.
Orchardgrass (*Dactylis glomerata*)‡,¶	Seeds	Jun–Aug	Dry, cool area	Mar–Sep	Entire U.S.	To 1.3 m	Clumped, perennial, hardy, full sun to shade	Prefers well-drained soils and does well in many soils, cultivated for grazing, hay, and silage.
Panic grass (*Panicum clandestinum*)‡	Seeds	Jun–Aug	Dry, cool area	Mar–Jun	Eastern and mid-U.S.	To 1.3 m	Dense clumped perennials, strong rhizomes, full sun	Prefers moist sandy soil.
Pearl millet (*Pennisetum glaucum*)¶	Seeds	Sep–Oct	Dry, cool area	Mar–Jun	MA, SE, SP, SW	To 2 m	Robust, summer annual, heavy seed producer, full sun	Cultivated for grain and silage, prefers moist soil but tolerates drought.

TABLE A.4 Selected Upland Plant Species for Habitat Development on Dredged-Material Sites and Various Other Areas (Continued)

Species	Best propagule type	Collection periods*	Temporary storage requirements	Planting periods	Range†	Mature height	Growth habits	Remarks
Grasses (Continued)								
Perennial ryegrass (*Lolium perenne*)‡,¶	Seeds	May–Jul	Dry, cool area	Sep–Nov	SE, MS, SP, FL	To 1 m	Hardy, dense root system, full sun	Good winter cover, good winter wildlife food and cattle forage in the south.
Prairie cordgrass (*Spartina pectinata*)‡,§,¶	Seeds	Jul–Oct	Dry, cool area	Apr–Jun	Entire U.S. except SE, FL, MS, CA	To 3 m	Tall perennial, full sun	Occurs in wet, coastal areas.
Proso millet (*Panicum milliaceum*)¶	Seeds	Sep–Oct	Dry, cool area	Mar–Jun	MW, SP	To 1.3 m	Summer annual, erect stems, full sun	Produces seeds in 4 months after planting, good food value, cultivated for grain.
Quackgrass (*Agropyron repens*)‡	Rootstock	Sep–Mar	In sand beds or pots of sand	Mar–Jun	Entire U.S.	To 1.3 m	Perennial, long, running rootstock, hardy, full sun	Pest plant, exotic.
Red fescue (*Festuca rubra*)‡,¶	Seeds	May–Aug (north)	Dry, cool area	Mar–May (north)	Entire U.S. except FL, SP, MS, SE	To 1 m	Hardy robust creeping grass forms a dense sod, shade to full sun	Cultivated extensively in mixed stands for pastures, lawns, and rights-of-way.
Redtop (*Agrostis alba*)‡,¶	Seeds	Aug–Oct	Dry, cool area	Apr–Jun	Entire U.S.	To 1 m	Tall hardy, stoloniferous, full sun	Cultivated for silage, hay, and grazing.
Reed canarygrass (*Phalaris arundinacea*)‡,¶	Seeds	Jun–Aug	Dry, cool area	Mar–Jun	Entire U.S.	To 2 m	Summer perennial, robust, fast growth, full sun	Prefers moist soil, but grows anywhere, cultivated on sewage areas and for pastures, good seed producer.
Rescue grass (*Bromus catharticus*)‡,¶	Seeds	Jul–Oct	Dry, cool area	Apr–Jun	SE, MA, CA, SW	To 1 m	Robust, summer perennial, full sun	Cultivated in south as forage.
Rice cutgrass (*Leersia oryzoides*)‡	Seeds	Aug–Oct	Dry, cool area	Apr–Jul	Entire U.S.	To 1.3 m	Dense culms, perennial, much-branched, shade to full sun	Prefers moist and wet soils.

Rye (Secale cereale)¶	Seeds	May–Jul	Dry, cool area	Sep–Nov (south) Apr–May (north)	Entire U.S.	To 1 m	Hardy cool-season annual, high seed producer	Cultivated extensively for grain, cover and green forage crops, especially in north.
Saltgrass (Distichlis spicata)‡,§,¶	Transplants, seeds	Sep–May Jul–Sep	In sand beds or in pots of sand	Mar–Jun	Entire U.S. in saline areas, except PNW, CA	To 0.3 m	Dense perennial, hardy, many rhizomes, good seed producer, full sun	Prefers moist, coastal areas, occurs in salt marshes and on sand dunes.
Saltmeadow cordgrass (Spartina patens)‡,§,¶	Transplants, seedlings	Year-round (south) Mar–Oct (north)	In wet sand beds or in sand pots	Feb–Jun	NE, MA, SE, FL, MS, SP	To 1 m	Densely rooted, summer perennial, spreads best from tillers	Occurs in flooded saline areas to dry sand dunes, occurs frequently, and is successfully planted on dredged material.
Sand dropseed (Sporobolus cryptandrus)‡	Seeds	Sep–Oct	Dry, cool area	Apr–Jul	Entire U.S.	To 1 m	Erect perennial, hardy, slow-growing, full sun	Prefers sandy soils, grows on prairie areas.
Sea oats (Uniola paniculata)‡,§,¶	Transplants, seeds	Sep–Mar (transplants) Aug–Oct (seeds)	In wet sand beds, dry, cool area	Mar–Jun	MA, SE, FL, MS	To 2 m	Robust perennial, dense roots, full sun	Prefers sandy, coastal areas, excellent dune stabilizer, tolerates salt spray.
Seashore bluegrass (Poa macantha)‡	Transplants	Sep–Mar	In wet sand beds or pots of sand	Mar–Jun	PNW, CA	To 0.4 m	Creeping rhizomous perennial with upright culms, full sun	Prefers coastal sand dunes.
Seashore paspalum (Paspalum vaginatum)‡	Transplants	Sep–Mar	In wet sand beds or pots of sand	Sep–Jun	SE, FL, MS	To 0.4 m	Dense perennial, fast-growing, full sun	Tolerates flooding and salt spray, occurs on dredged-material islands in dense stands.
Shoredune panic grass (Panicum amarulum)‡	Seeds	Sep–Oct	Dry, cool area	Mar–May	NE, MA, FL, MS, SP	To 2 m	Upright, coarse, perennial, fast-growing, full sun	Prefers sandy beach soils, tolerates salt sprays, occurs on dredged-material islands.

TABLE A.4 Selected Upland Plant Species for Habitat Development on Dredged-Material Sites and Various Other Areas (Continued)

Species	Best propagule type	Collection periods*	Temporary storage requirements	Planting periods	Range†	Mature height	Growth habits	Remarks
Grasses (Continued)								
Sixweeks fescue (*Festuca octoflora*)¶	Seeds	May–Jun	Dry, cool area	Mar–May	Entire U.S.	To 0.3 m	Annual, fast seed producers, full sun or shade	Cultivated as forage and hay crops.
Smooth crabgrass (*Digitaria ischaemum*)‡	Seeds	Jun–Sep	Dry, cool area	Apr–Sep	Entire U.S. except SW	To 0.3 m	Creeping, fast-growing, annual, full sun	Occurs in many soil types, a pest in cultivated fields and gardens.
Sorghum (*Sorghum vulgare*)¶	Seeds	Jul–Oct	Dry, cool area	Apr–Sep	Entire U.S.	To 1.5 m	Upright, summer annual, heavy seed producer, full sun	Cultivated extensively as grain and silage crop, tolerates wide range of soils.
Sudan grass (*Sorghum sudanese*)¶	Seeds	Jul–Oct	Dry, cool area	Apr–Jul	Entire U.S. except NP, NE, PNW	To 3 m	Wandering, upright, annual, hardy, fast-growing, full sun	Cultivated for hay and silage, tolerates wide range of soils.
Switchgrass (*Panicum virgatum*)‡,¶	Seeds	Jun–Sep	Dry, cool area	Apr–Sep	Entire U.S. except NP, PNW, CA	To 2 m	Summer perennial, fast-growing, hardy, full sun	Prefers moist soils, grows at water's edge, tolerant of salt spray.
Tall fescue (*Festuca arundinacea*)‡,§,¶	Seeds	Apr–Jun (south) May–Aug (north)	Dry, cool area	Oct–Nov (south) Mar–May (north)	Eastern U.S. except FL, MP, PNW	To 1.5 m	Cool-weather grass in south, summer grass in north, full sun	Cultivate for pastures.
Texas millet (*Panicum texanum*)	Seeds	Jul–Oct	Dry, cool area	Mar–Aug	MA, SE, FL, MS, SP	To 2 m	Summer annual with spreading stems, full sun	Fast-growing, considered crop weed, grows well on sand dunes.
Timothy (*Phleum pratense*)‡,§,¶	Seeds	Jul–Sep	Dry, cool area	Apr–Jun	Entire U.S. except SP, FL, MS	To 1 m	Summer perennial, fast-growing, erect, full sun	Cultivated extensively in north for hay.
Torpedo grass (*Panicum repens*)‡	Transplants	Sep–Mar	In wet soil beds or pots of sand	Sep–Jun	FL, MS, SP	To 0.1 m	Stout perennials, many rhizomes, dense cover, full sun	Sea beaches, prefers sandy moist soils, tolerates salt spray.

Grasses (Continued)

Vasey grass (*Paspalum urvillei*)‡	Seeds	Jul–Sep	Dry, cool area	Apr–Jun	FL, SE, MA, MS, SP, CA	To 2 m	Clumped, stout perennial, erect, hardy, full sun	Prefers moist soil, pasture grass, roadside cover.
Virginia dropseed (*Sporobolus virginicus*)‡	Seeds	Jun–Sep	Dry, cool area	Apr–Jun	MA, FL, MS	To 0.4 m	Perennial, branching rhizomes, erect culms, full sun	Occurs on sandy and muddy seashores, tolerates salt spray.
Walter's millet (*Echinochloa walteri*)‡,¶	Seeds	Jul–Sep	Dry, cool area	Apr–Sep	SP, MS, FL, SE, MA, NE, GL	To 3 m	Stiff stems, abundant seeds, annual, full sun	Occurs in all soils, cultivated for waterfowl food, prefers wet soils.
Wheat (*Triticum aestivum*)¶	Seeds	May–Jul	Dry, cool area	Oct–Nov (winter) Mar–May (spring)	Entire U.S.	To 1 m	Winter annual, good seed producer, hardy, full sun	Cultivated extensively, tolerates cold, good cover and food crop.
Wild rye (*Elymus virginicus*)‡	Seeds	May–Jul	Dry, cool area	Sep–Jun	Entire U.S. except CA	To 1.2 m	Perennial, tufted erect culms, heavy seeds, full sun	Prefers moist soils, good seed producer, tolerates salt spray somewhat.
Wooly panic grass (*Panicum lanuginosum*)‡	Seeds	Jul–Sep	Dry, cool area	Apr–Jun	MA, SE, FL, MS	To 0.7 m	Perennial, clumped, spreading shade and sun	Prefers moist soils, grows in woods and open areas, occurs on sea coast.
Yellow bristlegrass (*Setaria lutescens*)	Seeds	Jul–Oct	Dry, cool area	Apr–Jul	Entire U.S. except SW, CA	To 1 m	Summer annual, good seed producer, full sun	Occurs in many soil conditions, pest in crops, not palatable to browsers.
Forbs								
Alfalfa (*Medicago sativa*)¶	Seeds (inoculated)	Jul–Sep	Dry, cool area	Aug–Sep or Feb–Apr	Entire U.S.	To 0.5 m	Perennial, much-branched legume, full sun	Requires good seedbed preparation, occurs on most soils, prefers rich, moist areas.
Alsike clover (*Trifolium hybridum*)‡,¶	Seeds (inoculated)	Mar–Apr (south) Jun–Sep (north)	Dry, cool area	Nov–Feb (south) Mar–Jun (north)	Entire U.S.	To 0.5 m	Perennial, ascending branches, full sun	Prefers moist, acidic soils.

TABLE A.4 Selected Upland Plant Species for Habitat Development on Dredged-Material Sites and Various Other Areas (Continued)

Forbs (Continued)

Species	Best propagule type	Collection periods*	Temporary storage requirements	Planting periods	Range†	Mature height	Growth habits	Remarks
Arrow-leafed tearthumb (*Polygonum sagittatum*)	Transplants, seeds	Jul–Sep	Dry, cool area	Mar–Jun	Eastern and mid-U.S.	To 0.6 m	Viny, annual, weak-stemmed, spiny, full sun	Prefers moist soils.
Beach pea (*Lathyrus japonicus*)‡	Seeds (inoculated)	May–Sep	Dry, cool area	Feb–Jun	Entire coastal U.S.	To 0.3 m	Perennial viny plant, hardy, full sun	Prefers sandy moist soils, occurs on coastal beaches, dunes, and islands.
Beach strawberry (*Fragaria chiloensis*)	Transplants	Sep–Mar	In sand beds or in pots of sand	Mar–Jun	PNW, SW	To 0.2 m	Perennial plants with runners, full sun to shade	Prefers moist sandy soils.
Big filaree (*Erodium botrys*)	Seeds	Apr–Jul	Dry, cool area	Sep–Nov	CA	To 0.2 m	Winter annual, full sun	Pest plant, occurs in most well-drained soils.
Bird's foot trefoil (*Lotus corniculatus*)‡	Seeds (inoculated)	Jun–Sep	Dry, cool area	Mar–Jun	NE, MA	To 0.6 m	Long-rooted, perennial, full sun	Pest plant, occurs in most soils, common on coasts.
Bittersweet nightshade (*Solanum dulcamara*)‡	Seeds	May–Sep	Dry, cool area	Apr–May	NE, MA, NP	To 2.6 m	Perennial, climbing stem, full sun to shade	Prefers moist soils and in woods, but grows in open areas.
Black medic (*Medicago lupulina*)‡,¶	Seeds (inoculated)	Mar–Jun (south) Jun–Aug (north)	Dry, cool area	Nov–Feb (south) Mar–Jun (north)	Entire U.S.	To 0.3 m	Annual, shallow taproot, full sun	Prefers well-drained or dry soils, dormant in south in the summer.
Black nightshade (*Solanum nigrum*)‡	Seeds	Jul–Oct	Dry, cool area	Apr–Jun	Eastern U.S.	To 1 m	Erect, annual, hairy, hardy, full sun	Pest in cultivated areas, occurs in most soils.
Blackseed plantain (*Plantago rugelii*)‡	Seeds	Jun–Sep	Dry, cool area	Apr–Jun	Eastern and mid-U.S.	To 1 m	Perennial, rootstock stout, thick, erect, hardy, full sun or shade	Pest plant, occurs in woods, fields, and waste areas.

Forbs (Continued)

Bottlebrush (*Plantago arenaria*)‡	Seeds	May–Oct	Dry, cool area	Apr–Jun	Eastern U.S.	To 1 m	Annual, many-branched stem, full sun	Prefers well-drained open areas.
Bracted plantain (*Plantago aristata*)‡	Seeds	Jun–Oct	Dry, cool area	Apr–Jun	Entire U.S. except MW, PNW, CA, SW	To 0.5 m	Perennial, stout rootstock, erect, full sun	Prefers dry open areas.
Broadleaf plantain (*Plantago major*)‡	Seeds	May–Sep	Dry, cool area	Apr–Jun	Entire U.S.	To 0.2 m	Perennial, rootstock short, thick, erect, full sun	Occurs in most soils, in waste places.
Buckthorn plantain (*Plantago lanceolata*)‡	Seeds	Apr–Nov	Dry, cool area	Mar–Jun	Eastern U.S.	To 0.3 m	Perennial, pubescent, short rootstock, full sun	In fields and waste places.
Bush lupine (*Lupinus arboreus*)	Seeds	Jun–Sep	Dry, cool area, soak in hot water before planting	Apr–Jun	PNW, CA	To 0.6 m	Perennial, many-branched, shrubby, full sun	In dry, open areas.
Calandrinia (*Calandrinia maritima*)	Seeds	Jul–Sep	Dry, cool area	Mar–Jun	CA	—	—	In dry scrub areas, sandy coastal beaches.
Camphorweed (*Heterotheca subaxillaris*)‡	Seeds	Jul–Sep	Dry, cool area	Apr–Jun	MA, SE, FL, MS, SW, SP, MP	To 1 m	Biennial, many-branched, many-flowered, full sun	Prefers dry, sandy soils, sea beaches, occurs commonly on dredged-material islands.
Chufa (*Cyperus esculentus*)‡,§,¶	Tuber, seeds	Jul–Oct	Moist cold room (tubers); dry, cool area (seeds)	Mar–Jun	Entire U.S.	To 0.6 m	Perennial sedge, robust, fast-growing, numerous edible tubers, full sun	Prefers wet to moist soils prime wildlife food, extremely prolific.
Coast deervetch (*Lotus formosissimus*)	Seeds (inoculated)	Jun–Sep	Dry, cool area	Apr–Jun	PNW, CA	To 0.5 m	Perennial, long roots, slender stems, full sun	Prefers dry, well-drained soils.
Common chickweed (*Stellaria media*)‡	Seeds	Dec–Feb	Dry, cool area	Oct–Dec	Entire U.S.	To 0.5 m	Weak, tufted annual, much-branched, full sun	Pest plant in all agronomic situations.

TABLE A.4   Selected Upland Plant Species for Habitat Development on Dredged-Material Sites and Various Other Areas   (Continued)

Species	Best propagule type	Collection periods*	Temporary storage requirements	Planting periods	Range†	Mature height	Growth habits	Remarks
Forbs (Continued)								
Common filaree (*Erodium cicutarium*)‡	Seeds	Apr–Jul	Dry, cool area	Sep–Nov	NE, MA, SE, SP, GL, PNW, CA	To 0.2 m	Winter annual, taproots, many-branched, full sun	Pest plant, occurs in most soils, prefers well-drained soils.
Common lambsquarters (*Chenopodium album*)‡	Seeds	Jul–Oct	Dry, cool area	Apr–Jun	Entire U.S.	To 1.3 m	Annual, erect, bushy common, shade to full sun	Pest plant, occurs in most soils, occurs on dredged-material islands.
Common mullein (*Verbascum thapsus*)‡	Seeds	Jun–Sep	Dry, cool area	Apr–Jun	Entire U.S.	To 2.3 m	Erect, stout, biennial, full sun	Pest plant, occurs in open well-drained areas.
Common purslane (*Portulaca oleracea*)‡	Seeds	Jun–Sep	Dry, cool area	Apr–Jun	Entire U.S.	To 0.2 m	Annual, prostrate, free-branching, deep roots, full sun	Prefers dry sandy areas.
Common ragweed (*Ambrosia artimisiifolia*)‡	Seeds	Sep–Nov	Dry, cool area	Apr–Jun	Entire U.S.	To 2.3 m	Annual, shallow roots, robust, common, full sun	Pest plant, occurs in most soils, tolerates salt spray, occurs on dredged-material islands.
Common spikerush (*Eleocharis palustris*)‡	Transplants, seeds	Apr–Sep	In sand beds (transplants); moist, cool area	Apr–Sep	Entire U.S.	To 1 m	Perennial, upright, slender stems, full sun	Occurs in moist soils in interior areas.
Common threesquare (*Scirpus americanus*)‡	Transplants, seeds	Sep–Mar (transplants) Jul–Oct (seeds)	In sand beds (transplants); moist, cool area	Mar–Jun	Entire U.S. except SW	To 2 m	Perennial, upright, triangular stems, full sun	Occurs in moist soils in fresh and brackish areas, good wildlife food.
Cowpea (*Vigna sinensis*)‡,¶	Seeds (inoculated)	Jun–Sep	Dry, cool area	Mar–Sep	Entire U.S.	To 0.5 m	Summer annual, viny, fast-growing, good seed producer, full sun	Cultivated in most soils for human food, hay and forage, especially in the south.

Forbs (Continued)

Species	Propagation	Date	Site	Bloom	Range	Height	Characteristics	Remarks
Crimson clover (*Trifolium incarnatum*)¶	Seeds (inoculated)	Mar–Apr (south) Jun–Sep (north)	Dry, cool area	Dec–Feb (south) Mar–Jul (north)	Entire U.S.	To 0.5 m	Strong perennial in south, annual in north, procumbent stems, fast-growing	Cultivated on most soils for hay and grazing, and on rights-of-way.
Croton (*Croton californicus*)	Seeds	Aug–Oct	Dry, cool area	Apr–Jun	CA, SW	To 1 m	Many-branched, stout annual, robust, full sun	Occurs in waste areas and dry soils, pest plant.
Curly dock (*Rumex crispus*)‡	Seeds	Apr–Jul	Dry, cool area	Apr–Jun	Entire U.S.	To 1.3 m	Perennial, stout, deep taproot, erect, persistent, full sun	Pest plant, occurs in waste areas and crops and in most soils.
Deerweed (*Lotus scoparius*)	Seeds	Jun–Sep	Dry, cool area	Apr–Jun	CA	To 0.5 m	Perennial, long taproots, full sun	Occurs in waste areas, dry soils.
Dwarf spikerush (*Eleocharis parvula*)‡	Transplants, seeds	Mar–Nov (transplants) Jun–Sep (seeds)	In sand beds, dry, cool area	Mar–Jun	Entire U.S. except SW	To 1 m	Perennial, tiny stems, turflike, full sun	Occurs in moist soils in fresh, brackish areas.
Filaree (*Erodium obtusiplicatum*)	Seeds	Apr–Sep	Dry, cool area	Nov–May	PNW, CA	To 0.3 m	Annual, tufted, ascending stems, full sun	Occurs in most soils, waste places and fields, prefers well-drained areas.
Flat pea (*Lathyrus sylvestris*)‡,¶	Seeds (inoculated)	May–Sep	Dry, cool area	Feb–Jun	NE, MA, MRV, GL, PNW	To 2.3 m	Perennial, viny plant, forms mats, full sun to shade	Occurs in moist soils, very slow growing.
Flowering spurge (*Euphorbia corollata*)‡	Seeds	Apr–Oct	Dry, cool area	Mar–Jun	Eastern and mid-U.S	To 1 m	Perennial, long stout rootstock, erect, full sun	Prefers dry soils.
Giant ragweed (*Ambrosia trifida*)‡	Seeds	Jul–Oct	Dry, cool area	Apr–Jun	Entire U.S. except PNW, CA	To 0.5 m	Annual, stout, erect, persistent, full sun	Pest plant, prefers moist soil, tolerates salt spray, common on coasts.

Species	Best propagule type	Collection periods*	Temporary storage requirements	Planting periods	Range†	Mature height	Growth habits	Remarks
Forbs *(Continued)*								
Goosefoot (*Chenopodium murale*)‡	Seeds	Jun–Sep	Dry, cool area	Mar–Jun	Entire U.S.	To 1 m	Annual, scruffy, erect, branches, full sun	Pest plant, occurs in most soils, in waste places.
Hardstem bulrush (*Scirpus acutus*)‡,§	Rhizomes, transplants	Jun–Sep	Dry, cool area	Mar–Jun	Entire U.S.	To 2 m	Perennial, stout, sharp stem tips, persistent, full sun	Prefers moist soils, pest in ground pastures, extremely hardy.
Hairy vetch (*Vicia hirsuta*)¶	Seeds (inoculated)	Mar–Apr (south) Apr–Jul (north)	Dry, cool area	Nov–Feb (south) Mar–May (north)	Entire U.S.	To 1 m	Annual or biennial, viny, weak-stemmed, fast-growing, full sun	Cultivated for forage, occurs in most soils, excellent erosion control.
Hemp sesbania (*Sesbania exaltata*)‡	Seeds	Aug–Nov	Dry, cool area	Mar–Jun	SW, MA, SE, FL, MS, SP	To 4 m	Annual legume, widely branched, robust, full sun	Occurs in most soils, pest in soybean fields.
Hop clover (*Trifolium procumbens*)¶	Seeds (inoculated)	Jan–Mar (south) Mar–Jun (north)	Dry, cool area	Oct–Feb (south) Jan–Apr (north)	Entire U.S.	To 0.3 m	Winter annual, low, forms carpet, procumbent, full sun	Occurs on poor dry soils, excellent nitrogen-fixing legume, crowds out grasses.
Horse nettle (*Solanum carolinense*)‡	Seeds	May–Sep	Remove pulpy coat; dry, cool area	Apr–Jun	Eastern U.S. and SP	To 1.3 m	Perennial, erect, spiny, branched, full sun	Occurs in most dry soils, pest plant in agricultural situations.
Horseweed (*Erigeron canadensis*)‡	Seeds	Jun–Nov	Dry, cool area	Apr–Jun	Entire U.S.	To 3.3 m	Annual, stout, erect, fast-growing, full sun	Pest plant, occurs on most soils, tolerates salt spray, common on dredged-material islands.
Japanese clover (*Lespedeza striata*)¶	Seeds (inoculated)	May–Sep	Dry, cool area	Feb–Apr	Entire U.S.	To 1 m	Annual, erect, many-branched, full sun	Cultivated for forage, and silage, excellent on poor, well-drained soils.
Jerusalem artichoke (*Helianthus tuberosus*)	Seeds	Sep–Oct	Dry, cool area	Apr–Jun	Eastern U.S. mid-U.S.	To 4 m	Perennial, fleshy, rootstock tubers, stout, erect	Prefers moist soil, tubers are edible.

Forbs (Continued)

Common name (Scientific name)	Propagation	Season	Conditions	Planting time	Region	Height	Growth habit	Remarks
Korean clover (*Lespedeza stipulacea*)‡	Seeds (inoculated)	May–Sep	Dry, cool area	Feb–Apr	Entire U.S.	To 1 m	Annual, erect, many-branched, full sun	Cultivated for forage, hay, and silage, excellent on poor, well-drained soils.
Ladino clover (*Trifolium repens* var. *latum*)¶	Seeds (inoculated)	Mar–Apr (south) Apr–Jul (north)	Dry, cool area	Nov–Jan (south) Feb–Mar (north)	Entire U.S.	To 1 m	Perennial, fast-growing, fleshy stems, creeping, full sun	Cultivated for forage, hay, and silage, excellent on poor, well-drained soils.
Ladysthumb (*Polygonum persicaria*)‡	Seeds	Jun–Oct	Dry, cool area	Apr–Jun	Entire U.S.	To 0.6 m	Annual, ascending stems, variable branching, full sun	Prefers moist soils, in waste places, pest plant in some areas.
Lespedeza (*Lespedeza striata*)¶	Seeds (inoculated)	May–Sep	Dry, cool area	Feb–May	Entire U.S.	To 0.6 m	Perennial, shrubby, full sun	Cultivated for forage, hay, and silage, highway rights-of-way, well-drained soils.
Lupine (*Lupine polyphyllus*)	Seeds	May–Sep	Dry, cool area; soak with hot water prior to planting	Apr–Jun	PNW, CA, SW	To 0.5 m	Perennial, shrubby, full sun	Prefers dry, sandy soils.
Malta starthistle (*Centaurea melitensis*)	Seeds	Apr–Sep	Dry, cool area	Feb–Apr	Entire U.S.	To 1.3 m	Annual, much-branched, spiny yellow flowers, full sun	Occurs in most soils, waste and cultivated areas, pest plant.
Mapleleaf goosefoot (*Chenopodium hybridum*)‡	Seeds	Jul–Sep	Dry, cool area	Apr–Jun	Entire U.S. except PNW, CA	To 2.5 m	Annual, erect, bright green, branched, shade to full sun	Occurs in woods and thickets or in open, most soil types.
Marsh pea (*Lathyrus palustris*)‡	Seeds (inoculated)	May–Sep	Dry, cool area	Feb–Jun	Entire U.S.	To 1.3 m	Perennial, viny shrub, very persistent, full sun	Prefers moist areas.
Marsh pepper (*Polygonum hydropiper*)‡	Seeds	Jul–Sep	Dry, cool area	Mar–Jun	Entire U.S.	To 0.6 m	Annual, erect, reddish-green, may be branched, full sun	Occurs in moist waste places, sometimes in standing water.

TABLE A.4 Selected Upland Plant Species for Habitat Development on Dredged-Material Sites and Various Other Areas (Continued)

Species	Best propagule type	Collection periods*	Temporary storage requirements	Planting periods	Range†	Mature height	Growth habits	Remarks
Forbs (Continued)								
Maximillian's sunflower (Helianthus maximilliani)	Seeds	Aug–Nov	Dry, cool area	Apr–Jul	MA, SE, MS, SP, MP, NP, PNW	To 2 m	Upright, coarse, stout, annual, full sun	Occurs in most soils, attractive flowers.
Mexican tea (Chenopodium ambrosioides)‡	Transplants, seeds	Aug–Oct	Dry, cool area	Apr–Jun	Entire U.S.	To 1 m	Annual in north, perennial in south, much branched, erect, full sun	Pest plant, occurs in most soils, in cultivated and waste areas.
Musk filaree (Erodium moschatum)	Seeds	Feb–Jul	Dry, cool area	Nov–Apr	CA	To 0.5 m	Winter annual, semierect, full sun	Prefers dry well-drained soils.
Narrowleaf vetch (Vicia angustifolia)‡,¶	Seeds	Feb–Apr (south) Apr–Jun (north)	Dry, cool area	Oct–Dec (south) Feb–May (north)	Entire U.S.	To 1 m	Perennial, viny, trailing, spreading, full sun	Cultivated for pastures, hay, and silage.
Nodding smartweed (Polygonum lapthifolium)‡	Seeds	Jun–Sep	Dry, cool area	Mar–Jun	Entire U.S.	To 1 m	Annual, much branched, nodes swollen, good seed producer, full sun	Occurs in most soils and in waste and cultivated areas.
Nutsedge (Cyperus filiculmis)‡	Corms, seeds	Jun–Aug	Dry, cool area	Mar–Jun	NP, MP, SP, FL	To 0.5 m	Perennial, hard oblong corms, ascending, full sun	Occurs in dry fields and on hills.
Olney threesquare (Scirpus olneyi)‡	Transplants, seeds	Sep–Mar	In sand beds or in sand pots	Apr–Jun	Entire U.S. coastline	To 2.3 m	Perennial, upright, stems three-winged, full sun	Occurs in coastal and fresh moist areas, tolerates salinity.
Orache (Atriplex patula)‡	Seeds	Aug–Oct	Dry, cool area	Apr–Jun	Entire U.S. coastline	To 1 m	Annual, widely branched, fruiting bracts, fleshy, full sun	Occurs in salt meadows, along coasts, and inland areas.
Partridgepea (Cassia fasciculata)‡,¶	Seeds (inoculated)	Jul–Oct	Dry, cool area; soak seeds in water before planting	Apr–Jun	Eastern U.S.	To 1 m	Annual, widely branched, erect, spreading, full sun	In dry soils, common in south in cultivated fields and disturbed areas.

Forbs (Continued)

Pennsylvania smartweed (*Polygonum pennsylvanicum*)‡	Seeds	Jul–Sep	Dry, cool area	Mar–Jun	Eastern and mid-U.S.	To 1.3 m	Annual, ascending, branched stems, full sun	Occurs on most soils, prefers moist soil, a sometimes pest plant.
Pickleweed (*Rumex occidentalis*)‡	Seeds	May–Aug	Dry, cool area	Apr–Jun	CA, PNW, NE, SW	To 1 m	Perennial, stout stem, erect, unbranched, full sun	Prefers wet places.
Pokeberry (*Phytolacca americana*)‡	Seeds	Sep–Oct	Dry, cool area	Mar–Jun	Entire U.S. except NP, PNW, MW, SW	To 3 m	Robust perennial, with several purple stems, full sun to shade	Occurs in most soil types, and waste places.
Prostrate knotweed (*Polygonum aviculare*)‡	Seeds	Jun–Oct	Dry, cool area	Apr–Jun	Entire U.S.	To 0.6 m	Annual, prostrate or ascending stems, creeping, full sun	Pest plant in many areas, occurs in most soils.
Prostrate pigweed (*Amaranthus blitoides*)	Seeds	Jun–Oct	Dry, cool area	Apr–Jun	NE, GL, MRV, NP	To 0.6 m	Annual, many-branched, prostrate, spreading, full sun	Prefers well-drained soils, occurs in waste areas, pest plant.
Prostrate spurge (*Euphorbia supina*)	Seeds	May–Sep	Dry, cool area	Mar–Jun	Entire U.S.	To 0.5 m	Perennial, procumbent branches, stout at rootstock, full sun	Prefers well-drained soils.
Purple nutsedge (*Cyperus rotundus*)‡	Tubers, seeds	Jul–Sep	Moist, cool area (tubers); dry, cool area (seeds)	Mar–Jul	Entire U.S.	To 0.5 m	Perennial, extremely hardy and persistent, full sun	Pest plant in lawns, gardens, fields, pastures.
Purple vetch (*Vicia americanus*)‡	Seeds (inoculated)	Mar–May (south) May–Jul (north)	Dry, cool area	Nov–Feb (south) Mar–May (north)	Entire U.S.	To 1 m	Perennial, viny, trailing, spreading, full sun	Cultivated for pastures, hay, and silage.
Red clover (*Trifolium pratense*)‡,¶	Seeds (inoculated)	Mar–Apr (south) Apr–Sep (north)	Dry, cool area	Jan–Mar (south) Mar–Jun (north)	Entire U.S. except MW	To 0.6 m	Perennial, ascending stems, many-branched, full sun	Cultivated as forage and hay crops, soil conservation areas.

TABLE A.4 Selected Upland Plant Species for Habitat Development on Dredged-Material Sites and Various Other Areas *(Continued)*

Species	Best propagule type	Collection periods*	Temporary storage requirements	Planting periods	Range†	Mature height	Growth habits	Remarks
Forbs (*Continued*)								
Redroot pigweed (*Amaranthus retroflexus*)‡	Seeds	Jun–Oct	Dry, cool area	Mar–Jun	Entire U.S.	To 1 m	Coarse, summer annual, deep red taproot, very hardy and persistent, shade to full sun	Occurs on most soil types, pest plant in agronomic and feedlot situations.
Reseeding soybean (*Glycine ussuriensis*)¶	Seeds	Sep–Nov	Dry, cool area	Mar–Jun	SE, MS	To 4 m	Annual legume, viny stems, full sun	Cultivated as waterfowl food, occurs in most soils.
River bulrush (*Scirpus fluviatilis*)‡	Root-stock	Sep–Apr	In sand beds or pots of sand	Apr–Jun	NE, MA, SE, CA	To 2 m	Perennial, erect, widely spreading seed head, full sun	Occurs in moist areas and interior U.S.
Saltmarsh bulrush (*Scirpus robustus*)‡,§	Root-stock	Sep–Mar	In sand beds or pots of sand	Mar–Jun	MS, SP, CA, PNW	To 2 m	Perennial, spiny seed, triangular stems, full sun	Prefers marshes, occurs on dredged-material islands.
Saltwort (*Salsola kali*)‡	Trans-plants	Sep–Mar	In sand beds or in pots of sand	Mar–Jun	NE, MA, SE, FL	To 0.6 m	Annual, spiny, much-branched, gray leaves, full sun	Prefers coastal moist areas, tolerates brackish soils.
Schweinitz's nutsedge (*Cyperus schweintizii*)‡	Seeds	Aug–Oct	Dry, cool area	Apr–Jun	NE, GL, MRV, NP, MP	To 1 m	Perennial, thickened corms, slender stems, full sun	Prefers sandy soils, and moist areas.
Sea blite (*Suaeda maritima*)‡	Seeds	Jul–Sep	Dry, cool area	Mar–Jun	Entire U.S. in salt marshes	To 1 m	Annual, much-branched, full sun	Prefers coastal moist areas, tolerates salt spray.
Sea ox-eye (*Borrichia frutescens*)¶	Seeds, trans-plants	Jul–Sep (seeds) Sep–Mar (trans-plants)	Dry, cool area (seed); B&B or potted (trans-plants)	Feb–May	Eastern and southern U.S. coasts	To 0.5 m	Shrubby, fleshy, gray foliate, full sun	Occurs in sandy, coastal areas, tolerates salinity.
Seashore lupine (*Lupinus littoralis*)‡	Seeds	May–Sep	Dry, cool area, soak in water before planting	Mar–Jun	PNW, CA	To 0.5 m	Perennial, scrubby, full sun	Prefers sandy beaches and marshes.

Forbs (Continued)

Species	Propagation	Collection date	Storage	Planting period	Distribution	Height	Characteristics	Remarks
Seaside dock (*Rumex maritima*)‡	Seeds	Jul–Oct	Dry, cool area	Apr–Jun	Entire U.S. except SE, FL, MS	To 0.1 m	Perennial, deep roots, erect, fast-growing, full sun	Prefers moist sandy areas, tolerates salt spray.
Seaside goldenrod (*Solidago sempervirens*)‡	Seeds	Aug–Dec	Dry, cool area	Apr–Jun	Eastern and southern U.S. coasts	To 2.6 m	Perennial, stout, erect, very leafy, large flower, full sun	Occurs on coasts and dredged-material islands.
Seaside plantain (*Plantago maritima*)‡	Transplants, seeds	Mar–Oct (transplants) Jun–Sep (seeds)	In sand beds or pots, dry, cool area	Mar–Jun	Entire coastal U.S.	To 0.2 m	Annual and perennial, fleshy rootstock and stems, full sun	Prefers salt marshes and seashores, tolerates salinity.
Sericea lespedza (*Lespedeza cuneata*)¶	Seeds	Sep–Dec	Dry, cool area	Mar–Jun	FL, MP, MA, SE, MRV, SP, MS	To 1 m	Woody perennial, dense fine foliage, good seed production, full sun	Occurs in moist soils, used on rights-of-way, in pastures, hay fields, and conservation projects.
Sheep sorrel (*Rumex acetosella*)‡	Seeds	May–Jun	Dry, cool area	Feb–Apr	Entire U.S.	To 0.3 m	Perennial, basal rosette, full sun	Grows in infertile acid soils, will die in fertile soils.
Showy tick-trefoil (*Desmodium canadense*)‡	Seeds (inoculated)	Jul–Sep	Dry, cool area	Apr–Jun	Eastern U.S.	To 1.6 m	Perennial, erect, much-branched, pubescent, shade or sun	Prefers rich soils, grows in woods or open areas.
Silverleaf croton (*Croton punctatus*)‡	Seeds	Aug–Oct	Dry, cool area	Apr–Jun	FL, SE, MS	To 1 m	Annual, many-branched, silver leaves, full sun	Occurs in coastal soils, tolerates salt spray, tolerates drought.
Southern bulrush (*Scirpus californicus*)‡	Rootstock	Sep–Mar	In sand beds or pots of sand	Mar–Jun	SE, MS, FL, CA	To 4 m	Perennial, triangular stems, upright, droopy spikelets, full sun	Occurs in coastal moist areas, tolerates brackish soils.
Southern ragweed (*Ambrosia bidentata*)‡	Seeds	Jul–Oct	Dry, cool area	Apr–Jun	SE, MS, SP	To 1 m	Annual, hirsuite, many-branched, full sun	Occurs in dry upland soils, pest plant, occurs in waste areas.

TABLE A.4 Selected Upland Plant Species for Habitat Development on Dredged-Material Sites and Various Other Areas *(Continued)*

Forbs (*Continued*)

Species	Best propagule type	Collection periods*	Temporary storage requirements	Planting periods	Range†	Mature height	Growth habits	Remarks
Soybean (*Glycine max*)‡,§,¶	Seeds (inoculated)	Sep–Oct	Dry, cool area	Apr–Jul	Entire U.S.	To 0.6 m	Annual, fast-growing, high seed production, full sun	Cultivated extensively for beans, excellent wildlife food.
Spotted burclover (*Medicago arabica*)	Seeds (inoculated)	Feb–Apr (south) Apr–Jul (north)	Dry, cool area	Nov–Jan (south) Feb–May (north)	Entire U.S.	To 0.5 m	Annual, spreading, stout, spiny seeds, full sun	In poor, dry soils.
Spotted spurge (*Euphorbia maculata*)‡	Seeds	Jun–Nov	Dry, cool area	Apr–Jul	Entire U.S.	To 0.4 m	Annual, branched stem, prostrate, spreading, full sun	Prefers dry soils.
Squarestem spikerush (*Eleocharis quadrangulata*)	Transplants, seeds	Apr–Jul (transplants) Jun–Aug (seeds)	In sand beds or pots (transplants); dry, cool area (seeds)	Mar–Jul	Entire U.S.	To 1 m	Perennial, slender stems, square stems, full sun	Prefers moist areas, occurs on coasts in fresh water.
Sunflower (*Helianthus giganteus*)‡	Seeds	Jul–Oct	Dry, cool area	Apr–Jun	Eastern and mid-U.S.	To 4 m	Perennial, fleshy roots, creeping rootstock, branching, full sun	Prefers moist areas, stems often purple, showy flowers.
Tansymustard (*Descurainia pinnata*)‡	Seeds	May–Jul	Dry, cool area	Mar–May	Entire U.S. except SW	To 0.6 m	Annual, erect, branched, slender ascending branches, full sun	Prefers dry soils.
Tropic croton (*Croton glandulosus*)‡	Seeds	Aug–Oct	Dry, cool area	Apr–Jun	SE, FL, MS, SP, MA, MRV	To 1.5 m	Annual, rough, hardy, full sun	Pest in pasture areas, occurs in moist soils.
Tumbleweed (*Amaranthus albus*)‡	Seeds	Jun–Sep	Dry, cool area	Mar–Jun	Entire U.S.	To 1 m	Annual, pale green, erect, bushy branched	Occurs in most soils; prefers dry soils.
Virginia pepperweed (*Lepidium virginicum*)‡	Seeds	May–Nov	Dry, cool area	Mar–Jun	Entire U.S. except CA, PNW	To 0.5 m	Many-branched, hardy, full sun	In dry soils, pest plant in fields, on many dredged-material islands.

Forbs (Continued)

Species	Propagation	Season	Storage/Treatment	Planting	Region	Height	Growth habit	Notes
Western ragweed (*Ambrosia psilostachya*)‡	Seeds	Sep–Nov	Dry, cool area	Apr–Jun	MW, CA, SW, NE, GL, NP, MP, SP	To 2 m	Perennial, creeping rootstock, hardy, full sun	Prefers well-drained soils, a pest plant.
White clover (*Trifolium repens*)‡,§,¶	Seeds (inoculated)	Mar–May (south) May–Sep (north)	Dry, cool area	Jan–Mar (south) Mar–Jun (north)	Entire U.S. except MW	To 0.3 m	Shallow-rooted perennial with creeping branches, full sun	Cultivated as pasture and hay crops, occurs on moist soils.
White sweetclover (*Melilotus alba*)‡	Seeds (inoculated)	Apr–May (south) Jun–Nov (north)	Dry, cool area	Nov–Feb (south) Mar–May (north)	Eastern U.S.	To 3.3 m	Annual, erect or ascending, branching, full sun	Roadsides, pastures, lawns, occurs in moist soils.
Wild bean (*Strophostyles helvola*)‡	Seeds (inoculated)	Sep–Oct	Dry, cool area	Mar–Jun	Eastern and mid-U.S.	To 3 m	Summer annual legume, viny, full sun	Occurs on beaches, tolerates salt spray.
Wild buckwheat (*Polygonum convolvulus*)‡	Seeds	Jun–Nov	Dry, cool area	Mar–Jun	Entire U.S.	To 1 m	Annual, viny plant, rapid growth, full sun	Occurs in most soils, a pest plant in crops.
Wild sensitive pea (*Cassia nictitans*)	Seeds (inoculated)	Jun–Nov	Dry, cool area	Mar–Jun	Entire U.S.	To 0.3 m	Annual, erect, branching, full sun	Prefers dry soil.
Wild strawberry (*Fragaria virginiana*)	Seeds, transplants	Mar–May (south) May–Jul (north)	In sand beds (transplants); dry, cool area (seeds)	Sep–Feb	Eastern and mid-U.S.	To 0.1 m	Perennial, stout, slender stalks, shade or sun	Prefers dry, rich soil, edible berries.
Woolly croton (*Croton capitatus*)‡,¶	Seeds	Aug–Oct	Dry, cool area	Apr–Jun	MA, SE, MS, SP, MP, MRV	To 2.3 m	Robust, branching annual, good seed production, full sun	Pest in pastures, grows on most soils, prefers sandy areas.
Woolly indianwheat (*Plantago purshii*)‡	Seeds	May–Aug	Dry, cool area	Mar–Jun	MW, SP, NP, MP	To 0.3 m	Annual, ascending leaves, slender stems, full sun	Prefers dry plains and prairies, other dry areas.
Yellow starthistle (*Centaurea solstitialis*)‡	Seeds	Jul–Sep	Dry, cool area	Apr–Jun	NE, MA, MRV, MW, CA	To 0.6 m	Annual, branched, winged stems, full sun	Pest plant in cultivated areas.

TABLE A.4 Selected Upland Plant Species for Habitat Development on Dredged-Material Sites and Various Other Areas (Continued)

Species	Best propagule type	Collection periods*	Temporary storage requirements	Planting periods	Range†	Mature height	Growth habits	Remarks
Forbs (Continued)								
Yellow sweetclover (Melilotus officinalis)‡	Seeds (inoculated)	May–Jun (south) Jul–Nov (north)	Dry, cool area	Nov–Feb (south) Apr–Jun (north)	Eastern U.S.	To 0.3 m	Annual, erect or ascending, branching, full sun	Occurs in waste areas and fields, most soils.
Vines								
American bittersweet (Celastrus scandens)	Seeds	Sep–Nov	Dry, cool area	Mar–Jun	NE, MA, SP, SW, GL, MRV	To over 8 m	Twining, woody vine, ascending trees or trailing on ground	Prefers rich, moist soil.
Bamboo vine (Smilax laurifolia)	Tuber, seeds	Sep–Mar (tubers) Jun–Sep (seeds)	In soil beds: dry, cool area	Feb–Jun	MA, SE, FL, MS, SP	Long trailing stems	Tuber rootstocks, stout, hardy, evergreen, spines, shade	Prefers moist areas in woods and thickets.
Beach morning glory (Ipomoea stolonifera)‡	Rooted stems, seeds	Sep–Apr	In sand beds, dry, cool area	Mar–Jun	Eastern U.S. and SP	To 4 m	Perennial, twining, large roots	Prefers sandy beaches and dunes.
Common greenbrier (Smilax rotundifolia)‡	Seeds	May–Aug	Dry, cool area	Mar–Jun	Eastern and mid-U.S.	Long trailing stems	Woody, four-angled shoots, spiny, shade to sun	Prefers moist areas in woods and thickets, occurs in dry areas.
Crossvine (Bignonia capreolata)	Seeds	May–Aug	Dry, cool area	Mar–Jun	SE, MS, FL, MRV	To 20 m	Woody, cross visible in cross section, shade or sun	Prefers moist woods, occurs in moist open areas.
Fox grape (Vitis labrusca)‡	Seeds	Aug–Sep	Remove pulpy coat; dry, cool area	Mar–Jun	MA, NE, MRV, SE	To 30 m	Climbing, large stem, shade	Prefers thickets, native stock for cultivated grape hybrids.
Fringed catbrier (Smilax bona-nox)‡	Tuber, seeds	Sep–Mar (tubers) Apr–Jul (seeds)	In soil beds (tubers); dry, cool area (seeds)	Apr–Jun	Eastern and mid-U.S.	Long trailing stems	Woody, four-angled, large tubers, spiny leaves and stems, shade or sun	Prefers thickets, moist areas, occurs in dry habitats.
Frost grape (Vitis vulpina)‡	Transplants	Jun–Oct	Remove pulpy coat; dry, cool area	Mar–Jun	NE, MA, SE, MW	Long trailing stems	Climbing, pubescent, thin shining leaves, shade or sun	Prefers moist rocky areas, occurs in open moist areas.

Vines (Continued)

Japanese honeysuckle (*Lonicera japonica*)‡	Rootstock, transplants	Jun–Sep	Dry, cool area	Feb–Jun	Entire U.S.	Long climbing stems	Pubescent, fragrant, persistent, shade or sun	Pest plant in unkept areas, excellent forage plant.
Kudzu (*Pueraria lobata*)¶	Rootstock, transplants	Sep–Mar	In soil beds or pots of soil	Feb–Jun	Entire U.S.	Long climbing stems	Hairy, trifoliate leaves, sun or shade	Pest plant in unkept areas, excellent cover vine, ornamental.
Lanceleaf greenbrier (*Smilax smallii*)	Seeds	Apr–Aug	Dry, cool area	Mar–Jun	SE, FL, SP, MS	Long trailing stems	Woody, slender, no tubers or spines, shade or sun	Prefer dry thickets.
Muscadine grape (*Vitis rotundifolia*)‡,¶	Seeds, transplants	Aug–Oct	Remove pulpy coat; dry, cool area	Mar–Jun	SE, MA, FL, SP, MP, MS	Long trailing stems	Woody, slender stems, large leaves, shade or sun	Prefers moist sandy soil in thickets, occurs in silt and clay in open areas.
Peppervine (*Ampelopsis arborea*)‡	Seeds	Sep–Oct	Dry, cool area	Mar–Jun	Entire U.S.	Long climbing stems	Numerous tendrils, aerial roots, fast-growing, dense cover, sun or shade	Prefers wood and thickets, dry soil, but occurs in open areas.
Sawbrier (*Smilax glauca*)	Seeds	Sep–Mar (tubers) Jun–Aug (seeds)	In soil beds (transplants); dry, cool area (seeds)	Mar–May	Eastern U.S. and SP	Long trailing stems	Deep, tuberous rootstock, stout spines, shade or sun	Prefers dry sandy soil, also called sarsaparilla.
Summer grape (*Vitis aestivalis*)	Seeds	Sep–Oct	Remove pulpy coat; dry, cool area	Mar–Jun	SE, MS, FL	Long trailing vine	Evergreen, coarse-stemmed, persistent, sun or shade	Prefers dry soil in woods, occurs in open areas.
Supplejack (*Berchemia scandens*)‡	Seeds, transplants	May–Aug	Dry, cool area	Mar–Jun	MS, SE, FL, SP	High climbing stems	Shrub, tough, stout leaves and stems	Prefers moist woods, but occurs in open areas.
Virginia creeper (*Parthenocissus quinquefolia*)‡	Seeds	Aug–Oct	Remove pulpy coat; dry, cool areas	Mar–Jun	NE, MA, NRV, MS, SP, MP, NP	High climbing stems	Large leaves, bark loose and shreddy, tendrils, shade or sun	Prefers dry soil in thickets, occurs in the open.

TABLE A.4 Selected Upland Plant Species for Habitat Development on Dredged-Material Sites and Various Other Areas *(Continued)*

Species	Best propagule type	Collection periods*	Temporary storage requirements	Planting periods	Range†	Mature height	Growth habits	Remarks
Vines (Continued)								
Wild bamboo (*Smilax auriculata*)‡	Seeds	Oct–Nov	Remove pulpy coat; dry, cool area	Mar–Jun	SE, MS, FL	Long trailing vine	Evergreen, coarse-stemmed, persistent, sun or shade	Forms low thickets in the open or wooded areas.
Shrubs and small trees								
American elderberry (*Sambucus canadensis*)‡	Transplants, seeds	Sep–Mar Jul–Sep	In nursery; dry, cool place	Feb–Jun	Eastern and mid-U.S.	To 9 m	Deciduous, many-stemmed, large flowers, full sun	Prefers moist soils, but occurs over wide soil ranges.
American hornbeam (*Carpinus caroliniana*)	Transplants	Sep–Mar	B&B or potted in nursery	Feb–Jun	Eastern and mid-U.S.	To 9 m	Deciduous, round crown, partial or full shade	Prefers dry soils, often is understory in open woods.
American plum (*Prunus americana*)‡	Transplants, seeds	Sep–Mar Jul–Sep (seeds)	B&B or potted in nursery; dry, cool place	Feb–Jun	Eastern and mid-U.S.	To 9 m	Deciduous, spreading crown, full to partial sun	Prefers moist soils, occurs in dense thickets, edible fruit.
Arrowwood viburnum (*Viburnum dentatum*)	Transplants	Sep–Mar	B&B or potted in nursery	Feb–May	MS, SE	To 3 m	Deciduous, shrubby, large flowers, partial sun	Prefers moist soils, common as understory.
Autumn olive (*Elaeagnus umbellata*)‡,§,¶	Transplants	Sep–Mar	B&B or potted in nursery	Mar–Jun	MA, SE, MS, FL, SP	To 5 m	Evergreen in south, deciduous in north, full sun, shrub full to partial sun	Prefers dry soils, drought-resistant, very hardy.
Bayberry (*Myrica pensylvanica*)‡	Transplants	Sep–Mar	B&B or potted in nursery	Feb–Jun	NE, MA	To 3 m	Evergreen, very dense, full sun, shrub	Prefers sand soils, occurs in coastal areas, common on dredged material, important habitat plant.
Beach plum (*Prunus maritima*)‡	Transplants, seeds	Oct–Mar	B&B or potted in nursery	Feb–May	MA, NE	To 2 m	Deciduous, low, many-branched, full sun	Prefers sandy, coastal soils, edible fruit.

Shrubs and small trees (Continued)

Plant	Propagation	Collection	Treatment/storage	Planting	Region	Height	Characteristics	Remarks
Bearberry (*Arctostaphylos uva-ursi*)	Transplants, seedlings	Sep–Mar	B&B or potted in nursery, cleaned and stratified (seeds)	Feb–Jun	NE, MA, GL, MRV, NP, MW, CA, PNW	To 0.2 m	Evergreen, spreading shrubby, slow growth, shade to full sun	Occurs in dry, sandy, and rocky soils.
Beautyberry (*Callicarpa americana*)‡	Transplants, plants, seeds	Sep–Mar	B&B or potted in nursery	Feb–Jun	SE, MS, FL, MA	To 2.5 m	Deciduous, shrubby, abundant fruit, full sun to partial shade	Grows in variety of soil conditions, does best as understory plant.
Bicolor lespedeza (*Lespedeza bicolor*)	Transplants, plants	Sep–Nov, Mar–Jun	B&B or potted in nursery	Mar–Jun	MA, SE, FL, SP	To 3 m	Deciduous legume, irregular shrub, full sun	Tolerates poor soils and drought conditions, prefers well-drained, dry areas.
Black raspberry (*Rubus occidentalis*)‡	Transplants	Sep–Mar	Potted in nursery or soil bed	Feb–Jun	NE, MA, SE, SP, MP	To 4 m	Deciduous, spiny, glaucous, roots from stem tips, full sun	Occurs in most soils, persistent, pest plant in pastures.
Blue brush (*Ceanothus thryiflorus*)	Seeds	Jun–Aug	Dry, cool area	Feb–Jun	PNW, CA	To 1 m	Deciduous, shrubby, shade to sun	Occurs in dry, rocky, sandy areas, used for tea substitute by pioneers.
Blue elderberry (*Sambucus caerulea*)	Seeds	Jul–Oct	Cleaned and stratified seeds	Feb–Jun	SW, CA, PNW	To 8 m	Deciduous, many-stemmed, showy flowers, full sun	Occurs in most soils in open or in edges of woods.
Brazilian peppertree (*Schinus terebinthifolius*)‡	Cuttings, transplants	Oct–Apr	In rooting medium (cutting); B&B or potted (transplants)	Oct–Jun	FL	To 10 m	Evergreen, many-branched, tropical, show flowers, full sun	Occurs in most soils below freeze line in Florida, common on dredged-material islands.
Brewer saltbush (*Atriplex breweri*)	Seeds	Jun–Sep	Dry, cool area	Feb–Jun	CA, SW	To 0.5 m	Shrubby, dense, full sun	Occurs in dry, saline soil, also known as sagebrush.
Buffaloberry (*Shepherdia canadensis*)‡	Seeds	Jun–Sep	Cleaned and stratified	Mar–Jun	NE, MA, GL, NP, SW	To 2.5 m	Deciduous, shrubby, shade to sun	Occurs in moist soils.

TABLE A.4 Selected Upland Plant Species for Habitat Development on Dredged-Material Sites and Various Other Areas (*Continued*)

Shrubs and small trees (*Continued*)

Species	Best propagule type	Collection periods*	Temporary storage requirements	Planting periods	Range†	Mature height	Growth habits	Remarks
Bush lupine (*Lupinus albifrons*)	Seeds	Jul–Sep	Dry, cool area	Mar–Jun	PNW, CA	To 0.5 m	Perennial, shrubby, many seed pods, full sun to part shade	Occurs in dry and well-drained soils, both in open and in edges of woods.
California blackberry (*Rubus ursinus*)‡	Seeds, transplants	Sep–Apr (transplants) Jun–Jul (seeds)	B&B or potted in nursery (transplants), cleaned and stratified (seeds)	Feb–May	PNW, CA	To 1 m	Perennial, woody, many-branched, arching, full sun	Occurs in dry, well-drained areas in most soils, dense wood.
California buckthorn (*Rhamnus californica*)	Transplants	Sep–Mar	B&B or potted in nursery	Feb–May	PNW, CA	To 2 m	Deciduous, shrubby, thorny, full sun	Occurs in dry soils.
Canadian serviceberry (*Amelanchier canadensis*)‡	Seeds, transplants	Sep–Apr (transplants) May–Jun (seeds)	B&B or potted in nursery (transplants); cleaned and stratified (seeds)	Mar–Jun	SE, NE, MA	To 7 m	Deciduous, upright, shrubby, pubescent young twigs, full to partial sun	Prefers moist areas, occurs in most soils.
Carolina ash (*Fraxinus caroliniana*)	Transplants	Sep–Mar	B&B or potted in nursery	Mar–Jun	MA, SE, FL, MP, MS, SP	To 14 m	Deciduous, pubescent, five to seven leaflets, shade or sun	Occurs in moist or wet soils, in woods or in open.
Carolina rose (*Rosa carolina*)‡	Hips, cuttings	Jul–Oct (hips) Apr–Oct (cuttings)	Cleaned and stratified (hips); in rooting medium (cuttings)	Feb–Jun	Eastern and mid-U.S.	To 1.5 m	Deciduous, thorny, arching, fast-growing, full sun, open areas	Occurs in most soils, well-drained to dry.
Cascade buckthorn (*Rhamnus purshiana*)‡	Seeds	Jul–Sep	Cleaned and stratified	Apr–Jun	PNW, CA	To 7 m	Deciduous, shrubby, shade to full sun	Occurs in most soils, open areas or in woods.
Cherry laurel (*Prunus caroliniana*)‡,¶	Transplants, cuttings	Sep–Mar	B&B or potted in nursery	Mar–Jun	SE, MS, MA	To 10 m	Evergreen, shrubby, ascending branches, full sun to partial shade	Occurs in most soils, cultivated as an ornamental.

Shrubs and small trees *(Continued)*

Chickasaw plum (*Prunus angustifolia*)‡	Seeds	Jun–Jul	Cleaned and stratified	Feb–May	SE, MS, MA, SP	To 2 m	Deciduous, shrubby, thorny, large fruit, full sun	Ferns, thickets, occurs in most dry and well-drained soils.
Common buckthorn (*Rhamnus caroliniana*)	Trans-plants	Sep–Mar	B&B or potted in nursery	Feb–Jun	SE, FL, MS, SP	To 10 m	Deciduous, shrub or tree, seeds few, shade or sun	Prefers moist soils, in open or edges of woods.
Common chokecherry (*Prunus virginiana*)‡	Seeds	Aug–Sep	Cleaned and stratified	Mar–Jun	MS, MRV, GL, MP, MW, SW, PNW, CA	To 10 m	Deciduous, shrubby, underground stems, forms thickets, shade or sun	Occurs in most soils including sand dunes and rocky areas.
Common deerberry (*Vaccinium stamineum*)	Trans-plants, seeds	Sep–Mar (trans-plants) Apr–Jun (seeds)	B&B or potted, cleaned, and stratified	Feb–May	Eastern U.S.	To 2 m	Deciduous, much-branched, irregular, shade or sun	Occurs in dry soils in woody thickets and edges of woods.
Common juniper (*Juniperus communis*)‡	Seeds, seedlings	Sep–Mar (seedlings) Sep–Nov (seeds)	B&B or potted in nursery, stratified at 5°C	Mar–Jun	GL, MS, SE		Spreading, narrowleaf evergreen shrub, full sun	Used as an ornamental shrub over a large range, quite hardy, tolerates alkaline soils.
Common sweetleaf (*Symplocos tinctoria*)	Trans-plants	Sep–Mar	B&B or potted in nursery	Feb–May	MA, SE, MS	To 3 m	Deciduous, large waxy leaves, sweet taste, shade or sun	Occurs in woods and thickets, mostly in shade, sometimes in open areas.
Crabapple (*Malus angustifolia*)‡	Trans-plants, seeds	Sep–Mar (trans-plants) May–Jul (seeds)	B&B or potted (transplants), cleaned and stratified (seeds)	Feb–May	MA, SE, FA, MS	To 7 m	Deciduous, thorny, bit-ter fruit, showy flowers, full sun	Occurs in most dry soils, in open thickets.
Dahoon (*Ilex cassine*)‡	Trans-plants	Oct–Mar	B&B or potted in nursery	Feb–May	SE, FL, MS	To 8.5 m	Evergreen, thorny, slow-growing, full sun	Prefers sandy moist areas, in woods or open, in coastal areas.

595

TABLE A.4 Selected Upland Plant Species for Habitat Development on Dredged-Material Sites and Various Other Areas (*Continued*)

Species	Best propagule type	Collection periods*	Temporary storage requirements	Planting periods	Range†	Mature height	Growth habits	Remarks
Shrubs and small trees (*Continued*)								
Downy serviceberry (*Amelanchier arborea*)	Trans- plants	Sep–Mar	B&B or potted in nursery	Feb–Jun	SE, MS	To 14 m	Deciduous, large leaves, pubescent, shade or sun	Prefers dry soils in woods or open areas.
Eastern hophornbeam (*Ostrya virginiana*)‡	Trans- plants	Sep–Mar	B&B or potted in nursery	Feb–Jun	NE, GL, MP, SP, MRV, SE, MA, FL, MS	To 10 m	Deciduous, hardwood, leaves yellow-green, shade or sun	Prefers dry soils in woods or in open areas.
Elderberry (*Sambucus glauca*)‡	Seeds	Jun–Aug	Cleaned and stratified	Feb–Jun	MW, PNW, CA, SW	To 7 m	Deciduous, large seed heads, few branches	Occurs in dry soil.
Elderberry (*Sambucus callicarpa*)‡	Seeds	Jun–Aug	Cleaned and stratified	Feb–Jun	PNW, CA	To 7 m	Deciduous, shrubby	Occurs in dry soils.
Evergreen blackberry (*Rubus laciniatus*)‡	Seeds	Jun–Jul	Cleaned and replanted	Aug–Sep	Eastern U.S.	To 4 m	Stout, deciduous, arch- ing branches, persistent	Pest plant in pastures, cultivated for fruit.
Firethorn (*Pyracantha coccinea*)¶	Seeds, trans- plants	Sep–Jan (seeds) Sep–Mar (trans- plants)	Cleaned and stratified (seeds); B&B or potted (transplants)	Feb–May	MA, SE, SP, FL, MS	To 4 m	Evergreen, irregular, hardy showy flowers and fruit, full sun	Occurs in most soils, does well in wet or dry areas, cultivated as ornamental.
Flowering dogwood (*Cornus florida*)‡	Trans- plants	Oct–Feb	B&B or potted in nursery	Feb–Apr	Eastern U.S. and SP	To 15 m	Deciduous, bushy crown, showy flower, shade or sun	Occurs in dry soils, culti- vated as ornamental, in woods or in open areas.
Gallberry (*Ilex glabra*)‡	Trans- plants	Oct–Mar	B&B or potted in nursery	Feb–May	NE, MA, SE, FL, MS	To 2 m	Evergreen, shrubby, dot- ted underside of leaves, shade or sun	Prefers sandy soil, occurs on coasts.
Gray dogwood (*Cornus racemosa*)‡	Trans- plants	Sep–Mar	B&B or potted in nursery	Feb–May	Eastern and mid-U.S.	To 2 m	Dense, deciduous, shrubby, gray bark, shade or sun	Prefers moist soils, occurs in thickets, woods, open areas.

Shrubs and small trees (Continued)

Ground blueberry (*Vaccinium myrsinites*)‡	Seeds	May–Jun	Cleaned and stratified	Jan–Mar	SE, MS, MA	To 2 m	Evergreen, pubescent, few branches, shade or sun	Prefers moist areas, in woods or open areas.
Groundsel tree (*Baccharis halimifolia*)‡	Seeds, transplants	Sep–Nov	B&B or potted (transplants); dry, cool area (seeds)	Jan–May	SE, MA, MS, SP, NE	To 3. 5 m	Many-branched, deciduous, shrubby, full sun	Prefers moist areas, occurs on seacoasts, tolerates salinity.
Halberd-leaved willow (*Salix hastata*)‡,¶	Transplants	Sep–Mar	B&B or potted	Feb–Jun	Entire U.S.	To 10 m	Many-branched, deciduous, full sun	Cultivated to ornamental.
Hibiscus (*Hibiscus moscheutos*)‡	Seeds, transplants	Sep–Mar (transplants) Jun–Aug (seeds)	B&B or potted (transplants); dry, cool area (seeds)	Feb–Jun	NE, SE, MA, FL, MS, SP	To 2.3 m	Deciduous, many-branched, erect, large seed pods, full sun	Prefers moist soils, tolerates some salinity, occurs on coasts and inland.
Highbush blueberry (*Vaccinium corymbosum*)‡,¶	Seeds, cuttings	Jan–Feb (transplants) Jun–Aug (seeds)	Cooled, cleaned, and planted (seeds); layered in rooting medium (transplants)	Feb–Jun	NE, SE, MA, FL, MS	To 4 m	Deciduous, erect, hardy, many-branched, shade to full sun	Occurs in moist soils.
Hollyleaf cherry (*Prunus ilicifolia*)	Seeds, transplants	Jul–Sep	Cleaned and stratified	Nov–May	CA	To 8 m	Evergreen, serrated hollylike leaves, full sun	Prefers dry soils.
Honey mesquite (*Prosopis juliflora*)‡	Seeds	Aug–Sep	Dry, cool area	Feb–May	SP, SW	To 14 m	Deciduous, shrubby, thorny irregular crown, full sun	Prefers dry, sandy, or loam soils, pest plant in western pastures.
Hooker's willow (*Salix hookeriana*)‡	Cuttings	Year-round	Layered in rooting medium	Feb–Jun	PNW, CA	To 10 m	Deciduous, shrubby, pubescent, full sun	Prefers moist areas, tolerates shifting sand and flooding.
Japanese lespedeza (*Lespedeza japonica*)	Seeds, inoculated	May–Sep	Dry, cool area	Feb–Jun	Entire U.S.	To 1 m	Shrubby, woody, perennial, full sun	Cultivated for grazing.

TABLE A.4 Selected Upland Plant Species for Habitat Development on Dredged-Material Sites and Various Other Areas (Continued)

Species	Best propagule type	Collection periods*	Temporary storage requirements	Planting periods	Range†	Mature height	Growth habits	Remarks
Shrubs and small trees (*Continued*)								
Low blueberry (*Vaccinium vacillans*)	Seeds	Jun–Jul	Cleaned and stratified	Oct–May	SE, MA, MS	To 0.6 m	Shrubby, erect, rhizomous, stout, shade or sun	Prefers dry areas, thickets or woods.
Mapleleaf viburnum (*Viburnum acerifolium*)	Seeds	Jul–Oct	Cleaned and stratified	Feb–May	SE, MS, MA	To 1 m	Deciduous, shrubby, maple-shape leaf, shade or sun	Thickets or open areas.
Marsh elder (*Iva frutescens*)‡	Transplants	Oct–Apr	B&B or potted in nursery	Feb–May	NE, MA, SE, FL, MS, SP	To 4 m	Deciduous, many-branched, serrated leaves, full sun	Prefers sandy, moist areas, occurs on coastal islands, dunes and marshes.
Mountain blackberry (*Rubus allegheniensis*)	Seeds, rootstock	Jun–Jul (seeds) Year-round (rootstock)	Cleaned and replanted (seeds); in soil beds (rootstock)	Sep–Nov (seeds) Feb–May (rootstock)	NE, MA, GL, MRV	To 3.5 m	Deciduous, hardy, very robust, prolific fruiting, full sun, spiny	Pest plant in pastures, occurs and thrives almost anywhere.
Multiflora rose (*Rosa multiflora*)‡,§,¶	Transplants	Sep–Mar	B&B or potted in nursery	Feb–Jun	Entire U.S. except NP	To 4 m	Deciduous, arching, thorny, showy flowers, full sun	Pest plant in unkept pastures and fields, cultivated for windbreaks and cover.
Myrtle oak (*Quercus myrtifolia*)	Transplants	Oct–Mar	B&B or potted in nursery	Oct–Mar	FL	To 15 m	Evergreen, leathery, full sun	Prefers sandy coastal soils, tolerates salt spray.
Northern bayberry (*Myrica pensylvanica*)‡	Transplants	Oct–Mar	B&B or potted in nursery	Feb–Jun	NE, MA	To 15 m	Evergreen, pubescent, dense, dark green, full sun	Prefers sandy coastal soils, tolerates salt spray.
Oleander (*Nerium oleander*)‡,§,¶	Transplants	Oct–Mar	B&B or potted in nursery	Feb–Apr	SW, FL, MS	To 10 m	Evergreen, dense, upright stems, showy flowers, full sun	Prefers dry sandy soils, tolerates salt spray and drought, not freeze-tolerant.

598

Shrubs and small trees (*Continued*)

Pacific bayberry (*Myrica californica*)	Transplants	Sep–Mar	B&B or potted in nursery	Mar–Jun	PNW, CA	To 9 m	Evergreen, shrubby, dense foliage, full sun	Prefers sandy sites, occurs in coastal areas, tolerates salt spray.
Pacific dogwood (*Cornus nuttallii*)‡	Transplants	Sep–Mar	B&B or potted in nursery	Feb–Jun	PNW, CA	To 3 m	Deciduous, shrubby, erect, bushy, full sun and shade	Prefers well-drained areas.
Pacific wax myrtle (*Myrica californica*)	Transplants	Oct–Feb	B&B or potted in nursery	Feb–May	PNW, CA, coasts	To 11 m	Evergreen, thick shrubs, ascending branches, full sun	Prefers moist areas, occurs in marshes, gullies, sand dunes, islands.
Pacific willow (*Salix lasiandra*)‡	Cuttings, transplants	Year-round (cuttings) Sep–Mar (transplants)	In rooting medium (cuttings); B&B or in pots (transplants)	Feb–May	PNW, CA	To 4 m	Deciduous, shrubby, fast-growing, full sun	Prefers moist areas.
Poison ivy (*Rhus radicans*)‡	Transplants	Sep–Mar	B&B or in pots in nursery	Feb–Jun	Entire U.S.	To 5 m	Deciduous, fast-growing, full sun	Prefers moist areas, vine form not recommended for planting.
Possumhaw (*Ilex decidua*)‡,¶	Seeds	Sep–Dec	Cleaned and stratified	Mar–Jun	GL, SP, MP, MRV, SE, MS, MA, FL	To 10 m	Deciduous, red berries, very showy, shade or sun	Prefers moist areas, cultivated as ornamental.
Possumhaw viburnum (*Viburnum nudum*)	Seeds	Aug–Oct	Cleaned and stratified	Mar–Jun	SE, MS, MA, FL	To 8 m	Deciduous, large leaves, shade or sun	Occurs in moist soils, in woods or in open areas.
Purpleosier willow (*Salix purpurea*)	Transplants, cuttings	Sep–Mar	In rooting medium, B&B, or potted	Mar–Jun	MA, MRV, NE	To 4 m	Deciduous, purple stems, slender, full sun	Cultivated as an ornamental, prefers moist places, used in bank stabilization.
Pussy willow (*Salix discolor*)¶	Transplants, cuttings	Sep–Mar	B&B or potted in nursery	Mar–Jun	NE, NP, GL	To 8 m	Deciduous, shrubby, full sun	Prefers moist soils, widely used as an ornamental.
Quail brush (*Atriplex lentiformis*)	Seeds	Jul–Oct	Dry, cool area	Mar–May	SW	To 1 m	Deciduous, shrubby, pale green, full sun	Prefers dry, sandy soils, tolerates salinity.

TABLE A.4 Selected Upland Plant Species for Habitat Development on Dredged-Material Sites and Various Other Areas (Continued)

Species	Best propagule type	Collection periods*	Temporary storage requirements	Planting periods	Range†	Mature height	Growth habits	Remarks
Shrubs and small trees (Continued)								
Red alder (*Alnus rubra*)‡	Transplants, cuttings	Year-round (cuttings) Sep–Mar (transplants)	In rooting medium (cuttings); B&B or in pots (transplants)	Feb–May	PNW, CA	To 15 m	Deciduous, shrubby, upright branches, full sun	Occurs on most soils on cut over forestland, beaches, streams.
Red buckeye (*Aesculus pavia*)	Transplants, seeds	Aug–Oct (seeds) Sep–Mar (transplants)	Stratified (seeds), B&B, or in pots	Feb–May	SE, MS, SP	To 8 m	Deciduous, shrubby, shade or sun	Large fruit is inedible, occurs in most soils.
Redosier dogwood (*Cornus stolonifera*)‡,¶	Cuttings, transplants	Aug–Apr (cuttings) Sep–Apr (transplants)	In rooting medium, B&B, or potted	Apr–Jun	NE, MRV, GL, NP, SW, PNW, MW	To 2.3 m	Deciduous, shrubby, stoloniferous, full to partial sun	Occurs in moist soils, prefers moist poorly drained areas.
Riverflat hawthorn (*Crataegus opaca*)	Seeds	Apr–Jun	Cleaned and stratified	Mar–May	SE, MA, MS	To 5 m	Deciduous, leathery, thorny, shade or sun	Prefers dry soils, in woods or in open, red fruit.
Rough-leafed dogwood (*Cornus drummondii*)‡	Transplants	Sep–Mar	B&B or potted	Feb–May	SE, MA, MS, SP, NP, MP	To 5 m	Deciduous, showy flowers, fast-growing, sun or shade	Prefers moist areas, occurs in most soils.
Russian olive (*Elaeagnus angustifolia*)‡,§,¶	Seeds, transplants	Sep–Oct (seeds) Sep–Mar (transplants)	Cleaned and stratified (seeds); B&B or potted (transplants)	Mar–Jun	Entire U.S.	To 7 m	Evergreen, shrubby, spiny, irregular crown, full sun	Occurs in most soils, cultivated for windbreak, roadside, ornamental.
Rusty blackhaw (*Viburnum rufidulum*)	Seeds	Jul–Oct	Cleaned and stratified	Feb–Apr	SE, MS, MA, FL	To 3 m	Deciduous, leathery, shiny green, shade	Prefers dry areas, in woods, but occurs in thickets and open areas.

Shrubs and small trees (Continued)

Salal (*Gaultheria shallon*)‡,¶	Transplants, rootstock	Sep–Mar	B&B or potted in nursery	Feb–Jun	PNW, CA	To 2 m	Evergreen, dark shiny leaves, shade	Prefers moist areas, cultivated for florist industry.
Salmonberry (*Rubus spectabilis*)‡	Seeds	Jun–Aug	Cleaned and in dry, cool area	Mar–Jun	PNW	To 5 m	Deciduous, branching, leafy, shrubby, showy flowers, large fruit, shade	Occurs in moist areas, in woods and thickets.
Saltbush (*Atriplex polycarpa*)‡	Seeds	Jul–Oct	Dry, cool area	Feb–May	SW	To 1 m	Deciduous, shrubby, pale green, full sun	Prefers dry, sandy soils, tolerates drought and salinity.
Saltcedar (*Tamarisk parviflora*)‡,¶	Transplants	Oct–Mar	B&B or potted in nursery	Feb–May	MA, SW, SP, MS, FL	To 5 m	Evergreen, small foliage, irregular crown, full sun	Prefers dry, sandy soils, tolerates drought and salinity.
Sandbar willow (*Salix interior*)‡,¶	Transplants, cuttings	Sep–Mar	B&B or potted in nursery	Mar–Jun	NE, MRV, GL, MP, SP, MW	To 9 m	Deciduous, shrubby, dense, full sun	Prefers moist soils, riverbanks.
Sand blackberry (*Rubus cuneifolius*)‡	Seeds	May–Jul	Cleaned and stratified	Feb–Jun	MA, SE, FL	To 1 m	Deciduous, arching, erect, spiny, robust, full sun	Prefers dry, sandy areas.
Sand pine (*Pinus clausa*)‡,§,¶	Transplants, seedlings	Oct–mar	B&B or potted in nursery	Feb–May	FL, MS	To 6 m	Narrowleaf evergreen, shrubby, full sun	Grows in poor soils, tolerates droughty, sandy conditions, occurs on coasts.
Sawtooth oak (*Quercus acutissima*)‡,§,¶	Transplants	Sep–Mar	B&B or potted in nursery	Feb–May	SE, MS, FL, SP	To 10 m	Deciduous, irregular growth, full sun	Cultivated for wildlife food, occurs on most soils.
Scotch broom (*Cytisus scoparius*)‡,¶	Transplants	Sep–Mar	B&B or potted in nursery	Feb–May	PNW		Evergreen showy flowers, dense growth, full sun	Pest plant in some areas, cultivated as ornamental elsewhere.

TABLE A.4 Selected Upland Plant Species for Habitat Development on Dredged-Material Sites and Various Other Areas *(Continued)*

Species	Best propagule type	Collection periods*	Temporary storage requirements	Planting periods	Range†	Mature height	Growth habits	Remarks
Shrubs and small trees *(Continued)*								
Sharp-toothed blackberry *(Rubus argutus)*‡	Root-stock, seeds	Year-round (rootstock) Jun–Jul (seeds)	In soil beds (rootstock); cleaned and stratified (seeds)	Sep–Nov (seeds) Feb–May (rootstock)	SE, MA, FL, MS, MRV	To 2 m	Deciduous, hardy, very robust, prolific fruiting, full sun, spiny	Pest plant in pastures, occurs and thrives almost anywhere.
Shining sumac *(Rhus copallina)*‡	Seeds, rootstock	Sep–Nov Sep–Mar	Cleaned and stratified (seeds), in soil beds (rootstock)	Feb–Jun	Eastern and mid-U.S.	To 4 m	Deciduous, little branching, lateral spreading roots, forms thickets, full sun	Occurs in moist soils, in open areas.
Shore pine *(Pinus contorta)*‡	Transplants, cuttings	Sep–Mar	B&B or potted in nursery	Feb–May	PNW, CA	To 12 m	Narrowleaf evergreen, spreading, full sun	Coastal dunes plant, very hardy, can be grown from seeds.
Shrub verbena *(Lantana camara)*‡,¶	Seeds, transplants	May–Sep (seeds) Sep–Mar (transplants)	Dry, cool area (seeds), B&B or potted (transplants)	Jan–Apr	FL, SE, MS, SP	To 1 m	Deciduous, tropical, showy flowers, full sun	Cultivated as ornamental, prefers moist, sandy soils.
Silky dogwood *(Cornus amomum)*‡	Transplants	Sep–Mar	B&B or potted	Feb–Jun	Eastern and mid-U.S.	To 3.3 m	Deciduous, purplish stems, full sun	Prefers moist soils, in woods, and in open.
Silky willow *(Salix sericea)*‡	Transplants, cuttings	Year-round (cuttings) Sep–Mar (transplants)	In rooting medium, B&B or potted (transplants)	Mar–Jun	NE, MA, GL, MRV	To 4 m	Deciduous, purplish stems, pubescent, full sun	Prefers wet to moist soils, in open areas.
Sitka alder *(Alnus sinuata)*‡	Transplants, cuttings	Year-round (cuttings) Sep–Mar (transplants)	In rooting medium, B&B or potted (transplants)	Feb–May	PNW	To 10 m	Deciduous, shrubby, multistemmed, full sun	Prefers moist soils, in open areas.

Shrubs and small trees (Continued)

Species	Propagation	Collection	Treatment	Planting	Range	Size	Characteristics	Habitat
Smooth sumac (*Rhus glabra*)‡	Seeds	Sep–Feb	Cleaned and stratified	Feb–Jun	Entire U.S.	To 2 m	Deciduous, shrubby, few branches, forms thickets from roots, full sun	Occurs in most soils, in open areas.
Southern bayberry (*Myrica cerifera*)‡	Transplants	Sep–Mar	B&B or potted	Feb–May	SE, MA, FL, MS, SP	To 5 m	Evergreen, dense, upright branches, full sun	Prefers moist, sandy areas, occurs on seacoasts and islands.
Southern dewberry (*Rubus trivialis*)‡	Seeds, transplants	Apr–May (seeds) Year-round (transplants)	Cleaned and stratified (seeds), B&B or potted (transplants)	Jan–Mar	SE, MS, FL, SP	To 1 m	Deciduous, persistent, large fruit, full sun	Occurs in most soils, excellent wildlife food.
Sparkleberry (*Vaccinium arboreum*)	Seeds	May–Jul	Cleaned and stratified	Jan–May	SE, MA, SP, MS	To 10 m	Deciduous in north, evergreen in south, sprawling, shrubby, shade or full sun	Occurs in dry soils, in woods or open thickets.
Squaw huckleberry (*Vaccinium stamineum*)	Seeds	May–Jun	Cleaned and stratified	Feb–Jun	Eastern and mid-U.S.	To 5 m	Deciduous, leathery, shrubby shade or sun	Occurs in dry woods or open thickets, edges of woods.
Staghorn sumac (*Rhus typhina*)‡	Seeds	Oct–Dec	Cleaned and stratified	Feb–May	Eastern and mid-U.S.	To 4 m	Deciduous, few branches, showy fruit, full sun	Forms thicket, occurs in dry soils.
Summersweet (*Clethra alnifolia*)	Seeds	Sep–Nov	Cleaned and stratified	Feb–May	SE, MS	To 1.5 m	Deciduous, ascending stems, pubescent, shade or sun	Occurs in most soils, in woods and open areas, cultivated as ornamental.
Swamp privet (*Forestiera acuminata*)‡	Transplants	Sep–Mar	B&B or potted	Feb–May	SE, MS	To 8 m	Deciduous, many branches, shrubby, shade or sun	Prefers moist, bottomland-type soils (silt, clay).
Swamp rose (*Rosa palustris*)‡	Transplants	Sep–Mar	B&B or potted	Feb–Jun	MA, SE, MS	To 1 m	Deciduous, arching branches, full sun	Prefers moist soils.

TABLE A.4 Selected Upland Plant Species for Habitat Development on Dredged-Material Sites and Various Other Areas (Continued)

Species	Best propagule type	Collection periods*	Temporary storage requirements	Planting periods	Range†	Mature height	Growth habits	Remarks
Shrubs and small trees (Continued)								
Tag alder (Alnus serrulata)‡	Transplants, cuttings	Year-round (cuttings) Sep–Mar (transplants)	In rooting medium, B&B or potted	Feb–May	NE, MA, MS, SP, MRV	To 5 m	Deciduous, rusty, pubescent, shade or sun	Occurs in moist soils, in woods or in open areas.
Tartarian honeysuckle (Lonicera tartarica)‡	Transplants, rootstock	Sep–Mar	B&B, potted or in soil beds	Feb–Jun	Entire U.S.	To 2 m	Deciduous, showy flowers, full sun	Cultivated as ornamental shrub.
Texas huisache (Acacia smallii)‡	Seeds	Aug–Oct	Dry, cool area	Jan–Apr	SP, MS, SW	To 5 m	Deciduous, large seed pods, full sun	Prefers dry, sandy soils, tolerates drought and salinity.
Thorny elaeagmus (Elaeagnus pungens)‡,¶	Transplants, cuttings	Sep–Apr	B&B or potted in nursery	Mar–Jun	Entire U.S.	To 4 m	Evergreen, robust, thorny, spreading, arching, full sun	Cultivated as ornamental, tolerates poor soil and salt spray.
Toothache tree (Zanthoxylum clava-herculis)‡	Transplants	Sep–Mar	B&B or potted in nursery	Feb–May	SE, FL, MS, SP	To 12 m	Deciduous, fast-growing, spiny, full or partial sun	Prefers well-drained soils, occurs on dredged material in Texas and North Carolina.
Turkey oak (Quercus laevis)‡	Transplants, cuttings	Sep–Mar	B&B or potted in nursery	Feb–May	SE, MA, FL	To 10 m	Deciduous, large leathery leaves, full sun	Prefers sand coastal areas.
Waxmyrtle (Myrica cerifera)‡,¶	Transplants	Oct–Mar	B&B or potted in nursery	Mar–Jun	SE, FL, MS, MA, SP	To 3.3 m	Evergreen, dense, shrubby, ascending branches, full sun	Prefers moist areas, does well on poor, sandy coastal sites.
Western blackberry (Rubus vitifolius)	Transplants	Sep–Mar	B&B or potted	Feb–Jun	PNW, CA	To 1 m	Arching, deciduous, full sun	Occurs in dry soils, pest plant in pastures.
Western chokecherry (Prunus virginiana var. dimissa)	Seeds	Aug–Sep	Cleaned and stratified	Feb–May	CA, PNW	To 8 m	Deciduous, bushy, full sun	Occurs in most soils, smells bad.

Shrubs and small trees (Continued)

Western dogwood (*Cornus occidentalis*)	Transplants	Sep–Mar	B&B or potted	Feb–May	PNW, CA	To 5 m	Deciduous, irregular branches, shade or sun	Occurs in most soils, in woods or in open areas.
Western huckleberry (*Vaccinium ovatum*)	Transplants	Sep–Mar	B&B or potted in nursery	Feb–Jun	PNW, CA	To 2.5 m	Evergreen, erect, slow growth, shade to sun	Occurs in dry woods.
Wild apple (*Malus pumila*)	Seeds, transplants	Aug–Oct (seeds) Sep–Mar (transplants)	Cleaned and stratified, B&B or potted	Feb–May	Entire U.S.	To 7 m	Deciduous, thorny, showy flowers, large fruit, full sun	Occurs in most soils, parent stock of all commercial apple trees.
Wild black currant (*Ribes americanum*)‡	Transplants	Sep–Mar	B&B or potted	Feb–Jun	Northern U.S.	To 1 m	Deciduous, arching, erect branches, shade	Occurs in most soils.
Wild cherry (*Prunus emarginata*)	Seeds	Aug–Sep	Cleaned and stratified	Feb–Jun	PNW, CA, SW	To 10 m	Deciduous, bitter fruit, full sun	Occurs in most soils.
Wild indigo (*Baptisia leucophaea*)‡	Seeds, transplants	Sep–Oct	Dry, cool area (seeds) B&B or potted (transplants)	Jan–Mar	SP, MS, SE	To 1 m	Deciduous, tumbles, seedpods rattle, full sun	Occurs in dry soils, prefers sand or silt, tolerant of salt spray.
Wild rose (*Rosa rugosa*)‡,¶	Transplants, cuttings	Sep–Mar	B&B or potted in nursery (transplants), in rooting medium (cuttings)	Feb–Jun	MA, SE, MS, SP, FL	To 5 m	Deciduous, arching branches, thorns, profuse flowers, full sun	Prefers most soils, fast-growing, tolerant of wide range of soil conditions.
Wingscale (*Atriplex canescens*)	Seeds	Nov–Dec	Dry, cool place	Jan–May	MW, SW, CA	To 2.5 m	Evergreen, shrubby, much-branched, full sun	Tolerates drought and wide range of soil conditions, prefers dry sandy soil.
Winterberry (*Ilex verticillata*)¶	Transplants	Sep–Mar	B&B or potted in nursery	Mar–Jun	SE, MS	To 5 m	Deciduous, arching, rounded crown, full sun or shade	Wide range of soil conditions, prefers most soils.

TABLE A.4   Selected Upland Plant Species for Habitat Development on Dredged-Material Sites and Various Other Areas   (*Continued*)

Species	Best propagule type	Collection periods*	Temporary storage requirements	Planting periods	Range†	Mature height	Growth habits	Remarks
Shrubs and small trees (*Continued*)								
Witch-hazel (*Hamamelis virginiana*)	Transplants	Sep–Mar	B&B or potted in nursery	Feb–May	NE, MA, SE, MS, MP, GL, MRV	To 10 m	Deciduous, shrubby, partial sun to full shade	Prefers moist soils.
Yaupon (*Ilex vomitora*)‡,¶	Transplants	Oct–Mar	B&B or potted in nursery	Jan–Apr	SE, MA, MS, SP, FL	To 6 m	Evergreen, forms dense thickets, has ornamental dwarf form, full sun	Prefers sandy soils, grows on coast, tolerates salt spray.
Yellow paloverde (*Cercidium microphyllum*)¶	Transplants	Oct–Mar	B&B or potted in nursery	Jan–Apr	SW, CA	To 7 m	Deciduous, legume, shrubby, full sun	Tolerates extreme drought and some salinity, prefers sand soil.
Large trees								
American beech (*Fagus grandifolia*)‡,¶	Transplants	Sep–Mar	B&B or potted in nursery	Mar–Jun	NE, MA, SE, MS, GL, MRV, SP	To 30 m	Deciduous, with shallow root system, full sun	Best in moist conditions, poorly drained soils.
American sycamore (*Platanus occidentalis*)‡,¶	Transplants	Sep–Mar	B&B or potted in nursery	Mar–Jun	NE, MA, SE, MS, SP, MP, NP, GL, MRV	To 30 m	Deciduous, wide-spreading crown, full sun	Best in moist soils, but grows under a variety of conditions.
Australian pine (*Casuarina equisetifolia*)‡,¶	Transplants	Oct–Feb	B&B or potted in nursery	Dec–Apr	FL, CA	To 45 m	Narrowleaf evergreen, drooping branches, full sun	Grows well in sandy soils, exotic naturalized in U.S.
Black cherry (*Prunus serotina*)‡,¶	Transplants	Aug–Oct	B&B or potted in nursery	Mar–Jun	NE, MA, SE, FL, MS, SP, MP, NP, GL	To 18 m	Deciduous, upright crown, full sun	Can be grown from seed, wood highly prized for furniture.
Black cottonwood (*Populus trichocarpa*)‡,¶	Transplants, cuttings	Sep–Mar	B&B or ported in nursery (transplants), layered in rooting medium (cuttings)	Mar–Jun	PNW, SW, CA	To 38 m	Deciduous, fast-growing, large, full sun	Used for paper products, prefers moist soils, used for windbreaks and shade.

Large trees (Continued)

Blackgum (*Nyssa sylvatica*)‡,¶	Transplants	Sep–Mar	B&B or potted in nursery	Mar–Jun	NE, MA, SE, FL, MS, SP, MP, NP, MRV, GL	To 27 m	Deciduous, upright crown, slow growing, full sun	Prefers moist soil.
Black locust (*Robinia pseudoacacia*)‡,¶	Transplants	Sep–Mar	B&B or potted in nursery	Mar–Jun	MS, MA, MP	To 25 m	Deciduous, fragrant flowers, spiny, full sun	Tolerates drought and poor soil conditions, a legume.
Black walnut (*Juglans nigra*)‡,¶	Seeds, seedlings	Sep–Nov (seeds) Sep–Mar (seedlings)	Stratified (seeds), B&B or potted (transplants)	Mar–Jun	MA, SE, MS, SP, NP, MRV	To 30 m	Deciduous, edible, upright crown, sun to shade	Varied soil conditions, good food plant, excellent furniture wood, grows slowly.
Black willow (*Salix nigra*)‡	Transplants, cuttings	Oct–Mar	B&B or potted in nursery (transplants), layered in rooting medium	Feb–Jul	SE, MS, MA, SP, FL	To 12 m	Deciduous, shrubby, full sun	Very fast-growing, prefers moist and flooded soils.
Cow oak (*Quercus michauxii*)¶	Seeds, transplants	Sep–Nov (seeds) Oct–Mar (transplants)	Stratified at 5°C, B&B or potted in nursery	Mar–Jul	MA, SE, FL, MS, SP	To 24 m	Deciduous, large edible seed, full sun to part shade	Prefers moist soils, fast-growing.
Eastern cottonwood (*Populus deltoides*)‡,¶	Transplants, cuttings	Sep–Mar	B&B or potted in nursery (transplants), layered in rooting medium (cuttings)	Mar–Jun	MA, SE, GL, MRV, NP, MP, SP, MS	To 30 m	Deciduous, very fast-growing full sun	Used for paper products, shade, prefers moist soil.
Eastern redcedar (*Juniperus virginiana*)‡,¶	Transplants, seeds	Sep–Mar (transplants) Sep–Nov (seeds)	B&B, potted in nursery, (transplants), stratified at 5°C (seeds)	Feb–Jun	SE, MS, SP, MRV	To 12 m	Narrowleaf evergreen, drought-tolerant, full sun	Produced commercially by tree nurseries, tolerates alkaline soil, has shrub form under stressed conditions.
Eastern white pine (*Pinus strobus*)¶	Transplants	Sep–Mar	B&B or potted in nursery	Mar–Jun	NE, GL, MA	To 30 m	Narrowleaf evergreen, pyramidal crown, full sun	Prefers moist sandy soil.

TABLE A.4 Selected Upland Plant Species for Habitat Development on Dredged-Material Sites and Various Other Areas *(Continued)*

Species	Best propagule type	Collection periods*	Temporary storage requirements	Planting periods	Range†	Mature height	Growth habits	Remarks
Large trees (Continued)								
Green ash (*Fraxinus pennsylvanica*)‡	Transplants	Sep–Mar	B&B or potted in nursery	Mar–Jun	Eastern and mid-U.S.	To 24 m	Deciduous, full or partial shade	Prefers moist soils, tolerates poor soil conditions.
Hackberry (*Celtis occidentalis*)‡,¶	Transplants	Sep–Mar	B&B or potted in nursery	Feb–Jun	SE, MS, SP, MRV, MP	To 30 m	Deciduous, large spreading crown, full sun	Tolerates alkaline and sandy soils.
Honeylocust (*Gleditsia triacanthos*)‡,¶	Transplants	Sep–Mar	B&B or potted in nursery	Mar–Jun	SE, MA, GL, MRV, SP, MP, MS	To 24 m	Deciduous legume, spiny, full or partial sun	Prefers moist fertile soils.
Laurel oak (*Quercus laurifolia*)‡,¶	Transplants	Sep–Mar	B&B or potted in nursery	Jan–Mar	SE, SP, MS	To 30 m	Flat-topped crown, broadleaf evergreen, full sun	Prefers moist soils, occurs on coasts.
Live oak (*Quercus virginiana*)‡,¶	Transplants	Sep–Mar	B&B or potted in nursery	Jan–May	SE, SP, MS, MA	To 15 m	Evergreen, large spreading crown, full sun	Prefers sandy moist soils, and occurs on coasts, tolerates salt spray.
Loblolly pine (*Pinus taeda*)‡,¶	Transplants, seedlings	Sep–Mar	B&B or potted in nursery	Feb–Jun	SE, SP, MS, MA	To 21 m	Narrowleaf evergreen, large crown, full sun	Coastal and interior plant on sandy and silt soils (poorly drained).
Longleaf pine (*Pinus palustris*)‡,¶	Transplants, seedlings	Sep–Mar	B&B or potted in nursery	Feb–May	MA, SE, MS, FL, SP	To 37 m	Narrowleaf evergreen, tall open crown, full sun	Prefers sandy conditions, but occurs in other soils, occurs on coast.
Mockernut hickory (*Carya tomentosa*)¶	Transplants, seedlings	Sep–Mar	B&B or potted in nursery	Feb–May	NE, MA, SE, FL, MS, MRV, SP, MP	To 25 m	Deciduous, arching branches, full or partial sun	Prefers drier soils, edible nuts, hardy, common.
Paper mulberry (*Broussonetia papyrifera*)	Transplants	Sep–Mar	B&B or potted in nursery	Mar–Jun	Eastern U.S.	To 15 m	Deciduous, arching branches, full or partial sun	Exotic, naturalized in U.S., fast-growing, forms thickets.

Large trees (Continued)

Species	Propagation	Season	Nursery method	Flowering	Region	Height	Form	Remarks
Peachleaf willow (*Salix amygdaloides*)‡	Trans-plants, cuttings	Sep–Mar	B&B or potted in nursery (transplants), layered in rooting medium (cuttings)	Mar–Jun	GL, NP, MP, MW	To 18 m	Deciduous, drooping branches, full sun	Prefers moist soils, grown on dredged-material islands.
Pecan (*Carya illinoensis*)¶	Trans-plants, seedlings	Sep–Mar	B&B or potted in nursery	Feb–May	SE, MS, SP, MP	To 43 m	Deciduous, irregular crown, full sun	Prefers moist soils, but grows in wide range of soil conditions, edible nuts.
Persimmon (*Diospyros virginiana*)‡	Root-stock	Sep–Mar	In soil beds in nursery	Feb–Jun	MA, SE, FL, MS, SP, MP, MRV	To 18 m	Deciduous, drooping branches, full sun	Prefers moist, rich soils, but tolerates wide range of soil conditions, edible fruit.
Pignut hickory (*Carya glabra*)	Trans-plants, seedlings	Sep–Mar	B&B or potted in nursery	Feb–May	NE, MA, SE, FL, MS, MRV, SP, MP	To 23 m	Deciduous, open crown, full sun	Prefers drier soils than other hickories.
Redbay (*Persea borbonia*)‡	Trans-plants	Oct–Mar	B&B or potted in nursery	Feb–May	MA, FL, SE, MS, SP	To 18 m	Evergreen, upright branches, full or partial sun	Often occurs in dense woods, prefers moist soils.
Red maple (*Acer rubrum*)‡,¶	Trans-plants	Sep–Mar	B&B or potted in nursery	Feb–Jun	Entire eastern U.S.	To 25 m	Deciduous, upright branches, full or partial sun	Prefers moist soils, widely used as an ornamental.
Red mulberry (*Morus rubra*)‡,¶	Trans-plants	Sep–Mar	B&B or potted in nursery	Mar–Jun	Entire eastern U.S.	To 22 m	Deciduous, rounded dense crown, full or partial shade	Prefers moist, fertile soils, edible fruit.
River birch (*Betula nigra*)‡,¶	Trans-plants	Sep–Mar	B&B or potted in nursery	Feb–Jun	MA, SE, MS, SP, MP, MRV	To 25 m	Deciduous, irregular, multistemmed, full or partial sun	Prefers moist soils, used as ornamental, common in South.
Sassafras (*Sassafras albidum*)‡,¶	Trans-plants	Oct–Mar	B&B or potted in nursery	Feb–May	NE, MA, SE, MS, SP, MP, NP, GL, MRV	To 27 m	Deciduous, spreading branches, full or partial sun	Prefers upland soils but occurs over wide range of soil conditions, forms dense thicket.

Species	Best propagule type	Collection periods*	Temporary storage requirements	Planting periods	Range†	Mature height	Growth habits	Remarks
Large trees (Continued)								
Slash pine (*Pinus elliottii*)‡,¶	Transplants, seedlings	Oct–Mar	B&B or potted in nursery	Feb–May	SE, FL, MS	To 30 m	Narrowleaf evergreen, dense rounded crown, full sun	Grows rapidly, commercial forest tree, occurs on coast.
Southern red oak (*Quercus falcata*)¶	Transplants, seedlings	Oct–Mar	B&B or potted in nursery	Feb–May	MA, SE, MS, SP	To 25 m	Deciduous, rounded crown, full sun	Prefers poor upland soil, used as an ornamental.
Sugarberry (*Celtis laevigata*)‡,¶	Transplants	Oct–Mar	B&B or potted in nursery	Mar–Jun	SE, FL, MS, SP, MP	To 12 m	Deciduous, spiny, irregular crown, full sun	Prefers alkaline, well-drained soils.
Sugar maple (*Acer saccharum*)‡,¶	Transplants	Sep–Mar	B&B or potted in nursery	Mar–Jun	GL, NE, MRV, NP, MP, MA	To 30 m	Deciduous, rounded crown, full sun	Prefers moist soils, used for wood, furniture, as an ornamental, and for syrup.
Sweetbay (*Magnolia virginiana*)‡	Transplants	Oct–Mar	B&B or potted in nursery	Feb–May	MA, SE, FL, MS	To 18 m	Evergreen, shrub in north, tree in south, full sun to partial shade	Prefers moist soils, deciduous in north.
Sweetgum (*Liquidambar styraciflua*)‡	Transplants, seedlings	Sep–Mar	B&B or potted in nursery	Feb–Jun	MA, SE, FL, MS, SP, MRV	To 37 m	Deciduous, spreading, crown, fast-growing, full sun	Prefers well-drained soil, tolerates many soil conditions, used for furniture.
Tulip poplar (*Liriodendron tulipifera*)‡,¶	Transplants	Sep–Mar	B&B or potted in nursery	Feb–Jun	NE, MA, SE, MS, MRV, GL	To 46 m	Deciduous, fast-growing, full sun	Prefers moist soil.
Water oak (*Quercus nigra*)‡,¶	Transplants, seedlings	Oct–Mar	B&B or potted in nursery	Feb–May	SE, MA, FL, MS, SP	To 21 m	Deciduous, rounded crown, full sun	Prefers moist soil, fast-growing, produces abundant, small, bitter acorns.

Large trees (Continued)

White ash (*Fraxinus americana*)‡,¶	Transplants	Sep–Mar	B&B or potted in nursery	Mar–Jun	Eastern and mid-U.S.	To 24 m	Deciduous, upright crown, full sun	Prefers upland well-drained areas, fast-growing.
White oak (*Quercus alba*)¶	Transplants, seedlings	Sep–Mar	B&B or potted in nursery	Feb–Jun	NE, MA, SE, MS, GL, MRV, SP, MR, NP	To 30 m	Deciduous, spreading rounded crown, full sun	Tolerates wide range of soil and climatic conditions, edible acorns.
White poplar (*Populus alba*)¶	Transplants, cuttings	Sep–Mar	B&B or potted in nursery	Feb–Jun	Entire U.S.	To 24 m	Deciduous, multitrunked, full sun	Fast-growing, exotic, naturalized over much of U.S.

*Collection periods, storage requirements, and planting periods are only for best propagules. Many of these species may be handled in other ways for other propagule types not portrayed in this table.

†SE = southeast; MS = midsouth; SP = south plains; MP = mid plains; NP = north plains; NE = northeast; MA = mid Atlantic; PNW = Pacific northwest; SW = southwest; FL = Florida; GL = Great Lakes; MRV = Mississippi River Valley; CA = California; MW = midwest.

‡Known to occur on dredged material.
§Planted on dredged-material sites.
¶Known to be available commercially or from state and federal nurseries.
SOURCE: Hunt et al. (1978).

611

TABLE A.5   Characteristics of Some Upland Plant Species*

| | Region† | | | | | | | | | | | | | | Soil conditions pH | | |
Common name	SE	MS	SP	MP	NP	NE	MA	PNW	SW	FL	GL	MRV	CA	MW	Acid	Neu-tral	Alka-line
Grasses																	
American beachgrass						x	x				x					x	x
American dunegrass						x		x									
Bahiagrass	x	x				x				x						x	
Barley	x	x	x	x	x	x	x	x	x	x	x	x	x	x		x	
Barnyard grass	x	x	x	x	x	x	x	x	x		x	x	x	x	x	x	
Beach panic grass	x	x				x				x						x	x
Beaked panic grass	x	x	x	x			x			x		x				x	x
Big bluestem	x	x	x	x	x	x	x			x	x	x	x	x		x	
Bromegrass			x	x	x	x	x	x	x		x	x	x	x			x
Broomsedge	x	x	x			x	x			x	x	x	x	x	x		
Browntop millet	x	x				x				x					x	x	
Bull paspalum	x	x				x				x						x	
Bushy beardgrass	x	x	x			x	x	x	x			x					x
Calley Bermudagrass	x	x	x							x					x	x	
Coastal Bermudagrass	x	x	x			x				x					x	x	x
Common Bermudagrass	x	x	x	x		x			x	x	x	x	x		x	x	x
Common reed	x	x	x			x	x			x	x				x	x	x
Corn	x	x	x	x	x	x	x	x	x	x	x	x	x	x		x	
Dallisgrass	x	x	x			x			x	x					x	x	
Deertongue	x	x	x		x	x	x					x			x	x	
European beachgrass						x							x				
Fall panic grass	x	x	x	x		x	x		x	x	x	x	x	x	x	x	x
Foxtail millet	x	x		x	x	x	x	x	x		x	x				x	
Goose grass	x	x	x	x		x	x		x	x	x	x	x	x	x	x	x
Green bristlegrass	x	x	x	x	x	x	x	x	x	x	x	x	x	x	x	x	x
Italian ryegrass	x	x	x		x	x	x	x		x		x	x		x	x	x
Japanese millet	x	x	x	x	x	x	x	x	x			x	x	x	x	x	x

TABLE A.5   Characteristics of Some Upland Plant Species*   (Continued)

Common name	Soil conditions — Salinity: Fresh	Brackish	Saline	Moisture: Wet	Moist	Dry	Texture: Fine	Coarse	Wildlife value: Food	Cover	Nesting/ breeding	Aesthetic value	Soil stabilization and other soil benefits
Grasses													
American beachgrass		x	x		x			x	x	x			x
American dunegrass	x	x		x	x			x	x	x			x
Bahiagrass	x				x	x	x	x	x	x	?		x
Barley	x				x	x	x	x	x	x	?		x
Barnyard grass	x				x	x	?	x	x	x	?		
Beach panic grass		x	x	x	x			x	x	x			x
Beaked panic grass		x		x		?		x	x	x	?		
Big bluestem		x		x	x		x	x	x	x	?		
Bromegrass	x			x	x		x	x	x	x	?		
Broomsedge	x			x	x		x	x		x	x		
Browntop millet	x			x	x		x	?	x	x			x
Bull paspalum	x				x		x	x	x	x			
Bushy beardgrass	x				x		x	x		x	?		
Calley Bermudagrass	x				x		x	x	x	x			x
Coastal Bermudagrass	x	x		x	x	x	x	x	x	x			x
Common Bermudagrass	x			x	x	x	x	x	x	x	?	x	x
Common reed	x	x		x			x	x		x	x		x
Corn	x				x		x	?	x	x			x
Dallisgrass	x				x		x	x	x	x	?		x
Deertongue	x				x		x	x		x			
European beachgrass		x	x	x	x			x	x	x			x
Fall panic grass	x	x		x	x		x	x	x	x			
Foxtail millet	x				x		x	?	x	x	?		x
Goose grass	x			x	x		x	x	x				
Green bristlegrass	x			x	x	x	x	x		x			
Italian ryegrass	x			x	x		x	x	x	x	?	x	x
Japanese millet	x	x		x	x			x	x	x			x

TABLE A.5 Characteristics of Some Upland Plant Species* (*Continued*)

Region† columns: SE MS SP MP NP NE MA PNW SW FL GL MRV CA MW. Soil conditions → pH: Acid, Neutral, Alkaline.

Common name	SE	MS	SP	MP	NP	NE	MA	PNW	SW	FL	GL	MRV	CA	MW	Acid	Neutral	Alkaline
Grasses (*Continued*)																	
Johnson grass	x	x	x	x		x	x	x		x	x	x	x		x	x	x
Jungle rice	x	x	x	x		x	x	x	x	x	x	x	x		x	x	x
Large crabgrass	x	x	x	x		x	x	x	x	x	x	x	x	x	x	x	x
Little hairgrass						x	x					x			x	x	x
Oats	x	x	x	x	x	x	x	x	x	x	x	x	x	x	x	x	x
Orchardgrass	x	x	x	x	x	x	x	x	x	x	x	x	x	x	x	x	x
Panic grass	x	x	x	x	x	x	x			x					x	x	x
Pearl millet	x		x			x		x							x	x	x
Perennial ryegrass	x	x	x							x					x	x	x
Prairie cordgrass			x	x	x	x	x	x	x		x	x	x		x	x	
Proso millet			x											x	x	x	x
Quackgrass	x	x	x	x	x	x	x	x	x	x	x	x	x	x	x	x	x
Red fescue		x	x	x	x	x	x			x	x	x	x	x	x	x	x
Redtop	x	x	x	x	x	x	x	x	x	x	x	x	x	x	x	x	x
Reed canarygrass	x	x	x	x	x	x	x	x	x	x	x	x	x	x	x	x	x
Rescuegrass	x	x							x			x			x	x	
Rice cutgrass	x	x	x	x	x	x	x	x	x	x	x	x	x	x	x	x	x
Rye	x	x	x	x	x	x	x	x	x	x	x	x	x	x	x	x	x
Saltgrass	x	x	x	x	x				x	x	x	x		x	x	x	x
Saltmeadow cordgrass	x	x	x			x	x			x					x	x	x
Sand dropseed	x	x	x	x	x	x	x	x	x	x	x	x	x	x	x	x	x
Sea oats	x	x					x			x					x	x	x
Seashore bluegrass							x						x		x	x	x
Seashore paspalum	x	x								x					x	x	x
Shoredune panic grass			x	x		x	x			x					x	x	x
Sixweeks fescue	x	x	x	x	x	x	x	x	x	x	x	x	x	x	x	x	x
Smooth crabgrass	x	x	x	x	x	x	x	x		x	x	x	x	x	x	x	x
Sorghum	x	x	x	x	x	x	x	x		x	x	x	x	x	x	x	x
Sudan grass	x	x	x	x			x		x	x	x	x	x	x	x	x	x
Switchgrass	x	x	x	x		x	x		x	x	x	x		x	x	x	x
Tall fescue	x	x	x			x	x			x		x			x	x	x
Texas millet	x	x	x				x			x					x	x	x
Timothy	x			x	x	x	x	x	x		x	x	x	x		x	x
Torpedo grass			x	x						x					x	x	x
Vasey grass	x	x	x				x			x			x		x	x	x
Virginia dropseed		x					x			x					x	x	x
Walter's millet	x	x	x			x	x			x		x			x	x	x
Wheat	x	x	x	x	x	x	x	x	x	x	x	x	x	x	x	x	x

TABLE A.5   Characteristics of Some Upland Plant Species*   (*Continued*)

Common name		Salinity			Moisture			Texture		Wildlife value			Aesthetic value	Soil stabilization and other soil benefits
	Fresh	Brack-ish	Sa-line	Wet	Moist	Dry	Fine	Coarse	Food	Cover	Nesting/breeding		
Grasses (*Continued*)													
Johnson grass	x			x	x		x	x	x	x	?		x
Jungle rice	x	x			x	x		x	x	x	x		
Large crabgrass	x			x	x	x	x	x	x	x			
Little hair-grass	x	x			x	x		x		x			
Oats	x			x	x	x	x	x	x	x			x
Orchard-grass	x			x	x	x	x	x	x	x	?		x
Panic grass	x				x			x	?	x			x
Pearl millet	x				x	x	x	x	x	x			
Perennial ryegrass	x			x	x		x	x	x	x	?		x
Prairie cord-grass	x	x		x			x	x	x	x	?		x
Proso millet	x				x	x	x	x	x	x			x
Quackgrass	x			x	x	x	x	x		x			
Red fescue	x				x		x	x	x	x	?	x	x
Redtop	x			x	x		x	x	x	x	?	x	x
Reed canary-grass	x			x	x		x	x	x	x	x	x	x
Rescuegrass	x				x		x		x	x			x
Rice cutgrass	x			x	x		x	x	x	x	x		x
Rye	x				x		x	x	x	x		x	x
Saltgrass		x	x	x			x	x	x	x	x		x
Saltmeadow cordgrass		x		x			x	x	x	x	x		x
Sand drop-seed	x				x	x		x	?	x			x
Sea oats		x	x		x	x		x	x	x	x	x	x
Seashore bluegrass		x			x	x		x		x		x	x
Seashore paspalum		x	x	x				x	?	x	x		x
Shoredune panic grass		x			x	x		x	?	x	x		x
Sixweeks fescue	x				x			x	x	x			x
Smooth crabgrass	x			x	x	x	x	x	?	x			
Sorghum	x				x		x	x	x	x			x
Sudan grass	x				x		x	x	x	x	?		x
Switchgrass	x	x		x	x		x	x	x	x	?		x
Tall fescue	x				x		x	x	x	x	x		x
Texas millet	x				x		x	x	x	x			x
Timothy	x				x		x	x	x	x	?	x	x
Torpedo grass	x	x		x			x	x	x	x			x
Vasey grass	x			x	x		x	x	x	x			x
Virginia dropseed	x	x	x	x	x	x	x	x		x	?		x
Walter's millet	x			x			x	x	x	x			x
Wheat	x				x	x	x	x	x	x			x

TABLE A.5 Characteristics of Some Upland Plant Species* (*Continued*)

Common name	SE	MS	SP	MP	NP	NE	MA	PNW	SW	FL	GL	MRV	CA	MW	Acid	Neutral	Alkaline
(Region†)															*(Soil conditions — pH)*		
Grasses (*Continued*)																	
Wild rye	x	x	x	x	x	x	x	x	x	x	x	x		x	x	x	x
Woolly panic grass	x	x				x				x					x	x	x
Yellow bristlegrass	x	x	x	x	x	x	x	x		x	x	x		x	x	x	x
Herbs																	
Alfalfa	x	x	x	x	x	x	x	x	x	x	x	x	x	x		x	x
Alsike clover	x	x	x	x	x	x	x	x	x	x	x	x	x	x	x		
Arrow-leafed tearthumb	x	x	x	x	x	x	x			x	x	x		x	x	x	x
Beach pea	x	x	x			x	x	x		x		x			x	x	x
Beach strawberry								x	x						x	x	
Big filaree												x			x	x	x
Bird's foot trefoil						x	x								x	x	x
Bittersweet nightshade					x	x	x								x	x	
Black medic	x	x	x	x	x	x	x	x	x	x	x	x	x	x	x	x	x
Black nightshade	x	x	x			x	x			x		x			x	x	x
Blackseed plantain	x	x	x	x	x	x	x			x	x	x			x	x	x
Bottlebrush	x	x	x			x	x			x		x			x	x	x
Bracted plantain	x	x	x			x	x			x		x			x	x	x
Broadleaf plantain	x	x	x	x	x	x	x	x	x	x	x	x	x	x	x	x	x
Buckthorn plantain	x	x	x			x	x			x		x			x	x	x
Bush lupine						x						x			x		x
Calandrinia												x			x		x
Camphorweed	x	x	x	x		x			x	x					x	x	x
Chufa	x	x	x	x	x	x	x	x	x	x	x	x	x	x	x	x	
Coast deervetch								x				x			x		x
Common chickweed	x	x	x	x	x	x	x	x	x	x	x	x	x	x	x	x	x
Common filaree	x		x			x	x	x			x		x		x	x	x
Common lambsquarters	x	x	x	x	x	x	x	x	x	x	x	x	x	x	x	x	x
Common mullein	x	x	x	x	x	x	x	x	x	x	x	x	x	x	x	x	x
Common purslane	x	x	x	x	x	x	x	x	x	x	x	x	x	x	x	x	x
Common ragweed	x	x	x	x	x	x	x	x	x	x	x	x	x	x	x		x
Common spikerush	x	x	x	x	x	x	x	x	x	x	x	x	x	x	x	x	

TABLE A.5   Characteristics of Some Upland Plant Species*   (*Continued*)

| Common name | Soil conditions | | | | | | | | Wildlife value | | | Aesthetic value | Soil stabilization and other soil benefits |
| | Salinity | | | Moisture | | | Texture | | | | | | |
	Fresh	Brack-ish	Sa-line	Wet	Moist	Dry	Fine	Coarse	Food	Cover	Nesting/breeding		
Grasses (*Continued*)													
Wild rye	x	x			x		x	x	x	x			x
Woolly panic grass	x				x		x	x		x			
Yellow bristle-grass	x				x	x	x	x		x	?		x
Herbs													
Alfalfa	x				x		x	x	x	x	?		x
Alsike clover	x				x	x	x			x	?	x	x
Arrow-leafed tearthumb	x				x		x	x		x	?		x
Beach pea	x	x			x			x	?	x	?		x
Beach strawberry	x	x			x			x	x	x			
Big filaree	x				x		x	x		x			
Bird's foot trefoil	x				x		x	x	?	x			
Bittersweet nightshade	x				x		x	x	x				
Black medic	x				x	x	x	x	x	x		x	x
Black nightshade	x				x		x	x	x				
Blackseed plantain	x			x	x		x	x	x	x			
Bottlebrush	x					x	x	x		x			
Bracted plantain	x				x		x	x		x			
Broadleaf plantain	x				x		x	x		x			
Buckthorn plantain	x				x		x	x		x			
Bush lupine	x					x	x	x	?	x	?		x
Calandrinia	x	x			x			x		x			x
Camphor-weed	x					x		x		x	x		x
Chufa	x			x	x			x	x	x	?		x
Coast deervetch	x					x	x	x	x	x	?		x
Common chickweed	x				x	x	x	x		x			x
Common filaree	x				x	x	x	x		x	?		
Common lambs-quarters	x				x	x	x	x		x	x		x
Common mullein	x					x	?	x		x	?		x
Common purslane	x					x	?	x		x			x
Common ragweed	x	x			x	x	x	x		x	x		x
Common spikerush	x			x	x		x	x	x	x			x

TABLE A.5   Characteristics of Some Upland Plant Species*   (*Continued*)

In the table below, columns SE through MW are the **Region†** group; columns Acid, Neu-tral, and Alka-line are the **Soil conditions — pH** group.

Common name	SE	MS	SP	MP	NP	NE	MA	PNW	SW	FL	GL	MRV	CA	MW	Acid	Neu-tral	Alka-line
Herbs (*Continued*)																	
Common three-square	x	x	x	x	x	x	x		x	x	x	x	x	x	x	x	
Cow pea	x	x	x	x	x	x	x	x	x	x	x	x	x	x	x	x	x
Crimson clover	x	x	x	x	x	x	x	x	x	x	x	x	x	x	x	x	x
Croton									x			x			x	x	x
Curly dock	x	x	x	x	x	x	x	x	x	x	x	x	x	x	x	x	x
Deerweed													x			x	x
Dwarf spikerush	x	x	x	x	x	x	x	x		x	x	x	x	x	x	x	x
Filaree								x					x		x	x	x
Flat pea					x	x	x				x	x			x	x	x
Flowering spurge	x	x	x	x	x	x	x			x	x	x			x	x	x
Giant ragweed	x	x	x	x	x	x	x		x	x	x	x	x		x	x	x
Goosefoot	x	x	x	x	x	x	x	x	x	x	x	x	x	x	x	x	x
Hardstem bulrush	x	x	x	x	x	x	x	x	x	x	x	x	x	x	x	x	
Hairy vetch	x	x	x	x	x	x	x	x	x	x	x	x	x	x	x	x	x
Hemp sesbania	x	x	x			x			x	x					x	x	x
Hop clover	x	x	x	x	x	x	x	x	x	x	x	x	x	x	x	x	x
Horse nettle	x	x	x			x	x			x	x	x			x	x	
Horseweed	x	x	x	x	x	x	x	x	x	x	x	x	x	x	x	x	x
Japanese clover	x	x	x	x	x	x	x	x	x	x	x	x	x	x	x	x	x
Jerusalem artichoke	x	x	x	x	x	x	x			x	x	x			x	x	x
Korean clover	x	x	x	x	x	x	x	x	x	x	x	x	x	x	x	x	x
Ladino clover	x	x	x	x	x	x	x	x	x	x	x	x	x	x	x	x	x
Ladysthumb	x	x	x	x	x	x	x	x	x	x	x	x	x	x	x	x	
Lespedeza	x	x	x	x	x	x	x	x	x	x	x	x	x	x	x	x	x
Lupine									x	x		x			x	x	x
Malta star-thistle	x	x	x	x	x	x	x	x	x	x	x	x	x	x	x	x	x
Mapleleaf goosefoot	x	x	x	x	x	x	x			x	x	x		x	x	x	x
Marsh pea	x	x	x	x	x	x	x	x	x	x	x	x	x	x	x	x	x
Marsh pepper	x	x	x	x	x	x	x	x	x	x	x	x	x	x	x	x	x
Maximillian's sunflower	x	x	x	x	x	x	x								x	x	x
Mexican tea	x	x	x	x	x	x	x	x	x	x	x	x	x	x	x	x	x
Musk filaree													x		x	x	x
Narrow leaf vetch	x	x	x	x	x	x	x	x	x	x	x	x	x	x	x	x	x
Nodding smartweed	x	x	x	x	x	x	x	x	x	x	x	x	x	x	x	x	x
Nutsedge			x	x	x					x					x	x	x
Olney three-square	x	x	x			x	x			x			x		x	x	x

TABLE A.5 Characteristics of Some Upland Plant Species* (*Continued*)

| Common name | Soil conditions | | | | | | | | Wildlife value | | | Aesthetic value | Soil stabilization and other soil benefits |
| | Salinity | | | Moisture | | | Texture | | | | | | |
	Fresh	Brack-ish	Sa-line	Wet	Moist	Dry	Fine	Coarse	Food	Cover	Nesting/ breed-ing		
Herbs (*Continued*)													
Common three-square	x	x		x	x		x	x	x	x	x		x
Cow pea	x				x		x	x	x	x	?		x
Crimson clover	x				x		x	x		x	?	x	x
Croton	x				x	x	x	x	x	x			x
Curly dock	x			x	x		x	x	?	x			x
Deerweed	x					x	x	x	?	x			x
Dwarf spikerush	x	x		x	x		x	x	x	x			x
Filaree	x				x		x	x		x			
Flat pea	x				x		x	x	?	x			x
Flowering spurge	x					x	x	x		x			x
Giant ragweed	x	x		x	x		x	x	x	x	?		x
Goosefoot	x				x		x	x		x			
Hardstem bulrush	x	x		x	x		x	x	x	x	?		x
Hairy vetch	x				x	x	x	x	?	x			x
Hemp sesbania	x				x		x	x		x			x
Hop clover	x				x		x	x		x			x
Horse nettle	x				x	x	x	x	x				
Horseweed	x	x			x	x	x	x		x		x	x
Japanese clover	x				x	x	x	x	x	x	?		x
Jerusalem artichoke	x				x		x	x	x				
Korean clover	x				x	x	x	x	x	x			x
Ladino clover	x				x		x	x	x	x			x
Ladysthumb	x			x	x		x	x	x	x			x
Lespedeza				x	x	x	x	x	x	x		x	
Lupine	x				x	x	?	x		x	?		x
Malta star-thistle	x				x		x	x	?	x			
Mapleleaf goosefoot	x				x	x	x	x		x			
Marsh pea	x			x	x		x	x	x	x	x		x
Marsh pepper	x			x	x		x	x	x	x	?		
Maximillian's sunflower	x				x		x	x		x	?	x	x
Mexican tea	x				x		x	x	?	x	x		
Musk filaree	x				x	x	x	x		x			
Narrow leaf vetch	x				x		x	x	x	x			x
Nodding smartweed			x	x			x	x	x	x		x	
Nutsedge	x					x	x	x	?	x			
Olney three-square	x	x	x		x		x	x	x	x	x		x

TABLE A.5 Characteristics of Some Upland Plant Species* (*Continued*)

Common name	SE	MS	SP	MP	NP	NE	MA	PNW	SW	FL	GL	MRV	CA	MW	Acid	Neutral	Alkaline
Herbs (*Continued*)																	
Orache	x	x	x			x	x			x			x		x	x	x
Patridge pea	x	x	x			x	x			x	x	x			x	x	x
Pennsylvania smartweed	x	x	x	x	x	x	x			x	x	x			x	x	x
Pickleweed						x		x	x			x			x	x	x
Pokeberry	x	x	x	x		x	x			x	x	x	x		x	x	x
Prostrate knotweed	x	x	x	x	x	x	x	x	x	x	x	x	x	x	x	x	x
Prostrate pigweed					x	x						x	x		x	x	x
Prostrate spurge	x	x	x	x	x	x	x	x	x	x	x	x	x	x	x	x	x
Purple nutsedge	x	x	x	x	x	x	x	x	x	x	x	x	x	x	x	x	x
Purple vetch	x	x	x	x	x	x	x	x	x	x	x	x	x	x	x	x	x
Red clover	x	x	x	x	x	x	x	x	x	x	x	x		x	x	x	x
Redroot pigweed	x	x	x	x	x	x	x	x	x	x	x	x	x	x	x	x	x
Reseeding soybean	x	x													x	x	x
River bulrush	x					x	x					x			x	x	x
Saltmarsh bulrush		x	x				x					x			x	x	
Saltwort	x					x	x			x					x	x	x
Schweinitz's nutsedge				x	x	x					x	x			x	x	x
Sea blite	x	x	x			x	x	x	x	x			x	x	x	x	x
Sea ox-eye	x	x	x				x			x					x	x	x
Seashore lupine								x				x			x	x	x
Seaside dock		x	x	x	x	x	x	x	x		x	x	x	x	x	x	x
Seaside goldenrod	x	x	x				x			x					x	x	x
Seaside plantain	x	x	x			x	x	x		x		x			x	x	x
Sericea lespedeza	x	x	x	x			x			x		x			x	x	x
Sheep sorrel	x	x	x	x	x	x	x	x	x	x	x	x	x	x	x		
Showy tick-trefoil	x	x			x	x				x	x	x			x	x	x
Silverleaf croton	x	x								x					x	x	x
Southern bulrush	x	x								x			x		x	x	
Southern ragweed	x	x	x												x	x	x
Soybean	x	x	x	x	x	x	x	x	x	x	x	x	x	x	x	x	x
Spotted burclover	x	x	x	x	x	x	x	x	x	x	x	x	x	x	x	x	x
Spotted spurge	x	x	x	x	x	x	x	x	x	x	x	x	x	x	x	x	x
Squarestem spikerush	x	x	x	x	x	x	x	x	x	x	x	x	x	x	x	x	x

TABLE A.5 Characteristics of Some Upland Plant Species* *(Continued)*

| Common name | Soil conditions | | | | | | | | Wildlife value | | | Aesthetic value | Soil stabilization and other soil benefits |
| | Salinity | | | Moisture | | | Texture | | | | | | |
	Fresh	Brackish	Saline	Wet	Moist	Dry	Fine	Coarse	Food	Cover	Nesting/breeding		
Herbs (Continued)													
Orache		x	x	x			x	x	?	x			
Patridge pea	x				x	x	x	x	x	x		x	x
Pennsylvania smartweed	x			x	x		x	x	x	x	x		
Pickleweed	x			x			x	x		x			
Pokeberry	x				x		x	x	x	x			
Prostrate knotweed	x				x	x	x	x		x			x
Prostrate pigweed	x				x		x	x		x			
Prostrate spurge	x				x		x	x		x			
Purple nutsedge	x			x	x	x	x	x		x			
Purple vetch	x				x		x	x	x	x	x	x	x
Red clover	x				x		x	x	x	x		x	x
Redroot pigweed	x				x			x	?	x			x
Reseeding soybean	x				x		x	x	x	x			
River bulrush	x			x	x		x	x	x	x	x		
Saltmarsh bulrush	x	x	x	x	x		x	x	x	x	?		x
Saltwort	x	x			x		x	x		x			x
Schweinitz's nutsedge	x			x	x		x	x	x	x			
Sea blite		x	x	x	x		x	x		x	?		x
Sea ox-eye		x	x	x	x		x	x		x	x		x
Seashore lupine	x	x		x	x	x	x	x	?	x			x
Seaside dock	x	x		x		?	x	x	x	x			
Seaside goldenrod	x	x		x	x	x	x			x	x		
Seaside plantain	x	x	x	x	x	x		x	x		x		
Sericea lespedeza	x				x		x	x	x	x	?	x	x
Sheep sorrel	x				x		x	x		x			x
Showy tick-trefoil	x				x		x	x	x	x			
Silverleaf croton	x	x		x	x	x	x	x	x	x			
Southern bulrush	x	x		x	x		x	x	x	x	?		x
Southern ragweed	x				x	x	x	x		x	?		
Soybean	x				x		x	x	x	x			x
Spotted burclover	x				x	x	x	x		x			x
Spotted spurge	x					x	x	x		x			
Squarestem spikerush	x			x	x		x	x	x	x			

TABLE A.5   Characteristics of Some Upland Plant Species*   (Continued)

Common name	Region†														Soil conditions — pH		
	SE	MS	SP	MP	NP	NE	MA	PNW	SW	FL	GL	MRV	CA	MW	Acid	Neu-tral	Alka-line
Herbs (Continued)																	
Sunflower	x	x	x	x	x	x	x			x	x	x			x	x	x
Tansy mustard	x	x	x	x	x	x	x	x		x	x	x	x	x	x	x	x
Tropic croton	x	x	x			x				x		x			x	x	x
Tumbleweed	x	x	x	x	x	x	x	x	x	x	x	x	x	x	x	x	x
Virginia pepperweed	x	x	x	x	x	x	x			x	x	x	x		x	x	x
Western ragweed			x	x	x	x			x		x		x	x	x	x	x
White clover	x	x	x	x	x	x	x	x	x	x	x	x	x		x	x	x
White sweetclover	x	x	x	x	x	x	x	x	x	x	x	x	x	x	x	x	x
Wild bean	x	x	x	x	x	x	x			x	x	x			x	x	x
Wild buckwheat	x	x	x	x	x	x	x	x	x	x	x	x	x		x	x	x
Wild sensitive pea	x	x	x	x	x	x	x	x	x	x	x	x	x		x	x	x
Wild strawberry	x	x	x	x	x	x	x			x	x	x			x	x	x
Woolly croton	x	x	x	x			x					x			x	x	x
Woolly indianwheat			x	x	x								x			x	x
Yellow starthistle						x	x					x	x	x	x	x	x
Yellow sweetclover	x	x				x	x			x	x	x			x	x	x
Vines																	
American bittersweet			x			x	x				x	x		x	x	x	x
Bamboo vine	x	x	x			x				x					x	x	x
Beach morning glory	x	x	x			x	x			x	x	x			x	x	x
Common greenbrier	x	x	x	x	x	x	x			x	x	x			x	x	x
Crossvine	x	x								x		x			x	x	x
Fox grape	x					x	x					x			x	x	x
Fringed catbrier	x	x	x	x	x	x	x			x	x	x			x	x	x
Frost grape	x					x	x							x	x	x	x
Japanese honeysuckle	x	x	x	x	x	x	x	x	x	x	x	x	x	x	x	x	x
Kudzu	x	x	x	x	x	x	x	x	x	x	x	x	x	x	x	x	x
Lanceleaf greenbrier	x	x	x							x					x	x	x
Muscadine grape	x	x	x	x			x			x					x	x	x
Peppervine	x	x	x	x	x	x	x	x	x	x	x	x	x	x	x	x	x
Sawbrier	x	x	x		x	x				x	x	x			x	x	x
Summer grape	x	x								x					x	x	x

TABLE A.5 Characteristics of Some Upland Plant Species* (*Continued*)

Common name	Soil conditions								Wildlife value			Aesthetic value	Soil stabilization and other soil benefits
	Salinity			Moisture			Texture				Nesting/breeding		
	Fresh	Brackish	Saline	Wet	Moist	Dry	Fine	Coarse	Food	Cover			
Herbs (*Continued*)													
Sunflower	x			x			x	x		x		x	
Tansy mustard	x			x	x	x	x			x	x		
Tropic croton	x			x			x	x	x	x			
Tumbleweed	x			x	x	x	x			x			
Virginia pepperweed	x			x	x	x	x			x	x		
Western ragweed	x			x	x	x	x			x	?		
White clover	x			x			x	x	x	x	?	x	x
White sweetclover	x			x			x	x	x	x	?		x
Wild bean	x	x		x	x		x	x		x			x
Wild buckwheat	x			x			x	x		x			
Wild sensitive pea	x			x	x	x	x	x	x	x		x	x
Wild strawberry				x	x	x	x	x	x				
Woolly croton	x			x			x	x	x	x	?		
Woolly indianwheat	x				x	x	x			x			
Yellow starthistle	x			x			x	x	x	x			
Yellow sweetclover	x			x	x	x	x	x	x				x
Vines													
American bittersweet	x			x			x	x	x				
Bamboo vine	x			x			x	x	x				
Beach morning glory		x	x			x		x		x		x	x
Common greenbrier	x			x	x	x	x	x	x	x			
Crossvine	x			x			x	x		x			
Fox grape	x			x			x	x	x	x			
Fringed catbrier	x			x			x	x		x			
Frost grape	x			x			x	x	x	x			x
Japanese honeysuckle	x			x			x	x	x	x			x
Kudzu	x			x			x	x	x	x			x
Lanceleaf greenbrier	x			x	x	x	x	x		x			
Muscadine grape	x			x			x		x	x			
Peppervine	x			x	x			x		x			
Sawbrier	x			x	x			x		x			
Summer grape	x			x	x		x	x	x	x			

TABLE A.5   Characteristics of Some Upland Plant Species*   (Continued)

															Soil conditions		
																pH	
Common name							Region†								Acid	Neu-tral	Alka-line
	SE	MS	SP	MP	NP	NE	MA	PNW	SW	FL	GL	MRV	CA	MW			
Vines (Continued)																	
Supplejack	x	x	x							x					x	x	x
Virginia creeper		x	x	x	x	x	x					x			x	x	x
Wild bamboo	x	x								x					x	x	x
Shrubs and small trees																	
American elderberry	x	x	x	x	x	x	x			x	x	x			x	x	x
American hornbeam	x	x	x	x	x	x	x			x	x	x			x	x	x
American plum	x	x	x	x	x	x	x			x	x	x			x	x	x
Arrowwood viburnum	x	x													x	x	x
Autumn olive	x	x	x				x			x					x	x	x
Bayberry						x	x								x	x	x
Beach plum						x	x								x	x	x
Bearberry					x	x	x	x			x	x	x	x	x	x	x
Beautyberry	x	x					x			x					x	x	x
Bicolor lespedeza	x		x				x			x					x	x	x
Black rasp-berry	x		x	x		x	x								x	x	x
Blue brush							x					x			x	x	x
Blue elder-berry							x	x				x			x	x	x
Brazilian peppertree										x					x	x	x
Brewer saltbrush													x	x	x	x	
Buffaloberry					x	x	x		x		x				x	x	x
Bush lupine							x					x			x	x	x
California blackberry							x					x				x	x
California buckthorn							x					x			x	x	x
Canadian service-berry	x					x	x								x	x	x
Carolina ash	x	x	x	x			x			x					x	x	x
Carolina rose	x	x	x	x	x	x	x			x	x	x			x	x	x
Cascara buckthorn							x					x			x	x	x
Cherry laurel	x	x					x								x	x	x
Chickasaw plum	x	x	x				x								x	x	x
Common buckthorn	x	x	x							x					x	x	x
Common choke-cherry		x		x				x	x		x	x	x	x	x	x	x
Common deerberry	x	x				x	x			x	x	x			x	x	x

TABLE A.5   Characteristics of Some Upland Plant Species*   (*Continued*)

Common name	Soil conditions								Wildlife value			Aesthetic value	Soil stabilization and other soil benefits
	Salinity			Moisture			Texture				Nesting/breeding		
	Fresh	Brackish	Saline	Wet	Moist	Dry	Fine	Coarse	Food	Cover			
Vines (*Continued*)													
Supplejack	x				x		x	x		x			
Virginia creeper	x				x	x	x	x		x			
Wild bamboo	x				x		x	x		x			
Shrubs and small trees													
American elderberry	x				x	x	x	x	x	x	?	x	
American hornbeam	x				x	x	x	x	?	x	?		
American plum	x				x	x	x	x	x	x		x	
Arrowwood viburnum	x				x		x	x	x	x			
Autumn olive	x	x		x	x	x	x	x	x	x	x	x	x
Bayberry	x	x			x	x	?	x		x	x	x	x
Beach plum	x	x			x	x	?	x	x	x			x
Bearberry	x					x	?	x	x	x			x
Beautyberry	x				x		x	x	x	x		x	
Bicolor lespedeza	x				x	x	x	x	x	x			x
Black raspberry	x				x		x	x	x	x	?		
Blue brush	x					x		x	x	x			
Blue elderberry	x				x		x	x	x	x			
Brazilian peppertree	x	x			x	x	x	x		x	x	x	x
Brewer saltbrush		x	x		x	x	x			x			x
Buffaloberry	x				x		x	x	x	x	?		x
Bush lupine	x				x	x	x	x		x	?		x
California blackberry	x				x	x	x	x	x	x	?		x
California buckthorn	x					x	x	x		x			x
Canadian serviceberry	x				x	x	x	x	x	x	?		
Carolina ash	x			x	x		x	x	x	x	?	x	x
Carolina rose	x				x	x	x	x		x	x	x	x
Cascara buckthorn	x				x		x	x		x	?		
Cherry laurel	x				x		x	x		x	?	x	
Chickasaw plum	x				x	x	x	x	x	x	x	x	x
Common buckthorn	x				x		x	x		x			
Common chokecherry	x	x			x	x	x	x		x	?		x
Common deerberry	x					x	x	x	x	x			

TABLE A.5 Characteristics of Some Upland Plant Species* (*Continued*)

																Soil conditions		
																	pH	
Common name	Region†																Neu-tral	Alka-line
	SE	MS	SP	MP	NP	NE	MA	PNW	SW	FL	GL	MRV	CA	MW	Acid		
Shrubs and small trees (*Continued*)																	
Common juniper	x	x								x	x					x	x
Common sweetleaf	x	x				x									x	x	x
Crabapple	x	x				x				x					x	x	x
Dahoon	x	x								x					x	x	x
Downy service-berry	x	x													x	x	x
Eastern hophorn-beam	x	x	x	x		x	x			x	x	x			x	x	x
Elderberry (*glauca*)							x	x					x	x	x	x	x
Elderberry (*callicarpa*)							x						x		x	x	x
Evergreen blackberry	x	x				x	x			x	x	x			x	x	x
Firethorn	x	x	x				x			x					x	x	x
Flowering dogwood	x	x	x			x	x			x	x	x			x	x	
Gallberry	x	x				x	x			x					x	x	x
Gray dogwood	x	x	x	x	x	x	x			x	x	x			x	x	
Ground blueberry	x	x				x									x	x	x
Groundsel tree	x	x	x			x	x								x	x	x
Halberd-leaved willow	x	x	x	x	x	x	x	x	x	x	x	x	x	x	x	x	x
Hibiscus	x	x	x			x	x			x					x	x	x
Highland blueberry	x	x				x	x			x					x	x	
Hollyleaf cherry													x		x	x	x
Honey mesquite			x						x						x	x	x
Hooker's willow								x					x		x	x	x
Japanese lespedeza	x	x	x	x	x	x	x	x	x	x	x	x	x	x	x	x	x
Low blue-berry	x	x				x									x	x	
Mapleleaf viburnum	x	x				x									x	x	x
Marsh elder	x	x	x			x	x			x					x	x	x
Mountain blackberry						x	x					x	x		x	x	x
Multiflora rose	x	x	x	x		x	x	x	x	x	x	x	x	x	x	x	x
Myrtle oak										x					x	x	x
Northern bayberry						x	x								x	x	x
Oleander		x						x	x						x	x	x

TABLE A.5 Characteristics of Some Upland Plant Species* (*Continued*)

Common name	Soil conditions — Salinity: Fresh	Brackish	Saline	Moisture: Wet	Moist	Dry	Texture: Fine	Coarse	Wildlife value: Food	Cover	Nesting/breeding	Aesthetic value	Soil stabilization and other soil benefits
Shrubs and small trees (*Continued*)													
Common juniper	x				x		x	x		x	x	x	x
Common sweetleaf	x				x		x	x	x	x			
Crabapple	x				x		x	x	x	x		x	x
Dahoon	x	x			x	x		x		x	x	x	
Downy serviceberry	x				x	x	x	x	x	x			
Eastern hophornbeam	x				x	x	x	x		x	x		
Elderberry (*glauca*)	x				x	x	x	x	x	x			
Elderberry (*callicarpa*)	x				x	x	x	x	x	x			
Evergreen blackberry	x				x		x	x	x	x	x		x
Firethorn	x			x	x	x	x	x	x	x	x	x	x
Flowering dogwood	x				x	x	x	x	x	x		x	
Gallberry	x				x	x	x	x		x			
Gray dogwood	x				x		x	x	x	x			
Ground blueberry	x				x		x	x	x	x			
Groundsel tree	x	x	x		x	x	x	x		x	x		x
Halberd-leaved willow	x				x		x	x		x	x	x	
Hibiscus	x	x		x	x		x	x		x		x	
Highland blueberry	x				x		x	x	x	x			
Hollyleaf cherry					x		x		x			x	
Honey mesquite	x	x				x	x	x		x	x		x
Hooker's willow			x	x		x	x		x		?	x	
Japanese lespedeza	x				x		x	x	x	x		x	x
Low blueberry	x			x		x	x	x	x				
Mapleleaf viburnum	x			x		x	x	x	x		?		
Marsh elder	x		x	x			x		x	x		x	
Mountain blackberry	x			x		x	x	x	x	x		x	
Multiflora rose	x			x		x	x	x	x	x	x	x	
Myrtle oak	x			x		x	x	?	x	x	x		
Northern bayberry	x			x				x	x	x	x	x	
Oleander	x			x	x		x		x	x	x	x	

TABLE A.5   Characteristics of Some Upland Plant Species*   (*Continued*)

Common name	SE	MS	SP	MP	NP	NE	MA	PNW	SW	FL	GL	MRV	CA	MW	Acid	Neutral	Alkaline
Shrubs and small trees (*Continued*)																	
Pacific bayberry								x					x		x	x	x
Pacific dogwood								x					x		x	x	
Pacific wax myrtle								x					x		x	x	x
Pacific willow								x					x		x	x	
Poison ivy	x	x	x	x	x	x	x	x	x	x	x	x	x	x	x	x	x
Possumhaw	x	x	x	x			x			x	x	x			x	x	x
Possumhaw viburnum	x	x					x			x					x	x	x
Purple osier willow					x	x						x			x	x	x
Pussy willow				x	x							x			x	x	x
Quail brush									x						x	x	x
Red alder								x					x		x	x	x
Red buckeye	x	x	x												x	x	x
Red osier dogwood					x	x		x	x		x	x		x	x	x	x
Riverflat hawthorn	x	x					x								x	x	x
Rough-leafed dogwood	x	x	x	x	x		x								x	x	x
Russian olive	x	x	x	x	x	x	x	x	x	x	x	x	x	x	x	x	x
Rusty blackhaw	x	x					x			x					x	x	x
Salal								x					x		x	x	
Salmonberry								x							x	x	x
Saltbush														x	x	x	x
Saltcedar		x	x				x			x			x		x	x	x
Sandbar willow			x	x	x						x	x		x	x	x	x
Sand blackberry	x						x			x					x	x	x
Sand pine		x								x					x	x	x
Sawtooth oak	x	x	x							x					x	x	x
Scotch broom									x						x	x	x
Sharp-toothed blackberry	x	x					x			x	x				x	x	x
Shining sumac	x	x	x	x	x	x	x			x	x	x			x	x	x
Shore pine								x					x		x	x	x
Shrub verbena	x	x	x							x					x	x	x
Silky dogwood	x	x	x	x	x	x	x			x	x	x			x	x	
Silky willow					x	x					x	x			x	x	x
Sitka alder									x						x	x	x
Smooth sumac	x	x	x	x	x	x	x	x	x	x	x	x	x	x	x	x	x
Southern bayberry	x	x	x			x				x					x	x	x
Southern dewberry	x	x	x							x					x	x	x

TABLE A.5   Characteristics of Some Upland Plant Species*   (*Continued*)

Column groups: *Soil conditions* — Salinity (Fresh, Brackish, Saline), Moisture (Wet, Moist, Dry), Texture (Fine, Coarse); *Wildlife value* — Food, Cover, Nesting/breeding; Aesthetic value; Soil stabilization and other soil benefits.

Common name	Fresh	Brack-ish	Sa-line	Wet	Moist	Dry	Fine	Coarse	Food	Cover	Nesting/breeding	Aes-thetic value	Soil stabilization and other soil benefits
Shrubs and small trees (*Continued*)													
Pacific bayberry	x	x		x	x		x	x		x	?		
Pacific dogwood	x				x		x	x	x	x			
Pacific wax myrtle	x	x			x		x	x		x			x
Pacific willow	x			x	x		x	x		x	x	x	x
Poison ivy	x				x		x	x	x	x	x		
Possumhaw	x				x		x	x	x	x	x	x	
Possumhaw viburnum	x				x		x	x		x	?		
Purple osier willow	x			x	x		x	x				x	x
Pussy willow	x			x	x		x	x	x	x	?	x	x
Quail brush	x	x				x		x		x	x	x	x
Red alder	x				x		x	x		x	?	x	x
Red buckeye	x				x		x	x	x	x	x		
Red osier dogwood	x			x	x		x	x	x	x	x	x	x
Riverflat hawthorn	x				x	x	x	x	x	x	?		x
Rough-leafed dogwood	x			x	x		x	x	x	x	x	x	x
Russian olive	x				x	x	x	x		x	x	x	x
Rusty blackhaw	x				x	x	x	x	x	x			
Salal	x				x		x	x		x	?	x	
Salmonberry	x				x		x	x	x	x		x	x
Saltbush	x	x				x		x		x			
Saltcedar	x	x		x	x	x	x			x	x	x	x
Sandbar willow	x			x	x		x	x		x	x		x
Sand blackberry	x					x		x	x	x	?		x
Sand pine	x	x			x	x		x		x	?		x
Sawtooth oak	x					x	x	x	x	x	x	x	x
Scotch broom	x					x	x	x		x	x	x	x
Sharp-toothed blackberry	x				x	x	x	x	x	x	x		x
Shining sumac	x				x		x	x	x	x	?		x
Shore pine	x				x	x	x	x		x	?		x
Shrub verbena		x			x		x	x		x	x	x	x
Silky dogwood	x				x		x	x	x	x			
Silky willow	x			x	x		x	x		x	x		x
Sitka alder	x				x		x	x		x	x		x
Smooth sumac	x				x		x	x	x	x	?		
Southern bayberry	x	x			x		x	x		x	x		x
Southern dewberry	x				x		x	x	x	x	?		x

TABLE A.5 Characteristics of Some Upland Plant Species* (*Continued*)

Common name	SE	MS	SP	MP	NP	NE	MA	PNW	SW	FL	GL	MRV	CA	MW	Acid	Neutral	Alkaline
Region† spans SE–MW; Soil conditions / pH spans Acid–Alkaline																	

Shrubs and small trees (*Continued*)

Common name	SE	MS	SP	MP	NP	NE	MA	PNW	SW	FL	GL	MRV	CA	MW	Acid	Neutral	Alkaline
Sparkleberry	x	x	x				x								x	x	x
Squaw huckleberry	x	x	x	x	x	x	x			x	x	x			x	x	x
Staghorn sumac	x	x	x	x	x	x	x			x	x	x			x	x	x
Summersweet	x	x													x	x	x
Swamp privet	x	x													x	x	x
Swamp rose	x	x				x									x	x	x
Tag alder		x	x			x	x					x			x	x	x
Tartarian honeysuckle	x	x	x	x	x	x	x	x	x	x	x	x	x	x	x	x	x
Texas huisache		x	x						x						x	x	x
Thorny eleagnus	x	x	x	x	x	x	x	x	x	x	x	x	x	x	x	x	x
Toothache tree	x	x	x							x					x	x	x
Turkey oak	x	x								x					x	x	
Waxmyrtle	x	x	x			x				x					x	x	
Western blackberry								x					x		x	x	x
Western chokeberry								x					x		x	x	x
Western dogwood								x					x		x	x	x
Western huckleberry								x					x		x	x	x
Wild apple	x	x	x	x	x	x	x	x	x	x	x	x	x	x	x	x	x
Wild black currant					x	x					x	x			x	x	x
Wild cherry								x	x				x		x	x	x
Wild indigo	x	x	x												x	x	x
Wild rose	x	x	x			x			x						x	x	x
Wingscale									x				x	x	x	x	x
Winterberry	x	x													x	x	x
Witch-hazel	x	x	x			x	x				x	x			x	x	x
Yaupon	x	x	x			x			x						x	x	x
Yellow paloverde									x				x		x	x	x

Large trees

Common name	SE	MS	SP	MP	NP	NE	MA	PNW	SW	FL	GL	MRV	CA	MW	Acid	Neutral	Alkaline
American beech	x	x	x			x	x					x	x		x	x	x
American sycamore	x	x	x	x	x	x	x					x	x		x	x	x
Australian pine										x			x		x	x	x
Black cherry	x	x	x	x	x	x	x			x	x				x	x	x
Black cottonwood						x	x						x		x	x	x

TABLE A.5   Characteristics of Some Upland Plant Species*   (*Continued*)

Common name	Salinity Fresh	Brack-ish	Sa-line	Moisture Wet	Moist	Dry	Texture Fine	Coarse	Food	Cover	Nest-ing/ breed-ing	Aes-thetic value	Soil stabil-ization and other soil benefits
Shrubs and small trees (*Continued*)													
Sparkleberry	x				x	x	x		x	x			
Squaw huckle-berry	x				x	x	x		x	x			
Staghorn sumac	x				x	x	x		x	x	?		x
Summer-sweet	x				x	x	x			x		x	
Swamp privet	x			x	x		x		x	x	x		x
Swamp rose	x				x		x	x		x		x	
Tag alder	x				x		x	x		x	?		x
Tartarian honey-suckle	x				x		x	x		x		x	x
Texas huisache	x	x			x	x		x		x	x		x
Thorny eleagnus	x	x			x	x	x	x	x	x	x	x	x
Toothache tree	x						x	x		x	x		
Turkey oak	x				x	x		x	x	x	?	x	x
Waxmyrtle	x	x			x	x	x		x		x	x	x
Western blackberry	x				x		x	x	x	x	?		x
Western chokeberry	x				x		x	x	x	x	?		x
Western dogwood	x				x	x	x	x		x	?	x	
Western huckle-berry	x				x		x	x	x	x			
Wild apple	x				x		x	x	x	x			
Wild black currant	x				x		x	x	x	x			
Wild cherry	x				x		x	x	x	x	?		
Wild indigo	x	x			x	x	x	x		x	x		
Wild rose	x				x	x	x	x	x	x	x	x	x
Wingscale	x					x		x	x				x
Winterberry	x				x		x	x	x	x			
Witch-hazel	x				x		x	x	x	x			
Yaupon	x	x			x	x	x			x	x	x	
Yellow paloverde	x	x				x		x		x	?	x	x
Large trees													
American beech	x			x	x		x	x	x	x	x	x	x
American sycamore	x			x	x		x	x		x	x	x	x
Australian pine	x				x			x		x	x	x	x
Black cherry	x				x	x	x	x	x	x	x	x	
Black cotton-wood	x			x	x		x	x		x	x	x	x

TABLE A.5   Characteristics of Some Upland Plant Species* *(Continued)*

Common name	SE	MS	SP	MP	NP	NE	MA	PNW	SW	FL	GL	MRV	CA	MW	Acid	Neu-tral	Alka-line
Large trees (*Continued*)																	
Blackgum	x	x	x	x	x	x	x			x	x	x			x	x	x
Black locust		x		x			x								x	x	x
Black walnut	x	x	x		x		x					x			x	x	x
Black willow	x	x	x				x		x						x	x	x
Cow oak	x	x	x				x			x					x	x	x
Eastern cottonwood	x	x	x	x	x		x				x	x			x	x	x
Eastern redcedar	x	x	x									x			x	x	x
Eastern white pine						x	x				x				x	x	x
Green ash	x	x	x	x	x	x	x			x	x	x			x	x	x
Hackberry	x	x	x	x								x			x	x	x
Honeylocust	x	x	x	x			x				x	x			x	x	x
Laurel oak	x	x	x												x	x	x
Live oak	x	x	x				x								x	x	x
Loblolly pine	x	x	x				x								x	x	
Longleaf pine	x	x	x				x		x						x	x	
Mockernut hickory	x	x	x	x		x	x			x		x			x	x	x
Paper mulberry	x	x				x	x			x	x	x			x	x	x
Peachleaf willow	x			x	x							x		x	x	x	x
Pecan	x	x	x	x											x	x	x
Persimmon	x	x	x	x			x			x		x			x	x	x
Pignut hickory	x	x	x	x		x	x			x		x			x	x	x
Redbay	x	x	x				x			x					x	x	x
Red maple	x	x				x	x			x	x	x			x	x	x
Red mulberry	x	x				x	x			x	x	x			x	x	x
River birch	x	x	x	x			x					x			x	x	x
Sassafras	x	x	x	x	x	x	x				x	x			x	x	x
Slash pine	x	x								x					x	x	x
Southern red oak	x	x	x				x								x	x	x
Sugarberry	x	x	x	x						x					x	x	x
Sugar maple				x	x	x	x				x	x			x	x	x
Sweetbay	x	x					x			x					x	x	x
Sweetgum	x	x	x				x			x		x			x	x	x
Tulip poplar	x	x				x	x				x	x			x	x	x
Water oak	x	x	x				x			x					x	x	x
White ash	x	x	x	x	x	x	x			x	x	x			x	x	x
White oak	x	x	x	x	x	x	x				x	x			x	x	x
White poplar	x	x	x	x	x	x	x	x	x	x	x	x	x	x	x	x	x

*Table is coordinated with Table A.4.

†SE = Southeast, MS = mid-South, SP = south plains, MP = mid-plains, NP = north plains, NE = Northeast, MA = mid-Atlantic, PNW = Pacific Northwest, SW = Southwest, FL = Florida, GL = Great Lakes, MRV = Mississippi River Valley, CA = California, MW = Midwest.

SOURCE: Hunt et al. (1978).

TABLE A.5 Characteristics of Some Upland Plant Species* *(Continued)*

Common name	Soil conditions — Salinity: Fresh	Brack-ish	Sa-line	Moisture: Wet	Moist	Dry	Texture: Fine	Coarse	Wildlife value: Food	Cover	Nest-ing/breed-ing	Aes-thetic value	Soil stabil-ization and other soil benefits
Large trees (*Continued*)													
Blackgum	x				x	x	x	x			x	x	
Black locust	x				x		x	x	x	x	x	x	x
Black walnut	x				x		x	x	x	x	x	x	
Black willow	x			x			x	x	x	x	x		
Cow oak	x				x		x	x	x	x			
Eastern cottonwood	x			x	x		x			x	x	x	
Eastern redcedar	x				x	x	x	x	x	x	x	x	
Eastern white pine	x				x		x	x	?	x	?		
Green ash	x			x	x		x	x		x	x		x
Hackberry	x				x		x	x	x	x	x	x	
Honeylocust	x				x		x	x	?	x	?	x	x
Laurel oak	x				x	x	x	x		x	?		
Live oak	x	x			x		x	x	x	x	x	x	
Loblolly pine	x			x	x		x	x	x	x	x	x	x
Longleaf pine	x				x		x	x		x	x	x	x
Mockernut hickory	x	x				x	x	x	x	x	x	x	
Paper mulberry	x				x		x	x		x	?	x	
Peachleaf willow	x			x	x		x	x		x	x		x
Pecan	x				x		x	x	x	x	x	x	
Persimmon	x				x	x	x	x	x	x	x	x	
Pignut hickory	x				x	x	x	x	x	x	x	x	
Redbay	x				x		x	x		x			
Red maple	x			x	x		x	x	x	x	x	x	x
Red mulberry	x				x	x	x	x	x			x	
River birch	x			x	x		x	x		x		x	x
Sassafras	x				x	x	x	x		x	x	x	x
Slash pine	x				x		x	x	x	x	x	x	x
Southern red oak	x				x	x	x	x	x	x	x	x	x
Sugarberry	x				x		x	x	x	x	x	x	
Sugar maple	x				x		x	x	x		x	x	
Sweetbay	x				x		x	x	x	x			
Sweetgum	x				x	x	x	x	x	x	x	x	
Tulip poplar	x			x	x		x	x		x	x	x	
Water oak	x			x	x		x	x	x	x	x	x	x
White ash	x				x	x	x	x	?	x	x		
White oak	x				x	x	x	x	x	x	x	x	x
White poplar	x				x		x	x		x	x	x	

TABLE A.6 Characteristics of Trees and Shrubs Important in Maine Deeryards

Species	Soil and site requirements	Shade tolerance	Growth rate	Natural reproduction—seed	Natural reproduction—sprout	Apparent palatability	Resistance to browsing	Value as deer food
Conifers								
Balsam fir	Acid; moist, well-drained soils to swamps.	Tolerant. Nearly comparable to hemlock. Less so than red spruce.	Rapid	*Easy.* Good seed crops every 2–4 years. Seeds more abundantly and vigorously than other conifers listed.	Conifers do not sprout.	Medium, sometimes high.	Fair. More resistant than cedar.	Fair in combination with other foods. As sole diet will not maintain deer.
Spruce (3 species)	Neutral to acid; medium moist (red and white spruce) to wet soil (black spruce).	Red spruce very tolerant. More so than black spruce, white spruce, or fir.	Slow	*Difficult.* White spruce has good seed years more often (every 2–3 years) than red or black. Seedlings need abundant moisture.	Conifers do not sprout.	Very low.	Rarely browsed.	Practically none.
Northern white cedar	Neutral to slightly acid; moist, well-drained to wet soil.	Moderately tolerant.	Slow	*Easy.* Good seed crops about every 5 years. Seedlings come in under shade in moist decaying logs, stumps, or mineral soil.	Conifers do not sprout.	High. Usually preferred over other conifers.	Low. Optimum browsing rate is less than 25% of annual growth.	Best single browse species, but too palatable. Often browsed out before January.
Hemlock	Neutral to acid; medium moist soil. Frequent on swamp borders, moist benches, flats.	Very tolerant, more so than balsam fir.	Medium	*Easy.* Good seed crops every 2–3 years. Seedlings favor conditions like those for cedar. Reproduces in quantity only at long intervals.	Conifers do not sprout.	Medium	Fair. More resistant than cedar.	Fair in combination with other foods. Superior to fir.
Tamarack	Acid; swamps to well-drained uplands.	Very intolerant.	Slow	*Difficult.* Good seed crops every 5–6 years. Seedlings are seldom abundant. Best seeded is exposed, well-drained mineral soil.	Conifers do not sprout.	Low	Low	Low. Rarely available near deeryards because of site needs. Intolerant.

Conifers
(Continued)

Hardwoods —larger trees

Species	Soils	Shade tolerance	Growth rate	Reproduction	Sprouting			
White pine	Neutral; sandy to loam soils, best on dry uplands.	Moderately tolerant.	Medium	*Easy.* Seeds often, but requires openings. Does not reproduce under hardwoods.	Conifers do not sprout.	Low (except nursery stock).	Low	Low
Beech	Soils similar to those for sugar maple.	Very tolerant, about like sugar maple.	Slow	*Difficult.* Seed crops every 2–3 years. Germinates readily on leaf litter.	Sprouts vigorously from small stumps and also produces root suckers.	Low. Twigs are tough, hard to break.	Good, but seldom browsed heavily.	Low despite usual abundance.
Yellow birch	Acid to neutral; sandy loam to loam; tolerates poor drainage better than sugar maple; closely associated with hemlock.	Moderately tolerant; not typically climax.	Medium	*Easy.* Good crops every 2–3 years; requires openings, also moist seedbed of mineral soil or decayed wood; seedlings suffer in competition with maples.	Sprouts fairly vigorously from small stumps but water sprouts on large stumps usually die out.	Medium. But quite variable.	Good. Heavy use stimulates sprouting from the root collar.	Good in combination with other species.
Sugar maple	Neutral, well-drained fine sandy loam or loam but will grow on lighter and heavier soils.	Very tolerant; typically climax.	Medium	*Easy.* Seeds readily germinate on leaf litter; most aggressive reproducer among northern hardwoods. Good seed crops every 3–7 years, light crops other years.	Sprouts from stumps under 6 inches in diameter may develop into large trees but those from large stumps do not mature.	Medium	Good, but less than soft maples.	Good in combination with other species.

TABLE A.6   Characteristics of Trees and Shrubs Important in Maine Deeryards   (*Continued*)

Species	Soil and site requirements	Shade tolerance	Growth rate	Natural reproduction—seed	Natural reproduction—sprout	Apparent palatability	Resistance to browsing	Value as deer food
Hardwoods —larger trees (*Continued*)								
Red maple	Soil requirements similar to hemlock, but also occurs on well-drained uplands.	Moderately tolerant; not a climax species.	Medium	*Easy.* Spring seeder with crops almost every year. Germinates in early summer, soon after falling.	Vigorous sprouter, probably next to basswood in this respect.	Medium to high.	High. Browsing stimulates growth of lateral stems.	Good in combination with other species.
White birch	Neutral to acid; moist soil.	Intolerant; not a climax species.	Rapid	*Easy.* Good seed crops almost every year. Moist mineral soils and rotten logs make best seedbeds. Requires openings; reproduces best on burns.	Sprouts vigorously but new stems have high mortality.	Medium	Fair. Withstands repeated browsing of more than one-half of the annual growth.	Good combined with other species.
Black ash	Acid; wet; stream banks and swamps.	Intolerant.	Medium	*Easy.* Moist, well-drained loam makes the best seedbed.	Very vigorous.	Medium. But quite variable.	High. Withstands repeated browsing of all annual growth.	Good but usually not abundant.
Hardwoods —smaller trees								
Aspens	Acid, dry, exposed upland soil is best.	Very intolerant.	Rapid	*Easy.* Good seed crops every 4–5 years. Exposed mineral soil needed, as after fire.	Very vigorous from root suckers.	Medium— trembling aspen. High— bigtooth aspen.	Good, particularly where abundant.	Good, but grows out of reach in 3–6 years if not browsed heavily.
Pin (fire) cherry	Similar to aspens.	Very intolerant.	Rapid	*Easy.* After fire or logging. Needs exposed mineral soil. Birds distribute seeds widely.	Moderately, but seedlings usually more abundant.	Medium	Good. Withstands use of all annual growth.	Fair, seldom abundant near yards.

Hardwoods—smaller trees (Continued)

Gray birch	Acid; dry to wet soils. Does well on very infertile soil.	Intolerant.	Rapid	*Easy.* After fire, logging, farmland abandonment.	Sprouts abundantly, but new stems have high mortality.	Medium to low.	Good	Fair
Striped maple	Neutral to acid; moist, well-drained soils under shade.	Tolerant.	Very rapid	*Medium.* Requires moist mineral soil or hardwood leaf litter.	Very vigorous.	High	Very good.	Good, but growth is so rapid that stems soon grow out of reach if not heavily browsed.
Mountain maple	Neutral to acid; moist to dry soil under partial shade or open.	Tolerant.	Rapid	*Easy.* Particularly after logging in hardwoods or mixed growth.	Very vigorous; forms clumps.	High	Very good. Withstands use of all annual growth.	High. Exceeded only by willow in browse resistance and is more palatable than willow.
Alder	Acid; moist, well-drained soils to swamps and stream borders.	Intolerant.	Rapid	*Easy.* Particularly in very wet sites.	Vigorous; forms dense clumps.	Low	Fair, but seldom browsed.	Very low.

Shrubs

Sweet fern	Acid; dry, sterile soil after burns, logging, in old fields.	Intolerant.	—	*Easy.* Pioneer species along with brambles, aspen, fire cherry.	Forms dense colonies.	Medium but variable.	Good	Fair to good locally.

TABLE A.6 Characteristics of Trees and Shrubs Important in Maine Deeryards *(Continued)*

Species	Soil and site requirements	Shade tolerance	Growth rate	Natural reproduction—seed	Natural reproduction—sprout	Apparent palatability	Resistance to browsing	Value as deer food
Shrubs *(Continued)*								
Dogwoods	Redosier: poorly drained soils. Gray: well-drained soils.	Redosier: intolerant. Gray: moderately tolerant.	—	*Easy.*	Redosier sprouts vigorously from root stolons. Other species less vigorous.	High	Fair	Fair. Seldom abundant, damaged by repeated browsing.
Brambles (*Rubus* spp.)	Exposed mineral soil after fire, logging. Old fields.	Intolerant.	—	*Easy.* Seeds widely distributed by birds.	Branches touching the ground take root, send up new shoots.	Low to medium; varies with season.	Good	Fair summer food. Seldom used in winter.
Viburnums	Nearly neutral; drier soil (mapleleaf); well-drained to moist soils (other species).	Hobble bush very tolerant; others tolerant.	—	*Variable.* Most species reproduce well under shade.	Most species form dense clumps.	High	High. Browsing stimulates growth of lateral stems and root sprouts.	Good. Will survive under repeated browsing.
Willows	Very adaptable; most species tolerate moisture, wet sites.	Intolerant.	—	*Very easy.*	Very vigorous producers of suckers, shoots. Commonly form clumps or mats.	Medium to high; varies with season.	Very high.	Good. Thrives after repeated heavy browsing.
Beaked hazelnut	Neutral to acid; dry soil preferred.	Intolerant	—	*Medium.* Light seed crops nearly every year.	Sucker growth is common. Reproduces more from sprouts than seeds.	Medium	Good	Fair due to usual abundance.

SOURCE: Gill (1957).

TABLE A.7 Ratings of Some Tree Species for Values to Wildlife and as Firewood

Tree	Value to wildlife				Value as firewood	Remarks
	All wildlife	Song-birds	Upland game birds	Fur and game mammals		
Oaks *Quercus* spp.	Excellent	Excellent	Excellent	Excellent	Excellent	Retain a variety of species.
Black cherry *Prunus serotina*	Excellent	Excellent	Good	Good	Good	May have high timber value when mature.
Apples *Malus* spp.	Excellent	Good	Good	Good	Excellent	Rare; especially attractive to grouse.
Pines *Pinus* spp.	Excellent	Excellent	Fair	Good	Fair	Good as kindling.
Flowering dogwood *Cornus florida*	Excellent	Excellent	Good	Fair	Excellent	High aesthetic qualities.
Maples *Acer* spp.	Good	Good	Fair	Excellent	Excellent	High aesthetic qualities in the fall.
American beech *Fagus grandifolia*	Good	Fair	Fair	Excellent	Excellent	Aesthetic in the fall; important to squirrels.
Alders *Alnus* spp.	Good	Good	Good	Fair	Good	Locally important to song birds and game birds.
Aspens *Populus* spp.	Good	Fair	Good	Excellent	Fair	Especially attractive to grouse.
Birches *Betula* spp.	Good	Fair	Good	Good	Excellent	Important to northern wildlife.
Spruces *Picea* spp.	Good	Good	Fair	Good	Fair	Good as kindling; important to northern wildlife.
Hackberry *Celtis occidentalis*	Fair	Good	Fair	Fair	Excellent	Important winter food for songbirds.
Hickories *Carya* spp.	Fair	Fair	Fair	Good	Excellent	Especially attractive to squirrels.
Ashes *Fraxinus* spp.	Fair	Fair	Fair	Fair	Excellent	Supplies mast in the fall.

TABLE A.7   Ratings of Some Tree Species for Values to Wildlife and as Firewood   (Continued)

Tree	Value to wildlife				Value as firewood	Remarks
	All wildlife	Song-birds	Upland game birds	Fur and game mammals		
American basswood *Tilia americana*	Fair	Fair	Fair	Fair	Fair	Good as kindling.
Black walnut *Juglans nigra*	Fair	Fair	Fair	Fair	Excellent	May have high timber value when mature.
Black tupelo *Nyssa sylvatica*	Fair	Fair	Fair	Fair	Fair	Locally important to songbirds and game birds.
Eastern cottonwood *Populus deltoides*	Fair	Fair	Fair	Fair	Fair	Good as kindling.
Elms *Ulmus* spp.	Fair	Fair	Fair	Good	Fair	High water content when green; hard to split; cut if diseased.
Balsam fir *Abies balsamea*	Fair	Fair	Fair	Fair	Fair	Good as cover for snowshoe hares.
Eastern hemlock *Tsuga canadensis*	Fair	Fair	Fair	Fair	Fair	Attractive to northern wildlife.
Black locust *Robinia pseudoacacia*	Fair	Fair	Fair	Fair	Excellent	Low wildlife; high firewood; nitrogen fixer.
Magnolias *Magnolia* spp.	Fair	Fair	Fair	Fair	Good	Low wildlife; good firewood.
Eastern redcedar *Juniperus virginiana*	Fair	Good	Fair	Fair	Fair	Good as kindling; attractive to songbirds.
Sassafras *Sassafrass albidum*	Fair	Fair	Fair	Fair	Good	Berries eaten by insectivorous birds.
Sweetgum *Liquidambar styraciflua*	Fair	Fair	Fair	Fair	Fair	High water content when green; high aesthetic value.

Sycamore *Platanus occidentalis*	Fair	Fair	Fair	Fair	Aesthetic; high water content when green; hard to split.
Yellowpoplar *Liriodendron tulipifera*	Fair	Fair	Fair	Fair	Good as kindling; aesthetic.
Willows *Salix* spp.	Fair	Fair	Fair	Fair	Attractive to northern wildlife.

Note: Fur and game mammals = rabbits, squirrels, foxes, skunks, etc.
SOURCE: Carey and Gill (1980).

TABLE A.8   Forage Plants Commonly Seeded on Range and Other Perennial Pasture

Common and scientific name	Ease of establishment	Stand maintenance	Drought tolerance	Cold hardiness	Salinity tolerance	Soil adaptation			High water tolerance	Forage usability[c]					Grazing tolerance	Native or introduced
						Sandy	Silty	Clayey		Early spring	Late spring	Summer	Fall	Winter		
Alfalfa (*Medicago sativa* and *falcata*)	1	1–2	2	1–2	2	1	1	2	2	1–2	1	1	1	3	1–2	I
Bahiagrass (*Paspalum notatum* and *media*)	1	1–2	2	3	1	1	1	1	1	2	1	2	2	3	1	I
Bermudagrass (*Cynodon dactylon*)	1–2	1	1–2	3	1	1	1	2	1	3	1	1	2	2	1	I
Bitterbrush (*Purshia tridentata*)	1–2	1	1–2	1	2	2	1	1	3	1	1	1	1	1	1	N
Bluegrass, big (*Poa ampla*)	2	1–2	2	1	3	1	1	1	1–2	1	2	2	1	2	2	N
Bluegrass, bulbous (*Poa bulbosa*)	1	1	1	1	2	2	1	1	3	1	2	3	3	3	1	I
Bluegrass, Kentucky (*Poa pratensis*)	1–2	1	2	1	2–3	3	1	1	1–2	1	1	2	1	2	1	I
Bluestem, big (*Andropogon gerardi*)	2	1	2	1	2	2	1	1	2	2	1	1	1	2	1–2	N

TABLE A.8   Forage Plants Commonly Seeded on Range and Other Perennial Pasture (*Continued*)

Season of growth[d]	Regional adaptation[b]								Seeds per kg (thousands)[f]	Kg PLS per ha, seeding rate[f]	Principal cultivars[g]	Special considerations and adaptations
	Pacific Coast	Intermountain	Southwest	Northern Great Plains	Southern Great Plains	Midwest	Southeast	Northeast				
C–W	RI	RI	RI	RI	RI	R	R	R	462	4.6	Pasture types: Rambler, Teton, Rhizoma, Nomad, Travois, Drylander, Roamer, Kane, Spredor II, Sevelra, Victoria	Most widely used legume for range and pasture mixtures; a variable species complex. Adapted to irrigated pasture and dryland sites receiving 35cm precipitation or more; some varieties more drought-hardy.
W							R		365	5.8	Pensacola, Tifhi, Argentine, Wilmington	Keep young by grazing or mowing. Rhizomatous.
W	RI		RI		RI		R		3931	1.12	Midland, Coastal, Suwanee, Coastcross, NK 37, Tufcote	Keep young by grazing or mowing and ample fertilization. Named varieties must be grown from sprigs; only common and NK 37 can be seeded.
	R	R	R						33	32.5	Lassen	Principal browse species used in range seeding. Palatable to all grazing species. Some varieties layer, varieties mostly not persistent-leaved.
C	R	R	R						1980	1.7	Sherman	Seedling may be pulled up by grazing. Very early growth similar to crested wheatgrass. Seed in pure stands.
C	R	R							1012	2.1	P-4874	Good erosion control; withstands heavy grazing. Spreads by aerial bulblets and swollen stem bases. Low yield; unreliable producer.
C							R	R	4730	0.9	Delta, Troy, Cougar, Newport (many others)	Low production and summer dormancy limit use on range and pasture.
W				RI	RI	R			286	7.5	Kaw, Champ, Pawnee, Roundtree	Very palatable and productive on mesic sites. Seeded in warm-season mixtures.

TABLE A.8   Forage Plants Commonly Seeded on Range and Other Perennial Pasture

Common and scientific name	Ease of establishment	Stand maintenance	Drought tolerance	Cold hardiness	Salinity tolerance	Soil adaptation Sandy	Silty	Clayey	High water tolerance	Forage usability[c] Early spring	Late spring	Summer	Fall	Winter	Grazing tolerance	Native or introduced
Bluestem, Caucasian (*Bothriochloa caucasica*)	1	2	1–2	2	2	2	1	1	2	3	1	1	2	3	1	I
Bluestem, little (*Schizachyrium scoparium*)	2	1	1–2	1	3	1	1	1	2	3	1	1	2	2–3	2	N
Bluestem, sand (*Andropogon hallii*)	2	1	2	1	3	1	2	3	2	2	1	1	1	2	1–2	N
Bluestem, yellow (*Bothriochloa ischaemum*)	1	2	1–2	2–3	2	2	1	1	2	3	1	1	2	3	1	I
Brome, mountain (*Bromus marginatus*)	1	1–2	2	1	2	3	1	1	2	3	1	1	2	3	1–2	N
Brome, smooth (*Bromus inermis*)	1	1	2	1	2	2	1	1	2	1–2	1	1	2	3	1	I
Brome, meadow (*Bromus biebersteinii*)	1–2	1	2	1	2	2	1	1	2	1	1	1	2	3	1	N
Buffalograss (*Buchloe dactyloides*)	2	1	1	1	2	3	1	1	2	2	2	1	1	1	1	N
Buffelgrass (*Cenchrus ciliaris*)	1	1	1	3	3	1	1	2	2	2	1	1	1	2		I
Burnet, small (*Sanguisorba minor*)	2	2	2	1	3	2	1	2	3	1	1	2	2	2	2	I

TABLE A.8   Forage Plants Commonly Seeded on Range and Other Perennial Pasture (*Continued*)

Season of growth[d]	Pacific Coast	Intermountain	Southwest	Northern Great Plains	Southern Great Plains	Midwest	Southeast	Northeast	Seeds per kg (thousands)[e]	Kg PLS per ha, seeding rate[f]	Principal cultivars[g]	Special considerations and adaptations
					Regional adaptation[b]							
W					R			R	1892	1.7	Caucausian	Lower in palatability than King Ranch bluestem but is more winter hardy. Seeded on pure stands generally. An "Old World" bluestem.
W				R	R	R	R		561	3.8	Pastura, Blaze, Aldous, Camper, Cimarron	Widely used in warm-season grass mixtures on mesic and subhumid sites.
W				R	R				250	8.6	Woodward, Champ, Cherry, Elida, Garden, Goldstrike	Rhizomatous. Very palatable and productive on mesic, sandy soil.
W			R		R				1826	1.7	King Ranch, El Kan, Plains, Formosa, Ganada, WW-Spar	Seeded in pure stands; medium palatability. An "Old World" bluestem; also called Turkestan bluestem.
C	R	R							154	13.9	Bromar	Used in native grass mixtures on high mountain sites; used less now than formerly.
C	RI	RI	RI	RI	I	R	R	R	319	6.7	Lincoln, Southland, Manchar, Achenbach, Lancaster, Homesteader, Carlton, Magna, Baylor, Saratoga, Fischer, Polar, Elsberry	Rhizomatous. Important irrigated-pasture grass; adapted to mesic sites on dryland.
C		RI		RI					220	9.7	Regar	Less rhizomatous, quicker recovery, and longer growing season than smooth brome.
W				R	R				92	4.6[h]	Mesa, Texoka, Sharp's Improved	Low production. Seed only in mixtures. Seeded or transplanted by stolons.
W			R		RI				1760[i]	1.8[i]	Higgins, Nueces, Llano, Blue	Mostly rhizomatous; aggressive on adapted sites.
		R	R						121	8.8	Delar	Forb with persistent leaves; palatable but low-yielding.

TABLE A.8   Forage Plants Commonly Seeded on Range and Other Perennial Pasture

Common and scientific name	Ease of establishment	Stand maintenance	Drought tolerance	Cold hardiness	Salinity tolerance	Soil adaptation			High water tolerance	Forage usability[c]					Grazing tolerance	Native or introduced
						Sandy	Silty	Clayey		Early spring	Late spring	Summer	Fall	Winter		
Canarygrass, reed (*Phalaris arundinacea*)	2–3	1	2	1	2–3	2	1	1	1	1	1	2	2	3	1	N–I
Cliffrose, Stansbury (*Cowania mexicana*)	3	1	1	1	2	2	1	1	3	3	3	3	2	1	1	N
Clover, alsike (*Trifolium hybridum*)	1	2	3	1	2–3	2	1	1	1–2	2	1	1	2	2	1–2	I
Clover, crimson (*Trifolium incarnatum*)	1	2	3	1	2	1	1	1	3	1	2	2	1	1	1	I
Clover, Ladino white (*Trifolium repens*)	1	2	3	2	2–3	2	1	1	1–2	2	1	1	1	2	1	I
Clover, red (*Trifolium pratense*)	1	2	3	1	3	2	1	1	2	2	1	1	2	2	1–2	I
Clover, rose (*Trifolium hirtum*)	1	1–2	1	3	2	2	1	1	3	1	1	2	2	1	1	I
Clover, strawberry (*Trifolium fragiferum*)	1	1–2	3	2	1–2	2	1	1	1	2	1	1	2	2	1	I
Clover, subterranean (*Trifolium subterraneum*)	2	2	2	3	3	2	1	1	2	1	2	2	2	1	1	I
Cottontop, Arizona (*Digitaria californica*)			1–2	2	2	2	1	2		1	1	1			2	N
Dallisgrass (*Paspalum dilatatum*)	2	1–2	2	2	2	2	1	1	1	2	1	1	2	2	1–2	I
Dropseed, sand (*Sporobolus cryptandrus*)	2	2	1	1	2	1	1	2	2	3	2	2	2	3	1	N

TABLE A.8 Forage Plants Commonly Seeded on Range and Other Perennial Pasture (*Continued*)

Season of growth[d]	Regional adaptation[b]								Seeds per kg (thousands)[e]	Kg PLS per ha, seeding rate[f]	Principal cultivars[g]	Special considerations and adaptations
	Pacific Coast	Intermountain	Southwest	Northern Great Plains	Southern Great Plains	Midwest	Southeast	Northeast				
C	RI	RI		RI		R	R	R	1113	2.9	Ioreed, Frontier, Highland, Auburn, Rise, Vantage, Castor	Graze to prevent maturity. Pasture and hay on wet sites. Seeded or spread by sod or culm cuttings. Rhizomatous.
		R	R						141	7.6		Evergreen shrub palatable to deer; hybridizes with bitterbrush.
	RI	RI	I		R				1496	2.1	Aurora	Noncreeping. Adapted to cool, moist sites. Commonly used in irrigated-pasture mixtures.
W	R					R	R	R	308	6.9	Dixie, Autauga, Auburn, Talledaga, Chief, Kentucky	Winter annual legume. Readily reseeds itself.
	RI	RI	I	I	I	R	R	R	1870	1.7	Merit, Pilgrim	Used in pasture mixtures on mesic or irrigated sites. Creeping by stolons.
	RI	RI	I			R	R	R	594	3.6	Mammoth, Dollard, Midland, Lakeland, Kenland, Pennscott, Norlac, Kenstar	Short-lived perennial but readily reseeds under mesic conditions. Noncreeping.
	R						R		308	6.9	Wilton, Hykon, Sirint, Kondinin, Olympus, Wilton	Winter annual. Widely seeded in California on annual grassland and brush burns. Readily reseeds itself.
	RI	I	I						649	3.4	Salina	Creeping by rhizomes; low-growing. Best use is on wet, salty, or non-saline sites.
	R						R		143	15.0	Tallarook, Mr. Barker, Geraldton, Dinninup, Clare	Well adapted for interseeding mesic annual grasslands in California. Good winter growth. Winter annual.
C–W			R		R				2402	1.8		Seed sources limited.
W	RI		I		I		R		484	4.5		Long grazing period in Southeast.
W		R	R	R	R				11,000	0.4		Seeded on dry sites where better forages not adapted.

TABLE A.8   Forage Plants Commonly Seeded on Range and Other Perennial Pasture

| Common and scientific name | Ratings of plant characteristics[a] | | | | | Soil adaptation | | | High water tolerance | Forage usability[c] | | | | | Grazing tolerance | Native or introduced |
	Ease of establishment	Stand maintenance	Drought tolerance	Cold hardiness	Salinity tolerance	Sandy	Silty	Clayey		Early spring	Late spring	Summer	Fall	Winter		
Fescue, hard (*Festuca ovina* var. *duriuscula*)	2	1	2	1	3	2	1	1	3	2	2	3	2	3	1	N
Fescue, Idaho (*Festuca idahoensis*)	3	1	2	1	3	2	1	1	3	1	1	1	1	2	2	N
Fescue, tall (*Festuca arundinacea*)	1	1	2	1–2	1	2	1	1	1	2	1	2	2	2	1	I
Foxtail, meadow (*Aleopecurus pratensis*)	1–2	1	2–3	1	3	2	1	1	1	2	1	1	1	2	1	I
Galleta (*Hilaria jamesii*)	2	1	1	1	1	2	1	1	3	3	2	1	2	3	1–2	N
Grama, black (*Bouteloua eriopoda*)	2–3	1	1	2	3	1	1	3	3	2	1	1	1	1	2	N
Grama, blue (*Bouteloua gracilis*)	2	1	1	1	2	2	1	1	3	2	1	1	1	1	1	N
Grama, sideoats (*Bouteloua curtipendula*)	1	1	1–2	1	2	2	1	2	2	3	2	1	1	2	1	N
Hardinggrass (*Phalaris tuberosa* var. *stenopteta*)	2	1	2	2	2	2	1	1	2	1	1	1–2	1–2	1–2	1	I

TABLE A.8   Forage Plants Commonly Seeded on Range and Other Perennial Pasture (*Continued*)

Season of growth[d]	Regional adaptation[b]								Seeds per kg (thousands)[e]	Kg PLS per ha, seeding rate[f]	Principal cultivars[g]	Special considerations and adaptations
	Pacific Coast	Intermountain	Southwest	Northern Great Plains	Southern Great Plains	Midwest	Southeast	Northeast				
C	R	R		R					1243	2.6	Durar	Used mostly in erosion control; generally low palatability; robust form.
C	R	R							990	2.1	Nezpurs, Joseph	Lack of good seed yields restricts its use in range seeding.
C	RI	RI	I	RI	I	R	R	R	500	4.3	Ky. 31, Alta, Goar, Kenmont, Kenwell, Fawn, Asheville	Generally seeded in pure stands, occasionally in irrigated-pasture mixes. Winter-grazed in South.
C	RI	RI	I						1276	2.5		Creeping foxtail (*A. arundinaceus*) and meadow foxtail are well adapted to mountain meadows. Slightly rhizomatous.
W		R	R		R				350	6.2	Viva	Poor seed production.
W		R							2937	1.5	Flagstaff, Sonora, Nogal	Good-quality seed is scarce; rhizomatous.
W			R	R	R	R			6564	2.0	Capitan, Marfa, Lovington, Hachita	Low yields generally restrict seeding to more droughty portions of the Great Plains. Seeded in warm-season mixtures.
W			R	R	R	R			418	5.2	Premier, Butte, Trailway, Coronado, El Reno, Tucson, Vaughan, Ulvalde, Pierre, Van Horn, Haskell, Niner, Killdeer	Grows well in mixtures of warm-season grasses. Rhizomatous.
C	RI		I		R				770	2.8	Wintergreen (Texas)	Primary species for seeding California coastal and inland zones. Perla Koleagrass, an improved variety (var. *hirtiglumis*), has largely replaced the original variety.

TABLE A.8   Forage Plants Commonly Seeded on Range and Other Perennial Pasture

Common and scientific name	Ease of establishment	Stand maintenance	Drought tolerance	Cold hardiness	Salinity tolerance	Sandy	Silty	Clayey	High water tolerance	Early spring	Late spring	Summer	Fall	Winter	Grazing tolerance	Native or introduced
						Soil adaptation				Forage usability[c]						
Indiangrass (*Sorghastrum nutans*)	2	1	3	1	2	1	1	1–2	1–2	3	1	1	2	2	2	N
Johnson grass (*Sorghum halepense*)	1	1	1–2	2	2	1	1	1	1	2	1	1	1	2	1–2	I
Kleingrass (*Panicum coloratum*)	1	1	2	2–3	2	2	1	1	1	2	1	1	1	2	1–2	I
Kochia, prostrate or forage (*Kochia prostrata*)	1	1	1	1	1–2	1	1	1	3	2	1	1	1	1	1	I
Lovegrass, Boer (*Eragrostis chloromelas*)	2	1	1	2	2	1–2	1	2	3	1	1	1	1	1	1	I
Lovegrass, Lehmann (*Eragrostis lehmanniana*)	1	1	1	3	2	1	1	2	3	2	1	2	2	3	1	I
Lovegrass, sand (*Eragrostis trichodes*)	1	2	1	1–2	3	1	2	3	3	2	1	1	2	2	2	N
Lovegrass, weeping (*Eragrostis curvula*)	1	2	2	2	2	1	1	1	2	1	1	2	2	2	2	I
Milkvetch, cicer (*Astragalus cicer*)	2	2	2	1–2	2	1	1	1–2	2	2	1	1	2	2	2	I
Mountainmahogany, curlleaf (*Cercocarpus ledifolius*)	2	1	1	1	2	2	1	1	3	2	2	2	1	1	1–2	N

Ratings of plant characteristics[a]

TABLE A.8 Forage Plants Commonly Seeded on Range and Other Perennial Pasture (*Continued*)

| Season of growth[d] | Regional adaptation[b] | | | | | | | | Seeds per kg (thousands)[e] | Kg PLS per ha, seeding rate[f] | Principal cultivars[g] | Special considerations and adaptations |
	Pacific Coast	Intermountain	Southwest	Northern Great Plains	Southern Great Plains	Midwest	Southeast	Northeast				
W				RI	RI	R		R	374	5.7	Holt, Neb. 54, Cheyenne, Tejas, Llano, Oto, Osage, Rumsey, Lometa	Rhizomatous. Commonly seeded in warm-season mixtures on mesic sites.
W			R		R		R		260	8.3		Rhizomatous; prevent from spreading to cultivated lands. HCN potential. Very palatable and productive.
W			R		RI		R		1100	2.0	Kleingrass 75, Verde	Some varieties are rhizomatous.
		R							869	2.5	Immigrant	Useful as forage or in reclamation; competitive; broadcast or drill shallow.
W	R	R							6428	0.7	Catalina	Productive and nutritious.
W	R	R							9339	0.5	Puhuima A-68, Kalahari, Kuivato, Cold Hardy, Cochise (hybrid with *E. tricophera*)	Smaller and less cold tolerant than Boer and weeping lovegrass. Reseeds quickly after fire or other disturbance. Seeded generally in pure stands.
W				RI	RI				2860	1.5	Neb. 27, Bend, Mason	Seed in mixtures. Short-lived but readily reseeds itself.
W			R		R				3300	1.3	Ermelo, Morpa, Renner	Palatability low except when young. Seeded mostly in southern Great Plains and in pure stands.
W		R	R						319	6.7	Cicar, Lutana, Oxley, Monarch	Fair to good production on mountain range. Rhizomatous. Erratic in stand establishment. Nonbloating; does not accumulate selenium.
		R							1144	9.4		Evergreen. Important winter forage for deer and elk. May grow out of reach of grazing animals.

TABLE A.8 Forage Plants Commonly Seeded on Range and Other Perennial Pasture

Common and scientific name	Ratings of plant characteristics[a]					Soil adaptation			High water tolerance	Forage usability[c]					Grazing tolerance	Native or introduced
	Ease of establishment	Stand maintenance	Drought tolerance	Cold hardiness	Salinity tolerance	Sandy	Silty	Clayey		Early spring	Late spring	Summer	Fall	Winter		
Mountainmahogany, true (*Cercocarpus montanus*)	2	1	2	1	2	2	1	1	3	2	1	1	2	2	1–2	N
Needlegrass, green (*Stipa viridula*)	2	2	1–2	1	2	2	1	1	2	1	1	1–2	1–2	2	2	N
Oatgrass, tall (*Arrhenatherum elatius*)	1	2	2	2	2	1	1	1	2–3	2	1	2	2	3	2	I
Orchardgrass (*Dactylis glomerata*)	1	2	2–3	2	2–3	2	1	1	2–3	2	1	1	1–2	2	2	I
Pangolagrass (*Digitaria decumbens*)	1	2	3	3			1	1	2	1	1	1	2	3	1	I
Panic grass, blue (*Panicum antidotale*)	1–2	2	2	2	2	2	1	1	2–3	2	1	1	2	3	2	I
Redtop (*Agrostis alba*)	2	1	3	1	2	2	1	1	1	1	1	2	2	3	1	I
Rhodesgrass (*Chloris gayana*)	1–2	2	2	3	1	2	1	1	2							I
Ricegrass, Indian (*Oryzopsis hymenoides*)	2	1	1	1	2	1	1	2	3	1	1	2	2	1	1	N
Ryegrass, perennial (*Lolium perenne*)	1	2	3	2	2	2	1	1	2	1	1	2	2	3	1	I

TABLE A.8 Forage Plants Commonly Seeded on Range and Other Perennial Pasture (*Continued*)

Season of growth[d]	Regional adaptation[b]								Seeds per kg (thousands)[e]	Kg PLS per ha, seeding rate[f]	Principal cultivars[g]	Special considerations and adaptations
	Pacific Coast	Intermountain	Southwest	Northern Great Plains	Southern Great Plains	Midwest	Southeast	Northeast				
		R							130	8.3		Deciduous but hybridizes with curlleaf mountainmahogany. Hybrid has persistent leaves.
C			R						398	5.4	Green Stipagrass, Lodorm	Seeded in mixtures. Low seed quality; delayed germination.
C	RI	R	R			R		R	330	13.0	Tualatin	Rapid-developing, short-lived grass adapted to mesic sites. Now infrequently used in new seedings.
C–W	RI	RI	I	I	I	R	R	R	1188	2.7	Latar, Akaroa, Pomar, Pennlate, Potomac, Sterling, Chinook, Napier, Boone, Pennmead, Clatsop, Nordstern, Palestine, Paiute, Berber, Sandia	Adapted to irrigated or naturally mesic sites. Develops rapidly and is long-lived. Seeded in mixtures. Tolerates shade. Paiute is a drought-hardy variety.
W							R					Stoloniferous. Well adapted to tropical and subtropical areas. Established vegetatively by fresh stem and stolon cuttings.
W	RI		RI	RI					1445	2.2	Algerian, A-130	Rhizomatous. Highly productive on good sites.
C	I	I		I			R	R	10,978	0.4		Establishes well from broadcasting on wet soils. Widely adapted in mixtures on wet soils.
W	I					R		R	4715	0.9	Bell, Lubbock	High sodium tolerance.
C	R	R	R						414	5.1	Paloma, Nezpar	Hard, impermeable seed makes seeding success uncertain.
C	RI	R			I	R			543	3.9	Linn, Norlea, NK-100	Rapid-developing, short-lived perennial. Used as short-term pasture mostly.

TABLE A.8   Forage Plants Commonly Seeded on Range and Other Perennial Pasture

Common and scientific name	Ease of establishment	Stand maintenance	Drought tolerance	Cold hardiness	Salinity tolerance	Sandy	Silty	Clayey	High water tolerance	Early spring	Late spring	Summer	Fall	Winter	Grazing tolerance	Native or introduced
						Soil adaptation				Forage usability[c]						
Sacaton, alkali (*Sporobolus airoides*)	2	1	2	1	1	3	2	1	1	3	1	1	2	3	1	N
Sagebrush, big (*Artemisia tridentata*)	2	1	1	1	2	3	1	2	3	2	3	3	2	1–2	1	N
Sainfoin (*Onobrychis viciafolia*)	1–2	2	2	2	3				3						1	I
Saltbush, four wing (*Atriplex canescens*)	2	1	1	1	1	1	1	1	2	1	1	2	1	1	1	N
Sandreed, prairie (*Calamovilfa longifolia*)	2	1	1	1	3	1	2	3	3	3	2	1	1	2	1	N
Serviceberry (*Amelanchier alnifolia*)	2	1	2	1	3	3	1	2	3	2	1–2	1–2	2	2	2	N
Smilograss (*Oryzopsis mileacea*)	2	1	1–2	3		1	1	1	2	2	1	2	2	2	1	I
Sprangletop, green (*Leptochloa dubia*)	1	2–3	1	1	2	1	1	2							2	N
Sweetclover, white (*Melilotus alba*)	1	2–3	1–2	1	1–2	1	1	1	2	2	1	1	2	3	2	I
Sweetclover, yellow (*Melilotus officinalis*)	1	2	1	1	1–2	1	1	1	2	2	1	1	2	3	2	I

Ratings of plant characteristics[a]

TABLE A.8   Forage Plants Commonly Seeded on Range and Other Perennial Pasture (*Continued*)

Season of growth[d]	Regional adaptation[b]								Seeds per kg (thousands)[e]	Kg PLS per ha, seeding rate[f]	Principal cultivars[g]	Special considerations and adaptations
	Pacific Coast	Intermountain	Southwest	Northern Great Plains	Southern Great Plains	Midwest	Southeast	Northeast				
W		R	R	R	R				3850	1.1	Saltalk, Salado	Merits further study for range seeding on saline lowlands. Seed available from native harvest.
		R	R	R					5667	0.8	Hobblecreek	Seeding limited to critical deer winter range. Considered undesirable on most spring–fall and summer ranges. Palatability varies. Mostly evergreens.
		RI		RI					57[i]	18.8	Melrose, Eski, Remont, Onar, Runemex	Nonbloating legume; may be reduced by grass competition.
	R	R	R	R	R				132[i]	8.2	Rincon, Marana, Wytana	Provides outstanding winter forage. Leaves partially evergreen. Use adapted, local strains.
W			R						603	3.6	Goshen	Seeding limited by inadequate seed supplies and low seed quality. Seed common in native grass seed harvest. Rhizomatous.
	R	R							99	10.9		Seeding limited to big game range. Seeding success fair.
C	R								1945	1.7		Becomes stemmy with maturity. Adapted to broadcast seeding after fire. Used principally in California.
W			R		R				1184	2.7	Marfa	
	R	R	R	R	R	R		R	572	3.8	Spanish, Evergreen, Cumino, Hubam (an annual variety); Polara	Seed of sweetclover should be scarified. Used for green manure more than forage.
	R	R	R	R	R	R		R	572	3.8	Madrid, Goldtop, Yukon	More tolerant of drought and competition but has a shorter growth period than white sweetclover. Reseeds better than white sweetclover.

TABLE A.8   Forage Plants Commonly Seeded on Range and Other Perennial Pasture

Common and scientific name	Ease of establishment	Stand maintenance	Drought tolerance	Cold hardiness	Salinity tolerance	Soil adaptation			High water tolerance	Forage usability[c]					Grazing tolerance	Native or introduced
						Sandy	Silty	Clayey		Early spring	Late spring	Summer	Fall	Winter		
Switchgrass (*Panicum virgatum*)	1–2	1	2	1	2	1	1	1	1–2	3	1	1	2	2	2	N
Timothy (*Phleum pratense*)	1	2	3	1	2–3	2	1	1	2–3	2	1	1	1	2	3	I
Trefoil, bird's foot (*Lotus corniculatus*)	2–3	2	2–3	2–3	1–2	2	1	1	1–2	2	1	1	2	2	2	I
Vine mesquite (*Panicum obtusum*)	2	1	2	2	2	2	1	1	1	2	2	2	2	2	1	N
Wheatgrass, beardless (*Agropyron inerme*)	2	1–2	1–2	1	2	2	1	1	3	2	1	1	1	2	1–2	N
Wheatgrass, bluebunch (*Agropyron spicatum*)	2	1–2	1–2	1	2	2	1	1	3	2	1	1	1	2	1–2	N
Wheatgrass, Fairway crested (*Agropyron cristatum*)	1	1	1	1	2	2	1	1	2–3	1	1	2	1	3	1	I
Wheatgrass, intermediate (*Agropyron intermedium*)	1	1–2	2	1–2	2–3	2	1	1	2	2	1	1	1	2	2	I
Wheatgrass, pubescent (*Agropyron trichophorum*)	1	1–2	2	1–2	2–3	2	1	1	2	2	1	1	1	2	2	I
Wheatgrass, Siberian (*Agropyron sibiricum*)	1	1	1	1	2	2	1	1	2–3	1	1	2	1	3	1	I
Wheatgrass, slender (*Agropyron trachycalum*)	1	2	2	1	1–2	2	1	1	1–2	2	1	1	2	2	1–2	N

Ratings of plant characteristics[a]

TABLE A.8 Forage Plants Commonly Seeded on Range and Other Perennial Pasture (*Continued*)

Season of growth[d]	Regional adaptation[b]								Seeds per kg (thousands)[e]	Kg PLS per ha, seeding rate[f]	Principal cultivars[g]	Special considerations and adaptations
	Pacific Coast	Intermountain	Southwest	Northern Great Plains	Southern Great Plains	Midwest	Southeast	Northeast				
W				RI	R	R		R	880	2.5	Neb. 28, Blackwell, Caddo, Grenville, Kanlow, Summer, Pathfinder, Carthage, Alamo, Trailblazer, Sunburst, Cave-in-the-Rock	Rhizomatous. Widely seeded in warm-season grass mixes on mesic sites.
C	R	R		I		R		R	2706	1.6	Climax, Drummond, Essex, Champ, Bounty	Leafy and nutritious as forage but does not tolerate grazing well. Seeded in mixtures.
C–W	RI	I	I	I		R		R	895	2.4	Empire, Cascade, Granger, Tana, Viking, Douglas, Maitland, Kalo, Mackinaw	Does not cause bloat. Rhizomatous. Mostly used in irrigated pastures.
W			R		R				315	6.8		Stoloniferous. Used principally for erosion control.
C	R	R	R						312	6.8	Whitmar	
C		R							257	8.3	Secar	Adaptation and management similar to beardless wheatgrass but seed less available.
C		R	R	R	R				440	4.9	Fairway, Parkway, Ruff, Ephraim, Hycrest (hybrid with *A. elongatum*)	Stands thicken sooner and spread more than *A. desertorum*; also leafier and finer stemmed and grazed more uniformly. Seeded alone or with alfalfa. Ephraim is distinctly rhizomatous.
C	RI	RI	R	RI					205	10.5	Slate, Oahe, Greenar, Ree, Amur, Chief, Clarke, Tegmar	Productive on mesic sites and under irrigation. Rhizomatous.
C	R	R	R	R					198	10.9	Topar, Mandan, Luna, Utah 109, Greenleaf	A pubescent, possibly more drought-tolerant form of intermediate wheatgrass.
C	R	R	R	R					453	4.7	P-27	Similar to standard crested wheatgrass in adaptation and use but less widely used.
C		R	R	R					352	6.0	Primar, Revenue, San Luis	Short life limits use in range seeding. Seed in mixtures only.

TABLE A.8   Forage Plants Commonly Seeded on Range and Other Perennial Pasture

Common and scientific name	Ease of establishment	Stand maintenance	Drought tolerance	Cold hardiness	Salinity tolerance	Soil adaptation			High water tolerance	Forage usability[c]					Grazing tolerance	Native or introduced
						Sandy	Silty	Clayey		Early spring	Late spring	Summer	Fall	Winter		
Wheatgrass, standard crested (*Agropyron desertorum*)	1	1	1	1	2	2	1	1	2–3	1	1	2	1	3	1	I
Wheatgrass, tall (*Agropyron elongatum*)	1	1–2	2	1	1	3	1	1	1	3	1	1–2	2	2	1–2	I
Wheatgrass, thickspike (*Agropyron dasystachyum*)	2	1	1–2	1	2	2	1	2	1–2	2	1	2	2	2	1–2	N
Wheatgrass, western (*Agropyron smithii*)	2	1	1–2	1	1	3	1	1	1	2	1	2	2	2	1–2	N
Wildrye, Altai (*Elymus angustus*)	2	1	1	1	1	2	1	1	2	1	1	1–2	1	2	1	I
Wildrye, basin or giant (*Elymus cinereus*)	2	1	2	1	1–2	3	1	1	1–2	2	2	2	2	2	2	N
Wildrye, Canada (*Elymus canadensis*)	2	3	2	1	2	1	1	1	2	1	1	2	3	3	2	N
Wildrye, Russian (*Elymus junceus*)	2	1	1	1	1	3	1	1	2	1	1	1–2	1	2	1	I
Winterfat (*Ceratoides lanata*)	2	1	1	1	1	1	1	1	3	2	1	1	1	1	1	N

TABLE A.8 Forage Plants Commonly Seeded on Range and Other Perennial Pasture (*Continued*)

Season of growth[d]	Regional adaptation[b]								Seeds per kg (thousands)[e]	Kg PLS per ha, seeding rate[f]	Principal cultivars[g]	Special considerations and adaptations
	Pacific Coast	Intermountain	Southwest	Northern Great Plains	Southern Great Plains	Midwest	Southeast	Northeast				
C	R	R	R	R					385	5.6	Nordan, Summit, Neb. 10, Hycrest (hybrid with *A. cristatum*)	Refer to Fairway crested wheatgrass; full stands slightly more productive than Fairway.
C	RI	RI	RI	R					174	12.3	Alkar, Jose, Largo, Orbit, Platte	High sodium and salinity tolerance. Seed alone rather than in mixtures.
C		R		R					409	5.3	Elbee, Critana	Rhizomatous.
C		R	R	R	R	R			277	7.7	Rosana, Barton, Arriba, Walsh, Rodan, Flintlock	Seeded in mixtures or in pure stands. Tolerates alkalinity and silting. Rhizomatous.
C		R		R					385	5.6	Prairieland	Similar to Russian wildrye; deep root system.
C	R	R							209	10.3	Magnar	Vigorous, tall-growing bunchgrass. Limited use on bottomlands.
C		R		R					233	9.2	Mandan	Lack of stand maintenance and tolerance of grazing has limited its use.
C		R		R					385	5.6	Vinall, Sawki, Mayak, Cabree, Swift, Bozoisky-select, Synthetic A	Seed alone or with alfalfa. Early growth. Very hardy once established. Retains palatability after mature. Provide a weed-free seedbed.
			R	R					121	8.8	Hatch	Superior palatability, productivity, and adaptability; tolerates grass competition.

[a]1 = good; 2 = fair; 3 = poor.

[b]R = range and nonirrigated perennial pasture; I = irrigated and subirrigated pasture (western half of United States only).

[c]Forage usability by season considers green growth period, palatability, curing, and seasonal grazing tolerance.

[d]C = cool-season; W = warm-season.

[e]Seed weight information compiled from numerous printed sources.

[f]PLS is pure live seed or germinable units; seeding rates based on pure live seeds per 924 cm² drilled into prepared seedbeds on ordinary uplands as follows; 20 for medium size seeds (143 to 1100 thousand per kg), 10 for large (under 143 thousand), 30 for small (1100 to 2200 thousand), and 40 for very small (over 2200 thousand).

[g]A *cultivar*-derived from *culti*vated *var*iety—is distinguished by any morphological, physiological, cytological, or chemical characters and retains these distinguishing characters when reproduced; equivalent to named varieties; the term *cultivar* differs from *botanical variety*, a category below the species written in Latin form.

[h]Forty-three pure live burs per square meter

[i]Dewinged seed or shelled seed.

SOURCE: Vallentine (1989).

TABLE A.9   Ratings of Suitability, by Species Characteristics, for Use in Wildlife Habitat in Utah

Species‡	Initial establishment (1)	Growth rate (2)	Final establishment (3)	Persistence (4)	Germination (5)	Seed production and handling (6)	Ease of planting (7)	Natural spread (8)	Herbage yield (9)	Availability of current growth (10)	Soil stability (11)	Range of adaptation (12)
Shrubs												
Apacheplume	2	2	3	4	4	3	4	4	3	4	4	2
Barberry, creeping	2	2	3	4	2	2	4	4	3	2	3	3
Bitterbrush, antelope	4	3	4	4	5	5	5	2	4	4	4	4
Bitterbrush, desert	4	3	4	4	5	4	5	3	4	4	3	3
Blackbrush	1	1	1	4	4	1	5	3	3	3	3	1
Bladdersenna, common	3	4	4	3	5	4	5	1	3	3	3	2
Boxelder	4	4	2	2	5	4	4	3	2	2	3	2
Buffaloberry, roundleaf	2	2	3	3	2	1	4	3	3	3	4	2
Buffaloberry, silver	3	3	4	3	3	4	4	3	3	4	2
Ceanothus, Martin	3	3	5	5	3	1	3	4	4	3	5	4
Cherry, Bessey	4	4	2	2	4	4	4	1	2	4	3	2
Cherry, bitter	2	3	4	5	4	2	3	4	4	4	5	3
Chokecherry, black	2	3	4	5	4	5	4	4	5	4	5	3
Cinquefoil, bush	2	3	4	5	2	2	3	3	3	3	4	2
Cliffrose, Stansbury	3	3	3	4	4	4	4	4	4	4	3	2
Cotoneaster, Peking	2	2	3	4	2	4	4	2	3	4	4	3
Currant, golden	4	4	4	4	3	3	5	4	4	5	4	3
Currant, squaw	2	3	3	5	2	2	3	4	4	2	4	2
Currant, sticky	2	3	3	3	3	3	3	2	4	4	3	2
Cypress, Arizona	3	3	4	4	3	3	4	1	3	3	3	3
Elder, blueberry	2	5	5	5	1	3	4	3	5	4	4	4
Elder, redberry	2	5	5	5	1	3	4	3	5	4	4	2
Ephedra, green	4	2	4	5	5	3	5	3	3	4	4	4
Ephedra, Nevada	4	2	4	5	5	2	5	3	3	4	4	3
Eriogonum, Wyeth	3	3	4	5	4	0	5	4	3	3	4	4
Foresteria, New Mexican	2	3	4	5	3	4	4	2	2	3	3	3
Greasewood, black	1	2	4	5	5	3	4	2	3	3	3	2
Honeylocust	3	3	4	5	3	3	4	3	3	3	3	3
Honeysuckle, bearberry	1	3	4	5	2	2	2	3	4	4	4	2
Honeysuckle, Tartarian	2	3	4	5	5	3	4	4	3	3	4	4
Hopsage, spineless	4	3	2	4	5	3	4	3	3	3	4	3
Hopsage, spiny	1	2	2	5	5	2	4	1	2	2	2	3
Juniper, Rocky Mountain	1	2	4	4	2	3	5	5	3	4	3	4

TABLE A.9   Ratings of Suitability, by Species Characteristics, for Use in Wildlife Habitat in Utah   (*Continued*)

Palatability	Tolerance to grazing	Resistance to disease and insects	Compatibility with other plants	Palatable early spring growth	Palatable summer growth	Edible foliage retained—fall and winter	Ease of transplanting	Composite suitability index*	Vegetation type†
(13)	(14)	(15)	(16)	(17)	(18)	(19)	(20)	(21)	(22)
4	5	4	5	3	4	4	3	71	JP, BB, BS, MB
4	3	4	4	3	3	5	3	63	A, MB, JP, BS
5	5	4	5	3	4	3	3	80	JP, MB, BS, BB
4	5	4	4	3	3	4	4	77	JP, BS, BB, MB
3	5	5	3	3	4	3	2	58	BB, BS
2	3	3	3	3	3	1	4	62	MB, JP, A
2	4	4	3	4	4	1	5	64	MB, A, JP
3	4	4	3	3	3	4	2	58	JP, MB, BS
2	4	4	4	3	4	3	4	67	JP, BS, IS, BG, WM
4	5	5	4	3	4	3	4	75	MB, JP, A, BS
5	4	3	4	4	4	1	5	66	MB, JP, A
2	5	4	4	5	4	2	4	73	MB, JP, A, BS
3	5	3	4	5	4	3	3	78	MB, JP, A, SB, SA
2	4	4	4	4	4	3	4	65	SA, A, WM
4	5	4	5	3	4	5	2	74	JP, BS, MB, BB
4	3	4	3	3	4	3	4	65	MB, JP
4	4	3	4	5	5	2	4	78	MB, JP, BS, WM
2	4	4	4	4	4	3	3	64	SA, A, MB
2	4	4	4	4	4	3	3	63	SA, A, MB
3	4	4	3	3	5	4	4	67	MB, JP, BS
3	5	5	5	5	5	2	4	79	MB, JP, A, BS
4	5	5	4	5	5	2	4	77	A, SA, MB
3	5	5	4	4	5	5	3	80	JP, BS, MB, SS, BB
3	5	5	4	4	4	5	3	77	BS, JP, SS, BB, MB
3	4	4	4	3	4	4	2	74	MB, JP, BS, A, SA
3	4	4	4	2	5	3	4	67	MB, JP, BS
3	5	5	4	3	5	2	2	66	BG, SS, IS, BS
2	2	3	3	2	4	2	5	63	MB, JP
4	4	4	5	5	5	4	5	71	A, SA, WM, MB
3	4	5	3	5	4	1	5	74	MB, JP, BS
3	5	5	3	4	5	3	4	73	SS, BS, JP, BB
3	5	5	3	5	1	1	2	56	JP, BS, SS, BB
3	5	4	2	4	4	5	3	70	JP, MB, BS, A

TABLE A.9   Ratings of Suitability, by Species Characteristics, for Use in Wildlife Habitat in Utah   (*Continued*)

Species‡	Initial establishment (1)	Growth rate (2)	Final establishment (3)	Persistence (4)	Germination (5)	Seed production and handling (6)	Ease of planting (7)	Natural spread (8)	Herbage yield (9)	Availability of current growth (10)	Soil stability (11)	Range of adaptation (12)
Shrubs (*Continued*)												
Juniper, Utah	1	2	5	5	1	2	5	5	2	3	1	4
Lilac, common	1	3	4	5	3	3	3	2	4	4	4	3
Lilac, late	3	3	2	2	4	3	4	1	2	4	3	2
Locust, black	3	3	4	5	3	2	3	4	3	3	3	3
Maple, bigtooth	2	3	2	3	4	4	3	3	4	4	4	3
Maple, Manchurian	1	2	2	2	3	3	3	2	1	3	2	2
Maple, mountain	1	2	2	2	2	3	2	3	2	3	3	2
Matrimony-vine	2	4	4	4	3	2	4	4	3	3	5	4
Mountainmahogany, curlleaf	2	1	3	4	4	3	3	3	2	3	3	2
Mountainmahogany, littleleaf	2	1	2	4	4	3	4	3	3	4	3	2
Mountainmahogany, true or birchleaf	3	2	2	4	4	3	4	4	3	4	4	2
Oak, Gambel	3	3	2	4	4	3	2	2	3	4	5	2
Peachbrush, desert	5	3	4	5	5	4	4	4	3	3	3	3
Peashrub, Siberian	3	3	4	3	5	4	4	3	3	4	3	3
Plum, American	2	3	4	4	3	3	2	4	3	3	4	2
Rabbitbrush, Douglas	3	3	4	4	3	3	3	5	3	3	3	4
Rabbitbrush, dwarf	4	3	4	5	4	3	4	5	2	3	5	3
Rabbitbrush, Parry	3	3	4	4	4	3	4	4	5	3	4	3
Rabbitbrush, rubber	3	5	4	4	4	3	3	5	5	5	5	5
Rabbitbrush, small	4	3	4	5	4	3	4	5	3	3	4	2
Rose, Woods	3	4	4	5	2	2	4	3	4	3	4	3
Russian olive	2	3	4	5	3	4	4	3	3	4	3	3
Sagebrush, big	4	5	5	5	4	4	4	5	5	5	4	5
Sagebrush, black	3	4	5	5	4	3	4	5	3	3	4	3
Sagebrush, bud	1	3	4	4	2	2	3	4	2	2	2	2
Sagebrush, fringed	2	3	3	3	3	3	4	3	3	3	3	3
Sagebrush, silver	3	3	4	4	4	4	3	5	4	4	2
Saltbush, fourwing	3	5	3	5	3	5	5	3	5	4	4	5
Saltbush, Gardner	2	3	3	3	3	4	3	3	3	4	2
Saltbush, shadscale	1	3	2	3	2	2	4	3	3	3	4	3
Salt-tree, Siberian	3	3	3	4	4	3	4	4	3	3	4	3
Serviceberry, Saskatoon	3	3	3	4	4	3	5	3	3	4	4	3

TABLE A.9   Ratings of Suitability, by Species Characteristics, for Use in Wildlife Habitat in Utah   (*Continued*)

Palatability	Tolerance to grazing	Resistance to disease and insects	Compatibility with other plants	Palatable early spring growth	Palatable summer growth	Edible foliage retained—fall and winter	Ease of transplanting	Composite suitability index*	Vegetation type†
(13)	(14)	(15)	(16)	(17)	(18)	(19)	(20)	(21)	(22)
1	5	4	1	3	5	5	1	61	JP, BS, MB, BB, SS
4	4	5	3	5	5	2	5	72	MB, JP, BS, A
2	3	3	3	4	4	2	4	58	MB, JP
3	3	3	3	2	4	3	4	64	MB, JP, BS
4	3	4	5	5	4	2	3	69	MB, A, JP
2	2	3	2	4	4	1	4	48	MB, JP
2	3	3	2	4	4	1	2	48	MB, A
3	4	4	3	3	3	2	5	69	JP, MB, BS, SS
5	3	3	2	3	5	5	2	61	MB, JP
4	4	3	2	3	4	4	2	61	MB, JP
4	4	3	2	4	4	2	2	64	MB, JP, BS, A
3	5	4	3	1	5	2	1	61	MB, JP, A
1	4	3	3	5	4	1	4	71	JP, MB, BS, SS, BB
2	4	3	4	4	4	1	4	68	JP, MP, BS
4	4	4	3	4	4	1	3	64	WM, MB
3	4	4	4	3	4	3	4	70	BS, SS, JP, MB, A
4	5	4	4	4	4	4	5	69	MB, BS, JP, BB
2	5	4	4	4	4	4	5	76	SA, A, SS, MB
3	5	3	4	3	4	5	4	83	BS, MB, JP, SS, A, SA, BG, IS
2	5	5	3	3	4	4	5	75	SS, BS, JP
3	5	4	4	4	4	2	5	72	A, SA, MB, JP
2	4	4	3	4	4	2	5	69	MB, JP, IS, WM
4	4	3	3	3	4	5	5	86	BS, JP, SS, MB, BB, A, SA, BG
5	5	4	3	3	5	5	5	81	BS, JP, SS, MB
4	5	4	4	5	1	2	4	60	SS, BS
4	4	4	4	3	5	4	5	69	BS, JP, MB, SS
3	5	4	3	3	4	5	4	74	A, SA
5	5	2	5	3	5	5	4	84	SS, BS, JP, BB, MB, BG, IS
5	5	3	3	4	5	4	4	69	SS, BG, BS, JP, MB, IS
4	5	3	4	3	5	3	2	62	SS, BG, BS, BB
1	5	4	3	3	4	2	4	67	MB, JP, IS, BS
4	4	2	4	4	4	3	3	70	MB, JP, A, SA

TABLE A.9   Ratings of Suitability, by Species Characteristics, for Use in Wildlife Habitat in Utah (*Continued*)

Species‡	Initial establishment (1)	Growth rate (2)	Final establishment (3)	Persistence (4)	Germination (5)	Seed production and handling (6)	Ease of planting (7)	Natural spread (8)	Herbage yield (9)	Availability of current growth (10)	Soil stability (11)	Range of adaptation (12)
Shrubs (*Continued*)												
Serviceberry, Utah	3	3	4	4	4	3	5	3	3	4	4	4
Snowberry, longflower	3	4	4	4	3	2	4	4	4	4	4	2
Snowberry, mountain	4	4	5	5	4	3	5	4	4	4	5	3
Squaw-apple	3	2	3	5	4	3	5	3	4	4	4	3
Sumac, Rocky Mountain smooth	2	3	1	4	2	5	5	4	4	4	4	3
Sumac, skunkbush	2	3	4	5	2	3	5	3	3	3	4	3
Virginsbower, western	3	3	3	4	3	3	3	4	3	4	3	3
Willow, purpleosier	—	4	4	3	—	—	—	2	4	4	4	3
Willow, Scouler	—	3	3	4	—	—	—	4	4	4	4	2
Winterfat, common	4	5	4	4	5	3	2	4	4	3	3	4
Wormwood, oldman	1	5	4	2	1	1	3	2	3	3	3	3
Yellowbrush	3	4	4	4	4	3	3	5	3	3	3	4
Forbs												
Alfalfa, range type	5	5	4	4	5	5	5	2	4	3	4	5
Alfalfa, sickle	4	4	4	4	4	3	5	3	4	3	4	4
Alfileria	2	5	4	2	2	1	2	5	3	3	3	4
Angelica, small-leaf	5	5	3	3	4	5	5	5	4	3	3	2
Aster, alpine leafybracket	2	3	4	5	4	4	4	4	4	4	5	2
Aster, Engelmann	2	3	4	4	2	2	4	5	4	2	4	2
Aster, Pacific	2	3	4	5	4	3	4	5	4	3	5	5
Aster, smooth	4	4	5	5	5	3	3	5	4	3	5	5
Balsamroot, arrowleaf	3	2	5	5	4	4	5	4	4	4	3	4
Balsamroot, cutleaf	3	2	4	4	4	4	5	4	4	4	3	3
Bassia, fivehook	5	4	3	2	5	5	5	4	4	4	4	2
Bouncing-bet	4	4	4	5	5	4	5	3	4	3	5	4
Burnet, small	5	5	3	3	5	5	5	3	3	3	3	4
Checkermallow, Oregon	4	4	4	3	3	3	4	4	4	4	3	3
Clover, alsike	4	3	4	4	4	3	5	4	3	3	3	2
Clover, strawberry	4	3	4	5	5	4	5	5	2	2	4	2
Columbine, Colorado	3	4	4	3	4	3	4	3	4	3	4	2
Cowparsnip, common	2	3	4	3	4	3	4	3	4	3	4	2
Crownvetch, coronilla	4	4	4	4	4	4	4	5	4	4	5	3

TABLE A.9   **Ratings of Suitability, by Species Characteristics, for Use in Wildlife Habitat in Utah** *(Continued)*

Palatability	Tolerance to grazing	Resistance to disease and insects	Compatibility with other plants	Palatable early spring growth	Palatable summer growth	Edible foliage retained—fall and winter	Ease of transplanting	Composite suitability index*	Vegetation type†
(13)	(14)	(15)	(16)	(17)	(18)	(19)	(20)	(21)	(22)
4	4	3	4	4	4	3	3	73	JP, MB, BS, BB
3	4	4	4	5	3	2	4	71	JP, BB, BS, A
3	5	4	5	5	4	2	5	83	MB, A, SA, JP, BS
4	4	3	3	5	4	2	3	71	MB, JP, BS
2	4	4	4	3	4	3	3	67	MB, JP, BS
2	5	3	3	3	4	2	4	66	MB, JP, BS, BB
2	4	4	4	4	4	1	4	66	MB, JP, BS, BB
3	4	4	4	4	4	3	5	59	WM, MB, A
4	4	3	4	4	4	4	5	60	WM, SA, A
4	5	5	5	4	4	4	4	80	SS, BS, JP, BG, BB, MB, IS
3	4	5	3	3	5	3	5	62	MB, A, SA
2	5	4	4	3	4	2	4	80	MB, A, SA, BS
5	4	3	5	4	4	2	4	82	MB, JP, A, BS, SA, SS, BB, IS
5	4	4	5	4	3	2	5	78	MB, JP, A, BS, SA, SS, BB
4	4	5	4	5	3	5	2	68	BB, BS, SS, JP
5	3	3	5	5	4	1	1	74	A, SA, MB
4	4	4	3	4	5	4	5	78	A, SA, MB, WM
4	4	4	5	4	5	3	4	71	A, MB, SA
5	5	5	4	5	3	3	4	81	MB, A, JP, SA, BS, IS, WM
3	5	5	3	4	5	3	5	84	MB, A, SA, JP, BS
4	4	4	4	5	1	1	2	72	JP, MB, BS, A
4	4	4	4	5	1	1	2	69	MB, JP, A, BS
4	4	4	3	3	5	4	3	78	IS, BB, BS, JP
4	4	5	3	4	4	3	5	82	MB, JP, BS
5	4	3	4	5	3	2	3	76	JP, MB, BB, BS, SS
4	3	3	5	4	4	2	4	72	A, SA, MB, WM
4	4	4	3	4	4	3	3	71	WM
5	4	4	4	4	4	3	5	78	IS, WM, BB
4	3	4	4	4	4	2	4	70	A, SA, MB
5	3	3	4	4	4	3	3	68	A, SA, MB, WM
4	4	4	2	4	4	3	5	79	MB, JP

TABLE A.9 Ratings of Suitability, by Species Characteristics, for Use in Wildlife Habitat in Utah (*Continued*)

Species‡	Initial establishment (1)	Growth rate (2)	Final establishment (3)	Persistence (4)	Germination (5)	Seed production and handling (6)	Ease of planting (7)	Natural spread (8)	Herbage yield (9)	Availability of current growth (10)	Soil stability (11)	Range of adaptation (12)
Forbs (*Continued*)												
Cypress, Belvedere summer	5	4	4	3	5	4	5	5	5	4	4	4
Daisy, common oxeye	2	3	5	5	2	3	4	4	3	4	4	4
Eriogonum, cushion	3	3	4	5	4	3	5	4	3	2	4	5
Flax, Lewis (blue)	5	3	3	4	5	3	5	5	3	4	3	5
Geranium, sticky	2	4	4	5	3	2	4	4	4	3	3	2
Gianthyssop, nettleleaf	2	3	3	3	3	4	4	3	4	4	3	2
Globemallow, gooseberryleaf	3	4	4	4	3	3	4	4	4	4	4	4
Globemallow, stream	2	4	4	4	2	4	5	4	4	3	4	3
Goldeneye, Nevada showy	4	4	3	3	5	3	3	5	3	3	3	4
Goldeneye, showy	4	5	3	3	5	4	3	5	3	3	3	3
Goldenrod, Canada	2	3	3	4	3	2	3	4	3	4	4	3
Goldenrod, low	3	4	4	5	5	2	3	4	3	4	5	2
Goldenrod, Parry	3	4	5	5	5	3	3	4	4	4	5	4
Groundsel, butterweed	3	4	4	4	3	4	4	4	5	5	4	2
Helianthella, oneflower	4	3	4	4	5	4	4	4	3	4	3	4
Iris, German (common iris)	1	4	5	5	2	4	4	4	4	4	4	4
Leptotaenia, carrotleaf	2	2	4	5	4	3	3	3	4	3	3	3
Ligusticum, Porter	3	3	3	4	5	4	4	3	4	4	4	3
Lomatium, Nuttall	3	3	4	5	4	4	4	3	3	4	4	4
Lupine, mountain	3	3	2	4	5	4	5	5	4	3	4	3
Lupine, Nevada	3	3	3	4	5	3	5	4	4	3	4	4
Lupine, silky	3	3	3	4	5	3	5	4	4	3	4	4
Lupine, silvery	4	3	3	4	5	3	5	4	4	3	4	4
Medic, black	5	4	3	2	5	4	5	4	3	3	4	3
Milkvetch, chickpea	4	3	4	3	5	5	5	3	4	3	4	4
Milkvetch, sicklepod	4	3	4	3	4	5	5	3	4	4	3	3
Milkvetch, Snakeriver plains	3	3	4	5	3	5	5	4	4	3	3	4
Milkvetch, tall	4	4	4	4	4	5	5	3	5	5	4	2
Painted-cup, Northwestern	2	4	4	3	2	3	3	4	4	4	4	4
Peavine, flat	3	3	3	4	4	3	5	3	4	3	5	3
Peavine, perennial	2	3	3	4	4	4	5	3	3	4	3	3
Peavine, thickleaf	2	3	4	5	2	2	5	5	4	4	5	4
Peavine, Utah	2	3	4	4	2	2	5	5	4	2	4	3

TABLE A.9 Ratings of Suitability, by Species Characteristics, for Use in Wildlife Habitat in Utah (*Continued*)

Palatability (13)	Tolerance to grazing (14)	Resistance to disease and insects (15)	Compatibility with other plants (16)	Palatable early spring growth (17)	Palatable summer growth (18)	Edible foliage retained—fall and winter (19)	Ease of transplanting (20)	Composite suitability index* (21)	Vegetation type† (22)
4	4	4	4	3	4	4	4	87	KS, BG, BS, JP
3	4	5	3	4	5	3	4	74	MB, JP, BS
3	5	4	4	3	5	4	2	75	MB, A, SA, BS, JP
4	4	4	5	5	3	1	5	79	JP, MB, BS, A, SA, SS, WM
5	3	4	4	4	4	2	4	70	A, SA, MB
2	4	4	4	4	4	2	3	65	A, SA, MB
3	4	4	4	4	3	3	3	73	JP, BS, MB, BS, SS
4	3	3	4	4	4	4	3	72	A, SA, MB, JP
3	4	4	4	4	4	2	4	72	JP, MB, BS, BB
3	4	4	4	4	4	2	4	73	A, MB, SA, JP, BS
4	4	4	4	4	4	3	5	70	A, SA, MB
4	5	5	3	4	4	3	5	77	A, SA, MB
4	5	5	3	4	4	3	5	82	MB, JP, A
3	4	3	3	3	4	3	4	73	A, SA, MB
3	4	4	5	4	3	3	2	74	MB, JP, BS, A, SA
3	4	4	3	5	4	4	5	77	MB, JP, A, BS, SS, BB
5	4	4	4	5	1	0	1	63	MB, JP, BS
4	4	4	5	4	4	2	2	73	A, SA, MB
4	4	4	3	5	2	4	2	73	A, SA, MB, JP, BS
4	4	4	5	4	4	2	2	74	SA, A, MB
3	4	4	4	4	4	3	2	73	MB, JP, BS, A
3	4	4	4	4	4	3	2	73	A, MB, SA, JP, BS
3	4	4	4	4	4	3	2	74	MB, A, JP, BS
4	4	4	4	4	4	3	4	75	MB, A, JP, BS, IS
4	3	4	4	4	4	3	5	78	MB, A, SA, JP, BS
3	3	3	4	3	3	3	3	70	MB, JP, A, BS
4	4	4	5	4	4	3	2	76	MB, JP, BS
3	3	4	3	3	4	3	2	74	MB, JP
4	3	4	5	4	4	3	4	72	MB, A, JP, BS
2	3	4	5	4	4	4	4	73	A, SA, MB, JP
3	3	4	3	3	5	3	4	69	A, MB, JP
3	5	5	4	4	4	2	4	76	A, SA, MB, JP
5	3	3	5	5	5	2	3	71	A, MB, SA, JP

TABLE A.9   Ratings of Suitability, by Species Characteristics, for Use in Wildlife Habitat in Utah   (*Continued*)

Species‡	Initial establishment	Growth rate	Final establishment	Persistence	Germination	Seed production and handling	Ease of planting	Natural spread	Herbage yield	Availability of current growth	Soil stability	Range of adaptation
	(1)	(2)	(3)	(4)	(5)	(6)	(7)	(8)	(9)	(10)	(11)	(12)
Forbs (*Continued*)												
Penstemon, Eaton	5	3	4	3	4	5	5	5	3	3	3	4
Penstemon, littlecup	3	2	4	4	3	4	5	4	4	4	4	3
Penstemon, low	4	3	5	5	3	4	5	4	2	3	5	3
Penstemon, Palmer	4	4	3	3	4	4	5	4	4	4	3	4
Penstemon, Rydberg	2	3	3	4	3	4	5	4	3	2	4	2
Penstemon, sidehill	3	3	4	4	3	4	5	4	3	3	4	3
Penstemon, thickleaf	3	3	4	3	3	4	5	4	3	3	4	3
Penstemon, toadflax	2	3	4	4	3	4	5	4	3	2	3	3
Penstemon, Wasatch	4	4	3	3	4	4	5	4	4	4	4	4
Rhubarb, common	4	3	4	5	4	4	4	3	4	4	4	4
Sagebrush, Louisiana	1	3	4	4	3	3	5	5	3	5	3	4
Sagebrush, tarragon	1	4	4	4	2	2	3	5	3	3	5	4
Salsify, vegetable-oyster	5	5	3	3	4	3	3	5	3	3	3	4
Solomon-plume, fat	2	3	4	5	2	3	5	5	4	4	5	4
Sweetanise	4	3	4	4	5	4	3	4	4	4	4	3
Sweetclover, white	5	5	2	2	5	5	5	3	3	3	3	3
Sweetclover, yellow	5	5	2	2	5	5	5	4	4	4	3	4
Sweetroot, spreading	3	3	4	4	2	2	4	4	4	4	4	2
Sweetvetch, Utah	4	4	5	5	4	3	4	5	4	3	4	5
Valerian, edible	2	2	3	5	2	2	3	3	4	4	3	4
Vetch, American	2	2	4	5	4	3	5	5	3	3	4	3
Vetch, bramble	3	2	4	5	4	3	5	5	3	3	2	3

TABLE A.9 Ratings of Suitability, by Species Characteristics, for Use in Wildlife Habitat in Utah (Continued)

Palatability (13)	Tolerance to grazing (14)	Resistance to disease and insects (15)	Compatibility with other plants (16)	Palatable early spring growth (17)	Palatable summer growth (18)	Edible foliage retained—fall and winter (19)	Ease of transplanting (20)	Composite suitability index* (21)	Vegetation type† (22)
4	3	4	3	4	4	3	5	77	MB, JP, BS, A, BB, SS
3	3	4	3	3	4	4	4	72	MB, JP, BS
4	4	4	4	4	4	4	5	78	MB, JP, BS
4	4	4	3	3	4	4	4	76	MB, JP, BS, BB
3	4	4	2	4	3	1	4	64	SA, A, MB
4	4	4	4	3	3	3	4	72	MB, JP, BS
4	4	4	4	3	3	3	4	71	JP, BS, MB
4	4	4	4	4	3	4	4	71	MB, JP, BS, BB
4	4	4	4	3	2	3	4	75	MB, A, JP, BS
4	4	4	4	3	4	3	5	78	MB, JP, BS
3	5	4	4	4	4	3	5	75	MB, JP, BS, A
2	4	4	4	4	4	2	5	69	MB, JP, BS, A
4	3	4	3	4	3	2		69	JP, MB, BS, A
5	5	4	4	5	4	2	4	79	SA, MB, WM
4	4	4	4	4	4	1	2	73	A, SA, MB
3	3	4	3	3	4	4	5	74	MB, JP, BS, A
2	3	4	3	3	4	4	5	74	MB, JP, BS, A, SA, BG, IS
5	3	3	5	4	4	3	4	71	A, SA, MB
5	3	4	5	4	4	3	5	83	MB, JP, BS, A, SA
3	4	4	5	4	4	4	2	67	SA, A, MB, WM
4	4	3	5	4	4	2	4	73	A, MB, SA, BS
3	2	3	5	4	4	3	3	69	MB, JP, A, BS

*100 is possible.

†Type or community to which the species is adapted: JP = juniper-pinyon; MB = mountain brush; BS = big sagebrush; BG = black greasewood; SS = shadscale saltbush; BB = blackbrush; IS = inland saltgrass; A = aspen; SA = subalpine; WM = wet meadows.

‡Key to ratings: 1 = very poor; 2 = poor; 3 = medium or fair; 4 = good; 5 = very good.

SOURCE: Plummer et al. (1968).

TABLE A.10   Seeding Rates for Forages for Wildlife Habitat Projects in Alberta

Crop	Approx. no of seeds per kg	Seeding rate (kg/ha) to provide 80 seeds per meter of row in 15-cm row	Row spacing (cm)			
			15	30	60	90
Legumes						
Alfalfa	440,000	10.0	9.0	5.5		
Sweetclover	572,000	8.0	9.0	5.5		
Alsike clover	1,540,000	3.0	5.5	—		
Red clover	605,000	7.0	7.0	4.5		
White clover	1,760,000	2.5	4.5	—		
Bird's foot trefoil	825,000	5.0	9.0	7.0		
Sainfoin	66,000	65.0	35.0	20.0	10.0	
Cicer milkvetch	286,000	15.0	14.0	9.0		
Crown vetch	242,000	18.0	15.0	9.0		
Grasses						
Russian wildrye	385,000	11.0	—	5.5	3.5	2.5
Atai wildrye	112,000	38.0	—	13.5	9.0	4.5
Crested wheatgrass	385,000	11.0	—	5.5	2.5	
Northern wheatgrass	340,000	13.0	8.0	6.0	4.0	
Western wheatgrass	242,000	18.0	11.0	7.0	3.5	
Intermediate wheatgrass	194,000	22.0	11.0	7.0		
Pubescent wheatgrass	220,000	20.0	11.0	7.0	5.0	
Slender wheatgrass	350,000	12.0	9.0	6.0		
Streambank wheatgrass	344,000	12.0	9.0	6.0		
Tall wheatgrass	174,000	25.0	13.0	10.0		
Perennial ryegrass	500,000	8.5	9.0	6.0		
Italian ryegrass	500,000	9.0	9.0	6.0		
Kentucky bluegrass	4,800,000	0.9	7.0	5.0		
Smooth brome	300,000	14.0	9.0	6.0		
Meadow brome	176,000	24.0	12.0	7.0		
Creeping red fescue	1,353,000	3.0	5.5	3.5		
Meadow fescue	506,000	8.5	9.0	6.0		
Tall fescue	500,000	8.5	8.0	5.0		
Meadow foxtail	1,270,000	3.5	6.0	3.5		
Creeping foxtail	1,657,000	3.0	5.0	3.0		
Orchardgrass	1,439,000	3.0	6.0	4.0		
Timothy	2,710,000	1.6	5.0	4.0		
Reed canarygrass	1,175,000	3.5	6.0	3.5		

SOURCE: Alberta Fish and Wildlife Division (undated).

TABLE A.11   Suggested Grass-Legume Mixtures to Reclaim Disturbed Sites and Improve Wildlife Habitat

Grass mixtures	Seeding rate (kg/ha)	Adaptation
1. Alsike clover	4.5	Areas subject to prolonged
Reed canarygrass	3.4	flooding.
Timothy	1.1	
2. Alsike clover	4.5	For acidic soils subject to
Reed canarygrass	4.5	flooding.
3. Alfalfa	5.6	Areas of plentiful moisture.
Timothy	3.4	
Brome or Pubescent wheatgrass	7.8	
4. Alfalfa	3.4	Where moisture conditions are
Brome or Pubescent wheatgrass	5.6	variable.
Crested wheatgrass	3.4	
5. Alfalfa	2.2	For all but drier parts of
Bromegrass	6.7	province (prairies).
Creeping red fescue	3.4	
6. Crested wheatgrass or Russian wildrye	6.7	For moist to dry sites.
Alfalfa	5.6	
7. Crested wheatgrass or Russian wildrye	5.6	Driest sites.
Alfalfa	1.1	
8. Sweetclover	1.1	This is our all-purpose recipe
Alfalfa	2.2	we use on Buck for Wildlife
Crested wheatgrass*	2.2	projects. It provides excellent
Slender wheatgrass	2.2	nesting cover and high-quality
Intermediate wheatgrass	3.4	forage.

*Substitute tall wheatgrass in moist to wet areas.
SOURCE: Alberta Fish and Wildlife Division (undated).

TABLE A.12 Environmental Criteria for Selecting Various Grass and Legume Species for Wildlife Habitat

Species	Moisture requirement	Soil preference	pH tolerance (1–3) Acid	pH tolerance (1–3) Base	Salt tolerance (1–3)	Winter hardiness (1–3)	Palatability (1–5) General	Early spring	Fall–winter	Tolerance to grazing	Persistence	Forage yield	Remarks
Bent grass (redtop) (*Agrostis alba*)	Wet	Poorly drained, fine-textured, low-fertile.	2	1	1	2	2–3			3	4	4	Often grown with alsike clover and timothy. Useful to wildlife for cover.
Bluegrass, Kentucky (*Poa pratensis*)	Moist	Wide range, medium-textured soils.	2	2	1		5	5	4	5	5	3	Cool conditions. Does well on northern exposures and high elevations.
Bromegrass (*Bromus inermis*)	Dry to moist	Wide range.	2	2	2	Polar 3	5	5	3	5	4	5	Compatible in mixtures.
Fescue, hard (*Festuca ovina*)	Dry to moist	Well-drained sandy loams, clay—fair.	2	1	1	3	2	2	2	5	4	3	High use by mule deer. Medium use by elk and sheep, good fall pasture.
Fescue, meadow	Moist	Heavy soils.	2	1	?	1	4	4			2		Slow; often used in mixtures because others grazed in preference.
Fescue, red (*Festuca rubra*)	Moist to wet	Clay, loam, sandy soils, gray and black.	2	1	2	2	5	5	5	4	4	2	May eliminate alfalfa. Good in foothills area. Moose—low use.

Species	Moisture	Soil	1	2	3	4	5	6	7	8	9	Remarks
Fescue, tall (*Festuca arundinacea*)	Wet	Poorly drained.	2	2	2	3	4	2	4	4	4	Bighorn sheep—medium use. Mule deer—high use. Moose—low use.
Orchardgrass (*Dactylis glomerata*)	Moist	Well-drained.	2	1	Suba 3	Some varieties	3	3	5	3	4	Often planted with bird's foot trefoil, alfalfa, and white clover.
Reed canarygrass (*Phalaris arundinacea*)	Wet to moist	Heavy clay.	2	2	1	Suba, Castor, Frontier	3	2	5	3	4	Provides good cover for birds, fair forage for mule deer.
Russian wildrye (*Elymus junceus*)	Dry	Brown soils.	1	3	Sawki 3	2	5	4	5	5	4	
Ryegrass, perennial (*Lolium perenne*)	(750 mm + rainfall), moist	Gray, black, fertile soils.	1	2	2	2	4	?	?	5	2	Often sown with clovers.
Timothy (*Phleum pratense*)	Moist to wet	Dark brown, black, and gray soils.	2	1	1	2	3	2	4	4	3	Suited for low-lying peat area.
Wheatgrass, crested (*Agropyron cristatum*)	Dry	Brown, dark brown.	2	2	3	3	3	3	5	4	4	Compatible in mixtures; provides early spring forage.
Wheatgrass, streambank (*Agropyron riparium*)	Dry to moist	Brown, dark brown, well drained.	1	2	2	2	1	?	?	5	2	Because of its low palatability, may be suitable for highway use or where animal use discouraged.
Wheatgrass, tall (*Agropyron elongatum*)	Wet	Well drained to wet; high H$_2$O table preferred.	1	2	2	2	2	4	4	3	4	High palatability for bighorn sheep and elk; moderate palatability for moose; poor for mule deer.

TABLE A.12 Environmental Criteria for Selecting Various Grass and Legume Species for Wildlife Habitat (*Continued*)

Species	Moisture requirement	Soil preference	pH tolerance (1–3) Acid	pH tolerance (1–3) Base	Salt tolerance (1–3)	Winter hardness (1–3)	General	Early spring	Fall–winter	Tolerance to grazing	Persistence	Forage yield	Remarks
Alfalfa (*Medicago* spp.)	Dry to moist	Wide range—loam soils with high lime content.	1	2	2	1	5	4	2	4	4	4	Grim-Winterhardy variety. Good forage for antelope mule deer.
Sweetclover (*Melilotus* spp.)	Dry	Fertile, well-drained soils.	1	2	2	2	3	3	4	3	2	4	Good forage for mule deer, game birds and small mammals. Good cover for game birds and small mammals. Fair cover for mule deer.
Alsike clover (*Trifolium hybridum*)	Wet	Black and gray heavy moist alkaline soils.	1	2	2	2	4	4	3	4	4	3	Good forage for mule deer, game birds and small mammals. Poor cover for game birds. Poor cover for small mammals.
Red clover (*Trifolium pratense*)	Moist	Wide range—gray luvisoils, black soils.	1	2	2	1	4	?	3	3	2		Good forage for mule deer, small mammals, and game birds. Cover value for mule deer poor, game birds fair, small mammals good. Good yield produced when grown with timothy. Excellent fall pasture.

Palatability (1–5)

Species	Moisture	Soil											Comments
White clover (*Trifolium repens*)	Moist	Well-drained fine- to medium-textured soils.	2	1	1	2	5	4	?	5	3	3	Variable, depends (there are 3). Good forage for mule deer, small mammals, and game birds.
Wheatgrass, intermediate (*Agropyron intermedium*)	Moist	Dark brown and black.	1	2	1	2	4	5	3	5	5	5	Compatible with alfalfa.
Wheatgrass, pubescent (*Agropyron trichophorum*)	300 mm + ppn; moist to dry	Dark brown, black.	1	2	2	2	3	5	3	5	5	4	Competitive.
Wheatgrass, slender (*Agropyron trachycaulum*)	350 mm + ppn; moist	Prefers sandy loam, but wide range.	1	2	3	2	2	3	3	4	3	4	Preferred food of bighorn sheep, elk. Moderate palatability to moose.
Sanfoin (*Onobrychis viciafolia*)	Moist	Brown soils, then coarse 1 textured soils.	1	2	1	2	4	4		3	2		
Cicer milkvetch (*Astragalus cicer*)	Moist to wet	Dark brown and black soils, coarse-textured, well-drained.	2	2	2	2	3		3	2	4		
Crown vetch	Moist	Fertile, well-drained; does well on shifting soil.	1	3	1	4	3	4	4	4	4		Main use is in disturbed areas.
Bird's foot trefoil (*Lotus corniculatus*)	Moist to wet	Gray luvisoils.	1	3	2	1	5	4	4	4			Cannot tolerate nurse crops. Poor competitor (especially with timothy or bromegrass)

Note: Rating scales are from 1 to 3 or 1 to 5 as indicated; 1 is lowest rating.
SOURCE: Alberta Fish and Wildlife Division (undated).

TABLE A.13   Common Names and Trade Names of Insecticides (I), Acaricides (A), Nematocides (N), Herbicides (H), and Fungicides (F) Used in Virginia

Common name	Trade name	Use	Ref. no.*
acephate	Orthene	I	19
acifluorfen	Blazer, Tackle	H	102
alachlor	Lasso	H	75
aldicarb	Temik	I,A,N	51
allethrin	Allethrin, Pynamin	I	5
ametryn	Evik	H	88
amitrole	Weedazol	H	76
anilazine	Diyrenene	F	120
atrazine	Aatrex, Atrazine	H	81
azinphos-methyl	Guthion	I	33
Bacillus thuringiensis	Dipel, Thuricide, Biotrol	I	1
bendiocarb	Dycarb, Ficam, Turcam	I	26
benomyl	Benlate	F	136
bensulide	Betasan, Prefar, Pre-san	H	92
bentazon	Basagran	H	93
bromoxynil	Buctril, Brominal	H	107
butylate	Sutan	H	79
captan	Captan, Orthocide	F	119
carbaryl	Sevin	I	21
carbofuran	Furadan	I,N,A	57
carbophenothion	Trithion	I	39
carboxin	Vitavax	F	137
chlorimuron	Canopy, Classic, Gemini	H	70
chlorothalonil	Bravo, Daconil 2787, Exotherm	F	109
chlorpyrifos	Dursban, Lorsban, Killmaster II	I	35
copper sulfate + lime	Bordeaux Mixture	F	121
coumaphos	Co-Ral	I	43
crotoxyphos	Ciodrin	I	13
cyanazine	Bladex	H	101
cycloheximide	Acti-Dione	F	138
cypermethrin	Ammo, Cymbush	I	6
2,4-D	Formula 40, Dacamine Weed Rhap	H	103
2,4-DB	Butoxone, Butyrac	H	100
DCPA	Dacthal	H	62
demeton	Systox	I	47
diazinon	Diazinon, Spectracide	I	48
dicamba	Weedmaster, Banvel	H	94
dichlobenil	Casoron	H	87
dichlone	Phygon, Quintar	F	122
dichlorvos	DDVP, Vapona	I	37
diclofop-methyl	Hoelon	H	61
dicloran	Botran, DCNA	F	133
dicofol	Kelthane	A	15
dicrotophos	Bidrin	I	52
diflubenzuron	Dimilin	I	7
dikar	Dikar	F	115
dimethoate	Cygon, De-Fend, Rebelate	I	38
dinocap	Karathane	F	128
dioxathion	Delnav	I	16

TABLE A.13   Common Names and Trade Names of Insecticides (I), Acaricides (A), Nematocides (N), Herbicides (H), and Fungicides (F) Used in Virginia   (*Continued*)

Common name	Trade name	Use	Ref. no.*
diquat dibromide	Diquat	H	95
disulfoton	Di-Syston	I	44
diuron	Karmex	H	80
dodine	Cyprex	F	131
endosulfan	Thiodan	I	24
EPTC	Eptam	H	106
ethion	Ethion	I	22
ethoprop	Mocap	I,N	41
etridiazol	Terrazole, Truban, Koban	F	127
famphur	Warbex	I	49
fenchlorphos	Ronnel	I,N	20
fenoxaprop-ethyl	Whip, Furore	H	71
fensulfothion	Dasanit	I	55
fenthion	Baycid, Baytex, Tiguvon	I	50
fenvalerate	Pydrin, Ectrin	I	12
ferbam	Carbamate	F	117
fluazifop-butyl	Fusilade	H	60
fluvalinate	Mavrik	I	4
folpet	Phaltan	F	123
fonofos	Dyfonate	I	31
fosamine ammonium	Krenite	H	68
glyphosate	Kleenup, Roundup, Rodeo, Accord	H	74
hexazinone	Velpar	H	72
imazalil	Feundal	F	132
imazapyr	Arsenal	H	73
iprodione	Rovral	F	124
lindane	Gamma BHC, Lindane	I	18
linuron	Lorox	H	84
malathion	Cython	I	17
mancozeb	Dithane M-45, Fore	F	112
maneb	Dithane M-22, Manzate	F	113
MCPA	MCP, Rhonox	H	96
metalaxyl	Apron, Ridomil, Subdue	F	130
methamidophos	Monitor	I	36
methidathion	Supracide	I	34
methiocarb	Mesurol, Slug-Geta	I,A	40
methomyl	Lannate, Nudrin	I	32
methoxychlor	Marlate	I	8
methyl parathion	Penncap-M	I	45
metiram	Polyram	F	114
metolachlor	Dual	H	67
metribuzin	Lexone, Sencor	H	105
mevinphos	Phosdrin	I	53
monocrotophos	Azodrin	I	58
naled	Dibrom	I	23
napropamide	Devrinol	H	99
naptalam	Alanap, Ancrack, Klean Kropp	H	64
nicotine	Blackleaf 40	I	14
norflurazon	Zorial, Solicam	H	86
oryzalin	Surflan	H	98
oxadiazon	Ronstar	H	91

TABLE A.13   Common Names and Trade Names of Insecticides (I), Acaricides (A), Nematocides (N), Herbicides (H), and Fungicides (F) Used in Virginia   (*Continued*)

Common name	Trade name	Use	Ref. no.*
oxamyl	Vydate	I	46
oxydemeton-methyl	Metasystox-R	I	30
oxyfluorfen	Goal	H	65
paraquat	Gramoxone, Paraquat	H	104
parathion	Parathion	I	59
pendimethalin	Prowl	H	89
permethrin	Ambush, Pounce, Ectiban	I	3
phenamiphos	Nemacur	N	56
phorate	Thimet	I	54
phosmet	Imidan	I	28
picloram	Tordon	H	78
pronamide	Kerb	H	63
propanil	Stam, Stampede	H	85
propiconazole	Tilt, Banner	F	126
propoxur	Baygon	I	42
pyrethrin	Pyrethrin	I	2
quintozene	PCNB, Terrachlor	F	125
resmethrin	Resmethrin	I	9
rotenone	Prentox, Rotenone	I	11
sethoxydim	Poast	H	69
simazine	Princep, Amizene	H	66
streptomycin	Agri-strep, Agrimycin	F	111
sulfur	Brimstone, Magnetic 6	F	108
tebuthiuron	Spike	H	97
temephos	Abate	I	27
terbacil	Sinbar	H	90
terbufos	Counter	I	29
tertachlorvinphos	Gardona, Rabon	I	10
thiabendazole	Arbotect, Mertect	F	118
thiophanate-methyl	Topsin M	F	116
thiram	Thiram, Arasan	F	135
triadimefon	Bayleton	F	134
triadimenol	Baytan	F	129
triclopyr	Garlon	H	83
trichlorfon	Dylox, Proxol	I	25
trifluralin	Treflan	H	77
vernolate	Vernam	H	82
vinclozolin	Ronilan	F	110

*Use the reference number (Ref. no.) to look up toxicity data in Table A.15, A.16, or A.17.

TABLE A.14   Trade Names of Pesticides Used in Virginia, with Respective Common Names

Trade name	Common name	Ref. no.*	Trade name	Common name	Ref. no.*
Aatrex	atrazine	81	Counter	terbufos	29
Abate	temephos	27	Cygon	dimethoate	38
Accord	glyphosate	74	Cymbush	cypermethrin	6
Acti-Dione	cycloheximide	138	Cyprex	dodine	131
Agrimycin	streptomycin	111	Cythion	malathion	17
Agri-step	streptomycin	111	Dacamine	2,4-D	103
Alanap	naptalam	64	Daconil	chlorothalonil	109
Allethrin	allethrin	5	2787		
Ambush	permethrin	3	Dacthal	DCPA	62
Amizene	simazine	66	Dasanit	fensulfothion	55
Ammo	cypermethrin	6	DCNA	dicloran	133
Ancrack	naptalam	64	DDVP	dichlorvos	37
Apron	metalaxyl	130	De-Fend	dimethoate	38
Arasan	thiram	135	Delnav	dioxathion	16
Arbotect	thiabendazole	118	Devrinol	napropamide	99
Arsenal	imazapyr	73	Diazinon	diazinon	48
Atrazine	atrazine	81	Dibrom	naled	23
Azodrin	monocrotophos	58	Dikar	dikar	115
Banner	propiconazole	126	Dimilin	diflubenzuron	7
Banvel	dicamba	94	Dipel	Bacillus	1
Basagran	bentazon	93		thuringiensis	
Baycid	fenthion	50	Diquat	diquat dibromide	95
Baygon	propoxur	42	Di-Syston	disulfoton	44
Bayleton	triadimefon	134	Dithane	maneb	113
Baytan	triadimenol	129	M-22		
Baytex	fenthion	50	Dithane	mancozeb	112
Benlate	benomyl	136	M-45		
Betasan	bensulide	92	Diyrenene	anilazine	120
Bidrin	dicrotophos	52	Dodine	dodine	131
Biotrol	bacillus	1	Dual	metolachlor	67
	thuringiensis		Dursban	chlorpyrifos	35
Blackleaf	nicotine	14	Dycarb	bendiocarb	26
40			Dyfonate	fonofos	31
Bladex	cyanazine	101	Dylox	trichlorfon	25
Blazer	acifluorfen	102	Ectiban	permethrin	3
Bordeaux	copper sulfate	121	Ectrin	fenvalerate	12
Mixture	+ lime		Eptam	EPTC	106
Botran	dicloran	133	Ethion	ethion	22
Bravo	chlorothalonil	109	Evik	ametryn	88
Brimstone	sulfur	108	Exotherm	chlorothalonil	109
Brominal	bromoxynil	107	Feundal	imazalil	132
Buctril	bromoxynil	107	Ficam	bendiocarb	26
Butoxon	2,4-DB	100	Fore	mancozeb	112
Butyrac	2,4-DB	100	Formula	2,4-D	103
Canopy	chlorimuron	70	40		
Captan	captan	119	Furadan	carbofuran	57
Carbamate	ferbam	117	Furore	fenoxaprop-ethyl	71
Casoran	dichlobenil	87	Fusilade	fluazifop-butyl	60
Ciodrin	crotoxyphos	13	Gamma	lindane	18
Classic	chlorimuron	70	BHC		
Co-Ral	coumaphos	43			

TABLE A.14   Trade Names of Pesticides Used in Virginia, with Respective Common Names   (*Continued*)

Trade name	Common name	Ref. no.*	Trade name	Common name	Ref. no.*
Gardona	tetrachlorvin-phos, stirofos	10	Polyram	metiram	114
			Pounce	permethrin	3
Garlon	triclopyr	83	Prefar	bensulide	92
Gemini	chlorimuron	70	Prentox	rotenone	11
Goal	oxyfluorfen	65	Pre-san	bensulide	92
Gramoxone	paraquat	104	Princep	simazine	66
Guthion	azinphos-methyl	33	Prowl	pendimethalin	89
Hoelon	diclofop-methyl	61	Proxol	trichlorfon	25
Imidan	phosmet	28	Pydrin	fenvalerate	12
Karathane	dinocap	128	Pynamin	allethrin	5
Karmex	diuron	80	Pyrethrin	pyrethrin	2
Kelthane	dicofol	15	Quintar	dichlone	122
Kerb	pronamide	63	Rabon	tetrachlorvinphos, stirofos	10
Killmaster II	chlorpyrifos	35			
			Rebelate	dimethoate	38
Klean Krop	naptalam	64	Resmeth-rin	resmethrin	9
Kleenup	glyphosate	74	Rhonox	MCPA	96
Koban	etridiazol	127	Ridomil	metalaxyl	130
Krenite	fosamine ammonium	68	Rodeo	glyphosate	74
			Ronilan	vinclozolin	110
Lannate	methomyl	32	Ronnel	fenchlorphos	20
Lasso	alachlor	75	Ronstar	oxadiazon	91
Lexone	metribuzin	105	Rotenone	rotenone	11
Lindane	lindane	18	Roundup	glyphosate	74
Lorox	linuron	84	Rovral	iprodione	124
Lorsban	chlorpyrifos	35	Sencor	metribuzin	105
Magnetic 6	sulfur	108	Sevin	carbaryl	21
Manzate	maneb	113	Sinbar	terbacil	90
Marlate	methloxychlor	8	Slug-Geta	methiocarb	40
Mavrik	fluvalinate	4	Solicam	norflurazon	86
MCP	MCPA	96	Spectra-cide	diazinon	48
Mertect	thiabendazole	118			
Mesurol	methiocarb	40	Spike	tebuthiuron	97
Metasys-tox-R	oxydemeton-methyl	30	Stampede	propanil	85
			Subdue	metalaxyl	130
Mocap	ethoprop	41	Supracide	methidathion	34
Monitor	methamidophos	36	Surflan	oryzalin	98
Nemacur	phenamiphos	56	Sutan	butylate	79
Nudrin	methomyl	32	Systox	demeton	47
Orthene	acephate	19	Tackle	acifluorfen	102
Orthocide	captan	119	Temik	aldicarb	51
Paraquat	paraquat	104	Terrachlor	quintozene	125
Parathion	parathion	59	Terrazole	etridiazol	127
PCNB	quintozene	125	Thimet	phorate	54
Penncap-M	methyl parathion	45	Thiodan	endosulfan	24
Phaltan	folpet	123	Thiram	thiram	135
Phosdrin	mevinphos	53	Thuricide	Bacillus thur-ingiensis	1
Phygon	dichlone	122			
Poast	sethoxydim	69	Tiguvon	fenthion	50

TABLE A.14   Trade Names of Pesticides Used in Virginia, with Respective Common Names   (*Continued*)

Trade name	Common name	Ref. no.*	Trade name	Common name	Ref. no.*
Tilt	propiconazole	126	Vitavax	carboxin	137
Topsin M	thiophanate-methyl	116	Vydate	oxamyl	46
Tordon	picloram	78	Warbex	famphur	49
Treflan	trifluralin	77	Weedazol	amitrole	76
Trithion	carbophenothion	39	Weed-	dicamba	94
Truban	etridiazol	127	master		
Turcam	bendiocarb	26	Weed	2,4-D	103
Vapona	dichlorvos	37	Rhap		
Velpar	hexazinone	72	Whip	fenoxaprop-ethyl	71
Vernam	vernolate	82	Zorial	norflurazon	86

*Reference numbers can be used to look up toxicity data in Table A.15, A.16, or A. 17.

SOURCE: Stinson and Bromley (1991).

TABLE A.15   Acute-Toxicity Categories of Insecticides, Acaricides, and Nematocides

Ref. no.	Common name	LD_{50} (mg/kg)	Wildlife kills and cautions
	Relatively Nontoxic (LD_{50} > 5000 mg/kg Body Weight)		
1	Bacillus thur- ingiensis	Essentially nontoxic	Generally recognized as safe to fish and wildlife, to birds and mammals.
2	pyrethrin	7070–>10,000	Generally recognized as safe to birds and mammals.
	Slightly Toxic (LD_{50} = 1001–5000 mg/kg Body Weight)		
3	permethrin	3000–15,500	Moderately toxic to some mammals.
4	fluvalinate	>2510	Moderately toxic to some mammals.
5	allethrin	>2000	Moderately toxic to some mammals.
6	cypermethrin	>2000–>4640	Moderately toxic to some mammals.
7	diflubenzuron	>2000–>5000	Generally recognized as safe to birds and mammals.
8	methoxychlor	>2000	There are no published reports of wildlife kills due to methoxychlor.
9	resmethrin	>2000	Generally recognized as safe to birds and mammals.
10	tetrachlorvinphos	>2000	There are no published reports of wild-life kills from tetrachlorvinphos use.
11	rotenone	1680–≥2200	Highly toxic to some mammals.
12	fenvalerate	1600–>9932	Moderately toxic to some mammals.
	Moderately Toxic (LD_{50} = 201–1000 mg/kg Body Weight)		
13	crotoxyphos	790	There are no published reports of wildlife kills from crotoxyphos use.
14	nicotine	530–>2000	Highly toxic to some mammals.
15	dicofol	265	Dicofol is suspected of causing eggshell thinning in birds.
16	dioxathion	240–277	Extremely toxic to some mammals.
	Highly Toxic (LD_{50} = 41–200 mg/kg Body Weight)		
17	malathion	167–1485	Malathion is only moderately or slightly toxic to most birds and mammals tested. There are no published reports of wildlife kills from malathion use.
18	lindane	120–>2000	Highly toxic to some mammals.

TABLE A.15   Acute-Toxicity Categories of Insecticides, Acaricides, and Nematocides   (*Continued*)

Ref. no.	Common name	LD$_{50}$ (mg/kg)	Wildlife kills and cautions
19	acephate	106–852	Acephate can be converted to methamidophos in the environment and in the body. Methamidophos is more toxic than acephate.
20	fenchlorphos	80–>2000	There are no published reports of wildlife kills from fenchlorphos use.
21	carbaryl	56–3000	Carbaryl is only moderately or slightly toxic to most birds and mammals tested. There have been no published reports of wildlife kills from carbaryl use.
22	ethion	45–2560	Extremely toxic to some mammals.

Extremely Toxic (LD$_{50}$ ≤ 40 mg/kg Body Weight)

Ref. no.	Common name	LD$_{50}$ (mg/kg)	Wildlife kills and cautions
23	naled	37–120	There are no published reports of wildlife kills from naled use. Avoid applying naled to lakes, ponds, or wetlands during waterfowl nesting and brood rearing.
24	endosulfan	31–>320	There are no published reports of bird kills due to endosulfan use.
25	trichlorfon	22–123	There are no published reports of wildlife kills due to trichlorfon use. The toxicities of EPN, malathion, and azinophosmethyl are increased when these pesticides are used with trichlorfon.
26	bendiocarb	21–33	Extremely toxic to some mammals. Granules must be fully covered by soil to reduce wildlife exposure and hazard.
27	temephos	19–270	Hazardous to some species of aquatic invertebrates. Avoid applying temephos to lakes, ponds, or wetlands during waterfowl nesting and brood rearing.
28	phosmet	18–1830	Phosmet is only moderately toxic to most bird species tested.
29	terbufos	15–26	Avoid wildlife exposure. Extremely toxic to mammals. Granules must be fully covered by soil to reduce wildlife exposure and hazard.
30	oxydemeton-methyl	14–120	There are no published reports of wildlife kills from oxydemeton-methyl use.

TABLE A.15   Acute-Toxicity Categories of Insecticides, Acaricides, and Nematocides   *(Continued)*

Ref. no.	Common name	LD_{50} (mg/kg)	Wildlife kills and cautions
31	fonofos	10–42	Avoid wildlife exposure. Extremely toxic to some mammal species. Fonofos granules must be fully incorporated into the soil to reduce wildlife exposure and hazard.
32	methomyl	10–42	Avoid wildlife exposure. Extremely toxic to some mammal species, including deer.
33	azinphos-methyl	8.5–283	Avoid wildlife exposure. Extremely toxic to some mammal species, including deer. In a Washington field study, azinphos-methyl (35% wettable powder) killed birds when it was applied in apple orchards. Azinphos-methyl is relatively persistent in the environment.
34	methidathion	8.4–225	There are no published reports of wildlife kills from methidathion use.
35	chlorpyrifos	8.4–112	Avoid wildlife exposure. There have been reports of robins found dead or dying on lawns treated with chlorpyrifos. Chlorpyrifos is moderately persistent in the environment. In a recent study of contaminants in hunter-killed bobwhites in Virginia, chlorpyrifos was the most frequently found pesticide contaminant in bobwhites.
36	methamidophos	8.0–57	Avoid wildlife exposure. Extremely toxic to some mammals. House sparrows and killdeer have been killed by methamidophos application to cabbage fields. Sage grouse have been killed after methamidophos applications to potatoes. Its toxicity to wildlife is increased when it is used with malathion.
37	dichlorvos	7.8–17	Keep treated animal feeds away from wildlife.
38	dimethoate	6.6–63	Avoid wildlife exposure. Sage grouse occupying croplands sprayed with dimethoate have been killed.
39	carbophenothion	5.6–269	Avoid wildlife exposure. Extremely toxic to some mammals. Carbophenothion is environmentally persistent, highly toxic, and has a high bioconcentration potential.

TABLE A.15 **Acute-Toxicity Categories of Insecticides, Acaricides, and Nematocides** *(Continued)*

Ref. no.	Common name	LD$_{50}$ (mg/kg)	Wildlife kills and cautions
40	methiocarb	4.6–270	Extremely toxic to some mammals. When used for slug and snail control, methiocarb may be hazardous to birds that eat these species.
41	ethoprop	4.2–13	Avoid wildlife exposure. Ethoprop is relatively persistent in the environment. In one incident, American robins were found dead on a lawn treated with ethoprop 30 days before. Granules must be fully covered by soil to reduce wildlife exposure and hazard.
42	propoxur	3.6–120	Propoxur is extremely toxic to many bird species. However, there are no published reports of wildlife kills due to propoxur use.
43	coumaphos	3.5–32	Avoid wildlife exposure. Extremely toxic to birds and some mammal species. Coumaphos caused the die-off of more than 220 American widgeons found dead at ponds adjacent to a feedlot. Prevent wildlife access to coumaphos-treated animal feed.
44	disulfoton	3.2–>32	Avoid wildlife exposure. This insecticide is extremely toxic to birds and mammals. Application of disulfoton has killed birds, mammals, reptiles, and amphibians. This pesticide is highly toxic to wildlife both when eaten and when it contacts the skin.
45	methyl parathion	3.1–60	Avoid wildlife exposure. Methyl parathion is one of the most widely used pesticides in the United States. There have been relatively few documented die-offs reported for methyl parathion alone, however some kills have occurred when methyl parathion was used in addition to other insecticides.
46	oxamyl	2.6–9.4	Extremely toxic to birds and mammals. However, there are not published reports of wildlife kills due to oxamyl use.
47	demeton	2.4–22	Extremely toxic to birds and mammals both when eaten and when it contacts the skin.

TABLE A.15   Acute-Toxicity Categories of Insecticides, Acaricides, and Nematocides   (*Continued*)

Ref. no.	Common name	LD_{50} (mg/kg)	Wildlife kills and cautions
48	diazinon	2.0–110	Avoid wildlife exposure. There have been a number of bird kills in at least 17 states when diazinon has been confirmed or suspected as the poisoning agent. At least 23 bird species have been involved in these kills. Waterfowl were most often affected in kills and most waterfowl mortalities occurred on turf grass (lawns and golf courses). Wildlife kills have also occurred after diazinon application in corn and alfalfa. Over 800 birds have been killed in a single incident. In Virginia at least four wildlife die-offs have been caused by diazinon. Three of these cases involved waterfowl and one case involved songbirds.
49	famphur	1.8–9.9	Avoid wildlife exposure. Extremely toxic to birds and mammals. Red-tailed hawks, great horned owls, black-billed magpies, and robins are among those species that have been poisoned due to famphur applications to livestock for warble control. Hawks and owls have been killed after eating birds and rodents poisoned by famphur. Bald eagles have been poisoned by scavenging carcasses of livestock that had been previously treated with famphur. Residues of famphur on the hair of livestock can persist for several months after application. In one incident, birds associated with cattle were poisoned more than 3 months after cattle were treated with famphur and released into pastures. Famphur is extremely hazardous to birds. Prevent wildlife access to famphur-treated feed. Prevent wildlife access to carcasses of famphur-treated livestock.

TABLE A.15   Acute-Toxicity Categories of Insecticides, Acaricides, and Nematocides   (Continued)

Ref. no.	Common name	LD_{50} (mg/kg)	Wildlife kills and cautions
50	fenthion	1.8–26	Avoid wildlife exposure. Fenthion applied dermally to cattle has caused the deaths of insect-eating birds (black-billed magpies) associated with cattle 4 to 5 months after cattle were treated. Fenthion has caused secondary poisoning of owls and hawks when used to get rid of nuisance birds by charging perches with fenthion. In several instances, fenthion sprayed over ponds, lakes, and wetlands for mosquito and midge control has killed birds, including gulls, terns, stilts, herons, ducks, and songbirds. Some kills have been very large, involving an estimated 5000–25,000 birds. Do not spray fenthion over wetlands.
51	aldicarb	1.8–5.3	Avoid wildlife exposure. Aldicarb is extremely toxic to mammals. There are many documented cases of wildlife mortality caused by aldicarb use in Europe and Great Britain. In field studies, granular aldicarb used on citrus, cotton, and potatoes killed nontarget species including robins, opossums, rabbits, shrews, lizards, doves, mice, sparrows, and horned larks. Wildlife may be killed by eating aldicarb granules or contaminated insects. Granules must be fully covered by soil to reduce wildlife exposure and hazard.
52	dicrotophos	1.6–9.6	Avoid wildlife exposure. Extremely toxic to mammals, including deer.
53	mevinphos	0.7–4.6	Avoid wildlife exposure. Mevinphos is extremely toxic to birds and mammals. In one case, mevinphos killed about 120 songbirds when applied to cole crops.
54	phorate	0.6–21	Avoid wildlife exposure. Extremely toxic to birds and mammals. At least 17 wildlife kills have been attributed to phorate. Documented kills have included geese (95), ducks (556–581), raptors (23), other birds (2280–2300), and mammals. Raptor kills have included at least 8 bald eagles. Most known kills have occurred in or near wheat or alfalfa fields.

TABLE A.15   Acute-Toxicity Categories of Insecticides, Acaricides, and Nematocides   (*Continued*)

Ref. no.	Common name	LD$_{50}$ (mg/kg)	Wildlife kills and cautions
55	fensulfothion	0.5–2.4	Avoid wildlife exposure. Extremely toxic to birds and mammals. Fensulfothion has been implicated in a number of bird kills on golf courses and agricultural fields.
56	phenamiphos	0.5–2.4	Avoid wildlife exposure. Extremely toxic to birds and mammals. Phenamiphos was implicated in a kill of 400–500 cedar waxwings feeding on treated pyracantha bushes.
57	carbofuran	0.2–12	Avoid wildlife exposure. Extremely toxic to birds and mammals. Carbofuran has been associated with a substantial number of bird kills involving more than 70 species. The number of birds involved in any single kill has ranged up to at least 2450. In Virginia, carbofuran has been implicated in several wildlife kills. Since 1985, two bald eagle deaths in Virginia are known to have been caused by carbofuran poisoning, and at least four other bald eagle poisoning incidents are strongly suspected to have been caused by carbofuran. Other species poisoned by carbofuran in Virginia include redtailed hawk, American robin, eastern bluebird, northern cardinal, American goldfinch, red-winged blackbird, savannah sparrow, chipping sparrow, European startling, blue jay, and whitethroated sparrow. Carbofuran kills in Virginia have involved over 200 birds in a single die-off. Most documented kills in Virginia have been a result of using granular carbofuran in corn. Carbofuran has caused wildlife deaths even when applied in-furrow at lower than recommended rates. Granular carbofuran was canceled for use in Virginia in 1991.
58	monocrotophos	0.2–24	Avoid wildlife exposure. Extremely toxic to birds and mammals, including deer. Monocrotophos has been implicated as the poisoning agent in a number of bird deaths from both primary and secondary poisoning.

TABLE A.15   Acute-Toxicity Categories of Insecticides, Acaricides, and Nematocides   (*Continued*)

Ref. no.	Common name	LD_{50} (mg/kg)	Wildlife kills and cautions
59	parathion	0.1–24	Avoid wildlife exposure. Extremely toxic to birds and mammals, including deer. Nationwide, more wildlife die-offs have been attributed to parathion than any other organophosphate insecticide. In Virginia, parathion has poisoned purple martins and barn swallows.

Note: LD_{50} values are for multiple formulations and birds. A range of values for bird species is presented.

SOURCE: Stinson and Bromley (1991).

TABLE A.16 **Acute-Toxicity Categories of Herbicides**

Ref. no.	Common Name	LD_{50} (mg/kg)	Ref. no.	Common Name	LD_{50} (mg/kg)
	Relatively Nontoxic (LD_{50} > 5000 mg/kg Body Weight)		83	triclopyr	1698–4640
			84	linuron	[1500]
60	fluazifop-butyl	>17,000	85	propanil	[1384]
			86	norflurazon	>1250
61	diclofop-methyl	>10,000	87	dichlobenil	1189–>2000
62	DCPA	[>10,000]	88	ametryn	[1110]
63	pronamide	8700–20,000	89	pendimethalin	[1050]
64	naptalam	[8200]		Moderately Toxic (LD_{50} = 201–1000 mg/kg Body Weight)	
65	oxyfluorfen	[>5000]			
66	simazine	>5000	90	terbacil	Not highly toxic
67	metolachlor	Practically non-toxic to birds	91	oxadiazon	1000–6000
			92	bensulide	[770]
	Slightly Toxic (LD_{50} = 1001–5000 mg/kg Body Weight)		93	bentazon	720–2000
			94	dicamba	673–>2510
68	fosamine ammonium	4150	95	diquat di-bromide	564
69	sethoxydim	[3200]	96	MCPA	[550]
70	chlorimuron	>2510	97	tebuthiuron	>500–>2000
71	fenoxaprop-ethyl	[2357]	98	oryzalin	>500–1000
			99	napropamide	[>500]
72	hexazinone	2258	100	2,4-DB	[500]
73	imazapyr	>2150	101	cyanazine	445–>2400
74	glyphosate	>2000–3850	102	acifluorfen	325–2821
75	alachlor	>2000	103	2,4-D	200–>2000
76	amitrole	>2000		Highly Toxic (LD_{50} = 41–200 mg/kg Body Weight)	
77	trifluralin	>2000			
78	picloram	>2000	104	paraquat	199
79	butylate	>2000	105	metribuzin	164–168
80	diuron	>2000	106	EPTC	100
81	atrazine	2000–2510	107	bromoxynil	50–240
82	vernolate	[1800]			

Note: LD_{50} values are for multiple formulations and birds unless indicated otherwise. A range of values for bird species is presented, where data exist. Rat LD_{50} values are listed in brackets [ ] if bird LD_{50} data are unavailable.

SOURCE: Stinson and Bromley (1991).

TABLE A.17   Acute-Toxicity Categories of Fungicides

Ref. no.	Common Name	LD_{50} (mg/kg)	Ref. no.	Common Name	LD_{50} (mg/kg)
	Relatively Nontoxic (LD_{50} mg/kg Body Weight)		124	iprodione	[>2000]
			125	quintozene (PCNB)	>2000
108	sulfur	[Relatively non-toxic]	126	propiconazole	[1517]
109	chlorothalonil	[10,000]	127	etridiazol	[1077]
110	vinclozolin	[10,000]		**Moderately Toxic (LD_{50} = 201–1000 mg/kg Body Weight)**	
111	streptomycin	[9000]			
112	mancozeb	[>8000]	128	dinocap	[980]
113	maneb	[6750[	129	triadimenol	[700]
114	metiram	[6200]	130	metalaxyl	[669]
115	dikar	[>5000]	131	dodine	[660]
116	thiophanate-methyl	>5000	132	imazalil	510
			133	dicloran	500->2000
	Slightly Toxic (LD_{50} = 1001–5000 mg/kg Body Weight)		134	triadimefon	[363]
			135	thiram	300–2800
117	ferbam	[>4000]		**Highly Toxic (LD_{50} 41–200 mg/kg Body Weight)**	
118	thiabendazole	[3100]			
119	captan	>2000	136	benomyl	>100
120	anilazine	>2000	137	carboxin	42
121	copper sulfate + lime (Bordeaux Mixture)	>2000		**Extremely Toxic ($LD_{50} \leq$ 40 mg/kg Body Weight)**	
122	dichlone	>2000	138	cyclohexamide	[2.5]
123	folpet	>2000			

Note: LD_{50} values are for multiple formulations and birds unless indicated otherwise. A range of values for bird species is presented, where data exist. Rat LD_{50} values are listed in brackets [ ] if bird LD_{50} data are unavailable.
SOURCE: Stinson and Bromley (1991).

TABLE A.18 Comparison of Steel, Copper, and Plastic Pipe

Factors to consider	Galvanized steel (3-oz coating min.)
Underground soil corrosion—probable life expectancy*	30 plus years under most soil conditions. (If no corrosion inside pipe, life could extend to 100 years or more.)
	Waterlogged soils under most conditions—12–16 years. May be less than 10 years in very high acid soils.
Resistance to corrosion inside pipe	Will corrode in acid, alkaline, and hard waters or with electrolytic action.†
Resistance to deposits forming inside pipe	Will accumulate lime deposits from hard water.†
Effect of freezing	Bursts if frozen solidly.
Safe working pressures (lb/in²)	Adequate for pressures developed by small water systems.
Resistance to puncturing and rodents	Highly resistant to both.
Effect of sunlight	No effect.
Lengths available	21-ft lengths.
Ease of bending	Difficult to bend except for slight bends over long lengths.
Conductor of electricity	Yes

TABLE A.18   Comparison of Steel, Copper, and Plastic Pipe   (*Continued*)

Copper		Plastic
Type K (heavy duty)	Type L (standard)	
40–100 years under most conditions.	30–80 years under most conditions.	Experience indicates durability is satisfactory under most soil conditions.
14–20 years in high-sulfide conditions. May be less than 10 years in cinders.	12–14 years in high-sulfide conditions. May be less than 10 years in cinders.	
Normally very resistant. May corrode rapidly in water containing free carbon dioxide.		Very resistant.
Subject to lime scale and encrustation from suspended materials.		Resistant, but occasional deposits will form.‡
Will stand mild freezes.		PE—will stand some freezing. PVC—will stand mild freezes.
Adequate for pressures developed by small water systems.		Working pressures at 73°F: PE— 80 to 160. PVC—180 to 600.
Resistant to both.		PE—very limited resistance to puncture and rodents. PVC—resistant.
No effect.		PE—weakens with prolonged exposure. PVC—highly resistant.
Soft temper: 60-ft to 100-ft coils up to 1 in diameter 60-ft coils above 1 in diameter Hard temper: 12- and 20-ft lengths.		PE—usually in 100-ft coils or longer. PVC—usualy in 20-ft lengths.
Soft temper bends readily, will collapse on short bends. Hard temper difficult to bend except for slight bends over long lengths.		PE—bends readily, will collapse on short bends. PVC—rigid; bends on long radius.
Yes		No

Note: For metric equivalence, see metric conversion table in the front of the book.

*Derived from studies reported by Irving A. Dennison, and Melvin Romanoff, "Soil-corrosion studies, 1946 and 1948: Copper alloys, lead and zinc," Res. Pap. RP2077, Vol. 44, March 1950 and "Corrosion of galvanized steel in soils," Res. Pap. 2366, Vol. 49, No. 5, 1952, National Bureau of Standards, U.S. Dept. of Commerce.

†It is possible to greatly reduce corrosion and prevent lime scale in steel pipe by adding a phosphate material. It coats the inside of pipes, as well as the lining of all connected equipment. Prevents further lime scale and greatly reduces corrosion.

‡Elmer E. Jones, Jr., "New concepts in farmstead water system design," Am. Soc. of Agric. Eng., Pap. No. 67-216, 1967.

SOURCE: Brown and Karsky (1989).

TABLE A.19   A Summary of Fence Designs

Fence type	Advantages	Disadvantages	Main-tenance rating	Costs Material ($/mi)	Labor ($/mi)	Total ($/mi)
Conventional four-strand barbed wire	Skills & designs for construction readily available.	Labor and material costs high.	Medium	2100	2000	4100
Gancho four-strand barbed wire	Longer life than conventional barbed wire. 20–30% less expensive than conventional barbed wire. Lighter weight, less strain.	Wire less workable than conventional barbed wire.	Unknown	2000	2000	4000
Woven wire with top two-strand barbed wire	Skills and designs for construction readily, available. Good control of sheep and cattle.	Labor and material costs high.	Medium	2800	2000	4800
Let-down fence, four-strand barbed wire	Prevents fence damage in high snow pack and high wildlife concentration.	Labor and material costs high. Life span short because of wire corrosion.	High	3500	2300	5800
High-tensile eight-strand smooth wire	Durable. Less expensive to install and maintain than conventional barbed wire. Withstands more than other wire. No barbs.	Requires special equipment and techniques to install.	Low	1700	900	2600
High tensile ten-strand smooth wire	Very durable. Less expensive to install and maintain than conventional barbed wire. Withstands more than other wire. No barbs.	Requires special equipment and techniques to install.	Low	1900	1000	2900
Conventional barbed-wire suspension with wood stays	Few posts. Low costs. Long life. Alternative for interior and cross-fencing.	Not appropriate in rough, broken country or in areas of tall, dense vegetation. Won't detour cattle near water. Great down-fence distance with post breakage.	Low	1200	600	1800

TABLE A.19   A Summary of Fence Designs   (*Continued*)

Fence type	Advantages	Disadvantages	Main-tenance rating	Material ($/mi)	Labor ($/mi)	Total ($/mi)
Conventional barbed-wire suspension with wire stays	Fewer posts. Low costs. Long life. Alternative for interior and cross-fencing.	Not appropriate in rough, broken country or in areas of tall, dense vegetation. Won't detour cattle near water. Great down-fence distance with post breakage.	Low	900	500	1400
High-tensile smooth wire suspension with wood posts	Few posts. Low costs. Long life. Alternative for interior and cross-fencing.	Not appropriate in rough, broken country or in areas of tall, dense vegetation. Won't detour cattle near water. Great down-fence distance with post breakage.	Low	1100	600	1700
High-tensile smooth wire suspension with steel posts	Few posts. Low costs. Long life. Alternative for interior and cross-fencing.	Not appropriate in rough, broken country or in areas of tall, dense vegetation. Won't detour cattle near water. Great down-fence distance with post breakage.	Low	800	400	1200
Permanent electric con-ventional, barbed wire	Lower costs than conventional barbed wire. Long life. Versatile.	Not appropriate in rough, broken terrain.	Low	1000	300	1300
Portable twine and three-strand electric	Lightweight, port-able, easily adjust-able.	Weathers poorly. Don't use in lengths over 1000 ft.	High	1000	40	1040
Permanent electric high-tensile, smooth wire, post and stays.	Durable. Low cost. Good psychological barrier. Less main-tenance.	Not a physical barrier.	Low	800	400	1200
Jackleg—wire fence	Very durable. With-stands heavy snow-fall. Useful in areas where it is hard to dig or drive posts or on marshy ground with use of flotation boards.		Low	—	—	—
Rock jack and figure "4"	Useful in areas where it is hard to dig or drive posts. Good in light to heavy snow.	High material and labor costs.	Low	—	—	—

TABLE A.19   A Summary of Fence Designs   (*Continued*)

Fence type	Advantages	Disadvantages	Main-tenance rating	Costs		
				Material ($/mi)	Labor ($/mi)	Total ($/mi)
Jackleg—pole	Durable. Withstands heavy snowfall. Used in areas where digging or driving is impossible.	High material and labor costs.	Low	—	—	—
Post and pole	Durable. Withstands heavy snowfall.	High material and labor costs.	Low	—	—	—
Worm	Durable. Withstands heavy snowfall.	If logs not available, high material costs. Labor-intensive.	Low	—	—	—
Log and block	Durable. Withstands heavy snowfall.	If logs not available, high material costs. Labor-intensive.	Low	—	—	—
Suspension fence	Few posts, less cost. Little maintenance. Long lasting. Low-cost alternative for interior and cross-fencing.	Not appropriate in rough, broken country. Not suitable in tall, dense vegetation. Not an effective cattle deterrent near watering points. Greater down-fence distance with post breakage.	Low	850	450	1300
Semisuspension fence	Few posts. Low cost. An alternative for interior or cross-fencing.	Suitable only for flat or slightly undulating terrain. Not as good a cattle deterrent as suspension or conventional fences.	Low	—	—	—

Note: For metric equivalence, see metric conversion table in the front of the book.
SOURCE: Karsky (1988).

TABLE A.20   Fence Design Based on Site Conditions

Site condition	Fence design
Sandy soil	Double-end line and gate braces—spacing up to 80 rods ($\frac{1}{4}$ mi). Single-line braces—spacing up to 40 rods—spacing up to 40 rods ($\frac{1}{8}$ mi). Use of deadman on corner, end and gate braces. Use two diagonal braces or one horizontal brace with a diagonal brace on corner, end, or gate location. Need to strengthen groundholding capacity.
Marshy soil	Add mud sills (two long poles or boards) to the bottom of a jackleg, straddle jack, buck, or figure-four fence.
Rocky soil	Use rock jacks or rock cribs for braces. Use buck or jacklegs or figure-fours for line posts. May want to install steel or fiberglass posts.
Loam or clay soil	Single-end line and gate braces, spacing up to 80 rods.
Steep ground	Put line posts in perpendicular to the land.
Heavy snow	Jackleg, straddle jack, or buck fence with wire or pole fencing; post and pole fence; worm fence; log and block fence.
Ridgeline	Often a good fence line location. Easy to maintain and allows effective management. Consider a single-strand wire.
Water discharge	Infrequent—Normal fence construction with fence held in depressions with weights attached to the posts. Seasonal or frequent—Construct end braces on either side of depression. Construct independent braces for fence in depression. Build break-away fence in depression. Build swinging or floating water gap fence. Running stream—Construct end braces on either side of stream. Construct separate braces for holding swinging or floating water gap fence.
Wildlife exclusion fences	Deer—Electric fence designs: double deer fence; 6-ft, 6-in-high 10-strand high-tensile strength fence; 8-ft-high 15-strand high-tensile strength fence. Antelope—Electric fence designs: 6-ft, 6-in-high 10-strand high-tensile strength fence; 8-ft-high 15-strand high-tensile strength fence. Woven wire fence 32 in high with one barbed wire strand on the top. Elk—Power fence designs: 8-ft-high 15-strand high-tensile strength fence.
Visual impact	Wood fences are generally more pleasing in areas of high visitor use. Use standard fence designs for low visual impact.
Difficult accessibility	Use steel line posts for reduced weight and bulk, or consider fiberglass posts with a few wood posts for added strength.

TABLE A.20 **Fence Design Based on Site Conditions** *(Continued)*

Site condition	Fence design
Fences for wildlife	Deer—Fence height: min. 38 in to max. 42 in. Spacing between top and second wire, 12 in. Moveable top wire or two. Antelope—Cattle fence height: min. 38 in to max. 42 in. Bottom wire at least 18 in above the ground. Bottom wire should be a smooth wire. Sheep fence height: min. 38 in to max. 42 in. Bottom wire—smooth at least 10 in above the ground. Leave out fence stays in areas where antelope frequently cross. Provide small cattle guards at 1-mi intervals for antelope to jump over. Moveable bottom wire or two. Elk—Fence height: min. 38 in to max. 42 in. Attach wooden rail to top wire for visibility. Construct let-down fence. All fence posts should be wood.

Note: For metric equivalence, see metric conversion table in the front of the book.
SOURCE: **Karsky (1988).**

TABLE A.21 Common and Scientific Names of Animals Mentioned

Alphabetical by common name		Alphabetical by scientific name	
Common name	Scientific name	Scientific name	Common name
Abert squirrel	*Sciurus aberti*	*Accipiter cooperii*	Cooper's hawk
Acadian flycatcher	*Empidonax virescens*	*Aegolius acadicus*	Northern saw-whet owl, saw-whet owl
Alpomado falcon	*Falco femoralis*	*Agelaius phoeniceus*	Red-winged blackbird
American bison	*Bison bison*	*Aimophila cassinii*	Cassin's sparrow
American kestrel	*Falco sparverius*	*Aimophila ruficeps*	Rufous-crowned sparrow
American redstart	*Setophaga ruticilla*	*Aix sponsa*	Wood duck
American robin	*Turdus migratorius*	*Alces alces*	Moose
Ancient murrelet	*Synthli boramphus antiguus*	*Alectoris chukar*	Chukar partridge
Antelope jackrabbit	*Lepus alleni*	*Ammodramus bairdii*	Baird's sparrow
Arizona gray squirrel	*Sciurus arizonensis*	*Ammodramus henslowii*	Henslow's sparrow
Arizona pocket mouse	*Perognathus amplus*	*Ammodramus savannarum*	Grasshopper sparrow
Ash-throated flycatcher	*Myiarchus cinerascens*	*Ammospiza leconteii*	Le Conte's sparrow
Attwater's prairie chicken	*Tympanuchus cupido atwateri*	*Amphispiza bilineata*	Black-throated sparrow
Bachman's warbler	*Dendroica bachmanii*	*Amphizspiza belli*	Sage sparrow
Badger	*Taxidea taxus*	*Anolis carolinensis*	Green anole
Bailey pocket mouse	*Perognathus baileyi*	*Anthus spinoletta*	Water pipit
Baird's sparrow	*Ammodramus bairdii*	*Anthus spragueii*	Sprague's pipit
Bald eagle	*Haliaeetus leucocephalus*	*Antilocapra americana*	Pronghorn
Band-tailed pigeon	*Columbia fasciata*	*Antilocapra americana sonoriensis*	Sonoran pronghorn
Barn owl, common	*Tyto alba*	*Aphelocoma coerulescens*	Scrub jay
Barn swallow	*Hirundo rustica*	*Aphelocoma spp.*	Jay
Barred owl	*Strix varia*	*Aquila chrysaetos*	Golden eagle
Bear	*Ursus spp.*	*Arborimus longicaudus*	Red tree vole
Belted kingfisher	*Ceryle alcyon*	*Ardea herodias*	Great blue heron
Bewick's wren	*Thryomanes bewickii*	*Asio flammeus*	Short-eared owl
Bighorn sheep	*Ovis canadensis*	*Athene cunicularia*	Burrowing owl
Black bear	*Ursus americanus*	*Auriparus flaviceps*	Verdin
Black rat snake	*Elaphe obsoleta obsoleta*	*Bartramia lognicauda*	Upland sandpiper
Black-and-white warbler	*Mniotilta varia*	*Bassariscus astutus*	Ringtail
Black-bellied whistling duck	*Dendrocygna autumnalis*	*Bison bison*	American bison
Black-capped chickadee	*Parus atricapillus*	*Blarina brevicauda*	Northern short-tailed shrew
Black-capped vireo	*Vireo atricapillus*	*Blarina hylophaga*	Elliot's short-tailed shrew

TABLE A.21   Common and Scientific Names of Animals Mentioned   (Continued)

Alphabetical by common name		Alphabetical by scientific name	
Common name	Scientific name	Scientific name	Common name
Black-footed ferret	*Mustela nigripes*	*Bonasa umbellus*	Ruffed grouse
Black-headed grosbeak	*Pheucticus melanocephalus*	*Brachyramphus marmoratus*	Marbled murrelet
Black-shouldered kite	*Elanus caeruleus*	*Branta canadensis*	Canada goose
Black-tailed deer	*Odocoileus hemionus columbianus*	*Bubo virginianus*	Great horned owl
Black-tailed prairie dog	*Cynomys ludovicianus*	*Bucephala albeola*	Buffelhead
Black-throated blue warbler	*Dendroica caeruiescens*	*Bucephala clangula*	Common goldeneye
Black-throated gray warbler	*Dendroica nigrescens*	*Buteo jamaicensis*	Red-tailed hawk
Black-throated green warbler	*Dendroica virens*	*Buteo lagopus*	Rough-legged hawk
Black-throated sparrow	*Amphispiza bileneata*	*Buteo lineatus*	Red-shouldered hawk
Blacktailed jackrabbit	*Lepus californicus*	*Buteo regalis*	Ferruginous hawk
Blue grouse	*Dendragapus obscurus*	*Buteo swainsoni*	Swainson's hawk
Blue jay	*Cyanocitta cristata*	*Butorides striatus*	Green-backed heron
Blue-gray gnatcatcher	*Polioptila caerulea*	*Calamospiza melanocorys*	Lark bunting
Bluebird	*Siala* spp.	*Calcarius mccounii*	McCown's longspur
Bobolink	*Dolichonyx oryzivorus*	*Calcarius ornatus*	Chestnut-collared longspur
Bobwhite quail, northern	*Colinus virginianus*	*Callipepla californica*	California quail
Brainworm	*Parelaphostrongylus tenuis*	*Callipepla gambelii*	Gambel's quail
Brewer's sparrow	*Spizella breweri*	*Callipepla squamata*	Scaled quail
Broadhead skink	*Eumeces laticeps*	*Calypte costae*	Costa's hummingbird
Brown creeper	*Certhia americana*	*Campylorhynchus brunneicapillus*	Cactus wren
Brown-headed cowbird	*Molothrus ater*	*Canis* spp.	Wolf
Brown-headed nuthatch	*Sitta pusilla*	*Canis latrans*	Coyote
Buffelhead	*Bucephala albeola*	*Canis lupus*	Gray wolf
Burrowing owl	*Athene cunicularia*	*Cardinalis cardinalis*	Cardinal
Bushtit	*Psaltriperus minimus*	*Cardinalis sinuatus*	Pyrrhuloxia
Cactus wren	*Campylorhynchus brunneicapillus*	*Carpodacus mixicanus*	House finch
California quail	*Callipepla californica*	*Catharus fuscescens*	Veery
Canada goose	*Branta canadensis*	*Centrocercus urophosianus*	Sage grouse
Canada warbler	*Wilsonia canadensis*	*Certhia americana*	Brown creeper
Cardinal	*Cardinalis cardinalis*	*Cervus elaphus*	Elk
Caribou	*Rangifer tarandus*	*Ceryle alcyon*	Belted kingfisher
Carolina chickadee	*Parus carolinensis*	*Chamaea fasciata*	Wrentit

Common name	Scientific name
Carolina wren	*Thryothorus ludovicianus*
Cassin's sparrow	*Aimophila cassinii*
Cerulean warbler	*Dendroica cerulea*
Chestnut-collared longspur	*Calcarius ornatus*
Chestnut-sided warbler	*Dendroica pensylvanica*
Chickadee	*Parus* spp.
Chipping sparrow	*Spizella passerina*
Chukar partridge	*Alectoris chukar*
Clay-colored sparrow	*Spizella pallida*
Coast mole	*Scapanus orarius*
Common goldeneye	*Bucephala clangula*
Common merganser	*Mergus merganser*
Cooper's hawk	*Accipiter cooperii*
Costa's hummingbird	*Calypte costae*
Cottontail rabbit	*Sylvilagus floridanus*
Coues white-tailed deer	*Odocoileus virginianus couesi*
Cougar	*Felis concolor*
Coyote	*Canis latrans*
Crow, common	*Corvus brachyrhynchos*
Curve-billed thrasher	*Toxostoma curvirostre*
Dall sheep	*Ovis dalli*
Darkling beetle	*Coniontis porba*
Deer	*Odocoileus* spp.
Deer mouse	*Peromyscus maniculatus*
Desert bighorn sheep	*Ovis canadensis nelsoni*, *O. c. cremnobates, O. c. weemsi O. c. mexicana, O. c. texiana*
Desert cottontail rabbit	*Sylvilagus auduboni*
Desert mule deer	*Odocoileus hemionus crookii*
Desert tortoise	*Gopherus agassizi*
Dickcissel	*Spiza americana*
Downy woodpecker	*Picoides pubescens*
Dusky flycatcher	*Empidonax oberholseri*
Eastern bluebird	*Siala sialis*
Eastern meadowlark	*Sturnella magna*
Eastern wood pewee	*Contopus virens*
Killdeer	*Charadrius vociferus*
Green-tailed towhee	*Chlorura chlorura*
Lark sparrow	*Chondestes grammacus*
Spruce budworm	*Choristoneura fumiferana*
Northern harrier	*Circus cyaneus*
Short-billed marsh wren	*Cistothorus platensis*
Piute ground squirrel	*Citellus townsendi mollis*
Yellow-billed cuckoo	*Coccyzus americanus*
Common (northern) flicker	*Colaptes auratus*
Northern bobwhite quail	*Colinus virginianus*
Masked bobwhite quail	*Colinus virginianus ridgwayi*
Band-tailed pigeon	*Columbia fasciata*
Darkling beetle	*Coniontis proba*
Eastern wood pewee	*Contopus virens*
Raven	*Corvus* spp.
Common crow	*Corvus brachyrhynchos*
Blue jay	*Cyanocitta cristata*
Steller's jay	*Cyanocitta stelleri*
Prairie dog	*Cynomys* spp.
Black-tailed prairie dog	*Cynomys ludovicianus*
Mearn's (Montezuma) quail	*Cyrtonyx montezumae*
Blue grouse	*Dendragapus obscurus*
Black-bellied whistling duck	*Dendrocygna autumnalis*
Bachman's warbler	*Dendroica bachmanii*
Black-throated blue warbler	*Dendroica caeruiescens*
Cerulean warbler	*Dendroica cerulea*
Golden-cheeked warbler	*Dendroica chrysoparia*
Kirtland's warbler	*Dendroica kirtlandii*
Black-throated gray warbler	*Dendroica nigrescens*
Chestnut-sided warbler	*Dendroica pensylvanica*
Black-throated green warbler	*Dendroica virens*
June beetle	*Deplotaxis tenebrosa*
Opossum	*Didelphis virginiana*
Merriam's kangaroo rat	*Dipodomys merriami*
Bobolink	*Dolichonyx oryzivorus*
Pileated woodpecker	*Dryocopus pileatus*

TABLE A.21 Common and Scientific Names of Animals Mentioned (Continued)

Alphabetical by common name		Alphabetical by scientific name	
Common name	Scientific name	Scientific name	Common name
Eastern woodrat	*Neotoma floridana*	*Dumetella carolinensis*	Gray catbird
Elf owl	*Micrathene whiteneyi*	*Elanus caeruleus*	Black-shouldered kite
Elk	*Cervus elaphus*	*Elaphe* spp.	Rat snake
Elliot's short-tailed shrew	*Blarina hylophaga*	*Elaphe obsoleta lindheimeri*	Texas rat snake
English sparrow	*Passer domesticus*	*Elaphe obsoleta obsoleta*	Black rat snake
Ermine	*Mustela erminea*	*Empidonax hammondii*	Hammond's flycatcher
Ferruginous hawk	*Buteo regalis*	*Empidonax minimus*	Least flycatcher
Field sparrow	*Spizella pusilla*	*Empidonax oberholseri*	Dusky flycatcher
Fisher	*Martes pennanti*	*Empidonax virescens*	Acadian flycatcher
Five-lined skink	*Eumeces fasciatus*	*Empidonax wrightii*	Gray flycatcher
Flammulated owl	*Otus flammeolus*	*Eremophila alpestris*	Horned lark
Flicker, common northern	*Colaptes auratus*	*Eumeces* spp.	Skink
Florida panther	*Felis concolor coryi*	*Eumeces fasciatus*	Five-lined skink
Flying squirrel	*Glaucomys* spp.	*Eumeces inexpectatus*	Southeastern five-lined skink
Fox squirrel	*Sciurus niger*	*Eumeces laticeps*	Broadhead skink
Gambel's quail	*Callipepla gambelii*	*Eupoda montana*	Mountain plover
Golden eagle	*Aquila chrysaetos*	*Eutamias minimus*	Least chipmunk
Golden mouse	*Ochrotomys nuttalli*	*Falco columbarius*	Merlin
Golden-cheeked warbler	*Dendroica chrysoparia*	*Falco femoralis*	Alpomado falcon
Golden-fronted woodpecker	*Melanerpes aurifrons*	*Falco mexicanus*	Prairie falcon
Goldfinch	*Spinus* spp.	*Falco peregrinus*	Peregrine falcon
Gopher	*Geomys* spp.	*Falco sparverius*	American kestrel, sparrow hawk
Gopher	*Thomomys* spp.	*Felis concolor*	Cougar
Grackle, common	*Quiscalus quiscula*	*Felis concolor coryi*	Florida panther
Grasshopper sparrow	*Ammodramus savannarum*	*Geococcyx californianus*	Roadrunner
Gray catbird	*Dumetella carolinensis*	*Geomys* spp.	Gopher
Gray flycatcher	*Empidonax wrightii*	*Geothlypis trichas*	Common yellowthroat
Gray partridge	*Perdix perdix*	*Glaucomys* spp.	Flying squirrel
Gray squirrel, eastern	*Sciurus carolinensis*	*Glaucomys sabrinus*	Northern flying squirrel
Gray treefrog	*Hyla versicolor*	*Glaucomys volans*	Southern flying squirrel
Gray vireo	*Vireo vicinior*	*Gopherus agassizi*	Desert tortoise
Gray wolf	*Canis lupus*	*Gulo gulo*	Wolverine

Common name	Scientific name	Common name	Scientific name
Great Basin pocket mouse	*Perognathus parvus*	Bald eagle	*Haliaeetus leucocephalus*
Great blue heron	*Ardea herodias*	Worm-eating warbler	*Helmitheros vermivortes*
Great gray owl	*Strix nebulosa*	Barn swallow	*Hirundo rustica*
Great horned owl	*Bubo virginianus*	Green treefrog	*Hyla cinerea*
Great-crested flycatcher	*Myiarchus crinitus*	Squirrel treefrog	*Hyla squirella*
Greater prairie chicken	*Tympanuchus cupido*	Gray treefrog	*Hyla versicolor*
Green anole	*Anolis carolinensis*	Hermit thrush	*Hylocichla guttata*
Green treefrog	*Hyla cinerea*	Wood thrush	*Hylocichla mustelina*
Green-backed heron	*Butorides striatus*	Scott's oriole	*Icterus parisorum*
Green-tailed towhee	*Chlorura chlorura*	Junco	*Junco spp.*
Grizzly bear	*Ursus arctos*	Ptarmigan	*Lagopus spp.*
Ground squirrel	*Spermophilus spp.*	Willow ptarmigan	*Lagopus lagopus*
Gypsy moth	*Lymantria dispar*	Jackrabbit	*Lepus spp.*
Hairy woodpecker	*Picoides villosus*	Antelope jackrabbit	*Lepus alleni*
Hammond's flycatcher	*Empidonax hammondii*	Snowshoe hare	*Lepus americanus*
Harris' hawk	*Parabuteo unicinctus*	Blacktailed jackrabbit	*Lepus californicus*
Henslow's sparrow	*Ammodramus henslowii*	Rosy finch	*Leucosticte arctoa*
Hermit thrush	*Hylocichla guttata*	Hooded merganser	*Lophodytes cucullatus*
Hooded merganser	*Lophodytes cucullatus*	River otter	*Lutra canadensis*
Hooded warbler	*Wilsonia citrina*	Woodchuck	*Marmota monax*
Horned lark	*Eremophila alpestris*	Marten	*Martes americana*
House finch	*Carpodacus mixicanus*	Fisher	*Martes pennanti*
House sparrow	*Passer domesticus*	Golden-fronted woodpecker	*Melanerpes aurifrons*
House wren	*Troglodytes aedon*	Red-bellied woodpecker	*Melanerpes carolinus*
Jackrabbit	*Lepus spp.*	Redheaded woodpecker	*Melanerpes erythrocephalus*
Javelina	*Pecari angulatus*	Lewis woodpecker	*Melanerpes lewis*
Jay	*Aphelocoma spp.*	Turkey	*Meleagris gallopavo*
Junco	*Junco spp.*	Rio Grande turkey	*Meleagris gallopavo intermedia*
June beetle	*Deplotaxis tenebrosa*	Merriam's turkey	*Meleagris gallopavo merriami*
Kentucky warbler	*Oporornis formosus*	Skunk	*Mephitis spp.*
Killdeer	*Charadrius vociferus*	Common merganser	*Mergus merganser*
Kirkland's warbler	*Dendroica kirtlandii*	Elf owl	*Micrathene whiteneyi*
Kit fox	*Vulpes macrotis*	Mountain vole	*Microtus montanus*
Ladderback woodpecker	*Picoides scalaris*	Prairie vole	*Microtus ochrogaster*
Lark bunting	*Calamospiza melanocorys*	Meadow vole	*Microtus pennsylvanicus*
Lark sparrow	*Chondestes grammacus*	Mockingbird	*Mimus spp.*

TABLE A.21 Common and Scientific Names of Animals Mentioned (Continued)

	Alphabetical by common name		Alphabetical by scientific name
Common name	Scientific name	Scientific name	Common name
Lazuli bunting	*Passerina amoena*	*Mimus polyglottos*	Northern mockingbird
Le Conte's sparrow	*Ammospiza leconteii*	*Mniotilta varia*	Black-and-white warbler
Least chipmunk	*Eutamias minimus*	*Molothrus ater*	Brown-headed cowbird
Least flycatcher	*Empidonax minimus*	*Mustela erminea*	Ermine
Lecoute's thrasher	*Toxostoma lecontei*	*Mustela frenata*	Long-tailed weasel
Lesser prairie chicken	*Tympanuchus pallidicinctus*	*Mustela nigripes*	Black-footed ferret
Lewis woodpecker	*Melanerpes lewis*	*Myiarchus cinerascens*	Ash-throated flycatcher
Little pocket mouse	*Perognathus longimembris*	*Myiarchus crinitus*	Great-crested flycatcher
Long-billed curlew	*Numenius americanus*	*Neotoma* spp.	Woodrat
Louisiana waterthrush	*Seiurus motacilla*	*Neotoma floridana*	Eastern woodrat
Magpie	*Pica pica*	*Numenius americanus*	Long-billed curlew
Marbled murrelet	*Brachyramphus marmoratus*	*Nyctea scandiaca*	Snowy owl
Marten	*Martes americana*	*Ochrotomys nuttalli*	Golden mouse
Masked bobwhite quail	*Colinus virginianus ridgwayi*	*Odocoileus* spp.	Deer
Masked shrew	*Sorex cinereus*	*Odocoileus hemionus*	Mule deer
McCown's longspur	*Calcarius mccownii*	*Odocoileus hemionus columbianus*	Black-tailed deer
Meadow jumping mouse	*Zapus hudsonius*	*Odocoileus hemionus crookii*	Desert mule deer
Meadow vole	*Microtus pennsylvanicus*	*Odocoileus virginianus*	White-tailed deer
Meadowlark	*Sturnella* spp.	*Odocoileus virginianus couesi*	Coues white-tailed deer
Mearn's (Montezuma) quail	*Cyrtonyx montezumae*	*Ondatra zibethicus*	Muskrat
Merlin	*Falco columbarius*	*Oporornis formosus*	Kentucky warbler
Merriam's kangaroo rat	*Dipodomys merriami*	*Oporornis philadelphia*	Mourning warbler
Merriam's turkey	*Meleagris gallopavo merriami*	*Oreamnos americanus*	Mountain goat
Mockingbird	*Mimus* spp.	*Oreortyx pictus*	Mountain quail
Moose	*Alces alces*	*Oreoscoptes montanus*	Sage thrasher
Mountain bluebird	*Sialia currucoides*	*Otus asio*	Eastern screech owl
Mountain chickadee	*Parus gambeli*	*Otus asio kennicottii*	Western screech owl
Mountain goat	*Oreamnos americanus*	*Otus flammeolus*	Flammulated owl
Mountain plover	*Eupoda montana*	*Otus trichopsis*	Whiskered screech owl
Mountain quail	*Oreortyx pictus*	*Ovibos moschatus*	Muskox
Mountain sheep	*Ovis* spp.	*Ovis* spp.	Mountain sheep
Mountain vole	*Microtus montanus*	*Ovis canadensis*	Bighorn sheep

Common name	Scientific name
Mourning dove	*Zenaida macroura*
Mourning warbler	*Oporornis philadelphia*
Mule deer	*Odocoileus hemionus*
Muskox	*Ovibos moschatus*
Muskrat	*Ondatra zibethicus*
Northern flying squirrel	*Glaucomys sabrinus*
Northern harrier	*Circus cyaneus*
Northern mockingbird	*Mimus polyglottos*
Northern parula	*Parula americana*
Northern pocket gopher	*Thomomys talpoides*
Northern saw-whet owl	*Aegolius acadicus*
Northern short-tailed shrew	*Blarina brevicauda*
Northern waterthrush	*Seiurus noveboracensis*
Nuthatch	*Sitta* spp.
Opossum	*Didelphis virginiana*
Orange-crowned warbler	*Vermivora celata*
Osprey	*Pandion haliaetna*
Ovenbird	*Seiurus aurocapillus*
Peregrine falcon	*Falco peregrinus*
Phoebe, eastern	*Sayornis phoebe*
Pileated woodpecker	*Dryocopus pileatus*
Piute ground squirrel	*Citellus townsendi mollis*
Plain titmouse	*Parus inornatus*
Poorwill	*Phalaenoptilus nuttallii*
Prairie chicken	*Tympanuchus* spp.
Prairie dog	*Cynomys* spp.
Prairie falcon	*Falco mexicanus*
Prairie vole	*Microtus ochrogaster*
Pronghorn	*Antilocapra americana*
Prothonotory warbler	*Protonotaria citrea*
Ptarmigan	*Lagopus* spp.
Purple martin	*Progne subis*
Pygmy nuthatch	*Sitta pygmaea*
Pyrrhuloxia	*Cardinalis sinuatus*
Raccoon	*Procyon lotor*
Rat snake	*Elaphe* spp.

Scientific name	Common name
Ovis canadensis nelsoni, O. c. cremnobates, O. c. weemsi O. c. mexicana, O. c. texiana	Desert bighorn sheep
Ovis dalli	Dall sheep
Pandion haliaetna	Osprey
Parabuteo unicinctus	Harris' hawk
Parelaphostrongylus tenuis	Brainworm
Parula americana	Northern parula
Parus spp.	Chickadee, titmouse
Parus atricapillus	Black-capped chickadee
Parus bicolor	Tufted titmouse
Parus carolinensis	Carolina chickadee
Parus gambeli	Mountain chickadee
Parus inornatus	Plain titmouse
Passer domesticus	English sparrow, house sparrow
Passerculus sandwichensis	Savannah sparrow
Passerina amoena	Lazuli bunting
Pecari angulatus	Javelina
Perdix perdix	Gray partridge
Perognathus amplus	Arizona pocket mouse
Perognathus baileyi	Bailey pocket mouse
Perognathus intermedius	Rock pocket mouse
Perognathus longimembris	Little pocket mouse
Perognathus parvus	Great Basin pocket mouse
Peromyscus leucopus	White-footed mouse
Peromyscus maniculatus	Deer mouse
Phalaenoptilus nuttallii	Poorwill
Phasianus colchicus	Ring-necked pheasant
Pheucticus ludovicianus	Rose-breasted grosbeak
Pheucticus melanocephalus	Black-headed grosbeak
Pica pica	Magpie
Picoides borealis	Red-cockaded woodpecker
Picoides pubescens	Downy woodpecker
Picoides scalaris	Ladderback woodpecker
Picoides villosus	Hairy woodpecker
Pipilo erythrophthalmus	Rufous-sided towhee

TABLE A.21 Common and Scientific Names of Animals Mentioned (Continued)

Alphabetical by common name		Alphabetical by scientific name	
Common name	Scientific name	Scientific name	Common name
Raven	Corvus spp.	Piranga olivacea	Scarlet tanager
Red squirrel	Tamiasciurus hudsonicus	Piranga rubra	Summer tanager
Red tree vole	Arborimus longicaudus	Polioptila caerulea	Blue-gray gnatcatcher
Red-bellied woodpecker	Melanerpes carolinus	Pooecetes grammincus	Vesper sparrow
Red-breasted nuthatch	Sitta canadensis	Lymantria dispar	Gypsy moth
Red-cockaded woodpecker	Picoides borealis	Procyon lotor	Raccoon
Red-eyed vireo	Vireo olivaceous	Progne subis	Purple martin
Red-shouldered hawk	Buteo lineatus	Protonotaria citrea	Prothonotory warbler
Red-tailed hawk	Buteo jamaicensis	Psaltriperus minimus	Bushtit
Red-winged blackbird	Agelaius phoeniceus	Quiscalus quiscula	Common grackle
Redheaded woodpecker	Melanerpes erythrocephalus	Rangifer tarandus	Caribou, domestic reindeer
Reindeer, domestic	Rangifer tarandus	Rangifer tarandus caribou	Woodland caribou
Ring-necked pheasant	Phasianus colchicus	Reithrodontomys megalotis	Western harvest mouse
Ringtail	Bassariscus astutus	Rostrhamus sociabilis	Snail kite
Rio Grande turkey	Meleagris gallopavo intermedia	Salpinctes obsoletus	Rock wren
River otter	Lutra canadensis	Sayornis phoebe	Eastern phoebe
Roadrunner	Geococcyx californianus	Scapanus orarius	Coast mole
Rock pocket mouse	Perognathus intermedius	Sciurus aberti	Abert squirrel
Rock wren	Salpinctes obsoletus	Sciurus arizonensis	Arizona gray squirrel
Rose-breasted grosbeak	Pheucticus ludovicianus	Sciurus carolinensis	Eastern gray squirrel
Rosy finch	Leucosticte arctoa	Sciurus niger	Fox squirrel
Rough-legged hawk	Buteo lagopus	Scolopax minor	Woodcock
Ruffed grouse	Bonasa umbellus	Seiurus aurocapillus	Ovenbird
Rufous-crowned sparrow	Aimophila ruficeps	Seiurus motacilla	Louisiana waterthrush
Rufous-sided towhee	Pipilo erythrophthalmus	Seiurus noveboracensis	Northern waterthrush
Sage grouse	Centrocercus urophasianus	Setophaga ruticilla	American redstart
Sage sparrow	Amphizpiza belli	Siala spp.	Bluebird
Sage thrasher	Oreoscoptes montanus	Siala currucoides	Mountain bluebird
Savannah sparrow	Passerculus sandwichensis	Siala mexicana	Western bluebird
Saw-whet owl	Aegolius acadicus	Siala sialis	Eastern bluebird
Scaled quail	Callipepla squamata	Sitta spp.	Nuthatch
Scarlet tanager	Piranga olivacea	Sitta canadensis	Red-breasted nuthatch

Common name	Scientific name
Scott's oriole	*Icterus parisorum*
Screech owl, eastern	*Otus asio*
Scrub jay	*Aphelocoma coerulescens*
Sharp-tailed grouse	*Tympanuchus phasianellus*
Short-billed marsh wren	*Cistothorus platensis*
Short-eared owl	*Asio flammeus*
Skink	*Eumeces* spp.
Skunk	*Mephitis* spp.
Snail kite	*Rostrhamus sociabilis*
Snowshoe hare	*Lepus americanus*
Snowy owl	*Nyctea scandiaca*
Sonoran pronghorn	*Antilocapra americana sonoriensis*
Southeastern five-lined skink	*Eumeces inexpectatus*
Southern bog lemming	*Synaptomys cooperi*
Southern flying squirrel	*Glaucomys volans*
Sparrow hawk	*Falco sparverius*
Spotted owl	*Strix occidentalis*
Sprague's pipit	*Anthus spragueii*
Spruce budworm	*Choristoneura fumiferana*
Squirrel treefrog	*Hyla squirella*
Starling, European	*Sturnus vulgaris*
Steller's jay	*Cyanocitta stelleri*
Summer tanager	*Piranga rubra*
Swainson's hawk	*Buteo swainsoni*
Texas rat snake	*Elaphe obsoleta lindheimeri*
Thirteen-lined ground squirrel	*Spermophilus tridecemlineatus*
Titmouse	*Parus* spp.
Tree swallow	*Tachycineta bicolor*
Tufted titmouse	*Parus bicolor*
Turkey	*Meleagris gallopavo*
Upland sandpiper	*Bartramia lognicauda*
Veery	*Catharus fuscescens*
Verdin	*Auriparus flaviceps*
Vesper sparrow	*Pooecetes grammincus*
Violet-green swallow	*Tachycineta thalassina*
Virginia's warbler	*Vermivora virginiae*

Common name	Scientific name
White-breasted nuthatch	*Sitta carolinensis*
Brown-headed nuthatch	*Sitta pusilla*
Pygmy nuthatch	*Sitta pygmaea*
Masked shrew	*Sorex cinereus*
Ground squirrel	*Spermophilus* spp.
Thirteen-lined ground squirrel	*Spermophilus tridecemlineatus*
Yellow-bellied sapsucker	*Sphyrapicus varius*
Goldfinch	*Spinus* spp.
Dickcissel	*Spiza americana*
Brewer's sparrow	*Spizella breweri*
Clay-colored sparrow	*Spizella pallida*
Chipping sparrow	*Spizella passerina*
Field sparrow	*Spizella pusilla*
Great gray owl	*Strix nebulosa*
Spotted owl	*Strix occidentalis*
Barred owl	*Strix varia*
Meadowlark	*Sturnella* spp.
Eastern meadowlark	*Sturnella magna*
Western meadowlark	*Sturnella neglecta*
European starling	*Sturnus vulgaris*
Desert cottontail rabbit	*Sylvilagus auduboni*
Cottontail rabbit	*Sylvilagus floridanus*
Southern bog lemming	*Synaptomys cooperi*
Ancient murrelet	*Synthli boramphus antiguus*
Tree swallow	*Tachycineta bicolor*
Violet-green swallow	*Tachycineta thalassina*
Red squirrel	*Tamiasciurus hudsonicus*
Badger	*Taxidea taxus*
Gopher	*Thomomys* spp.
Northern pocket gopher	*Thomomys talpoides*
Bewick's wren	*Thryomanes bewickii*
Carolina wren	*Thryothorus ludovicianus*
Curve-billed thrasher	*Toxostoma curvirostre*
Lecoute's thrasher	*Toxostoma lecontei*
House wren	*Troglodytes aedon*
American robin	*Turdus migratorius*

TABLE A.21 Common and Scientific Names of Animals Mentioned (Continued)

Alphabetical by common name		Alphabetical by scientific name	
Common name	Scientific name	Scientific name	Common name
Virginia's warbler	*Vermivora virginiae*	*Tympanuchus* spp.	Prairie chicken
Water pipit	*Anthus spinoletta*	*Tympanuchus cupido*	Greater prairie chicken
Weasel, long-tailed	*Mustela frenata*	*Tympanuchus cupido attwateri*	Attwater's prairie chicken
Western bluebird	*Sialia mexicana*	*Tympanuchus pallidicinctus*	Lesser prairie chicken
Western harvest mouse	*Reithrodontomys megalotis*	*Tympanuchus phasianellus*	Sharp-tailed grouse
Western meadowlark	*Sturnella neglecta*	*Tyto alba*	Barn owl
Western screech owl	*Otus asio kennicottii*	*Ursus* spp.	Bear
Whiskered screech owl	*Otus trichopsis*	*Ursus americanus*	Black bear
White-breasted nuthatch	*Sitta carolinensis*	*Ursus arctos*	Grizzly bear
White-footed mouse	*Peromyscus leucopus*	*Verivora virginiae*	Virginia's warbler
White-tailed deer	*Odocoileus virginianus*	*Vermivora celata*	Orange-crowned warbler
Willow ptarmigan	*Lagopus lagopus*	*Vermivora virginiae*	Virginia's warbler
Wolf	*Canis* spp.	*Vireo atricapillus*	Black-capped vireo
Wolverine	*Gulo gulo*	*Vireo flavifrons*	Yellow-throated vireo
Wood duck	*Aix sponsa*	*Vireo olivaceous*	Red-eyed vireo
Wood thrush	*Hylocichla mustelina*	*Vireo vicinior*	Gray vireo
Woodchuck	*Marmota monax*	*Vulpes macrotis*	Kit fox
Woodcock	*Scolopax minor*	*Wilsonia canadensis*	Canada warbler
Woodland caribou	*Rangifer tarandus caribou*	*Wilsonia citrina*	Hooded warbler
Woodrat	*Neotoma* spp.	*Zapus hudsonius*	Meadow jumping mouse
Worm-eating warbler	*Helmitheros vermivortes*	*Zenaida macroura*	Mourning dove
Wrentit	*Chamaea fasciata*		
Yellowthroat, common	*Geothlypis trichas*		
Yellow-bellied sapsucker	*Sphyrapicus varius*		
Yellow-billed cuckoo	*Coccyzus americanus*		
Yellow-throated vireo	*Vireo flavifrons*		

Addendum

Bachman's sparrow	*Aimorphila aestivalis*	*Aimorphila aestivalis*	Bachman's sparrow
Collared lizard	*Crotaphytus collaria*	*Crotaphytus collaria*	Collared lizard
Grasshopper mouse	*Onychomys leucogaster*	*Onychomys leucogaster*	Grasshopper mouse
Pygmy rattlesnake	*Sistrutus miliarus*	*Peromyscus attwateri*	Texas brush mouse
Texas brush mouse	*Peromyscus attwateri*	*Sistrutus miliarus*	Pygmy rattlesnake

TABLE A.22 Common and Scientific Names of Plants Mentioned

Alphabetical by common name		Alphabetical by scientific name	
Common name	Scientific name	Scientific name	Common name
Acacia	*Acacia* spp.	*Abies* spp.	Fir
Acute willow	*Salix* spp.	*Abies amabilis*	Silver fir, Pacific
Agarito	*Berberis* spp.	*Abies balsamea*	Balsam fir
Agoseris	*Agoseris* spp.	*Abies concolor*	White fir
Alabama supplejack	*Berchemia scandens*	*Abies fraseri*	Fraser fir
Alaska yellow cedar	*Chamaecyparis nootkatensis*	*Abies grandis*	Grand fir
Alder	*Alnus* spp.	*Abies lasiocarpa*	Alpine fir
Alfalfa	*Medicago sativa*	*Abies lasiocarpa*	Subalpine fir
Alfileria	*Erodium cicutarium*	*Abies magnifica*	Red fir
Alkali sacaton	*Sporobolus airoides*	*Abies procera*	Noble fir
Alkaligrass	*Distichlis spicata*	*Acacia* spp.	Acacia
Alleghany menziesia	*Menziesia pilosa*	*Acacia berlandieri*	Guajillo acacia (guajillo)
Alligator juniper	*Juniperus deppeana*	*Acacia farnesiana*	Huisache
Allthorn goatbush (amargosa)	*Castela texana*	*Acacia greggii*	Catclaw (una de gato)
Alpine fir	*Abies lasiocarpa*	*Acacia rigidula*	Blackbrush acacia (chaparro prieto)
Alpine larch	*Larix lyalli*	*Acacia smallii*	Texas huisache
Alpine leafybracket aster	*Aster foliaceus*	*Acacia tortuosa*	Huisachillo (twisted acacia)
Alsike clover	*Trifolium hybridum*	*Acer* spp.	Maple
Altai wildrye	*Elymus angustus*	*Acer circinatum*	Vine maple
Alumroot	*Heuchera villosa*	*Acer ginnala*	Amur maple
Amargoso	*Castela texana*	*Acer glabrum*	Mountain maple (Rocky Mountain clump maple)
American arborvitae	*Thuja occidentalis*	*Acer grandidentatum*	Bigtooth maple
American basswood	*Tilia americana*	*Acer macrophyllum*	Bigleaf maple
American beachgrass	*Ammophila breviligulata*	*Acer manschuricum*	Manchurian maple
American beech	*Fagus grandifolia*	*Acer negundo*	Boxelder
American bittersweet	*Celastrus scandens*	*Acer pensylvanicum*	Striped maple
American chestnut	*Castanea dentata*	*Acer rubrum*	Red maple
American cupscale	*Sacciolepis striata*	*Acer saccharinum*	Silver maple (soft maple)
American dunegrass	*Elymus mollis*	*Acer saccharum*	Sugar maple
American elderberry	*Sambucus canadensis*	*Acer spicatum*	Mountain maple
American elm	*Ulmus americana*		

TABLE A.22 Common and Scientific Names of Plants Mentioned (Continued)

Alphabetical by common name		Alphabetical by scientific name	
Common name	Scientific name	Scientific name	Common name
American holly	*Ilex opaca*	*Achillea* spp.	Yarrow
American hophornbeam	*Carpinus caroliniana*	*Achillea lanulosa*	Western yarrow
American hornbeam	*Carpinus caroliniana*	*Achillea millefolium*	Common yarrow
American plum	*Prunus americana*	*Adenostoma fasiculatum*	Chamise
American sycamore	*Platanus occidentalis*	*Aesculus* spp.	Buckeye
American vetch	*Vicia americana*	*Aesculus pavia*	Red buckeye
Amur maple	*Acer ginnala*	*Agastache urticifolia*	Nettleleaf gianthyssop
Antelope bitterbrush	*Purshia tridentata*	*Agoseris* spp.	Agoseris
Apacheplume	*Fallugia paradoxa*	*Agropyron* spp.	Wheatgrass
Apple	*Malus* spp.	*Agropyron caninum*	Slender wheatgrass
Arizona sycamore	*Platanus wrightii*	*Agropyron cristatum*	Crested wheatgrass (fairway crested wheatgrass)
Arizona cottontop	*Digitaria californica*		
Arizona cypress	*Cupressus arizonica*	*Agropyron dasystachyum*	Northern wheatgrass (thickspike wheat grass)
Arizona white oak	*Quercus arizonica*		
Arnica	*Arnica* spp.	*Agropyron desertorum*	Desert wheatgrass (standard crested wheatgrass)
Arrow-leafed tearthumb	*Polygonum sagittatum*		
Arrowgrass	*Triglochin maritima*	*Agropyron elongatum*	Tall wheatgrass
Arrowleaf balsamroot	*Balsamorhiza sagittata*	*Agropyron inerme*	Beardless wheatgrass
Arrowwood viburnum	*Viburnum dentatum*	*Agropyron intermedium*	Intermediate wheatgrass
Ashe juniper	*Juniperus ashei*	*Agropyron repens*	Quackgrass
Ash	*Fraxinus* spp.	*Agropyron riparium*	Streambank wheatgrass
Aspen	*Populus* spp.	*Agropyron sibiricum*	Siberian wheatgrass
Aster	*Aster* spp.	*Agropyron smithii*	Western wheatgrass
Astragalus	*Astragalus* spp.	*Agropyron spicatum*	Bluebunch wheatgrass
Atlantic white cedar	*Chamaecyparis thyoides*	*Agropyron trichophorum*	Pubescent wheatgrass
Australian pine	*Casuarina equisetifolia*	*Agrostis alba*	Redtop
Austrian pine	*Pinus nigra*	*Aira praecox*	Little hairgrass
Autumn olive	*Elaeagnus umbellata*	*Alectoria* spp.	Old man's beard
Avens	*Geum* spp.	*Allium stellatum*	Wild onion
		Alnus spp.	Alder
		Alnus rubra	Red alder
		Alnus serrulata	Tag alder

Common name	Scientific name
Awnless bush sunflower	*Simsia calva*
Bahiagrass	*Paspalum notatum*
Bald cypress	*Taxodium distichum*
Balsam fir	*Abies balsamea*
Balsam poplar	*Populus balsamifera*
Balsamroot	*Balsamorhiza* spp.
Bamboo vine	*Smilax laurifolia*
Barberry	*Berberis* spp.
Barley	*Hordeum vulgare*
Barnyard grass	*Echinochloa crusgalli*
Basin big sagebrush	*Artemisia tridentata tridentata*
Basin wildrye	*Elymus cinereus*
Basswood	*Tilia* spp.
Bayberry, northern	*Myrica pensylvanica*
Beach morning glory	*Ipomoea stolonifera*
Beach panic grass	*Panicum ararum*
Beach pea	*Lathyrus japonicus*
Beach plum	*Prunus maritima*
Beach strawberry	*Frageria chiloensis*
Beaked hazelnut	*Corylus cornuta*
Beaked panic grass	*Panicum anceps*
Bear oak	*Quercus ilicifolia*
Bearberry	*Arctostaphylos uva-ursi*
Bearberry honeysuckle	*Lonicera involucrata*
Bearberry (manzanita)	*Arctostaphylos* spp.
Beardless wheatgrass	*Agropyron inerme*
Bearmat (misery mountain)	*Chamaebatia foliolosa*
Beautyberry	*Callicarpa americana*
Beech	*Fagus* spp.
Beggarweed (tick-trefoil)	*Desmodium* spp.
Beloperone	*Beloperone californica*
Belvedere summer cypress	*Kochia scoparia*
Bermudagrass	*Cynodon dactylon*
Bessey cherry	*Prunus besseyi*

Scientific name	Common name
Alnus sinuata	Sitka alder
Alopecurus arundinaceus	Creeping foxtail
Alopecurus pratensis	Meadow foxtail
Aloysia lycoides	Reventador (whitebrush)
Alyssum alyssoides	Pale alyssum
Amaranthus albus	Tumbleweed
Amaranthus blitoides	Prostrate pigweed
Amaranthus retroflexus	Redroot pigweed
Ambrosia spp.	Ragweed
Ambrosia artimisiifolia	Common ragweed
Ambrosia bidentata	Southern ragweed
Ambrosia dumosa	Bursage (white bursage)
Ambrosia psilostachya	Western ragweed
Ambrosia trifida	Giant ragweed (tall ragweed)
Amelanchier spp.	Serviceberry (juneberry)
Amelanchier alnifolia	Saskatoon (Saskatoon serviceberry, serviceberry)
Amelanchier arborea	Downy serviceberry
Amelanchier canadensis	Canadian serviceberry
Amelanchier utahensis	Utah serviceberry
Ammophila arenaria	European beachgrass
Ammophila breviligulata	American beachgrass
Amorpha canescens	Leadplant
Ampelopsis arborea	Peppervine
Anaphalis spp.	Pearly everlasting
Andropogon spp.	Bluestem
Andropogon gerardi	Big bluestem
Andropogon glomeratus	Bushy beardgrass
Andropogon hallii	Sand bluestem
Andropogon saccharoides	Silver bluestem
Andropogon virginicus	Broomsedge
Angelica pinnata	Small-leaf angelica
Antennaria spp.	Pussytoes, everlasting
Antennaria dimorpha	Low pussytoes

TABLE A.22 Common and Scientific Names of Plants Mentioned (Continued)

Alphabetical by common name		Alphabetical by scientific name	
Common name	Scientific name	Scientific name	Common name
Bicolor lespedeza	*Lespedeza bicolor*	*Antennaria microphylla*	Littleleaf pussytoes
Big bluegrass	*Poa ampla*	*Aphanostephus* spp.	Lady's tobacco
Big bluestem	*Andropogon gerardi*	*Aquilegia coerulea*	Colorado columbine
Big sagebrush	*Artemisia tridentata*	*Aralia spinosa*	Hercules club
Big-cone spruce	*Picea asperata*	*Aranaria utahensis*	Uinta sandwort
Bigberry manzanita	*Arctostaphylos glauca*	*Arbutus menziesii*	Madrone (Pacific madrone)
Bigleaf maple	*Acer macrophyllum*	*Arctium minus*	Common burdock
Bigtooth aspen	*Populus grandidentata*	*Arctostaphylos* spp.	Bearberry (manzanita)
Bigtooth maple	*Acer grandidentatum*	*Arctostaphylos ginnala*	Mariposa manzanita
Bir filaree	*Erodium botrys*	*Arctostaphylos glauca*	Bigberry manzanita
Birch	*Betula* spp.	*Arctostaphylos pungens*	Pointleaf manzanita
Birchleaf mountainmahogany	*Cercocarpus betuloides*	*Arctostaphylos uva-ursi*	Bearberry
Bird's foot trefoil	*Lotus corniculatus*	*Aristida* spp.	Threeawn
Bishop pine	*Pinus muricata*	*Aristida oligantha*	Prairie threeawn
Bitterbrush	*Purshia tridentata*	*Aristida stricta*	Pineland threeawn
Bittercherry	*Prunus emarginata*	*Arnica* spp.	Arnica
Bittersweet nightshade	*Solanum dulcamara*	*Arnica fulgens*	Orange arnica
Bitterweed	*Hymenoxys* spp.	*Aronia* spp.	Chokeberry
Black ash	*Fraxinus nigra*	*Arrhenatherum elatius*	Oatgrass (tall oatgrass)
Black cherry	*Prunus serotina*	*Artemisia* spp.	Sagebrush
Black cottonwood	*Populus trichocarpa*	*Artemisia arbuscula*	Low sagebrush
Black grama	*Bouteloua eriopoda*	*Artemisia cana*	Dwarf sagebrush (silver sagebrush)
Black Hills spruce	*Picea glauca densata*	*Artemisia drancunculus*	Tarragon sagebrush
Black locust	*Robinia pseudoacacia*	*Artemisia filifolia*	Sand sagebrush (sandsage)
Black medic	*Medicago lupulina*	*Artemisia frigida*	Fringed sagebrush
Black nightshade	*Solanum nigrum*	*Artemisia ludoviciana*	Louisiana sagebrush (prairie sagebrush, Louisiana sagewort)
Black oak	*Quercus velutina*		
Black raspberry	*Rubus occidentalis*	*Artemisia nova*	Black sagebrush
Black sagebrush	*Artemisia nova*	*Artemisia spinescens*	Bud sagebrush (budsage)
Black spruce	*Picea mariana*	*Artemisia tridentata*	Big sagebrush
Black tupelo	*Nyssa sylvatica*	*Artemisia tridentata tridentata*	Basin big sagebrush
Black walnut	*Juglans nigra*		

Common name	Scientific name	Scientific name	Common name
Black willow	*Salix nigra*	*Artemisia tridentata vaseyana*	Mountain big sagebrush (Vasey big sagebrush)
Blackberry	*Rubus* spp.	*Artemisia tridentata wyomingensis*	Wyoming big sagebrush
Blackbrush	*Coleogyne* spp.	*Artemisia tripartita*	Threetip sagebrush
Blackbrush acacia	*Acacia rigidula*	*Artemisia vulgaris*	Oldman wormwood
Blackgum (black tupelo, water tupelo)	*Nyssa sylvatica*	*Arundinaria gigantea*	Giant cane
Blackjack oak	*Quercus marilandica*	*Asclepias verticillata*	Whorled milkweed
Blackseed plantain	*Plantago rugelii*	*Aster* spp.	Aster
Blue ash	*Fraxinus quadrangulata*	*Aster chilensis*	Pacific aster
Blue brush	*Ceanothus thryiflorus*	*Aster engelmannii*	Englemann aster
Blue elderberry	*Sambucus caerulea*	*Aster foliaceus*	Alpine leafybracket aster
Blue grama	*Bouteloua gracilis*	*Aster glaucodes*	Smooth aster
Blue oak	*Quercus douglasii*	*Astragalus* spp.	Astragalus (locoweed, milkvetch)
Blue panicgrass	*Panicum antidotale*	*Astragalus cicer*	Cicer milkvetch (sicklepod milkvetch)
Blue spruce	*Picea pungens*		
Blue-beech	*Carpinus caroliniana*	*Astragalus convallarius*	Timber milkvetch
Blueberry elder	*Sambucus cerula*	*Astragalus falcatus*	Chickpea milkvetch
Blueberry (deerberry)	*Vaccinium* spp.	*Astragalus filipes*	Snakeriver plains milkvetch
Bluebunch wheatgrass	*Agropyron spicatum*	*Astragalus galegiformis*	Tall milkvetch
Bluegrass	*Poa* spp.	*Atriplex* spp.	Saltbush
Bluestem	*Andropogon* spp.	*Atriplex breweri*	Brewer saltbush
Bluewood	*Condalia obovata*	*Atriplex canescens*	Fourwing saltbush (wingscale)
Boer lovegrass	*Eragrostis chloromelas*	*Atriplex confertifolia*	Shadscale saltbush (shadscale)
Bottlebrush	*Plantago arenaria*	*Atriplex gardneri*	Gardner saltbush
Bottlebrush squirreltail	*Sitanion hystrix*	*Atriplex lahontanensis*	Lahontan saltbush
Bouncing-bet	*Saponaria officinalis*	*Atriplex lentiformis*	Quail brush
Boxelder	*Acer negundo*	*Atriplex patula*	Orache
Bracted plantain	*Plantago aristata*	*Atriplex polycarpa*	Saltbush
Bramble vetch	*Vicia tenuifolia*	*Avena sativa*	Oats
Bramble	*Rubus* spp.	*Baccharis halimifolia*	Groundsel tree
Brasil	*Condalia obovata*	*Balsamorhiza macrophylla*	Cutleaf balsamroot
Brazilian peppertree	*Schinus terebinthifolius*	*Balsamorhiza sagittata*	Arrowleaf balsamroot
Brewer saltbush	*Atriplex breweri*	*Balsamorhiza* spp.	Balsamroot
Bristle grass	*Setaria* spp.	*Baptisia leucophaea*	Wild indigo
Bristlecone pine	*Pinus aristata*	*Bassia hyssopifolia*	Fivehook bassia
Bristly locust	*Robinia hispida*	*Beloperone californica*	Beloperone

TABLE A.22 Common and Scientific Names of Plants Mentioned (Continued)

Alphabetical by common name		Alphabetical by scientific name	
Common name	Scientific name	Scientific name	Common name
Brittlebush	*Encelia* spp.	*Berberis* spp.	Agarito (barberry)
Broadleaf plantain	*Plantago major*	*Berberis aquifolium*	Oregon-grape
Brodiaea	*Brodiaea* spp.	*Berberis nervosa*	Tall Oregon-grape
Bromegrass	*Bromus inermus*	*Berberis repens*	Creeping barberry
Bromegrass	*Bromus* spp.	*Berchemia scandens*	Alabama supplejack (rattan, supplejack)
Broom snakeweed	*Xanthocephalum sarothrae*		
Broomcorn	*Sorghum vulgare*	*Betula* spp.	Birch
Broomsedge	*Andropogon virginicus*	*Betula alleghaniensis*	Yellow birch
Browntop millet	*Panicum ramosum*	*Betula lenta*	Sweet birch
Buckbrush	*Ceanothus* spp.	*Betula nigra*	River birch (red birch)
Buckeye	*Aesculus* spp.	*Betula papyrifera*	Paper birch (white birch)
Buckthorn	*Rhamnus* spp.	*Betula populifolia*	Gray birch
Buckthorn plantain	*Plantago lanceolata*	*Bignonia capreolata*	Crossvine
Buckwheat	*Eriogonum* spp.	*Borrichia frutescens*	Sea ox-eye
Bud sagebrush (budsage)	*Artemisia spinescens*	*Bothriochloa caucasica*	Caucasian bluestem
Buffaloberry	*Shepherdia canadensis*	*Bothriochloa ischaemum*	Yellow bluestem
Buffalograss	*Buchloe dactyloides*	*Bouteloua* spp.	Grama
Buffelgrass	*Cenchrus ciliaris*	*Bouteloua curtipendula*	Sideoats grama
Bulbous bluegrass	*Poa bulbosa*	*Bouteloua eriopoda*	Black grama
Bull paspalum	*Paspalum boscianum*	*Bouteloua gracilis*	Blue grama
Bulrush	*Scirpus americanus*	*Brassica* spp.	Mustard
Bumelia	*Bumelia* spp.	*Brodiaea* spp.	Brodiaea
Bundleflower	*Desmanthus* spp.	*Bromus* spp.	Bromegrass
Bur oak	*Quercus macrocarpa*	*Bromus catharticus*	Rescue grass
Burclover	*Medicago* spp.	*Bromus commutatus*	Meadow brome
Burdock, common	*Arctium minus*	*Bromus inermis*	Smooth brome (bromegrass)
Bursage	*Ambrosia dumosa*	*Bromus japonicus*	Japanese brome
Bush cinquefoil	*Potentilla fruticosa*	*Bromus marginatus*	Mountain brome
Bush honeysuckle	*Diervilla lonicera*	*Bromus mollis*	Soft chess
Bush lupine	*Lupinus albifrons*	*Bromus tectorum*	Cheatgrass brome
Bush lupine	*Lupinus arboreus*	*Broussonetia papyrifera*	Paper mulberry
Bushy beardgrass	*Andropogon glomeratus*	*Bryoria* spp.	Old man's beard

Common name	Scientific name
Buttercup	*Ranunculus* spp.
Butternut	*Juglans cinerea*
Butterweed groundsel	*Senecio serra*
Buttonbush	*Cephalanthus occidentalis*
Cabbage palmetto	*Sabal palmetto*
Cactus (pricklypear, cholla)	*Opuntia* spp.
Calandrinia	*Calandrinia maritima*
California black oak	*Quercus kelloggii*
California blackberry	*Rubus ursinus*
California buckthorn	*Rhamnus californica*
California coast live oak	*Quercus agrifolia*
California juniper	*Juniperus californica*
California laurel	*Umbellularia californica*
California live oak	*Quercus agrifolia*
California scrub oak	*Quercus dumosa*
California torreya	*Torreya californica*
California white oak	*Quercus lobata*
Calley Bermudagrass	*Cynodon dactylon* (hybrid)
Calliandra	*Calliandra* spp.
Calliandra (false-mesquite)	*Calliandra eriophylla*
Camphorweed	*Heterotheca subaxillaris*
Canada goldenrod	*Solidago canadensis*
Canada thistle	*Cirsium arvense*
Canada wildrye	*Elymus canadensis*
Canadian serviceberry	*Amelanchier canadensis*
Canyon live oak	*Quercus chrysolepis*
Capul	*Ilex* spp.
Caragana	*Caragana arborescens*
Cardinal russianolive	*Elaeagnus umbellata*
Carolina ash	*Fraxinus caroliniana*
Carolina hemlock	*Tsuga canadensis*
Carolina rose	*Rosa carolina*
Carrotleaf leptotaenia	*Lomatium dissectum*
Cascara buckthorn	*Rhamnus purshiana*
Catalpa	*Catalpa* spp.
Catclaw	*Acacia greggii*

Common name	Scientific name
Buffalograss	*Buchloe dactyloides*
Bumelia (coma, spiny bumelia)	*Bumelia* spp.
Purple pinegrass	*Calamagrostis purpurascens*
Prairie sandreed	*Calamovilfa longifolia*
Calandrinia	*Calandrinia maritima*
Calliandra	*Calliandra* spp.
Calliandra (false-mesquite)	*Calliandra eriophylla*
Beautyberry	*Callicarpa americana*
Poppymallow	*Callirhoe involucrata*
Pussypaws	*Calyptridium umbellatum*
Trumpet vine	*Campsis radicans*
Arizona cypress	*Cupressus arizonica*
Peashrub	*Caragana* spp.
Caragana (Siberian peashrub)	*Caragana arborescens*
Whitetop	*Cardaria draba*
Musk thistle	*Carduus nutans*
Sedge	*Carex* spp.
Douglas sedge	*Carex douglasii*
Threadleaf sedge	*Carex filifolia*
American hophornbeam (American hornbeam, blue-beech, ironwood)	*Carpinus caroliniana*
Safflower	*Carthamus* spp.
Hickory (pecan)	*Carya* spp.
Water hickory	*Carya aquatica*
Pignut hickory	*Carya glabra*
Pecan	*Carya illinoensis*
Shagbark hickory	*Carya ovata*
Mockernut hickory	*Carya tomentosa*
Partridgepea	*Cassia* spp.
Partridgepea	*Cassia fasciculata*
Wild sensitive pea (partridge pea)	*Cassia nictitans*
American chestnut	*Castanea dentata*
Golden chinkapin	*Castanopsis chrysophylla*
Allthorn goatbush (amargoso)	*Castela texana*
Indian paintbrush	*Castilleja* spp.
Northwestern painted-cup	*Castilleja hispida*

TABLE A.22 Common and Scientific Names of Plants Mentioned (Continued)

	Alphabetical by common name			Alphabetical by scientific name	
Common name	Scientific name			Scientific name	Common name
Cattail	*Typha* spp.			*Casuarina equisetifolia*	Australian pine
Caucasian bluestem	*Bothriochloa caucasica*			*Catalpa* spp.	Catalpa
Ceanothus	*Ceanothus* spp.			*Ceanothus* spp.	Jerseytea (deerbrush, buckbrush,
Cedar, red	*Juniperus* spp.				whitethorn, ceanothus, evergreen
Cedar	*Thuja* spp.				ceanothus)
Ceniza shrub	*Leucophyllum frutescens*			*Ceanothus americanus*	New Jersey tea
Centella	*Centella repanda*			*Ceanothus cuneatus*	Wedgeleaf ceanothus
Chamise	*Adenostoma fasiculatum*			*Ceanothus fendleri*	Fendler ceanothus
Chaparro prieto	*Acacia rigidula*			*Ceanothus greggii*	Desert ceanothus
Chapote	*Diospyros texana*			*Ceanothus integerrimus*	Deerbrush ceanothus
Cheatgrass brome	*Bromus tectorum*			*Ceanothus martinii*	Martin ceanothus
Checkerberry (wintergreen)	*Gaultheria procumbens*			*Ceanothus prostrata*	Mahala mat
Cherry laurel	*Prunus caroliniana*			*Ceanothus sanguineus*	Redstem ceanothus
Cherry (plum)	*Prunus* spp.			*Ceanothus thryiflorus*	Blue brush
Cherrybark oak	*Quercus falcata*			*Ceanothus velutinus*	Snowbrush ceanothus
Chestnut oak	*Quercus prinus*			*Celastrus scandens*	American bittersweet
Chickasaw plum	*Prunus angustifolia*			*Celtis* spp.	Palo blanco, hackberry
Chickpea milkvetch	*Astragalus falcatus*			*Celtis laevigata*	Sugarberry
Chickweed, common	*Stellaria media*			*Celtis occidentalis*	Hackberry
Chinaberry	*Melia azedarach*			*Celtis pallida*	Granjeno (spiny hackberry)
Chinese elm	*Ulmus parvifolia*			*Cenchrus ciliaris*	Buffelgrass
Chinese lettuce (prickly lettuce)	*Lactuca serriola*			*Centaurea melitensis*	Malta starthistle
Chinkapin	*Quercus muehlenbergii*			*Centaurea repens*	Russian knapweed
Chokeberry	*Aronia* spp.			*Centaurea solstitialis*	Yellow starthistle
Chokecherry	*Prunus virginiana*			*Centella repanda*	Centella
Cholla	*Opuntia imbricata*			*Cephalanthus occidentalis*	Buttonbush
Christmasfern, western	*Polystichum* spp.			*Ceratoides lanata*	Winterfat
Chufa	*Cyperus esculentus*			*Cercidium* spp.	Paloverde
Cicer milkvetch	*Astragalus cicer*			*Cercidium microphyllum*	Yellow paloverde
Cilindrillo	*Lycium berlandieri*			*Cercis canadensis*	Redbud
Cinquefoil	*Potentilla* spp.			*Cercocarpus* spp.	Hairy cercocarpus
Clapany	*Zizyphus obtusifolia*				(mountainmahogany)

Common name	Scientific name
Birchleaf mountainmahogany (western mountainmahogany)	*Cercocarpus betuloides*
Curlleaf mountainmahogany (true mountainmahogany, littleleaf mountainmahogany)	*Cercocarpus ledifolius*
Hairy mountainmahogany	*Cercocarpus montanus*
Saguaro	*Cereus giganteus*
Bearmat (misery mountain)	*Chamaebatia foliolosa*
Incense cedar	*Chamaecyparis* spp.
Port Orford cedar	*Chamaecyparis lawsoniana*
Alaska yellow cedar	*Chamaecyparis nootkatensis*
Atlantic white cedar	*Chamaecyparis thyoides*
Common lambsquarters	*Chenopodium album*
Mexican tea	*Chenopodium ambrosioides*
Mapleleaf goosefoot	*Chenopodium hybridum*
Goosefoot	*Chenopodium murale*
Desert-willow	*Chilopsis linearis*
Rhodesgrass	*Chloris gayana*
Common oxeye daisy	*Chrysanthemum leucanthemum*
Rabbitbrush (spineless rabbitbrush)	*Chrysothamnus* spp.
Dwarf rabbitbrush	*Chrysothamnus depressus*
Rubber rabbitbrush	*Chrysothamnus nauseosus*
Parry rabbitbrush	*Chrysothamnus parryi*
Small rabbitbrush	*Chrysothamnus stenophyllus*
Douglas rabbitbrush	*Chrysothamnus viscidiflorus*
Yellowbrush	*Chrysothamnus viscidiflorus*
Green rabbitbrush	*Chrysothamnus viscidiflorus*
Thistle	*Cirsium* spp.
Canada thistle	*Cirsium arvense*
Wavyleaf thistle	*Cirsium undulatum*
Fiddlewood	*Citharexylum* spp.
Reindeer moss	*Cladonia* spp.
Western virginsbower	*Clematis ligusticifolia*
Summersweet	*Clethra alnifolia*
Blackbrush	*Coleogyne* spp.
Colubrina (hogplum)	*Colubrina* spp.
Cliffrose	*Cowania ericaefolia*
Cliffrose (Stanbury cliffrose)	*Cowania mexicana*
Clover	*Trifolium* spp.
Coast deervetch	*Lotus formosissimus*
Colima	*Zanthoxylum fagara*
Colorado columbine	*Aquilegia coerulea*
Colubrina	*Colubrina* spp.
Columbia needlegrass	*Stipa columbiana*
Coma	*Bumelia* spp.
Comandra, common	*Comandra umbellata*
Common Bermudagrass	*Cynodon dactylon*
Common bladdersenna	*Coluta arborescens*
Common buckthorn	*Rhamnus caroliniana*
Common deerberry	*Vaccinium stamineum*
Common filaree	*Erodium cicutarium*
Common greenbrier	*Smilax rotundifolia*
Common juniper	*Juniperus communis*
Common lespedeza	*Lespedeza striata*
Common purslane	*Portulaca oleracea*
Common reed	*Phragmites australis*
Common spikerush	*Eleocharis palustris*
Common sweetleaf	*Symplocos tinctoria*
Common threesquare	*Scirpus americanus*
Condalia	*Condalia* spp.
Coralberry	*Symphoricarpos* spp.
Cordgrass	*Spartina* spp.
Corn	*Zea mays*
Coronilla crownvetch	*Coronilla varia*
Cotoneaster	*Cotoneaster* spp.
Cottonwood	*Populus* spp.
Coulter pine	*Pinus coulteri*
Cowparsnip, common	*Heracleum lanatum*
Cow oak	*Quercus michauxii*
Cow pea	*Vigna sinensis*
Coyote tobacco	*Nicotiana attenuata*
Coyotillo	*Karwinskia humboldtiana*

Alphabetical by common name		Alphabetical by scientific name	
Common name	Scientific name	Scientific name	Common name
Crabapple	*Malus angustifolia*	*Colubrina texensis*	Texas colubrina
Cranberry	*Viburnum trilobatum*	*Coluta arborescens*	Common bladdersenna
Creeping barberry	*Berberis repens*	*Comandra umbellata*	Common comandra
Creeping foxtail	*Alopecurus arundinaceus*	*Comptonia peregrina*	Sweet fern
Creeping red fescue	*Festuca rubra*	*Condalia arundinaceus*	Condalia
Creosotebush	*Larrea tridentata*	*Condalia obovata*	Brasil (bluewood)
Crested wheatgrass	*Agropyron cristatum*	*Condalia spathulata*	Squawbush
Crimson clover	*Trifolium incarnatum*	*Convolvulus arvensis*	Field bindweed
Crossvine	*Bignonia capreolata*	*Cordylanthus ramosus*	Plumeweed
Croton	*Croton californicus*	*Cornus* spp.	Dogwood
Crown vetch	*Vicia* spp.	*Cornus amomum*	Silky dogwood
Curlleaf mountainmahogany (true mountainmahogany)	*Cercocarpus ledifolius*	*Cornus canadensis*	Dwarf cornell (bunchberry)
Curly dock	*Rumex crispus*	*Cornus drummondii*	Rough-leafed dogwood
Currant	*Ribes* spp.	*Cornus florida*	Flowering dogwood
Cushion eriogonum	*Eriogonum ovalifolium*	*Cornus nuttallii*	Pacific dogwood
Cusick bluegrass	*Poa cusickii*	*Cornus occidentalis*	Western dogwood
Cutgrass	*Leersia* spp.	*Cornus racemosa*	Gray dogwood
Cutleaf balsamroot	*Balhsamorhiza macrophylla*	*Cornus stolonifera*	Redosier dogwood
Cypress	*Taxodium* spp.	*Coronilla varia*	Coronilla crownvetch
Dahoon (dahoon holly)	*Ilex cassine*	*Corylus* spp.	Hazel (hazelnut)
Dalea	*Dalea* spp.	*Corylus cornuta*	Beaked hazelnut
Dallisgrass	*Paspalum dilatatum*	*Cotoneaster* spp.	Cotoneaster
Dandelion	*Taraxacum vulgare*	*Cotoneaster acuminata*	Peking cotoneaster
Deer's tongue	*Trilisa odoratissima*	*Cowania ericaefolia*	Cliffrose
Deerbrush ceanothus	*Ceanothus integerrimus*	*Cowania mexicana*	Cliffrose (Stansbury cliffrose)
Deertongue	*Muhlenbergia rigens*	*Crataegus* spp.	Hawthorn
Deervetch	*Lotus* spp.	*Crataegus columbiana*	Thorn-apple
Deerweed	*Lotus scoparius*	*Crataegus opaca*	Riverflat hawthorn
Desert bitterbrush	*Purshia* spp.	*Crataegus phaenopyrum*	Washington hawthorn
Desert ceanothus	*Ceanothus greggii*	*Crepis acuminata*	Tapertip hawksbeard
Desert parsley	*Lomatium* spp.	*Croton californicus*	Croton
		Croton capitatus	Woolly croton

Common name	Scientific name
Desert peachbrush	*Prunus fasciculata*
Desert wheatgrass	*Agropyron desertorum*
Desert yaupon	*Ilex* spp.
Desert-willow	*Chilopsis linearis*
Dewberry	*Rubus* spp.
Diamondleaf (laurel) oak	*Quercus laurifolia*
Digger pine	*Pinus sabiniana*
Dog-tongue (wild buckwheat)	*Eriogonum* spp.
Dogwood	*Cornus* spp.
Douglas knotweed	*Polygonum douglasii*
Douglas rabbitbrush	*Chrysothamnus viscidiflorus*
Douglas sedge	*Carex douglasii*
Douglas-fir	*Pseudotsuga menziesii*
Downy serviceberry	*Amelanchier arborea*
Dwarf cornell (bunchberry)	*Cornus canadensis*
Dwarf huckleberry	*Gaylussacia dumosa*
Dwarf rabbitbrush	*Chrysothamnus depressus*
Dwarf sagebrush	*Artemisia cana*
Dwarf spikerush	*Eleocharis parvula*
Dwarf sumac	*Rhus copallina*
Eastern cottonwood	*Populus deltoides*
Eastern hemlock	*Tsuga canadensis*
Eastern hophornbeam	*Ostrya virginiana*
Eastern redcedar	*Juniperus virginiana*
Eastern white pine	*Pinus strobus*
Eaton penstemon	*Penstemon eatonii*
Edible valerian	*Valeriana edulis*
Elderberry	*Sambucus callicarpa*
Elderberry	*Sambucus glauca*
Elderberry	*Sambucus* spp.
Elm	*Ulmus* spp.
Emory oak	*Quercus emoryi*
Engelmann spruce	*Picea engelmannii*
Engelmann aster	*Aster engelmannii*
Eriogonum	*Eriogonum* spp.
European beachgrass	*Ammophila arenaria*
Tropic croton	*Croton glandulosus*
Silverleaf croton	*Croton punctatus*
Arizona cypress	*Cupressus arizonica*
Bermudagrass (common Bermuda-grass)	*Cynodon dactylon*
Calley Bermudagrass	*Cynodon dactylon* (hybrid)
Chufa	*Cyperus esculentus*
Nutsedge	*Cyperus filiculmis*
Purple nutsedge	*Cyperus rotundus*
Schweinitz's nutsedge	*Cyperus schweinitzii*
Swamp cyrilla (leatherwood)	*Cyrilla racemiflora*
Scotch broom	*Cytisus scoparius*
Orchardgrass	*Dactylis glomerata*
Dalea	*Dalea* spp.
Low larkspur	*Delphinium bicolor*
Tall larkspur	*Delphinium occidentale*
Tansymustard	*Descurainia* spp.
Pinnate tansymustard	*Descurainia pinnata*
Flaxweed tansymustard	*Descurainia sophia*
Bundleflower	*Desmanthus* spp.
Illinois bundleflower	*Desmanthus illinoensis*
Beggarweed (tick-trefoil)	*Desmodium* spp.
Showy tick-trefoil	*Desmodium canadense*
Bush honeysuckle	*Diervilla lonicera*
Arizona cottontop	*Digitaria californica*
Pangolagrass	*Digitaria decumbens*
Smooth crabgrass	*Digitaria ischaemum*
Large crabgrass	*Digitaria sanguinalis*
Arizona cottontop	*Digitaria californica*
Alkaligrass (saltgrass)	*Distichlis spicata*
Saltgrass	*Distichlis stricta*
Chapote (Texas persimmon)	*Diospyros texana*
Common persimmon	*Diospyros virginiana*
Jungle rice	*Echinochloa colonum*
Barnyardgrass (Japanese millet)	*Echinochloa crusgalli*
Walter's millet	*Echinochloa walteri*

TABLE A.22 Common and Scientific Names of Plants Mentioned (Continued)

Alphabetical by common name		Alphabetical by scientific name	
Common name	Scientific name	Scientific name	Common name
Evergreen blackberry	Rubus laciniatus	Elaeagnus angustifolia	Russian olive
Evergreen ceanothus	Ceanothus spp.	Elaeagnus pungens	Thorny eleagnus
Evergreen huckleberry	Vaccinium ovatum	Elaeagnus umbellata	Autumn olive (cardinal russianolive)
Fairway crested wheatgrass	Agropyron cristatum	Eleocharis spp.	Spikesedge
Fall panic grass	Panicum dichotomiflorum	Eleocharis palustris	Common spikerush
False hellebore	Veratrum viride	Eleocharis parvula	Dwarf spikerush
Fat solomon-plume	Smilacina racemosa	Eleocharis quadrangulata	Squarestem spikerush
Fendler ceanothus	Ceanothus fendleri	Eleusine indica	Goose grass
Fescue	Festuca spp.	Elymus spp.	Wildrye
Fiddlewood	Citharexylum spp.	Elymus angustus	Altai wildrye
Field bindweed	Convolvulus arvensis	Elymus canadensis	Canada wildrye
Filaree	Erodium obtusiplicatum	Elymus cinereus	Basin wildrye
Filaree (heronbill)	Erodium spp.	Elymus giganteus	Mammoth wildrye
Fir	Abies spp.	Elymus junceus	Russian wildrye
Firethorn	Pyracantha coccinea	Elymus mollis	American dunegrass
Fivehook bassia	Bassia hyssopifolia	Elymus virginicus	Wild rye
Flat pea	Lathyrus sylvestris	Encelia spp.	Brittlebush
Flat peavine	Lathyrus sylvestris	Ephedra spp.	Green ephedra
Flax	Linum spp.	Ephedra viridis	Mormon tea
Flaxleaf plainsmustard	Sisymbrium linifolium	Ephedra nevadensis	Nevada ephedra
Flaxweed tansymustard	Descurainia sophia	Epigaea repens	Trailing-arbutus (mayflower)
Fleabane	Erigeron spp.	Epilobium spp.	Willowweed (fireweed)
Flowering dogwood	Cornus florida	Equisetum spp.	Horsetail
Flowering spurge	Euphorbia corollata	Eragrostis chloromelas	Boer lovegrass
Foothill deathcamus	Toxicoscordium gramineum	Eragrostis curvula	Weeping lovegrass
Fourwing saltbush	Atriplex canescens	Eragrostis intermedia	Plains lovegrass
Fox grape	Vitis labrusca	Eragrostis lehmanniana	Lehmann lovegrass
Foxtail barley	Hordeum jubatum	Eragrostis trichodes	Sand lovegrass
Foxtail millet	Setaria italica	Eremocarpus setigerus	Turkey mullein
Foxtail pine	Pinus balfouriana	Erigeron spp.	Fleabane
Fragrant sumac	Rhus aromatic	Erigeron canadensis	Horseweed
Fraser fir	Abies fraseri	Erigeron concinnus	Hairy fleabane

720

Common name	Scientific name
Fremont cottonwood	*Populus fremontii*
Fringed bindweed	*Polygonum cilinode*
Fringed catbrier	*Smilax bona-nox*
Fringed sagebrush	*Artemisia frigida*
Frost grape	*Vitis vulpina*
Galax	*Galax aphylla*
Gallberry	*Ilex glabra*
Galleta	*Hilaria jamesii*
Gambel oak	*Quercus gambelii*
Gardner saltbush	*Atriplex gardneri*
Guajillo acacia	*Acacia berlandieri*
Gayophytum	*Gayophytum diffusum*
German iris	*Iris germanica*
Giant cane	*Arundinaria gigantea*
Giant ragweed	*Ambrosia trifida*
Goatsbeard	*Tragopogon spp.*
Golden chinkapin	*Castanopsis chrysophylla*
Golden currant	*Ribes aureum*
Golden willow	*Salix alba vitellina*
Goldenrod	*Solidago spp.*
Goose grass	*Eleusine indica*
Gooseberry	*Ribes spp.*
Gooseberryleaf globemallow	*Sphaeralcea grossulariaefolia*
Goosefoot	*Chenopodium murale*
Grama	*Bouteloua spp.*
Grand fir	*Abies grandis*
Granjeno	*Celtis pallida*
Grape	*Vitis spp.*
Gray birch	*Betula populifolia*
Gray dogwood	*Cornus racemosa*
Gray oak	*Quercus grisea*
Greasewood	*Sarcobatus vermiculatus*
Green ash	*Fraxinus pennsylvanica*
Green bristlegrass	*Setaria viridis*
Green ephedra	*Ephedra spp.*
Green needlegrass	*Stipa viridula*
Purpledaisy fleabane	*Erigeron corymbosus*
Eriogonum (buckwheat, dog-tongue, wild buckwheat)	*Eriogonum spp.*
Mat eriogonum	*Eriogonum caespitosum*
Wyeth eriogonum	*Eriogonum heracleoides*
Cushion eriogonum	*Eriogonum ovalifolium*
Wooly sunflower	*Eriophyllum spp.*
Filaree (heronbill)	*Erodium spp.*
Bir filaree	*Erodium botrys*
Alfileria	*Erodium cicutarium*
Common filaree	*Erodium cicutarium*
Musk filaree	*Erodium moschatum*
Filaree	*Erodium obtusiplicatum*
Strawberry bush (winterberry)	*Euonymus spp.*
White snakeroot	*Eupatorium rugosom*
Flowering spurge	*Euphorbia corollata*
Leafy spurge	*Euphorbia esula*
Spotted spurge	*Euphorbia maculata*
Prostrate spurge	*Euphorbia supina*
Winterfat	*Eurotia lanata*
Beech	*Fagus spp.*
American beech	*Fagus grandifolia*
Apacheplume	*Fallugia paradoxa*
Tall fescue	*Festuca arundinacea*
Fescue	*Festuca spp.*
Idaho fescue	*Festuca idahoensis*
Sixweeks fescue	*Festuca octoflora*
Hard fescue (sheep fescue)	*Festuca ovina*
Meadow fescue	*Festuca pratensis*
Creeping red fescue (red fescue)	*Festuca rubra*
Rough fescue	*Festuca scabrella*
Tar bush	*Flourensia cernua*
Swamp privet	*Forestiera acuminata*
New Mexican foresteria	*Forestiera neomexicana*
Strawberry	*Fragaria spp.*
Beach strawberry	*Frageria chiloensis*

TABLE A.22 Common and Scientific Names of Plants Mentioned (Continued)

Alphabetical by common name		Alphabetical by scientific name	
Common name	Scientific name	Scientific name	Common name
Green rabbitbrush	*Chrysothamnus viscidiflorus*	*Fragaria virginiana*	Wild strawberry
Green sprangletop	*Leptochloa dubia*	*Fraxinus* spp.	Ash
Greenbrier	*Smilax* spp.	*Fraxinus americana*	White ash
Ground blueberry	*Vaccinium myrsinites*	*Fraxinus caroliniana*	Carolina ash
Ground cherry	*Physalis* spp.	*Fraxinus latifolia*	Oregon ash
Ground juniper	*Juniperus horizontalis*	*Fraxinus nigra*	Black ash
Groundsel tree	*Baccharis halimifolia*	*Fraxinus pennsylvanica*	Green ash
Groundsmoke	*Galyophytum* spp.	*Fraxinus quadrangulata*	Blue ash
Grouse whortleberry	*Vaccinium scoparium*	*Galax aphylla*	Galax
Guajillo	*Acacia berlandieri*	*Galyophytum* spp.	Groundsmoke
Guayacan	*Porlieria angustifolia*	*Garrya* spp.	Silktassel
Gum	*Nyssa* spp.	*Garrya wrightii*	Wright silktassel
Gumweed	*Grindelia* spp.	*Gaultheria* spp.	Teaberry (wintergreen)
Hackberry	*Celtis occidentalis*	*Gaultheria procumbens*	Checkerberry (wintergreen)
Hairy cercocarpus (true)	*Cercocarpus* spp.	*Gaultheria shallon*	Salal
Hairy fleabane	*Erigeron concinnus*	*Gaylussacia* spp.	Huckleberry
Hairy mountainmahogany	*Cercocarpus montanus*	*Gaylussacia dumosa*	Dwarf huckleberry
Hairy vetch	*Vicia hirsuta*	*Gayophytum diffusum*	Gayophytum
Halberd-leaved willow	*Salix hastata*	*Gelsemium sempervirens*	Yellow jessamine
Halogeton	*Halogeton glomeratus*	*Geranium viscosissimum*	Sticky geranium
Hard fescue	*Festuca ovina*	*Geum* spp.	Avens
Hardinggrass	*Phalaris tuberosa stenopieta*	*Gleditsia triacanthos*	Honeylocust
Hardinggrass	*Phalaris tuberosa*	*Glycine max*	Soybean
Hardstem bulrush	*Scirpus acutus*	*Glycine ussuriensis*	Reseeding soybean
Hawthorn	*Crataegus* spp.	*Grayia spinosa*	Spiny hopsage
Hazel (hazelnut)	*Corylus* spp.	*Grindelia* spp.	Gumweed
Hemlock	*Tsuga* spp.	*Gymnocladus dioicus*	Kentucky coffee tree
Hemp sesbania	*Sesbania exaltata*	*Halimodendron halodendron*	Siberian salt-tree
Hercules club	*Aralia spinosa*	*Halogeton glomeratus*	Halogeton
Hibiscus	*Hibiscus moscheutos*	*Hamamelis virginiana*	Witch-hazel
Hickory (pecan)	*Carya* spp.	*Hedysarum boreale*	Utah sweetvetch
Highbush blueberry	*Vaccinium corymbosum*	*Helianthella uniflora*	Oneflower helianthella

Common name	Scientific name	Scientific name	Common name
Hoary phlox	*Phlox canescens*	*Helianthus* spp.	Sunflower
Hoary vervian	*Verbena stricta*	*Helianthus giganteus*	Sunflower
Hogplum	*Colubrina* spp.	*Helianthus maximilliani*	Maximillian's sunflower
Holly	*Ilex* spp.	*Helianthus tuberosus*	Jerusalem artichoke
Hollyleaf cherry	*Prunus ilicifolia*	*Heracleum lanatum*	Common cowparsnip
Honey mesquite	*Prosopis juliflora*	*Heteromeles arbutifolia*	Toyon (Christmas-berry)
Honeylocust	*Gleditsia triacanthos*	*Heterotheca subaxillaris*	Camphorweed
Honeysuckle	*Lonicera* spp.	*Heuchera villosa*	Alumroot
Hooker's willow	*Salix hookeriana*	*Hibiscus moscheutos*	Hibiscus
Hop clover	*Trifolium procumbens*	*Hieracium pilosella*	Mouseear (hawkweed)
Hoptree	*Ptelea trifoliata*	*Hilaria jamesii*	Galleta
Horse nettle	*Solanum carolinense*	*Hilaria mutica*	Tobosa (tobosagrass)
Horsebrush	*Tetradymia* spp.	*Holodiscus discolor*	Oceanspray
Horsetail	*Equisetum* spp.	*Hordeum jubatum*	Foxtail barley
Horseweed	*Erigeron canadensis*	*Hordeum vulgare*	Barley
Huckleberry	*Gaylussacia* spp.	*Hydrangea* spp.	Hydrangea
Huisache	*Acacia farnesiana*	*Hymenoxys* spp.	Bitterweed
Huisachillo	*Acacia tortuosa*	*Ilex* spp.	Capul (desert yaupon, holly)
Hydrangea	*Hydrangea* spp.	*Ilex cassine*	Dahoon (dahoon holly)
Idaho fescue	*Festuca idahoensis*	*Ilex coriacea*	Large gallberry
Illinois bundleflower	*Desmanthus illinoensis*	*Ilex decidua*	Possumhaw
Incense cedar	*Chamaecyporis* spp.	*Ilex glabra*	Gallberry (inkberry)
Incense-cedar	*Libocedrus decurrens*	*Ilex opaca*	American holly
Indian paintbrush	*Castilleja* spp.	*Ilex verticillata*	Winterberry
Indian ricegrass	*Oryzopsis hymenoides*	*Ilex vomitora*	Yaupon
Indiangrass	*Sorghastrum nutans*	*Impatiens carpensis*	Jewelweed
Indianpipe	*Monotropa* spp.	*Ipomoea stolonifera*	Beach morning glory
Inkberry	*Ilex glabra*	*Iris germanica*	German iris
Interior live oak	*Quercus wislizenii*	*Iva frutescens*	Marshelder (sumpweed)
Intermediate wheatgrass	*Agropyron intermedium*	*Juglans* spp.	Walnut
Ironwood	*Carpinus caroliniana*	*Juglans cinerea*	Butternut
Italian ryegrass	*Lolium multiflorum*	*Juglans nigra*	Black walnut
Jack pine	*Pinus banksiana*	*Juncus* spp.	Rush
Japanese brome	*Bromus japonicus*	*Juniperus* spp.	Red cedar
Japanese clover	*Lespedeza striata*	*Juniperus* spp.	Juniper
Japanese honeysuckle	*Lonicera japonica*	*Juniperus* spp.	Western redcedar

TABLE A.22 Common and Scientific Names of Plants Mentioned (Continued)

	Alphabetical by common name			Alphabetical by scientific name	
	Common name	Scientific name		Scientific name	Common name
	Japanese lespedeza	*Lespedeza japonica*		*Juniperus ashei*	Ashe juniper
	Japanese millet	*Echinochloa crusgalli*		*Juniperus californica*	California juniper
	Jeffrey pine	*Pinus jefferyi*		*Juniperus chinensis*	Pfitzer juniper
	Jerseytea (deerbrush, buckbrush, whitethorn)	*Ceanothus* spp.		*Juniperus communis*	Common juniper
				Juniperus deppeana	Alligator juniper
	Jerusalem artichoke	*Helianthus tuberosus*		*Juniperus horizontalis*	Ground juniper
	Jewelweed	*Impatiens carpensis*		*Juniperus monosperma*	One-seed juniper
	Johnsongrass	*Sorghum halepense*		*Juniperus occidentalis*	Western juniper
	Joshua tree	*Yucca brevifolia*		*Juniperus osteosperma*	Utah juniper
	Junegrass, prairie	*Koeleria cristata*		*Juniperus pinchotii*	Redberry (Pinchot) juniper
	Jungle rice	*Echinochloa colonum*		*Juniperus scopulorum*	Rocky Mountain juniper
	Juniper	*Juniperus* spp.		*Juniperus silicicola*	Southern redcedar
	Kentucky bluegrass	*Poa pratensis*		*Juniperus virginiana*	Eastern redcedar
	Kentucky coffee tree	*Gymnocladus dioicus*		*Kalmia angustifolia*	Lambkill
	Kleingrass	*Panicum coloratum*		*Kalmia latifolia*	Mountainlaurel
	Knobcone pine	*Pinus attenuata*		*Karwinskia humboldtiana*	Coyotillo
	Kochia	*Kochia prostrata*		*Kochia prostrata*	Kochia (prostrate kochia, forage kochia)
	Korean clover	*Lespedeza stipulacea*		*Kochia scoparia*	Belvedere summer cypress
	Korean lespedeza	*Lespedeza stipulucea*		*Koeleria cristata*	Prairie junegrass
	Kudzu	*Pueraria lobata*		*Lactuca* spp.	Lettuce (wild lettuce)
	Ladino clover	*Trifolium repens latum*		*Lactuca serriola*	Chinese lettuce (prickly lettuce)
	Lady's tobacco	*Aphanostephus* spp.		*Lantana* spp.	Lantana
	Ladysthumb	*Polygonum persicaria*		*Lantana camara*	Shrub verbena
	Lahontan saltbush	*Atriplex lahontanensis*		*Larix* spp.	Larch (tamarack)
	Lambkill	*Kalmia angustifolia*		*Larix laricina*	Tamarack
	Lambsquarters, common	*Chenopodium album*		*Larix lyalli*	Alpine larch
	Lambstongue groundsel	*Senecio integerrimus*		*Larix occidentalis*	Western larch
	Lanceleaf greenbrier	*Smilax smallii*		*Larrea tridentata*	Creosotebush
	Lantana	*Lantana* spp.		*Lathyrus* spp.	Peavine
	Larch (tamarack)	*Larix* spp.		*Lathyrus japonicus*	Beach pea
	Large crabgrass	*Digitaria sanguinalis*		*Lathyrus lanszwertii*	Thickleaf peavine
	Large gallberry	*Ilex coriacea*			

Common name	Scientific name
Laurel oak	*Quercus laurifolia*
Laurel willow	*Salix pentandra*
Leadplant	*Amorpha canescens*
Leafy spurge	*Euphorbia esula*
Lehmann lovegrass	*Eragrostis lehmanniana*
Lettuce	*Lactuca* spp.
Lewis flax	*Linum lewisii*
Lidzi	*Pueraria lobata*
Lilac	*Syringa* spp.
Lilac, common	*Syringa vulgaris*
Lilac, late	*Syringa villosa*
Limber pine	*Pinus flexilis*
Lime pricklyash	*Zanthoxylum fagara*
Little hairgrass	*Aira praecox*
Littlecup penstemon	*Penstemon sepalulus*
Littleleaf mountainmahogany	*Cercocarpus ledifolius*
Littleleaf pussytoes	*Antennaria microphylla*
Littleleaf sumac	*Rhus microphylla*
Live oak	*Quercus virginiana*
Loblolly pine	*Pinus taeda*
Locoweed	*Astragalus* spp.
Lodgepole pine	*Pinus contorta*
Lombardy poplar	*Populus nigra italica*
Longflower snowberry	*Symphoricarpos longiflorus*
Longleaf phlox	*Phlox longifolia*
Longleaf pine	*Pinus palustris*
Lotebush	*Ziziphus obtusifolia*
Louisiana sagebrush (sagewort)	*Artemisia ludoviciana*
Low blueberry	*Vaccinium vacillans*
Low goldenrod	*Solidago multiradiata*
Low larkspur	*Delphinium bicolor*
Low penstemon	*Penstemon humilis*
Low pussytoes	*Antennaria dimorpha*
Low sagebrush	*Artemisia arbuscula*
Ludwigia	*Ludwigia* spp.
Lupine	*Lupinus polyphyllus*

Scientific name	Common name
Lathyrus latifolius	Perennial peavine
Lathyrus palustris	Marsh pea
Lathyrus sylvestris	Flat pea
Lathyrus sylvestris	Flat peavine
Lathyrus utahensis	Utah peavine
Leersia spp.	Cutgrass
Leersia oryzoides	Rice cutgrass
Lepidium virginicum	Virginia pepperweed
Leptochloa dubia	Green sprangletop
Lespedeza spp.	Prostrate lespedeza
Lespedeza bicolor	Bicolor lespedeza (shrub lespedeza)
Lespedeza cuneata	Sericea lespedza
Lespedeza japonica	Japanese lespedeza
Lespedeza stipulacea	Korean clover
Lespedeza stipulucea	Korean lespedeza
Lespedeza striata	Common lespedeza (Japanese clover)
Leucophyllum frutescens	Ceniza shrub
Libocedrus decurrens	Incense-cedar
Ligusticum porteri	Porter ligusticum
Lindera benzoin	Spicebush
Linum spp.	Flax
Linum lewisii	Lewis flax
Liquidambar styraciflua	Sweetgum
Liriodendron tulipifera	Tulip poplar (yellowpoplar, tulip tree)
Lithocarpus densiflorus	Tanoak
Lolium spp.	Ryegrass
Lolium multiflorum	Italian ryegrass
Lolium perenne	Perennial ryegrass
Lomatium spp.	Desert parsley
Lomatium dissectum	Carrotleaf leptotaenia
Lomatium nuttallii	Nutall lomatium
Lonicera spp.	Honeysuckle (vining honeysuckle)
Lonicera involucrata	Bearberry honeysuckle

TABLE A.22 Common and Scientific Names of Plants Mentioned (Continued)

Alphabetical by common name		Alphabetical by scientific name	
Common name	Scientific name	Scientific name	Common name
Lupine	*Lupinus* spp.	*Lonicera japonica*	Japanese honeysuckle
Macartney rose	*Rosa bracteata*	*Lonicera tartarica*	Tartarian honeysuckle
Madrone, Pacific	*Arbutus menziesii*	*Lonicera utahenesis*	Utah honeysuckle
Magnolia	*Magnolia* spp.	*Lotus* spp.	Deervetch (trefoil)
Magnolia (cucumbertree)	*Magnolia acuminata*	*Lotus corniculatus*	Bird's foot trefoil
Mahala mat	*Ceanothus prostrata*	*Lotus formosissimus*	Coast deervetch
Malta starthistle	*Centaurea melitensis*	*Lotus scoparius*	Deerweed
Mammoth wildrye	*Elymus giganteus*	*Ludwigia* spp.	Ludwigia
Manchu cherry	*Prunus tomentosa*	*Lupinus* spp.	Lupine
Manchurian maple	*Acer manschuricum*	*Lupinus albifrons*	Bush lupine
Manzanita	*Arctostaphylos* spp.	*Lupinus alpestris*	Mountain lupine
Maple	*Acer* spp.	*Lupinus arboreus*	Bush lupine
Mapleleaf goosefoot	*Chenopodium hybridum*	*Lupinus argenteus*	Silvery lupine
Mapleleaf viburnum	*Viburnum acerifolium*	*Lupinus caudatus*	Tailcup lupine
Mariposa manzanita	*Arctostaphylos ginnala*	*Lupinus leucophyllus*	Velvet lupine
Marshelder	*Iva frutescens*	*Lupinus littoralis*	Seashore lupine
Marsh pea	*Lathyrus palustris*	*Lupinus nevadensis*	Nevada lupine
Marsh pepper	*Polygonum hydropiper*	*Lupinus polyphyllus*	Lupine
Martin ceanothus	*Ceanothus martinii*	*Lupinus sericeus*	Silky lupine
Mat eriogonum	*Eriogonum caespitosum*	*Lycium berlandieri*	Cilindrillo
Matrimony-vine	*Lycium halimifolium*	*Lycium berlandieri*	Wolfberry
Matroot penstemon	*Penstemon radicosus*	*Lycium halimifolium*	Matrimony-vine
Maximillian's sunflower	*Helianthus maximilliani*	*Lythrum salicaria*	Purple loosestrife
Meadow brome	*Bromus commutatus*	*Maclura pomifera*	Osage-orange
Meadow fescue	*Festuca pratensis*	*Madia* spp.	Tarweed
Meadow foxtail	*Alopecurus pratensis*	*Magnolia* spp.	Magnolia
Medic	*Medicago* spp.	*Magnolia acuminata*	Magnolia (cucumbertree)
Medusahead	*Taeniatherum caput-medusae*	*Magnolia grandiflora*	Southern magnolia
Melic	*Melica* spp.	*Magnolia virginiana*	Sweetbay
Mesquite	*Prosopis* spp.	*Malus* spp.	Apple
Mexican tea	*Chenopodium ambrosioides*	*Malus angustifolia*	Crabapple
Microsteris	*Microsteris gracilis*	*Malus pumila*	Wild apple

Milkvetch	*Astragalus* spp.	Sargent crabapple	*Malus sargenti*
Millet	*Setaria* spp.	Burclover (medic)	*Medicago* spp.
Mistletoe	*Phoradendron* spp.	Spotted burclover	*Medicago arabica*
Mockernut hickory	*Carya tomentosa*	Sickle alfalfa	*Medicago falcatus*
Mohr (shin) oak	*Quercus mohriana*	Black medic	*Medicago lupulina*
Monroe globemallow	*Sphaeralcea munroana*	Alfalfa	*Medicago sativa*
Monterey pine	*Pinus radiata*	Melic	*Melica* spp.
Moonseed	*Menispermum canadense*	Chinaberry	*Melia azedarach*
Mormon tea	*Ephedra viridis*	Sweetclover	*Melilotus* spp.
Mountain-ash	*Sorbus scopulina*	White sweetclover	*Melilotus alba*
Mountain big sagebrush	*Artemisia tridentata vaseyana*	Yellow sweetclover	*Melilotus officinalis*
Mountain blackberry	*Rubus allegheniensis*	Moonseed	*Menispermum canadense*
Mountain brome	*Bromus marginatus*	Alleghany menziesia	*Menziesia pilosa*
Mountain hemlock	*Tsuga mertensiana*	Microsteris	*Microsteris gracilis*
Mountainlaurel	*Kalmia latifolia*	Velvetpod mimosa	*Mimosa dysocarpa*
Mountain lupine	*Lupinus alpestris*	Partridgeberry	*Mitchella repens*
Mountain maple	*Acer glabrum*	Indianpipe	*Monotropa* spp.
Mountain maple	*Acer spicatum*	Mulberry	*Morus* spp.
Mountain muhly	*Muhlenbergia montana*	White mulberry (Russian mulberry)	*Morus alba*
Mountain snowberry	*Symphoricarpus oreophilus*	Red mulberry	*Morus rubra*
Mountainmahogany	*Cercocarpus* spp.	Stoneyhills muhly	*Muhlenbergia cuspidata*
Mountain-ash	*Sorbus* spp.	Mountain muhly	*Muhlenbergia montana*
Mouseear (hawkweed)	*Hieracium pilosella*	New Mexico muhly	*Muhlenbergia pauciflora*
Mulberry	*Morus* spp.	Deertongue	*Muhlenbergia rigens*
Mulesear	*Wyethia amplexicaulis*	Spike muhly	*Muhlenbergia wrightii*
Mullein, common	*Verbascum thapsus*	Waxmyrtle (bayberry)	*Myrica* spp.
Multiflora rose	*Rosa multiflora*	Pacific bayberry (Pacific waxmyrtle)	*Myrica californica*
Muscadine grape	*Vitis rotundifolia*	Southern bayberry (waxmyrtle)	*Myrica cerifera*
Musk filaree	*Erodium moschatum*	Northern bayberry	*Myrica pensylvanica*
Musk thistle	*Carduus nutans*	Common watercress	*Nasturtium officinale*
Mustard	*Brassica* spp.	Oleander	*Nerium oleander*
Mutton grass	*Poa fendleriana*	Coyote tobacco	*Nicotiana attenuata*
Myrtle oak	*Quercus myrtifolia*	Sacahuista	*Nolina microcarpa*
Nanking cherry	*Prunus tomentosa*	Sacahuista	*Nolina texana*
Nannyberry	*Viburnum lentago*	Waterlily	*Nymphaea odorata*
Narrowleaf vetch	*Vicia angustifolia*	Gum	*Nyssa* spp.

TABLE A.22 Common and Scientific Names of Plants Mentioned (Continued)

Alphabetical by common name		Alphabetical by scientific name	
Common name	Scientific name	Scientific name	Common name
Needle-and-thread	*Stipa comata*	*Nyssa aquatica*	Water tupelo
Needlegrass	*Stipa spp.*	*Nyssa sylvatica*	Blackgum (black tupelo, water tupelo)
Nettleleaf gianthyssop	*Agastache urticifolia*		
Nevada bluegrass	*Poa nevadensis*	*Nyssa sylvatica biflora*	Swamp tupelo
Nevada ephedra	*Ephedra nevadensis*	*Onobrychis viciafolia*	Sainfoin
Nevada lupine	*Lupinus nevadensis*	*Opuntia spp.*	Cactus (pricklypear, cholla)
Nevada showy goldeneye	*Viguiera multiflora nevadensis*	*Opuntia imbricata*	Cholla
New Jersey tea	*Ceanothus americanus*	*Opuntia leptocaulis*	Tasajillo
New Mexican foresteria	*Foresteria neomexicana*	*Oryzopsis hymenoides*	Indian ricegrass
New Mexico locust	*Robinia neomexicana*	*Oryzopsis miliacea*	Smilograss
New Mexico muhly	*Muhlenbergia pauciflora*	*Osmaronia cerasiformis*	Osoberry
Ninebark	*Physocarpus opulifolius*	*Osmorhiza chilensis*	Spreading sweetroot
Noble fir	*Abies procera*	*Osmorhiza occidentalis*	Sweetanise
Nodding smartweed	*Polygonum lapthifolium*	*Osmunda regalis*	Royal fern
Northern pin oak	*Quercus ellipsoidalis*	*Ostrya virginiana*	Eastern hophornbeam
Northern red oak	*Quercus rubra*	*Oxalis spp.*	Woodsorrel
Northern wheatgrass	*Agropyron dasystachyum*	*Oxydendron arboreum*	Sourwood
Northern white cedar	*Thuja occidentalis*	*Panicum spp.*	Panic grass
Northwestern painted-cup	*Castilleja hispida*	*Panicum amarulum*	Shoredune panic grass
Norway spruce	*Picea abies*	*Panicum anceps*	Beaked panic grass
Nutall lomatium	*Lomatium nuttallii*	*Panicum antidotale*	Blue panic grass
Nutsedge	*Cyperus fliculmis*	*Panicum ararum*	Beach panic grass
Oak	*Quercus spp.*	*Panicum clandestinum*	Panic grass
Oatgrass, tall	*Arrhenatherum elatius*	*Panicum coloratum*	Kleingrass
Oatgrass	*Stipa avenacca*	*Panicum dichotomiflorum*	Fall panic grass
Oats	*Avena sativa*	*Panicum lanuginosum*	Wooly panic grass
Oceanspray	*Holodiscus discolor*	*Panicum milliaceum*	Proso millet
Old man's beard	*Alectoria spp.*	*Panicum obtusum*	Vine mesquite
Old man's beard	*Bryoria spp.*	*Panicum ramosum*	Browntop millet
Old man's beard	*Usnea spp.*	*Panicum repens*	Torpedo grass
Oldman wormwood	*Artemisia vulgaris*	*Panicum texanum*	Texas millet
Oleander	*Nerium oleander*	*Panicum virgatum*	Switchgrass

Common name	Scientific name
Olney threesquare	*Scirpus olneyi*
One-seed juniper	*Juniperus monosperma*
Oneflower helianthella	*Helianthella uniflora*
Orache	*Atriplex patula*
Orange arnica	*Arnica fulgens*
Orchardgrass	*Dactylis glomerata*
Oregon ash	*Fraxinus latifolia*
Oregon checkermallow	*Sidalcea oregana*
Oregon white oak	*Quercus garryana*
Oregon-grape	*Berberis aquifolium*
Oriental arborvitae	*Thuja orientalis*
Osage-orange	*Maclura pomifera*
Osoberry	*Osmaronia cerasiformis*
Overcup oak	*Quercus lyrata*
Oxeye daisy, common	*Chrysanthemun leucanthemum*
Ozark rose	*Rosa arkansana*
Pacific aster	*Aster chilensis*
Pacific bayberry	*Myrica californica*
Pacific dogwood	*Cornus nuttallii*
Pacific waxmyrtle	*Myrica californica*
Pacific willow	*Salix lasiandra*
Pacific yew	*Taxus brevifolia*
Pale alyssum	*Alyssum alyssoides*
Palmer penstemon	*Penstemon palmeri*
Palmetto	*Sabal spp.*
Palo blanco	*Celtis spp.*
Paloverde	*Cercidium spp.*
Pangolagrass	*Digitaria decumbens*
Panic grass	*Panicum clandestinum*
Panic grass	*Panicum spp.*
Paper birch	*Betula papyrifera*
Paper mulberry	*Broussonetia papyrifera*
Paperflower	*Psilostrophe spp.*
Parry goldenrod	*Solidage parryi*
Parry rabbitbrush	*Chrysothamnus parryi*
Parthenium	*Parthenium spp.*

Common name	Scientific name
Retama	*Parkinsonia aculeata*
Whitlow-wart	*Paronychia spp.*
Parthenium	*Parthenium spp.*
Virginia creeper	*Parthenocissus quinquefolia*
Paspalum	*Paspalum spp.*
Bull paspalum	*Paspalum boscianum*
Dallisgrass	*Paspalum dilatatum*
Bahiagrass	*Paspalum notatum*
Vasey grass	*Paspalum urvillei*
Seashore paspalum	*Paspalum vaginatum*
Pearl millet	*Pennisetum glaucum*
Penstemon	*Penstemon spp.*
Wasatch penstemon	*Penstemon cyananthus*
Eaton penstemon	*Penstemon eatonii*
Low penstemon	*Penstemon humilis*
Toadflax penstemon	*Penstemon linarioides*
Rocky Mountain penstemon	*Penstemon montanus*
Thickleaf penstemon	*Penstemon pachyphyllus*
Palmer penstemon	*Penstemon palmeri*
Sidehill penstemon	*Penstemon platyphyllus*
Matroot penstemon	*Penstemon radicosus*
Rydberg penstemon	*Penstemon rydbergii*
Littlecup penstemon	*Penstemon sepalulus*
Squaw-apple	*Peraphyllum ramosissimum*
Redbay	*Persea borbonia*
Reed canarygrass	*Phalaris arundinacea*
Hardinggrass	*Phalaris tuberosa*
Hardinggrass	*Phalaris tuberosa stenopteta*
Syringa	*Philadelphus lewisi*
Timothy	*Phleum pratense*
Hoary phlox	*Phlox canescens*
Longleaf phlox	*Phlox longifolia*
Mistletoe	*Phoradendron spp.*
Common reed	*Phragmites australis*
Ground cherry	*Physalis spp.*
Ninebark	*Physocarpus opulifolius*

TABLE A.22 Common and Scientific Names of Plants Mentioned (Continued)

Alphabetical by common name		Alphabetical by scientific name	
Common name	Scientific name	Scientific name	Common name
Partridgepea	*Cassia fasciculata*	*Phytolacca americana*	Pokeweed (pokeberry)
Partridgeberry	*Mitchella repens*	*Picea* spp.	Spruce
Partridgepea	*Cassia* spp.	*Picea abies*	Norway spruce
Paspalum	*Paspalum* spp.	*Picea asperata*	Big-cone spruce
Peachleaf willow	*Salix amygdaloides*	*Picea engelmannii*	Engelmann spruce
Pearl millet	*Pennisetum glaucum*	*Picea glauca*	White spruce
Pearly everlasting	*Anaphalis* spp.	*Picea glauca densata*	Black Hills spruce
Peashrub	*Caragana* spp.	*Picea mariana*	Black spruce
Peavine	*Lathyrus* spp.	*Picea pungens*	Blue spruce
Pecan	*Carya illinoensis*	*Picea rubens*	Red spruce
Peking cotoneaster	*Cotoneaster acuminata*	*Picea sitchensis*	Sitka spruce
Pennsylvania smartweed	*Polygonum pennsylvanicum*	*Pinus* spp.	Pine
Penstemon	*Penstemon* spp.	*Pinus albicaulis*	Whitebark pine
Peppervine	*Ampelopsis arborea*	*Pinus aristata*	Bristlecone pine
Perennial peavine	*Lathyrus latifolius*	*Pinus attenuata*	Knobcone pine
Perennial ryegrass	*Lolium perenne*	*Pinus balfouriana*	Foxtail pine
Persimmon, common	*Diospyros virginiana*	*Pinus banksiana*	Jack pine
Persimmon, Texas	*Diospyros texana*	*Pinus clausa*	Sand pine
Pfitzer juniper	*Juniperus chinensis*	*Pinus contorta*	Lodgepole pine (shore pine)
Piñon pine (pinyon pine)	*Pinus edulis*	*Pinus coulteri*	Coulter pine
Pickleweed	*Rumex occidentalis*	*Pinus echinata*	Shortleaf pine
Pignut hickory	*Carya glabra*	*Pinus edulis*	Piñon pine (pinyon pine, pinyon)
Pin (fire) cherry	*Prunus pensylvanica*	*Pinus elliottii*	Slash pine
Pin oak	*Quercus palustris*	*Pinus flexilis*	Limber pine
Pine	*Pinus* spp.	*Pinus jefferyi*	Jeffrey pine
Pinehill bluestem	*Schizachyrium scoparius divergens*	*Pinus lambertiana*	Sugar pine
Pineland threeawn	*Aristida stricta*	*Pinus monticola*	Western white pine
Pinnate tansymustard	*Descurainia pinnata*	*Pinus muricata*	Bishop pine
Pinyon	*Pinus edulis*	*Pinus nigra*	Austrian pine
Pinyon ricegrass	*Piptochaetium fimbriatum*	*Pinus palustris*	Longleaf pine
Pitch pine	*Pinus rigida*	*Pinus ponderosa*	Ponderosa pine
Plains cottonwood	*Populus sargentii*	*Pinus radiata*	Monterey pine

Common name	Scientific name	Scientific name	Common name
Plains lovegrass	*Eragrostis intermedia*	*Pinus resinosa*	Red pine
Plantain	*Plantago* spp.	*Pinus rigida*	Pitch pine
Plumeweed	*Cordylanthus ramosus*	*Pinus sabiniana*	Digger pine
Pointleaf manzanita	*Arctostaphylos pungens*	*Pinus serotina*	Pond pine
Poison ivy	*Rhus radicans*	*Pinus strobus*	Eastern white pine (white pine)
Poison oak	*Rhus toxicodendron*	*Pinus sylvestris*	Scotch pine
Pokeweed (pokeberry)	*Phytolacca americana*	*Pinus taeda*	Loblolly pine
Pond pine	*Pinus serotina*	*Pinus virginiana*	Virginia pine
Pondcypress	*Taxodium distichum nutans*	*Piptochaetium fimbriatum*	Pinyon ricegrass
Ponderosa pine	*Pinus ponderosa*	*Plagiobothrys* spp.	Popcornflower
Popcornflower	*Plagiobothrys* spp.	*Plantago* spp.	Plantain
Poplar	*Populus* spp.	*Plantago arenaria*	Bottlebrush
Poppymallow	*Callirhoe involucrata*	*Plantago aristata*	Bracted plantain
Port Orford cedar	*Chamaecyparis lawsoniana*	*Plantago lanceolata*	Buckthorn plantain
Porter ligusticum	*Ligusticum porteri*	*Plantago major*	Broadleaf plantain
Possumhaw	*Ilex decidua*	*Plantago maritima*	Seaside plantain
Possumhaw viburnum	*Viburnum nudum*	*Plantago purshii*	Woolly indianwheat
Post oak	*Quercus stellata*	*Plantago rugelii*	Blackseed plantain
Prairie cordgrass	*Spartina pectinata*	*Platanus occidentalis*	American sycamore (sycamore)
Prairie sagebrush	*Artemisia ludoviciana*	*Platanus wrightii*	Arizona sycamore
Prairie sandreed	*Calamovilfa longifolia*	*Poa* spp.	Bluegrass
Prairie threeawn	*Aristida oligantha*	*Poa ampla*	Big bluegrass
Pricklypear	*Opuntia* spp.	*Poa bulbosa*	Bulbous bluegrass
Proso millet	*Panicum milliaceum*	*Poa cusickii*	Cusick bluegrass
Prostrate knotweed	*Polygonum aviculare*	*Poa fendleriana*	Mutton grass
Prostrate lespedeza	*Lespedeza* spp.	*Poa macantha*	Seashore bluegrass
Prostrate pigweed	*Amaranthus blitoides*	*Poa nevadensis*	Nevada bluegrass
Prostrate spurge	*Euphorbia supina*	*Poa pratensis*	Kentucky bluegrass
Protrate (forage) kochia	*Kochia prostrata*	*Poa secunda*	Sandberg bluegrass
Pubescent wheatgrass	*Agropyron trichophorum*	*Polygonum* spp.	Smartweed (knotweed)
Purple loosestrife	*Lythrum salicaria*	*Polygonum aviculare*	Prostrate knotweed
Purple nutsedge	*Cyperus rotundus*	*Polygonum cilinode*	Fringed bindweed
Purple willow	*Salix purpurea*	*Polygonum convolvulus*	Wild buckwheat
Purple pinegrass	*Calamagrostis purpurascens*	*Polygonum douglasii*	Douglas knotweed
Purple vetch	*Vicia americana*	*Polygonum hydropiper*	Marsh pepper
Purpledaisy fleabane	*Erigeron corymbosus*	*Polygonum lapthifolium*	Nodding smartweed

TABLE A.22 Common and Scientific Names of Plants Mentioned (Continued)

Alphabetical by common name		Alphabetical by scientific name	
Common name	Scientific name	Scientific name	Common name
Pussy willow	*Salix discolor*	*Polygonum pennsylvanicum*	Pennsylvania smartweed
Pussypaws	*Calyptridium umbellatum*	*Polygonum persicaria*	Ladysthumb
Pussytoes, everlasting	*Antennaria* spp.	*Polygonum sagittatum*	Arrow-leafed tearthumb
Quackgrass	*Agropyron repens*	*Polystichum* spp.	Western Christmasfern
Quail brush	*Atriplex lentiformis*	*Polystichum munitum*	Swordfern
Quaking aspen	*Populus tremuloides*	*Populus* spp.	Aspen (poplar)
Rabbitbrush	*Chrysothamnus* spp.	*Populus* spp.	Cottonwood
Ragweed	*Ambrosia* spp.	*Populus alba*	White poplar
Ragweed, common	*Ambrosia artimisiifolia*	*Populus balsamifera*	Balsam poplar
Rainbow plum	*Prunus angustifolia*	*Populus deltoides*	Eastern cottonwood
Raspberry	*Rubus* spp.	*Populus fremontii*	Fremont cottonwood
Rattan	*Berchemia scandens*	*Populus grandidentata*	Bigtooth aspen
Red alder	*Alnus rubra*	*Populus nigra italica*	Lombardy poplar
Red birch	*Betula nigra*	*Populus sargentii*	Plains cottonwood
Red buckeye	*Aesculus pavia*	*Populus tremuloides*	Quaking aspen
Red clover	*Trifolium pratense*	*Populus trichocarpa*	Black cottonwood
Red currant	*Ribes triste*	*Porliera angustifolia*	Texas porlieria
Red elder	*Sambucus pubens*	*Porlieria angustifolia*	Guayacan
Red fescue	*Festuca rubra*	*Portulaca oleracea*	Common purslane
Red fir	*Abies magnifica*	*Potentilla* spp.	Cinquefoil
Red globemallow	*Sphaeralcea coccinea*	*Potentilla fruiticosa*	Shrubby cinquefoil
Red maple	*Acer rubrum*	*Potentilla fruticosa*	Bush cinquefoil
Red mulberry	*Morus rubra*	*Prosopis* spp.	Mesquite
Red oak	*Quercus rubra*	*Prosopis juliflora*	Honey mesquite
Red pine	*Pinus resinosa*	*Prosopis glandulosa velutina*	Velvet mesquite
Red spruce	*Picea rubens*	*Prunus* spp.	Cherry (plum, wild plum, stonefruit)
Redbay	*Persea borbonia*	*Prunus americana*	American plum
Redberry (Pinchot) juniper	*Juniperus pinchotii*	*Prunus angustifolia*	Chickasaw plum (rainbow plum)
Redberry buckthorn	*Rhamnus crocea*	*Prunus besseyi*	Bessey cherry
Redberry elder (red elderberry)	*Sambucus racemosa*	*Prunus caroliniana*	Cherry laurel
Redbud	*Cercis canadensis*	*Prunus depressa*	Sand cherry
Redosier dogwood	*Cornus stolonifera*	*Prunus emarginata*	Bittercherry (wild cherry)

Common name	Scientific name
Redroot pigweed	*Amaranthus retroflexus*
Redstem ceanothus	*Ceanothus sanguineus*
Redtop	*Agrostis alba*
Redwood	*Sequoia sempervirens*
Reed canarygrass	*Phalaris arundinacea*
Reindeer moss	*Cladonia* spp.
Rescue grass	*Bromus catharticus*
Reseeding soybean	*Glycine ussuriensis*
Retama	*Parkinsonia aculeata*
Reventador	*Aloysia lycoides*
Rhodesgrass	*Chloris gayana*
Rhododendron	*Rhododendron* spp.
Rhubarb	*Rheum* spp.
Rice cutgrass	*Leersia oryzoides*
River birch	*Betula nigra*
River bulrush	*Scirpus fluviatilis*
Riverflat hawthorn	*Crataegus opaca*
Rock elm	*Ulmus thomasi*
Rocky Mountain clump maple	*Acer glabrum*
Rocky Mountain juniper	*Juniperus scopulorum*
Rocky Mountain penstemon	*Penstemon montanus*
Rocky Mountain smooth sumac	*Rhus glabra*
Rose	*Rosa* spp.
Rose clover	*Trifolium hirtum*
Rosebay (azalea)	*Rhododendron* spp.
Rough fescue	*Festuca scabrella*
Rough-leafed dogwood	*Cornus drummondii*
Roundleaf buffaloberry	*Shepherdia rotundiflora*
Royal fern	*Osmunda regalis*
Rubber rabbitbrush	*Chrysothamnus nauseosus*
Rush	*Juncus* spp.
Russian knapweed	*Centaurea repens*
Russian mulberry	*Morus alba*
Russian olive	*Elaeagnus angustifolia*
Russian thistle	*Salsola kali*
Russian wildrye	*Elymus junceus*
Desert peachbrush	*Prunus fasciculata*
Hollyleaf cherry	*Prunus ilicifolia*
Beach plum	*Prunus maritima*
Pin (fire) cherry	*Prunus pensylvanica*
Black cherry	*Prunus serotina*
Manchu (Nanking) cherry	*Prunus tomentosa*
Chokecherry	*Prunus virginiana*
Western chokecherry	*Prunus virginiana dirissa*
Douglas-fir	*Pseudotsuga menziesii*
Paperflower	*Psilostrophe* spp.
Hoptree	*Ptelea trifoliata*
Stinking ash	*Ptelea trifoliata*
Kudzu (Lidzi)	*Pueraria lobata*
Desert bitterbrush	*Purshia* spp.
Antelope bitterbrush (bitterbrush)	*Purshia tridentata*
Firethorn	*Pyracantha coccinea*
Oak	*Quercus* spp.
Sawtooth oak	*Quercus acutissima*
Western live oak (California live oak, California coast live oak)	*Quercus agrifolia*
White oak	*Quercus alba*
Arizona white oak	*Quercus arizonica*
Canyon live oak	*Quercus chrysolepis*
Scarlet oak	*Quercus coccinea*
Blue oak	*Quercus douglasii*
California scrub oak	*Quercus dumosa*
Northern pin oak	*Quercus ellipsoidalis*
Emory oak	*Quercus emoryi*
Southern red oak (cherrybark oak)	*Quercus falcata*
Gambel oak	*Quercus gambelii*
Oregon white oak	*Quercus garryana*
Gray oak	*Quercus grisea*
Shinnery oak (shin oak, sand shinnery oak)	*Quercus harvardii*
Bear oak	*Quercus ilicifolia*
California black oak	*Quercus kelloggii*
Turkey oak	*Quercus laevis*

TABLE A.22 Common and Scientific Names of Plants Mentioned (Continued)

Alphabetical by common name		Alphabetical by scientific name	
Common name	Scientific name	Scientific name	Common name
Rusty blackhaw	*Viburnum rufidulum*	*Quercus laurifolia*	Diamondleaf (laurel) oak
Rydberg penstemon	*Penstemon rydbergii*	*Quercus lobata*	California white oak
Rye	*Secale cereale*	*Quercus lyrata*	Overcup oak
Ryegrass	*Lolium* spp.	*Quercus macrocarpa*	Bur oak
Ryegrass, annual	*Secale cereale*	*Quercus marilandica*	Blackjack oak
Sacahuista	*Nolina microcarpa*	*Quercus michauxii*	Cow oak (swamp chestnut oak)
Sacahuista	*Nolina texana*	*Quercus mohriana*	Mohr (shin) oak
Sacaton	*Sporobolus* spp.	*Quercus muehlenbergii*	Chinkapin
Safflower	*Carthamus* spp.	*Quercus myrtifolia*	Myrtle oak
Sagebrush	*Artemisia* spp.	*Quercus nigra*	Water oak
Saguaro	*Cereus giganteus*	*Quercus palustris*	Pin oak
Sainfoin	*Onobrychis viciafolia*	*Quercus phellos*	Willow oak
Salal	*Gaultheria shallon*	*Quercus prinoides*	Scrub oak
Salmonberry	*Rubus spectabilis*	*Quercus prinus*	Chestnut oak
Saltbush	*Atriplex polycarpa*	*Quercus pungens vaseyana*	Vasey shinnery oak
Saltbush	*Atriplex* spp.	*Quercus rubra*	Northern red oak (red oak)
Saltcedar	*Tamarix parviflora*	*Quercus stellata*	Post oak
Saltcedar	*Tamarix* spp.	*Quercus undulata*	Wavyleaf oak
Saltgrass	*Distichlis spicata*	*Quercus velutina*	Black oak
Saltgrass	*Distichlis stricta*	*Quercus virginiana*	Live oak (shrub live oak)
Saltmarsh bulrush	*Scirpus robustus*	*Quercus wislizenii*	Interior live oak
Saltmeadow cordgrass	*Spartina patens*	*Ranunculus* spp.	Buttercup
Saltwort	*Salsola kali*	*Rhamnus* spp.	Buckthorn
Sand blackberry	*Rubus cuneifolius*	*Rhamnus californica*	California buckthorn
Sand bluestem	*Andropogon hallii*	*Rhamnus caroliniana*	Common buckthorn
Sand cherry	*Prunus depressa*	*Rhamnus crocea*	Redberry buckthorn
Sand dropseed	*Sporobolus cryptandrus*	*Rhamnus purshiana*	Cascara buckthorn
Sand lovegrass	*Eragrostis trichodes*	*Rheum* spp.	Rhubarb
Sand pine	*Pinus clausa*	*Rhododendron* spp.	Rhododendron (rosebay, azalea)
Sand sagebrush	*Artemisia filifolia*	*Rhus* spp.	Sumac
Sand shinnery oak	*Quercus harvardii*	*Rhus aromatic*	Fragrant sumac
Sandbar (coyote) willow	*Salix exigua*	*Rhus copallina*	Dwarf sumac (shining sumac)

Common name	Scientific name
Sandbar willow	*Salix interior*
Sandberg bluegrass	*Poa secunda*
Sandsage	*Artemisia filifolia*
Sargent crabapple	*Malus sargenti*
Saskatoon	*Amelanchier alnifolia*
Saskatoon serviceberry	*Amelanchier alnifolia*
Sassafras	*Sassafras albidum*
Saw-palmetto	*Serenoa repens*
Sawbrier	*Smilax glauca*
Sawtooth oak	*Quercus acutissima*
Scarlet globemallow	*Sphaeralcea coccinea*
Scarlet oak	*Quercus coccinea*
Schweinitz's nutsedge	*Cyperus schweinitzii*
Scotch broom	*Cytisus scoparius*
Scotch pine	*Pinus sylvestris*
Scouler willow	*Salix scouleriana*
Scrub oak	*Quercus prinoides*
Scrub palmetto	*Sabal* spp.
Sea blite	*Suaeda maritima*
Sea oats	*Uniola paniculata*
Sea ox-eye	*Borrichia frutescens*
Seashore bluegrass	*Poa macantha*
Seashore lupine	*Lupinus littoralis*
Seashore paspalum	*Paspalum vaginatum*
Seaside dock	*Rumex maritima*
Seaside goldenrod	*Solidago sempervirens*
Seaside plantain	*Plantago maritima*
Sedge	*Carex* spp.
Sequoia, giant	*Sequoiadendron giganteum*
Sericea lespedeza	*Lespedeza cuneata*
Serviceberry	*Amelanchier alnifolia*
Serviceberry (juneberry)	*Amelanchier* spp.
Shadscale	*Atriplex confertifolia*
Shadscale saltbush	*Atriplex confertifolia*
Shagbark hickory	*Carya ovata*
Sharp-toothed blackberry	*Rubus argutus*

Common name	Scientific name
Smooth sumac (Rocky Mountain smooth sumac)	*Rhus glabra*
Littleleaf sumac	*Rhus microphylla*
Sugar sumac	*Rhus ovata*
Poison ivy	*Rhus radicans*
Poison oak	*Rhus toxicodendron*
Skunkbush (skunkbush sumac, squawbush sumac)	*Rhus trilobata*
Staghorn sumac	*Rhus typhina*
Currant (gooseberry)	*Ribes* spp.
Wild black currant	*Ribes americanum*
Golden currant	*Ribes aureum*
Squaw currant	*Ribes cereum*
Red currant	*Ribes triste*
Sticky currant	*Ribes viscosissimum*
Bristly locust	*Robinia hispida*
New Mexico locust	*Robinia neomexicana*
Black locust	*Robinia pseudoacacia*
Rose	*Rosa* spp.
Ozark rose	*Rosa arkansana*
Macartney rose	*Rosa bracteata*
Carolina rose	*Rosa carolina*
Multiflora rose	*Rosa multiflora*
Swamp rose	*Rosa palustris*
Wild rose	*Rosa rugosa*
Woods rose	*Rosa woodsii*
Blackberry, raspberry, dewberry, bramble	*Rubus* spp.
Mountain blackberry	*Rubus alleghaeniensis*
Sharp-toothed blackberry	*Rubus argutus*
Sand blackberry	*Rubus cuneifolius*
Evergreen blackberry	*Rubus laciniatus*
Black raspberry	*Rubus occidentalis*
Salmonberry	*Rubus spectabilis*
Southern dewberry	*Rubus trivialis*
California blackberry	*Rubus ursinus*

TABLE A.22 Common and Scientific Names of Plants Mentioned   (Continued)

Alphabetical by common name		Alphabetical by scientific name	
Common name	Scientific name	Scientific name	Common name
Sheep fescue	*Festuca ovina*	*Rubus vitifolius*	Western blackberry
Sheep sorrel	*Rumex acetosella*	*Rumex acetosella*	Sheep sorrel
Shining sumac	*Rhus copallina*	*Rumex crispus*	Curly dock
Shinnery oak (shin oak)	*Quercus harvardii*	*Rumex maritima*	Seaside dock
Shore pine	*Pinus contorta*	*Rumex occidentalis*	Pickleweed
Shoredune panic grass	*Panicum amarulum*	*Sabal spp.*	Palmetto (scrub palmetto)
Shortleaf pine	*Pinus echinata*	*Sabal palmetto*	Cabbage palmetto.
Showy goldeneye	*Viguiera multiflora*	*Sacciolepis triata*	American cupscale
Showy tick-trefoil	*Desmodium canadense*	*Salix spp.*	Acute willow
Shrub lespedeza	*Lespedeza bicolor*	*Salix spp.*	Willow
Shrub live oak	*Quercus virginiana*	*Salix alba vitellina*	Golden willow
Shrub verbena	*Lantana camara*	*Salix amygdaloides*	Peachleaf willow
Shrubby cinquefoil	*Potentilla fruiticosa*	*Salix discolor*	Pussy willow
Siberian elm	*Ulmus pumila*	*Salix exigua*	Sandbar (coyote) willow
Siberian peashrub	*Caragana arborescens*	*Salix hastata*	Halberd-leaved willow
Siberian salt-tree	*Halimodendron halodendron*	*Salix hookeriana*	Hooker's willow
Siberian wheatgrass	*Agropyron sibiricum*	*Salix interior*	Sandbar willow
Sickle alfalfa	*Medicago falcatus*	*Salix lasiandra*	Pacific willow
Sicklepod milkvetch	*Astragalus cicer*	*Salix nigra*	Black willow
Sidehill penstemon	*Penstemon platyphyllus*	*Salix pentandra*	Laurel willow
Sideoats grama	*Bouteloua curtipendula*	*Salix purpurea*	Purpleosier willow
Silktassel	*Garrya spp.*	*Salix scouleriana*	Scouler willow
Silky dogwood	*Cornus amomum*	*Salix sericea*	Silky willow
Silky lupine	*Lupinus sericeus*	*Salsola kali*	Russian thistle (saltwort)
Silky willow	*Salix sericea*	*Sambucus spp.*	Elderberry
Silver bluestem	*Andropogon saccharoides*	*Sambucus caerulea*	Blue elderberry
Silver buffaloberry	*Shepherdia argentea*	*Sambucus callicarpa*	Elderberry
Silver fir, Pacific	*Abies amabilis*	*Sambucus canadensis*	American elderberry
Silver maple	*Acer saccharinum*	*Sambucus cerula*	Blueberry elder
Silver sagebrush	*Artemisia cana*	*Sambucus glauca*	Elderberry
Silverleaf croton	*Croton punctatus*	*Sambucus pubens*	Red elder
Silvery lupine	*Lupinus argenteus*	*Sambucus racemosa*	Redberry elder (red elderberry)

Common name	Scientific name
Sitka alder	*Alnus sinuata*
Sitka spruce	*Picea sitchensis*
Sixweeks fescue	*Festuca octoflora*
Skunkbush	*Rhus trilobata*
Skunkbush sumac	*Rhus trilobata*
Slash pine	*Pinus elliottii*
Slender wheatgrass	*Agropyron caninum*
Small burnet	*Sanguisorba minor*
Small rabbitbrush	*Chrysothamnus stenophyllus*
Small-leaf angelica	*Angelica pinnata*
Smartweed (knotweed)	*Polygonum spp.*
Smilograss	*Oryzopsis miliacea*
Smooth aster	*Aster glaucodes*
Smooth brome	*Bromus inermis*
Smooth crabgrass	*Digitaria ischaemum*
Smooth sumac	*Rhus glabra*
Snakeriver plains milkvetch	*Astragalus filipes*
Snowberry	*Symphoricarpos spp.*
Snowberry, common	*Symphoricarpos alba*
Snowbrush ceanothus	*Ceanothus velutinus*
Soapberry	*Sapindus spp.*
Soft chess	*Bromus mollis*
Soft maple	*Acer saccharinum*
Sorghum	*Sorghum vulgare*
Sourwood	*Oxydendron arboreum*
Southern bayberry	*Myrica cerifera*
Southern blackhaw	*Viburnum rufidulum*
Southern bulrush	*Scirpus californicus*
Southern dewberry	*Rubus trivialis*
Southern magnolia	*Magnolia grandiflora*
Southern ragweed	*Ambrosia bidentata*
Southern red oak	*Quercus falcata*
Southern redcedar	*Juniperus silicicola*
Soybean	*Glycine max*
Sparkleberry	*Vaccinium arboreum*
Speltz	*Triticum aestivum*

Scientific name	Common name
Sanguisorba minor	Small burnet
Saponaria officinalis	Bouncing-bet
Sapindus spp.	Soapberry
Sarcobatus vermiculatus	Greasewood (black greasewood)
Sassafras albidum	Sassafras
Schinus terebinthifolius	Brazilian peppertree
Schizachyrium scoparium divergens	Pinehill bluestem
Scirpus acutus	Hardstem bulrush (tule)
Scirpus americanus	Bulrush (common threesquare)
Scirpus californicus	Southern bulrush
Scirpus fluviatilis	River bulrush
Scirpus olneyi	Olney threesquare
Scirpus robustus	Saltmarsh bulrush
Secale cereale	Annual ryegrass (rye, winter rye)
Senecio integerrimus	Lambstongue groundsel
Senecio serra	Butterweed groundsel
Sequoia sempervirens	Redwood
Sequoiadendron giganteum	Giant sequoia
Serenoa repens	Saw-palmetto
Sesbania exaltata	Hemp sesbania
Setaria spp.	Bristle grass
Setaria spp.	Millet
Setaria italica	Foxtail millet
Setaria lutescens	Yellow bristlegrass
Setaria viridis	Green bristlegrass
Shepherdia argentea	Silver buffaloberry
Shepherdia canadensis	Buffaloberry
Shepherdia rotundiflora	Roundleaf buffaloberry
Sidalcea oregana	Oregon checkermallow
Simsia calva	Awnless bush sunflower
Sisymbrium linifolium	Flaxleaf plainsmustard
Sitanion spp.	Squirreltail
Sitanion hystrix	Bottlebrush squirreltail
Sitanion hystrix	Squirreltail
Smilacina racemosa	Fat solomon-plume
Smilax spp.	Greenbrier

TABLE A.22 Common and Scientific Names of Plants Mentioned (Continued)

Alphabetical by common name		Alphabetical by scientific name	
Common name	Scientific name	Scientific name	Common name
Spicebush	*Lindera benzoin*	*Smilax auriculata*	Wild bamboo
Spike muhley	*Muhlenbergia wrightii*	*Smilax bona-nox*	Fringed catbrier
Spikesedge	*Eleocharis* spp.	*Smilax glauca*	Sawbrier
Spineless rabbitbrush	*Chrysothamnus* spp.	*Smilax laurifolia*	Bamboo vine
Spiny bumelia	*Bumelia* spp.	*Smilax rotundifolia*	Common greenbrier
Spiny hackberry	*Celtis pallida*	*Smilax smallii*	Lanceleaf greenbrier
Spiny hopsage	*Grayia spinosa*	*Solanum carolinense*	Horse nettle
Spiraea	*Spiraea* spp.	*Solanum dulcamara*	Bittersweet nightshade
Spotted burclover	*Medicago arabica*	*Solanum nigrum*	Black nightshade
Spotted spurge	*Euphorbia maculata*	*Solidage parryi*	Parry goldenrod
Spreading sweetroot	*Osmorhiza chilensis*	*Solidago* spp.	Goldenrod
Spruce	*Picea* spp.	*Solidago canadensis*	Canada goldenrod
Squarestem spikerush	*Eleocharis quadrangulata*	*Solidago multiradiata*	Low goldenrod
Squaw currant	*Ribes cereum*	*Solidago sempervirens*	Seaside goldenrod
Squaw huckleberry	*Vaccinium stamineum*	*Sorbus* spp.	Mountain-ash
Squaw-apple	*Peraphyllum ramosissimum*	*Sorbus scopulina*	Mountain-ash
Squawbush	*Condalia spathulata*	*Sorghastrum nutans*	Indiangrass
Squawbush sumac	*Rhus trilobata*	*Sorghum halepense*	Johnsongrass
Squirreltail	*Sitanion hystrix*	*Sorghum sudanese*	Sudan grass
Squirreltail	*Sitanion* spp.	*Sorghum vulgare*	Sorghum (sudan grass, broomcorn)
Staghorn sumac	*Rhus typhina*	*Spartina* spp.	Cordgrass
Standard crested wheatgrass	*Agropyron desertorum*	*Spartina patens*	Saltmeadow cordgrass
Stansbury cliffrose	*Cowania mexicana*	*Spartina pectinata*	Prairie cordgrass
Sticky currant	*Ribes viscosissimum*	*Sphaeralcea coccinea*	Red globemallow (scarlet globe-mallow)
Sticky geranium	*Geranium viscosissimum*		
Stinking ash	*Ptelea trifoliata*	*Sphaeralcea grossulariaefolia*	Gooseberryleaf globemallow
Stonefruit	*Prunus* spp.	*Sphaeralcea munroana*	Monroe globemallow
Stoneyhills muhly	*Muhlenbergia cuspidata*	*Sphaeralcea rivularis*	Stream globemallow
Strawberry	*Fragaria* spp.	*Spiraea* spp.	Spiraea
Strawberry bush	*Euonymus* spp.	*Sporobolus* spp.	Sacaton
Strawberry clover	*Trifolium fragiferum*	*Sporobolus airoides*	Alkali sacaton
Stream globemallow	*Sphaeralcea rivularis*	*Sporobolus cryptandrus*	Sand dropseed

Common name	Scientific name	Scientific name	Common name
Streambank wheatgrass	*Agropyron riparium*	*Sporobolus virginicus*	Virginia dropseed
Striped maple	*Acer pensylvanicum*	*Stellaria media*	Common chickweed
Subalpine fir	*Abies lasiocarpa*	*Stipa* spp.	Needlegrass
Subalpine needlegrass	*Stipa columbiana*	*Stipa avenacca*	Oatgrass
Subterranean clover	*Trifolium subterraneum*	*Stipa columbiana*	Columbia needlegrass (subalpine needlegrass)
Sudan grass	*Sorghum sudanese*	*Stipa comata*	Needle-and-thread
Sudan grass	*Sorghum vulgare*	*Stipa leucotricha*	Texas wintergrass
Sugar maple	*Acer saccharum*	*Stipa occidentalis*	Western needlegrass
Sugar pine	*Pinus lambertiana*	*Stipa thurberiana*	Thurber needlegrass
Sugar sumac	*Rhus ovata*	*Stipa viridula*	Green needlegrass
Sugarberry	*Celtis laevigata*	*Strophostyles helvola*	Wild bean
Sumac	*Rhus* spp.	*Suaeda maritima*	Sea blite
Summer grape	*Vitis aestivalis*	*Symphoricarpos* spp.	Snowberry (coralberry)
Summersweet	*Clethra alnifolia*	*Symphoricarpos alba*	Common snowberry
Sunflower	*Helianthus giganteus*	*Symphoricarpos longiflorus*	Longflower snowberry
Sunflower	*Helianthus* spp.	*Symphoricarpos occidentalis*	Western snowberry
Supplejack	*Berchemia scandens*	*Symphoricarpus oreophilus*	Mountain snowberry
Swamp chestnut oak	*Quercus michauxii*	*Symplocos tinctoria*	Common sweetleaf
Swamp cyrilla (leatherwood)	*Cyrilla racemiflora*	*Syringa* spp.	Lilac
Swamp privet	*Forestiera acuminata*	*Syringa villosa*	Late lilac
Swamp rose	*Rosa palustris*	*Syringa vulgaris*	Common lilac
Swamp tupelo	*Nyssa sylvatica biflora*	*Sysimbrium loeselii*	Tumblemustard
Sweet birch	*Betula lenta*	*Taeniatherum caput-medusae*	Medusahead
Sweet fern	*Comptonia peregrina*	*Tamarix* spp.	Tamarisk (saltcedar)
Sweetanise	*Osmorhiza occidentalis*	*Tamarik parviflora*	Saltcedar
Sweetbay	*Magnolia virginiana*	*Taraxacum vulgare*	Dandelion
Sweetclover	*Melilotus* spp.	*Taxodium* spp.	Cypress
Sweetgum	*Liquidambar styraciflua*	*Taxodium distichum*	Bald cypress
Switchgrass	*Panicum virgatum*	*Taxodium distichum nutans*	Pondcypress
Swordfern	*Polystichum munitum*	*Taxus brevifolia*	Pacific yew
Sycamore	*Platanus occidentalis*	*Tecoma stans*	Trumpet bush
Syringa	*Philadelphus lewisi*	*Tetradymia* spp.	Horsebrush
Tag alder	*Alnus serrulata*	*Thuja* spp.	Cedar
Tailcup lupine	*Lupinus caudatus*	*Thuja occidentalis*	Northern white cedar (American arborvitae)
Tall fescue	*Festuca arundinacea*		
Tall larkspur	*Delphinium occidentale*		

TABLE A.22 Common and Scientific Names of Plants Mentioned (Continued)

Alphabetical by common name		Alphabetical by scientific name	
Common name	Scientific name	Scientific name	Common name
Tall milkvetch	*Astragalus galegiformis*	*Thuja orientalis*	Oriental arborvitae
Tall Oregon-grape	*Berberis nervosa*	*Thuja plicata*	Western redcedar
Tall ragweed	*Ambrosia trifida*	*Tilia* spp.	Basswood
Tall wheatgrass	*Agropyron elongatum*	*Tilia americana*	American basswood
Tamarack	*Larix laricina*	*Torreya californica*	California torreya
Tamarisk (saltcedar)	*Tamarix* spp.	*Toxicoscordium gramineum*	Foothill deathcamus
Tanoak	*Lithocarpus densiflorus*	*Tragopogon* spp.	Goatsbeard
Tansymustard	*Descurainia* spp.	*Tragopogon porrifolius*	Vegetable-oyster salsify
Tapertip hawksbeard	*Crepis acuminata*	*Trifolium* spp.	Clover
Tarbush	*Flourensia cernua*	*Trifolium fragiferum*	Strawberry clover
Tarragon sagebrush	*Artemisia drancunculus*	*Trifolium hybridum*	Alsike clover
Tartarian honeysuckle	*Lonicera tartarica*	*Trifolium incarnatum*	Crimson clover
Tarweed	*Madia* spp.	*Trifolium pratense*	Red clover (rose clover)
Tasajillo	*Opuntia leptocaulis*	*Trifolium procumbens*	Hop clover
Teaberry (wintergreen)	*Gaultheria* spp.	*Trifolium repens*	White clover
Texas colubrina	*Colubrina texensis*	*Trifolium repens latum*	Ladino clover
Texas huisache	*Acacia smallii*	*Trifolium subterraneum*	Subterranean clover
Texas millet	*Panicum texanum*	*Triglochin maritima*	Arrowgrass
Texas porlieria	*Porliera angustifolia*	*Trilisa odoratissima*	Deer's tongue (vanilla trilisa)
Texas wintergrass	*Stipa leucotricha*	*Triticosecale wittm*	Triticali
Thickleaf peavine	*Lathyrus lanszwertii*	*Triticum aestivum*	Wheat (speltz)
Thickleaf penstemon	*Penstemon pachyphyllus*	*Tsuga* spp.	Hemlock
Thickspike wheatgrass	*Agropyron dasystachyum*	*Tsuga canadensis*	Eastern hemlock (Carolina hemlock)
Thistle	*Cirsium* spp.		
Thorn-apple	*Crataegus columbiana*	*Tsuga heterophylla*	Western hemlock
Thorny eleagnus	*Elaeagnus pungens*	*Tsuga mertensiana*	Mountain hemlock
Threadleaf sedge	*Carex filifolia*	*Typha* spp.	Cattail
Threeawn	*Aristida* spp.	*Ulmus* spp.	Elm
Threetip sagebrush	*Artemisia tripartita*	*Ulmus americana*	American elm
Thurber needlegrass	*Stipa thurberiana*	*Ulmus parvifolia*	Chinese elm
Timber milkvetch	*Astragalus convallarius*	*Ulmus pumila*	Siberian elm
Timothy	*Phleum pratense*	*Ulmus thomasi*	Rock elm

Toadflax penstemon	*Penstemon linarioides*	California laurel	*Umbellularia californica*
Tobosa	*Hilaria mutica*	Sea oats	*Uniola paniculata*
Tobosagrass	*Hilaria mutica*	Old man's beard	*Usnea* spp.
Tongueleaf violet	*Viola nuttallii*	Blueberry (deerberry)	*Vaccinium* spp.
Toothache tree	*Zanthoxylum clavaherculis*	Sparkleberry	*Vaccinium arboreum*
Torpedo grass	*Panicum repens*	Highbush blueberry	*Vaccinium corymbosum*
Toyon (Christmas-berry)	*Heteromeles arbutifolia*	Ground blueberry	*Vaccinium myrsinites*
Trailing-arbutus (mayflower)	*Epigaea repens*	Evergreen huckleberry	*Vaccinium ovatum*
Trefoil	*Lotus* spp.	Western huckleberry	*Vaccinium ovatum*
Triticali	*Triticosecale wittm*	Grouse whortleberry	*Vaccinium scoparium*
Tropic croton	*Croton glandulosus*	Common deerberry	*Vaccinium stamineum*
Trumpet bush	*Tecoma stans*	Squaw huckleberry	*Vaccinium stamineum*
Trumpet vine	*Campsis radicans*	Low blueberry	*Vaccinium vacillans*
Tule	*Scirpus acutus*	Edible valerian	*Valeriana edulis*
Tulip poplar	*Liriodendron tulipifera*	False hellebore	*Veratrum viride*
Tumblemustard	*Sysimbrium loeselii*	Mullein (common mullein)	*Verbascum thapsus*
Tumbleweed	*Amaranthus albus*	Hoary vervian	*Verbena stricta*
Turkey mullein	*Eremocarpus setigerus*	Western ironweed	*Vernonia baldwinii*
Turkey oak	*Quercus laevis*	Viburnum	*Viburnum* spp.
Twisted acacia	*Acacia tortuosa*	Mapleleaf viburnum	*Viburnum acerifolium*
Uinta sandwort	*Aranaria utahensis*	Witherod	*Viburnum cassinoides*
Una de gato	*Acacia greggii*	Arrowwood viburnum	*Viburnum dentatum*
Utah honeysuckle	*Lonicera utahenesis*	Wayfaringbush	*Viburnum lantana*
Utah juniper	*Juniperus osteosperma*	Nannyberry	*Viburnum lentago*
Utah peavine	*Lathyrus utahensis*	Possumhaw viburnum	*Viburnum nudum*
Utah serviceberry	*Amelanchier utahensis*	Rusty blackhaw (southern blackhaw)	*Viburnum rufidulum*
Utah sweetvetch	*Hedysarum boreale*	Cranberry	*Viburnum trilobatum*
Vanilla trilisa	*Trilisa odoratissima*	Vetch (crown vetch)	*Vicia* spp.
Vasey big sagebrush	*Artemisia tridentata vaseyana*	American vetch (purple vetch)	*Vicia americana*
Vasey grass	*Paspalum urvillei*	Narrowleaf vetch	*Vicia angustifolia*
Vasey shinnery oak	*Quercus pungens vaseyana*	Hairy vetch	*Vicia hirsuta*
Vegetable-oyster salsify	*Tragopogon porrifolius*	Bramble vetch	*Vicia tenuifolia*
Velvet lupine	*Lupinus leucophyllus*	Cow pea	*Vigna sinensis*
Velvet mesquite	*Prosopis velutina*	Showy goldeneye	*Viguiera multiflora*
Velvetpod mimosa	*Mimosa dysocarpa*	Nevada showy goldeneye	*Viguiera multiflora nevadensis*
Vetch	*Vicia* spp.		

TABLE A.22 Common and Scientific Names of Plants Mentioned (Continued)

Alphabetical by common name		Alphabetical by scientific name	
Common name	Scientific name	Scientific name	Common name
Viburnum	Viburnum spp.	Viola spp.	Violet
Vine maple	Acer circinatum	Viola nuttallii	Tongueleaf violet
Vine mesquite	Panicum obtusum	Vitis spp.	Grape
Vining honeysuckle	Lonicera spp.	Vitis aestivalis	Summer grape
Violet	Viola spp.	Vitis labrusca	Fox grape
Virginia creeper	Parthenocissus quinquefolia	Vitis rotundifolia	Muscadine grape
Virginia dropseed	Sporobolus virginicus	Vitis vulpina	Frost grape
Virginia pepperweed	Lepidium virginicum	Wyethia amplexicaulis	Mulesear
Virginia pine	Pinus virginiana	Xanthocephalum sarothrae	Broom snakeweed
Walnut	Juglans spp.	Yucca spp.	Yucca
Walter's millet	Echinochloa walteri	Yucca brevifolia	Joshua tree
Wasatch penstemon	Penstemon cyananthus	Zanthoxylum clavaherculis	Toothache tree
Washington hawthorn	Crataegus phaenopyrum	Zanthoxylum fagara	Colima (lime pricklyash)
Water hickory	Carya aquatica	Zea mays	Corn
Water oak	Quercus nigra	Ziziphus obtusifolia	Lotebush (clapany)
Water tupelo	Nyssa aquatica		
Watercress, common	Nasturtium officinal		
Waterlily	Nymphaea odorata		
Wavyleaf oak	Quercus undulata		
Wavyleaf thistle	Cirsium undulatum		
Waxmyrtle	Myrica cerifera		
Waxmyrtle (bayberry)	Myrica spp.		
Wayfaringbush	Viburnum lantana		
Wedgeleaf ceanothus	Ceanothus cuneatus		
Weeping lovegrass	Eragrostis curvula		
Western blackberry	Rubus vitifolius		
Western chokecherry	Prunus virginiana dirissa		
Western dogwood	Cornus occidentalis		
Western hemlock	Tsuga heterophylla		
Western huckleberry	Vaccinium ovatum		
Western ironweed	Vernonia baldwinii		
Western juniper	Juniperus occidentalis		

Western larch	*Larix occidentalis*
Western live oak	*Quercus agrifolia*
Western mountainmahogany	*Cercocarpus betuloides*
Western needlegrass	*Stipa occidentalis*
Western ragweed	*Ambrosia psilostachya*
Western redcedar	*Juniperus* spp.
Western redcedar	*Thuja plicata*
Western snowberry	*Symphoricarpos occidentalis*
Western virginsbower	*Clematis ligusticifolia*
Western wheatgrass	*Agropyron smithii*
Western white pine	*Pinus monticola*
Western yarrow	*Achillea lanulosa*
Wheat	*Triticum aestivum*
Wheatgrass	*Agropyron* spp.
White ash	*Fraxinus americana*
White birch	*Betula papyrifera*
White bursage	*Ambrosia dumosa*
White cedar, northern	*Thuja occidentalis*
White clover	*Trifolium repens*
White fir	*Abies concolor*
White mulberry	*Morus alba*
White oak	*Quercus alba*
White pine	*Pinus strobus*
White poplar	*Populus alba*
White snakeroot	*Eupatorium rugosom*
White spruce	*Picea glauca*
White sweetclover	*Melilotus alba*
Whitebark pine	*Pinus albicaulis*
Whitebrush	*Aloysia lycoides*
Whitetop	*Cardaria draba*
Whitlow-wart	*Paronychia* spp.
Whorled milkweed	*Asclepias verticillata*
Wild apple	*Malus pumila*
Wild bamboo	*Smilax auriculata*
Wild bean	*Strophostyles helvola*
Wild black currant	*Ribes americanum*

TABLE A.22 Common and Scientific Names of Plants Mentioned (Continued)

Alphabetical by common name		Alphabetical by scientific name	
Common name	Scientific name	Scientific name	Common name
Wild buckwheat	*Polygonum convolvulus*		
Wild cherry	*Prunus emarginata*		
Wild indigo	*Baptisia leucophaea*		
Wild lettuce	*Lactuca* spp.		
Wild onion	*Allium stellatum*		
Wild plum	*Prunus* spp.		
Wild rose	*Rosa rugosa*		
Wild rye	*Elymus virginicus*		
Wild sensitive pea (partridge pea)	*Cassia nicitans*		
Wild strawberry	*Fragaria virginiana*		
Wildrye	*Elymus* spp.		
Willow	*Salix* spp.		
Willow oak	*Quercus phellos*		
Willowweed (fireweed)	*Epilobium* spp.		
Wingscale	*Atriplex canescens*		
Winter rye	*Secale cereal*		
Winterberry	*Euonymus* spp.		
Winterberry	*Ilex verticillata*		
Winterfat	*Ceratoides lanata*		
Winterfat	*Eurotia lanata*		
Witch-hazel	*Hamamelis virginiana*		
Witherod	*Viburnum cassinoides*		
Wolfberry	*Lycium berlandieri*		
Woods rose	*Rosa woodsii*		
Woodsorrel	*Oxalis* spp.		
Woolly croton	*Croton capitatus*		
Woolly indianwheat	*Plantago purshii*		
Wooly panic grass	*Panicum lanuginosum*		
Wooly sunflower	*Eriophyllum* spp.		
Wright silktassel	*Garrya wrightii*		
Wyeth eriogonum	*Eriogonum heracleoides*		
Wyoming big sagebrush	*Artemisia tridentata wyomingensis*		

Common name	Scientific name
Yarrow	*Achillea* spp.
Yarrow, common	*Achillea millefolium*
Yaupon	*Ilex vomitora*
Yellow birch	*Betula alleghaniensis*
Yellow bluestem	*Bothriochloa ischaemum*
Yellow bristlegrass	*Setaria lutescens*
Yellow jessamine	*Gelsemium sempervirens*
Yellow paloverde	*Cercidium microphyllum*
Yellow starthistle	*Centaurea solstitialis*
Yellow sweetclover	*Melilotus officinalis*
Yellowbrush	*Chrysothamnus viscidiflorus*
Yellowpoplar (tulip tree)	*Liriodendron tulipifera*
Yucca	*Yucca* spp.

Addendum

Common name	Scientific name
Alkali sagebrush	*Artemisia longiloba*
Arnica	*Arnica* spp.
Big sagebrush	*Artemisia tridentata xericensis*
Bigelow sagebrush	*Artemisia bigelovii*
Black chokecherry	*Prunus virginiana melanocarpa*
Bluebells	*Mertensia* spp.
Cochise lovegrass	*Eragrostis trichophera*
Cotoneaster	*Cotoneaster adultifolia*
Dwarf sagebrush	*Artemisia arbuscula arbuscula*
Goldenbush	*Aplopappus* spp.
Little bluestem	*Schizachyrium scoparium*
Missouri primrose	*Oenothera missourilusis*
Multiflowered false rhodesgrass	*Trichloris pluriflora*
Pink pappusgrass	*Pappophorum bicolor*
Puccoon	*Lithospermum* spp.
Red grama	*Bouteloua trifida*
Scapland sagebrush	*Artemisia rigida*
Sego lily	*Calochortus* spp.
Spineless hopsage	*Grayia brandegei*
Subalpine sagebrush	*Artemisia tridentata rothrockii*
Tamarisk (saltcedar)	*Tamarix hispida*

Scientific name	Common name
Aplopappus spp.	Goldenbush
Arnica spp.	Arnica
Artemisia arbuscula arbuscula	Dwarf sagebrush
Artemisia arbuscula thermopola	
Artemisia argilosa	
Artemisia bigelovii	Bigelow sagebrush
Artemisia longiloba	Alkali sagebrush
Artemisia pymaea	
Artemisia rigida	Scapland sagebrush
Artemisia tridentata rothrockii	Subalpine sagebrush
Artemisia tridentata xericensis	Big sagebrush
Artemisia tripartita rapicola	
Artemisia tripartita tripartita	Three-tip sagebrush
Bouteloua trifida	Red grama
Calochortus spp.	Sego lily
Cotoneaster adultifolia	Cotoneaster
Eragrostis trichophera	Cochise lovegrass
Grayia brandegei	Spineless hopsage
Lithospermum spp.	Puccoon
Mertensia spp.	Bluebells
Oenothera missourilusis	Missouri primrose

TABLE A.22 Common and Scientific Names of Plants Mentioned (Continued)

Alphabetical by common name		Alphabetical by scientific name	
Common name	Scientific name	Scientific name	Common name
Texas bristlegrass	*Setaria texana*	*Pappophorum bicolor*	Pink pappusgrass
Three-tip sagebrush	*Artemisia tripartita tripartita*	*Perideridia* spp.	Yampa
Yampa	*Perideridia* spp.	*Prunus virginiana melanocarpa*	Black chokecherry
	Artemisia arbuscula thermopola	*Schizachyrium scoparium*	Little bluestem
	Artemisia argilosa	*Setaria texana*	Texas bristlegrass
	Artemisia pymaea	*Tamarix hispida*	Tamarisk (saltcedar)
	Artemisia tripartita rapicola	*Trichloris pluriflora*	Multiflowered false rhodesgrass

References

Adams, L. W., and A. D. Geis. 1979. Roads and roadside habitat in relation to small mammal distribution and abundance. Pages 54-1 to 54-17 *in* D. Arner and R. E. Tillman, eds. Environmental concerns in rights-of-way management. EPRI WS-78-141, Elec. Power Res. Inst., Palo Alto, CA.

Adamus, P. R., and G. C. Clough. 1978. Evaluating species for protection in natural areas. Biol. Conserv. 13:165–178.

Agee, J. K., and D. R. Johnson, eds. 1988. Ecosystem management for parks and wilderness. Univ. Washington Press, Seattle. 237pp.

Alberta Fish and Wildlife Division. 1984. Developing wildlife habitat by planting trees and shrubs. Habitat Develop. Fact Sheet 1. ENR Rep. 1/121 No. 1. Alberta Fish Wildl. Div., Edmonton. 5pp.

Alberta Fish and Wildlife Division. Undated. Using grass-legume mixtures to improve wildlife habitat. Habitat Develop. Fact Sheet 2. ENR Rep. 1/121-No. 2. Alberta Fish Wildl. Div., Edmonton. 8pp.

Alexander, R. R., and C. B. Edminster. 1977. Regulation and control of cut under uneven-aged management. U.S. For. Serv. Res. Pap. RM-182. 7pp.

Allen, A. A. 1987a. Habitat suitability index models: gray squirrel. U.S. Fish Wildl. Serv. Biol. Rep. 82(10.135). 16pp.

Allen, A. W. 1987b. The relationship between habitat and furbearers. Pages 164–179 *in* M. Novak, J. A. Baker, M. E. Obbard, and B. Malloch, eds. Wild furbearer management and conservation in North America. Ontario Min. Nat. Resour., Toronto.

Allen, D. H. 1991. An insert technique for constructing artificial red-cockaded woodpecker cavities. U.S. For. Serv. Gen. Tech. Rep. SE-73. 19pp.

Allen, D. L. 1969. The farmer and wildlife. Wildl. Manage. Inst., Washington. 62pp.

Allen, H. L. 1987c. Forest fertilizers. J. For. 85:37–46.

Allen, J. A., and H. E. Kennedy, Jr. 1989. Bottomland hardwood reforestation in the lower Mississippi Valley. U.S. Fish Wildl. Serv. Natl. Wetlands Res. Cent., Slidell, LA, and U.S. For. Serv. South. For. Exp. Stn., Stoneville, MS. 28pp.

Alverson, W. S., D. M. Waller, and S. L. Solheim. 1988. Forests too deer: edge effects in northern Wisconsin. Conserv. Biol. 2:348–358.

Ambrose, R. E., C. R. Hinkle, and C. R. Wenzel. 1983. Practices for protecting and enhancing fish and wildlife on coal surface-mined land in the southcentral U.S. U.S. Fish Wildl. Serv. FWS/OBS-83/11. 229pp.

Ambuel, B., and S. A. Temple. 1983. Area-dependent changes in the bird communities and vegetation of southern Wisconsin. Ecology 64:1057–1068.

Anderson, M. A. 1988. Opportunities for habitat enhancement in commercial forestry practice. Pages 129–146 *in* G. P. Buckley, ed. Biological habitat reconstruction. Belhaven Press, New York.

Anderson, E. W., D. L. Franzen, and J. E. Melland. 1990. Forage quality as influenced by prescribed grazing. Pages 56–70 *in* K. E. Severson, tech. coord. Can livestock be used as a tool to enhance wildlife habitat? U.S. For. Serv. Gen. Tech. Rep. RM-194.

Anderson, J. R., E. E. Hardy, J. T. Raach, and R. E. Witmer. 1976. A land use and land cover classification system for use with remote sensor data. U.S. Geol. Surv. Prof. Pap. 964. 28pp.

Anderson, M. A.. 1988. Opportunities for habitat enhancement in commercial forestry practice. Pages 129-146 *in* G. P. Buckley, ed. Biological habitat reconstruction. Belhaven, New York.

Anderson, N. H., J. R. Sedell, L. M. Roberts, and F. J. Triska. 1978. The role of aquatic invertebrates in processing wood debris from coniferous forest streams. Am. Midl. Nat. 100:64–82.

Anderson, R. C., and A. J. Katz. 1993. Recovery of browse-sensitive tree species following release from white-tailed deer *Odocoileus virginianus* Zimmerman browsing pressure. Biol. Conserv. 63:203–208.

Anderson, S. H. 1985. Managing our wildlife resources. 2d ed. Prentice-Hall, Englewood Cliffs, NJ. 492pp.

Anderson, S. H., K. Mann, and H. H. Shugart, Jr. 1977. The effect of transmission-line corridors on bird populations. Am. Midl. Nat. 97:216–221.

Anderson, W. L. 1969. Making land produce useful wildlife. Farm. Bull. 2035. U.S. Dep. Agric., Washington. 29pp.

Andren, H., and P. Angelstam. 1988. Elevated predation rates as an edge effect in habitat islands: experimental evidence. Ecology 69:544–547.

Angelstam, P. 1986. Predation on ground-nesting birds' nests in relation to predator densities and habitat edge. Oikos 47:365–373.

Anthony, R. G., and R. Kozlowski. 1982. Heavy metals in tissues of small mammals inhabiting wastewater irrigated habitats. J. Environ. Qual. 11:20–22.

Archer, S. 1989. Have southern Texas savannas been converted to woodlands in recent history? Am. Nat. 134:545–561.

Archer, S., and F. A. Smeins. 1991. Ecosystem-level processes. Pages 109–139 *in* R. K. Keitschmidt and J. W. Stuth, eds. Grazing management: an ecological perspective. Timber Press, Portland, OR.

Armleder, H. M., R. J. Dawson, and R. N. Thomson. 1986. Handbook for timber and mule deer management co-ordination on winter ranges in the Cariboo Forest region. Land Manage. Handb. 13, British Columbia Min. For., Victoria. 98pp.

Armstrong, J. B. 1992. Bat management in Alabama. Coop. Ext. Serv., Auburn Univ., Auburn, AL. 4pp.

Arner, D. H. 1977. Transmission line rights-of-way management. U.S. Fish Wildl. Serv. FWS/OBS-76/20.2. 12pp.

Arnold, G. H. 1983. The influence of ditch and hedgerow structure, length of hedgerows, and area of woodland and gardens on bird numbers in farmland. J. Appl. Ecol. 20:731–750.

Ashton, F. M., and A. S. Crafts. 1981. Modes of action of herbicides. 2d ed. Wiley, New York. 525pp.

Askins, R. A., J. F. Lynch, and R. Greenberg. 1990. Population declines in migratory birds in eastern North America. Current Ornithol. 7:1–57.

Askins, R. A., M. J. Philbrick, and D. S. Sugeno. 1987. Relationship between the regional abundance of forest and the composition of forest bird communities. Biol. Conserv. 39:129–152.

Atlantic Waterfowl Council. 1972. Techniques handbook of waterfowl habitat development and management. 2d ed. Atlantic Waterfowl Counc., Bethany Beach, DE. 218pp.

Autenrieth, R., W. Molini, and C. Braun. 1982. Sage grouse management practices. West. States Sage Grouse Comm., Twin Falls, ID. 42pp.

Autenrieth, R. E. 1978. Guidelines for the management of pronghorn antelope. Proc. Pronghorn Antelope Workshop (Alberta Rec., Parks Wildl., Lethbridge) 8:473–526.

Avery, M. L., ed. 1978. Impact of transmission lines on birds in flight. U.S. Fish Wildl. Serv. FWS/OBS-78/48. 151pp.

Bailey, J. A. 1984. Principles of wildlife management. Wiley, New York. 373pp.

Bailey, J. A., and M. M. Alexander. 1960. Use of closed conifer plantations by wildlife. N. Y. Fish Game J. 7:130–148.

Bailey, R. G. 1977. A new map of the ecosystem regions of the United States. Pages 121–128 *in* Classification, inventory, and analysis of fish and wildlife habitat—the proceedings of a national symposium. U.S. Fish Wildl. Serv. FWS/OBS-78/76.

Bailey, R. G. 1978. Description of the ecoregions of the United States. U.S. For. Serv., Ogden, UT. 79pp.

Baker, D. L., and F. S. Guthery. 1990. Effect of continuous grazing on habitat and density of ground foraging birds in south Texas. J. Range Manage. 43:2-5.

Baker, M. F., and N. C. Frischnecht. 1973. Small mammals increase on recently cleared and seeded juniper rangeland. J. Range Manage. 26:101–103.

Baker, M. F., R. L. Eng, J. S. Gashwiler, M. H. Schroeder, and C. E. Braun. 1976. Observation committee report on effects of alteration of sagebrush communities on the associated avifauna. Wilson Bull. 88:165–171.

Balcom, R., C. A. Bowen, D. Wright, and M. Law. 1984. Effects on wildlife of at-planting corn applications of granular carbofuran. J. Wildl. Manage. 48:1353–1359.

Balda, R. P. 1975. Vegetation structure and breeding bird density. Pages 59–80 in D. R. Smith, tech. coord. Proceedings of the symposium on management of forests and range habitats for nongame birds. U.S. For. Serv. Gen. Tech. Rep. WO-1.

Balda, R. P., and N. Masters. 1980. Avian communities in the pinyon-juniper woodland: a descriptive analysis. Pages 146–169 in R. M. DeGraaf and N. G. Tilghman, eds. Workshop proceedings: management of western forests and grasslands for nongame birds. U.S. For. Serv. Gen. Tech. Rep. INT-86.

Baldwin, D. M., N. W. Hawkinson, and E. W. Anderson. 1974. High-rate fertilization of native rangeland in Oregon. J. Range Manage. 27:214–216.

Banasiak, C. 1961. Deer in Maine. Maine Dep. Inland Fish and Game Bull. 6. 159pp.

Bareiss, L. J., P. Schulz, and F. S. Guthery. 1986. Effects of short-duration and continuous grazing on bobwhite and wild turkey nesting. J. Range Manage. 39:259–260.

Barkalow, F. S., Jr., and R. F. Soots, Jr. 1965. An analysis of the effect of artificial nest boxes on a gray squirrel population. Trans. North Am. Wildl. Nat. Resour. Conf. 30:349–360.

Barnes, B. V., K. S. Pregitzer, T. A. Spies, and V. H. Spooner. 1982. Ecological forest site classification. J. For. 80:493–498.

Barnes, T. G. 1991. Bats: information for Kentucky homeowners. Coop. Ext. Serv., Univ. Kentucky, Lexington. 6pp.

Barnett, J. L., R. A. How, and W. F. Humphreys. 1978. The use of habitat components by small mammals in eastern Australia. Austral. J. Ecol. 3:277–285.

Barrett, M. W. 1979. Evaluation of fertilizer on pronghorn winter range in Alberta. J. Range Manage. 32:55–59.

Bartels, R., J. D. Dell, R. L. Knight, and G. Schaefer. 1985. Dead and down woody material. Pages 171–186 in E. R. Brown, ed. Management of wildlife and fish habitats in forests of western Oregon and Washington: Part 1—Chapter narratives. U.S. For. Serv., Portland, OR.

Bartolome, J. W., M. C. Stroud, and H. F. Heady. 1980. Influence of natural mulch on forage production on differing California annual range sites. J. Range Manage. 33:4–8.

Basile, J. V. 1970. Fertilizing to improve elk winter range in Montana. U.S. For. Serv. Res. Note INT-113. 6pp.

Baskett, T. S. 1985. Quality control in wildlife science. Wildl. Soc. Bull. 13:189–196.

Basore, N. S., L. B. Best, and J. B. Wooley. 1986. Bird nesting in Iowa no-tillage and filled cropland. J. Wildl. Manage. 50:19–28.

Bat Conservation International. 1991. Official bat-house builder's guide. Bat Conserv. Internat., Austin, TX. 4pp.

Baxter, W. L. 1982. Wildlife response to ecofallow in Nebraska. Pages 3–4 in R. B. Dahlgren, ed. Proceedings of the Midwest agricultural interfaces with fish and wildlife resources workshop. Iowa State Univ., Ames.

Baxter, W. L., and C. W. Wolfe. 1973. Life history and ecology of the ring-necked pheasant in Nebraska. Nebraska Game, Fish, Parks Comm., Lincoln. 58pp.

Bayoumi, M. A., and A. D. Smith. 1976. Response of big game winter range vegetation to fertilization. J. Range Manage. 24:44–48.

Beale, D. M., and A. D. Smith. 1970. Forage use, water consumption, and reproductivity of pronghorn antelope in western Utah. J. Wildl. Manage. 34:570–582.

Beardall, L. E., and V. E. Sylvester. 1976. Spring burning for removal of sagebrush competition in Nevada. Proc. Tall Timbers Fire Ecol. Conf. 14:539–547.

Beasom, S. L., M. Hernandez, M. Camargo, and C. D. Davis. 1991. Brush shelters to improve use of CRP lands by bobwhites. Page 8 *in* S. L. Beasom and B. Ware, eds. 1991–1992 annual report, Caesar Kleberg Wildlife Research Institute. Texas A&I Univ., Kingsville.

Beasom, S. L., J. M. Inglis, and C. J. Scifres. 1982. Vegetation and white-tailed deer responses to herbicide treatment of a mesquite drainage habitat type. J. Range Manage. 35:790–794.

Beasom, S. L., and C. J. Scifres. 1977. Population reactions of selected game species to aerial herbicide applications in south Texas. J. Range Manage. 30:138–142.

Beaufait, W., P. P. Laird, M. Newton, D. M. Smith, C. H. Tubbs, C. A. Wellner, and H. L. Williston. 1984. Silviculture. Pages 413–455 *in* K. F. Wenger, ed. Forestry handbook. 2d ed. Wiley, New York.

Beaver, D. L. 1976. Avian populations in herbicide treated brush fields. Auk 93:543–553.

Becker, D. Q., F. L. Bunnell, D. W. Janz, J. B. Nyberg, and E. L. Richardson. 1990. Techniques for managing habitat. Pages 133–195 *in* J. B. Nyberg and D. W. Janz, tech. eds. Deer and elk habitats in coastal forests of southern British Columbia. British Columbia Min. For., Victoria.

Bedell, T. E., and H. F. Heady. 1959. Rate of twig elongation of chamise. J. Range Manage. 12:116–118.

Behan, B., and B. L. Welch. 1985. Black sagebrush: mule deer winter preference and monoterpenoid content. J. Range Manage. 38:278–279.

Beier, P., and S. Loe. 1992. A checklist for evaluating impacts to wildlife movement corridors. Wildl. Soc. Bull. 20:434–440.

Bekele, E. 1980. Island biogeography and guidelines for the selection of conservation units for large mammals. Ph.D. thesis, Univ. Michigan, Ann Arbor.

Bell, K. L., and L. C. Bliss. 1973. Alpine disturbance studies: Olympic National Park. Biol. Conserv. 5:25–32.

Bellrose, F. C. 1980. Ducks, geese, and swans of North America. Stackpole Co., Harrisburg, PA. 540pp.

Belovsky, G. E. 1987. Extinction models and mammalian persistence. Pages 35–57 *in* M. E. Soulé, ed. Viable populations for conservation. Cambridge Univ. Press, New York.

Belt, G. H., J. O'Laughlin, and T. Merrill. 1992. Design of forest riparian buffer strips for the protection of water quality: analysis of scientific literature. Idaho For., Wildl. and Range Policy Advisory Group Rep. 8. Idaho For., Wildl. and Range Exp. Stn., Univ. Idaho, Moscow, 35pp.

Bendel, P. R., and J. E. Gates. 1987. Home range and microhabitat partitioning of the southern flying squirrel *Glaucomys volans*. J. Mammal. 68:243–255.

Bennett, A. L. 1962. Industrial forestry and wildlife—the Northeast. J. For. 60:18–20.

Bentley, J. R. 1967. Conversion of chaparral areas to grassland. U.S. Dept. Agric. Handb. 328. 35pp.

Bentley, J. R., and L. R. Green. 1954. Stimulation of native annual clovers through application of sulfur on California foothills range. J. Range Manage. 7:25–30.

Bergerud, A. T. 1978. Caribou. Pages 83–101 *in* J. L. Schmidt and D. L. Gilbert, eds. Big game of North America. Stackpole Books, Harrisburg, PA.

Bergerud, A. T., and F. Manuel. 1968. Moose damage to balsam fir-white birch forests in central Newfoundland. J. Wildl. Manage. 32:729–746.

Berner, A. L. 1987. Federal pheasants—impact of federal agricultural programs on pheasant habitat. Pages 45–93 *in* D. L. Hallett, W. R. Edwards, and G. V. Burger, eds. Pheasants: symptoms of wildlife problems on agricultural lands. Symp. Proc. 49th Midwest Fish Wildl. Conf. Milwaukee.

Berthelsen, P. S., L. M. Smith, and R. R. George. 1990. Ring-necked pheasant nesting ecology and production in CRP lands in the Texas southern high plains. Trans. North Am. Wildl. Nat. Resour. Conf. 55:46–56.

Best, L. B. 1972. First-year effects of sagebrush control on two sparrows. J. Wildl. Manage. 36:534–544.

Best, L. B. 1983. Conservation tillage: ecological traps for nesting birds? Wildl. Soc. Bull. 14:308–317.

Best, L. B. 1986. Bird use of fencerows: implications of contemporary fencerow management practices. Wildl. Soc. Bull. 4:343–347.

Bidwell, T. G., D. M. Engle, and P. L. Claypool. 1990. Effects of spring headfires and backfires on tallgrass prairie. J. Range Manage. 43:209–212.

Bilby, R. E., and L. J. Wasserman. 1989. Forest practices and riparian management in Washington state: data based regulation development. Pages 87–94 in R. E. Gresswell, B. A. Barton, and J. L. Kershner, eds. Practical approaches to riparian resource management. U.S. Bur. Land Manage., Billings, MT.

Biondini, M. E., A. A. Steuter, and C. E. Grygiel. 1989. Seasonal fire effects on the diversity patterns, spatial distribution and community structure of forbs in the northern mixed prairie, USA. Vegetatio 85:21–31.

Bird, W. M. 1977. Wildlife water basins. U.S. Bur. Land Manage. Tech. Note T/N 298. 7pp.

Bishop, R. C. 1981. Economic considerations affecting landowner behavior. Pages 73–87 in R. T. Dumke, G. V. Burger, and J. R. March, eds. Wildlife management on private lands. Wisconsin Chap. Wildl. Soc., Wisconsin Dep. Nat. Resour., Madison.

Bisson, P. A., R. E. Bilby, M. D. Bryant, C. A. Dolloff, G. B. Grette, R. A. House, M. L. Murphy, K. V. Koski, and J. R. Sedell. 1987. Large woody debris in forested streams in the Pacific Northwest: past, present, and future. Pages 143–190 in E. O. Salo and T. W. Cundy, eds. Streamside management: forestry and fishery interactions. Coll. For. Resour., Univ. Washington, Seattle.

Biswell, H. H. 1969. Prescribed burning for wildlife in California brushlands. North Am. Wildl. Nat. Resour. Conf. 34:438–446.

Biswell, H. H., H. R. Kallander, R. Komarek, R. J. Vogl, and H. Weaver. 1973. Ponderosa fire management: task force evaluation of controlled burning in ponderosa pine forests in central Arizona. Misc. Pub. 2, Tall Timbers Res. Stn., Tallahassee, FL. 49pp.

Biswell, H. H., A. M. Schultz, D. W. Hedrick, and J. I. Mallory. 1953. Frost heaving of grass and brush seedlings on burned chamise brushlands in California. J. Range Manage. 6:172–180.

Bjugstad, A. J., and C. F. Sorg. 1984. The value of wooded draws on the northern High Plains for hunting, furs, and woodcutting. Pages 5–9 in D. L. Noble and R. P. Winokur, eds. Wooded draws: characteristics and values for the northern Great Plains. South Dakota School Mines and Tech. Agric. Pub. 111, Rapid City.

Black, H., R. J. Scherzinger, and J. W. Thomas. 1976. Relationships of Rocky Mountain elk and Rocky Mountain mule deer habitat to timber management in the Blue Mountains of Oregon and Washington. Pages 11–31 in J. M. Peek, ed. Proceedings of the elk-logging-roads symposium. For., Wildl. and Range Exp. Stn., Univ. Idaho, Moscow.

Black, H. C., tech. ed. 1992. Silvicultural approaches to animal damage management in Pacific Northwest forests. U.S. For. Serv. Gen. Tech. Rep. PNW-GTR-287. 422pp.

Blair, R. M., R. Alcaniz, and A. Harrell. 1983. Shade intensity influences the nutrient quality and digestibility of southern deer browse leaves. J. Range Manage. 36:257–264.

Blair, R. M., and D. P. Feduccia. 1977. Midstory hardwoods inhibit deer forage in loblolly pine plantations. J. Wildl. Manage. 41:677–684.

Blaisdell, J. P. 1953. Ecological effects of planned burning of sagebrush-grass on the upper Snake River plains. U.S. Dep. Agric. Tech. Bull. 1075. 39pp.

Blakely, K. L., J. A. Crawford, R. S. Lutz, and K. M. Kilbride. 1990. Response of key foods of California quail to habitat manipulations. Wildl. Soc. Bull. 18:240–245.

Bleich, V. C., L. J. Coombes, and J. H. Davis. 1982. Horizontal wells as a wildlife habitat improvement technique. Wildl. Soc. Bull. 10:324–328.

Bleich, V. C., and S. A. Holl. 1982. Management of chaparral habitat for mule deer and mountain sheep in southern California. Pages 247–254 in C. E. Conrad and W. C. Oechel, tech. coords. Dynamics and management of Mediterranean-type ecosystems. U.S. For. Serv. Gen. Tech. Rep. PSW-58.

Bleich, V. C., and R. A. Weaver. 1983. "Improved" sand dams for wildlife habitat management. J. Range Manage. 36:133.

Blymer, J. R., and H. S. Mosby. 1977. Deer utilization of clearcuts in southwestern Virginia. South. J. Appl. For. 1:10–13.

Bock, C. E., and J. H. Bock. 1988. Effects of fire on wildlife in southwestern lowland habitats. Pages 50–64 *in* J. S. Krammes, tech. coord. Effects of fire management of southwestern natural resources. U.S. For. Serv. Gen. Tech. Rep. RM-191.

Bock, C. E., J. H. Bock, W. R. Kenney, and V. M. Hawthorne. 1984. Responses of birds, rodents, and vegetation to livestock exclusion in a semidesert grassland site. J. Range Manage. 37:239–242.

Bock, C. E., and B. Webb. 1984. Birds as grazing indicator species in southern Arizona. J. Wildl. Manage. 48:1045–1049.

Boer, A. 1978. Management of deer wintering areas in New Brunswick. Wildl. Soc. Bull. 6:200–205.

Bohm, R. T. 1977. Artificial nest platforms for raptors. Raptor Res. 11:97–99.

Bohmont, B. L. 1984. Pesticides and application methods. Pages 75B–79B *in* F. R. Henderson, ed. Guidelines for increasing wildlife on farms and ranches. Coop. Ext. Serv., Kansas State Univ., Manhattan.

Bohn, C., C. Galen, C. Maser, and J. W. Thomas. 1980. Homesteads—manmade avian habitats in the rangelands of southeastern Oregon. Wildl. Soc. Bull. 8:332–341.

Bormann, F. H., and G. E. Likens. 1979. Pattern and process in a forested ecosystem. Springer-Verlag, New York. 253pp.

Botkin, D. B. 1990. Discordant harmonies: a new ecology for the twenty-first century. Oxford Univ. Press, New York. 241pp.

Box, T. W. 1964. Changes in wildlife habitat composition following brush control practices in south Texas. North Am. Wildl. Nat. Resour. Conf. 29:432–438.

Box, T. W., J. Powell, and D. L. Drawe. 1967. Influence of fire on South Texas chaparral communities. Ecology 48:955–961.

Box, T. W., and R. S. White. 1969. Fall and winter burning of south Texas brush ranges. J. Range Manage. 22:373–376.

Boyce, D. A., C. M. White, R. E. F. Escano, and W. F. Lehman. 1982. Enhancement of cliffs for nesting peregrine falcons. Wildl. Soc. Bull. 10:380–381.

Boyd, R. J., A. Y. Cooperrider, P. C. Lent, and J. A. Bailey. 1986. Ungulates. Pages 519–564 *in* A. Y. Cooperrider, R. J. Boyd, and H. R. Stuart, eds. Inventory and monitoring of wildlife habitat. U.S. Bur. Land Manage., Denver.

Boyer, D. A., F. S. Guthery, and R. D. Brown. 1988. Evaluation of quail shelters. Page 32 *in* F. S. Guthery, B. D. Davis, and N. E. Koerth, eds. 1987–1988 annual report, Caeser Kleberg Wildlife Research Institute. Texas A&I Univ., Kingsville.

Bozzo, J. A., S. L. Beasom, and T. E. Fulbright. 1989. Effects of discing whitebrush communities on white-tailed deer use. Page 12 *in* F. S. Guthery, B. W. Davis, and N. E. Koerth, eds. 1988–1989 annual report, Caesar Kleberg Wildlife Research Institute. Texas A&I Univ., Kingsville.

Bradley, W. P. 1988. Riparian management practices on Indian lands. Pages 201–206 *in* K. J. Raedeke, ed. Streamside management: riparian wildlife and forestry interactions. Coll. For. Resour., Univ. Washington, Seattle.

Brady, S. J., and R. Hamilton. 1987. Wildlife opportunities within federal agricultural programs. Pages 95–109 *in* D. L. Hallett, W. C. Edwards, and G. V. Burger, eds. Pheasants: symptoms of wildlife problems on agricultural lands. Symp. Proc. 49th Midwest Fish Wildl. Conf., Milwaukee.

Brady, S. S. 1985. Important soil conservation techniques that benefit wildlife. Pages 55–62 *in* S. Schen, proj. dir. Technologies to benefit agriculture and wildlife. U.S. Off. Tech. Assess. OTA-BP-F-34.

Brady, W. W., M. R. Stromberg, E. F. Aldon, C. D. Bonham, and S. H. Henry. 1989. Response of a semidesert grassland to 16 years of rest from grazing. J. Range Manage. 42:284–288.

Branson, F. A. 1985. Vegetation changes on western rangeland. Range Monogr. 2. Soc. Range Manage., Denver.

Branson, F. A.,R. F. Miller, and R. S. McQueen. 1967. Geographical distribution and factors affecting the distribution of salt desert shrubs in the United States. J. Range Manage. 20:287–296.

Bratton, G. F. 1984. Wildlife habitat of small woodlands and woodland borders in the Great Plains. Pages 111B–116B *in* F. R. Henderson, ed. Guidelines for increasing wildlife on farms and ranches. Coop. Ext. Serv., Kansas State Univ., Manhattan.

Braun, C. E. 1980. Alpine bird communities in western North America: implications for management and research. Pages 280–291 *in* R. M. DeGraaf and N. G. Tilghman, eds. Workshop proceedings: management of western forests and grasslands for nongame birds. U.S. For. Serv. Gen. Tech. Rep. INT-86.

Braun, C. E., T. Britt, and R. O. Wallestad. 1977. Guidelines for the maintenance of sage grouse habitats. Wildl. Soc. Bull. 5:99–106.

Bridges, J. M., and D. McConnon. 1981. Nesting platforms for use with transmission or distribution structures. Pages 61-1 to 61-6 *in* D. Arner and R. E. Tillman, eds. Environmental concerns in rights-of-way management. EPRI WS-78-141. Elec. Power Res. Inst., Palo Alto, CA.

Bright, L. 1978. Weather stress differences between two levels of juniper canopy cover. Pages 91–95 *in* R. E. Martin, J. E. Dealy, and O. L. Carter, eds. Proceedings of the western juniper ecology and management workshop. U.S. For. Serv. Gen. Tech. Rep. PNW-74.

Brinkman, K. A., and E. I. Roe. 1975. Quaking aspen: silvics and management in the Lake States. U.S. For. Serv. Handb. 486. 52pp.

Brinson, M. M., B. L. Swift, R. C. Plantico, and J. S. Barclay. 1981. Riparian ecosystems: their ecology and status. U.S. Fish Wildl. Serv. FWS/OBS-81/17. 155pp.

Brittingham, M. C., and S. A. Temple. 1983. Have cowbirds caused forest songbirds to decline? BioScience 33:31–35.

Britton, C. M., and R. G. Clark. 1985. Effects of fire on sagebrush and bitterbrush. Pages 22–26 *in* K. Sanders and J. Durham, eds. Rangeland fire effects: a symposium. U.S. Bur. Land Manage., Boise, ID.

Britton, C. M., and H. A. Wright. 1971. Correlation of weather and fuel variables to mesquite damage by fire. J. Range Manage. 23:136–141.

Brocke, R. H., J. P. O'Pezio, and K. A. Gustafson. 1990. A forest management scheme mitigating impact of road networks on sensitive wildlife species. Pages 13–17 *in* R. M. DeGraaf and W. H. Healy, comps. Is forest fragmentation a management issue in the Northeast? U.S. For. Serv. Gen. Tech. Rep. NE-140.

Bromley, P. T., J. Starr, J. Sims, and D. Coffman. 1990. A landowner's guide to wildlife abundance through forestry. Pub. 420-138. Coop. Ext. Serv., Virginia Polytech. Inst. State Univ., Blacksburg. 26pp.

Bronson, F. A., R. F. Miller, and R. S. McQueen. 1967. Geographical distribution and factors affecting the distribution of salt desert shrubs in the United States. J. Range Manage. 20:287–296.

Brooks, C. 1991. The difference between dead trees and dying forests: tree farming revisited. Inner Voice 3(5):5,10.

Brooks, R. T. 1989. Use of forest site quality in evaluating wildlife habitat: an untested technology. Pages 49–55 *in* R. D. Briggs, W. B. Krohn, J. G. Trial, W. D. Ostrofsky, and D. B. Field, eds., Forest and wildlife management in New England—what can we afford? Maine Agric. Exp. Stn. Misc. Pub. 336. Coll. For. Resour., Univ. Maine, Orono.

Brown, D. 1977. Handbook of equipment for reclaiming strip-mined land. U.S. For Serv. Equipment Cent., Missoula, MT. 58pp.

Brown, D., and R. J. Karsky. 1989. Facilities for watering livestock and wildlife. U.S. Bur. Land Manage. and U.S. For. Serv. 2400-Range, MTDC 89-1. 70pp.

Brown, D. E. 1978. Grazing, grassland cover and gamebirds. Trans. North Am. Wildl. Nat. Resour. Conf. 43:477–485.

Brown, D. E. 1984a. The effects of drought on white-tailed deer recruitment in the arid southwest. Pages 7–12 *in* P. R. Krausman and N. S. Smith, eds. Deer in the southwest: a workshop. New Mexico State Univ., Las Cruces.

Brown, E. R., ed. 1985. Management of wildlife and fish habitats in forests of western Oregon and Washington. Part 2—Appendices. U.S. For. Serv., Portland, OR. 302pp.

Brown, E. R., and A. B. Curtis. 1985. Introduction. Pages 1–15 *in* E. R. Brown, ed. Management of wildlife and fish habitats in forests of western Oregon and Washington. Part 1—Chapter narratives. U.S. For. Serv., Portland, OR.

Brown, E. R., and J. H. Mandery. 1962. Planting and fertilizing as a possible means of controlling distribution of big game animals. J. For. 60:33–35.

Brown, M. T. 1984b. Habitat selection by Coues white-tailed deer in relation to grazing intensity. Pages 1–6 *in* P. R. Krausman and N. S. Smith, eds. Deer in the southwest: a workshop. New Mexico State Univ., Las Cruces.

Brown, M. T., and J. M. Schaefer. 1987. An evaluation of the applicability of upland buffers for the wetlands of the Wekiva Basin. Spec. Pub. SJ 87-SP7, Cent. for Wetlands, Univ. Florida, Gainesville. 163pp.

Brown, M. T., J. M. Schaefer, and K. H. Brandt. 1990. Buffer zones for water, wetlands, and wildlife in east central Florida. CFW Pub. 89-07, Cent. for Wetlands, Univ. Florida, Gainesville. 172pp.

Brown, R. L. 1982. Effects of livestock grazing on Mearns quail in southeastern Arizona. J. Range Manage. 35:727–732.

Brown, R. L. 1990. Effects of a Savory grazing method on big game. Arizona Game and Fish Dep. Tech. Rep. 3. 33pp.

Bryant, F. C. 1982. Grazing, grazing systems, and wildlife. Tech. Article T-9-297, Texas Tech Univ., Lubbock. 13pp.

Bryant, F. C. 1990. Managed habitats for deer in juniper woodlands of west Texas. Pages 56–75 *in* J. E. Rodiek and E.G. Bolen, eds. Wildlife and habitats in managed landscapes. Island Press, Washington.

Bryant, F. C., F. S. Guthery, and W. M. Webb. 1982. Grazing management in Texas and its impact on selected wildlife. Pages 94–112 *in* J. M. Peek and P. D. Dalke, eds. Symposium on wildlife-livestock relationships. For., Wildl., and Range Exp. Stn., Univ. Idaho, Moscow.

Bryant, F. C., G. K. Launchbaugh, and B. H. Koerth. 1983. Controlling mature Ashe juniper in Texas with crown fires. J. Range Manage. 37:165–168.

Bryant, F. C., and L. M. Smith. 1988. The role of wildlife as an economic input into a farming or ranching operation. Pages 95–98 *in* J. F. Mitchell, ed. Impacts of the conservation reserve program in the Great Plains. U.S. For. Serv. Gen. Tech. Rep. RM-158.

Bryant, F. C., C. A. Taylor, and L. B. Merrill. 1981. White-tailed deer diets from pastures in excellent and poor range condition. J. Range Manage. 34:193–200.

Buckley, G. P., ed. 1989. Biological habitat reconstruction. Belhaven Press, New York. 363pp.

Buckner, J. L., and J. L. Landers. 1980. A forester's guide to wildlife management in southern industrial pine forests. Tech. Bull. 10, Internat. Pap. Co., Bainbridge, GA. 16pp.

Budd, W. W., P. L. Cohen, P. R. Saunders, and F. R. Steiner. 1987. Stream corridor management in the Pacific Northwest: I. Determination of stream-corridor widths. Environ. Manage. 11:587–597.

Bull, E. L., R. S. Holthausen, and D. B. Marx. 1990. How to determine snag density. West. J. Appl. For. 5:56–58.

Bull, E. L., and E. C. Meslow. 1977. Habitat requirements of the pileated woodpecker in northwestern Oregon. J. For. 75:335–337.

Bull, E. L., and A. D. Partridge. 1986. Methods of killing trees for use by cavity users. Wildl. Soc. Bull. 14:142–146.

Bull, E. L., A. D. Partridge, and W. G. Williams. 1981. Creating snags with explosives. U.S. For. Serv. Res. Note PNW-393. 4pp.

Bull, E. L., A. D. Twombly, and T. M. Quigley. 1980. Perpetuating snags in managed mixed conifer forest of the Blue Mountains, Oregon. Pages 325–336 *in* R. M. DeGraaf, tech. coord. Workshop proceedings: management of western forests and grasslands for nongame birds. U.S. For. Serv. Gen. Tech. Rep. INT-86.

Bump, G., R. W. Darrow, F. C. Edminster, and W. F. Crissey. 1947. The ruffed grouse. New York State Conserv. Dep., Albany. 915pp.

Bunn, D. S., A. B. Warburton, and R. D. S. Wilson, 1982. The barn owl. Buteo Books, Vermillion, SD. 264pp.

Bunnell, F. L., R. S. McNay, and C. C. Shank. 1985. Trees and snow: the deposition of snow on the ground—a review and quantitative synthesis. IWIFR-17. British Columbia Min. For., Victoria. 439pp.

Bunting, S. C., L. F. Neuenschwander, and G. E. Gruell. 1985. Fire ecology of antelope bitterbrush in the northern Rocky Mountains. Pages 48–57 *in* J. E. Lotan and J. K. Brown, eds. Fire's effects on wildlife habitat. U.S. For. Serv. Gen. Tech. Rep. INT-186.

Bunting, S. C., and H. A. Wright. 1974. Ignition capabilities on nonflaming firebrands. J. For. 78:646–649.

Bunting, S. C., H. A. Wright, and L. F. Neuenschwander. 1980. Long-term effects of fire on cactus in the southern mixed prairie of Texas. J. Range Manage. 33:85–88.

Burger, G. V. 1969. Response of gray squirrels to nest boxes at Remington Farms, Maryland. J. Wildl. Manage. 33:796–801.

Burger, G. V. 1973. Practical wildlife management. Winchester Press, New York. 218pp.

Burger, G. V. 1985. Agricultural lands and wildlife: a perspective. Trans. North Am. Wildl. Nat. Resour. Conf. 50:133–134.

Burns, R. M., tech. comp. 1983. Silvicultural systems for the major forest types of the United States. U.S. For. Serv. Agric. Handb. 445. 191pp.

Burzlaff, D. F., G. W. Fick, and L. R. Rittenhouse. 1968. Effect of nitrogen fertilizer on certain factors of a western Nebraska range ecosystem. J. Range Manage. 21:21–24.

Busch, F. 1989. Integrated forest, farm and wildlife management. Circ. 646, Coop. Ext. Serv., Clemson Univ., Clemson, SC. 21pp.

Buttery, R. F., and P. W. Shields. 1975. Range management practices and bird habitat values. Pages 183–189 *in* D. R. Smith, tech. coord. Proceedings of the symposium on management of forests and range habitats for nongame birds. U.S. For. Serv. Gen. Tech. Rep. WO-1.

Byelich, J. D., J. L. Cook, and R. L. Blouch. 1972. Management for deer. Pages 120–125 *in* Aspen symposium proceedings. U.S. For. Serv. Gen. Tech. Rep. NC-1.

Cable, D. R. 1975. Range management in the chaparral type and its ecological basis: the status of our knowledge. U.S. For. Serv. Res. Pap. RM-155. 30pp.

Cacek, T. 1984a. Organic farming. Pages 85B–89B *in* F. R. Henderson, ed. Guidelines for increasing wildlife on farms and ranches. Coop. Ext. Serv., Kansas State Univ., Manhattan.

Cacek, T. 1984b. Opportunities with land set-aside programs. Pages 91b–92B *in* F. R. Henderson, ed. Guidelines for increasing wildlife on farms and ranches. Coop. Ext. Serv., Kansas State Univ., Manhattan.

California Department of Forestry and Fire Protection. 1991. California forest practice rules. California Dep. For. and Fire Protection, Sacramento, 150pp.

Call, M. 1979. Habitat management for birds of prey. U.S. Bur. Land Manage. Tech. Rep., Denver. 70pp.

Campbell, D. L., and L. E. Johnson. 1981. Guide for collecting and seeding native forbs for wildlife in Douglas-fir clearcuts. U.S. Fish Wildl. Serv. Wildl. Leafl. 513. 13pp.

Campbell, H., D. K. Martin, P. E. Ferkovick, and B. K. Harris. 1973. Effects of hunting and some other environmental factors on scaled quail in New Mexico. Wildl. Monogr. 34. 49pp.

Campbell-Kissock, L., L. H. Blankenship, and J. W. Stewart. 1985. Plant and animal foods of bobwhite and scaled quail in southwest Texas. Southwest. Nat. 30:543–553.

Campbell-Kissock, L., L. H. Blankenship, and L. D. White. 1984. Grazing management impacts on quail during drought in the northern Rio Grande Plain, Texas. J. Range Manage. 37:442–446.

Capel, S. 1984. Hedgerows and field border management. Pages 123B–126B *in* F. R. Henderson, ed. Guidelines for increasing wildlife on farms and ranches. Coop. Ext. Serv., Kansas State Univ., Manhattan.

Capel, S. W. 1988. Design of windbreaks for wildlife in the Great Plains of North America. Agric., Ecosystems, and Environ. 22/23:337–347.

Capp, J. C., and M. Mehl. 1984. Tree, tree stand, and wood volume characteristics for alternative silvicultural prescriptions. Pages 401–404 *in* R. L. Hoover and D. L. Wills, eds. Managing forested lands for wildlife. Colorado Div. Wildl., Denver.

Capp, J. C., W. W. Sandfort, and J. F. Lipscomb. 1984. Application—"Managing forested lands for wildlife"—Roaring Creek Management Area, Roosevelt National Forest. Pages 323–346 *in* R. L. Hoover and D. L. Wills, eds. Managing forested lands for wildlife. Colorado Div. Wildl., Denver.

Carey, A. B., and J. D. Gill. 1980. Firewood and wildlife. U.S. For. Serv. Res. Note NE-299. 5pp.

Carey, A. B., and J. D. Gill. 1983. Direct habitat improvements—some recent advances. Pages 80–87 in J. W. Davis, G. A. Goodwin, and R. A. Ockenfels, tech. coord. Snag habitat management: proceedings of the symposium. U.S. For. Serv. Gen. Tech. Rep. RM-99.

Carl, C. M., J. R. Donnelly, W. J. Gabriel, L. D. Garrett, R. A. Gregory, N. K. Huyler, W. L. Jenkins, R. E. Sendak, R. S. Walters, and H. W. Yawney. 1982. Sugar maple research: sap production, processing, and marketing of maple syrup. U.S. For. Serv. Gen. Tech. Rep. NE-72. 109pp.

Carlson, C. A. 1985. Wildlife and agriculture: can they coexist? J. Soil Water Conserv. 40:263–266.

Carothers, S. W., and R. R. Johnson. 1975. Water management practices and their effects on nongame birds in range habitats. Pages 210–222 in D. R. Smith, tech. coord. Proceedings of the symposium on management of forests and range habitats for nongame birds. U.S. For. Serv. Gen. Tech. Rep. WO-1.

Carpenter, L. H., and G. L. Williams. 1972. A literature review on the role of mineral fertilizers in big game range improvement. Colorado Div. Game, Fish Parks Spec. Rep. 28. 25pp.

Cassel, J. F., and J. M. Wiehe. 1980. Uses of shelterbelts by birds. Pages 78–87 in R. M. DeGraaf, tech. coord. Workshop proceedings: management of western forests and grasslands for nongame birds. U.S. For. Serv. Gen. Tech. Rep. INT-86.

Castrale, J. S. 1982. Effects of two sagebrush control methods on nongame birds. J. Wildl. Manage. 46:945–951.

Castrale, J. S. 1985. Responses of wildlife to various tillage conditions. Trans. North Am. Wildl. Nat. Resour. Conf. 50:142–156.

Chadwick, N. L., D. R. Progulske, and J. T. Finn. 1986. Effects of fuelwood cutting on birds in southern New England. J. Wildl. Manage. 59:398–405.

Chamrad, A. D., and J. D. Dodd. 1973. Prescribed burning and grazing for prairie chicken habitat manipulation in the Texas Coastal Prairie. Proc. Tall Timbers Fire Ecol. Conf. 12:257–276.

Chandler, C., P. Cheney, P. Thomas, L. Trabaud, and D. Williams. 1983a. Fire in forestry: forest fire behavior and effects. Wiley, New York. 540pp.

Chandler, C., P. Cheney, P. Thomas, L. Trabaud, and D. Williams. 1983b. Fire in forestry: forest fire management and organization. Wiley, New York. 298pp.

Chapman, J. A., and G. A. Feldhamer, eds. 1982. Wild mammals of North America: biology, management, and economics. Johns Hopkins Univ. Press, Baltimore. 1147pp.

Chapman, J. A., J. G. Hockman, and W. R. Edwards. 1982. Cottontails. Pages 83–123 in J. A. Chapman and G. A. Feldhamer, eds. Wild mammals of North America: biology, management, and economics. Johns Hopkins Univ. Press, Baltimore.

Chase, G., and C. W. Severinghaus. 1949. Winter deer feeding. New York Conserv. Dep. Fish Wildl. Inf. Bull. 3. 16pp.

Chasko, G. G., and J. E. Gates. 1982. Avian habitat suitability along a transmission-line corridor in an oak-hickory forest region. Wildl. Monogr. 82. 41pp.

Christensen, D. R., S. B. Monsen, and A. P. Plummer. 1966. Response of seeded and native plants six and seven years after eradication of Utah juniper. Proc. West Assoc. State Game and Fish Comm. 46:162–180.

Christensen, G. C. 1954. The chukar partridge in Nevada. Nevada Fish Game Comm. Biol. Bull. 1. 77pp.

Christensen, W. W., and A. E. Grafton. 1966. Characteristics, objectives, and motivations of woodland owners in West Virginia. Agric. Exp. Stn. Bull. 638, Univ. West Virginia, Morgantown. 28pp.

Cimon, N. 1983. A simple model to predict snag levels in managed forests. Pages 200–204 in J. W. Davis, G. A. Goodwin, and R. A. Ockenfels, tech. coord. Snag habitat management: proceedings of the symposium. U.S. For. Serv. Gen. Tech. Rep. RM-99.

Clark, W. R., and R. E. Young. 1986. Crop damage by small mammals in no-till corn-fields. J. Soil Water Conserv. 41:338–341.

Clary, W. P. 1986. Black sagebrush response to grazing in the east-central Great Basin. Pages 181–185 *in* E. D. McArthur and B. L. Welch, comps. Proceedings: symposium on the biology of Artemisia and Chrysothamnus. U.S. For. Serv. Gen. Tech. Rep. INT-200.

Clary, W. P. 1988. Plant density and cover response to several seeding techniques following wildfire. U.S. For. Serv. Res. Note INT-384. 6pp.

Cline, S. P., A. B. Berg, and H. M. Wight. 1980. Snag characteristics and dynamics in Douglas-fir forests, western Oregon. J. Wildl. Manage. 44:773–786.

Cohen, W. E., D. L. Drawe, F. C. Bryant, and L. C. Bradley. 1989a. Observations on white-tailed deer and habitat response to livestock grazing in south Texas. J. Range Manage. 42:361–365.

Cohen, W. E., R. J. Reiner, F. C. Bryant, D. L. Drawe, and L. C. Bradley. 1989b. Daytime activity of white-tailed deer in response to short duration and continuous grazing. Southwest. Nat. 34:428–431.

Collins, C. T., and R. E. Landry. 1977. Artificial nest burrows for burrowing owls. North Am. Bird Bander 2:151–154.

Collins, S. L., and D. J. Gibson. 1990. Effects of fire on community structure in tallgrass and mixed-grass prairie. Pages 81–98 *in* S. L. Collins and L. L. Wallace, eds. Fire in North American tallgrass prairies. Univ. Oklahoma Press, Norman.

Colvin, B. A. 1983. Nest boxes for barn owls. Ohio Dep. Nat. Resour. Div. Wildl. Publ. 346 (183).

Committee on Agricultural Land Use and Wildlife Resources. 1970. Land use and wildlife resources. Natl. Acad. Sci., Washington. 262pp.

Connecticut Department of Environmental Protection. 1988a. Openings for wildlife. Connecticut Dep. Environ. Prot. Wildl. Bur. Inf. Ser. TA-H-3. 4pp.

Connecticut Department of Environmental Protection. 1988b. Daylighting roads and trails to create edge. Connecticut Dep. Environ. Prot. Wildl. Bur. Inf. Ser. TA-H-2. 3pp.

Connecticut Department of Environmental Protection. 1988c. Rejuvenating old apple trees. Connecticut Dep. Environ. Prot. Wildl. Bur. Inf. Ser. TA-H-4. 3pp.

Connecticut Department of Environmental Protection. 1989. Guidelines for enhancing Connecticut's wildlife habitat through forestry operations. Connecticut Dep. Environ. Prot. Wildl. Bur. Pub. TA-H-9. 14pp.

Connell, D. L., G. Davis, and S. McCormick. 1973. The hospitable oak. U.S. For. Serv., San Francisco. 11pp.

Connell, J. H. 1978. Diversity in tropical rain forests and coral reefs. Science 199:1301–1310.

Connelly, J. W., W. J. Arthur, and O. D. Markham. 1981. Sage grouse leks on recently disturbed sites. J. Range Manage. 34:153–154.

Conner, R. N. 1978. Snag management for cavity nesting birds. Pages 120–128 *in* R. M. DeGraaf, tech. coord. Proceedings of the workshop: management of southern forests for nongame birds. U.S. For. Serv. Gen. Tech. Rep. SE-14.

Conner, R. N. 1981. Fire and cavity nesters. Pages 61–65 *in* G. W. Wood, ed. Prescribed fire and wildlife in southern forests. Belle W. Baruch For. Sci. Inst., Clemson Univ., Georgetown, SC.

Conner, R. N. 1988. Wildlife populations: minimally viable or ecologically functional? Wildl. Soc. Bull. 16:80–84.

Conner, R. N., J. G. Dickson, and B. A. Locke. 1981. Herbicide-killed trees infected by fungi: potential cavity sites for woodpeckers. Wildl. Soc. Bull. 9:308–310.

Conner, R. N., J. G. Dickson, B. A. Locke, and C. A. Segelquist. 1983a. Vegetation characteristics important to common songbirds in east Texas. Wilson Bull. 95:349–361.

Conner, R. N., J. G. Dickson, and J. H. Williamson. 1983b. Potential woodpecker nest trees through artificial inoculation of heart rots. Pages 68–72 *in* J. W. Davis, G. A. Goodwin, and R. A. Ockenfels, tech. coord. Snag habitat management: proceedings of the symposium. U.S. For. Serv. Gen. Tech. Rep. RM-99.

Conner, R. N., J. C. Kroll, and D. L. Kulhavy. 1983c. The potential of girdled and 2 4-D injected southern red oaks as woodpecker nesting and foraging sites. South. J. Appl. For. 7:125–128.

Conner, R. N., and D. C. Rudolph. 1989. Red-cockaded woodpecker and colony status on the Angelina, Davy Crockett, and Sabine national forests. U.S. For. Serv. Res. Pap. 50-250. 15pp.

Connors, M. A. Undated. Community wildlife involvement program field manual. Ontario Min. Nat. Resour., Toronto. Various pages.

Conroy, M. J., R. G. Oderwald, and T. L. Sharik. 1982. Forage production and nutrient concentrations in thinned loblolly pine plantations. J. Wildl. Manage. 46:719–727.

Cook, C. W. 1966. Development and use of foothill ranges in Utah. Utah Agric. Exp. St. Bull. 461. 47pp.

Cook, P. S., and T. T. Cable. 1990. The economic value of windbreaks for hunting. Wildl. Soc. Bull. 18:337–342.

Cooperrider, A. Y., R. J. Boyd, and H. R. Stuart, eds. 1986. Inventory and monitoring of wildlife habitat. U.S. Bur. Land Manage., Denver. 858pp.

Copelin, F. F. 1963. The lesser prairie chicken in Oklahoma. Oklahoma Wildl. Conserv. Dep. Bull. 6. 16pp.

Copeyon, C. K. 1990. A technique for constructing cavities for the red-cockaded woodpecker. Wildl. Soc. Bull. 18:303–311.

Cordell, H. K., L. M. Anderson, C. W. Berisford, Y. C. Berisford, L. Biles, P. E. Black, R. M. DeGraaf, F. Deneke, R. Dewers, J. E. Gallaher, G. W. Grey, D. L. Ham, L. Herrington, J. J. Kielbaso, G. Moll, and B. E. Mulligan. 1984. Urban forestry. Pages 887–983 in K. E. Wenger, ed. Forestry handbook. Wiley, New York.

Cosper, H. R., and J. R. Thomas. 1961. Influence of supplemental water and fertilizer on production and chemical composition of native forage. J. Range Manage. 14:292–297.

Cosper, H. R., J. R. Thomas, and A. Y. Alsayegh. 1967. Fertilization and its effect on range improvement in the Northern Great Plains. J. Range Manage. 20:216–227.

Countryman, C. M. 1971. Fire whorls...why, when, and where. U.S. For. Serv. Pac. Southwest For. Range Exp. Stn., Berkeley, CA. 11pp.

Coupland, R. T., ed. 1992. Ecosystems of the world 8A: Natural grasslands—introduction and Western Hemisphere. Elsevier, New York. 469pp.

Cowan, J. 1959. "Pre-fab" wire mesh cone gives doves better nest then they can build themselves. Outdoor Calif. 20(1):10–11.

Cowan, W. F. 1982. Waterfowl production on zero tillage farms. Wildl. Soc. Bull. 19:305–308.

Craig, G. R., and W. C. Andersen. 1978. Ferruginous hawk nesting studies. Colorado Div. Wildl., Job Prog. Rep., Proj. W-124-R:111–120.

Craven, S. 1981. Wisconsin woodlands: wildlife management. G3097, Coop. Ext. Serv., Univ. Wisconsin, Madison. 7pp.

Crawford, H. S., and R. M. Frank. 1987. Wildlife habitat responses to silvicultural practices in spruce-fir forests. Trans. North Am. Wildl. Nat. Resour. Conf. 52:92–100.

Crawford, H. S., and R. W. Titterington. 1979. Effects of silvicultural practices on bird communities in upland spruce-fir stands. Pages 110–119 in R. M. DeGraaf, tech. coord. Workshop proceedings: management of northcentral and northeastern forests for nongame birds. U.S. For. Serv. Gen. Tech. Rep. NC-51.

Crawford, J. A., and E. G. Bolen. 1976a. Effects of land use on lesser prairie chicken populations in west Texas. J. Wildl. Manage. 40:96–104.

Crawford, J. A., and E. G. Bolen. 1976b. Fall diet of lesser prairie chickens in west Texas. Condor 78:142–144.

Crawford, J. A., M. A. Gregg, M. S. Drut, and A. K. DeLong. 1992. Habitat use by female sage grouse during the breeding season in Oregon. Final rep. to Bur. Land Manage. Dep. Fish. Wildl., Oregon State Univ., Corvallis. 83pp.

Cross, D. C. 1984. The food habits of white-tailed deer on the Kerr Wildlife Management Area in conjunction with prescribed burning and rotational livestock grazing systems. M. S. thesis, Southwest Texas State Univ., San Marcos. 134pp.

Crow, T. R. 1991. Landscape ecology: the big picture approach to landscape management. Pages 55–65 in D. J. Decker. M. E. Krasny, G. R. Goff, C. R. Smith, and D. W. Gross, eds. Challenges in the conservation of biological resources: practitioner's guide. Westview Press, Boulder, CO.

Cuplin, P. 1986a. Fish. Pages 257–266 in A. Y. Cooperrider, R. J. Boyd, and H. R. Stuart, eds. Inventory and monitoring of wildlife habitat. U.S. Bur. Land Manage., Denver.

Cuplin, P. 1986b. Water quality. Pages 633–638 *in* A. Y. Cooperrider, R. J. Boyd, and H. R. Stuart, eds. Inventory and monitoring of wildlife habitat. U.S. Bur. Land Manage., Denver.

Curlin, J. W. 1962. Dogwood response to nitrogen fertilization. J. For. 69:718–719.

Curtis, J. T. 1959. The vegetation of Wisconsin. Univ. Wisconsin Press, Madison. 657pp.

Daddy, F., M. J. Trlica, and C. D. Bonham. 1988. Vegetation and soil water differences among big sagebrush communities with different grazing histories. Southwest. Nat. 33:413–424.

Dalke, P. D., D. B. Pyrah, D. C. Stanton, J. E. Crawford, and E. F. Schlatterer. 1963. Ecology, productivity, and management of sagegrouse in Idaho. J. Wildl. Manage. 27:811–841.

Daniel, T. W., J. A. Helms, and F. S. Baker. 1979. Principles of silviculture. 2d ed. McGraw-Hill, New York. 500pp.

Darr, G. W., and D. A. Klebenow. 1975. Deer, brush control, and livestock on the Texas Rolling Plains. J. Range Manage. 28:115–119.

Daubenmire, R., and J. B. Daubenmire. 1968. Forest vegetation of eastern Washington and northern Idaho. Washington Agric. Exp. Stn. Tech. Bull. 60. Washington State Univ., Pullman. 104pp.

David, L. M., and R. E. Warner. 1979. Roadside management for pheasants and song-birds in east-central Illinois. Pages 63-1 to 63-8 *in* D. Arner and R. E. Tillman, eds. Environmental concerns in rights-of-way management. EPRI WS-78-141. Elec. Power Res. Inst., Palo Alto, CA.

Davis, C. A., T. Z. Riley, R. A. Smith, H. R. Summiski, and M. J. Wisdom. 1979. Habitat evaluation of lesser prairie chickens in eastern Chaves County, New Mexico. Agric. Exp. Stn., Dep. Fish Wildl. Sci., New Mexico State Univ., Las Cruces. 141pp.

Davis, G. E. 1989. Design of a long-term ecological monitoring program for Channel Islands National Park, California. Nat. Areas J. 9:80–89.

Davis, J. N., and K. T. Harper. 1990. Weedy annuals and establishment of seeded species on a chained juniper-pinyon woodland in central Utah. Pages 72–79 *in* E. D. McArthur, E. M. Romney, S. D. Smith, and P. T. Tueller, comps. Cheatgrass invasion, shrub die-off, and other aspects of shrub biology and management. U.S. For. Ser. Gen. Tech. Rep. INT-276.

Davis, J. W. 1983. Snags are for wildlife. Pages 4–9 *in* J. W. Davis, G. A. Goodwin, and R. A. Ockenfels, tech. coord. Snag habitat management: proceedings of the symposium. U.S. For. Serv. Gen. Tech. Rep. RM-99.

Davis, R. B., and C. K. Winkler. 1968. Brush vs. cleared range as deer habitat in southern Texas. J. Wildl. Manage. 32:321–329.

Dawson, W. R., J. D. Ligon, J. R. Murphy, J. P. Myers, D. Simberloff, and J. Verner. 1987. Report of the Scientific Advisory Panel on the Spotted Owl. Condor 89:205–229.

Debano, L. F. 1990. Effects of fire on the soil resource in Arizona chaparral. Pages 65-77 *in* J. S. Krammes, tech. coord. Effects of fire management of southwestern natural resources. U.S. For. Serv. Gen. Tech. Rep. RM-191.

DeByle, N. V. 1985. Managing wildlife habitat with fire in the aspen ecosystems. Pages 73–82 *in* Proceedings of the symposium on fire's effects on wildlife habitat. U.S. For. Serv. Gen. Tech. Rep. INT-186.

deCalesta, D. S. 1983. Enhancing wildlife on private woodlands. Ext. Circ. 1122. Ext. Serv., Oregon State Univ., Corvallis. 6pp.

Decker, D. J., and G. R. Goff. 1987. Valuing wildlife. Westview, Boulder, CO. 424pp.

Decker, D. J., and J. W. Kelley. Undated. Enhancement of wildlife habitat on private lands. Inf. Bull. 181. Coll. Agric. Life Sci., Cornell Univ., Ithaca, NY. 40pp.

Decker, D. J., J. W. Kelley, T. W. Seamans, and R. R. Roth. 1983. Wildlife and timber from private land: a landowner's guide to planning. Inf. Bull. 193. New York State Coll. Agric. Life Sci., Cornell Univ., Ithaca, NY. 56pp.

DeGraaf, R. M., R. G. Bailey, and R. T. Brooks. 1988. A comparison of five national land classification maps. U.S. For. Serv. Agric. Handb. 672. 338pp.

DeGraaf, R. M., and A. L. Shigo. 1985. Managing cavity trees for wildlife in the northeast. U.S. For. Serv. Gen. Tech. Rep. NE-101. 21pp.

DeGraaf, R. M., M. Yamasaki, W. B. Leck, and J. W. Lanier. 1992. New England wildlife: management of forested habitats. U.S. For. Serv. Gen. Tech. Rep. NE-144. 271pp.

Dell, J. D., and F. R. Ward. 1970. Building firelines with liquid explosive. U.S. For. Serv. Res. Note PSW-200. 6pp.

Demarchi, D. A., and T. W. Chamberlain. 1978. The Canadian experience: an approach toward biophysical interpretation. Pages 145–155 *in* U.S. Fish and Wildlife Service. Classification, inventory, and analysis of fish and wildlife habitat. U.S. Fish Wildl. Serv. FWS/OBS-78/76.

DeVaney, T. E. 1967. Chemical vegetation control manual for fish and wildlife management programs. U.S. Fish Wildl. Serv. Resour. Publ. 48. 42pp.

Devlin, D., and J. Payne. Undated. Woodland wildlife management. Coop. Ext. Serv., Coll. Agric., Pennsylvania State Univ., University Park. 6pp.

Diamond, J. M. 1975. The island dilemma: lessons of modern biogeographic studies for the design of natural reserves. Biol. Conserv. 7:129–146.

Dickson, J. G. 1978. Forest bird communities of the bottomland hardwoods. Pages 66–73 *in* R. M. DeGraaf, tech. coord. Proceedings of the workshop of southern forests for nongame birds. U.S. For. Serv. Gen. Tech. Rep. SE-14.

Dickson, J. G. 1982. Impact of forestry practices on wildlife in southern pine forests. Pages 224–230 *in* Increasing forest productivity. Proc. 1981 Conv. Soc. Am. For., Bethesda, MD.

Dickson, J. G., and J. C. Huntley. 1987. Riparian zones and wildlife in southern forests: the problem and squirrel relationships. Pages 37–39 *in* J. G. Dickson and O. E. Maughan, eds. Managing southern forests for wildlife. U.S. For. Serv. Gen. Tech. Rep. 50–65.

Dickson, J. G., and R. E. Noble. 1978. Vertical distribution of birds in a Louisiana bottomland hardwood forest. Wilson Bull. 90:19–30.

Dickson, K. L., and D. Vance. 1981. Revegetating surface mined lands for wildlife in Texas and Oklahoma. U.S. Fish Wildl. Serv. FWS/OBS-81/25. 121pp.

Dimock, E. J., II. 1974. Animal populations and damage. Pages 01–028 *in* O. P. Cramer, ed. Environmental effects of forest residues management in the Pacific Northwest: a state-of-knowledge compendium. U.S. For. Serv. Gen. Tech. Rep. PNW-24.

Dodd, J. D. 1968. Mechanical control of pricklypear and other woody species on the Rio Grande plains. J. Range Manage. 21:366–370.

Dodd, N. L., and S. L. Adams. 1989. Integrating wildlife needs into national forest timber sale planning: a state agency perspective. Pages 131–140 *in* A. Tecle, W. W. Covington, and R. H. Hamre, tech. coords. Multiresource management of ponderosa pine forests. U.S. For. Serv. Gen. Tech. Rep. RM-185.

Dodd, N. L., and W. W. Brady. 1986. Cattle grazing influences on vegetation of a sympatric desert bighorn range in Arizona. Desert Bighorn Counc. Trans. 30:8–18.

Doerr, T. B. 1986a. Grass seeder. Sec. 8.4.5. U.S. Army Corps of Engineers wildlife resources management manual. U.S. Army Eng. Waterways Exp. Stn. Tech. Rep. EL-86-32. 7pp.

Doerr, T. B. 1986b. Pasture drills. Sec. 8.4.2. U.S. Army Corps of Engineers wildlife resources management manual. U.S. Army Eng. Waterways Exp. Stn. Tech. Rep. EL-86-48. 9pp.

Doerr, T. B. 1986c. Press seeder and punch seeder. Sec. 8.4.4. U.S. Army Corps of Engineers wildlife resources management manual. U.S. Army Eng. Waterways Exp. Stn. Tech. Rep. EL-86-49. 8pp.

Doerr, T. B. 1986d. Rangeland drill. Sec. 8.4.3. U.S. Army Corps of Engineers wildlife resources management manual. U.S. Army Eng. Waterways Exp. Stn. Tech. Rep. EL-86-41. 8pp.

Doerr, T. B. 1986e. Steep-slope seeder. Sec. 8.4.6. U.S. Army Corps of Engineers wildlife resources management manual. U.S. Army Eng. Waterways Exp. Stn. Tech. Rep. EL-86-50. 7pp.

Doerr, T. B. 1986f. Hydroseeders/mulchers. Sec. 8.4.7. U.S. Army Corps of Engineers wildlife resources management manual. U.S. Army Eng. Waterways Exp. Stn. Tech. Rep. EL-86-51. 8pp.

Doerr, T. B., M. C. Landin, and C. O. Martin. 1986. Mechanical site preparation techniques. Sec. 5.7.1. U.S. Army Corps of Engineers wildlife resources management manual. U.S. Army Eng. Waterways Exp. Stn. Tech. Rep. EL-86-17. 18pp.

Downey, T. 1976. Emphasizing the benefits of the environmental rehabilitation of natural gas pipeline rights-of-way. Pages 232–240 *in* R. Tillman, ed. Proceedings of the first national symposium on environmental concerns in rights-of-way management. Mississippi State Univ., Mississippi State.

Drawe, D. L. 1981. Wildlife responses to range management practices: the Welder Wildlife Refuge experience—implications for the future. Pages 86–92 *in* Proceedings of the international stockman's school. Beef Cattle Sci. Handb., Vol. 18. San Antonio, TX.

Drawe, D. L., and T. W. Box. 1969. High rates of nitrogen fertilizer influence coastal prairie range. J. Range Manage. 22:32–36.

Dressler, R. C., G. L. Storm, W. M. Tzilkowski, and W. E. Sopper. 1986. Heavy metals in cottontail rabbits on mined lands treated with sewage sludge. J. Environ. Qual. 15:278–281.

Dressler, R. C., and G. L. Wood. 1976. Deer habitat response to irrigation with municipal wastewater. J. Wildl. Manage. 40:639–644.

Driscoll, R. S., D. L. Merkel, D. L. Radloff, D. E. Snyder, and J. S. Hagihara. 1984. An ecological land classification framework for the United States. Misc. Pub. 1439. U.S. For. Serv., Washington.

Duffield, J. W. 1990. Forest regions of North America and the world. Pages 33–61 *in* R. A. Young and R. L. Giese, eds. Introduction to forest science. 2d ed. Wiley, New York.

Dumke, R. T. 1982. Habitat development for bobwhite quail on private lands in Wisconsin. Wisconsin Dep. Nat. Resour. Tech. Bull. 128. 46pp.

Dumke, R. T., G. V. Burger, and J. R. March, eds. 1981. Wildlife management on private lands. Wisconsin Chap. Wildl. Soc., Wisconsin Dep. Nat. Resour., Madison. 568pp.

Dumke, R. T., and C. M. Pils. 1979. Renesting and dynamics of nest site selection by Wisconsin pheasants. J. Wildl. Manage. 43:705–716.

Duncan, D. A. 1976. Frequent mowing increases turkey mullein on California foothill rangeland. Calif. Fish Game 62:117–122.

Duncan, D. A. 1980. Cattle and quail: we can have both on foothill rangelands. Abstr., Soc. Range Manage. Annu. Meet. 33:14.

Dunn, P. H. 1979. The distribution of leafy spurge (*Euphorbia esula*) and other weedy *Euphorbia* species in the United States. Weed Sci. 27:509–516.

Dunstan, T. C., and B. E. Harrell. 1973. Spatio-temporal relationships between breeding red-tailed hawks and great horned owls in South Dakota. Raptor Res. 7:49–54.

Dwyer, D. D. 1975. Response of livestock forage to manipulation of the pinyon-juniper ecosystem. Pages 97–103 *in* G. F. Gifford and F. E. Busby, eds. The pinyon-juniper ecosystem: a symposium. Coll. Nat. Resour., Utah State Univ., Logan.

Edgerton, P. J., and J. W. Thomas. 1978. Silvicultural options and habitat values in coniferous forests. Pages 56–65 *in* R. M. DeGraaf, tech. coord. Proceedings of the workshop on nongame bird habitat management in the coniferous forests of the western United States. U.S. For. Serv. Gen. Tech. Rep. PNW-64.

Ehrenfeld, D. 1976. The conservation of nonresources. Am. Scientist 64:648–656.

Ehrenfeld, D. 1988. Why put a value on biodiversity? Pages 212–216 *in* E. O. Wilson, ed. Biodiversity. Natl. Acad. Press, Washington.

Elder, J. B. 1954. Notes on summer water consumption by desert mule deer. J. Wildl. Manage. 18:540–541.

Elderkin, R. L., and J. Morris. 1989. Design for a durable and inexpensive guzzler. Wildl. Soc. Bull. 17:192–194.

Elliott, C. A. 1988. Riparian zones and wetlands. Pages 12–14 *in* C. A. Elliott, ed. A forester's guide to managing wildlife habitats in Maine. Coop. Ext. Serv., Univ. Maine, Orono.

Ellis, L. E., and J. Kellett. 1970. Experiment with artificial nests. Fla. Nat. 43:148–149.

Ellison, J. F. 1969. Mobility of white-tailed deer in south Texas. J. Wildl. Manage. 33:220–222.

Ellison, L. 1954. Subalpine vegetation of the Wasatch Plateau, Utah. Ecol. Monogr. 24:89–184.

Ellison, L. 1960. Influence of grazing on plant succession of rangelands. Bot. Rev. 26:1–78.

Emmingham, W. H., R. Holthausen, and M. Vomocil. 1992. Silvicultural systems and stand management. Pages 123–142 in H. C. Black, tech. ed. Silvicultural approaches to animal damage management in Pacific Northwest forests. U.S. For. Serv. Gen. Tech. Rep. PNW-GTR-287.

Eng, R. L. 1986. Upland game birds. Pages 407–428 in A. Y. Cooperrider, R. J. Boyd, and H. R. Stuart, eds. Inventory and monitoring of wildlife habitat. U.S. Bur. Land Manage., Denver.

Engle, D. M., T. G. Bidwell, J. F. Stritzke, and D. Rollins. 1990. Atrazine and burning in tallgrass prairie infested with prairie threeawn. J. Range Manage. 43:424–427.

Engle, D. M., J. F. Stritzke, and P. L. Claypool. 1987. Herbage standing crop around eastern redcedar trees. J. Range Manage. 40:237–239.

Erickson, L. R., and P. O. Currie. 1985. Rangeland machine for multiple renovation practices on semiarid rangeland. Trans. Am. Soc. Agric. Eng. 28:94–96.

Erman, D. C., J. D. Newbold, and K. B. Roby. 1977. Evaluation of streamside buffer-strips for protecting aquatic organisms. California Water Resour. Cent. Tech. Completion Rep. Contribution 165, Univ. California, Davis. 48pp.

Eubanks, S. 1989. Applied concepts of ecosystem management: developing guidelines for coarse woody debris. Pages 230–236 in D. A. Perry, R. Meurisse, B. Thomas, R. Miller, J. Boyle, J. Means, C. R. Perry, and R. F. Powers, eds. Maintaining the long-term, productivity of Pacific Northwest forest ecosystems. Timber Press, Portland, OR.

Evanko, A. N., and R. A. Peterson. 1955. Comparisons of protected and grazed mountain rangelands in southwestern Montana. Ecology. 36:71–82.

Evans, K. E., and R. N. Conner. 1979. Snag management. Pages 214–255 in R. M. DeGraff, tech. coord. Workshop proceedings: management of northcentral and northeastern forests for nongame birds. U.S. For Serv. Gen. Tech. Rep. NC-51.

Evans, R. A. 1988. Management of pinyon-juniper woodlands. U.S. For. Serv. Gen. Tech. Rep. INT-249. 34pp.

Evans, R. A., R. E. Eckert, and J. A. Young. 1975. The role of herbicides in management of pinyon-juniper woodlands. Pages 83–89 in G. F. Gifford and F. E. Busby, eds. The pinyon-juniper ecosystem: a symposium. Coll. Nat. Resour., Utah State Univ., Logan.

Evans, R. D. 1974. Wildlife habitat management program: a concept of diversity for the public forests of Missouri. Pages 73–83 in J. P. Slusher and T. M. Hinckley, eds. Timber-wildlife management symposium. Missouri Acad. Sci. Occ. Pap. 3, Univ. Missouri, Columbia.

Everest, F. M., N. B. Armantrout, S. M. Keller, W. D. Parante, J. R. Sedell, T. E. Nickelson, J. M. Johnston, and G. N. Haugen. 1985. Salmonids. Pages 199–230 in E. R. Brown, ed. Management of wildlife and fish habitats in forests of western Oregon and Washington. Part 1—Chapter narratives. U.S. For. Serv., Portland, OR.

Everitt, J. H. 1983. Effects of plant shredding on nutrient content of four south Texas deer forage species. J. Range Manage. 36:779–781.

Eyre, F. H., ed. 1980. Forest cover types of the United States and Canada. Soc. Am. For., Washington. 148pp.

Faaborg, J. 1980. Potential uses and abuses of diversity concepts in wildlife management. Trans. Missouri Acad. Sci. 14:41–49.

Fahnestock, G. R., and R. C. Hare. 1964. Heating of tree trunks in surface fires. J. For. 62:799–805.

Fairbanks, R. 1991. Fire, insects, and drought: eastern Oregon's failing forests. Inner Voice 3(5):7.

Ferguson, R. B. 1968. Survival and growth of young bitterbrush browsed by deer. J. Wildl. Manage. 32:769–772.

Ferguson, R. B., and J. V. Basile. 1966. Topping stimulates bitterbrush twig growth. J. Wildl. Manage. 30:839–841.

Field, N. H. 1971. Use of an eastern South Dakota shelterbelt by nesting birds. South Dak. Bird Notes 23:43–45.

Finch, D. M. 1991. Population ecology habitat requirements, and conservation of neotropical migratory birds. U.S. For. Serv. Gen. Tech. Rep. RM-205. 26pp.

Fitzgerald, R. D., and A. W. Bailey. 1983. Influence of grazing with cattle on establishment of forage in burned aspen brushland. Proc. Int. Grassland Cong. 14:564–566.

Fitzgerald, R. O. 1984. Silvicultural practices can provide diversity in a managed forest. Pages 263–266 *in* J. L. Cooley and J. H. Cooley, eds. Natural diversity in forest ecosystems: proceedings of the workshop. Inst. Ecol., Univ. Georgia, Athens.

Fitzgerald, S. M., and G. W. Tanner. 1992. Avian community response to fire and mechanical shrub control in south Florida. J. Range Manage. 45:396–400.

Fleming, W. J., D. R. Clark, Jr., and C. J. Henny. 1983. Organochlorine pesticides and PCB's: a continuing problem for the 1980's. Trans. North Am. Wildl. Nat. Resour. Conf. 48:186–199.

Flyger, V. F., and H. R. Cooper. 1967. The utilization of nesting boxes by gray squirrels. Proc. Southeast. Assoc. Game and Fish Comm. 21:113–117.

Forestry Canada. 1988. Canada's forest inventory, 1986. Can. Govt. Pub. Cent., Ottawa. 60pp.

Forman, R. T. T. 1983. Corridors in a landscape: their ecological structure and function. Ekologiya (CSSR) 2:375–387.

Forman, R. T. T. 1987. Emerging directions in landscape ecology and applications in natural resource management. Pages 59–88 *in* R. Herrmann and T. Bostedt-Craig, eds. Science in the national parks. Vol. 1. U.S. Natl. Park Serv. and George Wright Soc., Fort Collins, CO.

Forman, R. T.T. 1990. Landscape ecology plans for managing forests. Pages 27–32 *in* R. M. DeGraaf and W. M. Healy, comps. Is forest fragmentation a management issue in the northeast? U.S. For. Serv. Gen. Tech. Rep. NE-140.

Forman, R. T. T., and B. A. Elfstrom. 1975. Forest structure comparison of Hutcheson Memorial Forest and eight old woods on the New Jersey Piedmont. William L. Hutcheson Memorial Bull. 3:44–51.

Forman, R. T. T., and M. Godron. 1986. Landscape ecology. Wiley, New York. 619pp.

Forren, J. D. 1981. Artificial perch use by raptors on reclaimed surface mines in West Virginia. M. S. thesis, West Virginia Univ., Morgantown. 199pp.

Foss, T. 1991. Selection management revisited. Inner Voice 3(5):11.

Foster, M. L., and S. R. Humphrey. 1991. Effectiveness of wildlife crossing structures on alligator alley (I-75) for reducing animal/auto collisions. Florida Game and Fresh Water Fish Comm., Tallahassee. 62pp.

Frankel, O. H. 1983. The place of management in conservation. Pages 1–14 *in* C. M. Schoenwald-Cox, S. M. Chambers, B. MacBryde, and L. Thomas, eds. Genetics and conservation. Benjamin/Cummings, Menlo Park, CA.

Franklin, I. R. 1980. Evolutionary change in small populations. Pages 135–149 *in* M. E. Soulé and B. A. Wilcox, eds. Conservation biology: an evolutionary-ecological perspective. Sinauer Assoc., Sunderland, MA.

Franklin, J. F. 1976. Effects of uneven-aged management on species composition. Pages 64–70 *in* Uneven-aged silviculture and management in the western United States. Proc. In-service Workshop. Timber Manage. Res., U.S. For. Serv., Washington.

Franklin, J. F. 1989. Toward a new forestry. Am. For. Nov/Dec:37–44.

Franklin, J. F., K. Cromack, Jr., W. Denison, A. McKee, C. Maser, J. Sedell, F. Swanson, and G. Juday. 1981. Ecological characteristics of old-growth Douglas-fir forests. U.S. For. Serv. Gen. Tech. Rep. PNW-118. 48pp.

Franklin, J. F., and R. T. T. Forman. 1987. Creating landscape patterns by forest cutting: ecological consequences and principles. Landscape Ecol. 1:5–18.

Franklin, J. F., and T. A. Spies. 1984. Characteristics of old-growth Douglas-fir forests. Pages 328–334 *in* New forests for a changing world. Proc. 1983 Soc. Am. For. Natl. Conv., Soc. Am. For., Bethesda, MD.

Franklin, J. F., and T. A. Spies. 1991. Composition, function, and structure of old-growth Douglas-fir forests. Pages 71–80 *in* L. F. Ruggiero, K. B. Aubry, A. B. Carey, and M. H. Huff, tech. coord. Wildlife and vegetation of unmanaged Douglas-fir forests. U.S. For. Serv. Gen. Tech. Rep. PNW-GTR-285.

Fritschen, L. J., C. H. Driver, C. Avery, J. Buffo, R. Edmonds, R. Kinerson, and P. Schiess. 1971. Dispersion of air tracers into and within a forested area: 3. Res. and Dev. Tech. Rep. ECOM-68-G8-3, U.S. Army Elect. Command, Atmospheric Sci. Lab., Fort Huachuca, AZ.

Fulbright, T. E. 1987. Effects of repeated shredding on a guajillo (*Acacia berlandieri*) community. Texas J. Agric. Nat. Resour. 1:32–33.

Fulbright, T. E., and S. L. Beasom. 1987. Long-term effects of mechanical treatments on white-tailed deer browse. Wildl. Soc. Bull. 15:560–564.

Fulbright, T. E., L. Brothers, E. Montemayor, and B. J. Schat. 1989. Long-term effects of heavy discing on white-tailed deer browse. Page 12 *in* F. S. Guthery, B. W. Davis, and N. E. Koerth, eds. 1988–1989 annual report, Caesar Kleberg Wildlife Research Institute. Texas A&I Univ., Kingsville.

Fulbright, T. E., and A. Garza, Jr. 1991. Forage yield and white-tailed deer diets following live oak control. J. Range Manage. 44:451–455.

Furman, R. W., D. A. Haines, and D. R. Miller. 1984. Forest meteorology and climatology. Pages 97–141 *in* K. F. Wenger, ed. Forestry handbook. 2d ed. Wiley, New York.

Fyfe, R. W., and H. I. Armbruster. 1977. Raptor research and management in Canada. Pages 282–293 *in* R. D. Chancellor, ed. World conference on birds of prey: report of proceedings. Internal Count. Bird Preservation, Vienna, Austria.

Galli, A. E., C. F. Leck, and R. T.T. Forman. 1976. Avian distribution patterns in forest islands of different sizes in New Jersey. Auk 93:356–364.

Gano, R. D., Jr., and J. A. Mosher. 1983. Artificial cavity construction—an alternative to nest boxes. Wildl. Soc. Bull. 11:74–76.

Garrison, G. 1953. Effects of clipping on some range shrubs. J. Range Manage. 6:309–317.

Garrison, G. A., A. J. Bjugstad, D. A. Duncan, M. E. Lewis, and D. R. Smith. 1977. Vegetation and environmental features of forest and range ecosystems. U.S. For. Serv. Agric. Handb. 475. 68pp.

Garrison, G. A., and J. G. Smith. 1974. Habitat of grazing animals. Pages P1–P10 *in* O. P. Cramer, ed. Environmental effects of forest residues management in the Pacific Northwest: a state-of-knowledge compendium. U.S. For. Serv. Gen. Tech. Rep. PNW-24.

Gartner, F. R., and W. W. Thompson. 1972. Fire in the Black Hills forest-grass ecotone. Proc. Tall Timbers Fire Ecol. Conf. 12:37–68.

Gary, H. L., and M. J. Morris. 1980. Constructing wooden boxes for cavity-nesting birds. U.S. For. Serv. Res. Note RM-381. 7pp.

Gates, J. E. 1991. Powerline corridors, edge effects, and wildlife in forested landscapes of the central Appalachians. Pages 13–32 *in* J. E. Rodiek and E. G. Bolen, eds. Wildlife and habitats in managed landscapes. Island Press, Washington.

Gates, J. E., and L. W. Gysel. 1978. Avian nest dispersion and fledging success in field forest ecotones. Ecology 59:871–883.

Gates, J. E., and J. A. Mosher. 1981. A functional approach to estimating habitat edge width for birds. Am. Midl. Nat. 105:189–192.

Gates, J. M., and J. B. Hale. 1975. Reproduction of the east central Wisconsin pheasant population. Wisconsin Dep. Nat. Res. Tech. Bull. 85. 79pp.

Gehrken, G. A. 1975. Travel corridor technique of wild turkey management. Pages 113–117 *in* L. K. Hall, ed. Proceedings of the national wild turkey symposium. Texas Chap. Wildl. Soc., Austin.

Geist, J. M., P. J. Edgerton, and G. S. Strickler. 1974. Yukky to yummy with fertilizers. Rangeman's J. 1:39–41.

George, P. R. 1984. Reseeding pastures and rangeland for wildlife benefits in the central and southern Great Plains. Pages 37B–41B in F. R. Henderson, ed. Guidelines for increasing wildlife on farms and ranches. Coop. Ext. Serv., Kansas State Univ., Manhattan.

George, R., A. Farris, C. Schwartz, D. Humbert, and J. Coffey. 1979. Native prairie grass pastures as nest cover for upland birds. Wildl. Soc. Bull. 7:4–9.

George, R., J. Wooley, and J. Joens. 1981. Switchgrass cost-sharing program benefits Iowa wildlife and cattleman. Pages 540–541 *in* R. T. Dumke, G. V. Burger, and J. R. March, eds. Wildlife management on private lands. Wisconsin Chap. Wildl. Soc., Wisconsin Dep. Nat. Resour., Madison.

Germano, D. J., and C. R. Hungerford. 1981. Reptile population changes with manipulation of Sonoran Desert shrub. Great Basin Nat. 41:129–138.

Germano, D. J., C. R. Hungerford, and S. C. Martin. 1983. Responses of selected wildlife species to the removal of mesquite from desert grassland. J. Range Manage. 36:309–311.

Gibbens, R. P., and R. D. Pieper. 1962. The response of browse plants to fertilization. Calif. Fish Game. 48:268–281.

Gifford, G. F. 1975. Impacts of pinyon-juniper manipulation on watershed values. Pages 127–140 in G. F. Gifford and F. E. Busby, eds. The pinyon-juniper ecosystem: a symposium. Coll. Nat. Resour., Utah State Univ., Logan.

Giles, R. H. 1985. Planning the distribution of watering and similar developments for terrestrial wildlife. Wildl. Soc. Bull. 13:411–415.

Giles, R. H., Jr. 1978. Wildlife management. W. H. Freeman, San Francisco. 416pp.

Gill, J. D. 1957. Review of deer yard management 1956. Maine Dep. Inland Fish. Game Bull. 5. 61pp.

Gillen, R. L., F. T. McCollum, M. E. Hodges, J. E. Brummer, and K. W. Tate. 1991. Plant community responses to short duration grazing in tallgrass prairie. J. Range Manage. 44:124–128.

Gillis, A. M. 1990. The new forestry. BioScience 40:558–562.

Gilmer, D. S., and J. M. Wiehe. 1977. Nesting by ferruginous hawks and other raptors on high voltage powerline towers. Prairie Nat. 9:1–10.

Gittleman, J. L., and P. H. Harvey. 1982. Carnivore home-range size, metabolic needs and ecology. Behav. Ecol. Sociobiol. 10:57–63.

Giunta, B. C., D. R. Christensen, and S. B. Monsen. 1975. Interseeding shrubs in cheatgrass with a browse seeder-scalper. J. Range Manage. 28:398–402.

Glading, B. 1943. A self-filling quail watering device. Calif. Fish Game 29:157–164.

Glading, B. 1947. Game watering devices for the arid southwest. Trans. North Am. Wildl. Conf. 12:286–292.

Goerndt, D. L., S. D. Schemnitz, and W. D. Zeekyk. 1985. Managing common watercress and spring/seeps for Merriam's turkey in New Mexico. Wildl. Soc. Bull. 13:297–301.

Goetz, H. 1969. Composition and yields of native grassland sites fertilized at different rates of nitrogen. J. Range Manage. 22:384–390.

Goetz, H. 1975. Effect of site and fertilization on protein content of native grasses. J. Range Manage. 28:380–385.

Goldsmith, F. B., ed. 1991. Monitoring for conservation and ecology. Chapman and Hall, New York. 275pp.

Goodell, B. S., A. Kimball, and M. L. Hunter, Jr. 1986. Application of wood science to the creation and maintenance of snags for wildlife. Pages 135–139 in J. A. Bissonette, ed. Is good forestry good wildlife management? Misc. Publ. 689. Agric. Exp. Stn., Univ. Maine, Orono.

Goodrum, P. O., V. H. Reid, and C. E. Boyd. 1971. Acorn yields, characteristics and management criteria of oaks for wildlife. J. Wildl. Manage. 35:520–532.

Goodwin, J. G., Jr, and C. R. Hungerford. 1977. Habitat use by native Gambel's and scaled quail and released masked bobwhite quail in southern Arizona. U.S. For. Serv. Res. Pap. RM-197. 7pp.

Graff, W. 1980. Habitat protection and improvement. Pages 310–319 in G. Monson and L. Sumner, eds. The desert bighorn. Univ. Arizona Press, Tucson.

Graham, R. T., J. L. Kingery, and L. A. Volland. 1992. Livestock and forest management interactions. Pages 351–364 in H. C. Black, tech. ed. Silvicultural approaches to animal damage management in Pacific Northwest forests. U.S. For. Serv. Gen. Tech. Rep. PNW-GTR-287.

Graul, W. D. 1980. Grassland management practices and bird communities. Pages 38–47 in R. M. DeGraaf and N. G. Tilghman, eds. Workshop proceedings: management of western forests and grasslands for nongame birds. U.S. For. Serv. Gen. Tech. Rep. INT-86.

Graul, W. D., and G. C. Miller. 1984. Strengthening ecosystem management approaches. Wildl. Soc. Bull. 12:282–289.

Graul, W. D., J. Torres, and R. Denney. 1976. A species-ecosystem approach for nongame programs. Wildl. Soc. Bull. 4:79–80.

Gray, R. S. 1974. Lasting waters for bighorns. desert Bighorn Conc. Trans. 1974:25-27.

Greb, B. W. 1978. Millet production with limited water. Colorado State Univ. Exp. St. Prog. Rep. 15. 3 pp.

Green, J. E., and R. E. Salter. 1987. Methods for reclamation of wildlife habitat in the Canadian prairie provinces. Environ. Can., Edmonton, Alta. 114pp.

Green, L. R. 1970. An experimental prescribed burn to reduce fuel hazard in chaparral. U.S. For. Serv. Res. Note PSW-216. 6pp.

Greenberg, R. 1980. Demographic aspects of long-distance migration. Pages 493–504 *in* A. Keast and E. S. Morton, eds. Migrant birds in the Neotropics: ecology, behavior, distribution, and conservation. Smithsonian Inst. Press, Washington.

Greenhall, A. M. 1982. House bat management. U.S. Fish Wildl. Serv. Resour. Pub. 143. 33pp.

Grelen, H. E. 1975. Vegetative response to twelve years of seasonal burning on a Louisiana longleaf pine site. U.S. For. Serv. Res. Note S0-192. 4pp.

Gremaud, G. K., and R. B. Dahlgren. 1982. Biological farming: impacts on wildlife. Pages 38–39 *in* R. B. Dahlgren, ed. Proceedings of the Midwest agricultural interfaces with fish and wildlife resources workshop. Iowa State Univ., Ames.

Griffith, P. 1976. Introduction of problems. Pages 3–7 *in* R. W. Tinus ed. Proceedings of the symposium on shelterbelts on the Great Plains. Great Plains Agric. Counc. Pub. 78. Denver.

Gross, T. E., and D. P. Dykstra. 1989. Scheduling timber harvests for wildlife, allowing well-defined violations to age class nonadjacency constraints. Pages 165–175 *in* A. Tecle, W. W. Covington, and R. H. Hamre, tech. coords. Multiresource management of ponderosa pine forests. U.S. For. Serv. Gen. Tech. Rep. RM-185.

Grubb, T. G. 1980. An artificial bald eagle nest structure. U.S. For. Serv. Res. Note RM-383. 4pp.

Gruell, G. C., S. Bunting, and L. Neuenschwander. 1985. Influence of fire on curlleaf mountain-mahogany in the intermountain west. Pages 58–72 *in* J. E. Lotan and J. K. Brown, eds. Fire's effects on wildlife habitat. U.S. For. Serv. Gen. Tech. Rep. INT-186.

Grumbine, R. E. 1990a. Viable population, reserve size, and federal lands management: a critique. Conserv. Biol. 4:127–134.

Grumbine, R. E. 1990b. Protecting biological diversity through the greater ecosystem concept. Nat. Areas J. 10:114–120.

Grumbine, R. E. 1992. Ghost bears: exploring the biodiversity crisis. Island Press, Washington. 294pp.

Gruver, B. J. 1984. Management and live-brush density effects on avifauna in northwest Texas. Ph. D. thesis, Texas Tech Univ., Lubbock. 53pp.

Gruver, B. J., and F. S. Guthery. 1986. Effects of brush control and game-bird management on nongame birds. J. Range Manage. 39:251–253.

Guljas, E. Undated. Managing woodlands for wildlife. Indiana Dep. Nat. Resour. Manage. Ser. 3. 10pp.

Gullion, G. W. ca 1982. Managing woodlots for fuel and wildlife. Ruffed Grouse Soc., Coraopolis, PA. 18pp.

Gullion, G. W. 1984. Managing northern forests for wildlife. Ruffed Grouse Soc., Coraopolis, PA. 72pp.

Guthery, F. S. 1980. Bobwhites and brush control. Rangelands 5:202–204.

Guthery, F. S. 1986. Beef, brush, and bobwhites: quail management in cattle country. Caesar Kleberg Wildl. Res. Inst., Texas A&I Univ., Kingsville. 182pp.

Guthery, F. S., C. A. DeYoung, F. C. Bryant, and D. L. Drawe. 1990. Using short duration grazing to accomplish wildlife habitat objectives. Pages 41–55 *in* K. E. Severson, tech. coord. Can livestock be used as a tool to enhance wildlife habitat? U.S. For. Serv. Gen. Tech. Rep. RM-194.

Guthery, F. S., N. Kassinis, and C. A. Harveson. 1991. Bird use of quail hutches. Page 8 *in* S. L. Beasom and B. Ware, eds. 1991–1992 annual report, Caesar Kleberg Wildlife Research Institute, Texas A&I Univ., Kingsville.

Guthery, F. S., T. E. Shupe, L. J. Bareiss, and C. E. Russell. 1987. Responses of selected plants to herbicide treatment of disturbed soil. Wildl. Soc. Bull. 15:247–251.

Guthery, F. S., R. W. Whiteside, T. T. Taylor, and T. Shupe. 1984. How to manage pheasants in the southern high plains of Texas. Manage. Note 3, Texas Tech Univ., Lubbock. 5pp.

Gutiérrez, R. J., D. J. Decker, R. A. Howard, Jr., and J. P. Lassoie. 1984. Managing small woodlots for wildlife. Inf. Bull. 157, Coll. Agric. Life Sci., Cornell Univ., Ithaca, NY. 33pp.

Hadley, E. B. 1970. Net productivity and burning response of native eastern North Dakota prairie communities. Am. Midl. Nat. 84:121–135.

Hailey, T. L. 1979. Basics of brush management for white-tailed deer production. Pittman-Robertson Proj. W-109R, Texas Parks Wildl. Dep., Austin. 8pp.

Haines, D. A., and G. Updike. 1971. Fire whirlwind formation over flat terrain. U.S. For. Serv. Res. Pap. NC-71. 12pp.

Hair, J. D. 1980. Measurement of ecological diversity. Pages 269–275 in S. D. Schemnitz, ed. Wildlife management techniques manual. Wildl. Soc., Washington.

Hall, F. C., L. W. Brewer, J. F. Franklin, and R. L. Werner. 1985a. Plant communities and stand conditions. Pages 17–31 in E. R. Brown, ed. Management of wildlife and fish habitats in forests of western Oregon and Washington. U.S. For. Serv., Portland, OR.

Hall, F. C., C. McComb, and W. Ruediger. 1985b. Silvicultural options. Pages 291–306 in E. R. Brown, ed. Management of wildlife and fish habitats in forests of western Oregon and Washington. U.S. For. Serv., Portland, OR.

Hall, F. C., and J. W. Thomas. 1979. Silvicultural options. Pages 128–147 in J. W. Thomas, ed. Wildlife habitats in managed forests: the Blue Mountains of Oregon and Washington. U.S. For. Serv. Agric. Handb. 553.

Hall, T. R., W. E. Howard, and R. E. Marsh. 1981. Raptor use of artificial perches. Wildl. Soc. Bull. 9:296–298.

Hallisey, D. M., and G. W. Wood. 1976. Prescribed fire in scrub oak habitat in central Pennsylvania. J. Wildl. Manage. 40:507–516.

Halloran, A. F., and O. V. Deming. 1958. Water development for desert bighorn sheep. J. Wildl. Manage. 22:1–9.

Halls, L. K. 1973. Managing deer habitat in loblolly-shortleaf pine forest. J. For. 71:752–757.

Halls, L. K. 1977. Southern fruit-producing woody plants used by wildlife. U.S. For. Serv. Gen. Tech. Rep. S0-16. 235pp.

Halls, L. K., ed. 1984. White-tailed deer. Stackpole Books, Harrisburg, PA. 870pp.

Halls, L. K., D. S. deCalesta, R. L. Downing, F. H. Everest, R. F. Harlow, T. J. Harshbarger, J. C. Kroll, J. S. Lindzey, J. H. Meyer, and V. E. Scott. 1984. Forest wildlife and fish management. Pages 679–737 in K. F. Wenger, ed. Forestry handbook. 2d ed. Wiley, New York.

Hamel, P., H. LeGrand, Jr., M. Lennartz, and S. Gauthreaux, Jr. 1982. Bird-habitat relationships on southeastern forest lands. U.S. For. Serv. Gen. Tech. Rep. SE-22, 417pp.

Hamerstrom, F., F. N. Hamerstrom, and J. Hart. 1973. Nest boxes: an effective management tool for kestrels. J. Wildl. Manage. 37:400–403.

Hamilton, R. J. 1981. Effects of prescribed fire on black bear populations in southern forests. Pages 129–134 in G. W. Wood, ed. Prescribed fire and wildlife in southern forests. Belle W. Baruch For. Sci. Inst., Clemson Univ., Georgetown, SC.

Haney, A., and S. I. Apfelbaum. 1990. Structure and dynamics of Midwest oak savannas. Pages 19–30 in J. M. Sweeny, ed. Management of dynamic ecosystems. North Cent. Soc., Wildl. Soc., West Lafayette, IN.

Haney, A., S. I. Apfelbaum, and S. Packard. 1993. Restoration and management techniques for oak savannas. Unpub. rep. Coll. Nat. Resour., Univ. Wisconsin, Stevens Point. 14pp.

Hansen, A. J., T. A. Spies, F. J. Swanson, and J. L. Ohmann. 1991. Conserving biodiversity in managed forests: lessons from natural forests. BioScience 41:382–392.

Hansen, A. J., and F. di Castri, eds. 1992. Landscape boundaries: consequences for biotic diversity and ecological flows. Springer-Verlag, New York. 452pp.

Hansmire, J. A., D. L. Drawe, D. B. Wester, and C. M. Britton. 1988. Effect of winter burns on forbs and grasses of the Texas coastal prairie. Southwest. Nat. 33:333–338.

Hanson, W. R., and C. Y. McCulloch. 1955. Factors influencing mule deer in Arizona brushlands. Trans. North Am. Wildl. Conf. 20:568–588.

Harestad, A. S., and F. L. Bunnell. 1979. Home range and body weight—a re-evaluation. Ecology 60:389–402.

Harlow, R. F., B. A. Sanders, J. B. Whelan, and L. C. Chappel. 1980. Deer habitat on the Ocala National Forest: improvement through forest management. South. J. Appl. For. 4:98–102.

Harlow, R. F., and D. H. Van Lear. 1981. Silvicultural effects on wildlife habitat in the South (an annotated bibliography) 1953–1979. Dep. For. Tech. Pap. 14, Coll. For. Rec. Resour., Clemson Univ., Clemson, SC. 30pp.

Harlow, R. F., and D. H. Van Lear. 1987. Silvicultural effect on wildlife habitat in the South (an annotated bibliography) 1980–1985. Dep. For. Tech. Pap. 17, Coll. For. Rec. Resour., Clemson Univ., Clemson, SC. 30pp.

Harmel, D. E., W. E. Armstrong, T. Schumann, and K. McGinty. 1991. Land management practices on the Kerr Wildlife Management Area and the black-capped vireo. Special Status Rep. Texas Parks Wildl. Dep., Austin. 53pp.

Harmon, M. E., J. F. Franklin, F. J. Swanson, P. Sollins, S. V. Gregory, J. D. Lattin, N. H. Anderson, S. P. Cline, N. G. Aumen, J. R. Sedell, G. W. Leinkaemper, K. Cromack, Jr., and K. W. Cummins. 1986. Ecology of coarse woody debris in temperate ecosystems. Adv. Ecol. Res. 15:133–302.

Harmon, M. E., and J. F. Franklin. 1983. Age distribution of western hemlock and its relation to Roosevelt elk populations in the south fork of the Hoh Valley. Northwest Sci. 57:249–255.

Harper, K. T., F. J. Wagstaff, and L. M. Kunzler. 1985. Biology and management of the Gambel oak vegetative type: a literature review. U.S. For. Serv. Gen. Tech. Rep. INT-179. 31pp.

Harris, A. S. 1989. Wind in the forests of southeast Alaska and guides for reducing damage. U.S. For. Serv. Gen. Tech. Rep. PNW-GTR-224. 63pp.

Harris, B. L., J. N. Habinger, and Z. L. Carpenter. 1989. The conservation title: concerns and recommendations from the Great Plains. J. Soil Water Conserv. 44:371–375.

Harris, L. D. 1984. The fragmented forest: island biogeography theory and the preservation of biotic diversity. Univ. Chicago Press, Chicago. 211pp.

Harris, L. D. 1985. Conservation corridors: a highway system for wildlife. ENFO 85-5, Environ. Info. Cent., Florida Conserv. Found., Winter Park. 10pp.

Harris, L. D., and W. R. Marion. 1982. Forest stand scheduling for wildlife in the multiple use forest. Pages 209–214 in Increasing forest productivity. Proc. 1981 Conv. Soc. Am. For., Bethesda, MD.

Harris, L. D., C. Maser, and A. McKee. 1982. Patterns of old growth harvest and implications for Cascades wildlife. Trans. North Am. Wildl. Nat. Resour. Conf. 47:374–392.

Harris, L. D., and J. Scheck. 1991. From implications to applications: the dispersal corridor principle applied to the conservation of biological diversity. Pages 189–220 in D. A. Saunders and R. J. Hobbs, eds. Nature conservation 2: the role of corridors. Surrey Beatty & Sons, Chipping Norton, NSW, Australia.

Harris, L. D., and G. Silva-Lopez. 1992. Forest fragmentation and the conservation of biological diversity. Pages 197–237 in P. L. Fiedler and S. K. Jain, eds. Conservation biology: the theory and practice of nature conservation preservation and management. Chapman and Hall, New York.

Harris, L. D., and P. Skoog. 1980. Some wildlife habitat-forestry relationships in the southeastern coastal plain. Pages 103–119 in R. H. Chabreck and R. H. Mills, eds. Integrating timber and wildlife management in southern forests. Proc. 29th Annual Louisiana State Univ. Forestry Symp.

Harris, R. D. 1983. Decay characteristics of pileated woodpecker nest trees. Pages 125–129 in J. W. Davis, G. A. Goodwin, and R. A. Ockenfels, tech. coord. Snag habitat management: proceedings of the symposium. U.S. For. Serv. Gen. Tech. Rep. RM-99.

Harrison, K. G. 1977. Perch height selection of grassland birds. Wilson Bull. 89:486–487.

Harrison, R. L. 1992. Toward a theory of inter-refuge corridor design. Conserv. Biol. 6:293–296.

Hart, R. H., M. J. Samuel, P. S. Test, and M. A. Smith. 1988. Cattle, vegetation, and economic responses to grazing systems and grazing pressure. J. Range Manage. 41:282–286.

Hartley, D., and H. Kidd, ed. 1990. The agrochemicals handbook. 2d ed. Royal Soc. Chemistry Info. Serv., Cambridge, England. Various pages.

Hartman, H. T., and E. E. Kester. 1975. Plant propagation principles and practices. 3d ed. Prentice-Hall, Englewood Cliffs, NJ. 662pp.

Hassinger, J., L. Hoffman, M. J. Puglisi, T. D. Rader, and R. G. Wingard. 1979. Woodlands and wildlife. Coll. Agric., Pennsylvania State Univ., University Park. 67pp.

Hassinger, J., C. E. Schwartz, and R. G. Wingard. 1981. Timber sales and wildlife. Pennsylvania Game Comm., Harrisburg. 13pp.

Hastie, B. 1990. Being a bat host. Oregon Wildl. 46(6):14.

Hastings, H. R., and P. M. Turner. 1965. The changing mile. Univ. Arizona Press, Tucson. 317pp.

Hauke, H. H. 1975. Winter roost characteristics of the Rio Grande turkey in south Texas. Proc. Natl. Wild Turkey Symp. 3:164–169.

Hayes, T. D., D. H. Riskind, and W. L. Pace III. 1987. Patch-within-patch restoration of man-modified landscapes within Texas state parks. Pages 173–198 in M. G. Turner, ed. Landscape heterogeneity and disturbance. Springer-Verlag, New York. 239pp.

Hays, J. C. 1986. Intensive forest management for wildlife. Pages 181–185 in Foresters' future: leaders or followers? Proc. 1985 Soc. Am. For. Natl. Conv., Bethesda, MD.

Heady, H. F., and J. Bartolome. 1977. The Vale rangeland and rehabilitation programs: the desert repaired in southeastern Oregon. U.S. For. Serv. Res. Bull. PNW-70. 139pp.

Hedrick, D. W., D. N. Hyder, F. A. Sneva, and C. E. Poulton. 1966. Ecological response of sagebrush-grass range in central Oregon to mechanical and chemical removal of Artemisia. Ecology 47:432–439.

Hedrick, D. W., W. M. Moser, A. L. Steninger, and R. A. Long. 1969. Animal performance on crested wheatgrass pastures during May and June, Fort Rock, Oregon. J. Range Manage. 22:277–280.

Heidmann, L. J. 1984. Using herbicides for reforestation in the Southwest. U.S. For. Serv. Gen. Tech. Rep. RM-103. 12pp.

Heintzelman, D. S. 1971. Observations on the role of nest box sanitation in affecting egg hatchability of wild sparrow hawks in eastern Pennsylvania. Raptor Res. News 5:100–103.

Heirman, A. L., and H. A. Wright. 1973. Fire in medium fuels of west Texas. J. Range Manage. 26:331–335.

Heitschmidt, R. K., S. L. Dowhower, W. E. Pinchak, and S. K. Canon. 1989. Effects of stocking rate on quantity and quality of available forage in a southern mixed grass prairie. J. Range Manage. 42:468–473.

Heitschmidt, R. K., and J. W. Stuth. 1991. Grazing management and ecological perspectives. Timber Press, Portland, OR. 259pp.

Heliovaara, K., and R. Vaisanen. 1984. Effects of modern foresty on northwestern European forest invertebrates—a synthesis. Acta For. Fenn. 189:1–32.

Hemstrom, M. A., and J. F. Franklin. 1982. Fire and other disturbances of the forest in Mount Rainier National Park. Quaternary Res. 18:32–51.

Henderson, C. L. 1987. Landscaping for wildlife. Minnesota Dep. Nat. Resour., St. Paul. 145pp.

Henderson, C. L. 1988. Woodland landscaping for wildlife. Pages 13–17 in T. W. Hoekstra, comp. Integrating forest management for wildlife and fish. U.S. For. Serv. Gen. Tech. Rep. NC-122.

Henderson, C. L. 1992. Woodworking for wildlife: homes for birds and mammals. Minnesota Dep. Nat. Resour., St. Paul. 111pp.

Henderson, F. R., ed. 1984. Guidelines for increasing wildlife on farms and ranches. Coop. Ext. Serv., Kansas State Univ., Manhattan. 579pp.

Henderson, S. D., and J. B. Holt. 1962. Banding screech owls and kestrels at their nest boxes. EBBA News 25:93–104.

Herbel, C. H., and K. L. Anderson. 1959. Response of true prairie vegetation on major Flint Hills range sites to grazing treatment. Ecol. Monogr. 29:171–198.

Herbel, C. H., F. N. Ares, and R. A. Wright. 1972. Drought effects on a semidesert grassland range. Ecology 53:1084–1093.

Herricks, E. E., A. J. Krzysik, R. E. Szafoni, and D. J. Tazik. 1982. Best current practices for fish and wildlife on surface-mined lands in the eastern interior coal region. U.S. Fish Wildl. Serv. FWS/OBS-80/68. 212pp.

Hershey, F. A., and H. L. Wiegers. Undated. Forestry for wildlife habitat improvement. Coop. Ext. Serv., Univ. Nebraska, Lincoln. 12pp.

Heske, E. J., and M. Campbell. 1991. Effects of an 11-year livestock exclosure on rodent and ant numbers in the Chihuahuan Desert, Southeastern Arizona. Southwest. Nat. 36:89–93.

Hesselschwerdt, R. E. 1942. Use of den boxes in wildlife restoration on intensively farmed areas. J. Wildl. Manage. 6:31–37.

Hewitt, O. H., ed. 1967. The wild turkey and its management. Wildl. Soc., Washington. 589pp.

Hickman, M. V., C. G. Messersmith, and R. G. Lynn. 1990. Picloram release from leafy spurge roots. J. Range Manage. 43:442–445.

Higgins, K. F. 1975. Shorebird and game bird nests in North Dakota croplands. Wildl. Soc. Bull. 3:176–179.

Higgins, K. F., A. D. Kruse, and J. L. Piehl. 1989. Prescribed burning guidelines in the northern prairies. U.S. Fish Wildl. Serv. and Coop. Ext. Serv. Pub. EC760, South Dakota State Univ., Brookings. 36pp.

Hill, D. B. 1985. Small woodlot management in Kentucky. Coop. Ext. Serv., Coll. Agric., Univ. Kentucky, Lexington. 24pp.

Hillis, M. 1991. Biodiversity in western Montana: a landscape view. Inner Voice 3(5):6.

Hillman, C. N., R. L. Linder, and R. B. Dahlgren. 1979. Prairie dog distribution in areas inhabited by black-footed ferrets. Am. Midl. Nat. 102:185–187.

Hobbs, N. T., and R. A. Spowart. 1984. Effects of prescribed fire on nutrition of mountain sheep and mule deer during winter and spring. J. Wildl. Manage. 48:551–560.

Hobbs, R. J., and L. F. Huenneke. 1992. Disturbance, diversity, and invasion: implications for conservation. Conserv. Biol. 6:324–337.

Hocker, H. W., Jr. 1979. Introduction to forest biology. Wiley, New York. 467pp.

Hodorff, R. A., C. H. Sieg, and R. L. Linder. 1988. Wildlife response to stand structure of deciduous woodlands. J. Wildl. Manage. 52:667–673.

Hoffman, D. J., and P. H. Alders. 1984. Evaluation of potential embryotoxicity and teratogenicity of 42 herbicides, insecticides, and petroleum contaminants to mallard eggs. Arch. Environ. Contam. Toxicol. 13:15–27.

Hoffman, D. J., and W. C. Eastin, Jr. 1982. Effects of lindane, paraquat, toxaphane, and 2,4,5-trichlorophenoxyacetic acid on mallard embryo development. Arch. Environ. Contam. Toxicol. 11:79–86.

Hogg, D. 1990. Moose management: the forest habitat. Pages 30–33 in M. Buss and R. Truman, eds. The moose in Ontario: Book 1—moose biology, ecology and management. Ontario Min. Nat. Resour., Toronto.

Holbrook, H. L. 1974. A system for wildlife habitat management on southern national forests. Wildl. Soc. Bull. 2:119–123.

Holechek, J.L, R. D. Pieper, and C. H. Herbel. 1989. Range management principles and practices. Prentice-Hall, Englewood Cliffs, NJ. 501pp.

Holechek, J. L., R. Valdez, R. Pieper, S. D. Schemnitz, and C. Davis. 1982. Manipulation of grazing to improve or maintain wildlife habitat. Wildl. Soc. Bull. 10:204–210.

Holechek, J. L., M. Vavra, and J. Skovlin. 1981. Diet quality and performance of cattle on forest and grassland range. J. Anim. Sci. 53:291–298.

Holt, H. A., and B. C. Fischer, eds. 1981. Weed control in forest management. Dep. For. Nat. Resour., Purdue Univ., West Lafayette, IN. 305pp.

Honnas, R. C., B. L. Branscomb, and R. R. Humphrey. 1959. Effect of range fertilization on growth of three southern Arizona grasses. J. Range Manage. 13:88–91.

Hood, R. E., and J. M. Inglis. 1974. Behavioral responses of white-tailed deer to intensive ranching operations. J. Wildl. Manage. 38:488–498.

Hook, D. D., J. B. Baker, S. G. Boyce, S. B. Carpenter, T. W. Daniel, R. F. Fisher, J. S. Fralish, J. R. Gosz, C. A. Gresham, M. Newton, R. Pfister, A. F. Robinson, Jr., F.

Ronco, Jr., G. L. Switzer, T. Williams, G. W. Wood, and H. E. Young. 1984. Forest ecology. Pages 1–63 *in* K. F. Wenger, ed. Forestry handbook. 2d ed. Wiley, New York.

Hooper, J. F., J. P. Workman, J. B. Grumbles, and C. Wayne Cook. 1969. Improved livestock distribution with fertilizer—a preliminary economic evaluation. J. Range Manage. 22:108–110.

Hoose, P. M. 1981. Building an ark: tools for the preservation of natural diversity through land protection. Island Press, Covelo, CA. 221pp.

Hopkins, H., F. W. Albertson, and A. Riegel. 1948. Some effects of burning upon a prairie in west-central Kansas. Trans. Kan. Acad. Sci. 1:131–141.

Horejsi, R. G. 1982. Mule deer fawn survival on cattle-grazed and ungrazed desert ranges. Arizona Game and Fish Dep. Fed. Aid Rep. W-78-R, Work Plan 2, Job 17. 43pp.

Hormay, A. L. 1961. Rest-rotation grazing: a new management system for bunchgrass ranges. U.S. For. Serv. Production Res. Pap. 51. 43pp.

Hornbeck, J. W., and W. B. Leak. 1992. Ecology and management of northern hardwood forests in New England. U.S. For. Serv. Gen. Tech. Rep. NE-159. 44pp.

Horton, S. P., and R. W. Mannan. 1988. Effects of prescribed fire on snags and cavity-nesting birds in southeastern Arizona pine forests. Wildl. Soc. Bull. 16:37–44.

Houston, D. B. 1973. Wildfires in northern Yellowstone National Park. Ecology 54:1111–1117.

Howard, R. J., and J. A. Allen. 1989. Streamside habitats in southern forested wetlands: their role and implications for management. Pages 97–106 *in* D. D. Hook and R. Lea, eds. Proceedings of the symposium: the forested wetlands of the southern United States. U.S. For. Serv. Gen. Tech. Rep. SE-50.

Howard, R. P., and M. L. Wolfe. 1976. Range improvement practices and ferruginous hawks. J. Range Manage. 29:33–37.

Howard, R. P., and M. Hilliard. 1980. Artificial nest structures and grassland raptors. Raptor Res. 14:41–45.

Howard, V. W. 1991. Effects of electric predator-excluding fences on movements of mule deer in pinyon/juniper woodlands. Wildl. Soc. Bull. 19:331–334.

Howard, V. W., Jr., K. M. Cheap, R. H. Hier, T. G. Thompson, and J. A. Dimas. 1987. Effects of cabling pinyon-juniper on mule deer and lagomorph use. Wildl. Soc. Bull. 15:242–247.

Howard, V. W., Jr., J. R. Cox, and G. M. Southward. 1980. Response of wavyleaf oak to nitrogen fertilization. J. Range Manage. 33:457–459.

Howe, R. W. 1984. Local dynamics of bird assemblages in small forest habitat islands in Australia and North America. Ecology 65:1585–1601.

Hubbard, W. A., and J. L. Mason. 1967. Residual effects of ammonium nitrate and ammonium phosphate on some native ranges of British Columbia. J. Range Manage. 20:1–5.

Hudson, R. H., R. K. Tucker, and M. A. Haegele. 1984. Handbook of toxicity of pesticides to wildlife. 2d ed. U.S. Fish Wildl. Serv. Resour. Pub. 153. 90pp.

Huffine, W. W., and W. C. Elder. 1960. Effects of fertilizers on native grass pastures in Oklahoma. J. Range Manage. 13:34–36.

Hughes, L. E. 1982. A grazing system in the Mojave desert. Rangelands 4:256–258.

Hughes, L. E. 1990. Twenty years of rest-rotation grazing on the Arizona strip—an observation. Rangelands 12:173–176.

Hughes, R. H. 1975. The native vegetation in south Florida related to month of burning. U.S. For. Serv. Res. Note SE-222. 8pp.

Hummel, M. 1990. A conservation strategy for large carnivores in Canada. World Wildlife Fund Canada, Toronto.

Humphrey, R. R. 1962. Range ecology. Ronald Press, New York. 234pp.

Humphrey, R. R. 1963. The role of fire in the desert and desert grassland areas of Arizona. Proc. Tall Timbers Fire Ecol. Conf. 2:45–61.

Hungerford, C. R. 1960. Water requirements of Gambel's quail. Trans. North Am. Wildl. Nat. Resour. Conf. 25:231–240.

Hungerford, C. R. 1962. Adaptations shown in selection of food by Gambel's quail. Condor 64:213–219.

Hunt, L. J., A. W. Ford, M. C. Landin, and B. R. Wells. 1978. Upland habitat development with dredged material: engineering and plant propagation. U.S. Army Corps Eng. Tech. Rep. DS-78-17. 160pp.

Hunter, M. L., Jr. 1990. Wildlife, forests, and forestry: principles of managing forests for biological diversity. Prentice-Hall, Englewood Cliffs, NJ. 370pp.

Huntsinger, L., and L. P. Fortmann. 1990. California's privately owned oak woodlands: owners, use, and management. J. Range Manage. 43:147–152.

Husek, V. P. 1970. Wildlife land management for Ontario landowners. Ontario Min. Nat. Resour., Toronto. 21pp.

Hutchenson, A., J. T. Baccus, T. M. McClean, and P. J. Fonteyn. 1989. Response of herbaceous vegetation to prescribed burning in the Hill Country of Texas. Texas J. Agric. Nat. Resour. 3:42–47.

Hutchings, S. S., and G. Stewart. 1953. Increasing forage yields and sheep production on intermountain ranges. U.S. Dep. Agric. Circ. 925. 64pp.

Hyde, K. J., C. A. DeYoung, and A. Garza, Jr. 1987. Bed sites of white-tailed deer fawns in south Texas. Proc. Annu. Conf. Southeast. Assoc. Fish Wildl. Agencies 41:288–293.

Hyder, D. N., F. A. Sneva, and C. S. Cooper. 1955. Methods for planting crested wheatgrass. Pages 19–20 in 1955 field day report. Squaw Butte-Harney Range and Livestock Exp. Stn., Burns, OR.

Hynson, J., P. Adamus, S. Tibbetts, and R. Darnell. 1982. Handbook for protection of fish and wildlife from construction of farm and forest roads. U.S. Fish Wildl. Serv. FWS/OBS-82/18. 153pp.

Inglis, G., and A. J. Underwood. 1992. Comments on some designs proposed for experiments on the biological importance of corridors. Conserv. Biol. 6:581–585.

Inglis, J. M. 1985. Wildlife management and IBMS. Pages 35–40 in C. J. Scifres, ed. Integrated brush management systems for South Texas: development and implementation. Texas Agric. Exp. Stn. Bull. B-1493, Texas A&M Univ., College Station.

Inglis, J. M., B. A. Brown, C. A. McMahan, and R. E. Hood. 1986. Deer-brush relationships on the Rio Grande Plain, Texas. Caesar Kleberg Res. Program in Wildl. Ecol., Texas A&M, Univ., College Station. 80pp.

Institute for Land Rehabilitation. 1978. Rehabilitation of western wildlife habitat: a review. U.S. Fish Wildl. Serv. FWS/OBS-78/86. 238pp.

Isaacs, B., and D. Howell. 1988. Opportunities for enhancing wildlife benefits through the conservation reserve program. Trans. North Am. Wildl. Nat. Resour. Conf. 53:222–231.

Jackson, A. S. 1965. Wildfires in the Great Plains grasslands. Proc. Tall Timbers Fire Ecol. Conf. 4:241–259.

Jackson, A. S. 1969. Quail management handbook for west Texas Rolling Plains. Texas Parks Wildl. Bull. 48. 77pp.

Jackson, J. J., G. D. Walker, R. L. Shell, and D. Heighes. 1984. Managing timber and wildlife in the southern Piedmont. Bull. 845, Coop. Ext. Serv., Coll. Agric., Univ. Georgia, Athens.

Janzen, D. H. 1986. The eternal external threat. Pages 286–303 in M. E. Soulé, ed. Conservation biology. Sinauer, Sunderland, MA.

Jensen, C. H., A. D. Smith, and G. W. Scotter. 1972. Guidelines for grazing sheep on rangelands used by big game in winter. J. Range Manage. 25:346–352.

Jensen, H. P., D. Rollins, and R. L. Gillen. 1990. Effects of cattle stock density on trampling loss of simulated ground nests. Wildl. Soc. Bull. 18:71–74.

Jensen, I., and R. Hodder. 1979. Tubelings, condensation traps, native tree transplanting and root sprigging techniques for tree and shrub establishment in semiarid areas. Montana Agric. Exp. Stn. Res. Rep. 141. 105pp.

Jenson, W. F., T. K. Fuller, and W. L. Robinson. 1986. Wolf, Canis lupus, distribution on the Ontario-Michigan border near Sault Ste. Marie. Can. Wild-Nat. 100:363–366.

Jerry, D. G. 1984. Old-growth management in the Idaho Panhandle national forests. Pages 373–379 in W. R. Meehan, T. R. Merrell, Jr., and T. A. Hanley, eds. Fish and wildlife relationships in old-growth forests. Am. Inst. of Fish. Res. Biol., Rt. 4, Box 85, Morehead City, NC.

Johnsen, T. N., and R. S. Dalen. 1990. Managing individual juniper and pinyon infestations with pelleted tebuthiuron or picloram. J. Range Manage. 43:249–252.

Johnsgard, P. A. 1973. Grouse and quails of North America. Univ. Nebraska Press, Lincoln. 553pp.

Johnson, A. S., and J. L. Landers. 1978. Fruit production in slash pine plantations in Georgia. J. Wildl. Manage. 42:606–613.

Johnson, D. E., H. A.M. Mukhtar, R. Mapson, and R. R. Humphrey. 1962. The mortality of oak-juniper woodland species following wildfire. J. Range Manage. 15:201–205.

Johnson, D. H., and D. G. Follen, Sr. 1984. Barred owls and nest boxes. Raptor Res. 18:34–35.

Johnson, J. E., P. E. Pope, G. D. Mroz, and N. F. Payne. 1987. Environmental impacts of harvesting wood for energy. Counc. Great Lakes Governors, Chicago. 169pp.

Johnson, J. R., and G. F. Payne. 1968. Sagebrush reinvasion as affected by some environmental influences. J. Range Manage. 21:209–213.

Johnson, K. N., J. F. Franklin, J. W. Thomas, and J. Gordon. 1991. Alternatives for management of late-successional forests of the Pacific Northeast. Rep. to U.S. House of Representatives Comm. on Agric. Subcomm. on For., Family Farms and Energy, and Comm. on Merchant Marine and Fish. Subcomm. on Fish. and Wildl., Conserv., and Environ, Washington. 59pp.

Johnson, R., and S. Temple. 1986. Assessing habitat quality for birds nesting in fragmented tallgrass prairie. Pages 245–249 in J. A. Verner, M. Morrison, and C. Ralph, eds. Wildlife 2000: modeling habitat relationships of terrestrial vertebrates. Univ. Wisconsin Press, Madison.

Johnson, R. R., L. T. Height, M. M. Riffey, and J. M. Simpson. 1980. Brushland/steppe bird populations. Pages 98–112 in R. M. DeGraaf and N. G. Tilghman, eds. Workshop proceedings: management of western forests and grasslands for nongame birds. U.S. For. Serv. Gen. Tech. Rep. INT-86.

Johnson, S. A. 1992. Construction of an angle-iron gate in Wyandotte Cave, Indiana. Unpub. rep. Indiana Dep. Nat. Resour., Indianapolis. 15pp.

Johnson, T. R. 1983. Wildlife watering holes: their construction, value and use by amphibians. Missouri Dep. Conserv., Jefferson City. 4pp.

Johnson, T., and R. A. Jacobs. 1986. Gallinaceous guzzlers. Sec. 5.4.1. U.S. Army Corps of Engineers wildlife resources management manual. U.S. Army Eng. Waterways Exp. Stn. Tech. Rep. EL-86-8. 20pp.

Johnson, W. C., R. K. Schreiber, and R. L. Burgess. 1979. Diversity of small mammals in a powerline right-of-way and adjacent forest in east Tennessee. Am. Midl. Nat. 101:231–235.

Johnston, A., S. Smoliak, A. D. Smith, and L. E. Lutwick. 1967. Improvement of southeastern Alberta range with fertilizers. Can. J. Plant Sci. 47:671–678.

Johnston, W. F. 1977. Manager's handbook for northern white cedar in the north central states. U.S. For. Serv. Gen. Tech. Rep. NC-35. 18pp.

Johnston, W. F., and R. G. Booker. 1983. Northern white cedar. Pages 105–108 in R. M. Burns, ed. Silvicultural systems for the major forest types of the United States. U.S. For. Serv. Handb. 445.

Jones, J. R. 1985. Distribution. Pages 9–10 in N. V. DeByle and R. P. Winokur, eds. Aspen: ecology and management in the western United States. U.S. For. Serv. Gen. Tech. Rep. RM-119.

Jones, L. H. P., and K. Handreck. 1967. Silica in soils, plants, and animals. Adv. Agron. 19:107–149.

Jordan, W. R., III, R. L. Peters, II, and E. B. Allen. 1986. Ecological restoration as a strategy for conserving biological diversity. Environ. Manage. 12:55–72.

Joselyn, G. B., and G. M. Tate. 1972. Practical aspects of managing roadside cover for nesting pheasants. J. Wildl. Manage. 36:1–11.

Joselyn, G. B., and J. E. Warnock. 1964. Value of federal feed grain program to production of pheasants in Illinois. J. Wildl. Manage. 28:547–551.

Joselyn, G. B., J. E. Warnock, and S. L. Etter. 1968. Manipulation of roadside cover for nesting pheasants—a preliminary report. J. Wildl. Manage. 32:217–233.

Jourdonnais, C. S., and D. J. Bedunah. 1990. Prescribed fire and cattle grazing on an elk winter range in Montana. Wildl. Soc. Bull. 18:232–240.

Kahl, J. R. 1972. Better homes for feathered fisherman. Outdoor Calif. 33(3):4–6.

Kalmbach, E. R., and W. L. McAtee. 1969. Homes for birds. U.S. Fish Wildl. Serv. Conserv. Bull. 14. 18pp.

Kantrud, H. A. 1981. Grazing intensity effects on the breeding avifauna of North Dakota native grasslands. Can. Field-Nat. 95:404–417.

Kantrud, H. A. 1990. Effects of vegetation manipulation on breeding waterfowl in prairie wetlands—a literature review. Pages 93–123 in K. E. Severson, tech. coord. Can livestock be used as a tool to enhance wildlife habitat? U.S. For. Serv. Gen. Tech. Rep. RM-194.

Kantrud, H. A., and R. L. Kologiski. 1982. Effects of soils and grazing on breeding birds of uncultivated upland grasslands of the northern Great Plains. Wildl. Res. Rep. 15, U.S. Fish Wildl. Serv., Washington. 33pp.

Karr, J. R. 1981. An integrated approach to management of land resources. Pages 164–192 in R. T. Dumke, G. V. Burger, and J. R. March, eds. Wildlife management on private lands. Wisconsin Chap. Wildl. Soc., Wisconsin Dep. Nat. Resour., Madison.

Karr, J. R., and K. E. Freemark. 1985. Disturbance and vertebrates: an integrative perspective. Pages 153–168 in S. T. A. Pickett and P. S. White, eds. The ecology of natural disturbance and patch dynamics. Academic Press, Orlando, FL.

Karsky, R. 1988. Fences. U.S. Bur. Land Manage. and U.S. For. Serv. Tech. and Develop. Prog., 2400-Range, 8824 2803. 210pp.

Kartchner, R. J., J. R. Wight, J. L. Bishop, and R. A. Bellows. 1983. Beef and forage production on contour furrowed rangeland interseeded with alfalfa. J. Range Manage. 36:479–482.

Kaufman, D. W., E. J. Finck, and G. A. Kaufman. 1990. Small mammals and grassland fires. Pages 46–80 in S. L. Collins and L. L. Wallace, eds. Fire in North American tallgrass prairies. Univ. Oklahoma Press. Norman.

Kauffman, J. B., and W. C. Krueger. 1984. Livestock impacts on riparian ecosystems and streamside management implications...a review. J. Range Manage. 37:430–438.

Kay, B. L. 1969. Hardiness and annual legume production in the Sierra foothills. J. Range Manage. 22:174–177.

Kennedy, G. Undated. Wildlife management with trees and shrubs. Manage. Ser. 5, Indiana Dep. Nat. Resour., Indianapolis. 12pp.

Kerr, R. M. 1986. Habitat mapping. Pages 49–69 in A. Y. Cooperrider, R. J. Boyd, and H. R. Stuart, eds. Inventory and monitoring of wildlife habitat. U.S. Bur. Land Manage., Denver.

Kessler, W. B. 1984. Management potential of second-growth forest for wildlife objectives in southeast Alaska. Pages 381–384 in W. R. Meehan, T. R. Merrell, Jr., and T. A. Hanley, eds. Fish and wildlife relationships in old-growth forests. Am. Inst. Fish. Res. Biol., Rt. 4, Box 85, Morehead City, NC.

Kessler, W. B., H. Salwasser, C. W. Cartwright, Jr., and J. A. Caplan. 1992. New perspectives for sustainable natural resources management. Ecol. Appl. 2:221–225.

Keystone Center. 1991. Final consensus report of the Keystone policy dialogue on biological diversity on federal lands. The Keystone Cent., Keystone, CO. 96pp.

Kie, J. G., and E. R. Loft. 1990. Using livestock to manage wildlife habitat: some examples from California annual grassland and wet meadow communities. Pages 7–24 in K. E. Severson, tech. coord. Can livestock be used as a tool to enhance wildlife habitat? U.S. For. Serv. Gen. Tech. Rep. RM-194.

Kimmins, J. P. 1987. Forest ecology. Macmillan, New York. 531pp.

Kinch, G. 1989. Riparian area management: grazing management in riparian areas. Tech. Ref. 1737-4. U.S. Bur. Land Manage., Denver. 48pp.

Kirby, D. R., M. F. Pessin, and G. K. Clambey. 1986. Disappearance of forage under short duration and season long grazing. J. Range Manage. 39:496–500.

Kirby, S. B., K. M. Babcock, S. L. Sheriff, and D. J. Witter. 1981. Private land and wildlife in Missouri: a study of farm operator values. Pages 88–97 in R. T. Dumke, G. V. Burger, and J. R. March, eds. Wildlife management on private lands. Wisconsin Chap. Wildl. Soc., Wisconsin Dep. Nat. Resour., Madison.

Kirchhoff, M. D., and J. W. Schoen. 1987. Forest cover and snow: implications for deer habitat in Alaska. J. Wildl. Manage. 51:28–33.

Kirkpatrick, J. B., and M. J. Brown. 1991. Planning for species conservation. Pages 83–89 *in* C. R. Margules and M. P. Austin, eds. Nature conservation: cost effective biological surveys and data analysis. Australia CSIRO, East Melbourne.

Kirsch, L. M. 1974. Habitat management considerations for prairie chickens. Wildl. Soc. Bull. 2:124–129.

Kirsch, L. M., and A. D. Kruse. 1972. Prairie fires and wildlife. Proc. Tall Timbers Fire Ecol. Conf. 12:289–305.

Kjellsen, M. L., and K. F. Higgins. 1990. Grasslands: benefits from managing by fire. FS 857, U.S. Fish Wildl. Serv. and Coop. Ext. Serv., South Dakota State Univ., Brookings. 4pp.

Klebenow, D. A. 1970. Sage grouse versus sagebrush control in Idaho. J. Range Manage. 23:649–662.

Klebenow, D. A. 1980. The impacts of grazing systems on wildlife. Pages 153–162 *in* K. C. McDaniel and C. D. Allison, eds. Proceedings: grazing management systems for southwestern rangelands, a symposium. New Mexico State Univ., Las Cruces.

Klebenow, D. A. 1982. Livestock grazing interactions with sage grouse. Pages 113–123 *in* J. M. Peek and P. D. Dalke, eds. Symposium on wildlife-livestock relationships. For., Wildl., and Range Exp. Stn., Univ. Idaho, Moscow.

Klein, D. R. 1970. Tundra ranges north of the boreal forest. J. Range Manage. 23:8–14.

Klinger, R. C., M. J. Kutilek, and H. S. Shellhammer. 1989. Population responses of black-tailed deer to prescribed burning. J. Wildl. Manage. 53:863–871.

Knierim, P. G., K. L. Carvell, and J. D. Gill. 1971. Browse in thinned oak and cove hardwood stands. J. Wildl. Manage. 35:163–168.

Knight, D. H. 1987. Parasites, lightning, and the vegetation mosaic in wilderness landscapes. Pages 59–83 *in* M. G. Turner, ed. Landscape heterogeneity and disturbance. Springer-Verlag, New York.

Knopf, F. L. 1992. Faunal mixing, faunal integrity, and the biopolitical template for diversity conservation. Trans. North Am. Wildl. Nat. Resour. Conf. 57:330–342.

Kobayashi, S. 1985. Species diversity preserved in different numbers of nature reserves of the same total area. Res. Popul. Ecol. 27:137–143.

Kochert, M. N., K. Steenhof, J. Roope, and M. Mulrooney. 1984. Raptor and raven nesting on the PP&L Malin to midpoint 500 KV transmission line. Pages 20–39 *in* U.S. Bureau of Land Management, Boise District, Snake river birds of prey research project annual report. U.S. Bur. Land Manage., Boise, ID.

Koenig, W. D. 1988. On determination of viable population size in birds and mammals. Wildl. Soc. Bull. 16:230–234.

Koerth, B. H., W. M. Webb, F. C. Bryant, and F. S. Guthery. 1983. Cattle trampling of simulated ground nests under short duration and continuous grazing. J. Range Manage. 36:385–386.

Koerth, N. E.,and F. S. Guthery. 1990. Water requirements of captive northern bobwhites under subtropical seasons. J. Wildl. Manage. 54:667–672.

Koerth, N. E., and F. S. Guthery. 1991. Water restriction effects on northern bobwhite reproduction. J. Wildl. Manage. 55:132–137.

Koford, C. B. 1958. Prairie dogs, whitefaces, and blue grama. Wildl. Monogr. 3. 78pp.

Komarek, E. V. 1971. Effects of fire on wildlife and range habitats. Prescribed burning symposium proceedings. U.S. For. Serv., Southeast. For. Exp. Stn. Asheville, NC. 8pp.

Komarek, R. 1963. Fire and the changing wildlife habitat. Proc. Annu. Tall Timbers Fire Ecol. Conf. 2:35–43.

Komarek, R. 1966. A discussion of wildlife management, fire, and the wildlife landscape. Proc. Annu. Tall Timbers Fire Ecol. Conf. 5:177–194.

Kosciuk, J. R., and E. P. Peloquin. 1986. Elevated quail roosts. Sec. 5.1.5., U.S. Army Corps of Engineers wildlife resources management manual. U.S. Army Eng. Waterways Exp. Stn. Tech. Rep. EL-86-18. 15pp.

Kotar, J., J. Kovach, and C. Locey. 1988. Field guide to forest habitat types of northern Wisconsin. Dep. For., Univ. Wisconsin and Wisconsin Dep. Nat. Resour., Madison. 216pp.

Kothmann, M. M. 1980. Integrating livestock needs to the grazing system. Pages 65–83 *in* K. C. McDaniel and C. D. Allison, eds. Proceedings: grazing management systems for southwestern rangelands, a symposium. New Mexico State Univ., Las Cruces.

Kramp, B. A., D. R. Patton, and W. W. Brady. 1983. The effects of fire on wildlife habitat and species. RUN WILD Wildlife/Habitat Relationships Tech. Rep. U.S. For. Serv., Southwest. Reg., Albuquerque, NM. 29pp.

Krefting, L. W. 1941. Methods of increasing deer browse. J. Wildl. Manage. 5:95–102.

Krefting, L. W. 1962. Use of silvicultural techniques for improving deer habitat in the Lake States. J. For. 60:40–42.

Krohn, W. B., and R. B. Owen, Jr. 1988. Forestland raptors and herons. Pages 44–46 in C. A. Elliott, ed. A forester's guide to managing wildlife habitats in Maine. Coop. Ext. Serv., Univ. Maine, Orono.

Krueger, W. C. 1983. Cattle grazing in managed forests. Pages 29–41 in B. F. Roché, Jr., ed. Forestland grazing. Coop. Ext., Washington State Univ., Pullman.

Krusac, D. L., and E. D. Michael. 1979. Management of wildlife food plots: a regional comparison. Trans. Northeast Sect. Wildl. Soc. 36:88–96.

Kubisiak, J. F. 1985. Ruffed grouse habitat relationships in aspen and oak forests of Wisconsin. Wisconsin Dep. Nat. Resour. Tech. Bull. 151. 22pp.

Kuchler, A. W. 1964. Potential natural vegetation on the conterminous United States. Am. Geogr. Soc. Spec. Pub. 36. 116pp.

Kufeld, R. C. 1977. Improving gambel oak ranges for elk and mule deer by spraying with 2,4,5-TP. J. Range Manage. 30:53–57.

Kufeld, R. C. 1983. Responses of elk, mule deer, cattle, and vegetation to burning, spraying, and chaining of Gambel oak rangeland. Colorado Div. Wildl. Tech. Pub. 34. 47pp.

Kundaeli, J. N., and H. G. Reynolds. 1972. Desert cottontail use of natural and modified pinyon-juniper woodlands. J. Range Manage. 25:116–118.

Lacy, R. C. 1992. The effects of isolated populations: are minimum viable population sizes predictable? Pages 277–296 in P. L. Fiedler and S. K. Jain, eds. Conservation biology: the theory and practice of nature conservation preservation and management. Chapman and Hall, New York.

Laflen, J. M., and J. L. Baker. 1982. Farming practices: impacts on runoff quality and quantity. Pages 25–26 in R. B. Dahlgren, ed. Proceedings of the Midwest agricultural interfaces with fish and wildlife resources workshop. Iowa State Univ., Ames.

Lamb, S. H., and R. D. Pieper. 1971. Game range improvement in New Mexico. New Mexico Inter-Agency Range Comm. Rep. 9, Agric. Res. Serv., Las Cruces, NM. 18pp.

Lande, R., and G. F. Barrowclough. 1987. Effective population size, genetic variation, and their use in population management. Pages 87–123 in M. E. Soulé, ed. Viable populations. Cambridge Univ. Press, New York.

Landers, J. L. 1989. Fire in North American wildlands: a need for decision. 25th Paul L. Errington Memorial Lecture, Iowa State Univ., Ames. 19pp.

Landers, J. L. 1992. Integrating wildlife and timber management in southern pine forests. Wildl. Manage. Ser. 3, Internat. Pap. Co., Bainbridge, GA. 28pp.

Landres, P. B. 1992. Temporal scale perspectives in managing biological diversity. Trans. North Am. Wildl. Nat. Resour. Conf. 57:292–307.

Landres, P. B., J. Verner, and J. W. Thomas. 1988. Ecological uses of vertebrate indicator species: a critique. Conserv. Biol. 2:1–13.

Lansky, M. 1992. Beyond the beauty strip: saving what's left of our forests. Tilbury House, Gardiner, ME. 453pp.

Lantz, C. W., ed. 1984. Southern pine nursery handbook. U.S. For. Serv., Atlanta. 374pp.

Lanyon, W. E. 1981. Breeding birds and old field succession on fallow Long Island, New York farmland. Bull. Am. Mus. Nat. Hist. 168:1–60.

Larsen, J. S. 1974. Forest management practices and policies as related to wildlife. Pages 193–196 in H. C. Black, ed. Wildlife and forest management in the Pacific Northwest. School For., Oregon State Univ., Corvallis.

Larson, F. R., P. F. Ffolliott, and W. P. Clary. 1986. Managing wildlife habitat. J. For. 84:40–41.

Larson, J. E. 1980. Revegetation equipment catalog. U.S. For. Serv. Equip. Develop. Cent., Missoula, MT. 198pp.

Larson, J. S. 1967. Forests, wildlife, and habitat management—a critical examination of practice and need. U.S. For. Serv. Res. Pap. SE-30. 28pp.

Lauer, J. L., and J. M. Peek. 1976. Big game-livestock relationships on the bighorn sheep winter range, East Fork Salmon River, Idaho. Univ. Idaho For., Range, Wildl. Exp. Stn. Bull. 12. 44pp.

Launchbaugh, J. L. 1964. Effects of early spring burning on yields of native vegetation. J. Range Manage. 17:5–6.

Launchbaugh, J. L. 1976. Graze first-year native grass plantings. Kansas Agric. Exp. Stn. AES-23. Manhattan, KS. 2pp.

Launchbaugh, J. L., and C. E. Owensby. 1978. Kansas rangelands: their management based on a half-century of research. Kansas Agric. Exp. Stn. Bull. 622. 56pp.

Lavin, F. 1967. Fall fertilization of intermediate wheatgrass in the southwestern ponderosa pine zone. J. Range Manage. 20:16–20.

Lay, D. W. 1965. Quail management handbook for east Texas. Texas Parks Wildl. Dep. Bull. 34. 46pp.

Laycock, W. A. 1967. How heavy grazing and protection affect sagebrush-grass ranges. J. Range Manage. 20:206–213.

Laycock, W. A., and P. W. Conrad. 1981. Responses of vegetation and cattle to various systems of grazing on seeded and native mountain ranges in western Utah. J. Range Manage. 34:50–58.

Leak, W. B. 1980. Influence of habitat on silvicultural prescriptions in New England. J. For. 78:329–331.

Leak, W. B. 1982. Habitat mapping and interpretation in New England. U.S. For. Serv. Res. Pap. NE-496. 28pp.

Leckenby, D. A. 1978. Western juniper management for mule deer. Pages 137–161 *in* R. E. Martin, J. E. Dealy, and O. L. Carter, eds. Proceedings of the western juniper ecology and management workshop. U.S. For. Serv. Gen. Tech. Rep. PNW-74.

Leech, G. R. 1982. Controlled burning in Arizona from the ground up. Pages 15–20 *in* P. F. Ffolliott, L. K. Sowls, and J. C. Tash, eds. The effects of land management practices on fish and wildlife in southwestern conifer forests. Proc. workshop. Arizona Coop. Fish and Wildl. Res. Unit, Univ. Arizona, Tucson.

Leedy, D. L., and L. W. Adams. 1982. Wildlife considerations in planning and managing highway corridors. U.S. Fed. Highway Admin. Rep. FHWA-TS-82-212. 93pp.

Leege, T. A. 1969. Burning seral brush ranges for big game in northern Idaho. Trans. North Am. Wildl. Nat. Resour. Conf. 34:429–438.

Lehmann, V. W. 1965. Fire in the range of Attwater's prairie chicken. Proc. Tall Timbers Fire Ecol. Conf. 4:127–143.

Lehmkuhl, J. F. 1984. Determining size and distribution of minimum viable populations for land management planning and species conservation. Environ. Manage. 8:167–176.

Lehmkuhl, J. F., and L. F. Ruggiero. 1991. Forest fragmentation in the Pacific Northwest and its potential effects on wildlife. 35–46 *in* L. F. Ruggiero, K. B. Aubry, A. B. Carey, and M. H. Huff, tech. coords. Wildlife and vegetation of unmanaged Douglas-fir forests. U.S. For. Serv. Gen. Tech. Rep. PNW-GTR-285.

Lennartz, M. R., and R. A. Lancia. 1989. Old-growth wildlife in second-growth forests: opportunities for creative silviculture. Pages 74–103 *in* Proceedings of the national silviculture workshop: silviculture for all resources. Timber Manage., U.S. For. Serv., Washington.

Lent, P. C. 1978. Musk-ox. Pages 125–147 *in* J. L. Schmidt and D. L. Gilbert, eds. Big game of North America. Stackpole Books, Harrisburg, PA.

Lent, P. C. 1986. Tundra. Pages 149–168 *in* A. Y. Cooperrider, R. J. Boyd, and H. R. Stuart, eds. Inventory and monitoring of wildlife habitat. U.S. Bur. Land Manage., Denver.

Leopold, A. 1933. Game management. Charles Scribner's Sons, New York. 481pp.

Leopold, A. 1966. A sand county almanac, with other essays on conservation from Round River. Oxford Univ. Press, New York. 269pp.

Leopold, A. S. 1977. The California quail. Univ. California Press, Berkeley. 281pp.

Leopold, B. D., and P. R. Krausman. 1991. Factors influencing desert mule deer distribution and productivity in southwestern Texas. Southwest. Nat. 36:67–74.

Leopold, L. B., M. G. Wolman, and J. P. Miller. 1964. Fluvial processes in geomorphology. W. H. Freeman, San Francisco. 522pp.

Lesperance, A. L., P. T. Tueller, and V. R. Bohman. 1970. Symposium on pasture methods for maximum production in beef cattle: competitive use of the range forage resource. J. Anim. Sci. 30:115–121.

Levenson, J. B. 1981. Woodlots as biogeographic islands in southeastern Wisconsin. pages 13–39 in R. L. Burgess and D. M. Sharpe, eds. Forest island dynamics in man-dominated landscapes. Springer-Verlag, New York.

Lewis, C. E., G. W. Tanner, and W. S. Terry. 1985. Double vs. single-row pine plantations for wood and forage production. South. J. Appl. For. 9:55–61.

Lewis, J. B., D. A. Murphy, and J. Ehrenreich. 1964. Effects of burning dates on vegetation production on Ozark forests. Annu. Conf. Southeast Assoc. Game and Fish Comm. 18:1–10.

Lienkaemper, G. W., and F. J. Swanson. 1987. Dynamics of large woody debris in streams in old-growth Douglas-fir forests, Oregon. Can. J. For. Res. 17:150–156.

Lipscomb, J. F., J. C. Capp, S. P. Mealey, and W. W. Sandfort. 1984. Establishing wildlife goals and objectives. Pages 305–321 in R. L. Hoover and D. L. Wills, eds. Managing forested lands for wildlife. Colorado Div. Wildl., Denver.

Litton, G. W. 1977. Food habits of the Rio Grande turkey in the Permian Basin of Texas. Texas Parks Wildl. Dep. Tech. Bull. 18. 22pp.

Logan, W., E. R. Brown, D. Longrie, G. Herb, and R. A. Corthell. 1985. Edges. Pages 115–127 in E. R. Brown, ed. Management of wildlife and fish habitats in forests of western Oregon and Washington. U.S. For. Serv., Portland, OR.

Loney, B., and R. J. Hobbs. 1991. Management of vegetation corridors: maintenance, rehabilitation and establishment. Pages 229–311 in D. A. Saunders and R. J. Hobbs, eds. Nature conservation 2: the role of corridors. Surrey Beatty & Sons, Chipping Norton, NSW, Australia.

Long, S. G., J. K. Burrell, N. F. Laurenson, and J. H. Nyenhuis. 1984. Manual of revegetation techniques. U.S. For. Serv. Equip. Develop. Cent., Missoula, MT. 145pp.

Longhurst, W. M., M. B. Jones, R. R. Parks, L. W. Neubauer, and M. W. Cummings. 1962. Fences for controlling deer damage. California Agric. Exp. Stn. Circ. 514, Univ. California, Davis. 19pp.

Longhurst, W. M., H. K. Oh, M. B. Jones, and R. E. Kepner. 1968. A basis for the palatability of deer forage plants. Trans. North Am. Wildl. Nat. Resour. Conf. 34:181–192.

Loope, L. L., and G. E. Gruell. 1973. The ecological role of fire in the Jackson Hole area, northeastern Wyoming. Quaternary Res. 3:425–443.

Lovejoy, T. E., and D. C. Oren. 1981. The minimum critical size of ecosystems. Pages 7–12 in R. L. Burgess and D. M. Sharpe, eds. Forest island dynamics in man-dominated landscapes. Springer-Verlag, New York.

Lucich, G. C., and R. M. Hansen. 1981. Autumn mule deer foods on heavily grazed cattle ranges in northwestern Colorado. J. Range Manage. 34:72–73.

Luman, I. D., and W. A. Neitro. 1980. Preservation of mature forest seral stages to provide wildlife habitat diversity. Trans. North Am. Wildl. Nat. Resour. Conf. 45:271–277.

Lynch, J. F., and D. F. Whigham. 1984. Effects of forest fragmentation on breeding bird communities in Maryland, USA. Biol. Conserv. 28:287–324.

Lyon, L. J. 1983. Road density models describing habitat effectiveness for elk. J. For. 81:592–595, 613.

Lyon, L. J., and J. V. Basile. 1980. Influences of timber harvesting and residue management on big game. Pages 441–453 in Environmental consequences of timber harvesting in Rocky Mountain coniferous forests. U.S. For. Serv. Gen. Tech. Rep. INT-90.

MacArthur, R. H., and E. O. Wilson. 1967. The theory of island biogeography. Princeton Univ. Press, Princeton, NJ. 203pp.

MacClintock, L., R. Whitcomb, and B. Whitcomb. 1977. Evidence for the value of corridors and minimization of isolation in preservation of biotic diversity. Am. Birds 31:6–16.

MacCracken, J. G., and D. W. Uresk. 1984. Big game habitat use in southeastern Montana. Prairie Nat. 16:135–139.

Mace, G. M., and P. H. Harvey. 1983. Energetic constraints on home-range size. Am. Nat. 121:120–132.

MacGregor, W. G. 1950. An evaluation of California quail management. Proc. Annu. Conf. West. Assoc. State Game and Fish Comm. 33:157–160.

Mackie, R. J. 1970. Range ecology and relations of mule deer, elk, and cattle in the Missouri River breaks, Montana. Wildl. Monogr. 20. 79pp.

Mackie, R. J., and H. K. Buechner. 1963. The reproductive cycle of the chukar. J. Wildl. Manage. 27:246–260.

Mader, H. J. 1984. Animal habitat isolation by roads and agricultural fields. Biol. Conserv. 29:81–96.

Madsen, C. R. 1981. Wildlife habitat development and restoration programs. Pages 209–216 in R. T. Dumke, G. V. Burger, and J. R. March, eds. Wildlife management on private lands. Wisconsin Chap. Wildl. Soc., Wisconsin Dep. Nat. Resour., Madison.

Mannan, R. W., E. C. Meslow, and H. M. Wight. 1980. Use of snags by birds in Douglas-fir forests, western Oregon. J. Wildl. Manage. 44:787–797.

Mannon, R. W., M. L. Morrison, and E. C. Meslow. 1984. The use of guilds in forest bird management. Wildl. Soc. Bull. 12:426–430.

Manske, L. L., W. T. Barker, and M. E. Biondini. 1988. Effects of grazing management treatment on grassland plant communities and prairie grouse habitat. Pages 58–72 in A. J. Bjugstad, tech. coord. Prairie chickens on the Sheyenne National Grasslands. U.S. For. Serv. Gen. Tech. Rep. RM-159.

Manuwal, D. A., and M. H. Huff. 1987. Spring and winter bird populations in a Douglas-fir forest sere. J. Wildl. Manage. 51:586–595.

Mapston, R. D., R. S. ZoBell, K. B. Winter, and W. D. Dooley. 1970. A pass for antelope in sheep-tight fences. J. Range Manage. 23:457–459.

Marceau, J. P. 1981. Mechanical weed control in eastern Canada. Pages 94–101 in H. A. Holt and B. C. Fischer, eds. Proceedings: weed control in forest management. Dep. For. Nat. Resour., Purdue Univ., West Lafayette, IN.

Marcot, B. G., and R. Holthausen, 1987. Analyzing population viability of the spotted owl in the Pacific Northwest. Trans. North Am. Wildl. Nat. Resour. Conf. 52:333–347.

Marcot, B. G., and V. J. Meretsky. 1983. Shaping stands to enhance habitat diversity. J. For. 81:526–528.

Margules, C. R., and M. P. Austin, eds. 1991. Nature conservation: cost effective biological surveys and data analysis. Australia CSIRO, East Melbourne. 207pp.

Margules, C. R., A. J. Higgs, and R. W. Rafe. 1982. Modern biogeographic theory: are there any lessons for nature reserve design? Biol. Conserv. 24:115–128.

Margules, C. R., A. O. Nicholls, and R. L. Pressey. 1988. Selecting networks of reserves to maximise biodiversity. Biol. Conserv. 43:63–76.

Margules, C. R., R. L. Pressey, and A. O. Nicholls. 1991. Selecting native preserves. Pages 90–97 in C. R. Margules and M. P. Austin, eds. Nature conservation: cost effective biological surveys and data analysis. Australia CSIRO, East Melbourne.

Marion, W. R., and L. D. Harris. 1982. Relationships between increasing forest productivity and fauna in the flatwoods of the southeastern coastal plain. Pages 215–223 in Increasing forest productivity. Proc. Annu. Conf. Soc. Am. For., Bethesda, MD.

Marsh, R. E., and R. W. Steele. 1992. Pocket gophers. Pages 205–230 in H. C. Black, tech. ed. Silvicultural approaches to animal damage management in Pacific Northwest forests. U.S. For. Serv. Gen. Tech. Rep. PNW-GTR-287.

Marti, C. D., P. W. Wagner, and K. W. Denne. 1979. Nest boxes for the management of barn owls. Wildl. Soc. Bull. 7:145–148.

Martin, A. C., H. S. Zim, and A. L. Nelson. 1951. American wildlife and plants: a guide to wildlife food habits. McGraw-Hill, New York. 500pp.

Martin, C. D., W. A. Mitchell, and D. A. Hammer. 1986. Osprey nest platforms. Sec. 5.1.6., U.S. Army Corps of Engineers wildlife resources management manual. U.S. Army Eng. Waterways Exp. Stn. Tech. Rep. EL-86-21. 31pp.

Martin, C. O., and J. L. Steele, Jr. 1984. Brush structures for wildlife. Wildl. Resour. Notes, U.S. Army Corps of Eng. Inf. Exchange Bull. 2(2):1–2.

Martin, C. O., and J. L. Steele, Jr. 1986. Brush piles. Sec. 5.3.1, U.S. Army Corps of Engineers wildlife resources management manual. U.S. Army Eng. Waterways Exp. Stn. Tech. Rep. EL-86-14. 19pp.

Martin, J. P. 1981. Mechanical weed control in southern forests. Pages 102–107 *in* H. A. Holt and B. C. Fischer, eds. Weed control in forest management. Purdue Res. Found., Purdue Univ., West Lafayette, IN.

Martin, P., and G. F. Houf. 1993. Glade grasslands in southwest Missouri. Rangelands 15:70–73.

Martin, R. E., and J. D. Dell. 1978. Planning for prescribed burning in the inland Northwest. U.S. For. Serv. Gen. Tech. Rep. PNW-76. 67pp.

Martin, S. C., and D. R. Cable. 1974. Managing semidesert grass-shrub ranges: vegetation responses to precipitation, grazing, soil texture, and mesquite control. U.S. For. Serv. Tech. Bull. 1480, Washington. 45pp.

Martin, S. C., and D. E. Ward. 1976. Perennial grasses respond consistently to alternate year seasonal rest. J. Range Manage. 29:346–347.

Martin, S. G., D. A. Thiel, J. W. Duncan, and W. R. Lance. 1987. Effects of a paper industry sludge containing dioxin on wildlife in red pine plantations. Pages 363–377 *in* Proceedings of the 1987 TAPPI environmental conference. TAPPI Press, Atlanta.

Martin, T. E. 1980. Diversity and abundance of spring migratory birds using habitat islands in the Great Plains. Condor 82:430–439.

Martin, T. E., and P. A. Vohs. 1978. Configuration of shelterbelts for optimum utilization by birds. Pages 79–88 *in* R. W. Tinus, ed. Proceedings of the 30th annual Forestry Commission. Great Plains Agric. Counc. Pub. 87, Tulsa, OK.

Maser, C. 1988. The redesigned forest. R. & E. Miles, San Pedro, CA. 234pp.

Maser, C., R. G. Anderson, K. Cromack, Jr., J. T. Williams, and R. E. Martin. 1979a. Dead and down woody material. Pages 78–95 *in* J. W. Thomas, tech. ed. Wildlife habitats in managed forests: the Blue Mountains of Oregon and Washington. U.S. For. Serv. Agric. Handb. 553, Portland, OR.

Maser, C., and J. S. Gashwiler. 1978. Interrelationships of wildlife and western juniper. Pages 37–82 *in* R. E. Martin, J. E. Dealy, and O. L. Carter, eds. Proceedings of the western juniper ecology and management workshop. U.S. For. Serv. Gen. Tech. Rep. PNW-74.

Maser, C., J. M. Geist, D. M. Concannon, R. Anderson, and B. Lovell. 1979b. Wildlife habitats in managed rangelands—the Great Basin of southeastern Oregon, geomorphic and edaphic habitats. U.S. For. Serv. Gen. Tech. Rep. PNW-99. 84pp.

Maser, C., J. E. Rodiek, and J. W. Thomas. 1979c. Cliffs, talus, and caves. Pages 96–103 *in* J. W. Thomas, tech. ed. Wildlife habitats in managed forests: the Blue Mountains of Oregon and Washington. U.S. For. Serv. Agric. Handb. 553, Portland, OR.

Maser, C., R. F. Tarrant, J. M. Trappe, and J. F. Franklin, eds. 1988. From the forest to the sea: a story of fallen trees. U.S. For. Serv. Gen. Tech. Rep. PNW-229. 153pp.

Maser, C., J. W. Thomas, I. D. Luman, and R. Anderson. 1979d. Wildlife habitats in managed rangelands—the Great Basin of southeastern Oregon: manmade habitats. U.S. For. Serv. Gen. Tech. Rep. PNW-86. 39pp.

Maser, C., and J. M. Trappe, eds. 1984. The seen and unseen world of the fallen tree. U.S. For. Serv. Gen. Tech. Rep. PNW-164. 56pp.

Mason, J. L., and J. E. Miltimore. 1969. Yield increases from nitrogen on native range in southern British Columbia. J. Range Manage. 22:128–131.

McAninch, C. D., R. L. Hoover, and R. C. Kufeld. 1984. Silvicultural treatments and their effects on wildlife. Pages 211–241 *in* R. L. Hoover and D. L. Wills, eds. Managed forested lands for wildlife. Colorado Div. Wildl., Denver.

McCaffery, K. R., J. E. Ashbrenner, and J. C. Moulton. 1981. Forest opening construction and impacts in northern Wisconsin. Wisconsin Dep. Nat. Resour. Tech. Bull. 120. 41pp.

McCaffery, K. R., and W. A. Creed. 1969. Significance of forest openings to deer in northern Wisconsin. Wisconsin Dep. Nat. Resour. Tech. Bull. 44. 104pp.

McCarty, R. S. 1986. Handbook for successful planning, installation and monitoring of wildlife waterers. U.S. Bur. Land Manage. Tech Bull. 86-1. 23pp.

McCollum, F. T., R. L. Gillen, D. M. Engle, and G. W. Horn. 1990. Stocker cattle performance and vegetation response to intensive-early stocking of Cross Timbers rangeland. J. Range Manage. 43:99–103.

McComb, W. C. 1982. Forestry and wildlife habitat management in central hardwoods. J. For. 80:490–492.

McComb, W. C., S. A. Bonney, R. M. Sheffield, and N. D. Cost. 1986. Snag resources in Florida—are they sufficient for average populations of primary cavity-nesters? Wildl. Soc. Bull. 14:40–48.

McComb, W. C., and R. E. Noble. 1981. Nest-box and natural-cavity use in three mid-south forest habitats. J. Wildl. Manage. 45:93–101.

McComb, W. C., and R. L. Rumsey. 1983. Characteristics and cavity-nesting bird use of picloram-created snags in the central Appalachians. South. J. Appl. For. 7:34–37.

McConnell, B. R., and J. G. Smith. 1977. Influence of grazing on age-yield interactions in bitterbrush. J. Range Manage. 30:91–96.

McCormack, M. L., Jr., and C. H. Banks. 1983. An aerial technique to adjust spruce-fir density of stocking. Proc. Northeast. Weed Sci. Soc. 37:297–300.

McCormack, M. L., Jr., F. B. Knight, and R. A. Rogers. 1978. Glyphosate as a management tool for increasing forest productivity. Proc. Northeast. Weed Sci. Soc. 32:285–286.

McCulloch, C. Y. 1969. Some effects of wildfire on deer habitat in pinyon-juniper woodland. J. Wildl. Manage. 33:778–784.

McCulloch, C. Y. 1979. Pinyon-juniper woodland. Pages 48–65 in D. Neff, C. Y. McCulloch, D. Brown, C. Lowe, and J. Barstad, eds. Forest, range, and watershed management for enhancement of wildlife habitat in Arizona. Arizona Game and Fish Dep. Spec. Rep. 7.

McGinnes, B. S. 1969. How size and distribution of cutting units affect food and cover of deer. Pages 66–70 in White-tailed deer in the southern forest habitat. U.S. For. Serv. South. For. Exp. Stn., New Orleans.

McGinnies, W. J. 1968. Effects of nitrogen fertilizer on an old stand of crested wheatgrass. Agron. J. 60:560–562.

McKell, C. M. 1975. Shrubs and forbs for improvement of rangelands. Soc. Range Manage., Range Symp. Ser. 1:62–75.

McKell, C. M., J. Major, and E. R. Perrier. 1959. Annual-range fertilization in relation to soil moisture depletion. J. Range Manage. 12:189–193.

McKendrick, J. D. 1981. Response of arctic tundra to intensive musk-ox grazing. Agroborealis 13:49–55.

McKendrick, J. D., G. O. Batzli, K. R. Everett, and J. C. Swanson. 1980. Some effects of mammalian herbivores and fertilization on tundra soils and vegetation. Arctic and Alpine Res. 12:565–578.

McMurphy, W. E., and K. L. Anderson. 1965. Burning Fling Hills range. J. Range Manage. 18:265–269.

McNab, B. K. 1963. Bioenergetics and the determination of home-range size. Am. Nat. 97:133–140.

McNabb, F. M.A. 1969. A comparative study of water balance in three species of quail. I. Water turnover in the absence of temperature stress. Comp. Biochem. Phys. 28:1045–1058.

McPherson, G. R., G. A. Rasmussen, H. A. Wright, and C. M. Britton. 1986. Getting started in prescribed burning. Texas Tech Univ. Dep. Range Wildl. Manage. Note 9. 5pp.

McReynolds, H. E., R. W. Hollingsworth, and R. E. Radtke. 1983. A spacing system for location of management activities affecting riparian zones of the eastern national forests. Pages 224–232 in America's hardwood forests—opportunities unlimited. Proc. 1982 Conv. Soc. Am. For., Bethesda, MD.

Mead, T. L. 1973. Pheasant production on lands diverted for wildlife and other cover types. M.S. thesis. Univ. Nevada, Reno. 51pp.

Meagher, M. M. 1978. Bison. Pages 123–133 in J. L. Schmidt and D. L. Gilbert, eds. Big game of North America. Stackpole Books, Harrisburg, PA.

Mealey, S. P. 1984. Solving the diversity problem in forest planning. Pages 267–282 in J. L. Cooley and J. H. Cooley, eds. Natural diversity in forest ecosystems: proceedings of the workshop. Inst. Ecol., Univ. Georgia, Athens.

Mealey, S. P., and J. R. Horn. 1981. Integrating wildlife habitat objectives into the forest plan. Trans. North Am. Wildl. Nat. Resour. Conf. 46:488–500.

Mealey, S. P., J. P. Lipscomb, and K. N. Johnson. 1982. Solving the habitat dispersion problem in forest planning. Trans. North Am. Wildl. Nat. Resour. Conf. 47:142–153.

Mech, L. D., S. H. Fritts, G. L. Radde, and W. J. Paul. 1988. Wolf distribution and road density in Minnesota. Wildl. Soc. Bull. 16:85–87.

Medin, D. E. 1990. Birds of an upper sagebrush-grass zone habitat in east-central Nevada. U.S. For. Serv. Res. Pap. INT-433. 7pp.

Meffe, G. K., A. H. Ehrlich, and D. Ehrenfeld. 1993. Human population control: the missing agenda. Conserv. Biol. 7:1–3.

Mehl, M. S. 1992. Old-growth descriptions for the major forest cover types in the Rocky Mountain region. Pages 106–120 in M. R. Kaufmann, W. H. Moir, and R. L. Bassett, tech. coords. Old-growth forests in the Southwest and Rocky Mountain regions: proceedings of a workshop. U.S. For. Serv. Gen. Tech. Rep. RM-213.

Meister, R. P., ed. 1990. Farm chemicals handbook. Meister Pub. Co., Willoughby, OH. Various pages.

Melton, B. L., R. L. Hoover, R. L. Moore, and D. J. Pfankuch. 1984. Aquatic and riparian wildlife. Pages 261–301 in R. L. Hoover and D. L. Wills, eds. Managing forested lands for wildlife. Colorado Div. Wildl., Denver.

Merrill, E. H., H. F. Mayland, and J. M. Peek. 1982. Shrub response after fire in an Idaho ponderosa pine community. J. Wildl. Manage. 46:496–502.

Merrill, L. B. 1954. A variation of deferred rotation grazing for use under southwest range conditions. J. Range Manage. 7:152–154.

Mettler, L. E. 1984. Christmas tree brush piles. Wildl. Resour. Notes, U.S. Army Corps Eng. Inf. Exchange Bull. 2(2):7–8.

Michael, J. L., and D. G. Neary. 1990. Use, fate, and risk assessment of forestry herbicides in the southern United States. Pages 301–311 in Proceedings of XIXth IUFRO World Congress. Can. Internat. Union For. Res. Organ., Montreal.

Milchunas, D. G., W. K. Lauenroth, P. L. Chapman, and M. K. Kazempour. 1990. Community attributes along a perturbation gradient in a shortgrass steppe. J. Veg. Sci. 1:375–384.

Milchunas, D. G., O. E. Sala, and W. K. Lauenroth. 1988. A generalized model of the effects of grazing by large herbivores on grassland community structure. Am. Nat. 132:87–106.

Miles, D. W. R., and F. J. Swanson. 1986. Vegetation composition on recent landslides in the Cascade Mountains of western Oregon. Can. J. For. Res. 16:739–744.

Miller, A. V., and S. M. Craig, eds. 1979. Handbook for pesticide applicators and pesticide dispensers. British Columbia Min. Environ., Victoria. 233pp.

Miller, E., and D. R. Miller. 1980. Snag use by birds. Pages 337–356 in R. M. DeGraaf, tech. coord. Workshop proceedings: management of western forests and grasslands for nongame birds. U.S. For. Serv. Gen. Tech. Rep. INT-86.

Miller, J. P. 1934. The place of game management in New England forestry. J. For. 32:47–51.

Millsap, B. A., K. W. Cline, and B. A. Giron Pendleton. 1987. Habitat management. Pages 215–237 in B. A. Giron Pendleton, B. A. Millsap, K. W. Cline, and D. M. Bird, eds. Raptor management techniques manual. Natl. Wildl. Fed., Washington.

Minnesota Department of Natural Resources. 1985. Forestry-wildlife guidelines to habitat management. Minnesota Dep. Nat. Resour., St. Paul. 137pp.

Minser, W. G., and R. W. Dimmick. 1988. Bobwhite quail use of no-till versus conventionally planted crops in western Tennessee. J. Soil Water Conserv. 43:270–272.

Mitchell, W. A. 1988. Songbird nest boxes. Sect. 5.1.8., U.S. Army Corps of Engineers wildlife resources management manual. U.S. Army Eng. Waterways Exp. Stn. Tech. Rep. EL-88-19. 48pp.

Mooney, H. A., T. M. Bonnicksen, N. L. Christensen, J. E. Lotan, and W. A. Reiners, eds. 1981. Fire regimes and ecosystem properties. U.S. For. Serv. Gen. Tech. Rep. WO-26. 593pp.

Moore, W. H., and B. F. Swindel. 1981. Effects of site preparation on dry prairie vegetation in south Florida. South. J. Appl. For. 5:89–92.

Moore, W. H., B. F. Swindel, and W. S. Terry. 1982. Vegetative response to prescribed fire in a north Florida flatwoods forest. J. Range Manage. 35:386–389.

Monthey, R. W. 1984. Wildlife considerations in the management of fragmented older forests: the coast ranges of northwest Oregon. Pages 367–371 in W. R. Meehan, T. R.

Merrell, Jr., and T. A. Hanley, eds. Fish and wildlife relationships in old-growth forests. Proc. Symp. Am. Inst. Fish. Res. Biol., Rt. 4, Box 84, Morehead, NC.

Morgan, K. A., and J. E. Gates. 1983. Use of forest edge and strip vegetation by eastern cottontails. J. Wildl. Manage. 47:259–264.

Morris, L. A., W. L. Pritchett, and B. F. Swindel. 1983. Displacement of nutrients into windrows during site preparation of a flatwood forest. Soil Sci. Soc. Am. J. 47:591–594.

Morrison, M. L., B. G. Marcot, and R. W. Mannan. 1992. Wildlife-habitat relationships. Univ. Wisconsin Press, Madison. 343pp.

Morrison, M. L., and E. C. Meslow. 1983. Impacts of forest herbicides on wildlife: toxicity and habitat alteration. Trans. North Am. Wildl. Nat. Resour. Conf. 48:175–185.

Morrison, P. H., and F. J. Swanson. 1990. Fire history and pattern in a Cascade range landscape. U.S. For. Serv. Gen. Tech. Rep. PNW-GTR-254. 79pp.

Morrow, M. E. 1986. Ecology of Attwater's prairie chicken in relation to land management practices on the Attwater Prairie Chicken National Wildlife Refuge. Ph.D. thesis, Texas A&M Univ., College Station. 99pp.

Morton, H. L., and A. Melgoza. 1991. Vegetation changes following brush control in creosotebush communities. J. Range Manage. 44:133–139.

Morton, J. M., and J. B. Sedam. 1938. Cutting operations to improve wildlife environment on forest areas. J. Wildl. Manage. 2:206–214.

Mowrey, R. A., and J. C. Zasada. 1984. Den tree use and movements of northern flying squirrels in interior Alaska and implications for forest management. Pages 351–356 *in* W. R. Meehan, T. R. Merrell, Jr., and T. A. Hanley, eds. Fish and wildlife relationships in old-growth forests. Am. Inst. Fish. Res. Biol., Rt. 4, Box 85, Morehead City, NC.

Mueggler, W. F. 1950. Effects of spring and fall grazing by sheep on vegetation of the upper Snake River Plains. J. Range Manage. 3:308–315.

Mueggler, W. F. 1985. Vegetation associations. Pages 45–55 *in* N. V. DeByle and R. P. Winokur, eds. Aspen: ecology and management in the western United States. U.S. For. Serv. Gen. Tech. Rep. RM-119.

Mueggler, W. F., and J. P. Blaisdell. 1958. Effects on associated species of burning, rotobeating, spraying and railing sagebrush. J. Range Manage. 11:61–66.

Murphy, R. K., N. F. Payne, and R. K. Anderson. 1985. White-tailed deer use of an irrigated agriculture-grassland complex in central Wisconsin. J. Wildl. Manage. 49:125–128.

Mutz, J. L. 1980. Fire effects on deep sand range sites in south Texas. Pages 93–100 *in* C. W. Henselka, ed. Symposium: prescribed range burning in the coastal prairie and Rio Grande plains of Texas. Texas Agric. Exp. Stn., Texas A&M Univ., College Station.

Nason, G. 1984. Ecofarming. Pages 65B–68B in F. R. Henderson, ed. Guidelines for increasing wildlife on farms and ranches. Coop. Ext. Serv., Kansas State Univ., Manhattan.

National Audubon Society. 1969. Wildlife habitat improvement. Natl. Audubon Soc., New York. 96pp.

National Wildlife Federation. 1984. Wildlife planting guide. Natl. Wildl. Fed., Washington. 2pp.

Neal, D. L. 1982. Improvement of Great Basin deer winter range with livestock grazing. Pages 61–73 *in* J. M. Peek and P. D. Dalke, eds. Symposium on wildlife-livestock relationships. For., Wildl., Range Exp. Stn., Univ. Idaho, Moscow.

Neitro, W. A., V. W. Binkley, S. P. Cline, R. W. Mannan, B. G. Marcot, D. Taylor, and F. F. Wagner. 1985. Snags (wildlife trees). Pages 129–169 *in* E. R. Brown, ed. Management of wildlife and fish habitats in forests of western Oregon and Washington. Part 1—Chapter narratives. U.S. For. Serv., Portland, OR.

Nelle, S. 1984. Key food plants for deer—south Texas. Pages 277–291 *in* L. D. White and D. Guynn, eds. Proceedings of the 1984 International Ranchers Roundup, San Angelo, TX.

Nelson, M. W., and P. Nelson. 1976. Powerlines and birds of prey. Idaho Wildl. Rev. 28(5):3–7.

Nero, R. W., S. G. Sealy, and H. W. R. Copland. 1974. Great gray owls occupy artificial nest. Loon 46:161–165.

Newmark, W. D. 1985. Legal and biotic boundaries of western North American national parks: a problem of congruence. Biol. Conserv. 33:197–208.

Newmark, W. D. 1986. Mammalian richness, colonization, and extinction in western North American parks. Ph.D. thesis, Univ. Michigan, Ann Arbor. 172pp.

Newmark, W. D. 1987. A land-bridge island perspective on mammalian extinctions in western North American parks. Nature 325:430–432.

Newton, M., and E. C. Cole. 1987. A sustained-yield scheme for old-growth Douglas-fir. West. J. Appl. For. 2:22–25.

Newton, M., and F. B. Knight. 1981. Handbook of weed and insect control chemicals for forest resource managers. Timber Press, Beaverton, OR. 213pp.

Nicholls, A. O., and C. R. Margules. 1991. The design of studies to demonstrate the biological importance of corridors. Pages 49–61 in D. A. Saunders and R. J. Hobbs, eds. Nature conservation 2: the role of corridors. Surrey Beatty & Sons, Chipping Norton, NSW, Australia.

Nichols, J. T., and J. R. Johnson. 1969. Range productivity as influenced by biennial sweetclover in western South Dakota. J. Range Manage. 22:342–347.

Nicholson, A. J. 1941. The homes and social habitats of the woodmouse (Peromyscus leucopus noveboracensis) in southern Michigan. Am. Midl. Nat. 25:196–223.

Niering, W. A. 1987. Vegetation dynamics (succession and climax) in relation to plant community management. Conserv. Biol. 1:287–295.

Niering, W. A., and R. H. Goodwin. 1974. Creation of relatively stable shrublands with herbicides: arresting "succession" on rights-of-way and pastureland. Ecology 55:784–795.

Nixon, C. M., and R. W. Donohoe. 1979. Squirrel nest boxes—are they effective in young hardwood stands? Wildl. Soc. Bull. 7:283–284.

Nixon, C. M., and L. P. Hansen. 1987. Managing forests to maintain populations of gray and fox squirrels. Illinois Dep. Conserv. Tech. Bull. 5. 35pp.

Nixon, C. M., M. W. McClain, and K. R. Russell. 1970. Deer food habits and range characteristics in Ohio. J. Wildl. Manage. 34:870–886.

Noble, R. E., and R. B. Hamilton. 1975. Bird populations in even-aged loblolly pine forests of southeastern Louisiana. Proc. Annu. Southeast. Assoc. Game and Fish Comm. Conf. 29:441–450.

Norrgard, R. 1989. Woody cover plantings for wildlife. Minnesota Dep. Nat. Resour., St. Paul. 16pp.

Norton, B. G. 1987. Why preserve natural variety? Princeton Univ. Press, Princeton, NJ. 281pp.

Noss, R. F. 1985. On characterizing presettlement vegetation: how and why. Nat. Areas J. 5:5–19.

Noss, R. F. 1987a. From plant communities to landscapes in conservative inventories: a look at the Nature Conservancy (USA). Biol. Conserv. 41:11–37.

Noss, R. F. 1987b. Protecting natural areas in fragmented landscapes. Nat. Areas J. 7:1–13.

Noss, R. F. 1987c. Corridors in real landscapes: a reply to Simberloff and Cox. Conserv. Biol. 1:159–164.

Noss, R. F. 1990. Indicators for monitoring biodiversity: a hierarchical approach. Conserv. Biol. 4:355–364.

Noss, R. F. 1991a. Effects of edge and internal patchiness on avian habitat use in an old-growth Florida hammock. Nat. Areas J. 11:34–47.

Noss, R. F. 1991b. Wilderness recovery: thinking big in restoration ecology. Environ. Profess. 13:225–234.

Noss, R. F. 1992. The wildlands project land conservation strategy. Wild Earth. Special issue:10–25.

Noss, R. F., and L. D. Harris. 1986. Nodes, networks, and MUMs: preserving diversity at all scales. Environ. Manage. 10:299–309.

Noste, N. V., and J. K. Brown. 1981. Current practices of prescribed burning in the West. Pages 156–169 in H. A. Holt and B. C. Fisher, eds. Proceedings: weed control in forest management. Dep. For. Nat. Resour., Purdue Univ., West Lafayette, IN.

Nova Scotia Department of Lands and Forests. ca 1989. Forest/wildlife guidelines and standards for Nova Scotia. Nova Scotia Dep. Lands and For., Truro. 19pp.

Novak, M., J. A. Baker, M. E. Obbard, and B. Malloch, eds. 1987. Wild furbearer management and conservation in North America. Ontario Min. Nat. Resour., Toronto. 1150pp.

Nuzzo, V. A. 1986. Extent and status of Midwest oak savanna: presettlement and 1985.
Nat. Areas J. 6:6–36.

Nyberg, J. B., F. L. Bunnell, D. W. Janz, and R. M. Ellis. 1986. Managing young forests
as black-tailed deer winter range. Land Manage. Rep. 37, British Columbia Min.
For., Victoria. 49pp.

Nyberg, J. B., A. S. Harestad, and F. L. Bunnell. 1987. "Old-growth" by design: managing young forests for old-growth wildlife. Trans. North Am. Wildl. Nat. Resour. Conf.
52:70–81.

Nyberg, J. B., R. S. McNay, M. D. Kirchhoff, R. D. Forbes, F. L. Bunnell, and E. L.
Richardson. 1989. Integrated management of timber and deer: coastal forests of
British Columbia and Alaska. U.S. For. Serv. Gen. Tech. Rep. PNW-GTR-226. 65pp.

Oakley, A. L., J. A. Collins, L. B. Everson, D. A. Heller, J. C. Howerton, and R. E.
Vincent. 1985. Riparian zones and freshwater wetlands. Pages 57–80 *in* E. R.
Brown, ed. Management of wildlife and fish habitats in forests of western Oregon
and Washington. Part I—Chapter narratives. U.S. For. Serv., Portland, OR.

Odum, W. E., T. S. Smith III, and R. Dolan. 1987. Suppression of natural disturbance:
long-term ecological change on the outer banks of North Carolina. Pages 123–135 *in*
M. G. Turner, ed. Landscape heterogeneity and disturbance. Springer-Verlag, New
York.

Oelke, H. 1966. 35 years of breeding-bird census work in Europe. Audubon Field Notes
20:635–642.

Ohlsson, K. E., A. E. Robb, Jr., C. E. Guindon, Jr., D. E. Samuel, and R. L. Smith. 1982.
Best current practices for fish and wildlife on surface-mined land in the northern
Appalachian coal region. U.S. Fish Wildl. Serv. FWS/OBS-81/45. 305pp.

Ohman, L. F., H. O. Batzer, R. R. Buech, D. C. Lothner, D. A. Perala, A. L. Schipper,
Jr., and E. S. Veery. 1978. Some harvest options and their consequences for the
aspen, birch, and associated conifer forest types of the Lake States. U.S. For. Serv.
Gen. Tech. Rep. NC-48. 34pp.

Ohmart, R. D., and B. W. Anderson. 1986. Riparian habitat. Pages 169–199 *in* A. Y.
Cooperrider, R. J. Boyd, and H. R. Stuart, eds. Inventory and monitoring of wildlife
habitat. U.S. Bur. Land Manage., Denver.

Olawsky, C. D., and L. M. Smith. 1991. Lesser prairie-chicken densities on tebuthi-
uron-treated and untreated sand shinnery oak rangelands. J. Range Manage.
44:364–368.

Olendorff, R. R., A. D. Miller, and R. N. Lehman. 1981. Suggested practices for raptor
protection on power lines—the state of the art in 1981. Raptor Res. Rep. 111pp.

Olendorff, R. R., R. S. Motroni, and M. W. Call. 1980. Raptor management—the state of
the art in 1980. Pages 468–523 *in* R. M. DeGraaf and N. G. Tilghman, eds.
Workshop proceedings: management of western forests and grasslands for nongame
birds. U.S. For. Serv. Gen. Tech. Rep. INT-86.

Olendorff, R. R., and J. W. Stoddard. 1974. The potential for management of raptor
populations in western grasslands. Pages 47–88 *in* F. N. Hamerstrom, Jr., B. E.
Harrell, and R. R. Olendorff, eds. Management of raptors. Raptor Res. Rep. 2.

Oliver, C. D., and B. C. Larson. 1990. Forest stand dynamics. McGraw-Hill, New York.
467 pp.

Oliver, W. H. 1969. Riparian lands—icey habitat for upland birds. Washington Dep.
Game Bull. 21:3–5.

Oliveri, S. 1988. Forest openings. Pages 10–11 *in* C. A. Elliott, ed. A forester's guide to
managing wildlife habitats in Maine. Coop. Ext. Serv., Univ. Maine, Orono.

Olson, D., and C. Langer. 1990. Care of wild apple trees. Coop. Ext. Serv., Univ. New
Hampshire, Durham. 3pp.

O'Meara, T. E., J. B. Haufler, L. H. Stelter, and J. G. Nagy. 1981. Nongame wildlife
responses to chaining of pinyon-juniper woodlands. J. Wildl. Manage. 45:381–389.

Omernik, J. M. 1987. Ecoregions of the conterminous United States. Annals of Assoc. of
Am. Geographers 77:118–125.

Oregon Department of Forestry. 1991. Oregon forest practices rules. For. Practices
Sec., Oregon Dep. For., Salem. Various pages.

Orodho, A. B., M. J. Trlica, and C. D. Bonham. 1990. Long-term heavy grazing effects on soil and vegetation in the four corners region. Southwest. Nat. 35:9–14.

Owens, M. K., and B. E. Norton. 1990. Survival of juvenile basin-big sagebrush under different grazing regimes. J. Range Manage. 43:132–135.

Owens, R. A., and M. T. Myres. 1973. Effects of agriculture upon populations of native passerine birds of an Alberta fescue grassland. Can. J. Zool. 51:697–713.

Oxley, D. J., M. B. Fenton, and G. R. Carmody. 1974. The effects of roads on populations of small mammals. J. Appl. Ecol. 11:51–59.

Papendick, R. I., and L. F. Elliott. 1985. Different cropping systems in the United States and potential benefits to wildlife. Pages 63–68 *in* S. Shen, proj. dir. Technologies to benefit agriculture and wildlife. U.S. Off. Tech. Assess. OTA-BP-F-34.

Parker, L. R. 1990. Feasibility assessment for the reintroduction of North American elk, moose, and caribou into Wisconsin. Wisconsin Dep. Nat. Resour., Madison. 115pp.

Pase, C. P., and H. Granfelt. 1977. The use of fire on Arizona rangelands. Arizona Interagency Range Comm. Pub. 4. 15pp.

Pase, C. P., and A. W. Lindenmuth, Jr. 1971. Effects of prescribed fire on vegetation and sediment in oak-mountain mahogany chaparral. J. For. 69:800–805.

Patton, D. R. 1974. Patch cutting increases deer and elk use of a pine forest in Arizona. J. For. 72:764–766.

Patton, D. R. 1975. A diversity index for quantifying habitat "edge." Wildl. Soc. Bull. 3:171–173.

Patton, D. R. 1992. Wildlife habitat relationships in forested ecosystems. Timber Press, Portland, OR. 392pp.

Patton, D. R., and B. S. McGinnes. 1964. Deer browse relative to age and intensity of timber harvest. J. Wildl. Manage. 28:458–463.

Payne, N. F. 1992. Techniques for wildlife habitat management of wetlands. McGraw-Hill, New York. 549pp.

Payne, N. F., and F. Copes. 1988. Wildlife and fisheries habitat improvement handbook. U.S. For. Serv., Washington. 402pp.

Pearson, H. A., J. R. Davis, and G. H. Schubert. 1972. Effects of wildfire on timber and forage production in Arizona. J. Range Manage. 25:250–253.

Pechanec, J. F., A. P. Plummer, J. H. Robertson, and A. C. Hull, Jr. 1965. Sagebrush control on rangelands. U.S. Dep. Agric. Handb. 277. 40pp.

Pechanec, J. F., G. Stewart, and J. P. Blaisdell. 1954. Sagebrush burning—good and bad. Farmer's Bull. 1948. U.S. Dep. Agric., Washington. 32pp.

Peek, J. M. 1986. A review of wildlife management. Prentice-Hall, Englewood Cliffs, NJ. 486pp.

Peek, J. M., R. A. Riggs, and J. L. Lauer. 1979. Evaluation of fall burning on bighorn sheep winter range. J. Range Manage. 32:430–432.

Peek, J. M., D. L. Ulrich, and M. J. Mackie. 1976. Moose habitat selection and relationships to forest management in northeastern Minnesota. Wildl. Monogr. 48. 65pp.

Pegau, R. E. 1970. Effect of reindeer trampling and grazing on lichens. J. Range Manage. 23:95–97.

Pendry, B. M., and F. D. Provenza. 1987. Interplanting crested wheatgrass with shrubs and alfalfa: effects of competition and preferential clipping. J. Range Manage. 40:514–520.

Perala, D. A. 1977. Manager's handbook for aspen in the north central states. U.S. For. Serv. Gen. Tech. Rep. NC-37. 35pp.

Perala, D. A., and J. Russell. 1983. Aspen. Pages 113–115 *in* R. M. Burns, ed. Silvicultural systems for the major forest types of the United States. U.S. For. Serv. Agric. Handb. 445.

Perkins, W. C. Undated. Kentucky tree planting manual. Kentucky Dep. Nat. Resour. Environ. Prot., Frankfort. 104pp.

Perry, C., and R. Overly. 1976. Impact of roads on big game distribution in portions of the Blue Mountains of Washington. Pages 62–68 *in* J. M. Peek, ed. Proceedings of the elk-logging-roads symposium. For., Wildl., Range Exp. Stn., Univ. Idaho, Moscow.

Petersen, J. L., D. N. Ueckert, and M. W. Wagner. 1990. Herbicides to aid establishment of fourwing saltbush. Pages 305–309 *in* E. D. McArthur, E. M. Romney, S. D.

Smith, and P. T. Tueller, comps. Proceedings: symposium on cheatgrass invasion, shrub die-off, and other aspects of shrub biology and management. U.S. For. Serv. Gen. Tech. Rep. INT-276.

Peterson, K. L., and L. B. Best. 1987. Effects of prescribed burning on nongame birds in a sagebrush community. Wildl. Soc. Bull. 15:317–329.

Peterson, R. O. 1988. The pit or the pendulum: issues in large carnivore management in natural ecosystems. Pages 105–117 *in* J. K. Agee and D. R. Johnson, eds. Ecosystem management for parks and wilderness. Univ. Washington Press, Seattle.

Peterson, R. T. 1963. Birdhouses and feeders. Natl. Audubon Soc. Circ. 29, New York.

Petraitis, P. S., R. E. Latham, and R. A. Niesenbaum. 1989. The maintenance of species diversity by disturbance. Quart. Rev. Biol. 64:393–418.

Pfister, R. D., B. L. Kovalchik. S. F. Arno, and R. C. Presby. 1977. Forest habitat types of Montana. U.S. For. Serv. Gen. Tech. Rep. INT-34. 174pp.

PFRA Tree Nursery. Undated. Planting trees for wildlife habitat. PFRA Tree Nursery, Indian Head, Sask. 12pp.

Pickett, S. T.A., and J. N. Thompson. 1978. Patch dynamics and the design of nature reserves. Biol. Conserv. 13:27–37.

Pickett, S. T.A., and P. S. White, eds. 1985. The ecology of natural disturbance and patch dynamics. Academic Press, New York. 472pp.

Pielou, E. C. 1990. Depletion of genetic richness is not "harmless" consequence of clearcutting. For. Planning Can. 6(4):29.

Pieper, R. D. 1990. Overstory-understory relations in pinyon-juniper woodlands in New Mexico. J. Range Manage. 43:413–415.

Pieper, R. D., G. B. Donart, E. E. Parker, and J. D. Wallace. 1978. Livestock and vegetational response to continuous and four-pasture one-herd grazing systems in New Mexico. Proc. Internat. Rangeland Congr. 1:560–562.

Pieper, R. D., R. J. Kelsey, and A. B. Nelson. 1974. Nutritive quality of nitrogen fertilized and unfertilized bluegrama. J. Range Manage. 27:470–472.

Pierovich, J. M., E. H. Clarke, S. G. Pickford, and F. R. Ward. 1975. Forest residues management guidelines for the Pacific Northwest. U.S. For. Serv. Gen. Tech. Rep. PNW-33. 281pp.

Pimental, D., U. Stachow, D. A. Takacs, H. W. Brubaker, A. R. Dumas, J. J. Meaney, J. A. S. O'Neil, D. E. Onsi, and D. B. Corzilius. 1992. Conserving biological diversity in agricultural/forestry systems. BioScience 42:354–362.

Pletscher, D. H., and R. J. Robel. 1979. Possible use of 2,4-D in management of sunflower and ragweed. Wildl. Soc. Bull. 7:48–53.

Plummer, A. P., D. R. Christensen, and S. B. Monsen. 1968. Restoring big-game range in Utah. Utah Div. Fish Game Pub. 68-3. 183pp.

Plummer, A., A. D. Hull, Jr., G. Stewart, and J. H. Robertson. 1955. Seeding rangelands in Utah, Nevada, southern Idaho, and western Wyoming. U.S. Dep. Agric. Handb. 73. 71pp.

Podol, E. B. 1979. Utilization of windbreaks by wildlife. Pages 121–127 *in* Windbreak management workshop proceedings. Great Plains Agric. Counc. Pub. 92. Lincoln, NE.

Pojar, T. M., T. N. Woodland, and D. F. Reed. 1973. Deer underpass evaluation. Pages 177–184 *in* Game research report. Colorado Div. Wildl. Proj. W-38-R-27.

Pollio, C. A. 1991. Reclamation of abandoned mines at New River Gorge, Gauley River, and Bluestone. Park Serv. 11(2):8–10.

Porter, R. D. 1950. The Hungarian partridge in Utah. J. Wildl. Manage. 19:93–109.

Poston, H. J., and R. K. Schmidt. 1981. Wildlife habitat: a handbook for Canada's prairies and parklands. Can. Wildl. Serv., Edmonton, Alta. 51pp.

Postupalsky, S. 1978. Artificial nest platforms for ospreys and bald eagles. Pages 35–45 *in* S. A. Temple, ed. Endangered birds: management techniques for preserving threatened species. Univ. Wisconsin Press, Madison.

Postupalsky, S., and S. Stackpole. 1974. Artificial nesting platforms for ospreys in Michigan. Pages 105–117 *in* F. N. Hamerstrom, Jr., B. E. Harrell, and R. R. Olendorff, eds. Management of raptors. Raptor Res. Rep. 2.

Powell, J., and T. W. Box. 1967. Brush management influences preference values of south Texas woody species for deer and cattle. J. Range Manage. 19:212–214.

Powell, J., H. T. Zawi, J. J. Crockett, L. J. Croy, and R. D. Morrison. 1979. Central Oklahoma rangeland response to fire, fertilization, and grazing by sheep. Oklahoma State Univ. Agric. Exp. Stn. Bull. B-744. 25pp.

Powers, J. E. 1979. Planning for an optimal mix of agricultural and wildlife land use. J. Wildl. Manage. 43:493–502.

Powers, R. D., Jr. 1985. General cave gate considerations. Pages 77–79 in H. Thornton and J. Thornton, eds. Proceedings of the national cave management symposium. Harrisonburg, VA.

Prasad, N. L. N. S., and F. S. Guthery. 1986. Wildlife use of livestock water under short duration and continuous grazing. Wildl. Soc. Bull. 14:450–454.

Pressey, R. L., and A. O. Nicholls. 1991. Reserve selection in the western division of New South Wales: development of a new procedure based on land system mapping. Pages 98–105 in C. R. Margules and M. P. Austin, eds. Nature conservation: cost effective biological surveys and data analysis. Australia CSIRO, East Melbourne.

Preston, F. W., and R. T. Norris. 1947. Nesting heights of breeding birds. Ecology 28:241–273.

Prins, H. T. T., and G. R. Iason. 1989. Dangerous lions and nonchalant buffalo. Behaviour 108:262–296.

Probst, J. R., and T. R. Crow. 1991. Integrating biological diversity and resource management. J. For. 89:12–17.

Proctor, B. R., R. M. Thompson, J. E. Bunin, K. W. Fucik, G. R. Tamm, and E. G. Wolf. 1983a. Practices for protecting and enhancing fish and wildlife on coal mined land in the Uinta-southwestern Utah region. U.S. Fish Wildl. Serv. FWS/OBS-83/12. 250pp.

Proctor, B. R., R. W. Thompson, J. E. Bunin, K. W. Fucik, G. R. Tamm, and E. G. Wolf. 1983b. Practices for protecting and enhancing fish and wildlife on coal surface-mined land in the Powder River-Fort Union region. U.S. Fish Wildl. Serv. FWS/OBS-83/10. 246pp.

Pyle, W. H. 1992. Response of brood-rearing habitat of sage grouse to prescribed burning in Oregon. M. S. thesis. Oregon State Univ. Corvallis. 47pp.

Pyne, S. J. 1984. Introduction to wildland fire: fire management in the United States. Wiley, New York. 455pp.

Quinton, D. A., A. K. Montei, and J. T. Flinders. 1980. Brush control and Rio Grande turkeys in north-central Texas. J. Range Manage. 33:95–99.

Rabon, M. W., and R. Weyrick. 1989. Management of the riparian zone to maximize accumulation of large woody debris in streams. Pages 183–189 in R. D. Briggs, W. B. Krohn, J. G. Trial, W. D. Ostrofsky, and D. B. Fields, eds. Forest and wildlife management in New England—what can we afford? Maine Agric. Exp. Stn. Misc. Pub. 336, Coll. For. Resour., Univ. Maine, Orono.

Radvanyi, A. 1970. Small mammals and regeneration of white spruce forests in western Alberta. Ecology 51:1102–1105.

Radvanyi, A. 1973. Seed losses to small mammals and birds. Pages 67–74 in Proceedings of the direct seeding symposium. Can. For. Serv. Pub. 1339. Ottawa.

Radvanyi, A. 1974. Small mammal census and control on a hardwood plantation. Proc. Vertebrate Pest Conf. 6:9–19.

Rafaill, B. L., and W. G. Vogel. 1978. A guide for vegetating surface-mined lands for wildlife in eastern Kentucky and West Virginia. U.S. Fish Wildl. Serv. FWS/OBS-78/84. 89pp.

Ragotzkie, K. E., and J. A. Bailey. 1991. Desert mule deer use of grazed and ungrazed habitats. J. Range Manage. 44:487–490.

Rainville, R. P., S. C. Rainville, and E. L. Lider. 1986. Riparian silvicultural strategies for fish habitat emphasis. Pages 186–195 in Foresters' future: leaders or followers? Proc. 1985 Soc. Am. For. Natl. Conv., Bethesda, MD.

Range Seeding and Equipment Committee. 1970. Range seeding and equipment handbook. U.S. Dep. Agric. and Dep. Inter., Washington. 156pp.

Ranney, J. W., M. C. Bruner, and J. B. Levenson. 1981. The importance of edge in the structure and dynamics of forest islands. Pages 67–95 in R. L. Burgess and D. M. Sharpe, eds. Forest island dynamics in man-dominated landscapes. Springer-Verlag, New York.

Raphael, M. G., and M. White. 1984. Use of snags by cavity-nesting birds in the Sierra Nevada. Wildl. Monogr. 48. 66pp.

Rasmussen, W. O., and P. F. Ffolliott. 1983. A model to predict snag development. Wildl. Soc. Bull. 11:291–292.

Ratti, J. T., and K. P. Reese. 1988. Preliminary test of the ecological trap hypothesis. J. Wildl. Manage. 52:484–491.

Rauzi, F. 1979. Residual effects of phosphorus and high rates of nitrogen on shortgrass rangeland. J. Range Manage. 32:470–474.

Rauzi, F., R. L. Lang, and L. I. Painter. 1968. Effects of nitrogen fertilization on native rangeland. J. Range Manage. 21:287–291.

Reay, R. S., D. W. Blodgett, B. S. Burns, and S. J. Weber. 1990. Management guide for deer wintering areas in Vermont. Vermont Dep. Fish Wildl., Montpelier. 35pp.

Recher, H. F., J. Shields, R. Kavanaugh, and G. Webb. 1987. Retaining remnant mature forests for nature conservation at Eden, New South Wales: a review of theory and practice. Pages 177–194 in D. A. Saunders, G. W. Arnold, A. A. Burbridge, and A. J. M. Hopkins, eds. Nature conservation: the role of remnants of native vegetation. Surry Beatty, Sydney, Australia.

Reed, D. F., T. M. Pojar, and T. N. Woodward. 1974. Use of one-way gates by mule deer. J. Wildl. Manage. 38:9–15.

Reed, D. F., T. N. Woodward, and T. M. Pojar. 1975. Behavioral response of mule deer to a highway underpass. J. Wildl. Manage. 39:361–367.

Reed, J. M., P. D. Doerr, and J. R. Walters. 1986. Determining minimum population sizes for birds and mammals. Wildl. Soc. Bull. 14:255–261.

Reed, J. M., P. D. Doerr, and J. R. Walters. 1988. Minimum viable population size of the red-cockaded woodpecker. J. Wildl. Manage. 52:385–391.

Regelin, W. L., J. G. Nagy, and O. C. Wallmo. 1977. Effects of snowdrifts on mountain shrub communities. Trans. Internat. Congr. Game Biol. 13:414–419.

Reid, R. L., G. A. Jung, and S. J. Murray. 1966. Nitrogen fertilization in relation to the palatability and nutritive value of orchard grass. J. Anim. Sci. 25:636–645.

Reid, R. R., G. E. Grue, and N. J. Silvy. 1980. Competition between bobwhite and scaled quail for habitat in Texas. Proc. Annu. Conf. Southeast. Assoc. Fish Wildl. Agencies 33:146–153.

Reid, W. V., and K. R. Miller. 1989. Keeping options alive: the scientific basis for conserving biodiversity. World Resour. Inst., Washington. 128pp.

Reiner, R. J., and P. J. Urness. 1982. Effect of grazing horses managed as manipulators of big game winter range. J. Range. Manage. 35:567–571.

Reinert, S. E. 1984. Use of introduced perches by raptors: experimental results and management implications. Raptor Res. 18:25–29.

Remington, R., W. F. Werner, K. R. Rautenstrauch, and P. R. Krausman. 1984. Desert mule deer use of a new permanent water source. Pages 92–94 in P. R. Krausman and N. S. Smith, eds. Deer in the southwest: a workshop. New Mexico State Univ., Las Cruces.

Renwald, J. D., H. A. Wright, and J. T. Flinders. 1978. Effect of prescribed fire on bobwhite quail habitat in the Rolling Plains of Texas. J. Range Manage. 31:65–69.

Repenning, R. W., and R. F. Labisky. 1985. Effects of even-age timber management on bird communities of the longleaf pine forest in northern Florida. J. Wildl. Manage. 49:1088–1098.

Rever, M., and R. S. Miller. 1973. Common goldeneyes and the Emma Lake nest boxes. Blue Jay 31:27–30.

Reynolds, H. G. 1950. Relation of Merriam's kangaroo rats to range vegetation in southern Arizona. Ecology 31:456–463.

Reynolds, H. G. 1972. Wildlife habitat improvement in relation to watershed management in the southwest. Pages 10–17 in Proceedings of the 16th annual watershed symposium. Rep. 2, Arizona Water Comm. State Land Dep., Phoenix.

Reynolds, H. G., and S. C. Martin. 1968. Managing grass-shrub cattle ranges in the southwest. U.S. Dep. Agric. Handb. 162. 44pp.

Reynolds, J. G., and J. W. Bohning. 1956. Effects of burning on a desert grass-shrub range in southern Arizona. Ecology 37:769–777.

Rhodes, L. I. 1972. Success of osprey nest structures at Martin National Wildlife Refuge. J. Wildl. Manage. 36:1296–1299.

Rideout, C. B. 1978. Mountain goat. Pages 149–159 *in* J. L. Schmidt and D. L. Gilbert, eds. Big game of North America. Stackpole Books, Harrisburg, PA.

Riggs, R. A., P. J. Urness, and K. A. Gonzalez. 1990. Effects of domestic goats on deer wintering in Utah oakbrush. J. Range Manage. 43:229–234.

Ring, C. B., II, R. A. Nicholson, and J. L. Launchbaugh. 1985. Vegetational traits of patch-grazed rangeland in west-central Kansas. J. Range Manage. 38:51–55.

Ripley, T. H. 1980. Planning wildlife management investigations and projects. Pages 1–6 in S. D. Schemnitz, ed. Wildlife management techniques manual. Wildl. Soc., Washington.

Risser, P. G. 1988. Diversity in and among grasslands. Pages 176–179 *in* E. O. Wilson, ed. Biodiversity. Natl. Acad. Press, Washington.

Risser, P. G. 1990. Landscape processes and the vegetation of the North American grassland. Pages 133–146 *in* S. L. Collins and L. L. Wallace, eds. Fire in North American tallgrass prairies. Univ. Oklahoma Press. Norman.

Risser, P. G., E. C. Birney, H. D. Blocker, S. W. May, W. J. Parton, and J. A. Wiens. 1981. The true prairie ecosystem. U.S./IBP Synthesis Ser. 16, Hutchinson Ross Publ. Co., Stroudsburg, PA. 557pp.

Rizand, A. R., R. H. Marrs, M. W. Gough, and T. C. E. Wells. 1989. Long-term effects of various conservation management treatments on selected soil properties of chalk grassland. Biol. Conserv. 49:105–112.

Roach, B. A. 1974. Scheduling timber cutting for sustained yield of wood products and wildlife. Pages 33–43 *in* J. P. Slusher and T. M. Hinckley, eds. Timber-wildlife management symposium. Missouri Acad. Sci. Occ. Pap. 3., Univ. Missouri, Columbia.

Roach, B. A., and S. F. Gingrich. 1968. Even-aged silviculture for upland central hardwoods. U.S. For. Serv. Agric. Handb. 355. 39pp.

Robbins, C. S. 1979. Effect of forest fragmentation on bird populations. Pages 198–212 *in* R. M. DeGraaf and K. E. Evans, comps. Management of north central and northeastern forests for nongame birds. U.S. For. Serv. Gen. Tech. Rep. NC-51.

Robbins, C. S. 1984. Management to conserve forest ecosystems. Pages 101–107 *in* W. C. McComb, ed. Proceedings of the workshop on management of nongame species and ecological communities. Dep. For., Univ. Kentucky, Lexington.

Robbins, C. S. 1988. Forest fragmentation and its effects on birds. Pages 61–65 *in* J. E. Johnson, ed. Managing north central forests for non-timber values. Proc. 4th Soc. Am. For. Reg. V Tech. Conf., Soc. Am. For., Bethesda, MD.

Robbins, C. S., D. K. Dawson, and B. A. Dowell. 1989. Habitat area requirements of breeding forest birds of the middle Atlantic states. Wildl. Monogr. 103. 34pp.

Robbins, C. T. 1983. Wildlife feeding and nutrition. Academic Press, Orlando, FL. 343pp.

Robel, R. J. 1984. Food plots for wildlife. Pages 99B–103B in F. R. Henderson, ed. Guidelines for increasing wildlife on farms and ranches. Coop. Ext. Serv., Kansas State Univ., Manhattan.

Robel, R. J., A. R. Bisset, T. M. Clement, Jr., A. D. Dayton, and K. L. Morgan. 1979. Metabolizable energy of important foods of bobwhites in Kansas. J. Wildl. Manage. 43:982–987.

Robel, R. J., and N. G. Browning. 1981. Comparative use of woody plantings by nongame birds in Kansas. Wildl. Soc. Bull. 9:141–148.

Robel, R. J., R. M. Case, A. R. Bisset, and T. M. Clement, Jr. 1974. Energetics of food plots in bobwhite management. J. Wildl. Manage. 38:563–664.

Roberson, J. A. 1986. Sagegrouse-sagebrush relationships: a review. Pages 157–167 *in* E. D. McArthur and B. L. Welch, comps. Proceedings: symposium on the biology of Artemisia and Chrysothamnus. U.S. For. Serv. Gen. Tech. Rep. INT-200.

Roberts, R. F. 1977. Big game guzzlers. Rangeman's J. 4:80–82.

Robinson, S. K. 1990. Effects of forest fragmentation on nesting songbirds. Illinois Nat. Hist. Surv. Rep. 296. 2pp.

Robinson, W. L., and E. G. Bolen. 1989. Wildlife ecology and management. 2d ed. Macmillan, New York. 574pp.

Roby, G. A., and L. R. Green. 1976. Mechanical methods of chaparral modification. U.S. For. Serv. Agric. Handb. 487. 46pp.

Rodgers, R. D. 1981. Saving nests in fallow wheat fields. Pages 537–539 *in* R. T. Dumke, G. V. Burger, and J. R. March, eds. Wildlife management on private lands. Wisconsin Chap. Wildl. Soc., Wisconsin Dep. Nat. Resour., Madison.

Rodgers, R. D. 1985. Reducing wildlife losses to tillage in wheat production systems. Pages 69–76 *in* S. Shen, proj. dir. Technologies to benefit agriculture and wildlife. U.S. Off. Tech. Assess. OTA-BP-F-34.

Rodiek, J. E., and E. G. Bolen. 1991. Wildlife and habitats in managed landscapes. Island Press, Washington. 219pp.

Rogers, L. L., G. A. Wilker, and A. W. Allen. 1988. Managing northern forests for black bears. Pages 36–42 *in* T. W. Hoekstra and J. Capp, comps. Integrating forest management for wildlife and fish. U.S. For. Serv. Gen. Tech. Rep. NC-122.

Rollins, D., F. C. Bryant, D. D. Waid, and L. C. Bradley. 1988. Deer response to brush management in central Texas. Wildl. Soc. Bull. 16:277–284.

Romme, W. H., and D. H. Knight. 1982. Landscape diversity: the concept applied to Yellowstone Park. BioScience 32:664–670.

Rosenberg, K. V., and M. G. Raphael. 1986. Effects of forest fragmentation on vertebrates in Douglas-fir forests. Pages 263–272 *in* J. Verner, M. L. Morrison, and C. J. Ralph, eds. Wildlife 2000. Univ. Wisconsin Press, Madison.

Rosenfield, R. N., C. M. Morasky, J. Bielefeldt, and W. L. Loope. 1992. Forest fragmentation and island biogeography: a summary and bibliography. Natl. Park Serv. Tech. Rep. NPS/NRUW/NRTR-92/08. 52pp.

Rosenstock, S. S., S. B. Monsen, R. Stevens, and K. R. Jorgensen. 1989. Mule deer diets on a chained and seeded central Utah pinyon-juniper range. U.S. For. Serv. Res. Pap. INT-140. 4pp.

Rotzien, C. L. 1963. A cumulative report on winter bird population studies in eight deciduous shelterbelts of the Red River Valley, North Dakota. Proc. North Dak. Acad. Sci. 17:19–23.

Roundy, B. A., and G. L. Jordan. 1988. Vegetation changes in relation to livestock exclusion and rootplowing in southeastern Arizona. Southwest. Nat. 33:425–436.

Rowe, J. S. 1972. Forest regions of Canada. Can. For. Serv. Pub. 1300, Ottawa. 172pp.

Rudolph, D. C., and J. G. Dickson. 1990. Streamside zone width and amphibian and reptile abundance. Southwest. Nat. 35:472–476.

Runkle, J. R. 1985. Disturbance regimes in temperate forests. Pages 17–33 *in* S. T. A. Pickett and P. S. White, eds. The ecology of natural disturbance and patch dynamics. Academic Press, New York.

Russell, D. M. 1978. An option for wildlife development in reclamation. The Peabody Mag. Special issue:unpaged.

Russell, J. Undated. Artificial homes for wildlife. Indiana Dep. Nat. Resour., Indianapolis. 9pp.

Rutherford, W. H., and W. D. Snyder. 1983. Guidelines for habitat modification to benefit wildlife. Colorado Div. Wildl., Denver. 194pp.

Rutske, L. H. 1969. A Minnesota guide to forest game habitat improvement. Minnesota Dep. Conserv. Tech. Bull. 10. 68pp.

Ryder, R. A. 1980. Effects of grazing on bird habitats. Pages 51–66 *in* R. M. DeGraaf and N. G. Tilghman, eds. Workshop proceedings: management of western forests and grasslands for nongame birds. U.S. For. Serv. Gen. Tech. Rep. INT-86.

Sackett, S. S. 1975. Scheduling prescribed burns for hazard reduction in the Southwest. J. For. 73:143–147.

Salwasser, H. 1991. Roles for land and resource managers in conserving biological diversity. Pages 11–31 *in* D. J. Decker, M. E. Krasny, G. R. Goff, C. R. Smith, and D. W. Gross, eds. Challenges in the conservation of biological resources: a practitioner's guide. Westview Press, Boulder, CO.

Salwasser, H., C. Schonewald-Cox, and R. Baker. 1987. The role of interagency cooperation in managing for viable populations. Pages 147–173 *in* M. E. Soulé, ed. Viable populations. Cambridge Univ. Press, New York.

Salwasser, H., and J. C. Tappeiner II. 1981. An ecosystem approach to integrated timber and wildlife habitat management. Trans. North Am. Wildl. Nat. Resour. Conf. 46:473–487.

Sampson, A. W. 1913. Range improvement by deferred and rotation grazing. U.S. Dep. Agric. Bull. 34. 16pp.

Samson, F. B. 1980b. Island biogeography and the conservation of prairie birds. Proc. North Am. Prairie Conf. 7:293–299.

Samson, F. B. 1983. Minimum viable populations—a review. Nat. Areas J. 3:15–23.

Samson, F. B. 1992. Conserving biological diversity in sustained ecological systems. Trans. North Am. Wildl. Nat. Resour. Conf. 57:308–320.

Samson, F. B., P. Alaback, J. Christner, T. DeMeo, A. Doyle, J. Martin, J. McKibben, M. Orme, L. Suring, K. Thompson, B. G. Wilson, D. A. Anderson, R. W. Flynn, J. W. Schoen, L. G. Shea, and J. L. Franklin. 1989. Conservation of rain forests in southeast Alaska: report of a working group. Trans. North Am. Wildl. Nat. Resour. Conf. 54:121–133.

Samson, F. B., G. C. Iverson, R. M. Strauss, and J. C. Capp. 1991. New perspectives in Alaska forest management. Trans. North Am. Wildl. Nat. Resour. Conf. 56:652–661.

Samson, F. B., and F. L. Knopf. 1982. In search of a diversity ethic for wildlife management. Trans. North Am. Wildl. Nat. Resour. Conf. 47:421–431.

Samson, F. B., F. Perez-Trejo, H. Salwasser, L. F. Ruggiero, and M. L. Shaffer. 1985. On determining and managing minimum population size. Wildl. Soc. Bull. 13:425–433.

Samson, J. F., and L. E. Moser. 1982. Sod-seeding perennial grasses into eastern Nebraska pastures. Agron. J. 74:1055–1060.

Sanderson, H. R. 1975. Den-tree management for gray squirrels. Wildl. Soc. Bull. 3:125–131.

Sanderson, H. R., C. M. Nixon, R. W. Donohoe, and L. P. Hansen. 1980. Grapevines—an important component of gray and fox squirrel habitat. Wildl. Soc. Bull. 8:307–310.

Santillo, D. J. 1987. Response of small mammals and breeding birds to herbicide-induced habitat changes on clearcuts in Maine. M. S. thesis, Univ. Maine, Orono. 74pp.

Santillo, D. J. 1988. Herbicides. Pages 26–29 in C. A. Elliott, ed. A forester's guide to managing wildlife habitats in Maine. Coop. Ext. Serv., Univ. Maine, Orono.

Schacht, W., and J. Stubbendieck. 1985. Prescribed burning in the Loess Hills mixed prairie of southern Nebraska. J. Range Manage. 38:47–51.

Schaefer, P. R., S. Dronen, and D. Erickson. 1987. Windbreaks: a plains legacy in decline. J. Soil Water Conserv. 42:237–238.

Scharpf, R. W., and E. C. Dobler. 1985. Caves, cliffs, and talus. Pages 187–197 in E. R. Brown, ed. Management of wildlife and fish habitats in forests of western Oregon and Washington. Part 1—Chapter narratives. U.S. For. Serv., Portland, OR.

Schemnitz, S. D. 1961. Ecology of the scaled quail in the Oklahoma panhandle. Wildl. Monogr. 8. 47pp.

Schmutz, E. M. 1978. Deferred-rotation grazing-burning system for southwestern rangelands. Ariz. Agric. Ext. Q178. Univ. Arizona, Tucson. 2pp.

Schmutz, E. M., E. L. Smith, P. R. Ogden, M. L. Cox, J. O. Klemmedson, J. J. Norris, and L. C. Fierro. 1992. Desert grassland. Pages 337–362 in R. T. Copeland, ed. Natural grasslands: introduction and Western Hemisphere. Ecosystems of the world, Vol. 8A. Elsevier Sci. Publ., New York.

Schmutz, J. K. 1987. The effect of agriculture on ferruginous and Swainson's hawks. J. Range Manage. 40:438–440.

Schmutz, J. K., R. W. Fyfe, D. A. Moore, and A. R. Smith. 1984. Artificial nests for ferruginous and Swainson's hawks. J. Wildl. Manage. 48:1009–1013.

Schoen, J. W., and M. D. Kirchhoff. 1984. Sitka black-tailed deer/old-growth relationships in southeast Alaska: implications for management. Pages 315–319 in W. R. Meehan, T. R. Merrell, Jr., and T. A. Hanley, eds. Fish and wildlife relationships in old-growth forests. Proc. Symp. Am. Inst. Fish. Res. Biol., Rt. 4, Box 85, Morehead City, NC.

Schonewald-Cox, C. M. 1983. Conclusions: guidelines to management: a beginning attempt. Pages 414–445 in C. M. Schonewald-Cox, S. M. Chambers, B. MacBryde, and W. L. Thomas, eds. Genetics and conservation: a reference for managing wild plant and animal populations. Benjamin/Cummings, Menlo Park, CA.

Schonewald-Cox, C. M., and J. W. Bayliss. 1986. The boundary model: a geographical analysis of design and conservation of nature reserves. Biol. Conserv. 38:305–322.

Schonewald-Cox, C., and M. Buechner. 1992. Park protection and public roads. Pages 371–395 *in* P. L. Fiedler and S. K. Jain, eds. Conservation biology: the theory and practice of nature conservation preservation and management. Chapman and Hall, New York.

Schramm, H. L., Jr., L. M. Smith, F. C. Bryant, R. R. George, B. C. Thompson, S. A. Nelle, and G. L. Valentine. 1987. Managing for wildlife with the conservation reserve program. Manage. Note 11, Texas Tech Univ., Lubbock. 5pp.

Schreyer, R., and L. E. Royer. 1975. Impacts of pinyon-juniper manipulation on recreation and aesthetics. Pages 143–150 *in* G. F. Gifford and F. E. Busby, eds. The pinyon-juniper ecosystem: a symposium. Coll. Nat. Resour., Utah State Univ., Logan.

Schroeder, M. H., and D. L. Sturges. 1975. The effect on the Brewer's sparrow of spraying big sagebrush. J. Range Manage. 28:294–297.

Schroeder, R. L. 1983. Habitat suitability index models: black-capped chickadee. U.S. Fish Wildl. Serv. Rep. FWS/OBS-82/10.37. 12pp.

Schultz, A. M., H. N. Biswell, and J. Vlamis. 1958. Response of brush seedlings to fertilizers. Calif. Fish Game 44:335–348.

Schulz, P. A., and F. S. Guthery. 1987. Effect of short duration grazing on wild turkey home ranges. Wildl. Soc. Bull. 15:239–241.

Schweitzer, S. H. 1988. Evaluation of forage species for improving deer habitat in the rolling plains. M. S. thesis, Texas Tech Univ., Lubbock. 66pp.

Schweitzer, S. H., F. C. Bryant, and D. B. Wester. 1993. Potential forage species for deer in the southern mixed prairie. J. Range Manage. 46:70–75.

Scifres, C. J. 1980a. Integration prescribed burning with other practices in brush management systems. Pages 65–71 *in* C. W. Hanselka, ed. Prescribed range burning in the coastal prairie and Eastern Rio Grande Plains of Texas. Texas Agric. Exp. Stn., Texas A&M Univ., College Station.

Scifres, C. J. 1980b. Brush management: principles and practices for Texas and the southwest. Texas A&M Univ. Press, College Station. 360pp.

Scifres, C. J. 1986. Integrated management systems for improvement of rangeland. Pages 227–259 *in* M. A. Sprague and G. B. Triplett, eds. No-tillage and surface tillage agriculture: the tillage revolution. Wiley, New York.

Scifres, C. J., W. T. Hamilton, J. M. Englis, and J. R. Conner. 1983. Development of integrated brush management systems (IBMS): decision-making processes. Pages 97–104 *in* K. W. McDaniell, ed. Proceedings of the brush management symposium. Texas Tech Univ. Press, Lubbock.

Scifres, C. J., and B. H. Koerth. 1986. Habitat alterations in mixed brush from variable rate herbicide patterns. Wildl. Soc. Bull. 14:345–356.

Scott, D. R. M. 1980. The Pacific Northwest region. Pages 447–493 *in* J. W. Barrett, ed. Regional silviculture of the United States. 2d ed. Wiley, New York.

Scott, J. M., B. Csuti, and S. Caicco. 1991. Gap analysis: assessing protection needs. Pages 15–26 *in* W. E. Hudson, ed. Landscape linkages and biodiversity. Island Press, Washington.

Scott, J. M., F. Davis, B. Csuti, R. Noss, B. Butterfield, C. Groves, H. Anderson, S. Caicco, F. D'Erchia, T. S. Edwards, Jr., J. Ulliman, and R. G. Wright. 1993. Gap analysis: a geographic approach to protection of biological diversity. Wildl. Monogr. 123. 41pp.

Scott, M. D. 1992. Buck-and-pole fence crossings by 4 ungulate species. Wildl. Soc. Bull. 20:204–210.

Scott, V. E. 1978. Characteristics of ponderosa pine snags used by cavity-nesting birds in Arizona. J. For. 76:26–28.

Scott, V. E., and E. L. Boeker. 1977. Responses of Merriam's turkey to pinyon-juniper control. J. Range Manage. 30:220–223.

Scott, V. E., K. E. Evans, D. R. Patton, and C. P. Stone. 1977. Cavity-nesting birds of North American forests. U.S. For. Serv. Handb. 553. 510pp.

Scotter, G. W. 1980. Management of wild ungulate habitat in the western United States and Canada: a review. J. Range Manage. 33:16–27.

Seamans, R. A. 1951. Electric fences for the control of deer damage. Vermont Fish Game Serv. Bull. 16. 77pp.

Sedell, J. R., F. H. Everest, and D. R. Gibbons. 1989. Streamside vegetation management for aquatic habitat. Pages 115–125 *in* Proceedings of the national silvicultural workshop: silviculture for all resources. Timber Manage., U.S. For. Serv., Washington.

Sedgewick, J. A., and F. L. Knopf. 1986. Cavity-nesting birds and the cavity-tree resource in plains cottonwood bottomlands. J. Wildl. Manage. 50:247–252.

Seip, D. R., and F. L. Bunnell. 1985. Range burning, Stone's sheep, and the leaky bucket. Pages 44–47 *in* J. E. Lotan and J. K. Brown, eds. Fire's effects on wildlife habitat. U.S. For. Serv. Gen. Tech Rep. INT-186.

Severson, K. E., and L. F. Debano. 1991. Influence of Spanish goats on vegetation and soils in Arizona chaparral. J. Range Manage. 44:111–117.

Severson, K. E., and A. L. Medina. 1983. Deer and elk habitat management in the southwest. J. Range Manage. Monogr. 2. 74pp.

Severson, K. E., and J. N. Rinne. 1990. Increasing habitat diversity in southwestern forests and woodlands via prescribed fire. Pages 94–104 *in* J. S. Krammes, ed. Effects of fire management of southwestern natural resources. U.S. For. Serv. Gen. Tech. Rep. RM-191.

Severson, K. E., and P. J. Urness. 1993. Livestock grazing: a tool to improve wildlife habitat. Pages (in press) *in* M. Vavra, B. W. A. Laycock, and R. D. Pieper, eds. Ecological implications of livestock herbivory in the West. Soc. Range Manage., Denver.

Seymour, R. S., and M. L. Hunter, Jr. 1992. New forestry in eastern spruce-fir forests: principles and applications to Maine. Maine Agric. Exp. Stn. Misc. Pub. 716, Coll. For. Resour., Univ. Maine, Orono. 36pp.

Seymour, R. S., and M. L. McCormack, Jr. 1989. Having our forest and harvesting it too: the role of intensive silviculture in resolving forest land-use conflicts. Pages 207–213 *in* R. D. Briggs, W. B. Krohn, J. G. Trial, W. D. Ostrofsky, and D. B. Field, eds. Forest and wildlife management in New England—what can we afford? Maine Agric. Exp. Stn. Misc. Pub. 336, Coll. For Resour., Univ. Maine, Orono.

Shafer, C. L. 1990. Nature reserves: island theory and conservation practice. Smithsonian Inst. Press, Washington. 189pp.

Shaffer, M. 1987. Minimum viable populations: coping with uncertainty. Pages 69–86 *in* M. L. Soulé, ed. Viable populations for conservation. Cambridge Univ. Press, New York.

Shaffer, M. L. 1981. Minimum population sizes for species conservation. BioScience 31:131–134.

Shaffer, M. L. 1991. Population viability analysis. Pages 107–118 *in* D. J. Decker, M. E. Krasny, G. F. Goff, C. F. Smith, and D. W. Gross, eds. Challenges in the conservation of biological resources: a practitioner's guide. Westview Press, Boulder, CO.

Shalaway, S. D. 1985. Fencerow management for nesting birds in Michigan. Wildl. Soc. Bull. 13:302–306.

Sharma, M. P. 1986. Recognizing herbicide action and injury. 2d ed. Alberta. Agric. Agdex 641-7. 138pp.

Shaw, J. H., and T. S. Carter. 1990. Bison movements in relation to fire and seasonality. Wildl. Soc. Bull. 18:426–430.

Shaw, S. P. 1967. Woodlots, wildlife, and timber management. Trans. North Am. Wildl. Nat. Resour. Conf. 32:238–246.

Shaw, S. P. 1971. Wildlife and oak management. Pages 84–89 *in* Oak symposium proceedings. U.S. For. Serv. Northeast For. Exp. Stn., Upper Darby, PA.

Shaw, S. P. 1977. Timber cutting to enhance wildlife food supplies. Trans. Northeast Fish Wildl. Conf. 34:113–118.

Short, H. L. 1983. Wildlife guilds in Arizona desert habitats. U.S. Bur. Land Manage. Tech. Note 362. 258pp.

Short, H. L. 1986. Rangelands. Pages 93–122 *in* A. Y. Cooperrider, R. J. Boyd, and H. R. Stuart, eds. Inventory and monitoring of wildlife habitat. U.S. Bur. Land Manage., Denver.

Short, H. L., and K. P. Burnham. 1982. Techniques for structuring wildlife guilds to evaluate impacts on wildlife communities. U.S. Fish Wildl. Serv. Spec. Sci. Rep. Wildl. 244. 34pp.

Short, H. L., W. Evans, and E. L. Boeker. 1977. The use of natural and modified pinyon-juniper woodlands by deer and elk. J. Wildl. Manage. 41:453–559.

Short, H. L., and C. Y. McCulloch. 1977. Managing pinyon-juniper ranges for wildlife. U.S. For. Serv. Gen. Tech. Rep. RM-47. 10pp.

Shugart, H. H. 1984. A theory of forest dynamics. Springer-Verlag, New York. 278pp.

Shugart, H. H., and D. C. West. 1981. Long-term dynamics of forest ecosystems. Am. Scientist 69:647–652.

Shuman, T. W., R. J. Robel, A. D. Dayton, and J. L. Zimmerman. 1988. Apparent metabolizable energy content of foods used by mourning doves. J. Wildl. Manage. 52:481–483.

Sieg, C. H. 1988. The value of Rocky Mountain juniper (Juniperus scopulorum) woodlands in South Dakota as small mammal habitat. Pages 328–332 in R. C. Szaro and K. E. Severson, eds. Management of amphibians, reptiles, and small mammals in North America: symposium proceedings. U.S. For. Serv. Gen. Tech. Rep. RM-166.

Sieg, C. H. 1991. Rocky Mountain juniper woodlands: year-round avian habitat. U.S. For. Serv. Res. Pap. RM-296. 7pp.

Simberloff, D., and J. Cox. 1987. Consequences and costs of conservation corridors. Conserv. Biol. 1:63–71.

Simberloff, D., J. A. Farr, J. Cox, and D. W. Mehlman. 1992. Movement corridors: conservation bargains or poor investments? Conserv. Biol. 6:493–504.

Singer, F. J., and J. L. Doherty. 1985. Managing mountain goats at a highway crossing. Wildl. Soc. Bull. 13:469–477.

Sivils, B. E., and J. H. Brock. 1981. Sand dams as a feasible water development for arid regions. J. Range Manage. 34:238–239.

Skille, J. 1990. Stream and lake nutrient loading from burned logging slash. Water Quality Summary Rep. 26, Div. Environ. Quality, Water Quality Bur., Idaho Dep. Health and Welfare, Boise. 14pp.

Skousen, J. G., J. N. Davis, and J. D. Brotherson. 1989. Pinyon-juniper chaining and seeding for big game in central Utah. J. Range Manage. 42:98–104.

Skovlin, J. M., R. W. Harris, G. S. Strickler, and G. A. Garrison. 1976. Effects of cattle grazing methods on ponderosa pine-bunchgrass range in the Pacific Northwest. U.S. For. Serv. Tech. Bull. 1531. 40pp.

Slatkin, M. 1987. Gene flow and the geographic structure of natural populations. Science 236:787–792.

Small, M. F., and M. L. Hunter. 1988. Forest fragmentation and avian nest predation in forested landscapes. Oecologia 76:62–64.

Small, M. F., and W. N. Johnson, Jr. 1986. Wildlife management in riparian habitats. Pages 69–79 in J. A. Bissonette, ed. Is good forestry good wildlife management? Misc. Publ. 689, Agric. Exp. Stn., Univ. Maine, Orono.

Smith, A. D. 1949. Effects of mule deer and livestock upon a foothill range in northern Utah. J. Wildl. Manage. 13:421–423.

Smith, A. D., and P. Doell. 1968. Guidelines to allocating forage between cattle and big game winter range. Utah Div. Fish Game Pub. 68-11. 26pp.

Smith, A. D., A. Johnston, L. E. Lutwik, and S. Smoliak. 1968. Fertilizer response of fescue grassland vegetation. Can. J. Soil. Sci. 48:125–132.

Smith, D. M. 1980. The forests of the United States. Pages 1–23 in J. W. Barrett, ed. Regional silviculture of the United States. 2d ed. Wiley, New York.

Smith, D. M. 1986. The practice of silviculture. 8th ed. Wiley, New York. 527 pp.

Smith, E. D. 1985. Construction of artificial nesting sites for prairie falcons. Wildl. Soc. Bull. 13:543–546.

Smith, F., and L. Martin. 1974. Alteration in timber management practices which help to achieve the game management concept on Florida's wildlife management areas. Pages 84–88 in J. P. Slusher and T. M. Hinckley, eds. Timber-wildlife management symposium. Missouri Acad. Sci. Occ. Pap. 3, Univ. Missouri, Columbia.

Smith, G. E. 1963. Nutritional effects of big sagebrush (Artemisia tridentata) on deer. M. S. thesis, Oregon State Univ., Corvallis. 111pp.

Smith, G. J. 1987. Pesticide use and toxicology in relation to wildlife: organophosphorus and carbamate compounds. U.S. Fish Wildl. Serv. Res. Pub. 170. 171pp.

Smith, M. A., J. C. Malechek, and K. O. Fulgham. 1979. Forage selection by mule deer on winter range grazed by sheep in spring. J. Range Manage. 32:40–45.

Smith, N. S. 1984. Reproduction in Coues white-tailed deer relative to drought and cattle stocking rates. Pages 13–20 *in* P. R. Krausman and N. S. Smith, eds. Deer in the southwest: a workshop. New Mexico State Univ., Las Cruces.

Smith, R. L. 1958. Conifer plantations as wildlife habitat. N. Y. Fish Game J. 5:101–132.

Snyder, N. F. R., and H. A. Snyder. 1975. Raptors in range habitat. Pages 190–209 *in* D. R. Smith, tech. coord. Proceedings of the symposium on management of forests and range habitats for nongame birds. U.S. For. Serv. Gen. Tech. Rep. WO-1.

Snyder, W. D. 1984. Ring-necked pheasant nesting ecology and wheat farming on the high plains. J. Wildl. Manage. 48:878–888.

Soltero, S., F. C. Bryant, and A. Melgoza. 1989. Standing crop patterns under short duration grazing in northern Mexico. J. Range Manage. 42:20–21.

Soucy, L. J., Jr. 1980. Nest boxes for raptors: a helpful management technique. N.J. Audubon 6:18–20.

Soulé, M. E., ed. 1987a. Viable populations for conservation. Cambridge Univ. Press, New York. 189pp.

Soulé, M. E. 1987b. Where do we go from here? Pages 175–183 *in* M. E. Soulé, ed. Viable populations for conservation. Cambridge Univ. Press, New York.

Soulé, M. E. 1991. Theory and strategy. Pages 91–104 *in* W. E. Hudson, ed. Landscape linkages and biodiversity. Island Press, Washington.

Soulé, M. E., D. T. Bolger, A. C. Alberts, J. Wright, M. Sorice, and S. Hill. 1988. Reconstructed dynamics of rapid extinctions of chaparral-requiring birds in urban habitat islands. Conserv. Biol. 2:75–92.

Southern Forestry Fire Laboratory Personnel. 1976. Southern forestry smoke management guidebook. U.S. For. Serv. Gen. Tech. Rep. SE-10. 140pp.

Southwest Interagency Fire Council. 1968. Guide to prescribed fire in the Southwest. Watershed Manage. Dep., Univ. Arizona, Tucson. 58pp.

Sowell, B. B., B. H. Koerth, and F. C. Bryant. 1985. Seasonal nutrient estimates of mule deer diets in the Texas panhandle. J. Range Manage. 38:163–167.

Spencer, J. 1988. Managing woodlands for wildlife. Arkansas Game & Fish. 19(1):6–9.

Spies, T. A. 1991. Plant species diversity and occurrence in young, mature, and old-growth Douglas-fir stands in western Oregon and Washington. Pages 111–121 *in* L. F. Ruggiero, K. B. Aubry, A. B. Carey, and M. H. Huff, tech. coords. Wildlife and vegetation of unmanaged Douglas-fir forests. U.S. For. Serv. Gen. Tech. Rep. PNW-GTR-285.

Spies, T. A., and S. P. Cline. 1988. Coarse woody debris in forests and plantations of coastal Oregon. Pages 5–23 *in* C. Maser, R. F. Tarrant, J. M. Trappe, and J. F. Franklin, eds. From the forest to the sea: a story of fallen trees. U.S. For. Serv. Gen. Tech. Rep. PNW-GTR-229.

Spies, T. A., and J. F. Franklin. 1988. Old-growth and forest dynamics in the Douglas-fir region of western Oregon and Washington. Nat. Areas J. 8:190–201.

Spies, T. A., J. F. Franklin, and M. Klopsch. 1990. Canopy gaps in Douglas-fir forests of the Cascade Mountains. Can. J. For. Res. 20:649–658.

Spies, T. A., J. F. Franklin, and T. B. Thomas. 1988. Coarse woody debris in Douglas-fir forests of western Oregon and Washington. Ecology 69:1689–1702.

Spies, T. A., J. Tappeiner, J. Pojar, and D. Coates. 1991. Trends in ecosystem management at the stand level. Trans. North Am. Wildl. Nat. Resour. Conf. 56:628–639.

Spillet, J. J., J. B. Low, and D. Sill. 1967. Livestock fences—how they influence pronghorn antelope movements. Utah Agric. Exp. Stn. Bull. 470, Utah State Univ., Logan. 79pp.

Spowart, R. A., and F. B. Samson. 1986. Carnivores. Pages 475–496 *in* A. Y. Cooperrider, R. J. Boyd, and H. R. Stuart, eds. Inventory and monitoring of wildlife habitat. U.S. Bur. Land Manage., Denver.

Spowart, R. A., and N. T. Hobbs. 1985. Effects of fire on diet overlap between mule deer and mountain sheep. J. Wildl. Manage. 49:942–946.

Springer, M. D., T. E. Fulbright, and S. L. Beasom. 1987. Long-term response of live oak thickets to prescribed burning. Texas J. Sci. 39:89–95.

Springfield, H. W. 1970. Emergence and survival of winterfat seedlings from four planting depths. U.S. For. Serv. Res. Note RM-42. 8pp.

Sprugel, D. G. 1991. Disturbance, equilibrium and environmental variability: what is "natural" vegetation in a changing environment. Biol. Conserv. 58:1–18.

Stahlecker, D. W., and H. J. Griese. 1979. Raptor use of nest boxes and platforms on transmission towers. Wildl. Soc. Bull. 7:59–62.

Stalmaster, M. V., R. L. Knight, B. L. Holder, and R. J. Anderson. 1985. Bald eagles. Pages 269–290 *in* E. R. Brown, ed. Management of wildlife and fish habitats in forests of western Oregon and Washington. Part 1—Chapter narratives. U.S. For. Serv., Portland, OR.

Steele, J. L., Jr. 1984. Brush piles and bobwhites—a case history. Wildl. Resour. Notes, U.S. Army Corps Eng. Inf. Exchange Bull. 2(2):3–4.

Steele, J. L., Jr., and C. O. Martin. 1986. Half-cuts. Sec. 5.3.2, U.S. Army Corps of Engineers wildlife resources management manual. U.S. Army Eng. Waterways Exp. Stn. Tech. Rep. EL-86-14. 8pp.

Steinhoff, H. W. 1978. Management of Gambel oak associations for wildlife and livestock. Unpub. rep., U.S. For. Serv. Rocky Mountain region with Colorado State Univ., Ft. Collins. 119pp.

Steuter, A. A., and H. A. Wright. 1980. White-tailed deer densities and brush cover on the Rio Grande Plain. J. Range Manage. 33:328–331.

Stevens, R. 1986. Population dynamics of two sagebrush species and rubber rabbitbrush over 22 years of grazing use by three classes of animals. Pages 278–285 *in* E. D. McArthur and B. L. Welch, comps. Proceedings: symposium on the biology of Artemisia and Chrysothamnus. U.S. For. Serv. Gen. Tech. Rep. INT-200.

Stevens, R., B. C. Giunta, and A. P. Plummer. 1975. Some aspects in the biological control of juniper and pinyon. Pages 77–81 *in* G. F. Gifford and F. E. Busby, eds. The pinyon-juniper ecosystem: a symposium. Coll. Nat. Resour., Utah State Univ., Logan.

Stevens, R. W. L. Moden, Jr., and D. W. McKenzie. 1981. Interseeding and transplanting shrubs and forbs into grass communities. Rangelands 3:55–58.

Stinson, E. R., and P. T. Bromley. 1991. Pesticides and wildlife: guide to reducing impacts on animals and their habitat. Virginia Dep. Game Inland Fish. Pub. 420-004. 44pp.

Stoddard, H. L. 1931. The bobwhite quail: its habits, preservation and increase. Charles Scribner's Sons, New York. 559pp.

Stoddart, L. A., A. D. Smith, and T. W. Box. 1975. Range management. 3d ed. McGraw-Hill, New York. 532pp.

Stoeckler, J. H., J. M. Keener, and R. O. Strothman. 1958. Deer browse from felled trees in the northern hardwood-hemlock type. J. For. 56:416–421.

Stransky, J. J., and L. K. Halls. 1976. Browse quality affected by pine site preparation in east Texas. Proc. Annu. Conf. Southeast. Assoc. Game Fish Comm. 30:507–512.

Stransky, J. J., and L. K. Halls. 1980. Fruiting of woody plants affected by site preparation and prior land use. J. Wildl. Manage. 44:258–263.

Stransky, J. J., and R. F. Harlow. 1981. Effects of fire on deer habitat in the southeast. Pages 135–142 *in* G. W. Wood, ed. Prescribed fire and wildlife in southern forests. Belle W. Baruch For. Sci. Inst., Clemson Univ., Georgetown, SC.

Stransky, J. J., and J. H. Roese. 1984. Promoting soft mast for wildlife in intensively managed forests. Wildl. Soc. Bull. 12:234–240.

Stroehlein, J. L., P. R. Ogden, and B. Billy. 1968. Time of fertilizer application on desert grasslands. J. Range Manage. 21:86–89.

Stubblefield, T. C. 1980. Bird management—effects on timber management. Pages 302–310 *in* R. M. DeGraaf, tech. coord. Management of western forests and grasslands for nongame birds. U.S. For. Serv. Gen. Tech. Rep. INT-86.

Studier, D., R. Iff, J. Sessions, and W. B. Stuart. 1984. Logging. Pages 489–563 *in* K. F. Wenger, ed. Forestry handbook. 2d ed. Wiley, New York.

Stumpf, A. 1977. An experiment with artificial raptor hunting perches. Bird Watch 5:1–2.

Styskel, E. W. 1983. Problems in snag management implementation—a case study. Pages 24–27 *in* J. W. Davis, G. A. Goodwin, and R. A. Ockenfels, tech. coords. Snag habitat management: proceedings of the symposium. U.S. For. Serv. Gen. Tech. Rep. RM-99.

Sundstrom, C. 1968. Water consumption by pronghorn antelope and distribution related to water in Wyoming's Red Desert. Pages 39–46 *in* Proceedings of the 3rd biennial pronghorn antelope states workshop. Casper, WY.

Svenson, H. A. 1966. Vegetation management for rights-of-way. U.S. For. Serv. East. Reg., Milwaukee. 39pp.

Swallow, S. K., R. J. Gutiérrez, and R. A. Howard, Jr. 1986. Primary cavity-site selection by birds. J. Wildl. Manage. 50:576–583.

Swank, W. G. 1958. The mule deer in the Arizona chaparral. Arizona Game and Fish. Wildl. Bull. 3. 109pp.

Swanson, D. W. 1988. Effects of livestock grazing systems on grassland birds in south Texas. M. S. thesis, Texas A&M Univ., College Station. 50pp.

Swanson, F. J., J. F. Franklin, and J. R. Sedell. 1990. Landscape patterns, disturbance, and management in the Pacific Northwest, USA. Pages 191–213 in I. S. Zonneveld and R. T. T. Forman, eds. Changing landscapes: an ecological perspective. Springer-Verlag, New York.

Swanson, F. J., and G. W. Lienkaemper. 1978. Physical consequences of large organic debris in Pacific Northwest streams. U.S. For. Serv. Gen. Tech. Rep. PNW-69. 12pp.

Swift, B. L. 1984. Status of riparian ecosystems in the United States. Water Resour. Bull. 20:223–228.

Swihart, R. K., and R. H. Yahner. 1982. Habitat features influencing use of farmstead shelterbelts by eastern cottontails. Am. Midl. Nat. 107:411–414.

Swindel, B. F., W. R. Marion, L. D. Harris, L. A. Morris, W. L. Pritchett, L. F. Conde, H. Riekerk, and E. T. Sullivan. 1983. Multi-resource effects of harvest site preparation and planting in pine flatwoods. South. J. Appl. For. 7:6–15.

Sykes. P. W., Jr., and R. Chandler. 1974. Use of artificial nest structures by Everglade kites. Wilson Bull. 86:282–284.

Taber, R. D. 1973. Effects of even-age forest management on big game. Pages 59–74 in R. K. Hermann and D. P. Lavender, eds. Even-age management symposium. School For., Oregon State Univ., Corvallis.

Taber, R. D., R. A. Cooley, and W. F. Royce. 1970. The conservation of fish and wildlife. Pages 143–151 in H. D. Johnson, ed. No deposit—no return: man and his environment: a view toward survival. Addison-Wesley, Reading, MA.

Taber, R. D., and R. F. Dasmann. 1958. The black-tailed deer of the chaparral. Calif. Dep. Fish and Game Bull. 8. 163pp.

Taber, R. D., D. Manuwal, S. D. West, K. J. Raedeke, and D. deCalesta. 1981. Wildlife management in the mesic-temperate forest of Washington and Oregon. Pages 575–587 in Proceedings: Division 1, XVII IUFRO World Congress, Kyoto, Japan.

Takekawa, J. Y., E. O. Garton, and L. A. Langelier. 1982. Biological control of forest insect outbreaks: the use of avian predators. Trans. North Am. Wildl. Nat. Resour. Conf. 47:393–409.

Tanner, G. W., J. M. Inglis, and L. H. Blankenship. 1978. Acute impact of herbicide strip treatment on mixed-brush white-tailed deer habitat on the northern Rio Grande Plain. J. Range Manage. 31:386–391.

Taylor, M. A., and F. S. Guthery. 1980. Status, ecology, and management of the lesser prairie chicken. U.S. For. Serv. Gen. Tech. Rep. RM-77. 15 pp.

Taylor, M. W., C. W. Wolfe, and W. L. Baxter. 1978. Land-use changes and ring-necked pheasants in Nebraska. Wildl. Soc. Bull. 6:226–230.

Taylor, W. E., and R. G. Hooper. 1991. A modification of Copeyon's drilling technique for making artificial red-cockaded woodpecker cavities. U.S. For. Serv. Gen. Tech. Rep. SE-72. 31pp.

Teaford, J. W. 1986a. Eastern gray squirrel (Sciurus carolinensis). Sec. 4.7.1., U.S. Army Corps of Engineers wildlife resources management manual. U.S. Army Eng. Waterways Exp. Stn. Tech. Rep. EL-86-6. 36pp.

Teaford, J. W. 1986b. Squirrel nest boxes. Sec. 5.1.1., U.S. Army Corps of Engineers wildlife resources management manual. U.S. Army Eng. Waterways Exp. Stn. Tech. Rep. EL-86-11. 15pp.

Teensma, P. D. A. 1987. Fire history and fire regimes of the central western Cascades of Oregon. Ph.D. thesis, Univ. Oregon, Eugene. 235pp.

Telfer, E. S. 1978. Silviculture in the eastern deer yards. For. Chron. 54:203–208.

Telfer, E. S., and G. W. Scotter. 1975. Potential for game ranching in boreal aspen forests of western Canada. J. Range Manage. 28:172–180.

Temple, S. A. 1986. Predicting impacts of habitat fragmentation on forest birds: a comparison of two models. Pages 301–304 *in* J. Verner, M. L. Morrison, and C. J. Ralph, eds. Wildlife 2000. Univ. Wisconsin Press, Madison.

Temple, S. A. 1987. Predation of turtle nest increases near ecological edges. Copeia 1987:250–252.

Temple, S. A. 1988. When is a bird's habitat not habitat? Passenger Pigeon 50:37–41.

Temple, S. A. 1990. The nasty necessity: eradicating exotics. Conserv. Biol. 4:113–115.

Temple, S. A., and J. R. Cary. 1988. Modeling dynamics of habitat-interior bird populations in fragmented landscapes. Conserv. Biol. 2:340–347.

Terborgh, J., and S. Robinson. 1986. Guilds and their utility in ecology. Pages 65–90 *in* J. Kikkawa and D. J. Anderson, eds. Community ecology: pattern and process. Blackwell Sci. Publ., Boston.

Terrell, T. L. 1973. Mule deer use patterns as related to pinyon-juniper conversion in Utah. Ph.D. thesis, Utah State Univ., Logan. 145pp.

Terrell, T. L., and J. J. Spillet. 1975. Pinyon-juniper conversion: its impact on mule deer and other wildlife. Pages 105–120 *in* G. F. Gifford and F. E. Busby, eds. The pinyon-juniper ecosystem: a symposium. Coll. Nat. Resour., Utah State Univ., Logan.

Thie, J., and G. Ironsides, eds. 1976. Ecological (biophysical) land classification in Canada. Ecol. Land Classif. Ser. 1, Environ. Can. Lands Dir., Ottawa. 269pp.

Thiel, R. P. 1985. Relationship between road densities and wolf habitat suitability in Wisconsin. Am. Midl. Nat. 113:404–407.

Thilenius, J. F. 1979. Range management in the alpine zone. Pages 43–65 *in* D. A. Johnson, ed. Special management needs of alpine ecosystems. Range. Sci. Ser. 5, Soc. Range Manage., Denver.

Thilenius, J. F., and K. E. Hungerford. 1967. Browse use by cattle and deer in northern Idaho. J. Wildl. Manage. 31:141–145.

Thiollay, J. M., and B. U. Meyburg. 1988. Forest fragmentation and the conservation of raptors: a survey on the island of Java. Biol. Conserv. 44:229–250.

Thomas, C. D. 1990. What do real population dynamics tell us about minimum population sizes? Conserv. Biol. 4:324–327.

Thomas, J. R., H. R. Cosper, and W. Bever. 1964. Effects of fertilizers on the growth of grass and its use by deer in the Black Hills of South Dakota. Agron. J. 56:223–226.

Thomas, J. W. 1979a. Preface. Pages 6–7 *in* J. W. Thomas, tech. ed. Wildlife habitats in managed forests: the Blue Mountains of Oregon and Washington. U.S. For. Serv. Handb. 553, Portland, OR.

Thomas, J. W. 1979b. Introduction. Pages 10–21 *in* J. W. Thomas, tech. ed. Wildlife habitats in managed forests: the Blue Mountains of Oregon and Washington. U.S. For. Serv. Agric. Handb. 553, Portland, OR.

Thomas, J. W., R. G. Anderson, C. Maser, and E. L. Bull. 1979a. Snags. Pages 60–77 *in* J. W. Thomas, tech. ed. Wildlife habitats in managed forests: the Blue Mountains of Oregon and Washington. U.S. For. Serv. Agric. Handb. 553, Portland, OR.

Thomas, J. W., H. Black, Jr., R. J. Scherzinger, and R. J. Pedersen. 1979b. Deer and elk. Pages 104–127 *in* J. W. Thomas, tech. ed. Wildlife habitats in managed forests: the Blue Mountains of Oregon and Washington. U.S. For. Serv. Agric. Handb. 553, Portland, OR.

Thomas, J. W., C. Maser, and J. E. Rodiek. 1979c. Edges. Pages 48–59 *in* J. W. Thomas, tech. ed. Wildlife habitats in managed forests: the Blue Mountains of Oregon and Washington. U.S. For. Serv. Agric. Handb. 553, Portland, OR.

Thomas, J. W., R. J. Miller, C. Maser, R. G. Anderson, and B. E. Carter. 1979d. Plant communities and successional stages. Pages 22–39 *in* J. W. Thomas, tech. ed. Wildlife habitats in managed forests: the Blue Mountains of Oregon and Washington. U.S. For. Serv. Agric. Handb. 553, Portland, OR.

Thomas, J. W., E. D. Forsman, J. B. Lint, E. C. Meslow, B. R. Noon, and J. Verner. 1990. A conservation strategy for the northern spotted owl. U.S. For. Serv., U.S. Bur. Land Manage., U.S. Fish Wildl. Serv., U.S. Natl. Park Serv., Portland, OR. 427pp.

Thomas, J. W., D. A. Leckenby, L. J. Lyon, L. L. Hicks, and C. L. Marcum. 1988a. Integrated management of timber-elk-cattle: interior forests of western North America. U.S. For. Serv. Gen. Tech. Rep. PNW-225. 12pp.

Thomas, J. W., L. F. Ruggiero, R. W. Mannan, J. W. Schoen, and R. A. Lancia. 1988b. Management and conservation of old-growth forests in the United States. Wildl. Soc. Bull. 16:252–262.

Thomas, J. W., and D. E. Toweill, eds. 1982. Elk of North America. Stackpole Books, Harrisburg, PA. 698pp.

Thomas, J. W., and J. Verner. 1986. Forests. Pages 73–91 in A. Y. Cooperrider, R. J. Boyd, and H. R. Stuart, eds. Inventory and monitoring of wildlife habitat. U.S. Bur. Land Manage., Denver.

Thompson, F. R., III. 1986. Managing timber for people and wildlife. Missouri Conserv. 47(10):26–29.

Thompson, L. S. 1978. Transmission line wire strikes: mitigation through engineering design and habitat modification. Pages 27–52 in M. L. Avery, ed. Impacts of transmission lines on birds of flight. U.S. Fish Wildl. Serv. FWS/OBS-78/48.

Thornton, B. 1981. Response of deer to fuel management programs in Glenn and Colusa counties, California. Pages 255–257 in C. E. Conrad and W. C. Oechel, tech coords. Dynamics and management of Mediterranean-type ecosystems. U.S. For. Serv. Gen. Tech. Rep. PSW-58.

Titus, R. 1983. Management of snags and den trees in Missouri—a process. Pages 51–59 in J. W. Davis, G. A. Goodwin, and R. A. Ockenfels, tech. coords. Snag habitat management: proceedings of the symposium. U.S. For. Serv. Gen. Tech. Rep. RM-99.

Tour, J. 1991. New fireline explosives. U.S. For. Serv. Technol. Develop. Cent., Missoula, MT. 4 pp.

Towry, R. K., Jr. 1984. Wildlife habitat requirements. Pages 73–209 in R. L. Hoover and D. L. Wills, eds. Managing forested lands for wildlife. Colorado Div. Wildl., Denver.

Trautman, C. G. 1982. History, ecology and management of the ring-necked pheasant in South Dakota. South Dakota Dep. Game, Fish, Parks. Pierre. 118pp.

Trlica, M. J., Jr., and J. L. Schuster. 1969. Effect of fire on grasses of the Texas High Plains. J. Range Manage. 22:329–333.

Tubbs, C. H., R. M. DeGraaf, M. Yamasaki, and W. M. Healy. 1987. Guide to wildlife tree management in New England northern hardwoods. U.S. For. Serv. Gen. Tech. Rep. NE-118. 30pp.

Tubbs, C. H., and L. J. Verme. 1972. How to create wildlife openings in northern hardwoods. U.S. For. Serv., Upper Darby, PA. 5pp.

Tuttle, M. D. 1977. Gating as a means of protecting cave dwelling bats. Pages 77–82 in T. Aley and D. Rhodes, eds. Proceedings of the national cave management symposium. Speleobooks Adobe Press, Albuquerque, NM.

Ulrich, E. S. 1976. Selective clearing and maintenance of rights-of-way. Pages 206–219 in R. Tillman, ed. Proceedings of the first national symposium on environmental concerns in rights-of-way management. Mississippi State Univ., Mississippi State.

United Nations. 1973. International classification and mapping of vegetation. Ecol. Conserv. Ser. 6., U. N. Educ., Sci., Cult. Organ., Paris.

U.S. Army Corps of Engineers. 1977. General wildlife management measures. U.S. Army Eng. District, Fort Worth, TX. 38pp.

U.S. Army Corps of Engineers. 1979. Design memorandum for wildlife habitat development, Suppl. 1, Lower Snake River project. U.S. Army Eng. District, Walla Walla, WA. 178pp.

U.S. Bureau of Land Management. 1967. Engineering handbook and construction manual. U.S. Bur. Land Manage., Washington. Various pages.

U.S. Bureau of Land Management. 1974. Proceedings regional fencing workshop. U.S. Bur. Land Manage., Washington. 74pp.

U.S. Bureau of Land Management. 1975. Manual 1737—fencing. U.S. Bur. Land Manage., Washington. 17pp.

U.S. Bureau of Land Management. 1981. The need for wildlife habitat diversity on BLM-managed forest lands in western Oregon. U.S. Bur. Land Manage., Portland, OR. 21pp.

U.S. Department of Agriculture. 1968. Forest regions of the United States. National atlas map. U.S. For. Serv., Washington.

U.S. Department of Housing and Urban Development. 1984. Noise assessment guidelines. HUD-PDR-735(1). Off. Policy Develop. Res., U.S. Dep. Housing Urban Develop., Washington. 31pp.

U.S. Department of Transportation. 1981. Sound procedures for measuring highway noise: final report. FHWA-DP-45-1R, Demonstration Projects Prog., U.S. Dep. Transport., Washington. 105pp.

U.S. Environmental Protection Agency. 1974 plus updates. EPA compendium of registered pesticides. Vol. 1: Herbicides and plant regulations. U.S. Environ. Prot. Agency, Washington. 630pp.

U.S. Fish and Wildlife Service. 1985. Red-cockaded woodpecker recovery plan. U.S. Fish Wildl. Serv., Atlanta, GA. 88pp.

U.S. Forest Service. 1967. Section 74: geographic forest types. Pages 74–74.2-3 in U.S. Forest Service. Forest survey handbook. U.S. For. Serv. Handb. 4813.1.

U.S. Forest Service. 1969. Land treatment measures handbook. U.S. For. Serv. Handb. FSH 2509.11. 124pp.

U.S. Forest Service. 1971. Wildlife management handbook, Southern Region. FSH 2609.23R. U.S. For. Serv., Atlanta, GA. 189pp.

U.S. Forest Service. 1972. Structural range improvement handbook. U.S. For. Serv. Southwest Reg. Handb. 2209.22. Various pages.

U.S. Forest Service. 1973. Wildlife management guide for the national forests in Missouri. Mark Twain Natl. For., Rolla, MO. 42pp.

U.S. Forest Service. 1974a. Wildlife and patchcuts. U.S. For. Serv., San Francisco. 15pp.

U.S. Forest Service. 1974b. Watershed structural measures handbook. U.S. For. Serv. Handb. 2509.12. 103pp.

U.S. Forest Service. 1975. Fisheries and wildlife habitat management handbook— Ottawa, Hiawatha, and Huron-Manistee national forests, Michigan. FSH 2609.23R9. U.S. For. Serv. East. Reg., Milwaukee. Various pages.

U.S. Forest Service. 1981. An assessment of the forest and range land situation in the United States. U.S. For. Serv. For. Resour. Rep. 22. 352pp.

U.S. Forest Service. 1983. Slickrock water developments. No. 83-9. Intermt. Reg., Ogden, UT.

U.S. Forest Service. 1986. Guidelines for selecting live or dead standing tree wildlife habitat. U.S. For. Serv. Pac. Northwest Reg., Portland, OR. 6pp.

U.S. Geological Survey. 1967. Potential natural vegetation. U.S. Geol. Surv. Natl. Atlas Sheet 90.

U.S. Geological Survey. 1970. The national atlas of the United States of America. U.S. Geol. Surv., Washington. 417pp.

U.S. Rural Electrification Administration. 1972. Powerline contact by eagles and other large birds. REA Bull. 61-10, Washington. 6pp.

U.S. Soil Conservation Service. 1975. Establishing vegetation on utility rights-of-way. U.S. Soil Conserv. Serv., East Lansing, MI. 2pp.

Uresk, D. W. 1986. Food habits of cattle on mixed-grass prairie on the northern Great Plains. Prairie Nat. 18:211–218.

Uresk, D. W., and A. J. Bjugstad. 1983. Prairie dogs as ecosystem regulators on the northern High Plains. Proc. North Am. Prairie Conf. 7:91–94.

Uresk, D. W., W. H. Rickard, and J. F. Clint. 1980. Perennial grasses and their response to wildfire in south central Washington. J. Range Manage. 33:111–114.

Urness, P. 1990. Livestock as manipulators of mule deer winter habitats in northern Utah. Pages 25–40 in K. E. Severson, tech. coord. Can livestock be used as a tool to enhance wildlife habitat? U.S. For. Serv. Gen. Tech. Rep. RM-194.

Urness, P. J. 1974. Deer use changes after root plowing in Arizona chaparral. U.S For. Serv. Res. Note RM-255. 8pp.

Urness, P. J. 1979. Wildlife habitat manipulation in sagebrush ecosystems. Pages 164–178 in The sagebrush ecosystem: a symposium. Utah State Univ., Coll. Nat. Resour., Logan.

Urness, P. J. 1986. Value of crested wheatgrass for big game. Pages 147–153 in K. L. Johnson, ed. Crested wheatgrass: its values, problems and myths: symposium proceedings. Utah State Univ., Logan.

Usher, M. B. 1988. Biological invasions of nature reserves: a search for generalizations. Biol. Conserv. 44:119–135.

Vale, T. R. 1974. Sagebrush conversion projects: an element of contemporary environmental change in the western United States. Biol. Conserv. 6:274–284.

Valentine, K. A. 1967. Seasonal suitability, a grazing system for ranges of diverse vegetation types and condition classes. J. Range Manage. 20:395–397.

Valentine, K. A. 1970. Influence of grazing intensity on improvement of deteriorated black grama range. New Mexico Agric. Exp. Stn. Bull. 553. 21pp.

Vallentine, J. F. 1989. Range development and improvement. 3d ed. Brigham Young Univ. Press, Provo, UT. 524pp.

Vallentine, J. F. 1990. Grazing management. Academic Press, New York. 533pp.

VanCamp, L. F., and C. J. Henny. 1975. The screech owl: its life history and population ecology in northern Ohio. U.S. Fish Wildl. Serv. North Am. Fauna 71. 65pp.

Vance, D. R. 1976. Changes in land use and wildlife populations in southeastern Illinois. Wildl. Soc. Bull. 4:11–15.

Van Daele, C. J. 1980. Osprey and power poles in Idaho. Pages 104–112 *in* R. P. Howard and J. F. Gore, eds. Workshop on raptors and energy development. U.S. Fish Wildl. Serv., Boise, ID.

van der Maarel, E. 1971. Plant species diversity in relation to management. Pages 45–63 *in* E. Duffey and A. S. Watt, eds. The scientific management of animal and plant communities for conservation. Blackwell Scientific, Oxford, U.K.

Van Deusen, M., and D. W. Kaufman. 1977. Habitat distribution of *Peromyscus leucopus* within prairie woods. Trans. Kans. Acad. Sci. 70:151–154.

Van Epps, G. A., and C. M. McKell. 1977. Shrubs plus grass for livestock forage: a possibility. Utah Sci. 38:75–78.

Van Hoey, A. F. Undated. Wildlife management with herbaceous cover. Indiana Dep. Nat. Resour. Manage. Ser. 4. 10pp.

Van Lear, D. H. 1991. Integrating structural, compositional, and functional considerations into forest ecosystem management. Pages 117–127 *in* D. C. Le Master and G. R. Parker, eds. Ecosystem management in a dynamic society. Proc. Conf. in West Lafayette, Indiana. Dept. For. & Nat. Resour., Purdue Univ., West Lafayette, IN.

Varner, L. W., L. H. Blankenship, and G. W. Lynch. 1977. Seasonal changes in nutritive value of deer food plants in south Texas. Proc. Annu. Conf. Southeast. Assoc. Fish Wildl. Agencies 31:99–106.

Verme, L. J. 1965. Swamp conifer deeryards in northern Michigan—their ecology and management. J. For. 63:523–529.

Verme, L. J., and W. F. Johnston. 1986. Regeneration of northern white cedar deeryards in upper Michigan. J. Wildl. Manage. 50:307–313.

Verner, J. 1975. Avian behavior and habitat management. Pages 39–58 *in* D. R. Smith, tech. coord. Proceedings of the symposium on management of forests and range habitats for nongame birds. U.S. For. Serv. Gen. Tech. Rep. WO-1.

Verner, J. 1980. Birds of California oak habitats—management implications. Pages 246–264 *in* T. R. Plumb, tech. coord. Proceedings of the symposium on the ecology, management, and utilization of California oaks. U.S. For. Serv. Gen. Tech. Rep. PSW-44.

Verner, J. 1984. The guild concept applied to management of bird populations. Environ. Manage. 8:1–14.

Vestal, A. G., and M. F. Heermans. 1945. Size requirements for reference areas in mixed forest. Ecology 26:122–134.

Vogl, R. J. 1965. Effects of spring burning on yields of brush prairie savannah. J. Range Manage. 18:202–205.

Wade, D. D., and J. D. Lunsford. 1989. A guide for prescribed fire in southern forests. U.S. For. Serv. Tech. Publ. R8-TP 11. 56pp.

Wales, B. A. 1972. Vegetation analysis of north and south edges in a mature oak-hickory forest. Ecol. Monogr. 42:451–471.

Wallace, M. C., and P. R. Krausman. 1987. Elk, mule deer, and cattle habitats in central Arizona. J. Range Manage. 40:80–83.

Wallestad, R. 1975. Male sage grouse responses to sagebrush treatment. J. Wildl. Manage. 39:482–484.

Wallmo, O. C. 1969. Response of deer to alternate-strip clearcutting of lodgepole pine and spruce-fir timber in Colorado. U.S. For. Serv. Res. Note RM-141. 4pp.

Wallmo, O. C., ed. 1981. Mule and black-tailed deer of North America. Univ. Nebraska Press, Lincoln. 605pp.

Wallstad, J. D., and P. J. Kuch, eds. 1987. Forest vegetation management for conifer production. Wiley, New York. 523pp.

Warburton, D. B., and W. K. Klimstra. 1984. Wildlife use of no-till and conventionally tilled corn fields. J. Soil Water Conserv. 49:327–330.

Ward, A. L. 1973. Sagebrush control with herbicide has little effect on elk calving behavior. U.S. For. Serv. Res. Note RM-240. 4pp.

Ward, A. L. 1982. Mule deer behavior in relation to fencing and underpasses on Interstate 80 in Wyoming. Transport. Res. Record 859:8–10.

Warner, R. E., and S. L. Etter. 1989. Hay cutting and the survival of pheasants: a long-term perspective. J. Wildl. Manage. 53:458–461.

Warner, R. E., and G. B. Joselyn. 1986. Responses of Illinois ring-necked pheasant populations to block roadside management. J. Wildl. Manage. 53:455–461.

Warner, R. E., G. B. Joselyn, and S. L. Etter. 1987. Factors affecting roadside nesting by pheasants in Illinois. Wildl. Soc. Bull. 15:221–228.

Washington Department of Ecology. 1981. Western Washington urban stream assessment. Washington Dep. Ecol. Off. Water Prog., Olympia. 54pp.

Washington Forest Practices Board. 1988. Washington forest practices rules and regulations. Washington Dep. Nat. Resour., Olympia. 147pp.

Webb, W. M., and F. S. Guthery. 1982. Response of bobwhite to habitat management for northwest Texas. Wildl. Soc. Bull. 10:142–146.

Webb, W. M., and F. S. Guthery. 1983. Avian response to habitat management for northern bobwhites in northwest Texas. J. Wildl. Manage. 47:220–222.

Weed Science Society of America. 1989. Herbicide handbook of the Weed Science Society of America. 6th ed. Weed Sci. Soc. Am., Champaign, IL. 301pp.

Weiser, C., and D. J. Hlavinka. 1956. Comparison of breeding-bird populations of three deciduous shelterbelts. Am. Birds 10:416–419.

Welchert, W. T., and B. N. Freeman. 1973. "Horizontal" wells. J. Range Manage. 26:253–256.

Welsch, D. J. 1991. Riparian forest buffers: function and design for protection and enhancement of water resources. U.S. For. Serv. Pub. NA-PR-07-91. 24pp.

West, N. E. 1987. Intermountain deserts, shrubsteppes, and woodlands. Pages 209–230 in M. G. Barbour and W. B. Billings eds. North American terrestrial vegetation. Cambridge Univ. Press, New York.

West, N. E. 1993. Biodiversity of rangelands. J. Range Manage. 46:2-13.

West, N. E., K. E. Rea, and R. J. Tausch. 1975. Basic synecological relationships in the juniper-pinyon woodlands. Pages 41–52 in G. F. Gifford and F. E. Busby, eds. The pinyon-juniper ecosystem: a symposium. Coll. Nat. Resour., Utah State Univ., Logan.

West, S. D., R. D. Taber, and D. A. Anderson. 1981. Wildlife in sludge-treated plantations. Pages 115–122 in C. S. Bledsoe, ed. Municipal sludge application to Pacific Northwest forestlands. Coll. For. Resour., Univ. Washington, Seattle.

Western, D., and M. C. Pearl, eds. 1989. Conservation for the twenty-first century. Oxford Univ. Press, New York. 365pp.

Westman, W. E. 1985. Ecology, impact assessment, and environmental planning. Wiley, New York. 532pp.

Westman, W. E. 1990. Managing for biodiversity: unresolved science and policy questions. BioScience 40:26–33.

Whelan, T., ed. 1991. Nature tourism: managing for the environment. Island Press, Washington. 223pp.

Whisenant, S. G. 1987. Selective control of mountain big sagebrush (Artemisia tridentata spp. vaseyana) with clopyralid. Weed Sci. 35:120–123.

Whisenant, S. G., D. N. Ueckert, and C. J. Scifres. 1984. Effect of fire on Texas wintergrass communities. J. Range Manage. 37:387–391.

Whitcomb, R. F., C. S. Robbins, J. F. Lynch, B. L. Whitcomb, M. K. Klimkiewicz, and D. Bystrak. 1981. Effects of forest fragmentation on avifauna of the eastern deciduous forest. Pages 125–205 in R. L. Burgess and D. M. Sharpe, eds. Forest island dynamics in man-dominated landscapes. Springer-Verlag, New York.

White, C. M. 1974. Current problems and techniques in raptor management and conservation. Trans. North Am. Wildl. Nat. Resour. Conf. 39:301–311.

White, D. H. 1987. Testing of cave gate designs for use in protecting endangered bats. U.S. Fish Wildl. Serv. Res. Inf. Bull. 29–87. 2pp.

White, L. D. 1975. Ecosystem analysis of Paynes Prairie. Res. Rep. 24, School For. Resour. Conserv., Univ. Florida, Gainesville. 355pp.

White, L. P., L. D. Harris, J. E. Johnston, and D. G. Milchunas. 1975. Impact of site preparation on flatwoods wildlife habitat. Proc. Annu. Conf. Southeast. Game Fish Comm. 29:347–353.

White, P. S. 1987. Natural disturbance, patch dynamics, and landscape pattern in natural areas. Nat. Areas J. 7:14–22.

Whittaker, R. H. 1975. Communities and ecosystems. 2d ed. Macmillan, New York. 385pp.

Wiens, J. A., and M. I. Dyer. 1975. Rangeland avifaunas: their composition, energetics, and role in the ecosystem. Pages 146–182 in D. R. Smith, tech. coord. Proceedings of the symposium on management of forests and range habitats for nongame birds. U.S. For. Serv. Gen. Tech. Rep. WO-1.

Wiens, J. A., J. T. Rotenberry, and B. Van Horne. 1986. A lesson in the limitations of field experiments: shrubsteppe birds and habitat alteration. Ecology 67:365–376.

Wight, J. R. 1976. Range fertilization in the northern Great Plains. J. Range Manage. 29:180–185.

Wight, J. R., and A. L. Black. 1979. Range fertilization: plant response and water use. J. Range Manage. 32:345–349.

Wigley, B., and M. A. Melchoirs. 1987. State wildlife management programs for private lands. Wildl. Soc. Bull. 15:580–584.

Wilbert, D. E. 1963. Some effects of chemical sagebrush control on elk distribution. J. Range Manage. 16:74–78.

Wilcove, D. S. 1985. Nest predation in forest tracts and the decline of migratory songbirds. Ecology 66:1211–1214.

Wilcove, D. S. 1987. From fragmentation to extinction. Nat. Areas J. 7:23–29.

Wilcove, D. S. 1989. Protecting biodiversity in multiple-use lands: lessons from the U.S. Forest Service. Trends Ecol. Evol. 4:385–388.

Wilcove, D. S. 1990. Forest fragmentation as a wildlife management issue in the eastern United States. Pages 1–5 in R. M. DeGraaf and W. M. Healy, comps. Is forest fragmentation a management issue in the northeast? U.S. For. Serv. Gen. Tech. Rep. NE-140.

Wilcove, D. S, C. H. McLellan, and A. P. Dobson. 1986. Habitat fragmentation in the temperate zone. Pages 237–256 in M. Soulé, ed. Conservation biology: the science of scarcity and diversity. Sinauer Assoc., Sunderland, MA.

Wilcove, D. S., and F. B. Samson. 1987. Innovative wildlife management: listening to Leopold. Trans. North Am. Wildl. Nat. Resour. Conf. 52:321–329.

Wilcox, B. A., P. F. Brussard, and B. G. Marcot, eds. 1986. The management of viable populations: theory, applications, and case studies. Cent. for Conserv. Biol., Dept. Biol. Sci., Stanford Univ., Stanford, CA. 188pp.

Wiley, J. E. 1988a. Deer wintering areas. Pages 35–37 in C. A. Elliott, ed. A forester's guide to managing wildlife habitats in Maine. Coop. Ext. Serv., Univ. Maine, Orono.

Wiley, J. E., ed. 1988b. Wildlife guidelines for the public reserved lands of Maine. Maine Dep. Conserv., Augusta. 71pp.

Wilkins, K. T., and D. J. Schmidly. 1979. The effects of mowing highway rights-of-way on small mammals. Pages 55-1 to 55-13 in D. Arner and R. E. Tillman, eds. Environmental concerns in rights-of-way management. EPRI WS-78-141, Elec. Power Res. Inst., Palo Alto, CA.

Wilkins, N. 1988. Developing hunting enterprises on private lands. PB 1305, Agric. Ext. Serv., Univ. Tennessee, Knoxville. 12pp.

Williams, B. L., and B. G. Marcot. 1991. Use of biodiversity indicators for analyzing and managing forest landscapes. Trans. North Am. Wildl. Nat. Resour. Conf. 56:613–627.

Williams, R. D., and S. H. Hanks. 1976. Hardwood nurseryman's guide. U.S. For. Serv. Agric. Handb. 473. 78pp.

Williamson, S. J., and O. H. Hirth. 1985. An evaluation of edge use by white-tailed deer. Wildl. Soc. Bull. 13:252–257.

Williamson, S. J. Undated. Forester's guide to wildlife habitat improvement. Coop. Ext. Serv., Univ. New Hampshire, Durham. 56pp.

Willms, W., A. W. Bailey, A. McClean, and R. Tucker. 1981. The effects of fall defoliation on the utilization of bluebunch wheatgrass and its influence on the distribution of deer in spring. J. Range Manage. 34:16–18.

Willms, W. D., S. Smoliak, and G. B. Schaalje. 1986. Cattle weight gains in relation to stocking rate on rough fescue grassland. J. Range Manage. 39:182–187.

Wills, D. L. 1984. Creating wildlife habitat conditions. Pages 243–257 in R. L. Hoover and D. L. Wills, eds. Managing forested lands for wildlife. Colorado Div. Wildl., Denver.

Wilson, E. O., and E. O. Willis. 1975. Applied biogeography. Pages 522–534 in M. L. Cody and J. M. Diamond, eds. Ecology and evolution of communities. Belknap Press, Cambridge, MA.

Wilson, L. D., and D. Hannans. 1977. Guidelines and recommendations for design and modification of livestock watering developments to facilitate safe use by wildlife. U.S. Bur. Land Manage. Tech. Note 305. 20pp.

Wilson, J., and T. Schmidt. 1990. Controlling eastern redcedar on rangelands and pastures. Rangelands 12:156–158.

Wilson, W. L., and A. D. Johns. 1982. Diversity and abundance of selected animal species in undisturbed forest, selectively logged forest, and plantations in East Kalimantan, Indonesia. Biol. Conserv. 24:205–218.

Wilton, A. C., R. E. Ries, and L. Hofmann. 1978. The use and improvement of legumes for ranges. N. Dak. Farm Res. 36:29–31.

Windell, K. 1991. Tree shelters for seedling protection. U.S. For. Serv. Technol. & Develop. Prog., Missoula, MT. 142pp.

Wink, R. L., and H. A. Wright. 1973. Effects of fire on an ash-juniper community. J. Range Manage. 26:326–329.

Wisconsin Department of Natural Resources. 1990. Prescribed burn handbook. Wisconsin Dep. Nat. Resour., Madison. 47pp.

Witmer, G. W., M. Wisdom, E. P. Harshman, R. J. Anderson, C. Carey, M. P. Kuttel, I. D. Luman, J. A. Rochelle, R. W. Scharpf, and D. Smithey. 1985. Deer and elk. Pages 231–258 in E. R. Brown, tech. ed. Management of wildlife and fish habitats in forests of western Oregon and Washington. U.S. For. Serv., Portland, OR.

Woehler, E. E. 1982. Winter food and cover plots for farm wildlife. Wisconsin Dep. Nat. Resour. Res. Rep. 114. 24pp.

Woehler, E. E. 1987. Use of herbicides to control woody nuisance plants on public lands. Wisconsin Dep. Nat. Resour. Res. Manage. Findings 5. 4pp.

Woehler, E. E., and R. T. Dumke. 1982. Hedgerow establishment and maintenance for farm wildlife. Wisconsin Dep. Nat. Resour. Res. Rep. 113. 42pp.

Wong, M. 1985. Understory birds as indicators of regeneration in a patch of selectively logged West Malaysian rainforest. Pages 249–263 in A. W. Diamond and T. E. Lovejoy, eds. Conservation of tropical forest birds. Internat. Counc. for Bird Preserv. Tech. Publ. 4, Cambridge, U. K.

Wood, B. W., and J. D. Botherson. 1986. Ecological adaptation and grazing response of budsage (*Artemisia spinescens*) in southwestern Utah. Pages 75–92 in E. D. McArthur and B. L. Welch, comps. Proceedings: symposium on the biology of Artemisia and Chrysothamnus. U.S. For. Serv. Gen. Tech. Rep. INT-200.

Wood, J. E. 1969. Rodent populations and their impact on desert ranges. New Mexico State Univ. Agric. Exp. Stn. Bull. 555. 17pp.

Woodward, D. F. 1982. Acute toxicity of mixtures of range management herbicides to cutthroat trout. J. Range Manage. 35:539–540.

Wooley, J. B., L. B. Best, and W. R. Clark. 1985. Impacts of no-till row cropping on upland wildlife. Trans. North Am. Wildl. Nat. Resour. Conf. 50:157–169.

Wooley, J. B., R. George, B. Ohde, and W. Rybarczyk. 1982. Nesting evaluations of native grass pastures and narrow-row soybeans. Pages 5–6 in R. B. Dahlgren, ed. Proceedings of the Midwest agricultural interfaces with fish and wildlife resources workshop. Iowa State Univ., Ames.

Wright, H. A. 1970. Response of big sagebrush and three-tip sagebrush to season of clipping. J. Range Manage. 23:20–22.

Wright, H. A. 1973. Fire as a tool to manage tobosa grasslands. Proc. Annu. Tall Timbers Fire Ecol. Conf. 12:153–167.

Wright, H. A. 1974. Effect of fire on southern mixed prairie grasses. J. Range Manage. 27:417–419.

Wright, H. A., and A. W. Bailey. 1980. Fire ecology and prescribed burning in the Great Plains—a research review. U.S. For. Serv. Gen. Tech. Rep. INT-77. 61pp.

Wright, H. A., and A. W. Bailey, 1982. Fire ecology: United States and southern Canada. Wiley, New York. 501pp.

Wright, H. A., S. C. Bunting, and L. F. Neuenschwander. 1976. Effects of fire on honey mesquite. J. Range Manage. 29:467–471.

Wright, H. A., L. F. Neuenschwander, and C. M. Britton. 1979. The role and use of fire in sagebrush-grass and pinyon-juniper plant communities. U.S. Forest Serv. Gen. Tech. Rep. INT-58. 48pp.

Wright, H. A., and J. Stinson. 1970. Response of mesquite to season of top removal. J. Range Manage. 23:127–128.

Wunz, G. A. 1984. Establishment, maintenance and wildlife preference of herbaceous plant species planted in forest clearings. Northeast Fish Wildl. Conf. 41:130–141.

Wunz, G. A. 1987. Evaluation of methods for creating long-lasting forest clearings in Pennsylvania. Trans. Northeast Sect. Wildl. Soc. 44:61–71.

Wunz, G. A., A. H. Hayden, and R. R. Potts. 1983. Spring seep ecology and management. Trans. Northeast Sect. Wildl. Soc. 40:19–30.

Yahner, R. H. 1982a. Avian nest densities and nest-site selection in farmstead shelterbelts. Wilson Bull. 94:156–174.

Yahner, R. H. 1982b. Avian use of vertical strata and plantings in farmstead shelterbelts. J. Wildl. Manage. 46:50–60.

Yahner, R. H. 1982c. Microhabitat use by small mammals in farmstead shelterbelts. J. Mammal. 63:440–445.

Yahner, R. H. 1983a. Seasonal dynamics, habitat relationships, and management of avifauna in farmstead shelterbelts. J. Wildl. Manage. 47:85–104.

Yahner, R. H. 1983b. Small mammals in farmstead shelterbelts: habitat correlates of seasonal abundance and community structure. J. Wildl. Manage. 47:74–84.

Yahner, R. H. 1984. Effects of habitat patchiness created by a ruffed grouse management plan on avian communities. Am. Midl. Nat. 111:409–413.

Yahner, R. H. 1988. Changes in wildlife communities near edges. Conserv. Biol. 2:333–339.

Yahner, R. H., T. E. Morrell, and J. S. Rachael. 1989. Effects of edge contrast on depredation of artificial avian nests. J. Wildl. Manage. 53:1135–1138.

Yahner, R. H., and A. L. Wright. 1985. Depredation on artificial ground nests: effects of edge and plot age. J. Wildl. Manage. 49:508–513.

Yamasaki, M., and C. H. Tubbs. 1986. Wildlife tree management in New England northern hardwood forests. Pages 109–134 in J. A. Bissonette, ed. Is good forestry good wildlife management? Misc. Pub. 689, Agric. Exp. Stn., Univ. Maine, Orono.

Yarrow, G. K. 1990a. Wildlife management: farms and woodlands. Coop. Ext. Serv., Clemson Univ., Clemson, SC. 11pp.

Yarrow, G. K. 1990b. Wildlife management: incentives for the private landowner. Coop. Ext. Serv., Clemson Univ., Clemson, SC. 6pp.

Yarrow, G. K., and W. Smathers. 1990. Wildlife management: investment and income opportunities for the private landowner. Coop. Ext. Serv., Clemson Univ., Clemson, SC. 10pp.

Yoakum, J. 1986. Use of Artemisia and Chrysothamnus by pronghorns. Pages 176–180 in E. D. McArthur and B. L. Welch, comps. Proceedings: symposium on the biology of Artemisia and Chrysothamnus. U.S. For. Serv. Gen. Tech. Rep. INT-200.

Yoakum, J., W. P. Dasmann, H. R. Sanderson, C. M. Nixon, and H. S. Crawford. 1980. Habitat improvement techniques. Pages 329–403 in S. D. Schemnitz, ed. Wildlife management techniques manual. 4th ed. Wildl. Soc., Washington.

Yoakum, J. D. 1975. Antelope and livestock on rangelands. J. Anim. Sci. 40:985–992.

Yoakum, J. D. 1978. Pronghorn. Pages 103–121 in J. L. Schmidt and D. L. Gilbert, eds. Big game of North America. Stackpole Books, Harrisburg, PA.

Yonce, F. J. 1983. Forest ownership. Pages 222–229 *in* R. C. Davis, ed. Encyclopedia of American forest and conservation history. Vol. 1. Macmillan, New York.

Young, M. K., R. N. Schmal, and C. M. Sobszak. 1990. Railroad tie drives and stream channel complexity: past impacts, current status, and future prospects. Pages 126–130 *in* Forestry on the frontier. Proc. 1989 Soc. Am. For. Natl. Conv. Bethesda, MD.

Young, R. P. 1983. Fire as a vegetation management tool in rangelands of the intermountain region. Pages 18–31 *in* S. B. Monsen and N. Shaw, eds. Managing intermountain rangelands—improvement of range and wildlife habitats. U.S. For. Serv. Gen. Tech. Rep. INT-157.

Young, V. A., and G. F. Payne. 1948. Utilization of "key" browse species in relation to proper grazing practices in cutover western white pine lands in northern Idaho. J. For. 46:35–49.

Zackrisson, O. 1977. Influence of forest fires on the North Swedish boreal forest. Oikos 29:22–32.

Zasoski, R. J. 1981. Heavy metal mobility in sludge-amended soils. Pages 67–72 *in* C. S. Bledsoe, ed. Municipal sludge application to Pacific Northwest forestlands: proceedings of a symposium. Coll. For. Resour., Univ. Washington, Seattle.

Zedler, J., and O. L. Loucks. 1969. Differential burning response of *Poa praetensis* field and *Andropogon scoparius* prairies in central Wisconsin. Am. Midl. Nat. 81:341–352.

Zeleny, L. 1976. The bluebird: how you can help its fight for survival. Indiana Univ. Press, Bloomington. 170pp.

Zeleny, L. 1978. Nesting box programs for bluebirds and other passerines. Pages 55–60 *in* S. A. Temple, ed. Endangered birds: management techniques for preserving threatened species. Univ. Wisconsin Press, Madison.

Zillgitt, W. M. 1946. A quick method for estimating cull in northern hardwood stands. U.S. For. Serv. Lake States For. Exp. Stn. Tech. Note. 255. 1p.

Addendum

Crow, T. R., A. Haney, and D. M. Waller. 1993. Report of the scientific roundtable on biological diversity. U. S. For. Serv. TP-R9-CNF/NNF-92-1.

Gray, R. S. 1974. Lasting waters for bighorns. Desert Bighorn Counc. Trans. 1974:25–27.

Hasenyager, R. N., J. C. Pederson, and W. W. Heggen. 1979. Flammulated owl nesting in a squirrel box. West. Birds 10:224.

Idaho Department of Lands. 1990. Rules and regulations pertaining to the Idaho Forest Practices Act. Idaho Dep. Lands, Boise. 88pp.

K.ein, B. 1989. Effects of forest fragmentation on dung and carrion beetle communities in central Amazonia. Ecology 70:1715–1725.

Mapston, R. D., and R. S. ZoBell. 1972. Antelope passes: their value and use. Tech. Note D-360. U. S. Bur. Land Manage., Portland, OR. 11pp.

Nichol, A. A. 1936. The experimental feeding of deer. Trans. North Am. Wildl. Conf. 1:403–410.

Noss, R. F. 1983. A regional landscape approach to maintain diversity. BioScience 33:700–706.

Samson, F. B. 1980a. Use of montane meadows by birds. Pages 113–129 *in* R. M. DeGraaf and N. G. Tilghman, eds. Workshop proceedings: management of western forests and grasslands for nongame birds. U. S. For. Serv. Gen. Tech. Rep. INT-86.

Smith, H. R. 1975. Management of *Peromyseus leucopus* as part of an integrated program to control the gypsy moth. Trans. Northeast Sect. Wildl. Soc. Fish Wildl. Conf. 32:111–129.

Weed Science Society of America. 1983. Herbicide handbook of the weed science society of America. 5th ed. Weed Sci. Soc. Am., Champaign, IL. 515pp.

Index

ABOUT THE AUTHORS

NEIL F. PAYNE is a professor of wildlife in the College of Natural Resources, University of Wisconsin-Stevens Point (1975–present). He grew up in Sheboygan Falls, Wis., and received a bachelor of arts in biology from the University of Wisconsin-Madison (1961), a master of science in wildlife and forestry from Virginia Polytechnic Institute and State University (1964), and a doctor of philosophy in wildlife science from Utah State University (1975). He saw combat duty in Vietnam and was a captain with the U.S. Marine Corps (1964–67). He directed the bear and furbearer program for the Newfoundland and Labrador Wildlife Division (1967–71), and he was on the wildlife faculty at the University of Washington in Seattle (1973–75).

FRED C. BRYANT is a professor of range management in the Department of Range and Wildlife Management at Texas Tech University (1977–present). He was raised in Leon Valley near San Antonio, Texas. He received a bachelor of science in wildlife management from Texas Tech University (1970), a master of science in wildlife biology from Utah State University (1974), and a doctor of philosophy in range science from Texas A&M University (1977). He has directed research on habitat use and management of several ungulate species and Merriam's turkey, and on range–wildlife interrelationships, particularly livestock grazing and brush management.